Wolters Kluwer

MW01101064

Connect Online!

2017
U.S. Master™
Sales and Use
Tax Guide

Wolters Kluwer Editorial Staff Publication

Wolters Kluwer

Wolters Kluwer Editorial Staff Publication

Editor	Fred Conklin
Charts Editor	Brian Nudelman, J.D., Laura LeeLun, J.D.
Production Coordinator	Govardhan. L
Production	Jadunath Panigrahi

This publication is designed to provide accurate and authoritative information in regard to the subject matter covered. It is sold with the understanding that the publisher is not engaged in rendering legal, accounting, or other professional service. If legal advice or other expert assistance is required, the services of a competent professional person should be sought.

ISBN 978-0-8080-4571-7

2700 Lake Cook Road
Riverwoods, IL 60015
800 344 3734
CCHGroup.com

Printed in the United States of America

SUSTAINABLE FORESTRY INITIATIVE
Certified Sourcing
www.sfiprogram.org
SFI-01028

PREFACE

This Guide is designed as a quick-reference work on the sales and use taxes imposed by 46 states and the District of Columbia. It provides a snapshot of the basic elements of the laws. The amount of detail is kept to a minimum and is organized so that information can be found quickly and easily. The charts in this publication set forth the tax treatment of specific topics such as computers or mail-order sales, as well as an overview of aspects of the tax structure such as the basis of the taxes, penalties, interest, and remedies.

The arrangement of the state summaries is uniform from state to state, simplifying the reference of specific topics across states. The uniform arrangement follows the pattern of both the CCH MULTISTATE SALES TAX GUIDE and the in-depth sales and use tax coverage in CCH's series of state tax reporters, which should be consulted for details beyond the scope of this work.

The charts and state summaries relate to current law and to information received as of the publication date, except where there is specific reference to prior or future years.

April 2017

U.S. Master Sales and Use Tax Guide

TABLE OF CONTENTS

For the standard outline of the summaries for all states with a
state sales and use tax, see Alabama.

STATE SUMMARIES

Highlights of 2016 and Early 2017 Sales and Use Tax Changes

All States

Congressional Actions

• **Internet tax ban is now permanent**

The Internet Tax Freedom Act (ITFA) (P.L. 105-277), originally enacted in 1998 , was intended to prevent state taxes on Internet access, to ensure that multiple jurisdictions could not tax the same electronic commerce transaction, and to ensure that commerce over the Internet would not be singled out for discriminatory tax treatment. Congress extended the ITFA multiple times, but the moratorium was made permanent on February 24, 2016, as part of the "Trade Facilitation and Trade Enforcement Act of 2015." The ITFA was previously set to expire on October 1, 2016. (H.R. 644, 114th Congress, Laws 2015)

Alabama

• **Alabama increased estimated payment threshold in 2016**

Effective August 1, 2016, the average monthly tax liability for a taxpayer to be required to make estimated Alabama sales tax payments was increased from $1,000 or greater to $2,500 or greater during the preceding calendar year. (Act 316 (H.B. 151), Laws 2014) (AL ¶ 207)

• **4-R Act challenge to Alabama tax on railroad diesel continues**

On remand from the U.S. Supreme Court, the U.S. Court of Appeals for the Eleventh Circuit vacated its prior decision in *CSX Transportation, Inc. v. Alabama Department of Revenue,* 350 F. App'x 318 (11th Cir. 2009), in which it affirmed a federal district court's dismissal of a railroad's suit against the Alabama Department of Revenue that had alleged that the department's imposition of Alabama sales and use tax on diesel fuel used by railroads discriminated against railroad companies in violation of the federal Railroad Revitalization and Regulatory Reform Act (4-R Act).

The Supreme Court reversed the Eleventh Circuit in *CSX Transportation, Inc. v. Alabama Department of Revenue,* 131 S.Ct. 1101, Dkt. No. 09-520 (2011), holding that a railroad may, under the 4-R Act, challenge Alabama sales and use taxes that apply to rail carriers' purchases of diesel fuel, but exempt fuel purchases by rail competitors. In light of the Supreme Court's decision, the Eleventh Circuit also vacated the federal district court's order that dissolved the preliminary injunction, dismissed the taxpayer's case, and remanded the case to the district court for further proceedings consistent with the Supreme Court's Opinion. (*CSX Transportation, Inc. v. Alabama Department of Revenue,* U.S. Court of Appeals for the Eleventh Circuit, No. 09-10772, April 25, 2011, CCH ALABAMA TAX REPORTS, ¶ 201–551)

On remand from the U.S. Supreme Court, the U.S. District Court for the Northern District of Alabama held that the state's rail carriers did not suffer discriminatory sales and use tax treatment under the federal Railroad Revitalization and Regulatory Reform Act (4-R Act). Since there was no violation of the 4-R Act, the court entered an order dismissing the taxpayer's complaint with prejudice. (*CSX Transportation, Inc. v. Alabama Department of Revenue,* U.S. District Court, N.D. Alabama, No. 2:08-cv-655-AKK, August 24, 2012, CCH ALABAMA TAX REPORTS, ¶ 201–642; petition for certiorari filed October 30, 2013, *Alabama Department of Revenue v. CSX Transportation, Inc.,* U.S. Supreme Court, Dkt. No. 13-553)

In later action, the U.S. Supreme Court now has held that the Eleventh Circuit Court of Appeals properly concluded that an interstate rail carrier taxpayer's competitors are an appropriate comparison class for its claim that Alabama's asymmetrical sales tax treatment discriminates against a rail carrier in violation of the Railroad Revitalization and Regulation Reform Act (4-R Act). The state argued that the only appropriate comparison class for a subsection (b)(4) claim is all general commercial and industrial taxpayers. However, the high court disagreed and held that, although all general and commercial taxpayers may be an appropriate comparison class for such a claim, it is not the only comparison class. When a railroad alleges that a tax targets it for treatment that is worse than that provided to local businesses, all other commercial and industrial taxpayers are the comparison class. However, when a railroad alleges that a tax disadvantages it compared to its competitors in the transportation industry, the railroad's competitors in that jurisdiction are the comparison class.

Subsection (b)(4) also requires a showing of discrimination, a failure to treat similarly situated persons alike. A comparison class will support a discrimination claim only if it consists of individuals similarly situated to the claimant. In subsections (b)(1) to (b)(3) of the act that relate to prohibitions directed toward property taxes, the comparison class is limited to commercial and industrial property in the same assessment jurisdiction. However, subsection (b)(4) contains no such limitation, so the comparison class should be determined based on the theory of discrimination alleged in the claim. The category of similarly situated comparison classes must at least include the commercial and industrial taxpayers specified in the other subsections of the act, but it also can include a railroad's competitors. Discrimination in favor of that class both falls within the ordinary meaning of "discrimination" and also frustrates the 4–R Act's purpose of restoring the financial stability of the nation's railway system while fostering competition among all carriers by railroad and other modes of transportation.

In addition, the Eleventh Circuit erred in refusing to consider whether Alabama could justify its decision to exempt motor carriers from its sales and use taxes through its decision to subject motor carriers to a fuel excise tax. According to the Court, arguing that a tax discriminates against a rail carrier if a competitor who is exempt from that tax must pay another comparable tax from which the rail carrier is exempt does not agree with ordinary English usage since both competitors could then claim to be discriminated against relative to each other. The U.S. Supreme Court remanded the case to the Eleventh Circuit and instructed the court to consider:

> (1) whether Alabama's fuel excise tax is the rough equivalent of Alabama's sales tax as applied to diesel fuel that consequently justifies the motor carrier sales tax exemption; and

> (2) whether any of the state's alternative rationales justify that exemption.

(*Alabama Department of Revenue v. CSX Transportation, Inc.,* U.S. Supreme Court, Dkt. 13-553, March 4, 2015, CCH ALABAMA TAX REPORTS,¶ 201-802)

Arizona

• **Arizona enacts various tax exemptions**

The following sales and use tax exemptions have been enacted in Arizona, effective as noted: (AZ ¶ 233)

> — *Livestock and poultry feed:* Enacted Arizona legislation extends transaction privilege, use and municipal tax exemptions to include sales of livestock and poultry feed and other items to anyone who feeds their own livestock or board livestock noncommercially. The law includes animal feed grown or raised by a producer in the definition of "food product" and prohibits taxes, licenses and fees on purchases of food products from the producer. Further, the law removes the requirement for owners, proprietors, or tenants of agricultural lands or farms that sell livestock or poultry feed grown on their lands to obtain a Transaction Privilege Tax (TPT) exemption certificate or resale certificate when selling to anyone that:

(1) feeds their own livestock or poultry;

(2) produces livestock or poultry commercially; or

(3) feeds livestock or poultry commercially or board livestock noncommercially.

Existing TPT and use tax exemptions are extended to include sales of livestock and poultry feed, salts, vitamins and other additives for livestock and poultry consumption to persons who feed their own livestock or poultry or board livestock noncommercially. Further, the law exempts farmers who grow, package and market their own agricultural products from the presumption that they are engaged in retail business and subject to TPT. (Ch. 361 (H.B. 2326), Laws 2016, effective August 6, 2016)

— *Fine art:* Applicable to taxable periods beginning September 1, 2016, the sale of fine art at an auction or gallery to a nonresident for use outside the state is exempt from the TPT. A vendor must deliver the work of fine art to a destination outside Arizona in order to qualify for the exemption. (Ch. 368 (H.B. 2536), Laws 2016)

— *Agricultural aircraft:* An exemption from the TPT and use tax is enacted for "agricultural aircraft," which is defined as an aircraft that is built for agricultural use for the aerial application of pesticides or fertilizer or for aerial seeding. This provision is applicable retroactively to April 17, 1985. Taxpayers could file for a refund of up to $10,000, of TPT and use tax paid to the state between April 17, 1985, and December 31, 2016, on such aircraft. Any such refund claim had to be submitted to the Arizona Department of Revenue by December 31, 2016. (Ch. 181 (H.B. 2133), Laws 2016)

— *LP gas:* For taxable periods beginning on or after September 1, 2016, the sale of liquefied petroleum gas to a business that uses at least 51% of the liquefied petroleum gas in manufacturing or smelting operations is exempt from the utilities classification of the TPT and use tax. (Ch. 359 (H.B. 2025), Laws 2016)

— *Transportation of natural gas:* An exemption from the TPT and use tax is enacted, effective August 6, 2016, for gas transportation services. "Gas transportation services" means the services of transporting natural gas to a natural gas customer or to a natural gas distribution facility if the natural gas was purchased from a supplier other than the utility. Previously, these services were specifically excluded from the exemption for electricity and natural gas. (Ch. 357 (S.B. 1505), Laws 2016)

— *Transportation networks:* Effective July 1, 2016, a transaction privilege tax exemption is available for transportation network companies. Cities, towns and special taxing districts may not levy a transaction privilege, sales, use or other similar tax on:

(1) any amount attributable to fees collected by transportation network companies issued a permit;

(2) transporting for hire persons by transportation network companies issued a permit;

(3) transporting for hire persons by vehicle for hire companies issued a permit; and

(4) transporting for hire persons by vehicle for hire drivers on transactions involving vehicle for hire services.

The transporting classification specifically excludes (1) vehicles for hire companies issued a permit; and (2) vehicle for hire drivers operating under a company permit for transactions involving vehicle for hire services. (Ch. 171 (S.B. 1492), Laws 2016)

— *Billboards:* An exemption from the TPT and use tax is enacted for the leasing or renting of billboards that are designed, intended, or used to advertise or inform and that are visible from any street, road, or other highway. (Ch. 223 (S.B. 1310), Laws 2016, effective August 6, 2016)

• **Aircraft and manufacturing exemptions amended in Arizona**

The following sales and use tax exemptions have been amended in Arizona, effective as noted: (AZ ¶ 233)

— *Aircraft:* Arizona has amended its sales and use tax exemption for aircraft, navigational and communication instruments and other accessories and related equipment to include new provisions on who may qualify for the exemption. Under the amendments, effective June 30, 2017, purchasers may qualify for the exemption if they:

hold, or are exempt from holding, a federal certificate of public convenience and necessity;

are certified or licensed under federal aviation regulations (14 CFR parts 121 or 135) as a scheduled or unscheduled carrier or persons;

operate aircraft to transport persons for compensation or hire as an air carrier, foreign air carrier, a commercial operator, or under a restricted category; or

lease or transfer operational control of the aircraft, instruments or accessories to persons who meet one of the other exemption requirements.

The exemption applies to corporations not incorporated in Arizona if the corporations' principal corporate offices are located outside Arizona and the purchased property will not be used in Arizona. (Ch. 367 (H.B. 2533), Laws 2016)

— *Manufacturing:* The definition of "qualified manufacturing or smelting business" as it applies to the Arizona transaction privilege and use tax deduction of electricity and natural gas sales is expanded, effective January 1, 2017. In order for gross proceeds to be deducted from the tax base, the sales of electricity or natural gas must be to a "qualified manufacturing or smelting business." A "qualified manufacturing or smelting business" means a business that does one of the following:

manufactures or smelts tangible products in this state, of which at least 51% of the manufactured or smelted products will be exported out-of-state for incorporation into another product or sold out-of-state for a final sale;

derives at least 51% of its gross income from the sale of manufactured or smelted products manufactured or smelted by the business;

uses at least 51% of its square footage in Arizona for manufacturing or smelting and business activities directly related to manufacturing or smelting;

employs at least 51% of its workforce in Arizona in manufacturing or smelting and business activities directly related to manufacturing or smelting; or

uses at least 51% of the value of its capitalized assets in Arizona, as reflected on the business's books and records, for manufacturing or smelting and business activities directly related to manufacturing or smelting.

A utility that claims this deduction must report each month, on a form prescribed by the Department of Revenue, the name and address of each qualified manufacturing or smelting business for which this deduction is taken. A vendor must accept a certificate establishing a deduction in good faith. If the purchaser cannot establish the accuracy and completeness of the information provided in the certificate, then the purchaser is liable for the transaction privilege tax that the vendor would have been required to pay if the vendor had not accepted the certificate. (Ch. 374 (H.B. 2676), Laws 2016)

— *Computer data centers:* Various TPT and use tax relief provisions are amended for certified computer data centers, affecting exempt equipment, minimum investment requirements, certification revocation and recapture of tax benefits, and sustainable redevelopment projects, as follows: (Ch. 369 (H.B. 2584), Laws 2016, effective retroactively to September 12, 2013)

Equipment exemption, minimum investment.—The equipment exemption is expanded to include equipment that is leased or used pursuant to a contract for the right to use the equipment. The bill also eliminates the requirement that the owner, operator, or colocation tenant must present a certificate of qualification to a retailer at the time of purchase in order to receive the tax exemption. A data center's cost of improvements is included in determining whether it meets the minimum investment requirements to qualify for tax relief.

Certification, revocation, recapture of tax benefits.—If a computer data center's certification is revoked for failure to comply with minimum investment requirements, the Department of Revenue may recapture tax relief provided to the owners and operators. However, a qualified colocation tenant is not subject to recapture of any tax relief received, except that a contributing qualified colocation tenant may be subject to recapture if it is located in a computer data center that is certified from and after August 31, 2016. If a computer data center violates tax relief provisions by generating electricity for resale purposes or generating, providing, or selling electricity outside the computer data center, the center's certification must be revoked and the qualification period of any owner, operator, or qualified colocation tenant will automatically terminate. However, the Department may not recapture any tax relief provided to the owner, operator, or qualified colocation tenant before the date of revocation.

Sustainable redevelopment project.—For purposes of qualifying and continuing as a sustainable redevelopment project, a data center owner may substantially demolish an existing building to accommodate future data center use, and the demolition will not be a cause for loss of certification as a sustainable redevelopment project. An owner or operator may expand the boundaries of a certified computer data center by increasing the size of an existing building within a sustainable redevelopment project or by building additional improvements. Expansion activities do not prevent a facility from maintaining its classification as a sustainable redevelopment project. All construction activities and investments related to demolition and expansion are considered to be a part of the project.

- **Arizona adds TPT classification for online lodging marketplaces**

Effective January 1, 2017, a new Online Lodging Marketplace Classification is established for transaction privilege tax purposes for businesses operating an online lodging marketplace that are registered with the Arizona Department of Revenue for a license to collect tax. The tax base for the online lodging marketplace classification is the gross proceeds of sales or gross income derived from the business measured by the total amount charged for an online transient lodging transaction by the online lodging operator. The application tax rate is 5.5% of the tax base. Property tax managers who are licensed with the Department are permitted to file an electronic consolidated tax return monthly with respect to gross proceeds or gross income derived from the individual properties under management on behalf of the property owners. (Ch. 208 (S.B. 1350), Laws 2016) (AZ ¶ 231)

- **Arizona municipalities' tax on jet fuel limited to 10 million gallons per year**

Enacted Arizona legislation provides that for any municipal tax on jet fuel, the application of the tax is limited to amounts of not more than 10 million gallons purchased by each purchaser in each calendar year. The levy and measure of the tax must be structured to affirmatively exempt purchases in excess of 10 million gallons per purchaser per year. (H.B. 2064, Laws 2017, effective on the 91st day after adjournment of the first regular session) (AZ ¶ 235)

Arkansas

• Arkansas increases tax on candy and soft drinks, clarifies taxes on digital products and codes

Arkansas legislation effective January 1, 2018, increases the sales and use tax rate on candy and soft drinks, imposes sales and use tax on specified digital products and digital codes, and more. Details are as follows (Act 141 (H.B. 1162), Laws 2017):

Candy and soft drinks: Candy and soft drinks are excluded from the definition of "food and food ingredients," and thus will be subject to the full Arkansas sales and use tax rate instead of the 1.5% reduced rate applicable to food and food ingredients. "Candy" means a preparation of sugar, honey, or other natural or artificial sweeteners in combination with chocolate, fruits, nuts, or other ingredients or flavorings in the form of bars, drops, or pieces. "Candy" does not include a preparation that contains flour and requires no refrigeration. "Soft drink" means a nonalcoholic beverage that contains natural or artificial sweeteners. "Soft drink" does not include a beverage that contains milk or milk products, soy, rice, or similar milk substitutes, or that is greater than 50% of vegetable or fruit juice by volume. (AR ¶ 249)

Specified digital products; digital codes: Arkansas sales and use tax is imposed on sales of specified digital products sold to a purchaser who is an end user with the right of permanent or less than permanent use granted by the seller, regardless of whether the use is conditioned on continued payment by the purchaser, and on sales of digital codes, effective January 1, 2018. "Specified digital products" means digital audio works, digital audio-visual works, and digital books when they are transferred electronically. "Digital code" means a code that provides a purchaser with a right to obtain one or more specified digital products and that may be obtained by any means, including email or tangible means, regardless of its designation as a song code, video code, or book code. Definitions are also provided for the following terms: "digital audio works," "digital audio-visual works," "digital books," "end user," "ringtones," and "transferred electronically." (AR ¶ 246)

Sourcing: Concerning the sourcing of sales of specified digital products or digital codes for tax purposes, if none of the specific sourcing rules applies or if the seller lacks sufficient information, the location of the sale will be determined by the address from which the specified digital product or digital code was first available for transmission by the seller. (AR ¶ 246)

Instructional materials: The sales tax exemption for textbooks and instructional materials for public schools is amended to add that "instructional materials" includes specified digital products and a digital code that contains instructional information designed to be presented to students as part of a course of study. (AR ¶ 248)

Definitions: The definition of "tangible personal property" is amended to exclude specified digital products or a digital code. The definitions of "ancillary service" and "telecommunications service" for purposes of imposing sales tax does not include specified digital products or a digital code. (AR ¶ 246)

Conforming changes: The definitions of various sales tax terms, such as sale, gross receipts, sales price, and seller, and use tax terms, such as use, storage, purchase price, and purchaser, are amended to incorporate and apply to specified digital products and digital codes. Numerous sales and use tax provisions regarding imposition of tax, exemption, nexus, collection, liability, payment, reporting, vendors, contractors, registration, credit, and tax administration and enforcement for tangible personal property and/or services are amended to incorporate and apply to specified digital products and digital codes.

- **Incentive refund for nonprofit organizations repealed in Arkansas**

Arkansas has repealed the Nonprofit Incentive Act of 2005, which allowed qualified nonprofit organizations to receive refunds of Arkansas sales and use taxes as an incentive to locate in the state. (Act 208 (S.B. 160), Laws 2017, effective 90 days after adjournment of the 2017 Legislature) (AR ¶ 259)

- **Arkansas revises certain tax incentives**

Changes have been made to the Arkansas sales and use tax incentives under the Consolidated Incentive Act of 2003. Changes include:

— allowing an application for a retention tax credit for a qualified business only through June 30, 2017;

— allowing applications for increased refunds for major maintenance and improvement projects through June 30, 2022, and

— amendments to the sales tax refund for partial replacement and repair of certain machinery and equipment.

These amendments gradually increase the amount of refund available on the taxes levied until July 1, 2022, when qualified sales are exempt from sales tax. The procedures for claiming the refund of tax paid are also clarified. (Act 465 (S.B. 362), Laws 2017, effective March 13, 2017) (AR ¶ 259)

- **Exemption for aircraft sales amended in Arkansas**

The exemption from Arkansas sales tax for the sale of certain aircraft may be claimed by a seller in Arkansas that sells an aircraft that (1) has a certified maximum takeoff weight of more than 9,500 lbs. and (2) will be based outside Arkansas, even if the purchaser takes possession of the aircraft for the sole purpose of removing the aircraft from Arkansas under its own power. Formerly, the exemption was limited to aircraft sold by and to a nonresident who will base the aircraft outside Arkansas. (Act 595 (H.B. 2278), Laws 2017, effective March 23, 2017) (AR ¶ 248)

- **Arkansas amends exemption for vehicles purchased with federal funds**

An Arkansas sales and use tax exemption is allowed for new motor vehicles purchased with Federal (formerly, Urban Mass) Transit Administration funds. A former requirement for exemption, that the vehicles be purchased in lots of 10 vehicles or more and therefore are sold at fleet price by the manufacturer, has been deleted. (Act 661 (H.B. 1649), Laws 2017) (AR ¶ 248)

- **Exemption for beer kegs expanded in Arkansas**

A sale, lease, or rental (formerly, just sale) of a keg that is used to sell beer wholesale by a wholesale manufacturer of beer is exempt from Arkansas sales tax. (Act 672 (H.B. 2126), Laws 2017) (AR ¶ 248)

- **Arkansas clarifies exemption for sales by charities**

The statute that denies an Arkansas sales tax exemption for a charitable organization if sales by the organization compete with sales made by a for-profit business has been amended. A sale by a charitable organization does not compete with a sale by a for-profit business if the following three requirements are met:

(1) the sales transaction is conducted by a member of the charitable organization and not by a franchisee or licensee;

(2) all the proceeds derived from the sales transaction go to the charitable organization; and

(3) the sales transaction is not a continuing one and is held not more than three times a year.

A fourth requirement, that the dominant motive of a majority of purchasers was the making of a charitable contribution, with the purchase being merely incidental and secondary to the dominant purpose of making a gift to the charitable organization, has been deleted. (Act 665 (H.B. 1221), Laws 2017, effective on the first day of the calendar quarter following 90 days after adjournment of the 2017 Legislature) (AR ¶ 248)

California

• California medical cannabis patients and caregivers may claim exemption for marijuana products

The passage of Proposition 64 (The Control, Regulate and Tax Adult Use of Marijuana Act) at the November 8, 2016, election, exempts certain sales of medical marijuana from sales and use tax. Sales of medical cannabis to those who have a medical marijuana identification card (MMIC) issued on a county-by-county basis by the California Department of Public Health (CDPH) and a valid government-issued identification card are now exempt from sales and use tax. Consumers can obtain the CDPH-issued cards at their county health department at a cost that varies by county. A paper recommendation from a physician is not sufficient to qualify for this sales tax exemption. The county-issued MMIC will have the State of California seal and indicate whether the card holder is a "patient" or a "caregiver." The card will also contain the patient's or primary caregiver's photo, a nine-digit ID number, a CDPH website to verify the ID number, an expiration date, and the name of the county that issued the card. Cards are valid for the duration of the physician recommendation or up to one year, at which time the card must be renewed. Retailers should retain the purchaser's nine-digit ID number and expiration date, along with the related sales invoice or other record of sale, to support the exempt sale.

Exempted products include medical cannabis, medical cannabis concentrate, edible medical cannabis products, and topical cannabis as these terms are defined in Business and Professions Code Sec. 19300.5. Retailers should not collect sales tax reimbursement on qualifying exempt sales of medical marijuana. Retailers should claim a deduction on their sales and use tax returns for their qualifying exempt medical marijuana sales. Retailers may verify the validity of a nine-digit ID number on the CDPH website.

Sales of recreational marijuana will not start until January 1, 2018. Such sales will be subject to sales tax and an excise tax. A cultivator tax will also apply to marijuana beginning on that date. (Proposition 64, approved by the voters on November 8, 2016; *News Release 92-16-G,* California State Board of Equalization, November 17, 2016) (CA ¶ 265)

• Cannabis dispensaries may make payments by other than EFT in California

Before January 1, 2022, a person issued a seller's permit for a place of business that is a "dispensary," as defined in the Medical Cannabis Regulation and Safety Act, may remit California sales and use tax amounts due for retail sales at the dispensary by a means other than electronic funds transfer (EFT). During this period, a dispensary is not subject to the general requirement to remit amounts due by EFT if its estimated tax liability averages $10,000 or more per month. (Ch. 811 (A.B. 821), Laws 2016, effective January 1, 2017) (CA ¶ 267)

• California simplifies refund procedure for sales and use taxes, among others

For purposes of a variety of taxes, surcharges, and fees administered by the California State Board of Equalization, a claim for refund involving a case in which the amount of tax, surcharge, or fee determined has not been paid in full will be deemed to be a timely filed claim for refund with all subsequent payments applied to that determination. The changes are applicable to claims filed on or after January 1, 2017. (Ch. 98 (A.B. 1856), Laws 2016) (CA ¶ 274)

• Disaster extensions authorized for various California taxes

In the case of a disaster, the California State Board of Equalization (BOE) is authorized to extend the time for making any report or return or paying any BOE-administered tax or fee for a period not to exceed three months. This provision is applicable to the Sales and Use Tax (SUT) Law, the Motor Vehicle Fuel Tax Law, the Use Fuel Tax Law, the Cigarette and Tobacco Products Tax Law, the Alcoholic Beverage Tax Law, the Timber Yield Tax Law, the Energy Resources Surcharge Law, the Emergency Telephone Users Surcharge Act, the Hazardous Substances Tax Law, the Integrated Waste Management Fee Law, the Oil Spill Response, Prevention, and Administration Fees Law, the Underground Storage Tank Maintenance Fee Law, the Fee Collection Procedures Law, and the Diesel Fuel Tax Law. The extension may be granted at any time provided a request for relief is filed with the BOE within or before the period at issue. "Disaster" is defined as fire, flood, storm, tidal wave, earthquake, or similar public calamity, regardless of whether the disaster results from natural causes. (Ch. 257 (A.B. 1559), Laws 2016) (CA ¶ 267)

• California Supreme Court clarifies OTC liability for transient occupancy tax

Online travel companies (OTCs) are not operators of hotels within the meaning of the San Diego ordinance that imposes a local transient occupancy tax and, as such, the OTCs are not liable for the tax. Under the San Diego ordinance, in a merchant model type of transaction, a hotel operator is liable for a 6% tax on the wholesale price plus any additional amount for room rental the operator requires the OTC to charge the visitor under rate parity provisions of contracts between hotels and OTCs. (*In re Transient Occupancy Tax Cases,* California Supreme Court, No. S218400, December 12, 2016, CCH CALIFORNIA TAX REPORTS, ¶ 406-598) (CA ¶ 265)

Colorado

• Colorado exempts machinery for recycling

The Colorado sales and use tax exemption for machinery and machine tools used in manufacturing has been expanded to include equipment used for the processing of recovered materials. "Recovered materials" means those materials that have been separated, diverted, or removed from the waste stream for the purpose of remanufacturing, reuse, or recycling. To qualify under the new provision of the exemption, the business purchasing the machinery must be listed in the Department of Public Health and Environment's inventory of recyclers and solid waste processors. (Ch. 258 (S.B. 124), Laws 2016, applicable to sales after July 1, 2016) (CO ¶ 729)

• Exemption for residential energy sources clarified in Colorado

Effective June 10, 2016, the Colorado sales and use tax exemption for residential uses of electricity, coal, wood, gas, fuel oil, and coke applies when energy sources are resold or sold to persons who are not occupants of the residence. Under the previous law, the exemption only applied to energy sources sold to occupants of residences, and only when the energy sources would not be resold. The new provisions apply the exemption to all sales of energy sources for residential use, exempting from taxation energy sources that are purchased for a multifamily residential property and resold to individual resident households. Additionally, "residential use" is now presumed when an energy source is sold at a residential utility rate. (Ch. 315 (H.B. 1457), Laws 2016) (CO ¶ 278)

• Food for retirement communities' meal plans exempt in Colorado

Applicable July 1, 2016, food purchased and provided as part of a meal plan to residents of a Colorado retirement community is exempt from sales and use tax as food for domestic home consumption. Additionally, the packaging used in presenting the food to a resident of a retirement community is exempt from sales and use tax under the existing exemption for food packaging. (Ch. 205 (H.B. 1187), Laws 2016) (CO ¶ 278)

Connecticut

• **Connecticut adds sales and use tax changes to implement biennial budget**

Legislation regarding the 2016-2017 budget includes a number of Connecticut sales and use tax provisions, as follows (Act 3 (S.B. 502), Laws 2016, effective June 2, 2016, except as otherwise indicated):

— *Parking fees at government lots:* An exemption is enacted from Connecticut sales and use tax for non-metered motor vehicle parking in seasonal lots with 30 or more spaces operated by the United States, the state of Connecticut, or its political subdivisions and municipally-owned lots with 30 or more spaces. (CT ¶ 293)

— *Feminine hygiene products and diapers:* Effective July 1, 2018, and applicable to sales occurring on and after that date, an exemption is enacted for feminine hygiene products and disposable or reusable diapers. (CT ¶ 293)

— *Local option admissions surcharge:* A municipality is authorized, by ordinance, to impose a surcharge on admission charges to events held at facilities located in the municipality. The surcharge may be up to 5% of the admissions charge, except for the surcharge on events held at Dunkin' Donuts Park in Hartford, which may be up to 10%.

Municipalities are prohibited from imposing a surcharge on: (1) events from which all proceeds go exclusively to a federally tax-exempt organization, provided that organization actively engages in and assumes the financial risk of presenting the event; and (2) pari-mutuel or off-track betting facilities already subject to a local admissions tax. Any such municipal ordinance that is adopted under this provision may exclude additional events or facilities from the local option admissions surcharge. (CT ¶ 295)

— *Admissions tax exemptions:* Admissions tax exemptions are enacted for any event presented at the Dunkin' Donuts Park in Hartford on and after July 1, 2017, and any athletic event presented by a member team of the Atlantic League of Professional Baseball at the New Britain Stadium. (CT ¶ 293)

District of Columbia

• **DC's vehicle parking and storage tax may be increased**

The FY 2016 District of Columbia permanent budget bill may increase the tax rate for parking and motor vehicle storage services to 22% (currently 18%) after October 1, 2017, but only if estimated revenues are not sufficient to implement certain obligations. (Act 21-127 (D.C.B. 21-283), Laws 2015) (DC ¶ 324)

• **Exemptions for feminine hygiene products and diapers added in DC**

Washington D.C. has enacted sales tax exemptions for sales of feminine hygiene products and diapers. "Feminine hygiene products" mean sanitary napkins, sanitary towels, tampons, menstrual cups, or sanitary pads. A "diaper" is an absorbent incontinence product that is washable or disposable and worn by a person, regardless of age or sex, who cannot control bladder or bowel movements. (Act 21-557 (D.C.B. 21-696), Laws 2015, approved December 6, 2016) (DC ¶ 323)

Florida

• **Florida amends several sales and use tax provisions**

Various Florida sales and use tax credits, incentives, and exemptions are amended as follows (H.B. 33a, Laws 2015, effective July 1, 2015, except as otherwise noted):

Community contributions tax credit program: The sunset date for the community contribution tax credit is extended from June 30, 2016, to June 30, 2018. The total amount of tax credits that may be granted is $18.4 million for the 2015-2016 fiscal year, $21.4 million for the 2016-2017 fiscal year, and $21.4 million for the 2017-2018 fiscal year. (FL ¶ 345)

Business incentives: Effective January 1, 2016, a business that entered into a contract with the Department of Economic Opportunity for a project between January 1, 2012, and July 1, 2015, and the contract is still active within the boundaries of an enterprise zone as they existed on May 1, 2015, may apply for the following incentives:

— the sales and use tax refund for building materials used in the rehabilitation of real property located in an enterprise zone;

— the sales and use tax refund for business property used in an enterprise zone;

— the sales and use tax exemption for electrical energy used in an enterprise zone; or

— the enterprise zone jobs credit against sales and use tax.

Although the Florida Enterprise Zone Act ended on December 31, 2015, these incentives are treated as if they do not so expire, allowing businesses to apply for them for an additional three years, provided they meet the criteria. These provisions sunset December 31, 2018. (FL ¶ 345)

Agricultural exemptions: For purposes of the exemptions for sales of livestock by producers, sales of disinfectants and insecticides and similar products used to protect livestock, and sales of livestock feed, the definition of "livestock" is amended to include all aquaculture products, as defined. Also, the definition of "agricultural production," for purposes of the exemption for the sale of power farm equipment used in agricultural production, is amended to include the storage of raw products on a farm. (FL ¶ 338)

Power farm equipment: The exemption for the sale of power farm equipment used in agricultural production is amended to include irrigation equipment and replacement parts and accessories for power farm equipment or irrigation equipment. , an exemption is enacted for that portion of the sales price below $20,000 for a trailer weighing 12,000 pounds or less and purchased by a farmer for exclusive use in agricultural production or to transport farm products from his or her farm to the place where the farmer transfers ownership of the farm products to another. This exemption is not forfeited by using a trailer to transport the farmer's farm equipment. The exemption is inapplicable to the lease or rental of a trailer. In addition, the exemption for agricultural items is expanded to include stakes used by a farmer to support plants during agricultural production. (FL ¶ 338)

Gun club membership: Admissions to and membership fees for gun clubs are exempt from the sales and use tax on admissions. For purposes of the exemption, "gun club" is defined as an organization whose primary purpose is to offer its members access to one or more shooting ranges for target or skeet shooting. (FL ¶ 338)

Boat repairs: The maximum amount of sales and use tax that may be collected on each repair of a boat in Florida is capped at $60,000. (FL ¶ 338)

Prepaid college meal plans: The existing exemption for prepaid meal plans purchased from a college or other institution of higher learning by students currently enrolled at that college or other institution of higher learning is amended to specify that prepaid meal plans that contain a defined number of meals or a defined number of dollar equivalencies qualify for the exemption. However, the taxability of the dollar equivalencies of the prepaid meal plans is determined on the plan's use, and tax is due when the dollar equivalencies are used to make a purchase if that purchase is otherwise subject to sales and use tax. For these purposes, "dollar equivalencies" include university-specific dollars on a declining balance, such as "flex bucks" or "dining bucks." (FL ¶ 338)

School support organizations: In lieu of collecting sales and use tax from the purchaser, school support organizations may pay tax to their suppliers on the cost price of food, drink, and supplies necessary to serve such food and drink when the food, drink, and supplies are purchased for resale. "School support organization" is defined as an organization whose sole purpose is to raise funds to support extracurricular activities at public, parochial, or nonprofit schools that teach students in grades K through 12. (FL ¶ 342)

Tax holiday—certain textbooks: From July 1, 2015 through June 30, 2016, sales and use tax may not be collected on the retail sale of textbooks and instructional materials that are required or recommended for use in a course offered by a public postsecondary educational institution or a nonpublic postsecondary educational institution that is eligible to participate in a tuition assistance program. A student must provide qualifying information to the vendor. (FL ¶ 338)

Active duty military motor vehicles: The importation of a motor vehicle purchased and used for six months or more in a foreign country by an active member of the United States Armed Forces or his or her spouse is exempt from sales and use tax when the vehicle is imported, registered, or titled in Florida for personal use by the member or his or her spouse. Proof of the active status of the member, and, when applicable, proof of the spouse's relationship to the member, must be provided when the vehicle is titled and registered in Florida. (FL ¶ 338)

Prepaid calling arrangements: The definition of "prepaid calling arrangement" is amended to provide that the term means:

— a right to use communications services, other than mobile communications services, for which a separately stated price must be paid in advance, which are sold at retail in predetermined units that decline in number with use on a predetermined basis, and which consist exclusively of telephone calls originated by using an access number, authorization code, or other means that may be manually, electronically, or otherwise entered; or

— a right to use mobile communications services that must be paid for in advance and are sold at retail in predetermined units that expire or decline in number on a predetermined basis if: (1) the purchaser's right to use mobile communications services terminates upon all purchased units' expiring or being exhausted unless the purchaser pays for additional units; (2) the purchaser is not required to purchase additional units; and (3) any right of the purchaser to use units to obtain communications services other than mobile communications services is limited to services that are provided to or through the same handset or other electronic device that is used by the purchaser to access mobile communications services.

Predetermined units may be quantified as amounts of usage, time, money, or a combination of these or other means of measurement. (FL ¶ 336)

Therapeutic veterinary diets: Sales of therapeutic veterinary diets specifically formulated to aid in the management of illness and disease of a diagnosed health disorder in an animal that are only available from a licensed veterinarian are exempt from sales and use tax. (FL ¶ 338)

Community contribution tax credit: The sunset date of the community contribution tax credit is extended from June 30, 2015, to June 30, 2016. (FL ¶ 346)

School books and lunches: Prepaid meal plans purchased from a college or other institution of higher learning by students currently enrolled at that college or other institution of higher learning are exempt from sales and use tax. "Prepaid meal plans" are defined as advance payment to a college or institution of higher learning for the provision of a defined quantity of units that must expire at the end of an academic term, cannot be refunded to the student upon expiration, and that may only be exchanged for food. (FL ¶ 338)

Motor vehicle child restraints: A sales and use tax exemption is enacted for the sale of a child restraint system or booster seat for use in a motor vehicle. (FL ¶ 338)

Youth bicycle helmets: The sale of a bicycle helmet marketed for use by youth is exempt from sales and use tax. (FL ¶ 338)

Private-label credit card programs: A dealer may claim a credit for or obtain a refund of tax remitted by the dealer on the unpaid balance of consumer accounts or receivables found to be worthless or uncollectible provided:

— the accounts or receivables have been charged off as bad debt on the lender's books and records on or after January 1, 2014;

— a credit was not previously claimed and a refund was not previously allowed on any portion of the accounts or receivables; and

— the credit or refund is claimed within 12 months after the month in which the bad debt has been charged off by the lender for federal income tax purposes.

A "private-label credit card" is defined as a charge card or credit card that carries, refers to, or is branded with the name or logo of a dealer and can be used for purchases from that dealer or for purchases from the dealer's affiliates or franchises. (FL ¶ 345)

• Tax benefits available to out-of-state companies responding to disasters or emergencies in Florida

Out-of-state businesses operating in Florida solely to perform emergency-related work are not considered to have established a level of presence that would require the business to register, file, and remit state and local taxes or fees or be subject to any registration, licensing, or filing in the state, effective March 24, 2016. Activity conducted by such businesses during the disaster-related period must be disregarded with respect to any state or local tax on net or gross income or receipts, including any filing requirements for such taxes and specifically any filing required for a consolidated group. Taxes and registrations expressly subject to these provisions include: reemployment assistance tax; state or local professional or occupational licensing requirements or related fees; local business taxes; taxes on the operation of commercial vehicles; corporate income tax; and tangible personal property tax and use tax on certain equipment. (Ch. 99 (H.B. 1133), Laws 2016) (FL ¶ 344)

• Florida Supreme Court upholds tax on Internet sales by florists

A subsection of a Florida statute that imposes a sales and use tax on florists was not violative of the dormant Commerce Clause of the U.S. Constitution as applied to the taxpayer's Internet sales of flowers, gift baskets, and other tangible personal property. Moreover, the statute did not violate the Due Process Clause in that the taxpayer's activities had a substantial nexus to Florida. *(Florida Department of Revenue v. American Business USA Corp.,* Florida Supreme Court, No. SC14-2404, May 26, 2016, CCH FLORIDA TAX REPORTS, ¶ 206-181)

Georgia

• Transportation taxes increased in Atlanta

Georgia voters in Atlanta and Fulton County responded "Yes" to the following ballot questions posed in the election held on November 8, 2016 (Unofficial Results, Fulton County Board of Registration and Elections, November 10, 2016):

— *City of Atlanta Transportation-Special Purpose Local Option Sales and Use Tax (T-SPLOST) Referendum:* Shall an additional 0.4 percent sales tax be collected in the City of Atlanta for 5 years for the purpose of transportation improvements and congestion reduction? ("Yes," 67.91%)

— *Metropolitan Atlanta Rapid Transit Authority (MARTA) Sales and Use Tax Referendum:* Shall an additional sales tax of one-half percent be collected in the City of Atlanta for the purpose of significantly expanding and enhancing MARTA transit service in Atlanta? ("Yes," 71.34%)

• **Georgia extends hunger-related exemptions**

Georgia legislation extends by five years, to June 30, 2021, the sales and use tax exemption for sales of food and food ingredients to a qualified food bank. The exemption was previously scheduled to sunset on June 30, 2016. The legislation also adds the requirement that when a taxpayer applies for the exemption or renews it annually, they must electronically submit to the Georgia Department of Revenue the total number of clients served in the previous calendar year, the total pounds of food donated by retailers, and the total amount of exempt purchases made in the preceding year.

In addition, the legislation extends by one year, to June 30, 2021, the sales and use tax exemption for the use of food and food ingredients donated to a qualified nonprofit agency and used for hunger relief purposes. The exemption was previously scheduled to sunset on June 30, 2020. (Act 602 (H.B. 763), Laws 2016) (GA ¶ 353)

• **Job training organizations get temporary Georgia exemption for purchases**

A temporary sales and use tax exemption is available for sales of tangible personal property and services to a qualified job training organization. This exemption begins July 1, 2017, and ends June 30, 2020, and requires a qualifying job training organization to obtain an exemption determination letter from the state revenue commissioner to claim it. "Qualified job training organization" means an organization that:

(1) is located in Georgia;

(2) is exempt from income taxation under IRC Sec.501(c)(3);

(3) specializes in the retail sale of donated items;

(4) provides job training and employment services to individuals with workplace disadvantages and disabilities (such as re-entry citizens released from incarceration, persons with disabilities, and veterans); and

(5) uses a majority of its revenues for job training and placement programs.

The exemption applies only to state-level sales and use tax, expressly excluding any local sales and use taxes. A qualified job training organization that is granted the exemption must provide the Georgia Department of Revenue an annual report that includes information such as the number of individuals trained in the program, the number of individuals employed by the organization after receiving training, and the number of individuals employed in full-time positions outside the organization after training. (Act 571 (S.B. 379), Laws 2016) (GA ¶ 353)

Hawaii

• **Exemption for prescription drugs excludes marijuana in Hawaii**

Hawaii legislation amends the general excise tax exemption for amounts received by a licensed hospital, infirmary, medical clinic, health care facility, pharmacy, or practitioner for selling prescription drugs to provide that the exemption does not apply to sales of medical marijuana or manufactured medical marijuana products. (Act 230 (H.B. 2707), Laws 2016) (HI ¶ 368)

Idaho

• **Idaho extends exemption for vehicles sold to nonresidents**

Effective July 1, 2017, sales to nonresidents of motor vehicles, trailers, vessels, all-terrain vehicles (ATVs), utility type vehicles (UTVs), specialty off-highway vehicles (SOHVs), motorcycles intended for off-road use, and snowmobiles, for use outside Idaho, are exempt from Idaho sales and use tax, even though delivery is made in Idaho, provided that the vehicles or vessels are not used in Idaho more than 90 days in any 12-month period. The time limitation has been extended from 60 to 90 days. Other requirements for this exemption provide that the vehicles or vessels are taken from the delivery point in Idaho directly to an out-of-state point, are registered and titled immediately in the other state, and are not required to be titled in Idaho. (Ch. 53 (H.B. 32), Laws 2017) (ID ¶ 383)

- **Exemption for certain hand tools expanded in Idaho**

Hand tools, regardless of cost, may qualify for an Idaho sales tax exemption, effective July 1, 2016, when directly used in:

    (1) production of radio and television broadcasts,

    (2) production of certain free newspapers,

    (3) irrigation for agricultural production purposes, or

    (4) logging.

Formerly, hand tools with a unit price of $100 or less were specifically excluded from the exemptions for equipment directly used in the above activities. (Ch. 9 (H.B. 347), Laws 2016) (ID ¶ 383)

- **Idaho farming exemption expanded**

The Idaho sales and use tax exemption for tangible personal property directly used in a farming operation is amended to include items directly used or consumed in or during the removal of crops and other agricultural products from storage, effective March 17, 2016. (H.B. 386, Laws 2016) (ID ¶ 383)

- **Provisions regarding sales of park model RVs clarified in Idaho**

Effective July 1, 2017, the sales price of a new park model recreational vehicle shall include 100% of the sales price. Charges by a dealer for set up or transportation of a park model recreational vehicle shall be included in the sales price. Also, an allowance on merchandise accepted in payment of other merchandise shall not apply to the sale of a new park model recreational vehicle. The production exemption from sales tax shall not apply to sales of or repairs to a park model recreational vehicle as defined in Sec. 49-117. (H.B. 156, Laws 2017) (ID ¶ 383)

- **Paddleboards excluded from exemption for vessels sold to nonresidents for use outside Idaho**

Effective July 1, 2016, the Idaho sales tax exemption for vessels that are sold to nonresidents for use outside Idaho does not apply to sales of paddleboards, canoes, kayaks, inflatable boats or similar watercraft (formerly, canoes, kayaks, or inflatable boats) unless they are sold together with a motor. (Ch. 11 (H.B. 348), Laws 2016) (ID ¶ 383)

- **Idaho adds exemptions for wildfire aircraft used under government contract**

An Idaho sales and use tax exemption has been enacted, effective June 30, 2016 for the sale, lease, purchase, or use of fixed-wing aircraft primarily used as an air tactical group supervisor platform under contract with a governmental entity for wildfire activity, as well as for repair and replacement materials and parts in connection with the remodeling, repair, or maintenance of such aircraft. (Ch. 326 (H.B. 540), Laws 2016) (ID ¶ 383)

Illinois

- **Illinois exempts feminine hygiene products**

Beginning January 1, 2017, menstrual pads, tampons, and menstrual cups are exempt from Illinois sales and use tax. (P.A. 99-855 (S.B. 2746), Laws 2016) (IL ¶ 398)

• **Illinois taxes certain prescribed cancer treatment devices**

Effective August 19, 2016, Illinois imposes a 1% tax rate on sales of prescribed cancer treatment devices that are classified as Class III medical devices by the U.S. Food and Drug Administration (FDA), as well as any accessories and components related to those devices. (P.A. 99-858 (S.B. 3047), Laws 2015) (IL ¶ 399)

Indiana

• **Coins, bullion, and legal tender exempted in Indiana**

Indiana has enacted a sales and use tax exemption for the sale, lease and rental of storage for coins, bullion and legal tender, effective July 1, 2016. For a sale to qualify as exempt, the coins and bullion must be permitted investments by an individual retirement account or by an individually-directed account. Also enacted is an exemption for the sales of qualified precious metals bullion and currency by sellers outside Indiana that receive a 28-day temporary registration from the secretary of state. The temporary registration allows the foreign seller to make sales at trade fairs or coin shows when the seller is not already authorized to conduct business in Indiana. Foreign sellers will submit a $35 fee when applying for temporary registration.

"Precious metals bullion" means bars, ingots, or commemorative medallions of gold, silver, platinum, palladium, or a combination of these materials for which the value of the metal depends on its content and not its form. "Currency" means a coin made of gold, silver, or other metal or paper money that is, or has been, used as legal tender. (H.B. 1046, Laws 2016) (IN ¶ 413)

Iowa

• **Iowa expands exemptions for computers, machinery, and equipment**

Iowa has enacted legislation, effective March 21, 2016, modifying the sales tax exemptions related to the purchase of items used in manufacturing and other activities. The exemption for the sale or rental of certain computers, machinery and equipment, including materials used to construct them, now also includes replacement parts and supplies. The items must be directly and primarily used for any of the following:

— processing by a manufacturer,

— to maintain the integrity of the product or unique environmental conditions,

— in research and development of new products or processes, or

— recycling.

Items may also be pollution-control equipment, or computers used in processing or storage of data or information by an insurance company, financial institution, or commercial enterprise. (Ch. 1007 (H.F. 2433), Laws 2016) (IA ¶ 428)

• **Tax breaks for out-of-state disaster assistance providers added in Iowa**

Iowa legislation provides certain tax exemptions for out-of-state businesses and nonresident employees performing critical disaster relief work in Iowa during a state emergency declared by the governor or a presidential declaration of a major disaster, generally effective April 21, 2016. A disaster response period begins 10 calendar days before the declared emergency and extends for a period of 60 days after the end of the disaster or emergency. Details are as follows (Ch. 1095 (S.F. 2306), Laws 2016):

Sales and use tax provisions: A sales and use tax exemption and an equipment tax exemption are enacted for tangible personal property or equipment purchased outside Iowa and brought into the state to aid in disaster relief during a disaster response period, as long as the property or equipment does not remain in Iowa after the disaster response period has ended. Additionally, qualified out-of-state disaster relief companies are not required to obtain a sales or use tax permit, collect and remit sales and use tax, or make and file applicable sales or use tax returns.

Registration and income tax provisions: An out-of-state business that conducts operations within Iowa in response to a declared state disaster or emergency is not considered to have established a level of presence that would subject that business to any state or local registration, license, or similar authorization as a condition of doing business or engaging in an occupation in Iowa. An out-of-state employee will not be considered to have established residency or a presence in the state that would require that person to file and pay income taxes or to be subjected to tax withholding or to file and pay any other state or local tax or fee during the disaster response period. Further, a business will not be required to file income taxes or to withhold and remit income tax from out-of-state employees. An out-of-state business will also not need to be included in a consolidated return and will not increase the amount of net income that the out-of-state business allocates and apportions to Iowa. The income and withholding exemptions are applicable to taxable years beginning on or after January 1, 2016.

Property tax provisions: A property tax exemption is enacted as well for property of an out-of-state business that conducts operations within Iowa solely for the purpose of performing disaster or emergency-related work during a disaster response period. (IA ¶ 434)

Kansas

• Kansas waives taxes for repairing or replacing agricultural fences destroyed by wildfires

Kansas sales and use tax on sales of tangible personal property and services purchased during calendar years 2017 and 2018 necessary to reconstruct, repair, or replace any fence used to enclose land devoted to agricultural use that was destroyed by wildfires that occurred during calendar years 2016 and 2017 is waived through an exemption and refund program.

Any person who contracts for such reconstruction, repair, or replacement must get an exemption certificate from the Kansas Department of Revenue for the project involved. The exemption certificate will allow the person or contractor to purchase materials and lease machinery and equipment for such a project. In addition, persons or contractors who perform such work are required to provide the certificate number to all suppliers, and those suppliers are required to execute invoices with that certificate number. Upon completion of the project, the contractor must provide to the person that obtained the exemption certificate a sworn statement, on a form to be provided by the Director of Taxation, that all purchases made were entitled to the exemption.

Under the refund program, individuals who purchase fencing materials to be used in the reconstruction of fences surrounding agricultural land on or after January 1, 2017 through December 31, 2018, may apply for a sales tax refund. Those individuals will need a sales receipt or invoice that shows the amount of sales tax paid on the purchases. (H.B. 2387, Laws 2017) (KS ¶ 443)

Kentucky

• Kentucky restricts Tourism Development Act incentives

A tourism development project is not eligible for a sales tax incentive under the Kentucky Tourism Development Act if it includes material that is lewd, offensive, or deemed to have a negative impact on the tourism industry in the state. (H.B. 390, Laws 2017) (KY ¶ 465)

• Credit for aircraft fuel extended in Kentucky

The credit against Kentucky sales and use tax for certificated air carriers has been extended to include purchases of aircraft fuel by those that contract with at least one other certificated air carrier for the transportation of persons, property or mail. On or after the effective date, such taxpayer is entitled to the credit against the sales and use tax paid during a fiscal year on all purchases of aircraft fuel in excess of $1 million.

Previously, the credit did not include purchases of aircraft fuel under such contracts. (H.B. 368, Laws 2017, effective 90 days after adjournment of the legislative session) (KY ¶ 465)

• Kentucky constitutional exemption for charities applies to use tax as well as property tax

The Kentucky Court of Appeals has ruled that Sec. 170, Ky. Const., exempts an institution of purely public charity from the use tax imposed under KRS Sec. 139.310. Previously, the exemption provided by Sec. 170 was held to be limited to the property tax. (*Interstate Gas Supply, Inc. v. Finance and Administration Cabinet,* Kentucky Court of Appeals, No. 2013-CA-001766-MR, February 26, 2016, CCH KENTUCKY TAX REPORTS, ¶ 203-142) (KY ¶ 458)

Louisiana

• Louisiana temporarily increases state sales and use tax rate on sales, leases, and services

The Louisiana state sales and use tax rate on sales and leases of tangible personal property and sales of services is temporarily increased by 1%, from 4% to 5%, for the period beginning April 1, 2016, through June 30, 2018 (27 months). However, the temporary additional tax expired on July 1, 2016, for manufacturing equipment and machinery.

A new provision lists 65 items that are exempt or excluded from the 1% additional tax, including food for home consumption, prescription drugs, gasoline and other motor fuels, and materials for further processing (Sec. 321.1(F)). The transactions that are exempt from the 1% additional tax do not completely match the transactions that are exempt from the current 4% tax. (Act 26 (H.B. 62), Laws 2016, First Extraordinary Session; see also *Publication R-1002A,* Louisiana Department of Revenue, March 29, 2016, available on the Department of Revenue's website at **http://revenue.louisiana.gov/Publications/R-1002A%203-29-16.pdf**) (LA ¶ 474)

• List of allowable Louisiana sales and use tax exemptions temporarily limited

A new law enacts an exclusive list of over 30 transactions that will be the only allowable exemptions and exclusions from Louisiana state sales and use tax for the period April 1, 2016, through July 1, 2018. The exemptions include food for home consumption, prescription drugs, and materials for further processing. This list of exemptions will supersede and control over any conflicting provision during this period. (Act 25 (H.B. 61), Laws 2016, First Extraordinary Session) (LA ¶ 473)

• Louisiana enacts click-through and affiliate nexus for remote sales

Click-through and affiliate nexus provisions have been added to the Louisiana sales and use tax laws to require certain remote dealers to collect state tax on sales made in Louisiana, applicable to tax periods beginning on and after April 1, 2016. The provisions for establishing a person as a dealer for sales and use tax purposes may not be used in determining whether the person is liable for payment of Louisiana income and franchise taxes. Details are as follows (Act 22 (H.B. 30), Laws 2016, First Extraordinary Session):

Click-through nexus: The definition of a "dealer" for tax collection purposes is expanded to include any person soliciting business through an independent contractor or other representative pursuant to an agreement with a Louisiana resident or business under which the resident or business, for a commission, referral fee, or other consideration, directly or indirectly, refers potential customers to the seller, whether by link on an Internet website, an in-person oral presentation, telemarketing, or otherwise. (LA ¶ 471)

Affiliate nexus, substantial ownership interest: The law also expands the definition of a "dealer" to include any person who:

(1) Sells the same or a substantially similar line of products as a Louisiana retailer under the same or substantially similar business name, using the same trademarks, service marks, or trade names that are the same or substantially similar to those used by the Louisiana retailer.

(2) Solicits business and develops and maintains a market in Louisiana through an agent, salesman, independent contractor, solicitor, or other representative pursuant to an agreement with a Louisiana resident or business, under which the affiliated agent, for a commission, referral fee, or other consideration, engages in activities in Louisiana that benefits the person's development or maintenance of a market for its goods or services in the state. Such activities of the affiliated agent include referral of potential customers to the person, either directly or indirectly, whether by link on an Internet website or otherwise.

Also, a person is presumed to be a dealer if it holds a substantial ownership interest, directly or through a subsidiary, in a retailer maintaining sales locations in Louisiana, or is owned, in whole or in substantial part, by a retailer maintaining sales locations in Louisiana or by a parent or subsidiary thereof. "Substantial ownership interest" means affiliated persons with respect to each other where one of such persons has an ownership interest of more than five percent, whether direct or indirect, in the other, or where an ownership interest of more than five percent, whether direct or indirect, is held in each of such persons by another person or by a group of other persons that are affiliated persons with respect to each other. (LA ¶ 471)

Separate local use tax return: A taxpayer may elect to file a separate local use tax return with the parish tax collector or central collection commission and remit all local taxes due. If a dealer has withheld and remitted tax for a specific purchase from a taxpayer who subsequently files a paid local use tax return, the taxpayer may file an annual use tax refund request with the Department of Revenue in a manner to be determined by the Department, which may include electronic filing. (LA ¶ 477)

Administration: Persons who meet the definition of a dealer above must file sales and use tax returns and remittances through the electronic filing options.

If the U.S. Congress enacts legislation authorizing states to require a remote seller to collect sales and use taxes on taxable transactions, the federal law will preempt the provisions of the Louisiana law. (LA ¶ 471)

• New exemptions enacted in Louisiana

Effective July 1, 2016, the following transactions are exempt from the Louisiana sales tax imposed by Sec. 47:302 (2% rate) and Sec. 321.1 (new additional 1% rate) (Act 12 (H.B. 51), Laws 2016, Second Extraordinary Session):

(1) Sales of room rentals by a camp or retreat facility owned by a nonprofit organization;

(2) Sales of room rentals by a homeless shelter;

(3) Sales, leases, and rentals of tangible personal property and sales of services necessary to operate free hospitals;

(4) Sales, leases, or rentals of tangible personal property to Boys State of Louisiana, Inc. and Girls State of Louisiana, Inc.;

(5) Sales by nonprofit entities that sell donated goods;

(6) Isolated or occasional sales of tangible personal property by a person not engaged in such business;

(7) Sales of human tissue transplants;

(8) Sales of food items by a youth-serving organization chartered by the U.S. Congress;

(9) Sales and donations of tangible personal property by food banks;

(10) Sales or purchases of fire-fighting equipment by volunteer fire departments;

(11) Sales to, and leases, rentals, and use of educational materials and equipment used for classroom instruction by parochial and private elementary and secondary schools that comply with the court order from the *Dodd Brumfield* decision and IRC Sec. 501(c)(3);

(12) Sales by parochial and private elementary and secondary schools that comply with the court order from the *Dodd Brumfield* decision and IRC Sec. 501(c)(3);

(13) Certain admissions to athletic and entertainment events held for or by an elementary or secondary school and membership fees or dues of nonprofit, civic associations;

(14) Sales or use of materials used directly in the collection of blood;

(15) Sales or use of apheresis kits and leukoreduction filters;

(16) Sales or use of orthotic devices, prosthetic devices, hearing aids, eyeglasses, contact lenses, and wheelchairs prescribed by physicians, optometrists, or licensed chiropractors used exclusively by the patient for personal use;

(17) Sales or use of ostomy, colostomy, and ileostomy devices and equipment;

(18) Sales or use of adaptive driving equipment and motor vehicle modifications prescribed for personal use;

(19) Sales of meals by educational institutions, medical facilities, mental institutions, and occasional meals furnished by educational, religious, or medical organizations;

(20) Purchase or rental of kidney dialysis machines, parts, materials, and supplies for home use under a physician's prescription;

(21) Sales of admissions to entertainment events by Little Theater organizations;

(22) Sales of admissions to musical performances sponsored by nonprofit organizations;

(23) Sales of admissions to entertainment events sponsored by domestic nonprofit charitable, religious, and educational organizations;

(24) Sales of admissions, parking fees, and sales of tangible personal property at events sponsored by domestic, civic, educational, historical, charitable, fraternal, or religious nonprofit organizations;

(25) Sales of admissions and parking fees at fairs and festivals sponsored by nonprofit organizations;

(26) Purchases of fishing vessels, supplies, fuels, lubricants, and repairs for the vessels of licensed commercial fishermen;

(27) Sales of butane, propane, or other liquified petroleum gases for private, residential consumption;

(28) Sales and purchases by certain organizations that provide training for blind persons.

Note: The following transactions were already exempt from the additional 1% sales tax imposed by Sec. 321.1 and therefore are not included in the list of Sec. 321.1 exemptions in this bill: (3), (5), (6), (7), (8), (9), (14), and (15).

• Louisiana reimposes tax on short-term vehicle rentals

Effective April 1, 2016, a Louisiana 3% excise tax is imposed on short-term automobile rentals. The tax previously expired in 2012. The 3% tax (2.5% state, 0.5% local) is imposed on gross proceeds derived from the lease or rental of an automobile pursuant to an automobile rental contract, less any sales and use tax included in such contract. An automobile rental contract is an agreement for the rental of an automobile without a driver and designated to carry less than nine passengers for a period of not more than 29 calendar days. Rental agreements for a period of more than 29 calendar days will not be subject to the tax, unless the actual period of the rental agreement is less than 29 days as a result of the exercise of a cancellation clause. Exclusions and Exemptions Rentals of vehicles primarily for transport of freight or goods is not subject to the tax. In addition, the tax does not apply to any automobile rented by an insurance company as a replacement vehicle for a policyholder or by an automobile dealer as a replacement vehicle while a customer's vehicle is being serviced or repaired. Nor does the tax apply to any individual or business who rents a vehicle as a replacement vehicle while his vehicle is being repaired if the individual presents to the renter upon return of the rented vehicle a copy of the repair or service invoice. (Act 14 (H.B. 39), Laws 2016, First Extraordinary Session) (LA ¶ 471, ¶ 474)

• Hotel tax expanded to include certain rentals of private residences in Louisiana

Effective July 1, 2016, for purposes of the sales and use tax imposed on hotels that furnish occupancy to transient guests, the definition of a "hotel" has been expanded to include an establishment with any number of (formerly, six or more) sleeping rooms, cottages, or cabins and to include a residential location, including a house, apartment, condominium, camp, cabin, or other building structure used as a residence. However, a hotel does not include any establishment or person leasing apartments or single family dwelling on a month-to-month basis. Also, a "dealer" does not include persons leasing apartments or single family dwellings on a month-to-month basis. (Act 17 (H.B. 59), Laws 2016, First Extraordinary Session) (LA ¶ 471, ¶ 479)

• Louisiana requires electronic filing for certain refund claims

For taxable years beginning on and after January 1, 2016, a Louisiana law requires electronic filing of all schedules and invoices if a refund claim for an overpayment of sales tax is $25,000 or more or if the claim for refund is made by a tax preparer on behalf of the taxpayer, regardless of the amount of the refund. The requirement does not apply to the Louisiana Tax Free Shopping Program or to cases of a bad debt. (Act No. 446 (H.B. 756), Laws 2016) (LA ¶ 484)

• Out-of-state retailers must notify purchasers of use tax liability in Louisiana

Effective July 1, 2017, remote retailers must begin notifying Louisiana purchasers, at the time of sale, that:

(1) a purchase is subject to Louisiana use tax unless it is specifically exempt and

(2) there is no specific exemption for purchases made over the Internet, by catalog, or by other remote means.

The sale notice must also include a statement that Louisiana law requires that use tax liability be paid annually on the individual income tax return or through other means as may be required by administrative rule.

A "remote retailer" is a retailer that purposefully avails itself of the benefits of an economic market in Louisiana or who has any other minimum contacts with the state and who:

(1) is not required by law to register as a dealer or to collect Louisiana sales or use tax;

(2) makes retail sales of tangible personal property or taxable services in Louisiana and the cumulative annual gross receipts of the retailer and its affiliates from those Louisiana sales exceed $50,000 per calendar year; and

(3) does not collect and remit Louisiana sales and use tax on retail sales inLouisiana.

By January 31st of each year, a remote retailer must send to each Louisiana purchaser a notice containing the total amount paid by the purchaser to the retailer for property or taxable services in the preceding calendar year. The annual notice must list the dates and amounts of purchases if available, state whether the property or service is exempt from tax if known by the retailer, disclose the name of the retailer, and state that Louisiana use tax may be due.

The notification must be sent by first class mail, certified mail, or electronically at the purchaser's choice and shall not be included with any other shipment or mailing from the retailer. Further, the envelope containing the annual notice shall include the words "IMPORTANT TAX DOCUMENT ENCLOSED".

Also, by March 1st of each year, a remote retailer must file with the Department of Revenue an annual statement for each Louisiana purchaser that includes the total amount paid by the purchaser to that retailer for property or taxable services in the preceding calendar year. The statement must not contain detail as to the specific property or services purchased. The secretary may require the electronic filing of statements by a remote retailer who had sales in Louisiana in excess of $100,000 in the preceding calendar year. (Act 569 (H.B. 1121), Laws 2016) (LA ¶ 471)

• **Louisiana enterprise zone benefits limited and reduced**

Eligibility requirements for Louisiana enterprise zone contracts to receive sales tax rebates and income/franchise tax credits are amended to eliminate eligibility for all projects with a North American Industry Classification System (NAICS) Code of 44, 45, or 72 (which includes retailers, restaurants, and hotels) if the contract was not entered into before July 1, 2015. Projects that filed advanced notification prior to June 10, 2015, remained eligible for enterprise zone benefits, although they could not apply for benefits until July 1, 2016. (Act 114 (H.B. 466), Laws 2015) (LA ¶ 484)

Subsequent legislation provides that the amount of Louisiana corporate and personal income tax and sales tax benefits available to taxpayers who invest in projects located in an enterprise zone has been reduced. For projects for which advance notification is filed on or after April 1, 2016, the amount of sales and use tax rebates and the investment income tax credit may not exceed $100,000 per net new job created. (Act 18 (H.B. 71a), Laws 2016, First Extraordinary Session) (LA ¶ 484)

• **Dealer compensation limited in Louisiana**

The amount of compensation that a vendor or dealer is allowed for collecting and remitting Louisiana state sales and use taxes to the Department of Revenue has been capped at $1,500 per month ($18,000 per year) for a dealer who operates one or more business locations within the state. The compensation is only allowed on the original 4% state sales tax. Any additional sales tax levied by the state will not be used in calculating a vendor's compensation payment. These changes are effective and applicable to all taxable transactions occurring on or after April 1, 2016. (Act 15 (H.B. 43), Laws 2016, First Extraordinary Session) (LA ¶ 479)

• **Louisiana repeals SAVE tax credits for higher education**

Effective March 14, 2016, the Student Assessment for a Valuable Education (SAVE) credit against a student's (or the student's parent's or legal guardian's) individual income, sales and use, gasoline, and special fuels tax liability is repealed. Under the SAVE credit program, which was effective for tax years after 2014 until repeal, each student enrolled at a public institution of higher education was granted a credit equal to the amount of the SAVE assessment. (Act 21 (H.B. 2a), Laws 2016, First Extraordinary Session) (LA ¶ 480)

Maine

• Maine legalizes recreational marijuana but delays sales and taxation

Maine voters passed a statewide referendum that legalizes recreational marijuana for adults over the age of 21. The bill places a sales tax of 10% on retail sales of marijuana and marijuana products. (Question 1 (Ballot Initiative), passed by Maine voters, November 8, 2016)

Separate legislation postpones the effective date of the permissible sales and the tax on retail sales of marijuana and marijuana products to February 1, 2018. (L.D. 88 (H.P. 66), Laws 2017) (ME ¶ 486, 489)

• Tax exemptions added for health centers in Maine

Maine has enacted sales tax and service provider tax exemptions for incorporated nonprofit federally qualified health centers, effective August 1, 2016. A "federally qualified health center" is a health center that is qualified to receive funding under Section 330 of the federal Public Health Service Act, 42 United States Code, Section 254b and a so-called federally qualified health center look-alike that meets the requirements of Section 254b. (L.D. 1521 (H.P. 1046), Laws 2015) (ME ¶ 488)

• Maine revises taxation of satellite and cable radio and TV services

Effective March 10, 2016, a "retail sale" for Maine sales and use tax purposes includes satellite radio services and excludes extended cable services and extended satellite television services. Cable services and satellite television services remain within the definition of "retail sale." (L.D. 1551 (S.P. 607), Laws 2016) (ME ¶ 486, ¶ 487)

• Exemption for fuel expanded for agricultural uses in Maine

Fuel purchases made by persons engaged in commercial agricultural production, commercial fishing, commercial aquacultural production or commercial wood harvesting are tax-free, effective January 1, 2017, if that person holds an exemption certificate. Previously, only fuel purchases for use in a commercial fishing vessel were exempt from Maine sales tax. (L.D. 1606 (S.P. 647), Laws 2016) (ME ¶ 488)

Maryland

• Maryland changes taxation of park model trailers

Park model recreational vehicles are considered travel trailers, and therefore are not subject to Maryland sales tax. Instead, such vehicles are subject to the excise tax. (H.B. 922, Laws 2016, and S.B. 579, effective June 1, 2016) (MD ¶ 503)

Massachusetts

• Massachusetts enacts marijuana excise tax; local taxes authorized

Effective December 15, 2016, a marijuana excise tax is enacted on the sale of marijuana or marijuana products by a marijuana retailer, to anyone other than a marijuana establishment, at a rate of 3.75% of the total sales price received by the marijuana retailer. The excise tax is levied in addition to state sales tax.

In addition, any city or town may impose a local sales tax on the sale or transfer of marijuana or marijuana products by a marijuana retailer operating within the city or town, to anyone other than a marijuana establishment, at a rate not greater than 2% of the total sales price received by the marijuana retailer. (Ch. 334 (H.B. 3932), Laws 2016) (MA ¶ 515, ¶ 519, ¶ 520)

• Pilot voluntary disclosure program begins in Massachusetts

The Massachusetts Department of Revenue has announced a pilot voluntary disclosure program so that business taxpayers may settle uncertain tax issues and have related penalties waived. The program covers a variety of Massachusetts that are open for assessment, including the sales tax and the broadcast satellite services tax. Taxpayers with a potential uncertain tax liability of at least $100,000 are eligible to participate in the program, however, any tax issues under audit (pending or current) are not eligible. Uncertain tax issues arise when case law provides no clear guidance and the department has not issued any written guidance. In general, an "uncertain tax issue" is one in which taxpayers would be required to maintain a reserve in accordance with *ASC 740: Accounting for Uncertainty in Income Taxes* (formerly FIN 48). (*AP 637: Voluntary Disclosure Program for the Settlement of Uncertain Tax Issues,* Massachusetts Department of Revenue, March 2016, CCH MASSACHUSETTS TAX REPORTS, ¶ 401-577) (MA ¶ 526)

Michigan

• Michigan clarifies sourcing of direct mail

Michigan legislation effective September 6, 2016, clarifies how a seller or purchaser of advertising and promotional direct mail collects, pays, or remits sales tax or use tax and the sourcing of other direct mail in order to conform with the Streamlined Sales and Use Tax Agreement. The enacted law repeals existing sections of the General Sales Tax Act and the Use Tax Act (Acts) regarding the obligation of a seller or purchaser of direct mail to collect, pay, or remit sales or use tax, and enacts new provisions that:

— require a seller to source the sale of advertising and promotional direct mail to the jurisdictions to which the mail was to be delivered to recipients, and pay the applicable tax, if the purchaser provided that information;

— require the purchaser to source the sale of advertising and promotional direct mail to the jurisdictions to which it was to be delivered, and pay the applicable tax, if the purchaser provided the seller with a direct payment authorization or exemption form from the Department of Treasury;

— require a sale of advertising and promotional direct mail to be sourced as provided under the Acts, if the purchaser did not provide information about the delivery jurisdictions or provide a direct payment authorization or an exemption form;

— require the purchaser to source the sale of other direct mail and pay the applicable tax, if the purchaser provided the seller with a direct payment authorization or exemption form;

— require a sale of other direct mail to be sourced as provided in the Acts, if the purchaser did not provide a direct payment authorization or exemption form;

— relieve the seller of any obligation to collect, pay, or remit the applicable tax in situations in which the purchaser was required to pay the tax and source the sale; and

— describe the circumstances under which the provisions apply.

(Act 159 (H.B. 5132), Laws 2016 and Act 160 (H.B. 5133), Laws 2016) (MI ¶ 532)

• Use tax on certain medical services repealed in Michigan

Beginning January 1, 2017, medical services provided by Medicaid managed care organizations are no longer be subject to use tax. However, use tax could be reinstated on these services when the Health Insurance Claims Assessment (HICA) Act sunsets on July 1, 2020, when the HICA Act is repealed, or when the HICA rate is reduced to 0.0%, whichever occurs first. (Act 390 (S.B. 1172), Laws 2016) (MI ¶ 533)

• Michigan expands agricultural exemptions

The sales and use tax exemptions for personal property used in agriculture have been extended to include property used in draining. Tangible personal property affixed to a portable grain bin or grain drying equipment is also exempt. The sale or acquisition of agricultural land tile, subsurface irrigation pipe, portable grain bins, and grain drying equipment by a person in the business of construction is exempt to the extent such property is affixed to real estate and used for an exempt purpose. (Act 431 (H.B. 5889), Laws 2017 and Act 432 (H.B. 5890), Laws 2017) (MI ¶ 533)

• **Certain fundraising by veterans' organizations exempted in Michigan**

Effective April 5, 2017, sales of tangible personal property by a veterans' organization exempt from federal income tax under IRC Sec. 501(c)(19) are exempt from Michigan sales tax for the purpose of raising funds for the benefit of an active duty service member or a veteran. The exemption is limited to $25,000 in aggregate sales for each fund-raising event. (Act 503 (S.B. 106), Laws 2017) (MI ¶ 533)

• **Michigan exempts vehicle core charges**

Beginning January 1, 2017, the credit for a core charge attributable to a recycling fee, deposit, or disposal fee for a motor vehicle or recreational vehicle part or battery is excluded from the measure of Michigan sales or use tax as long as the fee is stated separately on the customer invoice. (Act 515 (S.B. 991) and Act 516 (H.B. 5928), Laws 2017) (MI ¶ 533)

Minnesota

• **Minnesota exemption for sales to certain local governments takes effect in 2017**

Minnesota legislation delayed the effective date of the sales and use tax exemption from January 1, 2016, to January 1, 2017 for sales to certain special districts; instrumentalities of statutory or home rule charter cities, counties, and townships; and certain joint powers boards or organizations. (Ch. 3 (H.F. 1a), Laws 2015, First Special Session) (MN ¶ 548)

• **Modular homes taxed at same rate as manufactured homes in Minnesota**

Beginning July 1, 2016, retail sales of modular homes for residential use are subject to Minnesota sales tax on 65% of the manufacturer's sales price of the modular home. Previously, that tax rate applied only to sales of manufactured homes and park trailers. (Ch. 189 (H.F. 2749), Laws 2016) (MN ¶ 549)

Mississippi

• **Mississippi expands tax breaks for certain large projects**

Mississippi has enacted legislation, in a special session, amending the Mississippi Major Economic Impact Act (Act) to authorize a package of corporate income tax, personal income tax, sales and use tax, and property tax benefits for tire or other related rubber or other automotive manufacturing plants and certain maritime fabrication and assembly facilities that meet specified investment and jobs creation requirements. The definition of a "project" under the Act is amended to include enterprises engaged in the manufacture of tires or other related rubber or automotive products for which construction of a plant begins after January 1, 2016, and is substantially completed no later than December 31, 2022. The project must have an initial capital investment of at least $1.45 billion and create at least 2,500 new full-time jobs. The average annual wages and taxable benefits of such jobs must be at least $40,000. Additionally, the definition of a "project" now includes enterprises owning or operating a maritime fabrication and assembly facility for which construction begins after February 1, 2016, and concludes not later than December 31, 2018. The project must have an initial capital investment of at least $68 million and create at least 1,000 new full-time jobs. The average annual wages and taxable benefits of such jobs must be at least $40,000.

Sales tax exemptions: In addition to specified withholding, income, and franchise tax benefits, a sales tax exemption is enacted for sales or leases of all personal property and fixtures to a tire or other related rubber or automotive product manufacturer that is part of a certified project, including sales or leases of the following:

— manufacturing machinery and equipment;

— special tooling such as dies, molds, jigs and similar items treated as special tooling for federal income tax purposes;

— component building materials, machinery, and equipment used in the construction of buildings and any other additions or improvements to the project site;

— nonmanufacturing furniture, fixtures and equipment (including all communications, computer, server, software and other hardware equipment); and

— fuel, supplies (other than nonmanufacturing consumable supplies and water), electricity, nitrogen gas and natural gas used directly in manufacturing/production operations or used to provide climate control for manufacturing/production areas.

All replacements of, repair parts for, or services to establish, support, operate, repair, and/or maintain the certified project are exempt.

Similar sales tax exemptions are enacted for sales or leases of specified items to a maritime fabrication and assembly facility that is part of a certified project (H.B. 1a, Laws 2016, First Extraordinary Session, effective February 8, 2016) (MS ¶ 563)

• **Exemption for agricultural products sold by producers clarified in Mississippi**

The Mississippi sales tax exemption for sales of agricultural products by producers has been amended, effective July 1, 2016, to clarify that the exemption applies to Christmas trees, hay, straw, fresh cut flowers, and similar products when

(1) grown in Mississippi and

(2) cut, severed, or otherwise removed from the farm, grove, garden, or other place of production and first sold from such place of production in the original state or condition of preparation for sale.

(H.B. 1677, Laws 2016) (MS ¶ 563)

Missouri

• **Missouri exempts Internet access**

Effective August 28, 2016, a state and local sales tax exemption applies to all Internet access or the use of Internet access, regardless of whether the tax is imposed on a provider or buyer of Internet access. The law defines various terms including "internet access," and gives examples of what is and is not included in "internet access." (S.B. 823, Laws 2016) (MO ¶ 578)

• **Durable medical equipment exempt in Missouri**

A Missouri sales tax exemption is available, effective August 28, 2016, for all sales, rentals, repairs, and parts of durable medical equipment, as well as for parts for certain other types of health care related equipment. (S.B. 794, Laws 2016) (MO ¶ 578)

• **Missouri exempts instructional classes**

Legislation enacted by a veto override provides that amounts paid for instructional classes are not subject to Missouri sales tax, effective October 14, 2016. "Instructional class" includes any class, lesson, or instruction intended or used for teaching. (S.B. 1025, Laws 2016) (MO ¶ 578)

Montana
• **Montana court holds online travel companies taxable**

A Montana appeals court held that charges made by online travel companies (OTCs) for accommodations are not subject to the lodging facility use tax, but are subject to sales tax, and the rental vehicle charges by OTCs are subject to sales tax. Fees charged by the owner or operator of a facility for use of the facility for lodging are subject to a lodging facility use tax.

The court held that the OTCs were not owners or operators for purposes of the tax, because they do not possess, run, control, manage, or direct the functioning of a hotel or rental agency. Sales tax is imposed on a purchaser and must be collected by the seller and is applied to the sales price. As fees received for services rendered, the amount of the charges the OTCs retained as compensation is subject to sales tax. Also, sales tax is imposed on the base charge for rental vehicles. The court found that "base rental charge" and "sales price" are synonyms for sales tax statutory purposes. (*Montana Department of Revenue v. Priceline.com, Inc.,* Montana Supreme Court, No. DA 14-0260, August 12, 2015, CCH MONTANA TAX REPORTS, ¶ 401-269) (MT ¶ 591)

• Proposed Montana constitutional amendment would prohibit state sales tax if approved by voters

Montana's governor is proposing a constitutional amendment to prohibit a statewide sales tax, subject to voter approval. Under legislation introduced in the Legislature, the constitution would be amended to end the possibility that future legislators and governors could impose a general sales tax. If passed, the measure would be submitted for voter approval in 2018. Currently, the state constitution limits a statewide general sales tax to 4%. (*Release,* Office of Governor Steve Bullock, March 23, 2017, **http://governor.mt.gov/Newsroom**)

Nebraska

• Nebraska clarifies exemption for food sold partially cooked

An exemption for certain food items has been revised in order to conform to the Streamlined Sales and Use Tax (SST) Agreement. Food that generally requires additional cooking in order to finish the product to its desired final condition is excluded from the definition of "prepared food," and is therefore exempt from Nebraska sales and use tax. (L.B. 776, Laws 2016) (NE ¶ 608)

• Exemption for C-BED energy projects amended in Nebraska

The Nebraska sales and use tax exemption for personal property used in a Community-Based Energy Development (C-BED) project have been amended. The definition of a "qualified owner" is expanded to include a public power district, a public power and irrigation district, a municipality, a registered group of municipalities, an electric cooperative, or an electric membership association. (L.B. 824, Laws 2016) (NE ¶ 608)

• Nebraska adds various exemptions

Legislation has been enacted that adds Nebraska sales and use tax exemptions for certain nonprofit and governmental organizations, effective October 1, 2016. Purchases by nonprofit centers for independent living and substance abuse treatment centers are exempt from sales and use tax. The legislation also provides an exemption for certain purchases of energy sources and fuels when more than 50% of the amount is purchased for use directly in the drying and aerating of grain in commercial agricultural facilities. Exemptions are also enacted for purchases by county agricultural societies and for purchases of animate or inanimate property by museums which have intrinsic cultural, historic, scientific, or artistic value. (L.B. 774, Laws 2016) (NE ¶ 608)

• Out-of-state disaster responders exempted from various Nebraska tax provisions

Nebraska has enacted the Facilitating Business Rapid Response to State Declared Disasters Act, which provides that an out-of-state business assisting in repairing, renovating, installing, or building infrastructure related to a declared state disaster or emergency is not subject to registration with the Secretary of State or withholding or income tax registration, filing, or remitting requirements. A declared state disaster or emergency is "a disaster or emergency event for which a Governor's state of emergency proclamation has been issued or that the President of the United States has declared to be a major disaster or emergency."

Under the Act, an out-of-state business or its out-of-state employees providing assistance in Nebraska related to a declared disaster or emergency during a disaster period are not subject to sales, use, or *ad valorem* tax on equipment brought into the state temporarily for use or consumption during the disaster period if such equipment does not remain in the state after the disaster period. (L.B. 913, Laws 2016) (NE ¶ 614)

Nevada

• Nevada counties increase tax rates

Effective April 1, 2017, Clark County's sales and use tax rate is increased to 8.25% (currently, 8.15%), and Washoe County's sales and use tax rate is increased to 8.265% (currently 7.725%). (*Press Release,* Nevada Department of Taxation, December 8, 2016)

New Jersey

• New Jersey reduces sales and use tax rate over two years

The New Jersey sales and use tax rate is reduced from 7% to 6.875% on January 1, 2017, and will be further reduced to 6.625% on January 1, 2018. Transitional provisions apply for taxing sales transactions that stretch across the tax rate change dates. (Ch. 57 (A.B. 12), Laws 2016) (NJ ¶ 654)

• Tax on limousine services originating in New Jersey repealed

Effective May 1, 2017, transportation services originating in New Jersey and provided by a limousine operator will no longer be subject to sales and use tax. (Ch. 27 (A.B. 3696), Laws 2017) (NJ ¶ 651)

• New Jersey issues audit procedure manual

The New Jersey Division of Taxation has issued an audit procedure manual, which provides an overview of the procedures and guidelines available to the Division of Taxation for completing all types of audits. Among other topics, the manual details audit preparations and procedures, confidentiality, and discussions of audits with respect to specific tax types. The manual can be accessed on the Division's website at **http:// www.state.nj.us/treasury/taxation/pdf/njmap.pdf**. (*New Jersey Manual of Audit Procedures,* New Jersey Division of Taxation, March 1, 2017)

New Mexico

• Gross receipts tax deductions for health services clarified in New Mexico

New Mexico has amended existing law to clarify which medical and health care service providers are permitted gross receipts tax deductions and the manner in which the deductions apply. More types of service providers are defined as health care practitioners under the amended provisions. In addition, receipts from payments made by federal programs and agencies must be deducted before receipts from a managed health care provider or health care insurer may be deducted. Failure to correctly report the deductions when preparing a return will result in a penalty of 20% on the amount distributed due to the improper deductions. (S.B. 6 a, Laws 2016, effective November 1, 2016) (NM ¶ 668)

• New Mexico adds disaster response legislation for out-of-state responders

Certain temporary corporate income, personal income, sales and property tax and registration exemptions are provided for out-of-state businesses and individuals who enter New Mexico to respond to declared disasters and perform work on critical infrastructure. An out-of-state business that conducts operations within New Mexico in response to a declared state disaster or emergency is not considered to have established a level of presence or nexus that would require that business to register, file or remit state or local taxes or fees, including gross receipts taxes or property tax on equipment brought into the state temporarily for use during the disaster response period and subsequently removed from New Mexico. Further, for purposes of the corporate income, personal income or sales taxes, all activity of the out-of-state business during the disaster response period conducted in New Mexico is disregarded with respect to any filing requirements. This includes the filing required for a unitary or combined group of which the out-of-state business may be a part. Finally, when apportioning income, revenue or receipts, the performance by an out-of-state business of any work during a disaster response period will not be sourced to or otherwise impact or increase the amount of income, revenue or receipts apportioned to New Mexico.

The legislation allows compensation to be allocated to the taxpayers' state of residence if the activities, labor or services are performed in New Mexico for disaster or emergency related critical infrastructure work, in response to a declared state disaster or emergency. An out-of-state employee will not be considered to have established residency or a presence in the state that would require that person or that person's employer to file and pay income taxes or to be subjected to tax withholdings or to file and pay any other state or local tax or fee during the disaster response period. (S.B. 19, Laws 2016) (NM ¶ 674)

New York

• New York's budget packages make several sales and use tax changes

New York's 2016-17 budget package includes a variety of sales and use tax provisions, including those detailed below (Ch. 60 (S.B. 6409), Laws 2016, effective April 13, 2016, except as noted):

Purchases of hotel room occupancies by room remarketers: An exemption is provided for the purchase of hotel room occupancies by room remarketers when those purchases are made from hotels for later resale, applicable to rent paid for hotel occupancies on or after June 1, 2016. A similar exemption applies to New York City's tax.

Prior to June 1, 2016, there is no exemption for room remarketers' purchases of hotel room occupancies they supplied to their customers, but room remarketers may seek a credit or refund for the tax they paid to the hotel operators if the room remarketers satisfy certain conditions. (NY ¶ 681, ¶ 683)

Fuel used in commercial and general aviation aircraft: Sales of fuel for use in commercial and general aviation aircraft are exempt from local sales taxes and from the prepayment of sales tax on motor fuels, effective December 1, 2017. (NY ¶ 683, ¶ 688)

Commercial fuel cell electricity generating systems equipment: An exemption is provided for commercial fuel cell electricity generating systems equipment and the service of installing and maintaining such systems, effective June 1, 2016. For purposes of the exemption, "fuel cell electricity generating systems equipment" means an electric generating arrangement or combination of components installed upon non-residential premises that utilize solid oxide, molten carbonate, proton exchange membrane or phosphoric acid fuel cell, or linear generator. (NY ¶ 683)

Also effective June 1, 2016, an exemption is provided for the sale of hydrogen gas or electricity by a person primarily engaged in the sale of fuel cell electricity generating system equipment and/or electricity generated by such equipment pursuant to written agreement under which the electricity is generated by commercial fuel cell electricity generating system equipment. The equipment must be: (NY ¶ 683)

— owned by a person other than the purchaser of such electricity;

— installed on the nonresidential premises of the purchaser of such electricity;

— placed in service; and

— used to provide heating, cooling, hot water or electricity to such premises.

Alternative fuels: The sunset date for the exemption for alternative fuels, including E85, Compressed Natural Gas (CNG), hydrogen, and B20, is extended from September 1, 2016 to September 1, 2021. (NY ¶ 683)

• **Feminine hygiene products exempted in New York**

Legislation has been enacted that creates a New York state and local sales and use tax exemption for feminine hygiene products, including but not limited to, sanitary napkins, tampons and panty liners, effective September 1, 2016. (Ch. 99 (A.B. 7555), Laws 2016) (NY ¶ 683)

• **New York exempts certain sales by veterans to benefit veterans' service organizations**

Effective March 1, 2017, a New York sales and use tax exemption is provided for tangible personal property manufactured and sold by a veteran for the benefit of a veteran's service organization, provided that such person or any member of his or her household does not conduct a trade or business in which similar items are sold. The exemption applies to the first $2,500 of receipts from such sales in a calendar year. (Ch. 478 (S.B. 4986), Laws 2016) (NY ¶ 683)

North Carolina

• **North Carolina budget amends sales and use tax provisions**

The 2016 North Carolina Appropriations Act makes a number of changes to sales and use tax provisions, as follows (Ch. 94 (H.B. 1030), Laws 2016):

Privilege taxes: Applicable retroactively to purchases made on or after July 1, 2013, the 1% privilege tax on certain purchases by companies located at ports facilities for waterborne commerce is expanded to apply to parts, accessories, or attachments used to maintain, repair, replace, upgrade, improve, or otherwise modify machinery and equipment that is used at the facility to unload or to facilitate the unloading or processing of bulk cargo to make it suitable for delivery to and use by manufacturing facilities.

Applicable to sales made on or after July 1, 2016, the privilege tax is expanded to apply to a person that gathers and obtains ferrous metals, nonferrous metals, and items that have served their original economic purpose, who converts them by processes, including sorting, cutting, classifying, cleaning, baling, wrapping, shredding, or shearing, into a new or different product for sale consisting of prepared grades for the purchase of equipment, or an attachment or repair part for the equipment, that meets certain requirements.

Effective July 1, 2016, the privilege tax applies to a company primarily engaged in processing tangible personal property for the purpose of extracting precious metals, to determine the value for potential purchase for the purchase of equipment, or an attachment or repair part for the equipment, that meets certain requirements. (NC ¶ 699)

Compromise of taxpayer's liability: The grounds that the North Carolina Secretary of Revenue may use to compromise a taxpayer's liability are expanded to include an assessment for sales tax that the taxpayer failed to collect or use tax the taxpayer failed to pay as a result of the change in the definition of "retailer" or the sales tax base expansion to: (1) service contracts; (2) repair, maintenance, and installation services; or (3) sales transactions for a person in retail trade. The secretary must determine that the taxpayer made a good-faith effort to comply with the sales and use tax laws. This provision is applicable to assessments for any reporting period beginning March 1, 2016, and ending December 31, 2022.

Definitions: Effective January 1, 2017, a number of definitions are added. "Clothing" is defined as all human wearing apparel suitable for general use. A "landscaping service" is a service to maintain or improve lawns, yards, or ornamental plants and trees. Examples include: the installation of trees, shrubs, or flowers; tree trimming; lawn mowing; and the application of seed, mulch, pesticide, or fertilizer to a lawn or yard. A "motor vehicle service contract" is a service contract sold by a motor vehicle dealer or by or on behalf of a motor vehicle service agreement company for a motor vehicle or for one or more components, systems, or accessories for a motor vehicle. "Real property" is defined as any one or more of the following: land; a building or structure on land; a permanent fixture on land; or a manufactured home or a modular home that is placed on a permanent foundation.

North Dakota

• North Dakota updates SST provisions

North Dakota legislation effective August 1, 2017, updates the state's conformity to the Streamlined Sales and Use Tax (SST) Agreement provisions regarding uniform tax returns, the taxability matrix, and administrative practices as follows (S.B. 2112, Laws 2017):

— The provision regarding uniform tax returns is amended to provide that web services must be adopted as the standardized process that allows for receipt of uniform tax returns and other formatted information as approved by the SST Governing Board.

— The provision regarding the taxability matrix is amended to reflect that sellers and certified service providers (CSPs) must be relieved from liability for having charged and collected the incorrect amount of sales or use tax resulting from the seller or CSP relying on erroneous data provided in the tax administration practices section of the taxability matrix.

— The provision regarding best practices is renamed "Tax administration practices" and is amended to reflect the addition of disclosed practices, which are tax practices that the SST Governing Board selects and requires each SST member state to disclose in the taxability matrix.

• Refund and credit provisions amended in North Dakota

North Dakota legislation includes changes to sales and use tax provisions regarding refunds and the credit for tax refunded to a customer, as follows (S.B. 2129, Laws 2017):

Refunds: Effective July 1, 2017, a taxpayer must file a claim for refund with the Tax Commissioner within three years after the due date of the return or the date the return was filed, whichever is later. For purposes of this provision, "taxpayer" means a person who is required under sales or use tax laws to file a return and who has remitted the tax for which a refund is claimed. Under prior law, a person who made an erroneous payment had to present a claim for refund or credit to the commissioner not later than three years after the due date of the return for the period for which the erroneous payment was made or one year after the erroneous payment was made, whichever was later. (ND ¶ 724)

Credit for tax refunded to customer: Effective July 1, 2017, retailers that collect excess sales or use taxes from a customer and then properly refund such excess taxes to the customer are required to file an amended return for the period the excess tax was collected and file a claim for refund. Under prior law, the statute authorized such retailers to claim a credit on their next return for the amount of excess sales or use taxes that were collected from a customer and later properly refunded to the customer. (ND ¶ 720)

Ohio

• Ohio budget expands nexus, adds exemptions

Ohio's fiscal year 2016-2017 state budget expands the presumption of "substantial nexus" and more, as follows (H.B. 64, Laws 2015).

Nexus: The legislation amends nexus provisions for use tax purposes, effective July 1, 2015. A seller is presumed to have substantial nexus with Ohio if the seller enters into an agreement with one or more residents under which the resident, for a commission or other consideration, directly or indirectly, refers potential customers, by a link on a website, in-person oral presentation, or otherwise, to the seller. The presumption requires that the cumulative gross receipts from sales by the seller to customers in Ohio who are referred to the seller be greater than $10,000 during the immediately preceding 12 months.

The presumption may be rebutted by demonstrating that the persons with whom the seller had agreements did not engage in activities that were significantly associated with the seller's ability to establish or maintain a market in Ohio. The presumption of substantial nexus for other specified activities performed by the seller or an affiliated person may also be rebutted if it can be shown that those activities did nothing to establish or maintain a market for the seller in Ohio.

The legislation expands the criteria for determining a presumption of substantial nexus to include:

(1) use of employees, agents or others to sell a similar line of products or use similar trade names or trademarks as the seller; and

(2) use of any person, except for a common carrier, to promote, advertise, facilitate customer sales, perform maintenance, delivery, and installation services for the seller's Ohio customers, or facilitate delivery by allowing customers to pick up property sold by the seller.

The following criteria no longer form the basis for a presumption of substantial nexus: (1) a seller's registration to do business in Ohio and (2) any other contact with Ohio that forms the basis of substantial nexus as permitted under the U.S. Constitution's Commerce Clause. (OH ¶ 726)

Exemption: Beginning October 1, 2015, sanitation services (cleaning) provided to a meat slaughtering or processing operation are exempt if the services are needed to comply with federal meat safety regulations. (OH ¶ 726)

Exemption: A rented motor vehicle that is transferred to the owner or lessee of a motor vehicle being repaired or serviced is exempt if the owner is reimbursed for the cost of the rented vehicle by the manufacturer, warrantor, or provider of a maintenance, service, or other contract with respect to the vehicle under repair. However, the abatement does not apply to a taxpayer who has unpaid tax liability as of September 1, 2015. (OH ¶ 728)

Vendor compensation: Retailers may no longer apply for compensation from county and transit authorities for the expense of adjusting cash registers when a new tax is imposed or increased on or after July 1, 2015.

• Ohio adds exemptions

The following ales and use tax exemptions have been added by recent legislation, effective as noted (OH ¶ 728):

— Sales of investment metal bullion and investment coins, effective January 1, 2017 (S.B. 172, Laws 2016);

— Sales of natural gas by a municipal gas utility, effective September 28, 2016 (H.B. 390, Laws 2016);

— Digital advertising services, effective October 12, 2016. "Digital advertising services" means providing access, via telecommunications equipment, to computer equipment that is used to enter, upload, download, review, manipulate, store, add, or delete data for the purpose of electronically displaying promotional advertisements to potential customers. (H.B. 466, Laws 2016).

Oklahoma

• Oklahoma amends nexus provisions for out-of-state retailers

Oklahoma has enacted the Oklahoma Retail Protection Act of 2016, concerning sales and use tax parity and nexus, effective November 1, 2016. Changes are as follows (Ch. 311 (H.B. 2531), Laws 2016) (OK ¶ 741):

Nexus: The definition of "maintaining a place of business in this state" is rebuttably presumed to include:

(1) (a) utilizing or maintaining in Oklahoma (directly or by subsidiary) an office, distribution house, sales house, warehouse, or other physical place of business, whether owned or operated by the vendor or any other person (other than a common carrier acting in its capacity as such), or

(b) having agents operating in Oklahoma, whether the place of business or agent is within the state temporarily or permanently or whether the person or agent is authorized to do business in the state; and

(2) the presence of any person (other than a common carrier acting in its capacity as such) who has substantial nexus in Oklahoma and who:

(a) sells a similar line of products as the vendor under the same or a similar business name;

(b) uses trademarks, service marks, or trade names in Oklahoma that are the same or substantially similar to those used by the vendor;

(c) delivers, installs, assembles, or performs maintenance services for the vendor;

(d) facilitates the vendor's delivery of property to customers in the state by permitting the vendor's customers to pick up property sold by the vendor at an office, distribution facility, warehouse, storage place, or similar place of business maintained by the person in Oklahoma; or

(e) conducts any other activities in Oklahoma that are significantly associated with the vendor's ability to establish and maintain a market in the state for the vendor's sale.

The presumption is rebuttable by showing that the person's activities in Oklahoma are not significantly associated with the vendor's ability to establish and maintain a market in the state for the vendor's sales.

In addition, the use tax code is amended no longer provide that a "retailer" includes making sales of tangible personal property to purchasers in Oklahoma by mail, telephone, the Internet, or other media who has contracted with an entity to provide and perform installation or maintenance services for the retailer's purchasers in Oklahoma. The use tax code is also amended to no longer state that the processing of orders electronically (including by facsimile, telephone, the Internet, or other electronic means) does not relieve a retailer of the duty to collect tax from the purchaser if the retailer is doing business in Oklahoma.

Retailer compliance initiatives: The legislation expands the state's out-of-state retailer use tax registration, collection, and remittance compliance initiatives to also apply with respect to sales tax. Under the initiative as amended, the Oklahoma Tax Commission will not seek payment of uncollected use taxes from an out-of-state retailer who registers to collect and remit applicable sales and use taxes on sales made to purchasers in Oklahoma prior to registration under the initiative, provided that the retailer was not registered in Oklahoma in the 12-month period preceding November 1, 2016.

Other changes concerning the compliance initiatives include the removal of provisions under former Sec. 1402(C)):

(1) prohibiting an out-of-state retailer's registration to collect use tax under the initiative as a factor in determining nexus for other Oklahoma taxes,

(2) allowing out-of-state retailers registering under the initiative a vendor discount for timely reporting and remittance of use tax, and

(3) prohibiting the charging of a registration fee against an out-of-state retailer who voluntarily registers to collect and remit use tax under the initiative.

Annual use tax notice requirements: Out-of-state retailers who are not required to collect Oklahoma use tax and who make sales of tangible personal property delivered to Oklahoma customers for use in the state, must, by February 1st of each year, provide each of these customers a statement of the total sales made to them during the preceding calendar year. The statement must contain language substantially similar to: *"You may owe Oklahoma use tax on purchases you made from us during the previous tax year. The amount of tax you owe is based on the total sales price of [insert total sales price] that must be reported and paid when you file your Oklahoma income tax return unless you have already paid the tax."* For reasons of confidentiality, the statement cannot contain any other information that would indicate, imply, or identify the class, type, description, or name of the products sold.

Pennsylvania

• Pennsylvania expands sales and use tax; adds exemptions, and more

Pennsylvania legislation imposes sales and use tax on downloaded videos, games, music, canned software, and other items; creates provisions authorizing a refund for sales or use tax on computer data center equipment; adds exemptions; amends the collection discount provision; and makes other changes, effective July 13, 2016, except as noted (Act 84 (H.B. 1198), Laws 2016; see also *Sales, Use & Hotel Occupancy Tax Bulletin 16-001,* Pennsylvania Department of Revenue, July 21, 2016, CCH PENNSYLVANIA TAX REPORTS, ¶ 204-544):

Tax on downloads: Effective August 1, 2016, sales and use tax is imposed on downloaded videos; photographs; books; any otherwise taxable printed matter; applications (commonly known as apps); games; music; any other audio, including satellite radio service; canned software; and any other otherwise taxable tangible personal property electronically or digitally delivered, streamed, or accessed. These items are taxable as tangible personal property and are considered tangible personal property whether they are electronically or digitally delivered, streamed, or accessed and whether they are purchased singly, by subscription, or in any other manner, including maintenance, updates, and support. (PA ¶ 771)

Refund for data centers: Beginning July 1, 2017, an owner, operator, or qualified tenant of a certified computer data center may apply to the Department of Revenue for a refund of sales or use tax paid on certain equipment that is used to outfit, operate, or benefit a computer data center and component parts, installations, refreshments, replacements, and upgrades to the equipment. The initial application must be filed by July 30, 2017, and subsequent applications must be filed by July 30 of the following years. The department will notify applicants of the amount of their tax refund by September 30, 2017, and by September 30 of the following years.

A computer data center must meet the requirements in either (1) or (2) below, after taking into account the combined investments made and annual compensation paid by the owner or operator of the computer data center or the qualified tenant:

(1) On or before the fourth anniversary of certification, the computer data center must create a minimum investment of (a) at least $25 million of new investment if the computer data center is located in a county with a population of 250,000 or fewer individuals or (b) at least $50 million of new investment if the computer data center is located in a county with a population of more than 250,000 individuals. "New investment" means the construction, expansion, or build out of data center space at either a new or an existing computer data center on or after January 1, 2014, and the purchase and installation of computer data center equipment, except software and related items.

(2) One or more taxpayers operating or occupying a computer data center, in the aggregate, must pay annual compensation of at least $1 million to employees at the certified computer data center site for each year of the certification after the fourth anniversary of certification.

The total amount of tax refunds cannot exceed $5 million in any fiscal year, and if the approved refunds exceed that amount the refunds will be allocated among all applicants. (PA ¶ 780)

Exemptions: The following exemptions have been added or clarified: (PA ¶ 773)

— *Timbering machinery and equipment.*—Effective July 1, 2017, machinery and equipment used in timbering and parts and supplies for such machinery and equipment are exempt from sales and use tax as agricultural property.

— *Returnable or reusable cartons.*—The exemption for cartons used for deliveries of tangible personal property applies to corrugated boxes used by manufacturers of snack food products to deliver the manufactured product, regardless of whether the boxes are returnable for potential reuse.

— *Services to property rented to certain exhibitors.*—After June 30, 2016, services related to the set up, tear down, or maintenance of tangible personal property rented by a Pennsylvania Convention Center Authority to exhibitors at a convention center or a public auditorium are exempt.

Collection discount: For sales and use tax returns due on or after August 1, 2016, the collection discount allowed to licensees as compensation for collecting and remitting the tax is the lesser of:

— 1% of the amount of tax collected or
— $25 per return for a monthly filer,
— $75 per return for a quarterly filer, or
— $150 per return for a semiannual filer.

Previously, the discount was a flat 1% of the amount of tax collected. (PA ¶ 777)

• Medical marijuana tax enacted in Pennsylvania

Pennsylvania imposes a 5% tax on the gross receipts of a grower/processor from the sale of medical marijuana to a dispensary, effective May 18, 2016. The tax is charged against and paid by the grower/processor and cannot be added as a separate charge or line item on any sales slip, invoice, receipt, or other statement or memorandum of the price paid by a dispensary, patient, or caregiver.

The tax is to be administered in the same manner as the state gross receipts tax, except that estimated tax payments under that law are not required. A grower/processor must make quarterly payments each calendar quarter; the tax is due and payable on the 20th day of January, April, July, and October for the preceding calendar quarter.

Medical marijuana is not subject to the state sales tax. Growers/processors must provide information as required by the Department of Revenue. (Act No. 2016-16 (S.B. 3), Laws 2016) (PA ¶ 771, ¶ 773, ¶ 774)

• Pennsylvania offers tax amnesty in 2017

The Pennsylvania Department of Revenue has issued guidelines informing taxpayers of the 2017 amnesty program which runs from April 21, 2017, until June 19, 2017 (the amnesty period). All taxes that are owed to Pennsylvania and administered by the Department of Revenue are eligible for the amnesty program, and the eligible periods are those where a known or unknown delinquency exists as of December 31, 2015.

Taxpayers who wish to participate must file an online amnesty return, file all delinquent tax returns, and make the required payment within the amnesty period. The notice provides a definition of the relevant terms, a list of taxes eligible for amnesty, a detailed overview of the notification process, the filing requirements, and other essential specifics required for taxpayers. (Act No. 84 (H.B. 1198), Laws 2016; *Notice, 2017 Tax Amnesty Program Guidelines,* Pennsylvania Department of Revenue, September 9, 2016, CCH PENNSYLVANIA TAX REPORTS, ¶ 204-555)

Rhode Island

• Rhode Island budget taxes transportation network companies

Rhode Island's Fiscal Year 2017 budget provides that transportation network companies, such as Uber, are subject to sales and use tax, effective July 1, 2016. "Transportation network companies" (TNC) are defined as entities that use a digital network to connect transportation network company riders to transportation network operators who provide prearranged rides. Any TNC operating in Rhode Island is a retailer that is required to file a business application and registration form, as well as obtain a permit to charge, collect, and remit Rhode Island sales and use tax. (P.L. 142 (H.B. 7454), Laws 2016) (RI ¶ 794)

South Carolina

• South Carolina enacts tax amnesty provisions

South Carolina legislation authorizes the South Carolina Department of Revenue to designate an amnesty period during which penalties and interest, or a portion of them, will be waived for taxpayers that voluntarily file and pay all taxes owed. If the department establishes an amnesty period, it must notify the South Carolina General Assembly of the amnesty period at least 60 days before the start of the amnesty period. Amnesty will be granted to taxpayers that request an amnesty form and voluntarily file all delinquent tax returns and pay in full all taxes due; voluntarily file an amended tax return to correct an incorrect or insufficient original return and pay all taxes due; or voluntarily pay in full all previously assessed tax liabilities due within an extended amnesty period as determined by the department. The department may set up installment agreements so long as all taxes are paid within this period. A taxpayer who has an appeal pending with respect to an assessment is eligible to participate in the amnesty program if the taxpayer pays all taxes owed. However, amnesty will not be granted to a taxpayer who is the subject of a state tax-related criminal investigation or criminal prosecution. (Act 85 (S.B. 526), Laws 2015) (SC ¶ 811)

• Exemptions added, amended in South Carolina

The following exemptions have been added or amended as follows: (SC ¶ 803)

Help for the needy: Construction materials used by a nonprofit corporation to build, rehabilitate, or repair a home for an individual or family in need are exempt from South Carolina sales and use taxes. Also exempt is children's clothing sold to a private charitable organization exempt from federal and state income tax for the sole purpose of distribution to needy children. The exemption does not apply to clothing sold to private schools. (SC ¶ 803)

Agricultural machines: Beginning July 1, 2016, machines used in agricultural packaging are exempt from South Carolina sales tax. (Act 256 (S.B. 427), Laws 2016)

Motor fuels: Natural gas sold to a person with a miscellaneous motor fuel user fee license is exempt from South Carolina sales tax if the person will use it to produce compressed natural gas or liquefied natural gas for use as a motor fuel. Also exempt is liquefied petroleum gas sold to a person with a miscellaneous motor fuel user fee license who will use the gas as a motor fuel. (H.B. 4328, Laws 2016, effective April 21, 2016)

• South Carolina budget reenacts exemptions

The South Carolina fiscal year 2016-2017 budget bill reenacted the following sales and use tax provisions, effective July 1, 2016 (H.B. 5001), Laws 2016):

College athletic tickets: The amount that an accredited college or university requires a season ticket holder to pay to a nonprofit athletic booster organization that is exempt from federal income taxes in order to receive the right to purchase athletic event tickets is exempt from admissions tax. (SC ¶ 803)

School property: For the current fiscal year, there is a use tax exemption for tangible personal property purchased for use in private primary and secondary schools, including kindergartens and early childhood education programs, that are exempt from income taxes pursuant to IRC § 501(c)(3). This exemption applies for sales occurring after 1995. However, no refund is allowed for use tax paid on such sales. (SC ¶ 803)

Medical items: The effective date of the sales and use tax exemption for prescription medicines used to prevent respiratory syncytial virus is January 1, 1999. However, no refund of sales and use tax may be claimed as a result of this exemption. Also, for the 2016-17 fiscal year, sales and use taxes on viscosupplementation therapies are again suspended. However, no refund or forgiveness of tax may be claimed as a result of this exemption. (SC ¶ 803)

• Heavy equipment rental surcharge replaced by heavy equipment rental fee in South Carolina

Effective January 1, 2017, the 3% surcharge on the rental of heavy equipment was discontinued and replaced by a 2.5% heavy equipment rental fee. The rental fee does not apply to the rental of heavy equipment property rented directly to the federal government, South Carolina, or any political subdivision of South Carolina. The rental fee is not subject to sales or use tax. Qualified heavy equipment property subject to the rental fee is also exempt from personal property tax. (Act 224 (H.B. 3891), Laws 2016) (SC ¶ 803, 804)

South Dakota

• South Dakota adds ½% to sales and use tax rate

The South Dakota sales and use tax rate was increased to 4.5% (previously 4%), effective June 1, 2016. The new tax rate applies to (H.B. 1182, Laws 2016) (SD ¶ 819):

(1) the sale, lease, or rental of tangible personal property, products transferred electronically, and services;

(2) the excise tax on the purchase of farm machinery;

(3) the amusement device tax; and

(4) special jurisdiction tax rates on Indian Country where there is a tax collection agreement.

• South Dakota bill to expand nexus provisions awaits judicial authorization

South Dakota enacted sales and use tax collection requirements for remote sellers who meet certain sales thresholds. It provides that a retailer is presumed to be liable for the collection of sales and use tax in South Dakota, even if the seller does not have a physical presence in state, if the seller meets either of the following criteria in the previous or current calendar year:

(1) the seller's gross revenue from the sale of tangible personal property, any product transferred electronically, or services delivered into South Dakota exceeds $100,000; or

(2) the seller sold tangible personal property, any product transferred electronically, or services for delivery into South Dakota in 200 or more separate transactions.

The legislation provides for an expedited appeals process for any challenges to the constitutionality of the law. (S.B. 106, Laws 2016) (SD ¶ 816)

Note: The legislation enacting this provision also provided for an automatic injunction if the law was challenged in court. A challenge invoking the injunction was filed on April 28, 2016. The injunction will be in effect throughout the court case. If the injunction is lifted or dissolved, the obligation to collect will begin from that day forward.

• South Dakota exempts nonprofit corporations for fire protection

A sales and use tax exemption has been enacted for nonprofit corporations controlled by any political subdivision of South Dakota and created for the purpose of fire protection. The exemption becomes effective July 1, 2016. (H.B. 1204, Laws 2016) (SD ¶ 818)

• Sales suppression devices prohibited in South Dakota

South Dakota legislation effective July 1, 2016, prohibits the use of certain automated sales suppression devices and phantom-ware designed to avoid or reduce perceived sales and use tax, contractors excise tax, or any other tax liability. An "automated sales suppression device" is a software program accessed through any method that falsifies the electronic records, transaction data, or transaction reports of electronic cash registers and other point-of-sale systems. "Phantom-ware" is defined as a programming option embedded in the operating system or hardwired into the electronic cash register that can be used to create a false till, or eliminate or manipulate transaction data before it is entered in the original till. Both civil and criminal penalties are provided. (H.B. 1051, Laws 2016)

Tennessee

• SST provisions delayed in Tennessee

Tennessee legislation has delayed the effective date of certain Streamlined Sales and Use Tax (SST) Agreement conformity provisions until July 1, 2017. (Ch. 273 (H.B. 95), Laws 2015) (TN ¶ 831):

Delayed SST conformity provisions include:

— requirements that sales delivered or shipped to the customer be sourced to the delivery or shipping destination;

— modifications to the single article limitation on local option sales taxes;

— use of a single sales and use tax return covering multiple dealer locations; and

— implementation of certain privilege taxes in lieu of sales tax.

• Tennessee exempts compressed natural gas

Effective July 1, 2016, a Tennessee sales and use tax exemption is available for compressed natural gas (CNG) that is subject to the taxes imposed on alternative fuels. (Ch. 1070 (H.B. 879), Laws 2016) (TN ¶ 833)

• Privilege tax imposed on fantasy sports operators in Tennessee

Effective July 1, 2016, a Tennessee privilege tax is imposed at the rate of 6% on all adjusted revenues of a fantasy sports contest offered by a fantasy sports operator to

Tennessee consumers. The tax is due on a quarterly basis. Each fantasy sports operator is required, on or before the 20th day immediately following the end of each calendar quarter, to transmit to the Tennessee Commissioner of Revenue returns that show all receipts derived from offering or providing consumers with any fantasy sports contests taxable under these provisions during the preceding calendar quarter. (Ch. 978 (S.B. 2109), Laws 2016) (TN ¶ 831)

• New tax filing website launched in Tennessee

As of March 2017, the Tennessee Department of Revenue has a new tax filing website, the Tennessee Taxpayer Access Point (TNTAP), to allow taxpayers to file sales and use tax returns, among others. For more information about the new tax filing website, taxpayers can visit **http://www.tntapinfo.com**. (*Press Release,* Tennessee Department of Revenue, December 30, 2016) (TN ¶ 837)

Utah

• Utah will impose transient room tax beginning in 2018

Effective January 1, 2018, Utah will impose a state transient room tax of 0.32% on transactions involving tourist home, hotel, motel, or trailer court accommodations and services that are regularly rented for less than 30 consecutive days. The Tax Commission will administer, collect, and enforce the tax.

Sellers collecting the tax may retain, as a commission, 6% of the amount the seller would otherwise remit. Certain sellers or service providers are not liable for failing to collect the tax when the seller or service provider relied on data provided by the Tax Commission or software certified for use by the Tax Commission. Similarly, a purchaser will not be liable for penalties on tax owed by the purchaser should the purchaser's seller or service provider rely on faulty data provided by the Tax Commission or software certified by the Tax Commission. The tax will be repealed on January 1, 2023. (S.B. 264, Laws 2017) (UT ¶ 861, 864, 867)

• Exemption limited for Utah sales of electricity from a new alternative energy source

The Utah sales and use tax exemption for sales or uses of electricity that are made under a tariff adopted by the Public Service Commission for the purchase of electricity produced from a new alternative energy source is amended to limit its application to electricity produced from a new alternative energy source built after January 1, 2016. Also, the provision has been amended to clarify that for a residential use customer, the exemption applies only to the portion of the tariff rate the customer pays that exceeds the rate the customer would have paid absent the tariff. (S.B. 242, Laws 2016) (UT ¶ 863)

• Utah revises provision for metro townships that impose sales and use taxes

The Utah State Tax Commission must treat metro townships that impose sales and use taxes the same as it treat cities, effective January 1, 2017. Previously, the law stated that a metro township that imposes sales and use tax must meet the same requirements that a city must meet. (S.B. 138, Laws 2017) (UT ¶ 865)

• Machinery and equipment exemptions enacted in Utah for auto manufacturers, hydrogen manufacturers

Utah has enacted separate sales and use tax machinery and equipment exemptions for automobile manufacturers and industrial gas manufacturers of hydrogen, effective July 1, 2017, as follows (S.B. 132, Laws 2017):

— *Automobile manufacturers:* An exemption is available for purchases or leases of certain machinery, equipment, or normal operating repair or replacement parts by qualifying automobile manufacturing facilities located in Utah. The machinery, equipment, or repair or replacement parts purchased must be used to manufacture an item sold as tangible personal property. In addition, the facility must be an "establishment" as defined by the State Tax Commission. (UT ¶ 863)

— *Hydrogen manufacturers:* An exemption also is available for purchases or leases of equipment or normal operating repair or replacement parts with an economic life of less than three years by industrial gas manufacturing facilities located in Utah. The equipment or repair or replacement parts must be used to manufacture hydrogen. (UT ¶ 863)

• **Utah adds exemption for exterior cleaning and washing of vehicles**

Utah legislation enacts a sales and use tax exemption for sales of vehicle cleaning and washing services when only the vehicle's exterior is washed, effective July 1, 2017. Sales of vehicle cleaning and washing are not exempt when the services also involve cleaning the inside of the vehicle. (S.B. 16, Laws 2017) (UT ¶ 863)

Vermont

• **Vermont adds requirements for out-of-state vendors, and more**

Vermont has enacted legislation that provides new sales and use tax notice requirements for certain noncollecting vendors, makes changes to the thresholds requiring certain out-of-state vendors to collect and remit sales and use taxes, clarifies requirements regarding improvements to real property, and more. Details are as follows (Act 134 (H.B. 873), Laws 2016):

Noncollecting vendor notice and annual statement requirements: Noncollecting vendors making sales into Vermont are required to notify certain purchasers that sales or use tax is due on nonexempt purchases from the vendor and that Vermont requires the purchaser to file a sales or use tax return. "Noncollecting vendor" is defined as a vendor that sells tangible personal property to purchasers who are not exempt from Vermont sales tax and that does not collect the tax.

The notice to purchasers must be provided by January 31 of each year to Vermont purchasers who have made purchases amounting to $500 or more from the noncollecting vendor in the previous calendar year. The notice must show the total amount paid by the purchaser for Vermont purchases made from the noncollecting vendor in the previous calendar year. Specific requirements are provided for the content and mailing of the notices, including a requirement that the notice must state that Vermont requires a sales or use tax return to be filed and tax to be paid on nonexempt purchases made by the purchaser from the noncollecting vendor. (VT ¶ 876)

Out-of-state vendor thresholds: The legislation changes thresholds that, if met, require certain out-of-state vendors to collect and remit Vermont sales and use tax. Persons making sales of tangible personal property from outside Vermont to a destination in Vermont and who do not maintain a place of business or other physical presence in Vermont meet the definition of "vendor" required to collect and remit Vermont sales or use tax if the person engages in regular, systematic, or seasonal solicitation of sales of tangible personal property in Vermont through various means of communication and has made sales from outside Vermont to destinations in Vermont of at least $100,000 or totaling at least 200 individual sales transactions during any 12-month period preceding the monthly period at issue. Previously, the threshold was sales from outside Vermont to destinations in Vermont of at least $50,000 during any 12-month period preceding the monthly or quarterly period at issue. (VT ¶ 876)

Manufacturers and retailers making real property improvements: Manufacturers and retailers that purchase materials and supplies to be used in erecting structures or otherwise improving, altering, or repairing real property are treated as contractors unless they elect, by filing a form with the Department of Taxes, to be treated as a retailer on their purchase of such materials and supplies. If the manufacturer or retailer makes the election, the purchase of such materials and supplies is not considered a retail sale. In addition, the provision imposing tax on tangible personal property used to improve, alter, or repair the real property of others by a manufacturer or retailer is repealed. (VT ¶ 876)

Vending machine sales: A provision specifying that food and beverages sold from a vending machine located at a restaurant are deemed to be sold by a restaurant would be repealed. (VT ¶ 879)

• Exemption for agricultural machinery amended in Vermont

Vermont's sales and use tax exemption for agricultural machinery and equipment has been amended, effective July 1, 2016, by changing the term "directly and exclusively" to "predominately" with respect to the use of the agricultural machinery or equipment. This change reduces the limitation percentage from 96% to 75%, making it easier to qualify for the sales tax exemption. Therefore, to qualify for the exemption the machinery and equipment must be used predominately, *i.e.,* 75% or more, of the time in the production for sale of tangible personal property on farms (including stock, dairy, poultry, fruit, and truck farms), orchards, nurseries, or in greenhouses or other similar structures used primarily for the raising of agricultural or horticultural commodities for sale. (Act 100 (H.B. 864), Laws 2016) (VT ¶ 878)

• Vermont clarifies tax on alcoholic beverages

Vermont legislation effective July 1, 2016, clarifies that alcoholic beverages sold or provided for immediate consumption are subject to meals and rooms tax and exempt from sales and use tax. (Act 144 (S.B. 250), Laws 2016) (VT ¶ 878)

• Motor vehicle purchase and use tax amended in Vermont

Changes have been enacted to the taxation of certain motor vehicles, as follows: (VT ¶ 879)

Heavy motor vehicles: The motor vehicle purchase and use tax cap on heavy motor vehicles is increased from $1,850 to $2,075, effective July 1, 2016. (Act 159 (H.B. 877), Laws 2016)

Tracked vehicles: The maximum sales and use tax on tracked vehicles is $1,320 for sales occurring between July 1, 2016, and June 30, 2018. The maximum tax is adjusted for inflation in even-numbered years and rounded to the nearest $10. If the sale of a tracked vehicle occurs in a municipality with a local option sales tax, the local option tax applies to the first $22,000 of the sales price of the vehicle. If the sales price of a tracked vehicle is more than $22,000, the local option tax is capped at $220. In such cases, the maximum state plus local tax is $1,540. (*Technical Bulletin TB-52,* Vermont Department of Taxes, June 14, 2016, CCH VERMONT TAX REPORTS, ¶ 200-984)

Virginia

• Virginia's biennial budget contains several sales and use tax provisions

Virginia's 2016-2017 budget includes the sales and use tax provisions discussed below (Ch. 780 (H.B. 30), Laws 2016, effective July 1, 2016, except as noted):

Sunset dates for exemptions: The sunset date on any existing sales tax exemption may not be extended beyond June 30, 2022. Any new sales tax exemption enacted prior to the 2021 regular legislative session must have a sunset date not later than June 30, 2022. However, this requirement does not apply to tax exemptions administered by the Department of Taxation for nonprofit entities and for exemptions with sunset dates after June 30, 2022, enacted or advanced during the 2016 session of the General Assembly. (VA ¶ 893)

Research and development exemption: The sales and use tax exemption for tangible personal property purchased or leased for use or consumption directly and exclusively in basic research or research and development in the experimental or laboratory sense will apply to such property used in a federally funded research and development center, regardless of whether the property is used by the purchaser, lessee, or another person or entity. (VA ¶ 893)

Accelerated sales tax payments: Any dealer or direct payment permit holder with taxable sales and purchases of $1 million or greater for a 12-month period beginning July 1 and ending June 30 of the immediately preceding calendar year is required to make a payment equal to 90% of the sales and use tax liability for the previous June. The payment must be made on or before June 30th, if payment is made by electronic funds transfer, or on or before June 25th, if payment is made by means other than electronic funds transfer. However, beginning with the tax payment to be remitted on or before June 25, 2017, if the payment is made by other than electronic fund transfers, and by June 30, 2017, if payments are made by electronic fund transfer, the accelerated sales tax payment provisions apply only to those dealers or permit holders with taxable sales and purchases of $10 million or greater for the 12-month period beginning July 1 and ending June 30 of the immediately preceding calendar year. Similar provisions apply to June 2018 payments, but the threshold is increased to $25 million. (VA ¶ 897)

• **Tax amnesty enacted in Virginia**

A Virginia tax amnesty program has been enacted that will occur during the period of July 1, 2017, through June 30, 2018, and will not last less than 60 nor more than 75 days. The exact dates of the program will be established by the Tax Commissioner. Any taxpayer required to file a return or to pay any tax administered or collected by the Department of Taxation will be eligible to participate in the Program, subject to certain requirements and guidelines. The Tax Commissioner may require participants to complete an amnesty application and other forms and to furnish any additional information necessary to make a determination regarding the validity of an amnesty application. With certain exceptions, all civil or criminal penalties assessed or assessable, and one-half of the interest assessed or assessable, that are the result of nonpayment, underpayment, nonreporting, or underreporting of tax liabilities, may be waived under the program upon receipt of the payment of the amount of taxes and interest owed. (Ch. 54 (H.B. 2246), Laws 2017; Ch. 433 (S.B. 1438), Laws 2017) (VA ¶ 901)

• **Virginia adds exemption requirement for cigarette wholesalers**

Effective January 1, 2018, purchasers of cigarettes for resale must apply for a special cigarette exemption certificate from the Virginia Department of Taxation in order to not be liable for the payment of sales and use tax at the time of purchase. The department will conduct a background investigation for taxpayers applying for the certificate, with a waiting period of at least 30 days, unless the taxpayer qualifies for an expedited process included in the legislation.

The legislation sets forth numerous requirements that a taxpayer must meet in order to qualify for a cigarette exemption certificate and establishes processes and procedures for the application (including a fee of up to $50), renewal, denial, suspension, and revocation of the certificates. A cigarette exemption certificate will be valid for five years.The department must develop guidelines regarding the exemption certificate, and must complete the process for issuing cigarette exemption certificates no later than December 31, 2017. The department must ensure that any taxpayer who qualifies under the expedited process prior to December 1, 2017, or applies for a cigarette exemption certificate prior to December 1, 2017, will be issued or denied the cigarette exemption certificate prior to January 1, 2018. (Ch. 112 (H.B. 1913), Laws 2017) (VA ¶ 893) (Sec. 58.1-623.2)

• **Tax penalties eased for Virginia small businesses**

Effective July 1, 2017, penalties related to taxes administered by the Virginia Department of Taxation will be waived for a small business during its first two years of operation, provided that such small business enters into an installment agreement with the Tax Commissioner. The legislation defines small business as an independently owned and operated business that has been organized pursuant to Virginia law or maintains a principal place of business in Virginia and has ten or fewer employees. (Ch. 718 (S.B. 793), Laws 2017)

• Beer-making equipment exempted in Virginia

An exemption from Virginia retail sales and use tax has been enacted for certain equipment and materials used by qualifying licensed brewers if the preponderance of their use is in the manufacturing of beer. The exemption would apply to:

— machinery, tools, equipment and repair and replacement parts, fuel, power, energy or supplies;

— materials for future processing, manufacturing or conversion into beer, where the materials either enter into the production of or become a component part of the beer; and

— materials, including containers, labels, sacks, cans, bottles, kegs, boxes, drums or bags for future use, for packaging the beer for shipment or sale.

The exemption is effective July 1, 2016. (Ch. 709 (H.B. 859), Laws 2016) (VA ¶ 893)

• Virginia exempts taxes on fuel for hunger relief vehicles

Effective July 1, 2016, a sales and use tax exemption and a motor fuel tax refund are provided for fuel used in highway vehicles owned and used by an exempt entity solely for the purpose of providing hunger relief services or food to the needy. (Ch. 34 (H.B. 23), Laws 2016) (VA ¶ 893)

• Alternative energy equipment exempt in Virginia

Effective January 1, 2017, a sales and use tax exemption is provided for machinery, tools, and equipment used by a public service corporation to generate energy derived from sunlight or wind. The exemption expires June 30, 2027. (Ch. 346 (H.B. 1305), Laws 2016) (VA ¶ 893)

• Virginia modifies exemption for veterans' organizations

Effective July 1, 2016, Virginia legislation provides that the sales and use tax exemption for certain nonprofit veterans organizations will not apply to tangible personal property used primarily for social and recreational activities for members or for providing insurance benefits to members or members' dependents. The legislation also permits nonprofit entities that are exempt from federal income taxation under IRC Sec. 501(c)(19), as well as organizations that have annual gross receipts below $5,000 and that are organized for one of the purposes set forth in IRC Sec. 501(c)(19), to obtain a sales and use tax exemption on purchases of tangible personal property. (Ch. 488 (H.B. 63), Laws 2016) (VA ¶ 893)

• Refunds of Virginia motor vehicle sales tax authorized for defective vehicles

Legislation effective July 1, 2017, allows a purchaser to be refunded any Virginia motor vehicle sales and use tax paid if the vehicle is returned pursuant to the Virginia Motor Vehicle Warranty Enforcement Act, or if the vehicle is returned within 45 days of purchase, and the purchase price is refunded, due to a mechanical defect or failure. A person claiming the refund under the Virginia Motor Vehicle Warranty Enforcement Act is required to provide a written statement stating that the vehicle was returned under the Act. A person claiming the refund due to a mechanical defect or failure is required to submit an affidavit to the Commissioner of the Department of Motor Vehicles stating that the vehicle was returned due to a mechanical defect or failure, the purchase price was refunded, the title was assigned to the person accepting the return, and the purchaser no longer has possession of the vehicle. (Ch. 552 (S.B. 1350), Laws 2017) (VA ¶ 904)

• Virginia adds exemption for aircraft parts

Beginning July 1, 2018, and ending July 1, 2022, a Virginia retail sales and use tax exemption is created for parts, engines, and supplies used for maintaining, repairing, or reconditioning aircraft or any aircraft's avionics system, engine, or component parts. For purposes of the exemption, "aircraft" includes both manned and unmanned systems. The exemption does not apply to tools and other equipment not attached to or that does not become a part of the aircraft. In addition, the exemption does not restrict the exemption available for tangible personal property sold or leased to an airline operating in intrastate, interstate or foreign commerce as a common carrier providing scheduled air service on a continuing basis to one or more Virginia airports. (Ch. 714 (H.B. 1738), Laws 2017) (VA ¶ 893)

• Numerous exemptions extended in Virginia

The sunset dates for various sales and use tax exemptions have been extended to July 1, 2022, as follows: (VA ¶ 893)

— Annual sales and use tax holidays (Ch. 446 (S.B. 1018), Laws 2017);

— Bullion (legal tender coins added effective 1/1/2018) (Ch. 445 (S.B. 934), Laws 2017);

— Machinery and tools, materials, and supplies used to drill, extract, or process natural gas or oil (Ch. 673 (S.B. 563), Laws 2016);

— Media-related exemptions (Ch. 412 (H.B. 1543), Laws 2017);

— Printing purchased by an advertising business for distribution outside Virginia (Ch. 441 (S.B. 804), Laws 2017).

Washington

• Washington clarifies nexus for trade show participants

Effective July 1, 2016, the participation of one or more representatives at a single trade convention per year in Washington is not considered a factor in the nexus determination. The safe harbor does not apply to persons making retail sales at a trade convention. (Ch. 137 (H.B. 2938), Laws 2016) (WA ¶ 906)

• Motor vehicle sales to tribes or tribal members in Indian country exempt in Washington

Effective June 9, 2016, the sale of a motor vehicle is exempt from Washington sales tax if it is delivered to a tribe or tribal member in Indian country or if the sale is made to a tribe or tribal member in Indian country. A tribal member is not required to reside in Indian country in order to qualify for exemption. In order to document the tribal member's exempt status, the seller must receive presentation of:

(1) the buyer's tribal membership or citizenship card;

(2) certificate of tribal enrollment, or

(3) a letter signed by a tribal official confirming the buyer's membership status.

In order to document delivery of a motor vehicle, a seller and buyer must complete and sign a declaration regarding the location of delivery and to the enrollment status of the tribal member. (Ch. 232 (S.B. 642)7, Laws 2016) (WA ¶ 908)

• Washington exempts sales for construction of new buildings for aircraft maintenance

Effective July 1, 2016, until January 1, 2027, Washington sales and use tax exemptions are available for charges for labor and services rendered for construction of new buildings made to an eligible maintenance repair operator engaged in maintenance of airplanes or a port district, political subdivision, or municipal corporation if the new building is to be leased to an eligible maintenance repair operator. Also exempt are sales of tangible personal property to be incorporated as a component of such buildings and charges made for labor and services performed in respect to the installation of fixtures not otherwise exempt.

The exemption is claimed in the form of a remittance. A person requesting a remittance may do so after the aircraft maintenance and repair station is operationally complete for four years, but not sooner than December 1, 2021. However, a person may request remittance of local sales and use taxes on and after July 1, 2016. (H.B. 2839, Laws 2016) (WA ¶ 908)

West Virginia

• West Virginia suspends medical equipment exemption for two years

The consumers' sales and service tax exemption for purchases of durable medical equipment by health care providers is suspended from July 1, 2016, through June 30, 2018, when the exemption is reestablished on and after July 1, 2018. (S.B. 421, Laws 2016) (WV ¶ 923)

• Hotel occupancy tax exemption for long-term stays eliminated in West Virginia

The exemption from hotel occupancy taxes for hotel stays of 30 or more consecutive days is eliminated, effective June 8, 2016. The legislation also excludes from the definition of "hotel," as the term is used with respect to hotel occupancy taxes, (1) sleeping accommodations rented on a month-to-month basis, or other rental arrangement for 30 or more days at the inception, at a boarding house, condominium, cabin, tourist home, apartment, or home; and (2) sleeping accommodations rented by a hotel operator to those persons directly employed by the operator for purposes of performing duties in support of the hotel's operation or related operations. (H.B. 4377, Laws 2016) (WV ¶ 923, ¶ 925)

• West Virginia exempts homeowners association dues

A consumers sales and service tax exemption is enacted, effective June 9, 2016, for membership dues, fees, and assessments paid to a homeowners' association by a member if for the purpose of permitting or funding the associations' payment of common expenses when acting in its representative capacity for its members. The exemption does not apply to purchases for resale of tangible personal property and services for use by the homeowners' association when acting in its representative capacity for its members. (S.B. 54, Laws 2016) (WV ¶ 923)

• Governor of West Virginia may negotiate reciprocal tax agreements with neighboring states and DC

Enacted West Virginia legislation authorizes the governor to enter into and renew reciprocity agreements with governors and other appropriate state governmental agencies from states that share contiguous borders with West Virginia, and the District of Columbia, in order to establish regulations, licensing requirements, and taxation for small businesses. (H.B. 4502, Laws 2016)

• West Virginia counties may impose transportation taxes for road and bridge projects

West Virginia legislation permits a county commission, with voter approval, to impose a transportation sales and use tax at a rate of up to 1% to finance the accelerated construction, upgrading, or modernization of roads and bridges within the county. Two or more county commissions may contract to share expenses and dedicate county funds or county transportation sales and use tax revenues, on a *pro rata* basis, to facilitate projects.

The tax base of a county transportation sales and use tax is generally the same as that of the state consumers sales and service tax and use tax, with some exceptions. However, county transportation sales and use taxes do not apply to:

(1) sales and uses of motor vehicles upon which the 5% consumers sales tax on motor vehicle sales was paid or is payable;

(2) sales and uses of motor fuel upon which the motor carrier road tax and motor fuel excise tax was paid or is payable;

(3) any sale of tangible personal property, sale of custom software, or furnishing of a service that is exempt from state consumers sales and service tax;

(4) any use of tangible personal property, use of custom software, or the results of a taxable service that is exempt from state use tax. However, this exception is not applicable to any use within the county when the state consumers sales and service tax was paid to the seller at the time of purchase but the county's transportation sales tax was not paid to the seller; and

(5) any sale or use of tangible personal property, custom software, or taxable service that the county is prohibited from taxing under federal law or the laws of West Virginia.

A vendor selling tangible personal property or custom software or furnishing a taxable service in a county that imposes a county transportation sales tax must collect the county's transportation sales tax from the purchaser at the same time and in the same manner that the consumers sales tax is collected from the customer. Special rules apply when purchases are made in a West Virginia county that does not impose county transportation sales and use taxes, and the items or services are used in a county that does impose the tax. (H.B. 4009, Laws 2016) (WV ¶ 925)

Wisconsin

• Wisconsin modifies credit card bad debt provision

Effective July 1, 2017, and first applicable to bad debts resulting from sales completed beginning on July 1, 2017, debt-collection expenses, which are excluded from the definition of "bad debt," do not include dual purpose credit debts and private label credit debts.

"Dual purpose credit debt" means accounts and receivables that result from credit sale transactions using a dual purpose credit card, but only to the extent the account or receivable balance resulted from purchases made from the seller whose name or logo appears on the card. "Dual purpose credit card" means a credit card that may be used as a private label credit card or to make purchases from persons other than the seller whose name or logo appears on the card or the seller's affiliates or franchisees, if the credit card issuer is able to determine the sales receipts of the seller and the seller's affiliates or franchisees apart from any sales receipts of unrelated persons.

"Private label credit debt" means accounts and receivables that result from credit sale transactions using a private label credit card, but only to the extent the account or receivable balance resulted from purchases made from the seller whose name or logo appears on the card. "Private label credit card" means any charge card or credit card that identifies a seller's name or logo on the card and that may be used only for purchases from that seller or from any of the seller's affiliates or franchisees.

Under the legislation, a seller may claim as a deduction the amount of any bad debt that the seller or lender writes off as uncollectible in the seller's or lender's books and records and that is eligible to be deducted as a bad debt for federal income tax purposes, regardless of whether the seller or lender is required to file a federal income tax return. A seller who claims this deduction must claim the deduction on the return that is submitted for the period in which the seller or lender writes off the amount of the deduction as uncollectible in the seller's or lender's books and records and in which that amount is eligible to be deducted as bad debt for federal income tax purposes. If the seller or lender subsequently collects all or part of any bad debt for which a bad debt deduction is claimed, the seller must include the amount collected in the return filed for the period in which the amount is collected and must pay the tax with the return. Also, "bad debt" means the portion of the sales price or purchase price that the seller has previously reported as taxable, and for which the seller has paid the tax, and that the seller or lender may claim as a deduction under IRC Sec. 166. Previously, lenders were not included in these provisions.

The legislation also allows sellers to compute their bad debt deduction using an estimate if the Department of Revenue approves the method for computing the estimate. (Act 229 (A.B. 644), Laws 2014, originally effective July 1, 2015, but delayed by Act 55 (S.B. 21), Laws 2015) (WI ¶ 945)

• **Wisconsin administrative provisions amended**

Wisconsin legislation effective March 3, 2016, amended sales and use tax provisions to specify the treatment of disregarded entities in various situations; amended statutes of limitations for assessments and refunds; and amended local tax provisions regarding sourcing of certain transactions. Details follow (Act 216 (S.B. 440), Laws 2016):

Disregarded entities: A provision regarding business tax registration is amended to provide that if a business owner elects to file a separate electronic return for each of the owner's disregarded entities, each disregarded entity must obtain a business tax registration certificate. A provision regarding applications for seller's permits is amended to provide that if an owner elects to file a separate electronic return for each of its disregarded entities, each disregarded entity is an applicant for a seller's permit. For a single-owner entity that is disregarded as a separate entity under Wisconsin income tax laws, the requirement to hold a seller's permit is satisfied if the seller's permit is in the name of either the disregarded entity or its owner. (WI ¶ 944)

Statutes of limitation: The statutes of limitations for assessments and refunds are amended to provide that the four-year limitations periods refer to the due date of the person's Wisconsin income or franchise return that corresponds to the date the sale or purchase was completed. Previously, the limitations periods referred to the due date of the Wisconsin income or franchise tax return or the corresponding Wisconsin income franchise tax return.

A provision regarding claims for refunds that are not passed along to customers, which provides a two-year statute of limitations for refund claims after an audit determination, is amended to provide that claims for refund are not allowed with regard to items that were not adjusted in the office audit or field audit. Previously, the provision disallowed refund claims for any tax self-assessed by the taxpayer. (WI ¶ 948)

Local taxes: For local sales and use tax purposes, single payment or lump-sum leases and rentals (*i.e.,* those that do not require recurring periodic payments) of certain motor vehicles, boats, recreational vehicles, and aircraft are to be sourced on the basis of the location where the customer receives the property (previously, where the motor vehicle, boat, recreational vehicle, or aircraft was customarily kept). (WI ¶ 937)

• **Wisconsin exempts sales of music used in jukeboxes**

Effective June 1, 2016, jukebox music sold in tangible form to a person in the business of providing taxable service through a jukebox is exempt from Wisconsin sales and use taxes. The music must be used exclusively for the jukebox. Music sold in a tangible form is a separate sale from the jukebox through which the music is played if the sales price of such property is indicated separately from the sales price of the jukebox on the invoice, bill of sale, or similar document that the seller gives to the purchaser. (Act 251 (S.B. 300), Laws 2016) (WI ¶ 938)

- **Online travel companies not taxable in Wisconsin**

A Wisconsin Court of Appeals determined that markup amounts collected by an online travel company as part of its reservation facilitation services were not subject to sales tax. The tax was imposed on the furnishing of rooms or lodging to transients by hotelkeepers, motel operators, and other persons furnishing accommodations available to the public. (*Wisconsin Department of Revenue v. Orbitz, LLC,* Court of Appeals of Wisconsin, District IV, No. 2015AP200, February 11, 2016, CCH Wisconsin Tax Reports, ¶ 402-040) (WI ¶ 936)

Wyoming

- **Wyoming sales tax imposed on remote sellers**

Effective July 1, 2017, a seller without a physical presence in Wyoming must remit sales tax on its sales of tangible personal property, admissions, or services delivered into Wyoming once the seller meets either of the following requirements in the current or preceding calendar year:

    (1)   the seller's gross revenue from such sales exceed $100,000 or

    (2)   the seller sold such items in 200 or more separate transactions.

The Department of Revenue may bring an action to obtain a declaratory judgment that the seller is obligated to remit sales tax. The term "vendor" is amended to include a remote seller. (H.B. 19, Laws 2017) (WY ¶ 951)

- **Manufacturing machinery exemption extended in Wyoming**

The sunset date for the manufacturing machinery exemption from Wyoming sales and use taxes has been extended from December 31, 2017, to December 31, 2027. This exemption includes the purchases, sales and leases of machinery used in Wyoming directly and predominantly in manufacturing tangible personal property. (Ch. 181 (S.F. 70), Laws 2017) (WY ¶ 953)

- **Wyoming clarifies refund or credit of erroneously collected tax**

Effective July 1, 2016, if a vendor erroneously collects Wyoming sales or use taxes from a taxpayer and remits those taxes to the Department of Revenue (DOR), the vendor may seek a refund or credit against subsequent tax liability only after the vendor has refunded the erroneously collected tax to the taxpayer that originally paid the tax to the vendor. If the taxpayer that originally paid the tax to the vendor cannot be identified, the tax will not be refunded or credited to the vendor.

Payment of erroneously collected tax: The tax must be remitted to the DOR after the vendor makes reasonable attempts to identify and refund the excess tax to the taxpayer that originally paid the tax.

Recomputation of tax: After a sales tax return is filed, if it appears from the information on the return that the tax to be remitted is incorrect, the DOR will recompute the tax. If the amount remitted exceeds that which is due from the recomputed return, the excess will be refunded or credited. (Ch. 33 (S.F. 20), Laws 2016) (WY ¶ 964)

Constitutional Issues

United States constitutional provisions that restrict the ability of states to levy sales and use taxes are discussed below.

Commerce and Due Process Provisions

Of the United States constitutional provisions that limit states' ability to tax, the Commerce and Due Process Clauses are the most frequently invoked to challenge sales and use tax laws.

Commerce Clause requirements

The Commerce Clause (Sec. 8, Cl. 3, Art. I, U.S. Const.) reserves to Congress the power to regulate commerce among the states, with foreign nations, and with Indian tribes. This provision at one time was interpreted as setting a virtual bar on a state's ability to tax interstate commerce. However, under the U.S. Supreme Court's current interpretation of the Commerce Clause, a state tax that impacts interstate commerce is valid if it meets the following requirements (*Complete Auto Transit, Inc. v. Brady* (1977, US SCt) 430 US 274, 97 SCt 1076):

1. it is applied to an activity with substantial connection (nexus) with the state;

2. it is fairly apportioned;

3. it does not discriminate against interstate commerce; and

4. it is fairly related to the services provided by the taxing state.

When international commerce is involved, in addition to the criteria above, a tax may not do either of the following (*Japan Line, Ltd., et al. v. County of Los Angeles, et al.* (1979, US SCt) 441 US 434, 99 SCt 1813):

1. create a risk of multiple taxation, or

2. prevent the federal government from speaking with one voice when regulating commercial relations with foreign governments.

In 1991, the U.S. Supreme Court affirmatively resolved the question of whether suits for violations of the Commerce Clause may be brought under the Civil Rights statute, 42 U.S.C. § 1983 (*Dennis v. Higgins, et al.* (1991, US SCt) 111 SCt 865). The statute provides that a party who uses a state law to deprive another of any rights, privileges, or immunities that are protected by the U.S. Constitution is liable to the injured party.

Due Process requirements

The Due Process Clause (Sec. 1, Amend. XIV, U.S. Const.) prevents the states from depriving any person of life, liberty, or property without due process of law. Not defined by the Constitution, the nature of due process itself has consequently been determined by case law. It has been held by the Supreme Court to require some definite link, some minimum connection, between a state and the person, property, or transaction it seeks to tax (*Miller Bros. Co. v. Maryland,* (1954, US SCt) 347 US 340). In essence, the tax imposed must be reasonably related to the protection, opportunities, and benefits given by the state (*Wisconsin v. J.C. Penney Co.* (1940, US SCt) 311 US 435, 61 SCt 246, *Moorman Mfg. Co. v. Bair* (1978, US SCt) 437 US 267).

Fair apportionment of tax

Connected with the principle that a tax must be reasonably related to the benefits provided by the taxing state is the requirement that the tax must be fairly apportioned.

This fairness requirement is an element of both the Commerce and Due Process Clauses, and according to the Supreme Court, it has two components (*Container Corp. of America v. FTB* (1983, US SCt) 463 US 159, 103 SCt 2933). First, the tax must have internal consistency; that is, the tax must be such that, if applied by every jurisdiction, it would result in no impermissible interference with free trade. Second, the tax must have external consistency that is, the factor or factors used in calculating the tax must actually reflect a reasonable sense of how the income being taxed is generated. In essence, the external consistency component requires an analysis of whether the income being taxed is in proportion to the activity being conducted within the taxing state.

The internal consistency component has been analyzed by the courts in sales and use tax cases dealing with tax statutes that on their face discriminate against interstate commerce. Discrimination against interstate commerce is discussed below.

Nexus Tests

"Nexus" is a requirement for taxation of interstate transactions under both the Commerce and Due Process Clauses. Under the first prong of the *Complete Auto* Commerce Clause test, a tax is valid only if it is applied to an activity having a substantial nexus with the taxing state. Under the Due Process Clause, there must be some minimum connection between a state and the person, property, or transaction it seeks to tax. However, although the two tests are similarly phrased and the courts at one time treated them as a single test, the U.S. Supreme Court in *Quill Corp.* (*Quill Corp. v. North Dakota* (1992, US SCt) 112 SCt 1904) confirmed that the Due Process Clause's minimum contacts requirement and the Commerce Clause's substantial nexus requirement are not identical.

Nexus tests distinguished

In *Quill*, the High Court ruled that the Commerce Clause, but not the Due Process Clause, barred North Dakota from requiring an out-of-state mail-order company to collect and pay use tax on goods sold to North Dakota customers when the company had no outlets, sales representatives, or other significant property in the state. In so ruling, the Court reaffirmed the portion of its landmark decision in *National Bellas Hess, Inc. v. Department of Revenue* (1967, US SCt) 386 US 753, 87 SCt 1389),that established under the Commerce Clause a bright-line rule that permits a state to compel those out-of-state mail-order sellers that have a physical presence in the state to collect its use taxes, but not those who do no more than communicate with customers in the state by mail or common carrier as part of a general interstate business.

However, the Court overturned *Bellas Hess* and its prior decisions to the extent that they indicate that the Due Process Clause requires a seller's physical presence in a state before the seller can be obligated to collect the state's use tax.

The distinction between the two nexus tests was grounded on the different constitutional concerns and policies that underlie the Due Process and Commerce Clauses. While due process primarily concerns the fundamental fairness of governmental activity, the Commerce Clause concerns the effects of state regulation on the national economy. The evolution of due process jurisprudence since *Bellas Hess* indicates that the focus of the minimum contacts test is whether a taxpayer has fair warning that its activity may subject it to a foreign sovereign's jurisdiction. In contrast, the substantial nexus test under the Commerce Clause is a means of limiting state burdens on interstate commerce.

Thus, although the *Quill* taxpayer's continuous and widespread solicitation of business—its economic presence—within North Dakota was more than sufficient to satisfy the minimum contact test, it was not, in the absence of the taxpayer's physical presence in the state, sufficient to satisfy the substantial nexus test. However, because Congress has the authority to regulate interstate commerce but not to modify the safeguards of the Due Process Clause, the Court's removal of the *Bellas Hess* due process objection frees Congress to decide whether, when, and to what extent the states may burden out-of-state mail-order companies with a duty to collect use taxes.

Physical presence as evidence of nexus

Under *Quill*, a taxpayer's physical presence in a state is required under the Commerce Clause before the state can impose use tax obligations on the taxpayer. A body of case law, very briefly summarized here, amplifies the factual elements that have been held to constitute physical presence.

Generally, having an office or other place of business in the state, employing individuals in the state, or holding property in the state constitutes physical presence sufficient to establish nexus under both the Commerce and Due Process Clauses. For example, nexus has been established by a single resident employee in the state (*Standard Pressed Steel Co. v. Department of Revenue* (1975, US SCt) 419 US 560), and the temporary storage of fuel to be withdrawn for consumption in interstate flights (*United Air Lines, Inc. v. Mahin, et al.* (1973, US SCt) 410 US 623). In *Scripto, Inc. v. Carson* (1960, US SCt) 362 US 207, 80 SCt 619), an out-of-state seller's nexus with Florida was established by independent brokers used by the seller to solicit sales in the state. The fact that the brokers, who were Florida residents, were independent contractors rather than employees was without constitutional significance.

Affiliate nexus: An out-of-state corporation that made online retail sales of tangible personal property was held liable for the collection and remittance of California use tax on all sales to California purchasers because its bricks-and-mortar affiliate acted as its agent when it accepted returns of merchandise purchased online. The activities of the bricks-and-mortar agent on behalf of its online retailer principal in, among other things, facilitating a return policy, were conducted for the purpose of selling the online retailer's goods. As such, the online retailer, through its agent's activities, had sufficient presence in California to justify the imposition of the use tax collection burden. In addition, every retailer engaged in business in the state is required to collect and remit use tax. The term "retailer engaged in business in the state" is statutorily defined, in part, as any retailer having any representative or agent (among other entities) operating in the state under the authority of the retailer for the purpose of selling (among other purposes). When the online retailer posted a return policy on its website that informed its customers that items purchased online could be returned to any of its affiliate's bricks-and-mortar stores, many of which were located in California, the bricks-and-mortar affiliate acted on behalf of the online retailer as its authorized agent or representative in California, and the online retailer became subject to California's use tax. (*Borders Online, LLC v. State Board of Equalization,* California Court of Appeal, First Appellate District, 129 Cal. App. 4th 1179, 29 Cal. Rptr. 3d 176 (2005)).

Click-through nexus: New York legislation enacted in 2008 creates a rebuttable presumption that certain sellers of taxable tangible personal property or services are sales tax vendors required to register for sales tax purposes and to collect state and local sales taxes (Sec. 1101(b)(8)(vi), Tax Law; TSB-M-08(3)S; TSB-M-08(3.1)S; TSB-M-08(9)S). Arkansas, California, Colorado, Connecticut, Georgia, Kansas, Louisiana, Maine, Michigan, Minnesota, Missouri, New Jersey, North Carolina, Ohio, Pennsylvania, Rhode Island, Tennessee, Vermont, and Washington have enacted similar "click-through nexus" legislation, and several other states are considering such legislation.

Specifically, under New York's so-called "Amazon law", a seller that makes taxable sales of tangible personal property or services in New York is presumed to be a vendor required to be registered for sales tax purposes and required to collect sales tax on all of its taxable sales in New York, if both of the following conditions are met:

—the seller enters into an agreement or agreements with a New York resident or residents under which, for a commission or other consideration, the resident representative directly or indirectly refers potential customers to the seller, whether by link on an Internet website or otherwise. A resident representative would be indirectly referring potential customers to the seller when, for example, the resident representative refers potential customers to its own website, or to another party's website, which then directs the potential customer to the seller's website, and

—the cumulative gross receipts from sales by the seller to customers in New York as a result of referrals to the seller by all of the seller's resident representatives under the type of contract or agreement described above total more than $10,000 during the preceding four quarterly sales tax periods.

The New York Supreme Court, New York County, dismissed a lawsuit filed by Amazon.com challenging the New York registration requirement. Amazon sought a declaratory judgment that the new statutory provision was invalid, illegal, and unconstitutional (facially and as applied to Amazon) on the grounds that it violated the Commerce Clause of the U.S. Constitution and the Due Process and Equal Protection Clauses of the U.S. and New York Constitutions. The court held that even accepting all the facts alleged by Amazon to be true, there was no basis upon which it could prevail. Thus, Amazon's complaint was dismissed in its entirety for failure to state a cause of action. (*Amazon.com LLC v. New York Department of Taxation and Finance,* New York Supreme Court, New York County, No. 601247/08, January 12, 2009, CCH NEW YORK TAX REPORTS, ¶ 406-287) However, the complaint was reinstated on appeal. The appellate court found that the statute is constitutional on its face in relation to the Commerce Clause and the Due Process Clause, and does not violate the Equal Protection Clause on its face or as applied. However, the court concluded that further discovery is required to evaluate the as-applied Commerce and Due Process Clause claims (*Amazon.com LLC v. Department of Taxation and Finance*, Appellate Division of the Supreme Court of New York, First Department, No. 601247/08, November 4, 2010, CCH NEW YORK TAX REPORTS, ¶ 407-041).

Under New York's Amazon law, a seller may rebut the presumption that it is soliciting sales in New York through resident representatives if the seller is able to establish that the only activity of its resident representative in New York on behalf of the seller is a link provided on the representatives' website to the seller's website and none of the resident representatives engage in any solicitation activity in the state targeted at potential New York customers on behalf of the seller. (Sec. 1101(b)(8)(vi), Tax Law; TSB-M-08(3)S). The inclusion of language in a contract or agreement between a seller and a resident representative that prohibits solicitation by the resident representative is not sufficient, by itself, to rebut the presumption that the seller is a vendor. In order to rebut the presumption, the seller must be able to demonstrate both that the prohibition has been established and that the resident representative has complied with it (TSB-M-08(3.1)S).

Related activity: A taxpayer's physical contacts with a state need not be related to the activity being taxed. In *National Geographic Society v. SBE* (1977, US SCt) 430 US 551), the U.S. Supreme Court held that the presence in California of advertising sales offices for the National Geographic magazine provided sufficient nexus for California to require National Geographic to collect the use tax on mail-order sales made to California by another division of the Society. Despite the fact that the two advertising sales offices had nothing to do with the mail-order division, the offices benefited from California services, and thus provided the connection with the state that allowed California to require the Society to collect the state's use tax. The Court applied similar reasoning in *D.H. Holmes Co., Ltd. v. McNamara* (1988, US SCt) 486 US 24), in which a company with retail outlets in the state was required to pay use tax on catalogs ordered from an out-of-state printer and sent by mail to company customers. However, two state supreme courts have refused to expand the reasoning of the *National Geographic* case to create nexus between a taxpayer and a state based on contacts between the state and a party related to the taxpayer (*SFA Folio Collections, Inc. v. Bannon* (1991, Conn SCt)

217 Conn 220, cert den US SCt, *Bloomingdale's By Mail, Ltd. v. Department of Revenue* (1989, Penn ComwthCt) 567 A2d 773, aff'd per curium Penn SCt, cert den US SCt).

Property ownership: A taxpayer's ownership of property in a state will not necessarily establish nexus if the property is insignificant. For example, in *Quill*, the U.S. Supreme Court refused to give constitutional significance to the fact that the taxpayer retained title to licensed software present in the state. In *Cally Curtis Co. v. Groppo* (1990, Conn SCt) 214 Conn 292), the Connecticut Supreme Court ruled that nexus was not established by the presence of films that a California firm rented to Connecticut customers for previewing prior to a customer's purchase of the film. This contact was found to be *de minimus*, as the rented films were only in the state for three-day periods.

Discrimination Against Interstate Commerce

The U.S. Supreme Court has traditionally held that states may not impose greater burdens on out-of-state business enterprises than on equivalent local business. An example of this discrimination is the Louisiana use tax, which was applied to oil service equipment that had been manufactured outside the state (*Halliburton Oil Well Cementing Co. v. Reily* (1963, US SCt) 373 US 64). The cost on which the tax was based included labor and shop overhead, but if equipment manufactured in Louisiana had been used, labor and overhead would have been excluded from the tax.

Exemptions offered to local businesses that are not available to out-of-state firms can also affect the constitutionality of a tax. In a Washington case, an exemption available only to in-state manufacturers who also engaged in wholesaling was deemed discriminatory in favoring local businesses (*Tyler Pipe Industries, Inc. v. Department of Revenue* (1987, US SCt) 483 US 232; *Armco Inc. v. Hardesty* (1984, US SCt) 467 US 638).

Credits and multiple taxation

Discrimination may also occur as a result of the structuring of credits, as was the case when Ohio granted a sales tax credit for ethanol produced in the state but not to ethanol produced in states that did not grant a tax advantage to Ohio-produced fuel (*New Energy Co. of Indiana v. Limbach et al.* (1988, US SCt) 486 US 269).

Subjecting a single transaction to the risk of multiple taxation is frequently cited as creating impermissible discrimination against interstate commerce (*AT&T Communications of the Mountain States v. Department of Revenue* (1989, Colo SCt) 778 P2d 677; Goldberg v. Sweet (1989, US SCt) 488 US 252)). However, the Wyoming Supreme Court has ruled that Wyoming was not required to grant a taxpayer a credit for use taxes previously paid to another state on pipe that under Wyoming law was also subject to the Wyoming use tax (*Exxon Corp. v. SBE* (1989, Wyo SCt) 783 P2d 685, cert den US SCt).

A utility excise levied upon interstate phone calls that originate or terminate in Illinois does not unconstitutionally burden interstate commerce, because a credit is provided for taxes paid in other states (*Goldberg v. Sweet* (1989, US SCt) 488 US 252). A like conclusion was reached that local telephone exchange access service is a local event properly subject to Colorado state taxation (*AT&T Communications of the Mountain States v. Department of Revenue* (1989, Colo SCt) 778 P2d 677).

The Equal Protection Clause

The Equal Protection Clause, which requires a state to offer equal protection to all persons within its jurisdiction, has been interpreted by the Supreme Court as preventing the states from making unfair classifications (Sec. 1, Amend. XIV, U.S. Const.). The Court has recognized such a number of acceptable reasons for classifying taxpayers in varying groups, however, that the provision has seldom been the sole basis for successful sales and use tax challenges. Typical of the few cases in which taxpayers prevailed under an Equal Protection challenge was that involving a Vermont use tax on cars purchased elsewhere and later registered in Vermont (*Williams et al. v. Vermont et al.* (1985, US SCt) 472 US 14). Vermont provided its own residents a credit for sales taxes that had been paid to other states but did not allow the credit to immigrating new residents. The Court could find no legitimate state purpose for such differing treatment in taxation.

The High Court declined to review an Arkansas Supreme Court decision upholding against an equal protection challenge Arkansas' gross receipts tax exemption for interstate wide-area telecommunications service (WATS) (*Bosworth, et al. v. Pledger, et al.*, 305 Ark 598, 810 SW2d 918, cert den US SCt). The Arkansas court rejected an argument that a compelling state interest was required to support the disparate treatment of WATS and non-WATS subscribers since the exemption violated free speech rights, and upheld the exemption as being rationally related to a legitimate government interest.

The Import-Export Clause

The Import-Export Clause forbids the imposition of an impost or duty on imports or exports without the consent of Congress (Sec. 10, Cl. 2, Art. I, U.S.). The original package doctrine, holding that imported goods that remain in the importer's possession in their original packages had not entered the stream of commerce and could not be taxed, was expressly overruled in 1976 when the Court sanctioned a nondiscriminatory property tax on imported tires stored in warehouses as wholesale inventory (*Michelin Tire Corp. v. Wages* (1976, US SCt) 423 US 276).

Shortly thereafter, the Court approved a business and occupation tax measured by the gross receipts from the service of stevedoring, an occupation that dealt with loading and unloading cargo in foreign commerce. The Court concluded that the tax did not violate any of the policies underlying the Import-Export Clause, which are that (1) the tax enables the federal government to speak with one voice on trade matters; (2) it prohibits the states from diverting customs revenues from the federal government; and (3) it prevents seaboard states from unfairly taxing goods that merely flow through their ports (*Association of Washington Stevedoring Cos. et al. v. Department of Revenue* (1978, US SCt) 435 US 734, 98 SCt 1388).

The Supremacy Clause

The Supremacy Clause (Art. VI, U.S. Const.) declares that the U.S. Constitution and laws are the supreme law of the land. One of the earliest U.S. Supreme Court cases, *McCulloch v. Maryland* (1819, US SCt) 17 US 316), held that this clause invalidated any state tax imposed directly on a federal instrumentality.

The declaration notwithstanding, the federal government has voluntarily relinquished portions of its constitutional immunity from taxation. The Public Salary Act of 1939, for example, permits the salaries of federal employees, including the military, to be taxed by the states (4 U.S.C. § 111). The 1940 Buck Act allows sales and use taxation on federal areas, providing the tax is not levied on the U.S. Government (4 U.S.C. § 105). Similarly, state taxation of motor fuel is authorized by the Federal Highway Act (4 U.S.C. § 104). The federal forum for state taxpayers has been reduced by the Anti-Injunction Act, which permits recourse to federal district courts for injunctions against state taxes only when there is no speedy, adequate, and efficient remedy available in state courts (28 U.S.C. § 1341).

Occasionally, a state tax statute will be contested on the grounds that it contravenes a federal law, regulation, or treaty. For example, in *Itel Containers International Corp. v. Huddleston*, 507 U.S. 60 (1993), the U.S. Supreme Court rejected a taxpayer's claim that Tennessee's imposition of its sales tax on leases of cargo containers used in international commerce was preempted by two international conventions to which the United States was a party and by federal laws and regulations granting favored status to international containers.

In 2015, the Supreme Court of the United States announced a successful Supremacy Clause challenge in *CSX Transportation v. Alabama DOR*, 562 U.S. 277

(2015). Under the Court's view, a discrimination claim was properly made under the Federal Railroad Revitalization Act. However, the lower court was left to evaluate whether discrimination had occurred.

The application of the Supremacy Clause has been considerably reduced over the passage of years. In relation to sales and use taxes, it is of particular importance in the areas of transactions with government contractors, bankruptcies, and financial institutions, as well as with Native Americans, discussed below.

Government contractors—Contemporary trends

Two U.S. Supreme Court decisions in the 1980's reflect contemporary interpretation of the Supremacy Clause as it affects federal contractors. The Supremacy Clause did not bar New Mexico from imposing its gross receipts and compensating use taxes on purchases made by cost-plus contractors that maintained and operated federally owned facilities in New Mexico under contracts with the U.S. Department of Energy (*United States v. New Mexico*(1982, US SCt) 455 US 736, 102 SCt 1373). The contractors, who had substantial autonomy in their operations, were not so closely connected to the federal government as to be considered its agency or instrumentality. A Washington sales and use tax statute imposed on all tangible property purchases of federal and nonfederal contractors was also upheld (*Washington v. United States* (1983, US SCt) 460 US 536, 103 SCt 1344). The tax, imposed at the same rate on both classes, was levied upon a narrower base on federal rather than on nonfederal contractors, who were taxed on the contract price rather than on actual purchases. The Court, examining the state's entire tax structure, upheld the tax, finding an absence of discrimination.

Another controversial phase of taxing contractors, that of contractor use of government-owned materials, has been decided in contradictory fashion by state courts. A California court of appeal found to be exempt project materials that vested in the U.S. Government before being used by the contractor, ruling that the materials fell within the statutory resale exemption (*Carson v. Roane-Anderson Co.; Carbide and Carbon Chemicals Corp.* (1952, US SCt) 342 US 232, 72 SCt 257).

Government contractors—Historical background

A landmark case in the field of federal tax immunity, leading to the contemporary interpretations of the Supremacy Clause, was that of *Dravo Contracting Co. (James v. Dravo Contracting Co.* (1937, US SCt) 302 US 134, 58 SCt 208). In this case, a West Virginia privilege tax on gross income had been levied on an independent contractor constructing dams for the U.S. Government. The U.S. Supreme Court found no justification for the distinction between property and other taxes, provided that they are not discriminatory. Of particular significance was the Court's finding that the legal incidence of the tax being upon the contractor made the tax acceptable, a finding that has become known as the legal incidence test.

The legal incidence test was also used in an Alabama case (*Alabama v. King & Boozer*(1941, US SCt) 314 US 1, 62 SCt 43). The Court looked to the Alabama Supreme Court's construction of who is the purchaser liable for the tax, rather than to where the ultimate economic burdens may fall, and found that the legal incidence of the tax was upon the contractor, not the federal government. When the contractor was merely the government's purchasing agent, with title to materials passing directly to the government, the legal incidence of the tax was found to fall on the United States, and, consequently, the tax was forbidden (*Kern-Limerick, Inc. v. Scurlock* (1954, US SCt) 347 US 110, 74 SCt 403).

States countered by enacting use taxes on a contractor's use of property, including government property, in performing contracts with others. In *United States v. Boyd* (1964, US SCt) 378 US 39, 84 SCt 1518), a Tennessee contractor's use tax was imposed on a contractor's use of government property in performing contracts with the Atomic

Energy Commission. The use of government property was for the contractor's own commercial advantage and was a distinct taxable event.

Federal common law: The fact that the federal government reimburses a contractor for state taxes does not alone create a federal common law cause of action to recover the taxes. In *United States v. California* (1993, US SCt) 113 SCt 1784), the federal government sought a refund of California sales and use taxes that had been assessed against a federal contractor and that the contractor had paid using funds the federal government provided pursuant to a cost reimbursement provision in the contract. The Supreme Court rejected the government's claim that it was entitled to the refund on the basis of a common law action for money had and received absent a contract implied in law between the federal government and the state.

Liquidation sales in bankruptcy

The U.S. Congress has been granted exclusive authority to establish a uniform system of bankruptcy laws (Sec. 8, Cl, 4, Art. I, U.S. Const.). In a 1989 California case, the U. S. Supreme Court clarified the issue of whether the doctrine of intergovernmental immunity prohibits state taxation of bankruptcy liquidations (*SBE v. Sierra Summit, Inc.* (1989, US SCt) 488 US 992, 109 SCt 554). In overturning long-standing precedent, the Court held that assessment of state sales or use tax does not place a burden on the federal bankruptcy court or discriminate against bankruptcy trustees or those with whom they deal, since a purchaser at a judicial sale is required to pay only the same tax that would have been charged by any other seller. Moreover, the bankruptcy trustee is a representative of the debtor's estate, not an arm of the federal government.

Taxation of national banks

It has long been settled by case law that states may tax national banks only if they are authorized to do so by Congress. In 1973, P.L. 91-156 authorized states to tax national banks in the same manner as state-chartered banks (12 U.S.C. § 548). Under this legislation, national banks are no longer specially treated, provided they are not subjected to discrimination.

Limitations Affecting Native Americans

The doctrine of federal preemption restricts taxes on transactions taking place on Native American reservations. Federal preemption is founded jointly upon the Supremacy Clause, which makes the federal government the highest authority among government bodies as discussed above, and the Commerce Clause, which specifies that Congress alone shall have power to regulate commerce with Indian tribes.

Under the doctrine of federal preemption, Arizona could not impose its transaction privilege (sales) tax on the sale of farm machinery by a corporation to a Native American tribe when the sale occurred on the reservation (*Central Machinery Co. et al. v. State Tax Commission* (1980, US SCt) 448 US 160); nor could Oklahoma tax cigarette sales to tribe members occurring on land held in trust for a recognized tribe (*Tax Commission v. Citizen Band Potawatomi Indian Tribe of Oklahoma* (1991, US SCt) 111 SCt 905). Similarly, New Mexico could not tax receipts received by a non-Native American construction company from a tribe's school board for the construction of a school on a New Mexico reservation (*Ramah Navajo School Board, Inc. et al. v. Bureau of Revenue* (1982, US SCt) 458 US 832). The U.S. Supreme Court upheld a decision that the Omaha Tribe may impose a 10% sales tax on alcohol sales from licensees in and around Pender, Nebraska because such establishments are located in Indian Country (Nebraska v. Parker, U.S. Supreme Court, Dkt. 14-1406, March 22, 2016, affirming Nebraska v. Parker, U.S. Court of Appeals, 8th Circuit, No.14-1642, December 19, 2014).

Despite the restriction on taxation of reservation sales to Native Americans, Native American retailers may be required to collect state taxes on sales to non-Native Americans (*Moe v. Confederated Salish and Kootenai Tribes of the Flathead Reservation* (1976, US SCt) 425 US 463).

A hotel occupancy tax imposed by the Navajo Nation of New Mexico on non-Indian guests on real property that was located within reservation boundaries, but owned by a non-Indian entity, was improper. The U.S. Supreme Court ruled there was no consensual relationship that would give rise to the imposition of the tax and that the tax was not necessary to protect tribal self-government or to control internal relations. (*Atkinson Trading Company, Inc. v. Shirley*, U.S. Supreme Court, 532 U.S. 645, May 29, 2001)

First Amendment

The First Amendment limits state authority to impose sales and use taxes that may discriminate against free speech or freedom of religion.

Free Speech Guarantee

The First Amendment protects freedom of speech and freedom of the press (Amend. I, U.S. Const.). A Minnesota use tax on ink and paper consumption in excess of $100,000 annually had the effect of taxing only a handful of large newspapers in the state and was invalidated by the U.S. Supreme Court (*Minneapolis Star & Tribune Co. v. Commissioner of Revenue* (1983, US SCt) 460 US 575). The Court found no adequate justification for singling out the press for special treatment and for the differential taxation of small and large newspapers.

The High Court also found a violation of free speech in an Arkansas tax scheme that subjected subscriptions to general magazines to the sales tax but exempted subscriptions to newspapers and religious, professional, trade, and sports journals (*Arkansas Writers' Project, Inc. v. Ragland* (1987, US SCt) 481 US 221). The Court noted that a genuinely nondiscriminatory tax on newspapers and magazines would be constitutionally permissible, but held that the Arkansas tax discriminated in favor of a few magazines on the basis solely of content. Arkansas failed to satisfy its heavy burden of proving both that the discriminatory tax scheme was necessary to serve a compelling state interest and that it was narrowly drawn to achieve that end.

First Amendment protection does *not* require that a tax be imposed equally on all forms of communication (*Leathers (formerly, Pledger) v. Medlock et al.* (1991, US SCt) 111 SCt 1438). The Court upheld the application of Arkansas' gross receipts tax to cable and satellite services even though print media remained exempt, saying that "the differential taxation of speakers, even members of the press, does not implicate the First Amendment unless the tax is directed at, or presents the danger of suppressing, particular ideas."

Religious Freedom—No Establishment Clause

First Amendment protection of religious freedom is two-sided: government may not establish religion, on the one hand, but it may not interfere with its free exercise, on the other (Amend. I, U.S. Const.). Both issues have been dealt with in recent major cases.

In 1989, the U.S. Supreme Court rejected a Texas sales tax exemption for religious periodicals as a violation of the Establishment Clause because the exemption exclusively benefited religious organizations (*Texas Monthly, Inc. v. Bullock, et al.* (1989, US SCt) 109 SCt 890).

In *Jimmy Swaggart Ministries v. Board of Equalization* (1990, US SCt) 110 SCt 688), the Court held that imposition of sales tax on sales of religious materials at evangelistic crusades within California did not violate the free exercise or no establishment of religion provisions under the First Amendment.

Streamlined Sales Tax Project

The Streamlined Sales Tax Project (SSTP) is an effort among the states to simplify and modernize sales and use tax laws and administration. The project promotes the use of technology for calculating, collecting, reporting, and paying the taxes through tax calculation service providers (CSP's) certified by the states, with the states assuming the costs of the system. In addition, it proposes uniform definitions and standardized audit and administration procedures for adoption by the states. A major goal of the project is to induce remote sellers to collect the tax of participating states. Proposed incentives include safe-harbor provisions for participating sellers, monetary collection incentives, and simplified registration, collection, and reporting.

The SSTP maintains a website at **http://www.streamlinedsalestax.org**.

Governing Board

The Streamlined Sales Tax Governing Board administers and operates the Streamlined Sales and Use Tax Agreement (SSUTA). The Board is empowered to admit new states, sanction states for falling out of compliance, and amend and interpret the Agreement.

The Governing Board is composed of representatives of the member states of the Agreement and it is advised in matters pertaining to the Agreement by a State and Local Advisory Council and Business Advisory Council. The State and Local Advisory Council includes representatives from both member and nonmember states, as well as representatives of local government. The Business Advisory Council is composed of private sector representatives.

Full members: A state that wishes to become a full member of the Agreement must certify that its laws, rules, regulations, and policies are compliant with each of the requirements of the Agreement. Full and associate members of the Governing Board include Arkansas, Georgia, Indiana, Iowa, Kansas, Kentucky, Michigan, Minnesota, Nebraska, Nevada, New Jersey, North Carolina, North Dakota, Ohio, Oklahoma, Rhode Island, South Dakota, Utah, Vermont, Washington, West Virginia, Wisconsin, and Wyoming.

Associate members: Associate members are states whose laws are in substantial compliance, but not full compliance, with the Agreement, or states whose complying laws have not yet taken effect. An Associate Member state is not allowed to vote on amendments to or interpretations of the Agreement. Each must successfully petition for full membership by a specific date or forfeit its position on the Governing Board. Tennessee is the only such state; full compliance legislation is currently scheduled to become effective July 1, 2017.

Contingent members: A state may be admitted to the Governing Board as a Contingent Member pursuant to terms and conditions adopted and made part of the Agreement. There are no such states as of March 31, 2017.

Advisory states: An Advisory State serves in an *ex officio* capacity on the Governing Board and as a member of the State and Local Advisory Council (SLAC). It does not have a vote on the Governing Board, but it may speak to any matter presented. An Advisory State may serve on standing committees, except for the Executive, Finance, and Compliance Review and Interpretations Committees. Any of the remaining states may become an Advisory State by enacting legislation or executing an official expression of intent to participate in the discussions.

The Advisory states are Alabama, Arizona, California, Connecticut, District of Columbia, Florida, Hawaii, Illinois, Louisiana, Maine, Maryland, Massachusetts, Mississippi, Missouri, New Mexico, New York, South Carolina, Texas, and Virginia.

Nonparticipating states: Colorado does not participate in the SST. Pennsylvania is a "project state" that is not an advisory state. The states of Alaska, Delaware, Montana, New Hampshire, and Oregon do not impose general sales and use taxes.

Streamlined Sales Tax Agreement

The Streamlined Sales and Use Tax Agreement (SSUTA) came into effect on October 1, 2005, and businesses can register online under the SST system to collect taxes in return for a limited amnesty.

The requirements of the Agreement include the following:

—state level administration of local sales and use taxes;

—a single state and local tax base in each state;

—a central online registration system for all member states, including a provision that registration cannot be used as a factor in determining if a seller has nexus in a state;

—an amnesty for uncollected or unpaid taxes for sellers who register to collect tax;

—adequate notice to sellers of changes in tax rates, the tax base, and jurisdictional boundaries;

—a single state and local tax rate per taxing jurisdiction, with the exception that a state (but not a locality) may have a second rate on food and drugs;

—uniform, destination-based sourcing rules;

—direct pay authority for holders of permits;

—limitations on exemptions to make them simpler to administer;

—uniform returns and remittances;

—uniform rules for bad debt deductions;

—limitations on sales tax holidays;

—the eventual elimination of most caps and thresholds;

—a uniform rounding rule;

—customer refund procedures that limit a purchaser's ability to sue for a return of over-collected tax from the seller;

—uniform definitions, including uniform product definitions;

—a books-and-records standard for certain bundled transactions;

—the use of new technology models for tax collection, including the certification of automated systems and service providers, offering sellers limitations on liability and the scope of audits;

—relief from liability for collecting the incorrect amount of tax as a result of relying on data that each member state must provide in the form of a taxability matrix; and

—monetary allowances to certified service providers.

Taxability matrices: Charts of the taxable status of various items in SST member states are accessible on each state's website and under "State info" on the SST's website at **http://www.streamlinedsalestax.org**.

Best practices matrices: To inform the general public of its practices regarding certain products, services, procedures or transactions, no later than January 1, 2016, each member statehad to complete the combined "Taxability/Best Practices Matrix" form.

Registration procedures and benefits

Sellers wishing to volunteer to collect under the Agreement and receive amnesty for uncollected or unpaid sales or use tax must register at **https:// www.sstregister.org**. The information provided will be sent to all of the full member states and to those associate members for which the seller chooses to collect. A registering seller is required to collect tax for all the full member states.

By registering on this site and collecting tax, a seller receives: a limited amnesty; a monetary allowance (determined by the technology model used for collection and remittance); a single, unique identification number for all member states; and the ability to update registration information in all member states at a single site.

Amnesty: A member state is required to provide amnesty to a seller that registers with it under the Agreement, provided the seller was not registered in that state in the 12 months preceding the state's participation in the Agreement and the seller has not been contacted for audit. The amnesty precludes assessment for uncollected or unpaid sales or use tax, together with penalty or interest, for sales made prior to the seller's registration. To qualify for the amnesty, a seller must register with a full member state within 12 months of the state's participation in the Agreement. An associate member state must provide amnesty from the time it joins as an associate member and until 12 months after it becomes a full member. A seller must maintain its registration and continue collecting taxes for at least 36 months in a member state or the amnesty may be voided by that state. The information obtained through registration may not be used by the states for determining whether a seller has nexus for any tax.

Certified technology models: When a seller registers under the Agreement, it must select the certified technology model it will be using (or it must select Model Four if it will not be using one of the three certified models). The models are the following:

Model One: Certified Service Provider (CSP), an agent certified under the Agreement to perform all the seller's sales and use tax functions;

Model Two: Certified Automated System (CAS), software certified under the Agreement to calculate the appropriate tax the seller must remit; or

Model Three: Certified System (CS), a proprietary automated sales tax system certified under the Agreement.

Model Four: A seller registered under the Agreement that is not a Model One, Model Two, or Model Three seller.

Databases: Each state that has local sales or use taxes must provide the following databases at no cost to the user:

—A database describing the boundary changes for all taxing jurisdictions and their effective dates;

—A database of all sales and use tax rates in the state identified by specified codes; and

—A database that assigns each ZIP code within a state to the proper tax rates and jurisdictions.

Some states also have the option of providing address-based boundary database records for assigning taxing jurisdictions and their associated rates.

States must relieve sellers and CSPs that use the ZIP code and address-based databases from liability for having collected the incorrect amount of tax as the result of relying on erroneous data provided by the state.

Federal legislation

The Agreement is a voluntary collection system as far as sellers without a physical presence in a given state are concerned. Collection by such remote sellers will become mandatory only if a court of competent jurisdiction rules that the concerns about complexity that led to the holding in *Quill Corp. v. North Dakota,* 504 U.S. 298 (1992), have been satisfied, or if federal legislation is enacted granting states collection authority over remote sellers.

Legislation has been introduced into both houses of Congress to authorize states to require remote sellers to collect use tax.

Sourcing of Sales

The general rule under the Agreement is that sales must be sourced on a destination basis under the following rules (Sec. 310, SSUTA):

(1) When the product is received by the purchaser at a business location of the seller, the sale is sourced to that business location.

(2) When the product is not received by the purchaser at a business location of the seller, the sale is sourced to the location where receipt by the purchaser (or the purchaser's donee, designated as such by the purchaser) occurs, including the location indicated by instructions for delivery to the purchaser (or donee), known to the seller.

(3) When (1) and (2) do not apply, the sale is sourced to the location indicated by an address for the purchaser that is available from the business records of the seller that are maintained in the ordinary course of the seller's business when use of this address does not constitute bad faith.

(4) When subsections (1), (2), and (3) do not apply, the sale is sourced to the location indicated by an address for the purchaser obtained during the consummation of the sale, including the address of a purchaser's payment instrument, if no other address is available, when use of this address does not constitute bad faith.

(5) When none of the previous rules apply, including the circumstance in which the seller is without sufficient information to apply the previous rules, then the location will be determined by the address from which tangible personal property was shipped, from which the digital good or the computer software delivered electronically was first available for transmission by the seller, or from which the service was provided (disregarding for these purposes any location that merely provided the digital transfer of the product sold).

Exceptions: The general sourcing rules do not apply to (1) transactions involving watercraft, modular homes, manufactured homes, or mobile homes, or (2) florist sales. These items must be sourced according to the requirements of each member state. Sales of motor vehicles, trailers, semi-trailers, or aircraft that do not qualify as transportation equipment are also sourced according to the requirements of each member state, but the Agreement includes provisions for sourcing the lease or rental of such items (Sec. 310(C), SSUTA).

Special sourcing rules apply to sales of telecommunications and ancillary services (Sec. 315, SSUTA) as well as to Internet access services (Sec. 314, SSUTA) and direct mail (Sec. 313, SSUTA).

Origin Sourcing

The Agreement was amended effective January 1, 2010, to provide that a state that has local jurisdictions that levy or receive sales or use tax may elect to source retail sales of tangible personal property or digital goods to the location where the order is received by the seller, rather than to the location where receipt by the purchaser occurs (or is presumed to occur) (Sec. 310.1, SSUTA). This provision does not apply to over-the-counter sales or leases and rentals. The order must be received in the same state by the seller where receipt of the product by the purchaser or its donee occurs (*i.e.,* it must be an intrastate sale). The location where receipt by the purchaser occurs is determined by the existing sourcing hierarchy in the Agreement. The seller's sales tax recordkeeping system must capture the location where the order is received to qualify.

A state making this election to source sales on an origin basis must comply with several requirements, as follows:

—Interstate sales must be sourced on a destination basis;

—When a sale is sourced on an origin basis, no additional tax may be levied based on where the product is delivered (*i.e.* a purchaser does not have any additional use tax liability). A purchaser also is not entitled to any refund if the rate is lower where the product is delivered;

—A state cannot require a seller to use a recordkeeping system that captures the location where an order is received;

—A purchaser has no additional liability for tax, penalty, or interest on a sale if it remits tax to the seller on the invoiced amount, so long as that amount is calculated at either the rate where receipt by the purchaser occurs or where the order is received by the seller;

—The location where the order is received is defined as "an established outlet, office, location or automated order receipt system operated by or on behalf of the seller where an order is initially received" and not where the order is subsequently accepted, completed, or fulfilled. An order is received when all the information necessary for acceptance has been received. The location from which a product is shipped cannot be used in determining the location where the order is received;

—A state must permit direct pay permits under specified circumstances. Purchasers using direct pay must remit tax at the rate in effect where receipt of the product occurs or the product is first used, as determined by state law.

An additional requirement is that a state elect either origin sourcing or destination sourcing for a transaction in which taxable services are sold with tangible personal property or digital products pursuant to a single contract or in the same transaction, are billed on the same statement, and would be sourced to different jurisdictions absent this requirement. The board may adopt a uniform methodology to address such sales in the future.

MPU Repealed

From its inception, the Agreement contained provisions relating to multiple points of use (MPU). Under the version that member states had until January 1, 2008, to enact, a business purchaser was required to deliver to the seller an exemption form claiming MPU if it was purchasing a digital good, computer software, or a service that would be concurrently available for use in more than one jurisdiction. The seller was then relieved of its collection obligation, and the purchaser had to remit tax on a direct pay basis.

These provisions fractured the business community. The differences largely arose from a perceived shifting of collection burdens from software sellers to business purchasers of software. There were also concerns that, as long as there are nonmember states, allowing the MPU would create undue complexity. The general consensus was that the MPU provisions were fatally flawed.

In response, the Board, in December 2006, approved the immediate repeal of the MPU provisions in the Agreement, in conjunction with the adoption of a new interpretive rule offered by the business community. The rule describes the application of the general (destination-based) sourcing provisions in the Agreement to transactions involving prewritten computer software, computer-related services, and software post-sale support agreements. Although the repeal was effective immediately, states that had to repeal the MPU provisions they had already enacted were given two years to do so.

Bundling Resolution

The Agreement contains a definition of "bundled transaction" that includes a *de minimis* test (and a related primary test for transactions including food, drugs, or medical equipment). If the taxable products represent 10% or less of the price of what would otherwise be considered a bundled transaction, then the sale falls outside the definition. At its meeting in August, 2006, the Board had directed the SLAC to prepare an interpretive rule on how to apply this definition, and to include in the rule a statement that the prices of any *de minimis* taxable products are not subject to tax. Several states, however, objected to the inclusion of any such taxability rules mandating state tax treatment. These states responded with a proposal to amend the Agreement to add a dollar cap on the *de minimis* test.

After lengthy negotiations, Nebraska withdrew its request for a dollar cap and a compromise version of the rule was approved. The taxability rules to which some states had objected were removed. In their place are limitations that prohibit a state, once a transaction has been determined not to be a bundled transaction, from (1) using thresholds to tax a portion of the sales price, (2) taxing the total sales or purchase price, or (3) requiring sellers to separately price the taxable products or itemize them on an invoice.

Meetings

The Board generally holds at least two in-person meetings a year: a Spring meeting in the Washington area that allows members to lobby Congress and a Fall meeting. Additional meetings are held by teleconference.

Charts

¶ 100 **CHARTS**

The following charts show the taxability of specific transactions and provide an overview of aspects of the tax structure, such as the tax base, penalties, interest, and remedies.

¶ 101   Administrative Appeals

The following chart describes the time period in which a taxpayer must file an appeal of a department decision with the appropriate administrative entity outside of the taxing authority. Appeals to the taxing authority or judicial entity are addressed in Department Appeals and Judicial Appeals.

State	Administrative Appeals	Comments	Citation
Alabama	State does not have administrative appeal body.		
Arizona	Petition must be filed with State Board of Tax Appeals within 30 days after receipt of the decision or order.		Ariz. Rev. Stat. § 42-1253
Arkansas	State does not have administrative appeal body.		
California	State does not have administrative appeal body.		
Colorado	State does not have administrative appeal body.		
Connecticut	State does not have administrative appeal body.		
District of Columbia	District does not have administrative appeal body.		
Florida	State does not have administrative appeal body.		
Georgia	State does not have administrative appeal body.		
Hawaii	Petition must be filed with District Board of Review within 30 days after mailing date of notice of assessment.		Haw. Rev. Stat. § 235-114(c), Haw. Rev. Stat. § 237-42
Idaho	Petition must be filed with Board of Tax Appeals within 91 days after notice of redetermination is received.		Idaho Code § 63-3049
Illinois	State does not have administrative appeal body.	Board of Appeals actions may be commenced within 180 days after liability has become final for relief from penalties and interest or for an offer in compromise; liability may not be contested.	Ill. Admin. Code tit. 86, § 210.101
Indiana	State does not have administrative appeal body.		
Iowa	Petition must be filed with Department and State Board of Tax Review within 30 days after decision rendered.		Iowa Code § 421.1
Kansas	Notice of appeal must be filed with State Board of Tax Appeals within 30 days after final decision.		Kan. Stat. Ann. § 74-2438

State	Administrative Appeals	Comments	Citation
Kentucky	Petition must be filed with the Kentucky Claims Commission (formerly the Kentucky Board of Tax Appeals) within 30 days after date of decision.		Ky. Rev. Stat. Ann. § 131.340
Louisiana	Petition must be filed with Board of Tax Appeals within 60 days after notice of deficiency or decision.		La. Rev. Stat. Ann. § 47:1565
Maine	State does not have administrative appeal body.		
Maryland	Petition must be filed with Tax Court within 30 days after mailing notice of decision.	Tax Court is an administrative, not judicial, entity.	Md. Code Ann. § 13-510(a)
Massachusetts	Petition must be filed with Appellate Tax Board within 60 days after date of notice of decision or within six months after application for abatement is deemed to be denied.		Mass. Gen. Laws ch. 62HC, § 39
Michigan	Petition must be filed with Tax Tribunal within 60 days after decision.	If the taxpayer has filed a request appointing an official representative to receive copies of letters and notices from the Department of Treasury, the 60 day period does not begin to accrue until both the taxpayer and its representative has been served with the final assessment.	Mich. Comp. Laws § 205.22, Mich. Comp. Laws § 205.8, Mich. Comp. Laws § 205.28
Minnesota	Notice of appeal must be filed with Tax Court within 60 days after Commissioner of Revenue's order.	Tax Court is an administrative, not judicial, entity.	Minn. Stat. § 271.06(2)
Mississippi	Petition must be filed with Board of Tax Appeals within 60 days from the date of the Board of Review's order.		Miss. Code. Ann. § 27-77-5
Missouri	Petition must be filed with Administrative Hearing Commission within 60 days after mailing or delivery of decision, whichever is earlier.		Mo. Rev. Stat. § 144.261
Nebraska	State does not have administrative appeal body.		
Nevada	Petition must be filed with Department and Tax Commission within 30 days after service of decision.		Nev. Rev. Stat. § 360.245
New Jersey	State does not have administrative appeal body.		
New Mexico	State does not have administrative appeal body.		

State	Administrative Appeals	Comments	Citation
New York	Petition must be filed with Tax Appeals Tribunal within 30 days after notice of decision.		N.Y. Tax Law, § 2006
North Carolina	Notice of intent to file a petition must be filed with Tax Review Board within 30 days after final decision.	Petition must be filed with Tax Review Board within 60 days after notice of intent.	N.C. Gen. Stat. § 105-241.2
North Dakota	State does not have administrative appeal body.		
Ohio	Petition must be filed with Board of Tax Appeals within 60 days after service of notice of decision.		Ohio Rev. Code Ann. § 5717.02
Oklahoma	State does not have administrative appeal body.		
Pennsylvania	Petition must be filed with Board of Finance and Revenue within 90 days after notice of decision.		72 P.S. § 9704
Rhode Island	State does not have administrative appeal body.		
South Carolina	Petition must be filed with Administrative Law Judge within 30 days after decision mailed or delivered.		S.C. Code Ann. § 12-60-460
South Dakota	State does not have administrative appeal body.		
Tennessee	State does not have administrative appeal body.		
Texas	State does not have administrative appeal body.		
Utah	State does not have administrative appeal body.		
Vermont	State does not have administrative appeal body.		
Virginia	State does not have administrative appeal body.		
Washington	Petition must be filed with Board of Tax Appeals within 30 days after mailing notice of decision.		Wash. Rev. Code § 82.03.190
West Virginia	Petition must be filed with Office of Tax Appeals within 60 days of receipt of assessment notice.		W. Va. Code § 11-10A-9
Wisconsin	Petition must be filed with Tax Appeals Commission within 60 days of Department of Revenue determination or redetermination.		Wis. Stat. § 73.01(5)
Wyoming	An appeal directly to the Board of Equalization must be filed within 30 days of decision.		Wyo. BOE Rule Ch. 2, § 5

¶ 102 **Bad Debts**

The following chart indicates whether bad debts may be claimed as a deduction, refund, or credit.

State	Bad Debts	Comments	Citation
Alabama	Refund or credit.		Ala. Admin. Code r. 810-6-4-.01
Arizona	Deduction		Ariz. Admin. Code § 15-5-2011
Arkansas	Deduction		Ark. Code Ann. § 26-52-309, Ark. Code Ann. § 26-53-111
California	Deduction		Cal. Rev. & Tax. Code § 6055, Cal. Rev. & Tax. Code § 6203.5
Colorado	Deduction		Colo. Code Regs. § 39-26-102.5, Colo. Code Regs. § 39-26-111
Connecticut	Credit		Conn. Gen. Stat. § 12-408(2)
District of Columbia	Deduction		D.C. Mun. Regs. t. 9, § 410.4
Florida	Refund or credit.		Fla. Stat. § 212.17(3)
Georgia	Deduction		Ga. Code Ann. § 48-8-45, Ga. Comp. R. & Regs. 560-12-1-.06
Hawaii	Deduction		Haw. Rev. Stat. § 237-3(b)
Idaho	Refund or credit.		Idaho Code § 63-3613(d), IDAPA 35.01.02.063(02)
Illinois	Credit.		Ill. Admin. Code tit. 86, § 130.1960(d)
Indiana	Deduction		Ind. Code § 6-2.5-6-9
Iowa	Deduction		Iowa Code § 423.21
Kansas	Deduction		Kan. Stat. Ann. § 79-3674
Kentucky	Deduction		Ky. Rev. Stat. Ann. § 139.350
Louisiana	Refund		La. Rev. Stat. Ann. § 47:315(B), La. Admin. Code tit. 61, § 4369
Maine	Credit		Me. Rev. Stat. Ann. tit. 36, § 1811-A
Maryland	Refund or credit.		Md. Code Regs. 03.06.03.07
Massachusetts	Refund		Mass. Gen. Laws ch. 64H, § 33
Michigan	Deduction		Mich. Comp. Laws § 205.54i
Minnesota	Deduction		Minn. Stat. § 297A.81
Mississippi	Credit		Miss. Code. Ann. § 27-65-33
Missouri	Refund or credit.		Mo. Code Regs. Ann. tit. 12, § 10-102.100

State	Bad Debts	Comments	Citation
Nebraska	Deduction	When the bad debt amount exceeds the taxable sales for the period in which the bad debt is written off, a refund claim may be filed.	Neb. Rev. Stat. § 77-2708(2)(j)
Nevada	Deduction	Prior to January 1, 2006, a bad debt credit was authorized.	Nev. Rev. Stat. § 372.368, Nev. Rev. Stat. § 374.373
New Jersey	Deduction		N.J. Stat. Ann. § 54:32B-12.1
New Mexico	Deduction		N.M. Stat. Ann. § 7-9-67
New York	Refund or credit.		N.Y. Tax Law, § 1132(e), N.Y. Comp. Code R. & Regs. tit. 20, § 534.7
North Carolina	Deduction		N.C. Gen. Stat. § 105-164.13(15)
North Dakota	Deduction		N.D. Cent. Code § 57-39.4-21, N.D. Admin. Code § 81-04.1-01-25
Ohio	Deduction	When the bad debt amount exceeds the taxable sales in a reporting period, a refund claim may be filed.	Ohio Rev. Code Ann. § 5739.121
Oklahoma	Deduction		Okla. Stat. tit. 68, § 1366, Okla. Admin. Code § 710:65-11-2
Pennsylvania	Refund		72 P.S. § 7247.1
Rhode Island	Deduction		R.I. Gen. Laws § 44-18.1-21, R.I. Code R. SU 87-6
South Carolina	Deduction		S.C. Code Ann. § 12-36-90(2)(h)
South Dakota	Deduction		S.D. Codified Laws § 10-45-30
Tennessee	Credit		Tenn. Code. Ann. § 67-6-507(e)
Texas	Deduction or refund.		Tex. Tax Code Ann. § 151.426, 34 Tex. Admin. Code § 3.302(d)(1)(B)
Utah	Deduction		Utah Code Ann. § 59-12-107
Vermont	Refund or credit.		Vt. Stat. Ann. tit. 32, § 9780
Virginia	Credit		Va. Code Ann. § 58.1-621
Washington	Refund or credit.	The refund or credit is limited to the seller.	Wash. Rev. Code § 82.08.037
West Virginia	Deduction		W. Va. Code § 11-15B-27(a)
Wisconsin	Deduction		Wis. Stat. § 77.585(1)
Wyoming	Credit		Wyo. Stat. Ann. § 39-15-107(a)(x)

¶ 103   Canned Software Delivered on Tangible Personal Property

State	Delivered on Tangible Personal Property	Comments	Citation
Alabama	Taxable		Ala. Admin. Code r. 810-6-1.37(4)
Arizona	Taxable		Ariz. Admin. Code § 15-5-154(B)
Arkansas	Taxable		Ark. Code Ann. § 26-52-304, Ark. Reg. GR-25
California	Taxable		Cal. Rev. & Tax. Code § 6010.9
Colorado	Taxable		Colo. Rev. Stat. § 39-26-104(1)(a), 1 Colo. Code Regs. § 201-5 (SR-7)
Connecticut	Taxable		Policy Statement 2006(8)
District of Columbia	Taxable		D.C. Mun. Regs. t. 9, § 474.4
Florida	Taxable	Software used predominantly for research and development may qualify for exemption.	Fla. Admin. Code Ann. r. 12A-1.032(4)
Georgia	Taxable		Ga. Code Ann. § 48-1-8
Hawaii	Taxable		Haw. Rev. Stat. § 237-13(2)(A)
Idaho	Taxable		Idaho Code § 63-3616(b)
Illinois	Taxable		35 ILCS 120/2-25, Ill. Admin. Code tit. 86 § 130.1935(a)
Indiana	Taxable		Information Bulletin #8 (II)(B)
Iowa	Taxable		Iowa Admin. Code r. 701-18.34(2)(c)(422,423)
Kansas	Taxable		Kan. Stat. Ann. § 79-3603(s)
Kentucky	Taxable		Ky. Rev. Stat. Ann. § 139.010(30), Ky. Rev. Stat. Ann. § 139.200(1)
Louisiana	Taxable		La. Rev. Stat. Ann. § 47:301(16)(e)
Maine	Taxable		Me. Rev. Stat. Ann. tit. 36, § 1752(17)
Maryland	Taxable		Md. Code Ann. § 11-101(h)(1)(i), Md. Code Ann. § 11-219(b)
Massachusetts	Taxable		Mass. Gen. Laws ch. 64H, § 1, TIR 05-15
Michigan	Taxable		Mich. Comp. Laws § 205.51a(o)

¶103

State	Delivered on Tangible Personal Property	Comments	Citation
Minnesota	Taxable		Minn. R. 8130.9910(2)
Mississippi	Taxable		Miss. Code Ann. § 27-65-23
Missouri	Taxable		Mo. Code Regs. Ann. tit. 12, § 10-109.050
Nebraska	Taxable		Neb. Rev. Stat. § 77-2701.16(3)(a)
Nevada	Taxable		Nev. Admin. Code § 372.880
New Jersey	Taxable		N.J. Stat. Ann. § 54:32B-2, N.J. Technical Bulletin TB-51R
New Mexico	Taxable		N.M. Admin. Code tit. 3, § 3.2.1.15(J)
New York	Taxable		N.Y. Tax Law, § 1101(b)(6)
North Carolina	Taxable		N.C. Gen. Stat. § 105-164.3(46)
North Dakota	Taxable		N.D. Admin. Code § 81-04.1-03-11(6)
Ohio	Taxable		Ohio Sales and Use Tax Information Release ST 2003-06
Oklahoma	Taxable		Okla. Admin. Code § 710:65-19-52(c)
Pennsylvania	Taxable		61 Pa. Code § 60.19
Rhode Island	Taxable		R.I. Gen. Laws § 44-18-16, R.I. Code R. SU 11-25
South Carolina	Taxable	Broadcasting software sold to a radio station, television station, or cable television system is exempt.	Revenue Ruling 03-5, Private Letter Ruling 12-1
South Dakota	Taxable		S.D. Admin. R. 64:06:02:79
Tennessee	Taxable	Exemptions may apply for the use of software developed and fabricated by an affiliated company or for fabrication of software by a person for that person's own use or consumption.	Letter Ruling No. 00-32, Tenn. Code Ann. § 67-6-231
Texas	Taxable		Tex. Tax Code Ann. § 151.009
Utah	Taxable		Utah Admin. Code r. 865-19S-92(B)

State	Delivered on Tangible Personal Property	Comments	Citation
Vermont	Taxable		Vt. Stat. Ann. tit. 32, § 9701(7), Vt. Stat. Ann. tit. 32, § 9771
Virginia	Taxable	Software used directly and exclusively in exempt research and development activities may qualify for exemption.	Va. Code Ann. § 58.1-602, Va. Code Ann. § 58.1-603
Washington	Taxable		Wash. Rev. Code § 82.04.050(6), Wash. Admin. Code § 458-20-15502
West Virginia	Taxable		W. Va. Code R. § 110-15-9.3.11.1
Wisconsin	Taxable		Wis. Stat. § 77.51(20), Wis. Stat. § 77.52(1)
Wyoming	Taxable		Wyo. Stat. Ann. § 39-15-103(a)(i)(O)

¶ 104 Canned Software Set-Up Sold Without Tangible Personal Property

State	Canned Software Set-Up Sold Without Tangible Personal Property	Comments	Citation
Alabama	Exempt		Ala. Admin. Code r. 810-6-1-.37, Ala. Admin. Code r. 810-6-1-.81
Arizona	Exempt		TPR 93-48
Arkansas	Exempt	If the software set-up qualifies as technical support for software, software programming service, or development of custom software.	Ark. Code Ann. § 26-52-304, Ark. Reg. GR-25(A)
California	Exempt		Reg. 1502(g), 18 CCR
Colorado	Exempt		Colo. Rev. Stat. § 39-26-104(1)(a)
Connecticut	Taxable	Software installation is taxed as a computer and data processing service and is taxed at a different rate than the sale of tangible personal property.	Conn. Gen. Stat. § 12-407(a)(37)(A), Policy Statement 2006(8)
District of Columbia	Taxable		D.C. Mun. Regs. t. 9, § 474.4
Florida	Taxable	If the software installed is modified, then it is a professional service and exempt.	Fla. Stat. § 212.02(16)
Georgia	Exempt	Must be separately stated.	Ga. Comp. R. & Regs. 560-12-2-.111
Hawaii	Taxable		Haw. Rev. Stat. § 237-13(6)
Idaho	Exempt	Must be separately stated.	IDAPA 35.01.02.011.02
Illinois	Exempt	Must be separately stated.	Ill. Admin. Code tit. 86, § 130.1935(b)
Indiana	Taxable		Information Bulletin #8 (II)(A)
Iowa	Exempt	If the service does not constitute an enumerated taxable service and it is separated stated.	Iowa Admin. Code r. 701-18.34(3)(e)
Kansas	Taxable		Kan. Stat. Ann. § 79-3603(p), Private Letter Ruling P-2005-011, Private Letter Ruling P-2002-091, E-mail from Kansas Department of Revenue, February 10, 2006
Kentucky	Exempt		103 Ky. Admin. Regs. 30:180

State	Canned Software Set-Up Sold Without Tangible Personal Property	Comments	Citation
Louisiana	Exempt	Caution: Numerous exemptions are suspended from April 1, 2016, to June 30, 2018. For chart of suspended exemptions and applicable tax rates, see Publication R-1002A.	La. Rev. Stat. Ann. § 47:301(14), LA DOR Publication R-1002A
Maine	Exempt	Must be separately stated.	Me. Rev. Stat. Ann. tit. 36, § 1752(14)(B)(4)
Maryland	Exempt		Md. Code Ann. § 11-101(l)(3)(i)(3)
Massachusetts	Exempt		Mass. Gen. Laws ch. 64H, § 1
Michigan	Taxable		Mich. Comp. Laws § 205.92(f)(v)
Minnesota	Taxable	Reinstallation of software is not taxable.	Minn. R. 8130.9910, Sales Tax Fact Sheet 134
Mississippi	Taxable		Miss. Code Ann. § 27-65-23, Miss. Rule 35.IV.5.06
Missouri	Taxable	The taxation of the purchase of software installation, training, and maintenance services shall be determined as follows: (1) Software maintenance agreements that are mandatory for canned software provided on a tangible medium are subject to tax, whether or not these charges are separately stated; (2) Software maintenance agreements that provide for canned software updates, upgrades, or enhancements delivered on a tangible medium are subject to tax. If the optional maintenance agreements do not provide for canned software updates, upgrades, or enhancements delivered on a tangible medium, then the separately stated cost of the maintenance agreement is not subject to tax; and (3) Charges for custom software maintenance agreements that provide for software updates, upgrades, or enhancements delivered on a tangible medium are not subject to tax.	Mo. Code Regs. Ann. tit. 12, § 10-109.050(F)

State	Canned Software Set-Up Sold Without Tangible Personal Property	Comments	Citation
Nebraska	Taxable	Charges to reinstall existing software are not taxable. Installation/setup includes providing software patches or security updates for virus protection.	Information Guide 6-511-2011
Nevada	Exempt	Must be separately stated.	Nev. Rev. Stat. § 372.025(3)(c)
New Jersey	Taxable		N.J. Stat. Ann. § 54:32B-3(b)(2), N.J. Technical Bulletin TB-51R
New Mexico	Taxable		N.M. Admin. Code tit. 3, § 3.2.1.18(A)
New York	Exempt	Services must be provided to a customer in conjunction with the sale of tangible personal property, and the charges must be reasonable and separately stated.	N.Y. Tax Law, § 1115(o)
North Carolina	Exempt	Must be separately stated.	N.C. Gen. Stat. § 105-164.13(49)
North Dakota	Exempt		N.D. Admin. Code § 81-04.1-01-22
Ohio	Taxable	The installation of system software is a taxable computer service if it is provided to support the sale, lease, or operation of taxable computer equipment used in business.	Ohio Admin. Code § 5703-9-46(2)(c)
Oklahoma	Exempt	Must be separately stated.	Okla. Admin. Code § 710:65-19-158
Pennsylvania	Taxable		61 Pa. Code § 31.1(4), 61 Pa. Code § 60.19
Rhode Island	Exempt		R.I. Code R. SU 11-25
South Carolina	Exempt		Revenue Ruling 03-5
South Dakota	Taxable		S.D. Admin. R. 64:06:02:78
Tennessee	Taxable		Tenn. Code Ann. § 67-6-231, Tenn. Code Ann. § 67-6-205(c)
Texas	Taxable		34 Tex. Admin. Code § 3.308(b)(2)
Utah	Taxable		Utah Admin. Code r. 865-19S-92(C)
Vermont	Exempt	Must be separately stated.	Vt. Stat. Ann. tit. 32, § 9701(4), Vt. Code R. 1.9701(4)-2(4)
Virginia	Exempt		Va. Code Ann. § 58.1-609.5

State	Canned Software Set-Up Sold Without Tangible Personal Property	Comments	Citation
Washington	Taxable		Wash. Admin. Code § 458-20-15502
West Virginia	Taxable		W. Va. Code R. § 110-15-114.2
Wisconsin	Taxable		Wis. Admin. Code § 11.71 (2) (b) (3)
Wyoming	Taxable		Wyo. BOE Rule Ch. 2, § 13

¶ 105

Clothing

Temporary sales tax holiday exemptions not included.

State	Clothing	Comments	Citation
Alabama	Taxable		Ala. Code § 40-23-2
Arizona	Taxable		Ariz. Rev. Stat. § 42-5008(A)
Arkansas	Taxable		Ark. Code Ann. § 26-52-301, Ark. Code Ann. § 26-52-444, Ark. Reg. 2011-2
California	Taxable	Exemptions allowed for (1) new children's clothing sold to nonprofit organizations for free distribution to elementary school children and (2) used clothing sold by certain thrift stores benefiting the chronically ill.	Cal. Rev. & Tax. Code § 6051
Colorado	Taxable		Colo. Rev. Stat. § 39-26-104
Connecticut	Taxable	Clothing and footwear that costs more than $1,000 is subject to the luxury goods tax. Certain exemptions apply.	Conn. Gen. Stat. § 12-408, Conn. Gen. Stat. § 12-412(119)
District of Columbia	Taxable		D.C. Code Ann. § 47-2002
Florida	Taxable		Fla. Admin. Code Ann. r. 12A-1.076
Georgia	Taxable		Ga. Code Ann. § 48-8-1
Hawaii	Taxable		Haw. Rev. Stat. § 237-13(2)
Idaho	Taxable	Exemption applies to purchases of clothes and footwear by nonsale clothiers that provide free clothes to the needy.	IDAPA 35.01.02.011.03(g), IDAPA 35.01.02.085
Illinois	Taxable		Ill. Admin. Code tit. 86, § 130.2040
Indiana	Taxable		Ind. Code § 6-2.5-2-1
Iowa	Taxable		Iowa Code § 423.2
Kansas	Taxable		Kan. Stat. Ann. § 79-3602
Kentucky	Taxable		Ky. Rev. Stat. Ann. § 139.260, Ky. Rev. Stat. Ann. § 139.470
Louisiana	Taxable		La. Rev. Stat. Ann. § 47:302(A)
Maine	Taxable		Me. Rev. Stat. Ann. tit. 36, § 1811
Maryland	Taxable		Md. Code Ann. § 11-102(a)(1)

State	Clothing	Comments	Citation
Massachusetts	Exempt	Exemption limited to clothing and footwear costing $175 or less. Certain clothing and footwear designed for athletic activity or protective use are taxable.	Mass. Gen. Laws ch. 64H, § 2, Mass. Gen. Laws ch. 64H, § 6(k)
Michigan	Taxable		Mich. Comp. Laws § 205.52(1)
Minnesota	Exempt	Accessories, most protective equipment, sports and recreational articles, and fur clothing are taxable.	Minn. Stat. § 297A.67(8)
Mississippi	Taxable	Clothing, footwear, and accessories used as wardrobes in production of motion pictures are exempt.	Miss. Code. Ann. § 27-65-17
Missouri	Taxable		Mo. Rev. Stat. § 144.020
Nebraska	Taxable		Neb. Rev. Stat. § 77-2703
Nevada	Taxable		Nev. Rev. Stat. § 372.105
New Jersey	Exempt	Fur clothing, clothing accessories or equipment, sport or recreational equipment, or protective equipment are taxable. Protective equipment is only exempt when purchased for the daily work of the user and worn as part of a work uniform or work clothing.	N.J. Stat. Ann. § 54:32B-8.4
New Mexico	Taxable		N.M. Stat. Ann. § 7-9-4
New York	Exempt	Exemption limited to clothing and footwear costing less than $110 per item or pair. Clothing and footwear costing $110 or more per item or pair are taxable.	N.Y. Tax Law, § 1115(a)(30), TSB-M-12(3)S, TSB-M-11(3)S, TSB-M-06(6)S, TSB-M-06(6.1)S, TSB-M-10(16)S
North Carolina	Taxable	Separately stated alteration charges in connection with the sale of clothing are exempt.	N.C. Gen. Stat. § 105-164.4
North Dakota	Taxable		N.D. Cent. Code § 57-39.2-02.1
Ohio	Taxable	Narrow exemption for protective clothing used exclusively in a regulated manufacturing area.	Ohio Rev. Code Ann. § 5739.02, Ohio Admin. Code § 5703-9-21
Oklahoma	Taxable		Okla. Admin. Code § 710:65-19-47

¶105

State	Clothing	Comments	Citation
Pennsylvania	Exempt	Accessories, fur articles, ornamental and formal wear, and sports clothing are taxable.	72 P.S. § 7204(26), 61 Pa. Code § 53.1, 61 Pa. Code § 53.2
Rhode Island	Exempt	Accessories and special clothing designed primarily for athletic or protective use are taxable. Effective October 1, 2012, exemption only applies to $250 of sales price per item.	R.I. Gen. Laws § 44-18-30(28)
South Carolina	Taxable	Certain protective clothing required for working in a clean room environment is exempt.	S.C. Code Ann. § 12-36-910, S.C. Code Ann. Regs. 117-302.5(B)
South Dakota	Taxable		S.D. Codified Laws § 10-45-2
Tennessee	Taxable	Exemption applies to used clothing sold by certain nonprofit organizations.	Tenn. Code. Ann. § 67-6-201
Texas	Taxable.		Tex. Tax Code Ann. § 151.051, Tex. Tax Code Ann. § 151.010
Utah	Taxable		Utah Code Ann. § 59-12-103(1)
Vermont	Exempt	Clothing accessories or equipment, protective equipment, and sport or recreational equipment are taxable.	Vt. Stat. Ann. tit. 32, § 9741(45)
Virginia	Taxable	Exemptions apply to: certain protective clothing furnished to employees engaged in research activities, mining, and manufacturing; and foul-weather clothing worn by commercial watermen.	Va. Code Ann. § 58.1-603
Washington	Taxable		Wash. Rev. Code § 82.08.020
West Virginia	Taxable		W. Va. Code § 11-15-3(a)
Wisconsin	Taxable		Wis. Stat. § 77.52(1)
Wyoming	Taxable		Wyo. Stat. Ann. § 39-15-103

¶ 106   **Collection Discounts Allowed**

The following chart indicates whether a state allows a collection discount that reimburses a seller for expenses incurred in acting as the collecting agent and remitting sales tax before it becomes delinquent. Where state law specifies the applicability of the discount to multiple locations, it is noted in the chart.

State	Collection Discounts Allowed	Comments	Citation
Alabama	5% of the first $100 of tax due and 2% of excess amount; maximum of $400 per month.	Single discount.	Ala. Admin. Code r. 810-6-4-.03
Arizona	Credit allowed equal to 1% of tax due, not to exceed $10,000 per calendar year.	Single discount.	Ariz. Rev. Stat. § 42-5017
Arkansas	2% of tax due; maximum of $1,000 per month.	Single discount.	Ark. Code Ann. § 26-52-503, Ark. Code Ann. § 26-52-512, Ark. Reg. GR-84
California	None		
Colorado	Effective July 1, 2011 through June 30, 2014, the vendor's fee is 2.22%.	Effective July 1, 2009 through June 30, 2011, the vendor's fee was temporarily eliminated.	Colo. Rev. Stat. § 39-26-106(2), Colo. Rev. Stat. § 39-26-105(3)(b)
Connecticut	None		
District of Columbia	None		
Florida	2.5% of the first $1,200 of tax due (mail order dealers may negotiate an allowance of up to 10%).	Per business location.	Fla. Admin. Code Ann. r. 12A-1.056(5), Fla. Stat. § 212.12
Georgia	3% of the first $3,000 of tax due and 0.5% of excess amount.	Per registration number.	Ga. Code Ann. § 48-8-50(b)
Hawaii	None		
Idaho	None		
Illinois	Greater of 1.75% of tax due or $5 per calendar year.		35 ILCS 120/3
Indiana	0.83% if total annual sales tax collected was less than $60,000; 0.6% if total annual sales tax collected was between $60,000 and $600,000; and 0.3% if total annual sales tax collected was more than $600,000.	Certain utilities not entitled to allowance. Effective for reporting periods beginning after June 30, 2008, collection allowances are: 0.73% if total sales tax collected was less than $60,000; 0.53% if total sales tax collected was between $60,000 and $600,000; and 0.26% if total sales tax collected was more than $600,000.	Ind. Code § 6-2.5-6-10
Iowa	None		
Kansas	None		

State	Collection Discounts Allowed	Comments	Citation
Kentucky	1.75% of the first $1,000 of tax due; through June 30, 2013, 1% of amount exceeding $1,000; effective July 1, 2013, 1.5% of amount exceeding $1,000. Through June 30, 2013, allowance is capped at $1,500 per reporting period; effective July 1, 2013, allowance is capped at $50 per reporting period.		Ky. Rev. Stat. Ann. § 139.570
Louisiana	0.935% of tax due.	Total vendor compensation is capped at $1,500 per month for dealers with one or more business locations, effective April 1, 2016. Compensation calculation is based only on state sales tax rate of 4% and not on the temporary additional 1% tax in effect from April 1, 2016, through June 30, 2018. Vendor compensation rate was reduced from 1.1% to 0.935%, effective with July 2013 return.	La. Rev. Stat. Ann. § 47:306(A)(3)(a)
Maine	None	However, retailers are allowed to retain "breakage" as compensation for collection of tax. Under the bracket system, when the tax due in a sales tax return is less than the actual tax collected from customers, the excess collected is "breakage".	
Maryland	Credit equal to 1.2% of first $6,000 of tax due and 0.9% of excess. Limited to $500 per return, or $500 for all returns for vendors eligible to file consolidated returns.	Credit does not apply to any sales and use tax that a vendor is required to pay for any taxable purchase or use made by the vendor.	Md. Code Ann. § 11-105
Massachusetts	None		
Michigan	Vendor may deduct greater of: (1) for payments made before the 12th day of the month, 0.75% of tax due at a rate of 4% for the preceding month (maximum $20,000 of tax due); for payments made between the 12th and the 20th, 0.5% of the tax due at a rate of 4% for the preceding month (maximum $15,000 of tax due); or (2) the tax collected at a rate of 4% on $150 of taxable purchase price for prior month.		Mich. Comp. Laws § 205.54
Minnesota	None		
Mississippi	2% of tax due; maximum of $50 per month and $600 per year.	Per business location.	Miss. Code. Ann. § 27-65-33(1)
Missouri	2% of tax due.		Mo. Rev. Stat. § 144.140

State	Collection Discounts Allowed	Comments	Citation
Nebraska	2.5% of the first $3,000 remitted each month.	Per business location.	Neb. Rev. Stat. § 77-2708(1)(d)
Nevada	Effective Jan. 1, 2009, the rate is 0.25% of tax due.	The 0.25% rate was set to be temporary and expire July 1, 2009, but the expiration date was later repealed. Prior to Jan. 1, 2009, the rate was 0.5%.	Nev. Rev. Stat. § 372.370
New Jersey	None		
New Mexico	None		
New York	Credit equal to 5% of tax due; maximum of $200 per quarterly (or longer) period.		N.Y. Tax Law, § 1137(f)
North Carolina	None		
North Dakota	1.5% of tax due; maximum of $110 per month	Per business location.	N.D. Cent. Code § 57-39.2-12.1, N.D. Cent. Code § 57-40.2-07.1
Ohio	0.75% of tax due.	A vendor that has selected a certified service provider as its agent is not entitled to the discount if the certified service provider receives a monetary allowance.	Ohio Rev. Code Ann. § 5739.12(B)
Oklahoma	1%; maximum of $2,500 per month.	Per permit.	Okla. Stat. tit. 68, § 1367.1, Okla. Admin. Code § 710:65-3-4
Pennsylvania	For returns due on or after August 1, 2016, discount is the lesser of: (1) 1% of the amount of tax collected or (2) $25 per return for a monthly filer, $75 per return for a quarterly filer, or $150 per return for a semiannual filer. For returns due before August 1, 2016, discount is 1% of tax due.		72 P.S. § 7227
Rhode Island	None		
South Carolina	2% of tax due (3% if tax due is less than $100); maximum discount is $3,000 per year ($3,100 if filing electronically; $10,000 for out-of-state taxpayers filing voluntarily).		S.C. Code Ann. § 12-36-2610
South Dakota	None	Effective July 1 after $10 million is accumulated in tax relief fund created from additional revenue received by state from sellers that voluntary register to collect under Streamlined Sales and Use Tax (SST) Agreement, monthly filers are allowed credit of 1.5% of gross amount of tax due (may not exceed $70 per month).	H.B. 1110, Laws 2006

State	Collection Discounts Allowed	Comments	Citation
Tennessee	2% of the first $2,500 and 1.15% of the excess amount per report (only allowed to out-of-state taxpayers filing voluntarily).		Tenn. Code Ann. § 67-6-509
Texas	0.5% of tax due plus 1.25% of the amount of any prepaid tax.	Discounts for timely filing do not apply to holders of direct pay permits.	Tex. Tax Code Ann. § 151.423, 34 Tex. Admin. Code § 3.286
Utah	1.31% of state tax and 1% of local, public transit, and municipal energy sales and use tax (monthly taxpayers).	Effective 7/1/07, monthly filers who remit the 2.75% tax collected on sales of food and food ingredients may retain an amount equal to the sum of (1) 1.31% of the amount the seller is required to remit under the provision imposing a 2.75% tax on food and food ingredients and (2) 1.31% of the difference between the amounts the seller would have remitted under the provision imposing a general 4.75% tax and the amounts the seller must remit under the provision imposing a 2.75% tax on food and food ingredients.	Utah Code Ann. § 59-12-108(3)(a)
Vermont	Seller who collects tax is allowed to retain any amount lawfully collected in excess of the tax imposed.		Vt. Stat. Ann. tit. 32, § 9776
Virginia	3% (4% food tax) if monthly taxable sales are less than $62,501; 2.25% (3% food tax) if $62,501 to $208,000; 1.5% (2% food tax) if over $208,000.	For returns filed for sales on and after 7/1/05, dealer is allowed a single discount at the percentages listed, applicable to the first 3% of state tax due for a given period.	Virginia Tax Bulletin No. 05-07, 23 Va. Admin. Code § 10-210-485(A)
Washington	None		
West Virginia	None		
Wisconsin	0.5% of the tax payable on retail sales or $10, whichever is greater, up to $1,000 for each reporting period, and not to exceed tax liability. Certified service providers ineligible.		Wis. Stat. § 77.61(4)(c)
Wyoming	Early payment credit, 1.95% of first $6,250 of taxes due, then 1% of amount over $6,250. Maximum credit of $500 per month.	Credit allowed only if taxes are remitted on or before 15th day of month that they are due. Effective January 1, 2012.	Wyo. Stat. Ann. § 39-15-107.1

¶ 107   **Coupons and Cash Discounts**

The following chart indicates whether or not coupons and cash discounts are included in the tax base.

State	Coupons and Cash Discounts	Comments	Citation
Alabama	Cash discounts, retailers coupons not included; manufacturers coupons included.		Ala. Code § 40-23-1(a), Ala. Admin. Code r. 810-6-1-.53, Ala. Admin. Code r. 810-6-1-.47, Revenue Ruling 02-020
Arizona	Cash discounts, retailers coupons not included; manufacturers coupons included.		Ariz. Rev. Stat. § 42-5001, Ariz. Admin. Code § 15-5-129
Arkansas	Cash discounts, retailers coupons, membership discounts not included; manufacturers coupons, motor vehicle rebates included.		Ark. Code Ann. § 26-53-102(1), Ark. Reg. GR-18
California	Retailer cash discounts and retailer coupons are not included. Where a manufacturer or third party reimburses the retailer (e.g. a manufacturer's coupon), the amount of the discount or coupon is included.		Cal. Rev. & Tax. Code § 6011(c)(1), Reg. 1671.1, 18 CCR
Colorado	Discounts, retailers coupons, discounts, rebates, credits not included; manufacturers coupons, early payment discounts included.		Colo. Code Regs. § 39-26-102.5, Colo. Code Regs. § 39-26-111, 1 Colo. Code Regs. § 201-5
Connecticut	Cash discounts and manufacturers and retailers coupons not included; rebate amounts included.		Conn. Gen. Stat. § 12-407(a)(8) and (9), Bulletin No. 24
District of Columbia	Cash discounts at time of sale, trade discounts, and quantity discounts at time of sale not included.		D.C. Mun. Regs. t. 9, § 406.2, D.C. Mun. Regs. t. 9, § 406.4, D.C. Mun. Regs. t. 9, § 406.5, D.C. Mun. Regs. t. 9, § 406.7
Florida	Cash discounts at time of sale, retailers coupons not included; manufacturers coupons included.		Fla. Stat. § 212.02(16), Fla. Admin. Code Ann. r. 12A-1.018
Georgia	The "sales price" does not include discounts, including cash, term, or coupons not reimbursed by a third party.		Ga. Code Ann. § 48-8-2(34)(B)
Hawaii	Cash discounts not included. Manufacturer-reimbursed coupons included.		Haw. Rev. Stat. § 237-3(a) and (b), Department of Taxation Response Regarding General Excise Tax Treatment of Coupons

State	Coupons and Cash Discounts	Comments	Citation
Idaho	Retailer discounts (to the extent they represent price adjustments), trade discounts, discounts offered as inducement to continue telecommunications services, retailers coupons, retailers rebates, and manufacturers rebates on motor vehicle sales not included; manufacturers coupons, manufacturers rebates (other than motor vehicle rebates), cash discounts offered as inducements for prompt payment included.		Idaho Code § 63-3613, IDAPA 35.01.02.051
Illinois	ROT, SOT: Discounts, retailers coupons not included; reimbursed coupons included.		Ill. Admin. Code tit. 86, § 130.420, Ill. Admin. Code tit. 86, § 130.2125, Ill. Admin. Code tit. 86, § 140.301
Indiana	Cash and term discounts, retailers coupons not included; manufacturers coupons included.		Ind. Code § 6-2.5-1-5, Information Bulletin #58
Iowa	Discounts, retailers coupons, motor vehicle rebates to purchasers not included; manufacturers coupons included.		Iowa Code § 423.1(47)(b)
Kansas	The "sales or selling price" does not include discounts, including cash, term, or coupons not reimbursed by a third party.		Kan. Stat. Ann. § 79-3602(ll)(3), Kan. Admin. Regs. § 92-19-46(b), Kan. Admin. Regs. § 92-20-4, Kan. Admin. Regs. § 92-19-16a
Kentucky	"Gross receipts" or "sales price" does not include cash discounts or include coupons not reimbursed by a third party.		Ky. Rev. Stat. Ann. § 139.010, 103 Ky. Admin. Regs. 31:080
Louisiana	Cash discounts, retailers coupons, motor vehicle rebates offered as price reductions not included; manufacturers coupons included.		La. Rev. Stat. Ann. § 47:301(13), La. Admin. Code tit. 47, § 4301
Maine	Discounts, retailers coupons not included; manufacturers coupons, manufacturers rebates included.		Me. Rev. Stat. Ann. tit. 36, § 1752(14)(B), Instruction Bulletin No. 25
Maryland	Discounts at time of sale and retailers coupons are not included. Early payment discounts, rebates to the buyer from a third party, and coupons for which vendor can be reimbursed or compensated in any form by a third party are included.		Md. Code Regs. 03-06-01-08
Massachusetts	Cash discounts at time of sale, trade discounts, manufacturers and retailers coupons not included; discounts for early payment included.		Mass. Gen. Laws ch. 64H, § 2, Mass. Regs. Code tit. 830, § 64H.1.4

State	Coupons and Cash Discounts	Comments	Citation
Michigan	Cash, trade, and quantity discounts given directly by the seller, retailers coupons not included; manufacturers coupons, manufacturers rebates included.		Mich. Admin. Code r. 205.22, RAB 1995-6
Minnesota	Discounts not reimbursed by third party, such as retailer coupons, not included; discounts reimbursed by third party, such as manufacturer coupons, included.		Minn. Stat. § 297A.61(7), Minn. R. 8130.0600(3)
Mississippi	Cash discounts, retailers coupons not included; manufacturers coupons included.		Miss. Code. Ann. § 27-65-3(i), Miss. Rule 35.IV.2.02
Missouri	Cash discounts, retailers coupons not included; manufacturers coupons excluded.		Mo. Rev. Stat. § 144.605(8), Mo. Code Regs. tit 12, § 10-103-555
Nebraska	Cash discounts, retailers coupons, motor vehicle rebates used to reduce the selling price not included; manufacturers coupons, cash rebates, deal-of-the day certificates included.		Neb. Rev. Stat. § 77-2701.35, Neb. Admin. Code § 1-020, Neb. Admin. Code § 1-024, Neb. Admin. Code § 1-037
Nevada	Cash discounts, retailers coupons not included; reimbursed coupons included.		Nev. Rev. Stat. § 372.025, Nev. Rev. Stat. § 372.065
New Jersey	Discounts that represent a price reduction, such as a trade discount, volume discount, or cash and carry discount, early payment discounts, and retailers coupons not included; reimbursed coupons, rebates included.		N.J. Stat. Ann. § 54:32B-2(oo), N.J. Admin. Code § 18:24-36.2, Publication ANJ-9
New Mexico	Cash discounts, retailers coupons not included; manufacturers coupons included.		N.M. Stat. Ann. § 7-9-3.5, N.M. Admin. Code tit. 3, § 3.2.1.14
New York	Discounts that represent a price reduction, such as a trade discount, volume discount or cash and carry discount, and retailers coupons are not included; manufacturer's coupons, reimbursed coupons, and early payment discounts included.		N.Y. Comp. Code R. & Regs. tit. 20, § 526.5
North Carolina	Cash discounts, trade discounts, retailers coupons not included; manufacturers coupons included.		N.C. Admin. Code tit. 17, § 17:07B.0108, N.C. Admin. Code tit. 17, § 17:07B.0122
North Dakota	Discounts, retailers coupons not included; manufacturers coupons, manufacturers rebates included if the seller receives consideration from the manufacturer and other criteria are met.		N.D. Cent. Code § 57-39.2-01(11), N.D. Admin. Code § 81-04.1-01-28

State	Coupons and Cash Discounts	Comments	Citation
Ohio	Cash and term discounts, retailers coupons not included; reimbursed coupons included.	The value of a gift card or certificate redeemed by a consumer in purchasing tangible personal property is excluded from tax if (1) the vendor is not reimbursed and (2) the gift card or certificate is distributed through a customer award, loyalty, or promotional program.	Ohio Rev. Code Ann. § 5739.01(H)(1), Ohio Admin. Code § 5703-9-15
Oklahoma	"Gross receipts," "gross proceeds," or "sales price" does not include cash discounts or include coupons not reimbursed by a third party.		Okla. Stat. tit. 68, § 1352, Okla. Admin. Code § 710:65-1-9
Pennsylvania	Discounts at time of sale and retailers and manufacturers coupons not included if separately stated; discounts after sale included.		72 P.S. § 7201(g), 16 Pa. Code § 33.2
Rhode Island	Discounts allowed by a seller, including cash, term, or coupons that are not reimbursed by a third party not included; consideration received by a seller from third parties, including manufacturer's coupons, included if certain criteria are met.		R.I. Gen. Laws § 44-18-12(b), R.I. Code R. SU 07-140
South Carolina	Cash discounts at time of sale, retailers coupons, discounts on the sale of items from the exchange of points from a customer loyalty awards program, not included; timely payment discounts deductible by retailer on subsequent report; manufacturers coupons and manufacturers rebates included.	When property is transferred to a customer, through a customer loyalty awards program, for no consideration, nominal consideration, or an amount significantly below cost, there is a rebuttable presumption that the property is a promotional item withdrawn from inventory, and the retailer is liable for sales tax based on the fair market value of the property.	S.C. Code Ann. § 12-36-90(2), S.C. Code Ann. § 12-36-130(2), Revenue Ruling 99-9, Private Letter Ruling 11-5, Private Letter Ruling 89-8
South Dakota	Discounts, retailers coupons not included; reimbursed coupons included.		S.D. Codified Laws § 10-45-1(3), S.D. Admin. R. 64:06:03:51
Tennessee	Discounts, including cash, term, or coupons not reimbursed by a third party that are allowed by seller not included.		Tenn. Code. Ann. § 67-6-102
Texas	Cash discounts and retailers and manufacturers coupons not included.		Tex. Tax Code Ann. § 151.007, 34 Tex. Admin. Code § 3.301
Utah	Cash discounts, retailers coupons, and term discounts not included; manufacturers coupons included.		Utah Code Ann. § 59-12-102

State	Coupons and Cash Discounts	Comments	Citation
Vermont	Discounts allowed by a seller, including cash, term, or coupons that are not reimbursed by a third party not included; consideration received by a seller from third parties included if certain criteria are met.		Vt. Stat. Ann. tit. 32, § 9701(4)
Virginia	Cash, trade, and early payment discounts, and retailers coupons not included; manufacturers coupons included.		23 Va. Admin. Code § 10-210-430, 23 Va. Admin. Code § 10-210-250
Washington	Discounts, retailers coupons not included; manufacturers coupons included.	The redemption of a deal-of-the-day voucher is taxed based on the amount paid for the voucher plus any other consideration received by the seller from the customer (e.g., cash, check, or credit card amount), provided the seller is not reimbursed by a third party.	Wash. Rev. Code § 82.08.010, Wash. Admin. Code § 458-20-108, Special Notice
West Virginia	The "sales price" does not include discounts, including cash, term, or coupons not reimbursed by a third party.		W. Va. Code § 11-15B-2(b), W. Va. Code R. § 110-15-95.1
Wisconsin	Discounts allowed by a seller, including cash, term, or coupons that are not reimbursed by a third party not included; consideration received by a seller from third parties included if certain criteria are met.		Wis. Stat. § 77.51(15b)(b)1. and (c), Wis. Admin. Code § 11.28(3) and (6), Wis. Admin. Code § 11.32(3)
Wyoming	Cash and term discounts and retailers coupons not included; manufacturers coupons included.		Wyo. Stat. Ann. § 39-15-101(a)(viii)

¶ 108   Custom Software Delivered on Tangible Personal Property

State	Delivered on Tangible Personal Property	Comments	Citation
Alabama	Exempt	Cost of tangible medium used to transfer custom software programming to customer taxable.	Ala. Admin. Code r. 810-6-1-.37
Arizona	Exempt		Ariz. Admin. Code § 15-5-154(C)
Arkansas	Taxable		Ark. Code Ann. § 26-52-304, Ark. Reg. GR-25
California	Exempt		Cal. Rev. & Tax. Code § 6010.9
Colorado	Exempt		1 Colo. Code Regs. § 201-5 (SR-7)
Connecticut	Taxable	Software taxable at 1% rate for computer and data processing services; tangible personal property taxable at general state sales/use tax rate. Custom software may be exempt if purchased in connection with exempt machinery under the biotechnology, manufacturing, or commercial printers/ publishers exemption.	Policy Statement 2006(8)
District of Columbia	Taxable		D.C. Mun. Regs. t. 9, § 474.4
Florida	Exempt	The charge that a computer technician makes for a customized software package that includes such items as instructional material, pre-punched cards, or programmed tapes is construed to be a service charge and exempt.	Fla. Admin. Code Ann. r. 12A-1.032(4), TAA No. 00A-082
Georgia	Exempt		Ga. Code Ann. § 48-8-3(22), Unofficial department guidance
Hawaii	Taxable		Haw. Rev. Stat. § 237-13
Idaho	Exempt		IDAPA 35.01.02.027(08)(a)
Illinois	Exempt		Ill. Admin. Code tit. 86, § 130.1935(c)
Indiana	Exempt		Ind. Admin. Code tit. 45, r. 2.2-4-2, Information Bulletin #8

State	Delivered on Tangible Personal Property	Comments	Citation
Iowa	Exempt	Custom software transferred in the form of written procedures, such as program instructions on coding sheets, and tangible personal property incidental to the sale of custom software are exempt. Material transferred in the form of typed or printed sheets is taxable if separately stated. If the cost for the typed or printed sheets is invoiced lump sum with the cost for custom software, the entire sale would become taxable.	Computers: Is yours exempt? (Pub. 78-575), August 2003
Kansas	Exempt		Notice 04-07, Rev. Ruling 19-2004-03
Kentucky	Exempt		Kentucky Sales Tax Facts, June 2006, Kentucky Taxability Matrix
Louisiana	Exempt	Caution: Numerous exemptions are suspended from April 1, 2016, to June 30, 2018. For chart of suspended exemptions and applicable tax rates, see Publication R-1002A.	La. Rev. Stat. Ann. § 47:301(16), LA DOR Publication R-1002A
Maine	Exempt		Me. Rev. Stat. Ann. tit. 36, § 1752
Maryland	Exempt		Md. Code Ann. § 11-219
Massachusetts	Exempt		Mass. Regs. Code tit. 830, § 64H.1.3(6)
Michigan	Exempt		Mich. Comp. Laws § 205.94a(d)
Minnesota	Exempt	When purchased with a computer, exempt only if charges for custom software are separately stated.	Minn. Stat. § 297A.61(3), Minn. R. 8130.9910(2)
Mississippi	Taxable		Miss. Code Ann. § 27-65-23, Miss. Rule 35.IV.5.06
Missouri	Exempt	Tax does not apply to the amount charged to the customer for customized software. The seller of the customized software is subject to tax on the purchase of any tangible personal property or taxable services used to provide the nontaxable service.	Mo. Code Regs. Ann. tit. 12, § 10-109.050(3)(C)

State	Delivered on Tangible Personal Property	Comments	Citation
Nebraska	Taxable		Neb. Rev. Stat. § 77-2701.16(3)(a), Neb. Admin. Code § 1-088
Nevada	Exempt	Exempt only if charges for custom software or programming are separately stated.	Nev. Admin. Code § 372.875(3)
New Jersey	Exempt	If a purchaser receives custom software in some tangible medium, the transfer of the disc or CD to the purchaser is deemed to be an incidental part of the sale of exempt software development and design services.	N.J. Technical Bulletin TB-51R, N.J. Stat. Ann. § 54:32B-8.56
New Mexico	Taxable		N.M. Admin. Code tit. 3, § 3.2.1.18(EE)
New York	Exempt		N.Y. Tax Law, § 1101(b), TSB-A-99(31)S
North Carolina	Exempt		Sales and Use Tax Technical Bulletin, Sec. 28-3
North Dakota	Exempt	When purchased with equipment, exempt only if charges for custom software are separately stated.	N.D. Admin. Code § 81-04.1-03-11(6)
Ohio	Exempt	Custom system software for business use is a taxable computer service. Programming of custom application software is not a taxable sale.	Ohio Rev. Code Ann. § 5739.01(B)(3)(e) and (Y)(1)(b), Ohio Admin. Code § 5703-9-46(A)(2)(c)
Oklahoma	Exempt	Exempt if tangible personal property transferred with custom software is incidental to sale of the software. If a computer is purchased with custom software and the charges are not separately stated, the entire purchase is taxable.	Okla. Admin. Code § 710:65-19-52(h)
Pennsylvania	Exempt		61 Pa. Code § 60.19
Rhode Island	Exempt		R.I. Code R. SU 11-25
South Carolina	Taxable	Broadcasting software sold to a radio station, television station, or cable television system is exempt.	117 S.C. Code Ann. Regs. 117-330, Revenue Ruling 03-5, Private Letter Ruling 12-1
South Dakota	Taxable		S.D. Admin. R. 64:06:02:80

State	Delivered on Tangible Personal Property	Comments	Citation
Tennessee	Taxable	Exemptions may apply for the use of software developed and fabricated by an affiliated company or for fabrication of software by a person for that person's own use or consumption.	Tenn. Code Ann. § 67-6-102, Tenn. Code Ann. § 67-6-231
Texas	Taxable		Tex. Tax Code Ann. § 151.009, 34 Tex. Admin. Code § 3.308
Utah	Exempt		Utah Admin. Code r. 865-19S-92(C)
Vermont	Exempt		Vt. Stat. Ann. tit. 32, § 9701(7), Vt. Stat. Ann. tit. 32, § 9771
Virginia	Exempt	Exempt if true object of sale is to provide exempt custom programming service and tangible personal property transferred is not critical to the transaction; separately stated charges for tangible personal property are taxable. Taxable if true object of sale is to provide tangible personal property. Information conveyed via tangible means (e.g., diskette, computer tape, report, etc.) generally is taxable except for information customized to a particular customer's needs and sold to that particular customer.	Va. Code Ann. § 58.1-609.5(7), 23 Va. Admin. Code § 10-210-4040(D)
Washington	Exempt		Wash. Admin. Code § 458-20-15502
West Virginia	Taxable		W. Va. Code § 11-15-3(a)
Wisconsin	Exempt		Wis. Stat. § 77.52, Wis. Admin. Code § 11.71(3)
Wyoming	Exempt		Wyo. BOE Rule Ch. 2, § 13

¶ 109   Custom Software Set-Up Sold Without Tangible Personal Property

State	Custom Software Set-Up Sold Without Tangible Personal Property	Comments	Citation
Alabama	Exempt		Ala. Admin. Code r. 810-6-1-.37, Ala. Admin. Code r. 810-6-1-.81
Arizona	Exempt		TPR 93-48
Arkansas	Exempt	If the software set-up qualifies as technical support for software, software programming service, or development of custom software.	Ark. Code Ann. § 26-52-304, Ark. Reg. GR-25(A)
California	Exempt		Reg. 1502(g), 18 CCR
Colorado	Exempt		Colo. Rev. Stat. § 39-26-104(1)(a)
Connecticut	Taxable	Software installation is taxed as a computer and data processing service and is taxed at a different rate than the sale of tangible personal property.	Conn. Gen. Stat. § 12-407(a)(37)(A), Policy Statement 2006(8)
District of Columbia	Taxable		D.C. Mun. Regs. t. 9, § 474.4
Florida	Exempt		Unoffical department guidance
Georgia	Exempt	Must be separately stated.	Ga. Comp. R. & Regs. 560-12-2-.111
Hawaii	Taxable		Haw. Rev. Stat. § 237-13(6)
Idaho	Exempt	Must be separately stated.	IDAPA 35.01.02.011.02
Illinois	Exempt	Must be separately stated.	Ill. Admin. Code tit. 86, § 130.1935(b)
Indiana	Taxable		Information Bulletin #8 (II)(A)
Iowa	Exempt	If the service does not constitute an enumerated taxable service and it is separated stated.	Iowa Admin. Code r. 701-18.34(3)(e)
Kansas	Exempt		Kan. Stat. Ann. § 79-3603, E-mail from Kansas Department of Revenue, February 10, 2006
Kentucky	Exempt		103 Ky. Admin. Regs. 30:180
Louisiana	Exempt	Caution: Numerous exemptions are suspended from April 1, 2016, to June 30, 2018. For chart of suspended exemptions and applicable tax rates, see Publication R-1002A.	La. Rev. Stat. Ann. § 47:301(14), LA DOR Publication R-1002A

State	Custom Software Set-Up Sold Without Tangible Personal Property	Comments	Citation
Maine	Exempt	Must be separately stated.	Me. Rev. Stat. Ann. tit. 36, § 1752(14)(B)(4)
Maryland	Exempt		Md. Code Ann. § 11-101(l)(3)(i)(3)
Massachusetts	Exempt	However, if the set-up service is a mandatory service, then taxable.	Mass. Regs. Code tit. 830, § 64H.1.3(4)(h)
Michigan	Exempt		Mich. Comp. Laws § 205.92(k), Mich. Comp. Laws § 205.54d(g)
Minnesota	Exempt	Reinstallation of software is not taxable.	Minn. R. 8130.9910, Sales Tax Fact Sheet 134
Mississippi	Taxable		Miss. Code Ann. § 27-65-23, Miss. Rule 35.IV.5.06
Missouri	Exempt	The taxation of the purchase of software installation, training, and maintenance services shall be determined as follows: (1) Software maintenance agreements that are mandatory for canned software provided on a tangible medium are subject to tax, whether or not these charges are separately stated; (2) Software maintenance agreements that provide for canned software updates, upgrades, or enhancements delivered on a tangible medium are subject to tax. If the optional maintenance agreements do not provide for canned software updates, upgrades, or enhancements delivered on a tangible medium, then the separately stated cost of the maintenance agreement is not subject to tax; and (3) Charges for custom software maintenance agreements that provide for software updates, upgrades, or enhancements delivered on a tangible medium are not subject to tax.	Mo. Code Regs. Ann. tit. 12, § 10-109.050(F)
Nebraska	Taxable	Charges to reinstall existing software are not taxable. Installation/setup includes providing software patches or security updates for virus protection.	Information Guide 6-511-2011
Nevada	Exempt	Must be separately stated.	Nev. Rev. Stat. § 372.025(3)(c)

State	Custom Software Set-Up Sold Without Tangible Personal Property	Comments	Citation
New Jersey	Exempt		N.J. Technical Bulletin TB-51R
New Mexico	Taxable		N.M. Admin. Code tit. 3, § 3.2.1.18(A)
New York	Exempt	Services must be provided to a customer in conjunction with the sale of tangible personal property, and the charges must be reasonable and separately stated.	N.Y. Tax Law, § 1115(o)
North Carolina	Exempt	Must be separately stated.	N.C. Gen. Stat. § 105-164.13(49)
North Dakota	Exempt		N.D. Admin. Code § 81-04.1-01-22
Ohio	Exempt		Ohio Rev. Code Ann. § 5739.01(Y)(2)(e), Ohio Admin. Code § 5703-9-46(2)(c)
Oklahoma	Exempt	Must be separately stated.	Okla. Admin. Code § 710:65-19-158
Pennsylvania	Exempt		61 Pa. Code § 60.19(c)(2)
Rhode Island	Exempt		R.I. Code R. SU 11-25
South Carolina	Exempt		Revenue Ruling 03-5
South Dakota	Taxable		S.D. Admin. R. 64:06:02:78
Tennessee	Taxable		Tenn. Code Ann. § 67-6-231, Tenn. Code Ann. § 67-6-205(c), Tenn. Code Ann. § 67-6-231
Texas	Taxable		34 Tex. Admin. Code § 3.308(b)(2)
Utah	Exempt		Utah Admin. Code r. 865-19S-92(C)
Vermont	Exempt	Must be separately stated.	Vt. Stat. Ann. tit. 32, § 9701(4), Vt. Code R. 1.9701(4)-2(4)
Virginia	Exempt		Va. Code Ann. § 58.1-609.5
Washington	Exempt		Wash. Admin. Code § 458-20-15502
West Virginia	Taxable		W. Va. Code R. § 110-15-114.2
Wisconsin	Exempt		Wis. Admin. Code § 11.71(3)(b)
Wyoming	Taxable		Wyo. BOE Rule Ch. 2, § 13

¶ 110   Department Appeals

The following chart describes the time period in which a taxpayer must file a protest or appeal of an assessment with the taxing authority. Appeals to other administrative or judicial entities are addressed in Administrative Appeals and Judicial Appeals.

State	Department Appeals	Comments	Citation
Alabama	Petition must be filed with the Department of Revenue, Administrative Law Division within 30 days after the date of entry of the assessment.		Ala. Code § 40-2A-7
Arizona	Petition must be filed with the Department of Revenue within 45 days after receipt of notice of deficiency assessment or within such additional time as the Department allows.		Ariz. Rev. Stat. § 42-1108
Arkansas	Petition must be filed with the Director of the Department of Finance and Administration within 30 days after receipt of the notice of assessment.		Ark. Code Ann. § 26-18-404
California	Petition for redetermination must be filed with the State Board of Equalization within 30 days after service of notice of deficiency assessment.		Cal. Rev. & Tax. Code § 6561
Colorado	Petition must be filed with the Executive Director of the Department of Revenue within 30 days after mailing of notice of deficiency.		Colo. Rev. Stat. § 39-21-103
Connecticut	Petition must be filed with the Commissioner of Revenue Services within 60 days after service of notice.		Conn. Gen. Stat. § 12-418
District of Columbia	Petition must be filed with the Mayor within 30 days after notice of deficiency.		D.C. Code Ann. § 47-2019
Florida	Petition must be filed with the Department of Revenue within 60 days after issuance of proposed assessment.		Fla. Admin. Code Ann. r. 12-6.003
Georgia	Petition must be filed with the Revenue Commissioner within 30 days after date of notice of assessment, or within another time limit specified with the notice.		Ga. Code Ann. § 48-2-46
Hawaii	Petition under expedited appeals and dispute resolution program must be filed after issuance of notice of proposed assessment.		Haw. Rev. Stat. § 231-7.5(b)
Idaho	Petition must be filed with the Tax Commission within 63 days after mailing notice of deficiency.		Idaho Code § 63-3631

State	Department Appeals	Comments	Citation
Illinois	Petition must be filed with the Department of Revenue within 60 days after issuance of notice of deficiency.		35 ILCS 120/4
Indiana	Petition must be filed with the Department of Revenue within 60 days after date of notice of assessment.		Ind. Code § 6-8.1-5-1
Iowa	Petition must be filed with the Director of Revenue within 60 days after date of notice of assessment.		Iowa Code § 423.37
Kansas	Informal conference may be requested with the Secretary of Revenue within 60 days after mailing of notice.		Kan. Stat. Ann. § 79-3226
Kentucky	Petition must be filed with the Revenue Cabinet within 45 days after date of notice of assessment.		Ky. Rev. Stat. Ann. § 131.110
Louisiana	Petition must be filed with the Secretary of Revenue and Taxation within 30 days after notice of deficiency or assessment.	15 days if notice based on failure to file return.	La. Rev. Stat. Ann. § 47:1563
Maine	Petition must be filed with the State Tax Assessor within 60 days after receipt of notice of assessment.		Me. Rev. Stat. Ann. tit. 36, § 151
Maryland	Petition must be filed with the Comptroller within 30 days after mailing notice of Comptroller's action.		Md. Code Ann. § 13-508
Massachusetts	Informal conference may be requested with the Commissioner of Revenue within 30 days of notice.		Mass. Gen. Laws ch. 62C, § 26
Michigan	Informal conference may be requested with the Department of Treasury within 60 days after receipt of notice of intent to assess.		Mich. Comp. Laws § 205.21
Minnesota	Petition must be filed with the Commissioner of Revenue within 60 days of notice of action.		Minn. Stat. § 270C.35
Mississippi	Petition must be filed with the Board of Review within 60 days from the date of the Department's action.		Miss. Code. Ann. § 27-77-5
Missouri	Petition for informal review must be filed with the Director of Revenue within 60 days after the assessment is delivered or sent by certified mail, whichever is earlier.		Mo. Rev. Stat. § 144.240

State	Department Appeals	Comments	Citation
Nebraska	Petition must be filed with the Tax Commissioner within 60 days after service of notice of deficiency.		Neb. Rev. Stat. § 77-2709
Nevada	Petition must be filed with the Department of Taxation within 45 days after service of notice of assessment.		Nev. Rev. Stat. § 360.360
New Jersey	Petition must be filed with the Director of the Division of Taxation within 90 days after service of notice of assessment.		N.J. Stat. Ann. § 54:32B-19
New Mexico	Petition must be filed with the Secretary of Taxation and Revenue within 90 days.		N.M. Stat. Ann. § 7-1-24
New York	Petition must be filed with the Division of Tax Appeals within 90 days after mailing notice of determination.		N.Y. Tax Law, § 1138
North Carolina	Petition must be filed with the Secretary of Revenue within 30 days after mailing or delivery of notice of proposed assessment.		N.C. Gen. Stat. § 105-241.1
North Dakota	Petition must be filed with the Tax Commission within 30 days after notice of determination.		N.D. Cent. Code § 57-39.2-15, N.D. Cent. Code § 28-32-42
Ohio	Petition must be filed with the Tax Commissioner within 60 days after service of notice of assessment.		Ohio Rev. Code Ann. § 5739.13
Oklahoma	Petition must be filed with the Tax Commission within 60 days after mailing of notice of assessment.		Okla. Stat. tit. 68, § 221
Pennsylvania	Notice of intention to file petition must be filed with the Department of Revenue within 90 days after mailing notice of assessment.		72 P.S. § 7232, 72 P.S. § 9702
Rhode Island	Petition must be filed with the Tax Administrator within 30 days after mailing notice of assessment.		R.I. Gen. Laws § 44-19-17
South Carolina	Petition must be filed with the Department of Revenue within 90 days after date of proposed assessment.		S.C. Code Ann. § 12-60-450
South Dakota	Petition must be filed with the Secretary of Revenue within 30 days after date of certification of assessment.		S.D. Codified Laws § 10-59-9
Tennessee	Informal conference may be requested with the Commissioner of Revenue within 30 days after date of notice of assessment.		Tenn. Code Ann. § 67-1-1801

State	Department Appeals	Comments	Citation
Texas	Petition must be filed with the Comptroller of Public Accounts within 30 days after issuance of notice of determination.		Tex. Tax Code Ann. § 111.009
Utah	Petition must be filed with the Tax Commission within 30 days after mailing notice of deficiency.		Utah Code Ann. § 59-12-114, Utah Code Ann. § 63-46b-12
Vermont	Petition must be filed with the Commissioner of Taxes within 60 days after notice of determination.		Vt. Stat. Ann. tit. 32, § 9777
Virginia	Petition must be filed with the Tax Commissioner within 90 days after notice of assessment.		Va. Code Ann. § 58.1-1821
Washington	Petition must be filed with the Department of Revenue within 30 days after issuance of notice of assessment.	The appeals division may grant an extension of time to file a petition if the taxpayer's request is made within the thirty-day filing period.	Wash. Rev. Code § 82.32.160
West Virginia	State does not have department appeal procedures. Taxpayer must file an administrative appeal.		
Wisconsin	Petition must be filed with the Department of Revenue within 60 days after receipt of notice of determination.		Wis. Stat. § 77.59(6)
Wyoming	State does not have department appeal procedures. Taxpayer must file an administrative appeal.		

¶ 111   **Direct Pay Permits**

The following chart indicates whether direct pay permits are allowed. Where limitations are placed on the issuance of permits, it is noted in the Comments column.

State	Direct Pay Permits	Comments	Citation
Alabama	Allowed	Limited to electric cooperatives, telephone companies, manufacturers, transportation companies, processors of tangible personal property and mining, quarrying, or compounding businesses.	Ala. Admin. Code r. 810-6-4-.13, Ala. Admin. Code r. 810-6-4-.14
Arizona	Allowed	Limited to taxpayers that made purchases of at least $500,000 during the calendar year preceding application.	Ariz. Rev. Stat. § 42-5167
Arkansas	Allowed		Ark. Code Ann. § 26-52-509
California	Allowed	Specified requirements must be met.	Cal. Rev. & Tax. Code § 7051.1
Colorado	Allowed	Limited to taxpayers that purchased at least $7 million of commodities, services, or tangible personal property subject to tax during the calendar year preceding application.	Colo. Rev. Stat. § 39-26-103.5
Connecticut	Allowed	Specified requirements must be met.	Conn. Gen. Stat. § 12-409a
District of Columbia	Not Allowed		
Florida	Allowed	Limited to certain specified taxpayers.	Fla. Admin. Code Ann. r. 12A-1.0911
Georgia	Allowed	Exceptions apply.	Ga. Comp. R. & Regs. 560-12-1-.16
Hawaii	Not Allowed		
Idaho	Allowed	Limited to sales of tangible personal property. Not applicable when engaging contractors improving real property.	IDAPA 35.01.02.112
Illinois	Allowed	Specified requirements must be met. Not applicable to food, beverages, property required to be titled or registered with government agency, or transactions subject to Service Occupation or Service Use Tax.	35 ILCS 120/2-10.5
Indiana	Allowed		Ind. Admin. Code tit. 45, r. 2.2-8-16

State	Direct Pay Permits	Comments	Citation
Iowa	Allowed	Limited to taxpayers accruing tax liability of more than $4,000 in semi-monthly period. Permit not applicable for sales of gas, electricity, heat, pay television service, communication service, tax on motor vehicles and on vehicles rented for 60 or fewer days.	Iowa Code § 423.36(8)(a)
Kansas	Allowed	Limited to taxpayers making annual purchases of at least $1 million of tangible personal property for business use and not for resale or purchasing substantial amounts of property for business use under circumstances making it difficult to determine whether property is taxable or exempt.	Kan. Admin. Regs. § 92-19-82
Kentucky	Allowed	Limited to certain specified taxpayers that meet specified requirements.	103 Ky. Admin. Reg. 31:030
Louisiana	Allowed	Limited to certain specified taxpayers that meet specified requirements.	La. Rev. Stat. Ann. § 47:303.1
Maine	Allowed	Limited to manufacturers and utilities. Not applicable to purchases of food, beverages, hotel accommodations, and telephone service, or to certain rentals and construction contracts.	Me. Rule 308
Maryland	Allowed	Limited to taxpayers that have effective rate agreements with the Comptroller of the Treasury.	Md. Code Ann. § 11-407
Massachusetts	Allowed	Specified requirements must be met.	Mass. Regs. Code tit. 830, § 64H.3.1
Michigan	Allowed		Mich. Comp. Laws § 205.98
Minnesota	Allowed	Not applicable to purchases of food, beverages, taxable lodgings, admissions to places of amusement athletic events or the privilege of use of amusement devices, motor vehicles, and certain taxable services.	Minn. Stat. § 297A.89, Minn. R. 8130.3400
Mississippi	Allowed	Limited to certain specified taxpayers. May be issued to public utilities, effective July 1, 2005.	Miss. Code. Ann. § 27-67-15

State	Direct Pay Permits	Comments	Citation
Missouri	Allowed	Limited to taxpayers making annual purchases over $750,000.	Mo. Rev. Stat. § 144.190.4
Nebraska	Allowed	Limited to taxpayers making annual purchases of at least $3 million, excluding purchases for which a resale certificate could be used. Direct pay permit holders must pay the tax on or before the 20th day of the month following the date of the taxable purchase, lease, or rental.	Neb. Rev. Stat. § 77-2705.01
Nevada	Allowed	Effective January 1, 2006, Nevada allows taxpayers to obtain direct pay permits.	Nev. Rev. Stat. § 360B.260
New Jersey	Allowed		N.J. Stat. Ann. § 54:32B-12
New Mexico	Not Allowed		
New York	Allowed		N.Y. Tax Law, § 1132(c)
North Carolina	Allowed	Limited to purchases of tangible personal property and telecommunications services.	N.C. Gen. Stat. § 105-164.27A
North Dakota	Allowed	Not applicable to purchases of food, beverages, taxable lodging, and admissions to places of amusement or athletic events or the privilege of use of amusement devices.	N.D. Cent. Code § 57-39.2-14.1, N.D. Admin. Code § 81-04.1-01-05
Ohio	Allowed	Limited to (1) taxpayers purchasing goods and services where its impossible to determine at the time of purchase whether purchases are taxable or exempt or (2) taxpayers whose number of purchase transactions of goods or services exceeds 5,000 annually or whose state sales and use tax paid on these purchases exceeds $250,000 annually.	Ohio Rev. Code Ann. § 5739.031, Ohio Sales and Use Tax Information Release ST 2003-01
Oklahoma	Allowed	Limited to taxpayers making purchases of at least $800,000 annually in taxable items.	Okla. Stat. tit. 68, § 1364.1

State	Direct Pay Permits	Comments	Citation
Pennsylvania	Allowed	Not applicable to purchases of certain motor vehicles, trailers, semi-trailers, or tractors; prepared food or beverages at any eating place; or occupancy or accommodations subject to hotel occupancy tax.	61 Pa. Code § 34.4, 72 P.S. § 7237(d)
Rhode Island	Allowed		R.I. Gen. Laws § 44-18-19.1
South Carolina	Allowed		S.C. Code Ann. § 12-36-2510
South Dakota	Allowed	Limited to taxpayers making purchases of at least $3 million annually in taxable goods and services. Not applicable to purchases of food, beverages, taxable lodgings, admissions to places of amusement and athletic events, motor vehicles, telecommunication services and utilities.	S.D. Codified Laws § 10-46-67, S.D. Admin. R. 64:01:01:34, S.D. Admin. R. 64:01:01:37
Tennessee	Allowed	Limited to exceptional circumstances or taxpayer hardship.	Tenn. Comp. R. & Regs. 1320-5-1-.68(4)
Texas	Allowed	Limited to taxpayers making purchases of at least $800,000 annually in taxable items for the taxpayer's own use and not for resale.	Tex. Tax Code Ann. § 151.417, 34 Tex. Admin. Code § 3.288
Utah	Allowed	Effective July 1, 2006, a direct pay permit may be issued to a seller that obtains a license, is subject to mandatory EFT, has a record of timely payment of taxes, and has the ability to determine the appropriate location of a transaction for each transaction for which the seller makes a purchase using the permit. Not applicable to purchases of food, accommodations, admissions, motor vehicles, common carrier or telecommunications services, or utilities.	Utah Code Ann. § 59-12-107.1
Vermont	Allowed		Vt. Stat. Ann. tit. 32, § 9745
Virginia	Allowed	Limited to manufacturers, mine operators, and public service corporations.	Va. Code Ann. § 58.1-624(A)

State	Direct Pay Permits	Comments	Citation
Washington	Allowed	Limited to taxpayers who make purchases of over $10 million per calendar year or have an expected cumulative tax liability of at least $240,000 in the current calendar year.	Wash. Rev. Code § 82.32.087
West Virginia	Allowed	Limited to certain specified taxpayers.	W. Va. Code § 11-15-9d, W. Va. Code R. § 110-15-9c
Wisconsin	Allowed	Specified requirements must be met.	Wis. Stat. § 77.52(17m)
Wyoming	Allowed	Limited to taxpayers making purchases of at least $5 million in a calendar year.	Wyo. Stat. Ann. § 39-15-107.1, Wyo. DOR Rule Ch. 2, § 6

¶ 112   **Downloaded Canned Computer Software**

This chart indicates whether sales or licenses of prewritten computer software delivered electronically are subject to tax.

State	Downloaded	Comments	Citation
Alabama	Taxable		Ala. Admin. Code r. 810-6-1.37
Arizona	Taxable		Ariz. Admin. Code § 15-5-154(B)
Arkansas	Exempt	Software delivered electronically or by "load and leave" not taxable.	Ark. Code Ann. § 26-52-304, Ark. Reg. GR-25
California	Exempt	Prewritten program transferred by remote telecommunications exempt, provided that purchaser does not obtain possession of any tangible personal property (such as storage media) in the transaction.	Reg. 1502(f)(1)(D), 18 CCR
Colorado	Exempt		Colo. Rev. Stat. § 39-26-102
Connecticut	Taxable	If no tangible personal property delivered to purchaser along with downloaded software, software is taxed at 1% rate applicable to computer and data processing services.	Policy Statement 2006(8)
District of Columbia	Taxable		Unofficial department guidance
Florida	Exempt		TAA No. 02A-052, Unofficial department guidance
Georgia	Exempt	Documentation must indicate method of delivery. If software is delivered both electronically and through a tangible medium, the transaction is treated as a taxable sale of tangible personal property unless the software qualifies as custom software.	Ga. Comp. R. & Regs. 560-12-2-.111
Hawaii	Taxable		Haw. Rev. Stat. § 237-13
Idaho	Exempt	Electronically delivered, remotely accessed (cloud), and "load and leave" software exempt.	Idaho Code § 63-3616(b)(i), IDAPA 35.01.02.027(04)(a)
Illinois	Taxable		Ill. Admin. Code tit. 86, § 130.1935(a)
Indiana	Taxable		Information Bulletin #8
Iowa	Exempt		Iowa Code § 423.3(66), Iowa Admin. Code r. 701-231.14

State	Downloaded	Comments	Citation
Kansas	Taxable		Kan. Stat. Ann. § 79-3603(s), Rev. Ruling 19-2004-03
Kentucky	Taxable		Ky. Rev. Stat. Ann. § 139.010, Kentucky Sales Tax Facts, Vol. 6, No. 1, April 2004
Louisiana	Taxable		Unofficial department guidance
Maine	Taxable		Me. Rev. Stat. Ann. tit. 36, § 1752(17)
Maryland	Exempt	Exempt as long as the transaction does not include the transfer of any tangible personal property.	Unofficial department guidance
Massachusetts	Taxable		Mass. Gen. Laws ch. 64H, § 1, TIR 05-15
Michigan	Taxable		RAB 1999-5
Minnesota	Taxable		Minn. Stat. § 297A.61(3)(f)
Mississippi	Taxable		Miss. Rule 35.IV.5.06
Missouri	Exempt		Mo. Code Regs. Ann. tit. 12, § 10-109.050(3)(A), LR 7074, LR 6991
Nebraska	Taxable		Neb. Rev. Stat. § 77-2701.16(3)(a), Neb. Admin. Code § 1-088
Nevada	Exempt		Nev. Admin. Code § 372.880
New Jersey	Taxable	Downloaded software is exempt only if used directly and exclusively in the conduct of the purchaser's business, trade, or occupation.	N.J. Technical Bulletin TB-51R, N.J. Stat. Ann. § 54:32B-8.56
New Mexico	Taxable		N.M. Admin. Code tit. 3, § 3.2.1.15
New York	Taxable		N.Y. Tax Law, § 1101(b)(6)
North Carolina	Taxable	Only computer software that meets certain descriptions is exempt.	N.C. Gen. Stat. § 105-164.13(43a)
North Dakota	Taxable		N.D. Admin. Code § 81-04.1-03-11(6)
Ohio	Taxable		Ohio Rev. Code Ann. § 5739.01(Y)(Y)
Oklahoma	Exempt		Okla. Stat. tit. 68, § 1357
Pennsylvania	Taxable		72 P.S. § 7201(m)(2)
Rhode Island	Taxable		R.I. Gen. Laws § 44-18-7, R.I. Code R. SU 11-25

State	Downloaded	Comments	Citation
South Carolina	Exempt	Exempt as long as no part of the software is transferred by tangible means.	Revenue Ruling 03-5
South Dakota	Taxable		Unofficial department guidance
Tennessee	Taxable		Tenn. Code Ann. § 67-6-231
Texas	Taxable		Tex. Tax Code Ann. § 151.009
Utah	Taxable		Utah Code Ann. § 59-12-103(1)(n), Utah Code Ann. § 59-12-102(82)(b)
Vermont	Taxable		Vt. Stat. Ann. tit. 32, § 9701(7), Vt. Stat. Ann. tit. 32, § 9771
Virginia	Exempt	Exempt as long as the transaction does not include the transfer of any tangible personal property.	Va. Code Ann. § 58.1-609.5(1)
Washington	Taxable		Wash. Rev. Code § 82.04.050(6), Wash. Admin. Code § 458-20-15502
West Virginia	Taxable	Exemptions may apply for high technology businesses, certain education software, software directly used in communications or incorporated into a manufactured product, or software used to provide data processing services.	W. Va. Code R. § 110-15-9.3.11.1
Wisconsin	Taxable		Wis. Stat. § 77.51(20), Wis. Stat. § 77.52(1)
Wyoming	Taxable		Wyo. Stat. Ann. § 39-15-103

¶ 113 **Downloaded Custom Computer Software**

This chart indicates whether sales or licenses of custom computer software delivered electronically are subject to tax.

State	Downloaded	Comments	Citation
Alabama	Exempt		Ala. Admin. Code r. 810-6-1.37
Arizona	Exempt		TPR 93-48
Arkansas	Exempt	Software delivered electronically or by "load and leave" not taxable.	Ark. Code Ann. § 26-52-304, Ark. Reg. GR-25
California	Exempt		Reg. 1502 (f) (2) (A), 18 CCR
Colorado	Exempt		1 Colo. Code Regs. § 201-5 (SR-7)
Connecticut	Taxable	If no tangible personal property delivered to purchaser along with downloaded software, software is taxed at 1% rate applicable to computer and data processing services.	Policy Statement 2004 (2), October 21, 2004
District of Columbia	Taxable		Unofficial department guidance
Florida	Exempt		TAA No. 02A-052, Unofficial department guidance
Georgia	Exempt		Ga. Comp. R. & Regs. 560-12-2-.111
Hawaii	Taxable		Haw. Rev. Stat. § 237-13
Idaho	Exempt		IDAPA 35.01.02.027 (08) (a)
Illinois	Exempt		Ill. Admin. Code tit. 86, § 130.1935 (c)
Indiana	Exempt		Information Bulletin #8
Iowa	Exempt		Iowa Code § 423.3 (66), Iowa Admin. Code r. 701-231.14
Kansas	Exempt		Kan. Stat. Ann. § 79-3603 (s), Rev. Ruling 19-2004-03
Kentucky	Exempt		Kentucky Taxability Matrix
Louisiana	Exempt	Caution: Numerous exemptions are suspended from April 1, 2016, to June 30, 2018. For chart of suspended exemptions and applicable tax rates, see Publication R-1002A.	La. Rev. Stat. Ann. § 47:301 (16) (e), LA DOR Publication R-1002A
Maine	Exempt		Me. Rev. Stat. Ann. tit. 36, § 1752 (17)

State	Downloaded	Comments	Citation
Maryland	Exempt		Unofficial department guidance, Md. Code Ann. § 11-219
Massachusetts	Exempt		Mass. Regs. Code tit. 830, § 64H.1.3(6)
Michigan	Exempt		RAB 1999-5
Minnesota	Exempt		Minn. Stat. § 297A.61(3), Minn. R. 8130.9910(2)
Mississippi	Taxable		Miss. Rule 35.IV.5.06
Missouri	Exempt	Tax does not apply to the amount charged to the customer for customized software. The seller of the customized software is subject to tax on the purchase of any tangible personal property or taxable services used to provide the nontaxable service.	Mo. Code Regs. Ann. tit. 12, § 10-109.050(3)(C)
Nebraska	Taxable		Neb. Admin. Code § 1-088
Nevada	Exempt		Nev. Admin. Code § 372.875(2)
New Jersey	Exempt		N.J. Technical Bulletin TB-51R
New Mexico	Taxable		N.M. Admin. Code tit. 3, § 3.2.1.18
New York	Exempt		Unofficial department guidance
North Carolina	Exempt		N.C. Gen. Stat. § 105-164.13(43a)
North Dakota	Exempt	When purchased with equipment, exempt only if charges for custom software are separately stated.	N.D. Admin. Code § 81-04.1-03-11(6)
Ohio	Exempt	Custom system software for business use is a taxable computer service. Programming of custom application software is not a taxable sale.	Ohio Rev. Code Ann. § 5739.01(B)(3)(e) and (Y)(1)(b), Ohio Admin. Code § 5703-9-46(A)(2)(c)
Oklahoma	Exempt		Okla. Admin. Code § 710:65-19-156
Pennsylvania	Exempt		61 Pa. Code § 60.19
Rhode Island	Exempt		R.I. Code R. SU 11-25

State	Downloaded	Comments	Citation
South Carolina	Exempt	Exempt as long as the transaction does not include the transfer of any tangible personal property.	Revenue Ruling 03-5
South Dakota	Taxable		Unofficial department guidance
Tennessee	Taxable	Exemptions may apply for the use of software developed and fabricated by an affiliated company or for fabrication of software by a person for that person's own use or consumption.	Tenn. Code Ann. § 67-6-231
Texas	Taxable		Tex. Tax Code Ann. § 151.009
Utah	Exempt		Utah Admin. Code r. 865-19S-92(2)
Vermont	Exempt		Vt. Stat. Ann. tit. 32, § 9701(7), Vt. Stat. Ann. tit. 32, § 9771
Virginia	Exempt	Exempt as long as the transaction does not include the transfer of any tangible personal property.	Va. Code Ann. § 58.1-609.5(1)
Washington	Exempt		Wash. Rev. Code § 82.04.050(6)
West Virginia	Taxable		W. Va. Code § 11-15-2(b)(16)
Wisconsin	Exempt		Wis. Stat. § 77.52, Wis. Admin. Code § 11.71(3)
Wyoming	Exempt		Wyo. BOE Rule Ch. 2, § 13

¶ 114   Drop Shipments

This chart indicates whether a state allows a seller with nexus to accept a resale exemption from a purchaser/re-seller without nexus on a transaction in which the seller drop ships property to a consumer in the state on behalf of the purchaser/re-seller.

State	Drop Shipments	Comments	Citation
Alabama	Yes		Ala. Admin. Code r. 810-6-3-.35, Unofficial department guidance
Arizona	Yes		Transaction Privilege Tax Ruling TPR 95-13
Arkansas	Yes		Ark. Reg. GR-5
California	No	California generally does not allow a seller with nexus to accept a resale exemption from a purchaser without nexus when the seller drop ships property to an in-state consumer. If an out-of-state retailer (true retailer) holds a permit, and it issues the drop shipper a resale certificate for the sale, the drop shipper is relieved of the responsibility to report and pay the tax.	Reg. 1706, 18 CCR, BOE Publication 121
Colorado	Yes		General Information Letter GIL 2007-31
Connecticut	No	Drop shipper required to collect tax if customer is not engaged in business in CT. However, the CT Supreme Court has held that a drop shipper did not deliver property in CT where property was shipped F.O.B. factory.	Conn. Gen. Stat. § 12-407(a)(3)(A), Steelcase, Inc. v. Commissioner
District of Columbia	No	If the reseller registers in the District, it may obtain and use a resale certificate.	D.C. Code Ann. § 47-2010

State	Drop Shipments	Comments	Citation
Florida	Depends on circumstances	Registered dealers located in Florida are required to collect tax. A registered nonresident dealer's sales of tangible personal property to an unregistered nonresident purchaser that are drop shipped into Florida are not subject to Florida sales and use tax unless: (1) the taxpayer ships the property to the Florida customer from the taxpayer's facility in Florida; (2) the taxpayer ships the property to the Florida customer from the taxpayer's facility located outside Florida, but uses transportation owned or leased by the taxpayer; or (3) the taxpayer ships the property to the Florida customer from the taxpayer's facility located outside Florida, but the terms of the delivery require the taxpayer to collect the sales price, in whole or in part, from the Florida customer at the time of delivery of the property to the customer.	Fla. Admin. Code Ann. r. 12A-1.091(10), TAA 09A-010
Georgia	Yes	Exceptions apply.	Sales and Use Tax Policy for Third-Party Drop Shipment Transactions
Hawaii	No	If purchaser/re-seller has nexus, drop shipper is subject to tax at wholesale rate. If purchaser/re-seller does not have nexus, drop shipper is subject to tax at retail rate.	Haw. Reg. 18-237-13-02.01
Idaho	Yes		IDAPA 35.01.02.022
Illinois	Yes		Ill. Admin. Code tit. 86, § 130.225
Indiana	Yes		Information Bulletin #57
Iowa	Yes		Iowa Admin. Code r. 701-18.55
Kansas	Yes		Kan. Stat. Ann. § 79-3651(c), Notice 07-03
Kentucky	Yes		103 Ky. Admin. Regs. 31:111-3, FAQ Sales and Use Tax
Louisiana	Yes		Revenue Ruling 05-006
Maine	Yes		Code Me. R. 301

State	Drop Shipments	Comments	Citation
Maryland	No		Md. Regs. Code tit. 3, § 03.06.01.14 (I)
Massachusetts	No		Mass. Gen. Laws ch. 64H, § 1, TIR 04-26
Michigan	Yes		Mich. Comp. Laws § 205.54k
Minnesota	Yes		Minn. Stat. § 297A.665
Mississippi	No	MS drop shipper must collect tax from out-of-state retailer except if MS consumer is: direct pay permit holder; licensed dealer making a purchase for resale; or exempt entity that provides an exemption certificate to drop shipper.	Miss. Rule 35.IV.3.05.303
Missouri	Yes		Letter Ruling LR 3726
Nebraska	Yes		Neb. Admin. Code § 1-013.11
Nevada	Yes		Nev. Rev. Stat. § 372.155
New Jersey	Yes		Bulletin S&U-5, Publication ANJ-10
New Mexico	Yes		N.M. Admin. Code tit. 3, § 3.2.13.9, N.M. Admin. Code tit. 3, § 3.2.201.13
New York	Yes		TSB-M-98(3)S
North Carolina	Yes		Technical Bulletin 42-4
North Dakota	Yes		N.D. Cent. Code § 57-39.4-18(1)(h)
Ohio	Yes		Information Release ST 1989-01
Oklahoma	Yes		Okla. Admin. Code § 710:65-13-200, Oklahoma SST Certificate of Compliance
Pennsylvania	Yes		Letter Ruling SUT 99-134
Rhode Island	Yes		R.I. Gen. Laws § 44-18.1-18(A)(8)
South Carolina	Yes		Revenue Ruling 98-8
South Dakota	Yes		S.D. Codified Laws § 10-45-61

State	Drop Shipments	Comments	Citation
Tennessee	No	If TN customer is exempt, purchaser/reseller may provide TN customer's exemption certificate or resale certificate along with the purchaser's home state resale certificate. Effective July 1, 2015, drop shipper may claim a resale exemption (included in definition of "resale").	Tenn. Code. Ann. § 67-6-102, Tenn. Comp. R. & Regs. 1320-5-1-.96, Unofficial Department guidance
Texas	Yes		34 Tex. Admin. Code § 3.285(d)
Utah	Yes		Publication 25
Vermont	Yes		Vt. Code R. 1.9701(5)-3
Virginia	Yes		Ruling of Commissioner, P.D. 98-142
Washington	Yes	Purchaser must provide SST exemption certificate, or MTC exemption certificate.	Wash. Admin. Code § 458-20-193, Wash. Admin. Code § 458-20-102
West Virginia	Yes		W. Va. Code R. § 11-15B-24(a)(8)
Wisconsin	Yes		Sales and Use Tax Report No. 1-10
Wyoming	Yes		Wyo. DOR Rule Ch. 2, § 15(i)

¶114

¶ 115   Electronic Filing

The following chart indicates whether a state allows taxpayers to file sales and use tax returns electronically.

State	Electronic Filing	Comments	Citation
Alabama	Yes	Required for all taxpayers.	Ala. Admin. Code r. 810-1-6-.12, Alabama Department of Revenue website
Arizona	Yes	Amended returns cannot be filed electronically.	Arizona Department of Revenue website
Arkansas	Yes		Arkansas Department of Finance and Administration website
California	Yes	Single-outlet retailer accounts and businesses with only one location that pre-pay on a quarterly basis may file electronically. Only Form BOE-401-A (with Schedules A and T only) and Form BOE-401-EZ may be filed electronically.	Cal. Rev. & Tax. Code § 6479.31, California State Board of Equalization website
Colorado	Yes		Colorado Department of Revenue website
Connecticut	Yes		Connectictut Department of Revenue Services website
District of Columbia	Yes		District of Columbia Office of Tax and Revenue website
Florida	Yes	Required for any taxpayer: (1) who has paid the tax or fee in the prior state fiscal year (July 1 through June 30) in an amount of $20,000 or more; (2) who files a consolidated return; or (3) who has two or more places of business for which the combined tax and/or fee payments equal or exceed $20,000 for the prior state fiscal year.	Florida Department of Revenue website
Georgia	Yes	Required for taxpayers who are required pay by EFT. Optional for other taxpayers.	Georgia Department of Revenue website
Hawaii	Yes		Haw. Rev. Stat. § 231-8.5, Hawaii Department of Taxation website
Idaho	Yes		Idaho State Tax Commission website
Illinois	Yes		Ill. Admin. Code tit. 86, § 760.100, Illinois Department of Revenue website

State	Electronic Filing	Comments	Citation
Indiana	Yes	Retail merchants that register with the department after December 31, 2009 are required to report and remit sales and use taxes using the department's online filing program.	Indiana Department of Revenue website
Iowa	Yes	Fuel tax returns are required by statute to be filed electronically.	Iowa Department of Revenue website
Kansas	Yes		Kansas Department of Revenue website
Kentucky	Yes	Consumer use tax returns cannot be filed electronically.	Kentucky Department of Revenue website
Louisiana	Yes	Required for motor vehicle leasing and rental businesses. Optional for other taxpayers.	Louisiana Department of Revenue website
Maine	Yes		Maine Revenue Services website
Maryland	Yes		Maryland Comptroller's website
Massachusetts	Yes	Required for taxpayers who had a combined tax liability in the preceding calendar year of at least $5,000 (previously, $10,000) in wage withholding, state and local room occupancy excise, and sales and use taxes (including sales taxes imposed on meals and telecommunications services). Businesses that registered after August 31, 2003 and taxpayers with zero tax returns must also file electronically. Optional for all other taxpayers.	TIR 10-18, TIR 04-30, Massachusetts Department of Revenue website
Michigan	Yes		Michigan Department of Treasury website
Minnesota	Yes	Required, unless taxpayer's religious beliefs prohibits use of electronics.	Minn. Stat. § 289A.11(1), Minnesota Department of Revenue website
Mississippi	Yes	The Mississippi Department of Revenue uses an online filing and payment system called Taxpayer Access Point (TAP).	Mississippi Taxpayer Access Point website

State	Electronic Filing	Comments	Citation
Missouri	Yes	The following types of businesses are allowed to file their sales and use tax returns electronically: those that owed no sales taxes and those with less than 150 locations.	Missouri Department of Revenue website
Nebraska	Yes	Amended returns cannot be filed electronically. As of July 1, 2011, the Tax Commissioner requires taxpayers subject to the EFT mandate for sales tax payments to also e-file their sales tax returns, Forms 10. Beginning July 2016, taxpayers are subject to EFT if they have made payments of $6,000 or more in the prior tax year. This threshold will be reduced in future years according to a specified schedule.	Nebraska Department of Revenue website
Nevada	Yes		Nevada Department of Taxation website
New Jersey	Yes	Required for all taxpayers.	New Jersey Division of Taxation website
New Mexico	Yes		New Mexico Department of Taxation and Revenue website
New York	Yes	Required for monthly and quarterly sales tax filers who meet these three conditions: (1) do not use a tax preparer to prepare the required filings; (2) use a computer to prepare, document or calculate the required filings or related schedules, or is subject to the corporation tax e-file mandate; and (3) have broadband Internet access. Tax preparers are also required to electronically file returns for annual sales tax filers.	New York Department of Taxation and Finance website, E-file mandate for tax preparers, New York Department of Taxation and Finance website, TB-ST-275
North Carolina	Yes		North Carolina Department of Revenue website
North Dakota	Yes		Office of State Tax Commissioner website
Ohio	Yes		Ohio Rev. Code Ann. § 5739.12

State	Electronic Filing	Comments	Citation
Oklahoma	Yes	Required for taxpayers who owed an average of $2,500 or more per month in total sales taxes in the previous fiscal year. Optional for other taxpayers.	Okla. Stat. tit. 68, § 1365, Oklahoma Taxpayer Access Point website
Pennsylvania	Yes	A third party preparer must e-file all sales, use, and hotel occupancy tax returns for all calendar years following a calendar year in which the preparer files 10 or more sales, use, and hotel occupancy tax returns.	Pennsylvania Department of Revenue website, 72 P.S. § 10
Rhode Island	Yes	Required for taxpayers who are required to pay by EFT. Optional for other taxpayers.	R.I. Code R. EFT 09-01, Rhode Island Division of Taxation website
South Carolina	Yes	Taxpayers owing $15,000 or more per month may be mandated to file electronically.	South Carolina Department of Revenue website, Electronic Services
South Dakota	Yes		South Dakota Department of Revenue and Regulation website
Tennessee	Yes	Required if tax required to be paid in connection with a return is $1,000 or more. Effective January 1, 2013, required if average sales tax liability is $500 or more. Optional for other taxpayers.	Tenn. Code Ann. § 67-6-504, Tenn. Code Ann. § 67-1-703(b), Tennessee Department of Revenue website
Texas	Yes	Required for taxpayers who are required to pay by EFT. Optional for other taxpayers.	34 Tex. Admin. Code § 3.9, Texas Comptroller's website
Utah	Yes		Utah State Tax Commission website
Vermont	Yes		Vermont Department of Taxes website

State	Electronic Filing	Comments	Citation
Virginia	Yes	Beginning with the July 2012 return (due August 20, 2012), monthly filers of the ST-9 and ST-9CO must submit their returns and payments electronically. Quarterly filers will be required to file and pay electronically beginning with the September 2013 return, due October 21, 2013. To meet this electronic filing requirement, the returns must be filed using eForms, Business iFile or Web Upload. Taxpayers that are unable to make the necessary changes to file and pay electronically may request a temporary waiver from the department. Such request must be in writing and provide the following information: business name, Virginia tax account number, contact person, phone number, e-mail address (optional), mailing address, the reason for the request, and the date when the retail sales taxes can be filed and paid electronically.	Virginia Department of Taxation website
Washington	Yes	All monthly and quarterly filers are required to file and pay electronically.	Wash. Rev. Code § 82.32.080
West Virginia	Yes	For tax years beginning on or after January 1, 2009, required for taxpayers who had a total annual remittance for any single tax type of $100,000 or more in the immediately preceding tax year. Effective for tax years beginning on or after January 1, 2013, this threshold is lowered to $50,000. The threshold amount is reduced to $25,000 for tax years beginning on or after January 1, 2014, and then to $10,000 for tax years beginning on or after January 1, 2015. For tax years beginning on or after January 1, 2016, the threshold is increased to $25,000.	W. Va. Code R. § 110-10D-9, West Virginia Tax Department website, W. Va. Code § 11-10-5z
Wisconsin	Yes		Wisconsin Department of Revenue website
Wyoming	Yes		Wyoming Department of Revenue website

¶ 116 **Electronic Payments**

The following chart indicates whether a state allows taxpayers to make sales and use tax payments electronically.

State	Electronic Payments	Comments	Citation
Alabama	Yes	Required for taxpayers making individual payments of $750 or more.	Ala. Code § 41-1-20
Arizona	Yes	Required for taxpayers whose tax liability in the prior year was $1 million or more.	Ariz. Admin. Code § 15-10-302
Arkansas	Yes	Required if average monthly tax liability for the preceding year exceeded $20,000.	Ark. Code Ann. § 26-19-105
California	Yes	Required if estimated monthly tax liability is $10,000 or more.	Cal. Rev. & Tax. Code § 6479.3, Reg. 1707, 18 CCR
Colorado	Yes	Required for taxpayers whose sales tax liability for the previous calendar year exceeded $75,000.	Colo. Rev. Stat. § 39-26-105.5
Connecticut	Yes	Required if prior year liability exceeded $10,000 for the 12-month period ending the preceding June 30.	Conn. Gen. Stat. § 12-686
District of Columbia	Yes	Required when the payment due for the tax period exceeds $25,000 and for payments made by third party bulk filers.	D.C. Code Ann. § 47-4402, D.C. Mun. Regs. t. 9, § 105.11, OTR Notice
Florida	Yes	Required if tax paid in the prior state fiscal year was $30,000 or more. All consolidated sales tax and solid waste and surcharge filers must remit payments electronically.	Fla. Stat. § 213.755, Tax Information Publication, No. 02A01-22
Georgia	Yes	For tax periods from Jan. 1, 2010 - Dec. 31, 2010, EFT required for payments exceeding $1,000; for tax periods from Jan. 1, 2011, forward, EFT required for payments exceeding $500.	Ga. Code Ann. § 48-2-32(f)(2.1), Ga. Comp. R. & Regs. 560-3-2-.26(3)(a)
Hawaii	Yes	Required for taxpayers whose annual tax liability exceeds $100,000 in any taxable year.	Haw. Rev. Stat. § 231-9.9, Haw. Reg. 18-231-9.9-03
Idaho	Yes	Required when the amount due is $100,000 or more.	Idaho Code § 67-2026

State	Electronic Payments	Comments	Citation
Illinois	Yes	Required for taxpayers whose state and local sales and use tax liability in the preceding calendar year was at least $200,000. Taxpayers who file electronic returns are also required to make electronic payments.	35 ILCS 105/9, 35 ILCS 110/9, 35 ILCS 120/3, Ill. Admin. Code tit. 86, § 750.300, Ill. Admin. Code tit. 86, § 760.220
Indiana	Yes	Required if taxpayer's estimated monthly tax liability for current tax year or the average monthly tax liability for the preceding year exceeds $10,000. Beginning January 1, 2010, the department may require a person who is paying outstanding tax using periodic payments to make the payments by electronic funds transfer through an automatic withdrawal from the person's account at a financial institution.	Ind. Code § 6-2.5-6-1(g), Information Bulletin #77, Indiana Department of State Revenue, November 2008
Iowa	Yes	Required for all taxpayers.	Iowa Code § 423.50
Kansas	Yes	Required if total sales tax liability exceeds $45,000 in any calendar year.	Kan. Stat. Ann. § 75-5151
Kentucky	Yes	Required if: (1) average payment per reporting period is at least $10,000; (2) payment is made on behalf of 100 or more taxpayers; (3) aggregate of funds to be remitted on behalf of others is at least $10,000 for each tax being remitted; or (4) average payment of sales tax per reporting period during 12-month period ending on September 30 of the year immediately preceding the current calendar year exceeds $25,000.	Ky. Rev. Stat. Ann. § 131.155, 103 Ky. Admin. Regs. 1:060
Louisiana	Yes	Required if tax due in connection a return exceeds $10,000. Threshold is $5,000 for tax periods beginning after 2007.	La. Rev. Stat. Ann. § 47:1519, La. Admin. Code tit. 61, § 4910
Maine	Yes	Required for any taxpayer with a combined tax liability of $100,000 or more for all tax types during the previous calendar year. Effective January 1, 2009, threshold decreases to $50,000; effective January 1, 2010, threshold decreases to $25,000.	Code Me. R. 102

¶116

State	Electronic Payments	Comments	Citation
Maryland	Yes	Required if tax of $10,000 or more is due in connection with a return.	Md. Code Ann. § 13-104, Md. Code Ann. § 13-105, Md. Code Regs. 03.01.02.01, Md. Code Regs. 03.01.02.05
Massachusetts	Yes	Required for taxpayers who are required to file electronic returns. Optional for other taxpayers.	TIR 10-18, TIR 04-30
Michigan	Yes	Required if total sales and use tax liability for preceding calendar year was at least $720,000.	Mich. Comp. Laws § 205.56(3), Mich. Comp. Laws § 205.96(3)
Minnesota	Yes	Taxpayers with sales and use tax liability of $10,000 or more during the preceding fiscal year ending June 30 must make all payments for periods in subsequent calendar years by EFT, unless prohibited by religious beliefs.	Minn. Stat. § 289A.20(4), Minnesota Department of Revenue website
Mississippi	Yes	The Mississippi Department of Revenue uses an online filing and payment system called Taxpayer Access Point (TAP). Required for taxpayers owing $20,000 or more in connection with a return and for taxpayers who have received notification from the Tax Commissioner.	Miss. Code Ann. § 27-3-81, Mississippi Taxpayer Access Point website
Missouri	Yes	May be required for taxpayers required to remit on a quarter-monthly basis.	Mo. Rev. Stat. § 144.081
Nebraska	Yes	Beginning July 2016, taxpayers are subject to EFT if they have made payments of $6,000 or more in the prior tax year. This threshold will be reduced in future years according to a specified schedule.	Neb. Rev. Stat. § 77-1784, Nebraska Department of Revenue website
Nevada	Yes		Nevada uncodified regulations, LCB File No. R062-05
New Jersey	Yes	Required for taxpayers whose tax liability for the prior year was $10,000 or more.	N.J. Stat. Ann. § 54:48-4.1
New Mexico	Yes	Taxpayers whose average tax payment during the previous calendar year was $25,000 or more are required to pay by EFT or another method specified by statute.	N.M. Stat. Ann. § 7-1-13.1

State	Electronic Payments	Comments	Citation
New York	Yes	Required if, on or after June 1, the taxpayer's liability for the June 1 through May 31 period immediately preceding was more than $500,000 for state and local sales and use taxes or more than $5 million for prepaid state and local sales and use taxes on motor fuel and diesel motor fuel.	N.Y. Tax Law, § 10
North Carolina	Yes	Required for taxpayers whose tax liability was at least $240,000 during a 12-month period.	N.C. Gen. Stat. § 105-241, N.C. Admin. Code tit. 17, § 17.01C.0504
North Dakota	Yes		N.D. Cent. Code § 57-39.4-20
Ohio	Yes	Taxpayers must use commissioner approved electronic method. Certain direct pay permit holders are required to use EFT.	Ohio Rev. Code Ann. § 5739.032, Ohio Rev. Code Ann. § 5739.122, Ohio Rev. Code Ann. § 5739.12
Oklahoma	Yes	Required for taxpayers who owed an average of $2,500 per month during previous fiscal year.	Okla. Stat. tit. 68, § 1365(C)
Pennsylvania	Yes	Required for payments of $1,000 or more.	61 Pa. Code § 5.3, 72 P.S. § 9
Rhode Island	Yes	Required if the seller's average monthly sales and use tax liability in the previous calendar year was at least $200.	R.I. Gen. Laws § 44-19-10.3
South Carolina	Yes	Taxpayers who paid $15,000 or more for any one filing period during the past year in sales, use, accommodations, local option, or special local taxes can be required to pay by EFT.	S.C. Code Ann. § 12-54-250
South Dakota	Yes		S.D. Codified Laws § 10-59-32
Tennessee	Yes	Required if tax required to be paid in connection with a return is $1,000 or more. Effective January 1, 2013, required if average sales tax liability is $500 or more.	Tenn. Code Ann. § 67-1-703(b)

State	Electronic Payments	Comments	Citation
Texas	Yes	Required for taxpayers who paid a total of $10,000 or more in a single category of payments or taxes during the preceding state fiscal year if the Comptroller reasonably anticipates the taxpayer will pay at least that amount during the current fiscal year.	Tex. Tax Code Ann. § 111.0625, 34 Tex. Admin. Code § 3.9
Utah	Yes	Required for taxpayers whose liability for state, local, public transit, municipal energy, and short-term leases and rentals of motor vehicles sales and use taxes was $96,000 or more in the previous tax year.	Utah Code Ann. § 59-12-108, Utah Admin. Code r. R865-19S-86
Vermont	Yes	May be required for any taxpayer required to pay a federal tax by EFT or for any taxpayer who has submitted to the Tax Department two or more protested or otherwise uncollectible checks with regard to any state tax payment in the prior two years.	Vt. Stat. Ann. tit. 32, § 9776
Virginia	Yes	Beginning with the July 2012 return (due August 20, 2012), monthly filers of the ST-9 and ST-9CO must submit their returns and payments electronically. Quarterly filers will be required to file and pay electronically beginning with the September 2013 return, due October 21, 2013. To meet this electronic filing requirement, the returns must be filed using eForms, Business iFile or Web Upload. Taxpayers that are unable to make the necessary changes to file and pay electronically may request a temporary waiver from the department. Such request must be in writing and provide the following information: business name, Virginia tax account number, contact person, phone number, e-mail address (optional), mailing address, the reason for the request, and the date when the retail sales taxes can be filed and paid electronically.	Virginia Department of Taxation website

State	Electronic Payments	Comments	Citation
Washington	Yes	Required for taxpayers filing returns on a monthly or quarterly basis.	Wash. Rev. Code § 82.32.080, Wash. Rev. Code § 82.32.085, Wash. Admin. Code § 458-20-22802
West Virginia	Yes	Effective for tax years prior to January 1, 2012, required for taxpayers with sales and use tax liability of $100,000 or more during the previous taxable year or reporting period; effective for tax years beginning on or after January 1, 2012, the threshold is reduced to $10,000; for tax years beginning on or after January 1, 2013, the threshold is increased to $50,000; for tax years beginning on or after January 1, 2014, the threshold is reduced to $25,000; for tax years beginning on or after January 1, 2015, the threshold is reduced to $10,000; for tax years beginning on or after January 1, 2016, the threshold is increased to $25,000. Required for both county and municipal special district excise taxes and for sales taxes collected within an economic opportunity development district, regardless of amount.	W. Va. Code R. § 110-10F-3, W. Va. Code R. § 110-39-3, W. Va. Code R. § 110-39-4
Wisconsin	Yes	Required if aggregate amount of general, county, and stadium sales and use taxes due in the prior calendar year was $300 or more.	Wis. Admin. Code § 1.12(4)(a)(3)
Wyoming	Yes		Wyoming Department of Revenue website

¶116

¶ 117   **Excise Taxes**

State	Excise Taxes	Comments	Citation
Alabama	Included, except for federal taxes retailers must collect from consumers, certain separately stated state taxes on alcoholic beverages, and municipal privilege tax.		Ala. Code § 40-23-1(a)(6), Ala. Code § 40-23-3, Ala. Admin. Code r. 810-6-1-.64, Ala. Admin. Code r. 810-6-2-.22.05, Ala. Admin. Code r. 810-6-4-.07.05, Ala. Admin. Code r. 810-6-1-.65, Ala. Admin. Code r. 810-6-1-.168, Ala. Admin. Code r. 810-6-1-.23, Ala. Admin. Code r. 810-6-1-.174
Arizona	Included, except for federal retail excise tax on autos, heavy trucks, and fuel.		Ariz. Rev. Stat. § 42-5061
Arkansas	Gross receipts, gross proceeds, or sales price includes any tax imposed on the seller but does not include any tax imposed directly on the consumer that is separately stated on the invoice or other document given to the purchaser.		Ark. Code Ann. § 26-52-103(a), Ark Reg. UT-3, Ark. Reg. GR-3
California	Federal excise taxes on retail sales, local rapid transit district sales and use taxes, state motor vehicle fees and taxes that are added to or measured by a vehicle's price, and diesel fuel excise tax not included; federal manufacturers and importers excise taxes on gasoline, diesel, or jet fuel for which the purchaser is entitled to a direct income tax credit or refund also not included; import duties not included if the importer of record is a consignee and the consignee is the buyer; state motor vehicle fuel license taxes included; other manufacturers and importers excise taxes included.		Cal. Rev. & Tax. Code § 6011, Cal. Rev. & Tax. Code § 6012, Reg. 1617, 18 CCR
Colorado	Direct federal taxes excluded and state sales and use taxes not included; indirect federal manufacturers taxes included.		Colo. Rev. Stat. § 39-26-102(7)
Connecticut	Federal taxes imposed on retail sales, state cabaret tax not included; federal manufacturers or importers excise taxes and all taxes imposed on a basis other than the proceeds from retail sales included.		Conn. Gen. Stat. § 12-407(a)(8)(B)(iii) and (a)(9)(B)(iii), Conn. Agencies Regs. § 12-426-21
District of Columbia	Separately stated federal retailers excise taxes not included.		D.C. Mun. Regs. t. 9, § 408.3

State	Excise Taxes	Comments	Citation
Florida	Separately stated federal retailers excise taxes, separately stated municipal public service taxes, separately stated motor vehicle warranty fee not included; federal manufacturers excise tax, municipal utility fees, state tire and battery fees, rental car surcharge included, state utility gross receipts tax included if the cost is separately itemized and passed on to customers; other taxes included.	Taxable admissions do not include any federal taxes.	Fla. Stat. § 212.05, Fla. Admin. Code Ann. r. 12A-1.022
Georgia	Excluded: (1) separately stated federal retailers' excise tax, (2) state motor fuel excise tax on gasoline and other motor fuel, (3) state excise tax on cigarettes. Included: federal excise taxes on (1) gasoline and diesel fuel; (2) tires, tubes, and accessories; and (3) cigarettes.		Ga. Code Ann. § 48-8-3(3), Ga. Comp. R. & Regs. 560-12-1-.35,
Hawaii	Certain state and federal liquid fuel taxes; state liquor tax; state cigarette and tobacco products taxes; federal excise taxes on articles sold at retail; federal taxes imposed on sugar manufactured in Hawaii; state rental motor vehicle surcharge taxes; state nursing home facility taxes not included.		Haw. Rev. Stat. § 237-24(8), (9), (10), (11), and (12), Haw. Rev. Stat. § 237-24.7(3) and (5)
Idaho	Federal importers and manufacturers excise taxes included; federal taxes on retail sales not included		Idaho Code § 63-3613(b)(5), IDAPA 35.01.02.060
Illinois	ROT: federal taxes collected from customer, federal excise taxes on retail sales, state motor fuel tax, state tire fee not included; federal excise taxes on manufacture, import taxes, tax on non-retail sale, state liquor tax, cigarette tax included.		Ill. Admin. Code tit. 86, § 130.435, Ill. Admin. Code tit. 86, § 130.2060
Indiana	Federal or state taxes collected as agent, federal retailers tax if imposed solely on sale of personal property and collected by a merchant as a separate item in addition to the price, manufacturers excise tax, and federal and state fuel tax not included.		Ind. Code § 6-2.5-5-24, Ind. Code § 6-2.5-4-1(f), Ind. Admin. Code tit. 45, r. 2.2-3-14, Ind. Admin. Code tit. 45, r. 2.2-5-48, Ind. Admin. Code tit. 45, r. 2.2-5-50, Ind. Admin. Code tit. 45, r. 2.2-5-51

State	Excise Taxes	Comments	Citation
Iowa	Taxes imposed on sales subject to Iowa sales and use tax, federal excise tax on first retail sale of a vehicle not included, federal excise tax on communication services of local and toll telephone and teletypewriter exchange services not included; federal excise taxes on alcohol, tobacco, fuel, and tires, and state cigarette tax included.		Iowa Admin. Code r. 701-15.12, Iowa Admin. Code r. 701-33.2
Kansas	Federal manufacturers' excise tax paid by manufacturer included; "sales or selling price" includes all taxes imposed on the seller but excludes separately stated taxes legally imposed directly on the consumer.		Kan. Admin. Regs. § 92-20-4, Kan. Stat. Ann. § 79-3602(ll)
Kentucky	"Gross receipts" or "sales price" includes all taxes imposed on the retailer but excludes separately stated taxes legally imposed directly on the purchaser; federal tax on retail sales excluded from tax base; federal manufacturers' excise tax or federal import duty included in tax base.		Ky. Rev. Stat. Ann. § 139.010(12), Ky. Rev. Stat. Ann. § 139.470(19)
Louisiana	Excise taxes included.		La. Rev. Stat. Ann. § 47:301(3), La. Admin. Code tit. 47, § 4301
Maine	Federal tax on retail sales not included; federal manufacturers, importers, alcohol, and tobacco excise taxes included.		Me. Rev. Stat. Ann. tit. 36, § 1752(14)
Maryland	Consumer excise taxes imposed directly on buyer, certain county utility taxes, admissions taxes, electricity surcharges, and certain taxes imposed on leased property not included.		Md. Code Ann. § 11-101(j), Md. Code Regs. tit. 3, § 03.06.01.08
Massachusetts	Federal retail excise tax on trucks not included; taxes with incidence on vendor included.		DOR-D No. 86-1
Michigan	Taxes legally imposed directly on the consumer that are separately stated on the invoice, bill of sale, or similar document, not included; taxes imposed on the seller and federal manufacturers' excise taxes, included.		Mich. Comp. Laws § 205.51, Mich. Comp. Laws § 205.92(f)
Minnesota	Separately stated taxes imposed directly on consumers, separately stated federal excise taxes imposed at retail level not included. Federal excise taxes imposed at the wholesale/lessor or other level included.		Minn. Stat. § 297A.61(7), Sales Tax Fact Sheet No. 125

State	Excise Taxes	Comments	Citation
Mississippi	Federal retailers excise tax, tax levied on income from transportation, telegraphic dispatches, telephone conversations, and electric energy, and certain state gasoline tax not included.		Miss. Code. Ann. § 27-65-109
Missouri	Federal manufacturers excise tax, excise tax on retail sales of fuel, vehicles, sporting goods, firearms, communications, and certain transportation, and state tobacco tax not included; local tobacco tax imposed on seller included.		Mo. Rev. Stat. § 144.030, Mo. Code Regs. Ann. tit. 12, § 10-103.555
Nebraska	Occupation taxes, import duties, manufacturer's excise taxes, property taxes included. Federal luxury excise tax excluded.		Neb. Rev. Stat. § 77-2701.35, Neb. Admin. Code § 1-007
Nevada	Federal taxes imposed on retail sales not included; manufacturers and importers excise taxes included.		Nev. Rev. Stat. § 372.025(3), Nev. Rev. Stat. § 374.070(3), Nev. Rev. Stat. § 372.065(3)
New Jersey	Excise taxes imposed on consumers not included; other federal, state, and local excise taxes included.		N.J. Stat. Ann. § 54:32B-2(d), N.J. Admin. Code § 18:24-36.2(a), N.J. Admin. Code § 18:24-7.5
New Mexico	Gross receipts taxes, federal communication excise tax, air transportation excise tax, not included; federal manufacturers excise tax, cigarette tax included.		N.M. Stat. Ann. § 7-9-3.5, N.M. Admin. Code tit. 3, § 3.2.1.14, N.M. Admin. Code tit. 3, § 3.2.1.15
New York	Excise taxes imposed on manufacturers, importers, producers, distributors, or distillers are included. Excise taxes imposed directly on consumers (other than cigarette taxes) not included (i.e., federal excise taxes on special motor fuels, communication services, taxable transportation, and state taxes on gasoline).		N.Y. Tax Law, § 1111(h), N.Y. Comp. Code R. & Regs. tit. 20, § 526.5
North Carolina	Separately stated taxes imposed directly on consumers not included; federal excise taxes imposed on manufacturer included.		N.C. Gen. Stat. § 105-164.3(37)(b), Sales and Use Tax Technical Bulletin, Sec. 1-2
North Dakota	Included		N.D. Cent. Code § 57-39.2-01(12)
Ohio	Excise taxes imposed on consumers not included; excise taxes imposed on manufacturers, distributors, wholesalers, and retailers, included.		Information Release ST 1995-05

State	Excise Taxes	Comments	Citation
Oklahoma	Under definitions of "gross receipts," "gross proceeds," and "sales price," separately stated taxes imposed directly on consumers not included. Federal excise taxes levied on retailers and manufacturers included.		Okla. Stat. tit. 68, § 1352, Okla. Admin. Code § 710:65-19-102
Pennsylvania	State taxes and taxes that represent cost to vendor, including manufacturers excise, gross receipts, and mercantile taxes, included.		72 P.S. § 7201(g)(1), 16 Pa. Code § 33.2
Rhode Island	Any taxes legally imposed directly on the consumer that are separately stated excluded; manufacturers, importers, and retailers excise taxes included.		R.I. Gen. Laws § 44-18-12(b)(4), R.I. Code R. SU 07-43
South Carolina	Federal taxes imposed on retail sales, local sales and use taxes, and local hospitality taxes and accommodations fees imposed directly on customers not included; federal manufacturers and importers excise taxes, local hospitality taxes and accommodations fees imposed on retailers included.		S.C. Code Ann. § 12-36-90(1)(b), 2(d), S.C. Code Ann. § 12-36-130(1)(b), 2(d), Revenue Ruling 97-20
South Dakota	Separately stated taxes imposed directly on consumers not included.		S.D. Codified Laws § 10-45-1(4), (6)
Tennessee	Separately stated taxes imposed directly on consumers not included.		Tenn. Code. Ann. § 67-6-102
Texas	Certain federal excise taxes included.		Tex. Tax Code Ann. § 151.007(c)(4)
Utah	Excise taxes included.		Utah Code Ann. § 59-12-102
Vermont	Separately stated taxes legally imposed directly on the consumer not included.		Vt. Stat. Ann. tit. 32, § 9701(4)
Virginia	Separately stated federal retailers excise tax, state and local sales and use taxes, and local excise taxes on meals and lodging not included; federal manufacturers excise tax and taxes on alcoholic beverages and tobacco included.		Va. Code Ann. § 58.1-602, 23 Va. Admin. Code § 10-210-5060
Washington	Any separately stated tax imposed on consumers not included; taxes imposed on sellers included.		Wash. Rev. Code § 82.08.010, Wash. Admin. Code § 458-20-195

State	Excise Taxes	Comments	Citation
West Virginia	"Sales price" does not include any taxes legally imposed directly on the consumer that are separately stated on the invoice. Any excise tax imposed before imposition of West Virginia sales tax included. Federal, state, and local taxes simultaneously imposed on the property or service purchased not included.		W. Va. Code § 11-15B-2, W. Va. Code R. § 110-15-2.35.1, W. Va. Code R. § 110-15-2.35.4
Wisconsin	Excluded from the basis are separately stated taxes legally imposed directly on the purchaser and separately stated taxes imposed on the seller, provided the seller may, but is not required to, pass on to and collect the tax from the user or consumer. These include the federal communications tax imposed upon telegraph service and telephone service; various local Wisconsin taxes; Wisconsin state vehicle rental fee; federal luxury tax; federal and Wisconsin motor vehicle excise taxes refunded; police and fire protection fee; low-income assistance fees; landline and wireless 911 charges; and state universal service fund fee. Included in the basis are the Wisconsin fermented malt beverage and intoxicating liquors taxes; federal stamp taxes and manufacturer's or importer's excise tax not imposed directly on the purchaser; federal, county, or municipal fuel taxes included in the price of alternate fuels and general aviation fuel subject to the sales tax; Wisconsin cigarette and tobacco products taxes; foreign export gallonage taxes on fuels; federal gas guzzler tax; federal medical device excise tax; federal universal service fund fee; dry cleaning and dry cleaning products fees; Wisconsin Public Service Commission fees; certain telephone and telecommunications surcharges; state-issued video service franchise fee; petroleum inspection fee; and Wisconsin motor fuel taxes.	Retroactively to September 1, 2014, any federal excise tax imposed on a seller of a heavy truck or trailer sold at retail is exempt from sales and use tax.	Wis. Stat. § 77.51(15b)(b)3., Wis. Admin. Code § 11.26(2) and (3), Sales and Use Tax Report No. 3-14
Wyoming	Separately stated taxes imposed directly on consumers not included; other taxes included.		Wyo. Stat. Ann. § 39-15-101(a)(viii)

¶ 118   Exemption Certificate Validity Periods

State	Exemption Certificate Validity Periods	Comments	Citation
Alabama	Valid as long as no change in character of purchaser's operation and the tangible personal property purchased is the kind usually purchased for the purpose indicated.		Ala. Admin. Code r. 810-6-5-.02
Arizona	Valid for the period set out on certificate.		Ariz. Admin. Code § 15-5-2214(C)
Arkansas	No stated expiration period.	Seller may require purchaser to complete Form ST391 to prove entitlement to exemption.	Ark. Reg. GR-74
California	Valid until revoked in writing by issuer, unless issued for specific transaction, in which case certificate is generally valid for one year.		Cal. Rev. & Tax. Code § 6421, Reg. 1667, 18 CCR
Colorado	Charitable exemption certificates do not expire. Contractor's exemption certificates expire at the end of the job.		Unofficial department guidance
Connecticut	Valid for three years from the issue date provided the exemption remains in effect.	An exemption certificate may be issued for a single exempt purchase or may be used for a continuing line of purchases of the same type provided the certificate is marked "Blanket Certificate." Most blanket certificates are valid for three years from the issue date if the exemption remains in effect.	Informational Publication 2006(11)
District of Columbia	Semipublic institution certificates are valid as long as the institution is located in the District. Contractor certificates are valid for purchases connected to the qualifying construction contract.		D.C. Code Ann. § 47-2005, D.C. Mun. Regs. t. 9, § 417.12, D.C. Mun. Regs. t. 9, § 438.8
Florida	Each sales tax exemption certificate expires five years after the date of issuance.	Upon expiration, the certificate is subject to review and reissuance procedures.	Fla. Stat. § 212.084
Georgia	Until revoked in writing.		Form ST-5
Hawaii	Does not expire.	New application must be filed if there is material change in facts.	Haw. Rev. Stat. § 237-23(d)
Idaho	No stated expiration period.		IDAPA 35.01.02.128
Illinois	Exemption certificate validity periods vary depending on the purchaser.	Manufacturers are not allowed to use blanket exemption certificates.	Information Bulletin FY 2013-16, Form ST-587

State	Exemption Certificate Validity Periods	Comments	Citation
Indiana	Does not expire.		Ind. Code § 6-2.5-8-5
Iowa	Exemption certificates valid up to 3 years.		Iowa Admin. Code r. 701-15.3(2)(b)(422,423)
Kansas	Exemption certificates are generally valid provided there is a recurring business relationship between the buyer and seller of no more than 12 months elapsing between sales. Tax-exempt entity exemption certificates contain an expiration date.		Kan. Stat. Ann. § 79-3651(c), Information Guide No. KS-1520
Kentucky	The Kentucky Department of Revenue recommends that certificates be updated every four years. The new and expanded industry certificate is project-specific.		Kentucky Sales Tax Facts, December 2012
Louisiana	Generally valid indefinitely	Direct pay, resale, and manufacturing exemption certificates automatically renewed for up to three years unless taxpayer no longer qualified for the exemption.	Unofficial department guidance, La. Rev. Stat. Ann. § 47:13
Maine	No stated expiration period.		Code Me. R. § 302(.02)(F), Code Me. R. § 303(.03)
Maryland	Expires five years after issuance.	Governmental entity certificates do not expire. All other exemption certificates will expire on September 30, 2017 and, upon reissuance, at 5-year intervals.	Md. Regs. Code tit. 3, § 03.06.01.22
Massachusetts	No stated expiration period.		Massachusetts Exempt Use Certificate (ST-12)
Michigan	Expires after four years unless shorter period is agreed upon.	Renewal of a blanket exemption certificate is not required if there is a recurring business relationship between buyer and seller. A "recurring business relationship" exists when a period of not more than 12 months elapses between sales transactions.	RAB 2002-15, Mich. Comp. Laws § 205.68, Mich. Comp. Laws § 205.97
Minnesota	Does not expire unless information changes; should be updated every three to five years.		2006 Sales and Use Tax Newsletter, 1995 Sales and Use Tax Newsletter
Mississippi	No stated expiration period.	Seller must obtain and maintain adequate records to substantiate exemption.	Miss. Rule 35.IV.3.01

State	Exemption Certificate Validity Periods	Comments	Citation
Missouri	Valid for 5 years.	Must be updated every 5 years or when the certificate expires by its terms, whichever is earlier.	Mo. Code Regs. Ann. tit. 12, § 10-107.100(3)
Nebraska	Valid indefinitely.	A blanket certificate remains valid if sales occur between the seller and purchaser at least once every 12 months.	Neb. Admin. Code § 1-014.07
Nevada	Valid for five years.		Nev. Admin. Code § 372.700
New Jersey	No stated expiration period.	Division of Taxation recommends that a seller request a new certificate from a buyer every few years.	N.J. Bulletin S&U-4, State Tax News, Vol. 36, No. 3
New Mexico	There is no stated validity period for a New Mexico nontaxable transaction certificate, other than that for utilities consumed in manufacturing (type 12).	Type 12 NTTCs expire after three years.	N.M. Stat. Ann. § 7-9-43(D)
New York	No stated expiration period.	A blanket certificate is valid until it is revoked in writing, the vendor knows it is fraudulent, or the department provides notice that the purchaser may not make exempt purchases.	Form ST-121
North Carolina	Blanket certificate remains valid provided purchaser is making recurring purchases.	If single purchase box is not checked on Form E-595E indicating certificate is being used for a single purchase, certificate will be treated as a blanket certificate. A blanket certificate continues in force as long as the purchaser is making recurring purchases (i.e., at least one purchase within a period of 12 consecutive months) or until it is otherwise cancelled by the purchaser.	Form E-595E, Streamlined Sales and Use Tax Agreement Certificate of Exemption, N.C. Gen. Stat. § 105-164.28
North Dakota	Valid until exemption no longer applies.		Application for Sales Tax Exemption Certificate (Form 21919); Certificate of Processing (Form SFN 21954); Contractor's Certificate (Form SFN 21946)
Ohio	No stated expiration period.		Form STEC B
Oklahoma	Blanket exemption certificates are valid provided there is a recurring business relationship between the buyer and seller of no more than 12 months elapsing between sales.		Okla. Admin. Code § 710:65-13-200, Okla. Stat. tit. 68, § 1361(A)(3)

State	Exemption Certificate Validity Periods	Comments	Citation
Pennsylvania	No expiration date.	A taxpayer claiming an exemption as a charitable, religious, or educational institution may be required to renew its exemption every three years.	61 Pa. Code § 32.2
Rhode Island	Blanket exemption certificates remain valid so long as the purchaser is making recurring purchases (at least one transaction within a period of 12 consecutive months) or until cancelled by the purchaser.		R.I. Gen. Laws § 44-18.1-18(C)(3)
South Carolina	There is no stated expiration period for an exemption certificate.	The Department advises that a certificate is valid as long as the business is in operation.	Unofficial department guidance, Form ST-8
South Dakota	Blanket certificates are valid indefinitely so long as the purchaser is making recurring purchases (at least one purchase within a period of 12 consecutive months) or until cancelled by the purchaser.		S.D. Tax Facts #154
Tennessee	Blanket exemption certificates remain valid so long as the purchaser is making recurring purchases (at least one transaction within a period of 12 consecutive months) or until cancelled by the purchaser.		Tenn. Code Ann. § 67-6-409
Texas	No stated expiration period.		34 Tex. Admin. Code § 3.287
Utah	There is no expiration period for a Utah exemption certificate if no more than a 12-month period elapses between sales transactions.		Utah Code Ann. § 59-12-106, Form TC-721
Vermont	Valid indefinitely.	Exemption certificate for fuel and electricity (Form S-3F) valid for three years. Exemption certificate for registerable motor vehicles other than cars and trucks (Form S-3V) valid for single purchase.	Exemption Certificate Forms S-3, S-3A, Form S-3C, S-3F, S-3M, and S-3V
Virginia	Valid until notice from Department of Taxation that certificate is no longer acceptable or is revoked.	Expiration date is stated on certificates for nonprofit organizations.	Va. Code Ann. § 58.1-623(B), 23 Va. Admin. Code § 10-210-280(A), Unofficial department guidance

¶118

State	Exemption Certificate Validity Periods	Comments	Citation
Washington	A blanket exemption certificate is valid as long as the purchaser has a "recurring business relationship" with the seller. Such a relationship is found where there is at least one sale transaction within a period of twelve consecutive months.		Wash. Rev. Code § 82.08.050(7), Wash. Admin. Code § 458-20-13601(4)(a), Form REV 27 0032, Form REV 27 0021e
West Virginia	Blanket certificates are effective so long as the purchaser makes at least one purchase within a period of 12 consecutive months, or until the certificate is otherwise cancelled by the purchaser.		Form F0003 Instructions
Wisconsin	Continuous certificates valid indefinitely but should be reviewed periodically.		Wis. Admin. Code § 11.14(5)
Wyoming	No stated expiration period.		SSTGB Form F0003

¶119 Finance Charges

If charges are excluded when separately stated, it is noted in the Comment column.

State	Finance Charges	Comments	Citation
Alabama	Excluded	Must be separately stated.	Ala. Admin. Code r. 810-6-1-.31
Arizona	Excluded	Must be separately stated.	Ariz. Admin. Code § 15-5-106
Arkansas	No specific provisions.		
California	Excluded	Must be separately stated.	Reg. 1641(a), 18 CCR
Colorado	Excluded	Must be separately stated.	Colo. Code Regs. § 39-26-102.7(a)
Connecticut	Included		Conn. Gen. Stat. § 12-407(a)(9)
District of Columbia	Excluded	Must be separately stated.	D.C. Mun. Regs. t. 9, § 408.4
Florida	Excluded	Must be separately stated.	Fla. Admin. Code Ann. r. 12A-1.017
Georgia	Excluded	Must be separately stated to be excluded from the "sales price."	Ga. Code Ann. § 48-8-2(34)(B)
Hawaii	Included		Haw. Rev. Stat. § 237-3
Idaho	Excluded		Idaho Code § 63-3613(b)(6)
Illinois	Excluded		Ill. Admin. Code tit. 86, § 130.420
Indiana	Excluded	Must be separately stated.	Ind. Code § 6-2.5-1-5
Iowa	Excluded	Must be separately stated.	Iowa Code § 423.1(47)
Kansas	Excluded	Must be separately stated to be excluded from the "sales or selling price."	Kan. Stat. Ann. § 79-3602, Kan. Admin. Regs. § 92-19-3a(d)
Kentucky	Excluded	Must be separately stated to be excluded from the "gross receipts" or "sales price."	Ky. Rev. Stat. Ann. § 139.010(12)
Louisiana	Excluded		La. Rev. Stat. Ann. § 47:301(13)
Maine	Excluded	Must be separately stated.	Me. Instructional Bulletin No. 20, Me. Instructional Bulletin No. 24
Maryland	Excluded	Must be separately stated.	Md. Code Ann. § 11-101(l)(3), Md. Regs. Code § 03.06.03.08
Massachusetts	Excluded	Must be separately stated.	Mass. Letter Ruling 1982-99
Michigan	Excluded	Must be separately stated.	Mich. Comp. Laws § 205.51(1)(d)
Minnesota	Excluded	Must be separately stated.	Minn. Stat. § 297A.61(7)(b)

State	Finance Charges	Comments	Citation
Mississippi	Excluded	Included prior to July 1, 2014. Excluded if credit extended by third-party creditor.	Miss. Code. Ann. § 27-65-3(h), Miss. Rule 35.IV.2.04
Missouri	Excluded		Mo. Code Regs. tit. 12, § 10-103.555(3)(I)
Nebraska	Excluded	Must be separately stated.	Neb. Admin. Code § 1-026
Nevada	Excluded	Must be separately stated.	Nev. Admin. Code § 372.050
New Jersey	Excluded		N.J. Admin. Code § 18:24-36.2(k)
New Mexico	Excluded		N.M. Stat. Ann. § 7-9-3.5
New York	Excluded		N.Y. Comp. Code R. & Regs. tit. 20, § 526.5(h)(1)
North Carolina	Excluded	Must be separately stated.	N.C. Gen. Stat. § 105-164.3(37)
North Dakota	Excluded	Must be separately stated.	N.D. Cent. Code § 57-39.2-01(12), N.D. Admin. Code § 81-04.1-01-11
Ohio	Excluded	Must be separately stated.	Ohio Rev. Code Ann. § 5739.01(H)(1)(c)
Oklahoma	Excluded	Must be separately stated to be excluded from the "gross receipts," "gross proceeds," or "sales price."	Okla. Stat. tit. 68, § 1352(12), Okla. Admin. Code § 710:65-19-103, Okla. Admin. Code § 710:65-19-341(e)
Pennsylvania	Excluded	Must be separately stated.	61 Pa. Code § 33.2(b)
Rhode Island	Excluded	Must be separately stated.	R.I. Gen. Laws § 44-18-12(b), R.I. Code R. SU 87-47
South Carolina	Excluded	Must be separately stated.	S.C. Code Regs. 117-318.2
South Dakota	Excluded	Must be separately stated.	S.D. Codified Laws § 10-45-1(4), (6)
Tennessee	Excluded	Must be separately stated.	Tenn. Comp. R. & Regs. 1320-5-1-.25
Texas	Excluded	Must be separately stated.	Tex. Tax Code Ann. § 151.007(c)(4)
Utah	Excluded	Must be separately stated.	Utah Code Ann. § 59-12-102
Vermont	Excluded	Must be separately stated.	Vt. Stat. Ann. tit. 32, § 9701(4)
Virginia	Excluded	Must be separately stated.	Va. Code Ann. § 58.1-602
Washington	Excluded	Must be separately stated.	Wash. Rev. Code § 82.08.010, Wash. Admin. Code § 458-20-109
West Virginia	Excluded	Must be separately stated to be excluded from the "sales price."	W. Va. Code § 11-15B-2(b), W. Va. Code R. § 110-15-3.4.2

State	Finance Charges	Comments	Citation
Wisconsin	Excluded	Must be separately stated.	Wis. Stat. § 77.51(12m)(b)2.
Wyoming	Excluded	Must be separately stated.	Wyo. Stat. Ann. § 39-15-101(a)(viii)

¶ 120 **Grocery Food**

The chart below sets forth the taxability of non-prepared grocery food. Many states that exempt grocery food exclude certain items such as soft drinks, candy, and confections. Food prepared by a grocery is taxable in all states as meals.

State	Grocery Food	Comments	Citation
Alabama	Taxable		Ala. Code § 40-23-2
Arizona	Exempt		Ariz. Rev. Stat. § 42-5061 (A) (15)
Arkansas	Taxable	Food and food ingredients taxed at reduced state rate of 1.5% beginning July 1, 2011, plus any applicable local rate. Food items ineligible for reduced rate taxed at regular state rate. State rate will fall from 1.5% to 0.125% if certain budget conditions met.	Ark. Code Ann. § 26-52-301, Ark. Code Ann. § 26-52-317, Ark. Code Ann. § 26-53-145
California	Exempt	Certain meals are taxed. Exceptions apply.	Cal. Rev. & Tax. Code § 6359
Colorado	Exempt	Certain items are taxable including carbonated water, chewing gum, seeds and plants to grow food, prepared salads and salad bars, cold sandwiches, deli trays, candy, soft drinks and hot/cold beverages served in unsealed cups through a vending machine.	Colo. Rev. Stat. § 39-26-114 (1) (a) (XX)
Connecticut	Exempt		Conn. Gen. Stat. § 12-412 (13)
District of Columbia	Exempt		D.C. Code Ann. § 47-2001 (n) (2) (E)
Florida	Exempt		Fla. Stat. § 212.08 (1)
Georgia	Exempt	This exemption for the sale of "food and food ingredients" to an individual consumer for off-premises human consumption does not apply to any local sales and use tax. "Food and food ingredients" does not include prepared food, alcoholic beverages, dietary supplements, drugs, over-the-counter drugs, or tobacco.	Ga. Code Ann. § 48-8-3 (57), Ga. Code Ann. § 48-8-2 (16)
Hawaii	Taxable	Food purchased with federal food coupons or vouchers exempt.	Haw. Rev. Stat. § 237-13 (2), Haw. Rev. Stat. § 237-24.3 (5)
Idaho	Taxable		Idaho Code § 63-3612 (2) (b)

State	Grocery Food	Comments	Citation
Illinois	Taxable	Taxed at reduced rate of 1%. Candy, soft drinks, alcoholic beverages, and food prepared for immediate consumption do not qualify for the 1% rate.	35 ILCS 105/3-10
Indiana	Exempt		Ind. Code § 6-2.5-5-20
Iowa	Exempt		Iowa Code § 423.3(57)
Kansas	Taxable	Certain exemptions may apply.	Kan. Stat. Ann. § 79-3603
Kentucky	Exempt	Exemption applies with regard to "food and food ingredients" for human consumption. "Food and food ingredients" does not include "candy," "tobacco," "alcoholic beverages," "soft drinks," "dietary supplements," "prepared food," or food sold through vending machines.	Ky. Rev. Stat. Ann. § 139.485
Louisiana	Exempt	Exemption applies to food sold for preparation and consumption in the home.	La. Rev. Stat. Ann. § 47:305(D)(1)(n)–(r)
Maine	Exempt	The exemption for food products for home consumption is limited to "grocery staples."	Me. Rev. Stat. Ann. tit. 36, § 1760(3)
Maryland	Exempt		Md. Code Ann. § 11-206(c)
Massachusetts	Exempt		Mass. Gen. Laws ch. 64H, § 6(h)
Michigan	Exempt		Mich. Comp. Laws § 205.54g
Minnesota	Exempt		Minn. Stat. § 297A.67(2)
Mississippi	Taxable		Miss. Code. Ann. § 27-65-17
Missouri	Taxable	Taxed at reduced rate.	Mo. Rev. Stat. § 144.014
Nebraska	Exempt		Neb. Rev. Stat. § 77-2704.24
Nevada	Exempt		Nev. Rev. Stat. § 372.284
New Jersey	Exempt		N.J. Stat. Ann. § 54:32B-8.2.
New Mexico	Exempt		N.M. Stat. Ann. § 7-9-92
New York	Exempt	The exemption does not apply to candy, confectionery, and certain drinks.	N.Y. Tax Law, § 1115
North Carolina	Exempt	Sales of food are subject to local taxes.	N.C. Gen. Stat. § 105-164.13B

State	Grocery Food	Comments	Citation
North Dakota	Exempt		N.D. Cent. Code § 57-39.2-04.1, N.D. Admin. Code § 81-04.1-03-03
Ohio	Exempt	All food, including prepared food, is exempt if sold for off-premises consumption.	Ohio Rev. Code Ann. § 5739.02(B)(2)
Oklahoma	Taxable	Exemptions apply to sales to and/or by churches, nonprofit schools, and certain nonprofit organizations serving the needy or elderly. Purchases of food using food stamps are also exempt.	Okla. Stat. tit. 68, § 1354(A)(1), Okla. Stat. tit. 68, § 1356(5), (65), Okla. Stat. tit. 68, § 1357(12), (13)
Pennsylvania	Exempt	Depends upon the type of food and the location from which food is sold.	72 P.S. § 7204(29), Policy Statement Sec. 60.7
Rhode Island	Exempt		R.I. Gen. Laws § 44-18-30(9)
South Carolina	Exempt	Unprepared food that can be purchased with federal food stamps is exempt from state sales and use tax, but may be subject to other local sales and use taxes.	S.C. Code Ann. § 12-36-2120
South Dakota	Taxable		S.D. Codified Laws § 10-45-2
Tennessee	Taxable	Food and food ingredients are taxed at reduced rate of 5.25%. Effective July 1, 2013, the rate is 5%. Prior to July 1, 2012, the rate was 5.5%.	Tenn. Code. Ann. § 67-6-228(a)
Texas	Exempt		Tex. Tax Code Ann. § 151.314
Utah	Taxable	Subject to local taxes. Food and food ingredients are taxed at reduced rate of 1.75%. In a bundled transaction involving both food/food ingredients and another taxable item of tangible personal property, the rate is 4.65%.	Utah Code Ann. § 59-12-103
Vermont	Exempt		Vt. Stat. Ann. tit. 32, § 9741(13)
Virginia	Taxable	Taxed at reduced rate of 1.5% (1% local option tax also applies).	Va. Code Ann. § 58.1-611.1
Washington	Exempt		Wash. Rev. Code § 82.08.0293

State	Grocery Food	Comments	Citation
West Virginia	Exempt	Sales and use tax ceased applying to sales of grocery food on July 1, 2013. Previously, the state-level rate applicable to sales of grocery food was 6% prior to January 1, 2006; 5% from January 1, 2006, through June 30, 2007; 4% from July 1, 2007, through June 30, 2008; 3% from July 1, 2008, through December 31, 2011; 2% from January 1, 2012, through June 30, 2012; and 1% from July 1, 2012, through June 30, 2013.	W. Va. Code § 11-15-3a(a)
Wisconsin	Exempt		Wis. Stat. § 77.54(20n)
Wyoming	Exempt	Food for domestic home consumption is exempt.	Wyo. Stat. Ann. § 39-15-105(a)(vi)(E), Wyo. Stat. Ann. § 39-15-101(a)(xli)

¶ 121   Installation Charges

If charges are excluded when separately stated, it is noted in the Comment column.

State	Installation Charges	Comments	Citation
Alabama	Excluded	Must be separately stated.	Ala. Admin. Code r. 810-6-1-.81
Arizona	Excluded	Must be separately stated.	Ariz. Admin. Code § 15-5-105
Arkansas	Excluded	Must be separately stated.	Ark. Reg. GR-18
California	Excluded		Cal. Rev. & Tax. Code § 6011
Colorado	Excluded	Must be separately stated.	Colo. Code Regs. § 39-26-102.7(a)
Connecticut	Excluded	Must be separately stated.	Conn. Gen. Stat. § 12-407(a)(8)
District of Columbia	Excluded	Must be separately stated.	D.C. Mun. Regs. t. 9, § 407.3
Florida	Included		Fla. Admin. Code Ann. r. 12A-1.016(3)
Georgia	Excluded	Must be separately stated.	Ga. Code Ann. § 48-8-2(34)(B), Ga. Comp. R. & Regs. 560-12-2-.88
Hawaii	Included		Haw. Rev. Stat. § 237-3
Idaho	Excluded	Must be separately stated.	Idaho Code § 63-3613(b)(4)
Illinois	Included	Excluded if separately contracted.	Ill. Admin. Code tit. 86, § 130.450
Indiana	Excluded	Must be separately stated.	Ind. Code § 6-2.5-1-5
Iowa	Included	Excluded if separately contracted.	Iowa Code § 423.1(47)
Kansas	Included	Certain installation services related to construction are excluded.	Kan. Stat. Ann. § 79-3603(p)
Kentucky	Excluded	Must be separately stated to be excluded from "gross receipts" or "sales price."	Ky. Rev. Stat. Ann. § 139.010(12)(c), 103 Ky. Admin. Regs. 30:180
Louisiana	Excluded	Must be separately stated.	La. Admin. Code tit. 61, § 4301
Maine	Excluded	Must be separately stated.	Me. Rev. Stat. Ann. tit. 36, § 1752(14)
Maryland	Excluded	Must be separately stated.	Md. Code Regs. 03.06.01.08
Massachusetts	Excluded		Mass. Gen. Laws ch. 64H, § 1
Michigan	Included, as long as they are incurred before the completion of the transfer of ownership of tangible personal property from the seller to the purchaser.		Mich. Comp. Laws § 205.51
Minnesota	Included		Minn. Stat. § 297A.61(7)(a)(5)

State	Installation Charges	Comments	Citation
Mississippi	Included		Miss. Code. Ann. § 27-65-3(h)
Missouri	Excluded	Must be separately stated or the price of the tangible personal property constitutes less than 10% of the total sale price.	Mo. Rev. Stat. § 144.010, Mo. Rev. Stat. § 144.605(8), Mo. Code. Regs. Ann. tit. 12, § 10-103.600(3)(B)
Nebraska	Included, as long as the property being installed is taxable.	Installation charges of sewer and water service providers are not gross receipts and are not taxable.	Neb. Rev. Stat. § 77-2701.16, Neb. Admin. Code § 1-066
Nevada	Excluded	Must be separately stated.	Nev. Rev. Stat. § 372.025(3), Nev. Admin. Code § 372.380
New Jersey	Included	Excluded if installation constitutes real property addition or capital improvement.	N.J. Stat. Ann. § 54:32B-3(b)(2)
New Mexico	Included		N.M. Admin. Code tit. 3, § 3.2.206.10
New York	Included	Excluded if installation constitutes real property addition, capital improvement, or in certain other situations.	N.Y. Tax Law, § 1105(c)(3)
North Carolina	Excluded	Must be separately stated. Effective March 1, 2016, the general sales and use tax rate applies to the sales price of, or the gross receipts derived from, repair, maintenance, and installation services. Certain exceptions apply.	N.C. Gen. Stat. § 105-164.3(33d) and (37), N.C. Gen. Stat. § 105-164.4(a)(15), N.C. Gen. Stat. § 105-164.13(49)
North Dakota	Excluded	Must be separately stated.	N.D. Cent. Code § 57-39.2-01(12), Guideline, Computers
Ohio	Included	Installation charges for exempt property or property that will become a part of a production, transmission, transportation, or distribution system for the delivery of a public utility service, are not taxable.	Ohio Rev. Code Ann. § 5739.01
Oklahoma	Excluded	Must be separately stated to be excluded from "gross receipts," "gross proceeds," or "sales price."	Okla. Stat. tit. 68, § 1352(12)(a), Okla. Admin. Code § 710:65-19-159
Pennsylvania	Included		61 Pa. Code § 31.1(4)
Rhode Island	Excluded	Must be separately stated.	R.I. Gen. Laws § 44-18-12(b)(ii)
South Carolina	Excluded	Must be separately stated.	S.C. Code Regs. 117-313.3

State	Installation Charges	Comments	Citation
South Dakota	Included		S.D. Codified Laws § 10-45-1(4), (6)
Tennessee	Included		Tenn. Comp. R. & Regs. 1320-5-1-.27
Texas	Included		Tex. Tax Code Ann. § 151.007
Utah	Excluded	Must be separately stated.	Utah Code Ann. § 59-12-102
Vermont	Excluded	Must be separately stated.	Vt. Stat. Ann. tit. 32, § 9701(4), Vt. Code R. 1.9701(4)-2
Virginia	Excluded	Must be separately stated.	Va. Code Ann. § 58.1-609.5(2)
Washington	Included		Wash. Rev. Code § 82.04.050
West Virginia	Included		W. Va. Code R. § 110-15-114
Wisconsin	Included		Wis. Stat. § 77.51(15b)(a)5.
Wyoming	Included		Wyo. Stat. Ann. § 39-15-101(a)(viii)(A)(V)

¶ 122   Installment Sales

State	Installment Sales	Comments	Citation
Alabama	Payments reported as received.	Lay-away sales taxable at transfer of title.	Ala. Code § 40-23-8, Ala. Admin. Code r. 810-6-2-.36.05, Ala. Admin. Code r. 810-6-4-.01
Arizona	Payments reported as received.	Lay-away sales taxable at transfer of title or when transaction nonrefundable.	Ariz. Rev. Stat. § 42-5011, Ariz. Admin. Code § 15-5-131
Arkansas	No specific provisions.		
California	Total sales price reported at time of sale.	Lay-away sales taxable at transfer of title.	Cal. Rev. & Tax. Code § 6006(a), Reg. 1641(c), 18 CCR
Colorado	Payments reported as received.		Colo. Rev. Stat. § 39-26-102(5), Colo. Rev. Stat. § 39-26-111
Connecticut	Total sales price reported at time of sale.		Conn. Form O-88 Return Instructions
District of Columbia	Total sales price reported at time of sale.		D.C. Mun. Regs. t. 9, § 409.1, D.C. Mun. Regs. t. 9, § 409.3
Florida	Total sales price reported at time of sale.		Fla. Stat. § 212.06(1)(a)
Georgia	No specific provisions.		
Hawaii	Reporting of payments depends on whether seller/lessor is cash or accrual basis taxpayer.	If seller/lessor is an accrual basis taxpayer, the transaction is reported by classifying purchase price as retailing income at inception of lease, and the finance charge is accrued as interest income ratably in accordance with the lease agreement, whether received by seller/lessor or not. If seller/lessor is a cash basis taxpayer, monthly payments received are reported by allocating the amount received between the purchase price of the property and the finance charge.	Tax Information Release No. 98-2
Idaho	Total sales price reported at time of sale.	Lay-away sales taxable at transfer of title.	Idaho Code § 63-3619(a), IDAPA 35.01.02.035
Illinois	Payments reported as received.		35 ILCS 120/1
Indiana	No specific provisions.		
Iowa	Total payment reported at time of delivery.		Iowa Admin. Code r. 701-213.3, Iowa Admin. Code r. 701-213.10

State	Installment Sales	Comments	Citation
Kansas	Payments reported as received.	If accrual basis, total sales price reported at time of sale.	Kan. Admin. Regs. § 92-19-3a(h)
Kentucky	Payments reported as received.	If accrual basis, total sales price reported at time of sale.	103 Ky. Admin. Regs. 28:020, 103 Ky. Admin. Regs. 31:011
Louisiana	Total sales price reported at time of sale.		La. Rev. Stat. Ann. § 47:301(12) and (13), La. Admin. Code tit. 61, § 4301.C.Sale, La. Admin. Code tit. 61, § 4307
Maine	Total sales price reported at time of sale.		Me. Rev. Stat. Ann. tit. 36, § 1952
Maryland	Total sales price reported at time of sale.		Md. Code Regs. 03.06.01.21
Massachusetts	Total sales price reported at time of sale.		Mass. Letter Ruling 1983-17, Mass. Letter Ruling 1983-18
Michigan	Total sales price reported at time of sale.		Mich. Comp. Laws § 205.52, Mich. Comp. Laws § 205.56
Minnesota	Payments reported as received.	If accrual basis, total sales price reported at time of sale.	Minn. Stat. § 297A.79
Mississippi	Total sales price reported at time of sale.		Miss. Code. Ann. § 27-65-33
Missouri	Payments reported as received.	If accrual basis, total sales price reported at time of sale. Lay-away sales taxed when sale complete.	Mo. Rev. Stat. § 144.100.3, Mo. Code Regs. tit. 12, § 10-103.555, Mo. Code Regs. tit. 12, § 10-103.560
Nebraska	Payments reported as received.	Retailers maintaining their books and records on the accrual basis, may choose to report such sales on a cash basis by deferring remittance of sales tax not yet collected on credit, conditional, and installment sales.	Neb. Rev. Stat. § 77-2708(1)(b)(iv), Neb. Admin. Code § 1-009
Nevada	No specific provisions.		
New Jersey	Total sales price reported at time of sale.		N.J. State Tax News
New Mexico	Payments reported as received.	Seller must elect to treat payments reported as received.	N.M. Stat. Ann. § 7-9-3.5
New York	Total sales price reported at time of sale.		N.Y. Tax Law, § 1132(d)

State	Installment Sales	Comments	Citation
North Carolina	Payments reported as received.	If accrual basis, total sales price reported at time of sale.	N.C. Admin. Code tit. 17, § 17:07B.4802, N.C. Admin. Code tit. 17, § 17.07B.4803
North Dakota	Payments reported as received when payment of principal sum is extended over a period longer than 60 days from date of sale.	Exception applies if purchaser is billed in full in intervals of less than 60 consecutive days, even though credit terms may allow purchaser to extend principal payments beyond 60 consecutive days.	N.D. Cent. Code § 57-39.2-30, N.D. Admin. Code § 81-04.1-01-25
Ohio	Total sales price reported at time of sale.		Ohio Admin. Code § 5703-9-19
Oklahoma	Total sales price reported at time of sale.		Okla. Admin. Code § 710:65-19-160
Pennsylvania	Seller must require purchaser to pay full amount of tax due on entire purchase price at time of purchase or within 30 days after purchase.		61 Pa. Code § 33.4
Rhode Island	No specific provisions.		
South Carolina	Payments reported as received or total sales price reported at time of sale, at taxpayer's election.	Lay-away payments taxed as received as long as title has been transferred to the property being held by the seller for the purchaser (e.g., as security). If both title and possession remain with the seller, sales tax on lay-away payments is remitted with the return for the month in which the item was transferred to the customer.	S.C. Code Ann. § 12-36-2560, S.C. Code Regs. 117-318.3, Private Letter Ruling 11-4
South Dakota	Payments reported as received.		S.D. Codified Laws § 10-45-2.3
Tennessee	Total sales price reported at time of sale.	Lay-away sales taxable upon delivery to customer.	Tenn. Comp. R. & Regs. 1320-5-1-.13, Tenn. Comp. R. & Regs. 1320-5-1-.75
Texas	Payments reported as received.	If accrual basis, total sales price reported at time of sale.	34 Tex. Admin. Code § 3.302(b)
Utah	Total sales price reported at time of sale.		Utah Admin. Code r. 865-19S-20
Vermont	Total sales price reported at time of sale.	Certain vendors may request permission to report payments as received.	Vt. Code R. 226-10
Virginia	Total sales price reported at time of sale.	Lay-away sales taxable upon delivery to customer.	23 Va. Admin. Code § 10-210-820, Va. Department of Taxation FAQ
Washington	Total sales price reported at time of sale.		Wash. Admin. Code § 458-20-198

State	Installment Sales	Comments	Citation
West Virginia	Total sales price reported at time of sale.	Lay-away sales taxable upon delivery to customer.	W. Va. Code R. § 110-15-4.4
Wisconsin	Payments reported when purchaser takes possession of the property.		Wis. Stat. § 77.51(14)(c), Wis. Admin. Code § 11.30(1)(a)
Wyoming	Total sales price reported at time of sale.	If title passes at a future date, payments taxed as received.	Wyo. Stat. Ann. § 39-15-107(b)(vi), Wyo. BOE Rule Ch. 2, § 15(f)

¶ 123 **Interest Rates on Overpayments—2017**

Rates listed are annual interest rates. NA denotes that the rate for a given period is not yet available.

State	Interest Rates on Overpayments - 2017	Comments	Citation
Alabama	Jan-Mar: 4% Apr-Jun: 4% July-Sep: NA Oct-Dec: NA		Ala. Code § 40-1-44(b), AL DOR website
Arizona	Jan-Mar: 4% Apr-Jun: 4%	Adjusted quarterly.	Ariz. Rev. Stat. § 42-1123
Arkansas	10%	Rate specified in statute.	Ark. Code. Ann. § 26-18-508
California	Jan-Jun: 0%	Adjusted semiannually.	Cal. Rev. & Tax Code § 6591.5, CA BOE website
Colorado			Colo. Rev. Stat. § 39-21-110.5
Connecticut	NA		Conn. Gen. Stat. § 12-39u, Conn. Gen. Stat. § 12-422
District of Columbia			D.C. Code Ann. § 47-4202
Florida	Jan-Jun: 7%	Adjusted semiannually.	Fla. Stat. ch. 213.235, Tax Information Publication No. 14ADM-01
Georgia	6.75%		Ga. Code Ann. § 48-2-35, Policy Bulletin ADMIN-2017-01, Georgia Department of Revenue, January 13, 2017
Hawaii	1/3 of 1% per month	Rate specified in statute.	Haw. Rev. Stat. § 231-23(d)
Idaho	3%	Adjusted annually.	Idaho Code § 63-3626(c)
Illinois	Jan-Jun 4%; Jul-Dec N/A		35 ILCS 735/3-2, IL DOR website
Indiana	3%	Adjusted annually.	Ind. Code § 6-8.1-10-1, Departmental Notice #3
Iowa			Iowa Code § 421.7
Kansas	5% (0.417% per month)	Adjusted annually.	Kan. Stat. Ann. § 79-2968, Penalty and Interest, Kansas Department of Revenue
Kentucky	1%	Adjusted annually.	Ky. Rev. Stat. Ann. § 131.183(2)
Louisiana	4.25%	Adjusted annually.	La. Rev. Stat. Ann. § 47:1624, La. Rev. Stat. Ann. § 13:4202
Maine	7%	Adjusted annually.	Me. Rev. Stat. Ann. tit. 36, § 186, Maine Interest Rates

State	Interest Rates on Overpayments - 2017	Comments	Citation
Maryland	12% or 3% above prime (greater of)	2018: 11.5% or 3% above prime (greater of). 2019: 11% or 3% above prime (greater of). 2020: 10.5% or 3% above prime (greater of). 2021: 10% or 3% above prime (greater of). 2022: 9.5% or 3% above prime (greater of). 2023 and after: 9% or 3% above prime (greater of).	Md. Code Ann. § 13-604
Massachusetts			Mass. Gen. Laws ch. 62C, § 40
Michigan	Jan-Jun: 4.5%	Adjusted semiannually.	Mich. Comp. Laws § 205.30, Mich. Comp. Laws § 205.23(2)
Minnesota	4%	Adjusted annually.	Minn. Stat. § 270C.40(5), Minn. Stat. § 270C.405
Mississippi	12%	Rate specified in statute.	Miss. Code Ann. § 27-65-53
Missouri	Jan-Mar: 0.6% Apr-Jun: 0.7% Jul-Sep: NA Oct-Dec: NA	Adjusted quarterly.	Mo. Rev. Stat. § 32.068, MO DOR website
Nebraska	3%	Adjusted biennially (every 2 years). Rate will remain at 3% through December 31, 2018.	Neb. Rev. Stat. § 45-104.02, Rev. Ruling 99-16-1
Nevada			Nev. Rev. Stat. § 372.660, Nev. Rev. Stat. § 360.2937
New Jersey	3.5%	Adjusted annually, with quarterly adjustments allowed if a cumulative change of more than one percentage point has occurred in the prime rate as of December 1 of prior year.	N.J. Stat. Ann. § 54:49-15.1, Technical Bulletin TB-21(R)
New Mexico	Jan- Mar 4% Apr-Jun 4%	Adjusted quarterly.	N.M. Stat. Ann. § 7-1-68
New York	Jan-Mar: 3% Apr-Jun: 3% Jul-Sep: NA Oct-Dec: NA	Adjusted quarterly.	N.Y. Tax Law, § 1142, NY State website
North Carolina	Jan-Jun: 5%	Adjusted semiannually.	N.C. Gen. Stat. § 105-241.21, NC DOR website
North Dakota	10%	Rate specified in statute.	N.D. Cent. Code § 57-39.2-18
Ohio	4%		Ohio Rev. Code Ann. § 5703.47, OH Dept. of Taxation website
Oklahoma	1.25% per month	Rate specified in statute.	Okla. Stat. tit. 68, § 217
Pennsylvania	2%	Adjusted annually.	72 P.S. § 806

State	Interest Rates on Overpayments - 2017	Comments	Citation
Rhode Island	3.5%	Adjusted annually.	R.I. Gen. Laws § 44-1-7
South Carolina	Jan-Mar: 1% April-June: 1%		S.C. Code Ann. § 12-54-25(D)
South Dakota			S.D. Codified Laws § 10-59-6
Tennessee	Jan-Jun: 7.5%		Tenn. Code Ann. § 67-1-801, TN DOR website
Texas	1.004	Adjusted annually.	Tex. Tax Code Ann. § 111.060, Texas Comptroller's website
Utah	3%	Adjusted annually.	Utah Code Ann. § 59-1-402, Publication 58, Interest and Penalties
Vermont	3.6% (0.3% per month)	Adjusted annually.	Vt. Stat. Ann. tit. 32, § 3108, Memorandum-2017 Interest Rates, Vermont Department of Taxes
Virginia	Jan-Mar: 6% Apr-Jun: 6% Jul-Sep: NA Oct-Dec: NA	Adjusted quarterly.	Va. Code Ann. § 58.1-15
Washington	3%		Wash. Rev. Code § 82.32.050(2)
West Virginia	Jan-Jun: 6.5%	Adjusted semiannually.	W. Va. Code § 11-10-17a(d), Administrative Notice 2016-28
Wisconsin	3%	Rate specified in statute.	Wis. Stat. § 77.60
Wyoming	State has no provisions for interest on overpayments.		Wyo. Stat. Ann. § 39-15-108(b)

¶ 124 **Interest Rates on Underpayments—2017**

Rates listed are annual interest rates. NA denotes that the rate for a given period is not yet available.

State	Interest Rates on Underpayments - 2017	Comments	Citation
Alabama	Jan-Mar: 4% Apr-Jun: 4% July-Sep: NA Oct-Dec: NA		Ala. Code § 40-1-44(b), AL DOR website
Arizona	Jan-Mar: 4% Apr-Jun: 4%	Adjusted quarterly.	Ariz. Rev. Stat. § 42-1123
Arkansas	10%	Rate specified in statute.	Ark. Code. Ann. § 26-18-508
California	Jan-Jun: 7%	Adjusted semiannually.	Cal. Rev. & Tax Code § 6591.5, CA BOE website
Colorado			Colo. Rev. Stat. § 39-21-110.5
Connecticut	1% per month		Conn. Gen. Stat. § 12-39u, Conn. Gen. Stat. § 12-422
District of Columbia			D.C. Code Ann. § 47-4202
Florida	Jan-Jun: 7%	Adjusted semiannually.	Fla. Stat. ch. 213.235, Tax Information Publication No. 14ADM-01
Georgia	6.75%		Ga. Code Ann. § 48-2-35, Policy Bulletin ADMIN-2017-01, Georgia Department of Revenue, January 13, 2017
Hawaii	2/3 of 1% per month	Rate specified in statute.	Haw. Rev. Stat. § 231-23(d)
Idaho	3%	Adjusted annually.	Idaho Code § 63-3626(c)
Illinois	Jan-Jun 4%; Jul-Dec N/A		35 ILCS 735/3-2, IL DOR website
Indiana	3%	Adjusted annually.	Ind. Code § 6-8.1-10-1, Departmental Notice #3
Iowa			Iowa Code § 421.7
Kansas	5% (0.417% per month)	Adjusted annually.	Kan. Stat. Ann. § 79-2968, Penalty and Interest, Kansas Department of Revenue
Kentucky	5%	Adjusted annually.	Ky. Rev. Stat. Ann. § 131.183(2)
Louisiana	7.25%	Adjusted annually.	La. Rev. Stat. Ann. § 47:1624, La. Rev. Stat. Ann. § 13:4202
Maine	7%	Adjusted annually.	Me. Rev. Stat. Ann. tit. 36, § 186, Maine Interest Rates

State	Interest Rates on Underpayments - 2017	Comments	Citation
Maryland	12% or 3% above prime (greater of)	2018: 11.5% or 3% above prime (greater of). 2019: 11% or 3% above prime (greater of). 2020: 10.5% or 3% above prime (greater of). 2021: 10% or 3% above prime (greater of). 2022: 9.5% or 3% above prime (greater of). 2023 and after: 9% or 3% above prime (greater of).	Md. Code Ann. § 13-604
Massachusetts			Mass. Gen. Laws ch. 62C, § 40
Michigan	Jan-Jun: 4.5%	Adjusted semiannually.	Mich. Comp. Laws § 205.30, Mich. Comp. Laws § 205.23(2)
Minnesota	4%	Adjusted annually.	Minn. Stat. § 270C.40(5), Minn. Stat. § 270C.405
Mississippi	8.4%	Rate specified in statute. For 2018, rate will be reduced to 7.2%, with additional rate reductions scheduled every year through 2019.	Miss. Code Ann. § 27-65-53
Missouri	4%	Adjusted annually.	Mo. Rev. Stat. § 32.068, MO DOR website
Nebraska	3%	Adjusted biennially (every 2 years). Rate will remain at 3% through December 31, 2018.	Neb. Rev. Stat. § 45-104.02, Rev. Ruling 99-16-1
Nevada			Nev. Rev. Stat. § 372.660, Nev. Rev. Stat. § 360.2937
New Jersey	6.5%	Adjusted annually, with quarterly adjustments allowed if a cumulative change of more than one percentage point has occurred in the prime rate as of December 1 of prior year.	N.J. Stat. Ann. § 54:49-15.1, Technical Bulletin TB-21(R)
New Mexico	4%		N.M. Stat. Ann. § 7-1-68
New York	Jan-Mar: 14.5% Apr-Jun: 14.5% Jul-Sep: NA Oct-Dec: NA	Adjusted quarterly. Rate may be reduced to 8% for this quarter if failure to pay or delayed payment is due to reasonable cause and not willful neglect.	N.Y. Tax Law, § 1142, NY State website
North Carolina	Jan-Jun: 5%	Adjusted semiannually.	N.C. Gen. Stat. § 105-241.21, NC DOR website
North Dakota	1% per month	Rate specified in statute.	N.D. Cent. Code § 57-39.2-18
Ohio	4%	Adjusted annually.	Ohio Rev. Code Ann. § 5703.47, OH Dept. of Taxation website

State	Interest Rates on Underpayments - 2017	Comments	Citation
Oklahoma	1.25% per month	Rate specified in statute.	Okla. Stat. tit. 68, § 217
Pennsylvania	4%	Adjusted annually.	72 P.S. § 806
Rhode Island	18%	Adjusted annually.	R.I. Gen. Laws § 44-1-7
South Carolina	Jan-Mar: 4% April-June: 4%		S.C. Code Ann. § 12-54-25(D)
South Dakota			S.D. Codified Laws § 10-59-6
Tennessee	Jan-Jun: 7.5%		Tenn. Code Ann. § 67-1-801, TN DOR website
Texas	4.75%	Adjusted annually.	Tex. Tax Code Ann. § 111.060, Texas Comptroller's website
Utah	3%	Adjusted annually.	Utah Code Ann. § 59-1-402, Publication 58, Interest and Penalties
Vermont	5.6%	Adjusted annually.	Vt. Stat. Ann. tit. 32, § 3108, Memorandum-2017 Interest Rates, Vermont Department of Taxes
Virginia	Jan-Mar: 6% Apr-Jun: 6% Jul-Sep: NA Oct-Dec: NA	Adjusted quarterly.	Va. Code Ann. § 58.1-15
Washington	3%		Wash. Rev. Code § 82.32.050(2)
West Virginia	Jan-Jun: 8%	Adjusted semiannually.	W. Va. Code § 11-10-17a(d), Administrative Notice 2016-28
Wisconsin	Delinquent taxes: 1.5% per month Non-delinquent taxes: 12% annually	Rates specified in statute.	Wis. Stat. § 77.60
Wyoming	7.38%	Adjusted annually.	Wyo. Stat. Ann. § 39-15-108(b)

¶ 125   Janitorial Services

The following chart indicates the taxability of janitorial services. Where a state's treatment of services that might be considered janitorial differs from the general treatment, it is noted in the Comments column.

State	Janitorial	Comments	Citation
Alabama	Exempt		Ala. Code § 40-23-1(a)(6), Ala. Code § 40-23-2
Arizona	Exempt		Ariz. Rev. Stat. § 42-5061
Arkansas	Taxable		Ark. Code Ann. § 26-52-301(3)(D), Ark. Reg. GR 9
California	Exempt		Cal. Rev. & Tax. Code § 6011
Colorado	Exempt		1 Colo. Code Regs. § 201-5 (SR-26)
Connecticut	Taxable	Janitorial or maintenance services performed on a casual-sale basis are not taxable. Janitorial services for the disabled may be exempt.	Conn. Agencies Regs. § 12-407(2)(i)(Y)-1, Conn. Agencies Regs. § 12-407(a)(37)(Y)
District of Columbia	Taxable		D.C. Mun. Regs. t. 9, § 472.6
Florida	Taxable	Nonresidential cleaning services, including janitorial services on a contract or fee basis, are taxable. Residential cleaning services are exempt.	Fla. Admin. Code Ann. r. 12A-1.0091
Georgia	Exempt	Not included in the definition of a taxable "retail sale."	Ga. Code Ann. § 48-8-30(f)(1), Ga. Code Ann. § 48-8-2(31)
Hawaii	Taxable		Haw. Rev. Stat. § 237-13(6)
Idaho	Exempt		IDAPA 35.01.02.011
Illinois	Exempt		35 ICLS 115/3
Indiana	Exempt		Ind. Admin. Code tit. 45, r. 2.2-4-2
Iowa	Taxable		Iowa Code § 423.2(6)
Kansas	Exempt	The waxing of floors is taxable.	Kan. Stat. Ann. § 79-3603, Information Guide: Janitorial Services Self-Audit Fact Sheet, Rev. Ruling 19-84-1
Kentucky	Exempt	Not expressly enumerated as taxable in the taxing statute.	Ky. Rev. Stat. Ann. § 139.200
Louisiana	Taxable	The furnishing of cleaning services, including the cleaning and renovation of furniture, carpets and rugs, is taxable. However, the cleaning and restoration of miscellaneous items other than furniture and structural cleaning are exempt provided certain conditions are met and the charge for each is separately stated.	Private Letter Ruling 01-006, La. Rev. Stat. Ann. § 301(14)(e)
Maine	Exempt		Me. Rev. Stat. Ann. tit. 36, § 1811

State	Janitorial	Comments	Citation
Maryland	Taxable	Cleaning of a commercial or industrial building is taxable. Cleaning for individuals is exempt.	Md. Code Ann. § 11-101
Massachusetts	Exempt		Mass. Gen. Laws ch. 64H, § 1
Michigan	Exempt		Mich. Comp. Laws § 205.51
Minnesota	Taxable		Minn. Stat. § 297A.61(3)(g)(6)(iii)
Mississippi	Exempt		Miss. Code Ann. § 27-65-23
Missouri	Exempt		Mo. Rev. Stat. § 144.020, Mo. Code Regs. Ann. tit. 12, § 10-103.600
Nebraska	Taxable		Neb. Rev. Stat. § 77-2701.16(4)
Nevada	Exempt		Nev. Rev. Stat. § 372.060
New Jersey	Taxable		N.J. Stat. Ann. § 54:32B-3(b)(4), Bulletin S&U-4
New Mexico	Taxable		N.M. Admin. Code tit. 3, § 3.2.1.18(A)
New York	Taxable	Interior cleaning and maintenance service agreements of 30 days or more are taxable.	N.Y. Tax Law, § 1105(c)(5), N.Y. Comp. Code R & Regs. tit. 20, § 527.7(c)
North Carolina	Exempt		N.C. Gen. Stat. § 105-164.4
North Dakota	Exempt		N.D. Cent. Code § 57-39.2-02.1, N.D. Admin. Code § 81-04.1-01-22
Ohio	Taxable		Ohio Rev. Code Ann. § 5739.01(B)(3)(j)
Oklahoma	Exempt	Not expressly enumerated as taxable in the taxing statute.	Okla. Stat. tit. 68, § 1354
Pennsylvania	Taxable		72 P.S. § 7201(k)(14)
Rhode Island	Exempt		R.I. Gen. Laws § 44-18-7
South Carolina	Exempt		S.C. Code Ann. Regs. 117-303.2
South Dakota	Taxable		S.D. Codified Laws § 10-45-5
Tennessee	Exempt	Cleaning real property, such as windows, walls, and carpeting is exempt. Cleaning personal property, including furniture, rugs, and draperies, is taxable.	Tenn. Comp. R. & Regs. 1320-5-1-.53
Texas	Taxable		Tex. Tax Code Ann. § 151.0048(a)(4)
Utah	Exempt	However, assisted cleaning or washing of tangible personal property is taxable.	Utah Code Ann. § 59-12-103(1)
Vermont	Exempt		Vt. Stat. Ann. Ann. tit. 32, § 9771
Virginia	Exempt		Va. Code Ann. § 58.1-603, 23 Va. Admin. Code § 10-210-4040

State	Janitorial	Comments	Citation
Washington	Exempt	Janitorial services does not include cleaning the exterior walls of buildings, the cleaning of septic tanks, special clean up jobs required by construction, fires, floods, etc., painting, papering, repairing, furnace or chimney cleaning, snow removal, sandblasting, or the cleaning of plant or industrial machinery or fixtures.	Wash. Rev. Code § 82.04.050 (2) (d), Wash. Admin. Code § 458-20-172
West Virginia	Taxable	Janitorial services performed on or in connection with new construction, reconstruction, alteration, expansion, or remodeling of a building are exempt.	W. Va. Code R. § 110-15-117.11, W. Va. Code R. § 110-15-9.3.4.2
Wisconsin	Exempt	Routine and repetitive janitorial services, including those provided by temporary employees, are exempt. Specialized cleaning of tangible personal property taxable; specialized cleaning of real property exempt. Janitor fees included in rental of certain school or government facilities may be taxable, depending on use of facility.	Wis. Stat. § 77.52 (2) (a) (10), Wis. Admin. Code § 11.03 (2), Wis. Admin. Code § 11.05 (2) (d), Tax Release, in Tax Bulletin No. 165, DOR Response to CCH Question Regarding Sales and Use Tax Treatment of Janitorial Services, Sales and Use Tax Report, 6-1980, Sales and Use Tax Report No. 3-14
Wyoming	Exempt	However, generally, services for repair, alteration, or improvement of tangible personal property are taxable.	Unofficial department guidance, Wyo. Stat. Ann. § 39-15-103 (a) (i) (J)

¶ 126   Judicial Appeals

The following chart describes the time period in which a taxpayer must seek judicial review of a department decision or decision by an administrative entity. Appeals to the taxing authority or administrative entity are addressed in Department Appeals and Administrative Appeals.

State	Judicial Appeals	Comments	Citation
Alabama	Suit must be filed with the Circuit Court within 30 days after the date of final assessment.		Ala. Code § 40-2A-7(b)
Arizona	Suit must be filed with the Tax Court within 30 days after the date of final decision.		Ariz. Rev. Stat. § 42-1254
Arkansas	Suit must be filed with the Circuit Court within one year after date of final determination.	Suit must be filed within 30 days if bond posted rather than tax paid.	Ark. Code Ann. § 26-18-406
California	Suit must be filed in a court of competent jurisdiction in a city or county in which the Attorney General has an office within 90 days after mailing of notice of Board's action.		Cal. Rev. & Tax. Code § 6933
Colorado	Suit must be filed with the District Court within 30 days after the mailing of the determination.		Colo. Rev. Stat. § 39-21-105
Connecticut	Suit must be filed with the Superior Court for the District of New Britain within one month after service of notice.		Conn. Gen. Stat. § 12-422
District of Columbia	Suit must be filed with the Superior Court within six months after date of final determination or denial of refund claim.		D.C. Code Ann. § 47-2021
Florida	Suit must be filed with the Circuit Court within 60 days after date of final assessment, in lieu of proceeding under the Administrative Procedure Act.	Appeal must be filed with the Appellate Court within 30 days of rendition of the order appealed from if proceeding under the APA.	Fla. Stat. § 72.011, Fla. Stat. § 120.68
Georgia	Suit must be filed with the Superior Court within 30 days after date of decision.		Ga. Code Ann. § 48-2-59
Hawaii	Notice of appeal must be filed with the Tax Appeal Court within 30 days after mailing date of notice of assessment if direct review.	Notice of appeal must be filed within 30 days after date decision was filed by State Board of Review if administrative review had been taken.	Haw. Rev. Stat. § 232-17, Haw. Rev. Stat. § 235-114(c), Haw. Rev. Stat. § 237-42
Idaho	Suit must be filed with the District Court within 91 days after notice of redetermination is received.	Within 28 days after Board of Tax Appeals decision is mailed.	Idaho Code § 63-3049, Idaho Code § 63-3812
Illinois	Suit must be filed with the Circuit Court within 35 days after date the administrative decision is served.		735 ILCS 5/3-103, 35 ILCS 120/12

State	Judicial Appeals	Comments	Citation
Indiana	Suit must be filed with the Tax Court within 180 days of issuance of letter of findings.		Ind. Code § 6-8.1-5-1
Iowa	Suit must be filed with the District Court within 30 days after date of State Board's decision.		Iowa Code § 17A.19
Kansas	Suit must be filed with the District Court within 30 days after rehearing order entered or denied by the State Board of Tax Appeals.		Kan. Stat. Ann. § 74-2426, Kan. Stat. Ann. § 77-613
Kentucky	Notice of appeal must be filed with the Kentucky Claims Commission (formerly the Kentucky Board of Tax Appeals) within 30 days of the final order. Statement of appeal must be filed with the Circuit Court within 30 days after notice of appeal is filed.		103 Ky. Admin. Regs. 1:010
Louisiana	Suit must be filed with the District Court within 30 days after decision of Board of Tax Appeals.		La. Rev. Stat. Ann. § 47:1434
Maine	Suit must be filed with the Superior Court within 60 days after receipt of notice.		Me. Rev. Stat. Ann. tit. 36, § 151
Maryland	Suit must be filed with the Circuit Court within 30 days after the latest of: date of action, date of agency's notice of action, or date taxpayer received notice.		Md. Code Ann. § 13-532, Md. Code Regs. 7-203
Massachusetts	Suit must be filed with the Appeals Court within 60 days of entry of judgment of the Board.		Mass. Gen. Laws ch. 58A, § 13, Administrative Procedure 630
Michigan	Suit must be filed with the Court of Claims within 90 days after assessment, decision, or order.	Decisions of the Court of Claims or Tax Tribunal may be appealed to the Court of Appeals.	Mich. Comp. Laws § 205.22(1)
Minnesota	Writ of certiorari must be obtained from the state Supreme Court within 60 days after Tax Court order entered.		Minn. Stat. § 271.10
Mississippi	Suit must be filed with the Chancery Court within 60 days from the date of the Board of Tax Appeal's order.		Miss. Code. Ann. § 27-77-7
Missouri	Suit must be filed with the Court of Appeals within 30 days after notice of final decision mailed or delivered.		Mo. Rev. Stat. § 621.189
Nebraska	Suit must be filed with the District Court within 30 days after service of final decision.		Neb. Rev. Stat. § 84-917

State	Judicial Appeals	Comments	Citation
Nevada	Suit must be filed with the District Court within 30 days of the Commission's decision.		Nev. Rev. Stat. § 360.390, Nev. Rev. Stat. § 233B.130(2)
New Jersey	Suit must be filed with the Tax Court within 90 days of the date of Director's decision.	Tax Court decisions may be appealed to the Appellate Division of the Superior Court.	N.J. Stat. Ann. § 54:51A-14
New Mexico	Suit must be filed with Court of Appeals within 30 days of mailing or delivery of administrative hearing decision.	If administrative hearing not held, suit must be filed with the District Court for Santa Fe County within 90 days after denial of claim or 90 days after expiration of Secretary's time for action.	N.M. Stat. Ann. § 7-1-25, N.M. Stat. Ann. § 7-1-26
New York	Suit must be filed with the Appellate Division of the Supreme Court, Third Division, within four months after notice of determination.		N.Y. Tax Law, § 1138(a)(4), N.Y. Tax Law, § 2016
North Carolina	Suit must be filed with the District Court within 30 days after receipt of decision.		N.C. Gen. Stat. § 105-241.3, N.C. Gen. Stat. § 105-241.4
North Dakota	Appeal must be filed with the District Court within 30 days after notice of Commissioner determination.		N.D. Cent. Code § 57-39.2-16
Ohio	Suit must be filed with the Court of Appeals or State Supreme Court within 30 days after entry of decision in Board's journal.		Ohio Rev. Code Ann. § 5717.04
Oklahoma	Suit must be filed with the State Supreme Court within 30 days after mailing of decision.		Okla. Stat. tit. 68, § 225
Pennsylvania	Appeal must be filed with the Commonwealth Court within 30 days after entry of the order by the Board of Finance and Revenue.		42 Pa. Cons. Stat. § 5571(b)
Rhode Island	Suit must be filed with the Sixth Division of the District Court within 30 days after mailing of notice of final decision.		R.I. Gen. Laws § 44-19-25, R.I. Gen. Laws § 8-8-25
South Carolina	Suit must be filed with the Circuit Court within 30 days of receipt of Administrative Law Judge's decision.		S.C. Code Ann. § 12-60-3380, S.C. Code Ann. § 1-23-610
South Dakota	Suit must be filed with the Circuit Court within 30 days after notice of final decision served.		S.D. Codified Laws § 1-26-31, S.D. Codified Laws § 1-26-31.1
Tennessee	Suit must be filed with the Chancery Court within 90 days after mailing notice of assessment.		Tenn. Code. Ann. § 67-1-1801

State	Judicial Appeals	Comments	Citation
Texas	Suit must be filed with the District Court within 30 days after denial of rehearing motion or within 90 days after filing protest.		Tex. Tax Code Ann. § 112.151, Tex. Tax Code Ann. § 112.052
Utah	Suit must be filed with the District Court within 30 days after mailing notice of agency action.		Utah Code Ann. § 59-1-504, Utah Code Ann. § 59-1-602
Vermont	Appeal must be filed with the Superior Court within 30 days after decision or action of Commissioner.		Vt. Stat. Ann. tit. 32, § 9817
Virginia	Suit must be filed with the Circuit Court within the later of three years after assessment or one year after Commissioner's determination.		Va. Code Ann. § 58.1-1825
Washington	An appeal of a Board of Tax Appeals decision must be filed with the Superior Court within 30 days after the decision. For a tax refund, the appeal must be filed to the superior court of Thurston county, within the time limitation for a refund provided in chapter 82.32 RCW or, if an application for refund has been made to the department within that time limitation, then within 30 days after rejection of the application, whichever is later.		Wash. Rev. Code § 82.03.180, Wash. Rev. Code § 82.32.180
West Virginia	Suit must be filed with the Circuit Court within 60 days after receipt of notice of decision.		W. Va. Code § 11-10-10, W. Va. Code § 11-10A-19
Wisconsin	Petition must be filed within 30 days after service of decision or disposition of rehearing request.		Wis. Stat. § 77.59(6)(b), Wis. Stat. § 227.53(1)
Wyoming	Suit must be filed with the District Court within 30 days after service of decision.		Wyo. Stat. Ann. § 16-3-114(a), Wyo. Rule App. Pro. Rule 12.04

¶ 127   Leases and Rentals of Tangible Personal Property

State	Tangible Personal Property	Comments	Citation
Alabama	Taxable	Subject to a privilege or license tax (rental tax)	Ala. Code § 40-12-222, Ala. Admin. Code r. 810-6-5-.09
Arizona	Taxable		Ariz. Rev. Stat. § 42-5071
Arkansas	Taxable	For rentals of less than 30 days, tax paid on basis of rental payments to lessor, regardless of whether lessor paid sales or use tax at time of purchase of property.	Ark. Code Ann. § 26-52-103, Ark. Code Ann. § 26-53-102
California	Taxable		Cal. Rev. & Tax. Code § 6006(g)
Colorado	Taxable	Exempt if lease/rental for 3 years or less and lessor paid sales/use tax upon acquisition.	Colo. Rev. Stat. § 39-26-102(23)
Connecticut	Taxable		Conn. Gen. Stat. § 12-407(a)(2)(J)
District of Columbia	Taxable		D.C. Code Ann. § 47-2001(n)(1)(F), D.C. Code Ann. § 47-2201(a)(1)(D)
Florida	Taxable		Fla. Stat. § 212.05
Georgia	Taxable		Ga. Code Ann. § 48-8-2(8)
Hawaii	Taxable		Haw. Rev. Stat. § 237-1, Haw. Rev. Stat. § 237-13
Idaho	Taxable		Idaho Code § 63-3612(2)(h)
Illinois	Exempt	Lessors pay use tax upon acquisition. Purported lease to nominal lessee may be subject to retailers' occupation tax.	Ill. Admin. Code tit. 86, § 130.2010(b), Ill. Admin. Code tit. 86, § 150.305(e)
Indiana	Taxable		Ind. Code § 6-2.5-4-10
Iowa	Taxable		Iowa Code § 423.1
Kansas	Taxable		Kan. Stat. Ann. § 79-3603(h), Kan. Admin. Regs. § 92-19-55b
Kentucky	Taxable		103 Ky. Admin. Regs. 28:051
Louisiana	Taxable		La. Rev. Stat. Ann. § 47:302(B)
Maine	Taxable	Only leases deemed by state tax assessor to be in lieu of purchase are treated as sales. In a "straight" lease, lessor pays tax on purchase price, no tax charged to lessee.	Me. Rev. Stat. Ann. tit. 36, § 1752(13)

State	Tangible Personal Property	Comments	Citation
Maryland	Taxable		Md. Regs. Code tit. 3, § 03.06.01.28
Massachusetts	Taxable		Mass. Gen. Laws ch. 64H, § 1
Michigan	Taxable	Lessor may elect to pay use tax on rental/lease receipts in lieu of payment of sales/ use tax on cost of property upon acquisition.	Mich. Comp. Laws § 205.51(1)(b), Mich. Comp. Laws § 205.95(4)
Minnesota	Taxable		Minn. Stat. § 297A.61(3) and (4), Minn. Stat. § 297A.62
Mississippi	Taxable		Miss. Code. Ann. § 27-65-23
Missouri	Taxable		Mo. Rev. Stat. § 144.020(1)(8)
Nebraska	Taxable		Neb. Rev. Stat. § 77-2701.33
Nevada	Taxable	Only leases deemed by Tax Commission to be in lieu of a transfer of title, exchange, or barter are treated as sales.	Nev. Rev. Stat. § 372.060
New Jersey	Taxable		N.J. Stat. Ann. § 54:32B-2
New Mexico	Taxable		N.M. Admin. Code tit. 3, § 3.2.1.17
New York	Taxable		N.Y. Tax Law, § 1101(b)(5)
North Carolina	Taxable		N.C. Gen. Stat. § 105-164.4(a)(2)
North Dakota	Taxable	Rental is not taxable if the lessor paid tax on the purchase of the property.	N.D. Cent. Code § 57-39.2-02.1, N.D. Cent. Code § 57-39.2-04(28)
Ohio	Taxable		Ohio Rev. Code Ann. § 5739.01(H)(1)
Oklahoma	Taxable		Okla. Stat. tit. 68, § 1354(A)(17)
Pennsylvania	Taxable		72 P.S. § 7201(k), 72 P.S. § 7237
Rhode Island	Taxable	Lessor may elect to pay tax on cost of property upon acquisition or collect tax on total rental/lease charges.	R.I. Gen. Laws § 44-18-7(1), R.I. Gen. Laws § 44-18-7.1(o)
South Carolina	Taxable	70% of gross proceeds from the rental of portable toilets are exempt.	S.C. Code Ann. § 12-36-100, S.C. Code Ann. § 12-36-2120(62)
South Dakota	Taxable		S.D. Codified Laws § 10-45-5, S.D. Codified Laws § 10-46-2.2
Tennessee	Taxable		Tenn. Code Ann. § 67-6-204

State	Tangible Personal Property	Comments	Citation
Texas	Taxable		Tex. Tax Code Ann. § 151.005
Utah	Taxable		Utah Code Ann. § 59-12-102
Vermont	Taxable	Rentals of furniture in furnished apartments or houses for residential use are exempt.	Vt. Stat. Ann. tit. 32, § 9701(4), Vt. Stat. Ann. tit. 32, § 9741(17)
Virginia	Taxable		Va. Code Ann. § 58.1-603
Washington	Taxable		Wash. Rev. Code § 82.04.050
West Virginia	Taxable		W. Va. Code § 11-15-2(b)(16)
Wisconsin	Taxable		Wis. Stat. § 77.52
Wyoming	Taxable		Wyo. Stat. Ann. § 39-15-103(a)(i)

¶ 128   **Managed Audit Programs**

The following chart indicates whether a state has a managed audit program. Managed audits allow a taxpayer (or qualified third party) to perform an audit under guidelines set by the state.

State	Managed Audit Programs	Comments	Citation
Alabama	No		
Arizona	Yes	Managed audit applications may be submitted beginning in 2006.	Ariz. Rev. Stat. § 42-2302
Arkansas	No		
California	Yes	Pilot program terminated 1/1/03. New program in effect beginning 1/1/04.	Cal. Rev. & Tax. Code § 7076
Colorado	Yes		Colorado Department of Revenue Website
Connecticut	Yes		Informational Publication 2001(8), Connecticut Department of Revenue Services, May 2001
District of Columbia	No		
Florida	Yes	State offers Certified Audit Program. Certified audits must be performed by qualified third parties.	Fla. Stat. § 213.285
Georgia	Yes	Managed audit agreement is unique for each taxpayer.	Audit Administrator, Georgia Department of Revenue
Hawaii	No		E-mail, Hawaii Department of Taxation
Idaho	Yes	Taxpayers seeking information on managed audits should contact Idaho State Tax Commission.	Unofficial department guidance
Illinois	No		
Indiana	No		
Iowa	No		
Kansas	Yes		Kan. Stat. Ann. § 79-3661
Kentucky	No		
Louisiana	No		
Maine	No	State has no formal provisions but Maine Revenue Services may make informal arrangements to permit the taxpayer to perform some audit procedures.	

State	Managed Audit Programs	Comments	Citation
Maryland	Yes		E-mail, Maryland Comptroller's Office, January 12, 2006, Revenews
Massachusetts	No		
Michigan	Yes	Taxpayers seeking information on managed audits should contact Department of Treasury Audit Discovery Division.	E-mail, Michigan Department of Treasury, November 2005
Minnesota	No	Field auditors may allow taxpayers to examine their own records during the course of a field audit if the auditor believes the taxpayer understands the issue to be examined.	E-mail, Minnesota Department of Revenue
Mississippi	No		
Missouri	No		
Nebraska	No		Managed Audit Survey, Nebraska Department of Revenue, December 20, 2016
Nevada	No		
New Jersey	No	New Jersey utilizes an "effective use tax rate program."	
New Mexico	Yes		N.M. Stat. Ann. § 7-1-11.1
New York	No		
North Carolina	Yes	Generally limited to businesses that do not make a large number of retail sales.	Unofficial department guidance
North Dakota	No		E-mail, North Dakota Office of State Tax Commissioner
Ohio	Yes		Managed Audits/Sales & Use Tax, Ohio Department of Taxation, April 1, 2001
Oklahoma	No		
Pennsylvania	Yes		Pennsylvania Tax Update No. 115, Sales and Use Tax Bulletin No. 2013-01
Rhode Island	Yes		R.I. Gen. Laws § 44-19-43
South Carolina	No		E-mail, South Carolina Department of Revenue, October 1, 2009
South Dakota	No		

¶ 129   Manufacturing—Machinery

The following chart does not include office equipment.

State	Machinery	Comments	Citation
Alabama	Taxable	Taxed at a reduced rate.	Ala. Code § 40-23-2(3)
Arizona	Exempt	Exempt if used directly in manufacturing, processing, fabricating, job printing, refining or metallurgical operations.	Ariz. Rev. Stat. § 42-5061(B)(1)
Arkansas	Taxable	Exemptions available for certain replacement and repair of machinery and equipment and purchases used in new or expanding facility.	Ark. Code Ann. § 26-52-402
California	Exempt	Operative July 1, 2014, and before July 1, 2022, an exemption is applicable to the gross receipts from the sale, storage, use, or other consumption in California of certain qualified tangible personal property, including machinery and equipment, purchased for use by certain qualified persons to be used primarily in any stage of manufacturing, processing, refining, fabricating, or recycling of tangible personal property.	Reg. 1525, 18 CCR, Cal. Rev. & Tax. Code § 6377.1
Colorado	Exempt	Purchase must be over $500. Exemption limited to $150,000 for qualifying purchases of used machinery.	Colo. Rev. Stat. § 39-26-114(11)
Connecticut	Exempt		Conn. Gen. Stat. § 12-412(34)
District of Columbia	Taxable		D.C. Code Ann. § 47-2001(n)(1)
Florida	Exempt	Florida provides an exemption for industrial machinery and equipment purchased by eligible manufacturing businesses. There are also exemptions for industrial M&E used exclusively for spaceport activities or to manufacture, process, compound, or produce tangible personal property for sale (limited to new or expanding businesses), industrial M&E used under federal procurement contracts, and industrial M&E used in semiconductor, defense, or space technology production.	Fla. Stat. § 212.05(1)(f), Fla. Stat. § 212.08(5)(b), (5)(d), (5)(j) and (7)(kkk)
Georgia	Exempt		Ga. Code Ann. § 48-8-3.2, Ga. Comp. R. & Regs. 560-12-2-.62
Hawaii	Taxable		Haw. Rev. Stat. § 237-13
Idaho	Exempt		Idaho Code § 63-3622D
Illinois	Exempt		35 ILCS 120/2-5
Indiana	Exempt		Ind. Code § 6-2.5-5-3

State	Machinery	Comments	Citation
Iowa	Exempt		Iowa Code 423.3(47)
Kansas	Exempt		Kan. Stat. Ann. § 79-3606(kk)
Kentucky	Taxable	Exemption available for purchases used in new and expanded industry. Refund available for purchases of energy-efficiency machinery or equipment used at a Kentucky manufacturing plant for an energy efficiency project.	Ky. Rev. Stat. Ann. § 139.480(10), Ky. Rev. Stat. Ann. § 139.518
Louisiana	Exempt	Caution: Numerous exemptions are suspended from April 1, 2016, to June 30, 2018. For chart of suspended exemptions and applicable tax rates, see Publication R-1002A.	La. Rev. Stat. Ann. § 47:301(13)(k), LA DOR Publication R-1002A
Maine	Exempt	Exemption available for specific activities.	Me. Rev. Stat. Ann. tit. 36, § 1760(31)
Maryland	Exempt		Md. Code Ann. § 11-210(b)(1)
Massachusetts	Exempt		Mass. Gen. Laws ch. 64H, § 6(s)
Michigan	Exempt		Mich. Comp. Laws § 205.54t
Minnesota	Exempt	Capital equipment exemption.	Minn. Stat. § 297A.68(5)
Mississippi	Taxable	Taxed at a reduced rate. Special rate for manufacturing machinery used at refinery.	Miss. Code. Ann. § 27-65-17(1), Miss. Code. Ann. § 27-65-24
Missouri	Exempt		Mo. Code Regs. tit. 12, § 10-111.010
Nebraska	Exempt	Exemption includes repair and replacement parts and purchases of installation, repair, or maintenance services performed on exempt machinery.	Neb. Rev. Stat. § 77-2704.22, Neb. Rev. Stat. § 77-2701.47, Neb. Admin. Code § 1-023.05, Information Guide 6-441-2005
Nevada	Taxable		Nev. Admin. Code § 372.370
New Jersey	Exempt		N.J. Stat. Ann. § 54:32B-8.13(a)
New Mexico	Taxable	Credit available for certain machinery.	N.M. Stat. Ann. § 7-9A-5
New York	Exempt		N.Y. Tax Law, § 1115(a)(12)
North Carolina	Taxable	Effective January 1, 2006, mill machinery and mill machinery parts and accessories exempt from sales and use tax but subject to privilege tax at rate of 1% of sales price, maximum $80 per article.	N.C. Gen. Stat. § 105-164.4(a)(1d)
North Dakota	Taxable	Exemption available for certain purchases used in new or expanding plant.	N.D. Cent. Code § 57-39.2-04.3
Ohio	Exempt		Ohio Rev. Code Ann. § 5739.011
Oklahoma	Exempt		Okla. Stat. tit. 68, § 1359

State	Machinery	Comments	Citation
Pennsylvania	Exempt		72 P.S. § 7201(k)(8)
Rhode Island	Exempt		R.I. Gen. Laws § 44-18-30(22)
South Carolina	Exempt		S.C. Code Ann. § 12-36-2120(17)
South Dakota	Taxable		S.D. Admin. R. 64:06:03:23
Tennessee	Exempt		Tenn. Code. Ann. § 67-6-206(a)
Texas	Exempt		Tex. Tax Code Ann. § 151.318
Utah	Exempt	Machinery and equipment that is used to manufacture an item sold as tangible personal property and that has an economic life of three or more years is exempt. Certain machinery and equipment used in the amusement industry.	Utah Code Ann. § 59-12-104
Vermont	Exempt		Vt. Stat. Ann. tit. 32, § 9741(14)
Virginia	Exempt		Va. Code Ann. § 58.1-609.3(2), 23 Va. Admin. Code § 10-210-920
Washington	Exempt	The exemption does not apply to machinery and equipment primarily used for activities taxable under the state public utility tax.	Wash. Rev. Code § 82.08.02565
West Virginia	Exempt		W. Va. Code § 11-15-2(b)(4)
Wisconsin	Exempt		Wis. Stat. § 77.54(6)
Wyoming	Exempt	Exemption effective beginning July 1, 2004.	Wyo. Stat. Ann. § 39-15-105(a)(viii)(O)

Manufacturing—Raw Materials

State	Raw Materials	Comments	Citation
Alabama	Exempt	Materials that do not become an ingredient or component of manufactured tangible personal property for sale are taxable.	Ala. Code § 40-23-1
Arizona	Exempt	Tax applies to materials that are consumed but not incorporated into manufactured property. Materials incorporated into manufactured property qualify for resale exemption.	Ariz. Rev. Stat. § 42-5159(A)(4), Ariz. Admin. Code § 15-5-122
Arkansas	Exempt	Resale exemption applies to materials that do become a recognizable integral part of the product. Other materials are taxable.	Ark. Code Ann. § 26-52-401(12), Ark. Reg. GR-53
California	Exempt	Tax applies to materials that are consumed but not incorporated into manufactured property manufactured.	Reg. 1525, 18 CCR, Reg. 1525.5, 18 CCR
Colorado	Exempt	Sales of materials that will become ingredients or components of manufactured property are wholesale sales. Materials used as an aid in manufacturing are taxable.	Colo. Rev. Stat. § 39-26-102(20), Colo. Code Regs. § 39-26-713.2
Connecticut	Exempt	Exemption applies to materials that become an ingredient or component of manufactured property or are used directly in an industrial plant in the actual fabrication of finished products to be sold.	Conn. Gen. Stat. § 12-412(18), Conn. Agencies Regs. § 12-412(18)-1
District of Columbia	Exempt	Resale exemption applies to materials that will be incorporated into manufactured property. Other materials are taxable.	D.C. Code Ann. § 47-2001(n)(1), D.C. Mun. Regs. t. 9, § 414.1
Florida	Exempt	Materials must become an ingredient component of the finished product.	Fla. Stat. § 212.02(14)(c), Fla. Admin. Code Ann. r. 12A-1.063
Georgia	Exempt		Ga. Code Ann. § 48-8-3.2, Ga. Comp. R. & Regs. 560-12-2-.62
Hawaii	Taxable	Sales to a licensed manufacturer of materials that will be incorporated into a saleable product are taxed at the wholesale rate.	Haw. Rev. Stat. § 237-4(a)(2)
Idaho	Exempt		Idaho Code § 63-3622D(b), IDAPA 35.01.02.079
Illinois	Exempt	Materials that are consumed but not physically incorporated into manufactured property are taxable.	35 ILCS120/1, Ill. Admin. Code tit. 86, § 130.210

State	Raw Materials	Comments	Citation
Indiana	Exempt		Ind. Code § 6-2.5-5-6, Ind. Admin. Code tit. 45, r. 2.2-5-14
Iowa	Exempt		Iowa Code § 423.3
Kansas	Exempt		Kan. Stat. Ann. § 79-3606(m), Kan. Admin. Regs. 92-19-54
Kentucky	Exempt		Ky. Rev. Stat. Ann. § 139.470(10)
Louisiana	Exempt	Caution: Numerous exemptions are suspended from April 1, 2016, to June 30, 2018. For chart of suspended exemptions and applicable tax rates, see Publication R-1002A.	La. Rev. Stat. Ann. § 47:301(10)(c), La. Admin. Code tit. 47, § 4301, LA DOR Publication R-1002A
Maine	Exempt		Me. Rev. Stat. Ann. tit. 36, § 1760(74)
Maryland	Exempt		Md. Code Ann. § 11-101
Massachusetts	Exempt		Mass. Gen. Laws ch. 64H, § 6(r)
Michigan	Exempt		Mich. Comp. Laws § 205.54t
Minnesota	Exempt		Minn. Stat. § 297A.68(2), Minn. R. 8130.5500
Mississippi	Exempt		Miss. Code. Ann. § 27-65-101(b), Miss. Rule 35.IV.7.03
Missouri	Exempt		Mo. Rev. Stat. § 144.030(2), Mo. Code Regs. Ann. tit. 12, § 10-110.200
Nebraska	Exempt		Neb. Admin. Code § 1-006, Neb. Admin. Code § 1-023
Nevada	Exempt		Nev. Rev. Stat. § 372.370
New Jersey	Exempt	Exemption applies to materials that become a component of a product and to essential materials used to cause a chemical or refining process.	N.J. Stat. Ann. § 54:32B-11(4), N.J. Stat. Ann. § 54:32B-8.20, N.J. Admin. Code § 18:24-4.5
New Mexico	Exempt		N.M. Stat. Ann. § 7-9-46
New York	Exempt		N.Y. Tax Law, § 1118(4)
North Carolina	Exempt	Materials must become an ingredient or component of manufactured property.	N.C. Gen. Stat. § 105-164.13(8)
North Dakota	Exempt		N.D. Cent. Code § 57-39.2-01(21)
Ohio	Exempt	Exemption applies to materials that are incorporated as components of manufactured property or are consumed directly in producing tangible personal property.	Ohio Rev. Code Ann. § 5739.02, Ohio Rev. Code Ann. § 5739.011
Oklahoma	Exempt		Okla. Stat. tit. 68, § 1359(1)

State	Raw Materials	Comments	Citation
Pennsylvania	Exempt	Exemption applies to property predominantly used directly in manufacturing. Materials that will be incorporated as ingredients or components of manufactured products qualify for resale exemption.	72 P.S. § 7201(k)(8), 61 Pa. Code § 32.32
Rhode Island	Exempt		R.I. Gen. Laws § 44-18-30(7), R.I. Code R. SU 07-58
South Carolina	Exempt		S.C. Code Ann. § 12-36-120, S.C. Code Ann. Regs. § 117-302.1
South Dakota	Exempt		S.D. Codified Laws § 10-46-9, S.D. Admin. R. 64:06:03:23
Tennessee	Exempt		Tenn. Comp. R. & Regs. 1320-5-1-.40
Texas	Exempt	Exemption applies to materials that become an ingredient or component of manufactured property. Materials directly consumed in manufacturing are exempt if they are necessary for the operation or cause a chemical or physical change to the product.	Tex. Tax Code Ann. § 151.318(a), 34 Tex. Admin. Code § 3.300
Utah	Exempt		Utah Code Ann. § 59-12-104(26)
Vermont	Exempt		Vt. Stat. Ann. tit. 32, § 9741(14), Vt. Code R. 1.9741(14)-1
Virginia	Exempt		Va. Code Ann. § 58.1-609.3(2), 23 Va. Admin. Code § 10-210-920
Washington	Exempt		Wash. Rev. Code § 82.04.050, Wash. Admin. Code § 458-20-113
West Virginia	Exempt		W. Va. Code § 11-15-3(a), W. Va. Code R. § 110-15-123.4.4.2
Wisconsin	Exempt		Wis. Stat. § 77.54(2), Wis. Admin. Code § 11.41
Wyoming	Exempt		Wyo. Stat. Ann. § 39-15-105(a)(iii)(A)

¶ 131   **Manufacturing—Utilities/Fuel**

State	Utilities/Fuel	Comments	Citation
Alabama	Taxable	Wood residue, coke, or coal sold to manufacturers, or stored by manufacturers, exempt.	Ala. Code § 40-23-4(a)(9), Ala. Code § 40-23-62(11), Ala. Code § 40-23-4(a)(14)
Arizona	Taxable		Ariz. Rev. Stat. § 42-5008(A)
Arkansas	Taxable	Natural gas and electricity used by manufacturers directly in manufacturing process or used by certain electric power generators taxed at reduced rate. Natural gas and electricity purchased for use in steel manufacturing or in tile manufacturing tile are exempt.	Ark. Code Ann. § 26-52-301, Ark. Code Ann. § 26-52-319
California	Exempt	Gas, electricity, and water, including steam, geothermal steam, brines, and heat are exempt when delivered to consumers through mains, lines, or pipes. Fuel oil is taxable.	Cal. Rev. & Tax. Code § 6353, SUTA Series 275
Colorado	Exempt	Temporarily taxable effective March 1, 2010 through June 30, 2012, with exceptions for (1) fuel or energy used for agricultural purposes, railroad transportation services, or the generation of electricity; (2) gas for electricity for residential use, and (3) gasoline and special fuel that is subject to excise tax.	Colo. Rev. Stat. § 39-26-102(21)
Connecticut	Exempt	Gas, electricity and heating fuel must be used in metered premises and 75% of gas electricity or fuel, or 75% of premises, must be used for manufacturing.	Conn. Gen. Stat. § 12-412(3)(A)
District of Columbia	Exempt		D.C. Code Ann. § 47-2005(11)
Florida	Exempt		Fla. Stat. § 212.08(7)(b), Fla. Stat. § 212.08(7)(ff)
Georgia	Taxable	Electricity used directly in manufacture of product is exempt if cost of electricity exceeds 50% of cost of all materials used in product, including electricity. From July 1, 2008, to December 31, 2010, partial exemption applies to certain fuels used in manufacturing or processing tangible personal property for resale.	Ga. Code Ann. § 48-8-3(35), Ga. Code Ann. § 48-8-2(6)(B)(ii), Ga. Code Ann. § 48-8-3(70.1)

State	Utilities/Fuel	Comments	Citation
Hawaii	Taxable	Certain utilities exempt from general excise tax, subject to public service company tax.	Haw. Rev. Stat. § 237-13, Haw. Rev. Stat. § 237-23(a)(1) and (2), Haw. Rev. Stat. § 239-5
Idaho	Exempt	Matter used to produce heat by burning, including wood, coal, petroleum and gas is exempt.	Idaho Code § 63-3622G
Illinois	Exempt		35 ILCS 105/3, 35 ILCS 110/2, 35 ILCS 115/2, 35 ILCS 120/2
Indiana	Exempt		Ind. Code § 6-2.5-2-1
Iowa	Exempt		Iowa Code § 423.3(47) and (51)
Kansas	Exempt		Kan. Stat. Ann. § 79-3606(n)
Kentucky	Exempt	Energy and energy producing fuels used in manufacturing, processing, refining, or fabricating exempt to the extent that cost of the energy or fuel exceeds 3% of the cost of production.	Ky. Rev. Stat. Ann. § 139.480(3)
Louisiana	Exempt	Purchases of electricity, natural gas, water, and steam are exempt. Fuel and gas are excluded from tax. Dyed diesel fuel for off-road use is taxable. Caution: Numerous exemptions are suspended from April 1, 2016, to June 30, 2018. For chart of suspended exemptions and applicable tax rates, see Publication R-1002A.	La. Rev. Stat. Ann. § 47:301(10)(C), LA DOR Publication R-1002A
Maine	Exempt	95% of sale price of fuel and electricity used at manufacturing facility exempt.	Me. Rev. Stat. Ann. tit. 36, § 1760(9-D)
Maryland	Exempt		Md. Code Regs. 03.06.01.10(A)
Massachusetts	Exempt		Mass. Gen. Laws ch. 64H, § 6(r)
Michigan	Exempt		Mich. Comp. Laws § 205.54t
Minnesota	Exempt	Transportation, transmission, or distribution of certain fuels through pipes, lines, tanks, or mains taxable.	Minn. Stat. § 297A.68(2)

State	Utilities/Fuel	Comments	Citation
Mississippi	Taxable	Reduced rate applies to electricity, current, power, steam, coal, natural gas, liquefied petroleum gas, or other fuel sold to or used by a qualified technology intensive enterprise. Fuel, electricity, and natural gas used directly in manufacture of motor vehicles exempt. Electricity used directly in electrolysis process in sodium chlorate production exempt. Effective July 1, 2014, exemption allowed for electricity, current, power, steam, coal, natural gas, liquefied petroleum gas, or other fuel sold to certain manufacturers; poultry, livestock, fish, milk, other food producers or processors; and commercial fishermen.	Miss. Code. Ann. § 27-65-101(1), Miss. Code. Ann. § 27-65-107(f), (g), (h)
Missouri	Exempt		Mo. Rev. Stat. § 144.030(12), Mo. Rev. Stat. § 144.054
Nebraska	Exempt	Electricity, gas, coal, corn and wood used as fuel, fuel oil, diesel fuel, propane, gasoline, coke, nuclear fuel, and butane exempt if more than 50% of amount purchased is used directly in processing, manufacturing, or refining.	Neb. Rev. Stat. § 77-2704.13
Nevada	Taxable	Gas, electricity, and water, when delivered to consumers through mains, lines, or pipes, are exempt. "Domestic fuels," including wood, coal, petroleum, and gas, are exempt. Purchases of tangible personal property that will be incorporated into a manufactured article to be sold are exempt.	Nev. Admin. Code § 372.370, Nev. Rev. Stat. § 372.295, Nev. Rev. Stat. § 374.300, Nev. Rev. Stat. § 372.300
New Jersey	Exempt	The purchase of natural gas distributed through a pipeline, electricity, and utility service is taxable.	N.J. Stat. Ann. § 54:32B-8.46, N.J. Admin. Code § 18:24-4.3
New Mexico	Exempt	100% of receipts received on or after January 1, 2017, and 80% of receipts received in calendar year 2016.	N.M. Stat. Ann. § 7-9-46
New York	Exempt		N.Y. Tax Law, § 1115(c)
North Carolina	Exempt	The exemption for electricity sold to a manufacturer is inapplicable to electricity used at a facility at which the primary activity is not manufacturing.	N.C. Gen. Stat. § 105-164.4, N.C. Gen. Stat. § 105-164.13(57)

State	Utilities/Fuel	Comments	Citation
North Dakota	Taxable	Exemptions include natural gas and fuels used for heating purposes, steam used for agricultural processing, electricity, and water.	N.D. Cent. Code § 57-39.2-02.1(1)(b), N.D. Cent. Code § 57-39.2-04(27), N.D. Cent. Code § 57-39.2-04(53), Guideline - Sales Tax Exemptions
Ohio	Exempt		Ohio Rev. Code Ann. § 5739.02
Oklahoma	Exempt		Okla. Admin. Code § 710:65-13-150.1
Pennsylvania	Exempt	Exempt if predominantly used directly in manufacturing or processing operations.	72 P.S. § 7201(k)(8), 61 Pa. Code § 32.32, 61 Pa. Code § 41.5
Rhode Island	Exempt		R.I. Gen. Laws § 44-18-30(7)
South Carolina	Exempt		S.C. Code Ann. § 12-36-2120
South Dakota	Taxable		S.D. Admin. R. 64:06:03:24
Tennessee	Taxable	Effective July 1, 2015, a special user privilege tax is imposed in lieu of sales and use tax. Until July 1, 2015, generally subject to tax at a reduced rate. Certain specified exemptions apply.	Tenn. Code Ann. § 67-6-206
Texas	Exempt	Gas and electricity directly used in manufacturing exempt.	34 Tex. Admin. Code § 3.300
Utah	Exempt		Utah Code Ann. § 59-12-104(42)
Vermont	Exempt		Vt. Stat. Ann. tit. 32, § 9741(34)
Virginia	Exempt		Va. Code Ann. § 58.1-609.3, 23 Va. Admin. Code § 10-210-920
Washington	Taxable		Wash. Admin. Code § 458-20-113
West Virginia	Exempt	Gasoline and special fuels taxable.	W. Va. Code § 11-15-9(b)(2)
Wisconsin	Exempt		Wis. Stat. § 77.54(30)(a)(6)
Wyoming	Exempt		Wyo. Stat. Ann. § 39-15-105(a)(iii)(A)

¶ 132   **Medical Devices**

The types of medical devices that are exempt vary greatly from state to state. Some states limit the exemption to prosthetic devices (which replace organic material), while others include durable medical equipment and mobility enhancing equipment in the exemption.

State	Medical Devices	Comments	Citation
Alabama	Taxable	Certain devices exempt if payment made by Medicare/Medicaid.	Ala. Code § 40-9-30, Ala. Admin. Code r. 810-6-3-.37.03
Arizona	Exempt	Prescription required.	Ariz. Rev. Stat. § 42-5061(A)
Arkansas	Exempt	Prescription required.	Ark. Code Ann. § 26-52-433
California	Exempt	Prescription required.	Cal. Rev. & Tax. Code § 6369
Colorado	Exempt	If price greater than $100, prescription required.	Colo. Rev. Stat. § 39-26-114(1)(a)(V)
Connecticut	Exempt		Conn. Gen. Stat. § 12-412(19)
District of Columbia	Exempt	Prescription required for some devices.	D.C. Code Ann. § 47-2005(15)
Florida	Exempt	Prescription required.	Fla. Stat. § 212.08(2)
Georgia	Exempt	Exemptions apply to the sale or use of any durable medical equipment or prosthetic device sold or used pursuant to a prescription, and to the sale or use of all mobility enhancing equipment prescribed by a physician.	Ga. Code Ann. § 48-8-3(54), (72)
Hawaii	Exempt	Prescription required.	Haw. Rev. Stat. § 237-24.3(6)(B)
Idaho	Exempt	Prescription required.	Idaho Code § 63-3622N(a)
Illinois	Taxable	Taxed at 1% reduced rate.	35 ILCS 120/2-10
Indiana	Exempt	Prescription required.	Ind. Code § 6-2.5-5-18
Iowa	Exempt	Prescription required for some devices.	Iowa Code § 423.3(60)
Kansas	Exempt	Prescription required.	Kan. Stat. Ann. § 79-3606(r)
Kentucky	Exempt	Prescription generally required.	Ky. Rev. Stat. Ann. § 139.472
Louisiana	Exempt	Prescription required. Caution: Numerous exemptions are suspended from April 1, 2016, to June 30, 2018. For chart of suspended exemptions and applicable tax rates, see Publication R-1002A.	La. Rev. Stat. Ann. § 47:305(D)(1)
Maine	Exempt		Me. Rev. Stat. Ann. tit. 36, § 1760

State	Medical Devices	Comments	Citation
Maryland	Exempt	A prescription is required for certain surgical or orthopedic devices.	Md. Code Regs. 3 03.06.01.09, Md. Code Ann. § 11-211
Massachusetts	Exempt	Prescription required for some devices.	Mass. Gen. Laws ch. 64H, § 6
Michigan	Exempt	Prescription required.	Mich. Comp. Laws § 205.54a(1)(h), Mich. Comp. Laws § 205.92b
Minnesota	Exempt	Durable medical equipment taxable unless sold for home use or if paid for or reimbursed by Medicare or Medicaid, regardless of whether sold for home use.	Minn. Stat. § 297A.67(7), Sales Tax Fact Sheet 117B
Mississippi	Exempt	Exemptions allowed for durable medical equipment, home medical supplies, prosthetics, orthotics, hearing aids, hearing devices, prescription eyeglasses, oxygen, and oxygen equipment if prescribed and if other requirements are met. Payment not required to be made by any particular person.	Miss. Code. Ann. § 27-65-105(g), Miss. Code. Ann. § 27-65-111(dd)
Missouri	Exempt	Effective August 28, 2016, all sales, rentals, repairs, and parts of durable medical equipment are also exempt, as well as for parts for certain types of health care related equipment.	Mo. Rev. Stat. § 144.030(19)
Nebraska	Exempt	For mobility enhancing equipment, a prescription is required. For durable medical equipment, home medical supplies, oxygen equipment, and prosthetic devices, a prescription is required and they must be of the type eligible for coverage under the medical assistance program established pursuant to the Medical Assistance Act.	Neb. Rev. Stat. § 77-2704.09
Nevada	Exempt		Nev. Rev. Stat. § 372.283, SST Matrix
New Jersey	Exempt		N.J. Stat. Ann. § 54:32B-8.1
New Mexico	Taxable	Exempt only if delivered by a licensed practitioner incidental to the provision of a service and the value of the device is included in the cost of the service.	N.M. Stat. Ann. § 7-9-73

State	Medical Devices	Comments	Citation
New York	Exempt		N.Y. Tax Law, § 1115(a)(3), (4)
North Carolina	Exempt	Prescription required for some devices.	N.C. Gen. Stat. § 105-164.13(12)
North Dakota	Exempt		N.D. Cent. Code § 57-39.2-04(26)
Ohio	Exempt	Prescription required. Medical oxygen and medical oxygen-dispensing equipment, not sold for home use, is also exempt when purchased by hospitals, nursing homes, or other medical facilities, regardless of whether the sale is made pursuant to a prescription.	Ohio Rev. Code Ann. § 5739.02(B)(19), Ohio Rev. Code Ann. § 5739.02(B)(18)
Oklahoma	Taxable	Some devices exempt; others exempt if prescribed and payment made under Medicare/Medicaid.	Okla. Stat. tit. 68, § 1357(22), Okla. Stat. tit. 68, § 1357.6
Pennsylvania	Exempt		72 P.S. § 7204(17)
Rhode Island	Exempt		R.I. Gen. Laws § 44-18-30(11), R.I. Code R. SU 07-30
South Carolina	Exempt	Some devices are exempt only if sold under a prescription.	S.C. Code Ann. § 12-36-2120
South Dakota	Exempt	Prescription required.	S.D. Codified Laws § 10-45-14.12
Tennessee	Exempt		Tenn. Code. Ann. § 67-6-314
Texas	Exempt	Prescription required for some devices.	Tex. Tax Code Ann. § 151.313
Utah	Exempt	Prescription required.	Utah Code Ann. § 59-12-104(38)
Vermont	Exempt		Vt. Stat. Ann. tit. 32, § 9741(2)
Virginia	Exempt		Va. Code Ann. § 58.1-609.7(15)
Washington	Taxable	Some devices exempt if sold under prescription.	Wash. Rev. Code § 82.08.0283
West Virginia	Exempt	Prescription required.	W. Va. Code § 11-15-9(a)(11)
Wisconsin	Exempt	Durable medical equipment must be for use in a person's home to qualify for exemption.	Wis. Stat. § 77.54(22b)
Wyoming	Exempt		Wyo. Stat. Ann. § 39-15-105(vi)(B)

Medical Services

State	Medical Services	Comments	Citation
Alabama	Exempt		Ala. Code § 40-23-2
Arizona	Exempt		Ariz. Rev. Stat. § 42-5061(A)
Arkansas	Exempt		Ark. Code Ann. § 26-52-301(3)
California	Exempt		Cal. Rev. & Tax. Code § 6051
Colorado	Exempt		Colo. Rev. Stat. § 39-26-104
Connecticut	Exempt		Conn. Gen. Stat. § 12-412(11)
District of Columbia	Exempt		D.C. Code Ann. § 47-2001(n)(2)(B)
Florida	Exempt		Fla. Stat. § 212.08(7)(v)
Georgia	Exempt		Ga. Code Ann. § 48-8-3(22)
Hawaii	Taxable		Haw. Rev. Stat. § 237-13(6)
Idaho	Exempt		IDAPA 35.01.02.011.02
Illinois	Exempt		Ill. Admin. Code tit. 86, § 130.120(d)
Indiana	Exempt		Ind. Admin. Code tit. 45 r. 2.2-4-2
Iowa	Exempt		Iowa Code § 423.2(6)
Kansas	Exempt		Kan. Stat. Ann. § 79-3603
Kentucky	Exempt		Ky. Rev. Stat. Ann. § 139.200
Louisiana	Exempt	Caution: Numerous exemptions are suspended from April 1, 2016, to June 30, 2018. For chart of suspended exemptions and applicable tax rates, see Publication R-1002A.	La. Rev. Stat. Ann. § 47:301(14), LA DOR Publication R-1002A
Maine	Exempt		Me. Rev. Stat. Ann. tit. 36, § 1752(17-A)
Maryland	Exempt		Md. Code Regs. 03.06.01.01(A)
Massachusetts	Exempt		Mass. Gen. Laws ch. 64H, § 1
Michigan	Exempt		Mich. Comp. Laws § 205.52(1), Mich. Comp. Laws § 205.93f
Minnesota	Exempt		Minn. Stat. § 297A.61(3)
Mississippi	Exempt		Miss. Code. Ann. § 27-65-23
Missouri	Exempt		Mo. Rev. Stat. § 144.020
Nebraska	Exempt		Neb. Admin. Code § 1-051.01

State	Medical Services	Comments	Citation
Nevada	Exempt		Nev. Rev. Stat. § 372.105
New Jersey	Exempt		N.J. Stat. Ann. § 54:32B-2(e)(4)(A)
New Mexico	Taxable	Receipts from payments by federal government exempt. Health care practitioners may deduct from gross receipts payments they receive from managed health care providers or health care insurers for commercial contract services or Medicare Part C services provided by a health care practitioner. Receipts from fee-for-service payments by a health care insurer do not qualify.	N.M. Stat. Ann. § 7-9-4, N.M. Stat. Ann. § 7-9-77.1, N.M. Stat. Ann. § 7-9-93
New York	Exempt		N.Y. Tax Law, § 1105(c)
North Carolina	Exempt		N.C. Gen. Stat. § 105-164.4
North Dakota	Exempt		N.D. Admin. Code § 81-04.1-01-22
Ohio	Exempt	Health care services provided or arranged by a Medicaid health-insuring corporation for Medicaid enrollees residing in Ohio under the corporation's contract with the state are taxable. The corporation will receive a direct payment permit and remit taxes directly to the state.	Ohio Rev. Code Ann. § 5739.01(B), Ohio Rev. Code Ann. § 5739.051
Oklahoma	Exempt		Okla. Stat. tit. 68, § 1354
Pennsylvania	Exempt		61 Pa. Code § 31.6
Rhode Island	Exempt		R.I. Code R. SU 87-77
South Carolina	Exempt		S.C. Code Ann. Regs. 117-308.1
South Dakota	Exempt		S.D. Admin. R. 64:06:02:53
Tennessee	Exempt		Tenn. Comp. R. & Regs. 1320-5-1-.47
Texas	Exempt		Tex. Tax Code Ann. § 151.0101
Utah	Exempt		Utah Code Ann. § 59-12-103
Vermont	Exempt		Vt. Stat. Ann. tit. 32, § 9771
Virginia	Exempt		23 Va. Admin. Code § 10-210-2060
Washington	Exempt		Wash. Admin. Code § 458-20-138

¶133

State	Medical Services	Comments	Citation
West Virginia	Exempt		W. Va. Code R. § 110-15-8
Wisconsin	Exempt		Wis. Admin. Code § 11.67(3)
Wyoming	Exempt		Wyo. Stat. Ann. § 39-15-103

¶ 134   **Medicines**

In all states except Illinois, prescription medicines are exempt from sales and use taxes. The chart below reflects the taxability of nonprescription medicines.

State	Medicines	Comments	Citation
Alabama	Taxable	Prescription medicine is exempt.	Ala. Code § 40-23-4.1
Arizona	Taxable	Prescription medicine is exempt.	Ariz. Rev. Stat. § 42-5061
Arkansas	Taxable	Prescription medicine is exempt.	Ark. Code Ann. § 26-52-406
California	Taxable	Prescription medicine is exempt.	Cal. Rev. & Tax. Code § 6369
Colorado	Taxable	Prescription medicine is exempt.	Colo. Rev. Stat. § 39-26-114(1)(a)(V)
Connecticut	Exempt	Prescription medicine is exempt. Applicable April 1, 2015, certain nonprescription drugs or medicines are exempt.	Conn. Gen. Stat. § 12-412(120)
District of Columbia	Exempt	Prescription and nonprescription medicine is exempt.	D.C. Code Ann. § 47-2005(14)
Florida	Taxable	Prescription medicine is exempt.	Fla. Admin. Code Ann. r. 12A-1.020(2)(a)
Georgia	Taxable	Prescription medicine is exempt. Over-the-counter drugs are taxable even if dispensed under a prescription or purchased on a physician's advice.	Ga. Comp. R. & Regs. 560-12-2-.30(3)(b), Ga. Code Ann. § 48-8-3(47)
Hawaii	Taxable	Prescription medicine is exempt.	Haw. Rev. Stat. § 237-13(2), Haw. Rev. Stat. § 237-24.3(6)
Idaho	Taxable	Prescription medicine is exempt.	Idaho Code § 63-3622N(a)
Illinois	Taxable	Prescription and nonprescription medicine is taxed at a lower rate.	35 ILCS 120/2-10
Indiana	Taxable	Prescription medicine is exempt.	Ind. Code § 6-2.5-5-19
Iowa	Taxable	Prescription medicine is exempt.	Iowa Code § 423.3(60)
Kansas	Taxable	Prescription medicine is exempt (excluding that used in the performance or induction of an abortion).	Kan. Stat. Ann. § 79-3603(a), Kan. Stat. Ann. § 79-3606(p)
Kentucky	Taxable	Prescription medicine is exempt. Over-the-counter drugs for which a prescription has been issued are exempt.	Ky. Rev. Stat. Ann. § 139.200(1)(a), Ky. Rev. Stat. Ann. § 139.472(1)

State	Medicines	Comments	Citation
Louisiana	Taxable	Prescription medicine is exempt.	La. Rev. Stat. Ann. § 47:305
Maine	Taxable	Prescription medicine is exempt.	Me. Rev. Stat. Ann. tit. 36, § 1760
Maryland	Exempt	Prescription and nonprescription medicine is exempt.	Md. Regs. Code tit. 3, § 03.06.01.09
Massachusetts	Taxable	Prescription medicine is exempt.	Mass. Gen. Laws ch. 64H, § 6
Michigan	Taxable	Medicine that can only be legally dispensed by prescription is exempt. The sale of over-the-counter drugs legally dispensed pursuant to a prescription is also exempt.	Mich. Comp. Laws § 205.54g, Mich. Comp. Laws § 205.94d
Minnesota	Exempt	Prescription and nonprescription medicine is exempt.	Minn. Stat. § 297A.67(7)
Mississippi	Taxable	Prescription medicine is exempt.	Miss. Code. Ann. § 27-65-111(h)
Missouri	Taxable	Prescription medicine is exempt. Nonprescription drugs purchased/used by disabled persons are also exempt.	Mo. Rev. Stat. § 144.030(18)
Nebraska	Taxable	Prescription medicine is exempt.	Neb. Rev. Stat. § 77-2704.09
Nevada	Taxable	Prescription medicine is exempt. Nonprescription medicine is exempt if furnished by medical personnel.	Nev. Rev. Stat. § 372.283(1)(d)
New Jersey	Exempt	Prescription and nonprescription medicine is exempt.	N.J. Stat. Ann. § 54:32B-8.1
New Mexico	Taxable	Prescription medicine is exempt.	N.M. Stat. Ann. § 7-9-73.2
New York	Exempt	Prescription and nonprescription medicine is exempt.	N.Y. Tax Law, § 1115(a)(3)
North Carolina	Taxable	Prescription medicine is exempt.	N.C. Gen. Stat. § 105-164.13(13)
North Dakota	Taxable	Prescription medicine is exempt.	N.D. Cent. Code § 57-39.2-04(7), N.D. Admin. Code § 81-04.1-04-23
Ohio	Taxable	Prescription medicine is exempt.	Ohio Rev. Code Ann. § 5739.02

State	Medicines	Comments	Citation
Oklahoma	Taxable	Prescription medicine is exempt.	Okla. Stat. tit. 68, § 1357(9), Okla. Stat. tit. 68, § 1357.6(A), Okla. Admin. Code § 710:65-13-170(a)
Pennsylvania	Exempt	Prescription and nonprescription medicine is exempt.	72 P.S. § 7204(17)
Rhode Island	Taxable	Prescription medicine is exempt.	R.I. Gen. Laws § 44-18-30(10), R.I. Code R. SU 07-60
South Carolina	Taxable	Prescription medicine is exempt. Over-the-counter drugs are exempt if sold to health care clinic that provides free medical and dental care to all of its patients. An exemption is available for injectable medicines and biologics.	S.C. Code Ann. § 12-36-2120
South Dakota	Taxable	Prescription medicine is exempt. Nonprescription medicine is exempt if furnished by medical personnel.	S.D. Codified Laws § 10-45-119
Tennessee	Taxable	Prescription medicine is exempt.	Tenn. Code. Ann. § 67-6-320
Texas	Exempt	Prescription medicine is exempt. Nonprescription medicine is exempt if required to be labeled with a "Drug Facts" panel in accordance with FDA regulations.	34 Tex. Admin. Code § 3.284(b)(3)
Utah	Taxable	Prescription medicine is exempt.	Utah Code Ann. § 59-12-104
Vermont	Exempt	Prescription and nonprescription medicine is exempt.	Vt. Stat. Ann. tit. 32, § 9741(2), Vt. Code R. 1.9741(2)-1(b)
Virginia	Exempt	Prescription and nonprescription medicine is exempt.	Va. Code Ann. § 58.1-609.7(15)
Washington	Taxable	Prescription medicine is exempt. Naturopathic medicines prescribed, dispensed or used by a licensed naturopath in the treatment of a patient are also exempt.	Wash. Rev. Code § 82.08.0281, Wash. Rev. Code § 82.08.0283
West Virginia	Taxable	Prescription medicine is exempt.	W. Va. Code § 11-15-9(a)(11), W. Va. Code R. § 110-15-92, W. Va. Code R. § 110-15-9.2.7

State	Medicines	Comments	Citation
Wisconsin	Taxable	Prescription medicine is exempt. Nonprescription medicine is exempt if furnished by medical personnel.	Wis. Stat. § 77.54(14)
Wyoming	Taxable	Prescription medicine is exempt.	Wyo. Stat. Ann. § 39-15-105

¶ 135   **Motor Vehicle Sales Tax Rates**

Rates listed below are the sales and use tax rates for motor vehicles.

State	Motor Vehicle Rates	Comments	Citation
Alabama	2%	Motor vehicle rentals are taxed at 1.5%.	Ala. Code § 40-23-101, Ala. Code § 40-12-222
Arizona	6.6%	5.6% prior to June 1, 2010, and after May 31, 2013.	Ariz. Rev. Stat. § 42-5010
Arkansas	6.5%	State rate increased from 6% to 6.5% effective July 1, 2013. No tax due if total consideration is under $4,000.	Ark. Code Ann. § 26-53-107, Ark. Code Ann. § 26-52-510
California	7.5%		Cal. Rev. & Tax. Code § 6051, Cal. Rev. & Tax. Code § 6051.2, Cal. Const. art. XIII § 35, Cal. Rev. & Tax. Code § 6051.3, Cal. Rev. & Tax. Code § 6051.5, Cal. Rev. & Tax. Code § 6201, Cal. Rev. & Tax. Code § 6051.7, Cal. Rev. & Tax. Code § 6201.7, Cal. Gov. Code § 99040
Colorado	2.9%		Colo. Rev. Stat. § 39-26-105
Connecticut	6.35%; 7% on motor vehicles that cost more than $50,000 (with certain exceptions)		Conn. Gen. Stat. § 12-408
District of Columbia	Exempt	Subject to an excise tax: Class I (3499 lbs. or less), 6%; Class II (3500 lbs.to 4,999 lbs) 7%, Class III (5,000 lbs. or more) 8%.	D.C. Code Ann. § 47-2005
Florida	6%		Fla. Stat. § 212.05
Georgia	Exempt	Effective March 1, 2013, exempt from sales and use tax other than any applicable transportation special purpose local option sales tax (T-SPLOST) imposed on the first $5,000 of a motor vehicle purchase. Effective March 1, 2013, title ad valorem tax (TAVT) applies.	Ga. Code Ann. § 48-5C-1(b)(1)(A), Ga. Code Ann. § 48-8-241(d)
Hawaii	4%		Haw. Rev. Stat. § 237-13
Idaho	6%		Idaho Code § 63-3619
Illinois	6.25%		35 ILCS 105/3-10
Indiana	7%		Ind. Code § 6-2.5-2-2
Iowa	6%	Subject to use tax.	Iowa Admin. Code r. 701-17.6(422,423)
Kansas	Taxable	6.5% effective July 1, 2015; 6.15% July 1, 2013 -June 30, 2015; 6.3% July 1, 2010 - June 30, 2013.	Kan. Stat. Ann. § 79-3603, Kan. Stat. Ann. § 79-3703, Kan. Admin. Regs. § 92-19-30a

State	Motor Vehicle Rates	Comments	Citation
Kentucky	Exempt	Taxable if motor vehicle usage tax has not been paid.	Ky. Rev. Stat. Ann. § 139.470(20)(a)
Louisiana	4%		La. Rev. Stat. Ann. § 47:302, La. Rev. Stat. Ann. § 47:331, La. Rev. Stat. Ann. § 51:1286, La. Rev. Stat. Ann. § 39:2006
Maine	5.5%	Effective from October 1, 2013, to June 30, 2015, Maine's sales tax rate increases from 5% to 5.5%.	Me. Rev. Stat. Ann. tit. 36, § 1811
Maryland	Exempt	Subject to 6% motor vehicle excise tax.	Md. Code Ann. § 11-221
Massachusetts	6.25%	5% prior to August 1, 2009	Mass. Gen. Laws ch. 64H § 2
Michigan	6%		Mich. Comp. Laws § 205.52
Minnesota	Exempt	Subject to 6.5% motor vehicle excise tax.	Minn. Stat. § 297A.67(30), Minn. Stat. § 297B.02
Mississippi	5% for autos and trucks with gross weight of 10,000 lbs. or less	3% for truck-tractors and semi-trailers. 5% for vehicles purchased from sellers who are not licensed dealers.	Miss. Code. Ann. § 27-65-17, Miss. Code. Ann. § 27-65-201, Miss. Rule 35.IV.11.02
Missouri	4%		Mo. Rev. Stat. § 144.020
Nebraska	5.5%		Neb. Rev. Stat. § 77-2701.02
Nevada	6.85%.	Prior to July 1, 2009 and after June 30, 2015, the rate is 6.5%. Rate is comprised of 2% state rate under general Sales and Use Tax Act, 2.6% state rate under Local School Support Tax Law (temporarily increased from 2.25% from July 1, 2009 through June 30, 2015), and 2.25% state-mandated local rate under City-County Relief Tax Law.	Nev. Rev. Stat. § 372.105, Nev. Rev. Stat. § 374.110, Nev. Rev. Stat. § 377.040
New Jersey	6.875%	Effective January 1, 2018, the rate will be 6.625%.	N.J. Stat. Ann. § 54:32B-3
New Mexico	Exempt	Subejct to 3% motor vehicle excise tax.	N.M. Stat. Ann. § 7-9-22
New York	4%	Additional tax imposed on certain passegner car rentals.	N.Y. Tax Law, § 1105, TB-ST-825
North Carolina	Exempt	Subejct to 3% highway use tax.	N.C. Admin. Code tit. 17, § 17: 07B.4614
North Dakota	Exempt	Subject to 5% motor vehicle excise tax.	N.D. Cent. Code § 57-39.2-04(13), N.D. Cent. Code § 57-40.3-02
Ohio	5.75%	Prior to September 1, 2013, the rate was 5.5%.	Ohio Rev. Code Ann. § 5739.02

State	Motor Vehicle Rates	Comments	Citation
Oklahoma	Exempt	Exempt if Oklahoma Motor Vehicle Excise Tax has been, or will be, paid. Subject to 3.25% excise tax for new vehicles; $20 excise tax on the first $1,500 or less of value of a used vehicle, plus 3.25% excise tax on the remaining value; $10 excise tax on any truck or truck-tractor with a laden weight or combined laden weight of at least 55,000 lbs.	Okla. Stat. tit. 68, § 1355(2), Okla. Admin. Code § 710:65-13-30(a), Okla. Stat. tit. 68, § 2103
Pennsylvania	6%		72 P.S. § 7202
Rhode Island	7%		R.I. Gen. Laws § 44-18-18
South Carolina	The maximum tax imposed on sales of motor vehicles is $300.		S.C. Code Ann. § 12-36-2110
South Dakota	Exempt	Subject to 3% motor vehicle excise tax.	S.D. Codified Laws § 32-5B-1
Tennessee	7%		Tenn. Code. Ann. § 67-6-203
Texas	6.25%		Tex. Tax Code Ann. § 152.021
Utah	4.7%		Utah Code Ann. § 59-12-103
Vermont	Exempt	Subject to 6% motor vehicle purchase and use tax. For any motor vehicle other than a pleasure car, motorcycle, motor home, and a vehicle weighing up to 10,099 pounds, the motor vehicle purchase and use tax is 6% or $1,850 (effective July 1, 2016, $2,075), whichever is less.	Vt. Stat. Ann. tit. 32, § 8903, Vt. Stat. Ann. tit. 32, § 9741(12)
Virginia	4.05%	A rate of 4.15% is being phased in over four years as follows: 3% through June 30, 2013; 4% beginning July 1, 2013, through June 30, 2014; 4.05% beginning July 1, 2014, through June 30, 2015; 4.1% beginning July 1, 2015, through June 30, 2016; and 4.15% beginning on and after July 1, 2016.	Va. Code Ann. § 58.1-2402
Washington	6.8%		Wash. Rev. Code § 82.08.020
West Virginia	Taxable	Taxed at reduced rate of 5%.	W. Va. Code § 11-15-3c
Wisconsin	5%		Wis. Stat. § 77.52
Wyoming	4%		Wyo. Stat. Ann. § 39-15-104

¶ 136   Multistate Certificates

The following chart indicates whether a state accepts the Multistate Tax Commission Uniform Multijurisdiction Exemption Certificate (MTC) and/or the Border States Uniform Sales for Resale Certificate (BSC) and any limitations on acceptance.

State	Multistate Certificates	Comments	Citation
Alabama	MTC	Retailer remains responsible to determine validity of exemption claim.	MTC Uniform Sales & Use Tax Certificate Footnote 1
Arizona	BSC, MTC	May only be used for sales for resale.	Transaction Privilege Tax Procedure TPP 00-3, MTC Uniform Sales & Use Tax Certificate
Arkansas	MTC		MTC Uniform Sales & Use Tax Certificate
California	BSC, MTC	May only be used for sales for resale.	Border States Uniform Sale for Resale Certificate, MTC Uniform Sales & Use Tax Certificate
Colorado	MTC	May not be used for sales for resale of taxable services.	MTC Uniform Sales & Use Tax Certificate Footnote 1
Connecticut	MTC	May only be used for sales for resale.	MTC Uniform Sales & Use Tax Certificate Footnote 4
District of Columbia	MTC	May only be used for sales for resale; must include purchaser's D.C. tax registration number.	MTC Uniform Sales & Use Tax Certificate Footnote 6
Florida	MTC	May only be used for sales for resale; must include purchaser's Florida tax registration number and registration date.	MTC Uniform Sales & Use Tax Certificate Footnote 23
Georgia	MTC	The purchaser's state of registration number will be accepted in lieu of Georgia's registration number when the purchaser is located outside Georgia, does not have nexus with Georgia, and the tangible personal property is delivered by drop shipment to the purchaser's customer located in Georgia.	MTC Uniform Sales & Use Tax Certificate & Instructions
Hawaii	MTC	May not be used for sales for resale of taxable services. May be used by seller to claim either lower tax rate or no tax.	Tax Information Release No. 93-5, MTC Uniform Sales & Use Tax Certificate
Idaho	MTC		IDAPA 35.01.02.128, MTC Uniform Sales & Use Tax Certificate
Illinois	MTC	May not be used for sales for resale of taxable services or for subsequent lease. Illinois registration or resale number must be included.	MTC Uniform Sales & Use Tax Certificate Footnotes 10

State	Multistate Certificates	Comments	Citation
Indiana	No		
Iowa	MTC		MTC Uniform Sales & Use Tax Certificate
Kansas	MTC		MTC Uniform Sales & Use Tax Certificate & Instructions
Kentucky	MTC	(1) Kentucky does not permit the use of the certificate to claim a resale exclusion for the purchase of a taxable service. (2) The certificate is not valid as an exemption certificate. Its use is limited to use as a resale certificate subject to the provisions of Ky. Rev. Stat. Ann. § 139.270 (Good Faith). (3) The use of the certificate by the purchaser constitutes the issuance of a blanket certificate in accordance with Ky. Admin. Reg. 103 § 31:111.	MTC Uniform Sales & Use Tax Certificate & Instructions, Ky. Rev. Stat. Ann. § 139.270, Ky. Admin. Reg. 103 § 31:111
Louisiana	No		
Maine	MTC	May not be used for sales for subsequent lease.	MTC Uniform Sales & Use Tax Certificate Footnote 12
Maryland	MTC	Vendors may accept resale certificates that bear the exemption number issued to a religious organization.	MTC Uniform Sales & Use Tax Certificate Footnote 13
Massachusetts	No		
Michigan	MTC	Effective for four years unless shorter period agreed to and stated on certificate.	MTC Uniform Sales & Use Tax Certificate Footnote 14
Minnesota	MTC	May not be used for sales for resale of taxable services in most situations. May be used for items to be used only once in production and never again.	MTC Uniform Sales & Use Tax Certificate
Mississippi	No		
Missouri	MTC	Improper use of certificate may subject purchaser to tax, penalty, and interest. Delivery outside of state may still subject transaction to Missouri tax.	MTC Uniform Sales & Use Tax Certificate Footnote 13
Nebraska	MTC	Blanket certificate valid for three years.	MTC Uniform Sales & Use Tax Certificate Footnote 17, Neb. Admin. Code § 1-013.11
Nevada	MTC		MTC Uniform Sales & Use Tax Certificate
New Jersey	MTC		MTC Uniform Sales & Use Tax Certificate

State	Multistate Certificates	Comments	Citation
New Mexico	BSC, MTC	May not be used for sales for resale of taxable services. May be used for sales for resale and purchases for ingredients or components if certificate not issued in state and buyer not required to be registered in state.	N.M. Admin. Code tit. 3, §3.2.201.13, N.M. Admin. Code tit. 3, §3.2.201.19, MTC Uniform Sales & Use Tax Certificate
New York	No		
North Carolina	MTC	May only be used for sales for resale, except may not be used by contractors who intend to use the property.	MTC Uniform Sales & Use Tax Certificate Footnote 25
North Dakota	MTC		MTC Uniform Sales & Use Tax Certificate
Ohio	MTC	Buyer must specify reason for exemption and deliver certificate before or during return period for filing returns.	MTC Uniform Sales & Use Tax Certificate Footnote 20, Information Release ST 2005-02
Oklahoma	MTC	Oklahoma allows this certificate in lieu of a copy of the purchaser's sales tax permit as one of the elements of "properly completed documents," which is one of the three requirements that must be met prior to a vendor being relieved of liability. The other two requirements are that the vendor must have the certificate in his possession at the time the sale is made, and must accept the documentation required under Okla. Admin. Code §710:65-7-6 in good faith. Absent strict compliance with these requirements, Oklahoma holds a seller liable for sales tax due on sales where the claimed exemption is found to be invalid, for whatever reason, unless the Oklahoma Tax Commission determines that the purchaser should be pursued for collection of the tax resulting from improper presentation of a certificate.	MTC Uniform Sales & Use Tax Certificate & Instructions, Okla. Admin. Code §710:65-7-6
Pennsylvania	MTC	May only be used for sales for resale; must include purchaser's Pennsylvania license number.	MTC Uniform Sales & Use Tax Certificate
Rhode Island	MTC	May only be used for sales for resale, where property will be resold in same form.	MTC Uniform Sales & Use Tax Certificate Footnote 17
South Carolina	MTC		MTC Uniform Sales & Use Tax Certificate

State	Multistate Certificates	Comments	Citation
South Dakota	MTC	May be used for sales of services for resale if not used by purchaser and delivered or resold to current customer without alteration.	MTC Uniform Sales & Use Tax Certificate Footnote 18
Tennessee	MTC		MTC Uniform Sales & Use Tax Certificate
Texas	BSC, MTC	Resale of items must be within the geographical limits of the U.S. (and its territories or possession).	MTC Uniform Sales & Use Tax Certificate Footnote 19, Border States Uniform Sale for Resale Certificate, 34 Tex. Admin. Code § 3.285(h)
Utah	MTC		MTC Uniform Sales & Use Tax Certificate
Vermont	MTC		MTC Uniform Sales & Use Tax Certificate
Virginia	No		
Washington	MTC	May be used for sales of chemicals to be used in processing. Must be renewed at least every four years.	MTC Uniform Sales & Use Tax Certificate Footnote 26
West Virginia	No		MTC Uniform Sales & Use Tax Certificate & Instructions
Wisconsin	MTC	May only be used for sales for resale.	MTC Uniform Sales & Use Tax Certificate
Wyoming	No		

¶ 137 **Nexus—General Rules**

This chart indicates when an out-of-state seller is required to collect tax. Note that state nexus statutes are subject to federal constitutional restrictions. In Quill Corp. v. North Dakota (504 U.S. 298 (1992)), the U.S. Supreme Court held that under the Commerce Clause, a seller must have a physical presence in a state in order for that state to require the seller to collect sales and use taxes.

State	General Rules	Comments	Citation
Alabama	Sellers maintaining a place of business in Alabama, or engaging in specific activities or business relationships, are required to collect the state's tax.	Applicable on or after January 1, 2016, out-of-state sellers who lack an Alabama physical presence but who are making retail sales of tangible personal property into the state have a substantial economic presence in Alabama for sales and use tax purposes and are required to register for a license with the department and to collect and remit tax, when: (a) the seller's retail sales of tangible personal property sold into the state exceed $250,000 per year based on the previous calendar year's sales; and (b) the seller conducts one or more of the activities described in Section 40-23-68, Code of Alabama.	Ala. Code § 40-23-68, Ala. Code § 40-23-190, Ala. Admin. Code r. 810-6-2-.90.03
Arizona	Retailers maintaining a place of business in the state are required to collect tax.		Ariz. Rev. Stat. § 42-5151, Arizona Nexus Brochure
Arkansas	Retailers doing business or engaging in business in the state are required to collect tax.		Ark. Code Ann. § 26-52-103, Ark. Code Ann. § 26-53-124, Ark. Reg. GR-5
California	Retailers engaged in business in this state are required to collect tax.		Cal. Rev. & Tax. Code § 6203, Reg. 1684, 18 CCR
Colorado	Retailers doing business in the state are required to collect tax.		Colo. Rev. Stat. § 39-26-102, Colo. Code Regs. § 39-26-102.3
Connecticut	Retailers engaged in business in the state are required to collect tax.		Conn. Gen. Stat. § 12-411(3), Conn. Gen. Stat. § 12-407(a)(15)(A)
District of Columbia	Retailers engaging in business in the District are required to collect tax.		D.C. Code Ann. § 47-2201(h)
Florida	Dealers making sales in the state are required to collect tax.		Fla. Stat. § 212.0596, Fla. Stat. § 212.06(3)(a)
Georgia	"Retailers," "dealers," and those engaging in certain activities in the state, must collect tax on taxable sales in Georgia.		Ga. Code Ann. § 48-8-2, Ga. Code Ann. § 48-8-30(b)(1), Ga. Code Ann. § 48-8-65(b)(2)

State	General Rules	Comments	Citation
Hawaii	Persons engaging in business in the state are required to collect tax.		Haw. Rev. Stat. § 237-2, Haw. Rev. Stat. § 237-13, Haw. Rev. Stat. § 238-2, Haw. Reg. 18-237-1
Idaho	Retailers engaged in business in the state are required to collect tax.		Idaho Code § 63-3611, Idaho Code § 63-3615A
Illinois	Retailers maintaining a place of business in the state are required to collect tax.		35 ILCS 105/3-45, 35 ILCS 105/2
Indiana	Retail merchants engaged in business in the state are required to collect tax.		Ind. Code § 6-2.5-3-1
Iowa	Retailers maintaining a place of business in the state are required to collect tax.		Iowa Code § 423.29, Iowa Code § 423.1
Kansas	Retailers doing business in the state are required to collect tax.		Kan. Stat. Ann. § 79-3702, Kan. Stat. Ann. § 79-3705c
Kentucky	Retailers engaged in business in this state are required to collect tax.		Ky. Rev. Stat. Ann. § 139.340
Louisiana	"Dealers" are required to collect tax.	Click-through and affiliate nexus provisions are applicable to remote sellers effective April 1, 2016.	La. Rev. Stat. Ann. § 47:301, La. Rev. Stat. Ann. § 47:304
Maine	Sellers with a substantial physical presence in the state are required to collect tax.		Me. Rev. Stat. Ann. tit. 36, § 1754-B(1)(G), Instructional Bulletin No. 43
Maryland	"Vendors" are required to collect tax.		Md. Code Ann. § 11-403, Md. Code Ann. § 11-101, Md. Code Ann. § 11-701
Massachusetts	Vendors engaged in business in the commonwealth are required to collect tax.		Mass. Gen. Laws ch. 64I, § 4, Mass. Gen. Laws ch. 64H, § 1, Technical Information Release 96-8
Michigan	Seller that engage in specified activities are required to collect tax.		Revenue Administrative Bulletin 1999-1, Revenue Administrative Bulletin 2015-22
Minnesota	Retailers maintaining a place of business in this state are required to collect tax.		Minn. Stat. § 297A.66
Mississippi	Sellers maintaining a place of business or doing business in the state are required to collect tax.		Miss. Code. Ann. § 27-67-3, Miss. Code. Ann. § 27-67-4
Missouri	Vendors engaged in business in Missouri, or having physical presence in or sufficient contact with the state, must collect tax.		Mo. Rev. Stat. § 144.605, Mo. Code Regs. Ann. tit. 12, § 10-114.100, Mo. Code Regs. Ann. tit. 12, § 10-4.085

State	General Rules	Comments	Citation
Nebraska	Sellers engaged in business in this state are required to collect tax.		Neb. Rev. Stat. § 77-2703(2)(b), Neb. Rev. Stat. § 77-2701.13, Neb. Admin. Code § 1-004
Nevada	Retailers maintaining a place of business in this state are required to collect tax. However, Nevada does not define the term "retailer maintaining a place of business."		Nev. Rev. Stat. § 372.195
New Jersey	"Sellers" are required to collect tax.	A person making sales of taxable tangible personal property, specified digital products, or services is presumed to be soliciting business through an independent contractor or other representative if the person making sales enters into an agreement with an independent contractor having physical presence in New Jersey or other representative having physical presence in New Jersey, for a commission or other consideration, under which the independent contractor or representative directly or indirectly refers potential customers, whether by a link on an Internet website or otherwise, and the cumulative gross receipts from sales to customers in New Jersey who were referred by all independent contractors or representatives that have this type of an agreement with the person making sales are in excess of $10,000 during the preceding four quarterly periods ending on the last day of March, June, September, and December (click-through nexus).	N.J. Stat. Ann. § 54:32B-2, TB-78
New Mexico	Sellers that attempts to exploit New Mexico's markets by carrying on an activity in the state are required to collect tax.		N.M. Stat. Ann. § 7-9-10
New York	Vendors making sales or maintaining a place of business in the state, and vendors engaged in specified activities, are required to collect tax in New York.	New York has a rebuttable presumption that certain Internet retailers of taxable tangible personal property or services are sales tax vendors required to register for sales tax purposes and collect state and local sales taxes.	N.Y. Tax Law, § 1101, N.Y. Comp. Code R. & Regs. tit. 20, § 526.10, TSB-M-08(3)S

State	General Rules	Comments	Citation
North Carolina	Retailers engaged in business in the state are required to collect tax.		N.C. Gen. Stat. § 105-164.8, N.C. Gen. Stat. § 105-164.3
North Dakota	Retailers maintaining a place of business in this state are required to collect tax.		N.D. Cent. Code § 57-40.2-07, N.D. Cent. Code § 57-40.2-01, Guideline - Out of State Retailers
Ohio	Sellers who have substantial nexus with the state are required to collect tax.		Ohio Rev. Code Ann. § 5741.17, Ohio Rev. Code Ann. § 5741.01, Information Release ST 2001-01
Oklahoma	A retailer must collect Oklahoma tax if it has a place of business in the state, is involved in certain activities or business relationships, or regularly solicits Oklahoma consumers.		Okla. Stat. tit. 68, § 1354.1, Okla. Stat. tit. 68, § 1354.2, Okla. Stat. tit. 68, § 1354.3, Okla. Stat. tit. 68, § 1406, Okla. Stat. tit. 68, § 1352, Okla. Stat. tit. 68, § 1401
Pennsylvania	Sellers maintaining a place of business in the state are required to collect tax.		72 P.S. § 7237, 72 P.S. § 7201(b)
Rhode Island	Retailers engaging in business in the state are required to collect tax.		R.I. Gen. Laws § 44-18-22, R.I. Gen. Laws § 44-18-23
South Carolina	Sellers that engage in specified activities, such as maintaining a place of business in South Carolina or soliciting sales by an agent or salesman, are required to collect tax.		S.C. Code Ann. § 12-36-1340, S.C. Code Ann. § 12-36-70, Revenue Ruling 14-4
South Dakota	Retailers maintaining a place of business in the state are required to collect tax.		S.D. Codified Laws § 10-46-1
Tennessee	"Dealers" are required to collect tax.		Tenn. Code. Ann. § 67-6-102, America Online, Inc. v. Johnson, Registering Your Business in Tennessee
Texas	Retailers engaged in business in this state are required to collect tax.		Tex. Tax Code Ann. § 151.103, Tex. Tax Code Ann. § 151.107, 34 Tex. Admin. Code § 3.286
Utah	Sellers that engage in specified activities are required to collect tax.		Utah Code Ann. § 59-12-107, Publication 37
Vermont	"Vendors" are required to collect tax.		Vt. Stat. Ann. tit. 32, § 9701
Virginia	Dealers maintaining a place of business in Virginia, or engaging in specified activities or business relationships, are required to collect tax.		Va. Code Ann. § 58.1-612

State	General Rules	Comments	Citation
Washington	Persons who maintain in the state a place of business or stock of goods or engage in business activities in the state are required to collect tax.		Wash. Rev. Code § 82.12.040, Wash. Admin. Code § 458-20-193
West Virginia	Retailers engaging in business in the state are required to collect tax.		W. Va. Code § 11-15A-6, W. Va. Code § 11-15A-1, W. Va. Code R. § 110-15-2
Wisconsin	Retailers engaged in business in the state are required to collect tax.		Wis. Stat. § 77.53(3), Wis. Stat. § 77.51, Wis. Admin. Code § 11.97
Wyoming	"Vendors" are required to collect tax.		Wyo. Stat. Ann. § 39-16-103(c)(v), Wyo. Stat. Ann. § 39-16-101(a)(x), Buehner Block Co. v. Wyoming Department of Revenue

¶ 138   **Nexus—Catalog Distribution**

This chart indicates whether the distribution of catalogs or other advertising material in a state can create nexus for a seller. Note that state nexus statutes are subject to federal constitutional restrictions. In Quill Corp. v. North Dakota (504 U.S. 298 (1992)), the U.S. Supreme Court held that under the Commerce Clause, a seller must have a physical presence in a state in order for that state to require the seller to collect sales and use taxes.

State	Catalog Distribution	Comments	Citation
Alabama	Yes	Statute indicates nexus may exist (i.e., seller distributes catalogs and by reason thereof receives and accepts orders from residents, within Alabama). However, in Quill Corp. v. North Dakota, the U.S. Supreme Court held that under the Commerce Clause, a vendor must have a physical presence in a state in order for that state to require the vendor to collect tax.	Ala. Code § 40-23-68, Ala. Code § 40-23-190
Arizona	No		Ariz. Rev. Stat. § 42-5151, Arizona Nexus Brochure
Arkansas	Yes	Promotional materials, such as catalogs, sent into Arkansas via interstate mail are considered to be distributed for purposes of the use tax.	Ark. Code Ann. § 26-52-103, Ark. Code Ann. § 26-53-124, Ark Reg. UT-3.D
California	No		Cal. Rev. & Tax. Code § 6203, Reg. 1684, 18 CCR
Colorado	No		Colo. Rev. Stat. § 39-26-102, Colo. Code Regs. § 39-26-102.3, FYI Sales 5

State	Catalog Distribution	Comments	Citation
Connecticut	Yes	Being engaged in business in Connecticut specifically includes, notwithstanding the fact that retail sales are made from outside Connecticut to a destination within the state and that a place of business is not maintained in Connecticut, engaging in regular or systematic solicitation of sales of tangible personal property in Connecticut by the distribution of catalogs, provided provided 100 or more retail sales from outside the state to destinations within the state are made during the 12-month period ended on the September 30 immediately preceding the monthly or quarterly period with respect to which liability for sales and use tax is determined. However, in Quill Corp. v. North Dakota, the U.S. Supreme Court held that under the Commerce Clause, a vendor must have a physical presence in a state in order for that state to require the vendor to collect tax.	Conn. Gen. Stat. § 12-411(3), Conn. Gen. Stat. § 12-407(a)(12)(G), Conn. Gen. Stat. § 12-407(a)(15)(A)
District of Columbia	No		D.C. Code Ann. § 47-2201(h)
Florida	Yes	Every dealer, as defined, who makes a mail order sale is subject to Florida's power to levy and collect tax when the dealer, by purposefully and systematically exploiting the market provided by Florida through any media, creates nexus with Florida.	Fla. Stat. § 212.0596
Georgia	No	A "dealer" required to collect sales tax does not include a person whose only activity in Georgia is advertising or solicitation by catalogs, direct mail, periodicals, advertising fliers, or print media.	Ga. Code Ann. § 48-8-2, Ga. Code Ann. § 48-8-30(b)(1)
Hawaii	No		Haw. Rev. Stat. § 237-13, Haw. Rev. Stat. § 238-2
Idaho	No		Idaho Code § 63-3611, Idaho Code § 63-3615A
Illinois	No		35 ILCS 105/3-45, 35 ILCS 105/2
Indiana	No		Ind. Code § 6-2.5-3-1

¶138

State	Catalog Distribution	Comments	Citation
Iowa	No		Iowa Code § 423.29, Iowa Code § 423.1, Iowa Admin. Code r. 701 30.1
Kansas	Yes		Kan. Admin. Regs. § 92-20-7
Kentucky	Yes	Nexus arises from the continuous, regular, or systematic solicitation of orders of tangible personal property or digital property from Kentucky residents when the solicitation of the order uses any print media located Kentucky. Also, remote seller use tax notice requirements apply to out-of-state catalog retailers who are not required to collect Kentucky use tax and who expect more than $100,000 in gross sales to Kentucky residents and businesses in the current calendar year.	Ky. Rev. Stat. Ann. § 139.340
Louisiana	No		La. Rev. Stat. Ann. § 47:301, La. Rev. Stat. Ann. § 47:304, LA DOR Sales Tax FAQ
Maine	No		Me. Rev. Stat. Ann. tit. 36, § 1754-B(1)(G)
Maryland	No		Md. Code Ann. § 11-403, Md. Code Ann. § 11-101, Md. Code Ann. § 11-701
Massachusetts	No		Mass. Gen. Laws ch. 64I, § 4, Mass. Gen. Laws ch. 64H, § 1, Technical Information Release 96-8
Michigan	No		Revenue Administrative Bulletin 1999-1
Minnesota	Yes	Statute indicates nexus may exist. However, in Quill Corp. v. North Dakota, the U.S. Supreme Court held that under the Commerce Clause, a vendor must have a physical presence in a state in order for that state to require the vendor to collect tax.	Minn. Stat. § 297A.66
Mississippi	Yes	Statute indicates nexus may exist. However, in Quill Corp. v. North Dakota, the U.S. Supreme Court held that under the Commerce Clause, a vendor must have a physical presence in a state in order for that state to require the vendor to collect tax.	Miss. Code. Ann. § 27-67-3, Miss. Code. Ann. § 27-67-4

State	Catalog Distribution	Comments	Citation
Missouri	No		Mo. Rev. Stat. § 144.605, Mo. Code Regs. Ann. tit. 12, § 10-114.100
Nebraska	No		Neb. Rev. Stat. § 77-2703(2)(b), Neb. Rev. Stat. § 77-2701.13, Neb. Admin. Code § 1-004
Nevada	May create nexus	Nevada does not provide any guidance on nexus for sales and use tax purposes.	Nev. Rev. Stat. § 372.195
New Jersey	No	However, a seller includes a person who solicits business by distribution of catalogs or other advertising matter and by reason thereof makes sales to persons within New Jersey of tangible personal property, specified digital products or services, the use of which is taxable.	N.J. Stat. Ann. § 54:32B-2, Bulletin S&U-5
New Mexico	No		N.M. Stat. Ann. § 7-9-10
New York	Yes	If the out-of-state seller has some additional connection with the state that satisfies the nexus requirement of the U.S. Constitution.	N.Y. Tax Law, § 1101(b)(8), N.Y. Comp. Code R. & Regs. tit. 20, § 526.10, TSB-M-08(3)S
North Carolina	Yes	A retailer who makes a remote sale is engaged in business in North Carolina and is subject to sales and use tax if the retailer, by purposefully or systematically exploiting the market provided by the state by any media-assisted, media-facilitated, or media-solicited means, including the distribution of catalogs, creates nexus with North Carolina. However, in Quill Corp. v. North Dakota, the U.S. Supreme Court held that under the Commerce Clause, a vendor must have a physical presence in a state in order for that state to require the vendor to collect tax.	N.C. Gen. Stat. § 105-164.3(9), N.C. Gen. Stat. § 105-164.8(b)(5)
North Dakota	Yes	Statute indicates nexus may exist. However, in Quill Corp. v. North Dakota, the U.S. Supreme Court held that under the Commerce Clause, a vendor must have a physical presence in a state in order for that state to require the vendor to collect tax.	N.D. Cent. Code § 57-40.2-07, N.D. Cent. Code § 57-40.2-01

State	Catalog Distribution	Comments	Citation
Ohio	No		Ohio Rev. Code Ann. § 5741.17, Ohio Rev. Code Ann. § 5741.01, Information Release ST 2001-01
Oklahoma	Yes	Tax must be collected on each sale or use of tangible personal property to or by a consumer-user in Oklahoma purchased from an out-of-state vendor who engages in business in Oklahoma through the continuous, regular, or systematic solicitation of retail sales by advertisement through mail order or catalog publications. Remote seller use tax notice requirements apply to out-of-state catalog retailers who are not required to collect Oklahoma use tax.	Okla. Stat. tit. 68, § 1354.1, Okla. Stat. tit. 68, § 1354.3, Okla. Stat. tit. 68, § 1406.1, Okla. Admin. Code § 710:65-21-8
Pennsylvania	No		72 P.S. § 7237, 72 P.S. § 7201(b), Bloomingdales By Mail, Ltd. v. Pennsylvania
Rhode Island	Yes	Statute indicates nexus may exist. However, in Quill Corp. v. North Dakota, the U.S. Supreme Court held that under the Commerce Clause, a vendor must have a physical presence in a state in order for that state to require the vendor to collect tax.	R.I. Gen. Laws § 44-18-15, R.I. Gen. Laws § 44-18-23
South Carolina	No	If mailing catalogs to South Carolina residents is the only activity with the state, no nexus is present. If the corporation also has property and solicitors in South Carolina, however, nexus may be present. In Quill Corp. v. North Dakota, the U.S. Supreme Court held that under the Commerce Clause, a vendor must have a physical presence in a state in order for that state to require the vendor to collect tax.	S.C. Code Ann. § 12-36-1340, S.C. Code Ann. § 12-36-70, Revenue Ruling 14-4
South Dakota	No		S.D. Codified Laws § 10-46-1
Tennessee	No		Tenn. Code. Ann. § 67-6-102, Bloomingdale's by Mail, Ltd. v. Huddleston

State	Catalog Distribution	Comments	Citation
Texas	Yes	Statute indicates nexus may exist. However, in Quill Corp. v. North Dakota, the U.S. Supreme Court held that under the Commerce Clause, a vendor must have a physical presence in a state in order for that state to require the vendor to collect tax.	Tex. Tax Code Ann. § 151.103, Tex. Tax Code Ann. § 151.107, 34 Tex. Admin. Code § 3.286
Utah	No		Utah Code Ann. § 59-12-107
Vermont	Yes	Statute indicates nexus may exist. However, in Quill Corp. v. North Dakota, the U.S. Supreme Court held that under the Commerce Clause, a vendor must have a physical presence in a state in order for that state to require the vendor to collect tax.	Vt. Stat. Ann. tit. 32, § 9701
Virginia	No		Va. Code Ann. § 58.1-612
Washington	No		Wash. Rev. Code § 82.12.040, Wash. Admin. Code § 458-20-193, E-mail, Washington Department of Revenue, September 13, 2010
West Virginia	Yes		W. Va. Code R. § 110-15-2.78.4, W. Va. Code R. § 110-15-128.1.5, W. Va. Code R. § 110-15-128.2.2.2.c, W. Va. Code § 11-15A-6(a)
Wisconsin	No		Wis. Stat. § 77.53(3), Wis. Stat. § 77.51, Wis. Admin. Code § 11.97
Wyoming	Yes	"Vendor" defined as including every person who engages in regular or systematic solicitation by three or more separate transmittances of advertisements in any 12 month period in a consumer market in Wyoming by the distribution of catalogs. Effective July 1, 2017, "vendor" includes remote sellers to the extent provided by Wyo. Stat. Ann. Sec. 39-15-501.	Wyo. Stat. Ann. § 39-16-103(c)(v), Wyo. Stat. Ann. § 39-16-101(a)(x), Wyo. Stat. Ann. § 39-15-501, Buehner Block Co. v. Wyoming Department of Revenue

¶138

¶ 139   Nexus—Delivery by Common Carrier

This chart indicates whether delivering property to a state by common carrier creates nexus for a seller.

State	Delivery by Common Carrier	Comments	Citation
Alabama	No		Ala. Code § 40-23-68(b), CCH Sales and Use Tax Nexus Survey
Arizona	No		Ariz. Rev. Stat. § 42-5151
Arkansas	No		Ark. Code Ann. § 26-52-103, Ark. Code Ann. § 26-53-124, Ark. Reg. GR-5
California	No		Cal. Rev. & Tax. Code § 6203, Reg. 1684, 18 CCR
Colorado	No		Colo. Rev. Stat. § 39-26-102, Colo. Code Regs. § 39-26-102.3
Connecticut	No		Conn. Gen. Stat. § 12-411(3), Conn. Gen. Stat. § 12-407(a)(15)(A)
District of Columbia	No		D.C. Code Ann. § 47-2201(h)
Florida	No		Fla. Stat. § 212.0596
Georgia	No	A "dealer" required to collect sales tax does not include a person whose only activity in Georgia is the delivery of tangible personal property within the state solely by common carrier.	Ga. Code Ann. § 48-8-2, Ga. Code Ann. § 48-8-30(b)(1)
Hawaii	No		Haw. Rev. Stat. § 237-13, Haw. Rev. Stat. § 238-2
Idaho	No		Idaho Code § 63-3611, Idaho Code § 63-3615A
Illinois	No		35 ILCS 105/3-45, 35 ILCS 105/2
Indiana	No		Ind. Code § 6-2.5-3-1, Information Bulletin #37, Indiana Department of State Revenue, June 2007
Iowa	No		Iowa Code § 423.29, Iowa Code § 423.1, Iowa Admin. Code r. 701 30.1
Kansas	No		Kan. Stat. Ann. § 79-3702(h)(2)(A)
Kentucky	No		Ky. Rev. Stat. Ann. § 139.340
Louisiana	No		La. Rev. Stat. Ann. § 47:301, La. Rev. Stat. Ann. § 47:304

State	Delivery by Common Carrier	Comments	Citation
Maine	No		Me. Rev. Stat. Ann. tit. 36, § 1754-B(1)(G), Instructional Bulletin No. 43
Maryland	No		Md. Code Ann. § 11-403, Md. Code Ann. § 11-101, Md. Code Ann. § 11-701
Massachusetts	No		Mass. Gen. Laws ch. 64I, § 4, Mass. Gen. Laws ch. 64H, § 1, Technical Information Release 96-8
Michigan	No		Revenue Administrative Bulletin 1999-1
Minnesota	No		Minn. Stat. § 297A.66
Mississippi	No		Miss. Code. Ann. § 27-67-3
Missouri	No		Mo. Rev. Stat. § 144.605, Mo. Code Regs. Ann. tit. 12, § 10-114.100(3)(B), Mo. Code Regs. Ann. tit. 12, § 10-4.085
Nebraska	No	Delivery of alcoholic beverages into Nebraska by common carrier by the holder of certain shipping licenses constitutes nexus.	Neb. Rev. Stat. § 77-2703(2)(b), Neb. Rev. Stat. § 77-2701.13, Neb. Admin. Code § 1-004
Nevada	No		Nev. Rev. Stat. § 372.195
New Jersey	No		N.J. Stat. Ann. § 54:32B-2, Bulletin S&U-5
New Mexico	No		N.M. Stat. Ann. § 7-9-10
New York	No		N.Y. Tax Law, § 1101, N.Y. Comp. Code R. & Regs. tit. 20, § 526.10, TSB-M-08(3)S
North Carolina	No		N.C. Gen. Stat. § 105-164.8
North Dakota	No		N.D. Cent. Code § 57-40.2-07, N.D. Cent. Code § 57-40.2-01
Ohio	No		Ohio Rev. Code Ann. § 5741.17, Ohio Rev. Code Ann. § 5741.01, Information Release ST 2001-01
Oklahoma	No		Okla. Stat. tit. 68, § 1407
Pennsylvania	No		72 P.S. § 7237, 72 P.S. § 7201(b)
Rhode Island	No		R.I. Gen. Laws § 44-18-22, R.I. Gen. Laws § 44-18-23
South Carolina	No		S.C. Code Ann. § 12-36-1340, S.C. Code Ann. § 12-36-70, Revenue Ruling 14-4

¶139

State	Delivery by Common Carrier	Comments	Citation
South Dakota	No		S.D. Codified Laws § 10-46-1
Tennessee	No		Tenn. Code. Ann. § 67-6-102
Texas	No		Tex. Tax Code Ann. § 151.103, Tex. Tax Code Ann. § 151.107, 34 Tex. Admin. Code § 3.286
Utah	No		Utah Code Ann. § 59-12-107
Vermont	No		Vt. Stat. Ann. tit. 32, § 9701
Virginia	No		Va. Code Ann. § 58.1-612(c)(4)
Washington	No		Wash. Rev. Code § 82.12.040, Wash. Admin. Code § 458-20-193
West Virginia	No		W. Va. Code § 11-15A-1(b)(8)(C), W. Va. Code R. § 110-15-2.78
Wisconsin	No		Wis. Stat. § 77.53(3), Wis. Stat. § 77.51, Wis. Admin. Code § 11.97
Wyoming	No	But see Buehner Block Co. v. Wyoming Department of Revenue.	Wyo. Stat. Ann. § 39-16-103(c)(v), Wyo. Stat. Ann. § 39-16-101(a)(x), Buehner Block Co. v. Wyoming Department of Revenue

¶ 140   Nexus—Delivery in Seller's Vehicle

This chart indicates whether making deliveries to a state using a company-owned vehicle can create nexus for a seller.

State	Delivery in Seller's Vehicle	Comments	Citation
Alabama	Yes		Ala. Code § 40-23-68, Ala. Admin. Code r. 810-6-2-.90.01(4)(a)
Arizona	Yes		Ariz. Rev. Stat. § 42-5151
Arkansas	Yes		Ark. Code Ann. § 26-52-103, Ark. Code Ann. § 26-53-124, Ark. Reg. GR-5
California	Yes		Cal. Rev. & Tax. Code § 6203, Reg. 1684, 18 CCR
Colorado	Yes		Colo. Rev. Stat. § 39-26-102, Colo. Code Regs. § 39-26-102.3
Connecticut	Yes		Conn. Gen. Stat. § 12-411(3), Conn. Gen. Stat. § 12-407(a)(3) and (a)(15)(A)
District of Columbia	Yes		D.C. Code Ann. § 47-2201(h)
Florida	Yes		Fla. Stat. § 212.0596
Georgia	Yes	A "dealer" includes a person who has distributed tangible personal property in Georgia and who cannot prove that tax has been paid.	Ga. Code Ann. § 48-8-2(8)(A), Ga. Code Ann. § 48-8-30(b)(1)
Hawaii	Yes		Haw. Rev. Stat. § 237-13, Haw. Rev. Stat. § 238-2
Idaho	Yes		Idaho Code § 63-3611, Idaho Code § 63-3615A
Illinois	Yes		35 ILCS 105/3-45, 35 ILCS 105/2
Indiana	Yes		Ind. Code § 6-2.5-3-1
Iowa	Yes		Iowa Code § 423.29, Iowa Code § 423.1, Iowa Admin. Code r. 701 30.1
Kansas	Yes	Retailers doing business in Kansas must register to collect use tax on tangible personal property sold for use, storage, or consumption in Kansas by any salesperson, representative, trucker, peddler, canvasser, or agent, regardless of whether delivery is made by the salesperson, representative, trucker, peddler, canvasser, or agent.	Kan. Admin. Regs. § 92-20-7(b)

State	Delivery in Seller's Vehicle	Comments	Citation
Kentucky	Yes		Ky. Rev. Stat. Ann. § 139.340, 103 Ky. Admin. Regs. 25:050(2)
Louisiana	Yes		La. Rev. Stat. Ann. § 47:301, La. Rev. Stat. Ann. § 47:304
Maine	Yes		Me. Rev. Stat. Ann. tit. 36, § 1754-B(1)(G), Instructional Bulletin No. 43
Maryland	Yes		Md. Code Ann. § 11-403, Md. Code Ann. § 11-101, Md. Code Ann. § 11-701
Massachusetts	Yes		Mass. Gen. Laws ch. 64I, § 4, Mass. Gen. Laws ch. 64H, § 1, Technical Information Release 96-8
Michigan	Yes		Revenue Administrative Bulletin 1999-1
Minnesota	Yes		Minn. Stat. § 297A.66
Mississippi	Yes		Miss. Code. Ann. § 27-67-3, Miss. Code. Ann. § 27-67-4
Missouri	Yes	If seller makes deliveries regularly.	Mo. Rev. Stat. § 144.605, Mo. Code Regs. Ann. tit. 12, § 10-114.100, Mo. Code Regs. Ann. tit. 12, § 10-4.085
Nebraska	Yes		Neb. Rev. Stat. § 77-2703(2)(b), Neb. Rev. Stat. § 77-2701.13, Neb. Admin. Code § 1-004
Nevada	Yes		Nev. Rev. Stat. § 372.195
New Jersey	Yes		N.J. Stat. Ann. § 54:32B-2, Bulletin S&U-5, CCH Sales and Use Tax Nexus Survey
New Mexico	Yes		N.M. Stat. Ann. § 7-9-10
New York	Yes	If deliveries are made regularly or systematically.	N.Y. Tax Law, § 1101, N.Y. Comp. Code R. & Regs. tit. 20, § 526.10
North Carolina	Yes		N.C. Gen. Stat. § 105-164.3(9), N.C. Gen. Stat. § 105-164.8
North Dakota	Yes		N.D. Cent. Code § 57-40.2-07, N.D. Cent. Code § 57-40.2-01
Ohio	Yes		Ohio Rev. Code Ann. § 5741.17, Ohio Rev. Code Ann. § 5741.01, Information Release ST 2001-01
Oklahoma	Yes		Okla. Stat. tit. 68, § 1407

¶140

State	Delivery in Seller's Vehicle	Comments	Citation
Pennsylvania	Yes	If delivery includes unpacking, positioning, placing, or assembling the property.	72 P.S. § 7237, 72 P.S. § 7201(b)
Rhode Island	Yes		R.I. Gen. Laws § 44-18-23, R.I. Code R. SU 07-56
South Carolina	Yes		S.C. Code Ann. § 12-36-1340, S.C. Code Ann. § 12-36-70, Revenue Ruling 14-4
South Dakota	Yes		S.D. Codified Laws § 10-46-1
Tennessee	Yes		Tenn. Code. Ann. § 67-6-102, Tenn. Code. Ann. § 67-6-203
Texas	Yes		Tex. Tax Code Ann. § 151.103, Tex. Tax Code Ann. § 151.107, 34 Tex. Admin. Code § 3.286
Utah	Yes		Utah Code Ann. § 59-12-107
Vermont	Yes		Vt. Stat. Ann. tit. 32, § 9701
Virginia	Yes	If regular deliveries (more than 12 times during a calendar year to deliver goods) are made within Virginia by means other than common carrier.	Va. Code Ann. § 58.1-612(C)(4)
Washington	Yes		Wash. Rev. Code § 82.12.040, Wash. Admin. Code § 458-20-193
West Virginia	Yes	Under the state's affiliate nexus provisions, "retailer engaging in business in this state" includes a retailer who is related to or part of a unitary business with a related entity, business, or person who (or by an agent, representative, or employee) performs a "service" in West Virginia in connection with items or services sold by the retailer or any related entity, where "service" includes delivery services by means other than common carrier or the U.S. Postal Service.	W. Va. Code § 11-15A-1(b)(8)(C), W. Va. Code R. § 110-15-2.78
Wisconsin	Yes		Wis. Stat. § 77.53(3), Wis. Stat. § 77.51, Wis. Admin. Code § 11.97
Wyoming	Yes		Wyo. Stat. Ann. § 39-16-103(c)(v), Wyo. Stat. Ann. § 39-16-101(a)(x)

¶ 141   Nexus—Employee Making Sales

This chart indicates whether nexus is created by the presence in a state of an employee who makes sales.

State	Employee Making Sales	Comments	Citation
Alabama	Yes		Ala. Code § 40-23-68
Arizona	Yes	If employee is present in Arizona for more than 2 days per year.	Ariz. Rev. Stat. § 42-5151
Arkansas	Yes		Ark. Code Ann. § 26-52-103, Ark. Reg. GR-5
California	Yes		Cal. Rev. & Tax. Code § 6203, Reg. 1684, 18 CCR
Colorado	Yes		Colo. Rev. Stat. § 39-26-102, Colo. Code Regs. § 39-26-102.3
Connecticut	Yes		Conn. Gen. Stat. § 12-411(3), Conn. Gen. Stat. § 12-407(a)(12) and (a)(15)(A)
District of Columbia	Yes		D.C. Code Ann. § 47-2201(h)
Florida	Yes		Fla. Stat. § 212.0596
Georgia	Yes	A "dealer" required to collect sales tax includes persons who solicit business by an employee or agent. However, a "dealer" excludes a person (including the dealer's representatives, agents, salespersons, canvassers, independent contractors, and solicitors) (1) whose only activity in the state is to engage in trade show activities, (2) who engages in a trade show for five or fewer days during 12 months, and (3) who earned no more than $100,000 of net income from the activities in the state during the prior calendar year.	Ga. Code Ann. § 48-8-2(8)(H)-(I), Ga. Code Ann. § 48-8-30(b)(1)
Hawaii	Yes		Haw. Rev. Stat. § 237-13, Haw. Rev. Stat. § 238-2
Idaho	Yes		Idaho Code § 63-3611, Idaho Code § 63-3615A
Illinois	Yes		35 ILCS 105/3-45, 35 ILCS 105/2
Indiana	Yes		Ind. Code § 6-2.5-3-1
Iowa	Yes		Iowa Code § 423.29, Iowa Code § 423.1, Iowa Admin. Code r. 701 30.1

State	Employee Making Sales	Comments	Citation
Kansas	Yes		Kan. Stat. Ann. § 79-3702(h)(1)
Kentucky	Yes		Ky. Rev. Stat. Ann. § 139.340
Louisiana	Yes	Click-through and affiliate nexus provisions are applicable to remote sellers effective April 1, 2016.	La. Rev. Stat. Ann. § 47:301, La. Rev. Stat. Ann. § 47:304
Maine	Yes		Me. Rev. Stat. Ann. tit. 36, § 1754-B(1)(G), Instructional Bulletin No. 43
Maryland	Yes		Md. Code Ann. § 11-403, Md. Code Ann. § 11-101, Md. Code Ann. § 11-701
Massachusetts	Yes		Mass. Gen. Laws ch. 64I, § 4, Mass. Gen. Laws ch. 64H, § 1, Technical Information Release 96-8
Michigan	Yes		Revenue Administrative Bulletin 1999-1
Minnesota	Yes		Minn. Stat. § 297A.66
Mississippi	Yes		Miss. Code. Ann. § 27-67-3, Miss. Code. Ann. § 27-67-4, Miss. Code. Ann. § 27-65-9
Missouri	Yes		Mo. Rev. Stat. § 144.605, Mo. Code Regs. Ann. tit. 12, § 10-114.100(2)(B), Mo. Code Regs. Ann. tit. 12, § 10-4.085(2)(C)
Nebraska	Yes		Neb. Rev. Stat. § 77-2703(2)(b), Neb. Rev. Stat. § 77-2701.13, Neb. Admin. Code § 1-004
Nevada	Yes		Nev. Rev. Stat. § 372.195
New Jersey	Yes		N.J. Stat. Ann. § 54:32B-2, TB-78
New Mexico	Yes		N.M. Stat. Ann. § 7-9-10
New York	Yes		N.Y. Tax Law, § 1101(b)(8), N.Y. Comp. Code R. & Regs. tit. 20, § 526.10(a), TSB-M-08(3)S
North Carolina	Yes		N.C. Gen. Stat. § 105-164.3(9), N.C. Gen. Stat. § 105-164.8
North Dakota	Yes		N.D. Cent. Code § 57-40.2-07, N.D. Cent. Code § 57-40.2-01
Ohio	Yes		Ohio Rev. Code Ann. § 5741.17, Ohio Rev. Code Ann. § 5741.01, Information Release ST 2001-01

State	Employee Making Sales	Comments	Citation
Oklahoma	Yes		Okla. Admin. Code § 710:65-1-8(b), Okla. Stat. tit. 68, § 1406, Okla. Admin. Code § 710:65-21-4(b)
Pennsylvania	Yes		72 P.S. § 7237, 72 P.S. § 7201(b)
Rhode Island	Yes		R.I. Gen. Laws § 44-18-23
South Carolina	Yes		S.C. Code Ann. § 12-36-1340, S.C. Code Ann. § 12-36-70, Revenue Ruling 14-4
South Dakota	Yes		S.D. Codified Laws § 10-46-1
Tennessee	Yes		Tenn. Code. Ann. § 67-6-102
Texas	Yes		Tex. Tax Code Ann. § 151.103, Tex. Tax Code Ann. § 151.107, 34 Tex. Admin. Code § 3.286
Utah	Yes		Utah Code Ann. § 59-12-107
Vermont	Yes		Vt. Stat. Ann. tit. 32, § 9701
Virginia	Yes		Va. Code Ann. § 58.1-612(C)(2)
Washington	Yes	An employee's visits to the state to make wholesale sales are not associated with the taxpayer's ability to establish and maintain a market for its product if the products never enter the Washington marketplace, but are delivered outside the state for retail sale outside the state.	Wash. Rev. Code § 82.12.040, Wash. Admin. Code § 458-20-193, Tax Determination No. 11-0225, Washington Department of Revenue, June 28, 2012
West Virginia	Yes		W. Va. Code § 11-15A-1(b)(8)(A), W. Va. Code R. § 110-15-2.78.1
Wisconsin	Yes		Wis. Stat. § 77.53(3), Wis. Stat. § 77.51, Wis. Admin. Code § 11.97
Wyoming	Yes		Wyo. Stat. Ann. § 39-16-103(c)(v), Wyo. Stat. Ann. § 39-16-101(a)(x)

¶ 142   **Nexus—Independent Sales Agent**

This chart indicates whether the use of an independent agent to solicit sales in a state creates nexus for a seller.

State	Independent Sales Agent	Comments	Citation
Alabama	Yes		Ala. Code § 40-23-68
Arizona	Yes		Ariz. Rev. Stat. § 42-5151
Arkansas	Yes		Ark. Code Ann. § 26-52-103, Ark. Reg. GR-5
California	Yes		Cal. Rev. & Tax. Code § 6203, Reg. 1684, 18 CCR
Colorado	Yes		Colo. Rev. Stat. § 39-26-102, Colo. Code Regs. § 39-26-102.3
Connecticut	Yes		Conn. Gen. Stat. § 12-411(3), Conn. Gen. Stat. § 12-407(a)(12) and (a)(15)(A)
District of Columbia	Yes		D.C. Code Ann. § 47-2201(h)
Florida	Yes		Fla. Stat. § 212.0596
Georgia	Yes		Ga. Code Ann. § 48-8-65(b)(2)
Hawaii	Yes		Haw. Rev. Stat. § 237-13, Haw. Rev. Stat. § 238-2
Idaho	Yes		Idaho Code § 63-3611, Idaho Code § 63-3615A
Illinois	Yes		35 ILCS 105/3-45, 35 ILCS 105/2
Indiana	Yes		Ind. Code § 6-2.5-3-1
Iowa	Yes		Iowa Code § 423.29, Iowa Code § 423.1, Iowa Admin. Code r. 701 30.1
Kansas	Yes		Kan. Stat. Ann. § 79-3702(g)-(h), Kan. Stat. Ann. § 79-3705c, Kan. Admin. Regs. § 92-20-7, In the Matter of the Appeal of Family Eagles, Ltd.
Kentucky	Yes		Ky. Rev. Stat. Ann. § 139.340
Louisiana	Yes	Click-through and affiliate nexus provisions are applicable to remote sellers effective April 1, 2016.	La. Rev. Stat. Ann. § 47:301, La. Rev. Stat. Ann. § 47:304
Maine	Yes		Me. Rev. Stat. Ann. tit. 36, § 1754-B, Instructional Bulletin No. 43
Maryland	Yes		Md. Code Ann. § 11-403, Md. Code Ann. § 11-101, Md. Code Ann. § 11-701

State	Independent Sales Agent	Comments	Citation
Massachusetts	Yes		Mass. Gen. Laws ch. 64I, § 4, Mass. Gen. Laws ch. 64H, § 1, Technical Information Release 96-8
Michigan	Yes		Revenue Administrative Bulletin 1999-1
Minnesota	Yes		Minn. Stat. § 297A.66
Mississippi	Yes		Miss. Code. Ann. § 27-67-3, Miss. Code. Ann. § 27-67-4, Miss. Code. Ann. § 27-65-9
Missouri	Yes		Mo. Rev. Stat. § 144.605, Mo. Code Regs. Ann. tit. 12, § 10-114.100, Mo. Code Regs. Ann. tit. 12, § 10-4.085
Nebraska	Yes		Neb. Rev. Stat. § 77-2703(2)(b), Neb. Rev. Stat. § 77-2701.13, Neb. Admin. Code § 1-004
Nevada	Yes		Nev. Rev. Stat. § 372.195
New Jersey	Yes	Depending upon relationship to the seller. A person making sales of taxable tangible personal property, specified digital products, or services is presumed to be soliciting business through an independent contractor or other representative if the person making sales enters into an agreement with an independent contractor having physical presence in New Jersey or other representative having physical presence in New Jersey, for a commission or other consideration, under which the independent contractor or representative directly or indirectly refers potential customers, whether by a link on an Internet website or otherwise, and the cumulative gross receipts from sales to customers in New Jersey who were referred by all independent contractors or representatives that have this type of an agreement with the person making sales are in excess of $10,000 during the preceding four quarterly periods ending on the last day of March, June, September, and December.	N.J. Stat. Ann. § 54:32B-2, Bulletin S&U-5, TB-78, Unofficial Department Guidance
New Mexico	Yes		N.M. Stat. Ann. § 7-9-10

State	Independent Sales Agent	Comments	Citation
New York	Yes		N.Y. Tax Law, § 1101, N.Y. Comp. Code R. & Regs. tit. 20, § 526.10, TSB-M-08(3)S
North Carolina	Yes		N.C. Gen. Stat. § 105-164.3(9), N.C. Gen. Stat. § 105-164.8
North Dakota	Yes		N.D. Cent. Code § 57-40.2-07, N.D. Cent. Code § 57-40.2-01
Ohio	Yes		Ohio Rev. Code Ann. § 5741.17, Ohio Rev. Code Ann. § 5741.01, Information Release ST 2001-01
Oklahoma	Yes		Okla. Stat. tit. 68, § 1352(13), Okla. Admin. Code § 710:65-1-8(b)
Pennsylvania	Yes		72 P.S. § 7237, 72 P.S. § 7201(b)
Rhode Island	Yes		R.I. Gen. Laws § 44-18-15, R.I. Gen. Laws § 44-18-23
South Carolina	Yes		S.C. Code Ann. § 12-36-1340, S.C. Code Ann. § 12-36-70, Revenue Ruling 14-4
South Dakota	Yes		S.D. Codified Laws § 10-46-1
Tennessee	Yes		Tenn. Code. Ann. § 67-6-102
Texas	Yes		Tex. Tax Code Ann. § 151.103, Tex. Tax Code Ann. § 151.107, 34 Tex. Admin. Code § 3.286
Utah	Yes		Utah Code Ann. § 59-12-107
Vermont	Yes		Vt. Stat. Ann. tit. 32, § 9701
Virginia	Yes		Va. Code Ann. § 58.1-612
Washington	Yes		Wash. Rev. Code § 82.12.040, Wash. Admin. Code § 458-20-193
West Virginia	Yes		W. Va. Code § 11-15A-1(b)(8), W. Va. Code R. § 110-15-2, W. Va. Code R. § 110-15-2.78
Wisconsin	Yes		Wis. Stat. § 77.53(3), Wis. Stat. § 77.51, Wis. Admin. Code § 11.97
Wyoming	Yes		Wyo. Stat. Ann. § 39-16-103(c)(v), Wyo. Stat. Ann. § 39-16-101(a)(x)

Nexus—Internet Sales

This chart indicates whether using a website to make sales to a state's residents can create nexus for a seller. Note that state nexus statutes are subject to federal constitutional restrictions. In Quill Corp. v. North Dakota (504 U.S. 298 (1992)), the U.S. Supreme Court held that under the Commerce Clause, a seller must have a physical presence in a state in order for that state to require the seller to collect sales and use taxes.

State	Internet Sales	Comments	Citation
Alabama	No		Ala. Code § 40-23-68
Arizona	No		Ariz. Rev. Stat. § 42-5151
Arkansas	Yes	Click-through nexus: There is a presumption of nexus if seller enters into agreement with Arkansas resident under which resident, for a consideration, refers purchasers, via link on Internet website or otherwise, to seller.	Ark. Code Ann. § 26-52-103, Ark. Code Ann. § 26-52-117, Ark. Code Ann. § 26-53-124(a)(3)
California	Yes	Click-through (and affiliate) nexus provisions are operative September 15, 2012. The definition of "retailer engaged in business in this state" includes, effective September 15, 2012, any retailer who enters into an agreement under which a person in California, for a commission or other consideration, directly or indirectly refers potential purchasers of tangible personal property to the retailer, whether by an Internet-based link, a website, or otherwise, provided two conditions are met. Those conditions are: (1) that the total cumulative sales price from all of the retailer's sales within the preceding 12 months of tangible personal property to purchasers in California that are referred pursuant to such an agreement is in excess of $10,000; and (2) the retailer has total cumulative sales of tangible personal property to California purchasers in excess of $1 million within the preceding 12 months.	Cal. Rev. & Tax. Code § 6203, Reg. 1684, 18 CCR
Colorado	Yes		Colo. Rev. Stat. § 39-26-102, Colo. Code Regs. § 39-26-102.3

State	Internet Sales	Comments	Citation
Connecticut	Yes	Click-through nexus is imposed applicable to sales that occur on or after May 4, 2011. The definition of "retailer" includes every person who makes sales of tangible personal property or services through an agreement with another person located in Connecticut under which that person located in the state, for a commission or other consideration that is based on the sale of tangible personal property or services by the retailer, directly or indirectly refers potential customers to the retailer, whether by a link on an Internet website or otherwise, and the cumulative gross receipts from sales by the retailer to Connecticut customers who are referred to the retailer by all such persons with this type of an agreement with the retailer, is in excess of $2,000 during the preceding four quarterly periods ending on the last day of March, June, September, and December. In addition, the definition of "engaged in business in the state" includes selling tangible personal property or services through an agreement with a person located in Connecticut, under which that person, for a commission or other consideration that is based on the sale of tangible personal property or services by the retailer, directly or indirectly refers potential customers, whether by a link on an Internet website or otherwise, to the retailer, provided the cumulative gross receipts from sales by the retailer to Connecticut customers who are referred to the retailer by all such persons with this type of agreement with the retailer is in excess of $2,000 during the four preceding four quarterly periods ending on the last day of March, June, September, and December.	Conn. Gen. Stat. § 12-411(3), Conn. Gen. Stat. § 12-407(a)(12) and (a)(15)(A)
District of Columbia	No		D.C. Code Ann. § 47-2201, D.C. Code Ann. § 47-3932
Florida	Yes	Every dealer who makes a mail order sale is subject to the power of the state to levy and collect sales and use tax when the dealer, by purposefully or systematically exploiting the market provided by Florida by any media-assisted, media-facilitated, or media-solicited means, including computer-assisted shopping, creates nexus with Florida.	Fla. Stat. § 212.0596

State	Internet Sales	Comments	Citation
Georgia	May create nexus	"Click-through" nexus provisions apply. Effective July 18, 2012, the definition of "dealer"; was expanded to include any person who enters into an agreement with one or more persons who are Georgia residents under which the resident(s), for a commission or other consideration, based on completed sales, directly or indirectly refers potential customers (whether by a link on an Internet website, an in-person oral presentation, telemarketing, or otherwise) to the person, if the cumulative gross receipts from sales by the person to customers in Georgia who are referred to the person by all residents with this type of an agreement with the person is more than $50,000 during the preceding 12 months. The presumption that such a person qualifies as a "dealer" in Georgia is rebuttable.	Ga. Code Ann. § 48-8-65(b)(2), Ga. Code Ann. § 48-8-2(8)(M), Ga. Code Ann. § 48-8-30(b)(1)
Hawaii	No	Hawaii has not adopted a "click-through nexus" policy.	Haw. Rev. Stat. § 237-13, Haw. Rev. Stat. § 238-2, HI DOT Response to CCH Survey Regarding Click-Through Nexus
Idaho	No		Idaho Code § 63-3611, Idaho Code § 63-3615A
Illinois	No	The Illinois Supreme Court declared the click-through nexus definition provisions found in 35 ILCS 105/2(1.1) and 35 ILCS 110/2(1.1) to be void in an opinion dated October 13, 2013. The statute was applicable July 1, 2011.	35 ILCS 105/2, 35 ILCS 110/2, Ill. Admin. Code tit. 86, § 160.130
Indiana	No		Ind. Code § 6-2.5-3-1
Iowa	No		Iowa Code § 423.29, Iowa Code § 423.1, Iowa Admin. Code r. 701 30.1
Kansas	May create nexus	"Click-through" nexus provisions apply. There is a rebuttable presumption that a retailer is a "retailer doing business in this state" if the retailer enters into an agreement with one or more Kansas residents under which the resident, for a commission or other consideration, directly or indirectly refers potential customers, whether by a link or an Internet website, by telemarketing, by an in-person oral presentation, or otherwise, to the retailer, if the cumulative gross receipts from sales by the retailer to customers in Kansas who are referred to the retailer by all residents with this type of an agreement with the retailer is more than $10,000 during the preceding 12 months.	Kan. Stat. Ann. § 79-3702(h)(2)(C)
Kentucky	No		Ky. Rev. Stat. Ann. § 139.340

State	Internet Sales	Comments	Citation
Louisiana	Yes	Click-through and affiliate nexus provisions are applicable to remote sellers effective April 1, 2016.	La. Rev. Stat. Ann. § 47:301, La. Rev. Stat. Ann. § 47:304, LA DOR Sales Tax FAQ
Maine	No		Me. Rev. Stat. Ann. tit. 36, § 1754-B(1)(G)
Maryland	No		Md. Code Ann. § 11-403, Md. Code Ann. § 11-101, Md. Code Ann. § 11-701
Massachusetts	May create nexus	Statute indicates nexus may exist. However, in Quill Corp. v. North Dakota, the U.S. Supreme Court held that under the Commerce Clause, a vendor must have a physical presence in a state in order for that state to require the vendor to collect tax.	Mass. Gen. Laws ch. 64I, § 4, Mass. Gen. Laws ch. 64H, § 1, Technical Information Release 96-8
Michigan	Yes	There is a rebuttable presumption that a retailer is engaged in business in Michigan if the retailer enters into an agreement with one or more Michigan residents under which the resident, for a commission or other consideration, directly or indirectly refers potential customers, whether by a link or an Internet website, by an in-person oral presentation, or otherwise, to the retailer, if the cumulative gross receipts from sales by the retailer to customers in Michigan who are referred to the retailer by all residents with this type of an agreement with the retailer is more than $10,000 during the preceding 12 months. Also, the seller's total cumulative gross receipts from sales to customers in Michigan must be greater than $50,000 during the immediately preceding 12 months	Revenue Administrative Bulletin 1999-1, Revenue Administrative Bulletin 2015-22, Mich. Comp. Laws § 205.52b
Minnesota	Yes	Statute indicates nexus may exist. However, in Quill Corp. v. North Dakota, the U.S. Supreme Court held that under the Commerce Clause, a vendor must have a physical presence in a state in order for that state to require the vendor to collect tax. Click-through nexus provision (Internet sales resulting from referral agreements with in-state residents creates nexus) is effective for sales and purchases made after June 30, 2013.	Minn. Stat. § 297A.66, subd. 4a
Mississippi	May create nexus	Nexus may exist if person purposefully or systematically exploits consumer market in Mississippi via computer-assisted shopping or other electronic media and if other requirements are met (Sec. 27-67-4(2)(e)). However, in Quill Corp. v. North Dakota, the U.S. Supreme Court held that under the Commerce Clause, a vendor must have a physical presence in a state in order for that state to require the vendor to collect tax.	Miss. Code. Ann. § 27-67-3, Miss. Code. Ann. § 27-67-4

¶143

State	Internet Sales	Comments	Citation
Missouri	Yes	Click-through nexus: There is a presumption of nexus if a vendor enters into an agreement with a state resident, under which the resident, for a commission or other consideration, refers potential customers, through a link on an Internet website or otherwise, to the vendor, and the vendor's cumulative gross receipts from sales to Missouri customers referred by residents with such an agreement exceeded $10,000 in the preceding 12 months. This presumption may be rebutted by showing that the Missouri resident did not engage in activity within Missouri that was significantly associated with the vendor's market in Missouri in the preceding 12 months.	Mo. Rev. Stat. § 144.605, Mo. Code Regs. Ann. tit. 12, § 10-114.100
Nebraska	No		Neb. Rev. Stat. § 77-2703(2)(b), Neb. Rev. Stat. § 77-2701.13, Neb. Admin. Code § 1-004
Nevada	May create nexus	Nevada does not provide statutory or regulatory guidance on nexus for sales and use tax purposes. However, in Quill Corp. v. North Dakota, the U.S. Supreme Court held that under the Commerce Clause, a vendor must have a physical presence in a state in order for that state to require the vendor to collect tax.	Nev. Rev. Stat. § 372.195

State	Internet Sales	Comments	Citation
New Jersey	Yes	Click-through nexus: A person making sales of taxable tangible personal property, specified digital products, or services is presumed to be soliciting business through an independent contractor or other representative if the person making sales enters into an agreement with an independent contractor having physical presence in New Jersey or other representative having physical presence in New Jersey, for a commission or other consideration, under which the independent contractor or representative directly or indirectly refers potential customers, whether by a link on an Internet website or otherwise, and the cumulative gross receipts from sales to customers in New Jersey who were referred by all independent contractors or representatives that have this type of an agreement with the person making sales are in excess of $10,000 during the preceding four quarterly periods ending on the last day of March, June, September, and December. This presumption may be rebutted by proof that the independent contractor or representative with whom the person making sales has an agreement did not engage in any solicitation in New Jersey on behalf of the person that would satisfy the nexus requirements of the U.S. Constitution during the four quarterly periods in question.	N.J. Stat. Ann. § 54:32B-2, Bulletin S&U-5, TB-78
New Mexico	No		N.M. Stat. Ann. § 7-9-10
New York	Yes	Click-through nexus: New York has a rebuttable presumption that certain Internet retailers of taxable tangible personal property or services are sales tax vendors required to register and collect state and local sales taxes. Specifically, New York's statutes define a vendor required to collect tax to include a seller that enters into a commission agreement with a New York resident under which the resident directly or indirectly refers potential customers, whether by a link on an internet website or otherwise, to the seller and such referrals result in gross receipts in excess of $10,000 during the preceding four quarterly periods. The presumption is deemed rebutted where the seller is able to establish that the only activity of its resident representative in New York on behalf of the seller is a link provided on the representatives' Web site to the seller's Web site and none of the resident representatives engage in any solicitation activity in the state targeted at potential New York customers on behalf of the seller.	N.Y. Tax Law, § 1101, N.Y. Comp. Code R. & Regs. tit. 20, § 526.10, TSB-M-08(9)S, TSB-M-08(3)S

State	Internet Sales	Comments	Citation
North Carolina	Yes	Click-through nexus is imposed. A retailer is presumed to be soliciting or transacting business by an independent contractor, agent, or other representative if the retailer enters into an agreement with a North Carolina resident who, pursuant to the agreement and for a commission or other consideration, directly or indirectly refers potential customers, whether by link on an Internet Web site or otherwise, to the retailer. The presumption applies only if the cumulative gross receipts from sales by the retailer to North Carolina purchasers who are referred to the retailer by all residents with this type of agreement with the retailer is in excess of $10,000 during the preceding four quarterly periods. The presumption may be rebutted by proof that the resident with whom the retailer has an agreement did not engage in any solicitation in North Carolina on behalf of the seller that would satisfy the nexus requirement of the U.S. Constitution during the four quarterly periods in question.	N.C. Gen. Stat. § 105-164.8(b)(3)
North Dakota	Yes	Statute indicates nexus may exist. However, in Quill Corp. v. North Dakota, the U.S. Supreme Court held that under the Commerce Clause, a vendor must have a physical presence in a state in order for that state to require the vendor to collect tax.	N.D. Cent. Code § 57-40.2-07, N.D. Cent. Code § 57-40.2-01, Guideline - Out of State Retailers, ND Office of State Tax Commissioner Response to CCH Survey Regarding Click-Through Nexus
Ohio	Yes	Click-through nexus: There is a rebuttable presumption of substantial nexus if seller enters into agreement with Ohio resident under which resident, for a consideration, refers purchasers, via link on Internet website or otherwise, to seller. The presumption requires that the cumulative gross receipts from sales by the seller to customers in Ohio who are referred to the seller be greater than $10,000 during the immediately preceding 12 months.	Ohio Rev. Code Ann. § 5741.17, Ohio Rev. Code Ann. § 5741.01, Information Release ST 2001-01
Oklahoma	May create nexus	Any retailer making sales of tangible personal property to purchasers in Oklahoma by the Internet that has contracted with an entity to provide and perform installation or maintenance services for the retailer's purchasers in Oklahoma comes within the definition of a "retailer."	Okla. Admin. Code § 710:65-19-156, Okla. Stat. tit. 68, § 1352, Okla. Stat. tit. 68, § 1401(9)(e)

State	Internet Sales	Comments	Citation
Pennsylvania	Yes	Click-through nexus: The DOR has stated that a remote seller has nexus if the seller: has a contractual relationship with an entity or individual physically located in PA whose website has a link that encourages purchasers to place orders with the remote sellers, and the in-state entity or individual receives consideration for the contractual relationship with the remote seller; or regularly solicits orders from PA customers via the website of an entity or individual physically located in PA, such as via click-through technology.	72 P.S. § 7237, 72 P.S. § 7201(b), Sales and Use Tax Bulletin 2011-01
Rhode Island	Yes	Click-through nexus: There is a presumption of nexus if a retailer enters into an agreement with a state resident, under which the resident, for a commission or other consideration, refers potential customers, through a link on an Internet website or otherwise, to the retailer, if the retailer's cumulative gross receipts from sales to Rhode Island customers referred by residents with such an agreement exceeded $5,000 during the preceding 4 quarterly periods. The presumption can be rebutted by proof that the state resident did not engage in any solicitation on behalf of the seller that would satisfy the nexus requirements of the U.S. Constitution during the four quarterly periods in question.	R.I. Gen. Laws § 44-18-23, R.I. Gen. Laws § 44-18-15
South Carolina	No	A business that sells tangible personal property over the Internet and operates a website maintained on a server owned by the business and located in South Carolina, has nexus. Other exceptions may also apply.	S.C. Code Ann. § 12-36-1340, Revenue Ruling 14-4
South Dakota	No		S.D. Codified Laws § 10-46-1
Tennessee	Effective July 1, 2015, yes.	Effective July 1, 2015, a dealer is presumed to have a representative, agent, salesperson, canvasser, or solicitor operating in Tennessee for the purpose of making sales and is presumed to have a substantial nexus with Tennessee provided: (a) the dealer enters into an agreement or contract with one or more persons located in Tennessee under which the person, for a commission or other consideration, directly or indirectly refers potential customers to the dealer, whether by a link on an Internet website or any other means; and (b) the dealer's cumulative gross receipts from retail sales made by the dealer to customers in Tennessee who are referred to the dealer by all residents with this type of an agreement with the dealer exceed $10,000 during the preceding 12 months.	Tenn. Code. Ann. § 67-6-102, Tenn. Code. Ann. § 67-6-520, Bloomingdale's by Mail, Ltd. v. Huddleston

¶143

State	Internet Sales	Comments	Citation
Texas	Yes	Statute indicates nexus may exist. However, in Quill Corp. v. North Dakota, the U.S. Supreme Court held that under the Commerce Clause, a vendor must have a physical presence in a state in order for that state to require the vendor to collect tax. A person whose only activity in Texas is conducted as a user of Internet hosting is not engaged in business in Texas.	Tex. Tax Code Ann. § 151.103, Tex. Tax Code Ann. § 151.107, Tex. Tax Code Ann. § 151.108, 34 Tex. Admin. Code § 3.286
Utah	No		Utah Code Ann. § 59-12-107
Vermont	Yes	Statute indicates nexus may exist if seller made at least $50,000 in sales in Vermont within a 12-month period. However, in Quill Corp. v. North Dakota, the U.S. Supreme Court held that under the Commerce Clause, a vendor must have a physical presence in a state in order for that state to require the vendor to collect tax. Also, Vermont has enacted a click-through nexus provision that is effective as of October 13, 2015, with remote sellers required to register and to collect and remit sales tax as of December 1, 2015.	Vt. Stat. Ann. tit. 32, § 9701(9), Updated: Statement of Vermont Department of Taxes on Vermont Click Through Nexus Law
Virginia	No	Virginia has legislation that requires certain remote sellers that utilize in-state facilities to collect Virginia sales tax. The law establishes a presumption that a dealer has nexus with the state if any commonly controlled person maintains a distribution center, warehouse, fulfillment center, office, or similar location in Virginia that facilitates the delivery of tangible personal property sold by the dealer to its customers. The presumption may be rebutted by demonstrating that the activities conducted by the commonly controlled person in Virginia are not significantly associated with the dealer's ability to establish or maintain a market in the state. The law takes effect on the earlier of September 1, 2013, or the effective date of federal legislation authorizing the states to require a seller to collect taxes on sales of goods to in-state purchasers without regard to the location of the seller. If, however, such federal legislation is enacted prior to August 15, 2013, and the effective date of that federal legislation is after September 1, 2013, but on or before January 1, 2014, then the provisions become effective on January 1, 2014.	Va. Code Ann. § 58.1-612

State	Internet Sales	Comments	Citation
Washington	Yes	A seller is presumed to have substantial nexus with Washington if the seller enters into an agreement with one or more residents under which the resident, for a commission or other consideration, directly or indirectly, refers potential customers, by a link on an Internet website or otherwise, to the seller. The presumption requires that the cumulative gross receipts from sales by the seller to customers in this state who are referred to the seller be greater than $10,000 during the preceding calendar year.	Wash. Rev. Code § 82.12.040, Wash. Admin. Code § 458-20-193, Section 202, S.B. 6138, Laws 2015
West Virginia	Yes	Sellers who purposefully or systematically exploit the market in the state by any media-assisted, media-facilitated, or media-solicited means, including computer-assisted shopping, create nexus with the state for purposes of sales and use tax.	W. Va. Code R. § 110-15-128.1.5
Wisconsin	No	Nexus may be created under certain circumstances, for example if website data is stored on server owned by company and located in Wisconsin.	Wis. Stat. § 77.53(3), Wis. Stat. § 77.51, Wis. Admin. Code § 11.97, CCH Sales and Use Tax Nexus Survey
Wyoming	Yes	"Vendor" defined as including every person who engages in regular or systematic solicitation by three or more separate transmittances of advertisements in any 12 month period in a consumer market in Wyoming by the distribution of catalogs. Effective July 1, 2017, "vendor" includes remote sellers to the extent provided by Wyo. Stat. Ann. Sec. 39-15-501.	Wyo. Stat. Ann. § 39-16-103(c)(v), Wyo. Stat. Ann. § 39-16-101(a)(x), Wyo. Stat. Ann. § 39-15-501, Buehner Block Co. v. Wyoming Department of Revenue

¶ 144   Nexus—Related Entity

This chart indicates whether the presence of a related entity in a state can create nexus for a seller. Note that state nexus statutes are subject to federal constitutional restrictions. In Quill Corp. v. North Dakota (504 U.S. 298 (1992)), the U.S. Supreme Court held that under the Commerce Clause, a seller must have a physical presence in a state in order for that state to require the seller to collect sales and use taxes.

State	Related Entity	Comments	Citation
Alabama	Yes	Nexus is established if an out-of-state vendor and an in-state business maintaining one or more locations within Alabama are related parties and they: (1) use an identical or substantially similar name, tradename, trademark, or goodwill, to develop, promote, or maintain sales; (2) pay for each other's services contingent upon the volume or value of sales; (3) share a common business plan or substantially coordinate their business plans; or (4) the in-state business provides services to, or that inure to the benefit of, the out-of-state business related to developing, promoting, or maintaining the in-state market.	Ala. Code § 40-23-68, Ala. Code § 40-23-190, Ala. Admin. Code r. 810-6-2-.90.01
Arizona	Yes	If the related entity's activities help establish or maintain a market for the seller.	Ariz. Rev. Stat. § 42-5151
Arkansas	Yes	If seller: (1) holds a substantial ownership interest in, or is substantially owned by a parent or subsidary of, a retailer maintaining sales locations in Arkansas; and (2) sells a substantially similar line of products under a substantially similar business name, or facilities or employees of the Arkansas retailer are used to advertise or promote sales by the seller to Arkansas purchasers.	Ark. Code Ann. § 26-52-103, Ark. Code Ann. § 26-52-117, Ark. Code Ann. § 26-53-124(a)(3)
California	Yes	Affiliate nexus provisions are operative September 15, 2012. The term "retailer" includes an entity affiliated with a retailer within the meaning of IRC § 1504. In addition, the term "retailer engaged in business in this state" includes any retailer that is a member of a commonly controlled group and a combined reporting group, both as defined, that includes another member of the retailer's commonly controlled group that, pursuant to an agreement with or in cooperation with the retailer, performs services in California in connection with tangible personal property to be sold by the retailer, including but not limited to the design and development of tangible personal property sold by the retailer, or the solicitation of sales of tangible personal property on behalf of the retailer.	Cal. Rev. & Tax. Code § 6203, Reg. 1684, 18 CCR, Borders Online, LLC v. SBE
Colorado	Yes	If subsidiary of seller is located in the state. A retailer who does not collect Colorado sales tax and is part of a "controlled group of corporations" that has a "component member" who has a retail presence in the state is presumed to be doing business in the state.	Colo. Rev. Stat. § 39-26-102, Colo. Code Regs. § 39-26-102.3

State	Related Entity	Comments	Citation
Connecticut	Yes	If the related entity is a retailer engaged in a similar line of business in the state.	Conn. Gen. Stat. § 12-411(3), Conn. Gen. Stat. § 12-407(a)(15)(A)
District of Columbia	Yes	If the related entity acts on behalf of the seller.	D.C. Code Ann. § 47-2201(h)
Florida	Yes	If the seller is a member of an affiliated group eligible to file a consolidated federal income tax return, and any corporation in the affiliated group has nexus with the state.	Fla. Stat. § 212.0596
Georgia	Yes	With certain exceptions, the definition of "dealer" includes an affiliate that sells at retail, offers for sale at retail in Georgia, or engages in the regular or systematic solicitation of a consumer market in Georgia through a related dealer located in Georgia. There is rebuttable presumption that a "dealer" is one who makes sales of tangible personal property or services that are subject to sales and use tax if a "related member" (other than a common carrier acting in its capacity as such) that has substantial nexus in Georgia (1) sells a similar line of products as the person and does so under the same or a similar business name; or (2) uses trademarks, service marks, or trade names in Georgia that are the same or substantially similar to those used by the person.	Ga. Code Ann. § 48-8-2(8)(J)-(K), Ga. Code Ann. § 48-8-30(b)(1)
Hawaii	Yes	If the related entity acts on behalf of the seller.	Haw. Rev. Stat. § 237-13, Haw. Rev. Stat. § 238-2
Idaho	Yes	If the seller that had at least $100,000 in sales in Idaho in the previous year and other statutory requirements are met.	Idaho Code § 63-3611, Idaho Code § 63-3615A
Illinois	Yes	Having or maintaining in Illinois, directly or by a subsidiary, an office, distribution house, sales house, warehouse or other place of business constitutes maintaining a business.	35 ILCS 105/3-45, 35 ILCS 105/2
Indiana	No		Indiana Information Bulletin No. ST37, Ind. Code § 6-2.5-3-1
Iowa	Yes	If the related entity acts on behalf of the seller.	Iowa Code § 423.29, Iowa Code § 423.1, Iowa Admin. Code r. 701 30.1
Kansas	Yes	"Affiliate nexus" provisions apply.	Kan. Stat. Ann. § 79-3702(h)(2), Kan. Stat. Ann. § 79-3705c
Kentucky	Yes	The definition of "retailer engaged in business in this state" includes a retailer who maintains, operates, or uses in Kentucky an office, place of distribution, sales or sample room, warehouse, storage place, or other place of business through a subsidiary or any other related entity.	Ky. Rev. Stat. Ann. § 139.340

State	Related Entity	Comments	Citation
Louisiana	Yes	Click-through and affiliate nexus provisions are applicable to remote sellers effective April 1, 2016.	La. Rev. Stat. Ann. § 47:301, La. Rev. Stat. Ann. § 47:304, St. Tammany Parish Tax Collector v. Barnesandnoble.com
Maine	Yes	If the related entity acts on behalf of the seller.	Me. Rev. Stat. Ann. tit. 36, § 1754-B
Maryland	Yes	If the related entity acts on behalf of the seller.	Md. Code Ann. § 11-403, Md. Code Ann. § 11-101, Md. Code Ann. § 11-701, Md. Code Regs. 06.01.33
Massachusetts	Yes	If the related entity's activities help create or maintain a market for the seller.	Mass. Gen. Laws ch. 64I, § 4, Mass. Gen. Laws ch. 64H, § 1, Letter Ruling 05-7
Michigan	Yes	If the related entity acts on behalf of the seller.	Revenue Administrative Bulletin 1999-1, Revenue Administrative Bulletin 2015-22, Mich. Comp. Laws § 205.52b
Minnesota	Yes	If the related entity or affiliate acts on behalf of the seller. An affiliate includes a related party that uses the retailer's facilities or employees in Minnesota to advertise, promote, or facilitate sales of items by the retailer to purchasers in Minnesota or for the provision of services to the retailer's purchasers in Minnesota, such as accepting returns of purchases for the retailer, providing assistance in resolving customer complaints of the retailer, or providing other services.	Minn. Stat. § 297A.66, subd. 1, Minn. Stat. § 297A.66, subd. 4
Mississippi	Yes	If the related entity acts on behalf of the seller.	Miss. Code. Ann. § 27-67-3
Missouri	Yes	Presumption of nexus if the affiliated entity: sells a similar line of products under a similar business name; maintains a place of business that facilitates the delivery of property or services sold by the vendor or allows the vendor's customers to pick up property sold by the vendor; delivers, installs, assembles, or performs maintenance services for the vendor's customers in the state; or conducts any other activities in the state that are significantly associated with the vendor's ability to maintain a market in the state.	Mo. Rev. Stat. § 144.605, Mo. Code Regs. Ann. tit. 12, § 10-114.100
Nebraska	Yes	If the seller is owned or controlled by the same interests that own or control a retailer engaged in a similar line of business in the state. However, in Quill Corp. v. North Dakota, the U.S. Supreme Court held that under the Commerce clause, a vendor must have a physical presence in a state in order for that state to require the vendor to collect tax.	Neb. Rev. Stat. § 77-2703(2)(b), Neb. Rev. Stat. § 77-2701.13, Neb. Admin. Code § 1-004

State	Related Entity	Comments	Citation
Nevada	Yes		Nev. Rev. Stat. § 372.195
New Jersey	Yes	A seller includes a person who solicits business either by employees, independent contractors, agents or other representatives or by distribution of catalogs or other advertising matter and by reason thereof makes sales to persons within the State of tangible personal property, specified digital products or services, the use of which is taxed by this act. A person making sales of taxable tangible personal property, specified digital products, or services is presumed to be soliciting business through an independent contractor or other representative if the person making sales enters into an agreement with an independent contractor having physical presence in New Jersey or other representative having physical presence in New Jersey, for a commission or other consideration, under which the independent contractor or representative directly or indirectly refers potential customers, whether by a link on an Internet website or otherwise, and the cumulative gross receipts from sales to customers in New Jersey who were referred by all independent contractors or representatives that have this type of an agreement with the person making sales are in excess of $10,000 during the preceding four quarterly periods ending on the last day of March, June, September, and December. Also, when in the opinion of the director it is necessary for the efficient administration of this act to treat any salesman, representative, peddler or canvasser as the agent of the seller, distributor, supervisor or employer under whom the agent operates or from whom the agent obtains tangible personal property or a specified digital product sold by the agent or for whom the agent solicits business, the director may, treat such agent as the seller jointly responsible with the agent's principal, distributor, supervisor or employer for the collection and payment over of the tax. A person is an agent of a seller in all cases, but not limited to such cases, that: (A) the person and the seller have the relationship of a "related person" N.J. Stat. Ann. § 54:10A-5.5; and (B) the seller and the person use an identical or substantially similar name, tradename, trademark, or goodwill, to develop, promote, or maintain sales, or the person and the seller pay for each other's services in whole or in part contingent upon the volume or value of sales, or the person and the seller share a common business plan or substantially coordinate their business plans, or the person provides services to, or that inure to the benefit of, the seller related to developing, promoting, or maintaining the seller's market.	N.J. Stat. Ann. § 54:32B-2, Bulletin S&U-5, TB-78

State	Related Entity	Comments	Citation
New Mexico	Yes	If the related entity acts on behalf of the seller.	N.M. Stat. Ann. § 7-9-10, N.M. Admin. Code tit. 3, § 3.2.13.8
New York	Yes	If the related entity acts on behalf of the seller and certain conditions are met. Under certain conditions, a vendor includes out-of-state sellers (remote affiliates) of taxable tangible personal property or services that are affiliated with businesses in New York (New York affiliates). In such a situation, a New York business and an out-of-state seller are affiliated with each other if one owns, directly or indirectly, more than 5% of the other or if more than 5% of each is owned, directly or indirectly, by the same person or by an affiliated group of persons. Remote affiliates are vendors and must register for sales tax purposes and begin to collect and remit sales tax when they are affiliated with a business in New York and either of the following conditions is met: —Condition I: A New York affiliate who is a sales tax vendor uses a trademark, service mark, or trade name in New York that is the same as that used in New York by the remote affiliate, or —Condition II: A New York affiliate engages in activities in New York that benefit the remote affiliate in its development or maintenance of a market for its goods or services in New York, to the extent that those activities are sufficient for the remote affiliate to satisfy the nexus requirements of the U.S. Constitution. For purposes of determining whether this condition is met, the Department will consider whether the direct or indirect ownership exceeds 50%, (i.e., if one owns, directly or indirectly, more than 50% of the other or if more than 50% of each person is owned, directly or indirectly, by the same person or by an affiliated group of persons). Condition II will be considered to be met if the percentage of direct or indirect ownership exceeds 50% and the New York affiliate engages in any activities that are more than de minimis and that promote the development or maintenance of a market for the remote affiliate's products or services in New York.	N.Y. Tax Law, § 1101, N.Y. Comp. Code R. & Regs. tit. 20, § 526.10, TSB-M-08(3)S, TSB-M-09(3)S
North Carolina	Yes	If the related entity transacts business on behalf of the seller.	N.C. Gen. Stat. § 105-164.8, N.C. Gen. Stat. § 105-164.3
North Dakota	Yes	If the related entity acts on behalf of the seller.	N.D. Cent. Code § 57-40.2-07, N.D. Cent. Code § 57-40.2-01
Ohio	Yes	If the seller is a member of an affiliated group with least one member that has nexus, and the activities of that member establish or maintain a market in Ohio for the seller.	Ohio Rev. Code Ann. § 5741.17, Ohio Rev. Code Ann. § 5741.01, Information Release ST 2001-01

State	Related Entity	Comments	Citation
Oklahoma	May create nexus	"Maintaining a place of business in this state" includes having or maintaining in Oklahoma permanently or temporarily (including through a subsidiary) a physical place of business. "Affiliate nexus" provisions also apply.	Okla. Stat. tit. 68, § 1352(13), Okla. Admin. Code § 710:65-1-8(b), Okla. Stat. tit. 68, § 1401(9)(b), (d)
Pennsylvania	Yes	If the related entity acts on behalf of the seller, or provides services that benefit, support or complement the remote seller's business activity.	72 P.S. § 7237, 72 P.S. § 7201(b), Bloomingdales By Mail, Ltd. v. Pennsylvania, Sales and Use Tax Bulletin 2011-01
Rhode Island	Yes	If the related entity acts on behalf of the seller.	R.I. Gen. Laws § 44-18-15, R.I. Gen. Laws § 44-18-23
South Carolina	Yes	If the related entity/affiliate sells similar merchandise and uses common trade names, trademarks or logos or if the South Carolina affiliate is used to accept returns, take orders, perform customer service, or distribute advertising materials on the corporation's behalf. Also, the corporation has nexus if it authorizes an affiliated company to install, deliver, service, or repair merchandise in South Carolina. A corporation also has nexus if it uses an affiliated company to investigate, handle or resolve customer issues, or provide training or technical assistance.	S.C. Code Ann. § 12-36-1340, S.C. Code Ann. § 12-36-80, Revenue Ruling 14-4
South Dakota	Yes	If the related entity acts on behalf of the seller.	S.D. Codified Laws § 10-46-1
Tennessee	Yes	If the related entity acts on behalf of the seller.	Tenn. Code. Ann. § 67-6-102, America Online, Inc. v. Johnson, Registering Your Business in Tennessee
Texas	Yes	(1) If retailer holds a substantial ownership interest in, or is substantially owned by, a person with a business location in Texas and either (a) sells a substantially similar line of products under a substantially similar business name as the person located in Texas or (b) uses facilities or employees of the Texas business to advertise, promote sales, or perform other activity to establish a marketplace in Texas; (2) if retailer holds a substantial ownership interest in, or is substantially owned by, a person that (a) maintains a distribution center, warehouse, or similar location in Texas and (b) delivers property sold by the retailer to consumers.	Tex. Tax Code Ann. § 151.103, Tex. Tax Code Ann. § 151.107, 34 Tex. Admin. Code § 3.286

State	Related Entity	Comments	Citation
Utah	Yes	If the related entity engages in advertising, marketing, or sales activities on behalf of the seller.	Utah Code Ann. § 59-12-107, Publication 37
Vermont	Yes	If the seller owns or controls a person engaged in the same manner or similar line of business in the state.	Vt. Stat. Ann. tit. 32, § 9701
Virginia	Yes	If the seller and the related entity are owned or controlled by the same interests. Virginia has legislation that requires certain remote sellers that utilize in-state facilities to collect Virginia sales tax. The law establishes a presumption that a dealer has nexus with the state if any commonly controlled person maintains a distribution center, warehouse, fulfillment center, office, or similar location in Virginia that facilitates the delivery of tangible personal property sold by the dealer to its customers. The presumption may be rebutted by demonstrating that the activities conducted by the commonly controlled person in Virginia are not significantly associated with the dealer's ability to establish or maintain a market in the state. A "commonly controlled person" means any person that is a member of the same "controlled group of corporations," as defined in IRC § 1563(a), as the dealer or any other entity that bears the same ownership relationship to the dealer as a corporation that is a member of the same controlled group of corporations. The law took effect on September 1, 2013 (the law provided that it is effective on the earlier of September 1, 2013, or upon passage of federal legislation granting states the authority to require remote sellers to collect taxes on goods shipped to in-state purchasers. Because no such federal legislation has been enacted, the effective date is September 1, 2013.)	Va. Code Ann. § 58.1-612, VTB 13-11
Washington	Yes	An affiliated company that performs activities significantly associated with the out-of-state taxpayer's ability to establish or maintain a market in Washington creates nexus.	Wash. Rev. Code § 82.12.040, Wash. Admin. Code § 458-20-193, E-mail, Washington Department of Revenue, September 13, 2010, Det No. 10-0057, Washington Department of Revenue, December 20, 2011

State	Related Entity	Comments	Citation
West Virginia	Yes	A retailer is considered to do business in West Virginia if it (1) solicits orders by mail, has physical presence in the state, and economically benefits from an authorized installation, servicing, or repair facility in the state owned or operated by a related person; (2) has a franchisee or licensee operating in the state under its trade name; or (3) has, maintains, occupies, or uses through a subsidiary an office, distribution house, sales house, warehouse, or other place of business in the state. "Affiliate nexus" provisions also apply.	W. Va. Code § 11-15A-6a, W. Va. Code § 11-15A-1(b)(8), W. Va. Code R. § 110-15-2.78
Wisconsin	Yes	If the seller's affiliate in Wisconsin uses facilities or employees in Wisconsin to advertise, promote, or facilitate sales of items by the seller to purchasers in Wisconsin or for providing services to the seller's purchasers in Wisconsin, including accepting returns of purchases or resolving customer complaints.	Wis. Stat. § 77.53(3), Wis. Stat. § 77.51(13g), Wis. Admin. Code § 11.97
Wyoming	Yes	If the related entity acts on behalf of seller.	Wyo. Stat. Ann. § 39-16-103(c)(v), Wyo. Stat. Ann. § 39-16-101(a)(x)

¶145   **Nexus—Warehouse**

This chart indicates whether having a warehouse in a state creates nexus for a seller.

State	Warehouse	Comments	Citation
Alabama	Yes		Ala. Code § 40-23-68
Arizona	Yes		Ariz. Rev. Stat. § 42-5151
Arkansas	Yes		Ark. Code Ann. § 26-52-103, Ark. Code Ann. § 26-53-124, Ark. Reg. GR-5
California	Yes		Cal. Rev. & Tax. Code § 6203, Reg. 1684, 18 CCR, SBE Publication 77
Colorado	Yes		Colo. Rev. Stat. § 39-26-102, Colo. Code Regs. § 39-26-102.3
Connecticut	Yes		Conn. Gen. Stat. § 12-411(3), Conn. Gen. Stat. § 12-407(a)(15)(A)
District of Columbia	Yes		D.C. Code Ann. § 47-2201(h)
Florida	Yes		Fla. Stat. § 212.0596, Fla. Stat. § 212.06(3)(a)
Georgia	Yes		Ga. Code Ann. § 48-8-2(8)(E), Ga. Code Ann. § 48-8-30(b)(1)
Hawaii	Yes		Haw. Rev. Stat. § 237-13, Haw. Rev. Stat. § 238-2, Haw. Reg. 18-237-8.6-02
Idaho	Yes		Idaho Code § 63-3611, Idaho Code § 63-3615A
Illinois	Yes		35 ILCS 105/3-45, 35 ILCS 105/2
Indiana	Yes		Ind. Code § 6-2.5-3-1
Iowa	Yes		Iowa Code § 423.29, Iowa Code § 423.1, Iowa Admin. Code r. 701 30.1
Kansas	Yes		Kan. Stat. Ann. § 79-3702(h)(1), Kan. Stat. Ann. § 79-3705c, Kan. Admin. Regs. § 92-20-7
Kentucky	Yes		Ky. Rev. Stat. Ann. § 139.340
Louisiana	Yes		La. Rev. Stat. Ann. § 47:301, La. Rev. Stat. Ann. § 47:304
Maine	Yes		Me. Rev. Stat. Ann. tit. 36, § 1754-B
Maryland	Yes		Md. Code Ann. § 11-403, Md. Code Ann. § 11-101, Md. Code Ann. § 11-701

State	Warehouse	Comments	Citation
Massachusetts	Yes		Mass. Gen. Laws ch. 64I, § 4, Mass. Gen. Laws ch. 64H, § 1, Technical Information Release 96-8
Michigan	Yes		Revenue Administrative Bulletin 1999-1
Minnesota	Yes		Minn. Stat. § 297A.66
Mississippi	Yes		Miss. Code. Ann. § 27-67-3, Miss. Code. Ann. § 27-67-4
Missouri	Yes		Mo. Rev. Stat. § 144.605, Mo. Code Regs. Ann. tit. 12, § 10-4.085 (2) (A), Mo. Code Regs. Ann. tit. 12, § 10-114.100
Nebraska	Yes		Neb. Rev. Stat. § 77-2703 (2) (b), Neb. Rev. Stat. § 77-2701.13, Neb. Admin. Code § 1-004
Nevada	Yes		Nev. Rev. Stat. § 372.195
New Jersey	Yes		N.J. Stat. Ann. § 54:32B-2, Bulletin S&U-5, TB-78
New Mexico	Yes		N.M. Stat. Ann. § 7-9-10
New York	Yes		N.Y. Tax Law, § 1101, N.Y. Comp. Code R. & Regs. tit. 20, § 526.10 (a) (2)
North Carolina	Yes		N.C. Gen. Stat. § 105-164.3 (9), N.C. Gen. Stat. § 105-164.8
North Dakota	Yes		N.D. Cent. Code § 57-40.2-07, N.D. Cent. Code § 57-40.2-01
Ohio	Yes		Ohio Rev. Code Ann. § 5741.17, Ohio Rev. Code Ann. § 5741.01, Information Release ST 2001-01
Oklahoma	Yes		Okla. Stat. tit. 68, § 1352 (13), Okla. Admin. Code § 710:65-1-8 (b)
Pennsylvania	Yes		72 P.S. § 7237, 72 P.S. § 7201 (b)
Rhode Island	Yes		R.I. Gen. Laws § 44-18-23
South Carolina	Yes		S.C. Code Ann. § 12-36-1340, S.C. Code Ann. § 12-36-70, S.C. Code Ann. § 12-36-2691, Revenue Ruling 14-4
South Dakota	Yes		S.D. Codified Laws § 10-46-1
Tennessee	Yes		Tenn. Code. Ann. § 67-6-102 (25) (G)

State	Warehouse	Comments	Citation
Texas	Yes		Tex. Tax Code Ann. § 151.103, Tex. Tax Code Ann. § 151.107, 34 Tex. Admin. Code § 3.286
Utah	Yes		Utah Code Ann. § 59-12-107
Vermont	Yes		Vt. Stat. Ann. tit. 32, § 9701
Virginia	Yes	Also, legislation created a rebuttable presumption that a dealer has nexus with the state if any commonly controlled person maintains a distribution center, warehouse, fulfillment center, office, or similar location in Virginia that facilitates the delivery of tangible personal property sold by the out-of-state dealer to its customers. The presumption may be rebutted by demonstrating that the activities conducted by the commonly controlled person in Virginia are not significantly associated with the dealer's ability to establish or maintain a market in the state. The legislation provides that it is effective on the earlier of September 1, 2013, or upon passage of federal legislation granting states the authority to require remote sellers to collect taxes on goods shipped to in-state purchasers. Because no such federal legislation has been enacted, the effective date for this legislation is September 1, 2013. Thus, all affected out-of-state dealers must begin collecting sales and use taxes on sales made into Virginia on September 1, 2013.	Va. Code Ann. § 58.1-612, 23 Va. Admin. Code § 10-210-2070, VTB 13-11
Washington	Yes		Wash. Rev. Code § 82.12.040, Wash. Admin. Code § 458-20-193
West Virginia	Yes		W. Va. Code § 11-15A-1(b)(8), W. Va. Code R. § 110-15-2.78
Wisconsin	Yes		Wis. Stat. § 77.53(3), Wis. Stat. § 77.51, Wis. Admin. Code § 11.97
Wyoming	Yes		Wyo. Stat. Ann. § 39-16-103(c)(v), Wyo. Stat. Ann. § 39-16-101(a)(x)

¶ 146   **Nexus—Warranty Repairs**

This chart indicates whether performing warranty repairs in a state can create nexus for a seller.

State	Warranty Repairs	Comments	Citation
Alabama	Yes		Ala. Code § 40-23-68
Arizona	Yes	If employee is present in state for more than 2 days per year.	Ariz. Rev. Stat. § 42-5151
Arkansas	Yes		Ark. Code Ann. § 26-52-103, Ark. Reg. GR-5
California	Yes	But not if the person performing the repair is an unrelated independent contractor. A retailer is not "engaged in business in this state" based solely on its use of a representative or independent contractor in California to perform warranty or repair services on tangible personal property sold by the retailer, provided that the ultimate ownership (i.e., a stock holder, bond holder, partner, or other person holding an ownership interest) of the representative or independent contractor and the retailer is not substantially similar.	Cal. Rev. & Tax. Code § 6203, Reg. 1684, 18 CCR
Colorado	Yes		Colo. Rev. Stat. § 39-26-102, Colo. Code Regs. § 39-26-102.3
Connecticut	Yes		Conn. Gen. Stat. § 12-411(3), Conn. Gen. Stat. § 12-407(a)(15)(A), Dell Catalog Sales v. Commissioner of Revenue Services
District of Columbia	Yes		D.C. Code Ann. § 47-2201(h)
Florida	Yes		Fla. Stat. § 212.0596
Georgia	Yes		Ga. Code Ann. § 48-8-65(b)(2), Ga. Code Ann. § 48-8-2, Ga. Code Ann. § 48-8-30(b)(1), CCH Sales and Use Tax Nexus Survey, Georgia Department of Revenue, August 6, 2010
Hawaii	Yes		Haw. Rev. Stat. § 237-13, Haw. Rev. Stat. § 238-2, National Nexus Program Bulletin 95-1
Idaho	Yes		Idaho Code § 63-3611, Idaho Code § 63-3615A

State	Warranty Repairs	Comments	Citation
Illinois	Yes		35 ILCS 105/3-45, 35 ILCS 105/2
Indiana	Yes		Ind. Code § 6-2.5-3-1
Iowa	Yes		Iowa Code § 423.29, Iowa Code § 423.1, Iowa Admin. Code r. 701 30.1
Kansas	Yes		Kan. Stat. Ann. § 79-3702(h)(1), Kan. Stat. Ann. § 79-3705c
Kentucky	May create nexus	"Retailer engaged in business in this state" includes any retailer soliciting orders for tangible personal property or digital property from Kentucky residents on a continuous, regular, systematic basis if the retailer benefits from an agent or representative operating in Kentucky under the authority of the retailer to repair or service tangible personal property or digital property sold by the retailer.	Ky. Rev. Stat. Ann. § 139.340(2)(e)
Louisiana	Yes		La. Rev. Stat. Ann. § 47:301, La. Rev. Stat. Ann. § 47:304, Louisiana v. Dell International, Inc.
Maine	Yes		Me. Rev. Stat. Ann. tit. 36, § 1754-B(1)(G), Instructional Bulletin No. 43
Maryland	Yes		Md. Code Ann. § 11-403, Md. Code Ann. § 11-101, Md. Code Ann. § 11-701
Massachusetts	Yes		Mass. Gen. Laws ch. 64I, § 4, Mass. Gen. Laws ch. 64H, § 1, Technical Information Release 96-8
Michigan	Yes		Revenue Administrative Bulletin 1999-1
Minnesota	Yes		Minn. Stat. § 297A.66
Mississippi	Yes		Miss. Code. Ann. § 27-67-3, Miss. Code. Ann. § 27-65-9
Missouri	Yes		Mo. Rev. Stat. § 144.605, Mo. Code Regs. Ann. tit. 12, § 10-114.100, Mo. Code Regs. Ann. tit. 12, § 10-4-085, Letter Ruling LR3476
Nebraska	Yes		Neb. Rev. Stat. § 77-2703(2)(b), Neb. Rev. Stat. § 77-2701.13, Neb. Admin. Code § 1-004

State	Warranty Repairs	Comments	Citation
Nevada	Yes		Nev. Rev. Stat. § 372.195
New Jersey	Yes		N.J. Stat. Ann. § 54:32B-2, Bulletin S&U-5, TB-78
New Mexico	Yes		N.M. Stat. Ann. § 7-9-10, Dell Catalog Sales L.P. v. New Mexico Taxation and Revenue Department
New York	Yes		N.Y. Tax Law, § 1101, N.Y. Comp. Code R. & Regs. tit. 20, § 526.10, TSB-M-08(3)S
North Carolina	Yes		N.C. Gen. Stat. § 105-164.8, Secretary of Revenue Decision No. 2005-75
North Dakota	Yes		N.D. Cent. Code § 57-40.2-07, N.D. Cent. Code § 57-40.2-01
Ohio	Yes		Ohio Rev. Code Ann. § 5741.17, Ohio Rev. Code Ann. § 5741.01, Information Release ST 2001-01
Oklahoma	Yes		Okla. Stat. tit. 68, § 1401(10), Okla. Admin. Code § 710:65-1-8(b)
Pennsylvania	Yes		72 P.S. § 7237, 72 P.S. § 7201(b)
Rhode Island	Yes		R.I. Gen. Laws § 44-18-15, R.I. Gen. Laws § 44-18-23
South Carolina	Yes		S.C. Code Ann. § 12-36-1340, S.C. Code Ann. § 12-36-70, Revenue Ruling 14-4
South Dakota	Yes		S.D. Codified Laws § 10-46-1
Tennessee	Yes		Tenn. Code. Ann. § 67-6-102, Registering Your Business in Tennessee
Texas	Yes		Tex. Tax Code Ann. § 151.103, Tex. Tax Code Ann. § 151.107, 34 Tex. Admin. Code § 3.286, Decision Hearing No. 41,140
Utah	Yes	If seller regularly services property in the state.	Utah Code Ann. § 59-12-107
Vermont	Yes	May create nexus under certain circumstances, for example when the value of the tangible personal property transferred with the repair service is 10% or more of the total charge for the transaction and no separate charge is made for materials.	Vt. Stat. Ann. tit. 32, § 9701, Vt. Stat. Ann. tit. 32, § 9741(35)

State	Warranty Repairs	Comments	Citation
Virginia	Yes		Va. Code Ann. § 58.1-612
Washington	Yes		Wash. Rev. Code § 82.12.040, Wash. Admin. Code § 458-20-193
West Virginia	Yes		W. Va. Code § 11-15A-1 (b) (8) (A)-(C), W. Va. Code § 11-15A-6a(a) (3), W. Va. Code R. § 110-15-2.78
Wisconsin	Yes		Wis. Stat. § 77.53(3), Wis. Stat. § 77.51, Wis. Admin. Code § 11.97
Wyoming	Yes		Wyo. Stat. Ann. § 39-16-103 (c) (v), Wyo. Stat. Ann. § 39-16-101 (a) (x)

Occasional Sales

State	Occasional Sales	Comments	Citation
Alabama	Exempt	Includes exemption provisions for a retailer selling property, if the transaction is not in the regular course of business.	Ala. Admin. Code r. 810-6-1-.33(1)
Arizona	Exempt	Includes exemption provisions for a retailer selling property, if the transaction is not in the regular course of business.	Ariz. Rev. Stat. § 42-5001(1), Ariz. Admin. Code § 15-5-102, Ariz. Admin. Code § 15-5-2312
Arkansas	Exempt		Ark. Code Ann. § 26-52-401(17)
California	Exempt		Cal. Rev. & Tax. Code § 6367
Colorado	Taxable		Colo. Rev. Stat. § 39-26-114
Connecticut	Exempt	Includes exemption provisions for a retailer selling property, if the transaction is not in the regular course of business.	Conn. Agencies Regs. § 12-426-17
District of Columbia	Exempt		D.C. Code Ann. § 47-2005(7)
Florida	Exempt	Includes exemption provisions for a retailer selling property, if the transaction is not in the regular course of business.	Fla. Stat. § 212.02(2)
Georgia	Exempt	Includes exemption provisions for a retailer selling property, if the transaction is not in the regular course of business.	Ga. Comp. R. & Regs. 560-12-1-.07
Hawaii	Exempt	Includes exemption provisions for a retailer selling property, if the transaction is not in the regular course of business.	Haw. Rev. Stat. § 237-2
Idaho	Exempt		Idaho Code § 63-3622K
Illinois	Exempt	Includes exemption provisions for a retailer selling property, if the transaction is not in the regular course of business.	35 ILCS 120/1, 35 ILCS 105/2
Indiana	Exempt	Includes exemption provisions for a retailer selling property, if the transaction is not in the regular course of business.	Ind. Admin. Code tit. 45, r. 2.2-1-1
Iowa	Exempt	Includes exemption provisions for a retailer selling property, if the transaction is not in the regular course of business.	Iowa Code § 423.3(39)

State	Occasional Sales	Comments	Citation
Kansas	Exempt	Includes exemption provisions for a retailer selling property, if the transaction is not in the regular course of business.	Kan. Stat. Ann. § 79-3606(l)
Kentucky	Exempt		Ky. Rev. Stat. Ann. § 139.470(4)
Louisiana	Exempt	Includes exemption provisions for a retailer selling property, if the transaction is not in the regular course of business.	La. Rev. Stat. Ann. § 47:301
Maine	Exempt	Includes exemption provisions for a retailer selling property, if the transaction is not in the regular course of business.	Me. Rev. Stat. Ann. tit. 36, § 1752
Maryland	Exempt	Exemption applies only if the sale price is less than $1,000 and the sale is not made through an auctioneer or dealer.	Md. Code Ann. § 11-209(a)
Massachusetts	Exempt	Includes exemption provisions for a retailer selling property, if the transaction is not in the regular course of business.	Mass. Gen. Laws ch. 64H, § 6(c)
Michigan	Exempt	No use tax exemption. Includes exemption provisions for a retailer selling property, if the transaction is not in the regular course of business.	Mich. Comp. Laws § 205.54d
Minnesota	Exempt	Includes exemption provisions for a retailer selling property, if the transaction is not in the regular course of business.	Minn. Stat. § 297A.67(23)
Mississippi	Exempt		Miss. Rule 35.IV.3.02
Missouri	Exempt	Exemption does not apply if gross receipts from all such sales in calendar year exceed $3,000. Includes exemption provisions for a retailer selling property, if the transaction is not in the regular course of business.	Mo. Rev. Stat. § 144.010(1)(2)
Nebraska	Exempt		Neb. Admin. Code § 1-022
Nevada	Exempt		Nev. Rev. Stat. § 372.320, Nev. Rev. Stat. § 374.325
New Jersey	Exempt		N.J. Stat. Ann. § 54:32B-8.6

State	Occasional Sales	Comments	Citation
New Mexico	Exempt	Includes exemption provisions for a retailer selling property, if the transaction is not in the regular course of business.	N.M. Stat. Ann. § 7-9-28
New York	Exempt	Exemption applies only to first $600 of receipts from such sales in calendar year.	N.Y. Tax Law, § 1115(a)(18)
North Carolina	Exempt		N.C. Gen. Stat. § 105-164.3(1)
North Dakota	Exempt	Includes exemption provisions for a retailer selling property, if the transaction is not in the regular course of business.	N.D. Admin. Code § 81-04.1-01-16
Ohio	Exempt	Exemption does not include motor vehicles; watercraft or outboard motors that are required to be titled under Sec. 1548.06, Ohio R.C.; watercraft documented with the U.S. Coast Guard; or snowmobiles or all-purpose vehicles.	Ohio Rev. Code Ann. § 5739.02(B)(8)
Oklahoma	Taxable		Okla. Stat. tit. 68, § 1354
Pennsylvania	Exempt	Includes exemption provisions for a retailer selling property, if the transaction is not in the regular course of business.	72 P.S. § 7204(1)
Rhode Island	Exempt	Includes exemption provisions for a retailer selling property, if the transaction is not in the regular course of business.	R.I. Code R. SU 07-17
South Carolina	Exempt		S.C. Code Ann. Regs. 117-322
South Dakota	Exempt		S.D. Codified Laws § 10-45-1(11)
Tennessee	Exempt	Excluded from the definition of "business." Occasional sales of aircraft, motor vehicles, and vessels are taxable.	Tenn. Code. Ann. § 67-6-102
Texas	Exempt		Tex. Tax Code Ann. § 151.304
Utah	Exempt	Includes exemption provisions for a retailer selling property, if the transaction is not in the regular course of business.	Utah Code Ann. § 59-12-104(13)
Vermont	Exempt		Vt. Stat. Ann. tit. 32, § 9741(4)

State	Occasional Sales	Comments	Citation
Virginia	Exempt	Includes exemption provisions for a retailer selling property, if the transaction is not in the regular course of business.	Va. Code Ann. § 58.1-609.10(2)
Washington	Exempt	No use tax exemption. Includes exemption provisions for a retailer selling property, if the transaction is not in the regular course of business.	Wash. Rev. Code § 82.08.0251
West Virginia	Exempt	Includes exemption provisions for a retailer selling property, if the transaction is not in the regular course of business.	W. Va. Code § 11-15-9(a)(14)
Wisconsin	Exempt	Exemption applies to persons not required to hold a seller's permit only if gross receipts for calendar year are less than $1,000 ($1,000 threshold does not apply to nonprofit organizations). A sale of any tangible personal property or taxable services is not considered an occasional sale if at the time of such sale the seller holds or is required to hold a seller's permit. However, a sale of business assets after cessation of business may qualify for exemption.	Wis. Stat. § 77.51(9), Wis. Stat. § 77.54(7), Wis. Admin. Code § 11.33
Wyoming	Taxable	Exemption applies only to occasional sales by religious or charitable organizations.	Wyo. Stat. Ann. § 39-15-105(a)(iv)(C)

¶ 148   Occasional Sales of Motor Vehicles

State	Occasional Sales of Motor Vehicles	Comments	Citation
Alabama	Exempt	Exempt from general sales/use tax, but subject to separate tax.	Ala. Code § 40-23-101, Ala. Code § 40-23-102
Arizona	Exempt		Ariz. Admin. Code § 15-5-102, Ariz. Admin. Code § 15-5-2312
Arkansas	Taxable		Ark. Code Ann. § 26-52-510, Ark. Code Ann. § 26-53-126
California	Taxable	Motor vehicle sales specifically excluded from occasional sales exemption. Separate sales tax exemption exists for sales by non-dealers, but purchaser subject to use tax. Use tax exemptions may apply for certain family and/or corporate transfers/sales.	Cal. Rev. & Tax. Code § 6367, Cal. Rev. & Tax. Code § 6292
Colorado	Taxable		Colo. Rev. Stat. § 39-26-113, Colo. Rev. Stat. § 39-26-208
Connecticut	Taxable	Motor vehicle sales specifically excluded from occasional sales exemption. Separate sales tax exemption exists for sales by non-dealers, but purchaser subject to use tax. Use tax exemptions may apply for certain family and/or corporate transfers/sales.	Conn. Gen. Stat. § 12-431
District of Columbia	Exempt	Exempt from general sales/use tax, but subject to separate tax.	D.C. Code Ann. § 47-2005(13)
Florida	Taxable	Exemptions may apply for certain family and/or corporate transfers/sales.	Fla. Stat. § 212.05
Georgia	Exempt		Ga. Comp. R. & Regs. 560-12-1-.07
Hawaii	Exempt		Haw. Rev. Stat. § 237-2
Idaho	Taxable	Exemptions may apply for certain family and/or corporate transfers/sales.	Idaho Code § 63-3622K
Illinois	Exempt	Sales by individuals and non-dealers are exempt from retailers' occupation tax and general use tax, but are subject to vehicle use tax.	625 ILCS 5/3-1001
Indiana	Taxable	Exemptions may apply for certain family and/or corporate transfers/sales.	Ind. Code § 6-2.5-3-2(b)

State	Occasional Sales of Motor Vehicles	Comments	Citation
Iowa	Taxable	Exempt from sales tax, but purchaser subject to use tax. Use tax exemptions may apply for certain family and/or corporate transfers/sales. Motor vehicles sales specifically excluded from occasional sales exemption.	Iowa Admin. Code r. 701-17.6
Kansas	Taxable	Exemptions may apply for certain family, corporate, or LLC transfers/sales.	Kan. Stat. Ann. § 79-3603(o)
Kentucky	Exempt	Exempt from general sales/use tax, but subject to separate tax.	Ky. Rev. Stat. Ann. § 139.050(3)(f)
Louisiana	Taxable		La. Rev. Stat. Ann. § 47:303(B)(4)
Maine	Taxable	Exemptions may apply for certain family and/or corporate transfers/sales.	Me. Rev. Stat. Ann. tit. 36, § 1764
Maryland	Exempt	Exempt from general sales/use tax, but subject to motor vehicle excise tax. Short-term rentals are taxable.	Md. Code Ann. § 11-221(a)
Massachusetts	Taxable	Exemptions may apply for certain family and/or corporate transfers/sales.	Mass. Gen. Laws ch. 64H, § 6(c), Mass. Gen. Laws ch. 64I, § 7(b)
Michigan	Taxable	Exemptions may apply for certain family and/or corporate transfers/sales.	Mich. Admin. Code r. 205.135
Minnesota	Exempt	Exempt from general sales/use tax, but subject to separate tax.	Minn. Stat. § 297A.67(30)
Mississippi	Taxable	Effective July 1, 2005, taxed at 5% rate (3% prior to that date). Exemptions may apply for certain family and/or corporate transfers/sales.	Miss. Code. Ann. § 27-65-201
Missouri	Taxable		Mo. Rev. Stat. § 144.070
Nebraska	Taxable	Exemptions may apply for certain corporate transfers/ sales.	Neb. Rev. Stat. § 77-2701.24
Nevada	Taxable	Exemptions may apply for certain family and/or corporate transfers/sales.	Nev. Rev. Stat. § 374.040(2)
New Jersey	Taxable	Exemptions may apply for certain family and/or corporate transfers/sales.	N.J. Stat. Ann. § 54:32B-8.6
New Mexico	Exempt	Exempt from general sales/use tax, but subject to separate tax.	N.M. Stat. Ann. § 7-9-22, N.M. Stat. Ann. § 7-9-23
New York	Taxable	Exemptions may apply for certain family and/or corporate transfers/sales.	N.Y. Tax Law, § 1105(a)(18)

State	Occasional Sales of Motor Vehicles	Comments	Citation
North Carolina	Exempt	Exempt from general sales/use tax, but subject to separate tax.	N.C. Gen. Stat. § 105-164.13(32)
North Dakota	Exempt	Exempt from general sales/use tax, but subject to separate tax.	N.D. Cent. Code § 57-39.2-04(13)
Ohio	Taxable		Ohio Rev. Code Ann. § 5739.02(B)
Oklahoma	Exempt	Exempt from general sales/use tax, but subject to separate tax.	Okla. Stat. tit. 68, § 1354
Pennsylvania	Taxable	Exemptions may apply for certain family and/or corporate transfers/sales.	72 P.S. § 7204(1)
Rhode Island	Taxable	Exemptions may apply for certain family and/or corporate transfers/sales.	R.I. Code R. SU 07-18
South Carolina	Exempt	Exempt from general sales/use tax, but subject to casual excise tax. Exemptions may apply for certain family and/or corporate transfers/sales.	S.C. Code Ann. § 12-36-1710
South Dakota	Exempt	Exempt from general sales/use tax, but subject to separate tax.	S.D. Codified Laws § 32-5B-1
Tennessee	Taxable	Exemptions may apply for certain family and/or corporate transfers/sales.	Tenn. Code. Ann. § 67-6-102
Texas	Exempt	Exempt from general sales/use tax, but subject to separate tax.	Tex. Tax Code Ann. § 151.308(a)(5)
Utah	Taxable		Utah Code Ann. § 59-12-104(13)
Vermont	Exempt	Exempt from general sales/use tax, but subject to separate tax.	Vt. Stat. Ann. tit. 32, § 9741(12)
Virginia	Exempt	Exempt from general sales/use tax, but subject to separate tax.	Va. Code Ann. § 58.1-609.1(2), Va. Code Ann. § 58.1-2402
Washington	Taxable		Wash. Admin. Code § 458-20-178
West Virginia	Exempt		W. Va. Code R. § 110-15-9.2.24.2
Wisconsin	Taxable	Exemptions may apply for certain family and/or corporate transfers/sales.	Wis. Stat. § 77.54(7)(b)
Wyoming	Taxable		Wyo. Stat. Ann. § 39-15-103

¶ 149   **Packaging**

This chart deals with whether packaging materials are taxable or exempt. Packaging materials include, but are not limited to, the following: containers, pallets, drums, and other items used to ship merchandise to customers, and supplies used in shipping, such as bubble wrap, tape, rope, plastic peanuts, foam, cardboard pads, wrapping, and packaging slips.

State	Packaging	Comments	Citation
Alabama	Exempt		Ala. Code § 40-23-1, Ala. Code § 40-23-60, Ala. Admin. Code r. 810-6-1-.69
Arizona	Exempt	If transferred with the contents in a subsequent sale. Pricing tags, shipping tags and advertising material are taxable	Ariz. Admin. Code § 15-5-134, Ariz. Admin. Code § 15-5-136
Arkansas	Exempt	Taxable if owned by and returned to the manufacturer or if it does not become part of the finished product received by the consumer (e.g., returnable pallets).	Ark. Reg. GR-53
California	Exempt	Packaging materials used by packers, loaders and shippers are taxable when they are used to condition, preserve, or protect merchandise for shipment or as containers of the shipped merchandise.	Cal. Rev. & Tax. Code § 6364, Reg. 1589, 18 CCR
Colorado	Exempt	Sales and purchases of nonessential food items and packaging provided with purchased food and beverage items are subject to the state sales tax.	1 Colo. Code Regs. § 9, Colo. Rev. Stat. § 39-26-707
Connecticut	Taxable	Unless resale exclusion met or purchases of certain non-returnable containers and packaging materials is made by manufacturers, fabricators and processors.	Conn. Gen. Stat. § 12-412(14), Policy Statement 94(1)
District of Columbia	Exempt	When purchased for delivery of other tangible goods. Tax applies if (1) the packaging is purchased for consumption by the vendee and not for further delivery; (2) when the vendor uses a returnable container and the vendor retains title to it; (3) when used in the business of rendering tax-exempt services; (4) when there are charges for retaining possession of a container (a.k.a. demurrage)	D.C. Mun. Regs. t. 9, § 439.1, D.C. Mun. Regs. t. 9, § 439.2, D.C. Mun. Regs. t. 9, § 439.3, D.C. Mun. Regs. t. 9, § 439.4, D.C. Mun. Regs. t. 9, § 439.5, D.C. Mun. Regs. t. 9, § 439.6

State	Packaging	Comments	Citation
Florida	Exempt	Sales of boxes, wrapping paper, twine, tape, and similar articles to people who use such them in connection with services rendered and who are not required to collect tax upon receipt of the services; containers such as barrels, boxes, bags, kegs, drums, cartons, sacks, and cans that are to be returned to the seller and that are intended by the seller to provide a means of containing the merchandise while it is delivered to the purchaser; and containers, sacks, or bags used more than one time for packaging tangible personal property for ship for sale are all taxable.	Fla. Stat. § 212.02(15), Fla. Admin. Code Ann. r. 12A-1.040(1)
Georgia	Exempt	The packaging items must be used solely for packaging and cannot be purchased for reuse. The exemption applies to nonreturnable packaging materials only.	Ga. Code Ann. § 48-8-3(94), Ga. Comp. R. & Regs. 560-12-2-.25
Hawaii	Taxable		Haw. Rev. Stat. § 237-4(a)(12), Haw. Rev. Stat. § 237-13(2)
Idaho	Taxable	Containers generally exempt, but containers used by persons who provide a service rather than sell a product are taxable.	Idaho Code § 63-3622E, IDAPA 35.01.02.084
Illinois	Exempt	If transferred to customers along with the tangible personal property. Sales of paper bags, wrapping paper, string, and other property as an incident to the rendering of a wrapping service are subject to Service Occupation Tax.	Ill. Admin. Code tit 86, § 130.2070
Indiana	Exempt	Labels are taxable.	Ind. Code § 6-2.5-5-9, Ind. Code § 6-2.5-3-7(a)
Iowa	Exempt	Labels, tags, and nameplates attached to products for the benefit of the vendor, such as shipping, price tags, and instructions to cashiers, are taxable unless they are sold to manufacturers and retailers for packaging or facilitating the transportation of tangible personal property sold at retail.	Iowa Code § 423.3(44), Iowa Admin. Code r. 701-18.7

State	Packaging	Comments	Citation
Kansas	Exempt	Exemption applies to nonreturnable packaging materials only.	Kan. Stat. Ann. § 79-3606(m), Kan. Stat. Ann. § 79-3602(p), Kan. Admin. Regs. § 92-19-54(a)
Kentucky	Exempt	Unless sold for use in connection with the provision of a service.	103 Ky. Admin. Regs. 30:170, Unofficial Department Guidance
Louisiana	Exempt	If qualified for resale. Also, leases or rentals of pallets used in packaging products produced by a manufacturer are exempt. Caution: Numerous exemptions are suspended from April 1, 2016, to June 30, 2018. For chart of suspended exemptions and applicable tax rates, see Publication R-1002A.	La. Rev. Stat. Ann. § 47:301, LA DOR Publication R-1002A
Maine	Exempt	Exemption applies to both returnable and nonreturnable packaging materials. Certain exceptions to the exemption apply.	Me. Rev. Stat. Ann. tit. 36, § 1760(12-A)
Maryland	Exempt	Purchases of containers which will not be used to package tangible personal property for sale are taxable.	Md. Code Ann. § 11-201(a), Md. Regs. Code tit. 3. § 03.06.01.15
Massachusetts	Exempt	If used by the vendor's customers to carry food or drink off the premises. However, tax applies when used on the premises by the vendor's customers.	Mass. Gen. Laws ch. 64H, § 6(q), Mass. Regs. Code tit. 830, § 64H.6.5(8)
Michigan	Exempt	Taxable if not sold for resale; sold to persons regularly engaged in rendering services; sales or purchases for a single use; and sales of containers to a person who uses the containers to ship or deliver goods and retains the ownership or legal right of possession of the container.	Mich. Admin. Code r. 205.68
Minnesota	Exempt	Exempt if used in industrial or agricultural production for use in packaging, shipping, or delivering tangible personal property to customers; or used in providing certain taxable services. Returnable containers exempt only if used for food and beverages.	Minn. Stat. § 297A.62(1), Minn. Stat. § 297A.68(2) and (3), Minn. Stat. § 297A.69(2), Minn. R. 8130.5500(6)
Mississippi	Exempt		Miss. Code. Ann. § 27-65-5(3), Miss. Code. Ann. § 27-65-101(1)(a)

State	Packaging	Comments	Citation
Missouri	Exempt		Mo. Rev. Stat. § 144.011, Mo. Code. Regs. Ann. tit. 12, § 10-103.700, Mo. Code. Regs. Ann. tit. 12, § 10-103.220
Nebraska	Exempt	Tax is imposed on the sale of returnable containers without contents to persons who place the contents in the containers.	Neb. Rev. Stat. § 77-2704.47, Neb. Admin. Code. § 1-043
Nevada	Exempt	Certain exceptions apply, including packaging provided for the storage of personal property and outright sales of packaging materials.	Nev. Rev. Stat. § 372.290, Nev. Rev. Stat. § 374.295, Nev. Admin. Code § 372.310, Nev. Admin. Code § 585
New Jersey	Exempt		N.J. Stat. Ann. § 54:32B-8.15
New Mexico	Exempt		N.M. Admin. Code tit. 3, § 3.2.205.13
New York	Exempt	Taxable items include returnable containers bought at retail by a person who does not transfer ownership of the container; cartons or other packaging materials bought by vendor for his/her own use; racks, trays, or similar devices used to facilitate delivery of a product if not transferred with the product; and packaging material used in conjunction with the rendition of exempt services.	N.Y. Tax Law, § 1115(a)(19), N.Y. Comp. Code R & Regs. § 528.20
North Carolina	Exempt		N.C. Gen. Stat. § 105-164.13(23)
North Dakota	Exempt	Title to the packaging materials must pass to the customer for the exemption to apply. Returnable containers are taxed to the seller of the item being sold in the returnable container. Businesses rendering services are taxed on packaging materials used by them.	N.D. Admin. Code § 81-04.1-01-13
Ohio	Exempt		Ohio Rev. Code Ann. § 5739.02(B)(15)
Oklahoma	Taxable	Sales of packaging materials to agricultural producers and manufacturers are exempt.	Okla. Stat. tit. 68, § 1359(10), Okla. Admin. Code § 710:65-13-15(k)(58)-(59), Okla. Admin. Code § 710:65-13-150.1(b)(5)-(6), Okla. Admin. Code § 710:65-19-191

State	Packaging	Comments	Citation
Pennsylvania	Exempt	Exempt if the use is incidental to the delivery of personal property. The sale or use of returnable containers is generally taxable unless the purchaser is engaged in the business of manufacturing, processing, dairying or farming and the returnable container is used in the delivery of the product to the ultimate consumer.	72 P.S. § 7204(13), 31 Pa. Code § 31.3(5), 32 Pa. Code § 32.6
Rhode Island	Taxable	Exemptions allowed for nonreturnable containers sold to persons who place contents in the containers and sell the contents with the containers; returnable containers when sold with contents in a retail sale; and containers sold with exempt contents.	R.I. Gen. Laws § 44-18-30(4), R.I. Code R. SU 87-26
South Carolina	Exempt		S.C. Code Ann. § 12-36-120, S.C. Code Ann. Regs. 117-312.3
South Dakota	Exempt	If the packaging is used to hold tangible personal property sold by a retailer and is provided free to the customer as a convenience. Tax applies to containers that are used to hold property that is not subject to sales tax or used by a service business to perform a service of the business.	S.D. Codified Laws § 10-45-14.5, S.D. Codified Laws § 10-46-9.4, S.D. Admin. R. 64:06:03:09, S.D. Admin. R. 64:09:01:06
Tennessee	Exempt	If used to package property sold directly to the consumer or if the packaging is incidental to the sale. Packaging used to render exempt services is taxable.	Tenn. Code. Ann. § 67-6-329, Tenn. Comp. R. & Regs. 1320-5-1-.11, Tenn. Comp. R. & Regs. 1320-5-1-.21
Texas	Taxable	Exemptions for packaging supplies used in manufacturing, in newspaper printing, by export packers, and by laundries and dry cleaners. Also, exemptions for containers sold with exempt contents, empty nonreturnable containers sold to persons who fill the containers and sell the containers and contents, and returnable containers sold with contents or resold for refilling.	Tex. Tax Code Ann. § 151.302, Tex. Tax Code Ann. § 151.318, Tex. Tax Code Ann. § 151.322, 34 Tex. Admin. Code § 3.314

State	Packaging	Comments	Citation
Utah	Exempt	Taxable when sold to the final user or consumer or to a manufacturer, processor, wholesaler, or retailer, for use as a container that is ordinarily returned and reused or for internal transportation or accounting control purposes.	Utah Code Ann. § 59-12-104(22)
Vermont	Exempt	Exempt if sold to a manufacturer or distributor for packing, packaging, or shipping goods, or for resale. Packaging materials sold to retail stores to pack items purchased by their customers are taxable. Packaging materials sold to persons rendering a service are taxable.	Vt. Stat. Ann. tit. 32 § 9771, Vt. Stat. Ann. tit. 32 § 9741(16), Vt. Code R. 1.9741, Vt. Code R. 226-6(II)
Virginia	Exempt	If the items are marketed with the product being sold and become the property of the purchaser. Certain exceptions apply.	Va. Code Ann. § 58.1-609.3(2), 23 Va. Admin. Code § 10-210-400
Washington	Exempt	Sales of packing materials to people engaged in the business of custom or commercial packing are considered taxable sales for consumption. Sales of containers to vendors for use as returnable containers, following the purchase by a customer of the item contained therein, are deemed to be taxable sales for consumption.	Wash. Admin. Code § 458-20-115
West Virginia	Exempt	Sales of returnable containers are taxable.	W. Va. Code § 11-15B-2, W. Va. Code R. § 110-15-32.1
Wisconsin	Exempt	Containers used in the incidental transfer of property to customers by persons providing services are taxable.	Wis. Stat. § 77.54(6), Wis. Admin. Code § 11.15
Wyoming	Exempt	Reusable shipping materials are not exempt.	Wyo. Stat. Ann. § 39-15-105(a)(iii)(A), Wyo. Stat. Ann. § 39-16-105(a)(iii)(A), Wyo. BOE Rule Ch. 2, § 7

¶149

¶ 150   **Penalties (Civil)—Failure to File**

This chart describes the civil penalty for failure to file a return.

State	Failure to File	Comments	Citation
Alabama	Greater of 10% of tax due or $50.		Ala. Code § 40-2A-11(a)
Arizona	4.5% of tax due per month or fraction (maximum 25%).	25% of tax due if return not filed after notice and demand.	Ariz. Rev. Stat. § 42-1125(A) and (B)
Arkansas	5% of tax due per month or fraction (maximum 35%).		Ark. Reg. GR-84
California	10% of tax due.		Cal. Rev. & Tax. Code § 6591(b)
Colorado	Greater of 10% of tax due plus 0.5% of tax due per month (maximum 18%) or $15.		Colo. Rev. Stat. § 39-26-118(2)
Connecticut	Greater of 15% of tax due or $50.		Conn. Gen. Stat. § 12-416(a)
District of Columbia	5% of tax due per month or fraction (maximum 25%).		D.C. Code Ann. § 47-4213(a)(1)
Florida	10% of tax due (minimum of $50).		Fla. Stat. § 212.12(2)(a)
Georgia	Greater of 5% of tax due or $5 per 30 days (maximum 25% or $25).		Ga. Code Ann. § 48-8-66
Hawaii	5% of tax due per month or fraction (maximum 25%).		Haw. Rev. Stat. § 231-39((b)(1)
Idaho	Greater of 5% of tax due per month (maximum 25%) or $10.		Idaho Code § 63-3046(c)(1), (f), and (g)
Illinois	2% of tax due (maximum $250).	Greater of 2% of tax due or $250 (maximum $5,000) additional penalty for failure to file after notice of non-filing.	35 ILCS 735/3-3
Indiana	10% of tax due.		Ind. Code § 6-8.1-10-2.1
Iowa	10% of tax due.		Iowa Code § 421.27(1)
Kansas	1% of tax due per month or fraction (maximum 24%).		Kan. Stat. Ann. § 79-3615(d), Kan. Stat. Ann. § 79-3706(e)
Kentucky	Greater of 2% of tax due per 30 days or fraction (maximum 20%) or $10.		Ky. Rev. Stat. Ann. § 131.180(1)
Louisiana	5% of tax due per 30 days or fraction (maximum 25%).		La. Rev. Stat. Ann. § 47:1602(A)(1)
Maine	Greater of 10% of tax due or $25.	100% of tax due if return not filed within 60 days of demand from assessor.	Me. Rev. Stat. Ann. tit. 36, § 187-B(1)
Maryland	No penalty for failure to file by due date	25% of tax due if not filed and paid within period required under a notice and demand.	Md. Code Ann. § 13-708(a), Unofficial department guidance
Massachusetts	1% of tax due per month or fraction (maximum 25%).		Mass. Gen. Laws ch. 62C, § 33(a)

State	Failure to File	Comments	Citation
Michigan	5% of tax due if filed within two months and additional 5% of tax due per month or fraction after two months (maximum 25%).		Mich. Comp. Laws § 205.24(2)
Minnesota	5% of tax due.	25% of tax due if notice of repeated failure has been given.	Minn. Stat. § 289A.60(2) and (5a)
Mississippi	10% of tax due.	If persistent, willful, or recurring.	Miss. Code. Ann. § 27-65-33(7)
Missouri	5% of tax due per month or fraction (maximum 25%).	No late penalty given for first month if liability is over $250.	Mo. Rev. Stat. § 144.250(1)
Nebraska	Greater of 10% of tax due or $25.		Neb. Rev. Stat. § 77-2708(c)
Nevada	10% of tax due.	An amnesty program is in effect from July 1-September 30, 2008.	Nev. Rev. Stat. § 360.300(4), Nevada Tax Commission Website
New Jersey	$100 plus 5% of tax due per month or fraction (maximum of 25%).		N.J. Stat. Ann. § 54:49-4
New Mexico	Greater of 2% of tax due per month or fraction (maximum 20%) or $5.		N.M. Stat. Ann. § 7-1-69(A)
New York	10% of tax due for the first month plus 1% per month or fraction (maximum 30% and minimum of $50), if the return is late by 60 days or less.	If return more than 60 days late, the penalty is the greater of (1) 10% of the tax due for the first month or part of a month, not to exceed 30% of the tax due; (2) $100 or 100% of tax due, whichever is less; or (3) $50.	N.Y. Tax Law, § 1145(a)(1), TB-ST-805
North Carolina	5% of tax due if the failure is for not more than one month, with an additional 5% for each additional month, or fraction (maximum 25% in aggregate) or $5, whichever is greater.	Effective January 1, 2014, the $5 minimum and the "whichever is greater" language is eliminated.	N.C. Gen. Stat. § 105-236(a)(3)
North Dakota	Greater of 5% of tax due per month or fraction (maximum 25%) or $5.		N.D. Cent. Code § 57-39.2-18(1)(b)(1)
Ohio	Greater of 10% of tax due or $50.	Additional penalty of up to 50% of tax due may be added to assessment.	Ohio Rev. Code Ann. § 5739.12(D), Ohio Rev. Code Ann. § 5739.133
Oklahoma	25% of tax due if not filed within 10 days after written demand.		Okla. Stat. tit. 68, § 217(E)
Pennsylvania	Greater of 5% of tax due per month or fraction (maximum 25%) or $2.		72 P.S. § 7266(a)
Rhode Island	10% of tax due.		R.I. Gen. Laws § 44-19-14
South Carolina	5% of tax due if the failure is for not more than one month, with an additional 5% for each additional month or fraction of the month (maximum 25%).		S.C. Code Ann. § 12-54-43(C)
South Dakota	Greater of 10% of tax due or $10.		S.D. Codified Laws § 10-59-6

State	Failure to File	Comments	Citation
Tennessee	Greater of 5% of tax due per 30 days or fraction (maximum 25%) or $15.		Tenn. Code. Ann. § 67-1-804(a)(1)
Texas	Greater of 5% (plus additional 5% if more than 30 days late) or $1.		Tex. Tax Code Ann. § 151.703
Utah	Greater of 10% of tax due or $20.		Utah Code Ann. § 59-1-401(1)
Vermont	5% of tax due per month or fraction (maximum 25%).	If return more than 60 days late, minimum penalty is $50.	Vt. Stat. Ann. tit. 32, § 3202(b)(1)
Virginia	Greater of 6% of tax due per month or fraction (maximum 30%) or $10.		Va. Code Ann. § 58.1-635(A)
Washington	Assessment penalty applies - 5% of tax the department has determined to be due, increased to 15% if not paid by the date in the notice, and increased to 25% if not paid by 30 days following the due date in the notice (minimum $5).		Wash. Rev. Code § 82.32.100, Wash. Rev. Code § 82.32.090(2), Wash. Admin. Code § 458-20-228(5)
West Virginia	5% of tax due per month or fraction (maximum 25%).		W. Va. Code § 11-10-18(a)(1)
Wisconsin	5% of tax due per month or fraction (maximum 25%). If return not filed and DOR estimates tax, penalty is 25% of estimate.	Delinquent returns also subject to $20 late filing fee.	Wis. Stat. § 77.59(9), Wis. Stat. § 77.60(2), Wis. Stat. § 77.60(4)
Wyoming	$10 ($25 if not filed within 30 days of notice to file).		Wyo. Stat. Ann. § 39-15-108(c)(xiii)

¶ 151   **Penalties (Civil)—Failure to Pay**

This chart describes the civil penalty for failure to pay tax.

State	Failure to Pay	Comments	Citation
Alabama	10% of tax due.		Ala. Code § 40-2A-11(b)
Arizona	0.5% of tax due per month or fraction (maximum 10%)		Ariz. Rev. Stat. § 42-1125(D)
Arkansas	5% of tax due per month or fraction (maximum 35%).		Ark. Reg. GR-84
California	10% of tax due.	Effective January 1, 2007, a person who collects and fails to remit sales tax reimbursement or use tax is subject to a penalty of 40% of the amount not remitted.	Cal. Rev. & Tax. Code § 6591(a), Cal. Rev. & Tax. Code § 6597
Colorado	Greater of 10% of tax due plus 0.5% of tax due per month (maximum 18%) or $15.		Colo. Rev. Stat. § 39-26-118(2)
Connecticut	Greater of 15% of tax due or $50.		Conn. Gen. Stat. § 12-419(a)
District of Columbia	5% of tax due per month or fraction (maximum 25%).		D.C. Code Ann. § 47-4213(a)(2)
Florida	10% of tax due (minimum of $50).		Fla. Stat. § 212.12(2)(a)
Georgia	Greater of 5% of tax due or $5 per 30 days (maximum 25% or $25).		Ga. Code Ann. § 48-8-66
Hawaii	Up to 25% of tax due.	Up to 20% of tax due if tax not paid within 60 days of timely filed return.	Haw. Rev. Stat. § 231-39(b)
Idaho	0.5% of tax due per month (maximum 25%).		Idaho Code § 63-3046(c)(2) and (g)
Illinois	2% of tax due if paid within 30 days; 10% of tax due if paid after 30 days but within 90 days; 15% of tax due if paid after 90 days but within 180 days; 20% of tax due if paid after 180 days.		35 ILCS 735/3-3
Indiana	10% of tax due.		Ind. Code § 6-8.1-10-2.1
Iowa	5% of tax due.		Iowa Code § 421.27(2)
Kansas	1% of tax due per month or fraction (maximum 24%).		Kan. Stat. Ann. § 79-3615(d), Kan. Stat. Ann. § 79-3706(e)
Kentucky	Greater of 2% of tax due per 30 days or fraction (maximum 20%) or $10.		Ky. Rev. Stat. Ann. § 131.180(2)
Louisiana	5% of tax due per 30 days or fraction (maximum 25%).		La. Rev. Stat. Ann. § 47:1602(A)(2)
Maine	1% of tax due per month or fraction (maximum 25%).	25% of tax due if review unavailable and not paid within 10 days of notice of demand.	Me. Rev. Stat. Ann. tit. 36, § 187-B(2)

State	Failure to Pay	Comments	Citation
Maryland	Up to 10% of tax due.	25% of tax due if not paid within 10 days of notice of demand.	Md. Code Ann. § 13-701, Md. Code Ann. § 13-709(a)
Massachusetts	1% of tax due per month or fraction (maximum 25%).		Mass. Gen. Laws ch. 62C, § 33(b) and (c)
Michigan	5% of tax due if paid within two months and additional 5% of tax due per month or fraction after two months (maximum 25%).		Mich. Comp. Laws § 205.24(2)
Minnesota	5% of tax due per 30 days or fraction (maximum 15%).	25% of tax due if notice of repeated failure has been given.	Minn. Stat. § 289A.60(1)(e) and (5a)
Mississippi	10% of tax due for first offense; 15% of tax due for second; 25% of tax due for third; 50% of tax due for any subsequent offense.	15% of tax due for first offense; 25% of tax due for second; 50% of tax due for any subsequent offense if not paid after notice.	Miss. Code. Ann. § 27-65-39
Missouri	5% of tax due.		Mo. Rev. Stat. § 144.250(2)
Nebraska	Greater of 10% of tax due or $25.		Neb. Rev. Stat. § 77-2708(c)
Nevada	Up to 10% of tax due.	An amnesty program is in effect from July 1-September 30, 2008.	Nev. Rev. Stat. § 360.417, http://gov.state.nv.us/ PressReleases/2008/2008-06 -02-TaxAmnestyProgram.htm
New Jersey	5% of tax due.		N.J. Stat. Ann. § 54:49-4
New Mexico	Greater of 2% of tax due per month or fraction (maximum 20%) or $5.		N.M. Stat. Ann. § 7-1-69(A)
New York	10% of tax due for the first month plus 1% per month or fraction (maximum 30%).	If more than 25% of the taxes required to be shown on the return are omitted, the penalty is 10% of the tax failed to be reported.	N.Y. Tax Law, § 1145(a)(1), TB-ST-805
North Carolina	10% of tax due subject to a $5 minimum.	Effective January 1, 2014, the $5 minimum is eliminated.	N.C. Gen. Stat. § 105-236(a)(4)
North Dakota	Greater of 5% of tax due or $5.		N.D. Cent. Code § 57-39.2-18(1)(b)(2)
Ohio	Greater of 10% of tax due or $50.	Additional penalty of up to 50% of tax due may be added to assessment.	Ohio Rev. Code Ann. § 5739.12(D), Ohio Rev. Code Ann. § 5739.133
Oklahoma	10% of tax due if not paid within 15 days of delinquency.	Prior to December 11, 2014, waived if tax remitted within 30 days of proposed assessment or voluntarily paid with amended return. Effective December 11, 2014, waived if tax (and interest) remitted within 60 days of proposed assessment or voluntarily paid with amended return.	Okla. Stat. tit. 68, § 217(C)
Pennsylvania	3% of tax due per month (maximum 18%).		61 Pa. Code § 35.2(b)(2)

¶151

State	Failure to Pay	Comments	Citation
Rhode Island	10% of tax due.		R.I. Gen. Laws § 44-19-12
South Carolina	0.5% of tax due for first month, additional 0.5% per each additional month or fraction of month (maximum 25%).		S.C. Code Ann. § 12-54-43(D)
South Dakota	No provisions.		
Tennessee	Greater of 5% of tax due per 30 days or fraction (maximum 25%) or $15.		Tenn. Code. Ann. § 67-1-804(a)(1)
Texas	Greater of 5% (plus additional 5% if more than 30 days late) or $1.		Tex. Tax Code Ann. § 151.703
Utah	Greater of 2%, 5% or 10% of tax due or $20.	Applicable percentage depends on the lateness of the payment.	Utah Code Ann. § 59-1-401(2)
Vermont	5% of tax due per month or fraction (maximum 25%).		Vt. Stat. Ann. tit. 32, § 3202(b)(3)
Virginia	Greater of 6% of tax due per month or fraction (maximum 30%) or $10.		Va. Code Ann. § 58.1-635(A)
Washington	9% of tax due, increased to 19% if not paid by end of month following due date, and increased to 29% if not paid by second month following due date (minimum $5).		Wash. Rev. Code § 82.32.090(1)
West Virginia	0.5% of tax due per month or fraction (maximum 25%).		W. Va. Code § 11-10-18(a)(2)
Wisconsin	5% of tax owed per month or fraction (maximum 25%).		Wis. Stat. § 77.60(4)
Wyoming	10% of tax due.		Wyo. Stat. Ann. § 39-15-108(c)(i)

¶152   Penalties (Civil)—Intent to Evade

This chart describes the civil penalty for fraud or intent to evade tax.

State	Intent to Evade	Comments	Citation
Alabama	Up to 100% of tax due.		Ala. Code § 40-29-73
Arizona	50% of tax due.		Ariz. Rev. Stat. § 42-1125(G)
Arkansas	50% of tax due.		Ark. Reg. GR-85
California	25% of tax due.		Cal. Rev. & Tax. Code § 6485
Colorado	100% of tax due plus additional 3% per month.		Colo. Rev. Stat. § 39-26-115
Connecticut	25% of tax due.		Conn. Gen. Stat. § 12-415(d)
District of Columbia	75% of tax due that is attributable to fraud.		D.C. Code Ann. § 47-4212(a)
Florida	100% of tax due plus additional penalty of 200% of tax evaded.		Fla. Stat. § 212.12(2)(d), Fla. Stat. § 213.29
Georgia	50% of tax due.		Ga. Code Ann. § 48-8-66
Hawaii	Up to 50% of tax due.		Haw. Rev. Stat. § 231-39(b)(2)(B)
Idaho	50% of tax due (minimum $10).		Idaho Code § 63-3046(b) and (f)
Illinois	50% of tax due that is attributable to fraud.		35 ILCS 735/3-3
Indiana	100% of tax due.		Ind. Code § 6-8.1-10-4
Iowa	75% of tax due.		Iowa Code § 421.27(4)
Kansas	50% of tax due.		Kan. Stat. Ann. § 79-3615(e), Kan. Stat. Ann. § 79-3706(f)
Kentucky	50% of tax due.		Ky. Rev. Stat. Ann. § 131.180(8)
Louisiana	50% of tax due.		La. Rev. Stat. Ann. § 47:1604
Maine	Greater of 75% of tax due that is attributable to fraud or $75.		Me. Rev. Stat. Ann. tit. 36, § 187-B(2)
Maryland	100% of tax due.		Md. Code Ann. § 13-703, Md. Code Ann. § 13-704
Massachusetts	Up to 100% of tax due.		Mass. Gen. Laws ch. 62C, § 28
Michigan	100% of tax due.		Mich. Comp. Laws § 205.23(5)
Minnesota	50% of tax due.		Minn. Stat. § 289A.60(6)
Mississippi	50% of tax due.		Miss. Code. Ann. § 27-65-39
Missouri	25% of tax due.		Mo. Rev. Stat. § 144.500
Nebraska	Greater of 25% of tax due or $50.		Neb. Rev. Stat. § 77-2709(4)
Nevada	25% of tax due.		Nev. Rev. Stat. § 360.340

State	Intent to Evade	Comments	Citation
New Jersey	50% of tax due.		N.J. Stat. Ann. § 54:49-9.1
New Mexico	Greater of 50% of tax due or $25.		N.M. Stat. Ann. § 7-1-69(D)
New York	Twice the amount of tax due.	Plus interest on the unpaid tax.	N.Y. Tax Law, § 1145(a)(2), TB-ST-805
North Carolina	50% of tax due.		N.C. Gen. Stat. § 105-236(6)
North Dakota	No provisions.		
Ohio	up to 50% of the amount assessed		Ohio Rev. Code Ann. § 5739.133
Oklahoma	50% of tax due.		Okla. Stat. tit. 68, § 217(F)
Pennsylvania	50% of tax due.		72 P.S. § 7267(b)
Rhode Island	50% of tax due.		R.I. Gen. Laws § 44-19-14
South Carolina	75% of tax due that is attributable to fraud and 50% of interest due.		S.C. Code Ann. § 12-54-43(G)
South Dakota	No provisions.		
Tennessee	100% of tax due.		Tenn. Code. Ann. § 67-1-804(c)(1)
Texas	50% of tax due.		Tex. Tax Code Ann. § 111.061(b)
Utah	Greater of 100% of tax due or $500.		Utah Code Ann. § 59-1-401(5)
Vermont	100% of tax due.		Vt. Stat. Ann. tit. 32, § 3202(b)(5)
Virginia	50% of tax due.		Va. Code Ann. § 58.1-635(A)
Washington	50% of tax due.	This penalty cannot be applied in combination with the penalty for disregarding specific written instructions or the penalty for engaging in a disregarded transaction.	Wash. Rev. Code § 82.32.090(7)
West Virginia	50% of tax due.		W. Va. Code § 11-10-18(d)
Wisconsin	50% of tax due.		Wis. Stat. § 77.60(5)
Wyoming	25% of tax due.		Wyo. Stat. Ann. § 39-15-108(c)(ii)

State	Labor Only	Comments	Citation
Alabama	Exempt	Labor charges are not taxable when billed for labor expended in repairing or altering existing tangible personal property belonging to another in order to restore the property to its original condition or usefulness without producing new parts. When repair work includes the sale of repair parts in conjunction with repairs to existing tangible personal property belonging to another, only the sales price of the repair parts is taxable provided the charges for the repair parts and the charges for the repair labor are billed separately on the invoice to the customer. If a repairman fabricates repair parts which are used in conjunction with repairs to existing tangible personal property belonging to another, the total charge for the parts, including any labor charges incurred in making, producing, or fabricating the parts, is taxable even if the fabrication labor charges are billed to the customer as a separate item.	Ala. Admin. Code r. 810-6-1-.84(2)
Arizona	Exempt	Repairs to tangible personal property permanently attached to real property are taxable under the contracting classification.	Ariz. Rev. Stat. § 42-5061(A)(3)
Arkansas	Taxable	Special exemptions apply.	Ark. Code Ann. § 26-52-301(3)(B), Ark. Code Ann. § 26-52-418
California	Exempt		Reg. 1546, 18 CCR
Colorado	Exempt		1 Colo. Code Regs. § 201-5 (SR-28), 1 Colo. Code Regs. § 201-5 (SR-4)
Connecticut	Taxable	Special exemptions apply.	Conn. Agencies Regs. § 12-407(2)(i)(DD)-1, Conn. Gen. Stat. § 12-407(a)(37)
District of Columbia	Taxable		D.C. Code Ann. § 47-2001(n)(1)(I), D.C. Mun. Regs. t. 9, § 463.1(a)

State	Labor Only	Comments	Citation
Florida	Taxable	Charges for repairs of tangible personal property that require labor or service only are taxable unless the repairer can establish that repairer furnished no tangible personal property that was incorporated into or attached to the repaired item.	Fla. Admin. Code Ann. r. 12A-1.006(4)
Georgia	Exempt		Ga. Code Ann. § 48-8-3(23), Ga. Comp. R. & Regs. 560-12-2-.88, Ga. Comp. R. & Regs. 560-12-2-.78(1)
Hawaii	Taxable		Haw. Rev. Stat. § 237-13(6)
Idaho	Exempt		IDAPA 35.01.02.062.02
Illinois	Exempt		35 ICLS 115/3
Indiana	Exempt		Ind. Admin. Code tit. 45, r. 2.2-4-2 (a)
Iowa	Taxable	The tax applies to labor for "enumerated services." Most repairs of tangible personal property fall under an enumerated service. Where the repair is not an enumerated service, the charge for labor is exempt if separately stated.	Iowa Code § 423.2(6), Iowa Admin. Code r. 701 26.1(422)
Kansas	Taxable	Exceptions apply.	Kan. Stat. Ann. § 79-3603(q), Kan. Stat. Ann. § 79-3603(p)
Kentucky	Exempt		103 Ky. Admin. Regs. 27:150(1)
Louisiana	Taxable	Special exemptions apply. Caution: Numerous exemptions are suspended from April 1, 2016, to June 30, 2018. For chart of suspended exemptions and applicable tax rates, see Publication R-1002A.	La. Rev. Stat. Ann. § 47:301(14)(g)(i), La. Rev. Stat. Ann. § 47:302(C), LA DOR Publication R-1002A
Maine	Exempt		Instructional Bulletin No. 39, Code Me. R. § 320
Maryland	Exempt		Md. Code Regs. 03.06.01.03(A)
Massachusetts	Exempt		Mass. Regs. Code tit. 830, § 64H.1.1(2)(a)(1)
Michigan	Exempt		Mich. Admin. Code r. 205.117 (Rule 67)
Minnesota	Exempt		Minn. Stat. § 297A.61(3), Minn. R. 8130.0200(4)

State	Labor Only	Comments	Citation
Mississippi	Taxable	An exclusion is allowed for repair services when the repaired property is delivered to the customer in another state by common carrier or in the seller's equipment.	Miss. Code Ann. § 27-65-11(i), Miss. Code Ann. § 27-65-23
Missouri	Exempt		Mo. Code. Regs. Ann. tit. 12, § 10-103.600(3)(B)
Nebraska	Taxable	Charges for repair labor are taxable when the item of property being repaired is taxable and is not annexed to real property. Most charges for labor to repair motor vehicles are not taxable.	Neb. Admin. Code § 1-082
Nevada	Exempt		Nev. Admin. Code § 372.390(1)
New Jersey	Taxable		N.J. Stat. Ann. § 54:32B-3(b)(2)
New Mexico	Taxable		N.M. Stat. Ann. § 7-9-4
New York	Taxable	Certain exceptions apply.	N.Y. Tax Law, § 1105(c)(3), N.Y. Comp. Code R. & Regs. tit. 20, § 527.5(a)
North Carolina	Exempt	Effective March 1, 2016, the general sales and use tax rate applies to the sales price of, or the gross receipts derived from, repair, maintenance, and installation services. Certain exceptions apply.	N.C. Gen. Stat. § 105-164.3(33d) and (37), N.C. Gen. Stat. § 105-164.4(a)(15), N.C. Admin. Code tit. 17, § 17.07B.0806(a)
North Dakota	Exempt		N.D. Admin. Code § 81-04.1-01-22
Ohio	Taxable	Repair services for exempt tangible personal property is not taxable.	Ohio Rev. Code Ann. § 5739.01(B)(3)(a), Ohio Rev. Code Ann. § 5739.02(B)
Oklahoma	Exempt		Okla. Stat. tit. 68, § 1354, Okla. Admin. Code § 710:65-19-11, Okla. Stat. tit. 68, § 1357(28), Okla. Admin. Code § 710:65-19-310
Pennsylvania	Taxable	Certain exemptions exist for the repair of wearing apparel, shoes, and exempt tangible personal property, and repairs involving real estate.	72 P.S. § 7201(k)(4), 61 Pa. Code § 31.5
Rhode Island	Exempt		R.I. Code R. SU 07-92
South Carolina	Exempt		S.C. Code Ann. Regs. 117-306
South Dakota	Taxable		S.D. Codified Laws § 10-45-5

State	Labor Only	Comments	Citation
Tennessee	Taxable		Tenn. Comp. R. & Regs. 1320-5-1-.54
Texas	Taxable	Certain exemptions exist for the repair of aircraft, certain ships and boats, motor vehicles, and computer programs.	Tex. Tax Code Ann. § 151.0101(a)(5), Tex. Tax Code Ann. § 151.058(b), 34 Tex. Admin. Code § 3.292
Utah	Taxable	May be exempt if the tangible personal property being repaired is exempt.	Utah Code Ann. § 59-12-103(1)(g)
Vermont	Exempt		Vt. Stat. Ann. tit. 32, § 9771
Virginia	Exempt		Va. Code Ann. § 58.1-609.5, 23 Va. Admin. Code § 10-210-3050(A), 23 Va. Admin. Code § 10-210-4040(C)(3)
Washington	Taxable		Wash. Admin. Code § 458-20-173
West Virginia	Taxable	Exceptions apply. Repairs that result in a capital improvement to a building or other structure or to real property are tax-exempt contracting services.	W. Va. Code R. § 110-15-33.6, W. Va. Code § 110-15-117, W. Va. Code § 11-15-9(a)(33)
Wisconsin	Taxable	Repairs of aircraft and aircraft parts are exempt.	Wis. Stat. § 77.52(2)(a)(10)
Wyoming	Taxable		Wyo. Stat. Ann. § 39-15-103(a)(i)(A)

Resale Certificate Validity Periods

State	Resale Certificate Validity Periods	Comments	Citation
Alabama	Resale certificates not required.		Unofficial department guidance
Arizona	Valid for the period set out on certificate.		Ariz. Admin. Code § 15-5-2214(C)
Arkansas	No stated expiration period.		Ark. Reg. GR-53(C)
California	Valid until revoked in writing by the issuer.		Cal. Rev. & Tax. Code § 6091, Reg. 1668, 18 CCR
Colorado	Colorado does not have an official resale certificate form.		Unofficial department guidance
Connecticut	Must be renewed every three years from the date it was issued.	A resale certificate may be issued for one purchase or may be issued as a blanket certificate for a continuing line of purchases. To use a resale certificate for a continuing line of purchases, the purchaser must mark the certificate a "Blanket Certificate." The certificate must be renewed at least every three years from the date it is issued.	Conn. Agencies Reg. § 12-426-1, Informational Publication 2009(15)
District of Columbia	Until cancelled by purchaser.		Unofficial department guidance
Florida	Annual resale certificates are issued each year.	Annual resale certificates expire each year on December 31. Active and registered dealers automatically receive a new Florida Annual Resale Certificate for Sales Tax (Form DR-13) every year.	Fla. Admin. Code Ann. r. 12A-1.039(2)(a)
Georgia	Until revoked in writing.		Form ST-5
Hawaii	Until revoked in writing.		Haw. Reg. 18-237-13-02(d)
Idaho	No stated expiration period.		IDAPA 35.01.02.128
Illinois	Valid indefinitely, but should be updated at least every three years.		Ill. Admin. Code tit. 86, § 130.1405(c)(1)
Indiana	Does not expire.		Ind. Code § 6-2.5-8-5
Iowa	Certificate valid for up to 3 years.		Iowa Admin. Code r. 701-15.3(2)(b)(422,423)
Kansas	The resale certificate is valid provided there is a recurring business relationship between the buyer and seller of no more than 12 months elapsing between sales.		Form ST-28A

State	Resale Certificate Validity Periods	Comments	Citation
Kentucky	Valid provided there is no change in the character of the purchaser's operation and the purchases are of tangible personal property of the kind usually purchased by the purchaser for resale.		103 Ky. Admin. Regs. 31:111(1)
Louisiana	Valid for the period indicated on the certificate.	Sale for resale exemption certificates automatically renewed for up to three years unless taxpayer no longer qualified for the exemption.	Unofficial department guidance, La. Rev. Stat. Ann. § 47:13
Maine	Valid for five years	Provisional resale certificates issued between January 1st and September 30th effective for the duration of the calendar year in which it is issued and for the two subsequent calendar years. Provisional resale certificates issued between October 1st and December 31st effective until the end of the third succeeding calendar year. Beginning September 14, 2013, the assessor will issue a resale certificate to the retailer effective for five calendar years if certain conditions are met. Before September 14, 2013, the Assessor will issue a resale certificate, on or before the expiration date, effective for the next three calendar years. Any subsequent annual resale certificate issued effective for the next five calendar years.	Me. Rev. Stat. Ann. tit. 36, § 1754-B(2-B), Me. Rev. Stat. Ann. tit. 36, § 1754-B(2-C)
Maryland	Valid until revoked by either taxpayer or Comptroller.		Unofficial department guidance
Massachusetts	No stated expiration period.		Mass. Regs. Code tit. 830, § 64H.8.1(5)
Michigan	Expires after four years unless shorter period agreed to.	Renewal of a blanket exemption certificate is not required if there is a recurring business relationship between buyer and seller. A "recurring business relationship" exists when a period of not more than 12 months elapses between sales transactions.	RAB 2002-15
Minnesota	Does not expire unless information changes; should be updated every three to five years.		2006 Sales and Use Tax Newsletter, 1995 Sales and Use Tax Newsletter

State	Resale Certificate Validity Periods	Comments	Citation
Mississippi	No stated expiration period. Contractor's Material Purchase Certificate is valid for the job identified on the certificate.	Seller must obtain and maintain adequate records to substantiate resale exemption.	Miss. Rule 35.IV.3.01
Missouri	Valid as long as no change in character of purchaser's operation, and the purchases are of tangible personal property or taxable services of a sort that the purchaser usually purchases for resale.		Mo. Code Regs. Ann. tit. 12, § 10-107.100(3)
Nebraska	Valid indefinitely	A blanket resale certificate remains valid if sales occur between the seller and purchaser at least once every 12 months.	Neb. Admin. Code § 1-013.06
Nevada	Valid until revoked in writing.	Department recommends updating every two to three years.	Nev. Admin. Code § 372.730, Tax Notes No. 130
New Jersey	No stated expiration period.	Division of Taxation recommends that a seller request a new certificate from a buyer every few years.	N.J. Bulletin S&U-4, State Tax News, Vol. 36, No. 3
New Mexico	New Mexico resale certificates have no stated expiration period.		Unofficial department guidance
New York	No stated expiration period.	Must be delivered to vendor within 90 days of transaction and be properly completed (all required entries were made).	N.Y. Comp. Code R. & Regs. tit. 20, § 532.4(d), Form ST-120
North Carolina	Blanket certificate remains valid provided purchaser is making recurring purchases.	If single purchase box is not checked on Form E-595E indicating certificate is being used for a single purchase, certificate will be treated as a blanket certificate. A blanket certificate continues in force as long as the purchaser is making recurring purchases (i.e., at least one purchase within a period of 12 consecutive months) or until it is otherwise cancelled by the purchaser.	Form E-595E, Streamlined Sales and Use Tax Agreement Certificate of Exemption, N.C. Gen. Stat. § 105-164.28
North Dakota	New certificate should be taken every two years.		N.D. Sales and Use Tax Requirements
Ohio	No stated expiration period.		Form STEC B
Oklahoma	Blanket certificates are valid provided there is a recurring business relationship between the buyer and seller of no more than 12 months elapsing between sales.		Okla. Stat. tit. 68, § 1361(A)(3)
Pennsylvania	No expiration date.	Sales tax license must be renewed every five years.	61 Pa. Code § 32.2

State	Resale Certificate Validity Periods	Comments	Citation
Rhode Island	Resale certificates have no stated expiration period.		Rhode Island Resale Certificate
South Carolina	Valid until cancelled or revoked in writing.		Form ST8A
South Dakota	New certificate should be requested each year.		S.D. Tax Facts #154
Tennessee	Valid until revoked writing by the purchaser.		Tennessee Blanket Resale Certificate
Texas	No stated expiration period.		34 Tex. Admin. Code § 3.285(c)
Utah	Valid indefinitely.	Department recommends updating every year.	Unofficial department guidance
Vermont	Valid indefinitely.		Exemption and Resale Certificate Form S-3
Virginia	Valid until notice from Department of Taxation that certificate is no longer acceptable or is revoked.		23 Va. Admin. Code § 10-210-280(A), Unofficial department guidance
Washington	Permits issued to other qualifying businesses are valid for a period of 48 months. A reseller permit issued to a business with limited contacts with the Department of Revenue is valid for 24 months. Reseller permits issued to qualifying contractors after July 1, 2013 will be valid for 24 months. As of July 1, 2011, the department may issue, renew, or reinstate permits to contractors for a period of 24 months if it is satisfied that the contractor is entitled to make wholesale purchases.	Resale certificates have been replaced by Department-issued reseller permits.	Wash. Admin. Code § 458-20-102(3), Wash. Rev. Code § 82.32.783
West Virginia	Blanket certificates are effective so long as the purchaser makes at least one purchase within a period of 12 consecutive months, or until the certificate is otherwise cancelled by the purchaser.		W. Va. Code § 11-15-9, Form F0003 Instructions
Wisconsin	Valid indefinitely, but should be reviewed periodically.		Wis. Admin. Code § 11.14(5)
Wyoming	No stated expiration period.		SSTGB Form F0003

¶154

¶ 155   **Return Due Dates**

This chart lists sales and use tax return due dates.

State	Return Due Dates	Comments	Citation
Alabama	20th of month following reporting period.		Ala. Code § 40-23-7
Arizona	20th of month following reporting period.		Ariz. Rev. Stat. § 42-5014
Arkansas	20th of month following reporting period.		Ark. Code Ann. § 26-52-501
California	Last day of month following reporting period.		Cal. Rev. & Tax. Code § 6452, Cal. Rev. & Tax. Code § 6455
Colorado	20th of month following reporting period.	If taxpayer's accounting period does not end on the last day of the month, return is due on 20th day following the last day of the accounting period.	Colo. Rev. Stat. § 39-26-105, 1 Colo. Code Regs. § 39-26-105.1(a)(6)
Connecticut	Last day of the month following the end of the applicable monthly, quarterly, or annual period.	Effective October 1, 2015, and applicable to periods ending on or after December 31, 2015, the deadline for remittance of sales and use taxes and the filing of returns is the last day of the month following the applicable monthly, quarterly, or annual period.	Conn. Gen. Stat. § 12-414, Special Notice 2014(3)
District of Columbia	20th of month following reporting period.		D.C. Code Ann. § 47-2015, D.C. Mun. Regs. t. 9, § 420.11
Florida	20th of month following reporting period.		Fla. Stat. § 212.11, Fla. Admin. Code Ann. r. 12A-1.056
Georgia	20th of month following reporting period.		Ga. Code Ann. § 48-8-49, Ga. Comp. R. & Regs. 560-12-1-.22
Hawaii	General excise tax and use tax return due 20th day of month following reporting period.		Haw. Rev. Stat. § 237-30, Haw. Rev. Stat. § 238-5
Idaho	20th of month following reporting period.		Idaho Code § 63-3623, IDAPA 35.01.02.105
Illinois	20th of month following reporting period.		35 ILCS 105/9, 35 ILCS 110/9, 35 ILCS 120/3, 35 ILCS 115/9

State	Return Due Dates	Comments	Citation
Indiana	Monthly filers: (1) 20th of month following reporting period if average monthly sales and use tax liability in preceding year exceeded $1,000, or if filing combined sales/withholding tax return and withholding tax return is due by 20th; (2) 30th of month following reporting period if average monthly sales and use liability in preceding year did not exceed $1,000. Annual filers: last day of month following reporting period.		Ind. Code § 6-2.5-6-1(a), (d)
Iowa	Last day of month following reporting period.		Iowa Code § 423.31(1), Iowa Code § 423.32(2)
Kansas	25th of month following reporting period.		Kan. Stat. Ann. § 79-3607(a), Kan. Stat. Ann. § 79-3706(a), Kan. Admin. Regs. § 92-20-6
Kentucky	20th of month following reporting period.	If the average monthly tax liability exceeds $10,000, the due date is the 25th day of the current month for the period from the 16th of preceding month through the 15th of current month.	Ky. Rev. Stat. Ann. § 139.540, Ky. Rev. Stat. Ann. § 139.550, 103 Ky. Admin. Regs. 25:131
Louisiana	20th of month following reporting period.		La. Rev. Stat. Ann. § 47:306, La. Admin. Code tit. 61, § 4351
Maine	15th of month following reporting period.		Me. Rev. Stat. Ann. tit. 36, § 1951-A, Code Me. R. 304
Maryland	20th of month following reporting period.		Md. Code Ann. § 11-502
Massachusetts	20th of month following reporting period.		Mass. Gen. Stat. ch. 62C, § 16, Mass. Regs. Code tit. 830, § 62C.16.2
Michigan	20th of month following reporting period.		Mich. Comp. Laws § 205.56
Minnesota	20th of month following reporting period.		Minn. Stat. § 289A.20, subd. 4
Mississippi	Monthly, quarterly filers: 20th of month following reporting period. 4-week accounting period filers: 20th day following end of reporting period.		Miss. Code Ann. § 27-65-33(1), Miss. Rule 35.IV.1.02
Missouri	Monthly filers: 20th of month following reporting period. Quarterly, annual filers: last day of month following reporting period.		Mo. Code Regs. Ann. tit. 12, § 10-104.030
Nebraska	20th of month following reporting period.		Neb. Rev. Stat. § 77-2708(1)

State	Return Due Dates	Comments	Citation
Nevada	Last day of month following reporting period.		Nev. Rev. Stat. § 372.355, Nev. Rev. Stat. § 372.380, Nev. Rev. Stat. § 374.360, Nev. Rev. Stat. § 374.385
New Jersey	20th of month following reporting period.		N.J. Admin. Code § 18:24-11.2
New Mexico	25th of month following reporting period.		N.M. Stat. Ann. § 7-1-13, N.M. Stat. Ann. § 7-9-11
New York	Monthly filers: 20th of month following reporting period. Quarterly filers: last day of month following reporting period.		N.Y. Tax Law, § 1136
North Carolina	Monthly filers: 20th of month following reporting period. Quarterly filers: last day of month following quarter.		N.C. Gen. Stat. § 105-164.16
North Dakota	Last day of month following quarter.		N.D. Cent. Code § 57-39.2-11
Ohio	23rd of month following reporting period.		Ohio Rev. Code Ann. § 5739.12(A), Ohio Admin. Code § 5703-9-13(D)
Oklahoma	20th of month following reporting period.		Okla. Stat. tit. 68, § 1365, Okla. Stat. tit. 68, § 1405, Okla. Admin. Code § 710:65-3-1
Pennsylvania	20th of month following reporting period.		72 P.S. § 7217
Rhode Island	Monthly filers: 20th of month following reporting period. Quarterly filers: last day of month following reporting period.		R.I. Gen. Laws § 44-19-10, R.I. Code R. SU 89-94
South Carolina	20th of month following reporting period.		S.C. Code Ann. § 12-36-2570, S.C. Code Ann. § 12-36-2580
South Dakota	20th of month following reporting period. EFT remitters: 23rd of month following reporting period.		S.D. Codified Laws § 10-45-27.3
Tennessee	20th of month following reporting period.		Tenn. Code Ann. § 67-6-504(a), Tenn. Comp. R. & Regs. 1320-5-1-.74
Texas	20th of month following reporting period.		Tex. Tax Code Ann. § 151.401, 34 Tex. Admin. Code § 3.286(f)
Utah	Last day of month following reporting period.		Utah Code Ann. § 59-12-107(3), Utah Code Ann. § 59-12-108(1), Utah Admin. Code r. R865-19S-12
Vermont	25th (23rd of February) of month following reporting period.		Vt. Stat. Ann. tit. 32, § 9775

State	Return Due Dates	Comments	Citation
Virginia	20th of month following reporting period.		Va. Code Ann. § 58.1-615, 23 Va. Admin. Code § 10-210-480
Washington	Monthly filers: 25th of month following reporting period. Other filing periods: last day of month following reporting period.		Wash. Rev. Code § 82.32.045
West Virginia	20th of month following reporting period.		W. Va. Code § 11-15-16, W. Va. Code § 11-15A-10, W. Va. Code § 11-15-20
Wisconsin	Last day of month following reporting period.	20th of month following reporting period if sales and use tax liability exceeds $3,600 per quarter and Department of Revenue provides written notice of earlier due date.	Wis. Stat. § 77.58
Wyoming	Last day of month following reporting period.		Wyo. Stat. Ann. § 39-15-107, Wyo. DOR Rule Ch. 2 § 7

¶ 156   Returns and Repossessions

Where treatment differs for repossessed goods, it is noted in the Comments column.

State	Returns and Repossessions	Comments	Citation
Alabama	Deductible, if full sales price refunded.	A deduction or credit is allowed for the unpaid purchase price of repossessed property.	Ala. Code § 40-23-1(a)(6), Ala. Admin. Code r. 810-6-1-.147, Ala. Admin. Code r. 810-6-4-.01(7)
Arizona	Not included in gross receipts.	No specific provisions on repossessions.	Ariz. Rev. Stat. § 42-5001
Arkansas	Deductible, if full purchase price and tax were returned to customer.	A deduction is not allowed for property that has been repossessed or voluntarily returned without a full refund.	Ark. Reg. GR-18
California	Deductible, if the purchaser receives a full refund of the sales price including tax, and the purchaser is not required to purchase other property at a price greater than the returned merchandise in order to obtain a refund or credit.	Repossessions are deductible if the entire amount paid by the purchaser is refunded, or if a credit for a worthless account is allowable.	Cal. Rev. & Tax. Code § 6011, Reg. 1641, 18 CCR
Colorado	Deductible, if full sale price and tax refunded.	A deduction is allowed for the uncollected selling price of repossessed property.	Colo. Rev. Stat. § 39-26-102(5), 1 Colo. Code Regs. § 201-5 (SR-38)
Connecticut	Not included in gross receipts, if property is returned within 90 days from the purchase date.	No specific provisions on repossessions.	Conn. Gen. Stat. § 12-407(a)(8)
District of Columbia	A refund is allowed, if property is returned within 90 days of sale and full purchase price including tax is refunded to purchaser.	No deduction or refund is allowed for repossessed property.	D.C. Mun. Regs. t. 9, § 409.4, D.C. Mun. Regs. t. 9, § 409.5
Florida	Deductible if tax has not been remitted. If tax has been remitted, a credit is allowed.	A deduction is allowed for the unpaid balance of repossessed property.	Fla. Stat. § 212.17, Fla. Admin. Code Ann. r. 12A-1.012
Georgia	Deductible, if the property is returned within 90 days from the sale date, and the entire sales price is refunded to the purchaser. For property returned after 90 days, dealer may request a credit memorandum.	No specific provisions on repossessions.	Ga. Code Ann. § 48-8-58
Hawaii	Amount refunded not included in gross proceeds.	No specific provisions on taxability of repossessions. Repossession services are taxable.	Haw. Rev. Stat. § 237-3(b), Haw. Rev. Stat. § 237-13(6)
Idaho	Deductible, if the sale price is refunded, and the purchaser is not required to purchase other merchandise at a greater price.	A bad debt adjustment is allowed for property that is repossessed and seasonally resold.	Idaho Code § 63-3613(b)(3), IDAPA 35.01.02.063

State	Returns and Repossessions	Comments	Citation
Illinois	Deductible, if the amount charged including tax is refunded to the purchaser.	A credit is allowed for the uncollected portion of the sale price of repossessed property.	35 ILCS 105/9, Ill. Admin. Code tit. 86, § 140.305, Ill. Admin. Code tit. 86, § 130.1960
Indiana	No specific provisions.		
Iowa	Amount refunded not included in gross receipts.	A seller may claim a bad debt credit for repossessed merchandise.	Iowa Code § 423.2, Iowa Admin. Code r. 701 15.2
Kansas	Deductible, if the amount charged including tax is refunded to the purchaser.	Resales of repossessed goods by a retailer are reportable as part of the retailer's gross receipts; retailers and financial institutions accrue tax on the use of repossessed goods other than for retention, demonstration, or display in the regular course of business.	Kan. Stat. Ann. § 79-3602, Kan. Admin. Regs. § 92-19-49b, Kan. Admin. Regs. § 92-19-3c
Kentucky	Property repossessed by the seller may not be classed as returned goods or deductible bad debt.		Ky. Rev. Stat. Ann. § 139.350(2), 103 Ky. Admin. Regs. 31:050
Louisiana	Deductible before tax has been remitted; refund allowed after tax has been remitted.	No deduction or refund is allowed for repossessed property.	La. Rev. Stat. Ann. § 47:315, La. Admin. Code tit. 47, § 4369
Maine	Deductible, if the full sale price is refunded.	A deduction is not allowed for repossessed property unless the retailer incurs a loss, based on either the fair market value of the property or the resale price.	Me. Rev. Stat. Ann. tit. 36, § 1752(14), Instructional Bulletin No. 29
Maryland	Deductible	A credit is allowed for repossessed property. The amount is the difference between the tax on the unpaid balance and the tax on the value of the item at the time of repossession.	Md. Code Regs. 03.06.03.05, Md. Code Regs. 03.06.03.07
Massachusetts	Deductible, if the property is returned within 90 days from the sale date (180 days for motor vehicles), and the entire amount charged, less vendor's handling fees, has been refunded.	No specific provisions on repossessions.	Mass. Gen. Laws ch. 64H, § 1, Mass. Regs. Code tit. 830, § 64H.25.1(12)
Michigan	Deductible	No specific provisions on repossessions.	Mich. Comp. Laws § 205.60
Minnesota	Deductible, if the sales tax is refunded to the purchaser.	A repossession is not considered a deductible return.	Minn. R. 8130:1700(6)
Mississippi	Deductible, if the total sales price is refunded to the purchaser.	A deduction is allowed for the uncollected portion of the selling price of repossessed property.	Miss. Code. Ann. § 27-67-3, Miss. Rule 35.IV.11.02, Miss. Rule 35.IV.11.03, Miss. Rule 35.IV.10.03

State	Returns and Repossessions	Comments	Citation
Missouri	Deductible, if the full sales price including tax is refunded to the purchaser.	No specific provisions on repossessions.	Mo. Rev. Stat. § 144.130
Nebraska	Deductible	A credit is allowed for the unpaid balance of repossessed property. A credit is not allowed if the retailer remitted the tax on a cash accounting basis or collected the full tax from the purchaser at the time of purchase.	Neb. Admin. Code § 1-025, Neb. Admin. Code § 1-027
Nevada	Deductible, if the full sales price is refunded, and the purchaser is not required to purchase other property at a greater price than the returned property in order to obtain a refund.	No specific provisions on repossessions.	Nev. Rev. Stat. § 372.025
New Jersey	Not deductible; a regulation allowing a deduction has been authorized but not implemented.	A retailer may file a refund claim for overpaid sales tax on repossessed property; a deduction is not allowed.	N.J. Stat. Ann. § 54:32B-12(c)
New Mexico	Deductible	A retailer that reports on an accrual basis may deduct amounts written off as uncollectible debt for the amount credited to a buyer from whom property was repossessed.	N.M. Stat. Ann. § 7-9-67, N.M. Admin. Code tit. 3, § 3.2.227.11
New York	Tax that has not been remitted may be deducted during current reporting period. A credit or a refund is allowed for tax that has already been remitted.	No specific provisions on repossessions.	N.Y. Comp. Code R. & Regs. tit. 20, § 534.6
North Carolina	A refund or a credit is allowed if the entire amount charged including tax is refunded to the purchaser.	A deduction is not allowed for repossessed property.	N.C. Admin. Code tit.17, § 17:07B.3002, N.C. Admin. Code tit.17, § 17:07B.3003
North Dakota	A credit is allowed, if the purchase price including tax is refunded to the purchaser.	A credit is allowed for tax paid on the unpaid balance of the original sale of the repossessed property.	N.D. Admin. Code § 81:04.1-01-20
Ohio	Amounts refunded not included in receipts.	No specific provisions on repossessions.	Ohio Rev. Code Ann. § 5739.01, Ohio Admin. Code § 5703-9-11
Oklahoma	Deductible, if the full purchase price including tax is refunded to the purchaser.	A credit is allowed for the unpaid portion of repossessed property.	Okla. Admin. Code § 710:65-19-89, Okla. Admin. Code § 710:65-11-2
Pennsylvania	Deductible, if the sale amount and tax have been refunded to the purchaser.	A deduction is not allowed for repossessed property.	16 Pa. Code § 33.3

State	Returns and Repossessions	Comments	Citation
Rhode Island	Deductible, if the full sale price including tax but excluding handling charges is refunded to the purchaser, and the merchandise is returned within 120 from the purchase date.	A deduction is not allowed for repossessed property.	R.I. Gen. Laws § 44-18-30(58), R.I. Code R. SU 87-96
South Carolina	Amounts refunded not included in gross proceeds.	No specific provisions on repossessions.	S.C. Code Ann. § 12-36-90, S.C. Code Ann. § 12-36-130
South Dakota	Amounts refunded not included in gross receipts.	No specific provisions on repossessions.	S.D. Codified Laws § 10-45-29, S.D. Admin. R. 64:06:01:37, S.D. Admin. R. 64:06:01:41
Tennessee	Deductible, if the purchase price including tax is refunded to the purchaser.	If the unpaid purchase price of repossessed property exceeds $500, a dealer may claim a credit equal to the difference between the sales tax paid at the time of the original purchase and the amount of sales tax that would be owed for the portion of the purchase price that was paid by the purchaser, plus the sales tax on the first $500 of the unpaid balance.	Tenn. Code. Ann. § 67-6-507(c) and (d), Tenn. Comp. R. & Regs. 1320-5-1-.52
Texas	Credit allowed for tax on fully refunded amount.	A credit is allowed for the unpaid portion of the purchase price of repossessed property.	Tex. Tax Code Ann. § 151.007, Tex. Tax Code Ann. § 151.426(c), 34 Tex. Admin. Code § 3.302(e)
Utah	Adjustment and credit allowed if tax reported and paid in full. Credit amount may not exceed sales tax on portion of purchase price remaining unpaid at time the goods are returned.	Credit allowed to seller of a motor vehicle for tax that the seller collected on vehicle that has been repossessed and that the seller resells. Credit is equal to the product of the portion of the vehicle's purchase price that was subject to tax and remains unpaid after resale of the vehicle, and the tax rate.	Utah Admin. Code r. 865-19S-20, Utah Code Ann. § 59-12-104.3
Vermont	Deductible, if the full price including tax is refunded to the purchaser.	A vendor may apply for a refund for tax paid on the unpaid balance of repossessed property.	Vt. Stat. Ann. tit. 32, § 9780, Vt. Code R. 226-13
Virginia	Deductible, if the sales price is refunded or credited to the account of the purchaser.	The unpaid balance on repossessed property is deductible.	23 Va. Admin. Code § 10-210-3080, 23 Va. Admin. Code § 10-210-3060, Va. Code Ann. § 58.1-620

State	Returns and Repossessions	Comments	Citation
Washington	Deductible, if the full selling price including tax is refunded to the purchaser. If property is not returned within the guaranty period or if the full selling price is not refunded, a presumption is raised that the property returned is not returned goods but rather an exchange or repurchase by the vendor.	No specific provision on repossessions.	Wash. Admin. Code § 458-20-278
West Virginia	Deductible	No specific provisions on repossessions.	W. Va. Code § 11-15-2(b)(8), W.Va. Code St. R. § 110-15-2.35
Wisconsin	Deduction allowed for the amount of the purchase price refunded to the buyer if tax refunded to buyer.	Repossession of property not included in tax base if the only consideration is cancellation of the purchaser's obligation to pay the remaining balance of the purchase price. A deduction for repossessed property is not allowed unless the entire consideration paid by the purchaser is refunded, or a deduction for worthless accounts is allowable.	Wis. Stat. § 77.51(14g)(f), Wis. Admin. Code § 11.30(1)(b), Publication No. 216
Wyoming	Deductible, if the full sales price including tax is refunded to the purchaser.	A deduction is not allowed for repossessed property.	Wyo. BOE Rule Ch. 2, § 5, Wyo. BOE Rule Ch. 8, § 10

Room and Lodgings

State	Room Rentals	Comments	Citation
Alabama	Taxable	Exempt from general sales/use tax, but subject to separate state occupancy tax.	Ala. Code § 40-26-1
Arizona	Taxable	For rooms rented for less than 30 consecutive days. Owner-occupied bed-and-breakfast establishments that lease no more than four rooms are exempt if average annual occupancy rate is 50% or less. For calendar years 2006 through 2010, leases or rentals of lodging space to a motion picture production company may qualify for exemption.	Ariz. Rev. Stat. § 42-5070
Arkansas	Taxable	For rooms rented on less than a month-to-month basis. Subject to additional tourism gross receipts tax.	Ark. Code Ann. § 26-52-301(3)(B)
California	Exempt	Exempt from general sales/use tax, but local transient occupancy taxes may apply.	Cal. Rev. & Tax. Code § 7280
Colorado	Taxable		Colo. Rev. Stat. § 39-26-102(11)
Connecticut	Taxable	For rooms rented for 30 consecutive days or less. Special tax rate applies.	Conn. Gen. Stat. § 12-407(a)
District of Columbia	Taxable	For rooms rented for 90 consecutive days or less. Special tax rate applies.	D.C. Code Ann. § 47-2001(n)(1)(C)
Florida	Taxable	For rooms rented for 6 months or less.	Fla. Stat. § 212.03, Fla. Admin. Code Ann. r. 12A-1.061
Georgia	Taxable	Tax applies to rooms rented for fewer than 90 consecutive days. Effective July 1, 2015, $5-per-night fee also applies to first 30 days of stay.	Ga. Code Ann. § 48-8-2(6)(C), Ga. Code Ann. § 48-13-50.3, Ga. Comp. R. & Regs. 560-13-2-.01
Hawaii	Taxable	Subject to general excise tax and transient accommodations tax.	Haw. Rev. Stat. § 237-13, Haw. Rev. Stat. § 237D-2
Idaho	Taxable	For rooms rented for 30 consecutive days or less. Additional 2% travel and convention tax imposed. However, if room rented for purpose other than sleeping, travel and convention tax does not apply.	Idaho Code § 63-3612(2)(g)
Illinois	Taxable	Exempt from general sales/use tax, but subject to separate state occupancy tax.	35 ILCS 145/3

State	Room Rentals	Comments	Citation
Indiana	Taxable	For rooms rented for less than 30 consecutive days.	Ind. Code § 6-2.5-4-4
Iowa	Taxable	Exempt from general sales/use tax, but subject to separate state occupancy tax.	Iowa Code § 423.2
Kansas	Taxable	Applies to rooms rented for 28 days or less.	Kan. Stat. Ann. § 79-3603(g)
Kentucky	Taxable	For rooms rented for less than 30 consecutive days.	Ky. Rev. Stat. Ann. § 139.200(2)(a)
Louisiana	Taxable	For rooms rented for less than two consecutive months. If more than half of guests are permanent, establishment is not classified as a hotel. Room rentals in houses, apartments, and condos as well as establishments with less than 6 sleeping rooms are subject to tax effective July 1, 2016.	La. Rev. Stat. Ann. § 47:301(14)
Maine	Taxable	Rentals for 28 consecutive days or more exempt if occupant does not maintain primary residence at another location or is away from primary residence for employment or education. As of July 1, 2005, casual rentals of living quarters for more than 14 days in a calendar year taxable.	Me. Rev. Stat. Ann. tit. 36, § 1811
Maryland	Taxable	Rentals on monthly basis or to permanent residents exempt. All rentals for 4 months or less in resort areas taxable.	Md. Code Regs. 03.06.01.23
Massachusetts	Taxable	Exempt from sales tax, but subject to room occupancy tax. Applies to rentals of up to 90 consecutive days.	Mass. Gen. Laws ch. 64G, § 3
Michigan	Taxable	For rooms rented for one month or less. Subject to use tax.	Mich. Comp. Laws § 205.93a(1)(b)
Minnesota	Taxable	For rooms rented for less than 30 consecutive days.	Minn. Stat. § 297A.61(3)(g)(2)
Mississippi	Taxable	Charges for non-transient guests exempt. To be considered non-transient guest, guest must enter into a contract at beginning of stay for a period of at least three consecutive complete months or for a minimum of 90 consecutive days.	Miss. Code. Ann. § 27-65-23
Missouri	Taxable	For rooms rented for less than 30 consecutive days. Room rentals on permanent basis to certain businesses, including airlines, taxable.	Mo. Rev. Stat. § 144.010, Mo. Code Regs. Ann. tit. 12, § 10-110.220

State	Room Rentals	Comments	Citation
Nebraska	Taxable	For rooms rented for less than 30 consecutive days. An additional 1% state lodging tax applies to the total consideration charged for hotel room occupancy. A county lodging tax may also apply.	Neb. Rev. Stat. § 77-2701.33, Neb. Rev. Stat. § 81-3715
Nevada	Exempt	Exempt from general sales/use tax, but local transient lodging taxes may apply.	Nev. Rev. Stat. § 244.3352, Nev. Rev. Stat. § 268.096
New Jersey	Taxable	For rooms rented for less than 90 consecutive days. Exempt for permanent residents or if total amount of rent is $2.00 per day or less. Additional hotel/motel occupancy fees apply.	N.J. Stat. Ann. § 54:32B-3(d), N.J. Stat. Ann. § 54:32D-31(a)
New Mexico	Taxable		N.M. Stat. Ann. § 7-9-53
New York	Taxable	For rooms rented for less than 90 consecutive days. Exempt if total amount of rent is less than $2.00 per day.	N.Y. Tax Law, § 1105(e)
North Carolina	Taxable	Certain exemptions apply.	N.C. Gen. Stat. § 105-164.4(a)(3), N.C. Gen. Stat. § 105-164.4F
North Dakota	Taxable	For rooms rented for less than 30 consecutive days.	N.D. Cent. Code § 57-39.2-02.1(1)(e), N.D. Cent. Code § 57-39.2-04(22)
Ohio	Taxable	For rooms rented for less than 30 consecutive days.	Ohio Rev. Code Ann. § 5739.01(B)(2), (N)
Oklahoma	Taxable		Okla. Stat. tit. 68, § 1354(A)(6)
Pennsylvania	Taxable	Exempt from general sales/use tax, but subject to hotel occupancy tax.	72 P.S. § 7202, 72 P.S. § 7210
Rhode Island	Taxable	Subject to sales tax and hotel tax. Applies to rooms rented for 30 consecutive days or less.	R.I. Gen. Laws § 44-18-7(11), R.I. Gen. Laws § 44-18-36.1, R.I. Code R. SU 16-97
South Carolina	Taxable	For rooms rented for less than 90 consecutive days. Exempt if facility is individual's residence in which fewer than 6 sleeping rooms are rented or if the facility is an individual's residence and is rented for fewer than 15 days in a year.	S.C. Code Ann. § 12-36-920(A)
South Dakota	Taxable	For rooms rented for less than 28 consecutive days. Rentals for 10 days or less in calendar year exempt. In June-September, additional seasonal tax imposed.	S.D. Codified Laws § 10-45-7, S.D. Codified Laws § 10-45D-2
Tennessee	Taxable	For rooms rented for less than 90 consecutive days.	Tenn. Code. Ann. § 67-6-102

State	Room Rentals	Comments	Citation
Texas	Taxable	Exempt from general sales/use tax, but subject to separate state occupancy tax.	Tex. Tax Code Ann. § 156.051
Utah	Taxable	For rooms rented for less than 30 consecutive days.	Utah Code Ann. § 59-12-103(1)(i)
Vermont	Taxable	Exempt from general sales/use tax, but subject to meals and rooms tax.	Vt. Stat. Ann. tit. 32, § 9241, Vt. Stat. Ann. tit. 32, § 9741(9)
Virginia	Taxable	For rooms rented for less than 90 consecutive days. Exempt if rentals are for 90 continuous days or more.	Va. Code Ann. § 58.1-602, Va. Code Ann. § 58.1-609.5(8)
Washington	Taxable	For rooms rented for less than 30 consecutive days.	Wash. Rev. Code § 82.04.050(2)(f)
West Virginia	Taxable	Prior to June 8, 2016, hotel occupancy tax did not apply to hotel stays of 30 or more consecutive days.	W. Va. Code R. § 110-15-38, W. Va. Code R. § 110-15-33.5, W. Va. Code § 7-18-1
Wisconsin	Taxable	For rooms rented for less than one month.	Wis. Stat. § 77.52(2)(a)(1)
Wyoming	Taxable	For rooms rented for less than 30 consecutive days.	Wyo. Stat. Ann. § 39-15-103(a)(i)(G)

¶ 158   **Sales Tax Holidays—2017**

The following chart indicates whether a state authorizes a sales tax holiday during 2017.

State	Sales Tax Holidays - 2017	Comments	Citation
Alabama	Yes	August 4-6: clothing (not accessories or protective or recreational equipment) with sales price of $100 or less per item; single purchases, with a sales price of $750 or less, of computers, computer software, school computer equipment; noncommercial purchases of school supplies, school art supplies, and school instructional materials with sales price of $50 or less per item; noncommercial book purchases with sales price of $30 of less per book. February 24-26: severe weather preparedness items that cost $60 or less, except for portable generators and power cords used to provide light or communications or preserve food in the event of a power outage, which are covered as long as they cost $1,000 or less.	Ala. Code Sec. 40-23-210, Ala. Code Sec. 40-23-211, Ala. Admin. Code r. 810-6-3-.65, Alabama Department of Revenue website, Act 256 (H.B. 436), Laws 2012
Arizona	No		
Arkansas	Yes	Aug. 5-6: clothing items under $100, clothing accessory or equipment under $50, school art supply, school instructional material, and school supply.	Ark. Code. Ann. § 26-52-444, Ark. Reg. 2012-2
California	No		
Colorado	No		
Connecticut	Yes	August 20-26: clothing and footwear (not athletic or protective clothing or footwear, jewelry, handbags, luggage, umbrellas, wallets, watches, and similar items) that cost less than $300 per item.	Conn. Gen. Stat. § 12-407e, Informational Publication 2012(12)
District of Columbia	No		
Florida	No		
Georgia	No		
Hawaii	No		
Idaho	No		
Illinois	No		
Indiana	No		

State	Sales Tax Holidays - 2017	Comments	Citation
Iowa	Yes	August 4-5: clothing and footwear (not accessories, rentals, athletic or protective) with sales price of less than $100 per item.	Iowa Code § 423.3(68), Iowa Admin. Code r. 701-231.15
Kansas	No		
Kentucky	No		
Louisiana	Yes	May 27-28: first $1,500 of sales price of hurricane preparedness items. Excludes items purchased at airports, hotels, convenience stores, or entertainment complexes. Aug 4-5: first $2,500 of sales price of noncommercial purchases (not leases) of items of tangible personal property (not vehicles or meals). Does not apply to local taxes. However, St. Charles Parish will waive its local Louisiana sales tax during the same weekend as the state holiday. Sept 1-3: noncommercial purchases of firearms, ammunition, and hunting supplies. Does not include purchases of animals for the use of hunting.	La. Rev. Stat. Ann. § 47:305.54, La. Rev. Stat. Ann. § 47:305.58, La. Rev. Stat. Ann. § 47:305.62, La. Rev. Stat. Ann. § 47:337.10(L)
Maine	No		
Maryland	Yes	February 18-20: Energy Star products and solar water heaters. August 13-19: Items of clothing (not accessories) and footwear with a taxable price of $100 or less.	Md. Code Ann. § 11-228, Md. Regs. Code tit. 3, § 03.06.01.37, Md. Code Ann. § 11-226
Massachusetts	No		
Michigan	No		
Minnesota	No		
Mississippi	Yes	July 28-29: Clothing or footwear (not accessories, rentals, or skis, swim fins, or skates) with sales price under $100 per item. Aug 25-27: Firearms, ammunition, and hunting supplies, including archery equipment	Miss. Code Ann. § 27-65-111(bb) and (ff)

State	Sales Tax Holidays - 2017	Comments	Citation
Missouri	Yes	August 4-6: noncommercial purchases of clothing (not accessories) with taxable value of $100 or less per item; school supplies up to $50 per purchase; computer software with taxable value of $350 or less; and personal computers and computer peripherals up to $3,500. Localities may opt out. If less than 2% of retailer's merchandise qualifies, retailer must offer a tax refund in lieu of tax holiday. Effective August 28, 2015, graphing calculators with a taxable value of $150 or less will qualify, and the amount allowed for a personal computer or computer peripheral device to qualify is lowered from $3,500 to $1,500. April 19-25: Retail sales of Energy Star certified new appliances of up to $1,500 per appliance.	Mo. Rev. Stat. § 144.049, Mo. Rev. Stat. § 144.526
Nebraska	No		
Nevada	No		
New Jersey	No		
New Mexico	Yes	August 4-6: footwear and clothing (not accessories or athletic or protective clothing) with sales price of less than $100 per item; school supplies with sales price of less than $30 per item; computers with sales price of $1,000 or less per item; computer peripherals with sales price of $500 or less per item; book bags, backpacks, maps and globes with sales price less than $100 per item; and handheld calculators with sales price of less than $200 per item. Retailers are not required to participate.	N.M. Stat. Ann. § 7-9-95, N.M. Admin. Code tit. 3, § 3.2.242.7
New York	No	Items of clothing and footwear sold for less than $110 are exempt from the state's sales and use tax.	
North Carolina	No	The annual back-to-school and Energy Star sales tax holidays are repealed effective July 1, 2014.	N.C. Gen. Stat. § 105-164.13C, N.C. Gen. Stat. § 105-164.13D, Sec. 3.4(a), Ch. 316 (H.B. 998), Laws 2013
North Dakota	No		
Ohio	No		

State	Sales Tax Holidays - 2017	Comments	Citation
Oklahoma	Yes	August 4-6, 2017. Applies to the sale of any article of clothing or footwear (excluding accessories, rentals, and athletic or protective clothing) that is designed to be worn on or about the human body and that has a sales price of less than $100.	Okla. Stat. tit. 68, § 1357.10, Okla. Admin. Code § 710:65-13-511
Pennsylvania	No		
Rhode Island	No		
South Carolina	Yes	August 4-6: clothing (not rentals), clothing accessories, footwear, school supplies, computers, printers, printer supplies, computer software, bath wash clothes, bed linens, pillows, bath towels, shower curtains, bath rugs.	S.C. Code Ann. § 12-36-2120(57)
South Dakota	No		
Tennessee	Yes	July 28-30: clothing (not accessories), school supplies, and school art supplies with sales price of $100 or less per item; computers with sales price of $1,500 or less per item.	Tenn. Code Ann. § 67-6-393

State	Sales Tax Holidays - 2017	Comments	Citation
Texas	Yes	April 22-24: Emergency preparation items: (i) a portable generator used to provide light or communications or to preserve perishable food in the event of a power outage, provided the sales price of the generator is less than $3,000; (ii) a storm protection device manufactured, rated, and marketed specifically to prevent damage to a glazed or non-glazed opening during a storm or an emergency or rescue ladder, provided that the sales price of the device or ladder is less than $300; or (iii) a reusable or artificial ice product; a portable, self-powered light source; a gasoline or diesel fuel container; a AAA cell, AA cell, C cell, D cell, 6 volt, or 9 volt battery, or a package containing more than one battery, other than an automobile or boat battery; a nonelectric cooler or ice chest for food storage; a tarpaulin or other flexible waterproof sheeting; a ground anchor system or tie-down kit; a mobile telephone battery or battery charger; a portable self-powered radio, including a two-way radio or weatherband radio; a fire extinguisher, smoke detector, or carbon monoxide detector; a hatchet or axe; a self-contained first aid kit; or a nonelectric can opener, provided that the sales price of the item listed in (3) is less than $75. May 27-29: the following Energy Star products: air conditioners (sales price up to $6,000), clothes washers, ceiling fans, dehumidifiers, dishwashers, incandescent or fluorescent lightbulbs, programmable thermostats, and refrigerators (sales price up to $2,000). May 27-29: Water-conserving products purchased for residential property and WaterSense-labeled products purchased for personal or business purposes. Aug 11-13: Clothing and footwear (not accessories, athletic, protective, or rentals), school supplies, and school backpacks with sales price of less than $100 per item.	Tex. Tax Code Ann. § 151.326, Tex. Tax Code Ann. § 151.327, Tex. Tax Code Ann. § 151.333, 34 Tex. Admin. Code § 3.365
Utah	No		

State	Sales Tax Holidays - 2017	Comments	Citation
Vermont	No		
Virginia	Yes	August 4-6: Combined annual tax holiday for school supplies and clothing, Energy Star and WaterSense products, and hurricane preparedness items. School supplies and clothing: clothing and footwear with selling price of $100 or less per item, and school supplies with selling price of $20 or less per item. Energy Star and WaterSense: noncommercial purchases of Energy Star and WaterSense qualified products with a sales price of $2,500 or less per item. Hurricane preparedness: portable generators with selling price of $1,000 or less, gas-powered chain saws with a sales price of $350 or less, chainsaw accessories with a sales price of $60 or less per item, and other hurricane preparedness items with selling price of $60 or less.	Va. Code Ann. § 58.1-611.2, Va. Code Ann. § 58.1-611.3, Va. Code Ann. § 58.1-609.1(18), P.D. 15-149
Washington	No		
West Virginia	No		
Wisconsin	No		
Wyoming	No		

Services Generally

This chart indicates whether services are subject to sales and use tax.

State	Services Generally	Comments	Citation
Alabama	Services are generally not taxable.		Ala. Code § 40-23-2
Arizona	Specified services are taxable.		Ariz. Rev. Stat. § 42-5061.A.1
Arkansas	Specified services are taxable.		Ark. Code Ann. § 26-52-316(a)
California	Services are generally not taxable.		Cal. Rev. & Tax. Code § 6006
Colorado	Specified services are taxable.		Colo. Rev. Stat. § 39-26-104
Connecticut	Specified services are taxable.		Conn. Gen. Stat. § 12-407(a)(2), Conn. Gen. Stat. § 12-412(11)
District of Columbia	Specified services are taxable.		D.C. Code Ann. § 47-2001(n)
Florida	Specified services are taxable.		Fla. Stat. § 212.05
Georgia	Specified services are taxable.		Ga. Code Ann. § 48-8-30(f)(1), Ga. Code Ann. § 48-8-2(31)
Hawaii	Services are taxable unless specifically exempted.		Haw. Rev. Stat. § 237-13(6)
Idaho	Specified services are taxable.		Idaho Code § 63-3612, IDAPA 35.01.02.011
Illinois	Services are generally not taxable.	Service Occupation Tax (SOT) is imposed on tangible personal property that is transferred incidental to a service transaction.	Ill. Admin. Code tit. 86, § 130.120(d), Ill. Admin. Code tit. 86, § 140.125(c)
Indiana	Services are generally not taxable.		Ind. Admin. Code tit. 45, r. 2.2-4-2
Iowa	Specified services are taxable.		Iowa Code § 423.2(6)
Kansas	Specified services are taxable.		Kan. Stat. Ann. § 79-3603
Kentucky	Specified services are taxable.		Ky. Rev. Stat. Ann. § 139.200
Louisiana	Specified services are taxable.		La. Rev. Stat. Ann. § 47:301, La. Admin. Code tit. 61, § 4301
Maine	Specified services are taxable.		Me. Rev. Stat. Ann. tit. 36, § 1811, Me. Rev. Stat. Ann. tit. 36, § 2552
Maryland	Specified services are taxable.		Md. Code Ann. § 11-101
Massachusetts	Specified services are taxable.		Mass. Gen. Laws ch. 64H, § 1
Michigan	Specified services are taxable.		Mich. Comp. Laws § 205.51(1)(b)
Minnesota	Specified services are taxable.		Minn. Stat. § 297A.61, subd 3(g)
Mississippi	Specified services are taxable.		Miss. Code. Ann. § 27-65-23, Miss. Rule 35.IV.5.07
Missouri	Specified services are taxable.		Mo. Rev. Stat. § 144.010

State	Services Generally	Comments	Citation
Nebraska	Specified services are taxable.		Neb. Rev. Stat. § 77-2701.16
Nevada	Specified services are taxable.		Nev. Rev. Stat. § 372.105, Nev. Rev. Stat. § 374.110, Nev. Rev. Stat. § 374.190
New Jersey	Specified services are taxable.		N.J. Stat. Ann. § 54:32B-2(e)(4)(A), N.J. Stat. Ann. § 54:32B-3(b)
New Mexico	Services are taxable unless specifically exempted.		N.M. Admin. Code tit. 3, § 3.2.1.18(A)
New York	Specified services are taxable.		N.Y. Tax Law, § 1105(c)
North Carolina	Specified services are taxable.		N.C. Gen. Stat. § 105-164.4
North Dakota	Specified services are taxable.		N.D. Cent. Code § 57-39.2-02.1
Ohio	Specified services are taxable.		Ohio Rev. Code Ann. § 5739.01(B)
Oklahoma	Specified services are taxable.		Okla. Stat. tit. 68, § 1354
Pennsylvania	Specified services are taxable.		72 P.S. § 7201(k)
Rhode Island	Specified services are taxable.		R.I. Gen. Laws § 44-18-7
South Carolina	Specified services are taxable.		S.C. Code Ann. § 12-36-910
South Dakota	Services are taxable unless specifically exempted.		S.D. Codified Laws § 10-45-5
Tennessee	Specified services are taxable.		Tenn. Code. Ann. § 67-6-102, Tenn. Code. Ann. § 67-6-205
Texas	Specified services are taxable.		Tex. Tax Code Ann. § 151.0101(a)(3)
Utah	Specified services are taxable.		Utah Code Ann. § 59-12-103
Vermont	Specified services are taxable.		Vt. Stat. Ann. tit. 32, § 9771
Virginia	Specified services are taxable.		Va. Code Ann. § 58.1-609.5, 23 Va. Admin. Code § 10-210-4040
Washington	Specified services are taxable.		Wash. Rev. Code § 82.04.050, Wash. Admin. Code § 458-20-138
West Virginia	Taxable	Services are taxable unless specifically exempted.	W. Va. Code § 11-15-2(b)(17)-(18), W. Va. Code § 11-15-8, W. Va. Code R. § 110-15-8, W. Va. Code R. § 110-15-33, W. Va. Code R. § 110-15-9
Wisconsin	Specified services are taxable.		Wis. Stat. § 77.52(2)
Wyoming	Specified services are taxable.		Wyo. Stat. Ann. § 39-15-103, Wyo. BOE Rule Ch. 2, § 13

¶ 160 — **Shipping Charges**

The following chart indicates whether shipping and postage charges in conjunction with the sale of tangible personal property are included in the tax base.

State	Shipping Charges	Comments	Citation
Alabama	Excluded if (1) charges are separately stated and paid directly or indirectly by the purchaser, and (2) delivery is by common carrier or the U.S. Postal Service.	Transportation charges are not separate and identifiable if included with other charges and billed as "shipping and handling" or "postage and handling."	Ala. Admin. Code r. 810-6-1-.178
Arizona	Excluded if charges are separately stated.		Ariz. Admin. Code § 15-5-133
Arkansas	Included	If shipment includes both exempt and taxable property, the seller should allocate the delivery charge and must tax the percentage allocated to the taxable property. Charges billed to buyer by a carrier other than the seller are excluded.	Ark. Reg. GR-18
California	Excluded if charges are separately stated and delivery is made directly to the purchaser by independent contractor, common carrier or the U.S. Postal Service.	Charges imposed by the seller to transport property, and property sold for a "delivered price," are not subject to tax, provided that (1) delivery charges are stated as a separate entry on the invoice or other bill of sale; and (2) goods are shipped to the purchaser via U.S. mail, independent contractor, or common carrier, rather than the seller's vehicles; and (3) transportation occurs after the property is sold. Tax does not apply to separately stated charges for transportation of land fill material if (1) the charges are reasonable; (2) consideration received is solely for the transport of the material to a specific site; and (3) the material is transferred without charge.	Reg. 1628, 18 CCR
Colorado	Excluded if charges are (1) separable from the sales transaction, and (2) separately stated.		Special Reg. 18
Connecticut	Included	Charges to deliver exempt items are excluded.	Conn. Gen. Stat. 12-407 (a)(8)
District of Columbia	Excluded if charges are separately stated and delivery occurs after the sale.		D.C. Code Ann. § 47-2001(n)
Florida	Excluded if charges are (1) separately stated, and (2) optional.	Separately stated charges for transportation after title passes to the buyer are also excluded.	Fla. Admin. Code Ann. r. 12A-1.045

State	Shipping Charges	Comments	Citation
Georgia	Included	Exceptions apply.	Ga. Code Ann. § 48-8-2(34)(A), Ga. Code Ann. § 48-8-2(10), Ga. Comp. R. & Regs. 560-12-2-.45
Hawaii	Included	Charges for items shipped outside the state are excluded.	Haw. Rev. Stat. § 237-3(a), Haw. Rev. Stat. § 237-13(1)(C)
Idaho	Excluded if charges are separately stated.	Charges by a manufactured homes dealer to transport the home to a buyer are included.	Idaho Code § 63-3613(b)(7)
Illinois	Excluded if charges are separately contracted for.		Ill. Admin. Code tit. 86, § 130.415
Indiana	Included		Ind. Code § 6-2.5-1-5(a)(4)
Iowa	Excluded if charges are separately contracted for and separately stated.	If shipment includes both exempt and taxable property, the seller should allocate the delivery charge and must tax the percentage allocated to the taxable property.	Iowa Code § 423.1(47)
Kansas	Included	If shipment includes both exempt and taxable property, the seller should allocate the delivery charge and must tax the percentage allocated to the taxable property.	Kan. Stat. Ann. § 79-3602(ll), Kan. Admin. Regs. § 92-19-46(b)
Kentucky	Included		Ky. Rev. Stat. Ann. § 139.010(4)
Louisiana	Excluded if charges are separately stated and delivery occurs after the sale.		La. Admin. Code tit. 61, § 4301
Maine	Excluded if (1) shipment is made direct to the purchaser, (2) charges are separately stated, and (3) the transportation occurs by means of common carrier, contract carrier or the United States mail.		Me. Rev. Stat. Ann. tit. 36, § 1752(14)(B)(7)
Maryland	Excluded if charges are separately stated.		Md. Code Regs. 03.06.01.08
Massachusetts	Excluded if charges (1) reflect the costs of preparing and delivering goods to a location designated by the buyer, (2) are separately stated on the invoice to the buyer, and (3) are set in good faith and reasonably reflect the actual costs incurred by the vendor.		Department of Revenue Directive 04-5, Massachusetts Department of Revenue, July 7, 2004

State	Shipping Charges	Comments	Citation
Michigan	Included	Charges are excluded: (1) if the retailer is engaged in a separate delivery business; or (2) if incurred after the transfer of ownership. If shipment includes both exempt and taxable property, the seller should allocate the delivery charge and must tax the percentage allocated to the taxable property.	Mich. Comp. Laws § 205.51(1)(d), RAB 2015-17, Mich. Admin. Code r. 205.124
Minnesota	Included	Shipping charges are excluded if the product being shipped is exempt. If shipment includes both exempt and taxable property, the seller should allocate the delivery charge on the basis of the sales price or weight of the property being delivered and must tax the percentage allocated to the taxable property.	Minn. Stat. § 297A.61(7)(a)
Mississippi	Included		Miss. Rule 35.IV.2.03
Missouri	Included	Included if the charge is part of the sale of tangible personal property, whether or not it is separately stated. Also included if charge is not part of the sale of tangible personal property but is separately stated. Excluded if the charge is not part of the sale of tangible personal property if separately stated. If parties intend delivery charges to be part of the sale of tangible personal property, it is included even when the delivery charge is separately stated.	Mo. Code. Regs. Ann. tit. 12, § 10-103.600, Missouri Department of Revenue website
Nebraska	Included	If shipment includes both exempt and taxable property, the seller should allocate the delivery charge and must tax the percentage allocated to the taxable property. Delivery charges are exempt when the charges relate to the sale of exempt property or the purchaser paid the delivery charge to a delivery/freight company separately.	Neb. Rev. Stat. § 77-2701.35, Neb. Admin. Code § 1-079
Nevada	Excluded if (1) charges are separately stated, and (2) title passes to the purchaser before shipment pursuant to a written agreement.	If shipment includes both exempt and taxable property, the seller should allocate the delivery charge and must tax the percentage allocated to the taxable property.	Nev. Admin. Code § 372.101

State	Shipping Charges	Comments	Citation
New Jersey	Included	Regardless if separately stated. Delivery charges are not taxable if the sale itself is not taxable. If a shipment includes both exempt and taxable property, the seller should allocate the delivery charge by using: (1) a percentage based on the total sales price of the taxable property compared to the total sales price of all property in the shipment; or (2) a percentage based on the total weight of the taxable property compared to the total weight of all property in the shipment. The seller must tax the percentage of the delivery charge allocated to the taxable property but is not required to tax the percentage allocated to the exempt property.	N.J. Stat. Ann. § 54:32B-2(oo)(1)(D), N.J. Admin. Code § 18:24-27.2
New Mexico	Included	If the transportation costs are paid by the seller to the carrier.	N.M. Admin. Code tit. 3, § 2.1.15
New York	Included	Separately stated charges to ship promotional materials are excluded.	N.Y. Tax Law, § 1101, N.Y. Tax Law, § 1115(n)(3)
North Carolina	Included	If shipment includes both exempt and taxable property, the seller should allocate the delivery charge and must tax the percentage allocated to the taxable property.	N.C. Gen. Stat. § 105-164.3(37), Sales and Use Tax Technical Bulletin Sec. 38-2, North Carolina Department of Revenue
North Dakota	Included	Shipping charges are excluded if the product being shipped is exempt. If shipment includes both exempt and taxable property, the seller should allocate the delivery charge on the basis of the sales price or weight of the property being delivered and must tax the percentage allocated to the taxable property.	N.D. Cent. Code § 57-39.2-01, N.D. Admin. Code § 81-04.1-01-10
Ohio	Included	If shipment includes both exempt and taxable property, the seller should allocate the delivery charge and must tax the percentage allocated to the taxable property. Charges paid by customer to delivery company (not imposed/collected by retailer) are not taxable.	Ohio Rev. Code Ann. § 5739.01(H)(1)(a)(iv), Ohio Admin. Code § 5703-9-52

State	Shipping Charges	Comments	Citation
Oklahoma	Included	If shipment includes both exempt and taxable property, the seller should allocate the delivery charge and must tax the percentage allocated to the taxable property. Excluded where separately stated.	Okla. Stat. tit. 68, § 1352(12)
Pennsylvania	Included	Charges made in conjunction with nontaxable transactions are excluded. Charges for delivery made and billed by someone other than seller of item being delivered not taxable.	72 P.S. § 7201(g)(1), 61 Pa. Code § 54.1
Rhode Island	Included, if the property sold is taxable.	If the property sold is exempt, delivery charges are not taxable. If a shipment includes both exempt and taxable property, the seller should allocate the delivery charges by using: (1) a percentage based on the total sales prices of the taxable property compared to the total sales prices of all property in the shipment; or (2) a percentage based on the total weight of the taxable property compared to the total weight of all property in the shipment. The seller must tax the percentage of the delivery charge allocated to the taxable property but does not have to tax the percentage allocated to the exempt property.	R.I. Gen. Laws § 44-18-12(a)(iv), R.I. Code R. SU 07-33
South Carolina	Included	Charges for transportation after title has passed to the purchaser are excluded.	S.C. Code Ann. Regs. 117-310
South Dakota	Included	If shipment includes both exempt and taxable property, the seller should allocate the delivery charge and must tax the percentage allocated to the taxable property. Freight charges paid directly to freight company (not to seller) by purchaser are exempt.	S.D. Admin. R. 64:06:02:34
Tennessee	Included	Delivery charges paid by buyer to an independent third-party hired by buyer are excluded.	Tenn. Code. Ann. § 67-6-102

State	Shipping Charges	Comments	Citation
Texas	Included	Shipping charges incident to the sale or lease/rental of taxable tangible personal property or the performance of taxable services that are billed by the seller/lessor to the purchaser/lessee are taxable. A third-party carrier that only provides transportation and does not sell the item being delivered is not responsible for collecting tax.	Tex. Tax Code Ann. § 151.007
Utah	Excluded if charges are separately stated.		Utah Code Ann. § 59-12-102
Vermont	Included	Separately stated delivery charges for direct mail excluded.	Vt. Stat. Ann. tit. 32, § 9701(4), (26)
Virginia	Excluded if charges are separately stated.		Va. Code Ann. § 58.1-609.5, 23 Va. Admin. Code § 10-210-6000
Washington	Included	Charges incurred after purchaser has taken receipt of the goods and charges to deliver exempt items are excluded.	Wash. Rev. Code § 82.08.807, Wash. Admin. Code § 458-20-110
West Virginia	Included	Excluded if (1) separately stated, (2) delivery is by common carrier, and (3) customer pays the delivery charge directly to the carrier.	W. Va. Code § 11-15B-2(b)(48)(A), W. Va. Code R. § 110-15-89
Wisconsin	Included.	Separately stated delivery charges for direct mail excluded. If shipment includes both exempt and taxable property, the seller should allocate the delivery charge on the basis of the sales price or weight of the property being delivered and must tax the percentage allocated to the taxable property.	Wis. Stat. § 77.51(15b)(a)4., Wis. Stat. § 77.51(15b)(b)4.
Wyoming	Excluded if charges are separately stated		Wyo. Stat. Ann. § 39-15-105(a)(ii)(A)

¶ 161   Solar Energy Equipment

The following chart indicates whether a state provides an exemption for solar energy equipment.

State	Solar Energy Equipment	Comments	Citation
Alabama	No		
Arizona	Yes	Deductions are allowed from retail, personal property and prime contracting classifications for the gross proceeds of sales or gross income derived from a contract to provide and install a solar energy device.	Ariz. Rev. Stat. § 42-5061(N), Ariz. Rev. Stat. § 42-5071(B)(2), Ariz. Rev. Stat. § 42-5075(B)(14), Ariz. Rev. Stat. § 42-5001(15)
Arkansas	No		
California	Yes	Exemption applies to transfers between the California Alternative Energy and Advanced Transportation Financing Authority and any participating party of title to tangible personal property that constitutes a project. Effective March 24, 2010, an exemption is provided for any tangible personal property that is used for the design, manufacture, production, or assembly of advanced transportation technologies or alternative source products, components, or systems.	Cal Rev. & Tax. Code § 6010.8, Cal Pub. Res. Code § 26003, Cal Pub. Res. Code § 26011.8
Colorado	Yes	An exemption is available for components.	Colo. Rev. Stat. § 39-26-724, Colo. Rev. Stat. § 25-6.5-201(2), Colo. Rev. Stat. § 39-26-502
Connecticut	Yes		Conn. Gen. Stat. § 12-412(117)
District of Columbia	No		
Florida	Yes		Fla. Stat. § 212.08(7)(hh)
Georgia	No		
Hawaii	No		
Idaho	No		
Illinois	No		
Indiana	No		
Iowa	Yes		Iowa Code § 423.3(89)
Kansas	No		
Kentucky	No		

State	Solar Energy Equipment	Comments	Citation
Louisiana	No		
Maine	No		
Maryland	Yes		Md. Code Ann. § 11-230, Md. Code Regs. 03.06.01.43
Massachusetts	Yes	Exemption applies to equipment relating to a solar energy system in an individual's principal residence.	Mass. Gen. Laws ch. 64H, § 6(dd)
Michigan	No		
Minnesota	Yes		Minn. Stat. § 297A.67(29)
Mississippi	No		
Missouri	No		
Nebraska	Yes		Neb. Rev. Stat. § 77-2704.57
Nevada	No		
New Jersey	Yes		N.J. Stat. Ann. § 54:32B-8.33
New Mexico	Yes		Ch. 204 (S.B. 463), Laws 2007
New York	Yes	Exemption applies to residential and commercial solar energy system equipment. Municipalities are authorized but not required to grant the same exemption. Effective December 1, 2015, the existing exemption is expanded to include electricity generated by such equipment that is sold under a power purchase agreement.	N.Y. Tax Law, § 1115(ee), N.Y. Tax Law, § 1210(a)(1) and (n), N.Y. Tax Law, § 1115(hh)
North Carolina	No		
North Dakota	No		
Ohio	Yes		Ohio Rev. Code Ann. § 5739.02, Ohio Rev. Code Ann. § 5727.01
Oklahoma	No		
Pennsylvania	No		
Rhode Island	Yes		R.I. Gen. Laws § 44-18-30(57)
South Carolina	No		
South Dakota	No		
Tennessee	No		

State	Solar Energy Equipment	Comments	Citation
Texas	No		
Utah	Yes	Exemption applies to machinery or equipment used in construction of a renewable energy production facility that became operational after June 30, 2004, or had its generation capacity increased by one or more megawatts after June 30, 2004, as a result of the use of the machinery or equipment.	Utah Code Ann. § 59-12-104, Utah Code Ann. § 59-12-102
Vermont	Yes	Exemption applies to certain tangible personal property incorporated into a hot water heating system that converts solar energy into thermal energy used to heat water.	Vt. Stat. Ann. tit. 32, § 9741 (46)
Virginia	Yes	Effective July 1, 2017, an exemption is provided for machinery, tools, and equipment used by a public service corporation to generate energy derived from sunlight or wind (the exemption expires June 30, 2027).	Va. Code Ann. § 58.1-609.3 (2)
Washington	Yes		Wash. Rev. Code § 82.08.963, Wash. Rev. Code § 82.08.962
West Virginia	No		
Wisconsin	Yes	Exemption applies to product whose power source is direct radiant energy received from the sun; product must produce at least 200 watts of alternating current or 600 British thermal units per day; exemption not applicable to uninterruptible power source designed primarily for computers.	Wis. Stat. § 77.54 (56)
Wyoming	No	Previous exemption for solar energy equipment expired on December 31, 2011, or June 30, 2012, depending on net rating capacity of project.	Wyo. Stat. Ann. § 39-15-105 (a) (viii) (N), Wyo. Stat. Ann. § 39-16-105 (a) (viii) (C)

¶ 162   Sourcing—Interstate Sales

The following chart indicates whether a state follows origin-based sourcing or destination-based sourcing for general interstate retail sales.

State	Interstate Sales	Comments	Citation
Alabama	Destination		Ala. Code § 40-23-1(a)(5), Ala. Admin. Code r. 810-6-3-.35.02
Arizona	Origin	An interstate sale is sourced to the delivery location if the order is received from outside Arizona. Effective December 31, 2014, retail sales of tangible personal property are sourced: (1) to the seller's business location if the seller receives the order at a business location in-state; (2) to the purchaser's location in-state if the seller receives the order at a business location outside Arizona.	Ariz. Admin. Code § 15-5-170, Arizona Transaction Privilege Tax Ruling TPR 08-1
Arkansas	Destination	Streamlined Sales Tax sourcing rules.	Ark. Code Ann. § 26-52-521
California	Origin		Cal. Rev. & Tax. Code § 6396, Cal. Rev. & Tax. Code § 7205, Reg. 1620, 18 CCR
Colorado	Destination		1 Colo. Code Regs. § 39-26-704.2
Connecticut	Destination		Informational Publication 2006(11)
District of Columbia	Destination		D.C. Mun. Regs. t. 9, § 404.3, D.C. Mun. Regs. t. 9, § 404.4
Florida	Destination	Mail order sellers are not required to collect local option surtax unless the seller is located in a county that imposes a surtax, the order is placed at that location, and the property is delivered to a county that imposes a surtax.	Fla. Stat. § 212.06(5)(a)1, Fla. Stat. § 212.054(3), Fla. Stat. § 212.0596(6), Fla. Admin. Code Ann. r. 12A-1.0015
Georgia	Destination	Streamlined Sales Tax sourcing rules.	Ga. Code Ann. § 48-8-77
Hawaii	Destination		Haw. Rev. Stat. § 237-13, Haw. Reg. 18-237-13-02.01, Information Release 98-5
Idaho	Destination		Idaho Code § 63-3622Q, IDAPA 35.01.02.092, IDAPA 35.01.02.069
Illinois	Destination		Ill. Admin. Code tit. 86, § 130.605

State	Interstate Sales	Comments	Citation
Indiana	Destination	Streamlined Sales Tax sourcing rules.	Ind. Code § 6-2.5-13-1
Iowa	Destination	Streamlined Sales Tax sourcing rules	Iowa Code § 423.15
Kansas	Destination	Streamlined Sales Tax sourcing rules.	Kan. Stat. Ann. § 79-3670
Kentucky	Destination	Streamlined Sales Tax sourcing rules.	Ky. Rev. Stat. Ann. § 139.105
Louisiana	Destination		La. Rev. Stat. Ann. § 47:305(E)
Maine	Destination		Me. Rev. Stat. Ann. tit. 36, § 1760(82)
Maryland	Destination		Md. Code Regs. 03.06.01.25
Massachusetts	Destination		Mass. Gen. Laws ch. 64H, § 6(b), Mass. Regs. Code tit. 830, § 64H.6.7
Michigan	Destination	Streamlined Sales Tax sourcing rules	Mich. Comp. Law § 205.69
Minnesota	Destination	Streamlined Sales Tax sourcing rules	Minn. Stat § 297A.668
Mississippi	Destination		Miss. Rule 35.IV.3.05
Missouri	Destination		Mo. Code Regs. Ann. tit. 12, § 10-113.200(3), Mo. Code Regs. Ann. tit. 12, § 10-117.100
Nebraska	Destination	Streamlined Sales Tax sourcing rules	Neb. Rev. Stat. § 77-2703.01
Nevada	Destination	Streamlined Sales Tax sourcing rules	Nev. Rev. Stat. § 360B.360
New Jersey	Destination	Streamlined Sales Tax sourcing rules.	N.J. Stat. Ann. § 54:32B-3.1
New Mexico	Origin	Some exceptions.	FYI-200
New York	Destination		N.Y. Comp. Code R. & Regs. tit. 20, § 525.2(a)(3)
North Carolina	Destination	Streamlined Sales Tax sourcing rules.	N.C. Gen. Stat. § 105-164.4B
North Dakota	Destination	Streamlined Sales Tax sourcing rules	N.D. Gen. Stat. § 57-39.4-11
Ohio	Destination	Streamlined Sales Tax sourcing rules	Ohio Rev. Code Ann. § 5739.033
Oklahoma	Destination	Streamlined Sales Tax sourcing rules.	Okla. Stat. tit. 68, § 1354.27, Okla. Admin. Code § 710:65-18-3

State	Interstate Sales	Comments	Citation
Pennsylvania	Destination		61 Pa. Code § 32.5, 53 P.S. § 12720.504, 16 P.S. § 6153-B, Policy Statement 60.16
Rhode Island	Destination	Streamlined Sales Tax sourcing rules.	R.I. Gen. Laws § 44-18.1-11
South Carolina	Destination		S.C. Code Ann. Regs. 117-334, Revenue Ruling No. 09-9
South Dakota	Destination	Streamlined Sales Tax sourcing rules	S.D. Codified Laws § 10-45-108, S.D. Admin. R. 64:06:01:63
Tennessee	Destination	Streamlined Sales Tax sourcing rules, effective July 1, 2017.	Tenn. Code Ann. § 67-6-902, Tenn. Comp. R. & Regs. 1320-5-2-.05
Texas	Destination		Tex. Tax Code Ann. § 151.330, Tex. Tax Code Ann. § 321.203
Utah	Destination	Streamlined Sales Tax sourcing rules.	Utah Code Ann. § 59-12-211, Utah Code Ann. § 59-12-212
Vermont	Destination	Streamlined Sales Tax sourcing rules	Vt. Code R. 1.9701(8)-2, Vt. Code R. 1.9701(8)-3
Virginia	Destination		23 Va. Admin. Code § 10-210-780
Washington	Destination	Streamlined Sales Tax sourcing rules	Wash. Rev. Code § 82.32.730, Wash. Admin. Code § 458-20-145
West Virginia	Destination	Streamlined Sales Tax sourcing rules.	W. Va. Code § 11-15B-15
Wisconsin	Destination	Streamlined Sales Tax sourcing rules	Wis. Stat. § 77.522
Wyoming	Destination	Streamlined Sales Tax sourcing rules.	Wyo. Stat. Ann. § 39-15-104(f), Wyo. BOE Rule Ch. 2, § 5

¶ 163   Sourcing—Intrastate Sales

The following chart indicates whether a state follows origin-based sourcing or destination-based sourcing for general intrastate retail sales.

State	Intrastate Sales	Comments	Citation
Alabama	Destination		Ala. Code § 40-23-1(a)(5), Ala. Admin. Code r. 810-6-3-.35.02
Arizona	Origin	Effective December 31, 2014, retail sales of tangible personal property are sourced: (1) to the seller's business location if the seller receives the order at a business location in-state; (2) to the purchaser's location in-state if the seller receives the order at a business location outside Arizona.	Arizona Transaction Privilege Tax Ruling TPR 96-5
Arkansas	Destination	Streamlined Sales Tax sourcing rules.	Ark. Code Ann. § 26-52-521, Ark. Reg. GR-91
California	Origin		Cal. Rev. & Tax. Code § 6010.5, Cal. Rev. & Tax. Code § 7205, Cal. Rev. & Tax. Code § 7262, Cal. Rev. & Tax. Code § 7263, Reg. 1802, 18 CCR
Colorado	Destination		1 Colo. Code Regs. § 39-26-704.2
Connecticut	N/A	Connecticut has no provisions that authorize municipalities or other political subdivisions to levy local sales and use taxes.	Conn. Gen. Stat. § 12-408, Informational Publication 2006(11)
District of Columbia	N/A		
Florida	Destination	Mail order sellers are not required to collect local option surtax unless the seller is located in a county that imposes a surtax, the order is placed at that location, and the property is delivered to a county that imposes a surtax.	Fla. Stat. § 212.06(5)(a)1, Fla. Stat. § 212.054(3), Fla. Stat. § 212.0596(6), Fla. Admin. Code Ann. r. 12A-1.0015
Georgia	Destination	Streamlined Sales Tax sourcing rules.	Ga. Code Ann. § 48-8-77
Hawaii	Destination		Haw. Rev. Stat. § 237-13, Haw. Reg. 18-237-8.6-02, Haw. Reg. 18-237-13-02.01
Idaho	Destination		Idaho Code § 63-3622Q, IDAPA 35.01.02.092, IDAPA 35.01.02.069

State	Intrastate Sales	Comments	Citation
Illinois	Origin		Ill. Admin. Code tit. 86, § 130.605, Ill. Admin. Code tit. 86, § 220.115, ST 07-0043-GIL
Indiana	Destination	Streamlined Sales Tax sourcing rules. No local sales and use taxes.	Ind. Code § 6-2.5-13-1
Iowa	Destination	Streamlined Sales Tax sourcing rules	Iowa Code § 423.15
Kansas	Destination	Streamlined Sales Tax sourcing rules.	Kan. Stat. Ann. § 79-3670
Kentucky	Destination	Streamlined Sales Tax sourcing rules. No local sales and use taxes.	Ky. Rev. Stat. Ann. § 139.105
Louisiana	Destination		La. Rev. Stat. Ann. § 47:305(E)
Maine	Destination	No local sales and use taxes.	Me. Rev. Stat. Ann. tit. 36, § 1760(82)
Maryland	Destination	No local sales and use taxes	Md. Code Regs. 03.06.01.25
Massachusetts	Destination	No local sales and use taxes	Mass. Gen. Laws ch. 64H, § 6(b), Mass. Regs. Code tit. 830, § 64H.6.7
Michigan	Destination	Streamlined Sales Tax sourcing rules No local sales and use taxes.	Mich. Comp. Law § 205.69
Minnesota	Destination	Streamlined Sales Tax sourcing rules	Minn. Stat § 297A.668
Mississippi	Origin		Miss. Code. Ann. § 27-65-3(f), Miss. Rule 35.IV.3.05
Missouri	Origin	Origin for sales tax. Destination for use tax.	Mo. Code Regs. Ann. tit. 12, § 10-113.200(1), Mo. Code Regs. Ann. tit. 12, § 10-117.100
Nebraska	Destination	Streamlined Sales Tax sourcing rules	Neb. Rev. Stat. § 77-2703.01
Nevada	Destination	Streamlined Sales Tax sourcing rules	Nev. Rev. Stat. § 360B.360
New Jersey	Destination	Streamlined Sales Tax sourcing rules.	N.J. Stat. Ann. § 54:32B-3.1
New Mexico	Origin	Some exceptions.	FYI-200
New York	Destination		N.Y. Comp. Code R. & Regs. tit. 20, § 525.2(a)(3)
North Carolina	Destination	Streamlined Sales Tax sourcing rules.	N.C. Gen. Stat. § 105-164.4B
North Dakota	Destination	Streamlined Sales Tax sourcing rules	N.D. Gen. Stat. § 57-39.4-11

¶163

State	Intrastate Sales	Comments	Citation
Ohio	Origin		Ohio Rev. Code Ann. § 5739.033
Oklahoma	Destination	Streamlined Sales Tax sourcing rules.	Okla. Stat. tit. 68, § 1354.27, Okla. Admin. Code § 710:65-18-3
Pennsylvania	Origin		61 Pa. Code § 32.5, 53 P.S. § 12720.504, 16 P.S. § 6153-B, Policy Statement 60.16
Rhode Island	Destination	Streamlined Sales Tax sourcing rules.	R.I. Gen. Laws § 44-18.1-11
South Carolina	Destination		S.C. Code Ann. Regs. 117-334, Revenue Ruling No. 09-9
South Dakota	Destination	Streamlined Sales Tax sourcing rules	S.D. Codified Laws § 10-45-108, S.D. Admin. R. 64:06:01:63
Tennessee	Origin	Destination (Streamlined Sales Tax rules), effective July 1, 2017.	Tenn. Code Ann. § 67-6-902, Tenn. Comp. R. & Regs. 1320-5-2-.05
Texas	Origin		Tex. Tax Code Ann. § 321.203
Utah	Origin		Utah Code Ann. § 59-12-211, Utah Code Ann. § 59-12-212
Vermont	Destination	Streamlined Sales Tax sourcing rules	Vt. Code R. 1.9701(8)-2, Vt. Code R. 1.9701(8)-3
Virginia	Origin		23 Va. Admin. Code § 10-210-2070
Washington	Destination	Streamlined Sales Tax sourcing rules	Wash. Rev. Code § 82.32.730, Wash. Admin. Code § 458-20-145
West Virginia	Destination	Streamlined Sales Tax sourcing rules.	W. Va. Code § 11-15B-15
Wisconsin	Destination	Streamlined Sales Tax sourcing rules	Wis. Stat. § 77.522
Wyoming	Destination	Streamlined Sales Tax sourcing rules.	Wyo. Stat. Ann. § 39-15-104(f), Wyo. BOE Rule Ch. 2, § 5

State	State Contacts	Comments	Citation
Alabama	Alabama Department of Revenue Office of the Commissioner P.O. Box 327001 Montgomery, AL 36132-7001 (334) 242-1175 ADOR Website		
Arizona	Arizona Department of Revenue Taxpayer Information and Assistance P.O. Box 29086 Phoenix, AZ 85038-9086 (602) 255-3381 or (800) 352-4090 AZ DOR Website		
Arkansas	Arkansas Department of Finance and Administration Sales and Use Tax Unit P.O. Box 1272 Little Rock, AR 72203-1272 (501) 682-1895 E-mail: sales.tax@rev.state.ar.us AR DFA Website		
California	California State Board of Equalization 450 N Street P.O. Box 942879 Sacramento, CA 94279-001 (800) 400-7115 CA SBE Website		
Colorado	Colorado Department of Revenue 1375 Sherman St. Denver, CO 80261 (303) 238-7378 DOR Website		
Connecticut	Connecticut Department of Revenue Services 25 Sigourney St. Hartford, CT 06106-5032 (860) 297-5962 or (800) 382-9462 (in CT) CT DRS Website		
District of Columbia	Office of Tax and Revenue Office of the Chief Financial Officer 941 N. Capitol St. NE 8th Fl. Washington, DC 20002 (202) 727-4829 E-mail: otr.ocfo@dc.gov DC OTR Website		
Florida	Florida Department of Revenue Taxpayer Services 1379 Blountstown Hwy. Tallahassee, FL 32304-2716 (800) 352-3671 FL DOR Website		
Georgia	Georgia Department of Revenue 1800 Century Blvd, NE Atlanta, GA 30345 (877) 423-6711, option 1 GA DOR Website		

State	State Contacts	Comments	Citation
Hawaii	Hawaii Department of Taxation Oahu District Office Princess Ruth Keelikolani Building 830 Punchbowl Street Honolulu, HI 96813-5094 (808) 587-4242 or (800) 222-3229 HI DOT Website		
Idaho	Idaho State Tax Commission P.O. Box 36 800 Park Blvd., Plaza IV Boise, ID 83722-0410 (208) 334-7660 or (800) 972-7660 ID Tax Commission Website		
Illinois	Illinois Department of Revenue P.O. Box 19044 62794-9044 (217) 524-4772 or (800) 732-8866 IL DOR Website		
Indiana	Indiana Department of Revenue 100 N. Senate Ave. Indianapolis, IN 46204 Phone: (317) 233-4015 IN DOR Website		
Iowa	Iowa Department of Revenue Taxpayer Services P.O. Box 10457 Des Moines, IA 50306-0457 (515) 281-3114 or (800) 367-3388 (Iowa, Rock Island, Moline, Omaha) E-mail: idr@iowa.gov IA DOR Website		
Kansas	Kansas Department of Revenue Tax Assistance Docking State Office Building Room 150 915 SW Harrison Street Topeka, KS 66612 (785) 368-8222 KS DOR Website		
Kentucky	Kentucky Department of Revenue 200 Fair Oaks Ln. Frankfort, KY 40602 (502) 564-8139 KY DOR Website		
Louisiana	Louisiana Department of Revenue Sales Tax Division P.O. Box 3138 Baton Rouge, LA 70821-3138 (225) 219-7356 LA DOR Website		
Maine	Maine Department of Revenue Services Sales, Fuel & Special Tax Division P.O. Box 1065 Augusta, ME 04332-1605 (207) 626-9693 Email: sales.tax@maine.gov ME DRS Website		

State	State Contacts	Comments	Citation
Maryland	Comptroller of Maryland 110 Carroll St. Annapolis, MD 21411 (410) 260-7980 or (800) MD-TAXES E-mail: taxprohelp@comp.state.md.us MD Comptroller's Website		
Massachusetts	Massachusetts Department of Revenue P.O. Box 7010 Boston, MA 02204 (617) 887-6367 or (800) 392-6089 (within MA) MA DOR Website		
Michigan	Michigan Department of Treasury Lansing, MI 48922 (517) 636-6925 E-mail: treasSUW@michigan.gov MI Dept. of Treasury Website		
Minnesota	Minnesota Department of Revenue 600 North Robert Street St. Paul, MN 55101 (651) 556-3000 MN DOR Website		
Mississippi	Mississippi Department of Revenue P.O. Box 1033 Jackson, MS 39215-1033 (601) 923-7000 MS DOR Website		
Missouri	Missouri Department of Revenue P.O. Box 3300 Jefferson City, MO 65105-3300 (573) 751-2836 E-mail: salesuse@dor.mo.gov MO DOR Website		
Nebraska	Nebraska Department of Revenue Nebraska State Office Building 301 Centennial Mall South P.O. Box 94818 Lincoln, NE 68509-4818 (402) 471-5729 or (800) 742-7474 (in NE & IA) NE DOR Website		
Nevada	Nevada Department of Taxation 1550 College Pkwy., Ste. 115 Carson City, NV 89706 (866) 962-3707 NV DOT Website		
New Jersey	New Jersey Division of Taxation P.O. Box 281 Trenton, NJ 08695-0281 (609) 292-6400 NJ DOT Website		
New Mexico	New Mexico Taxation and Revenue Department 1100 S. St. Francis Dr. P.O. Box 630 Santa Fe, NM 87504-0630 (505) 827-0700 NM TRD Website		

State	State Contacts	Comments	Citation
New York	New York State Department of Taxation and Finance W.A. Harriman Campus Albany, NY 12227 (518) 485-2889 or (800) 698-2909 (in NY) DTF Website		
North Carolina	North Carolina Department of Revenue Sales and Use Tax Division P.O. Box 871 Raleigh, NC 27640-0640 (877) 252-3052 NC DOR Website		
North Dakota	North Dakota Office of State Tax Commissioner 600 E. Boulevard Ave. Bismarck, ND 58505-0599 (701) 328-7088 ND Tax Dept. Website		
Ohio	Ohio Department of Taxation Sales and Use Tax Division 4485 Northland Ridge Blvd. Columbus, OH 43229 (888) 405-4039 Fax: (206) 339-9305 OH Dept. of Taxation Website		
Oklahoma	Oklahoma Tax Commission 2501 North Lincoln Boulevard Oklahoma City, OK 73194 (405) 521-3160 OK Tax Commission Website		
Pennsylvania	Pennsylvania Department of Revenue Bureau of Business Trust Fund Taxes P.O. Box 280901 Harrisburg, PA 17128-0901 (717) 787-1064 PA DOR Website		
Rhode Island	Rhode Island Division of Taxation One Capitol Hill Providence, RI 02908 (401) 222-2950 DOT Website		
South Carolina	South Carolina Department of Revenue 300A Outlet Pointe Boulevard PO Box 125 Columbia, SC 29214 Phone: 803-898-5000 DOR Website		
South Dakota	South Dakota Department of Revenue and Regulation Attn: Business Tax Division 445 East Capitol Ave. Pierre, SD 57501 (605) 773-3311 or (800) 829-9188 Fax: (605) 773-6729 Email: bustax@state.sd.us SD DRR Website		

¶164

State	State Contacts	Comments	Citation
Tennessee	Tennessee Department of Revenue Andrew Jackson Building, Room 1200 500 Deaderick St. Nashville, TN 37242-1099 (615) 253-0600 or (800) 342-1003 (within TN) E-mail: TN.Revenue@tn.gov TN DOR Website		
Texas	Texas Comptroller of Public Accounts P.O. Box 13528, Capitol Station Austin, TX 78711-3528 (800) 252-5555 (Sales and Use Tax) or (877) 662-8375 (Customer Service) E-mail: tax.help@cpa.state.tx.us; ombudsman@cpa.state.tx.us TX Comptroller Website		
Utah	Utah State Tax Commission 210 North 1950 West Salt Lake City, UT 84134 Phone: (801) 297-2200 or (800) 662-4335 TDD: (801) 297-2020 UT State Tax Commission Website		
Vermont	Vermont Department of Taxes 133 State St. Montpelier, VT 05633 (802) 828-5787 VT DOT Website		
Virginia	Virginia Department of Taxation P.O. Box 1115 Richmond, VA 23218-1115 (804) 367-8037 VA DOT Website		
Washington	Washington State Department of Revenue Taxpayer Account Administration P.O. Box 47476 Olympia, WA 98504-7476 Phone: (800) 647-7706 WA DOR Website		
West Virginia	West Virginia State Tax Department 1206 Quarrier St. Charleston, WV 25301 Phone: (304) 558-3333 or (800) WVA-TAXS (982-8297) WV Tax Dept. Website		
Wisconsin	Wisconsin Department of Revenue 2135 Rimrock Road Madison, WI 53713 (608) 266-2772 WI DOR Website		
Wyoming	Wyoming Department of Revenue Excise Tax Division 122 W. 25th St. Herschler Bldg., 2nd Floor West Cheyenne, WY 82002-0110 (307) 777-5200 or (307) 777-3745 E-Mail: dor@wy.gov WY DOR Website		

¶ 165 **State Rates—2017**

Rate listed below is the general state rate. Most states authorize additional local sales and use taxes, which are not included.

State	2017 Rates	Comments	Citation
Alabama	4%		Ala. Code § 40-23-26
Arizona	5.6%		Ariz. Rev. Stat. § 42-5010
Arkansas	6.5%	Food rate is 1.5%.	Ark. Code. Ann. § 26-52-302
California	7.25%	The 7.25% current total statewide base includes 0.25% that goes to county (local) transportation funds and 1% that goes to city or county (local) operations.	Cal. Rev. & Tax Code § 6051, Cal. Rev. & Tax Code § 6051.2, Cal. Const. art. XIII, § 35, Cal. Const. art. XIII, § 36, Cal. Rev. & Tax Code § 6051.3, Cal. Rev. & Tax Code § 6051.5, Cal. Rev. & Tax Code § 6201, Cal. Rev. & Tax Code § 6051.7, Cal. Rev. & Tax Code § 6201.7, Cal. Gov. Code § 99040
Colorado	2.9%	An additional state sales tax rate applies to sales of marijuana and marijuana products.	Colo. Rev. Stat. § 39-26-105
Connecticut	6.35%	7.75% on motor vehicles that cost more than $50,000 (with certain exceptions), jewelry that costs more than $5,000, and certain clothing, footwear, and other items that cost more than $1,000.	Conn. Gen. Stat. § 12-408, Conn. Gen. Stat. § 12-411
District of Columbia	5.75%		D.C. Code Ann. § 47-2002
Florida	6%		Fla. Stat. ch. 212.05
Georgia	4%	Effective July 1, 2015, sales of motor fuel for highway use exempt from 4% state sales and use tax rate. Prior to July 1, 2015, sales of motor fuel for highway use exempt from first 3% of state sales and use tax, but subject to remaining 1% of state sales and use tax.	Ga. Code. Ann. § 48-8-30, Ga. Code. Ann. § 48-8-3.1
Hawaii	4%	0.5% rate for wholesalers/manufacturers.	Haw. Rev. Stat. § 237-13
Idaho	6%		Idaho Code § 63-3619
Illinois	6.25%	Grocery food, drugs, medical appliances, and modifications to make a motor vehicle usable by a disabled person are taxed at 1%.	35 ILCS 105/3-10
Indiana	7%		Ind. Code § 6-2.5-2-2
Iowa	6%		Iowa Code § 423.2

State	2017 Rates	Comments	Citation
Kansas	6.5%	6.15% July 1, 2013 - June 30, 2015.	Kan. Stat. Ann. § 79-3603, Kan. Stat. Ann. § 79-3703
Kentucky	6%		Ky. Rev. Stat. Ann. § 139.200, Ky. Rev. Stat. Ann. § 139.310
Louisiana	5%	Total state rate is temporarily increased from 4% to 5% effective April 1, 2016, through June 30, 2018. The temporary additional 1% tax has its own exclusive list of exemptions and exclusions. Numerous exemptions are suspended during this period. For chart of suspended exemptions and applicable tax rates, see Publication R-1002A.	La. Rev. Stat. Ann. § 47:302, La. Rev. Stat. Ann. § 47:331, La. Rev. Stat. Ann. § 51:1286, La. Rev. Stat. Ann. § 47:321, LA DOR Publication R-1002A
Maine	5.5%	Rate remains at 5.5% after June 30, 2015.	Me. Rev. Stat.Ann. tit.36, § 1811
Maryland	6%		Md. Code Ann. § 11-104(a)
Massachusetts	6.25%		Mass. Gen. Laws ch. 64H, § 2
Michigan	6%		Mich. Comp. Laws § 205.52(1)
Minnesota	6.875%		Minn. Stat. § 297A.62(1) and (1a), Minn Const Art. XI, § 15
Mississippi	7%		Miss. Code. Ann. § 27-65-17
Missouri	4.225%	Total rate of 4.225% consists of general sales/use tax of 4%, additional sales tax of 0.10% for soil/water conservation and state parks, and additional sales tax of 0.125% for wildlife conservation. Grocery food taxed at reduced rate of 1.225%.	Mo. Rev. Stat. § 144.020, Mo. Const. art. IV, § 43(a), Mo. Const. art. IV, § 47(a)
Nebraska	5.5%	Adjusted biennially.	Neb. Rev. Stat. § 77-2701.02
Nevada	6.85%		Nev. Rev. Stat. § 372.105, Nev. Rev. Stat. § 374.110, Nev. Rev. Stat. § 377.040
New Jersey	6.875%	Effective January 1, 2018, the rate will be 6.625%.	N.J. Stat. Ann. § 54:32B-3
New Mexico	5.125%	Compensating tax rate on services is 5%.	N.M. Stat. Ann. § 7-9-4
New York	4%		N.Y. Tax Law, § 1110
North Carolina	4.75%		N.C. Gen. Stat. § 105-164.4
North Dakota	5%		N.D. Cent. Code § 57-39.2-02.1

State	2017 Rates	Comments	Citation
Ohio	5.75%		Ohio Rev. Code Ann. § 5739.02
Oklahoma	4.5%		Okla. Stat. tit. 68, § 1354, Okla. Stat. tit. 68, § 1402
Pennsylvania	6%		72 P.S. § 7202
Rhode Island	7%		R.I. Gen. Laws § 44-18-18
South Carolina	6%		S.C. Code Ann. § 12-36-910, S.C. Code Ann. § 12-36-1110
South Dakota	4%		S.D. Codified Laws § 10-45-2
Tennessee	7%	The rate on food is 5%. Additional tax of 2.75% imposed on any single item sold in excess of $1,600 but not more than $3,200.	Tenn. Code. Ann. § 67-6-202
Texas	6.25%		Tex. Tax Code Ann. § 151.051
Utah	4.7%	Food and food ingredients are taxed at reduced rate of 1.75%.	Utah Code Ann. § 59-12-103(2)
Vermont	6%		Vt. Stat. Ann. tit. 32, § 9771
Virginia	4.3%	Additional 1% local rate imposed in all localities. Additional 0.7% state tax imposed in the localities that make up Northern Virginia and Hampton Roads regions. Grocery food taxed at reduced rate of 2.5% (1.5% state tax and 1% local option tax).	Va. Code. Ann. § 58.1-603
Washington	6.5%		Wash. Rev. Code § 82.08.020
West Virginia	6%	Reduced rates apply to long-term vehicle lease payments, and to sales and uses of motor vehicles, gasoline, and certain fuels.	W. Va. Code § 11-15-3(b), W. Va. Code § 11-15A-2
Wisconsin	5%		Wis. Stat. § 77.52(1)
Wyoming	4%		Wyo. Stat. Ann. § 39-15-104

¶ 166   Statutes of Limitations—Assessments

This chart states the period in which sales and use taxes may be assessed. Generally, there is no limitation period for assessments where no return was filed or a fraudulent return was filed.

State	Assessments	Comments	Citation
Alabama	3 years from later of return due date or return filing date.	If base understated by more than 25%, 6 years from later of return due date or return filing date.	Ala. Code § 40-2A-7
Arizona	4 years from later of return due date or return filing date.	If receipts understated by more than 25%, 6 years from return filing date.	Ariz. Rev. Stat. § 42-1104
Arkansas	3 years from later of return due date or return filing date.	If receipts understated by more than 25%, six years from the date the return was filed.	Ark. Code Ann. § 26-18-306
California	3 years from later of the end of the calendar month following the quarterly period for which the assessment relates, or the return filing date.	8 years from the end of the calendar month following the quarterly period if no return was filed.	Cal. Rev. & Tax. Code § 6487(a)
Colorado	3 years from later of tax due date or return filing date.		Colo. Rev. Stat. § 39-26-125, Colo. Rev. Stat. § 39-21-107
Connecticut	3 years from the later the end of the calendar month following the tax period, or the date the return was filed.		Conn. Gen. Stat. § 12-415(f)
District of Columbia	3 years from return filing date.	6 years from return filing date if tax understated by more than 25%.	D.C. Code Ann. § 47-4301
Florida	3 years from later of return due date, tax due date, or return filing date, or any time a right to a refund or credit is available to the taxpayer.		Fla. Stat. § 95.091(3)
Georgia	3 years from later of return due date or return filing date.		Ga. Code Ann. § 48-2-49
Hawaii	3 years from later of annual return due date or filing date.		Haw. Rev. Stat. § 237-40
Idaho	3 years from later of return due date or return filing date.	7 years from return due date if no return was filed.	Idaho Code § 63-3633
Illinois	3 years from the month or period in which the taxable gross receipts were received (assessments issued on January 1 or July 1).		Ill. Admin. Code tit. 86, § 130.815
Indiana	3 years from later of the return filing date or the end of the calendar year containing the period for which the return was filed.		Ind. Code § 6-8.1-5-2
Iowa	3 years from return filing date.		Iowa Code § 423.37

State	Assessments	Comments	Citation
Kansas	3 years from return filing date.	In the case of a false or fraudulent return, 2 years from the date fraud was discovered.	Kan. Stat. Ann. § 79-3609(b), Kan. Admin. Regs. § 92-19-63
Kentucky	4 years from later of return due date or return filing date.		Ky. Rev. Stat. Ann. § 139.620(1)
Louisiana	3 years from the end of the calendar year in which the tax payment was due.		La. Const. Art. VII, § 16, La. Rev. Stat. Ann. § 47:1580
Maine	3 years from later of return due date or return filing date. If tax understated by 50% or more, 6 years from return filing date.		Me. Rev. Stat. Ann. tit. 36, § 141
Maryland	4 years from tax due date.	No limitations period if proof of fraud or gross negligence.	Md. Code Ann. § 13-1102
Massachusetts	3 years from later of return due date or return filing date.		Mass. Gen. Laws ch. 62C, § 26
Michigan	4 years from later of return due date or return filing date.	For cases involving fraud, 2 years from the date fraud was discovered.	Mich. Comp. Laws § 205.27a(2)
Minnesota	3.5 years from later of return due date or return filing date.	If taxes underreported by more than 25%, 6.5 years from later of return due date or return filing date.	Minn. Stat. § 289A.38
Mississippi	3 years from return filing date.		Miss. Code. Ann. § 27-65-42
Missouri	3 years from later of return due date or return filing date.		Mo. Rev. Stat. § 144.220
Nebraska	3 years from later of date the return was filed or the last day of the calendar month following the tax period.	For cases where a return has not been filed, a false or fraudulent return has been filed with the intent to evade the tax, or an amount has been omitted from a return that is in excess of 25% of the amount of tax stated, 6 years after the last day of the calendar month following the period in which the amount is proposed to be determined.	Neb. Rev. Stat. § 77-2709
Nevada	3 years from later of return filing date or the last day of the calendar month following the tax period.	8 years from the last day of the month following the tax period if no return is filed.	Nev. Rev. Stat. § 360.355
New Jersey	4 years from return filing date.		N.J. Stat. Ann. § 54:32B-27(b), N.J. Stat. Ann. § 54:49-6

State	Assessments	Comments	Citation
New Mexico	3 years from the end of the calendar year in which the tax payment was due.	If taxes underreported by more than 25%, 6 years from the end of the calendar year in which the tax payment was due. 7 years from the end of the calendar year in which the tax payment was due if no return was filed. 10 years from the end of the calendar year in which the tax payment was due if fraudulent return was filed.	N.M. Stat. Ann. § 7-1-18
New York	3 years from later of return due date or return filing date.		N.Y. Tax Law, § 1147(b)
North Carolina	3 years from later or return due date or return filing date.		N.C. Gen. Stat. § 105-241.1(e)
North Dakota	3 years from later of return due date or return filing date.	If tax understated by 25% or more, 6 years from later of return due date or return filing date. 6 years from return due date if no return was filed.	N.D. Cent. Code § 57-39.2-15
Ohio	4 years from later of return due date or return filing date.	Statute of limitations period does not apply if the taxpayer has not filed a return, if the commissioner has information that the taxpayer has collected taxes but failed to remit to the state, or the taxpayer and commissioner have waived the limitations period in writing.	Ohio Rev. Code Ann. § 5739.16(A), Ohio Rev. Code Ann. § 5703.58
Oklahoma	3 years from later of return due date or return filing date.		Okla. Stat. tit. 68, § 223
Pennsylvania	3 years from later of return filing date or the end of the year in which the liability arose.		72 P.S. § 7258
Rhode Island	3 years from later of return filing date or the 15th day of the month following the month in which the return was due.		R.I. Gen. Laws § 44-19-13
South Carolina	3 years from later of date the return was filed or due to be filed.	3 year statute of limitations period does not apply (i) if there is a fraudulent intent to evade taxes; (ii) a taxpayer has failed to file a return, (iii) there has been an understatement of tax by 20% or more; (iv) taxpayer has given consent in writing to waive limitation; and (v) tax imposed is a use tax and assessment is based on information obtained from state, local, regional or national tax administration organization.	S.C. Code Ann. § 12-54-85

State	Assessments	Comments	Citation
South Dakota	3 years from return filing date.		S.D. Codified Laws § 10-59-16
Tennessee	3 years from the end of the calendar year in which the return was filed.		Tenn. Code. Ann. § 67-1-1501(b)
Texas	4 years from tax due date.	No limitation period if tax understated by 25% or more.	34 Tex. Admin. Code § 3.339(a)
Utah	3 years from return filing date.		Utah Code Ann. § 59-12-110(6)
Vermont	3 years from later of return due date or return filing date.	If tax understated by 20% or more, 6 years from return filing date.	Vt. Stat. Ann. tit. 32, § 9815(b)
Virginia	3 years from tax due date.	6 years from tax due date if no return was filed or fraudulent return was filed.	Va. Code Ann. § 58.1-634
Washington	4 years from the close of the tax year in which the liability arose.	Statute of limitations period does not apply to a taxpayer that has not registered, that has committed fraud or misrepresentation, or has executed a written waiver of the limitation.	Wash. Rev. Code § 82.32.050(4)
West Virginia	3 years from later of return due date or return filing date.		W. Va. Code § 11-10-15
Wisconsin	Generally 4 years from return filing date.	Period may be extended if taxpayer consents in writing.	Wis. Stat. § 77.59(3), Wis. Stat. § 77.59(3m)
Wyoming	3 years from the date of delinquency.		Wyo. Stat. Ann. § 39-15-110(b)

¶ 167   **Statutes of Limitations—Refunds**

This chart states the sales and use tax refund claim period.

State	Refunds	Comments	Citation
Alabama	Later of 3 years from return filing date or 2 years from payment date.		Ala. Code § 40-2A-7
Arizona	Later of 4 years from return due date, 4 years from return filing date, or 6 months from payment date for payments due to deficiency assessments.		Ariz. Rev. Stat. § 42-1104, Ariz. Rev. Stat. § 42-1106
Arkansas	Later of 3 years from return filing date or 2 years from payment date.		Ark. Code Ann. § 26-18-306, Ark. Reg. GR-81.1
California	Later of 3 years from the end of the calendar month following the quarterly period for which the overpayment was made. For taxes collected through enforcement procedures, 3 years from overpayment date. For refunds relating to determinations, later of 6 months from date determination becomes final or six overpayment date.		Cal. Rev. & Tax. Code § 6902, Cal. Rev. & Tax. Code § 6902.3
Colorado	Later of 3 years from return due date or 1 year from overpayment date.		Colo. Rev. Stat. § 39-26-703
Connecticut	3 years from the end of the calendar month following the period in which the overpayment was made, or for deficiency assessments 6 months after an assessment becomes final.		Conn. Gen. Stat. § 12-425
District of Columbia	3 years from payment date.		D.C. Code Ann. § 47-2020
Florida	3 years from payment date.		Fla. Stat. § 215.26(2)
Georgia	3 years from payment date.		Ga. Code Ann. § 48-2-35(c)
Hawaii	3 years from the later of the date the annual return was filed or was due. 3 years from later of the payment date or the due date if an annual return is not filed or is filed more than 3 years after the due date.		Haw. Rev. Stat. § 237-40
Idaho	3 years from the later of the payment date, or for payments resulting from deficiency assessments the date the deficiency is resolved.		Idaho Code § 63-3636
Illinois	A refund claim filed on or after January 1 and July 1 is not valid unless the erroneous payment was made within three years prior to January 1 and July 1 of the year of the claim.		35 ILCS 120/6, Ill. Admin. Code tit. 86, § 130.1501

State	Refunds	Comments	Citation
Indiana	3 years from the later of the payment date or the end of the calendar year containing the period for which the return was filed.		Ind. Code § 6-8.1-9-1
Iowa	Later of 3 years from payment due date or 1 year from payment date.		Iowa Code § 423.37
Kansas	3 years from return due date.		Kan. Stat. Ann. § 79-3609(b)
Kentucky	4 years from later of return due date or payment date.		Ky. Rev. Stat. Ann. § 139.580
Louisiana	Later of 3 years from the end of the calendar year in which tax was due or 1 year from payment date.		La. Rev. Stat. Ann. § 47:1623
Maine	3 years from overpayment date.		Me. Rev. Stat. Ann. tit. 36, § 2011
Maryland	4 years from payment date.		Md. Code Ann. § 13-1104
Massachusetts	Later of 3 years from return filing date, 2 years from assessment date, or 1 year from payment date.	If a return has not been timely filed, refund is requested by filing the overdue return by the later of 3 years from return due date including extensions or 2 years from payment date.	Mass. Gen. Laws ch. 62C, § 36, Mass. Gen. Laws ch. 62C, § 37
Michigan	4 years from return due date.	90 days from return due date for claims based on the validity of a tax law under federal law or the U.S. or Michigan constitution.	Mich. Comp. Laws § 205.27a(2), (7)
Minnesota	Later of 3.5 years from return due date (including extensions if return is filed during extended period), or 1 year from the date of an assessment order, order determining an appeal, or return made by the Commissioner, upon payment in full of the tax, penalties, and interest shown on the order or return made by the commissioner.		Minn. Stat. § 289A.40
Mississippi	36 months from the later of filing date or assessment date.		Miss. Code. Ann. § 27-65-42
Missouri	3 years from overpayment date.		Mo. Rev. Stat. § 144.190
Nebraska	Later of 3 years from required filing date following the period in which overpayment was made, 6 months after determination becomes final, or 6 months after overpayment with respect to a determination.		Neb. Rev. Stat. § 77-2708
Nevada	3 years from the end of the month following the close of the period for which overpayment was made.		Nev. Rev. Stat. § 372.365

State	Refunds	Comments	Citation
New Jersey	4 years from payment date.		N.J. Stat. Ann. § 54:32B-20
New Mexico	3 years from the later of the end of the calendar year in which the payment was due or the overpayment resulted from an assessment.	1 year from payment date if tax was not paid within general refund period. 1 year from assessment date if assessment applies to a period ending at least 3 years prior to the beginning of the year in which the assessment was made.	N.M. Stat. Ann. § 7-1-26
New York	Later of 3 years from filing date or 2 years from payment date.		N.Y. Tax Law, § 1139(c)
North Carolina	Later of 3 years from return due date or 2 years from payment date.		N.C. Gen. Stat. § 105-241.6
North Dakota	Effective July 1, 2017, the later of three years after the due date of the return or the date the return was filed.	Through June 30, 2017, the later of three years from return due date or one year from payment date.	Uncodified Sec. 5, S.B. 2129, Laws 2017, N.D. Cent. Code § 57-39.2-24 (repealed effective 7/1/17)
Ohio	4 years from payment date.		Ohio Rev. Code Ann. § 5739.07(D)
Oklahoma	2 years from payment date.		Okla. Stat. tit. 68, § 227
Pennsylvania	Later of 3 years from payment date or 6 months from mailing date of notice for payments resulting from assessments, determinations, settlements, or appraisements.		72 P.S. § 10003.1
Rhode Island	Later of 3 years from 15th of month after the close of the month for which overpayment was made, or 6 months from overpayment date for payments resulting from determinations.		R.I. Gen. Laws § 44-19-26
South Carolina	Later of 3 years from return filing date or 2 years from payment date.		S.C. Code Ann. § 12-54-85
South Dakota	3 years from earlier of payment date or return due date.		S.D. Codified Laws § 10-59-19
Tennessee	3 years from the end of the calendar year in which tax was paid.		Tenn. Code. Ann. § 67-1-1802(a)
Texas	Later of 4 years from tax due date, or 6 months after deficiency determination becomes final.		34 Tex. Admin. Code § 3.325(b)
Utah	Later of 3 years from return due date or 2 years from payment date.		Utah Code Ann. § 59-1-1410
Vermont	3 years from return due date.		Vt. Stat. Ann. tit. 32, § 9781
Virginia	3 years from the tax due date.		23 Va. Admin. Code § 10-210-3040

State	Refunds	Comments	Citation
Washington	No refund is allowed for tax, interest, or penalties paid more than 4 years before the beginning of the calendar year in which a refund application is made or examination of records by the Department is completed.		Wash. Rev. Code § 82.32.060, Wash. Admin. Code § 458-20-229
West Virginia	Later of 3 years from return due date or 2 years from payment date.		W. Va. Code § 11-10-14
Wisconsin	4 years from the due date of taxpayer's state income or franchise tax return that corresponds to the date the sale or purchase was completed, or for taxpayers not subject to income or franchise tax, 4 years from the 15th day of the 4th month following the end of the year fthat corresponds to the date the sale or purchase was completed.	2 years from determination date for tax resulting from determination if taxpayer does not protest by filing petition for redetermination and refund will not be not passed along to customers.	Wis. Stat. § 77.59(4)
Wyoming	3 years from overpayment date.		Wyo. Stat. Ann. § 39-15-109(c)

¶ 168 **Streamlined Sales Tax Membership**

The following chart indicates whether a state is a member of the Streamlined Sales and Use Tax Agreement.

State	Streamlined Sales Tax Membership	Comments	Citation
Alabama	Advisor State		Act 418 (S.B. 185), Laws 2002
Arizona	Advisor State		Ch. 289 (H.B. 2178), Laws 2002
Arkansas	Member State		Ark. Code Ann. § 26-20-103
California	Advisor State		Cal. Rev. & Tax. Code § 6025
Colorado	Not currently participating.		
Connecticut	Not currently participating.		
District of Columbia	Advisor State		D.C. Law 14-156, Laws 2002
Florida	Advisor State		Fla. Stat. § 213.256
Georgia	Full Member effective July 1, 2011	Associate Member January 1, 2011 - June 30, 2011; Advisor State prior to January 1, 2011.	Ga. Code Ann. § 48-8-162
Hawaii	Advisor State		Haw. Rev. Stat. § 255D-1
Idaho	Not currently participating.		
Illinois	Advisor State		35 ILCS 171/5
Indiana	Member State		Ind. Code § 6-2.5-11-5
Iowa	Member State		Iowa Code § 423.9
Kansas	Member State		Kan. Stat. Ann. § 79-3665
Kentucky	Member State		Ky. Rev. Stat. Ann. § 139.783
Louisiana	Advisor State		La. Rev. Stat. Ann. § 47:335.2
Maine	Advisor State		Sec. 7124, Ch. 496 (H.B. 668), Laws 2002
Maryland	Advisor State		Md. Code Ann. § 11-106
Massachusetts	Advisor State		Sec. 82, Ch. 4 (S.B. 1949), Laws 2003
Michigan	Member State		Mich. Comp. Laws § 205.809
Minnesota	Member State		Minn. Stat. § 297A.995
Mississippi	Advisor State		Sec. 4, Ch. 338 (S.B. 2089), Laws 2003
Missouri	Advisor State		Mo. Rev. Stat. § 144.1006
Nebraska	Member State		Neb. Rev. Stat. § 77-2712.03
Nevada	Member State		Nev. Rev. Stat. § 360B.010
New Jersey	Member State		N.J. Stat. Ann. § 54:32B-46

State	Streamlined Sales Tax Membership	Comments	Citation
New Mexico	Advisor State		Ch. 225 (H.B. 575), Laws 2005
New York	Advisor State		N.Y. Tax Law, § 1173
North Carolina	Member State		N.C. Gen. Stat. § 105-164.42C
North Dakota	Member State		N.D. Cent. Code § 57-39.4-01
Ohio	Member State		Ohio Rev. Code Ann. § 5740.02
Oklahoma	Member State		Okla. Stat. tit. 68, § 1354.18
Pennsylvania	Represented on State and Local Advisory Council.		
Rhode Island	Member State		R.I. Gen. Laws § 44-18.1-1
South Carolina	Advisor State		S.C. Code Ann. § 12-35-50
South Dakota	Member State		S.D. Codified Laws § 10-45C-3
Tennessee	Associate Member State	Tennessee will become a full member when remaining conforming provisions become effective. These change are currently scheduled to take effect on July 1, 2015.	Tenn. Code Ann. § 67-6-803
Texas	Advisor State		Tex. Tax Code Ann. § 142.005
Utah	Associate Member State		Utah Code Ann. § 59-12-102.2
Vermont	Member State		Ch. 144 (H.B. 771), Laws 2002
Virginia	Advisor State		Ch. 476 (S.B. 688), Laws 2002
Washington	Member State		Wash. Rev. Code § 82.02.210
West Virginia	Member State		W. Va. Code § 11-15B-3
Wisconsin	Member State		Wis. Stat. § 77.65
Wyoming	Member State		Wyo. Stat. Ann. § 39-15-403

¶ 169   **Trade-Ins**

The following chart indicates whether or not the value of a trade-in is included in the sales price for sales tax purposes.

State	Trade-Ins	Comments	Citation
Alabama	Included	Certain exclusions.	Ala. Code § 40-23-103, Ala. Admin. Code r. 810-6-1-.22
Arizona	Excluded		Ariz. Rev. Stat. § 42-5001(6)
Arkansas	Included	Exclusion allowed for certain items, e.g. vehicles, trailers, and aircraft.	Ark. Code Ann. § 26-52-505, Ark. Code Ann. § 26-52-510(b)
California	Included		Cal. Rev. & Tax. Code § 6012(b)(3)
Colorado	Excluded		Colo. Rev. Stat. § 39-26-104(1)(b)
Connecticut	Excluded		Conn. Gen. Stat. § 12-407(a)(8)(B)(v)
District of Columbia	Included		D.C. Mun. Regs. t. 9, § 466.2
Florida	Excluded		Fla. Stat. § 212.09
Georgia	Excluded		Ga. Code Ann. § 48-8-2(34)(B), Ga. Code Ann. § 48-8-44
Hawaii	Excluded		Haw. Rev. Stat. § 237-3(b)
Idaho	Excluded	Exclusion not allowed on sale of a new manufactured home or a modular building.	Idaho Code § 63-3613(b)(2)
Illinois	Excluded		Ill. Admin. Code tit. 86, § 130.425
Indiana	Excluded		Ind. Code § 6-2.5-1-5
Iowa	Excluded		Iowa Code § 423.3(59)
Kansas	Excluded		Kan. Stat. Ann. § 79-3602(o)
Kentucky	Excluded		Ky. Rev. Stat. Ann. § 139.010(10)
Louisiana	Excluded		La. Rev. Stat. Ann. § 47:301(13)
Maine	Included	Exclusion allowed for certain items, e.g. vehicles, boats, aircraft, chain saws, and trailers. Separately stated charges are excluded.	Me. Rev. Stat. Ann. tit. 36, § 1765
Maryland	Included		Md. Code Regs. 03.06.01.08(B)(2)(a)
Massachusetts	Included	Exclusion allowed for certain items, e.g. vehicles, boats, and aircraft.	Mass. Gen. Laws ch. 64H, § 26, Mass. Gen. Laws ch. 64H, § 27A

State	Trade-Ins	Comments	Citation
Michigan	Included	Credit for the agreed-upon value of a titled watercraft used as part payment of the purchase price of a new or used watercraft is excluded. The agreed-upon value of a motor vehicle or recreational vehicle (up to a specified maximum limit) used as part payment of the purchase price of a new or used motor vehicle or a new or used recreational vehicle, is excluded. Beginning March 29, 2017, credit for the core charge attributed to a recycling fee, deposit, or disposal fee for a motor vehicle or recreational vehicle part or battery is excluded.	Mich. Admin. Code r. 205.15, Mich. Comp. Laws § 205.51
Minnesota	Excluded		Minn. Stat. § 297A.67(26)
Mississippi	Excluded		Miss. Code. Ann. § 27-65-3(h)
Missouri	Excluded	Exclusion not applicable to certain manufactured home sales.	Mo. Rev. Stat. § 144.025
Nebraska	Excluded		Neb. Rev. Stat. § 77-2701.35
Nevada	Excluded		Nev. Rev. Stat. § 372.025(2), Nev. Rev. Stat. § 374.030(3)
New Jersey	Excluded	Credit for trade-in on property of the same kind accepted in part payment and intended for resale if the amount is separately stated on the invoice, bill of sale, or similar document given to the purchaser is specifically excluded from the sales price. Exclusion not allowed on certain sales of manufactured or mobile homes.	N.J. Stat. Ann. § 54:32B-2, N.J. Admin. Code § 18:24-7.19(a)(1)(iii)
New Mexico	Excluded	Exclusion not allowed on trade-in of manufactured home.	N.M. Stat. Ann. § 7-9-71
New York	Excluded		N.Y. Comp. Code R. & Regs. tit. 20, § 526.5(f)
North Carolina	Included		N.C. Admin. Code tit. 17, § 17:07B.3001
North Dakota	Excluded	Exclusion not allowed on trade-in of used mobile home.	N.D. Cent. Code § 57-39.2-01, N.D. Admin. Code § 81-04.1-01-19

State	Trade-Ins	Comments	Citation
Ohio	Included	Exclusion allowed on sales of certain items, e.g. watercraft and new vehicles.	Ohio Rev. Code Ann. § 5739.01 (H)
Oklahoma	Included		Okla. Stat. tit. 68, § 1352(12), Okla. Admin. Code § 710:65-19-72
Pennsylvania	Excluded		72 P.S. § 7201 (g) (2)
Rhode Island	Included	Certain exclusions apply.	R.I. Gen. Laws § 44-18-30, R.I. Code R. SU 11-109
South Carolina	Excluded		S.C. Code Ann. § 12-36-90(2)
South Dakota	Excluded		S.D. Codified Laws § 10-45-1(4), (6), S.D. Tax Facts #177
Tennessee	Excluded		Tenn. Code. Ann. § 67-6-510
Texas	Excluded		Tex. Tax Code Ann. § 151.007 (c) (5)
Utah	Excluded		Utah Code Ann. § 59-12-104
Vermont	Excluded		Vt. Stat. Ann. tit. 32, § 9701 (4)
Virginia	Excluded		Va. Code Ann. § 58.1-602, 23 Va. Admin. Code § 10-210-5070
Washington	Excluded		Wash. Rev. Code § 82.08.010(1)
West Virginia	Excluded		W. Va. Code R. § 110-15-2.35
Wisconsin	Excluded	Exclusion not allowed on sale of certain manufactured or modular homes.	Wis. Stat. § 77.51 (15b) (b) 5., 7., and 8.
Wyoming	Excluded		Wyo. Stat. Ann. § 39-15-101 (a) (ix) (A)

¶ 170   **Transportation**

The following chart indicates the taxability of services related to intrastate transportation of persons or property. The chart does not include transportation/delivery services in connection with the sale of tangible personal property.

State	Transportation	Comments	Citation
Alabama	Exempt	Exemption limited to transportation services of the kind and nature that would be regulated by the state Public Service Commission or similar regulatory body if sold by a public utility.	Ala. Code § 40-23-4 (a) (8)
Arizona	Taxable	Taxpayers subject to motor carrier fee or light motor vehicle fee exempt. Certain transportation services provided by railroads, ambulances, dial-a-ride programs, or special needs programs exempt.	Ariz. Rev. Stat. § 42-5062
Arkansas	Exempt		Ark. Code Ann. § 26-52-301 (2)
California	Exempt		Cal. Rev. & Tax. Code § 6051
Colorado	Exempt		Colo. Rev. Stat. § 39-26-104
Connecticut	Exempt	Effective July 1, 2011, certain intrastate transportation services provided by livery services are taxable.	Conn. Gen. Stat. § 12-407
District of Columbia	Exempt		D.C. Code Ann. § 47-2001 (n) (2) (A)
Florida	Taxable	Certain intrastate transportation services provided by livery services are taxable. Certain exceptions apply.	Fla. Stat. § 212.04 (1) (d), Fla. Stat. § 212.05, Fla. Stat. § 212.08 (9) (b)
Georgia	Exempt	Charter and sightseeing services provided by urban transit systems taxable. Common carrier charges for the intrastate transport of persons taxable. Fares for taxicabs and cars for hire taxable.	Ga. Code Ann. § 48-8-3 (4)- (5), (18), Ga. Comp. R. & Regs. 560-12-2-.19 (9), Ga. Comp. R. & Regs. 560-12-2-.84
Hawaii	Taxable	Certain inter-island transport of agricultural commodities, stevedoring and towing services, county transportation system services, and helicopter rides not taxable.	Haw. Rev. Stat. § 237-7, Haw. Rev. Stat. § 237-18 (h), Haw. Rev. Stat. § 237-24.3 (1), Haw. Rev. Stat. § 237-24.3 (3), Tax Information Release No. 89-10
Idaho	Taxable	Intrastate unscheduled air transportation for hire of freight and passengers generally taxable. Interstate transportation services exempt.	Idaho Code § 63-3612 (2) (i)
Illinois	Exempt		35 ICLS 115/3

State	Transportation	Comments	Citation
Indiana	Exempt		Ind. Admin. Code tit. 45, r. 2.2-4-2
Iowa	Exempt	Limousine services taxable.	Iowa Code § 423.2(6)
Kansas	Exempt	Not expressly enumerated as taxable in the taxing statute.	Kan. Stat. Ann. § 79-3603
Kentucky	Exempt	Not expressly enumerated as taxable in the taxing statute.	Ky. Rev. Stat. Ann. § 139.200
Louisiana	Exempt	Caution: Numerous exemptions are suspended from April 1, 2016, to June 30, 2018. For chart of suspended exemptions and applicable tax rates, see Publication R-1002A.	La. Rev. Stat. Ann. § 47:301(14), LA DOR Publication R-1002A
Maine	Exempt		Me. Rev. Stat. Ann. tit. 36, § 1752(17-B)
Maryland	Exempt		Md. Code Ann. § 11-223
Massachusetts	Exempt		Mass. Gen. Laws ch. 64H, § 1
Michigan	Exempt		Mich. Comp. Laws § 205.51, Mich. Comp. Laws § 205.93a
Minnesota	Exempt		Minn. Stat. § 297A.61(3)(g), Minn. R. 8130.0900(6)
Mississippi	Exempt		Miss. Code Ann. § 27-65-23
Missouri	Taxable	Exempt if provided on contract basis, when no ticket is issued. Transportation by limousines, taxis, and buses that are not required to be licensed by the Division of Motor Carrier and Railroad Safety are exempt. Federal law prohibits taxation of receipts from the intrastate transportation of persons for hire in air commerce.	Mo. Rev. Stat. § 144.020, Mo. Code Regs. Ann. tit. 12, § 10-108.600
Nebraska	Exempt		Neb. Rev. Stat. § 77-2701.16
Nevada	Exempt		Nev. Rev. Stat. § 372.105
New Jersey	Exempt	However, the following transportation charges are taxable: transportation services originating in New Jersey and provided by a limousine operator, except such services provided in connection with funeral services; transportation or transmission of natural gas and electricity (utility service); and delivery charges. Effective May 1, 2017, transportation services originating in New Jersey and provided by a limousine operator will no longer be subject to tax.	N.J. Stat. Ann. § 54:32B-8.11, N.J. Stat. Ann. § 54:32B-3(13), N.J. Admin. Code § 18:24-27.1

State	Transportation	Comments	Citation
New Mexico	Taxable		N.M. Admin. Code tit. 3, § 3.2.1.18, N.M. Admin. Code tit. 3, § 3.2.206.14
New York	Taxable	Sales tax is imposed on specified transportation services, whether or not any tangible personal property is transferred in conjunction therewith, and regardless of whether the charge is paid in New York or out-of-state, as long as the service is provided in New York. Certain exceptions apply.	N.Y. Tax Law, § 1105(c)(10), N.Y. Tax Law, § 1101(b)(34), TSB-M-09(7)S
North Carolina	Exempt		N.C. Gen. Stat. § 105-164.4
North Dakota	Exempt	Passenger transportation and freight transportation by common carrier specifically exempt.	N.D. Cent. Code § 57-39.2-02.1, N.D. Cent. Code § 57-39.2-04(2)
Ohio	Taxable	Transportation of persons by aircraft or motor vehicle, except ambulance or transit bus, is taxable. Charges by delivery companies that are not making sales of tangible personal property generally exempt.	Ohio Rev. Code Ann. § 5739.01(B)(3)(s), Ohio Rev. Code Ann. § 5739.02(B)(11), Ohio Admin. Code § 5703-9-06
Oklahoma	Taxable	Exceptions apply.	Okla. Stat. tit. 68, § 1354(A)(3), Okla. Admin. Code § 710:65-19-328, Okla. Stat. tit. 68, § 1357(2), (36)
Pennsylvania	Exempt		61 Pa. Code § 31.6(a)(6)
Rhode Island	Taxable	Tax applies to taxicab services, limousine services, and other road transportation services, including charter bus service and all other transit and ground passenger transportation. Certain exceptions apply.	R.I. Gen. Laws § 44-18-7, R.I. Code R. SU 12-151
South Carolina	Exempt		S.C. Code Ann. § 12-36-910
South Dakota	Taxable	Certain railroad, river/canal, and air transportation; trucking and courier services; and local and suburban passenger transportation, except limousine service, exempt.	S.D. Codified Laws § 10-45-4.1, S.D. Codified Laws § 10-45-12.1
Tennessee	Exempt		Tenn. Code Ann. § 67-6-102
Texas	Exempt	Transportation services provided on a stand-alone basis exempt. Transportation services that are incident to the performance of a taxable service are taxable.	Tex. Tax Code Ann. § 151.0101(a), Tex. Tax Code Ann. § 151.007
Utah	Taxable		Utah Code Ann. § 59-12-103(1)

State	Transportation	Comments	Citation
Vermont	Exempt		Vt. Stat. Ann. tit. 32, § 9771(2)
Virginia	Exempt	Separately stated transportation charges are exempt.	Va. Code Ann. § 58.1-609.5(3), 23 Va. Admin. Code § 10-210-4040(C)(4)
Washington	Exempt	Towing services, and similar automotive transportation services, are taxable. Charges for moving existing structures/ buildings are taxable.	Wash. Rev. Code § 82.04.050, Wash. Admin. Code § 458-20-180
West Virginia	Taxable	Businesses regulated by the Public Service Commission exempt.	W. Va. Code § 11-15-8, W. Va. Code R. § 110-15-8
Wisconsin	Exempt		Wis. Stat. § 77.52(2)
Wyoming	Taxable	Transportation by ambulance or hearse and certain transportation of freight/property, raw farm products, and drilling rigs exempt. Transportation of employees to/from work exempt when paid or contracted for by employee or employer.	Wyo. Stat. Ann. § 39-15-103(a)(i)(D)

¶ 171   Vending Machine—Food

The following chart indicates the taxability of sales of food made through vending machines but does not specify upon whom the liability for the tax falls.

State	Food	Comments	Citation
Alabama	Taxable	Food, food products, coffee, milk, milk products, and substitutes for these products taxed at reduced rate.	Ala. Code § 40-23-2(5)
Arizona	Exempt	Food for consumption on premises is taxable.	Ariz. Rev. Stat. § 42-5102(A)(6)
Arkansas	Exempt	Registered vending device operators exempt from general gross receipts tax, but subject to either special vending device sales/use tax or vending device decal fee.	Ark. Code Ann. § 26-57-1002(d)
California	Taxable	33% of cold food receipts taxable.	Cal. Rev. & Tax. Code § 6359.2
Colorado	Exempt	Certain items are taxable including carbonated water, chewing gum, seeds and plants to grow food, prepared salads and salad bars, cold sandwiches, deli trays, candy, soft drinks and hot/cold beverages served in unsealed cups through a vending machine.	Colo. Rev. Stat. § 39-26-114(7.5), Colo. Rev. Stat. § 39-26-714
Connecticut	Exempt	Candy, carbonated and alcoholic beverages, cigarettes, tobacco products, and items not intended for human consumption are not considered food products and are taxable. All sales for 50 cents or less exempt.	Conn. Gen. Stat. § 12-412(27)
District of Columbia	Taxable		D.C. Code Ann. § 47-2001(n)(1)(A)(ii)
Florida	Taxable	Sales for less than 10 cents exempt. Food/drink sales in school cafeterias, food/drink sales for 25 cents or less through coin-operated machines sponsored by certain charitable organizations, and receipts from machines operated by churches exempt.	Fla. Stat. § 212.0515
Georgia	Taxable		Ga. Code Ann. § 48-8-3
Hawaii	Taxable		Haw. Rev. Stat. § 237-18(a)

State	Food	Comments	Citation
Idaho	Taxable	Sales for 11 cents or less exempt. Sales for 12 cents through $1 taxed at 117% of vendor's acquisition cost. Sales for more than $1 taxed on retail sales price.	IDAPA 35.01.02.058.01
Illinois	Taxable	Reduced tax rate of 1% applies to food sold through vending machines, except soft drinks, candy, and hot foods are subject to the full tax rate. Bulk vending machine sales of unsorted food items (e.g, nuts) are exempt.	35 ILCS 120/2-10, 35 ILCS 105/3-10
Indiana	Taxable	Sales for 8 cents or less exempt. Sales may be exempt because of tax-exempt status of person or organization that makes the sale.	Ind. Code § 6-2.5-5-20(c)
Iowa	Taxable	Applies to items sold for consumption on premises, items prepared for immediate consumption off premises, candy, candy-coated items, candy products, and certain beverages.	Iowa Code § 423.3(57), Iowa Admin. Code r. 701 231.3
Kansas	Taxable		Kan. Stat. Ann. § 79-3603(f)
Kentucky	Taxable	Sales of 50 cents or less through coin-operated bulk vending machines exempt.	Ky. Rev. Stat. Ann. § 139.485
Louisiana	Exempt	Sales to dealer for resale through coin-operated vending machines taxable; subsequent resale exempt. Food products sold through a distributor's own vending machines are subject to use tax on the distributor's cost of the items sold. Caution: Numerous exemptions are suspended from April 1, 2016, to June 30, 2018. For chart of suspended exemptions and applicable tax rates, see Publication R-1002A.	La. Rev. Stat. Ann. § 47:301(10)(b), Revenue Ruling 05-007, LA DOR Publication R-1002A
Maine	Taxable	Exemption for sales of products for internal human consumption when sold through vending machines operated by a person more than 50% of whose retail gross receipts are from sales through vending machines.	Me. Rev. Stat. Ann. tit. 36, § 1760(34)

¶171

State	Food	Comments	Citation
Maryland	Taxable	Taxed at special rate. Snack food, milk, fresh fruit/ vegetables, and yogurt are exempt.	Md. Code Ann. § 11-104(b), Md. Code Ann. § 11-206
Massachusetts	Taxable	Exempt if machine sells only snacks and/or candy with a sales price of less than $3.50.	Mass. Gen. Laws ch. 64H, § 6(h)
Michigan	Taxable	Food or drink heated or cooled to an average temperature above 75 degrees Fahrenheit or below 65 degrees Fahrenheit before sale is taxable. Milk, juices, fresh fruit, candy, nuts, chewing gum, cookies, crackers, chips, and nonalcoholic beverages in sealed container exempt.	Mich. Comp. Laws § 205.54g
Minnesota	Taxable		Minn. Stat. § 297A.61(3)(d)
Mississippi	Exempt	Food/drinks sold through vending machines serviced by full-line vendors exempt.	Miss. Code. Ann. § 27-65-111(m)
Missouri	Taxable	Sales made on religious, charitable, and public elementary or secondary school premises exempt.	Mo. Rev. Stat. § 144.012
Nebraska	Taxable		Neb. Rev. Stat. § 77-2704.24
Nevada	Taxable	Prepared food intended for immediate consumption taxable.	Nev. Rev. Stat. § 372.284
New Jersey	Taxable	Taxed at 70% of retail vending machine price. Sales for 25 cents or less by retailer primarily engaged in coin-operated machine sales exempt. Food/drink sold in school cafeterias and milk exempt.	N.J. Stat. Ann. § 54:32B-3(c)(4)
New Mexico	Taxable		N.M. Admin. Code tit. 3, § 3.2.1.14(K)
New York	Taxable	Sales for 10 cents or less by vendor primarily engaged in vending machine sales exempt. Candy and certain beverages sold for 75 cents or less (effective June 1, 2014, $1.50 or less) are exempt. Certain sales intended for off-premises consumption and certain bulk vending machine sales exempt.	N.Y. Comp. Code R. & Regs. tit. 20, § 527.8(g)
North Carolina	Taxable	Taxed at 50% of sales price. Sales for one cent exempt.	N.C. Gen. Stat. § 105-164.13B

State	Food	Comments	Citation
North Dakota	Taxable	Sales for 15 cents or less exempt.	N.D. Cent. Code § 57-39.2-03.3
Ohio	Taxable	Sales of food for off-premises consumption exempt. Sales of automatic food vending machines that preserve food with a shelf life of forty-five days or less by refrigeration and dispense it to the consumer, are exempt.	Ohio Rev. Code Ann. § 5739.02(B)(2),(35)
Oklahoma	Taxable	Sales from coin-operated devices for which certain license fees have been paid are exempt.	Okla. Stat. tit. 68, § 1354(A)(16)
Pennsylvania	Exempt	Specific items taxable, including soft drinks, meals, sandwiches, hot beverages, and items dispensed in heated form or served cold but normally heated in operator-provided oven/microwave. Sales on school or church premises exempt.	61 Pa. Code § 31.28
Rhode Island	Taxable	Sales in school areas designated primarily for students/teachers exempt.	R.I. Code R. SU 04-59
South Carolina	Taxable	Vendors making sales solely through vending machines are deemed to be users or consumers of certain property they purchase for sale through vending machines (not cigarettes or soft drinks in closed containers, which are subject to business license tax at wholesale level).	S.C. Code Ann. § 12-36-110(1)(g)
South Dakota	Taxable		S.D. Admin. R. 64:06:03:41
Tennessee	Taxable	Certain nonprofit entities may pay gross receipts tax in lieu of sales tax.	Tenn. Code. Ann. § 67-6-202
Texas	Taxable	Taxed on 50% of receipts. Candy and soft drinks fully taxable. Sales of food, candy, gum, or items designed for a child's use/play for 50 cents or less through coin-operated bulk vending machines exempt.	Tex. Tax Code Ann. § 151.007(d)
Utah	Taxable	For food, beverages, and dairy products sold for $1 or less, operators may pay tax on total sales or 150% of cost of goods sold.	Utah Code Ann. § 59-12-104(3)

State	Food	Comments	Citation
Vermont	Exempt	Food sold through vending machines is exempt from sales and use tax but subject to meals and rooms tax.	Vt. Stat. Ann. tit. 32, § 9202(10), Vt. Stat. Ann. tit. 32, § 9741(10)
Virginia	Taxable	Rate and base vary depending on placement/ use of machine.	Va. Code Ann. § 58.1-614
Washington	Taxable	Taxed on 57% of receipts. Hot prepared foods and soft drinks are fully taxable.	Wash. Rev. Code § 82.08.0293(4)
West Virginia	Taxable		W. Va. Code R. § 110-15-126.1.3
Wisconsin	Exempt	Candy, soft drinks, dietary supplements, and prepared food are taxable.	Wis. Stat. § 77.54(20n)(a)
Wyoming	Taxable, except food that qualifies as food for domestic home consumption is exempt beginning July 1, 2011		Wyo. BOE Rule Ch. 2, § 15(kk), Wyo. Stat. Ann. § 39-15-101(a)(xli)

¶ 172   Vending Machine—Merchandise

The following chart indicates the taxability of sales made through vending machines but does not specify upon whom the liability for the tax falls.

State	Merchandise	Comments	Citation
Alabama	Taxable		Ala. Admin. Code r. 810-6-1-.183.02
Arizona	Taxable		Ariz. Rev. Stat. § 42-5071
Arkansas	Exempt	Registered vending device operators exempt from general gross receipts tax, but subject to either special vending device sales/use tax or vending device decal fee. Devices that sell only cigarettes, newspapers, magazines, or postage stamps not taxable as vending devices.	Ark. Code Ann. § 26-57-1002(d)
California	Taxable		Reg. 1574, 18 CCR
Colorado	Taxable	Sales for 15 cents or less exempt.	Colo. Rev. Stat. § 39-26-114(7)
Connecticut	Taxable	Sales for 50 cents or less exempt.	Conn. Gen. Stat. § 12-407(a)(2)(A)
District of Columbia	Taxable		D.C. Mun. Regs. t. 9, § 437.1
Florida	Taxable	Sales for less than 10 cents exempt. Receipts from machines operated by churches exempt.	Fla. Stat. § 212.0515
Georgia	Taxable		Ga. Comp. R. & Regs. 560-12-1-.06
Hawaii	Taxable		Haw. Rev. Stat. § 237-18(a)
Idaho	Taxable	Sales for 11 cents or less exempt. Sales for 12 cents through $1 taxed at 117% of vendor's acquisition cost. Sales for more than $1 taxed on retail sales price.	IDAPA 35.01.02.058.01
Illinois	Taxable	Bulk vending machine sales exempt.	35 ILCS 120/2-10, 35 ILCS 105/3-10
Indiana	Taxable	Sales for 8 cents or less exempt. Sales may be exempt because of tax-exempt status of person or organization that makes the sale.	Ind. Code § 6-2.5-5-20(c)
Iowa	Taxable		Iowa Code § 423.1(33), Iowa Code § 423.3(57)
Kansas	Taxable		Kan. Stat. Ann. § 79-3603(f)
Kentucky	Taxable	Sales of 50¢ or less through coin-operated bulk vending machines are exempt.	Ky. Rev. Stat. Ann. § 139.485(4), Ky. Rev. Stat. Ann. § 139.470(6), 103 Ky. Admin. Regs. 27:180

State	Merchandise	Comments	Citation
Louisiana	Exempt	Sales of tangible personal property to dealer for resale through coin-operated vending machines taxable. Subsequent resale exempt. Caution: Numerous exemptions are suspended from April 1, 2016, to June 30, 2018. For chart of suspended exemptions and applicable tax rates, see Publication R-1002A.	La. Rev. Stat. Ann. § 47:301(10)(b), LA DOR Publication R-1002A
Maine	Taxable	Items sold through vending machines (other than items for internal human consumption) are taxable retail sales. Chewing gum is not considered an item for internal human consumption.	Instruction Bulletin No. 8
Maryland	Taxable	Taxed at special rate. Sales for 75 cents or less through bulk vending machines exempt.	Md. Code Ann. § 11-104(b), Md. Code Ann. § 11-201.1
Massachusetts	Taxable	Sales for 10 cents or less exempt.	Mass. Gen. Laws ch. 64H, § 6(t)
Michigan	Taxable		Mich. Admin. Code r. 205.126
Minnesota	Taxable		Minn. Stat. § 297A.61(4), Minn. Stat. § 297A.62
Mississippi	Taxable		Miss. Rule 35.IV.4.03
Missouri	Taxable	Photocopies, tobacco products, and sales made on religious, charitable, and public elementary or secondary school premises exempt.	Mo. Rev. Stat. § 144.012
Nebraska	Taxable		Neb. Admin. Code § 1-007.01
Nevada	Taxable		Nev. Admin. Code § 372.500
New Jersey	Taxable	Sales for 25 cents or less by retailer primarily engaged in coin-operated machine sales exempt.	N.J. Admin. Code § 18:24-16.1
New Mexico	Taxable		N.M. Admin. Code tit. 3, § 3.2.1.14(K)
New York	Taxable	Sales for 10 cents or less and bulk vending machine sales for 50 cents or less exempt if vendor primarily engaged in vending machine sales.	N.Y. Comp. Code R. & Regs. tit. 20, § 528.14
North Carolina	Taxable	Taxed at 50% of sales price. Tobacco products fully taxable. Newspapers and sales for one cent exempt.	N.C. Gen. Stat. § 105-164.13(50)
North Dakota	Taxable	Sales for 15 cents or less exempt.	N.D. Cent. Code § 57-39.2-03.3
Ohio	Taxable		Ohio Rev. Code Ann. § 5739.02

State	Merchandise	Comments	Citation
Oklahoma	Taxable	Sales from coin-operated devices for which certain license fees have been paid are exempt.	Okla. Stat. tit. 68, § 1354(A)(16)
Pennsylvania	Taxable		61 Pa. Code § 31.28
Rhode Island	Taxable	Sales made from machines located in certain facilities by licensed operators who are blind are exempt.	R.I. Code R. SU 87-116
South Carolina	Taxable	Vendors making sales solely through vending machines are deemed to be users or consumers of certain property they purchase for sale through vending machines (not cigarettes or soft drinks in closed containers, which are subject to business license tax at wholesale level).	S.C. Code Ann. § 12-36-110(1)(g)
South Dakota	Taxable		S.D. Admin. R. 64:06:03:41
Tennessee	Taxable	Certain nonprofit entities may pay gross receipts tax in lieu of sales tax.	Tenn. Code. Ann. § 67-6-202
Texas	Taxable	Candy and soft drinks fully taxable. Sales of food, candy, gum, or items designed for a child's use/play for 50 cents or less through coin-operated bulk vending machines exempt.	Tex. Tax Code Ann. § 151.305
Utah	Taxable		Utah Admin. Code r. 865-19S-74
Vermont	Taxable		Vt. Stat. Ann. tit. 32, § 9771
Virginia	Taxable	Rate and base vary depending on placement/use of machine.	Va. Code Ann. § 58.1-614
Washington	Taxable		Wash. Admin. Code § 458-20-187(4)
West Virginia	Taxable		W. Va. Code R. § 110-15-46
Wisconsin	Taxable		Wis. Admin. Code § 11.52
Wyoming	Taxable	Postage stamps exempt.	Wyo. BOE Rule Ch. 2, § 15(kk)

¶ 173 **Web Hosting Services**

This chart indicates whether web hosting fees are subject to sales and use tax.

State	Web Hosting	Comments	Citation
Alabama	Exempt		Ala. Code § 40-23-2
Arizona	Exempt	Extranet hosting service directly related to software lease/rental may be taxable.	Ariz. Rev. Stat. § 42-5061, Private Taxpayer Ruling LR 04-010
Arkansas	Exempt		Ark. Code Ann. § 26-52-301(3)
California	Exempt	Exempt if no tangible personal property is transferred to the customer.	Reg. 1540(b)(1)(E), 18 CCR
Colorado	Exempt		FYI Sales 80
Connecticut	Taxable	Effective October 1, 2015, services in connection with the creation, development, hosting, or maintenance of a website are taxable.	Conn. Gen. Stat. § 12-407(a)(37)(A), Special Notice 2015(5)
District of Columbia	Taxable		D.C. Mun. Regs. t. 9, § 474.1
Florida	Exempt		TAA No. 98A-076, TAA No. 01A-019
Georgia	Exempt	Charges must be separately stated from any charges for taxable software sales.	Ga. Comp. R. & Regs. 560-12-2-.111
Hawaii	Taxable		Haw. Rev. Stat. § 237-13
Idaho	Exempt		IDAPA 35.01.02.011
Illinois	Exempt		General Info Letters ST 98-0072
Indiana	Exempt		Ind. Admin. Code tit. 45, r. 2.2-4-2, Information Bulletin #8
Iowa	Exempt		Iowa Code § 423.2(6), Policy Letter 01300016
Kansas	Exempt	Charges by a web page provider for remote administrative and monitoring services are exempt if the customer is not contractually required to purchase or lease computer hardware or software. A web page host must pay sales tax on charges for use of a server located in Kansas.	Information Guide No. EDU-71R
Kentucky	Exempt		Ky. Rev. Stat. Ann. § 139.200

¶173

State	Web Hosting	Comments	Citation
Louisiana	Exempt	Caution: Numerous exemptions are suspended from April 1, 2016, to June 30, 2018. For chart of suspended exemptions and applicable tax rates, see Publication R-1002A.	La. Rev. Stat. Ann. § 47:301(14), La. Admin. Code tit. 61, § 4301, LA DOR Publication R-1002A
Maine	Exempt		Me. Rev. Stat. Ann. tit. 36, § 1752(17-B)
Maryland	Exempt		Md. Code Ann. § 11-101
Massachusetts	Exempt	Taxable if the service is a mandatory part of a taxable sale of computer hardware or prewritten software.	Mass. Regs. Code tit. 830, § 64H.1.3(14)(b)
Michigan	Exempt		Mich. Comp. Laws § 205.52
Minnesota	Exempt		Minn. Stat. § 297A.61(3), Minn. R. 8130.0500(2)
Mississippi	Exempt		Miss. Code Ann. § 27-65-23
Missouri	Exempt		Letter Ruling LR 5416
Nebraska	Exempt		Rev. Ruling 1-10-2, Information Guide 6-511-2011
Nevada	Exempt		Nev. Rev. Stat. § 372.025
New Jersey	Exempt		N.J. Bulletin S&U-9, TB-72
New Mexico	Exempt		N.M. Stat. Ann. § 7-9-56.2
New York	Exempt		N.Y. Tax Law, § 1105, TSB-A-01(21)S, TB-ST-405
North Carolina	Exempt		N.C. Gen. Stat. § 105-164.4C(c)(12), Sales and Use Tax Technical Bulletin, Sec. 28-3(B)
North Dakota	Exempt		N.D. Admin. Code § 81-04.1-01-22
Ohio	Taxable	Taxable only if the service is sold for use in a business.	Ohio Rev. Code Ann. § 5739.01, Ohio Admin. Code § 5703-9-46
Oklahoma	Exempt		Okla. Admin. Code § 710:65-19-156
Pennsylvania	Exempt		72 P.S. § 7201(k)
Rhode Island	Exempt		R.I. Gen. Laws § 44-18-7
South Carolina	Exempt		S.C. Code Ann. § 12-36-910
South Dakota	Taxable		S.D. Admin. R. 64:06:02:78
Tennessee	Exempt		Tenn. Code Ann. § 67-6-205, Tenn. Code Ann. § 67-6-102

State	Web Hosting	Comments	Citation
Texas	Taxable	Web host provider is taxed on 80% of the charge as a data processing service. A person whose only activity in Texas is conducted as a user of Internet hosting is not engaged in business in the state for tax nexus purposes.	Tex. Tax Code Ann. § 151.0035, Tex. Tax Code Ann. § 151.108, Tex. Tax Code Ann. § 151.351, 34 Tex. Admin. Code § 3.330, Letter No. 200009685L
Utah	Exempt		Private Letter Ruling, Opinion No. 01-030
Vermont	Exempt		Vt. Stat. Ann. tit. 32, § 9701 (9) (H)
Virginia	Exempt		Va. Code Ann. § 58.1-609.5(1), Ruling of Commissioner, P.D. 06-138
Washington	Exempt	The provision of space on a server for web hosting is not considered a digital automated service. Services beyond mere storage are taxable.	Wash. Rev. Code § 82.04.050, Wash. Admin. Code § 458-20-15503
West Virginia	Taxable	Taxable as a data generation service.	Decision No. 02-308C, West Virginia Office of Tax Appeals
Wisconsin	Exempt		Wis. Stat. § 77.52(2) (a), Wisconsin Tax Bulletin 148
Wyoming	Exempt		Wyo. Stat. Ann. § 39-15-103

¶ 174   **Web Page Design**

This chart indicates whether charges for designing a website are subject to sales and use tax.

State	Web Page Design	Comments	Citation
Alabama	Exempt		Ala. Code § 40-23-1, Ala. Code § 40-23-2
Arizona	Exempt		Ariz. Admin. Code § 15-5-154
Arkansas	Exempt		Ark. Code Ann. § 26-52-301, Ark. Code Ann. § 26-52-103 (a) (3) (E)
California	Exempt	Exempt provided no tangible personal property is transferred to the client.	Reg. 1540 (b) (1) (E), 18 CCR
Colorado	Exempt		Colo. Rev. Stat. § 39-26-104, Colo. Rev. Stat. § 39-26-102 (10), (11), (12)
Connecticut	Taxable	Effective October 1, 2015, services in connection with the creation, development, hosting, or maintenance of a website are taxable.	Conn. Gen. Stat. § 12-407 (a) (37) (A), Special Notice 2015 (5)
District of Columbia	Taxable		D.C. Code Ann. § 47-2001 (n) (1) (N), Unofficial department guidance
Florida	Exempt		Fla. Stat. § 212.08 (7) (v), TAA No. 98A-076, Unofficial department guidance
Georgia	Exempt	Must be separately stated.	Ga. Comp. R. & Regs. 560-12-2-.111
Hawaii	Taxable		Haw. Rev. Stat. § 237-13 (6), Unofficial department guidance
Idaho	Exempt		IDAPA 35.01.02.011
Illinois	Exempt		General Info Letters ST 98-0072
Indiana	Exempt		Ind. Admin. Code tit. 45, r. 2.2-4-2, Information Bulletin #8
Iowa	Exempt		Iowa Code § 423.2 (6), Policy Letter 01300016
Kansas	Exempt		Information Guide No. EDU-71R
Kentucky	Exempt		Ky. Rev. Stat. Ann. § 139.200

State	Web Page Design	Comments	Citation
Louisiana	Exempt	Caution: Numerous exemptions are suspended from April 1, 2016, to June 30, 2018. For chart of suspended exemptions and applicable tax rates, see Publication R-1002A.	La. Rev. Stat. Ann. § 47:301(14), LA DOR Publication R-1002A
Maine	Exempt		Me. Rev. Stat. Ann. tit. 36, § 1752 (17-B)
Maryland	Exempt		Md. Code Ann. § 11-101, Md. Code Ann. § 11-219
Massachusetts	Exempt		Mass. Regs. Code tit. 830, § 64H.1.3(14)(b)
Michigan	Exempt		Mich. Comp. Laws § 205.52
Minnesota	Exempt		Minn. Stat. § 297A.61(3), Minn. R. 8130.9700(4)
Mississippi	Taxable		Miss. Rule 35.IV.5.06
Missouri	Exempt		Mo. Rev. Stat. § 144.020, Mo. Code Regs. Ann. tit. 12, § 10-109.050, Letter Ruling LR 9899, Letter Ruling LR 3865
Nebraska	Exempt	Charges are taxable only if the website is transferred to the customer on a tangible storage medium.	Information Guide 6-511-2011, Rev. Ruling 1-10-2
Nevada	Exempt		Nev. Rev. Stat. § 372.227(3)
New Jersey	Exempt		N.J. Bulletin S&U-4, N.J. Bulletin S&U-9
New Mexico	Taxable	Receipts of an eligible software development company from the sale of software development services, including the design and development of websites, may be deducted from gross receipts tax if they are performed in a qualified area.	N.M. Stat. Ann. § 7-9-57.2
New York	Exempt		N.Y. Tax Law, § 1105(c), TSB-A-02(13)S
North Carolina	Exempt		N.C. Gen. Stat. § 105-164.4
North Dakota	Exempt		N.D. Admin. Code § 81-04.1-01-22, N.D. Sales Tax Newsletter, Vol. 24, No. 4
Ohio	Exempt		Ohio Rev. Code Ann. § 5739.01(B), (Y)
Oklahoma	Exempt		Okla. Admin. Code § 710:65-19-156

State	Web Page Design	Comments	Citation
Pennsylvania	Exempt		72 P.S. § 7202, Sales and Use Tax Ruling SUT-99-021
Rhode Island	Exempt		R.I. Gen. Laws § 44-18-7
South Carolina	Exempt		S.C. Code Ann. § 12-36-910(c)
South Dakota	Taxable	Exempt as an advertising service if the web page is both designed and placed on the Internet by the same firm.	S.D. Admin. R. 64:06:02:78, S.D. Admin. R. 64:06:02:03
Tennessee	Taxable		Tenn. Code Ann. § 67-6-205, Letter Ruling No. 97-54
Texas	Taxable	Taxed on 80% of the charge as a data processing service.	34 Tex. Admin. Code § 3.330, Letter No. 200204975L
Utah	Exempt		Private Letter Ruling, Opinion No. 01-030
Vermont	Exempt		Vt. Stat. Ann. tit. 32, § 9771
Virginia	Exempt		Va. Code Ann. § 58.1-609.5(1), Ruling of Commissioner, P.D. 02-94
Washington	Exempt		Wash. Rev. Code § 82.04.050, Tax Topics
West Virginia	Taxable	Taxable as a data generation service.	Decision No. 02-308C, West Virginia Office of Tax Appeals
Wisconsin	Exempt		Wis. Stat. § 77.52(2)(a), Private Letter Ruling No. W9745007
Wyoming	Exempt		Wyo. Stat. Ann. § 39-15-103

¶ 200   ALABAMA

¶ 201   Scope of Tax

Source.—Statutory references are to Title 40, Chapter 23, of the Code of Alabama of 1975, as amended to date. Details are reported in the CCH ALABAMA TAX REPORTS starting at ¶ 60-000.

The Alabama sales and use tax is a privilege or license tax levied on the gross proceeds or the gross receipts from the businesses of selling at retail or renting tangible personal property (Sec. 40-12-222, Sec. 40-23-2(1)) or of furnishing entertainment (Sec. 40-23-2(2)). Services, other than entertainment, are not taxable. The sales or use tax is in addition to other taxes (Sec. 40-23-28). The use tax on storage, use, or consumption of tangible personal property in the state is a complementary tax and does not apply in situations in which the sales tax is collected (Sec. 40-23-62(1)).

Lease tax: A privilege or license tax is levied on persons engaging in the business of leasing or renting tangible personal property (Sec. 40-12-222, Code). The tax is based on the gross proceeds of lease or rental transactions (Sec. 40-12-220(4)). Charges for maintenance contracts that are required as a condition of a lease are included in the gross receipts, the basis for the tax (Rule 810-6-5-.09.01(3)(a)).

The Alabama Tax Tribunal has held that proceeds from lease-to-own agreements were subject to lease or rental tax, not sales tax (*Hallman Enterprises, LLC v. Alabama Department of Revenue,* Alabama Tax Tribunal, No. S. 15-1210, March 16, 2016, CCH ALABAMA TAX REPORTS, ¶ 201-859).

Prepaid calling cards or services: The sale of prepaid wireless service that is evidenced by a physical card constitutes the sale of a prepaid telephone calling card, and the sale of prepaid wireless service that is not evidenced by a physical card constitutes the sale of a prepaid authorization number, both of which are subject to Alabama sales and use tax. (Sec. 40-23-1(a)(13, (14)), Code; Sec. 40-23-60(13), (14), Code; Rule 810-6-5-.36.01)

- **Incidence of tax**

The sales tax is imposed on retailers, including operators of places of amusement (Sec. 40-23-2). It is presumed to be a direct tax on the consumer, collected from the retailer only for convenience (Sec. 40-23-26). Retailers may not absorb the tax, which remains a debt of the retailer to the state until paid.

Privilege or license taxes may be passed on to lessees, except that the authority to pass on a privilege or license tax does not apply to the leasing or renting of tangible personal property to the state or an Alabama county or municipality, unless the flat amount collected by the lessor includes both the tax and the leasing fee (Sec. 40-12-222, Code).

The incidence of the use tax is on the consumer (Sec. 40-23-63). Consumers are liable for the tax unless they have a receipt showing payment of the tax to a retailer.

- **Services subject to tax**

With the exception of businesses that furnish entertainment or amusement, services are not subject to the sales and use tax (Sec. 40-23-2). In the fields of repair or installation, services may be included in the measure of tax if the services are not separately stated on the bill. If separated, however, they are not taxable. Incidental services that are customarily performed in connection with the sale of property are part of the measure of tax (Reg. 810-6-1-.84).

Sales of dental appliances to dentists are considered sales of services (*Haden v. McCarty,* Ala.Sup.Ct., 151 So. 2d 141 (1963); see also *Smartsmiles Orthodontics, P.C. v. Alabama DOR,* Alabama Department of Revenue, Administrative Law Division, S. 05-772, December 29, 2005, CCH ALABAMA TAX REPORTS, ¶ 201-101).

- **Use tax**

The use tax is imposed on the use, storage, or consumption of tangible personal property in Alabama; this tax complements the sales tax and is not levied when the sales tax is imposed (Sec. 40-23-61). The use tax operates to protect Alabama merchants from discrimination arising from the state's inability to impose its sales tax on sales made outside the state of Alabama to Alabama residents by merchants of other states. The withdrawal of tax-exempt items from inventory for the merchant's own use is treated as a retail sale and is subject to the sales tax rather than the use tax (Sec. 40-23-1(a)(10), Sec. 40-23-60(5), Reg. 810-6-1-.89.02, Reg. 810-6-1-.196).

- **Responsibility for collecting tax**

Sales tax: The sales tax, collected by the seller from the purchaser, is presumed to be a direct tax on the retail consumer, precollected by the retailer only for the purpose of convenience (Sec. 40-23-26). It is unlawful for the retailer to refund or absorb the tax or to advertise that it will refund or absorb the tax.

Use tax: Retailers who have sufficient contacts with Alabama to constitute substantial nexus with the state are required to collect the use tax, which is to be separately stated, from purchasers to be remitted to the Department of Revenue (Sec. 40-23-67). The tax remains a liability of the purchaser, however, until paid, unless the purchaser has a receipt showing payment of the tax to the retailer (Sec. 40-23-63). Retailers who pay the tax are required to give receipts to the purchasers (Sec. 40-23-67).

- **Nexus**

Out-of-state retailers are required to collect and remit the use tax on sales of personal property for storage, use, or consumption in Alabama when they meet any of the following conditions (Sec. 40-23-68; Rule 810-6-2-.90.01):

     — maintaining a place of business in the state;

     — qualifying to do business in the state or registering to collect sales and use tax in the state;

     — soliciting and receiving orders by any representative, agent, salesmen, canvasser, solicitor, or installer in the state;

     — soliciting and receiving orders through broadcasters or publishers located in Alabama that are disseminating advertising primarily to Alabama consumers;

     — soliciting orders for tangible personal property by mail if the solicitations are substantial and recurring and if the retailer benefits from any banking, financing, debt collection, telecommunication, or marketing activities occurring in the state or benefits from the location in the state of authorized installation, servicing, or repair facilities;

     — having, under a franchise or licensing arrangement or contract, a franchisee or licensee operating under its trade name;

     — soliciting, pursuant to a contract with a cable television operator located in the state, orders for tangible personal property by means of advertising that is transmitted or distributed over a cable television system in the state;

     — soliciting orders for tangible personal property by means of a telecommunication or television shopping system that is intended to be broadcast to Alabama consumers by cable television or other means of broadcasting; or

     — maintaining any other contact with Alabama that would allow the state to require the seller to collect and remit tax due under the provision of the constitution and laws of the United States; and

     — distributing catalogs or other advertising matter and thereby receiving and accepting orders from residents of the state.

Large remote sellers: Out-of-state sellers who lack an Alabama physical presence but who are making retail sales of tangible personal property into the state have a substantial economic presence in Alabama for sales and use tax purposes and are required to register for a license with the department and to collect and remit tax when (Rule 810-6-2-.90.03):

(a) the seller's retail sales of tangible personal property sold into Alabama exceed $250,000 per year based on the previous calendar year's sales; and

(b) the seller conducts one or more of the activities described in Sec. 40-23-68 (above).

Affiliate nexus: A seller may have substantial nexus with Alabama due to the business activities conducted in the state by the seller's affiliates. A seller has substantial nexus with the state for the collection of use tax if (Sec. 40-23-190; Rule 810-6-2-.90.01):

— the seller and an in-state business maintaining one or more locations within the state are related parties; and

— the seller and the in-state business use an identical or substantially similar name, trade name, trademark, or goodwill, to develop, promote, or maintain sales, or the in-state business and the seller pay for each other's services in whole or in part contingent upon the volume or value of sales, or the in-state business and the seller share a common business plan or substantially coordinate their business plans, or the in-state business provides services to, or that inure to the benefit of, the business related to developing, promoting, or maintaining the in-state market.

• Streamlined Act status

Alabama is one of the Streamlined Sales Tax Advisor States and has enacted an abridged version of the Uniform (Simplified) Sales and Use Tax Administration Act. A commission will examine Alabama's tax laws to see what changes are necessary to come into compliance with the Agreement. The recommendations of the commission, if ratified by the Alabama Legislature, will not be implemented until and unless federal legislation adopting the SST Agreement becomes law. (Act 563 (H.B. 355), Laws 2011)

¶ 202   Tax Base

Generally included in the tax base are all the costs of the property sold, including delivery charges prior to sale and any consumer excise taxes that are included in the sales price of the property sold (Sec. 40-23-1(a)(5), Sec. 40-23-1(a)(6), Sec. 40-23-1(a)(8)). The basis of the sales tax is gross proceeds of sales for sales of tangible personal property and gross receipts for receipts from places of amusement (Sec. 40-23-1(a)(6), Sec. 40-23-1(a)(8)). The basis of the use tax is sales price (Sec. 40-23-60(10)).

• Basis definitions

"Gross proceeds of sales" and "gross receipts" are both defined as the value proceeding from the sale of tangible personal property without deduction for the cost of the property sold or any consumer excise taxes that may be included within the sales price of the property sold (Sec. 40-23-1(a)(6), Sec. 40-23-1(a)(8)). "Sales price" is the total amount for which tangible personal property is sold, including any services such as transportation that are a part of the sale without any deduction for the cost of the property sold (Sec. 40-23-60(10)).

¶ 203   List of Exemptions, Exceptions, and Exclusions

Unless otherwise indicated, the statutory exemptions, exceptions, and exclusions listed below apply to both sales and use taxes; those applicable only to the lease tax are listed separately. Items that are excluded from the sales or use tax base are treated at ¶ 202, "Tax Base."

Exemption certificates: All persons or companies (except government agencies) that are statutorily exempt from the payment of Alabama sales, use, and lodgings taxes, other than governmental entities, must annually obtain a certificate of exemption (Form STE-1, *State Sales and Use Tax Certificate of Exemption*) from the Department of Revenue. This requirement only applies to entities that have been granted a general exemption from sales, use, or lodgings taxes. The requirements are not triggered by the purchase of tangible personal property that is exempt from sales and use tax. (Uncodified Act 534 (S.B. 24b), First Special Session, Laws 2015; Rules 810-6-5-.02 and 810-6-5-.02.01, see also **http://revenue.alabama.gov/salestax/notices.cfm**)

Back to school sales tax holiday: A state sales tax holiday exempts certain clothing and school supplies from Alabama state sales and use tax during the first full weekend in August of each year. The exemption applies to (1) articles of clothing with a sales price of $100 or less per article; (2) a single purchase, with a sales price of $750 or less, of computers, computer software, and school computer supplies; (3) noncommercial purchases of school supplies, school art supplies, and school instructional material, up to a price of $50 per item; and (4) other books up to $30 each. The sales tax holiday covers items during the period from 12:01 a.m. on the first Friday in August of each year to midnight the following Sunday (Sec. 40-23-210; Sec. 40-23-211; Rule 810-6-3-.65).

Local governments may choose to participate in the annual holiday, to participate for a specific year, or not to participate. A local participation chart may be found on the Department's website at **http://revenue.alabama.gov/salestax/STholiday.cfm**.

Severe weather preparedness sales tax holiday: There is also an annual state sales tax holiday for severe weather preparedness items, which is held during the last full weekend of February. Items related to severe weather preparedness will be exempt from state sales and use taxes. Counties and municipalities are allowed to join the state by removing their own local sales and use taxes from the same items during the same weekend. Items generally exempt during the tax holiday include specified batteries, radios, portable self-powered light sources, tarpaulins, plastic sheeting, ground anchor systems, duct tape, plywood, window film or other materials specifically designed to protect window openings, non-electric food storage cooler or water storage containers and can openers, artificial ice, first aid kits, fire extinguishers, smoke or carbon monoxide detectors, and gas or diesel containers (Rule. 810-6-3-.66). The covered items must cost $60 or less, except for portable generators and power cords used to provide light or communications or preserve food in the event of a power outage, which are covered as long as they cost $1,000 or less.

Local governments may choose to participate in the annual holiday, to participate for a specific year, or not to participate. A chart listing localities that have notified the Department of Revenue regarding their participation in the severe weather preparedness tax holiday can be found on the department's website at **http://revenue.alabama.gov/salestax/WPholiday.cfm**.

- **Sales and use tax exemptions, exceptions, and exclusions**

Admissions, professional golf events	Sec. 40-23-5(q)
Agricultural products	Sec. 40-23-4(a)(3), Sec. 40-23-4(a)(5), Sec. 40-23-62(6), Sec. 40-23-62(8)
Air carrier with hub operation	Sec. 40-12-223(13), Sec. 40-23-4(a)(40), Sec. 40-23-62(32)
Aircraft conversion, reconfiguration, or general maintenance on out-of-state aircraft	Sec. 40-23-4(a)(46)
Aircraft moved out of state	Sec. 40-23-4(a)(37)

Aviation jet fuel used by a certificated carrier in international all-cargo operations . . . . Sec. 40-23-4(a)(42)

Alabama governmental entities, sales to . . . . Sec. 40-23-2(1),
Sec. 40-23-4(a)(11),
Sec. 40-23-62(13)

Bagging and ties for marketing cotton . . . . Sec. 40-23-1(a)(9g),
Sec. 40-23-60(4g)

Barges, sold by builders . . . . Sec. 40-23-2(1),
Sec. 40-23-4(a)(12),
Sec. 40-23-4(a)(13),
Sec. 40-23-61(a),
Sec. 40-23-62(14),
Sec. 40-23-62(17)

Bingo games operated by qualified charities . . . . Sec. 40-23-4(a)(43)

Bonds . . . . Sec. 40-12-220(8)

Books sold by public schools . . . . Sec. 40-23-2(1)

Chicks . . . . Sec. 40-23-4(a)(3),
Sec. 40-23-62(6)

Commercial fishing vessels, sold by builders; materials and supplies; component parts . . . . Sec. 40-23-2(1),
Sec. 40-23-4(a)(12),
Sec. 40-23-4(a)(13),
Sec. 40-23-61(a),
Sec. 40-23-62(14),
Sec. 40-23-62(17)

Containers for delivering chicks or eggs . . . . Sec. 40-23-1(a)(9f),
Sec. 40-23-60(4f)

Contractors' purchases for brownfield development property . . . . . . Sec. 40-9C-4

Contractors' purchases for private user industrial property . . . . Sec. 40-9B-4,
Sec. 40-9G-2

Cottonseed . . . . Sec. 40-23-4(a)(6),
Sec. 40-23-62(9)

Delivery containers and labels . . . . Sec. 40-23-1(a)(9c),
Sec. 40-23-60(4c)

Diabetes treatment items . . . . Sec. 40-9-27.1

Domestic coal products . . . . Sec. 40-23-4(a)(45),
Sec. 40-23-62(34)(e)

Drugs . . . . Sec. 40-9-27,
Sec. 40-23-4(a)(30),
Sec. 40-23-4.1,
Sec. 40-23-62(30)

Durable medical equipment and oxygen . . . . Sec. 40-9-30

Educational institutions, public and private, sales to and by . . . . . . Sec. 40-23-4(a)(15), (49)
Sec. 40-23-62.9(16), (38)

Educational or cultural productions . . . . Sec. 40-23-4(a)(24)

Energy projects, alternative and renewable (abatements) . . . . Sec. 40-9B-3; Sec. 40-9B-4

Entertainment production companies (rebate) . . . . Sec. 41-7A-43

Exports to foreign countries (tax refund) . . . . Sec. 40-23-39(a)

Feed for commercial fish . . . . Sec. 40-23-1(a)(9i)

Feed for livestock and poultry	Sec. 40-23-4(a)(4), Sec. 40-23-62(8)
Fertilizer	Sec. 40-23-4(a)(2), Sec. 40-23-62(5)
Film production	Sec. 40-23-4(a)(46), Sec. 40-23-62(35)
Food stamp purchases	Sec. 40-23-4.2
Fuel, agricultural and commercial fishing	Sec. 40-23-4(a)(27), Sec. 40-23-4(a)(33), Sec. 40-23-4(a)(38), Sec. 40-23-62(27), Sec. 40-23-62(31)
Fuel and supplies, vessels used in foreign or interstate commerce . .	Sec. 40-23-4(a)(10), Sec. 40-23-62(12)
Fuel, manufacturing	Sec. 40-23-4(a)(9), Sec. 40-23-4(a)(14), Sec. 40-23-62(11), Sec. 40-23-62(15)
Fuel used in refining	Sec. 40-23-1(a)(6), Sec. 40-23-1(a)(8)
Ingredient of manufactured product	Sec. 40-23-1(a)(6), Sec. 40-23-1(a)(9b), Sec. 40-23-60(4)(b)
Insecticides	Sec. 40-23-4(a)(4), Sec. 40-23-62(7)
Insurance	Sec. 40-12-220(8)
Intangibles	Sec. 40-12-220(8)
Lease items	Sec. 40-23-1(a)(9j), Sec. 40-23-60(4i)
Leases, vessels and railroad equipment used in interstate or foreign commerce	Sec. 40-12-223(12)
Livestock	Sec. 40-23-4(a)(5), Sec. 40-23-62(8)
Lodging in excess of 180 days	Sec. 40-26-1(b)
Lubricating oil and gasoline	Sec. 40-23-4(a)(1), Sec. 40-23-62(4)
Lumber sold for resale	Sec. 40-23-1(c)
Machinery, agricultural (reduced rate of tax)	Sec. 40-23-37, Sec. 40-23-63
Machinery, manufacturing (reduced rate of tax)	Sec. 40-23-2(3), Sec. 40-23-61(b)
Manufactured product, ingredient	Sec. 40-23-1(a)(6), Sec. 40-23-1(a)(9b), Sec. 40-23-60(4)(b)
Meals by airlines, hub operators	Sec. 40-23-4(a)(41), Sec. 40-23-62(33)
Meals for patients or inmates of certain Alabama institutions	Sec. 40-23-4(a)(19)
Meals served to needy persons by Christian Service Mission	Sec. 40-23-5(n)
Medical equipment (durable), prosthetic devices, and supplies	Sec. 40-9-30(d)

Medicines for fish, livestock, and poultry	Sec. 40-23-4(a)(29), Sec. 40-23-62(29)
Metals (other than gold or silver) purchased for investment	Sec. 40-23-4(a)(46), Sec. 40-23-62(35)
Mobile homes (reduced rate of tax)	Sec. 40-23-2(4), Sec. 40-23-61(c), Sec. 40-23-101
Motor fuels	Sec. 40-23-4(a)(1), Sec. 40-23-62(4)
Motor vehicles (reduced rate of tax)	Sec. 40-23-2(4), Sec. 40-23-101
Motorboats (reduced rate of tax)	Sec. 40-23-101, Sec. 40-23-102, Sec. 40-23-103, Sec. 40-23-104, Sec. 40-23-106
National championship sporting events	Sec. 40-23-4(a)(39)
Nonprofit entities and organizations, specified	Sec. 40-23-5
Offshore oil exploration, supplies	Sec. 40-23-4(a)(42), Sec. 40-23-62(34)
Packaging	Sec. 40-23-1(a)(9c), Sec. 40-23-60(4c)
Park and recreational facilities, construction of	Sec. 11-86A-18
Petroleum pipelines	Sec. 40-9B-3(6)
Pollution control and cleanup equipment	Sec. 40-23-4(a)(16), Sec. 40-23-62(18)
Property of nonresidents	Sec. 40-23-62(3)
Public schools and nonprofit affiliated groups, sales by	Sec. 40-9-31
Public and private schools, sales to and by	Sec. 40-23-4(a)(15), (49) Sec. 40-23-62.9(16), (38)
Railroad cars, sold by manufacturer	Sec. 40-23-2(1), Sec. 40-23-4(a)(12), Sec. 40-23-4(a)(13), Sec. 40-23-61(a), Sec. 40-23-62(14), Sec. 40-23-62(17)
Religious publications (use tax exemption)	Sec. 40-23-62(20)
Resales	Sec. 40-23-1(a)(9a), Sec. 40-23-60(4a), Sec. 40-23-60(5)
Sausage casings	Sec. 40-23-1(a)(9h), Sec. 40-23-60(4k)
Seeds	Sec. 40-23-4(a)(3), Sec. 40-23-62(6)
Services (other than entertainment)	Sec. 40-23-2
Sod sold by producers	Sec. 40-23-4(a)(31)
Sporting events, national championships	Sec. 40-23-4(a)(39)

State nurseries, seed and seedlings	Sec. 40-23-4(a)(34), Sec. 40-23-4(a)(35), Sec. 40-23-4(a)(36)
Stocks	Sec. 40-12-220(8)
Tomato production materials	Sec. 40-23-4(a)(32)
Transportation services regulated by state regulatory bodies	Sec. 40-23-4(a)(8), Sec. 40-23-62(10)
Tube sections for vehicular tunnels	Sec. 40-23-4(a)(23), Sec. 40-23-62(24)
U.S. government, sales to	Sec. 40-23-4(a)(17), Sec. 40-23-62(2)
Utilities	Sec. 40-21-50, Sec. 40-21-53, Sec. 40-21-56— Sec. 40-21-60, Sec. 40-23-4(a)(7)
Vehicles moved out of state	Sec. 40-23-2(4)
Vending machines, food sales (reduced rate of tax)	Sec. 40-23-2(5)
Vessels, sold by manufacturer	Sec. 40-23-2(1), Sec. 40-23-4(a)(12), Sec. 40-23-4(a)(13), Sec. 40-23-61(a), Sec. 40-23-62(14), Sec. 40-23-62(17)
Volunteer fire and rescue organizations	Sec. 40-9-13, Sec. 40-23-5(o), (r)
Wholesale sales	Sec. 40-23-1(a)(9a), Sec. 40-23-60(4a), Sec. 40-23-60(5)
Wrapping paper used in wrapping poultry products	Sec. 40-23-4(a)(20), Sec. 40-23-62(21)

• Exemptions, exceptions, and exclusions applicable only to the lease tax

Apartment or motel fixtures	Sec. 40-12-223(3), Sec. 40-12-223(5)
Constitutional exemptions	Sec. 40-12-223(6)
Demurrage charges	Rule 810-6-5-.09
Docks	Sec. 40-12-223(2)
Durable medical equipment	Sec. 40-9-30
Film	Sec. 40-12-223(1)
Intercompany transactions	Sec. 40-12-223(11)
Nuclear material	Sec. 40-12-223(7)
Pollution control equipment	Sec. 40-12-223(10)
Regulated motor carriers	Sec. 40-12-223(9)
Subleases	Sec. 40-12-223(4)
Truck leased with operator	Sec. 40-12-223(8)

¶ 204 Rate of Tax

The general rate of the Alabama sales and use tax, except when a different amount is specified, is 4% of the gross proceeds of sales or rentals of tangible personal property and of the proceeds from any business of providing amusement (Sec. 40-12-222, Sec. 40-23-61).

Rate exceptions: The rental of linens and garments is taxed at a rate of 2% (Sec. 40-12-222). Food and food products sold through vending machines are taxed at the rate of 3% (Sec. 40-23-2). Sales of motor vehicles, mobile homes and motorboats, including set-up materials, are taxed at 2%, whether sold by dealers or through casual sales (Sec. 40-23-2(4), Sec. 40-23-61(c), Sec. 40-23-101). Sales of agricultural, mining, and manufacturing machinery and equipment are taxed at the rate of 1.5% (Sec. 40-23-2, Sec. 40-23-37, Sec. 40-23-61(b), Sec. 40-23-63). Street and highway contractors are taxed at the rate of 5% on the gross receipts from contracts to build or reconstruct public highways, roads, or bridges (Sec. 40-23-50).

Rate changes: The correct rate of tax due on credit sales made prior to the effective date of a rate increase is the old rate in effect prior to the rate change (Reg. 810-6-4-.21).

Collection discount: For sales tax, the vendors' discount is 5% of the first $100 of tax collected and 2% over $100. The discount for monthly filers is based on the amount collected per calendar quarter or calendar year. The maximum discount to any license holder is $400 per month, regardless of the number of retail locations the retail license holder has within the state. No discount is allowed on taxes that are not paid before delinquency. (Sec. 40-23-36; Rule 810-6-4-.03) The sales tax discount applies to state sales tax and to all county and municipal sales taxes administered by the Department.

No discount is available to use tax filers (Rule 810-6-5-.19.01).

Motor vehicle drive-outs: Alabama sales tax due on a motor vehicle that will be registered or titled for use in another state and removed from Alabama within 72 hours may not exceed the amount of sales tax that would have otherwise been due in the state where the vehicle will be registered or titled for first time use. Each January 1, the Alabama Department of Revenue must publish on the state's website a list of states that do not allow drive-out provisions to Alabama residents. (Sec. 40-23-2(4)); see the relevant discussion at **http://revenue.alabama.gov/salestax/whatsnew.cfm**.

Lease tax: The general rate of the privilege tax on leases or rentals of tangible personal property is 4%; however, motor vehicle rentals are taxed at 1.5% (Sec. 40-12-222).

¶ 205 Local Taxes

For the most current local tax rates for all counties and cities in Alabama, go to the lookup feature on the DOR's website at **http://www.ador.state.al.us/salestax/sales/index.cfm**. Sales tax rates for a specific address may be looked up at **https://www.alabamainteractive.org/ador_taxrate_lookup/welcome.action**.

Appropriate taxing jurisdiction: The Alabama Attorney General has opined that local sales and use tax is due in the jurisdiction where title to the goods is transferred, which will be at the time of delivery, unless explicitly agreed otherwise. If parties to a retail sales transaction are not using a common carrier for delivery and agree to allow title to transfer at the place of the sale, then local tax is due in the jurisdiction where the sale takes place. However, if a common carrier is the method of delivery, then local tax is due in the jurisdiction where delivery is completed, regardless of any agreement to allow title to transfer at the place of the sale. (*Opinion No. 2017-001*, Alabama Attorney General, October 5, 2016, CCH ALABAMA TAX REPORTS, ¶ 201-884)

¶ 206   Bracket Schedule

Bracket schedules are provided by the Department of Revenue at **http://reve-nue.alabama.gov/salestax/brackets.cfm**.

¶ 207   Returns, Payments, and Due Dates

Returns for the state sales and use tax; lodgings tax; rental tax; contractor's gross receipts tax; and state-administered local sales, use, rental, and lodgings taxes must be filed electronically by the 20th of each month and must include payment of the taxes for the previous calendar month period (Sec. 40-23-7; Rule 810-1-6-.12). Payments are accelerated, however, for taxpayers with larger liabilities. Use tax returns also must be filed electronically on the 20th of the month following the month during which the use triggering the tax occurred (Sec. 40-23-68). Returns are not required to be made under oath (Sec. 40-23-10).

Taxpayers whose average monthly tax liability is less than $200 may file quarterly (Sec. 40-23-7(d), Reg. 810-6-5-.30).

Taxpayers may file electronically using the Internet. Circumstances that may result in a waiver of the electronic filing requirements include lack of a computer, lack of Internet access, incompatible computer hardware, no access to a telephone, or any special circumstance deemed worthy of a waiver (Rule 810-1-6-.12).

My Alabama Taxes (MAT) is the State's electronic filing and remittance system used for the filing of state and some city and county sales, use, rental, and lodgings taxes. Alabama retailers may file and pay all city/county sales, use, and rental taxes in MAT, using the Optional Network Election for Single Point Online Transactions or "ONE SPOT" program. Effective October 1, 2016, lodging taxes also may be remitted using ONE SPOT. For additional information, see **https://myalaba-mataxes.alabama.gov** or **http://www.revenue.alabama.gov/salestax/ONE_SPOT.cfm**.

Bulk filing: Approved third-party bulk filers must submit returns and payments for taxes required to be filed electronically in a timely manner over the Internet using the Alabama Paperless Filing System for taxpayers having a valid account with the Department. They are required to submit separate electronic payments for each return, account, or filing period; permit the Department to conduct audits of their books and records; provide the Department with copies of client contracts upon request; and electronically provide the Department with monthly updated client lists (Rule 810-1-6-.13).

• **Simplified reporting for remote sellers**

The Simplified Sellers Use Tax Remittance Program is designed to allow an eligible seller who participates in the program to collect, report, and remit a simplified Alabama sellers use tax instead of the sales and use taxes otherwise due by or on behalf of Alabama customers who have purchased items from the eligible seller that were shipped or otherwise delivered into Alabama by the eligible seller (Sec. 40-23-191, *et seq*; Rule 810-6-2-.90.02). Effective October 1, 2015, the simplified sellers use tax due under the program is 8% of the sales price on any tangible personal property sold or delivered into Alabama by an eligible seller participating in the program (Sec. 40-23-193). The collection and remittance of simplified sellers use tax relieves the eligible seller and the purchaser from any additional state or local sales and use taxes on the transaction.

An "eligible seller" is an individual, trust, estate, fiduciary, partnership, limited liability company (LLC), limited liability partnership, corporation or other legal entity that sells tangible personal property or a service, but does not have a physical presence in Alabama or is not otherwise required to be subject to requirements for collecting and remitting state and local sales or use tax for sales delivered into the state (Sec. 40-23-191(b)(2)). In order to participate in the program, an eligible seller must apply to the Department of Revenue (Sec. 40-23-192). Applications are available at **http://revenue.alabama.gov/salestax/pdf/SSUT-Application_(9-15).pdf**.

The simplified sellers use tax collected by the eligible seller must be electronically reported on or before the 20th day of the month next succeeding the month in which the tax accrues. The eligible seller should remit the tax at the required rate or the amount of the tax collected, whichever is greater. The required monthly reporting from the eligible seller will only include statewide totals of the simplified sellers use taxes collected and remitted and will not require information related to the location of purchasers or amount of sales into a specific locality. No eligible seller will be required to collect the tax at a rate greater than 8%, regardless of the combined actual tax rates that may otherwise be applicable. Also, no sales for which the simplified sellers use tax is collected will be subject to any additional sales or use tax from any locality levying a sales or use tax with respect to the purchase or use of the property, regardless of the actual tax rate that might have otherwise been applicable. (Sec. 40-23-193)

An eligible seller must collect the tax on all purchases delivered into Alabama unless the purchaser furnishes the eligible seller with a valid exemption certificate, sales tax license, or direct pay permit issued by the department. The eligible seller must provide the purchaser with a statement or invoice showing that the simplified sellers use tax was collected and is to be remitted on the purchaser's behalf. (Sec. 40-23-193(d); Rule 810-6-2-.90.02)

Amnesty: An eligible seller participating in the program is granted amnesty for any uncollected remote use tax that may have been due on sales made to purchasers in Alabama for the 12-month period preceding the effective date of the eligible seller's participation in the program. (Sec. 40-23-199)

Discount: An eligible seller may deduct and retain a discount of 2% of the simplified sellers use tax properly collected and then remitted to the department (Sec. 40-23-194).

Refund or credit: Any taxpayer who pays a simplified sellers use tax through this program that is higher than the actual state and local sales or use tax levied in the locality where the sale was delivered may file for a refund or credit of the excess amount paid to the eligible seller participating in the program. A business taxpayer who has a registered consumer use tax account with the department may claim credit for the overpayment of simplified use tax on its consumer use tax return. All other taxpayers may file a petition for refund in the manner prescribed by the department. (Sec. 40-23-196)

Change in federal law: In the event that a change in federal law removes current federal limitations on states' ability to enforce their sales and use tax jurisdiction against businesses that lack an in-state physical presence, the provisions of this law will be inapplicable as to any eligible seller who is not registered with the department as a participant in the program at least six months prior to the date of such change in law. In such event, the provisions of this law will continue to apply to any eligible seller who has been approved by the department as a participant in the program at least six months prior to the change in law and to any taxpayer who has paid or pays the simplified sellers use tax provided the eligible seller continues to collect, report, and remit the simplified sellers use tax and otherwise complies with all procedures and requirements of the program. (Sec. 40-23-198)

• **Electronic funds transfer**

The threshold for making payments by electronic funds transfer (EFT) of Alabama taxes, fees, and other obligations collected by the Department of Revenue is $750. This provision also applies to local government business entity taxes and fees that are collected by the Department. Governing bodies of self-administered counties or cities may elect to require electronic payments at this threshold. In addition, the funds must be immediately available on the first banking day following the due date of payment (Sec. 41-1-20; Regs. 810-13-1-.01 *et seq.*).

The Automated Clearing House (ACH) debit payment method is the primary method to be used by taxpayers to make electronic funds transfers (Rule 810-13-1-.08) but the ACH credit method may be used with ADOR approval; see (**https:// myalabamataxes.alabama.gov**).

¶ 208   **Prepayment of Taxes**

Taxpayers whose average monthly liability exceeded $1,000 during the preceding year are required to make estimated payments of tax by the 20th of each month (Sec. 40-23-7(3)). The amount of the payment is the lesser of two-thirds of the amount of the liability for the corresponding month in the previous year or two-thirds of the current year's estimated liability. Necessary adjustments to the estimated amounts are made on the final return, filed in the following month.

Effective August 1, 2016, the average monthly tax liability for a taxpayer to be required to make estimated Alabama sales tax payments will increase from $1,000 or greater to $2,500 or greater during the preceding calendar year (Sec. 40-23-7(3)).

¶ 209   **Vendor Registration**

Persons in the business of making retail sales or in the business of leasing or renting tangible personal property are required to have a license issued by the Department of Revenue (Sec. 40-12-221, Sec. 40-23-6). Out-of-state retailers who meet any of the following qualifications within the state are similarly required to register with the Department and furnish specified information (Sec. 40-23-66): (a) maintaining a place of business; (b) being qualified to do business; (c) soliciting and receiving orders from agents or salespersons; or (d) distributing catalogues or advertising matter and receiving orders therefrom.

Contracting restriction: Alabama state departments and agencies may not contract for the purchase or lease of tangible personal property unless vendors, contractors, or their affiliates are registered with the Alabama Department of Revenue to collect and remit all state and local sales, use, and lease taxes. Vendors, contractors, and affiliates that sell or lease tangible personal property to a state department or agency must collect and remit tax due on their sales and leases into Alabama (Sec. 41-4-116).

¶ 210   **Sales or Use Tax Credits**

Taxpayers who paid a legally imposed sales or use tax to another state or any of its subdivisions may claim a credit against the Alabama use tax due, regardless of whether that jurisdiction allows a credit for sales and use taxes paid to Alabama or its subdivisions (Reg. 810-6-5-.04). Reciprocal credit is also offered within Alabama for county and municipal sales and use taxes on a "city to city" and "county to county" basis (Reg. 810-6-5-.04.01).

¶ 211   **Deficiency Assessments**

When the Department of Revenue determines that an amount of tax reported is incorrect or when no return is filed, the Department is authorized to calculate the correct tax based on the most accurate and complete information reasonably obtainable (Sec. 40-2A-7(b)). The Department may then enter a preliminary assessment for the correct tax, including any applicable penalty and interest.

If the amount of tax reported is not disputed by the Department, or if the taxpayer gives written consent to the amount of any deficiency, determination of value or preliminary assessment, the Department may immediately enter a final assessment for the amount of tax, plus applicable penalty and interest.

Additional tax may be assessed by the Department within any applicable period allowed, notwithstanding that a preliminary or final assessment has been previously entered against the same taxpayer for the same or a portion of the same tax period.

A taxpayer who disagrees with a preliminary assessment may file a written petition for review with the Department within 30 days from the date of entry of the preliminary assessment describing specific objections. The Department must schedule a conference with the taxpayer for the purpose of allowing both sides to present their respective positions, discuss any omissions or errors, and to attempt to agree upon any changes or modifications to their respective positions.

• **Final assessment**

When a written petition for review is not timely filed, or when the petition is properly filed but the Department, upon further review, determines the preliminary assessment is due to be upheld in whole or in part, the Department may make the assessment final in the amount of tax due as computed, with applicable interest and penalty computed to the date of entry of the final assessment (Sec. 40-2A-7(b)).

¶ 212   Audit Procedures

The Department of Revenue and self-administered counties or municipalities are authorized to examine and audit a taxpayer's records and books, as well as other relevant information maintained by the taxpayer or any other person for the purpose of computing and determining the correct amount of tax (Sec. 40-2A-7(a), Sec. 40-2A-13). Generally, audits may not be conducted more frequently than once every three years (Sec. 40-2A-13(b)).

Alabama may not enter into a contract or arrangement for examination of a taxpayer's books and records or collection of tax if part of the compensation paid or payable for the services of the person, firm, or corporation conducting the examination or collecting the tax is contingent upon, or otherwise related to, the amount of tax, interest, court cost, or penalty assessed against, or collected from, the taxpayer (Sec. 40-2A-6). Any such contract or arrangement is void and unenforceable, and an assessment or preliminary assessment of taxes, penalties, or interest under a contingent fee arrangement is likewise null and void. However, the state may enter into contracts or arrangements for the collection of tax, interest, court costs, or penalties if the person, firm, or corporation making collection has no authority to determine the amount of tax, interest, court cost, or penalty owed the state.

Private auditing or collecting firms must disclose to the Department of Revenue and local taxing agencies, and to taxpayers being audited, the names of the taxing jurisdictions they represent (Sec. 40-2A-13).

• **Voluntary disclosure**

A voluntary disclosure program encourages businesses that are not in compliance with the Alabama tax laws to come forward voluntarily to register and bring their accounts into compliance. In order to be considered for the voluntary disclosure program, the applicant must not have been contacted by the Department or an agent of the Department, such as the Multistate Tax Commission, nor filed a tax return for seven years prior to the initial written request for voluntary disclosure. Each proposal for voluntary disclosure is evaluated on a case-by-case basis. The only taxes eligible for the voluntary disclosure program are business privilege, corporate income, withholding, and sales and use. The program has a mandatory three-year look-back period that is calculated by determining the last three past-due tax years. Taxpayers who wish to participate in the voluntary disclosure program must send a written request/proposal to the Department. (*Voluntary Disclosure Program,* Alabama Department of Revenue, July 2008). For more information see the department's website at **http://revenue.alabama.gov/analysis/voluntary-disclosure.cfm**.

¶ 213   **Statute of Limitations**

A preliminary assessment must be entered within three years from the later of the due date of the return or the date the return is filed (Sec. 40-2A-7(b)(2)). However, a preliminary assessment may be entered at any time if a required return is not filed, or if a false or fraudulent return is filed with the intent to evade tax. For returns that omit more than 25% of the correct taxable base required to be shown on the return, a preliminary assessment may be entered within six years from the later of the due date of the return or the date the return is filed. The taxable base is the gross income, gross proceeds from sales, gross receipts, capital employed, or other amounts on which the tax paid with a return is computed (Sec. 40-2A-7(b)(2)).

Suspension of limitations period: The running of the limitations period for entering a preliminary assessment is suspended for the time period that the taxpayer or the taxpayer's assets are involved in a bankruptcy case, plus a period of six months, or for the period that the assets of the taxpayer are in the control of a court in any proceeding, plus a period of six months (Sec. 40-2A-7(b)(2)).

• **Levy of property and collection suits**

When an assessment of tax has been started or made within the proper period of limitation, tax may be collected by levy or by a proceeding in court if commenced within 10 years after the final assessment of the tax, or prior to the expiration of any period for collection agreed upon in writing by the Commissioner of Revenue and the taxpayer before the expiration of the 10-year period (or, if there is a release of levy, after the 10-year period and before the release) (Sec. 40-29-51). The period agreed upon may be extended by subsequent written agreements made before the expiration of the period formerly decided. The period during which a tax may be collected by levy may not be extended or curtailed by reason of a judgment against the taxpayer. The date on which a levy on property or rights to property is made is the date on which the notice of seizure is given.

¶ 214   **Application for Refund**

A taxpayer may file a petition for refund with the Department of Revenue for any overpayment of tax or other amount erroneously paid to the Department (Sec. 40-2A-7(c)). However, when a final assessment has been entered by the Department, a petition for refund of all or a portion of the tax may be filed only if the final assessment plus applicable interest has been paid in full prior to, or with the filing of, the petition for refund. A petition for refund of sales or use taxes must be filed jointly by the taxpayer who collected and paid the tax to the Department and the purchaser who paid the tax to the taxpayer. However, a direct petition may be filed if the taxpayer never collected the tax from the purchaser, or if the tax has been credited or repaid to the consumer/purchaser by the taxpayer.

• **Time for filing petition for refund**

A petition for refund must be filed with the Department, or a credit allowed, either within three years from the date the return was filed or within two years from the date of payment of the tax, whichever is later (Sec. 40-2A-7(c)).

¶ 215   ALASKA

¶ 216   **State Tax Not Imposed**

There are no sales or use taxes imposed by the state of Alaska. However, local jurisdictions may impose the taxes. For details, consult the CCH Alaska STATE TAX REPORTS.

¶ 231   Scope of Tax

Source.—Statutory references are to sections of the Arizona Revised Statutes, as amended to date and reflecting the recodification of Title 42. Details are reported in the CCH ARIZONA TAX REPORTS starting at ¶ 60-000.

The Arizona transaction privilege tax is a tax on the privilege of doing business in the state. The tax is measured by the amount or volume of business transacted by persons on account of their business activities; the incidence of the tax is on the seller, not the buyer (Sec. 42-5008(A), Reg. R15-5-2002). The tax is imposed on the following "classifications" of business:

Amusement classification (Sec. 42-5073);

Job printing classification (Sec. 42-5066);

Mining classification (Sec. 42-5072);

Online lodging marketplace (eff. 01/01/2017) (Sec. 42-5076);

Owner-builder sales classification (Sec. 42-5076);

Personal property rental classification (Sec. 42-5071);

Pipeline classification (Sec. 42-5071);

Prime contracting classification (Sec. 42-075);

Private car line classification (Sec. 42-5068);

Publication classification (Sec. 42-5065);

Restaurant classification (Sec. 42-5074);

Retail classification (Sec. 42-5061);

Telecommunications classification (Sec. 42-5064);

Transient lodging classification (Sec. 42-5070);

Transporting classification (Sec. 42-5062); and

Utilities classification (Sec. 42-5063).

Counties may impose a local commercial lease tax.

Federal government: Because the Arizona transaction privilege tax is imposed directly on the seller of tangible personal property (or on the seller of services covered under the above classifications) the state has successfully applied the tax to sales to the federal government, arguing that even though the United States may ultimately pay the tax, the tax is not imposed directly on the United States.

• **Use tax**

The use tax is an excise tax on the storage, use, or consumption in Arizona of tangible personal property purchased from a retailer (Sec. 42-5154) or a utility business (Sec. 42-5155). The use tax is imposed at the same rate that is applied to retailers and utility businesses according to their transactions privilege tax classification for the same type of transaction or business activity (Sec. 42-5155(B)). The use tax complements the transactions privilege tax because only one of the taxes can apply to a given transaction (Sec. 42-5159(A)(1), Reg. R15-5-2306).

If a purchase from an out-of-state retailer is subject to another state's sales tax, then the purchaser may take a credit against the use tax equal to the amount of sales tax paid in the state of purchase (Reg. R15-5-2305).

• **Responsibility for the tax**

The transaction privilege tax is the responsibility of persons carrying on business activities that fit within taxable classifications, most commonly the retail classification (Sec. 42-5008, Sec. 42-5024, Reg. R15-5-2002). If the seller imposes an added charge to cover the tax, or a charge identified as being to cover the tax, the seller cannot remit less than the amount collected to the state (Sec. 42-5002).

The use tax is the responsibility of the person who is storing, using, or consuming tangible personal property in the state, and the responsibility is not extinguished until the tax has been paid to the state (Sec. 42-5155(D), Sec. 42-5160). However, every retailer that maintains a place of business in Arizona is required to collect the use tax from the purchaser or user at the time of a taxable sale (Sec. 42-5160, Sec. 42-5161). The tax remains a liability of the purchaser until the tax is paid to the state, although a receipt showing the tax paid issued by an Arizona retailer or a retailer authorized to collect the tax extinguishes the purchaser's liability for the tax (Sec. 42-5155(D), Sec. 42-5155(E)).

Remote sales: A ruling clarifies the imposition of transaction privilege tax on sales of tangible personal property by out-of-state mail-order or Internet-based ("remote") vendors and the responsibility for use tax collection by such vendors. Ascertaining whether a remote vendor is liable for transaction privilege tax, is responsible for collecting use tax, or has no liability for either tax requires a determination of the vendor's nexus with the state. (*Arizona Transaction Privilege Tax Ruling TPR 08-1*, Arizona Department of Revenue, July 30, 2008, CCH ARIZONA TAX REPORTS, ¶ 400-955)

Sourcing of sales: A remote vendor that is liable for Arizona transaction privilege tax or collection of Arizona use tax must charge, collect, and remit the tax based on the rate in effect at the physical location of the customer. The vendor may rely on the shipping address provided for a transaction to determine the customer's physical location. (*Arizona Transaction Privilege Tax Ruling TPR 08-1,* Arizona Department of Revenue, July 30, 2008, CCH ARIZONA TAX REPORTS, ¶ 400-955).

Contractors: A contractor may be subject to the transaction privilege tax on its contracting business under either the prime contracting classification or the owner-builder sales classification. Materials purchased by a TPT-licensed contractor for incorporation into a construction project are not subject to retail TPT at the time of purchase from a retailer, because such projects are subject to prime contracting TPT.

A "prime contractor" is a contractor that is responsible for the completion of the contract and that supervises, performs, or coordinates the modification of any building, highway, road, railroad, excavation, manufactured building or other structure, project, development or improvement including contracting with any subcontractors or specialty contractors. Generally, a person who owns real property, who engages contractors to modify that real property and who does not itself modify that real property, is not a prime contractor regardless of the existence of a contract for sale or the subsequent sale of that real property; see Secs. 42-5075(A) and (F).

Effective January 1, 2015, nonconstruction or service contractors, are exempted from prime contracting on both the state and city levels. Contractors who only enter into "MMRA" contracts with owners of real property to maintain, repair, replace, or alter their property must pay tax at the point of purchase on the building materials used in those projects. See *Transaction Privilege Tax Notice 15-1,* Arizona Department of Revenue, April 9, 2015, CCH ARIZONA TAX REPORTS, ¶ 401-270.

• **Nexus**

Retailers maintaining a place of business in Arizona and utility businesses must collect the use tax on their sales of tangible personal property for storage, use, or other consumption in the state (Sec. 42-5161). The term "retailer" is defined to include every person engaged in the business of making sales of tangible personal property for storage, use, or other consumption. The term also includes persons that solicit orders for tangible personal property by mail if the solicitations are substantial and recurring and that benefit from any banking, financing, debt collection, telecommunication, television shopping system, cable, optic, microwave, or other communication system or marketing activities in the state or benefit from the location of authorized installation, servicing, or repair facilities in the state. (Sec. 42-5151(17)).

- **Streamlined Act status**

Arizona has enacted an abridged version of the Uniform (Simplified) Sales and Use Tax Administration Act (H.B. 2178, Laws 2002). Arizona is an Advisor Member of the Agreement because, although it has enacted legislation authorizing it to enter into the Agreement, it has not enacted the changes to its laws necessary to comply with the Agreement's requirements.

¶ 232   **Tax Base**

Arizona's transaction privilege (sales) taxes are assessed against specific "classifications" of business, like the retail or restaurant classifications. Each of these classifications has its own statutory tax base.

In most cases, the tax base is the gross proceeds of sales or the gross income derived from the business. "Gross income" means the gross receipts of a taxpayer derived from trade, business, commerce or sales and the value accruing from the sale of tangible personal property or service, or both, without any deduction on account of losses (Sec. 42-5001(4)).

"Gross proceeds of sales" is defined as the value accruing from the sale of tangible personal property without any deduction on account of the cost of the property sold, expense of any kind, or losses (Sec. 42-5001(5)).

"Gross receipts" means the total amount of the sale, lease or rental price of the retail sales of retailers, including any services that are part of the sales, valued in money, whether received in money or otherwise, including all receipts, cash, credits and property of every kind or nature without deduction for cost of the property sold, materials used, labor, interest, losses or any other expenses (Sec. 42-5001(7)). A regulation specifically provides that the cost of labor employed in manufacturing, processing, or fabricating tangible personal property is not allowed as a deduction from the gross receipts derived from a sale of such property (Reg. R15-5-126). A similar use tax regulation disallows a deduction from the purchase price for the cost of labor employed in manufacturing, processing, or fabricating the tangible personal property (Reg. R15-5-2326).

Excluded from gross income, gross receipts, or gross proceeds of sales are any amounts from transactions or activities that would not be taxable if engaged in by a person not subject to any classification of the transaction privilege tax, and transactions or activities that would not be taxable under any classification due to an exemption, exclusion, or deduction (Sec. 42-5002(C)).

- **Use tax basis**

The tax base of the use tax is the sales price paid to a retailer (Sec. 42-5155). The "purchase price" or "sales price" means the total amount for which tangible personal property is sold, including any services that are a part of the sale, valued in money, whether paid in money or otherwise (Sec. 42-5151(4)). The use tax rate is the same as the transaction privilege (sales) tax rate applied to retailers.

Direct mail advertising: A taxpayer in the business of selling cooperative direct mail advertising was not subject to Arizona use tax. Under both the dominant purpose test and the common understanding test, the court found that the taxpayer's business consisted of the nontaxable services of designing, mailing, and printing, not the taxable selling of tangible personal property; therefore, the transaction was not subject to the use tax. (*Val-Pak East Valley, Inc. v. Arizona Department of Revenue,* Arizona Court of Appeals, Div. One, No. 1 CA-TX 10-0005, March 13, 2012, CCH ARIZONA TAX REPORTS, ¶ 401-122).

¶ 233   List of Exemptions, Exceptions, and Exclusions

Unless otherwise indicated, the statutory exemptions, exceptions, and exclusions listed below apply to both sales and use taxes; those applicable only to the use tax are listed separately. Items that are excluded from the sales or use tax base are discussed at ¶ 232, "Tax Base."

• **Sales and use tax exemptions, exceptions, and exclusions**

Advertising	Sec. 42-5065(B)(1)
Agriculture	Sec. 42-5061, Sec. 42-5159
Agricultural aircraft	Sec. 42-5061(B)(13), Sec. 42-4159(B)(13)
Aircraft repair or maintenance	Sec. 42-5061(B)(8), Sec. 42-5159(B)(8)
Aircraft and related equipment	Sec. 42-5061(B)(7), Sec. 42-5159(B)(7)
Alternative fuels	Sec. 42-6004(A)(9)
Amusement classification exemptions	Sec. 42-5073
Arizona exposition and state fair board	Sec. 42-5073(A)(3)
Arizona health sciences center food	Sec. 42-5102(B)
Auction sales of motor vehicles to nonresidents	Sec. 42-5061(A)(44)
Bed and breakfast establishments	Sec. 42-5070(B)(3)
Billboards (leasing or renting)	Sec. 42-5071
Book publishing	Sec. 42-5065(A)(1)
Breeding animals	Sec. 42-5061(B)(5), Sec. 42-5159(B)(5)
Bullion	Sec. 42-5061(A)(21)
Buses	Sec. 42-5061(B)(11), Sec. 42-5159(B)(11)
Cable television services	Sec. 42-5064
Charitable organizations	Sec. 42-5061(A)(4), Sec. 42-5159(A)(15)(a)
Chemicals used in manufacturing, mining, and research and development	Sec. 42-5061(A)(39), Sec. 42-5061(A)(40), Sec. 42-5159(A)(31), Sec. 42-5159(A)(35)
Chemicals used in printing	Sec. 42-5061(A)(40), Sec. 42-5159(A)(35)
Child and adult day care centers food	Sec. 42-5102(C)(2), Sec. 42-5102(C)(3)
Child Nutrition Act	Sec. 42-5061(A)(16), Sec. 42-5159(A)(23)
Cleanrooms	Sec. 42-5061(B)(17), Sec. 42-5159(B)(17)
Coin-operated amusement devices	Sec. 42-5073(A)

Eyeglasses and contact lenses (prescription)	Sec. 42-5061(A)(11), Sec. 42-5159(A)(18)
Fine art, sales at an auction or gallery to nonresidents for delivery out of state	H.B. 2536, Laws 2016
Food	Sec. 42-5061(A)(5), Sec. 42-5061(A)(15)
Food and nonalcoholic drinks served gratuitously to hotel guests . . .	Sec. 42-5061(A)(47), Sec. 42-5159(A)(33)(k)
Food sold to airlines for service to passengers	Sec. 42-5061(A)(50), Sec. 42-5159(A)(43)
Food sold for service at schools	Sec. 42-5074(B)(11), Sec. 42-5159(A)(26)
Food sold from vending machines and consumed off premises	Sec. 42-5102
Food sold or consumed at prisons	Sec. 42-5061(A)(42), Sec. 42-5159(A)(36)
Food stamps (Supplemental Nutrition Assistance), purchases with . .	Sec. 42-5061(A)(16), Sec. 52-5106, Sec. 42-5159(A)(23)
Football, intercollegiate and Super Bowl	Sec. 42-5073(A)(7)
Forest products (biomass); construction and equipment	Sec. 42-5061(B)(22), Sec. 42-5071(B)(2)(b)(ii), Sec. 42-5075(B)(18), Sec. 42-5159(B)(22)
Fraternal benefit societies	Sec. 20-883
Fuel for on-site power and utilities of environmental technology facilities	Sec. 42-5061(A)(39), Sec. 42-5063(C)(4), Sec. 42-5159(A)(31)
Fuel, locomotive diesel in fuel tanks	Sec. 42-5166
Funeral services	Sec. 42-5061(A)(1), Sec. 42-5061(A)(2)
Gas (liquefied petroleum) in manufacturing or smelting operations . .	Sec. 42-5159(G)(1)
Gas (natural) transportation services	Sec. 42-5063(c)(6), Sec. 42-5159(G)(1)
Groundwater measuring devices	Sec. 42-5061(B)(12), Sec. 42-5075(B)(2), Sec. 42-5159(B)(12)
Hazardous waste cleanup	Sec. 42-5075(B)(6)
Health club fees at resort hotels	Sec. 42-5073(B)(1), Sec. 42-5073(C)(1)
Health club membership fees	Sec. 42-5073(B)
Healthy forest enterprises (various incentives)	Sec. 41-1516, 42-5061(B)(21), 42-5159(B)(21),
Hearing aids	Sec. 42-5061(A)(12), Sec. 42-5071(B)(2)(a), Sec. 42-5159(A)(20)

Hospital beds . . . . Sec. 42-5061(A)(13),
Sec. 42-5071(B)(2)(a),
Sec. 42-5159(A)(15),
Sec. 42-5159(A)(21)

Hospitals (qualified) . . . . Sec. 42-5001(10),
Sec. 42-5001(11),
Sec. 42-5061(A)(25)(a),
Sec. 42-5063(C)(3)(a),
Sec. 42-5065(B)(2)(a),
Sec. 42-5066(B)(3)(a)

Housing, charitable organizations that provide federally subsidized
    apartments for seniors . . . . Sec. 42-5061(A)(25)(f),
Sec. 42-5075(B)(12),
Sec. 42-5159(A)(13)(l)

Ice and dry ice used in packaging food . . . . Sec. 42-5106(B)(2)

Ignition interlock devices (breathalyzers), leased or rented . . . . Sec. 42-5071(A)(8),
Sec. 42-6004(A)(13)

Installation of machinery or equipment . . . . Sec. 42-5075(B)(7)

Insulin . . . . Sec. 42-5061(A)(10),
Sec. 42-5159(A)(19)

Internet access . . . . Sec. 42-5064

Interstate and foreign transactions . . . . Sec. 42-5061(A)(24),
Sec. 42-5061(A)(36)

Intrastate telecommunications services . . . . Sec. 42-5064

Job printing classification exemptions . . . . Sec. 42-5066

Lawn maintenance services . . . . Sec. 42-5075(I)

Launch site construction . . . . Sec. 42-5075(B)(14)

Leasing or renting (various exemptions) . . . . Sec. 42-5071(A)

Leasing mineral rights . . . . Sec. 42-5069(C)(17)

Leasing or renting property for religious worship . . . . Sec. 42-5069(C)(11)

Liquidation sales . . . . Sec. 42-5061(A)(41),
Sec. 42-5159(A)(40)

Liquor wholesalers . . . . Sec. 42-5061(A)(51)

Livestock and poultry feed . . . . Sec. 42-5061(A)(44),
Sec. 42-5159(A)(8)

Lottery tickets . . . . Sec. 42-5061(A)(20),
Sec. 42-5159(A)(27)

Low-income apartment providers . . . . Sec. 42-5159(A)(13)(l)

Machinery and equipment used in agriculture . . . . Sec. 42-5061(B)(20),
Sec. 42-5159(B)(20)

Machinery and equipment used in computer data centers . . . . Sec. 42-5061(A)(59),
Sec. 42-5159(A)(54),
Sec. 42-6004(A)(13)

Machinery and equipment used in job printing . . . . Sec. 42-5061(B)(1),
Sec. 42-5159(B)(1)

Machinery and equipment used in producing or transmitting electric
    power . . . . Sec. 42-5061(B)(4),
Sec. 42-5159(B)(4)

Machinery and equipment used in satellite television or data
transmission facilities . . . .   Sec. 42-5061(B)(16),
Sec. 42-5061(C)(4),
Sec. 42-5061(P),
Sec. 42-5064(B)(1)(b),
Sec. 42-5064(B)(4),
Sec. 42-5159(B)(16),
Sec. 42-5159(C)(4)

Maintenance or repair contracts with a homeowner . . . .   Sec. 42-5075(O),
Sec. 42-6004(A)(13)

Manufacturers sales made direct to U.S. government . . . .   Sec. 42-5061(K),
Sec. 42-5159(A)(39)

Manufacturing machinery or equipment . . . .   Sec. 42-5061(B)(1),
Sec. 42-5061(C)(1),
Sec. 42-5071(B)(2)(b),
Sec. 42-5159(B)(1),
Sec. 42-5159(C)(1)

Medical oxygen and equipment . . . .   Sec. 42-5061(A)(8),
Sec. 42-5159(A)(16)

Medical supplies and drugs . . . .   Sec. 42-5061(A)(8)—
Sec. 42-5061(A)(13),
Sec. 42-5159(A)(16)—
Sec. 42-5159(A)(21)

Military reuse zones (construction) . . . .   Sec. 42-5075(B)(4),
Sec. 42-5075(B)(5)

Milk extracting and cooling equipment . . . .   Sec. 42-5061(B)(13),
Sec. 42-5159(B)(13)

Mining classification exemptions . . . .   Sec. 42-5072,
Sec. 42-5061(B)(2),
Sec 42-5061(S),
Sec 42-5072(F),
Sec. 42-5159(A)(54),
(B)(2),
Sec 42-6004(A)(14)

Motion pictures leased to theaters covered by amusement
classification . . . .   Sec. 42-5071(A)(1)

Motor fuel . . . .   Sec. 42-5061(A)(22),
Sec. 42-5071(B)(3),
Sec. 42-5159(A)(5)

Motor vehicles, alternative fuel . . . .   Sec. 42-5061(A)(51),
Sec. 42-5159(A)(44),
Sec. 42-6004(A)(9)

Motor vehicles sold to nonresidents . . . .   Sec. 42-5061(A)(28), (46)

Motor vehicles sold to Native Americans living on reservations . . . .   Sec. 42-5061(A)(28)(b)

Natural gas and liquified petroleum gas . . . .   Sec. 42-5061(A)(36), (38),

Sec. 42-5061(R),
Sec. 42-5063(B)(2),
Sec. 42-5067(A),
Sec. 42-5159(A)(33),
45(B)

Television, satellite broadcasting facilities	Sec. 42-5061(B)(16),
	Sec. 42-5061(C)(4),
	Sec. 42-5061(P),
	Sec. 42-5064(B)(1),
	Sec. 42-5064(B)(4),
	Sec. 42-5159(B)(16),
	Sec. 42-5159(C)(4)
Textbooks (college)	Sec. 42-5061(A)(17),
	Sec. 42-5159(A)(28)
Tourist magazines	Sec. 42-5065(A)(2),
	Sec. 42-5159(A)(29)
Tractors	Sec. 42-5061(B)(13),
	Sec. 42-5159(B)(13)
Training for persons with disabilities	Sec. 42-5061(A)(29)
Transient lodging classification exemptions	Sec. 42-5070
Transportation facilities	Sec. 28-7705(A),
	Sec. 28-7705(B),
	Sec. 42-5069(C)(16)
Transportation network companies	Sec. 42-5062(A)(1),
	Sec. 42-6004(C)
Transporting classification exemptions	Sec. 42-5062
United States sales (50% reduction)	Sec. 42-5061(L)
University or college food	Sec. 42-5102(B)
Urban mass transit vehicles	Sec. 42-5061(B)(11),
	Sec. 42-5071(B)(2),
	Sec. 42-5159(B)(11)
Used manufactured building, sale of	Sec. 42-5075(A, K)
Utilities classification exemptions	Sec. 42-5061(B)(4),
	Sec. 42-5159(B)(4)
Vehicles purchased for rental	Sec. 42-5061(A)(43),
	Sec. 42-5159(A)(37)
Veterinary drugs and medicines	Sec. 42-5061(A)(8),
	Sec. 42-5061(A)(45),
	Sec. 42-5159(A)(7)
Warranty or service contracts	Sec. 42-5061(A)(3)

• Exemptions, exceptions, and exclusions applicable only to the use tax

Breeding stock	Sec. 42-5159(B)(5)
Disaster recovery: infrastructure temporarily brought into Arizona during the disaster period	Sec. 42-1130(B)(2)
Livestock, poultry feed and supplies used by farmers and ranchers . .	Sec. 42-5159(A)(8)
Materials for libraries, unavailable in Arizona	Sec. 42-5159(A)(12)
Motor vehicles provided by dealer for charitable or educational organizations, public schools, or state universities	Sec. 42-5159(A)(32)
Newspaper advertising supplements	Sec. 42-5159(A)(11)
Nonresident's property (first used outside Arizona)	Sec. 42-5159(A)(6)
Property already subject to tax by other states, including advertising supplements	Sec. 42-5159(A)(11)
Property incorporated into manufactured product	Sec. 42-5159(A)(4)

Property purchased by certain nonprofit institutions . . . .   Sec. 42-5159(A)(13)

Purchases for personal use from out of state (limit $200) . . . .   Sec. 42-5159(A)(10)

School district or charter school purchases (local exemption only) . .   Sec. 42-6004(F)

¶ 234   Rate of Tax

Tax rates for the transaction privilege (sales) tax and the use tax are provided below.

• Transaction privilege tax

The rate of tax is 5.6% of the tax base on the business classifications listed below beginning June 1, 2013. The rate was temporarily increased to 6.6% on the below classifications from June 1, 2010, until May 31, 2013. The rate is scheduled to decrease to 5% on July 1, 2021. (Sec. 42-5010(A))

Amusements;

Job printing;

Online lodging marketplace;

Owner builder sales;

Personal property rentals;

Pipelines;

Prime contracting;

Private car lines;

Publications;

Restaurants;

Retail;

Telecommunications;

Transporting; and

Utilities.

Other classifications are taxed at the following rates:

Mining—$3\frac{1}{8}$%;

Transient lodging—$5\frac{1}{2}$%.

Rental vehicle surcharge: Persons in Arizona engaged in the business of renting motor vehicles without drivers must collect a 5% surcharge when the rental is for a period of 180 days or less. "Rental vehicle" means (Sec. 28-5810):

(1) a passenger vehicle designed to transport 15 or fewer passengers and that is rented without a driver, or

(2) a truck, trailer, or semitrailer with a gross weight of less than 26,000 pounds that is rented without a driver and used to transport personal property.

The surcharge is not imposed on pickup trucks or utility trailers that are rented for hauling property and that are subject to proportional registration. The surcharge does not apply to the lease or rental of a motor vehicle used in an employee vanpool arrangement for a group of at least seven, but not more than 14, passengers including a driver (Sec. 5-839(D)(2)).

The surcharge is based on the total amount stated in the rental contract, less any transaction privilege (sales) taxes and county stadium district surtaxes. Further, the surcharge is not subject to either of these two taxes. The amount of the surcharge must be noted on the rental contract (Sec. 28-5810).

Commercial leases: This classification remains in the statutes (Sec. 42-5069), even though the tax rate has been 0% since 1997.

Contracting: The tax base for the prime contracting classification is 65% of the gross proceeds of sales or gross income derived from the business, after specified deductions (Sec. 42-5075(B)). For information on 2015 amendments to taxation of contractors, see *Transaction Privilege Tax Notice 14-1,* Arizona Department of Revenue, November 18, 2014, CCH Arizona Tax Reports, ¶ 401-263.

- **Use tax rate**

The use tax is imposed at the same rate as the transaction privilege tax applied to retailers and utility businesses (Sec. 42-5155(C)). The use tax rate is also applied to tangible personal property provided under the terms of a warranty or service contract (Sec. 42-5156).

¶ 235   Local Taxes

Arizona counties and cities are authorized to levy local transaction privilege (sales) taxes. Any Arizona county, with voter approval, may levy a transportation excise tax and/or a transportation excise tax for roads (Sec. 42-6106).

Residential rentals: Towns or cities may not impose or increase the tax rate for residential rental property unless the change is approved by voters at a regular municipal election. However, this does not apply to health care facilities, long-term care facilities, or transient lodging businesses such as hotels and motels. (Sec. 42-6011)

Cable TV limitation: The total of the rates of local license fees and local transaction privilege taxes on gross revenues from providing cable television service in a local jurisdiction may not exceed 5% (Sec. 9-506).

Local tax rates for Arizona counties and most cities *(i.e.,* program cities) are available on the Department of Revenue's website at **https://www.azdor.gov/ Portals/0/TPTRates/01012017_RateTable.pdf**.

- **Nonprogram cities**

Although the Arizona Department of Revenue generally collects the sales taxes imposed by Arizona cities, certain cities in the state administer their own sales taxes. The Department of Revenue has compiled a list of telephone numbers for these nonprogram cities (see below) so that taxpayers can contact each nonprogram city directly for information about its sales tax. The discussion immediately below outlines the taxes imposed by Phoenix and Tucson, which are the largest nonprogram cities.

Phoenix privilege license tax: Phoenix levies a city privilege license tax that is administered locally. The city rates are as follows (Phoenix Tax Code): 0.5% for advertising; 2.0% for retailing, construction contracting, timbering and other extractions, job printing, publishing, transportation, restaurants, bars, caterers, rental of tangible personal property, rental of residential real property (including lodging over 30 days), amusements, speculative builders, owner-builders, and manufactured buildings; 2.1% for rental of nonresidential real property; 2.7% for utilities, wastewater removal services; 4.0% for short-term motor vehicle leasing; 5.0% for lodging of 30 days or less; and 4.7% for cable television and telecommunications services. The city also levies a 2.0% use tax and a sales and use tax of .732 cents per gallon of jet fuel. State, county, and city combined rates are available on the website of the City of Phoenix at **https:// www.phoenix.gov/financesite/Documents/107710.pdf**.

Tucson transaction privilege tax: Tucson levies a privilege tax at the rate of 2% on the gross income of those engaged in the following businesses (Sec. 19-400, Tucson City Code): amusements; construction contracting; job printing; timbering, and extracting oil or natural gas; publishing; leasing or renting real property; leasing or renting tangible personal property; food and drink establishments; retailing; telecommunication services; transporting for hire; and utility services. The rate for mining is 0.1%. For additional information, see the website of the City of Tucson at **https:// www.tucsonaz.gov/files/finance/Revenue/TaxRates2016.pdf**.

Tax rates: Tax rates and additional information for cities and counties is available at **https://www.azdor.gov/TransactionPrivilegeTax(TPT)/ RatesandDeductionCodes.aspx**.

¶ 236   **Bracket Schedule**

Arizona does not use a bracket schedule.

¶ 237   **Returns, Payments, and Due Dates**

Transaction privilege (sales) taxes must be paid and reported to the Department of Revenue every month using a combined sales, use, and severance tax return (Sec. 42-5014, *General Tax Procedure GTP 96-2*, Dept. of Revenue, Oct. 15, 1996). The Arizona Department of Revenue has authority to allow taxpayers to replace monthly payments of transaction privilege (sales) taxes with quarterly or annual payments (Sec. 42-5014(B), Sec. 42-5162(B)). Effective January 1, 2015, taxpayers with annual liabilities between $2,000 and $8,000 must pay taxes quarterly, and taxpayers with liabilities of less than $2,000 must pay annually. Previously, taxpayers with liabilities of less than $500 had to pay taxes annually, and taxpayers with liabilities between $500 and $1,250 were allowed to pay quarterly. (Sec. 42-5014(B)). All other taxpayers must continue to pay sales taxes monthly.

Monthly reports: The due date for monthly payments and returns is the 20th day of the month after the month in which sales tax liability arises (Sec. 1-218, Sec. 1-301). The Arizona Department of Revenue will consider mailed transaction privilege tax payments delinquent if they are not postmarked by the 25th of the month or if the payment is not received on or before the second to last business day of the month in which the tax is due (Sec. 42-5014(A)(2)).

Electronic filing: Taxpayers subject to Arizona transaction privilege (sales) and use tax may file their returns electronically. Rules provide definitions and procedures for taxpayers to register for electronic filing through the Department of Revenue's website at **https://www.aztaxes.gov/Home**. A Registration Signature Card must be executed and submitted to the Department indicating the accuracy of the taxpayer's signature and the signature of a duly authorized representative if one is appointed to act on behalf of the taxpayer. For each transaction privilege (sales) and use tax return, the record retention requirement is six years (R15-10-502 and R15-10-504).

Electronic payment (EFT): Taxpayers whose total transaction privilege (sales) tax liability in the preceding tax year was $20,000 or more are required to transmit their tax payments to the Arizona Department of Revenue electronically through the EFT (Electronic Funds Transfer) program (Sec. 42-1129; R15-10-302). Taxpayers with a lower tax liability in the preceding year may voluntarily pay taxes electronically (R15-10-303). For additional information, see *Publication 650, Electronic Funds Transfer,* Arizona Department of Revenue, rev. December 2016, CCH Arizona Tax Reports, ¶ 401-345.

A penalty of 5% of the tax due is imposed if a taxpayer fails to make a payment by electronic funds transfer (EFT) when required to do so, unless it is due to reasonable cause and not willful neglect (Sec. 42-1125(O)).

The department has modified the online portal so that taxpayers can pay any and all state, county, or municipality TPT and affiliated excise taxes online (Sec. 42-5015). The department will administer the online portal, and cities and towns who do not have an intergovernmental contract or agreement with the department as of January 1, 2013, will be responsible for the costs. Taxpayers who are required to pay municipal TPT to a city or town without a DOR agreement are allowed to pay the tax through a DOR-administered online portal. Taxpayers who do not pay the required taxes through the portal must pay taxes to the department, provided that the DOR has developed electronic and non-electronic means to capture data with sufficient specificity to meet taxing jurisdictions' needs. For additional information, go to **https:// www.aztaxes.gov/Home**. Users of business services may register at **https:// www.aztaxes.gov/Security/Register**.

Rental vehicles surcharge: On or before February 15 of each year, persons engaged in the business of renting motor vehicles must file a report with the Assistant Director of the Arizona Motor Vehicle Division stating the total vehicle license tax paid the previous year, the total amount of vehicle rental revenues for the previous year, and the amount by which the surcharge exceeds the amount of the vehicle license tax. Any excess surcharges collected by the taxpayer are to be paid to the local registering officer in the same manner and under the same provisions as the vehicle license tax (Sec. 28-5810).

Direct payment permits: The Department of Revenue will issue an Arizona use tax direct payment permit to qualified taxpayers who spent at least $500,000 in the previous year on tangible personal property for the taxpayer's own use (Sec. 42-5167, A.R.S.).

Arizona purchasers that make recurring purchases from out-of-state sources may apply to the Department of Revenue for a registration certificate and remit payment directly to the state on a monthly report form in lieu of remitting use tax to the out-of-state vendor (Reg. R15-5-2310).

Use tax: Taxpayers may be authorized by the Director of Taxation to use a percentage based reporting method to determine the amount of use tax due.

A taxpayer using a percentage based reporting method must (Sec. 42-5168(A) and (G)(2)):

— categorize its purchase transactions according to the standards specified in a letter of authorization issued to the taxpayer by the Director;

— review approved sample invoices for each category of transactions when determining the percentage of taxable transactions; and

— use that percentage to calculate the amount of use tax due.

¶ 238   **Prepayment of Taxes**

Business entities must make an estimated payment of tax by June 20 each year if the taxpayer has an annual total tax liability of $1 million or more under the transaction privilege tax (sales) tax, telecommunications services excise tax, and the county excise tax (Sec. 42-5014(D)). Annual tax liability for purposes of the estimated tax does not include use or severance taxes. Taxpayers who are required, or have elected, to pay tax electronically or through any method that makes a tax payment immediately available to the Department of Revenue must pay estimated tax by June 25 each year.

To calculate annual total tax liability, the taxpayer must aggregate all relevant taxes owed by the business entity under which the taxpayer reports and pays its state income tax.

Even if a taxpayer's annual total tax liability in the preceding calendar year was less than $1 million, the taxpayer may still be required to make an estimated payment of tax in June if the taxpayer reasonably anticipates that its annual total tax liability for the current year will be at least $1 million.

The estimated tax payment due by June 20 or June 25 must equal either (1) one-half of the actual tax liability for May of the current calendar year, or (2) the actual tax liability for the first 15 days of June. The estimated tax payment made in June is credited against the actual June tax liability as computed on the return filed in July. "Tax liability" for these purposes does not include use or severance taxes, but does include the transaction privilege tax, the telecommunications services excise tax, and county excise taxes. (Sec. 42-5014(D))

¶ 239   Vendor Registration

Every person receiving gross proceeds of sales or gross income upon which the transaction privilege (sales) tax is imposed must obtain a privilege license from the Department of Revenue (Sec. 42-5005(A)). The fee for the license is $12 and there is no expiration date.

Retailers required to collect the use tax must also register (Sec. 42-5154, Reg. R15-5-2220). Users of business services may register at **https://www.aztaxes.gov/ Security/Register**.

A person engaged in business at more than one location, or under more than one business name, must obtain a license for each location or business name, and any change of ownership, location, mailing address, or trade name used by the business requires application for a new license. These rules apply to both transaction privilege tax and use tax licenses (Sec. 42-5005; Reg. R15-5-2202—R15-5-2204).

¶ 240   Sales or Use Tax Credits

Use tax credits are allowed in many instances for sales or use taxes paid to other states. The general use tax offset given for sales tax paid in other states is discussed at ¶ 231. A credit in the form of a prompt payment discount is given for collection of the tax. Taxpayers are entitled to credits for excess taxes paid (Sec. 42-1118).

¶ 241   Deficiency Assessments

If a person required to file a transaction privilege (sales) tax return fails or refuses to do so, state law directs the Department of Revenue to obtain facts and information on which to base the tax by examining books, records and papers and taking evidence under oath (Sec. 42-5026). When sufficient information has been obtained, a public hearing is held for the purpose of ascertaining the amount of tax payable. At least 10 days' written notice must be given of the time and place of the hearing. Notice is mailed to the taxpayer at his last known address, or served personally. The assessment of tax after this hearing is final as to any person who fails or refuses to file a return.

In addition to audit provisions found in the transaction privilege (sales) tax statutes, the general administrative provisions on audits, deficiency and jeopardy assessments, penalties, appeals and remedies, as well as the tax lien and levy procedures, apply to transaction privilege (sales) and use taxes (Sec. 42-1101, Sec. 42-1108(A), Sec. 42-1151, Sec. 42-1201).

Collections: Information on the collection process is available in *Publication 2, Collections Process,* Arizona Department of Revenue, January 2014, CCH ARIZONA TAX REPORTS, ¶ 401-219.

¶ 242   Audit Procedures

A transaction privilege (sales) tax provision permits audits if no return is filed (Sec. 42-5026). A general administrative provision permits similar audits if a taxpayer files a false or fraudulent return or fails to file a return within 15 days after the Department's written demand (Sec. 42-1109).

• **General administrative provisions**

A general administrative provision, Sec. 42-1108, also authorizes audits if the Department of Revenue is not satisfied with a return or tax payment. Unless the taxpayer appeals to the Department in writing for a hearing, correction, or redetermination within 45 days after receipt of the Department's deficiency assessment following an audit, the assessment becomes final and is due and payable after ten days from the notice and demand (Sec. 42-1108, Sec. 42-1251). Confidential information related to TPT collected by the department from any jurisdiction may be disclosed, subject to statutory guidelines, to any county, city or town tax official if it relates to a taxpayer who is subject to a department audit (Sec. 42-2003(H)).

• **Transaction privilege (sales) tax provisions**

Taxpayers may be subject only to a single audit, eliminating possible subsequent or joint audits by cities or towns. The department director and cities and towns that levy TPT must enter into agreements with each other to provide for unified or coordinated licensing, collection, and auditing programs. (Sec. 42-6001; Sec. 42-6002)

A transaction privilege (sales) tax statute provides that any additional tax found due following an audit under Sec. 42-1108, is payable within 30 days after receipt of the assessment, or if an appeal is filed with the Department, within ten days after the Department's decision on the appeal becomes final (Sec. 42-5021).

• **Managed audits**

A taxpayer may apply for a managed audit agreement with the Department of Revenue. The Department Director has sole discretion whether to enter into a managed audit agreement with the taxpayer. Such an agreement would allow for an audit by the taxpayer of certain business activities for a specified time period (Sec. 42-2302).

¶ 243   **Statute of Limitations**

The Department of Revenue must mail notices of additional tax due (deficiency assessments) within four years after the report or return was required to be filed or was actually filed, whichever is later (Sec. 42-1104).

If a taxpayer omits in excess of 25% of gross income or gross receipts from the amount stated in the return, the tax may be assessed at any time within six years after the return was filed.

In the case of false or fraudulent returns filed with intent to evade tax, or failure to file a return, the Department of Revenue can assess the tax at any time.

The statutes of limitation on assessments also apply to claims for credit or refund except that the limitations period for a credit or refund claim based on accounts that subsequently became a bad debt is seven years from the date prescribed for filing the return with respect to which the claim is made (Sec. 42-1106).

Tax levies must be made and collection suits must be initiated by the Department of Revenue within ten years following the date on which the amount of tax determined to be due becomes final (Sec. 42-1114, Sec. 42-1201). The taxpayer and the Department may extend the time by executing a written agreement before expiration of the limitation period.

¶ 244   **Application for Refund**

If the Department of Revenue determines that any amount of tax, penalty or interest has been paid in excess of the amount actually due, it is to credit the excess amount against any tax it administers or refund that amount (Sec. 42-1118(A)). Interest is added to all overpayments of tax (Sec. 42-1123).

A claim for refund must be in writing and must specify the grounds for the claim (Sec. 42-1118(D)). Claims must specify the amount of refund requested and the tax years involved in addition to the claimant's name, address, and tax identification number. Denial of a refund claim by the Department of Revenue is final unless the taxpayer appeals to the Department for redetermination in writing within the time and in the manner prescribed by Sec. 42-1251 for appealing a deficiency assessment (Sec. 42-1119). The Department's failure to act on a taxpayer's refund claim within six months is deemed a denial of the claim for appeal purposes (Sec. 42-1119).

Claims for refund must be filed within the period set by the statute of limitations on assessments or within six months of payment of a deficiency assessment, whichever period is later (Sec. 42-1106, Sec. 42-1251).

¶ 246   Scope of Tax

Source.—Statutory references are to Chapters 52 and 53 of Title 26 of the Arkansas Code Annotated, as amended to date. Details are reported in the CCH ARKANSAS TAX REPORTS starting at ¶ 60-000.

The Arkansas gross receipts (sales) tax is an excise tax on gross receipts from the sale of tangible personal property and specified services. The compensating (use) tax is a complementary tax and does not apply in situations where the sales tax is collected (Sec. 26-53-112). The sales tax is in addition to other taxes (Sec. 26-52-104).

Digital products: Tax applies to the sale of a subscription for digital audio-visual work and digital audio work if the end user does not have the right of permanent use granted by the seller and the use is contingent on continued payments by the purchaser. "Digital audio-visual work" means an electronically transferred series of related images that when shown in succession, impart an impression of motion, together with accompanying sounds, if any. "Digital audio work" means an electronically transferred work that results from the fixation of a series of musical, spoken, or other sounds, including ringtones. (Sec. 6-52-301(3)(C))

If a commercial software development company delivers software to its customers electronically rather than on a CD, a flash drive, or some other tangible medium, the sale of the software is not subject to Arkansas sales tax. (*Revenue Legal Opinion,* No. 20160107, Arkansas Department of Finance and Administration, January 29, 2016, CCH ARKANSAS TAX REPORTS, ¶ 400-614)

Effective January 1, 2018, the definition of "tangible personal property" is amended to exclude specified digital products or a digital code (Sec. 26-52-103(21)). Also, the definitions of "ancillary service" and "telecommunications service" for purposes of imposing sales tax do not include specified digital products or a digital code (Sec. 26-52-315(e)(2)(B); Sec. 26-52-315(e)(19)(C)(x)). However, sales and use tax is specifically imposed on sales of specified digital products sold to a purchaser who is an end user with the right of permanent or less than permanent use granted by the seller, regardless of whether the use is conditioned on continued payment by the purchaser, and on sales of digital codes (Sec. 26-52-301(1)(B)). "Specified digital products" means digital audio works, digital audio-visual works, and digital books when they are transferred electronically (Sec. 26-52-103(33)). "Digital code" means a code that provides a purchaser with a right to obtain one or more specified digital products and that may be obtained by any means, including email or tangible means, regardless of its designation as a song code, video code, or book code (Sec. 26-52-103(29)).

Concerning the sourcing of sales of specified digital products or digital codes for tax purposes, if none of the specific sourcing rules applies (see ¶ 252) or if the seller lacks sufficient information, the location of the sale will be determined by the address from which the specified digital product or digital code was first available for transmission by the seller. (Sec. 26-52-521(b)(5))

Software and software maintenance contracts: Sales of computer software, including prewritten computer software, are taxed as sales of tangible personal property (Sec. 26-52-304(a)). Gross receipts or gross proceeds derived from the sale of a computer software maintenance contract are not taxable (Sec. 26-52-304(d)). "Computer software maintenance contract" means a contract that obligates a software vendor to provide a customer with software updates or upgrades, software support services, or both.

For additional information, see *Revenue Legal Opinion,* No. 20150908, Arkansas Department of Finance and Administration, January 14, 2016, CCH ARKANSAS TAX REPORTS, ¶ 400-620.

- **Services subject to tax**

The definition of "sale" does not include the furnishing or rendering of services, except for services specifically mentioned by statute, including certain utility services, telephone or telecommunications services, lodging, cleaning services, cable television services, printing services, photography and admission to places of amusement (Sec. 26-52-301). If a taxable service is performed in Arkansas, the gross receipts tax is due even if the customer is from another state.

The following services are subject to the gross receipts (sales) tax: (1) wrecker and towing; (2) collection and disposal of solid wastes; (3) cleaning parking lots and gutters; (4) dry cleaning and laundry; (5) industrial laundry; (6) body piercing, tattooing, and electrolysis; (7) pest control; (8) security and alarm monitoring; (9) boat storage and docking fees; (10) furnishing camping spaces or trailer spaces at public or privately-owned campgrounds, except federal campgrounds, on less than a month-to-month basis; (11) locksmith; and (12) pet grooming and kennel services (Sec. 26-52-316; Reg. 2004-1). The regulation provides exemptions, guidelines for the collection of state and local taxes, and related definitions for each service subject to tax.

Prepaid telecommunications: Sales of a prepaid calling service or a prepaid wireless calling service and the recharge of a prepaid calling service or a prepaid wireless calling service are subject to Arkansas gross receipts (sales) and compensating (use) tax (Sec. 26-52-314).

- **Compensating (use) tax**

The compensating (use) tax complements the gross receipts tax, protecting Arkansas merchants from discrimination arising from the inability of the state to impose the gross receipts tax on out-of-state purchases by Arkansas residents. It is not imposed in situations where the gross receipts tax has already been paid or where a transaction would be exempt from the gross receipts tax (Sec. 26-53-112(2)). In addition, if another state's gross receipts (or sales) tax is paid, the Arkansas compensating (use) tax is imposed only to the extent that the Arkansas levy exceeds that imposed by the other state (Sec. 26-53-131).

The compensating (use) tax is imposed on the privilege of storing, using, distributing, or consuming within Arkansas any article of tangible personal property once that property has finally come to rest in Arkansas or become commingled with the general mass of property in the state (Sec. 26-53-106, Reg. UT-4).

The compensating use tax does not apply to services performed outside the state (Reg. UT-12). The tax does apply to any tangible personal property that is a part of a sale of services if the property is subsequently brought into Arkansas for storage, use, distribution, or consumption. Moreover, if the charge for the services and the charge for the property are not separately stated, the tax will be due on the entire consideration for the sale.

- **Incidence of gross receipts tax**

The seller of tangible personal property, the collector of admissions to places of amusement or entertainment, or the provider of taxable services must pay the tax to the Department of Finance and Administration (Sec. 26-52-508). The seller or person furnishing services may pass on the tax to the purchaser, but the "seller" is the "taxpayer" and liable to remit the tax (Reg. GR-3).

- **Incidence of compensating (use) tax**

"Every person storing, using, or consuming tangible personal property purchased from a vendor" is liable for the tax and this liability is not extinguished until the tax has been paid to the state (Sec. 26-53-123). Only a valid receipt from a vendor will relieve a purchaser from further liability for paying the compensating (use) tax.

¶246   Arkansas

Out-of-state vendors: Internet and other out-of-state sellers are required to collect Arkansas use tax on their sales to Arkansas customers if they are affiliated with a business that has a physical presence in Arkansas (Sec. 26-53-124). The law provides that the processing of orders over the Internet or by fax, mail, telephone, or otherwise does not relieve the seller of the obligation to collect tax if (1) the vendor directly or indirectly owns or is owned by a retailer that maintains sales locations in Arkansas, and (2) the vendor either sells the same or a substantially similar line of products as the Arkansas retailer under the same or a similar business name, or the facilities or employees of the Arkansas retailer are used to advertise or promote sales by the vendor to Arkansas purchasers.

Although vendors making sales of tangible personal property for use, storage or consumption in the state are required to collect the compensating (use) tax from their customers (Sec. 26-53-124), the Commerce Clause, Due Process Clause, and other provisions of the U.S. Constitution, and court cases interpreting them, limit the extent to which a state can compel vendors or service providers located in other states to collect its use tax.

To facilitate collection of the compensating (use) tax, there is a presumption that tangible personal property shipped, mailed or brought into the state by the purchaser was purchased for storage, use, or consumption in the state (Sec. 26-53-106).

Drop shipments: The taxability of drop shipments in Arkansas depends on the location of the purchaser (also known as the second seller or the reseller) and the consumer. The location of the first seller (also known as the drop shipper) is irrelevant because the sale from the first seller to the second seller is an exempt sale for resale. (Reg. GR-5; see also *Revenue Legal Counsel Opinion,* No. 20160104, Arkansas Department of Finance and Administration, February 9, 2016, CCH Arkansas Tax Reports, ¶ 400-632)

• Nexus

Arkansas requires every vendor making a sale of tangible personal property directly or indirectly for the purpose of storage, use, distribution, or consumption in the state to collect compensating (use) tax from the purchaser and to remit such amounts to the state. This provision includes all out-of-state vendors that deliver merchandise into Arkansas in their own conveyance, where such merchandise will be stored, used, distributed, or consumed within Arkansas. (Sec. 26-53-124) In addition, certain out-of-sellers are deemed to be doing business in Arkansas and are therefore responsible for collecting and remitting use tax if they come under the state's "affiliate nexus" or "click-through nexus" provisions (see below).

Doing business or engaging in business: "Doing business or engaging in business" is defined as any and all local activity regularly and persistently pursued by any seller or vendor through agents, employees, or representatives, with the object of gain, profit, or advantage, and which results in a sale, delivery, or the transfer of the physical possession of any tangible personal property by the vendor to the vendee. The transfer of the physical possession can be at or from any point within Arkansas, whether from a warehouse, store, office, storage point, rolling store, motor vehicle, delivery conveyance, or by any method or device under the control of the seller effecting such local delivery, without regard to the terms of sale with respect to the point of acceptance of the order, point of payment, or any other condition. (Sec. 26-52-103)

Affiliate nexus: A seller is presumed to be engaged in selling property or taxable services for use in Arkansas if an affiliated person is subject to Arkansas sales and use tax jurisdiction and one of the following conditions exists (Sec. 26-52-117(b)):

(1) the seller sells a similar line of products as the affiliated person and sells the products under the same or a similar business name;

(2) the affiliated person uses its in-state employees or in-state facilities to advertise, promote, or facilitate sales by the seller to consumers;

(3) the affiliated person maintains an office, distribution facility, warehouse or storage place, or similar place of business to facilitate the delivery of property or services sold by the seller to the seller's business;

(4) the affiliated person uses trademarks, service marks, or trade names in the state that are the same or substantially similar to those used by the seller; or

(5) the affiliated person delivers, installs, assembles, or performs maintenance services for the seller's purchasers within the state.

"Affiliated person" means (1) a person that is a member of the same controlled group of corporations as the seller or (2) another entity that bears the same ownership relationship to the seller as a corporation that is a member of the same controlled group of corporations (Sec. 26-52-117(a)). The seller may rebut the affiliate nexus presumption with certain proof (Sec. 26-52-117(c)).

Click-through nexus: If there is no affiliated person, a seller is presumed to be engaged in selling property or taxable services for use in Arkansas if the seller enters into an agreement with one or more Arkansas residents under which the residents, for a commission or other consideration, directly or indirectly refer potential purchasers, whether by a link on an Internet website or otherwise, to the seller (Sec. 26-52-117(d)). The click-through nexus presumption applies only if the cumulative gross receipts from sales by the seller to purchasers in Arkansas who are referred to the seller as described above exceed $10,000 during the preceding 12 months. The seller may rebut the click-through nexus presumption with certain proof. (Sec. 26-52-117(e))

• **Streamlined Act status**

Arkansas is a full member of the Streamlined Sales Tax Governing Board. Arkansas adopted the Uniform Sales and Use Tax Administration Act in 2001 (Secs. 26-20-101 *et seq.*) See also ¶ 252.

¶ 247   Tax Base

The sales tax is imposed on the "gross proceeds" or "gross receipts" derived from sales of tangible personal property and taxable services (Sec. 26-52-301, Sec. 26-52-302, Reg. GR-4). The use tax is imposed on the "sales price" of tangible personal property purchased for storage, use, distribution, or consumption in the state (Sec. 26-53-106, Sec. 26-53-107, Sec. 26-53-108, Reg. UT-4).

In general, "gross receipts" and "gross proceeds" are defined as the total amount of consideration, whether in money or otherwise, for the sale of tangible personal property or a taxable service (Sec. 26-52-103(a)(4), Reg. GR-3). No deduction from the tax base is permitted for the cost of property sold, labor service performed, interest paid, losses, or other expenses.

The "sales price" is the consideration paid or given, or contracted to be paid or given, by the purchaser to the vendor for an article of tangible personal property and for services that are a part of the sale (Sec. 26-52-102, Reg. UT-3). The "sales price" includes any amount for which credit is given to the purchaser by the vendor, and no deduction is permitted for the cost of property sold, labor service performed, interest paid, losses, or other expenses.

Vehicles: The Director is authorized to adopt an alternative method for determining the total consideration to be used as the tax base for sales of manufactured, modular, or mobile homes; aircraft; and motor vehicles, trailers, or semitrailers. If the consideration stated by the parties to the sale is less than the amount determined under the alternative method, the latter amount is presumed to be the total consideration for the sale unless the taxpayer provides evidence establishing that the true consideration is less than the amount determined under the alternative method. (Sec. 26-52-514)

The initial sale of a new manufactured home or modular home is subject to Arkansas sales tax on 62% of the home's sales price (Sec. 26-52-802). No tax is due on the sale of a mobile home or on any subsequent sale of a manufactured or modular home.

¶ 248   List of Exemptions, Exceptions, and Exclusions

Unless otherwise indicated, the statutory exemptions, exceptions, and exclusions listed below apply to both sales and use taxes; those applicable only to the use tax are listed separately. Items that are excluded from the sales or use tax base are treated at ¶ 247, "Tax Base."

Contingent exemption: Gross receipts from the sale of food and food ingredients will not be subject to sales and use tax if and when (1) federal law authorizes the state to collect sales and use tax from sellers who have no physical presence within Arkansas, and (2) the Director of the Department of Finance and Administration determines, during a six-month consecutive period, that the amount of revenues attributable to the collection of tax from sellers who do not have a physical presence in Arkansas is 150% or more of the sales and use tax imposed on food and food ingredients. However, the taxation of food and food ingredients by cities and counties will not change (Sec. 26-52-317; Sec. 26-53-145).

Tax holiday: Certain clothing and school-related items are exempt from Arkansas sales and use tax if sold during the period beginning 12:01 a.m. on the first Saturday in August each year and ending 11:59 p.m. on the following Sunday (Sec. 26-52-444; Reg. 2011-2). State and local sales tax will not be collected during this 48-hour period on the sale of:

> (1) Clothing and footwear if the sales price is less than one hundred dollars ($100) per item;

> (2) Clothing accessories and equipment if the sales price is less than fifty dollars ($50) per item;

> (3) School supplies;

> (4) School art supplies; and

> (5) School instructional materials.

• Sales and use tax exemptions, exceptions, and exclusions

Admission fees at state or local fairs or at any nonprofit rodeo	Sec. 26-52-401(15)
Admission tickets sold by municipalities or counties for places of amusement and athletic, recreational and entertainment events	Sec. 26-52-411
Admission tickets sold for athletic and interscholastic events of elementary and secondary schools	Sec. 26-52-411, Sec. 26-52-412
Advertising space or billboard space	Sec. 26-52-401(13)
Agricultural gas and electricity	Sec 26-52-446, Sec. 26-52-450
Agricultural implements	Sec. 26-52-403(b)
Agricultural products (raw) sold directly to the consumer; cotton; seed	Sec. 26-52-401(18)(A), Sec. 26-52-401(18)(B), Sec. 26-52-401(18)(C)
Agriculture, aquaculture, horticulture—electricity and gas utilities used in	Sec. 26-52-446, Sec. 26-52-450

¶248   Arkansas

Fill materials	Sec. 26-52-401(31)
Food sold for free distribution	Sec. 26-52-401(19), Sec. 26-52-421, Sec. 26-53-127
Food or food ingredients or prepared food sold for teachers and pupils in public school or college nonprofit cafeterias or lunch rooms	Sec. 26-52-401(3)
Food stamp or WIC purchases	Sec. 26-52-401(27)
Fort Smith Clearinghouse	Act 913, Laws 1993
4-H or FFA Clubs (sales to)	Sec. 26-52-401(10)
Fuel-packaging materials, machinery, and equipment	Sec. 26-52-401(37)
Habitat for Humanity, sales to	Sec. 26-52-401(32)
Hospitals or sanitariums, charitable or nonprofit	Sec. 26-52-401(21)
Humane societies	Sec. 26-52-414
Intermodal facilities and their lessees	Sec. 14-143-121
Isolated sales	Sec. 26-52-401(17)
Livestock and poultry products	Sec. 26-52-401(18)(D), Sec. 26-52-401(18)(F)
Livestock reproduction equipment and products	Sec. 26-52-438
Lodging furnished on a month-to-month basis	Sec. 26-52-301(3)(B)
Manufacturing chemicals	Sec. 26-52-401(35)
Manufacturing machinery and equipment (new or improved); repair or replacement (partial refund)	Sec. 26-52-402, Sec. 26-52-447
Medical equipment (durable), mobility-enhancing equipment, prosthetic devices, and disposable medical supplies	Sec. 26-52-433
Medical equipment sold or rented in conjunction with certain Medicare or Medicaid programs	Sec. 26-52-401(20)
Motor fuel on which gasoline or motor vehicle fuel tax previously paid	Sec. 26-52-401(11)
Motor fuels for consumption by vessels, barges and other commercial watercraft and railroads	Sec. 26-52-401(11)
Motor fuels sold for use in municipal buses	Sec. 26-52-417
Motor vehicles and adaptive equipment purchased under certain Veterans Administration programs for disabled veterans (limited exemption)	Sec. 26-52-401(6)
Motor vehicles and school buses sold to political subdivisions	Sec. 26-52-410, Sec. 26-52-420
Motor vehicles, trailers, and semitrailers, new or used, sold for less than $4,000	Sec. 26-52-510(b)
Museums	Sec. 26-52-438, Sec. 26-53-145
Natural gas used in manufacturing glass, steel, tile, tires, agriculture	Sec. 15-4-2401 *et seq.*; Sec. 26-3-310, Sec. 26-52-423, Sec. 26-52-441, Sec. 26-52-446
Newspapers	Sec. 26-52-401(4)

Orphans' or children's homes . . . . Sec. 26-52-413

Poets' Roundtable of Arkansas . . . . Sec. 26-52-401(9)

Pollution control, machinery and equipment required by law . . . . . . Sec. 26-52-401(36),
Sec. 26-52-402,
Sec. 26-53-114

Prescription drugs and oxygen . . . . Sec. 26-52-406

Radio and television companies' purchase of services for use in their
programming . . . . Sec. 26-52-301(D)(ii)

Railroad parts, cars, or equipment brought into Arkansas for repair,
modification or conversion . . . . Sec. 26-52-428,
Sec. 26-53-115

Religious, professional, trade, and sports journals and publications sold
through regular subscriptions . . . . Sec. 26-52-401(14)

Resale sales prohibited from taxation by constitution or law . . . . Sec. 26-52-401(16),
Sec. 26-53-112(1)

Resales . . . . Sec. 26-52-401(12)(A)

Sales that cannot be taxed under the Constitution or laws of the United
States or Arkansas . . . . Sec. 26-52-401(16),
Sec. 26-53-112(1)

Services not specifically mentioned by statute . . . . Sec. 26-52-301

Tea and coffee, specified ingredients for preparing . . . . Sec. 26-72-905(3)

Telephone repair for out-of-state telephones . . . . Sec. 26-52-418

Telephone services obtained with a prepaid calling card . . . . Sec. 26-52-301(3)(A)(iv)(d)

Textbooks, library books, and instructional materials for public
schools . . . . Sec. 26-52-437

Timber harvesting equipment (may be administered as a rebate) . . . Sec. 26-52-431

Trade-ins . . . . Sec. 26-52-401(22)

U.S. government, sales to . . . . Sec. 26-52-401(5)

Unprocessed crude oil . . . . Sec. 26-52-401(23)

Vehicles purchased with Federal Transportation Administration funds
. . . . Sec. 26-52-420

Vessels (limited exemption) . . . . Sec. 26-52-407,
Sec. 26-53-116

Veterans Home of Arkansas . . . . Sec. 26-52-401(25)

Waste fuel . . . . Sec. 26-52-425

Watch and clock repair if the watches and clocks are received by mail
or common carrier from outside Arkansas and returned by mail
or common carrier . . . . Sec. 26-52-301(3)(C)

- **Exemptions, exceptions, and exclusions applicable only to the use tax**

Sales tax paid . . . . Sec. 26-52-401(29)

¶ 249   Rate of Tax

Effective July 1, 2013, the Arkansas general gross receipts (sales) tax rate was increased from 6% to 6.5%. The half-cent rate increase will be collected for approximately 10 years and will terminate when there are no bonds outstanding to which tax collections have been pledged (HJR 1001, Laws 2011; Ballot Issue 1, November 6, 2012, election). The total tax rate is comprised of a basic rate of 3% (Sec. 26-52-301) plus several additional rates (Sec. 26-52-302(a)-(d); Sec. 26-53-107(a)-(d); Reg. GR-4; Sec. 2, Amend. 75, Ark. Const.).

¶249   Arkansas

The compensating (use) tax is imposed at the same rate as the gross receipts tax (Sec. 26-53-106(a), Sec. 26-53-107).

Food and food ingredients: The Arkansas state sales and use tax rate on food and food ingredients is 1.5% (Sec. 26-52-317; 26-53-145). The state rate consists of a 1⅜% statutory rate plus the ⅛% constitutional rate. Food and food ingredients are subject to any applicable local sales and use tax.

Effective January 1, 2018, candy and soft drinks are excluded from the definition of "food and food ingredients," and thus will be subject to the full Arkansas sales and use tax rate instead of the 1.5% reduced rate. (Sec. 26-53-102(5)(B))

The statutory state rate of 1.375%, will be reduced to 0% if the Director of the Department of Finance and Administration determines either (1) that federal law authorizes the collection of sales and use taxes from remote (out-or-state) sellers and that collections will increase by a specified percentage or (2) that certain costs currently incurred by the state have declined by at least $35 million during a six-month period as compared with the same six-month period in the prior year (Sec. 26-52-317(3)).

The 0.125% constitutional tax rate and any local county and city sales and use taxes would remain in effect and continue to apply to food and food ingredients.

Beginning July 1, 2013, the director will begin making a monthly determination as to whether the conditions for the rate reduction under (2) above have been met. In making this determination, the director must consider all economic factors, including pending litigation. If the director finds that the conditions for the rate reduction have been met, the statutory state rate on food and food ingredients will fall to 0% beginning on the first day of the calendar quarter that is at least 30 days following the Director's determination. (Sec. 26-52-317(2)(a))

The term "food and food ingredients" is defined as substances, whether in liquid, concentrated, solid, frozen, dried, or dehydrated form, that are sold for ingestion or chewing by humans and are consumed for their taste or nutritional value (Sec. 26-52-317; 26-53-145). The term does not include alcoholic beverages, candy, soft drinks, tobacco, dietary supplements, or prepared food. These items are therefore not included in the 3% state rate. "Prepared food" is defined as: (1) food sold in a heated state or heated by the seller; (2) two or more food ingredients mixed or combined by the seller for sale as a single item; or (3) food sold with an eating utensil provided by the seller, including a plate, knife, fork, spoon, glass, cup, napkin, or straw. "Prepared food" does not include food that is only cut, repackaged, or pasteurized by the seller, or eggs, fish, meat, poultry, and foods containing these raw animal foods requiring cooking by the consumer to prevent food borne illnesses (Sec. 26-52-317; 26-53-145).

Short-term rentals: Short-term rentals (*i.e.,* rentals of tangible personal property (except motor vehicles, trailers, and farm machinery) for less than 30 days) are subject to a 1% tax that is in addition to the general 6% tax (Sec. 26-52-310, Reg. GR-4). Rental taxes are imposed as special excise taxes under Sec. 26-63-301 *et seq.*

Rental vehicle taxes: Short-term rentals of motor vehicles are subject to a 5% tax that is in addition to the gross receipts or compensating use taxes imposed on the transaction (Sec. 26-52-311, Reg. GR-4). Short-term rentals of gasoline or diesel powered trucks rented or leased for residential moving or shipping are subject to a residential moving tax imposed at the rate of 4.5% (Sec. 26-52-312). Rental taxes are imposed as special excise taxes under Sec. 26-63-301 *et seq.*

Prior to July 1, 2015, long-term rentals of vehicles (30 days or more) were subject to a 1.5% tax on the gross receipts or gross proceeds from the rentals on the basis of the rental or lease payments made to the lessor during the time of the lease or rental. Excluded from the tax were diesel trucks used in commercial shipping, farm machinery and equipment, and gasoline or diesel trucks used for residential moving or shipping. Rental taxes are imposed as special excise taxes under Sec. 26-63-301 *et seq.*

Electricity and natural gas used in manufacturing or electric power generation: The sales and use tax rate on the sale of natural gas and electricity to a manufacturer for use or consumption directly in the actual manufacturing process is 0.625%, effective July 1, 2015 (previously, 1.625%; see below) plus any local rate. Natural gas and electricity subject to the reduced tax rate must be separately metered from natural gas and electricity used for any other purpose by the manufacturer. A "manufacturer" means a manufacturer classified within sectors 31 through 33 of the North American Industry Classification System, as in effect on January 1, 2007. The Department of Finance and Administration may require a seller of natural gas or electricity to obtain a certificate from the consumer certifying that the latter is eligible to purchase natural gas and electricity at the reduced tax rate (Sec. 26-52-319(a)).

Beginning January 1, 2015, the state sales and use tax rate on natural gas and electricity used by an electric power generator to operate a new or existing facility using combined-cycle gas turbine technology was decreased to 1% from the 2014 rate of 2.625%. (Sec. 26-52-319(c)(2))

Bingo: Bingo receipts are subject to Arkansas gross receipts (sales) tax, which applies to the total gross receipts derived from the retail sale of any device used in playing bingo and any charge for admittance to facilities or for the right to play bingo or other games of chance regardless of whether the activity might otherwise be prohibited by law (Sec. 26-52-301). A bingo excise tax equal to three-tenths of one cent ($0.003) is imposed on the sale of each bingo face sold by a licensed distributor to a licensed authorized organization in Arkansas. Items subject to this tax are exempt from the general sales and use tax. (Sec. 23-114-601)

Vending machines: Special decal fees are imposed in lieu of the gross receipts tax on vending machine operators.

¶ 250   Local Taxes

Cities, incorporated towns, and counties are authorized to levy a 1% sales tax and a special sales tax of .25% with voter approval. In addition, certain cities are authorized to impose taxes on lodging and prepared (restaurant) food at various rates. First class cities can also impose a Tourism Promotion Tax of up to 3%. Local tax rates are reproduced in the chart below.

SST conformity: In conformity with the Streamlined Sales Tax Agreement, purchasers may claim a credit or rebate for local sales and use taxes paid in excess of the tax due on the first $2,500 of gross receipts or gross proceeds from a qualifying purchase of goods or services in a single transaction. The purchaser must file a claim with the Department of Finance and Administration within one year from the date of the qualifying purchase or date of payment, whichever is later. Definitions are provided for "qualifying purchase" and "single transaction" (Sec. 26-52-523).

Rate changes: If a state tax rate change takes effect less than 30 days from the enactment of the statute providing the rate change, a seller is relieved of liability for failing to collect tax at the new rate if, absent fraud, the seller collected tax at the rate in effect before the rate change and the seller's failure to collect tax at the new rate does not extend beyond 30 days after the date of enactment. (Sec. 26-21-106)

Sourcing of telecommunications charges: Arkansas has conformed to the federal Mobile Telecommunications Sourcing Act (Act), P.L. 106-2522. All charges for mobile telecommunications services are considered to be provided by the customer's home service provider and sourced to the customer's place of primary use (Sec. 26-52-301(3)(A)(vi)). All such charges are subject to gross receipts (sales) tax based on the customer's place of primary use.

The service provider will be held harmless for an error in assigning wireless services to a jurisdiction if it utilizes an electronic database provided by the state or a designated entity, or, if the state has not provided or designated a database, if it utilizes a database that makes assignments based on a nine-digit zip code.

- **Border cities, local rates**

A different tax rate is authorized for certain border cities, including Texarkana (Sec. 26-52-303). The maximum state and local gross receipts (sales) tax rate that may be applied in specified border cities is the state tax rate imposed in the adjoining state, not to exceed the state tax rate as levied by the Arkansas General Assembly, initiatives enacted by Arkansas voters, and amendments to the Arkansas Constitution. See ¶ 249 for the current state tax rate. However, if voters in a border city choose to impose an additional 1% gross receipts (sales) tax rate in lieu of paying Arkansas personal income taxes, the maximum state and local gross receipts (sales) tax rate that may be imposed is 1% above the Arkansas state gross receipts (sales) tax rate (previously, 6%).

These special tax rates apply to an Arkansas city or incorporated town in which (1) a state line divides the city or town from an incorporated city or town in an adjoining state, (2) the population in the city or town in the adjoining state is greater than the Arkansas city or town population, and (3) the tax imposed in such adjoining state is in the nature of a selective sales tax or limited to specific items as a special excise tax (Sec. 26-52-303).

Rate and boundary changes

Local sales and use taxes may not be newly imposed or changed except to be effective on the first day of a calendar quarter period after a minimum of 90 days notice to the Director and at least 60 days notice from the Director to sellers or, for purchases from printed catalogs, on the first day of a calendar quarter after a minimum of 120 days notice to the seller. (Sec. 26-74-211(b), (c))

A local boundary change becomes effective on the first day of a calendar quarter after a minimum of 60 days' notice by the director to sellers (Sec. 26-74-211(d)).

- **Tourism taxes**

Certain cities may impose a tourism promotion tax of up to 3% (Sec. 26-75-602).

- **State and local tax chart**

Local sales taxes may be looked up by address or ZIP code on the state's website at **http://www.arkansas.gov/dfa/excise_tax_v2/st_zip.html**. A city and county tax rate table, updated on the first of every month, is also available.

¶ 251   **Bracket Schedule**

SST conformity: In accordance with the SST Agreement, sales and use tax computation must be carried to the third decimal place and rounded to the nearest whole cent, rounding up if the third decimal place is greater than four (Sec. 26-21-108; Reg. GR-71).

¶ 252   **Returns, Payments, and Due Dates**

Gross receipts tax returns and payments are due monthly except that certain large retailers are required to make payments in advance of monthly returns and small retailers are allowed to file quarterly or yearly returns, depending on the amount of their monthly tax liability (Sec. 26-52-501(h), Sec. 26-52-501(i), Sec. 26-52-512).

Once a taxpayer becomes liable to file a report, the taxpayer must continue to file, even though no tax is due, until the taxpayer notifies the Director of the Department of Finance and Administration in writing that he or she is no longer liable for the tax (Sec. 26-52-501(a)).

An extension of the filing deadline may be granted up to 120 days for good cause, which includes, but is not limited to, disasters declared by the Governor or by the President of the United States, and an additional 60 day extension may be granted in extraordinary circumstances (Sec. 26-18-505).

Vendors' or consumers' use tax returns are due monthly (Sec. 26-52-125).

Special events: Vendors must collect sales tax from purchasers of tangible personal property and remit the tax daily, along with a daily sales tax report, to the promoter or organizer. Within 30 days after the event, the organizer or promoter must forward all daily reports and payments to the Department of Finance and Administration along with a completed sales tax report combining all taxable sales and sales tax due (Sec. 26-52-518).

Discount for timely payment: A taxpayer who submits a timely report and payment may claim a discount of 2% of the amount of tax due, up to $1,000 per month (Sec. 26-52-503). The $1,000 per month limitation does not apply to city and county taxes.

- **Gross receipts tax returns and payments due dates**

Multiple business locations—Combined report: Taxpayers with multiple business locations in Arkansas must file a single sales tax report combining all gross receipts and gross proceeds from sales made at all of the locations (Sec. 26-52-501). The business locations must be registered under the same federal employer's identification number or social security number. This single report requirement applies to individuals, corporations, partnerships, limited liability companies, and other entities with multiple business locations.

Monthly returns and payments: Gross receipts tax returns and payments are due by the 20th day of each month for the preceding calendar month if the retailer's total tax liability for any month exceeds $100 (Sec. 26-52-501, Reg. GR-77). Taxes from the previous month that remain unpaid as of the due date are considered delinquent. The date a return is postmarked is deemed to be the date of delivery (Reg. GR-77).

Quarterly returns and payments: Quarterly, instead of monthly, reports and payments may be made on or before July 20, October 20, January 20, and April 20 of each year for the preceding three-month period if the total amount of tax for which a retailer is liable for any month does not exceed $100 (Sec. 26-52-501(h), Reg. GR-77).

Yearly returns and payments: If the total amount of tax for which a retailer is liable for any month does not exceed $25, gross receipts tax returns and payments may be made annually on or before January 20 of each year for the preceding 12-month period (Sec. 26-52-501(i), Reg. GR-77).

Out-of-state sellers: A seller that makes a taxable sale sourced to Arkansas must file a return on or before the 20th day of the month following the sale. A registered seller that does not have a legal requirement to register in Arkansas must be given a minimum of 30 days' notice before the department establishes a tax liability based solely on the seller's failure to timely file (Sec. 26-53-101(e)(1)).

- **Direct payment**

If the Commissioner of Revenues approves, a consumer or user may be permitted to accrue and remit gross receipts taxes directly to the Division, instead of paying the taxes to the seller (Sec. 26-52-509). The agreement is subject to revocation by the Commissioner. Direct payment permittees must report and remit the tax by the 20th day of the month for the previous month's taxable purchases (Sec. 26-52-509; Reg. GR-87) A retailer or vendor selling to the holder of a valid direct pay permit is not responsible for collection of the tax.

Limited direct pay permit: The Department of Finance and Administration may issue a limited direct pay permit that allows a user or consumer to accrue and remit sales and use taxes on "eligible purchases" of property or services related to a partial replacement and repair of machinery and equipment that is eligible for a tax refund. The seller should not collect and remit taxes on purchases that include eligible purchases. The limited direct pay permit holder is responsible for remitting any taxes due to the state. If a seller relies on the limited direct pay permit and fails to properly collect tax on sales other than eligible purchases, the limited direct pay permit holder shall remit the proper amount of tax to the state. A person who has entered into a limited direct pay agreement and makes purchases of property or services without paying the taxes due on those purchases is responsible for remitting the proper amount of tax due. (Sec. 26-52-509(a))

Replacement of manufacturing equipment: A partial tax refund is allowed on machinery and equipment purchased to modify, replace, or repair existing machinery or equipment used directly in manufacturing at a plant or facility in Arkansas (Secs. 26-52-447 and 26-53-149). Under one option, a refund of 1% is allowed for taxpayers who hold a direct pay or limited direct pay tax permit. Under a second option, an increased refund of 5.875% is available to eligible taxpayers who undertake and expend at least $3 million on an approved major maintenance and improvement project.

• Electronic filing and payment

An enhanced online service called Arkansas Taxpayer Access Point (ATAP) is available for taxpayers to report and pay Arkansas sales and use taxes over the Internet. An online tutorial and list of frequently asked questions are available on the ATAP Web site at **https://atap.arkansas.gov/_/**.

Taxpayers having monthly tax liabilities of more than $20,000 during the preceding calendar year are required to remit taxes by electronic funds transfer (EFT) (Sec. 26-19-105; Reg. 2000-5). Payment of taxes by EFT does not relieve a taxpayer from filing returns or complying with other requirements of the tax laws.

Taxpayers with monthly tax liability of $2,500 or more may voluntarily agree to make payments by EFT.

Taxpayers remitting taxes by EFT are required to make the transfer no later than the day before the due date for payment of the taxes so that payment is received on or before the due date. The failure to remit taxes by EFT when required to do so subjects a taxpayer to a penalty of 5% of the amount of taxes due. Moreover, the taxpayer is ineligible for the prompt payment discount.

If the Federal Reserve Bank is closed on a due date that prohibits a taxpayer from being able to make a payment through electronic funds transfer, the payment and any accompanying return shall be accepted as timely if they are made and filed on the next day the Federal Reserve Bank is open (Sec. 26-52-512(c)).

• Uniform Sales Tax Administration Act

Arkansas has enacted the Uniform Sales and Use Tax Administration Act and is a full member of the Streamlined Sales Tax Governing Board (Secs. 26-20-101 *et seq.*). Legislation conforming Arkansas law to the Streamlined Sales and Use Tax Agreement became effective January 1, 2008. See also ¶ 246.

Taxability matrix: A chart of the taxable status of various items is accessible at **http://www.streamlinedsalestax.org/otm/**.

Selected provisions conforming to the Streamlined Sales Tax Agreement are as follows:

Filing and payment: See Sec. 26-53-125.

Vendor registration; returns: Vendors that register for an Arkansas permit are not required to sign the application if they register electronically (Sec. 26-52-202). Vendors may register through an agent if the registration is filed with the Director and is made in writing. Vendors that do not have a legal requirement to register under either the

Gross Receipts (Sales) Tax or the Compensating (Use) Tax Acts and are not using a certified service provider (CSP) or a certified automated system (CAS) are required to submit an initial sales and use tax return anytime within one year of the month of initial registration. Future returns may be required on an annual basis in succeeding years, and the vendor may be required to submit returns in the month following any month in which it has accumulated state and local tax funds in the total amount of $1,000 or more. After registration, the Director must provide the vendor the required Arkansas returns.

Sourcing of sales: Sales will be sourced generally to the destination of the product sold, with a default to origin-based sourcing in the absence of that information. Special sourcing rules apply to sales of vehicles and telecommunications. The following general sourcing rules apply (Sec. 26-52-521(b)):

— When the product or service is received by the purchaser at a business location of the seller, the sale is sourced to that business location;

— When the product or service is not received by the purchaser at a business location of the seller, the sale is sourced to the location where receipt by the purchaser or the purchaser's designated donee occurs;

— If neither of the above apply, the sale is sourced to the location indicated by an address for the purchaser that is available from the business records of the seller that are maintained in the ordinary course of the seller's business when use of this address does not constitute bad faith;

— If none of the above apply, the sale is sourced to the location indicated by an address for the purchaser obtained during the consummation of the sale, including the address of a purchaser's payment instrument, if no other address is available, when use of this address does not constitute bad faith;

— If none of the other rules apply, including the circumstance in which the seller is without sufficient information to apply the previous rules, then the location will be determined by the address from which tangible personal property was shipped or from which the service was provided.

Special rules apply to the sourcing of telecommunications services and the sourcing of leases and rentals.

Bad debts: A bad debt deduction may be claimed on the return for the period during which the bad debt is written off as uncollectable in the taxpayer's books and records and is eligible to be deducted for federal income tax purposes (Sec. 26-52-309(a)(1) and (b)(1); Sec. 26-53-111(a)(1) and (b)(1)). If the taxpayer subsequently collects a debt, in whole or in part, for which a deduction had been claimed, the tax on the amount collected must be reported and claimed on the return filed for the period in which the collection was made (Sec. 26-52-309(e); Sec. 26-53-111(e)). When the filing responsibilities have been assumed by a CSP, the service provider will be allowed to claim, on behalf of the taxpayer, any bad debt allowance, but the CSP must credit or refund to the taxpayer the full amount of any bad debt allowance or refund received (Sec. 26-52-309(f); Sec. 26-53-111(f)).

Exemption certificates: A seller may accept a blanket exemption certificate from a purchaser with which the seller has a recurring business relationship. A seller is not required to renew blanket certificates or update exemption certificate information or data elements when there is a recurring business relationship between the purchaser and seller. A recurring business relationship exists when a period of no more than 12 months elapses between sales transactions. (Sec. 26-52-517(d))

Confidentiality: With very limited exceptions, a certified service provider must perform its tax calculation, remittance, and reporting functions without retaining the personally identifiable information of consumers. The Department of Finance and Administration may not retain any personally identifiable information when it is no longer required for the purposes of verifying the validity of an exemption. If personally

¶252 Arkansas

identifiable information regarding an individual is retained by the department, the individual must be provided reasonable access to his or her own information and a right to correct any inaccurately recorded information. If a third party seeks to discover personally identifiable information, a reasonable and timely effort must be made to notify the individual of the request. (Sec. 26-21-115)

Local taxes: See ¶ 250.

¶ 253 **Prepayment of Taxes**

All retailers with average net sales of more than $200,000 per month during the preceding calendar year must make prepayment of sales tax according to one of the following payment options:

(1) The taxpayer may elect to make two advance payments for the current calendar month, each equal to 40% of the tax due on the monthly average net sales (Sec. 26-52-512(a), Reg. GR-77). The advance payments must be made on or before the 12th day and 24th day of each month. The remaining 20% is paid with the regular report on the 20th day of the following month.

(2) The taxpayer may elect to pay an amount equal to or exceeding 80% of the tax due for the current month on or before the 24th day of each month. The remaining 20% is paid with the regular report on the 20th day of the following month.

Prepayment by EFT: Retailers that have average net sales of more than $200,000 per month for the preceding calendar year must prepay their sales tax by electronic funds transfer (EFT) (Sec. 26-52-512(a)). If an EFT due date falls on a Saturday, Sunday or legal holiday, the transfer must be made on the next succeeding business day.

Discount available: A taxpayer who timely remits the required prepayments and who timely files and pays the monthly gross receipts tax report is entitled to a discount that is the lesser of 2% of the reported monthly gross tax, or $1,000 (Sec. 26-52-512(b)(1)).

¶ 254 **Vendor Registration**

It is unlawful for any taxpayer to transact business in Arkansas prior to issuance and receipt of a gross receipts tax permit from the Commissioner of Revenues (Sec. 26-52-201). A separate permit is needed for each business location (Reg. GR-72).

Permits cannot be assigned (Sec. 26-52-204), and conspicuous display of the permit at the place of business is required (Sec. 26-52-205).

Vendors selling tangible personal property for storage, use, or consumption in Arkansas must also register and give the names and addresses of all agents operating in the state, as well as the location of any and all distribution or sales offices in the state (Sec. 26-53-121(a), Reg. UT-5).

Special event promoters: Organizers and promoters of special entertainment, amusement, recreation, and marketing events (*e.g.,* gun, boat, or auto shows; carnivals or fairs; flea markets), held at a single location on an irregular basis must register for sales tax collectionand provide each vendor with tax reporting forms and other information (Sec. 26-52-518).

• **Application and deposit**

The application must be signed by the owner of the business, or a corporate officer, in the case of a corporation (Sec. 26-52-202). A nonrefundable fee of $50 must be remitted with each new application for a permit (Sec. 26-52-203).

Anyone doing retail business in the state without a permanent business domicile in Arkansas must make a deposit or bond sufficient to cover one year's sales (Sec. 26-52-203).

These requirements do not affect permits already in effect (Reg. GR-89).

Registration online: See **https://atap.arkansas.gov/_/#2**.

• Cessation of business

All permits expire at the time of cessation of business at the permit location (Sec. 26-52-206).

When business is discontinued, the permit must be returned for cancellation along with a remittance of any unpaid or accrued taxes (Sec. 26-52-207, Reg. GR-72).

• Out-of-state businesses responding to a declared disaster or emergency

Out-of-state businesses and their employees who enter Arkansas on a temporary basis to provide help and assistance in response to a declared state disaster or emergency are exempt from certain taxes and regulatory requirements (Sec. 12-88-104). Such an out-of-state business is exempt from registering, filing, and remitting state or local taxes and from complying with state and local licensing, certification, and registration requirements, including without limitation: unemployment insurance contributions; state and local occupational licensing fees and privilege taxes; state and local income taxes; and state and local sales and use taxes on property temporarily brought into the state for use during the disaster response period and subsequently removed from the state. The exemptions do not apply to an out-of-state business or out-of-state employee who remains in Arkansas after a disaster response period with respect to activities conducted in Arkansas after the disaster response period (Sec. 12-88-104(b)) . A disaster response period extends for 60 days following a disaster or emergency declaration by the Governor of Arkansas or the President of the United States (Sec. 12-88-103(4)).

For purposes of a state or local tax on or measured by, in whole or in part, net or gross income or receipts, all activity of the out-of-state business that is conducted in Arkansas is exempt from filing requirements for the state or local tax, including without limitation any filing required by a unitary or combined group of which the out-of-state business may be a part. (Sec. 12-88-104(a)(3)(A))

For the purpose of apportioning income, revenue, or receipts, the performance of an out-of-state business of disaster-related or emergency-related work will not be sourced to or otherwise impact or increase the amount of income, revenue, or receipts apportioned to Arkansas (Sec. 12-88-104(a)(3)(B)).

During a disaster response period, an out-of-state employee:

    (1) is not required to file or pay Arkansas income taxes;

    (2) is not subject to Arkansas income tax withholding; and

    (3) is not required to file or pay any other state or local tax or fee, including related state or local employer withholding and remittance obligations, but not including transaction taxes or fees.

An out-of-state business and an out-of-state employee must pay any applicable *ad valorem* taxes (Sec. 12-88-104(c)), as well as certain state and local transaction taxes and fees, including without limitation motor fuel taxes; distillate special fuel taxes; sales and use taxes on materials and services consumed or used in Arkansas; hotel taxes; car rental taxes and fees; and any other tax or fee that applies to goods or services that the out-of-state business or out-of-state employee purchases for use or consumption in Arkansas during the disaster response period, unless the tax or fee is otherwise exempt during the disaster response period (Sec. 12-88-105).

• Revocation or suspension

If a permit holder fails to comply with the Gross Receipts Act, the Commissioner may issue notice of intention to revoke the permit (Sec. 26-52-208). The taxpayer may apply within 10 days for a hearing, the results of which can be appealed to a chancery court within 30 days and, ultimately, to the Arkansas Supreme Court.

¶ 255 Sales or Use Tax Credits

The main credits are the economic investment tax credit, the tourism project credits, and the credit for taxes paid to other states. For discussion of the Consolidated Incentive Act of 2003, see ¶ 259.

Technology-based enterprises may earn a credit against the corporate income, personal income, or sales and use taxes based on new investment made (Sec. 15-4-2706(b)(7)). The business must create new payroll of at least $250,000 and pay wages that are equal to or greater than 175% of the county average hourly wage. The credit amount ranges from 2% to 8% depending on the amount of investment made. The taxpayer may elect to use the credit against either the income tax or the sales tax.

SST conformity: Local taxes on qualifying purchases that exceed $2,500 in a single transaction may be credited or refunded. See ¶ 250.

• **Taxes paid to other states**

Arkansas has adopted the Multistate Tax Compact's tax credit provisions (Sec. 26-5-101). Purchasers liable for use tax on tangible personal property are entitled to full credit for sales or use taxes paid to another state on the same property.

The compensating (use) tax statutes specifically grant a credit for tax paid to another state to the extent that the tax paid is not less than the Arkansas tax due on the transaction (Sec. 26-53-131, Sec. 26-53-203). The tax credit under these sections is available only if the other state grants a similar credit for Arkansas taxes.

However, no credit is allowed for taxes paid to other states on motor vehicles, trailers, or semitrailers that are first registered in Arkansas by the purchaser (Sec. 26-53-131, Sec. 26-52-510).

• **Economic investment sales and use tax credit (InvestARK)**

A manufacturers' investment credit is allowed against a manufacturer's state sales and use tax liability equal to 7% of the total cost of any project subject to the limits set by Sec. 26-52-705 (Sec. 26-52-704).

Along with manufacturers, the list of businesses and projects eligible for the credit includes various nonretail computer-related businesses, motion picture production companies, certain research businesses, and administrative support facilities, such as distribution centers and corporate headquarters (Sec. 26-52-702).

Refunds of sales and use taxes are authorized under the Arkansas Enterprise Zone Act of 1993 (Sec. 15-4-1704), but recipients of benefits under the Economic Investment Tax Credit Act are precluded from receiving benefits under the Enterprise Zone Act for the same project (Sec. 26-52-703).

• **Tourism project credits**

A credit is available to approved companies investing at least $500,000 in qualified Arkansas tourism projects. The credit may be used to offset a portion of the taxpayer's "increased state sales tax liability," which is the portion of an approved company's reported gross receipts tax liability resulting from taxable sales at the tourist attraction for any monthly sales tax reporting period occurring after certification of approved costs that exceeds the reported sales tax liability for the same month in the calendar year preceding certification. (Sec. 15-11-503).

Amount of credit: An approved company that expends approved costs of more than $500,000 but less than $1 million is entitled to a sales tax credit equal to 10% of the approved costs (Sec. 15-11-507(b)(1)(A)). The company may use 100% of the issued credit to offset its increased state sales tax liability during the first year of eligibility if the company's tax liability is equal to or greater than the amount issued in the Department of Finance and Administration's state sales tax credit memorandum to the company (Sec. 15-11-507(c)(2)(B)).

An approved company that expends approved costs in excess of $1 million is entitled to a sales tax credit equal to 25% of the approved costs (Sec. 15-11-507(b)(1)(B)). Any unused credits may be carried forward to a subsequent year (Sec. 15-11-507(c)(2)(A)).

- **Motion picture and digital production rebates**

An approved production company may apply for a rebate of 15%, with no cap per production, on all qualified production costs in connection with the production of a state-certified film project. An additional rebate of 10% will be granted for the payroll of below-the-line employees who are full-time residents of Arkansas. To qualify for a production or post-production rebate, the production company must submit an application to the Arkansas Economic Development Commission and spend at least $50,000 within a six-month period in connection with the production or post-production of one project. (Sec. 15-4-2001 *et seq.*)

Post-production rebates: A qualifying production company may apply for a rebate of 15%, with no cap per production, on all qualified production costs in connection with the post-production of a state-certified film project. An additional rebate of 10% will be granted for the payroll of below-the-line employees who are full-time residents of Arkansas. (Sec. 15-4-2006)

¶ 256   Deficiency Assessments

If any taxpayer fails to file a return, or files a deficient return and the Director determines that the tax is less than adequate, the Director will propose the assessment of additional tax plus penalties (Sec. 26-18-403).

If, upon audit or examination, the Commissioner of Revenues determines that an additional tax is due, the Commissioner must prepare a schedule reflecting the amount of additional tax, interest and penalties payable and must give a copy to the taxpayer (Reg. GR-81). A "Notice of Proposed Assessment" and a copy of the "Taxpayer's Bill of Rights" must also be mailed to the address listed in the retail permit application or to the actual business address of the taxpayer.

¶ 257   Audit Procedures

The statutes relating to collection of tax give the Commissioner of Revenues power to conduct audits or examinations to determine whether additional taxes are due.

The Commissioner of Revenues may audit and compute the state tax payable by any taxpayer subject to taxation under any state tax law (Sec. 26-18-301).

The Commissioner of Revenues may, when conducting an audit, examine the records and files of any person, except where privileged by law, any business, institution, financial institution, the records of any state agency, agency of the United States Government, or agency of any other state where permitted by agreement or reciprocity (Sec. 26-18-305). Sampling is authorized with the taxpayer's consent.

Accurate and complete records reflecting the amounts of cash sales and credit sales must be kept by the taxpayer. These records must be open for audit by the Commissioner of Revenues (Reg. GR-78).

A taxpayer subject to an audit may file an amended return or verified claim for credit or refund of an overpayment of an Arkansas tax that occurred at any time during the time period for which the audit is performed. However, the total refund of overpayments for the extended audit period will not be more than the total amount assessed for the extended audit period. (Sec. 26-18-306(i)(1)(C))

Local audits: To reduce costs, two or more Arkansas cities that have enacted an advertising and promotion sales and use tax may employ a joint auditor to perform a joint audit of a taxpayer to determine the accuracy of a return or establish tax liability. In performing the audit, the joint auditor is authorized to examine books, records, and relevant property or stock of merchandise in possession of the taxpayer or a third party as well as tax information from the books and records of the Department of Finance and Administration concerning the taxpayer. (Sec. 26-75-619(b))

¶ 258   Statute of Limitations

The general statute of limitations on assessments is three years from the date the return was required to be filed or was actually filed, whichever is later (Sec. 26-18-306). If no return is filed, no statute of limitations applies.

The time within which a final assessment may be made can be extended by mutual agreement between the Commissioner of Revenues and the taxpayer (Sec. 26-18-306).

• Understatement of tax by 25% or more

If the tax is understated by 25% or more, an assessment may be made within six years from the date the return was due or was actually filed, whichever is later (Sec. 26-18-306).

• Fraudulent return or failure to file return

In the case of a fraudulent return or failure to file a return, there is no statute of limitations; a tax assessment may be issued anytime (Sec. 26-18-306).

• Statute of limitations on criminal indictments

The statute of limitations for criminal indictments under state tax law is six years (Sec. 26-18-306).

¶ 259   Application for Refund

If an examination of a return indicates that a taxpayer has overpaid the amount of tax required, the excess can be credited against a subsequent tax or refunded, at the option of the taxpayer. Overpaid taxes can also be refunded on the filing of an amended return or a verified claim for refund (Reg. GR-83).

In general, a claim for a refund (or credit) must be filed within three years from the filing of the return or two years from the time the tax was paid, whichever is later (Sec. 26-18-306). However, if a taxpayer fails to file a return, the claim must be filed within three years from the date the return was originally due. In the case of an individual taxpayer, the running of the periods specified for filing an amended return or verified claim for credit or refund is suspended during any period that an individual is financially disabled (Sec. 26-18-306(k)). A credit or rebate of local sales and use tax will not be paid for a claim filed after one year after the date of the qualified purchase or the date of payment, if later (Sec. 26-52-523(d)).

The refund claim should specify the name of the taxpayer, the time when the tax was paid, the period for which the tax was paid, the amount of the tax claimed to have been erroneously overpaid, and the grounds upon which a refund is claimed (Sec. 26-18-507, Reg. GR-83). The Commissioner must respond within six months with a written determination. Any refund can be paid to the taxpayer or credited against taxes due or to become due. The standard of proof for taxpayers to establish facts supporting their claims is clear and convincing evidence (Sec. 26-18-313).

Judicial relief is available if the Commissioner refuses the refund or does not answer the request within six months (Sec. 26-18-507).

• Interest on overpayment or refund

Interest is paid on overpaid taxes at the rate of 10% (Reg. GR-83). However, no interest is allowed if the Commissioner refunds the tax within 90 days after the return due date, including any extension of time for filing the return, or 90 days after the date the return is filed, whichever occurs later.

• Consolidated Incentive Act of 2003

The Consolidated Incentive Act of 2003 combined several existing economic development tax incentives and created two new incentives in regard to Arkansas corporate income and gross receipts (sales) and compensating (use) taxes (Secs. 15-4-2701—15-4-2714).

The act established a tier system that offers increased benefits to businesses that locate in less economically prosperous counties. All 75 Arkansas counties are ranked by the Arkansas Department of Economic Development (ADED) into four divisions on the basis of economic prosperity by taking into account the county's unemployment and poverty rates, per capita income, and population growth. Payroll requirements are highest in the more prosperous Tier 1 counties.

Choice of benefits: Eligible businesses that signed a financial incentive agreement with the ADED before March 3, 2003, are eligible only for benefits for which they are qualified under any of the following existing incentives:

— the Biotechnology Training and Development Act;

— the Economic Development Incentive Act of 1993;

— the Arkansas Enterprise Zone Act of 1993;

— the Arkansas Economic Development Act of 1995;

— the Economic Investment Tax Credit Act; and

— the Arkansas Emerging Technology Development Act of 1999.

Eligible businesses that sign an agreement after March 3, 2003, receive only benefits for which they are qualified under the Consolidated Incentive Act of 2003. Under no circumstances is an eligible business entitled to receive incentives or benefits for a project under both this act and the incentives listed above.

Retention credit: A retention tax credit established in the act replaces provisions in the Arkansas Economic Development Act of 1995 that authorize a refund of state and local sales and use taxes paid on certain purchases of material, machinery, and equipment made by certain businesses that spend at least $5 million on a project to construct or expand a plant or facility in Arkansas and hire at least 100 net new full-time permanent employees within 24 months after committing to the project. The new version however, allows a credit as opposed to a refund, in the amount of 0.5% above the state sales and use tax rate in effect at the time a financial incentive agreement is signed. A credit taken cannot exceed 50% of the direct pay sales and use tax liability of the business for taxable purchases in any one year following the year of the expenditures. An application for a retention tax credit for a qualified business may be filed through June 30, 2017.

Partial refund for replacement or repair of manufacturing machinery and equipment: A partial refund of Arkansas sales and use tax is allowed on machinery and equipment purchased to modify, replace, or repair, either in whole or in part, existing machinery or equipment used directly in producing, manufacturing, fabricating, assembling, processing, finishing, or packaging articles of commerce at a manufacturing or processing plant or facility in Arkansas. The refund also applies to services relating to the initial installation, alteration, addition, cleaning, refinishing, replacement, or repair of the above machinery or equipment. (Sec. 26-52-447; Sec. 26-53-149) Two sales tax refund options are provided:

¶259   **Arkansas**

(1) *Refund of 1%.*—Under the first option, a tax refund will be allowed for taxes paid in excess of 4.875%. To be eligible for this option, the taxpayer must hold a direct pay permit and claim the tax refund under the permit. (Sec. 26-52-447; Sec. 26-53-149)

(2) *Refund of 5.875%.*—Under the second option, a taxpayer that undertakes an approved major maintenance and improvement project may be eligible for a 5.875% tax refund (6.5% total state rate less the 0.625% rate not subject to refund) on purchases to replace or repair manufacturing machinery and equipment. The taxpayer must enter into a financial incentive agreement with the Arkansas Economic Development Commission and must expend at least $3 million on an approved project. The increased refund is discretionary and not available unless offered by the AEDC (Sec. 15-4-3501). A taxpayer must hold and use a direct pay or a limited direct pay permit from the Department of Finance and Administration (Sec. 26-52-447(f); Sec. 26-53-149(f)). Applications for increased refunds for major maintenance and improvement projects are allowed through June 30, 2022.

Construction refund ("Tax Back"): A sales and use tax refund on the purchase of material used in the construction of a building or buildings or any addition, modernization, or improvement for housing any new or expanding qualified business, as well as machinery and equipment to be located in or in connection to such a building, will be authorized by the Director of the DFA if the municipality or county has authorized the refund of municipal or county sales and use taxes in an endorsement resolution (Sec. 15-04-2706(d)). A business must meet specific investment and payroll requirements based on the tier system in order to qualify for the refund.

Local tax refunds for targeted businesses: Certain targeted businesses may claim a refund of sales and use taxes imposed by a municipality or county on qualified expenditures (Sec. 15-4-2706(e)). A targeted business must have a payroll of at least $200,000, an equity investment of at least $500,000, and pay more than the average state or county wage as determined by the tier system, in order to qualify for the refund. For example, a targeted business would have to pay 180% of the lesser of the state or county average wage in a Tier 1 county, in addition to meeting the other requirements. This refund incentive is discretionary and is not available unless offered by the ADED.

Targeted businesses include those in the following sectors:

— advanced materials and manufacturing systems;

— agriculture, food, and environmental sciences;

— biotechnology, bioengineering, and life sciences;

— information technology;

— transportation logistics; and

— bio-based products.

- **Nonprofit Incentive Act of 2005 (repealed)**

Prior to repeal by Act 208 (S.B. 160), Laws 2017, effective 90 days after adjournment of the 2017 Legislature, certain nonprofit corporations could receive refunds of sales and use taxes as an incentive to locate in Arkansas. Nonprofit organizations that had a payroll of new, full-time permanent employees in excess of $1 million dollars annually could apply. In order to qualify, however, the nonprofit organization had to pay wages that average in excess of 110% of the lesser of the county or state average wage and receive a minimum of 75% of its income from out-of-state sources. Hospitals, medical clinics, accredited academic educational institutions, and churches were specifically excluded (Former Sec. 15-4-3201; Former Sec. 15-4-3204).

To qualify for the sales and use tax refund, a qualified nonprofit organization had to spend in excess of $500,000 on buildings, machinery, and equipment in a new or improved facility. The nonprofit also had to sign a financial incentive agreement with the Department of Economic Development (Former Sec. 15-4-3204; Former Sec. 15-4-3205).

- **Incentive refunds for manufacturers**

Manufacturing machinery and equipment: A partial refund of Arkansas sales and use tax is allowed on machinery and equipment purchased to modify, replace, or repair, either in whole or in part, existing machinery or equipment used directly in producing, manufacturing, fabricating, assembling, processing, finishing, or packaging articles of commerce at a manufacturing or processing plant or facility in Arkansas. The refund will also apply to services relating to the initial installation, alteration, addition, cleaning, refinishing, replacement, or repair of the above machinery or equipment. (Sec. 26-52-446)

The taxes subject to refund are the statutory taxes in excess of the following rates (Sec. 26-52-446(b)(1)):

— Beginning July 1, 2013, 4.875%;

— Beginning July 1, 2014, 3.875%;

— Beginning July 1, 2015, 2.875%;

— Beginning July 1, 2016, 1.875%; and

— Beginning July 1, 2017, 0.875%.

On and after July 1, 2018, 100% of the taxes are refundable (Sec. 26-52-446(b)(3)). However, the 1/8% excise tax under Amendment 75 to the Arkansas Constitution and the temporary 0.5% excise tax under Amendment 91 (effective July 1, 2013) are not subject to the refund.

To claim the tax refund, a taxpayer must hold a direct pay permit and claim the tax refund under the permit.

¶ 261   Scope of Tax

Source.—Statutory references are to Division 2 of the Revenue and Taxation Code of California, unless otherwise indicated, as amended to date. Details are reported in the CCH CALIFORNIA TAX REPORTS starting at ¶ 60-000.

The sales tax is imposed on every retailer for the privilege of making retail sales of tangible personal property in the state (Sec. 6051, Rev. & Tax. Code). The legal incidence of the sales tax is on the retailer, not the purchaser. Payment of sales tax reimbursement by the purchaser is entirely a matter of agreement between the purchaser and seller, although certain conditions create a presumption that the purchaser agreed to pay the tax reimbursement (Sec. 1656.1, Civ. Code, Reg. 1700).

The tax is applied to the gross receipts from the sale of tangible personal property in the state. Sales tax generally does not apply to services. With some specific exceptions, leases of tangible personal property in California are treated as "sales" and are taxed either on their sale, as measured by the purchase price, or on their use, as measured by the rental receipts.

Tax on sales of health services: Sales tax is imposed on sellers of Medi-Cal managed care plans in California. Counties, cities, and districts are prohibited from imposing a sales or use tax on such gross receipts. The sales tax becomes inoperative on July 1, 2016, and is repealed effective January 1, 2017. (Sec. 6174, Rev. & Tax. Code; *Special Notice L-359,* California State Board of Equalization, August 2013; *Special Notice L-367,* California State Board of Equalization, October 2013)

Special assessments: There are special assessments imposed on sales of certain products; see ¶ 264.

Electronic commerce: Transfers solely by remote telecommunication are not regarded as sales of tangible personal property. If the transaction does not involve any transfer of tangible personal property to the customer, then it is not a sale subject to sales or use tax (Reg. 1502(f)(1)(D)).

Support services: Sales tax is imposed on providers of support services at retail measured by the gross receipts from the sale of those services. (Sec. 6151, Rev. & Tax. Code).

Mobile food vendors: Taxable sales by mobile food vendors *(i.e.,* food truck operators) are presumed to include California sales tax, unless a separate sales tax amount is added to the charged price. This presumption is inapplicable when mobile food vendors make sales as caterers hired by a private party to provide food and/or drink on the customer's premises. (Reg. 1603; *Special Notice L-383,* California State Board of Equalization, June 2014)

Medical marijuana: Sales of medical marijuana are subject to California sales and use taxes, and may be subject to county privilege taxes (see ¶ 265). Vendors are required to register (see ¶ 267). See also the Board of Equalization's *Tax Guide for Medical Cannabis Businesses* at **http://www.boe.ca.gov/industry/ medical_cannabis.html.**

Winemakers: A tax guide for winemakers is available from the BOE at **http:// www.boe.ca.gov/industry/sales-tax-guide-for-winemakers.html.**

• **Application of use tax**

The use tax is imposed on every person who stores, uses, or otherwise consumes in California tangible personal property purchased from a retailer (Sec. 6202, Rev. & Tax. Code). Transactions that are exempt from sales tax or on which sales tax has been paid (except for leases, to which special provisions may apply) are exempt from use tax (Sec. 6401, Rev. & Tax. Code). Purchasers or lessees of property that is subject to use tax must pay the tax to the seller or lessor if the seller or lessor holds a seller's permit or a "Certificate of Registration—Use Tax" (Sec. 6202, Rev. & Tax. Code, Reg. 1685). If the seller or lessor lacks such a permit or certificate, the purchaser or lessor is liable for and should make payment to the State Board of Equalization. Purchasers and lessees, as a general rule, are liable for payment of tax to the Board unless a receipt is obtained from sellers or lessors holding a seller's permit or a Certificate of Registration—Use Tax. Out-of-state retailers are required to collect and remit use tax on their retail sales if they are "engaged in business in this state" (Sec. 6203, Rev. & Tax. Code; Reg. 1684).

Online retailer: An out-of-state corporation that made online retail sales of tangible personal property was properly held liable for the collection and remittance of California use tax on all sales to California purchasers because its brick-and-mortar affiliate acted as its agent when it accepted returns of merchandise purchased online. The activities of the brick-and-mortar agent on behalf of its online retailer principal in, among other things, facilitating a return policy, were conducted for the purpose of selling the online retailer's goods. As such, the online retailer, through its agent's activities, had sufficient presence in California to justify the imposition of the use tax collection burden (*Borders Online, LLC v. SBE,* California Court of Appeal, First Appellate District, No. A105488, May 31, 2005, CCH CALIFORNIA TAX REPORTS, ¶ 403-800). For additional information on nexus and registration requirements, see ¶ 269.

Vehicles, vessels, and aircraft: A vehicle, vessel, or aircraft bought outside of California that is brought into California within 12 months from the date of its purchase and that is subject to California motor vehicle registration is presumptively subject to California use tax (Sec. 6248, Rev. & Tax. Code). Vessels, vehicles, and aircraft purchased outside of California are presumptively subject to California use tax if (1) the vehicle, vessel, or aircraft was purchased by a California resident (including a closely held corporation or limited liability company (LLC) if 50% or more of the shares or membership interests are held by shareholders or members who are California residents); (2) the vehicle is subject to California motor vehicle registration during the first 12 months of ownership; or (3) the vehicle, vessel, or aircraft is used or stored in California more than one-half of the time during the first 12 months of ownership. A vehicle owner may present documentary evidence to rebut the presumption. The presumption is inapplicable to: (1) any vehicle, vessel, or aircraft used in interstate or foreign commerce; and (2) any aircraft or vessel brought into California for the purpose of repair, retrofit, or modification performed by a qualifying licensed repair facility for vessels or by a certified repair station or manufacturer's maintenance facility for aircraft. For additional information, see *BOE Publication 52, Vehicles and Vessels: How to Request a Use Tax Clearance for DMV Registration,* California State Board of Equalization, August 2014, CCH CALIFORNIA TAX REPORTS, ¶ 406-200.

• **Nexus**

Every retailer engaged in business in California and making sales of tangible personal property for storage, use, or other consumption in California, not otherwise exempted, must collect sales or use tax from the purchaser. "Retailer engaged in business in this state" specifically includes but is not limited to any retailer who (Sec. 6203, Rev. & Tax Code; Reg. 1684(a)):

— maintains, occupies, or uses, permanently or temporarily, directly or indirectly, or through a subsidiary, or agent, by whatever name called, an office, place of distribution, sales or sample room or place, warehouse or storage place, or other place of business;

— has any representative, agent, salesperson, canvasser, independent contractor, or solicitor operating in California under the authority of the retailer or its subsidiary for the purpose of selling, delivering, installing, assembling, or the taking of orders for any tangible personal property;

— derives rentals from a lease of tangible personal property situated in California;

— is a member of a commonly controlled group and a combined reporting group that includes another member of the retailer's commonly controlled group that, pursuant to an agreement with or in cooperation with the retailer, performs services in California in connection with tangible personal property to be sold by the retailer, including but not limited to the design and development of tangible personal property sold by the retailer, or the solicitation of sales of tangible personal property on behalf of the retailer.

Because Congress has not authorized states to compel the collection of state sales and use tax by out-of-state retailers, the definition does not include retailers that solicit qualifying orders by mail and that benefit from either specified activities occurring in this state or the location in California of authorized facilities.

"Click-through" nexus: California imposes click-through and affiliate nexus. "Retailer engaged in business in this state" includes any retailer who enters into an agreement under which a person in California, for a commission or other consideration, directly or indirectly refers potential purchasers of tangible personal property to the retailer, whether by an Internet-based link, a website, or otherwise, provided two conditions are met. Those conditions are (Sec. 6203(c)(5)(A), Rev. & Tax Code):

(1) that the total cumulative sales price from all of the retailer's sales within the preceding 12 months of tangible personal property to purchasers in California that are referred pursuant to such an agreement is in excess of $10,000; and

(2) the retailer has total cumulative sales of tangible personal property to California purchasers in excess of $1 million within the preceding 12 months.

An "agreement," for purposes of this provision, does not include any agreement under which a retailer:

— purchases advertisements from a person in California, to be delivered on television, radio, in print, on the Internet, or by any other medium, unless the advertisement revenue paid consists of commissions or other consideration that is based upon sales of tangible personal property (Sec. 6203(c)(5)(B), Rev. & Tax Code); or

— engages a person in California to place an advertisement on a website operated by that person, or operated by another person in the state, unless the person entering the agreement with the retailer also directly or indirectly solicits potential customers in California through the use of flyers, newsletters, telephone calls, electronic mail, blogs, micro blogs, social networking sites, or other means of direct and indirect solicitation specifically targeted at potential customers in the state (Sec. 6203(c)(5)(C), Rev. & Tax Code).

Affiliate nexus. In addition, the term "retailer" includes an entity affiliated with a retailer within the meaning of IRC Sec. 1504. These provisions are inapplicable if the retailer can demonstrate that the person in California with whom the retailer has an agreement did not engage in referrals in the state on behalf of the retailer that would satisfy the requirements of the Commerce Clause of the U.S. Constitution. (Sec. 6203, Rev. & Tax Code).

The term "retailer engaged in business in this state" also includes any retailer that is a member of a commonly controlled group and a combined reporting group that includes another member of the retailer's commonly controlled group that, pursuant to an agreement with or in cooperation with the retailer, performs services in California in connection with tangible personal property to be sold by the retailer, including but not limited to the design and development of tangible personal property sold by the retailer, or the solicitation of sales of tangible personal property on behalf of the retailer (Sec. 6203(c)(4), Rev. & Tax Code). In addition, the definition includes a retailer that has substantial nexus with California for purposes of the Commerce Clause of the U.S. Constitution and any retailer upon whom federal law permits the state to impose a use tax collection duty.

Affiliate nexus does not apply if a retailer can demonstrate that all of the persons with whom the retailer has agreements, as described, did not directly or indirectly solicit potential customers for the retailer in California. In addition, a retailer can demonstrate that an agreement is not an agreement subject to the affiliate nexus provision if (Reg. 1684):

— the retailer's agreement prohibits persons operating under the agreement from engaging in any solicitation activities in California that refer potential customers to the retailer including but not limited to distributing flyers, coupons, newsletters and other printed promotional materials or electronic equivalents, verbal soliciting (*e.g.*, in-person referrals), initiating telephone calls, and sending emails;

— the person or persons operating under the agreement in California certify annually (Form BOE-232 Affiliate Nexus Information), under penalty of perjury, that they have not engaged in any prohibited solicitation activities in California at any time during the previous year; and

— the retailer accepts the certification or certifications in good faith, and the retailer does not know or have reason to know that the certification or certifications are false or fraudulent.

A retailer can demonstrate that an agreement with an organization, such as a club or nonprofit group, is not subject to the affiliate nexus provision if, in addition to the above requirements, the agreement provides that the organization will maintain information on its website alerting its members to the prohibition against each of the solicitation activities described above, and the retailer obtains an annual certification from the organization under penalty of perjury that includes a statement certifying that its website includes information directed at its members alerting them to the prohibition against the solicitation activities described above. (Reg. 1684)

Annual certification: A person may complete Form BOE-232, Annual Certification of No Solicitation, or any document that satisfies the regulatory requirements, to annually certify under penalty of perjury that the person has not engaged in any prohibited solicitation activities in California at any time during the previous year. An organization may complete the Additional Statement from Organization section of Form BOE-232, or any document that satisfies the regulatory requirements, to annually certify under penalty of perjury that its website includes information directed at its members alerting them to the prohibition against the solicitation activities described above. (Reg. 1684)

Trade shows. An out-of-state retailer is not engaged in business in California based solely on the physical presence of the retailer or its agents at convention or trade show activities (as described in IRC Sec. 513(d)(3)(A)) for 15 or fewer days in any 12-month period that did not derive more than $100,000 of net income from those activities in California during the prior calendar year. However, that retailer must collect use tax on any sales of tangible personal property at those activities and with respect to any such sale made pursuant to an order taken at those activities. (Sec. 6203(d), Rev. & Tax Code; Reg. 1684(d)(3))

Independent contractors: A retailer also is not "engaged in business" in California based solely on its use of a representative or independent contractor in California to perform warranty or repair services on tangible personal property sold by the retailer, provided the ultimate ownership (*i.e.,* stock holder, bond holder, partner, or other person who holds an ownership interest) of the representative or independent contractor and the retailer is not substantially similar (Reg. 1684(d)(2)).

¶261   California

Prior law: Nexus provisions in effect prior to September 15, 2012, and legislative actions resulting in the above nexus provisions are discussed in the 2012 edition of this Guide and at ¶ 60-025 in CCH CALIFORNIA TAX REPORTS.

• Streamlined Act status

California is one of the Advisor States (Ch. 702 (S.B. 157), Laws 2003). The legislation authorizes the state to participate in the ongoing discussions to refine the Streamlined Sales and Use Tax Agreement approved in 2002. It does not make the substantive changes to California law required to conform to the existing Agreement.

¶ 262   Tax Base

"Gross receipts," upon which the sales tax is imposed, and "sales price," upon which the use tax is imposed, are similarly defined (Sec. 6011, Rev. & Tax. Code, Sec. 6012, Rev. & Tax. Code) as the total amount for which tangible personal property is sold, leased, or rented, valued in money (whether paid in money or otherwise), without any deduction for the following: (a) the cost of the property sold; (b) the cost of materials used, labor or service costs, interest paid ("interest charged" for use tax purposes), losses, or any other expenses; or (c) the cost of transporting the property, except as otherwise provided. The "total amount for which property is sold, leased, or rented" includes the following: (1) any services that are a part of the sale; (2) any amount for which credit is given to the purchaser by the seller; and, in the definition of "gross receipts," (3) all receipts, cash, credits, and property of any kind.

Sales tax does not apply to automated teller machine (ATM) charges when an access device (*e.g.,* a debit card or credit card) is issued to make a cash withdrawal from, or to engage in any other transaction that is not subject to tax, at an ATM (Reg. 1643). In addition, gross receipts from a retail sale of tangible personal property do not include debit card charges collected by the retailer if (1) the debit card charges are separately stated, (2) the consumer would not otherwise incur the charge if he or she did not use the debit card, (3) the fee is not calculated as a percentage of the amount of the purchase, and (4) the charge is reasonably related to the cost of the transaction to the retailer.

Taxes imposed by a California Indian tribe and measured by a percentage of the sales or purchase price are excluded from the tax base for California sales and use tax purposes (Sec. 6011, Rev. & Tax. Code).

Internet tax freedom: Under the federal Internet Tax Freedom Act (ITFA) and its amendments (P.L. 105-277, amended by P.L. 107-75, P.L. 108-435, P.L. 110-108, P.L. 113-164 and P.L. 113-235), state and local governments are barred from imposing multiple or discriminatory taxes on electronic commerce and taxes on Internet access, except for Internet access taxes allowed under grandfather clauses. The most recent extension of the moratorium expires on September 30, 2016.

¶ 263   List of Exemptions, Exceptions, and Exclusions

Unless otherwise indicated, the statutory exemptions, exceptions, and exclusions listed below apply to both sales and use taxes; those applicable only to the use tax are listed separately. Items that are excluded from the sales or use tax base are treated at ¶ 262, "Tax Base."

Tax holidays: There are no statewide tax holidays, but some municipalities have declared various sales tax holiday periods that affect only local taxes.

• Sales and use tax exemptions, exceptions, and exclusions

Aircraft gasoline . . . . Sec. 6357, Rev. & Tax. Code, Sec. 6357.5, Rev. & Tax. Code, Sec. 6385, Rev. & Tax. Code

Aircraft leased or sold to common carriers . . . . Sec. 6366, Rev. & Tax. Code, Sec. 6366.1, Rev. & Tax. Code

Aircraft leased or sold to nonresidents or foreign governments . . . . Sec. 6366, Rev. & Tax. Code, Sec. 6366.1, Rev. & Tax. Code

Alternative energy and advanced transportation projects . . . . Sec. 6010.8, Rev. & Tax. Code

Animals . . . . Sec. 6010.40, Rev. & Tax. Code, Sec. 6010.50, Rev. & Tax. Code, Sec. 6358, Rev. & Tax. Code, Sec. 6358.5, Rev. & Tax. Code, Sec. 6366.5, Rev. & Tax. Code

Artworks purchased or leased for specified purposes . . . . Sec. 6365, Rev. & Tax. Code

Artworks sold at certain social gatherings . . . . Sec. 6010.30, Rev. & Tax. Code

Auction sale by nonprofit organizations . . . . Sec. 6363.2, Rev. & Tax. Code

Aviation gasoline on which gas tax has been paid . . . . Sec. 6357, Rev. & Tax. Code, Sec. 6480(b), Rev. & Tax. Code

Bracelets sold by charitable organizations . . . . Sec. 6359.3, Rev. & Tax. Code

California Lottery . . . . Sec. 8880.68, Govt. Code

Carbon dioxide packing . . . . Sec. 6359.8, Rev. & Tax. Code

Cargo containers purchased for interstate or out-of-state use . . . . . . Sec. 6388.5, Rev. & Tax. Code

Charitable donations to exempt organizations . . . . Sec. 6403, Rev. & Tax. Code

Charitable organizations . . . . Sec. 6375, Rev. & Tax. Code

Clothing donated to needy children . . . . Sec. 6375.5, Rev. & Tax. Code

Coins and gold or silver bullion . . . . Sec. 6354, Rev. & Tax. Code; Sec. 6355, Rev. & Tax. Code

Common carriers: sales to, for use outside state . . . . Sec. 6012.5, Rev. & Tax. Code, Sec. 6357.5, Rev. & Tax. Code, Sec. 6385, Rev. & Tax. Code, Sec. 6396, Rev. & Tax. Code

Commuter vehicles, sale and purchase . . . . Sec. 6010.11, Rev. & Tax. Code

Computer programs that are custom made . . . . Sec. 6010.9, Rev. & Tax. Code

Construction contractors: sales to, for use outside state . . . . Sec. 6386, Rev. & Tax. Code

Containers and labels . . . . Sec. 6364, Rev. & Tax. Code, Sec. 6364.5, Rev. & Tax. Code

Delivery to export packers . . . . Sec. 6387, Rev. & Tax. Code

Direct mail advertising materials . . . . Sec. 6379.5, Rev. & Tax. Code

Drugs administered to animals . . . . Sec. 6358.4, Rev. & Tax. Code

Electricity . . . . Sec. 6353, Rev. & Tax. Code

Factory-built housing . . . . Sec. 6012.7, Rev. & Tax. Code

Factory-built school buildings . . . . Sec. 6012.6, Rev. & Tax. Code

Family members: sales of vehicles . . . . Sec. 6285, Rev. & Tax. Code

Farm equipment and machinery (partial exemption) . . . . Sec. 6356.5, Rev. & Tax. Code

Feed and medicine for certain animals . . . . Sec. 6358, Rev. & Tax. Code

Fertilizer . . . . Sec. 6358, Rev. & Tax. Code, Sec. 6358.2, Rev. & Tax. Code

Food products . . . . Sec. 6358, Rev. & Tax. Code, Sec. 6359, Rev. & Tax. Code, Sec. 6359.1, Rev. & Tax. Code, Sec. 7282.3, Rev. & Tax. Code

Food stamp purchases . . . . Sec. 6373, Rev. & Tax. Code

Fuel and petroleum . . . . Sec. 6357, Rev. & Tax. Code, Sec. 6357.5, Rev. & Tax. Code, Sec. 6358.1, Rev. & Tax. Code

Fuel (diesel) used in farming and food processing (partial exemption) . . . . Sec. 6357.1, Rev. & Tax. Code

Fuel used in space flight . . . . Sec. 6380, Rev. & Tax. Code

Gas . . . . Sec. 6353, Rev. & Tax. Code

Gold . . . . Sec. 6354, Rev. & Tax. Code

Green manufacturing exclusion (exp. 1/1/2021)	Sec. 6010.8, Rev. & Tax. Code; Sec. 26003, Pub. Res. Code; Sec. 26011.8, Pub. Res. Code
Hospitals and health or care institutions	Sec. 6363.6, Rev. & Tax. Code
Ice used in packing or shipping foods	Sec. 6359.7, Rev. & Tax. Code
Insurers: sales by (sales tax exemption only)	Sec. 12204, Rev. & Tax. Code
Interstate and foreign commerce	Sec. 6396, Rev. & Tax. Code
Lapel pins sold by certain veterans' organizations	Sec. 6360.1, Rev. & Tax. Code
Leases, certain items	Sec. 6016.3, Rev. & Tax. Code
Leases of property outside California	Sec. 6390, Rev. & Tax. Code
Low-emission motor vehicles: incremental costs of	Sec. 6356.5, Rev. & Tax. Code
Machinery and equipment for use in manufacturing or R&D (eff. July 1, 2014, until July 1, 2022)	Sec. 6377.1, Rev. & Tax. Code
Mailing lists	Sec. 6379.8, Rev. & Tax. Code
Master tapes and records	Sec. 6362.5, Rev. & Tax. Code
Meals served by certain organizations or social clubs	Sec. 6361, Rev. & Tax. Code, Sec. 6363.5, Rev. & Tax. Code, Sec. 6363.8, Rev. & Tax Code, Sec. 6374, Rev. & Tax. Code
Meals served in health care facilities or boarding houses	Sec. 6363.6, Rev. & Tax. Code, Sec. 6363.7, Rev. & Tax. Code
Meals served to low-income elderly	Sec. 6374, Rev. & Tax. Code, Sec. 6376.5, Rev. & Tax. Code, Sec. 6363.7, Rev. & Tax. Code
Meals served to students	Sec. 6363, Rev. & Tax. Code
Medical cannabis sold to authorized patients	Proposition 64, app. 11/08/2016; Special Notice L-486, California State Board of Equalization, November 2016

Pets adopted from certain organizations . . . . Sec. 6010.40, Rev. & Tax. Code

Plants and seeds . . . . Sec. 6358, Rev. & Tax. Code, 6366.5, Rev. & Tax. Code

Pollution control equipment . . . . Sec. 6010.10, Rev. & Tax. Code

Poultry litter . . . . Sec. 6358.2, Rev. & Tax. Code

Prescription medicines . . . . Sec. 6369, Rev. & Tax. Code, Sec. 6369.1, Rev. & Tax. Code, Sec. 6359(c), Rev. & Tax. Code

Printing materials, sales and purchase . . . . Sec. 6010.3, Rev. & Tax. Code

Property donated by retailer . . . . Sec. 6403, Rev. & Tax. Code

Property sold at auction to fund homeless shelters . . . . Sec. 6363.2, Rev. & Tax. Code

Property used in space flight . . . . Sec. 6380, Rev. & Tax. Code

Prosthetic devices and equipment . . . . Sec. 6369, Rev. & Tax. Code

Race horse breeding stock (partial exemption) . . . . Sec. 6358.5, Rev. & Tax. Code

Rail freight cars . . . . Sec. 6368.5, Rev. & Tax. Code

Recycling equipment purchased by certain start-up entities . . . . Sec. 6377, Rev. & Tax. Code

Resales . . . . Sec. 6092, Rev. & Tax. Code

Research equipment purchased by certain start-up entities . . . . Sec. 6006, Rev. & Tax. Code, Sec. 6377, Rev. & Tax. Code, Sec. 6902.2, Rev. & Tax. Code

Retail sales . . . . Sec. 6359, Rev. & Tax. Code

"Safe-harbor" sale and leaseback transactions . . . . Sec. 6010.11, Rev. & Tax. Code, Sec. 6018.8, Rev. & Tax. Code, Sec. 6368.7, Rev. & Tax. Code

San Diego Aerospace Museum . . . . Sec. 6366.4, Rev. & Tax. Code

School yearbooks and catalogs . . . . Sec. 6361.5, Rev. & Tax. Code

Seeds . . . . Sec. 6358, Rev. & Tax. Code

Space flight . . . . Sec. 6380, Rev. & Tax. Code

Stocks, bonds, and other securities . . . . Sec. 50026.5, Govt. Code

Telegraph and telephone lines	Sec. 6016.5, Rev. & Tax. Code
Teleproduction service equipment	Sec. 6378, Rev. & Tax. Code
Thrift stores operated by certain nonprofit organizations (exp. 1/1/2019)	Sec. 6363.3, Rev. & Tax. Code
Thrift store sales on military bases (exp. 1/1/2024)	Sec. 6363.4, Rev. & Tax. Code
Timber harvesting machinery, equipment, and parts (partial exemption)	Sec. 6356.6, Rev. & Tax. Code
Transportation equipment, sale and leaseback by public agency	Sec. 6368.8, Rev. & Tax. Code
Transportation technologies; alternative source products	Sec. 6010.8, Rev. & Tax. Code; Sec. 26011.8, Public Resources Code
Trucks and trailers for out-of-state use	Sec. 6388, Rev. & Tax. Code, Sec. 6388.5, Rev. & Tax. Code
U.S. contractors	Sec. 6384, Rev. & Tax. Code
U.S. flags sold by nonprofit veterans organizations	Sec. 6359.3, Rev. & Tax. Code
U.S. government: transactions with	Sec. 6381, Rev. & Tax. Code, Sec. 6402, Rev. & Tax. Code
Vehicles for physically disabled persons	Sec. 6369.4, Rev. & Tax. Code
Vehicles purchased by foreigners	Sec. 6366.2, Rev. & Tax. Code
Vending machines	Sec. 6359.2, Rev. & Tax. Code, Sec. 6359.4, Rev. & Tax. Code, Sec. 6359.45, Rev. & Tax. Code
Vessels and watercraft	Sec. 6356, Rev. & Tax. Code, Sec. 6368, Rev. & Tax. Code, Sec. 6368.1, Rev. & Tax. Code
Veterinarians	Sec. 6018.1, Rev. & Tax. Code
Water	Sec. 6353, Rev. & Tax. Code
Water, bottled	Sec. 6359, Rev. & Tax. Code

- ## Use tax exemptions, exceptions, and exclusions

Demonstration and display prior to resale	Sec. 6094, Rev. & Tax. Code, Sec. 6244, Rev. & Tax. Code
Imports: Property purchased in a foreign country and personally hand-carried into California (first $800)	Sec. 6405, Rev. & Tax. Code
Green manufacturing exclusion (California Alternative Energy and Advanced Transportation Financing Authority) (exp. 1/1/2021)	Sec. 6010.8, Rev. & Tax. Code; Sec. 26003, Public Resources Code; Sec. 26011.8, Public Resources Code
Loans of property to educational institutions	Sec. 6404, Rev. & Tax. Code
Medical health information and health and safety materials	Sec. 6408, Rev. & Tax. Code, Sec. 6409, Rev. & Tax. Code
Military members' purchases prior to receipt of transfer orders to California	Sec. 6412, Rev. & Tax. Code
Railroad equipment component parts	Sec. 6411, Rev. & Tax. Code
Trailers or semitrailers moved under "one-trip permit"	Sec. 6410, Rev. & Tax. Code
U.S. government: property purchased from	Sec. 6402, Rev. & Tax. Code

¶ 264   Rate of Tax

Effective January 1, 2017, the total statewide sales and use tax rate was reduced to 7.25% (previously, 7.5%) (Sec. 36(f)(1)(A), Rev. & Tax Code; Art. XIII, Cal. Const.). The statewide base sales and use tax rate of 6.25% represents a total of six separate sales and use tax rates. Every California county has adopted the sales and use tax provided under the Bradley-Burns Law and therefore, the uniform statewide rate is 7.25%. Local taxes may add up to 2% to the rate (see ¶ 265). The statewide rate consists of the following components:

— a permanent rate of 4.75% (Sec. 6051, Rev. & Tax. Code, Sec. 6201, Rev. & Tax. Code);

— a 0.5% sales and use tax that is permanent unless the California Supreme Court or a California court of appeal determines that although the tax revenues from the increase are deposited in the Local Revenue Fund, they are actually General Fund proceeds or allocated local tax proceeds under Article VI, Sec. 8, of the California Constitution, in which case this 0.5% tax will become inoperative on the first day of the first month of the following calendar quarter (Sec. 6051.2, Rev. & Tax. Code, Sec. 6201.2, Rev. & Tax. Code);

— a permanent 0.5% sales and use tax (local public safety fund) imposed by the California Constitution and effective January 1, 1994 (Sec. 35, Art. XIII, Cal. Const.);

— a temporary 0.25% state sales and use tax was imposed beginning July 1, 2004, in addition to any other sales and use taxes imposed (Secs. 6051.5, 6201.5, Rev. and Tax. Code). Revenues from the temporary tax were dedicated to the repayment of state deficit financing bonds under the California Economic Recovery Bond Act (ERBA). However, also beginning July 1, 2004, the 1% rate of tax that could be levied by local governments under the Bradley-Burns Uniform Sales and Use Tax Law was reduced by 0.25% to 0.75%, meaning that the combined state and local sales and use tax rate in any taxing jurisdiction remained unchanged (Sec. 7203.1, Rev. and Tax. Code). ERBA expired at the end of 2015, and as a result, local agencies will receive their 1% Bradley-Burns local sales and use tax for sales and purchases within their jurisdictions beginning in 2016.

— a 0.25% sales and use tax that expires on January 1 of any calendar year after the Director of Finance certifies that the amount in the state's Special Fund for Economic Uncertainties exceeds specified levels for prior and current fiscal years, but is revived on any January 1 following certification by the Director that the amount in the Fund fails to exceed the specified level for the current and immediately preceding fiscal years (Sec. 6051.3, Rev. & Tax. Code, Sec. 6051.4, Rev. & Tax. Code, Sec. 6201.3, Rev. & Tax. Code, Sec. 6201.4, Rev. & Tax. Code). This 0.25% tax was not in effect for the 2001 tax year, but was revived effective January 1, 2002, and continues in effect.

Note: A temporary 0.25% increase in the general fund portion of the state sales and use tax (Proposition 30), which became effective January 1, 2013, became inoperative by its own terms on January 1, 2017 (Sec. 36(f)(1)(A), Rev. & Tax Code; Art. XIII, Cal. Const.).

Lumber and engineered wood products: In addition to any other California sales and use taxes imposed by law, an assessment is imposed on a person who purchases a lumber product or an engineered wood product for storage, use, or other consumption in California, at the rate of 1% of the sales price (Sec. 4629.5, Pub. Res. Code; *Publication 256, Lumber Products and Engineered Wood Products,* California State Board of Equalization, August 2014, CCH CALIFORNIA TAX REPORTS, ¶ 406-189).

A "lumber product" is defined as a product in which wood or wood fiber is a principal component part, including but not limited to a solid wood product, or an engineered wood product, that is identified in regulations adopted by the board. The definition does not include furniture, paper products, indoor flooring products such as hardwood or laminated flooring, bark or cork products, firewood, or other products not typically regarded as lumber products. "Engineered wood product" is defined as a building product, including but not limited to veneer-based sheeting material, plywood, laminated veneer lumber (LVL), parallel-laminated veneer (PLV), laminated beams, I-joists, edge-glued material, or composite material such as cellulosic fiberboard, hardboard, decking, particleboard, waferboard, flakeboard, oriented strand board (OSB), or any other panel or composite product where wood is a component part, that is identified in regulations adopted by the board. The definition only includes products that consist of at least 10% wood. (Sec. 4629.5, Pub. Res. Code)

The retailer is required to charge the purchaser the amount of the assessment as a charge that is separate from, and not included in, any other fee, charge, or other amount paid by the purchaser. The retailer is also required to separately state the amount of the assessment on the sales receipt given by the retailer to the person at the time of sale. (Sec. 4629.5, Pub. Res. Code)

Effective January 1, 2015, a California retailer with *de minimis* sales of qualified lumber products and engineered wood products of less than $25,000 during the previous calendar year is not a retailer for purposes of the provisions regarding the assessment. An excluded retailer is required to provide a notice to a purchaser of qualified lumber products or engineered wood products regarding the purchaser's obligation to remit the assessment to the California State Board of Equalization (BOE). (Sec. 4629.5, Pub. Res. Cod)

The lumber products assessment is due and payable to the BOE quarterly on or before the last day of the month next succeeding each quarterly period. On or before the last day of the month following each quarterly period, a return for the preceding quarterly period is required to be filed with the BOE using electronic media, in the form prescribed by the BOE.

A retailer required to collect the lumber products assessment may retain no more than $250 per location as reimbursement for startup costs associated with the collection of the assessment. Such reimbursement is to be taken on the retailer's first return on which the assessment is reported, or, if the amount of the collected assessment is less than the allowed reimbursement, on the retailer's next consecutive returns until the allowed reimbursement amount is retained. (Reg. 2000)

Motor vehicle fuel and diesel fuel: Effective July 1, 2016, through June 30, 2017, the excise tax rates decreased to $0.278 per gallon from $0.30 per gallon for gasoline and increased to $0.16 per gallon from $0.13 per gallon for diesel fuel. For additional information, including special provisions for sales of dyed diesel fuel, see *BOE Publication 388,* State Board of Equalization, September 2016, CCH CALIFORNIA TAX REPORTS, ¶ 406-553.

The statewide sales and use tax rates for aircraft jet fuel and diesel fuel will decrease by 0.25% on January 1, 2017 (*Special Notice L-480,* California State Board of Equalization, December 2016). Sales and use tax rates for these fuels are as follows:

— aircraft jet fuel: 7.5% July 1, 2016, through December 31, 2016; and 7.25% January 1, 2017, through June 30, 2017;

— diesel fuel: 9.25% July 1, 2016, through December 31, 2016; and 9% January 1, 2017, through June 30, 2017.

The 0.25% reductions effective January 1, 2017, reflect the expiration of the temporary statewide sales tax increase under Proposition 60, as discussed above.

Fruit trees, nut trees, olive trees, and grapevines: An annual 1% special assessment is levied on the gross sales of all deciduous pome and stone fruit trees, nut trees, olive trees, and grapevines that are produced and sold within California or produced within and shipped from the state by any licensed nursery dealer. The assessment covers seeds, seedlings, rootstocks, and topstock and included ornamental varieties of apple, apricot, crabapple, cherry, nectarine, peach, pear, and plum. (Sec. 6981, Food & Agric. Code)

The assessment (1) applies at the point of sale where the nursery stock is sold by a producer to a nonproducer; (2) is based on gross sales for the previous fiscal year; and (3) is due and payable to the Secretary of the Department of Food and Agriculture by March 10 of each year. (Sec. 6982, Food & Agric. Code; Sec. 6983, Food & Agric. Code)

Sales of health services: From July 1, 2013, until July 1, 2016, sales tax was imposed on sellers of Medi-Cal managed care plans at a rate of 3.9375% of the gross receipts of any seller from the sale of all such plans in California. Counties, cities, and districts are prohibited from imposing a sales or use tax on such gross receipts. (Former Sec. 6174, Rev. & Tax. Code)

Surcharge on prepaid phone services: For calendar years 2016 through 2019, a prepaid mobile telephony services (MTS) surcharge will be imposed and must be collected by a seller from a prepaid consumer at the time of a retail transaction in California. The prepaid MTS surcharge is a percentage of the sales price of each retail transaction that occurs in California and is in lieu of any charges imposed pursuant to the emergency telephone users surcharge act and the Public Utilities Commission (PUC) surcharges for prepaid mobile telephony services. The surcharge rate will be calculated annually by the Board of Equalization (BOE) no later than November 1, beginning in 2015, by adding the emergency telephone users surcharge rate and the

PUC reimbursement fee and surcharges. (Sec. 319, Public Utilities Code; Sec. 41020, Rev. & Tax.Code; Sec. 42001 *et seq.*, Rev. & Tax. Code) See also ¶ 265.

Contractors: The California State Board of Equalization (BOE) advises construction contractors that they may be able to purchase and/or sell materials and fixtures at a partial sales and use tax rate (3.3125%, plus applicable district taxes) for certain jobs when contracted by qualified companies engaged in manufacturing or Research and Development (R&D). Legislation made effective July 1, 2014, allows certain companies engaged in manufacturing or R&D to make annual purchases up to $200 million of qualifying property at a reduced sales and use tax rate. The partial exemption also applies to qualifying property purchased for use in constructing or reconstructing a special purpose building. The BOE advises that the law is unusual because qualified companies can authorize the construction contractor to make purchases of materials and fixtures for the special purpose building at a reduced tax rate and pass the tax savings back to the qualified manufacturing or R&D company. (*Special Notice L-430,* California State Board of Equalization, January 2016, **http://www.boe.ca.gov/pdf/l430.pdf**)

• **Tax rate changes—Application to fixed-price contracts and leases**

When there is a change in the sales and use tax rate, the rate of tax that applies to sales and purchases made under an existing contract or lease depends on whether there is an increase or decrease in the tax rate and whether the contract or lease meets certain conditions. If the new rate is higher, an existing contract or lease will qualify for an exclusion from the tax rate increase and the tax rate or amount specified in the contract or lease will continue to apply provided the following conditions are met: (1) all costs are fixed at the outset; (2) neither party has an unconditional right to terminate the contract or lease; (3) the tax amount or rate is specifically stated in the contract or lease agreement; and (4) there is no provision in the contract or lease for an increase in the amount of tax (*Tax Information Bulletin,* BOE, June 1997). If the new rate is lower, the lower rate will apply for taxable transactions that occur on and after the effective date of the rate change.

¶ 265   Local Taxes

All California cities and counties impose local sales and use taxes at the rate of 1%, as authorized by the Bradley-Burns Uniform Local Sales and Use Tax Law (Sec. 7200, Rev. & Tax. Code—Sec. 7212, Rev. & Tax. Code). Therefore, the rate of tax anywhere in California is at least 7.5% (the 6.5% state rate plus 1% Bradley-Burns local rate). Revenues are divided between city and county governments.

In addition, a transactions and use tax is imposed, at a maximum rate of 2%, within the boundaries of various transit, traffic, or other districts where allowed by state law.

Online travel companies: Under the plain language of the San Francisco ordinance that imposes a California local transient occupancy tax of 6% of the rent charged by the operator on transients for the privilege of occupancy of any hotel, online travel companies (OTCs) had no tax liability. The appellate court held that the ordinance does not impose a tax on the service fees and markups charged by the OTCs. Rather, the tax is imposed on the rent charged by the hotel operator, and the tax obligations are only imposed on transients and hotel operators. The ordinance includes no provision that imposes any tax liability on any entity other than the hotel operator or the transient. (*In re Transient Occupancy Tax Cases,* Court of Appeal of California, Second District, No. B243800, March 27, 2014, CCH CALIFORNIA TAX REPORTS, ¶ 406-088)

Online travel companies (OTCs) are not operators of hotels within the meaning of the San Diego ordinance that imposes a California local transient occupancy tax and, as such, the OTCs are not liable for the tax. Under the San Diego ordinance, in a merchant model type of transaction, a hotel operator is liable for a 6% tax on the wholesale price plus any additional amount for room rental the operator requires the OTC to charge the visitor under rate parity provisions of contracts between hotels and OTCs.

Under the merchant model, OTCs contract with hotels to advertise and rent rooms to the general public, and they handle all financial transactions related to the hotel reservations, but they do not own, operate, or manage hotels. The price the hotel charges the OTC for the room is the wholesale price and rate parity provisions in most contracts between OTCs and hotels bar the OTC from selling a room for a rent lower than what the hotel quotes its customers directly. The OTC offers rooms to the public at retail prices and charges customers a "tax recovery charge," which represents the OTC's estimate of what the hotel will owe in transient occupancy tax based on the wholesale price of the room as charged by the hotel to the OTC. The hotel bills the OTC for the wholesale price of the room plus the transient occupancy tax the hotel will have to pay based on the room's wholesale price, and the OTC remits the charged amount to the hotel, which in turn remits the tax to San Diego, and the OTC retains its markup and service fees. San Diego Transient Occupancy Tax Ordinance The San Diego ordinance provides that, for the privilege of occupancy in any hotel located in San Diego, each transient must pay a tax in the amount of 6% of the rent charged by the operator. "Operator" is defined as the person who is the proprietor of the hotel, whether in the capacity of owner, lessee, sublessee, mortgagee in possession, licensee, or any other capacity.

The California Supreme Court held that the ordinance imposes the tax on the amount charged by the operator; it does not refer to amounts received or collected by the operator. To the extent a hotel determines the markup, such as by contractual rate parity provisions requiring the OTC to quote and charge the customer a rate not less than what the hotel is quoting on its own website, it effectively charges that amount, regardless of whether it ultimately receives or collects any portion of the markup, and that amount is therefore subject to the tax. The fact that the OTCs act as hotel agents or intermediaries for the limited purpose of charging and collecting rent does not subject the OTCs to assessment as an operator or make any undifferentiated portion of the charge representing the amount unilaterally set by the OTCs rent charged by the operator. Under the contracts between the hotels and the OTCs, the OTCs agreed to be responsible for any taxes assessed by any governmental authority on the markup, to collect and remit room tax, and to assume liability to San Diego for nonpayment or underpayment of the tax. However, these provisions allocate responsibility as between the hotels and the OTCs for properly assessed room taxes but they do not create liability for the tax; only the ordinance can do that, and the ordinance imposes assessment of the transient occupancy tax on hotel operators. (*In re Transient Occupancy Tax Cases,* California Supreme Court, No. S218400, December 12, 2016, CCH CALIFORNIA TAX REPORTS, ¶ 406-598)

Sourcing of telecommunications charges: California conforms to the federal Mobile Telecommunications Sourcing Act, P.L. 106-252. All charges for mobile telecommunications services are considered to be provided by the customer's home service provider and sourced to the customer's place of primary use (Sec. 41020, Rev. and Tax Code). All such charges are subject to sales tax based on the customer's place of primary use.

The service provider will be held harmless for an error in assigning wireless services to a jurisdiction if it utilizes an electronic database provided by the state or a designated entity, or, if the state has not provided or designated a database, if it utilizes a database that makes assignments based on a nine-digit zip code.

Surcharge on prepaid phone services: For calendar years 2016 through 2019, any local charge imposed by a local agency on prepaid mobile telephones ervice (MTS) must be collected from the prepaid consumer by a seller at the same time and manner as the prepaid state MTS surcharge is collected (see ¶ 264). Further, the authority of any city and/or county to impose a utility user tax on the consumption of prepaid MTS is suspended and the rate on prepaid MTS is a specified percentage of the utility user tax as set by ordinance. (Sec. 42001 *et seq.*, Rev. & Tax. Code)

Medical marijuana: Effective January 1, 2016, California counties may impose a tax—not a fee or special assessment—on the privilege of cultivating, dispensing, producing, processing, preparing, storing, providing, donating, selling, or distributing medical cannabis or medical cannabis products by a licensee. In addition, another law requires the State Board of Equalization (BOE) to adopt a system for reporting the movement of commercial cannabis products throughout the distribution chain. (Ch. 689 (A.B. 266), Laws 2015; Ch. 719 (S.B. 643), Laws 2015)

County tax: A county board of supervisors must specify in an ordinance subject to voter approval the activities subject to tax, the applicable rate or rates, the method of apportionment, and the manner of collection of the tax. They may provide for the collection of the tax in the same manner as for other charges and taxes fixed and collected by the counties. The tax may be imposed on any or all of the activities listed above regardless whether the activity either is undertaken individually, collectively, or cooperatively or is for compensation or gratuitous. This law does not limit or prohibit the levy or collection of any other fee, charge, or tax, or a license or service fee or charge upon, or related to, the activities relating to medical marijuana tax. It also is not a limitation upon the taxing authority of a county as provided by law. However, the law does not authorize a county to impose a sales or use tax in addition to other authorized sales and use taxes. (CA ¶ 265)

Monitoring distribution: The BOE monitoring system must employ secure packaging and be capable of providing information to the BOE. Specific information to be provided is, at a minimum, the amount of tax due; the name, address, and license number of the designated entity remitting the tax; the name, address, and license number of the succeeding entity receiving the product; the transaction date; and any other information deemed necessary by the BOE for the taxation and regulation of marijuana and marijuana products. (CA ¶ 267)

Exemption for marijuana patients: The passage of Proposition 64 (The Control, Regulate and Tax Adult Use of Marijuana Act) at the November 8, 2016, election, exempts certain sales of medical marijuana from sales and use tax. Sales of medical cannabis to those who have a medical marijuana identification card (MMIC) issued on a county-by-county basis by the California Department of Public Health (CDPH) and a valid government-issued identification card are now exempt from sales and use tax. Consumers can obtain the CDPH-issued cards at their county health department at a cost that varies by county. A paper recommendation from a physician is not sufficient to qualify for this sales tax exemption. The county-issued MMIC will have the State of California seal and indicate whether the card holder is a "patient" or a "caregiver." The card will also contain the patient's or primary caregiver's photo, a nine-digit ID number, a CDPH website to verify the ID number, an expiration date, and the name of the county that issued the card. Cards are valid for the duration of the physician recommendation or up to one year, at which time the card must be renewed. Retailers should retain the purchaser's nine-digit ID number and expiration date, along with the related sales invoice or other record of sale, to support the exempt sale. Exempted products include medical cannabis, medical cannabis concentrate, edible medical cannabis products, and topical cannabis as these terms are defined in Business and Professions Code Sec. 19300.5. Retailers should not collect sales tax reimbursement on qualifying exempt sales of medical marijuana. Retailers should claim a deduction on their sales and use tax returns for their qualifying exempt medical marijuana sales. Retailers may verify the validity of a nine-digit ID number on the CDPH website. Sales of recreational marijuana will not start until January 1, 2018. Such sales will be subject to sales tax and an excise tax. A cultivator tax will also apply to marijuana beginning on that date. (Proposition 64, approved by the voters on November 8, 2016; *News Release 92-16-G,* California State Board of Equalization, November 17, 2016)

• **Local tax rates**

The most current local tax rates are available on the Board of Equalization's website at **http://www.boe.ca.gov/sutax/pam71.htm**.

Local and district taxes collected within each county are reported on Form BT-401-A (State, Local and District Sales and Use Tax Return) and Schedule A (Computation Schedule for District Tax).

Mobile web rate lookup: Taxpayers can find a tax rate using their phone's GPS system or by searching for a city or county on the Internet at **www.geotax.com.**, which hosts an application that will enable taxpayers to find their sales tax rate based on an address. This enables taxpayers and consumers to find the tax rate for any address in the state. The web application is available on the BOE's website at **www.boe.ca.gov**.

¶ 266   **Bracket Schedule**

The California Civil Code provides that whether a retailer can add sales tax reimbursement to the sales price of property sold at retail to a purchaser depends on the terms of the agreement of sale (Sec. 1656.1, Civ. Code).

It is rebuttably presumed that the parties agree to the addition of sales tax to the price if (1) the agreement of sale expressly provides for such addition of sales tax reimbursement, (2) sales tax reimbursement is shown on the sales check or other proof of sale, or (3) the retailer posts in a visible location (or includes on a price tag or other printed materials) a notice to the effect that the sales tax will be added to the sales price.

It is rebuttably presumed that the price includes the tax if the retailer posts a sign indicating that prices of taxable items (or of a particular item) includes sales tax reimbursement.

• **Sales tax reimbursement schedules**

The schedules for various rates are available from the State Board of Equalizaton at **http://www.boe.ca.gov/sutax/streimsched.htm**.

¶ 267   **Returns, Payments, and Due Dates**

Returns must be filed by sellers and by every person liable for sales tax. Out-of-state retailers engaged in business in the state and consumers subject to use tax who have not paid it to a retailer must also file returns (Sec. 6452, Rev. & Tax. Code). Returns may be filed by electronic media.

Sales and use tax is due and payable to the State Board of Equalization (BOE) quarterly, on or before the last day of the month following each quarterly period (Sec. 6451, Rev. & Tax. Code). Taxpayers are permitted to use credit cards or other payment devices to remit sales and use tax payments (Sec. 6163, Govt. Code). For information, phone the BOE at 1-800-272-9829.

Taxpayers can request special reporting periods for the sales and use tax. Businesses are generally required to file their tax returns for regular calendar periods, but if the business has established accounting periods that do not correspond to the calendar, the BOE may be able to customize the taxpayer's reporting periods. Form BOE-715 is used if the taxpayer would like to file sales and use tax returns and pay the tax based on special reporting periods.

Virtual currencies: Retailers who accept virtual currencies, such as Bitcoin, Litecoin, Dogecoin, or Peercoin, as payment are instructed to retain documentation on the amount for which they regularly sell the same or similar property to their customers when payment is made in United States dollars (cash, check, credit or debit card). The BOE does not accept virtual currencies as a payment method for any tax or fee program. (*Special Notice L-382,* California State Board of Equalization, June 2014)

¶266   California

Penalty for untimely payment: Any person who knowingly collects California sales tax reimbursement or use tax, as defined, and who fails to timely remit those amounts to the California State Board of Equalization is liable for a penalty of 40% of the amount not timely remitted. The penalty, however, is inapplicable to any person whose liability for unremitted sales tax reimbursement or use tax averages $1,000 or less per month or does not exceed 5% of the total amount of tax liability for which the tax reimbursement was collected for the period in which tax was due, whichever is greater. In addition, relief from the penalty is provided to a person whose failure to timely remit sales tax reimbursement or use tax was due to a reasonable cause or circumstances beyond the person's control and occurred notwithstanding the exercise of ordinary care and the absence of willful neglect (Sec. 6597, Rev. and Tax. Code).

Simplified use tax reporting: Under the Alternative Method for Reporting Use Tax (AMRUT) program, taxpayers may report use tax using a formula based on the percentage of their sales for which the use tax typically applies. However, the BOE must approve the type of purchase and percentage allowed prior to the use of the percentage formula. In addition, an Audit Sampling Plan (Form BOE-472) must be completed prior to using the percentage reporting method.

To participate in this program, a taxpayer must submit a written application, have an account that is in good standing, and maintain acceptable accounting records and internal controls. Interested individuals may obtain additional information and order a copy of the AMRUT guidelines by calling (916) 324-2883. (Tax Information Bulletin, California State Board of Equalization.)

Returns for specially designated periods: The BOE may require returns and tax payments for periods other than calendar quarters in order to ensure payment and facilitate collection (Sec. 6455, Rev. & Tax. Code). Reports for these "designated" periods must be filed on or by the last day of the month following each such period.

Disaster extensions: The BOE is authorized, in the case of a disaster, to extend the time for making any report or return or paying any BOE-administered tax or fee for a period not to exceed three months. This provision is applicable to the Sales and Use Tax (SUT) Law, the Motor Vehicle Fuel Tax Law, the Use Fuel Tax Law, the Cigarette and Tobacco Products Tax Law, the Alcoholic Beverage Tax Law, the Timber Yield Tax Law, the Energy Resources Surcharge Law, the Emergency Telephone Users Surcharge Act, the Hazardous Substances Tax Law, the Integrated Waste Management Fee Law, the Oil Spill Response, Prevention, and Administration Fees Law, the Underground Storage Tank Maintenance Fee Law, the Fee Collection Procedures Law, and the Diesel Fuel Tax Law. The extension may be granted at any time provided a request for relief is filed with the BOE within or before the period at issue. "Disaster" is defined as fire, flood, storm, tidal wave, earthquake, or similar public calamity, regardless of whether the disaster results from natural causes. (Sec. 6459(c), Rev. & Tax. Code)

Self-reporting of use tax: Persons not required to hold a seller's permit or to register with the BOE may self-report their qualified use tax liabilities on their timely filed original personal income or corporation franchise (income) tax returns. Payments remitted with income tax returns are applied first to income taxes, penalties, and interest and, second, to qualified use tax liabilities. Notwithstanding a person's election to self-report, the BOE would still be entitled to make determinations for understatement of use tax (Sec. 6452.1, Rev. & Tax. Code; Reg. 1685.5).

The BOE has approved a use tax lookup table to use in the calculation and reporting of estimated California use tax on individuals' state income tax returns. According to the BOE, the intent of the table is to make it convenient for taxpayers who are not registered with the BOE to comply with their use tax obligations by providing them the option to report their estimated use tax liabilities by using the table instead of calculating and reporting their actual unpaid use tax liabilities. The BOE is required to annually calculate the estimated amount of use tax due based on a person's California adjusted gross income (AGI). The 2016 use tax lookup table is available at **https:// www.boe.ca.gov/info/use_tax_table.html**.

Application of payments: Payments and credits on a California personal income tax, corporation franchise or income tax, partnership, limited liability company, estate or trust tax, or information return of a taxpayer that reports California use tax on the return must be applied first to satisfy the use tax liability, with any excess amount then being applied to any outstanding taxes, penalties, and interest owed to the Franchise Tax Board (Sec.6452.1, Rev. & Tax. Code).

• Electronic funds transfer

Persons, other than those who collect use tax voluntarily, whose estimated tax liability averages $10,000 or more per month must remit the tax due by an electronic funds transfer (Sec. 6479.3, Rev. & Tax. Code; Reg. 1707). Persons whose estimated tax liability is less than the threshold amounts and those who voluntarily collect use tax may remit tax due by electronic funds transfer with the approval of the SBE. The State Board of Equalization may permit the filing of quarterly California sales and use tax returns by electronic media (Sec. 6452, Rev. & Tax. Code, Sec. 6479.31, Rev. & Tax. Code). Electronic funds transfers must be made in compliance with the usual due dates. Payment is deemed timely if the transmission is completed on or before the due date of the return. The E-file system may be accessed at **http://www.boe.ca.gov**.

Internet payment: Taxpayers may make their EFT payments over the Internet if they are currently registered as EFT taxpayers and use the automated clearing house (ACH) debit payment method. Taxpayers that are not registered to make ACH debit payments or that desire to change to this method must complete Form BOE-555-EFT, Authorization Agreement for Electronic Funds Transfer, or call the EFT Helpline at 916-327-4229.

BOE ePay: The BOE is offering a free application, BOE ePay, that allows owners of most mobile devices to make payments to their BOE tax and fee accounts. The application enables taxpayers to use their credit card, checking, or savings account to make "ePayments," view their ePayment history and register, and manage their "eClient" accounts. Taxpayers must register as an eClient to use all application features, and an express login code is available to taxpayers who simply want to make ePayments. BOE ePay is available at **https://www.boe.ca.gov/mobile/**.

Cannabis dispensaries: Before January 1, 2022, a person issued a seller's permit for a place of business that is a "dispensary," as defined in the Medical Cannabis Regulation and Safety Act, may remit sales and use tax amounts due for retail sales at the dispensary by a means other than electronic funds transfer (EFT). During this period, a dispensary is not subject to the general requirement to remit amounts due by EFT if its estimated tax liability averages $10,000 or more per month. (Sec. 6479.3(k), Rev. & Tax. Code)

¶ 268   Prepayment of Taxes

Persons whose estimated taxable receipts average $17,000 or more per month (this threshold may increase to $50,000; see below) must file a quarterly prepayment report and prepay the tax (Sec. 6471, Rev. & Tax. Code, Sec. 6472, Rev. & Tax. Code). Once notified by the State Board of Equalization (BOE) that prepayments are required, prepayments must be made until further notification by the BOE. The BOE may consider previously filed tax returns, as well as any other information it has or may receive, to determine whether a taxpayer's taxable receipts do in fact exceed the above threshold amount (Sec. 6474, Rev. & Tax. Code). The prepaid amount is treated as a credit for the tax due for the quarter (Sec. 6473, Rev. & Tax. Code). The prepayment provisions do not apply to persons filing returns for other than quarterly periods (Sec. 6470, Rev. & Tax. Code).

The $17,000 threshold amount would increase to $50,000 whenever the Attorney General certifies to the legislature and to the BOE that a court has upheld the constitutionality of Sec. 6203(d), Rev. & Tax. Code through Sec. 6203(h), Rev. & Tax. Code, as added by 1987 and 1988 legislation, requiring use tax collection by out-of-state retailers that solicit sales in California through telecommunications and other specified means, and the Department of Finance certifies to the legislature that revenues attributable to these provisions are being remitted to the SBE.

Holders of direct payment permits: Businesses that hold "direct payment permits" are required to make prepayments of tax (Reg. 1699.5(f)). The prepayment due dates are five days earlier than those for prepaying taxpayers in general.

Prepayment on fuels: Effective July 1, 2016, through June 30, 2017, the sales tax prepayment rates (per gallon) for fuels are as follows: (1) 5¢ for motor vehicle fuel (gasoline); (2) 7¢ for aircraft jet fuel; and (3) 17¢ for diesel fuel. The California State Board of Equalization is required to establish the prepayment tax rate for such fuels by March 1 of each year.

¶ 269   **Vendor Registration**

Retailers that have substantial nexus with California (see ¶ 261) should register for a permit by applying online (see below). A retailer is considered engaged in business in California and required to register with the State Board of Equalization (BOE) to collect California use tax if the retailer:

(1) maintains, occupies, or uses a place of business in California;

(2) has persons operating in California under its authority for the purpose of selling, delivering, installing, assembling, or the taking of orders for tangible personal property; or

(3) derives rentals from a lease of tangible personal property situated in California.

Additional information is available in *Special Notice L-324,* California State Board of Equalization, August 2012.

Any person that wants to conduct business as a seller in California must apply for a permit from the State Board of Equalization (BOE) for each place of business (Sec. 6066, Rev. & Tax. Code). The application must be on a prescribed form and be signed by the owner, partner, or corporate officer, with the signatory certifying that the applicant will actively conduct business as a seller of tangible personal property. Permit applications may be filed using electronic media under rules prescribed by the BOE (Sec. 6066, Rev. & Tax. Code).

California cities and counties may collect California sales and use tax seller's permit application information from persons desiring to engage in the business of selling tangible personal property in the jurisdiction and may submit that information to the California State Board of Equalization (BOE) (Sec. 6066.3, Rev. & Tax. Code). The information submitted to the BOE serves as all of the following: (1) the preliminary application for a seller's permit; (2) notice to the BOE by the local jurisdiction of a person desiring to engage in the business of selling tangible personal property in the jurisdiction; and (3) notice to the BOE for purposes of the redistribution of tax between counties. The local jurisdiction may not charge a fee for collecting and transmitting the information.

Online registration: Businesses can use a BOE website, **http://www.boe.ca.gov/ elecsrv/esrvcont.htm#Register**, that allows users to get a seller's permit and perform several other actions, such as:

     — register for a special tax or fee account, such as International Fuel Tax Agreement (IFTA) accounts and cigarette and tobacco products licenses;

     — add a new business location;

— view the status of a user's account online; and

— access BOE reference materials, forms, and publications.

Withdrawal: The BOE has issued guidance regarding closing out a seller's permit for sales and use tax purposes. Topics discussed include notifying the BOE, filing a final tax return, taxable sales after closing out a permit, successor's liability and tax clearance, and changes in ownership (*BOE Publication 74, Closing Out Your Seller's Permit,* California State Board of Equalization, December 2010, CCH CALIFORNIA TAX REPORTS, ¶ 405-321).

Marijuana vendors: Sellers of medical cannabis, including growers and dispensaries, are required to register with the BOE for a seller's permit for sales and use tax purposes. Once registered, sellers, growers, and dispensaries must file sales and use tax returns and pay any tax due. Sales and use tax returns are filed using the BOE's online filing service. (*Special Notice L-421,* California State Board of Equalization, October 2015); see also the BOE's *Tax Guide for Medical Cannabis Businesses* at **http:// www.boe.ca.gov/industry/medical_cannabis.html**.

• **Permit requirements**

A separate, nonassignable permit must be held for each place of business and conspicuously displayed at each such place (Sec. 6067, Rev. & Tax. Code). A permit holder who changes a business address will be issued a new permit after notifying the BOE of the new address; a new application need not be filed (Sec. 6068, Rev. & Tax. Code).

• **Use tax registration requirements**

Every retailer selling tangible personal property for storage, use, or other consumption in California must register with the BOE and give the name and address of all agents operating in the state and the location of all distribution or sales houses, offices, or other business places in the state (Sec. 6226, Rev. & Tax. Code, Reg. 1684). Such retailers must hold seller's permits since they are considered to be engaging in business in the state. Retailers not "engaged in business in the state" may apply for a Certificate of Registration—Use Tax (Reg. 1684(b)). Holders of such a certificate are required to collect use tax from, and give use tax receipts to, purchasers and to remit the tax to the SBE.

Service businesses: Service business owners that meet the statutory definition of a "qualified purchaser" are required to register with the BOE, file returns by April 15 of each year, and report all purchases subject to use tax from the previous calendar year (Sec. 6225, Rev. & Tax. Code). A "qualified purchaser" is a business that receives at least $100,000 in gross receipts per year from business operations, is not required to hold a seller's permit with the BOE, is not a holder of a use tax direct payment permit, is not required to be registered with the BOE, and is not otherwise registered with the BOE to report use tax. Businesses that do not meet the $100,000 gross receipts threshold are still required to report and pay use tax, but are not required to register with the BOE for that purpose. Persons that have multiple businesses with the same ownership must register if the aggregate gross receipts of those businesses meet or exceed the $100,000 threshold.

• **Restriction on state contracting**

A state department or agency may not enter into a contract for the purchase of tangible personal property from any vendor, contractor, or affiliate of a vendor or contractor unless the vendor, contractor, and all affiliates that make sales for delivery into California have a valid seller's permit or are registered with the California State Board of Equalization (BOE) for California sales and use tax purposes (Sec. 10295.1, Pub. Contracts Code). An exception is provided if the contract is necessary to meet a compelling state interest.

¶269   California

• Sellers treated as consumers

Certain sellers are treated as consumers in order to minimize compliance burdens, as follows:

— Certain itinerant U.S. Armed Forces veteran vendors are regarded as consumers rather than retailers of tangible personal property owned and sold by the qualified itinerant vendors, except for alcoholic beverages or items sold for more than $100. The law is scheduled to sunset on January 1, 2022. (Sec. 6018.3, Rev. & Tax. Code);

— A nonprofit membership organization is characterized as a consumer rather than as a retailer in regards to specified tangible personal property that the organization provides or sells to its members. Such property includes sales at cost or less of limited quantities of nonpolitical items that bear the logo of the organization. (Sec. 6018.9, Rev. & Tax. Code).

¶ 270   Sales or Use Tax Credits

A credit is allowed against California use tax for sales or use taxes paid to another state prior to the use, storage, or consumption of the property in California. A credit or refund is also allowed for erroneous or overpaid taxes (Sec. 6901, Rev. & Tax. Code, Sec. 6901.5, Rev. & Tax. Code).

Film and television credit: A motion picture production credit (the credit is also referred to as the "film and television credit") is available against personal income tax, corporation franchise and income taxes, and state sales and use taxes. The credit may be claimed by qualified taxpayers for a percentage of qualified expenditures paid or incurred by the taxpayer in California in the production of a qualified motion picture, as defined. Taxpayers may make an irrevocable election to claim a sales and use tax credit in lieu of the personal income or corporation franchise and income tax credit. (Sec. 6902.5, Rev. & Tax Code; Secs. 17053.85, 17053.95, Rev. & Tax. Code; Secs. 23685, 23695, Rev. & Tax. Code; Reg. 5502, 10 CCR Reg. 5503). The California Film Commission must allocate the new credit to applicants in one or more allocation periods per fiscal year on or after July 1, 2015, and before July 1, 2016, and in two or more allocation periods per fiscal year on or after July 1, 2016, and before July 1, 2020.

Irrevocable elections to apply unused certified credits against qualified sales and use taxes must be made in the form prescribed by the BOE and include a copy of the credit certificate certifying the credits being claimed. (Sec. 6902.5, Rev. & Tax Code; *Special Notice, Legislation Affecting the California Film and Television Tax Credit Programs,* California State Board of Equalization, April 2015, CCH CALIFORNIA TAX REPORTS, ¶ 406-326)

¶ 271   Deficiency Assessments

If unsatisfied with a tax return or payment, the State Board of Equalization (BOE) may determine the required payment from facts in the return or from any information the BOE may obtain (Sec. 6481, Rev. & Tax. Code). One or more deficiency determinations may be made for one or more periods. A deficiency determination for a discontinued business may be made at any time prior to expiration of the statute of limitations, even if prior to the filing due date that would have applied had the business not been discontinued.

In making deficiency determinations, the BOE may offset overpayments and related interest against underpayments and related penalties and interest (Sec. 6483, Rev. & Tax. Code).

Deficiency determinations when no return is made: The above provisions also apply when required returns have not been filed. The BOE, on the basis of available information, estimates the gross receipts or, if applicable, the sales price of property bought or sold and subject to use tax, and imposes an automatic 10% penalty on the estimated required payment (Sec. 6511, Rev. & Tax. Code, Sec. 6512, Rev. & Tax. Code, Sec. 6515, Rev. & Tax. Code).

Collection: Both the BOE and the FTB must make available as a matter of public record a list of the 500 largest tax delinquencies in excess of $100,000 (Sec. 31, Bus. & Prof. Code; Sec. 494.5, Bus. & Prof. Code). The SBE must post the delinquencies quarterly and the FTB must post them at least twice a year. In addition, state agencies generally are prohibited from entering into any contract for the acquisition of goods or services with a contractor whose name appears on either of the lists (Sec. 10295.4, Pub. Cont. Code).

Both the BOE and the FTB are authorized to enter into an agreement to collect any delinquent tax debt due to the IRS or any other state imposing an income tax, a tax measured by income, sales and use tax, or a similar tax, provided that the IRS and the other states agree to collect delinquent tax debts due to the BOE and the FTB (Sec. 6835, Rev. & Tax. Code). Under any such agreement, the California Controller would offset any delinquent tax debt due to that other state from a person or entity against any refund to that person or entity under the California sales and use tax law, personal income tax law, or corporation tax law.

¶ 272   Audit Procedures

The State Board of Equalization (BOE) or its authorized representatives may examine the books, papers, records, and equipment of any seller of tangible personal property or of any person liable for use tax and may investigate the character of the business to verify the accuracy of the tax returns or, if no returns are filed, to determine the proper tax amount due (Sec. 7054, Rev. & Tax. Code; Reg. 1698.5).

• **Managed audit program**

Under the managed audit program (MAP), taxpayers may self-audit their books and records, with guidance from the BOE (Sec. 7076.1, Rev. & Tax. Code). The program features a reduced interest rate of one-half the regular rate on liabilities covered by the audit period (Sec. 7076.5, Rev. & Tax. Code).

At the discretion of the BOE and in a manner consistent with the efficient use of audit resources, a taxpayer is eligible for the MAP only if all of the following criteria are met:

— the taxpayer's business involves few or no statutory exemptions;

— the taxpayer's business involves a single or small number of clearly defined taxability issues;

— the taxpayer is taxed pursuant to the MAP and agrees to participate in the MAP; and

— the taxpayer has the resources to comply with the MAP instructions provided by the SBE.

The MAP does not preclude the taxpayer from reliance on the statute that provides relief of tax, interest, and penalties in cases in which a taxpayer relied on erroneous advice from the SBE.

For additional information, see *Publication 53, Managed Audit Program.*

¶ 273   Statute of Limitations

The Board must mail notices of deficiencies within three years after the later of (1) the end of the calendar month following the quarterly period to which the deficiency determination relates or (2) the date on which the return was filed (Sec. 6487, Rev. & Tax. Code). If no return has been filed, the limitations period is generally extended to eight years after the end of the calendar month following the quarterly period. For taxpayers who file annual returns, a notice of deficiency must be mailed within three years after the later of (1) the end of the calendar month following the one-year reporting period or (2) the date on which the return was filed; if no return has been filed, the notice must be mailed within eight years after the end of the calendar month following the one-year reporting period at issue.

The limitation periods do not apply when there has been fraud or attempted evasion of tax (Sec. 6487, Rev. & Tax. Code). Also, the taxpayer may waive the limitation periods by written consent (Sec. 6488, Rev. & Tax. Code).

• Self-reported use tax

Under the voluntary use tax reporting program, the statute of limitations for California use tax deficiency assessments against qualifying purchasers is limited to three years for the collection of unreported use tax on specified purchases if it is determined that the failure to report and pay the tax was due to reasonable cause. These limitation provisions, however, do not apply to purchases of vehicles, vessels, or aircraft (Sec. 6487.06, Rev. & Tax. Code). "Qualifying purchaser" means a person who voluntarily files an individual use tax return for tangible personal property that is purchased out of state for storage, use, or other consumption in California and that meets certain other requirements (Sec. 6487.05, Rev. & Tax. Code).

• Personal liability

A statute of limitations applies to the issuance of deficiency determinations against corporate officers and other responsible persons liable for the unpaid California sales and use taxes of a business. A notice of deficiency determination must be mailed within the earlier of: (1) three years after the last day of the calendar month following the quarterly period in which the State Board of Equalization (BOE) obtains actual knowledge, through its audit or compliance activities, or by written communication by the business or its representative, of the termination, dissolution, or abandonment of the business of the corporation, partnership, limited partnership, limited liability partnership, or limited liability company; or (2) eight years after the last day of the calendar month following the quarterly period in which the entity was terminated, dissolved, or abandoned. If a business or its representative files a notice of termination, dissolution, or abandonment of its business with a state or local agency other than the BOE, the filing will not constitute actual knowledge of the SBE. (Sec. 6829(f), Rev. & Tax. Code)

¶ 274 Application for Refund

Refund claims for erroneous or overpaid taxes, penalties, or interest must be in writing and state the specific grounds on which the claims are founded (Sec. 6904, Rev. & Tax. Code). The factual and legal bases of the claim should be stated as completely as possible because any subsequent court action against the State Board of Equalization (BOE) will be limited to the grounds specified (Sec. 6933, Rev. & Tax. Code, *Javor v. SBE,* 73 CalApp3d 939, 141 CalRptr 226 (1977)). The BOE must serve notice on the claimant within 30 days after disallowing a refund claim in whole or in part (Sec. 6906, Rev. & Tax. Code). The claimant has 90 days from service of the notice in which to bring court action. If the claimant does not receive notice of the BOE's action within six months after the claim is filed, the taxpayer may consider the claim disallowed and may bring court action (Sec. 6934, Rev. & Tax. Code).

Veterans as itinerant vendors: A "qualified veteran," as defined, may receive from the state a qualified repayment of certain California state and local sales and use taxes, interest, or penalties paid during the eight-year period beginning on and after April 1, 2002, and before April 1, 2010. A "qualified veteran" is defined as a person who met the requirements of a "qualified itinerant vendor" during the period in which the sales were made and who paid taxes and associated penalties and interest imposed under the Sales and Use Tax Law, Section 35 of Article XIII of the California Constitution, the Bradley-Burns Uniform Local Sales and Use Tax Law, and the Transactions and Use Tax Law during the eight-year period, for which no sales tax reimbursement was collected from customers. (Sec. 6018.2, Rev. & Tax. Code)

A qualified veteran may file a claim for a qualified repayment with the BOE before January 1, 2016. The claim must be on Form BOE-101 and include proof of payment of the tax, interest, or penalties. The total amount of money available to make qualified repayments cannot exceed $50,000. (*Special Notice L-399,* California State Board of Equalization, December 2014)

Time limits on filing: A refund claim must be filed within three years from the due date of the return for which the overpayment is alleged (Sec. 6902, Rev. & Tax. Code). However, a taxpayer has three years from the date of overpayment to file a claim for refund of an overpayment of any tax, penalty, or interest collected by the BOE through the use of a levy, lien, or other enforcement procedure (Sec. 6902.3, Rev. & Tax. Code). After deficiency determinations, determinations when no return is filed, or jeopardy determinations, a refund claim must be filed within six months from the time the determination becomes final or from the date of overpayment, whichever is later. Failure to file a claim within the prescribed time is a waiver of any demand against the state (Sec. 6905, Rev. & Tax. Code).

For purposes of a variety of taxes, surcharges, and fees administered by the California State Board of Equalization, a claim for refund involving a case in which the amount of tax, surcharge, or fee determined has not been paid in full will be deemed to be a timely filed claim for refund with all subsequent payments applied to that determination (Sec. 6209.6, Rev. & Tax. Code). The law change applies to claims filed on or after January 1, 2017, for refunds of the following:

— sales and use tax;

— use fuel tax;

— alcoholic beverage tax;

— energy resources surcharge;

— emergency telephone users surcharge;

— hazardous substances tax;

— integrated waste management fee;

— oil spill response, prevention, and administration fees;

— underground storage tank maintenance fee;

— diesel fuel tax; and

— cigarette and tobacco products tax;

Disability: The limitations period for filing a California sales tax refund claim is suspended during the period that a person is unable to manage financial affairs because of a physical or mental impairment that is life threatening or that is expected to last for at least 12 months (Sec. 6902.4, Rev. & Tax. Code). There is no waiver for individuals who are represented in their financial matters by their spouses or other persons.

Lemon Law: The BOE may reimburse a manufacturer of a new motor vehicle for the use tax the manufacturer refunds to a buyer or lessee when the new motor vehicle is reacquired by the manufacturer pursuant to California's "Lemon Law" (Sec. 1793.25, Civil Code; Reg. 1655).

Local ordinances preempted: An Internet service provider that had improperly charged its customers taxes for Internet access and who had unsuccessfully sought refunds of those taxes from the cities and counties to which the taxes had been remitted, had standing to bring an action for a tax refund. The cities and counties argued that the claims at issue were barred by local ordinances that allow a service supplier, such as the Internet service provider, to file a refund claim only when the service supplier has already refunded the disputed taxes from its own funds to its customers. However, the "refund first" local ordinances are preempted by the Government Claims Act (in the California Government Code), which provides that a claim may be presented by the claimant or a person acting on his or her behalf. The act does not require that the claim be presented only by an entity that has repaid the taxes to its customers. The appellate court held that the cities and counties may not impose a refund first requirement that circumscribes the class of persons that may bring a claim on another's behalf. As such, the Internet service provider had standing to present claims to the cities and counties on behalf of its customers who were charged the Internet access taxes. (*Sipple v. City of Hayward,* Court of Appeal of California, Second District, No. B242893, April 8, 2014, CCH CALIFORNIA TAX REPORTS, ¶ 406-106)

Consumer protection: The California Supreme Court held that a consumer protection lawsuit filed to address a sales tax question is inconsistent with the method established by the Legislature to determine whether a transaction is subject to sales tax. The use of consumer protection statutes to challenge a retailer's collection of a sales tax reimbursement is inconsistent with sales tax code provisions, especially those provisions that assign the Board of Equalization (BOE) the role of resolving sales tax issues and which state that all sales are taxable unless otherwise demonstrated to the satisfaction of the BOE. (*Loeffler et al. v. Target Corp.,* California Supreme Court, No. S173972, May 1, 2014, CCH CALIFORNIA TAX REPORTS, ¶ 406-132)

Source.—Statutory references are to Title 39, Article 26, Colorado Revised Statutes, as amended to date. Details are reported in the CCH COLORADO STATE TAX REPORTS starting at ¶ 60-000.

The sales tax is imposed on sales and purchases of tangible personal property at retail (Sec. 39-26-104(1)(a)) and is collected from retailers making sales of commodities or specified services (Sec. 39-26-105(1)(a)). The use tax applies to the privilege of storing, using, or consuming tangible personal property in Colorado that has been purchased at retail (Sec. 39-26-202(1)) and is supplementary to the sales tax (Sec. 39-26-203(1)). The sales tax and use tax are complementary taxes (Reg. 26-202). The use tax is not imposed on sales that are subject to the sales tax (Sec. 39-26-203(1)(a)). No tax is due on the storage, use, or consumption of tangible personal property the sale or use of which has already been subjected to a tax equal to or in excess of the use tax (Sec. 39-26-203(1)(k), Reg. 26-203.1(a)).

"Person" subject to tax includes an individual, firm, limited liability company, partnership, joint adventure, corporation, estate, or trust, or any group or combination acting as a unit (Sec. 39-26-102(6), Sec. 39-26-201(2)). The use tax definition also includes within the definition of "person" an association and a receiver (Sec. 39-26-201(2)).

The sales tax is in addition to all other taxes (Sec. 39-26-119).

Computer software: The definition of "tangible personal property" excludes standardized software. Computer software is subject to tax only if it is prepackaged for repeated sale or license, governed by a tear-open nonnegotiable license agreement, and delivered to the customer in a tangible medium. (Sec. 39-26-102(15(c)); Reg. 39-26-102.13). License renewal fees are taxable even if the renewal is done electronically (*GIL 13-014,* Colorado Department of Revenue, August 7, 2013, CCH COLORADO TAX REPORTS, ¶ 201-238).

Software maintenance agreements: Standardized software does not include agreements for the maintenance of standardized software. However, if the price of the maintenance agreement includes the price of standardized software, then the maintenance agreement must contain a reasonable, separately stated charge for the standardized software. Additionally, if the value of the standardized software included with the maintenance agreement is less than 25% of the price of the maintenance agreement, then the maintenance agreement will not be deemed to include standardized software. (Reg. 39-26-102.13)

Sales and use tax applies to multiple point of use (MPU) software, and special apportionment rules apply. The regulation provides specific apportionment rules and also provides some examples (Reg. 39-26-102.13).

• **Taxes on recreational marijuana**

Colorado voters approved a constitutional amendment in 2012 to regulate and tax marijuana in the same manner as alcohol (Amendment 64, approved by the voters at the November 6, 2012, general election). The initiative provides for the General Assembly to enact an excise tax to be levied upon marijuana sold or transferred at a rate not to exceed 15% prior to January 1, 2017, and at a rate determined by the General Assembly after that.

At the November 2013 statewide election, voters approved provisions creating the excise tax and a special sales tax levied on retail marijuana sales beginning January 1, 2014. These taxes are not imposed on sales to or by medical marijuana centers.

The excise tax rate is 15% of the average market rate of the unprocessed retail marijuana on its first sale or transfer from a cultivation facility to a retail store, product manufacturing facility, or other cultivation facility (Sec. 39-28.8-302). Retail marijuana cultivation facilities must file a return with the Department of Revenue by the 20th day of the month following the month reported and remit the amount of tax due.

The special sales tax is equal to 10% (reduced to 8% beginning July 1, 2017) of the amount of the sale (Sec. 39-28.8-202). This tax is imposed in addition to state and local sales taxes. The department may require electronic filing and payment of the tax, and penalties are imposed for filing a false or fraudulent return or for the willful evasion of tax.

For additional information, see *FYI Sales 93,* Colorado Department of Revenue, January 2014, CCH COLORADO TAX REPORTS, ¶ 201-240.

• Services

The sales tax is imposed on only those services specifically made subject to tax (Sec. 39-26-104, Reg. 42). Services specifically taxed are telephone and telegraph services; gas, electric, and steam services; service of food or drink; and furnishing of rooms or accommodations.

Persons engaged in the business of rendering service are consumers, not retailers, of the tangible personal property that they use incidentally in rendering service and are, therefore, subject to tax on the purchase of such property (Reg. 42). If such persons regularly sell tangible personal property to consumers, in addition to rendering service, they are retailers with respect to such sales and must collect and remit the tax.

The basic distinction in determining whether a transaction is a sale of tangible personal property or the transfer of tangible personal property incidental to the performance of a service is one of the true objects of the contract: if the real object sought by the buyer is service, the transaction is not subject to tax even though some tangible personal property is transferred.

The Colorado Supreme Court has held that electricity is treated as a service rather than tangible personal property under the sales and use tax statutes (*Department of Revenue v. Public Service Co.,* Colorado Supreme Court, No. 11SC759, June 30, 2014, CCH COLORADO TAX REPORTS, ¶ 201-265).

• Incidence of sales tax

The sales tax is imposed on the sale of tangible personal property at retail and is applicable whether the transaction is between a licensed vendor and a vendee or between private parties (Sec. 39-26-104(1)(a), Reg. 26-102.16). The tax is imposed on the purchaser but if the transaction involves a licensed vendor it is the vendor's duty to add the tax to the sales price and remit the tax to the state (Reg. 26-104.1(a)). If no licensed vendor is involved in the transaction or the vendor fails to collect the tax, the purchaser must pay the tax directly to the Department of Revenue. Also, if the vendor fails to collect the tax from the purchaser, the Department of Revenue may assess the tax due against the vendor or the purchaser at its option.

• Incidence of use tax

The use tax is imposed on persons storing, using, or consuming in Colorado tangible personal property purchased at retail (Sec. 39-26-202). The obligation for payment of the tax is on the user whether the tax is called a "sales tax" or a "use tax" (Reg. 26-202).

• Nexus

Colorado requires any retailer doing business in Colorado and making sales of tangible personal property for storage, use, or consumption in Colorado to collect use tax from the purchaser, regardless of whether title to the goods passes within or without Colorado, and give the purchaser a receipt. A retailer collecting the tax becomes a trustee for any tax collected and is responsible as an agent of Colorado. (Sec. 39-26-204(2); Reg. 39-26-204.2)

"Doing business in this state" means selling, leasing, or delivering in Colorado or performing any activity in Colorado in connection with the selling, leasing, or delivering of tangible personal property by a retail sale for use, storage, distribution, or consumption within Colorado and includes the following (Sec. 39-26-102(3); Reg. 39-26-102.3):

(1) maintaining in Colorado, directly or indirectly or by a subsidiary, an office, distributing house, sales room or house, warehouse, or other place of business; and

(2) soliciting by direct or indirect representatives or manufacturers' agents, by distribution of catalogs or other advertising, by use of any communications media such as the newspaper, radio, or television advertising media, or by any other means of business from persons residing in Colorado and consequently receiving orders from, or selling or leasing tangible personal property to, such persons for use, consumption, distribution, and storage for use or consumption in Colorado.

Online retailers: A nexus presumption bill was enacted in Colorado, effective March 1, 2010, targeting out-of-state online retail sales and imposing reporting and notification requirements. Specifically, a retailer who does not collect Colorado sales tax and is part of a controlled group of corporations that has a component member with a retail presence in Colorado is presumed to be doing business in the state (Sec. 39-26-102(3)(b)(ii); Regs. 39-21-112.3.5 (1 CCR 201-1) and 39-26-102.3 (1 CCR 201-4)). The terms "controlled group of corporations" and "component member" are both defined as having the same meaning as set forth in the Internal Revenue Code of 1986, as amended. The presumption can be rebutted by proving that the component member with an in-state presence did not engage in constitutionally sufficient solicitation on behalf of the retailer who does not collect Colorado sales tax. The presumption is similar, but not identical, to New York's so-called "Amazon law."

A retailer subject to this law who does not collect Colorado sales tax must notify Colorado purchasers that sales or use tax is due on all purchases made from the retailer and the purchaser is required to file a sales or use tax return. Retailers who fail to provide the required notification can be penalized $5 for each failure. (Sec. 39-21-112(b), (c))

In addition, a retailer who does not collect Colorado sales tax must notify Colorado purchasers by January 31 of the year following any purchases made from the retailer that sales or use tax is due. The notification should include, if available, the dates of purchases, the amounts of each purchase, and the category of the purchase, including, if known by the retailer, whether the purchase is taxable or exempt. The notification requirements specify that the notice must be a separate first class mailing and can not be included with other shipments. (Sec. 39-21-112(d))

The Department of Revenue may require a retailer who does not collect Colorado sales tax to notify the department through an annual statement of purchases made by each Colorado resident summarizing the total Colorado purchases made by each purchaser. The annual statement must be made by March 1 of each year and if the retailer's total Colorado sales exceeds $100,000 in a year, that report has to be made by magnetic media or another machine readable form. A penalty of $10 for each purchaser that should have been included on the annual statement is provided. (Sec. 39-21-112)

Presumption of physical presence: Effective July 1, 2014, the Colorado Marketplace Fairness and Small Business Protection Act (H.B. 1269, Laws 2014) creates a rebuttable presumption that an out-of-state retailer has substantial nexus and codifies the types of business activities that create taxable sales for a controlled group of corporations. A person is presumed to be doing business in Colorado if that person enters into an agreement or arrangement with a person who has physical presence in Colorado, other than a common carrier, and the person who has physical presence (Sec. 39-26-102(3)(e)(i)):

(1) sells under the same or a similar business name tangible personal property or taxable services similar to those sold by the person against whom the presumption of physical presence is asserted;

(2) maintains an office, distribution facility, salesroom, warehouse, storage place, or other similar place of business in the state to facilitate the delivery of tangible personal property or taxable services sold by the person against whom the presumption is asserted to such person's in-state customers;

(3) delivers, installs, or assembles tangible personal property in the state, or performs maintenance or repair services on tangible personal property that is sold to in-state customers by the person against whom the presumption is asserted; or

(4) facilitates the delivery of tangible personal property to in-state customers of the person against whom the presumption is asserted by allowing such customers to pick up tangible personal property sold by such person at an office, distribution facility, salesroom, warehouse, storage place, or other similar place of business maintained in Colorado.

The presumption may be rebutted by proof that the person, during the calendar year in question, did not engage in any activities in Colorado that are sufficient under U.S. Constitutional standards to establish nexus (Sec. 39-26-102(3)(e)(ii)). However, the presumption does not apply to certain agreements or arrangements concerning advertising, affiliate marketing, and small businesses. (Sec. 39-26-102(3)(e)(iii))

Controlled groups: A person is presumed to be doing business in Colorado if that person is part of a controlled group of corporations, and that controlled group has a component member, other than a common carrier, that has physical presence in Colorado, and the person who has physical presence (Sec. 39-26-102(3)(d)(i)):

— sells under the same or a similar business name tangible personal property or taxable services similar to those sold by the person against whom the presumption of physical presence is asserted;

— maintains an office, distribution facility, salesroom, warehouse, storage place, or other similar place of business in this state to facilitate the delivery of tangible personal property or taxable services sold by the person against whom the presumption is asserted to such person's in-state customers;

— uses trademarks, service marks, or trade names in Colorado that are the same or substantially similar to those used by the person against whom the presumption is asserted;

— delivers, installs, or assembles tangible personal property in Colorado, or performs maintenance or repair services on tangible personal property that is sold to in-state customers by the person against whom the presumption is asserted; or

— facilitates the delivery of tangible personal property to in-state customers of the person against whom the presumption is asserted by allowing such customers to pick up tangible personal property sold by such person at an office, distribution facility, salesroom, warehouse, storage place, or other similar place of business maintained in Colorado.

The presumption may be rebutted by proof that the person, during the calendar year in question, did not engage in any activities in Colorado that are sufficient under U.S. Constitutional standards to establish nexus (Sec. 39-26-102(3)(d)(iii)).

Litigation: The reporting and notification requirements were initially declared unconstitutional and were permanently enjoined by a federal District Court judge in the case of *The Direct Marketing Association v. Huber,* (U.S. District Court for the District of

Colorado, U.S. District Court, D. Colorado, Dkt. 10-cv-01546-REB-CBS, March 30, 2012, CCH COLORADO TAX REPORTS, ¶ 201-089). In its opinion, the federal District Court concluded that the reporting and notification provisions directly regulated and discriminated against out-of-state retailers and, therefore, interstate commerce. The District Judge held that the state failed to demonstrate that its legitimate interests in collecting sales and use tax could not be served adequately by reasonable nondiscriminatory alternatives. Additionally, the court held that the statute and regulations improperly burdened interstate commerce because they imposed a use tax collection burden on a retailer with no physical presence in the state, in violation of the safe harbor established by the U.S. Supreme Court in *Quill*. Although the burden of the notice-and-reporting requirements may be somewhat different than the burden of collecting and remitting tax, the sole purpose of the burden imposed by the provisions was the collection of use tax in instances when sales tax cannot be collected. (*The Direct Marketing Association v. Huber,* supra)

The U.S. Court of Appeals remanded the case to the federal district court to dismiss the plaintiff's claims and to lift the permanent injunction. In the decision, the court cited the Tax Injunction Act (28 U.S.C. § 1341), which states that federal courts should not enjoin, suspend or restrain any state tax assessments or collections if the disputed matter can be resolved by lower courts. (*Direct Marketing Association v. Brohl,* U.S. Court of Appeals, Tenth Circuit, Dkt. 12-1175, August 20, 2013, CCH COLORADO TAX REPORTS, ¶ 201-1752; *The Direct Marketing Association v. Huber,* U.S. District Court for the District of Colorado, Dkt. No. 10-cv-01546-REB-DBS, December 10, 2013; petition for certiorari filed February 25, 2014, *Direct Marketing Association v. Brohl,* petition for certiorari granted July 1, 2014, U.S. Supreme Court, Dkt. 13-1032)

The U.S. Supreme Court held that the federal district court has jurisdiction over the taxpayer lawsuit challenging the constitutionality of the Colorado law that imposes notice and reporting requirements on out-of-state retailers and may enjoin enforcement of the requirements. The federal district court's enjoinder of the state law does not prevent Colorado from assessing, levying, or collecting tax, as prohibited under the federal Tax Injunction Act (Act), because the notice and reporting requirements involve information gathering, not tax assessment, levy or collection. The lawsuit does not restrain assessment, levy or collection of tax merely because it might inhibit Colorado's ability to assess and collect the taxes. (*Direct Marketing Association v. Brohl,* U.S. Supreme Court, No. 13-1032, March 3, 2015)

The U.S. District Court of Appeals then held that the notification and reporting requirements did not violate the dormant Commerce Clause because they did not discriminate or unduly burden interstate commerce. The court held that *Quill Corp v. North Dakota,* 504 US 298 (1992), applied only to the collection of sales and use taxes, and Colorado's notification and reporting obligations did not require the collection or remittance of sales and use taxes. Instead, the Colorado law only imposed notice and reporting obligations. Therefore, the *Quill* ruling, which DMA relied upon in its claims, did not apply to the Colorado notification and reporting requirements. The district court's order granting summary judgment was reversed and remanded. (*Direct Marketing Association vs. Brohl,* U.S. Court of Appeals, Tenth Circuit, Dkt. 12-1175, February 22, 2016, CCH COLORADO TAX REPORTS, ¶ 201-323; *Direct Marketing Association v. Brohl,* U.S. Supreme Court, Dkt. 16-267, petition for certiorari denied December 12, 2016; *Brohl v, Direct Marketing Association,* U.S. Supreme Court, Dkt. 16-458, conditional cross-petition for certiorari denied December 12, 2016)

• **Streamlined Act status**

Colorado has not enacted the Uniform Sales and Use Tax Act or similar legislation, and does not participate in the Steamlined Sales Tax Project. Colorado legislation has been enacted that complies with requirements of the federal Marketplace Fairness Act of 2013 (S. 743), as passed by the U.S. Senate on May 4, 2013, which generally would allow states to require out-of-state retailers to collect state and local sales and use taxes on remote sales of more than $1 million (Ch. 314 (H.B. 1295), Laws 2013).

¶ 277   **Tax Base**

The tax base for the sales tax is the purchase price paid or charged on the sale and purchase of tangible personal property at retail (Sec. 39-26-104). The tax base for the use tax is the storage or acquisition charges or costs of storing, using, or consuming tangible personal property in Colorado purchased at retail (Sec. 39-26-202).

"Purchase price" means the price to the consumer, exclusive of any direct federal tax or the Colorado sales and use tax (Sec. 39-26-102(7), Reg. 26-102.7(a)). In the case of retail sales involving the exchange of property, "purchase price" includes the fair market value of the property exchanged at the time and place of the exchange; however, the term does not include the fair market value of the exchanged property if (1) the exchanged property is to be sold thereafter in the usual course of the retailer's business or (2) the exchanged property is a vehicle, including a vehicle operating on public highways, off-highway recreation vehicle, watercraft, or aircraft, that is exchanged for another vehicle and both vehicles are subject to licensing, registration, or certification (Sec. 39-26-104, Sec. 39-26-102(7)). Any money or other consideration paid over and above the value of the exchanged property is subject to tax (Reg. 26-102.7(b)).

"Sale" or "sale and purchase" include the sale or exchange of property for money; an installment or credit sale; every transaction, conditional or otherwise, constituting a sale; and the sale or furnishing of electrical energy, gas, steam, telephone, or telegraph services (Sec. 39-26-102(10)). "Sale" or "sale and purchase" do not include the transfer of assets in a corporate reorganization or similar transactions.

"Acquisition charges or costs" includes "purchase price" (Sec. 39-26-201(1)).

• **Basis for remitting taxes**

Retailers are liable for the payment of an amount equivalent to 3% of all sales made by them of commodities and specified services (Sec. 39-26-105(1)). "Gross taxable sales" means the total amount received in money, credits, or property, excluding the fair market value of exchanged property that is to be sold thereafter in the usual course of a retailer's business, and other consideration valued in money from sales and purchases at retail (Sec. 39-26-102(5), Reg. 26-102.5).

Retailers who supply tangible personal property and services in connection with the maintenance or servicing of such property are required to pay tax on the full contract price unless they apply to the Executive Director of the Department of Revenue for permission to use a percentage basis of reporting the property sold and service supplied under such contract (Sec. 39-26-105(2)). The Executive Director is authorized to determine the percentage based on the property included in the consideration in proportion to the total of the consideration paid under the combination contract or sale subject to tax.

¶ 278   **List of Exemptions, Exceptions, and Exclusions**

Unless otherwise indicated, the statutory exemptions listed below apply to both sales and use taxes. Items that are excluded from the sales or use tax base are treated at ¶ 277, "Tax Base."

A DOR publication discusses how to document sales to retailers, tax-exempt organizations, and direct pay permit holders for sales and use tax purposes. Topics covered include: general information, purchases for resale, purchases by charitable and religious organizations, purchases by government agencies, tax-exempt construction projects, affidavit of exempt sales and purchases made with a direct pay permit. *(FYI Sales 1,* Colorado Department of Revenue, April 2016, CCH COLORADO TAX REPORTS, ¶ 201-331)

• Sales and use tax exemptions, exceptions, and exclusions

Advertising, cooperative direct mail	Sec. 39-26-102(2.7)
Agricultural compounds and pesticides	Sec. 39-26-716
Air carriers, machinery and tools used in enterprise zones	Sec. 39-30-106(2)
Aircraft, commercial, used in interstate commerce	Sec. 39-26-114(1)(a)(XXII), Sec. 39-26-203(1)(aa)
Aircraft sold to nonresident	Sec. 39-26-711.5
Bedding for livestock and poultry	Sec. 39-26-114(8)
Bingo raffle equipment	Sec. 39-26-114(24)
Biogas production equipment (until July 1, 2019)	Sec. 39-26-724, Sec. 29-2-109
Biotechnology research property (refund)	Sec. 39-26-401, Sec. 39-26-402
Bullion and coins	Sec. 39-26-114(17), Sec. 39-26-203(1)(bb)
Carbon electrodes (manufacturing)	Sec. 39-26-114(14)
Charitable organizations	Sec. 39-26-102(2.5), Sec. 39-26-114(1)(a)(II), Sec. 39-26-203(1)(e)
Computer software (standardized)	Sec. 39-26-102(15)(c)(I)
Construction and building materials, sales to interstate common carriers by rail	Sec. 39-26-114(1)(a)(XI)
Construction and building materials for ski area tramways (local use tax exemption)	Sec. 29-2-109
Construction materials used and owned by charitable organizations .	Sec. 39-26-114(1)(a)(XIX), Sec. 39-26-203(1)(w)
Containers for food	Sec. 39-26-114(1)(a)(XVI), Sec. 39-26-114(1)(a)(XVII), Sec. 39-26-203(1)(t), Sec. 39-26-203(1)(u)
Containers used incident to sale of property	Sec. 39-26-102(20), Sec. 39-26-203(1)(f)
Cooperative direct mail advertising	Sec. 39-26-102(2.7)
Corporate reorganization transfers of assets	Sec. 39-26-102(10)
Direct mail advertising materials (local exemption only)	Sec. 39-26-102(15), Sec. 39-26-102(2.7), Sec. 39-26-102(2.8)
Drugs, prescription	Sec. 39-26-114(1)(a)(V)
Electricity, fuel, or steam used in construction	Sec. 39-26-102(21), Sec. 39-26-203(1)(g)
Electricity, fuel, or steam used by manufacturers and miners	Sec. 39-26-102(21), Sec. 39-26-203(1)(g)
Electricity, fuel, or steam used for residential purposes	Sec. 39-26-114(1)(a)(XXI), Sec. 39-26-203(1)(z)

Electricity, coal, wood, gas, fuel oil, or coke sold for residential purposes .... Sec. 39-26-114(1)(a)(XXI), Sec. 39-26-203(1)(z), Sec. 39-26-715

Electricity, fuel, or steam used in irrigation; street and railroad transportation; or telephone, telegraph, and radio communication .... Sec. 39-26-102(21), Sec. 39-26-203(1)(g)

Electricity, machinery to produce from renewable sources .... Sec. 39-26-709(1)(a)(III)

Eyeglasses and contact lenses .... Sec. 39-26-114(1)(a)(V)

Factory-built housing (partial exemption) .... Sec. 24-32-703(3), Sec. 39-26-114(10)

Farm close-out sales .... Sec. 39-26-102(4), Sec. 39-26-114(5)

Farm equipment .... Sec. 39-26-114(20), Sec. 39-26-203(1)(hh)

Feed for livestock and poultry .... Sec. 39-26-114(6)

Fish .... Sec. 39-26-114(5)

Food .... Sec. 39-26-102(4.5), Sec. 39-26-114(1)(a)(XX), Sec. 39-26-203(1)(v.1), Sec. 39-26-203(1)(x)

Food, meals, and beverages (excludes nonessential items) .... Sec. 39-26-707

Food stamps and supplemental food programs .... Sec. 39-26-114(15), Sec. 39-26-114(16)

Foreclosures .... Sec. 39-26-102(10)(j)

Fraternal benefit societies .... Sec. 10-14-401, Sec. 10-14-504

Fuel (agricultural) .... Sec. 39-26-114(1)(a)(XV), Sec. 39-26-203(1)(c)(I), Sec. 39-27-201(8)

Fuel (construction) .... Sec. 39-26-102(21), Sec. 39-26-203(1)(g)

Fuel (manufacturing and mining) .... Sec. 39-26-102(21), Sec. 39-26-203(1)(g)

Fuel (motor) .... Sec. 39-26-114(1)(a)(VII), Sec. 39-26-203(1)(c)

Fuel (residential purposes) .... Sec. 39-26-114(1)(a)(XXI), Sec. 39-26-203(1)(z) Sec. 39-26-715

Fuel (street and railroad transportation) .... Sec. 39-26-102(21), Sec. 39-26-203(1)(g)

Fuel (telephone, telegraph, and radio communication) .... Sec. 39-26-102(21), Sec. 39-26-203(1)(g)

Government contractors .... Sec. 39-26-114(1)(a)(XIX), Sec. 39-26-203(1)(w)

Government transactions	Sec. 39-26-114(1)(a)(I), Sec. 39-26-203(1)(e)
Hearing aids	Sec. 39-26-114(1)(a)(V)
Household effects of nonresidents	Sec. 39-26-203(1)(d), Sec. 39-26-203(1)(*l*)
Inorganic materials used in processing vanadium-uranium ores	Sec. 39-26-114(14)
Insulin and insulin measuring and injecting devices	Sec. 39-26-114(1)(a)(V)
Internet access services	Sec. 24-79-102
Interstate transactions	Sec. 39-26-114(1)(a)(III)
Leases (three year or less)	Sec. 39-26-114(1)(a)(XII)
Livestock	Sec. 39-26-114(5), Sec. 39-26-203(1)(h)
Lottery tickets	Sec. 24-35-214
Lodging, occupancy period of 30 or more days	Sec. 39-26-114(1)(a)(VI)
Machinery in excess of $500 that comprises a cleanroom (exp. 6/30/2016)	Sec. 39-26-722
Machinery and tools (air carriers)	Sec. 39-30-106(2)
Machinery and tools (enterprise zones)	Sec. 39-30-106
Machinery and tools (manufacturing)	Sec. 39-26-114(11), Sec. 39-26-203(1)(y), Sec. 39-30-106(1)(b)
Machinery used to produce electricity from renewable sources	Sec. 39-26-709(1)(a)(III)
Manufacturing—ingredient or component parts of processing	Sec. 39-26-102(20), Sec. 39-26-203(1)(f)
Meals to employees	Sec. 39-26-104(1)(e), Sec. 39-26-203(1)(v.1)
Medical marijuana, sales to indigent patients	Sec. 39-26-726
Medicine, prescription sales	Sec. 39-26-114(1)(a)(V) Sec. 39-26-717
Mergers	Sec. 39-26-102(10)
Mobile homes (partial)	Sec. 24-32-703(3), Sec. 39-26-114(10), Sec. 39-26-203(1)(o), Sec. 42-1-102(82)(b)
Motor fuel	Sec. 39-26-114(1)(a)(VII), Sec. 39-26-203(1)(c)
Motor vehicles sold to nonresidents	Sec. 39-26-113(5), Sec. 39-26-114(1)(a)(IX), Sec. 39-26-203(1)(m), Sec. 39-26-203(1)(p)
Motor vehicles, large, low-emission	Sec. 39-26-114(20)(a), Sec. 39-26-203(1)(hh)
Native Americans	Sec. 39-26-114(1)(a)(III)
Newspapers	Sec. 39-26-102(15)
Newsprint	Sec. 39-26-102(21), Sec. 39-26-203(1)(i)

Vending machine sales of food	Sec. 39-26-102(4.5),
	Sec. 39-26-114(7.5),
	Sec. 39-26-203(1)(hh)
Veterans' organizations' special events	Sec. 39-26-102(2.5),
	Sec. 39-26-114(1)(a)(II),
	Sec. 39-26-203(1)(e)
Wheelchairs and hospital beds	Sec. 39-26-114(1)(a)(V)
Wood products from salvaged wood	Sec. 39-26-723

¶ 279   Rate of Tax

The state sales and use taxes are imposed at the rate of 2.9% of the tax base (Sec. 39-26-105, Sec. 39-26-106, Sec. 39-26-202).

Commercial trucks: If certain conditions exist regarding state revenues, the sales tax imposed on the sale of a new or used commercial truck, truck tractor, tractor, semitrailer, or vehicle that has a gross vehicle weight rating in excess of 26,000 pounds will be imposed at a rate of .01% for the fiscal year (Sec. 39-26-106(3)(a)).

Waste tire fee: A recycling fee of $1.50 is imposed on every waste motor vehicle tire that is delivered or transferred by its owner to a new tire retailer for disposal. The fee is collected on any waste motor vehicle tire for any passenger vehicle, including motorcycles and any truck, when the vehicle or truck weighs less than 15,000 pounds. The fee is also collected on tires of trucks, including truck tractors, trailers, and semitrailers, that weigh more than 15,000 pounds. No fee is collected on tires that are recapped or otherwise reprocessed for use (Sec. 25-17-202).

The waste tire recycling fee is considered part of the purchase price of a tire as of August 5, 2009 (*FYI General 13,* Colorado Department of Revenue, July 2009, CCH COLORADO TAX REPORTS, ¶ 200-906).

Marijuana: Sales of marijuana are subject to an excise tax and a special sales tax. The excise tax rate is 15% of the average market rate of the unprocessed retail marijuana on its first sale or transfer from a cultivation facility to a retail store, product manufacturing facility, or other cultivation facility (Sec. 39-28.8-302). The excise tax is not imposed on sales to a medical marijuana center.

The special sales tax is equal to 8% (10% before September 17, 2015) of the amount of the sale (Sec. 39-28.8-202). This tax is imposed in addition to the state sales tax of 2.9%. The special sales tax is not imposed on sales by a medical marijuana center.

The Colorado Court of Appeals held that Adam County's special sales tax on the sale of retail marijuana was invalid. Although the County held a valid election approving the special sales tax, the County was not authorized by the General Assembly or the Colorado Constitution to impose such a tax, and therefore, the tax was invalid. (*City of Northglenn v. Board of County Commissioners, Adams County,* Colorado Court of Appeals, No. 15CA1743, December 15, 2016, CCH COLORADO TAX REPORTS, ¶ 201-355)

¶ 280   Local Taxes

Various local sales and use taxes are imposed by counties, cities, towns, and various districts. For rates, see **https://www.colorado.gov/revenueonline/_/#1**.

Sourcing of telecommunications charges: Colorado has conformed to the federal Mobile Telecommunications Sourcing Act (Sec. 39-26-104; Sec. 29-1-1002). Charges for wireless telecommunications are sourced to the customer's "place of primary use," which means the residential or primary business address of the customer within the licensed service area of the home service provider. The jurisdiction in which the place of primary use is located is the only jurisdiction that may tax the communications services, regardless of the customer's location when a call is placed or received.

Although not part of the federal act, the Colorado law provides that a taxpayer may dispute the assignment of primary place of use or taxing jurisdiction within two years after the date the bill was issued (Sec. 29-1-1002). The notification of the dispute to the home service provider must be in writing and the home service provider has 60 days after receipt of the notice from the customer to send the customer a refund, issue a credit, or provide a written explanation of the assignment, if it determines no error was made. A customer may file a claim in district court only after complying with the above steps.

- **County lodging tax**

The county lodging tax for the purpose of advertising and marketing local tourism may not exceed 2% of the purchase price paid or charged for rooms or accommodations (Sec. 30-11-107.5). For localities and rates, see **https://www.colorado.gov/pacific/ sites/default/files/DR1002.pdf**.

- **County rental tax**

The county tax on the rental of personal property is limited to 1% of the amount of the rental payment (Sec. 30-11-107.7). For rates, see **https://www.colorado.gov/ pacific/sites/default/files/DR1002.pdf**.

- **Local improvement district**

A local improvement district (LID) sales tax is imposed within designated areas of various counties. For rates, see **https://www.colorado.gov/pacific/sites/default/ files/DR1002.pdf**.

- **County mass transit system**

A mass transportation system tax may be levied by a county outside the jurisdiction of the Regional Transportation District. For rates, see **https://www.colorado.gov/ pacific/sites/default/files/DR1002.pdf**.

- **County water rights**

Counties are authorized to impose a county sales and use tax of up to 1% for the purposes of recovering costs in connection with the development, management, and maintenance of water rights (Sec. 29-2-103.7). Counties may levy the special tax subject to approval of the county voters at a general election. For rates, see **https:// www.colorado.gov/pacific/sites/default/files/DR1002.pdf**.

- **Denver Metro Area**

The Denver Metro Area Special Taxing District consists of three separate tax districts with similar boundaries: the Regional Transportation District, the Cultural and Scientific Facilities District, and the Metropolitan Football Stadium District. The combined tax rate in all three districts is 1.2%, and their tax bases generally conform to the state tax base. However, low-emitting motor vehicles, power sources, and related parts; machinery or machine tools; and vending machine sales of food, excluding candy and soft drinks, are taxable by the RTD and the SCFD but exempt from the state sales and use tax.

The City of Denver's sales and use tax rate is imposed on the retailer's gross taxable sales of commodities, services, or tangible personal property, (Denver Rev Mun. Code Sec. 53-28, 98-106; Denver Rev Mun. Code Sec. 53-99). The retailer bears the burden of proving that the retailer is exempt from remitting any tax otherwise due. (Denver Rev Mun. Code Sec. 53-28, 98-106; Denver Rev Mun. Code Sec. 53-99)

Lodging: The Denver lodger's tax did not apply to the fees charged by online travel companies who facilitated booking reservations. The online travel companies booked travel reservations for hotel accommodations and other travel-related services. When booking a hotel room through an online travel company, a traveler paid a total price that included the rate charged by the hotel to the online travel companies. The total price

¶280   Colorado

also included the online companies' markup and service fees. The Court of Appeals found that the city and county's lodger's tax did not apply to the fees charged by the online travel companies because (1) the online travel companies were not vendors within the meaning of the ordinance because they did not furnish lodging, and (2) the online travel companies' fees were not included in the purchase price for lodging under the ordinance, because the fees were not directly connected with the furnishing of lodging. (*Expedia, Inc. v. City and County of Denver,* Colorado Court of Appeals, No. 13CA0779, July 3, 2014, CCH COLORADO TAX REPORTS, ¶ 201-270)

• **Local Marketing District**

The Local Marketing District levies a tax of on lodging services including hotels, motels, condominiums and camping spaces in certain resort areas. Tax is remitted quarterly to the Department of Revenue on Form DR 1490, Local Marketing District Tax Return. For rates, see **https://www.colorado.gov/pacific/sites/default/files/ DR1002.pdf.**

• **Rural Transportation Authority**

Certain cities impose a Rural Transportation Authority (RTA) tax (Sec. 43-4-605; Sec. 43-4-612). For rates, see **https://www.colorado.gov/pacific/sites/default/files/ DR1002.pdf.**

• **Public safety**

Montrose County has a public safety improvements tax of 0.75% with no exemptions. Use tax is not allowed. The tax is reported in the special districts column of sales tax return, DR 0100.

• **Multi-jurisdictional housing authority**

Summit County has a multi-jurisdictional housing authority sales tax with certain exemptions. The tax is filed in the Special Districts column of the sales tax return, DR 0100. For rates, see **https://www.colorado.gov/pacific/sites/default/files/ DR1002.pdf.**

• **Local tax rates**

The total tax rate for any jurisdiction must be computed by adding all taxes applicable to that jurisdiction and the particular transaction, including the 2.9% state tax, the Regional Transportation District tax, the Scientific and Cultural Facilities District tax, etc. A chart that lists the Colorado cities and counties that impose local sales and use taxes and their rates is available at **https://www.colorado.gov/pacific/sites/ default/files/DR1002.pdf.**

¶ 281   **Bracket Schedule**

Colorado does not use a bracket schedule. The tax is to be computed in accordance with schedules or systems approved by the Executive Director of the Department of Revenue (Sec. 39-26-106, Sec. 39-26-202). The schedules or systems must be designed so that no tax is charged on any sale of 17¢ or less.

A sales tax rate calculator is located under "Sales Tax Rate Charts" at **https:// www.colorado.gov/revenueonline/_/#5.**

¶ 282   **Returns, Payments, and Due Dates**

Retailers liable for the sales and use tax must file returns with the Executive Director of the Department of Revenue on or before the 20th day of the month following the month in which the tax accrued, accompanied by the tax due (Sec. 39-26-105(1), Sec. 39-26-204(3), Reg. 26-105.1(a), Reg. 26-122, Reg. 26-204.2). If the 20th day of the month is a Saturday, Sunday, or holiday, the return is due on the next following business day (Reg. 26-105.1(a)). Returns must be filed on forms and contain information prescribed by the Executive Director (Sec. 39-26-105(1)). Amounts must be rounded to the nearest dollar (Reg. 26-109, Reg. 26-204.1, Reg. 26-204.2). Taxpayers with a monthly tax liability of less than $15 may file annually, by January 20 of the following year, if they have received prior approval to do so from the Department. A person who uses, stores, or consumes tangible personal property outside the conduct of a business and who has not paid the sales or use tax due to a retailer is required to file a return and pay the tax on an annual basis at the time the Colorado income tax return of such person is due.

Filing methods: The Colorado Department of Revenue has developed a computer system to manage Colorado sales, use, and wage withholding taxes. Spreadsheet filing for multiple location/jurisdiction filers is no longer accepted, and those filers must choose one of the following methods for filing: (1) contact software companies or vendors to use their services; (2) use the department's e-file format which is in XML; or (3) file a separate DR 0100 paper return for each branch (physical) business location. (*FYI Sales 58,* Colorado Department of Revenue, June, 2012)

Zero tax filing: A taxpayer who files a Colorado Combined Sales Tax Return must file the return, with a zero entered on each line that applies to the sales tax account, if no tax is due. Failure to file a return, even when no tax is due, can result in the Department being notified the taxpayer is a non-filer.

Direct payment: The Colorado Department of Revenue is authorized to issue sales and use tax direct payment permit numbers to qualified purchasers (Sec. 39-26-103.5). To be eligible for a permit, a taxpayer must have purchased at least $7 million in taxable goods and services during the preceding 12 months. A vendor or retailer is not responsible for collecting sales and use taxes on sales to qualified purchasers who provide a direct payment permit number (Sec. 39-26-105(1)). A qualified purchaser who uses a direct payment permit number when making a purchase must, before the 20th day of the month following the purchase, make a return and remit the sales tax owed.

Marijuana businesses: Owners of both a medical marijuana business and a retail marijuana business must file two separate Colorado sales tax returns. The regular Form DR0100 sales tax return must show the state sales tax plus any state-collected local sales tax, and Form DR 4200 is used to report the retail marijuana sales tax. See *Marijuana Tax Filing and Payment Tips,* Colorado Department of Revenue, March 2014, CCH COLORADO TAX REPORTS, ¶ 201-257.

- **Electronic filing and payment**

Any vendor whose sales tax liability for the previous calendar year exceeded $75,000 is required to use electronic funds transfers (EFT) to remit collected taxes to the Department of Revenue (Sec. 39-26-105.5). Taxpayers who submit sales taxes by electronic funds transfers are not required to remit sales taxes prior to the deadline for those taxpayers who remit sales taxes by other means.

In order to be considered timely, EFT payments must be made by 4:00 PM Mountain Time on the due date to be credited on that day, and such payments made after 4:00 PM Mountain Time on the due date will be considered late. The EFT system is available at **https://www.colorado.gov/revenueonline/_/#1**.

ACH Debit and ACH Credit are two free methods of EFT payment. Either or both methods may be selected. The ACH debit service is accessible through the department's website, by telephone, or through the banking system using a standard format. Taxpayers must be registered for EFT with the department to use either service. Detailed information about ACH Debit and ACH Credit is available on the department's website at **https://www.colorado.gov/tax/node/37451**.

- **Colorado certified rate database**

Vendors that collect Colorado sales and use tax and use an electronic database of addresses certified by the Department of Revenue to determine the amount of tax are not liable for collecting the incorrect amount of tax or for any tax, charge, or fee imposed by any Colorado taxing jurisdiction that otherwise would be due (Sec. 39-26-105.3).

¶282   Colorado

• Vendor service fee

Colorado generally allows vendors to keep a portion of the taxes collected as compensation for the administrative costs of collecting sales tax (Sec. 39-26-105). The service fee (also known as the vendor's fee or discount fee) has been restored to a rate of 3.33% for timely filed returns filed on or after July 1, 2014. The service fee was 2.22% from July 1, 2011, to June 30, 2014. The service fee rate affects state sales tax, state retailer's use tax, aviation sales tax, and RTD/CD (Denver metro area) special district taxes.

¶ 283   Prepayment of Taxes

There are no specific Colorado provisions requiring prepayment of taxes.

¶ 284   Vendor Registration

Retailers must obtain a license from the Executive Director of the Department of Revenue for each separate place of business (Sec. 39-26-103, Reg. 49-102; *FYI Sales 9*, Colorado Department of Revenue). The cost for each license is $16, payable at the time of application. The license fee is prorated in increments of six months for licenses issued after June 30. A $50 deposit must also be paid with the initial license application as a credit against the Colorado sales tax to be remitted; however, a person who sells products that are subject only to local taxes may petition the Department to waive the deposit. Out-of-state retailers required to collect the Colorado sales or use tax must obtain a Colorado retailer's license (Sec. 39-26-303) but there is no charge for such license (Reg. 26-204.2). No license is required of a person who sells exclusively commodities that are exempt from taxation (Sec. 39-26-103).

Charitable organizations and persons conducting a singular sales event for a temporary period of time may apply for a license to engage in the business of selling at retail upon the payment of an $8 fee. Wholesalers may apply to the Department of Revenue for a wholesalers' license; the license fee is $16 and the licensing provisions applicable to retailers also apply to wholesalers.

The application for a license must show the name and address of the applicant, the name of the business and its location, and any other information that the Executive Director may require. The license is valid until December 31 of the year following the year in which it was issued, unless revoked, and must be renewed every two years on or before January 1 of the second year following the year of issuance or renewal. However, when there are no retail sales activities for any period of twelve consecutive months, the license may not be renewed because such inactivity is considered to be a proof that the licensee is not in the business of selling at retail. Licenses are not transferable.

New businesses can apply for state sales tax and personal income withholding accounts electronically through a consolidated, online service called Colorado Business Express (CBE). CBE (**https://www.colorado.gov/apps/jboss/cbe/**) eliminates the need for new business owners to use paper forms to register separately with different state agencies. In one transaction, the service consolidates business registration information required by multiple government departments and automatically updates state regulatory systems for the business filer.

Vendors of medical marijuana: The Colorado Department of Revenue has issued guidelines regarding the sales tax licensing and reporting requirements for vendors of medical marijuana. Businesses selling medical marijuana must file Form CR 0100, Colorado Business Registration, to set up a sales tax account and receive a license. A fee and a sales tax deposit are required with the license application. The form may be taken to a Colorado Taxpayer Service Division service center where the account will be set up for immediate issuance of a temporary license. The department will mail the final, paper license in four to six weeks. Businesses are required to collect sales tax once the sales tax account is set up. Forms relating to sales of medical marijuana are available on the department's Web site at **http://www.colorado.gov/revenue**.

¶ 285 **Sales or Use Tax Credits**

See ¶ 289 for incentive programs, which are treated as refunds.

The amount of sales or use tax paid to another state on the purchase or use of tangible personal property in that state is allowed as a credit against any use tax imposed on that property in Colorado (Sec. 39-26-203(1)(k), Reg. 26-203.1(k)).

Restaurant operators whose use of gas and electricity to prepare meals is exempt may claim a credit for sales tax paid on their purchases of gas and electricity to process food for immediate consumption as follows: if the sales of processed food exceed 25% of the total sales revenue, credit is based on 55% of the Colorado sales tax paid; if the sales of processed food are 25% or less of the total sales revenue or the restaurant is metered for gas and electricity purposes as part of another business operation, such as a hotel, bowling alley, or gas station, the allowable credit is based on ½ of 1% of the total Colorado processed food sales by the restaurant (Reg. 19). The second method may be used even though the applicable percentage of food sales exceeds 25%.

Tax paid under dispute: A credit may be allowed to a purchaser who paid tax under dispute arising between the purchaser and a retailer regarding the exempt status of a sale, service, or commodity.

Overpayment of tax: In the case of overpayment of tax because of error in computation or canceled sales, a retailer may take a credit on a subsequent return, in lieu of filing a claim for a refund, for the amount of overpayment (Reg. 26-102.5, Reg. 26-114.2(3)(e)).

When the price on which tax was computed and paid to the state is subsequently adjusted prior to payment of the tax by the purchaser, the retailer may take a credit against the tax due on the next return (Reg. 26-102.5).

¶ 286 **Deficiency Assessments**

The Executive Director of the Department of Revenue may estimate the tax liability of a person who fails to file a return and remit the tax due (Sec. 39-26-118(2), Sec. 39-26-204(5)). The Executive Director must give written notice to the delinquent taxpayer regarding the estimated taxes, penalty, and interest, and this notice becomes a notice of deficiency (Sec. 39-26-118(2), Sec. 39-21-103).

The tax due may be assessed against either the vendor or the purchaser (Reg. 26-104.1(a)).

• **List of delinquent taxpayers**

The Colorado Department of Revenue is required to publicly disclose an annual list of taxpayers that are delinquent on more than $20,000 in Colorado taxes, including penalties and interest, for a period of six months from the time the taxes were assessed or became final (Sec. 24-35-117). Unpaid taxes are not considered delinquent for purposes of annual disclosure if the tax liability is the subject of an administrative hearing, administrative review, judicial review, or an appeal of any such proceedings.

¶ 287 **Audit Procedures**

To ascertain the correctness of any return or to make an estimate of delinquent tax, the Executive Director of the Department of Revenue may examine any records pertaining to information that is required to be included in returns (Sec. 39-21-112(10)). Books, invoices, and other records must be open at any time for examination by the Executive Director of the Department of Revenue or the Executive Director's authorized agent (Sec. 39-26-116, Reg. 26-116).

Managed audits: Colorado does not currently have a managed audit program.

¶285 Colorado

¶ 288   Statute of Limitations

Taxes, penalties, or interest must be assessed within three years of their due date or the date the sales or use tax return was filed, whichever is later (Sec. 39-26-125, Sec. 39-26-210). The three-year statute of limitations also applies to the filing of lien notices, issuance of distraint warrants, and commencement of collection suits. No lien may continue beyond the three-year limitation period except for taxes assessed and notices of lien filed before the expiration of such period; in such cases, the lien will continue only for one year after the filing of the notice. However, taxes, penalties, and interest, may be assessed, or proceedings for the collection of such amounts may be begun, at any time when a fraudulent return is filed with the intent to evade tax. A taxpayer and the Executive Director of the Department of Revenue may agree in writing to extend the limitation period, and the extended period may be extended again by subsequent agreements in writing.

The statute of limitations does not apply whenever a use tax return required to be filed is not filed (Reg. 26-210).

¶ 289   Application for Refund

When a seller disputes a purchaser's claim that a certain sale is exempt from tax, the purchaser must pay the tax to the seller and then may apply to the Executive Director of the Department of Revenue for a refund of the tax paid (Sec. 39-26-703). Applications for refund must be made within three years after the date of purchase or the initial date of the storage, use or consumption in Colorado and must be made on forms prescribed by the Executive Director (Sec. 39-26-703(2)(d)). The right to a refund is not assignable, and the application for a refund must be made by the person who purchased the goods and paid the tax.

A vendor may claim a refund on behalf of any purchaser if: (1) the purchaser could timely file a claim for a refund on his or her own behalf; and (2) the vendor establishes to the satisfaction of the executive director that the amount claimed, including any interest, has been or will actually be paid by the vendor to the purchaser. Vendors cannot be required to file a refund claim, and so long as the vendor has properly paid all collected taxes over to the department, the vendor has a complete defense to any claim brought against it by a purchaser for any erroneously collected taxes. (Sec. 39-26-703(2.5))

Warrants for tax refunds become void if not presented for payment within six months of issuance (Sec. 39-28-108(7)). Such warrants are presumed to be abandoned and will be turned over to the State Treasurer as unclaimed property. However, there is no time limit for claiming unclaimed property.

Overpayment of tax: When the Executive Director discovers that a taxpayer has paid a tax, penalty, or interest in excess of the amount due, a refund must be issued to the taxpayer (Sec. 39-21-108(2)).

A vendor who remits tax in excess of the amount due may claim a credit on a subsequent return in lieu of applying for a refund, unless the vendor is no longer engaged in business (Sec. 39-26-703(2.5)(a)).

• TABOR refunds

The sales tax TABOR refund is available to (1) full-year Colorado residents 18 years of age or older, and (2) full-year residents under age 18, but only if they are required to file a Colorado personal income tax return.

Amount of refund: The amount of the refund is based on the federal adjusted gross income as reported on the Colorado personal income tax return.

Claiming the refund: The refund may be claimed either on the Colorado personal income tax return or on the Property Tax/Rent/Heat Rebate form 104PTC.

• Incentive refunds

Biotechnology, clean technology, and medical device research property refund: A refund is available for all state sales and use tax paid on the storage, use, or consumption of tangible personal property to be used in Colorado directly and predominantly in research and development of biotechnology (Sec. 39-26-401). To claim the refund, a taxpayer must submit a refund application to the Colorado Department of Revenue, on a form provided by the Department, during the period from January 1 through April 1 of the calendar year following the calendar year for which the refund is claimed (Sec. 39-26-402). The application must be accompanied by proof of payment of Colorado sales and use taxes and additional information required by the Department.

Also, qualified clean technology and medical device firms are eligible to receive refunds on their purchases of equipment used in research and development (Sec. 39-26-403). The firms must be headquartered in Colorado and have no more than 35 employees (50 employees prior to 2015). Each taxpayer may not receive more than a $50,000 refund in any calendar year. These refunds are effective for sales tax paid on or after January 1, 2009, through December 31, 2019. Clean technology firms include those engaged in the research and development of renewable energy and/or products that mitigate the impact of humans on the environment (Sec. 39-26-401). Medical technology firms include those engaged in the research and development of a therapeutic or diagnostic tool used to improve human or animal health (Sec. 39-26-401). Equipment upon which a refund could be collected includes capital equipment, instruments, apparatus, and supplies used in laboratories, including, but not limited to, microscopes, machines, glassware, chemical reagents, computers, computer software, and technical books and manuals.

Pollution control property refund: Subject to certain state revenue limitations, a refund is available for the purchase, storage, use, or consumption of pollution control equipment (Sec. 39-26-501). To claim the refund, a taxpayer must submit a refund application to the Colorado Department of Revenue, on a form provided by the Department, during the period from January 1 through April 1 of the calendar year following the calendar year for which the refund is claimed (Sec. 39-26-502(3)). The application must be accompanied by proof of payment of Colorado sales and use taxes and additional information required by the Department.

Research and development refunds: Subject to certain state revenue limitations, a qualified taxpayer may claim a refund in the following year equal to 100% of Colorado sales and use taxes paid on the sale, purchase, storage, use or consumption of tangible personal property, including machinery, used directly or predominantly for research and development (Sec. 39-26-601). To claim the refund, the taxpayer must submit an application to the Department of Revenue between January 1 and April 1 of the state fiscal year immediately following the fiscal year for which the refund is claimed.

Renewable energy: Any Colorado county or municipality may offer a property tax or sales tax credit or rebate to a residential or commercial property owner who installs a renewable energy fixture upon his or her property. "Renewable energy fixture" is defined as any fixture, product, system, device, or interacting group of devices that produces electricity from renewable resources, including, but not limited to, photovoltaic systems, solar thermal systems, small wind systems, biomass systems, or geothermal systems (Sec. 30-11-101.3; Sec. 30-11-107.3).

Sales of new tractor trailers: Under certain conditions, the sales and use taxes paid on new Class A vehicles will be refunded over a five-year period based on the proration of annual specific ownership taxes paid on the vehicles. The refund is limited to model year 2010 or newer truck tractors weighing greater than 54,000 pounds. The refund program will only take effect if a sustainable source of revenue has been identified. The refund would be claimed as follows (Sec. 39-26-113.5):

— 10% in the calendar year in which the truck tractor is purchased, stored, or used;

— 15% in the second year after the truck tractor was purchased, stored, or used;

— 25% in the third year after the truck tractor was purchased, stored, or used;

— 25% in the fourth year after the truck tractor was purchased, stored, or used; and

— 25% in the fifth year after the truck tractor was purchased, stored, or used.

To claim a refund, the taxpayer must submit a refund application to the Department of Revenue on a prescribed form. Proof of payment of Colorado sales and use tax by the taxpayer must accompany the application, as well as any additional information that the Department may require by regulation. For additional information, see FYI Sales 90, Department of Revenue, August 2013, at **https://www.colorado.gov/pacific/sites/default/files/Sales90.pdf.**

¶ 291   Scope of Tax

Source.—Statutory references are to Title 12, Chapter 219, of the General Statutes of Connecticut, as amended to date. Details are reported in the CCH CONNECTICUT TAX REPORTS starting at ¶ 60-000.

The sales tax is a tax on the privilege of making retail sales for a consideration in Connecticut (Sec. 12-408(1)).

The use tax is an excise tax on (1) the storage, acceptance, consumption, or any other use in Connecticut of tangible personal property purchased from any retailer, (2) the acceptance or receipt of any services constituting a sale, or (3) the storage, acceptance, consumption, or any other use in Connecticut of tangible personal property that has been manufactured, fabricated, assembled, or processed from materials by a person (either within or without the state) for storage, acceptance, consumption, or any other use by such person in the state (Sec. 12-411(1)).

Nature of Connecticut sales and use tax: The Connecticut sales and use tax is a general tax that extends to all leases and sales at retail (as defined under the law) of tangible personal property. A specific constitutional or statutory exemption must exist for the transaction not to be subject to tax. For Connecticut sales and use tax purposes, "sale" or "purchase" includes exchange or barter (Sec. 12-407(a)(2), Sec. 12-407(a)(7)). On the other hand, since the law lists the services that are subject to tax (Sec. 12-407(a)(2)), services not listed are exempt.

Sales or use tax applies even on property acquired out of state if such property would have been subject to sales tax had the sale occurred within Connecticut (Sec. 12-430(5)). In such cases, a credit for tax paid to another state may be allowed.

If the gross receipts from the sale of services or property stored, accepted, consumed, or used in Connecticut are required to be included in the measure of the sales tax, such receipts are exempt from the use tax (Sec. 12-413(1)). However, use tax may be imposed upon purchases that are subject to sales tax, but for which no sales tax is collected (*e.g.,* in-state retail purchases for which no sales tax is collected or paid by the retailer).

Sale-leaseback transactions: A sale is not taxable if it is part of a sale-leaseback transaction in which the lease is subject to tax (Sec. 12-407(a)(3)(B)).

Admissions: Admissions are generally subject to the Connecticut admissions and dues tax, a tax distinct from the sales and use tax and separately imposed (Sec. 12-540, G.S.).

Medical Marijuana: Effective October 1, 2012, sales of marijuana by licensed dispensaries are subject to sales and use taxes; the sales and use tax exemption for prescription medicine will not apply. Licensed dispensaries may purchase the marijuana from licensed producers on a resale basis.

Licensed producers may be able to claim a sales tax exemption under the provision commonly called the farmer tax exemption. This exemption allows entities engaged in agricultural production as a trade or business to be exempt from the sales and use tax for purchases of tangible personal property used exclusively for agricultural production (*Special Notice 2012(5),* Connecticut Department of Revenue Services, August 28, 2012, CCH CONNECTICUT TAX REPORTS, ¶ 401-605)

• **The sales tax**

Incidence of tax: The Connecticut sales tax is a privilege tax imposed on the retailer (lessor or service provider) measured by gross receipts as defined by law (Sec. 12-408(1)). However, the retailer is entitled to collect reimbursement of the tax from the purchaser (Sec. 12-408(2)). When the tax is added to the original purchase price, the tax becomes a debt of the purchaser and is subsequently recoverable as a debt from the purchaser by the retailer. The debt of sales tax from the consumer to the retailer, when recovered at law, is deemed to be a special fund in trust for the state of Connecticut.

Space rented for the storage of personal property is subject to tax (Sec. 12-407). The tax only applies to businesses engaged in the business of renting space and does not apply to residential spaces.

Services that constitute a sale: The following services are deemed taxable sales (Sec. 12-407(a)(2)(L) and Sec. 12-407(a)(37), Sec. 12-407(a)(2)(K), Sec. 12-407(a)(2)(*l*)):

— Business analysis, management, and management consulting;

— Car wash services, including coin-operated car washes;

— Community antenna television services;

— Computer and data processing services (including Internet website services, effective October 1, 2015);

— Cosmetic medical procedures, excluding reconstructive surgery;

— Credit information and reporting services;

— Employment and personnel agency services;

— Exterminating services;

— Flight instruction and chartering services by a certificated air carrier;

— Furniture reupholstering and repair services;

— Health and athletic club services;

— Janitorial services;

— Landscaping and horticultural services, except those provided by a licensed landscape architect;

— Lobbying or political special interest group consulting services;

— Locksmith services;

— Maintenance services;

— Manicure, pedicure, and all other nail services;

— Motor vehicle parking, storage (excluding self-storage units);

— Motor vehicle repair;

— Motor vehicle towing and road services;

— Packing and crating (other than that provided by retailers in connection with the sale of tangible personal property);

— Painting and lettering services;

— Painting, staining, and wallpapering services;

— Paving services;

— Personal services included in industry group 729 of the Standard Industrial Classification Manual (other than certain massage services);

— Pet grooming, boarding (other than grooming or boarding provided as an integral part of veterinarian services), and obedience services;

— Photographic studio services;

— Private investigation, protection, patrol work, security, and armored car services;

— Repair or maintenance services to any item of tangible personal property including any contract of warranty or service related to any such item;

— Services in connection with the sale of tangible personal property;

— Services providing "piped-in" music;

¶291　Connecticut

— Services to industrial, commercial, or income-producing real property;

— Spa services, including body waxing and wraps, peels, scrubs, and facials;

— Stenographic services;

— Swimming pool cleaning and maintenance services;

— Telecommunications services;

— Telephone answering services;

— Transportation services (intrastate) provided by livery services, including limousines, community cars or vans, with a driver, but excluding such services provided by taxis, buses, ambulances, scheduled public transportation, and funerals;

— Window cleaning services.

- **The use tax**

Incidence of tax: The Connecticut use tax is imposed on the storage, acceptance, consumption, or any other use in Connecticut of tangible personal property purchased from any retailer; the acceptance or receipt of taxable services; and the storage, acceptance, consumption, or any other use in Connecticut of tangible personal property that has been manufactured, fabricated, assembled, or processed from materials by a person, either within or without the state (Sec. 12-411(1)). The use tax on fabricated goods is measured by the sales price of the materials.

The Connecticut Department of Revenue Services provides guidance regarding individual use tax. Topics discussed include the imposition of the tax on certain goods and services, rates, and exemptions. (*Informational Publication 2016(19),* Connecticut Department of Revenue Services, January 5, 2017, CCH CONNECTICUT TAX REPORTS, ¶ 401-812)

Nexus

Every retailer engaged in business in Connecticut and making sales or leases of tangible personal property for use, storage, or other consumption, or rendering taxable services in Connecticut, not otherwise exempted, must collect sales or use tax from the purchaser (Sec. 12-411(3)).

Remote sales: Connecticut imposes a so-called "Amazon" provision. Applicable to sales that occur on or after May 4, 2011, the term "retailer" includes every person making sales of tangible personal property or services through an agreement with another person located in Connecticut under which the person, for a commission or other consideration that is based on the sale of tangible personal property or services by the retailer, directly or indirectly refers potential customers to the retailer, whether by a link on an Internet website or otherwise; and the cumulative gross receipts from sales by the retailer to Connecticut customers who are referred to the retailer by all such persons with this type of agreement with the retailer are in excess of $2,000 during the preceding four quarterly periods ending on the last day of March, June, September, and December. (Sec. 12-407(a)(12))

Moreover, and also applicable to sales that occur on or after May 4, 2011, the definition of "engaged in business in the state" is amended to include selling tangible personal property or services through an agreement with a person located in Connecticut under which the person, for a commission or other consideration that is based on the sale of tangible personal property or services by the retailer, directly or indirectly refers potential customers to the retailer, whether by a link on an Internet website or otherwise, and the cumulative gross receipts from sales by the retailer to Connecticut customers who are referred to the retailer by all such persons with this type of agreement with the retailer are in excess of $2,000 during the preceding four quarterly periods ending on the last day of March, June, September, and December. (Sec. 12-407(a)(15))

Drop shipment rule: Connecticut law imposes liability for sales tax on third parties (usually the manufacturer or a wholesaler of the goods) who deliver goods into Connecticut on behalf of retailers not engaged in business in the state. The drop shipment rule applies when a registered out-of-state seller (generally a wholesaler or a manufacturer, and referred to as "wholesaler") sells tangible personal property to an unregistered out-of-state seller ("unregistered seller") and the wholesaler either delivers the tangible personal property with its own vehicles to the unregistered seller's customer in Connecticut or ships it F.O.B. destination. The wholesaler must charge tax to the customer on the goods delivered in Connecticut unless the customer establishes that the purchase is not taxable. The location of the inventory does not change the applicability of the drop shipment rule. (*Policy Statement 2013(3),* Connecticut Department of Revenue Services, June 19, 2013, CCH CONNECTICUT TAX REPORTS, ¶ 401-640)

• **Streamlined Act status**

Connecticut is a participating state in the Streamlined Sales Tax Project (SSTP) (Executive Order No. 27, March 17, 2003).

Legislation necessary to implement the SST Agreement has not been enacted.

¶ 292   **Tax Base**

The sales tax is measured by the gross receipts from retail sales, from the rendering of any services constituting a sale, or from the total rent received from the rental of rooms in a hotel or lodging house (Sec. 12-408(1)).

Use tax: The use tax is measured by the sales price of the tangible personal property stored, consumed, or otherwise used or on the consideration for the rendition of any services constituting a sale (Sec. 12-411(1)). For property that is manufactured, fabricated, assembled, or processed for use in Connecticut, the use tax is based on the sales price of the materials.

Alternative calculation of basis: Taxpayers who have not segregated the tax collections from the sales receipts (but rather billed customers "tax included") may compute the gross receipts from sales exclusive of the taxes collected to be equal to 94.3% of the gross receipts (Sec. 12-414(3)).

• **"Gross receipts" and "sales price" defined**

"Gross receipts" or "sales price" is the total amount for which tangible personal property is sold, the total amount of rent received for occupancy, the total amount received for any service rendered, or the total amount of payment or periodic payments received for leasing or rental of tangible personal property (Sec. 12-407(a)(8)). Sales price includes (1) any services that are a part of the sale, (2) all receipts, cash, credits, and property of any kind, (3) any amount for which credit is allowed by the seller to the purchaser, and (4) all compensation and all employment related expenses (whether or not separately stated) paid to or on behalf of employees of a retailer of any taxable service (Sec. 12-407(a)(9)).

"Sales price" does not include the following: (1) cash discounts allowed and taken on sales; (2) any portion of the amount charged for property returned by purchasers, which upon rescission of the contract of sale is refunded either in cash or credit, provided the property is returned within ninety days from the date of purchase; (3) federal taxes, other than manufacturers' or importers' excise taxes, imposed by the United States upon or with respect to retail sales; (4) separately stated charges for installation labor; (5) trade-in allowances; (6) the face value of any coupon used to reduce the price of tangible personal property; (7) certain separately stated management services; (8) separately stated compensation, fringe benefits, workers' compensation and payroll taxes or assessments paid to or on behalf of a leased employee; or (9) refundable deposits (Sec. 12-407(a)(8)).

¶ 293   List of Exemptions, Exceptions, and Exclusions

Unless otherwise indicated, the statutory exemptions, exceptions, and exclusions listed below apply to both sales and use taxes; those applicable only to the use tax are listed separately. Items that are excluded from the sales or use tax base are discussed at ¶ 292, "Tax Base."

Sales tax holiday: Certain clothing and footwear sold for less than $100 is exempt from sales and use taxes each year for the week beginning with the third Sunday in August and ending on the following Saturday, inclusive. The exemption does not apply to athletic or protective clothing and footwear, jewelry, handbags, luggage, umbrellas, wallets, watches and similar items (Sec. 12-407d).

• **Sales and use tax exemptions, exceptions, and exclusions**

Admissions, entertainment, and dues	Sec. 12-407(a)(37)(DD), Sec. 12-541
Advertising and public relations; media and direct mail advertising . .	Sec. 12-407(a)(2)(L), Sec. 12-407(a)(37)(U)
Affiliated business entities, sales between	Sec. 12-412(58), (62)
Agriculture, including fishing, forestry, and animal farming	Sec. 12-412(63)
Aircraft, certain services pertaining to	Sec. 12-412(22)
Air pollution control facilities	Sec. 12-412(22)
Artwork sold on consignment	Sec. 12-407(a)(2)(L), Sec. 12-407(a)(37)
Auctions	Sec. 12-412(24)
Aviation fuel	Sec. 12-412(59), Sec. 12-412(75)
Bicycle helmets	Sec. 12-412(102)
Biotechnology industry	Sec. 12-412(89)
Calibration services for manufacturing machinery	Sec. 12-412(104)
"Call before you dig" program services	Sec. 12-412(106)
Caskets used for burial	Sec. 12-412(55)
Child car seats	Sec. 12-412(108)
Cleaning and maintenance services for disabled	Sec. 12-412(85)
Clothing and footwear (during sales tax holiday)	Sec. 12-407d
Clothing sold on consignment	Sec. 12-407(a)(37)(S)
Coin and currency services provided to a financial service company by or through another financial services company	Sec. 12-407(a)(37)(D)
Coin-operated amusement devices—see Vending machines	
Cold storage locker rental	Sec. 12-407(a)(37)(CC)
Commercial aircraft, repair parts and services	Sec. 12-412(76), Sec. 12-412(77), Sec. 12-412(78)
Commercial photographers' processing equipment	Sec. 12-412(88)
Computer and data processing services (selected)	Sec. 12-412(74)
Computer disc cleaning equipment	Sec. 12-412(64)
Connecticut credit unions, sales to (eff. July 1, 2016)	Sec. 12-412(120)
Consignment services	Sec. 12-407(a)(2)(L), Sec. 12-407(a)(37)
Contractor, purchasing for exempt organizations	Sec. 12-412(29)

Cooperative direct mail advertising	Sec. 12-407(a)(2)(L), Sec. 12-407(a)(37)
Credit unions, sales to and storage by	Sec. 12-412(121)
Diabetes treatment items	Sec. 12-412(54)
Diapers (disposable or reusable) (eff. 7/1/2018)	Sec. 12-412(1232)
Diesel fuel used in certain portable power system generators	Sec. 12-412(107)
Diplomatic personnel and missions	Sec. 12-412(2)
Drugs (nonprescription, as specified)	Sec. 12-412(120)
Drugs (prescription)	Sec. 12-412(48)
Educational institutions	Sec. 12-412(9)
Energy (solid waste to energy systems)	Sec. 12-412(95)
Energy-efficient systems (solar, geothermal)	Sec. 12-412(117)
Enterprise zones	Sec. 12-412(43)
Environmental consulting and clean up services	Sec. 12-407(a)(2)(L), Sec. 12-407(a)(37)
Equipment—see specific types	
Feed, seed, fertilizers, and food-bearing plants used in agricultural production by farmers	Sec. 12-412(63)
Feminine hygiene products (eff. 7/1/2018)	Sec. 12-412(122)
Financial institutions, specific	Sec. 36-84
Firearm safety devices	Sec. 12-412(101)
Flags	Sec. 12-412(23)
Food	Sec. 12-412(13)
Food products from vending machines	Sec. 12-412(13), Sec. 12-412(27)
Food products sold in schools	Sec. 12-412(9)
Food stamps	Sec. 12-412(57), Sec. 12-412e
Fuel cell manufacturing facility, sales of machinery and equipment to	Sec. 12-412(113)
Funeral services, up to $2,500	Sec. 12-412(55)
Gold or silver valued at $1,000 or more	Sec. 12-412(45)
Government transactions	Sec. 12-412(1), Sec. 12-412(2)
Hospitals and nursing homes, sales to and by	Sec. 12-412(5), (9), (56)
Housing: owner-occupied residential property with no more than three units; for low- or moderate-income taxpayers	Sec. 12-407(a)(2)(L), Sec. 12-407(a)(37)
Hybrid passenger cars	Sec. 12-412(115)
Ice storage systems	Sec. 12-412(118)
Industrial waste removal	Sec. 12-412(21)
Internet access services	Sec. 12-408(1)
Joint ventures, sales between participants	Sec. 12-412(58)
Land surveying services	Sec. 12-407(a)(2)(L), Sec. 12-407(a)(37)
Landscaping services for disabled	Sec. 12-412(85)
Libraries	Sec. 12-412(24)

¶293   **Connecticut**

¶293 **Connecticut**

• **Exemptions, exceptions, and exclusions applicable only to the use tax**

Property not exceeding $25 purchased out of state by a returning
resident . . . . Sec. 12-413(3)

Property or services, the gross receipts of which are required to be
included in the basis of the sales tax . . . . Sec. 12-407(a)(5),
Sec. 12-411(1)

Property purchased by a United States agency or instrumentality . . . Sec. 12-413

Property withdrawn from inventory and donated to the state or federal
government or an IRC Sec. 501(c)(3) organization . . . . Sec. 12-413(4)

Vessels brought into Connecticut exclusively for storage, maintenance,
or repair . . . . Sec. 12-413a

¶ 294   Rate of Tax

The sales and use tax is imposed at the rate of 6.35% of the applicable tax base, except in the following situations (Sec. 12-408(1); Sec. 12-411(1)):

Computer and data processing services: Computer and data processing services are subject to a reduced tax rate of 1%. Internet website services are exempt. (Sec. 12-408(1)(D)). Effective October 1, 2015, the types of computer and data processing services subject to tax include the creation, development, hosting, and maintenance of a website.

Hotel occupancies: Gross receipts from certain hotel occupancies are taxed at the rate of 15%. (Sec. 12-408(1)(B))

Motor vehicle sales: Gross receipts from the sale of any motor vehicle to a member or the spouse of a member of the U.S. Armed Forces who is on full-time active duty in Connecticut and who is considered to be a resident of another state under federal law are taxed at 4.5% (Sec. 12-408(1)(C), *Special Notice SN 98(8)*, Dept. of Revenue Services, June 11, 1998). "Full-time active duty" does not include service as a reservist or national guardsman (Reg. Sec. 12-426-16a(e), *Bulletin No. 21,* Dept. of Revenue Services, June 27, 1984). An affidavit is required (Reg. Sec. 12-426-16a(i)).

Motor vehicle rentals: The rental or leasing of a passenger motor vehicle for 30 consecutive calendar days or less is subject to a sales and use tax rate of 9.35% (Sec. 12-408(1)(G), as well as a 3% surcharge (see below)).

Luxury goods tax: The sales and use tax rate applicable to certain luxury goods is increased from 7% to 7.75% effective July 1, 2015. This rate applies to the full sales price of the following items that cost more than:

      — $50,000 for a motor vehicle (with certain exceptions);

      — $5,000 for jewelry, whether real or imitation; and

      — $1,000 for an article of clothing or footwear intended to be worn on or about the human body, a handbag, luggage, umbrella, wallet, or watch. (Sec. 12-408(1)(H))

Motor vehicles excluded from the luxury goods tax are those that: (1) are purchased by an active duty U.S. military member stationed in Connecticut; (2) weigh over 12,500 pounds; or (3) weigh 12,500 pounds or less, are not used for private passenger purposes but are designed or used to transport merchandise, freight, or persons in connection with any business enterprise, and are issued a commercial or more specific type of registration by the Department of Motor Vehicles. (Sec. 12-408(1)(H))

Applicable to sales that occur on or after July 1, 2013, the luxury goods tax (sales and use tax) rate on vessels with a sales price in excess of $100,000 is reduced from 7% to 6.35%.

Admissions and dues: A 10% admissions tax rate is imposed on admission charges to any place of amusement, entertainment or recreation. The tax rate on admission charges to motion picture shows is 6%. (Sec. 12-541, G.S.)

A 10% dues or initiation fees tax rate is imposed on any amount paid as dues or initiation fees to a social, athletic or sporting club. The tax is imposed upon the club, which is to collect it from the member. (Sec. 12-543(a), G.S.) However, private clubs that are owned or operated by their members are only subject to the tax if their dues or initiation fees are more than $100 per year. Clubs that are sponsored or controlled by a charitable organization, governmental agency, or a nonprofit educational institution are exempt from dues tax (*Policy Statement 2001(11)*, Connecticut Department of Revenue Services, September 21, 2001, CCH CONNECTICUT TAX REPORTS, ¶ 400-580).

• **Dry-cleaning surcharge**

Although the laundering or dry cleaning of clothes are not listed as taxable services (see ¶ 291), each eligible dry-cleaning establishment must pay a surcharge of 1% of its gross receipts at retail for dry cleaning services performed at retail. An "eligible dry cleaning establishment" is defined as any place of business engaged in the cleaning of clothing or other fabrics using tetrachlorethylene, Stoddard solvent or other chemicals, or any place of business that accepts clothing or other fabrics to be cleaned by another establishment using such chemicals. (Sec. 12-263m, G.S.; see ¶ 299 for registration requirements)

• **Passenger motor vehicle, truck, and machinery rental surcharges**

A surcharge of 3% of the total contract price is imposed upon leases, less than 31 days, of passenger motor vehicles, trucks of 26,000 lbs. gross vehicle weight or less used for nonbusiness purposes, and trailers of 6,000 lbs. or less (Sec. 12-692). In addition, there is a $1 per day tourism fund surcharge on automobile rentals for periods of up to 30 days (Sec. 12-666(a)).

Machinery: A 1.5% surcharge is imposed on heavy machinery (including but not limited to bulldozers, earth-moving equipment, well-drilling machinery and equipment, and cranes) rented without an operator within the state by a rental company for a period of fewer than 31 days (Sec. 12-692). the scope of the surcharge is expanded, effective July 1, 2015, to apply to: (1) all equipment a rental company owns; and (2) rentals of 364 days or less. For additional information, see *Policy Statement 2007(3)*, Connecticut Department of Revenue Services, September 12, 2007, CCH CONNECTICUT TAX REPORTS, ¶ 401-256.

Rental companies: A company must receive at least 51% of its total annual revenue from rental income, excluding retail or wholesale sales of rental equipment, in order to be required to collect the surcharge; see *OCG-1*, Office of Counsel Guidance Regarding the Rental Surcharge, Connecticut Department of Revenue Services, October 16, 2015, CCH CONNECTICUT TAX REPORTS, ¶ 401-757.

• **Rate changes**

Upon enactment of a new rate, the new rate applies to all retail sales on and after the effective date of the new rate (Sec. 12-408(1), Sec. 12-411(1)). However, the old rate applies to any sales transaction involving a binding sales contract without an escalator clause entered into prior to the effective date of the new rate if delivery is made within 90 days after the effective date of the new rate.

• **Payment of tax to another state**

If sales or use tax has been paid to another state or political subdivision, the rate of tax applicable will be the difference between the rate imposed by Connecticut and the rate at which the tax to the other state was computed (Sec. 12-430(5)). If the other state's tax rate is equal to or more than the Connecticut rate, no tax will be due to Connecticut.

¶294   **Connecticut**

• Sourcing of telecommunications charges

Connecticut has conformed to the federal Mobile Telecommunications Sourcing Act (Act), P.L. 106-252. All charges for mobile telecommunications services are considered to be provided by the customer's home service provider and sourced to the customer's place of primary use (Sec. 12-407a). All such charges are subject to sales tax based on the customer's place of primary use.

¶ 295   Local Taxes

Connecticut has no general provision enabling municipalities and other political subdivisions to levy local sales and use taxes.

Local option admissions surcharge: A municipality is authorized, by ordinance, to impose a surcharge on admission charges to events held at facilities located in the municipality. The surcharge may be up to 5% of the admissions charge, except for the surcharge on events held at Dunkin' Donuts Park in Hartford, which may be up to 10%.

Municipalities are prohibited from imposing a surcharge on:

(1) events from which all proceeds go exclusively to a federally tax-exempt organization, provided that organization actively engages in and assumes the financial risk of presenting the event; and

(2) pari-mutuel or off-track betting facilities already subject to a local admissions tax.

Any such municipal ordinance that is adopted under this provision may exclude additional events or facilities from the local option admissions surcharge. (Sec. 186, Act 3 (S.B. 502), Laws 2016)

¶ 296   Bracket Schedule

A bracket or rate schedule is prescribed by statute (Sec. 12-408(3)). Presumably, this schedule does not apply to transactions entitled to the special rates, as discussed above.

Amount of Sale		Amount of Tax
$0.00 to	$0.07 inclusive	No tax
0.08 to	0.23 inclusive	1¢
0.24 to	0.39 inclusive	2¢
0.40 to	0.55 inclusive	3¢
0.56 to	0.70 inclusive	4¢
0.71 to	0.86 inclusive	5¢
0.87 to	1.02 inclusive	6¢
1.03 to	1.18 inclusive	7¢

On all sales above $1.18, the tax is computed at the rate of 6.35% (Sec. 12-408(3)).

Coin-operated telephone service: The tax on coin-operated telephone service is computed on the nearest multiple of 5¢, except that if the tax is midway between multiples of 5¢, the next higher multiple applies (Sec. 12-408(7)).

¶ 297   Returns, Payments, and Due Dates

The Department of Revenue Services has prescribed a combined sales and use tax return (Form OS-114) for reporting all transactions for which the sales or use tax was collected by the retailer. For the payment of use tax not paid to the seller, a different return (Form OP-186) is used.

Retailers with sales in more than one Connecticut town must file additional information with their tax return. The additional information must disaggregate the town in which sales occurred for which the retailer collected sales and use tax, along with an indication of the amount of tax collected in each town. See *Informational*

Publication 2007(23), Connecticut Department of Revenue Services, September 1, 2007, CCH CONNECTICUT TAX REPORTS, ¶ 401-253.

Alternative methods of reporting gross receipts: Gross receipts must be reported exclusive of the tax collected; however if the tax collections have not been segregated, the Commissioner of Revenue Services may permit the alternative form of reporting gross receipts including the tax reimbursement (Sec. 12-414(3)).

Direct payment: A direct payment permit allows a business to purchase most taxable goods and services without paying Connecticut sales tax and to remit the use tax due directly to the DRS. To qualify for a direct payment permit, taxpayers must remit sales and use taxes using EFT (Electronic Funds Transfer) technology. To apply, the taxpayer must complete Form AU-620, Direct Payment Permit Application, and remit the $20 permit fee to DRS. Additional information is available in *Informational Publication 2004(7),* DRS, February 10, 2004.

Electronic filing: Taxpayers who are required to pay by electronic funds transfer (EFT) are also required to file their returns electronically through the Taxpayer Service Center.

• **Taxpayers required to file returns**

Sales tax: Every seller must file sales tax returns (Sec. 12-414(2)).

Use tax: The following are required to file use tax returns: (1) every retailer engaged in business in Connecticut; (2) every person purchasing services or tangible personal property, the storage, acceptance, consumption, or other use of which is subject to use tax, who has not paid the use tax to a retailer (Sec. 12-414(2)); and (3) individuals who have made aggregate purchases of more than $25 brought into Connecticut at one time by a resident for personal use (Instructions to Form OP-186, Connecticut Individual Use Tax Return; see also *Informational Publication 2015(21),* Connecticut Department of Revenue Services, September 2015, CCH CONNECTICUT TAX REPORTS, ¶ 401-743).

Sellers of cigarettes: Applicable to sales that occur on or after July 1, 2013, stampers and non-stamping licensed cigarette distributors are required to collect sales and use tax on cigarettes they sell to licensed dealers and remit the tax at the same time as other sellers (*i.e.,* retailers). Licensed dealers are required to collect the tax when selling cigarettes to a customer but may claim a credit against the sales and use tax equal to the amount of taxes they paid to the distributor or stamper (Sec. 12-430(8); *Special Notice 2013(4),* Connecticut Department of Revenue Services, June 28, 2013, CCH CONNECTICUT TAX REPORTS, ¶ 401-641). Previously, stampers and distributors could claim a resale exemption when selling to licensed dealers.

A "stamper" is defined as anyone who is lawfully allowed to buy unstamped packages of cigarettes and required to place cigarette tax stamps on those packages (Sec. 12-430(8)(A)(ii)). When a stamper sells stamped packages of cigarettes to a licensed dealer, the sale must be treated as a retail sale and not a sale for resale. The stamper is subject to the sales and use tax on its gross receipts from such sales and is required to (Sec. 12-430(8)(B)(i)):

— collect reimbursement for the tax from the licensed dealer even if the dealer presents a valid resale certificate;

— separately state the tax on its invoice to the licensed dealer; and

— file sale and use tax returns and remit the tax in the same way as other sellers.

When a licensed dealer purchases stamped packages of cigarettes from a stamper, the subsequent sale of those packages must be treated as a retail sale and not as a sale for resale. The licensed dealer is subject to the sales and use tax on its gross receipts from such sales and is required to collect reimbursement for the tax from each customer. When calculating the sales price, dealers cannot include the tax amount paid to the stamper. The dealer is allowed a credit against the sales and use tax due during a reporting period on its retail cigarette sales equal to the amount of tax it paid to the stamper during the same reporting period. (Sec. 12-430(8)(B)(ii))

When a stamper sells stamped packages of cigarettes to a nonstamping distributor who then sells them to a licensed dealer, the sale must be treated as a retail sale and not a sale for resale. The nonstamping distributor is subject to the sales and use tax on its gross receipts from such sales and is subject to the above requirements. (Sec. 12-430(8)(C)(i))

When a licensed dealer purchases stamped packages of cigarettes from a non-stamping distributor, the subsequent sale of such packages must be treated as a retail sale and not a sale for resale. The licensed dealer is subject to the sales and use tax on its gross receipts from such sales and is required to collect reimbursement for the tax from each customer. When calculating the sales price, dealers cannot include the tax amount paid to the nonstamping distributor. The dealer is allowed a credit against the sales and use tax due during a reporting period on its retail cigarette sales equal to the amount of tax it paid to the nonstamping distributor during the same reporting period. (Sec. 12-430(8)(C)(ii))

- **Due dates**

Monthly returns: Effective for tax periods ending on or after December 31, 2015, taxpayers must file a return and pay the tax on a monthly or quarterly basis, on or before the last day (formerly, the 20th day) of the month following the month covered by the return (Sec. 12-414(a)). Taxpayers whose Connecticut tax liability is less than $1,000 for the 12-month period ending on September 30 must file an annual return by January 31 of the following year. See Reg. 12-426-24.

Quarterly returns: Every person whose total tax liability for the twelve-month period ending on the preceding June 30 was less than $4,000 must remit tax on a quarterly basis (Sec. 12-414(a)).

Weekly returns: The Commissioner may require any person who is delinquent to remit the tax collected during a weekly period on a weekly basis (Sec. 12-414(e)(2)(A)). "Weekly period" is defined as the seven-day period beginning on a Saturday and ending the following Friday. Any person who is required to remit tax for a weekly period is required to remit the tax to the commissioner on or before the Wednesday next succeeding the weekly period. The requirement to remit tax on a weekly basis does not alter a person's obligation to file monthly or quarterly returns, as the case may be. When the end of one month and the beginning of the following month fall within the same weekly period, each person required to remit tax on a weekly basis is required to report all of the tax collected and remitted during that weekly period, regardless of the month, along with the corresponding gross receipts, on the return covering the monthly period that ended during such weekly period. (Sec. 12-414(e)(2)(A))

The commissioner is required to send a written notice informing each person required to remit tax on a weekly basis (Sec. 12-414(e)(2)(B)). Any person so required must remit tax on a weekly basis for one year beginning on the date indicated in the written notice. The notice must also contain information regarding the manner and method of such remittal. Any person who fails to remit tax on a weekly basis is subject to all penalties imposed under the sales and use tax laws, including revocation of such person's permit. (Sec. 12-414(e)(2)(C))

The Commissioner of Revenue Services may require the filing of returns and payment of taxes for periods other than monthly or quarterly periods if the Commissioner deems this action necessary in order to ensure collection of the tax (Sec. 12-414(e)(1)).

Taxpayers are required to file returns even if no tax is due. The return must be completed by showing "zero sales" and "zero taxes due" (*Informational Publication IP 92(1.1),* Dept. of Revenue Services, June 19, 1992).

Use tax: Taxpayers filing returns for use tax due on purchases for personal use or consumption, and not for use or consumption in carrying on a trade, occupation, business, or profession, may also file a return and pay the tax on an annual basis (Sec. 12-414(2)). Such returns are due April 15th of the following year.

• **Payment of tax**

Generally, remittance of the sales and use tax must be made to the Commissioner of Revenue Services at the same time as the filing of the return (Sec. 12-414(1)). Electronic payment may be made by any of the following methods (*Informational Publication 2011(22),* Connecticut Department of Revenue Services, January 23, 2012, CCH CONNECTICUT TAX REPORTS, ¶ 401-573):

— the ACH debit method through the DRS Taxpayer Service Center (TSC). The TSC may be acessed online at **www.ct.gov/TSC** or by telephone at 860-289-4829.

— the ACH credit method through any financial institution; or

— by credit card.

Payment by credit card: There are three ways to pay by credit card (American Express, Discover, Master Card or Visa) or comparable debit card:

(1) Log in to the Taxpayer Service Center (TSC) and select Make Payment by Credit Card;

(2) Visit **www.officialpayments.com** and select State Payments; or

(3) Call Official Payments Corporation toll-free at 800-2PAY-TAX (1-800-272-9829) and follow the instructions. Connecticut's Jurisdiction Code is 1777.

Delinquent taxpayers: Applicable to taxable periods that commence on or after October 1, 2013, and prior to April 1, 2014, the commissioner may require a taxpayer who is delinquent in paying sales taxes to remit electronically the tax due on each sale made during the tax period by consumer credit or debit card or electronic transfer (Sec. 80, Act 184 (H.B. 6704), Laws 2013). In order to be approved by the commissioner, a processor of consumer credit or debit card payments or electronic transfers must:

— use the specific file format prescribed by the commissioner;

— make available to the commissioner any information the commissioner requires;

— identify the specific software, including any third-party software, being used by the processor, as well as the software and processing specifications; and

— provide assurance to the commissioner that the software and processing will provide record transactions sufficient for collecting and auditing taxable sales.

A taxpayer who fails to comply with these provisions will be subject to any and all penalties imposed under the sales and use tax laws, including revocation of its permit.

• **Electronic funds transfer**

Monthly or quarterly filers: The Commissioner of Revenue Services may require persons who file a sales or use tax return on a monthly or quarterly basis to pay the tax by electronic funds transfer (EFT) if their tax liability was more than $4,000 for the 12-month period ending the preceding June 30, or for the preceding taxable year for annual filers (Sec. 12-686(a)(1)). See *Informational Publication 2014(15),* Connecticut Department of Revenue Services, November 12, 2014, CCH CONNECTICUT TAX REPORTS, ¶ 401-695.

¶297 **Connecticut**

Timeliness: Tax payments required to be made by EFT are timely if the taxpayer initiates the EFT on or before the payment due date. Specifically, taxpayers may initiate timely ACH Debit payments up until midnight on the payment due date, and taxpayers using the ACH Credit method must initiate payment on or before the due date, and the department's bank account must receive payment on or before the next business day following the due date of the return.

Tax payments that are required to be made by EFT and are not so made are treated as payments not made in a timely manner and are subject to a 10% penalty. Late electronic fund transfers are subject to a 2% penalty if the payment is not more than five days late, a 5% penalty if the payment is more than five days but not more than 15 days late, and a 10% penalty if the payment is more than 15 days late. (*Announcement 2011(7)*, Connecticut Department of Revenue Services, December 29, 2011)

Persons electing to pay tax by electronic funds transfer: Any person who files a sales or use tax return on a monthly, quarterly, or annual basis and who is not required to pay tax by electronic funds transfer may, at any time, submit a request to the Department for permission to pay tax by means of such method (Sec. 12-688(a)(1), Sec. 12-688(a)(2)). Persons permitted to pay tax by electronic funds transfer are regarded, for the period for which permission is granted, as persons required to pay tax by electronic funds transfer (Sec. 12-688(b)). Such persons must give notice, by certified mail, to the Department, at least 60 days before the expiration of the period, that they no longer choose to pay tax by electronic funds transfer beyond such period.

¶ 298 Prepayment of Taxes

Connecticut does not have any provisions regarding prepayment of taxes.

¶ 299 Vendor Registration

Every person desiring to engage in or transact business as a seller within Connecticut must secure a permit for each place of business before starting the business (Sec. 12-409(1)). The fee for the five-year permit is $100. The permit must be displayed conspicuously at all times at the place of business for which it is issued. A permit is not assignable and is valid only for the person in whose name it is issued and for the transaction of business at the place designated on it (Sec. 12-409(4)). Accordingly, if the ownership or structure of the business changes (for example, if a sole proprietorship becomes a partnership or corporation), a new permit is required.

Anyone who fails to get or renew a sales tax permit is subject to a civil penalty of $250 for the first day and $100 for each subsequent day that the person conducts business without a permit (Sec. 12-409(h)(2)).

Dry-cleaning establishments: Effective July 1, 2015, each dry-cleaning establishment registered with the Connecticut Commissioner of Revenue Services is required to renew its registration by October 1, 2015, and annually thereafter. Any such establishment that fails to register with the commissioner will pay a $1,000 penalty, which cannot be waived. Moreover, any dry-cleaning establishment that fails to renew within 45 days of the nonrenewal notice will be liable for a penalty of $200, which the commissioner may waive if the failure to register was due to reasonable cause and was not intentional or due to neglect. (Sec. 12-263m, G.S.)

- **Registration to collect use tax**

Connecticut law requires every retailer selling services or tangible personal property for storage, acceptance, consumption, or other use in Connecticut to register with the Commissioner of Revenue Services to collect the use tax (Sec. 12-411(8)).

- **State contractors**

Vendors and their affiliates that have no nexus with Connecticut and that enter into contracts for state agency purchases must to agree to collect use tax on all Connecticut sales during the term of the contract (Uncodified Sec. 105, Act 1 (H.B. 6802), Laws 2003).

¶ 300 **Sales or Use Tax Credits**

Use tax credits are allowed in many instances for sales taxes paid to other states or counties. If sales or use tax has been paid to another state or political subdivision, a credit is effectively allowed for such payment by reducing the applicable Connecticut tax rate by the rate of tax of the other state.

Tax previously paid: A credit (in lieu of a refund) may be obtained for the same grounds and under the same circumstances that would justify filing a claim for refund.

Returned goods: The sales tax on returned goods is credited by excluding from the tax base the sales price of the returned goods (Sec. 12-407(a)(8), Sec. 12-407(a)(9)).

Bad debts: The sales tax on uncollectible amounts may be credited within three years after the tax was remitted. The bad debt deduction or credit is not assignable (*DaimlerChrysler Services of North America, LLC v. Commissioner of Revenue Services,* Connecticut Supreme Court, No. 17277, June 28, 2005, CCH CONNECTICUT TAX REPORTS, ¶ 401-069).

Use tax credit for e-commerce education: A use tax credit is available to a direct pay permit holder in an amount equal to the amount of use tax liability on qualified purchases of computer equipment to be used in Connecticut public or private colleges or universities for instruction in electronic commerce (Sec. 12-413b).

Industrial reinvestment projects: Certain large manufacturers proposing "industrial reinvestment projects" (IRPs) in the state may exchange unused Connecticut research and development (R&D) tax credits for payments from the state that could be in the form of offsets or refunds of the Connecticut corporation business tax or sales and use tax. A manufacturer qualifies for such an exchange if it meets specified criteria and agrees to spend at least $100 million over five years on an IRP, which may consist of activities ranging from constructing new plants to hiring and training employees. The Department of Economic and Community Development (DECD) must:

 (1) certify that manufacturers and their proposed IRPs meet the legislation's criteria, and

 (2) enter into reinvestment contracts providing payments for the unused R&D credits in exchange for undertaking the IRP.

The DECD's authority to enter into the contracts ends June 30, 2015. To the extent that payments involve the offset or refund of state taxes, the DECD must consult with the Department of Revenue Services. (Act 2 (H.B. 5465), Laws 2014)

CCH Note: The legislation supports an agreement Connecticut reached in February 2014 with United Technologies Corporation (UTC) under which the company will invest up to $500 million to upgrade and expand its aerospace research and development and manufacturing facilities over the next five years. During the same time period, UTC expects to invest up to $4 billion in research and other capital expenditures in Connecticut, impacting more than 75,000 jobs in the state. For UTC, exchanged R&D credits will be offset with tax reductions over a 14-year period, with the final amount based on the company's level of jobs, wages, and investments.

¶ 301 **Deficiency Assessments**

A deficiency assessment may be issued by the Commissioner of Revenue Services if he or she is not satisfied with the return filed or the amount of tax paid (Sec. 12-415(1)) or if a taxpayer fails to file a return (Sec. 12-416(1)).

Assessment when tax return filed: If a return made or any amount paid is not satisfactory, the Commissioner may recompute the amount required to be paid on the basis of the return filed or of any information that the Commissioner has or that may come into the Commissioner's possession (Sec. 12-415(1)).

Assessment when no return filed: If a person fails to make a return, the Commissioner may estimate the amount of gross receipts or the amount of the total sales price on the basis of any information that the Commissioner has or may come into the Commissioner's possession (Sec. 12-416(1)).

The Commissioner may not make more than one assessment for a tax period for which a return has been filed, except in cases of fraud or intent to evade tax. However, the Commissioner may make a single supplemental assessment within the period otherwise prescribed for assessment upon written finding that an earlier assessment was imperfect or incomplete in any material respect (Sec. 12-415(1), Sec. 12-416(1)).

Offsets: In making an assessment, the Commissioner may offset overpayments, plus interest thereon, for one period against any underpayment, plus interest, for another period (Sec. 12-415(3), Sec. 12-416(2), Sec. 5, Act 48, Laws 1999).

¶ 302 Audit Procedures

The Commissioner of Revenue Services may examine the books, papers, records, and equipment of any person selling services or tangible personal property and any person liable for the use tax (Sec. 12-426(4)). The character of the business may also be investigated in order to verify the accuracy of any return made or to determine any amount to be paid if no return was filed.

The Commissioner may, by written notice order a hearing and require a taxpayer or any other person believed to be in possession of relevant information concerning the taxpayer to appear with any specified books of account, papers or other documents for examination under oath (Sec. 12-421).

The Commissioner may authorize any person to perform the examination function (Sec. 12-426(4)) and designate representatives to conduct hearings or perform any other duties (Sec. 12-426(2)).

Voluntary disclosure: The Voluntary Disclosure Program allows taxpayers who are not in compliance with Connecticut tax laws to voluntarily come forward and bring their accounts into compliance in exchange for a penalty waiver, a limited look-back period, and an avoidance of discovery through Connecticut's investigative and audit processes. Taxpayers must submit a written request to the department to participate in the program. The written request must include the type of tax involved, a description of the applicant's activities in the state, the starting date of the applicant's activities in the state, the reasons for noncompliance, the amount of the potential tax liability, and an admission of liability for the tax type at issue. Each request is considered on its own merits. For additional information, see *Informational Publication 2010(18),* Connecticut Department of Revenue Services, September 28, 2010, CCH CONNECTICUT TAX REPORTS, ¶ 401-476.

¶ 303 Statute of Limitations

Deficiency assessments: A notice of deficiency assessment must generally be mailed within three years after the last day of the month following the period to which the deficiency relates, or within three years after the return is filed, whichever expires later (Sec. 12-415(7)).

Refunds: A claim for refund or credit of overpaid taxes must be filed with the Commissioner within three years from the last day of the month following the close of the period for which the overpayment was made. A claim for refund of deficiency assessments paid must be filed within six months after the assessments become final (Sec. 12-425(2), *Policy Statement 91-3,* Dept. of Revenue Services).

No time limit in special cases: The right to assess is without time limit in certain cases, namely, fraud, intent to evade sales or use tax law or regulation, failure to make returns, or in cases of additional amounts assessed before the original assessment becomes final (Sec. 12-415(7)).

The three-year time limit does not apply to a sales or use tax assessment when notice of a deficiency assessment has been given (Sec. 12-415(7)).

¶ 304   **Application for Refund**

Before a refund or credit of sales and use tax can be allowed, a written claim must be filed with the Commissioner of Revenue Services stating the specific grounds upon which the claim is founded (Sec. 12-425(4)).

The claim must be filed within the three-year statutory period or, in the case of deficiency or estimated assessments, within six months after the assessments become final, unless the statute of limitations has been waived (Sec. 12-425(2), *Policy Statement 91-3,* Dept. of Revenue Services). Failure to file a timely claim constitutes a waiver of any demand for refund of an overpayment (Sec. 12-425(5)).

Grounds for refund: A refund or credit may be allowed on the grounds that the tax, penalty, or interest (1) has been paid more than once or (2) has been erroneously or illegally collected or computed (Sec. 12-425(1)).

Equitable refund: The Comptroller, upon application of any state department or commission, may draw an order upon the Treasurer in favor of any person equitably entitled to a refund of any money paid to the state (Sec. 4-37). The Attorney General must approve any such refund that exceeds $100.

Financial disability: The running of the statute of limitations for an individual to file a refund claim may be suspended during any period that an individual is financially disabled, provided the individual proves the existence of the financial disability as required by the Connecticut Commissioner of Revenue Services (Sec. 12-39t). An individual is defined as "financially disabled" if the person is unable to manage his or her financial affairs because of a medically determinable physical or mental impairment that can be expected to result in death or that has lasted or can be expected to last for a continuous period of at least 12 months. A person is not considered financially disabled during any period that the person's spouse or any other person is authorized to act on behalf of the individual in financial matters (Sec. 12-39t).

¶ 305   DELAWARE

¶ 306   Scope of Tax

Source.—Unless otherwise specified, statutory references are to Title 30 of the Delaware Code of 1974, as amended to date. Details are reported in the CCH DELAWARE TAX REPORTS starting at ¶ 64-001.

Delaware does not have a general sales tax. However, a person engaging in contracting, manufacturing, wholesaling, retailing, food processing, commercial feed dealing, restaurant retailing, or farm machinery retailing is subject to a gross receipts tax.

A use tax is imposed on every lessee under a lease of tangible personal property for use in Delaware (Sec. 4302(a)).

• **Streamlined Act status**

Delaware is not a participant in the Streamlined Sales Tax Project.

¶ 307   Tax Base

In general, the basis of the tax is the gross receipts of the taxpayer.

The term "gross receipts" does not include amounts received as a result of a transaction with a related entity (Sec. 2120(b)). Entities are related when (1) more than 80% in value of the stock, partnership interest, beneficial trust interest, or other ownership interest of each entity is owned directly, indirectly, or beneficially by the same five or fewer individuals, or (2) 100% of each entity is owned by a member or members of one family.

• **Contractors**

The gross receipts of a contractor (including architects, engineers, and construction managers), other than a real estate developer, include all sums received by the contractor for any work done or materials supplied in connection with any real property located in Delaware. However, contractors are not required to include receipts from subcontractors subject to license fees in computing their gross receipts (Sec. 2501).

Real estate developer: A real estate developer's gross receipts include all sums received from the sale of real property with structures, minus (1) the cost of the land and improvements to the land that are not structures, (2) miscellaneous expenses, and (3) sums paid to licensed subcontractors pursuant to a written agreement, provided these sums do not include payments for labor and materials related to nonstructural improvements (Sec. 2501).

Nonresident contractors providing disaster assistance: Out-of-state businesses that enter Delaware at the request of a registered Delaware business solely to provide infrastructure-related services during a state-declared emergency do not establish nexus, a presence in the state, or residency that would require such business or its out-of-state employees to register, file, or remit state or local taxes during the emergency period, including corporate income taxes, personal income and withholding tax, sales and use taxes, and *ad valorem* taxes on equipment. Such businesses and employees are not exempt from transaction taxes and fees, including without limitation, fuel taxes, sales and use taxes on materials or services, hotel taxes, and car rental taxes or fees, unless such taxes are otherwise exempted during a state-declared emergency. (Sec. 3102)

The tax safe harbor period begins within five days of the first day of a state-declared emergency and extends for a period of 60 calendar days after the end of such emergency declaration, unless a longer period is authorized (Sec. 3101(b)). An out-of-state business or any affiliate that enters Delaware during an emergency period must provide the Delaware Division of Revenue, upon request, a written statement that the business is in the state for purposes of performing emergency-related work (Sec. 3104). If an out-of-state business or any employee remains in Delaware after the emergency period, it is subject to the state's normal standards for establishing presence, residency, or doing business in the state and responsible for all the resulting state and local registration, licensing, and tax filing requirements (Sec. 3103).

• Manufacturers

All proceeds received by Delaware manufacturers for products manufactured for sale in whole or in part in Delaware, or the fair market value of any products consumed by the manufacturer or any person affiliated with it, are included in gross receipts (Sec. 2701(1)). When a manufacturer manufactures a product partially in Delaware and partially elsewhere, the gross receipts realized on the ultimate sale, transfer, or consumption of the product are apportioned to Delaware in the proportion that the cost of manufacturing in Delaware bears to the full cost of manufacturing the product. In addition, gross receipts do not include proceeds from products used in the manufacture of other products in Delaware. These products are considered to be included in the ultimate product manufactured, whether they are in an altered or unaltered form.

• Retailers

In the case of a retailer, "gross receipts" includes the total consideration received for all goods sold or services rendered within Delaware, but does not include the following: (1) tobacco products taxes or motor fuel taxes paid or payable to Delaware; (2) gasoline and special fuel taxes paid or payable to the federal government under IRC Sec. 4041 or IRC Sec. 4081; or (3) receipts derived from the sale of petroleum products, provided the petroleum products were sold to the retailer by a person who is licensed under Ch. 29, Tit. 30, Code, and the sale is described in the definition of "gross receipts" with regard to the retailer (Sec. 2901(2)(a)).

• Wholesalers

In the case of a wholesaler, "gross receipts" includes the total consideration received from sales of tangible personal property physically delivered in Delaware to a purchaser or its agent (Sec. 2901(2)(b)). However, in the case of a wholesaler, the definition of "gross receipts" excludes the sale of any product that is placed on a common carrier and shipped to an out-of-state purchaser (*KMC Foods, Inc. v. Director of Revenue,* Delaware Superior Court, New Castle, No. 02A-02-003 RSG, August 30, 2002, CCH DELAWARE TAX REPORTS, ¶ 200-622).

• Use tax

The use tax is based on the rent payable under leases of tangible personal property (Sec. 4302(a)).

¶ 308   List of Exemptions, Exceptions, and Exclusions

The exemptions listed below apply to the licenses and taxes based on gross receipts, discussed at ¶ 307, "Tax Base."

• Contractors

Real estate developers	Sec. 2501(5)
Sums paid to subcontractors	Sec. 2501(5)
Transactions with a related entity	Sec. 2120(b)

• Manufacturers

Aircraft weighing 12,500 lbs. or more	Sec. 2909(*l*)
Transactions with a related entity	Sec. 2120(b)
Utilities and farm products	Sec. 2703

• Wholesalers

Agricultural products	Sec. 2909(a)
Aircraft (12,500 lbs. or more)	Sec. 2909(l)
Alcoholic liquor retail sales	Sec. 2909(c)
Commercial crabbers	Sec. 2909(g)
Exchanges between wholesalers	Sec. 2909(k)
Farm wineries, microbreweries, and brewery-pubs	Sec. 2901(2)(b)(iii),
Foreign wholesalers selling pharmaceutical ingredients	Sec. 2901(2)(b)(vii)[viii]
Handicapped peddlers	Sec. 2909(e)
Horse racing licensees	Sec. 2909(i)
Individual artists and craftsmen	Sec. 2909(f)
Motor vehicles	Sec. 2909(b)
Nonprofit organizations	Sec. 2909(j)
Out-of-state sales	Sec. 2909(d)
Petroleum products, intermediate sales of	Sec. 2901(4)
Pharmaceutical products and ingredients	Sec. 2901(2)(b)(vii)[viii] Sec. 2901(4)
Printing contracts awarded by Dept. of Administrative Services	Sec. 2901(2)(b)(vi)[vii]
Transactions with a related entity	Sec. 2120(b)

• Retailers

Agricultural products	Sec. 2909(a)
Aircraft (12,500 lbs. or more)	Sec. 2909(l)
Alcoholic liquor retail sales	Sec. 2909(c), Tit. 30, Code
Commercial crabbers	Sec. 2909(g)
Handicapped peddlers	Sec. 2909(e)
Horse racing licensees	Sec. 2909(i)
Individual artists and craftsmen	Sec. 2909(f)
Motor vehicles	Sec. 2909(b)
Nonprofit organizations	Sec. 2909(j)
Out-of-state sales	Sec. 2909(d)
Transactions with a related entity	Sec. 2120(b)

• Use tax exemptions

The following items are exempt from the use tax on leases of tangible personal property (Sec. 4302(a)):

— household furniture, household fixtures or household furnishing;

— hospital equipment and any and all medical and remedial equipment, aids and devices leased by or to elderly, ill, injured or handicapped persons for their own use;

— manufacturing equipment under leveraged leases in which rental payments are guaranteed, wholly or partially by the Economic Development Administration of the United States Department of Commerce pursuant to P.L. 89-136, as amended;

— equipment, machinery, fixtures, buildings, or nonregistered vehicles used by farmers in raising crops or animals;

— motion picture films leased by a nonprofit film society.

　　　　　　　　　　　　　Rate of Tax

Each licensee pays a $75 annual fee for each place of business, and a tax imposed on aggregate gross receipts at varying rates depending upon the occupation.

• Contractors

Since January 1, 2014, the tax rate for contractors (including architects, engineers, and construction managers) is $75 (Sec. 2502(a)) plus 0.6472% (previously, 0.6537%) of the aggregate gross receipts (Sec. 2502(c)(1)). In computing the fee due each month, a deduction of $100,000 is allowed from the aggregate gross receipts of an enterprise.

• Manufacturers

Since January 1, 2014, the tax rate for manufacturers is $75 (Sec. 2702(a)) plus 0.126% (previously, 0.1886%) of the aggregate gross receipts. In computing the fee due each month, a deduction of $1.25 million is allowed from the aggregate gross receipts of an enterprise.

Automobile manufacturers: For automobile manufacturers, the gross receipts tax rate since January 1, 2014, is 0.0945% (previously, 0.1414%) (Sec. 2703).

Clean energy device manufacturers: For manufacturers of solar, wind, fuel cell, and geothermal power devices, the gross receipts tax rate since January 1, 2014, is 0.0945% (previously, 0.1458%) (Sec. 2702(b)(2)).

• Wholesalers

Since January 1, 2014, the rate for wholesalers is $75 (Sec. 2902(b)) plus 0.3983% (previously, 0.4023%) of the aggregate gross receipts (Sec. 2902(c)(1)). In computing the fee due each month, a deduction of $100,000 is allowed from the aggregate gross receipts of an enterprise.

Petroleum products: An additional tax of 0.9% (hazardous substances cleanup tax) is imposed until 2022 on aggregate gross receipts derived from the sale of petroleum products in excess of $100,000 per month. Wholesalers are also subject to a surtax of 0.2489% (0.2514% before January 1, 2014) on the sale of petroleum products (Sec. 2902(c)(1)).

Effective for gross receipts received after June 30, 2007 and before January 1, 2015, the gross receipts surtax on petroleum and petroleum products was not imposed on gross receipts from a sale of petroleum or petroleum products by a wholesaler, if the petroleum or petroleum products were sold to the wholesaler by a person who is licensed under Delaware gross receipts tax provisions and the sale was included in the seller's gross receipts (Secs. 9114(a) and (d), Tit. 7, Code).

• Food processors

Since January 1, 2014, the rate of tax for food processors is $75 (Sec. 2903(b)) plus 0.1991% (previously, 0.2012%) of the aggregate gross receipts (Sec. 2903(c)(1)). In computing the fee due each month, a deduction of $100,000 is allowed from the aggregate gross receipts of an enterprise.

Persons 65 years of age or older whose gross receipts are less than $5,000 per year pay one-fourth of the annual license fee (Sec. 2908(h)).

• Commercial feed dealers

Since January 1, 2014, the rate of tax for commercial feed dealers is $75 (Sec. 2904(b)) plus 0.0996% (previously, 0.1006%) of the aggregate gross receipts (Sec. 2904(c)(1)). In computing the fee due each month, a deduction of $100,000 is allowed from the aggregate gross receipts of an enterprise.

Persons 65 years of age or older whose gross receipts are less than $5,000 per year pay one-fourth of the annual license fee (Sec. 2908(h)).

• Occupations requiring licenses

Since January 1, 2014, the rate of tax for persons engaged in numerous specified occupations that require licenses is a fixed tax in varying amounts, plus a tax on aggregate gross receipts at the rate of 0.3983% (previously, 0.4147%) (Sec. 2901). In computing the fee due each month, a deduction of $100,000 is allowed from the aggregate gross receipts of an enterprise.

Persons 65 years of age or older whose gross receipts are less than $5,000 per year pay one-fourth of the annual license fee (Sec. 2908(h)).

• Lessors

The license fee for lessors of tangible personal property is $75 plus $25 for each additional place of business located in Delaware (Sec. 4305(a)). In addition, since January 1, 2014, an annual license tax of 0.2987% (previously, 0.3017%) is also imposed (Sec. 4305(b)). However, the rate for leases of motor vehicles remains at 0.288%. In computing the fee due each month, a deduction of $300,000 is allowed from the aggregate gross receipts of an enterprise to be applied first to receipts from leases of tangible property other than motor vehicles and any remainder applied to receipts from leases of motor vehicles.

• Retailers

The rate of tax for retailers is $75 and an additional $25 for each separate branch or business location (Sec. 2905(a)). In addition, since January 1, 2014, 0.7468% (previously, 0.7543%) of the aggregate gross receipts is taxed. In computing the fee due each month, a deduction of $100,000 is allowed from the aggregate gross receipts of an enterprise.

Persons 65 years of age or older whose gross receipts are less than $5,000 per year pay one-fourth of the annual license fee (Sec. 2908(h)).

Petroleum products: An additional tax of 0.9% (hazardous substances cleanup tax) is imposed on aggregate gross receipts in excess of $100,000 per month. Retailers are exempt from the additional fee if the hazardous substances cleanup tax was paid to their supplier.

Local event taxes: Delaware municipalities with a population of 50,000 or more may impose an event tax up to $2.50 on admission tickets exceeding $10 (Sec. 907, Tit. 22, Code). The tax is limited to sporting, cultural, recreational, or other entertainment events. Further, the tax cannot be imposed on school-sponsored events (as approved by the State Department of Public Education or any government agency authorized to operate a school) or political fund-raising events.

• Restaurant retailers

The rate of tax for restaurant retailers is $75, plus $25 for each separate branch or location (Sec. 2906(b)). In addition, since January 1, 2014, the tax rate is 0.6272% (previously, 0.6537%) of the aggregate gross receipts. In computing the tax due each month, a deduction of $100,000 is allowed from the aggregate gross receipts of an enterprise.

Persons 65 years of age or older whose gross receipts are less than $5,000 per year pay one-fourth of the annual license fee (Sec. 2908(h)).

• Farm machinery, supplies, or materials retail

Since January 1, 2014, the rate for farm machinery, supplies, or materials retailers is $75 (Sec. 2907(b)) plus 0.0996% (previously, 0.1006%) of the aggregate gross receipts (Sec. 2907(c)(1)). In computing the fee due each month, a deduction of $100,000 is allowed from the aggregate gross receipts of an enterprise.

Persons 65 years of age or older whose gross receipts are less than $5,000 per year pay one-fourth of the annual license fee (Sec. 2908(h)).

• **Transient retailers**

Since January 1, 2014, the rate of tax for transient retailers is $25 (Sec. 2905(f)) plus 0.7468% (previously, 0.7543%) of the aggregate gross receipts attributable to all goods sold or services rendered that exceed $3,000 (Sec. 2905(g)). Persons 65 years of age or older whose gross receipts are less than $5,000 per year pay one-fourth of the annual license fee (Sec. 2908(h)).

• **Grocery supermarket retailers**

Grocery supermarket retailers are not subject to the provisions of Sec. 2905, which are applicable to general retailers. Instead, they are required to pay an annual license fee, renewable on December 31st of each year, in the amount of $75 for the first location, and $25 for each separate location. In addition, since January 1, 2014, gross receipts are taxed monthly at 0.3267% (previously, 0.33%) of the aggregate gross receipts (Sec. 2908). In computing the fee due on aggregate gross receipts for each month, a $100,000 deduction is allowed. For purposes of determining the rate of taxation and the exclusion, all branches or entities comprising an enterprise with common ownership or common direction and control are considered as one, and allowed one exclusion.

• **Use tax on lessees**

Since January 1, 2014, a use tax equal to 1.9914% (previously, 2.0114%) of the rent is imposed on lessees of tangible personal property (other than motor vehicles, household furniture, household fixtures or household furnishings, hospital equipment and medical and remedial equipment, aids and devices leased by or to elderly, ill, injured or handicapped persons for their own use, including television sets leased to patients in a health care facility, and manufacturing equipment under certain leveraged leases guaranteed by the federal Economic Development Administration) (Sec. 4302(a)).

The use tax on leases of motor vehicles is also equal to 1.9914% (previously, 2.0114%) of the rent under the lease (Sec. 4302(b)).

• **Local lodging taxes**

Delaware municipalities, with a population in excess of 50,000, may impose a lodging tax not to exceed 3% of rent for a room or rooms at a hotel, motel, or tourist home (Sec. 908, Tit. 22, Code). The municipal tax is in addition to the state-imposed lodging tax.

The Kent County Levy Court is authorized to impose by ordinance a local lodging tax on rooms in a Delaware hotel, motel, or tourist home if the annual operating revenue of the Dover Civic Center is insufficient during the debt repayment period to cover the principal and interest payments for the general obligation bonds issued by the Levy Court. The Levy Court, with assistance by the State Treasurer and Secretary of Finance, will establish the rate and duration of any lodging tax. Authority to levy this lodging tax will sunset once all the principal and interest associated with the bond issuance has been repaid. (Uncodified Ch. 329 (H.B. 500), Laws 2010)

• **E911 prepaid wireless charge**

Effective January 1, 2015, a Delaware prepaid wireless E911 surcharge of 60¢ must be collected by the seller from the consumer (Sec. 10101 *et seq.*, Tit. 16, Code).

• **Some municipal taxes require state legislative authorization**

On or after June 15, 2014, a municipality may only impose a tax within its jurisdiction if such tax is expressly authorized by an Act of the Delaware General Assembly. Any provision in a municipal charter granting the municipal corporation "all powers" cannot be construed as exempting the municipal corporation from the limitation. However, "new tax enacted" does not include the increase or continuation of existing taxes that were in existence prior to June 15, 2014, and the limitation is not applicable to any municipal corporation that obtained a home rule charter prior to June 1, 1966. (Sec. 1901, Tit. 22, Code)

¶ 310   Returns, Payments, and Due Dates

All reports are filed with the Department of Finance.

The license tax report based on taxable gross receipts of the previous month is due on or before the 20th of the succeeding month. If a licensee's taxable gross receipts during the lookback period (between July 1 and June 30 immediately preceding the taxable year) do not exceed the statutory threshold (generally, $1,500,000, but $8 million forcommercial feed dealers and farm machinery dealers), the return and license fee is due by the last day of the first month following the close of the quarter (Sec. 2122).

The penalty for the failure to file any Delaware tax return under Title 30 (State Taxes) is 5% per month, capped at 50% of the amount of tax required to be shown on the unfiled return. If the failure to file the return is due to fraudulent behavior, the amount is 75% of the tax shown on the unfiled return. (Sec. 534)

Use tax: Every person required to obtain a lessors license from the Department of Finance is required to file a return that shows the amount of rental payments received during the period covered by the return that are subject to the use tax on leases of tangible personal property and the amount of taxes required to be collected (Sec. 4307(a)). Returns must contain information that the Department of Finance deems necessary for the proper administration of the use tax.

Every person required to collect the use tax on leases of tangible personal property is required to collect the tax from the lessee when collecting the rent under the lease to which the tax applies (Sec. 4303(a)). The tax must be paid to the person required to collect it as trustee for Delaware.

In order to prevent tax evasion and properly administer the use tax, it is presumed that all rental payments under leases are subject to the tax until the contrary is established. The burden of proving that any rental payment is not taxable rests with the person required to collect the tax or the lessee (Sec. 4303(a)).

• Electronic filing of returns

The Director may permit the filing of returns by electronic means (Telephone conversation, Delaware Division of Revenue, September 19, 2001).

¶ 311   Prepayment of Taxes

Delaware does not have any provisions requiring prepayment of taxes.

¶ 312   Vendor Registration

Any person conducting business activities is required to register with and obtain a business license from the Division of Revenue. A vendor is required to complete a Combined Registration Application (Form CRA) and pay the appropriate license fee before operations begin. Fees for many license categories may be prorated for the first year of activity.

¶ 313   Tax Credits

Business finder's fee (BFF) credit: Refundable business finder's fee tax credits are available to both a Delaware business entity that sponsors an out-of-state business relocating to Delaware (sponsor firm) and the out-of-state business (new business firm) if the relocation results in the creation of new jobs by the new business firm. The new employees must be employed for at least three months prior to the date the firms apply for the credits. The credits may be claimed against the Delaware corporate income tax, personal income tax, bank franchise tax, insurance gross premiums and privilege taxes, gross receipts tax, lessee use tax, lodging tax, or business occupational license fees. (Sec. 2092; Sec. 2094)

Both the sponsor firm and the new business firm must be either a corporation, partnership, limited liability company, statutory trust, or sole proprietorship that has been in business for at least three years at the time they apply for the BFF credit. Affiliated firms are not eligible for the credit. In addition, real estate agencies and developers cannot be sponsor firms. Likewise, a sponsor firm cannot be a landlord for the new business firm, or a bank or other lender that provides financing for the new business firm to establish a Delaware business location.

Credit amount.—The BFF credit that may be claimed by the sponsor firm and the new business firm is equal to $500 multiplied by the total number of full-time Delaware employees of the new business firm each tax year (Sec. 2092). The tax credit may be claimed for each of the three tax years from the anniversary of the new business certification date (Sec. 2094).

The maximum amount of credits available to all sponsor and new business firms is $3 million in any state fiscal year. Credits are awarded in chronological order based upon the date and time of each application. If a credit award results in exceeding the state limitation for the fiscal year, the amount by which such credit award exceeds the limitation will carry over and receive priority in the next fiscal year.

Application and filing requirements.—The sponsor and new business firms must submit a joint BFF credit application to the Delaware Economic Development Office (DEDO) on or after the anniversary of the date it was certified that the firms satisfied the eligibility and job creation requirements ("new business certification date") (Sec. 2093). The application must indicate the tax against which each firm seeks to apply a credit.

In order to claim the credit, the sponsor firm and new business firm must attach the DEDO's authorization for the approved application to the Delaware tax return against which the credit is claimed. (Sec. 2094)

• Reduction in manufacturers' and wholesalers' license fee

A taxpayer, other than a public utility, that qualifies for the Delaware corporate income tax credit for its qualified investment in business facilities in the state also is eligible for a reduction in the license taxes, other than the tax imposed under the Hazardous Substance Cleanup Act, for the same 10-year period for which the income tax credit is allowed. The reduction is allowed in an amount equal to 90% of the fee for the first year graduated down to a 5% reduction in the 10th year (Sec. 2010).

• Travelink Program

Employers that participate in a Department-certified Travelink Program are eligible for a credit against the aggregate gross receipts of the license requirements and taxes for the following industries (Sec. 2033): manufacturer; wholesaler; food processor; restaurant retailer; commercial feed dealer; retailer; farm machinery retailer.

¶314   Deficiency Assessments

When a taxpayer fails to pay the full amount of tax due, the Division of Revenue will send the taxpayer a tax advisory notice explaining what is owed, the penalties and interest charged on the unpaid balance.

The Director of Revenue may direct the Division of Professional Regulation (DPR) to deny or suspend any taxpayer's professional or occupation license issued under Sec. 8735, Tit. 29, Code for the failure to pay any amount owed for taxes, including any interest, additional amounts, and assessable penalties, that exceeds $1,000 and that has been reduced to a judgment pursuant to Sec. 554, Tit. 30, Code. The director will notify the DPR to deny or suspend the license within 20 days of the notice to the debtor of the intent to deny or suspend unless the debt is satisfied in full, the delinquent taxpayer has entered into a written agreement with the director for payment of the debt, or the taxpayer has requested a hearing with the division of revenue. The debtor will remain ineligible for the issuance, renewal, or reinstatement of any license until the director of revenue provides written certification to the DPR within 30 days of satisfaction of the debt that the grounds for denial or suspension of a license no longer exist. (Sec. 547)

¶ 315   **Audit Procedures**

Delaware law provides that the Director of Revenue must examine returns as soon as practicable after any return is filed to determine the correct amount of tax due (Sec. 521).

If the Director finds that the amount of tax shown on the return is less than the correct amount, the Director will notify the taxpayer in writing of the amount of the deficiency proposed to be assessed. If the Director finds that the tax that has been paid by the taxpayer is more than the correct amount, the Director must credit the overpayment and refund the difference to the taxpayer (Sec. 521(a)).

If a taxpayer fails to file any return of tax required to be filed, the Director must estimate from any available information the taxpayer's taxable amount, the tax due, and notify the taxpayer in writing of the amount proposed to be assessed against the taxpayer as a deficiency (Sec. 521(b)).

¶ 316   **Statute of Limitations**

A notice of proposed assessment must be mailed to the taxpayer within three years after the return is filed. No deficiency will be assessed or collected with respect to the taxable period for which a return was filed unless the notice was mailed within the three-year period or within a period otherwise prescribed (Sec. 531(a)). In the case of a license fee deficiency, a notice of proposed assessment must be mailed within three years after the expiration date of the license (Sec. 531(b)).

No return filed or false or fraudulent return: If a taxpayer fails to file a return or filed a false or fraudulent return with the intent to evade tax, a notice of proposed assessment may be mailed to the taxpayer at any time (Sec. 531(c)).

¶ 317   **Application for Refund**

On satisfactory proof of erroneous payment and upon recommendation of the Department of Finance, an application for refund may be made, but must be made within three years from the time that the return was filed or within two years from the time that the tax was paid, whichever is later. If no return was filed, the claim must be filed within two years from the time the tax was paid. Further, the refund claim must be made in writing, filed with the Director of Revenue, and state the specific grounds upon which it is founded. A claim may not be amended after the last date prescribed by the limitation provision if the net effect would be an increase in the amount of the overpayment (Sec. 539).

¶ 320   DISTRICT OF COLUMBIA

¶ 321   Scope of Tax

Source.—Statutory references are to Title 47 of the District of Columbia Code, as amended to date. Details are reported in the CCH DISTRICT OF COLUMBIA TAX REPORTS starting at ¶ 60-000.

Generally, the sales tax applies to retail sales of tangible personal property and specified services (Sec. 47-2002). The use tax applies to tangible personal property and services stored, used, or consumed in the District and on which no sales tax was paid when purchased (Sec. 47-2202, Sec. 47-2206(1)).

Property purchased for resale and property purchased to be incorporated as a material or part of another item of tangible personal property is not considered to have been purchased at retail, and such sales are therefore exempt (Sec. 47-2001(n)(1)). Items that are exempt from the sales tax when purchased are exempt also from the use tax (Sec. 47-2206(2)).

The sales tax is based on the gross receipts from sales or charges for tangible personal property and services. The use tax is based on the sales price of the property and services purchased (Sec. 47-2002, Sec. 47-2202).

Digitized products: Sales of digitized products delivered over the Internet are generally taxable as sales of data processing or information service. Examples include downloaded music, videos, newspapers, pictures, greeting cards, noncustomized software, and tax research products.

• **Services subject to sales and use taxes**

Taxable services include sales of or charges for (Sec. 47-2001; Reg. Secs. 423 - 429):

— storage of household goods through renting or leasing space for self-storage, including rooms, compartments, lockers, containers, or outdoor space, except general merchandise warehousing and storage and coin-operated lockers;

— carpet and upholstery cleaning, including the cleaning or dyeing of used rugs, carpets, or upholstery, or for rug repair;

— health club services or a tanning studio;

— car washing, including cleaning, washing, waxing, polishing, or detailing an automotive vehicle, except for coin-operated, self-service car washes; and

— the service of a bowling alley or a billiard parlor.

• **Incidence of tax**

The sales tax is imposed on all vendors for the privilege of selling tangible personal property at retail and for the privilege of selling specified services (Reg. Sec. 400.1). "Vendor" includes a person or retailer selling taxable property or rendering taxable services (Sec. 47-2002). "Retailer" includes persons engaged in the business of making sales at retail. Liability for tax occurs when purchase and delivery occur in the District, even if the property is subsequently used, stored, or consumed outside the District (Reg. Sec. 405.2).

A use tax is imposed on vendors engaging in business in the District and on purchasers on the use, storage, or consumption of any tangible personal property and on services sold or purchased at retail sale (Sec. 47-2202).

Online travel companies (OTCs) and room remarketers: Sales and use tax is imposed on charges for transient accommodations made by persons other than the retailer, including charges received from Internet transactions by online travel companies (Sec. 47-2002(2)(B); Sec. 47-2002.02(1)(B); Sec. 47-2202(2)(B); Sec. 47-2202.01(1)(B)). The definition of "retail sales" for sales and use tax purposes includes net charges and additional charges for any room or rooms, lodgings, or accommodations furnished to transients by any room remarketer, as well as by any hotel, inn, tourist camp, tourist cabin, or any other place in which rooms, lodgings, or accommodations are regularly furnished, to transients for consideration (Sec. 47-2001(n)(1)(C)). "Net sale" or "net charges" means the sale or charge receipts for any room or rooms, lodgings, or accommodations furnished to transients, received from a room remarketer by the operator of a hotel, inn, tourist camp, tourist cabin, or any other place in which rooms, lodgings, or accommodations are regularly furnished to transients for a consideration. "Additional charges" means the excess of the sale or charge receipts received by a room remarketer over the net charges. "Room remarketer" means any person, other than the retailer, having any right, access, ability, or authority, through an Internet transaction or any other means whatsoever, to offer, reserve, book, arrange for, remarket, distribute, broker, resell, or facilitate the transfer of rooms the occupancy of which is subject to sales tax.

The room remarketer must remit tax on, and file returns for, the "additional charges." The operator must remit tax and file returns on the "net charges" it receives from room remarketers. (Sec. 47-2015(a-1); see also *Expedia, Inc. v. District of Columbia,* District of Columbia Court of Appeals, Nos. 14-CV-308 and 14-CV-309, July 23, 2015, CCH DISTRICT OF COLUMBIA TAX REPORTS, ¶ 200-753, holding that the OTCs were not liable for tax due on amounts they paid to hotels as sales tax reimbursements)

Sales in federal buildings and by federal enterprises or organizations: Sales and use taxes are imposed on sales made in federal buildings and by government-sponsored enterprises and corporations, institutions, and organizations (Act 19-0381 (D.C.B. 19-742), Laws 2012); (Act 20-370 (D.C.B. 20-749), Laws 2014). Taxable sales include sales that are made to

— the general public, whether the establishment is operated by the federal government, an agent of the federal government, or a contractor; and

— other than the general public, if operated by an agent of the federal government or a contractor.

Taxable sales also include sales of goods and services by government-sponsored enterprises and corporations, institutions, and organizations established by federal statute or regulation, including, but not limited to, the Smithsonian Institution, National Gallery of Art, National Building Museum, Federal National Mortgage Association, and Federal Home Loan Mortgage Corporation, if the federal enterprise or organization is otherwise exempt, to the extent such sales would otherwise be subject to District sales and use tax if the federal enterprise or organization were organized as a nonprofit corporation under District law and as an exempt IRC Sec. 501(c)(3) organization.

• **Use tax**

The use tax is imposed on the storage, use, or consumption of tangible personal property and services in the District; this tax complements the sales tax and is not levied when the sales tax is imposed (Sec. 47-2202, Sec. 47-2206(1)). The use tax operates to protect District merchants from discrimination arising from the District's inability to impose its sales tax on sales made outside the District to D.C. residents by merchants of other jurisdictions.

Sales that are exempt from the sales tax are generally exempt from the use tax (Sec. 47-2206(2)).

Also exempt from the use tax is the sale of tangible personal property that is purchased or acquired by a nonresident before coming into the District and establishing or maintaining a residence or business in the District (Sec. 47-2201(a)(2)(C)).

• **Responsibility for sales and use tax collection**

The tax is imposed on the vendor, nexus vendor, or remote vendor, but the vendor is authorized to collect reimbursement for the tax from the purchaser on all taxable

¶321   **District of Columbia**

sales (Sec. 47-2203, Sec. 47-2206(3)). Purchasers are liable for the tax in the event that the vendor has not been reimbursed; this occurs generally in connection with the use tax (Sec. 47-2205).

Vendors and nexus-vendors are responsible for collecting the use tax on use, storage, or consumption (Sec. 47-2202, Sec. 47-2203). For purposes of the use tax, "vendor" includes persons engaging in business in the District and making sales at retail for immediate or future delivery of tangible personal property or performance of services (Sec. 47-2201(g)). "Vendor" may include agents of dealers or distributors if necessary for the administration of the tax.

When specified conditions have been met (see below), remote-vendors will be required to collect and remit tax (Sec. 47-3932).

• Nexus

The District of Columbia requires any retailer "engaging in business" in the District to collect and remit sales or use tax. Engaging in business in the District includes any activity in connection with the selling, delivering, or furnishing in the District of tangible personal property or services sold at retail. The term specifically includes the following acts or methods (Sec. 47-2201(h)):

— the maintaining, occupying or using, permanently or temporarily, directly or indirectly, or through a subsidiary or agent, of any office, place of distribution, sales or sample room or place, warehouse or storage place, or other place of business; and/or

— the having of any representative, agent, salesman, canvasser, or solicitor in the District for the purpose of making sales at retail, or the taking of orders for such sales.

Nexus vendors: Internet sales of tangible personal property or services by a nexus vendor are taxable (Sec. 47-2001(h-2)). A "nexus-vendor" is a vendor that has a physical presence within the District, such as property or retail outlets, selling property or rendering services via the Internet to a purchaser in the District. Tangible personal property sold under a contract is not taxable if the property (1) is not in the District when the contract is executed and (2) is not sold by a nexus-vendor. (Sec. 47-2001(h-2),(n),(w))

Remote vendors: A seller that is a remote vendor is required to collect and remit "remote sales taxes" to the District if it has a specified level of cumulative gross receipts from Internet sales to purchasers in the District (Sec. 47-3932(a)). "Remote sales taxes" are sales and use taxes applied to a property or service sold by a vendor via the Internet to a purchaser in the District. A "remote-vendor" is a seller, whether or not it has a physical presence or other nexus within the District, selling property or rendering a service via the Internet to a purchaser in the District (Sec. 47-3931(3)). Before the District can require collection, however, it must pass local laws establishing a registry with specified provisions, including (Sec. 47-3932):

— a registry, with privacy and confidentiality controls, where each remote vendor will register;

— appropriate protections for consumer privacy;

— a means for a remote-vendor to determine the current District sales and use tax rate and taxability;

— a formula and procedure that permits a remote-vendor or a third-party service provider hired by the remote-vendor to deduct reasonable compensation for expenses incurred in the administration, collection, and remittance of remote sales taxes;

— the date that the collection of remote sales taxes will commence;

— a small-vendor exemption, including a process for an exempted vendor to apply for a certificate of exemption;

— the products and types of products that shall be exempt from the remote sales taxes;

— rules (1) for accounting for bad debts and rounding, (2) that address refunds and credits for remote sales taxes relating to customer returns, restocking fees, discounts and coupons, (3) for allocating shipping and handling and discounts that apply to multiple items, (4) regarding notice and procedural requirements for registry enrollment by remote-vendors, and (5) that the Mayor determines are necessary or appropriate to further the purposes of the collection responsibilities and enforcement laws; and

— a plan to substantially reduce the administrative burdens associated with sales and use taxes, including remote sales taxes.

These provisions do not require the District to exempt or to impose a tax on any product or to adopt any particular type of tax, or to impose the same tax rate as any other taxing jurisdiction that collects remote sales taxes. In addition, nothing in these provisions permits or prohibits the District from (1) licensing or regulating a person, (2) requiring a person to qualify to transact remote selling, (3) subjecting a person to District taxes not related to the sale of goods or services, or (4) exercising authority over matters of interstate commerce.

An "exempted vendor" is a remote vendor that, in accordance with local law, has a specified level of cumulative gross receipts from Internet sales to buyers in the District that exempts it from the requirement to collect remote sales taxes. (Sec. 47-3931(3))

• **Streamlined Act status**

The District of Columbia has enacted the Uniform (Simplified) Sales and Use Tax Administration Act, the product of the Streamlined Sales Tax Project (SSTP) (D.C. Law 14-156, Laws 2002). The District is included as one of the Advisor States. See also ¶ 327.

¶ 322   Tax Base

The sales tax is imposed on vendors for the privilege of selling certain tangible personal property and selected services at retail (Sec. 47-2002, Reg. Sec. 400.2). It is measured by the gross receipts from the sales of or charges for such tangible personal property and services.

"Gross receipts" means the total amount of the sales prices of the retail sales of vendors, valued in money, whether received in money or otherwise (Sec. 47-2001(h)).

The Director of the Department of Finance and Revenue may prescribe methods for determining the gross proceeds from sales made or services rendered and for allocating such sales into taxable and nontaxable sales (Sec. 47-2024(3), Sec. 47-2213).

The use tax is imposed on every vendor engaging in business in the District and every purchaser on the use, storage, or consumption of tangible personal property and service sold at retail (Sec. 47-2202, Reg. Sec. 405.1). The tax is measured by the sales price of the tangible personal property and service sold or purchased.

Federal sales: Sales and use tax is imposed on certain sales made in federal buildings and by government-sponsored enterprises and corporations, institutions, and organizations1. Taxable sales include sales at gift shops, souvenir shops, kiosks, convenience stores, food shops, cafeterias, restaurants, and similar establishments in federal buildings, including, but not limited to, memorials and museums, that are made to:

— the general public, whether the establishment is operated by the federal government, an agent of the federal government, or a contractor; and

— other than the general public, if operated by an agent of the federal government or a contractor.

Taxable sales also include sales of goods and services by government-sponsored enterprises and corporations, institutions, and organizations established by federal statute or regulation, including, but not limited to, the Smithsonian Institution, National Gallery of Art, National Building Museum, Federal National Mortgage Association, and Federal Home Loan Mortgage Corporation, if the federal enterprise or organization is otherwise exempt from such taxation, but only to the extent that such sales would otherwise be subject to District sales and use tax if the federal enterprise or organization were organized as a nonprofit corporation under District law and as an exempt § 501(c)(3) organization. (Sec. 206, Act 18-0657 (D.C.B. 18-1101), Laws 2010)

• **Sales price**

In computing gross receipts, "sales price" means the total amount paid by a purchaser to a vendor as consideration for a retail sale, valued in money, whether paid in money or otherwise (Sec. 47-2001(p)(1), Sec. 47-2001(j)). Deductions are not allowed for the following:

(1) cost of property sold;

(2) cost of materials used, labor or service cost, interest charged, losses, or any other expenses;

(3) cost of transportation of the property before its sale at retail. Total sales price includes any services that are part of the sale and any amount for which credit is given to the purchaser by the vendor; and

(4) amounts charged for cover, minimum, entertainment, or other service in hotels, restaurants, cafes, bars, and other establishments where meals, food, drink, or other like tangible personal property is furnished for a consideration.

"Sales price" does *not* include the following (Sec. 47-2001(p)(2), Reg. Sec. 408.1—Reg. Sec. 408.4):

(1) cash discounts on sales;

(2) amounts charged for property returned upon rescission of contracts if entire amounts charged are refunded (either in cash or credit) and if the property is returned within 90 days from the date of sale;

(3) amounts charged for labor or services in installing or applying property sold, except as otherwise provided by statute;

(4) amounts of reimbursement of taxes paid by the purchaser to the vendor, if stated separately from the sales price;

(5) transportation charges, separately stated, if the transportation occurs after the sale of property is made;

(6) amounts of federal retailer's excise taxes, if stated separately from the sales price; and

(7) amounts paid by the purchaser as interest, finance charge, or carrying charge, if stated separately from the amount paid for the tangible personal property or services.

¶ 323   List of Exemptions, Exceptions, and Exclusions

Unless otherwise indicated, the statutory exemptions, exceptions, and exclusions listed below apply to both sales and use taxes; those applicable only to the use tax are listed separately. Items that are excluded from the sales or use tax base are treated at ¶ 322, "Tax Base."

Negotiated exemptions: The District of Columbia Housing Authority (DCHA) is empowered to negotiate sales and use tax exemption agreements with organizations involved in for-profit activities relating to DCHA housing properties (Sec. 5, D.C. Act 13-259, Laws 2000). The agreement must be approved by the District of Columbia City Council and cannot exceed a maximum duration of five years.

Incentive grants: See ¶ 330.

Nonprofit organizations: A nonprofit organization that intends to conduct activities in the District of Columbia, which may subject the organization to franchise, sales and use, or personal property tax, should submit its tax exemption application (Form FR-164) to the District's Office of Tax and Revenue (OTR) no later than the time that its activities commence. Any exemption granted cannot take effect prior to the filing of the requisite application. The sales and use tax exemption becomes effective when the applicable exemption certificate is issued. Any exemption generally applies only to those activities that further the organization's exempt purposes. Unrelated business activities remain subject to tax. Note that a determination of federal tax exempt status does not, by itself, confer an exemption from District tax. A letter or certificate of exemption from District tax must be specifically secured from the OTR (*OTR Tax Notice 2007-2,* District of Columbia Office of Tax and Revenue, November 29, 2007, CCH DISTRICT OF COLUMBIA TAX REPORTS, ¶ 200-689).

Sales in federal buildings: Sales and use taxes are imposed on sales made in federal buildings and by government-sponsored enterprises and corporations, institutions, and organizations. Taxable sales include sales at gift shops, souvenir shops, kiosks, convenience stores, food shops, cafeterias, restaurants, and similar establishments in federal buildings, including, but not limited to, memorials and museums, that are made to (1) the general public, whether the establishment is operated by the federal government, an agent of the federal government, or a contractor; and (2) other than the general public, if operated by an agent of the federal government or a contractor. (Sec. 316(1), Act 20-370 (D.C.B. 20-749), Laws 2014)

Sales by federal enterprises or organizations: Taxable sales also include sales of goods and services by government-sponsored enterprises and corporations, institutions, and organizations established by federal statute or regulation, including, but not limited to, the Smithsonian Institution, the National Gallery of Art, the National Building Museum, the Federal National Mortgage Association, and the Federal Home Loan Mortgage Corporation, if the federal enterprise or organization is otherwise exempt, to the extent that such sales would otherwise be subject to sales and use tax if the federal enterprise or organization were organized as a nonprofit corporation under District law and as an exempt Sec. 501(c)(3) organization. (Sec. 316(2), Act 20-370 (D.C.B. 20-749), Laws 2014)

- **Sales and use tax exemptions, exceptions, and exclusions**

Admission charges by semipublic institutions	Sec. 47-2001(n)(1)(H)
Admissions to certain public events, and use fees	Sec. 47-2201(a)(1)(F)
Boats	Sec. 47-2005(21)
Building inspection	Sec. 47-2001(n)(1)(M), Sec. 47-2201(a)(1)(J)
Cable television services and commodities	Sec. 47-2005(26)
Carpet cleaning	Sec. 47-2001(n)(1)(M), Sec. 47-2201(a)(1)(J)
Casual or isolated sales of semipublic institutions	Sec. 47-2001(n)(1)(H)
Charitable institutions	Sec. 47-2001(r), Sec. 47-2005(7), Sec. 47-2005(22)
Cigarettes and cigars	Sec. 47-2002

Common carriers and sleeping car companies: purchase of repair parts	Sec. 47-2001(n)(2)(D)
Communication services other than data processing, information, and local telephone services	Sec. 47-2001(n)(2)(A), Sec. 47-2201(a)(2)(A)
Computer-related sales to and by qualified nology companies	Sec. 47-2005(31)
Construction: CareFirst project	Sec. 47-4602
Construction: Carver 2000 housing project	Sec. 47-4601
Construction: DC-USA project	Sec. 47-4608
Construction: Jenkins Row project	Sec. 47-4603
Construction: Lincoln Square Theatre	Sec. 47-4601
Construction: Parkside Terrace Project	Sec. 47-4607
Construction materials or equipment temporarily stored in DC	Sec. 47-2005(31-a), Sec. 47-2206(4)
Construction services performed	Sec. 47-2001(n)(1)(M), Sec. 47-2201(a)(1)(J)
Contracts made before May 1949	Sec. 47-2005(10)
Data processing services among affiliated corporations	Sec. 47-2001(n)(1)(N), Sec. 47-2201(a)(1)(K)
Dental materials	Sec. 47-2005(15)(A)
Diapers	Sec. 47-2005(39)
Digital audio radio satellite service companies, purchases by	Sec. 47-2005(5)
Educational institutions	Sec. 47-2001(r), Sec. 47-2005(3), Sec. 47-2005(22)
Eyeglasses	Sec. 47-2005(15)(A)
Federal government transactions	Sec. 47-2005(1), Sec. 47-2206
Feminine hygiene products	Sec. 47-2005(38)
Food and drink delivered and sold by nonprofit volunteer organization to homebound	Sec. 47-2005(18)
Food and drink for home preparation	Sec. 47-2001(n)(1)(A), Sec. 47-2001(n)(2)(E), Sec. 47-2201(a)(1)(E)
Food purchased with food stamps	Sec. 47-2005(23)
Food sold in trains, aircraft, or boats in interstate commerce	Sec. 47-2005(9)
Fuel: natural or artificial gas used for refrigeration in a restaurant	Sec. 47-2005(11A)
Hearing aids	Sec. 47-2005(15)(A)
Hospitals	Sec. 47-2001(r), Sec. 47-2005(3), Sec. 47-2005(22)
Hotel charges to nontransients	Sec. 47-2001(n)(1)(C)
House of Representatives: food and drink sold by or to persons operating cloakrooms	Sec. 47-2005(8)
House of Representatives: materials and services used in operating cloakrooms	Sec. 47-2005(4)
Inconsequential sales as part of services	Sec. 47-2001(n)(2)(B), Sec. 47-2201(a)(2)(B)

¶323   **District of Columbia**

Scientific institutions . . . . Sec. 47-2001(r),
                                                  Sec. 47-2005(3),
                                                  Sec. 47-2005(22)

Semipublic institutions . . . . Sec. 47-2001(r),
                                                  Sec. 47-2005(3),
                                                  Sec. 47-2005(22)

Senior citizen meals . . . . Sec. 47-2005(19)

State and local government transactions . . . . Sec. 47-2005(2),
                                                  Sec. 47-2206

Supermarkets areas (including restaurants and retail stores),
    construction materials . . . . Sec. 47-2005(28)

Telecommunication company purchases of property . . . . Sec. 47-2005(5)

Telephone: coin-operated local telephone, toll telephone, or private
    communication services . . . . Sec. 47-2001(n)(1)(G)

Telephone: installation of equipment for local telephone service . . . . Sec. 47-2001(n)(1)(G)

Trailers . . . . Sec. 40-703(j),
                                                  Sec. 47-2005(13)

Transportation services . . . . Sec. 47-2001(n)(2)(A),
                                                  Sec. 47-2201(a)(2)(A)

Utilities used by a restaurant or hotel restaurant . . . . Sec. 47-2005(11A)

Utility company purchases of property . . . . Sec. 47-2005(5)

Utility sales for manufacturing . . . . Sec. 47-2005(11),
                                                  Sec. 47-2201(a)(1)(B)

Utility sales for resale . . . . Sec. 47-2201(a)(1)(B)

Valet parking services . . . . Sec. 47-2001(n)

War memorials . . . . Sec. 47-2005(16)

Wheelchairs and crutches . . . . Sec. 47-2005(15)(B)

• Exemptions, exceptions, and exclusions applicable only to the use tax

Common carrier or sleeping car company: tangible personal property
    used or stored in the District but held mainly for use in
    interstate commerce as part of a train, aircraft, or boat . . . . . . Sec. 47-2201(a)(2)(E)

Sales on which the sales tax was properly collected . . . . Sec. 47-2202,
                                                  Sec. 47-2206(1)

Sales that are exempt from the sales tax . . . . Sec. 47-2206(2)

Tangible personal property acquired by a nonresident before coming
    into the District and establishing a residence or business in the
    District . . . . Sec. 47-2201(a)(2)(C),
                                                  Sec. 47-2201(a)(2)(D)

Temporary storage of personal property for less than 90 days for the
    purpose of subsequently transporting the property outside the
    District for use outside the District . . . . Sec. 47-2206(4)

¶ 324   Rate of Tax

Since October 1, 2013, the sales tax and the use taxes are imposed at the rate of 5.75% (previously, 6%), but special rates apply to certain transactions (Sec. 47-2002.1, Sec. 47-2201.1).

The 5.75% rate applies in general to sales of tangible personal property and services (Sec. 47-2002). It applies also to the following sales:

(1) vending-machine sales of food, drink, and tangible personal property (Reg. Sec. 437.2, Reg. Sec. 437.3);

(2) real property maintenance services;

(3) landscaping services;

(4) armored car, private investigation and security services;

(5) data processing services; and

(6) information services.

• **Special rates**

Special tax rates apply to the following (Sec. 47-2001, Sec. 47-2002, Sec. 47-2002.1, Sec. 47-2202, Sec. 47-2202.1):

(1) *Off-sale alcoholic beverages:* 10% of gross receipts from sales of, or charges for, spirituous or malt liquor, beer, and wines sold for consumption off the premises;

(2) *Prepared food or drink:* 10% of gross receipts (a 9% base rate plus an additional 1% tax) from (a) food or drink prepared for immediate consumption or sold by restaurants, lunch counters, cafeterias, hotels, snack bars, caterers, boarding houses, carryout shops, and similar places of business; (b) spirituous or malt liquor, beer, and wine sold for on-premise consumption; and (c) rentals of vehicles and utility trailers (see also *"Convention Center surtax,"* below);

(3) *Transient lodging:* 14.55% of gross receipts (a 10.05% base rate plus an additional 4.5% tax) from charges for rooms, lodgings, or accommodations furnished to transients (see also *"Convention Center surtax,"* below);

(4) *Parking and motor vehicle storage:* 18% (may increase to 22% on 10/01/2017) of gross receipts from parking charges not specifically exempted (*e.g.,* valet parking); and

(5) *Tobacco products:* A tax of 12% of gross receipts is imposed on sales of other tobacco products (Sec. 47-2002(a)(5), (6)). An "other tobacco product" is any product containing, made, or derived from tobacco, other than a cigarette or a premium cigar, that is intended or expected to be consumed, but does not include an e-cigarette (Sec. 47-2001(h-3)). Vapor products are subject to a separate excise tax (Sec. 47-2402.01).

(6) *Rental vehicles:* 10% of gross receipts from the charges for the rental or leasing of rental vehicles and utility trailers. The 10% rate is composed of a basic 9% tax and a separate and additional 1% tax. Sec. 47-2002(3); Sec. 47-2202(3)

(7) *Prepaid phone cards:* 10% of gross receipts from the sale of a prepaid telephone calling card. The 10% rate is composed of a basic 9% tax and a separate and additional 1% tax. Sec. 47-2001(n)(1)(T); Sec. 47-2002(3)(A); Sec. 47-2002.02(2)(A).

(8) *Prepaid wireless telecommunication charges:* In addition to a 10% charge on sales of prepaid wireless telecommunications services, sellers also must collect a separately stated 2% charge if the service sold allows a caller to dial 911. Sellers must remit the 911 charges collected to the Office of Tax and Revenue, but may retain 3% of the total 911 charges collected as a collection fee.

(9) *Legitimate theaters:* 5.75% of gross receipts from the sale of or charges for tangible personal property or services by legitimate theaters, or by entertainment venues with 10,000 or more seats. However, the provision excludes any such theaters or entertainment venues from which such taxes are applied to pay debt services on tax-exempt bonds.

Convention Center surtax: The 1% additional tax on vehicle rentals and certain foods and beverages (see (2), above) and the 4.5% additional tax on transient lodgings

¶324   District of Columbia

(see (3), above) are imposed to provide funding for the Washington Convention Center Authority (the Authority). If the required annual audit of the Authority's accounts and operations indicates that projected revenues from the taxes imposed by the Act are insufficient to meet the Authority's projected expenditures and reserve requirements for the upcoming fiscal year, the Mayor is required to impose a surtax on each of those taxes dedicated to the Authority, excluding the tax on sales of restaurant meals and alcoholic beverages (Sec. 47-2002.1, Sec. 47-2201.1).

Baseball stadium tax: A 4.25% additional sales tax is imposed on the gross receipts from sales of tickets to any public event at the baseball stadium (other than a live performance of ballet, dance or choral performance, concert, play, opera, or readings and exhibitions of paintings, sculpture, photography, graphic and craft arts). The tax also applies to tickets sold to professional baseball games and professional baseball-related events and exhibitions held at Robert F. Kennedy Stadium.

A 4.25% additional sales tax is also imposed on the gross receipts from sales of tangible personal property and services at the new stadium and at Robert F. Kennedy Stadium during times reasonably related to the performance of baseball games or baseball-related events or exhibitions. However, the tax does not apply to sales of food and beverages prepared for immediate consumption; sales of spirituous or malt liquors, beer, and wine sold for consumption on the premises; or charges for the service of parking motor vehicles (Sec. 47-2002.05).

Verizon Center: A temporary additional sales tax of 4.25% is imposed on gross receipts from the sale at the Verizon Center of taxable tangible personal property or services. The tax expires on the first day of the month after the date that the bonds authorized by the Bond Act (Sec. 47-2002.06(b)(1)) have been paid in full. Exempt from this additional tax are:

— the sale of food and beverages subject to the tax under Sec. 47-2002(3);

— the sale of charge for the services of parking motor vehicles subject to the tax under Sec. 47-2002(1); and

— the sale of tangible personal property or services by the following businesses: Urban Adventures at Gallery Place, LLC (doing business as Vida Fitness); Urban Salon, Inc. (doing business as Bang Salon); and Shimba Hills Coffee, Inc., (doing business as Shimba Hills Coffee).

Futhermore, an additional sales tax of 4.25% is imposed on the gross receipts from the sale of tickets to any public event sponsored by a person (or any affiliate of that person) that is to be performed at the Verizon Center, regardless of whether the ticket is sold to a person who resells the ticket to another person or to a person who uses for admission. (Sec. 47-2002.06(b)(1))

• **Computation of tax**

On all sales subject to tax, the vendor adds the tax to the sales price and collects reimbursement for the tax from the purchaser (Sec. 47-2003, Reg Sec. 413.1, Reg. Sec. 413.2).

For determining the amounts to be collected, a bracket schedule is used (Sec. 47-2004, Reg. Sec. 413.2). The schedule is reproduced at ¶ 326, "Bracket Schedule." It applies to the use tax as well as the sales tax (Sec. 47-2203).

¶ 325   Local Taxes

No local sales and use taxes are imposed within the District.

The District has conformed to the federal Mobile Telecommunications Sourcing Act (P.L. 106-252), under which wireless telecommunications are sourced to the customer's primary place of use, which is the residential or primary business address of the customer and which must be located in the service provider's licensed service area (Sec. 47-3922).

¶ 326   Bracket Schedule

Bracket schedules are not available for collection of tax at the 5.75%.

For each sale or charge subject to the sales tax at the 6% rate, the vendor must collect the following reimbursement (Reg. Sec. 413.5):

Range of Sale Price or Charge	Tax
(a) 9¢ to 24¢	1¢
(b) 25¢ to 41¢	2¢
(c) 42¢ to 58¢	3¢
(d) 59¢ to 74¢	4¢
(e) 75¢ to 91¢	5¢
(f) 92¢ to $1.08	6¢

(g) For amounts over $1.08, compute the tax based on 6 cents on each dollar or multiple of a dollar plus the amount due on any additional fraction of a dollar based on (a)—(f) of this section.

¶ 327   Returns, Payments, and Due Dates

Sales and use tax returns are due monthly unless the taxpayer's tax liability is less than $50 per month, in which case returns may be filed annually (Sec. 47-2015, Reg. Sec. 420.10—Reg. Sec. 420.12). A taxpayer not placed on an annual basis must file monthly returns (Reg. Sec. 412.5, Reg. Sec. 413.1). Sales tax reporting provisions apply also to the use tax (Sec. 47-2210, Reg. Sec. 400.4).

The form of returns is prescribed by the Director of the Department of Finance and Revenue (Sec. 47-2015, Reg. Sec. 420.9). It is the responsibility of the vendor or retailer to obtain the necessary forms from the Department if they are not received by mail (Reg. Sec. 420.7). The District uses a tax return system similar to the federal depository system for sales and use taxes (Reg. Sec. 400.7).

• **Monthly returns**

Sales and use tax returns must be filed with the Department of Finance and Revenue by the 20th day of the month following the calendar month or other reporting period (Sec. 47-2015, Sec. 47-2211, Reg. Sec. 420.17, Reg. Sec. 420.1).

The return must show the total gross proceeds of the vendor's business for the month for which the return is filed, the gross receipts on which the tax is computed, the amount of tax for which the vendor is liable, and any other information needed to compute and collect the tax (Sec. 47-2210, Sec. 47-2015).

Returns may be permitted or required to be made for other periods and on other dates, but the gross receipts during any tax year are to be included in returns covering only that year (Sec. 47-2210, Sec. 47-2015).

A purchaser's use tax return must show the total sales price of the tangible personal property and services purchased at retail on which sales tax has not been paid and the amount of tax for which the purchaser is liable (Sec. 47-2211).

• **Annual returns**

The annual filing period is from October through September. Annual returns must be filed by October 20 (Reg. Sec. 420.11).

If all monthly returns have been filed, the vendor is deemed to have complied with the annual return requirement (Reg. Sec. 420.2). That presumption does not apply, however, if the total taxable gross receipts for the tax year exceed the total amount reported on the vendor's monthly returns. If those receipts exceed the total amount reported, the vendor must notify the Director within 30 days after the end of the vendor's tax year, show the excess amount of receipts, and pay the tax on the excess (Reg. Sec. 420.3—Reg. Sec. 420.5).

¶326   **District of Columbia**

- **Time for tax payments**

Sales and use tax payments are due and payable to the D.C. Treasurer at the time the returns are due to be filed, regardless of whether a return is actually filed or whether a return that is filed correctly shows the amount of gross receipts and taxes due (Sec. 47-2210, Sec. 47-2011, Sec. 47-2016).

Any return or payment falling due on a Saturday, Sunday, or legal holiday may be filed or paid on the first business day following (Reg. Sec. 400.6).

- **Electronic filing and payment**

The District of Columbia Office of Tax and Revenue's Electronic Funds Transfer (EFT) Payment Guide, which outlines methods of paying District of Columbia taxes electronically on its web portal, **MyTax.DC.gov.**

The EFT payment Guide notes the four methods of EFT payments: ACH debit, electronic check (e-check), ACH credit, and credit/debit card. The guide also outlines payment reporting, international ACH transactions, mandatory electronic payments, debit blocks, and payment options. The Guide is available on the District of Columbia Office and Tax and Revenue website at **http://otr.cfo.dc.gov/sites/default/files/dc/ sites/otr/publication/attachments/2017%20EFT%20guide%20110416.pdf**.

- **Street vendors**

Licensed street vendors who have collected less than $375 in sales tax in a quarter must file a return and remit a $375 minimum sales tax payment for the quarter being reported (Sec. 47-2002.01). Street vendors who collect more than $375 must file a return and remit the sales tax collected for the quarter. If an individual street vendor holds a license as an employee of a business vendor, the employee license holder is not individually responsible for filing a return or remitting the minimum sales tax of $375. If a business vendor files a single consolidated return, reporting and remitting all sales tax collected by all employee license holders, the business vendor must report the vending license number for each employee license holder whose information is included in the return. The business vendor is responsible for maintaining all books and records of sales made by its employee license holders and must file its consolidated sales tax return electronically. A business vendor includes corporations, limited liability companies, partnerships or other business entities that are the beneficial owner of a vending license held by an employee license holder. (Sec. 47-2002.01)

- **Use tax returns by employers**

Any employer that is required to file a District withholding tax return, but is not required to collect and remit sales tax, must file an annual use tax return. The return must be filed on or before October 20 of each year, and use taxes due must be remitted with the return. The Chief Financial Officer may permit or require such returns to be made for other periods and filed on other dates. However, the gross receipts during any tax year must be included in returns covering that year. (Sec. 47-2211(g))

- **Uniform Sales Tax Administration Act**

The District has enacted the Uniform Sales and Use Tax Administration Act, the product of the Streamlined Sales Tax Project (SSTP), along with modifications recommended by the National Conference of State Legislators (NCSL). The SSTP developed the Act and the related Streamlined Sales and Use Tax (SST) Agreement to simplify and modernize sales and use tax administration in order to substantially reduce the burden of tax compliance for all sellers and for all types of commerce.

The District of Columbia is not a member of the Agreement because, although it has enacted legislation authorizing it to enter into the Agreement (D.C. Law 14-156,

Laws 2002, effective June 25, 2002), it has not yet enacted the changes to its laws necessary to comply with the Agreement's requirements. However, as one of the SST Advisor States, it will, for a period of time, continue to provide advice to the Governing Board.

¶ 328   Prepayment of Taxes

Prepayment of tax is not required.

¶ 329   Vendor Registration

Every vendor engaged in the business of making taxable retail sales, including a manufacturer, wholesaler, or jobber, must obtain a certificate of registration (Sec. 47-2026, Reg. Sec. 415.1). Also, every person purchasing tangible personal property for resale or for any other nontaxable purpose must apply for a certificate of registration.

• Certificate of registration

Each vendor or purchaser must apply for a certificate of registration before starting business or opening a new place of business (Reg. Sec. 415.2). A single retail establishment operated by two or more persons constituting a single vendor may be operated under one certificate of registration (Sec. 47-2026).

The lack of a certificate does not relieve a vendor or purchaser from the duty of collecting and paying the tax (Reg. Sec. 415.4).

The sales tax requirements regarding certificates of registration apply to the use tax as well, but a holder of a certificate of registration for sales tax purposes need not obtain a separate certificate for use tax purposes (Sec. 47-2212).

An out-of-District vendor or retailer who is authorized to pay the tax is entitled to a permit without charge (Sec. 47-2204). The permit may be revoked at any time upon proper notice. A person who does not engage in business in the District but who makes purchases from wholesalers, distributors, dealers, retailers, or others in the District for the purpose of resale may register under the District sales and use tax provisions (Reg. Sec. 415.5).

In the case of vendors selling from vehicles, each vehicle is deemed to be a retail establishment requiring a certificate of registration (Sec. 47-2026). If a vendor has no fixed place of business and does not sell from a vehicle, the application must show an address to which a notice may be sent, and that place will constitute a retail establishment for tax purposes.

The registration certificate, which is not transferable, must be displayed in the applicant's place of business and surrendered to the Director if the vendor ceases doing business at the place named in the certificate (Sec. 47-2026, Reg. Sec. 415.6). The Director may, upon proper notice, cancel a certificate for noncompliance with the law or regulations (Sec. 47-2024(6), Reg. Sec. 415.7).

¶ 330   Sales or Use Tax Credits and Other Incentives

A credit is allowed vendors for expenses incurred in collecting and remitting sales and use tax (Sec. 47-2004(b), Reg. Sec. 420.18). The credit is the lesser of $5,000 or 1% of the gross tax to be remitted and may be credited against the amount of tax payable.

The purchaser may claim a credit or refund for the use tax paid on the portion of personal property that the taxpayer proves to have been initially purchased solely for use or consumption outside the District if the following can be substantiated by adequate and acceptable records (Reg. Sec. 405.14):

(a) the date of purchase of the item;

(b) the purchase price of the item and the amount of tax paid; and

(c) the fact that the item was never used or consumed inside the District, was actually shipped outside the District, and was used or consumed outside the District.

A claim for credit or refund must be filed with the Department of Finance and Revenue within three years from the date of payment (Sec. 47-2020, Sec. 47-2213).

When a refund is due a taxpayer, a credit is allowed for any payments due from the taxpayer (Sec. 47-2020, Sec. 47-2213).

Under specified circumstances, credit may be taken against taxable gross sales for accounts found to be worthless and charged off for income tax or franchise tax purposes (Sec. 47-2020, Sec. 47-2213).

Museum: A sales and use tax credit is available to the National Law Enforcement Officers Memorial Fund, Inc. and its vendors, against gross receipts at the National Law Enforcement Museum.

¶ 331 Deficiency Assessments

The Director of the Department of Finance and Revenue may assess, determine, revise, and readjust the amount of sales and use taxes due (Sec. 47-2024(5), Sec. 47-2213). The Director is authorized to determine the tax where no return is filed or where an incorrect or insufficient return is filed (Sec. 47-2019, Sec. 47-2213). Notice of such a determination is to be given to the taxpayer.

To aid in making these determinations, the Director may examine records and witnesses (Sec. 47-2025, Sec. 47-2213). The Director may also request information from the Internal Revenue Service about any person, and the Internal Revenue Service is authorized to supply the information requested (Sec. 47-2024(2)).

¶ 332 Audit Procedures

To ascertain the correctness of a return or make a return where none was made, the Department of Finance and Revenue may examine books, papers, records, or memoranda (Sec. 47-2025, Sec. 47-2213). The Department may also examine persons and summon them to appear and produce materials. A notice of proposed audit changes must be sent at least 30 days before a notice of proposed assessment is issued.

A person who refuses or hinders an examination of such materials is subject to a fine of up to $500 or imprisonment of up to six months, or both.

¶ 333 Statute of Limitations

The Department's determination, redetermination, assessment, or reassessment of the tax may be made at any time within five years of the filing of the return (Sec. 47-2029, Sec. 47-2213). In the case of a fraudulent return or failure to file a return, the assessment may be made at any time.

Extensions: The five-year period may be extended if the taxpayer consents in writing to the extension before the period expires (Sec. 47-2032, Sec. 47-2213). Further extensions may be made upon subsequent written consents before the expiration of the extended period.

Collection suits: Suits to recover unpaid taxes must be brought by the District within three years from the time the tax was due (Sec. 47-2011, Sec. 47-2207).

Bonds and prepayments: With respect to certain bonds or prepayments with surety authorized by regulations governing vending businesses in public space, refunds are made provided the application is filed within six years from the date the vendor filed the bond or prepayment (Sec. 47-2020(d), Sec. 47-2213).

¶ 334 **Application for Refund**

Any tax erroneously or illegally collected is refunded if application is made within three years from the date of payment (or within six years for refunds of bonds or prepayments, discussed below) (Sec. 47-2020(a), Sec. 47-2213). Application must be made by the person on whom the tax was imposed and who actually paid the tax. No refund is made to a vendor until the vendor has repaid to the purchaser the amount that has been applied for as a refund. Refunds may also be made upon the certificates of the Director of the Department of Finance and Revenue and the D.C. Treasurer. In lieu of a refund, a credit may be allowed on payments due from the applicant.

Application for a refund or credit is treated as an application for a revision of tax, penalty, or interest, and the Director may take evidence to aid in making a determination (Sec. 47-2020(c), Sec. 47-2213).

¶ 335   FLORIDA

¶ 336   Scope of Tax

Source.—Statutory references are to Chapter 212 of the Florida Statutes, as amended to date. Details are reported in the CCH Florida State Tax Reports starting at ¶ 60-000.

The Florida sales and use taxes are imposed on every person who does the following:

(1) engages in the business of renting or leasing living quarters (Sec. 212.03(1));

(2) leases or rents parking or storage spaces for motor vehicles, docking or storage space for boats, or tie-down or storage space for aircraft (Sec. 212.03(6), Rule 12A-1.070);

(3) leases or rents real property (Sec. 212.031);

(4) sells admissions (Sec. 212.04);

(5) engages in the business of selling tangible personal property in the state, including the business of making mail order sales (Sec. 212.05);

(6) rents or furnishes any taxable things or services (Sec. 212.05);

(7) stores for use or consumption in the state any item of tangible personal property (Sec. 212.05);

(8) leases or rents tangible personal property in the state (Sec. 212.05);

(9) unlawfully sells, uses, consumes, distributes, manufactures, derives, produces, transports, or stores any medicinal drug, cannabis, or controlled substance in the state (Sec. 212.0505); or

(10) engages in the state in the business of soliciting or issuing any service warranty (Sec. 212.0506).

The sales and use taxes apply to each sale, admission, use, storage, consumption, or rental set forth in the statute, except those specifically exempted or void (Sec. 1, Art. VII, Fla. Const., Sec. 212.21).

The sales tax and the use tax complement one another and provide a uniform tax upon the sale at retail or the use of all tangible personal property irrespective of where it may have been purchased (Rule 12A-1.091(4)).

• **Services subject to sales and use tax**

Some services are taxable, including transportation and public utility services, detective and other protection services, fingerprinting, nonresidential cleaning (except cleaning of transportation equipment), nonresidential pest control services, telecommunications, and the provision of electrical power.

Professional and personal services generally are not taxable, e.g., *Technical Assistance Advisement,* No. 14A-008, Florida Department of Revenue, March 20, 2014, CCH Florida Tax Reports, ¶ 205-919; *Technical Assistance Advisement,* No. 14A-007, Florida Department of Revenue, March 14, 2014, CCH Florida Tax Reports, ¶ 205-918.

Communication services are subject to a separate tax.

Prepaid calling arrangements: Sales and use tax on calls made with a prepaid telephone calling card or other prepaid calling arrangement (as defined at Sec. 202.11) must be collected and remitted at the time a dealer sells or recharges the card or calling arrangement. If the sale or recharge does not take place at the dealer's place of business, it will be deemed to take place at the customer's shipping address or, if no item is shipped, at the customer's address or the location associated with the customer's mobile telephone number. The sale or recharge is treated as a sale of tangible personal property in Florida and subjects the dealer to Florida jurisdiction for sales tax purposes (Sec. 212.05(e)(1)(a)).

Timeshare accommodations and exchanges: Florida local option tourist development tax, tourist impact tax, transient rentals tax, and convention development tax is imposed on certain timeshare resort products (Sec. 125.0104(3)(a); Sec. 125.0108(1)(b); Sec. 212.0305(3)(a)).

The exchange of a timeshare unit for the use of another timeshare unit and a membership fee or transaction fee paid by the timeshare owner to an exchange program for a timeshare exchange are not taxable. A timeshare inspection package purchased in Florida is subject to tax, unless the consideration is applied to the purchase of a timeshare estate. Tax is due on the last day of occupancy. These provisions apply to vacation clubs only if the club meets the definition of a "multisite timeshare plan," as specified. Vacation clubs that do not meet this definition are unaffected by these provisions. (*Tax Information Publication, No. 09A01-04,* Florida Department of Revenue, June 18, 2009, CCH FLORIDA TAX REPORTS, ¶ 205-348)

• **Legal incidence of the sales and use tax**

The sales and use tax is collected from all dealers on the sale at retail, the use, the consumption, the distribution, or the storage for use or consumption in the state of tangible personal property or taxable services (Sec. 212.06(1)(a)). Although dealers are liable for the tax, they are required to collect it from the purchaser or consumer (Sec. 212.07(1)(a)).

Drop shipments: An out-of-state dealer who is registered in Florida is required to collect sales tax on a sale to an unregistered out-of-state buyer when the merchandise will be drop-shipped to the buyer's customer in Florida from a vendor/drop shipper's Florida facility. The dealer is required to collect the tax from the out-of-state buyer's Florida customer because the merchandise is in Florida at the time of sale and the unregistered out-of-state buyer cannot collect the tax and remit it to the state when the merchandise is resold to the Florida customer (*Technical Assistance Advisement, No. 07A-043,* Department of Revenue, November 8, 2007, CCH FLORIDA TAX REPORTS, ¶ 205-135).

A registered nonresident dealer's sales to an unregistered nonresident purchaser of tangible personal property that are drop shipped into Florida are not subject to Florida sales and use tax. Such a transaction does not qualify as a taxable Florida sale unless (*Technical Assistance Advisement, No. 09A-010,* Department of Revenue, March 2, 2009, CCH FLORIDA TAX REPORTS, ¶ 205-316):

> — the taxpayer ships the property to the Florida customer from the taxpayer's facility in Florida;

> — the taxpayer ships the property to the Florida customer from the taxpayer's facility located outside Florida, but uses transportation owned or leased by the taxpayer; or

> — the taxpayer ships the property to the Florida customer from the taxpayer's facility located outside Florida, but the terms of the delivery require the taxpayer to collect the sales price, in whole or in part, from the Florida customer at the time of delivery of the property to the customer.

See also *Technical Assistance Advisement, No. 13A-017,* Florida Department of Revenue, August 14, 2013, CCH FLORIDA TAX REPORTS, ¶ 205-880; *Technical Assistance Advisement, No. 15A-020,* Florida Department of Revenue, December 7, 2015, CCH FLORIDA TAX REPORTS, ¶ 206-154.

• **Use tax**

The use tax includes the use, consumption, distribution, and storage as defined in sales tax (Sec. 212.02(21)), and is levied on the exercise of any right of ownership over tangible personal property except a sale at retail in the regular course of business (Sec. 212.02(20)).

The following transactions are specifically subject to the use tax:

(1) out-of-state purchases that would have been subject to sales tax if purchased from a Florida vendor, provided that it is presumed that property used in another state for six months or longer before being imported into Florida was not purchased for use in Florida (Sec. 212.06(8)(a), Rule 12A-1.091);

(2) the rental or lease of tangible personal property used or stored in Florida, without regard to its prior use or to tax paid on the purchase of the property outside Florida (Sec. 212.06(8)(a), Rule 12A-1.091);

(3) the solicitation of business by dealers, either directly or through representatives, and the reception of orders for property from consumers in Florida for use, consumption, distribution, or storage (Rule 12A-1.091);

(4) the repair of items sent out of Florida and later returned, but not the repair of items shipped into Florida and later shipped back to their owners in other states (Rule 12A-1.091);

(5) the importing of property for use, consumption, distribution, or storage for consumption in the state, after it has come to rest and become a part of the general mass of property in the state (Sec. 212.06(6), Rule 12A-1.091);

(6) the purchase from a sales officer in Florida of goods shipped to a Florida customer by a factory in another state (Rule 12A-1.091);

(7) the sale of goods by a Florida manufacturer to an unregistered out-of-state dealer, and delivery to the customer in Florida (Rule 12A-1.091);

(8) the delivery to Florida customers by an out-of-state supplier of law and medical books, accounting manuals, tax service books, and similar publications (Rule 12A-1.091);

(9) the importing of a fabricated building built in the owner's plant in another state (Rule 12A-1.091); and

(10) the failure to prove that tax has been paid on the use, consumption, distribution, or storage for consumption in the state of tangible personal property, admissions, communication services, or leases of property (Rule 12A-1.091).

If a similar tax that was equal to or greater than Florida use tax was paid in another state, no Florida use tax is due (Sec. 212.06(7), Rule 12A-1.091(3)).

• Nexus

Florida sales or use tax is imposed on all dealers engaged in the sale, lease, or rental of tangible personal property sold at retail in the state or all persons that use, consume, distribute, or store tangible personal property in the state (Sec. 212.05(1)(b); Rule 12A-1.091(2)(a)). An out-of-state dealer is engaged in business in Florida if (Sec. 212.0596):

(1) the dealer is a resident, domiciliary, citizen, or corporation doing business under the laws of Florida;

(2) the dealer maintains retail establishments in Florida;

(3) the dealer solicits or transacts business in Florida through agents;

(4) property is delivered in Florida in fulfillment of a contract entered into in Florida when a person in Florida accepts an offer by ordering the property;

(5) the dealer purposefully or systematically advertises in Florida;

(6) the dealer is in a state that supports Florida's taxing power;

(7) the dealer consents, expressly or by implication, to the imposition of the tax;

(8) the dealer is subject to the service of process;

(9) the dealer is subject to Florida tax under a federal statute;

(10) the dealer owns real property or tangible personal property that is physically located in Florida;

(11) the dealer is a corporation that is eligible to file a consolidated federal tax return, and one of the affiliated corporations has nexus with Florida; or

(12) the dealer has some other sufficient connection with Florida to create a nexus that will allow the state to collect the tax.

• **Streamlined Act status**

Florida is one of the Streamlined Sales Tax Advisor states (see ¶ 342).

¶ 337   **Tax Base**

Sales tax is levied on the sales price of an item of tangible personal property purchased (Sec. 212.05(1)(a)). Real property that is leased, let, or rented is taxed on the total rental charged (Sec. 212.03(1), Sec. 212.03(1)(c)). Tangible personal property that is leased or rented is taxed on the gross proceeds (Sec. 212.05(1)(c)) or the rental price paid (Sec. 212.05(1)(d)). Admissions are taxed on the net sum of money charged after the deduction of any federal taxes paid (Sec. 212.02(1), Sec. 212.04).

Use tax is levied on the cost price or fair market value of property that is not sold, but is used, consumed, distributed, or stored for use or consumption in Florida (Sec. 212.05(4)). Property manufactured, produced, compounded, processed, or fabricated for a person's own use is also taxed on the cost of the product (Sec. 212.06(1)(b)). Asphalt manufactured for a person's own use is taxed on the cost of the materials and transportation, in addition to a tax per ton of asphalt (Sec. 212.06(1)(c)).

"Sales price" means the total amount paid for the property, including any services (valued in money) that are a part of the sale (Sec. 212.02(17)). It may also include any amount for which credit is given to the purchaser by the seller, but not the cost of the property sold, the cost of the materials used, labor or service costs, interest charged, losses or any other expenses.

Credits given for used items taken as trade-ins are not included in the sale price (Sec. 212.09; see also *Gamestop, Inc. v. Department of Revenue,* Florida Department of Revenue, DOAH Case No. 09-5759RX, May 4, 2010, CCH FLORIDA TAX REPORTS, ¶ 205-475).

"Cost price" means the actual cost of articles of tangible personal property, without any deduction for expenses such as materials, labor, services, or transportation charges (Sec. 212.02(4)).

Direct materials on which sales tax has been paid are not included when computing the tax on the cost price of items of tangible personal property manufactured, produced, compounded, processed, or fabricated (Rule 12A-1.043(1)(c)). Exempt direct materials may be purchased by people who manufacture, produce, compound, process, or fabricate tangible personal property items for resale or for their own use, but they must include the costs of the materials when computing tax on the cost price of the items created for their own use.

"Gross sales" mean the sum total of all sales of tangible personal property or services, without any deduction except as provided by statute (Sec. 212.02(15)(d)).

Contractors: Statutory definitions assist contractors in deciding which materials are taxable to the customer as a sale of tangible personal property and which are taxable to the contractor as materials used in the performance of a real property contract (Sec. 212.06(14); Rule 12A-1.051). "Real property" is land, improvements to land, and fixtures. "Fixtures" are "items that are an accessory to a building, other structure, or land and that do not lose their identity as accessories when installed but that do become permanently attached to realty." Although the determination of whether an item is exempt as a fixture requires review of all the facts and circumstances, a prerequisite is that it must be attached to the real property in some manner, indicating that it has become part of the real property and will remain in place indefinitely.

Online travel companies: A Florida local option tourist development tax applies only to the amount the property owner receives for the rental of transient accommodations and not to the amount of consideration received by an online travel company (OTC) from tourists who reserve accommodations using the OTC's website. After review of the relevant statutes, the Florida Supreme Court found no clear legislative intent to require taxation on the total monetary charges incurred by customers who get reservations for hotel room rentals through an OTC's website. The court also found nothing in the legislative history of the statutes which demonstrates that the Legislature intended that the tax pertain to anything other than the amount hotels charge for the room rentals.

The counties argued that under the merchant model transactions, the full amount of charges the OTCs require of their customers is subject to tax. The court disagreed and found that the amount the OTCs charge their customers for facilitating Florida hotel room reservations is fully negotiated between the OTC and the hotel, and under merchant model transactions, the markup portion of the total charges reflects the agreed-upon remuneration for the services an OTC provides through its website.

After noting that the Legislature has repeatedly declined to revise the transient rental statutes, the court held that the statutes are not ambiguous and concern only the amount of funds a hotel requires for a customer to occupy the hotel room it rents on a transient basis, and it is irrelevant which actors are involved and what roles they play in transactions for facilitating transient hotel room reservations. Only the transient rental rate, set by the hotel and collected by the OTC under its contract with the hotel, is subject to taxation pursuant to the tourist development tax. (*Alachua County v. Expedia, Inc.,* Florida Supreme Court, No. SC13-838, June 11, 2015, CCH FLORIDA TAX REPORTS, ¶ 206-038)

¶ 338   List of Exemptions, Exceptions, and Exclusions

Unless otherwise indicated, the statutory exemptions, exceptions, and exclusions listed below apply to both sales and use taxes; those applicable only to the use tax are listed separately. Items that are excluded from the sales or use tax base are treated at ¶ 337, "Tax Base."

Tax holiday—Back-to-School: A sales and use tax holiday for the sale of books and clothing is in effect from August 5 through August 7, 2016, on the sale of clothing (excluding watches, watchbands, jewelry, umbrellas, and handkerchiefs), footwear (excluding skis, swim fins, roller blades, and skates), wallets, or bags (including handbags, backpacks, fanny packs, and diaper bags, but excluding briefcases, suitcases, and other garment bags) having a sales price of $60 or less per item; and school supplies (pens, pencils, erasers, crayons, notebooks, notebook filler paper, legal pads, binders, lunch boxes, construction paper, markers, folders, poster board, composition books, poster paper, scissors, cellophane tape, glue or paste, rulers, computer disks, protractors, compasses, and calculators) having a sales price of $15 or less per item, purchased for noncommercial home or personal use. The tax holiday exemptions do not apply to sales within a theme park or entertainment complex, a public lodging establishment, or an airport. (Uncodified Ch. 220 (H.B. 7099), Laws 2016)

Tax holiday—certain textbooks: From July 1, 2015 through June 30, 2016, sales and use tax may not be collected on the retail sale of textbooks and instructional materials that are required or recommended for use in a course offered by a public postsecondary educational institution or a nonpublic postsecondary educational institution that is eligible to participate in a tuition assistance program. In order to demonstrate that a sale is not subject to tax, a student must provide to the vendor the student's identification number and an applicable course syllabus or list of required and recommended textbooks and instructional materials. In addition, vendors must maintain proper documentation, as prescribed by department rule, to identify the complete transaction or portion of the transaction that involves the sale of textbooks that are not subject to tax. These exemptions are inapplicable to sales within a theme park, entertainment complex, public lodging establishment, or airport, all as defined. (Uncodified Sec. 29, Ch. 221 (H.B. 33a), Laws 2015; *Tax Information Publication, No. 15A01-06,* Florida Department of Revenue, June 26, 2015, CCH FLORIDA TAX REPORTS, ¶ 206-064)

Hurricane victims: Purchases made with Red Cross client assistance cards by hurricane victims are exempt from Florida sales and use tax. However, the exemption does not apply to purchases of taxable items made directly by storm victims using personal funds, including cash obtained by accessing funds through the client assistance cards. Purchases made with Federal Emergency Management Agency (FEMA) assistance cards are not exempt from tax. Because the cards can be used as debit cards and converted directly into cash, purchases made with FEMA assistance cards are considered to be the equivalent of cash purchases and are fully taxable. Retailers should confirm that a Red Cross client assistance card is being used to pay for the items purchased and should make a notation in a manner that can be traced to the record of the purchase.

Vouchers issued by the Red Cross and FEMA function as direct purchases by those organizations and are exempt from tax. However, purchases made with funds received through checks issued by the Red Cross or FEMA are not exempt from tax (*Tax Information Publication, No. 05A01-17,* Florida Department of Revenue, November 30, 2005, CCH FLORIDA TAX REPORTS, ¶ 204-803).

• **Sales and use tax exemptions, exceptions, and exclusions**

Note: Some exemptions are available in the form of refunds; see ¶ 345.

Accessible taxicabs	Sec. 212.08(7)(iii)
Admissions imposed by sponsoring nonprofit organizations	Sec. 212.04(2)(a)(2)
Admissions paid by students participating in school required activities	Sec. 212.04(2)(a)(1), Sec. 212.04(2)(a)(3)
Admissions to athletic events sponsored by schools	Sec. 212.04(2)(a)(1)
Admissions to athletic or other events sponsored by governmental entities	Sec. 212.04(2)(a)(6)
Admissions to live theater, opera, or ballet sponsored by charitable organizations	Sec. 212.04(2)(a)(7)
Admissions to museums or historic buildings	Sec. 212.04(2)(a)(2)
Admissions to certain sports championship or all-star games	Sec. 212.04(2)(a)(5)
Admissions to physical fitness facilities owned by a hospital	Sec. 212.02(1)
Advertising circulars	Sec. 212.08(7)(w)
Advertising services	Sec. 212.08(7)(yy)
Agricultural equipment (power)	Sec. 212.08(3)
Agricultural electricity	Sec. 212.08(5)(e)2
Agricultural products sold directly by the farmer	Sec. 212.07(5)
Agricultural products used by farmer, family, or employees	Sec. 212.07(6)
Agricultural items used for processing, propagation, protection, etc.	Sec. 212.07(7), Sec. 212.08(5)(a)
Aircraft, fractional ownership	Sec. 212.08(7)(hhh)
Aircraft modification	Sec. 212.08(5)(i)
Aircraft temporarily in Florida	Sec. 212.08(7)(ggg)

Aircraft and aircraft repair parts and labor charges	Sec. 212.08(7)(ee), (rr), (ss)
Aircraft and gas turbine engine manufacturing equipment and materials	Sec. 212.08(7)(hhh)
Aircraft repair and maintenance equipment	Sec. 212.08(7)(uu)
Aircraft sold or leased to common carrier	Sec. 212.08(7)(vv)
Aircraft sold to nonresidents (partial exemption)	Sec. 212.08(11)
Alcoholic beverages for tasting purposes	Sec. 212.08(7)(s)
Altar paraphernalia	Sec. 212.06(9)
Animal shelters	Sec. 212.08(7)(o)(2)(b)(VII)
Animals, poultry, or bees for breeding purposes	Sec. 212.07(5)
Artificial limbs	Sec. 212.08(2)
Artwork used for educational purposes	Sec. 212.08(7)(cc)
Banks and trust companies	Sec. 213.12(1)
Bibles, hymnals, textbooks, and prayer books	Sec. 212.06(9)
Bicycle helmets (youth)	Sec. 212.08(7)(mmm)
Blue or stone crab bait	Sec. 212.08(7)(c)
Boats (tax cap of $18,000); boat repairs (tax cap of $60,000)	Sec. 212.05(5)
Boat temporarily in Florida	Sec. 212.08(7)(t)
Boiler fuels	Sec. 212.08(7)(b)
Brownfield sites (bonus refund; see ¶ 345)	Sec. 212.08(5), Sec. 288.107(2)
Bookstore operations at colleges	Sec. 212.08(7)(eee)
Building materials for qualified housing in certain areas	Sec. 212.08(5)(n)
Building materials to rehabilitate enterprise zone property	Sec. 212.08(5)(g)
Bullion and coin sales exceeding $500	Sec. 212.05(1)(k)(4), Sec. 212.08(7)(zz)
Business purchases in an enterprise zone	Sec. 212.08(5)(h)
Butane, propane, and liquefied gas for farm purposes	Sec. 212.08(5)(e)
Cattle, performance- or growth-enhancing products	Sec. 212.08(5)(l)
Cemetery maintenance organizations	Sec. 212.08(7)(bb)
Chambers of Commerce	Ch. 98-296, Laws 1998
Charitable organizations	Sec. 212.08(7)(o)
Chartered fishing vessel admissions	Sec. 212.08(7)(y)
Child restraint systems or booster seats for motor vehicle use	Sec. 212.08(7)(lll)
Churches	Sec. 212.08(7)(o)(2)(a)
Coal	Sec. 212.08(7)(j)
Coast Guard auxiliaries	Sec. 212.08(7)(cc)
Commemorative flowers sold by veterans organizations	Sec. 212.08(7)(a)
Communication services	Sec. 202.12
Community newspapers, shoppers, free circulated magazines	Sec. 212.08(7)(w)
Condominiums, lease of common elements by the association	Sec. 212.031(1)(a)(4)
Containers for agricultural uses	Sec. 212.08(5)(a)
Credit unions	Sec. 213.12(2)

Fuel, renewable energy equipment, materials, and pump retrofits
(refund) (exp. 7/1/16) . . . . Sec. 212.08(7)(hhh)

Fuel used by a utility to generate electricity . . . . Sec. 212.08(4)(a)(2)

Fuel used for agricultural, aquacultural, or fishing purposes . . . . . . Sec. 212.06.41(4)(c)(3),
Sec. 212.08(4)(a)

Fuel used to manufacture property . . . . Sec. 212.08(7)(b)

Fuel used by vessels in interstate commerce . . . . Sec. 212.08(4)(a)2

Funeral services . . . . Sec. 212.08(2)

Fungicides . . . . Sec. 212.08(5)(a)

Golf tournament sponsors . . . . Sec. 212.08(7)(gg)

Government contractors, sales to (requires certificate of entitlement) Sec. 212.08(17)

Government sales or purchases . . . . Sec. 212.08(6),
Sec. 212.08(17)

Groceries . . . . Sec. 212.08(1)

Growing stock for farms and nurseries . . . . Sec. 212.08(5)(a)

Guide dogs for the blind . . . . Sec. 212.08(7)(h)

Gun clubs, admission and membership fees . . . . Sec. 212.04(2)(a)(11)

Herbicides . . . . Sec. 212.08(5)(a)

Hospital food . . . . Sec. 212.08(7)(i)

Hospital room rentals and meals . . . . Sec. 212.08(7)(i)

Household fuels . . . . Sec. 212.08(7)(j)

Industrial fuels . . . . Sec. 212.08(7)(b)

Insecticides . . . . Sec. 212.08(5)(a)

Irrigation equipment for farm or forest use . . . . Sec. 212.08(3)

Insurance services . . . . Sec. 212.08(7)(v)

Interstate commerce sales . . . . Sec. 212.06(7)

Lease of street for utility . . . . Sec. 212.031(1)(a)(5)

Lease or rental of skyboxes or luxury seats at high school or college
athletic events . . . . Sec. 212.031(9)

Library cooperatives . . . . Sec. 212.08(7)(xx)

Livestock . . . . Sec. 212.07(5),
Sec. 212.07(6)

Lodging . . . . Sec. 212.03(7)

Machinery and equipment used in semiconductor production . . . . . Sec. 212.08(5)(j)

Machinery and equipment used in defense or space technology . . . . Sec. 212.08(5)(j)

Machinery and equipment used in production of electrical or steam
energy . . . . Sec. 212.06(1)(b),
Sec. 212.08(5)(c),
Sec. 212.08(7)(ff)(2)

Manufacturing equipment for new or expanded plant . . . . Sec. 212.08(5)(b)(1),
Sec. 212.08(5)(b)(2)

Manufacturing machinery and equipment . . . . Sec. 212.08(7)(kkk)

Master tapes . . . . Sec. 212.08(12)(a)

Meals furnished as part of a packaged room rate . . . . Sec. 212.08(7)(mm)

Meal plans, prepaid college . . . . Sec. 212.08(7)(r)

- **Transactions taxed at other rates**

Coin-operated amusements: A 4% tax is imposed on charges for the use of coin-operated amusement machines (Sec. 212.05(1)(j)(1)). The method used to calculate the charges is detailed under "Industry tax rate," below.

Energy: EElectrical power or energy is taxed at the rate of 4.35% (Sec. 212.05(1)(e)(1)(c)). A seller of electrical power or energy may collect a combined rate of 6.95%, which consists of the 4.35% sales and use tax and a 2.6% gross receipts tax on utility services (*Tax Information Publication,* No. 14A01-07, Florida Department of Revenue, June 20, 2014).

Asphalt: In addition to the tax on the cost of materials and transportation, a tax of 75¢ per ton is due on asphalt manufactured by the contractor for his or her own use during the period from July 1, 2016, through June 30, 2017 (Sec. 212.06(1)(c)). This tax rate is adjusted annually. Sixty percent of the cost of asphalt used for state or local government public works projects is exempt from tax, so the tax is paid at the rate of 30¢ per ton on these projects (*Tax Information Publication, No. 16A01-04,* Florida Department of Revenue, June 9, 2016). The indexed tax rate on manufactured asphalt used in public works projects of the federal, state, and local governments is being phased out over three years. Beginning July 1, 2016, the indexed tax rate ws reduced by 60%, beginning July 1, 2017, the rate is reduced by 80%, and beginning July 1, 2018, the tax will be eliminated.

Motor vehicles: A surcharge of $2 per day is imposed for the first 30 days of the term upon the lease or rental of a motor vehicle licensed for hire and designed to carry less than nine passengers (Sec. 212.0606(1)).

A motor vehicle dealer must pay an annual use tax of $27 for each dealer license plate purchased in addition to the license tax (Sec. 212.0601).

When the purchaser of a motor vehicle gives the dealer a notarized statement stating that the car will be registered in another state within 45 days of the purchase, the dealer will collect Florida tax at (1) the lesser of the rate imposed in the state in which the vehicle will be registered (if the other state offers a credit for taxes paid to Florida) or (2) the Florida rate. Currently, Arkansas, Mississippi, and West Virginia impose a sales tax on motor vehicles, but do not allow a credit for taxes paid to Florida (Sec. 212.08(10); Rule 12A-1.007(8)(a); *Tax Information Publication, No. 16A01-01R2,* Florida Department of Revenue, March 22, 2015, CCH FLORIDA TAX REPORTS, ¶ 206-167).

Car-sharing services: A member of a car-sharing service who uses a motor vehicle for less than 24 hours under an agreement with a car-sharing service is required to pay a Florida surcharge of $1 per usage. A member of a car-sharing service who uses the same motor vehicle for 24 hours or more must pay a surcharge of $2 per day or any part of a day. (Sec. 212.0606(2))

A "car-sharing service" is defined as a membership-based organization or business, or a division of either, that requires the payment of an application or membership fee and provides member access to motor vehicles:

— only at locations that are not staffed by car-sharing service personnel employed solely for the purpose of interacting with car-sharing service members;

— 24 hours a day, seven days a week;

— only through automated means, including but not limited to smartphone applications or electronic membership cards;

— on an hourly basis or for a shorter increment of time;

— without a separate fee for refueling the motor vehicle;

— without a separate fee for minimum financial responsibility liability insurance; and

— owned or controlled by the car-sharing service or its affiliates.

Prior to the enactment of Sec. 212.0606(2), rentals of cars to members of a car-sharing service were subject to the rental car surcharge because the taxpayer who offers the service is deemed to be engaged in the rental of motor vehicles. (*Technical Assistance Advisement, No. 12A-022*, Florida Department of Revenue, September 17, 2012, CCH FLORIDA TAX REPORTS, ¶ 205-784)

Communication services: See discussion below.

- **Industry tax rate**

When it is impracticable, due to the nature of the business practice within an industry, to separately state Florida tax on the bill of sale, the Department of Revenue may establish an effective tax rate for the industry (Sec. 212.07(2)). The Department may amend this effective tax rate as industry's pricing or practices change.

Vendors at carnivals, for example, are taxed at 6.59% of gross sales (Rule 12A-1.080). To compute the tax, the vendor must divide the total receipts by 1.0659 and subtract the quotient from total receipts.

Coin-operated amusement devices: The generally applicable rate of sales tax to be paid on the charges for the use of coin-operated amusement machines is 4.0%; however, for counties with a 6.5% sales tax, the rate is 4.5%, and for counties with a 7.0% sales tax, the rate is 5.0% (Sec. 212.05(1)(i)).

Vending machines: The generally applicable rate of sales tax to be paid on items sold in vending machines is 6.45% for beverages and food and 6.59% for other items of tangible personal property; however, the rate must reflect any local option tax component as follows (Sec. 212.0515(2)):

— for counties imposing a 0.5% sales surtax, the rate is 6.86% for beverage and food items and 7.07% for other items of tangible personal property;

— for counties imposing a 0.75% sales surtax, the rate is 7.07% for beverage and food items and 7.27% for other items of tangible personal property;

— for counties imposing a 1% sales surtax, the rate is 7.26% for beverage and food items and 7.49% for other items of tangible personal property; and

— for counties imposing a 1.5% sales surtax, the rate is 7.67% for beverage and food items and 7.91% for other items of tangible personal property.

Sales of natural fluid milk, homogenized milk, pasteurized milk, whole milk, chocolate milk, or similar milk products and natural fruit or vegetable juices sold in vending machines are taxable at the rate for food.

Concessionaires: Dealers operating concession stands who cannot separately state tax must remit tax at the rate of 6.59% of the total taxable sales of food and drink items, unless the records of the dealer clearly demonstrate a lesser rate. To compute the correct amount of tax due, the dealer should divide the total receipts by 1.0659 to compute the taxable sales and then subtract this amount from total receipts to arrive at the amount of tax due. The 6.59% rate takes into account the variations that may result from multiple sales transactions (Rule 12A-1.011(4)(a)). Such dealers must maintain accurate records of the tax collected, and the exact amount of tax due must be remitted to the state (Rule 12A-1.011(4)(b)).

Alcoholic beverage dealers: For the privilege of deviating from the standard taxing procedures, a dealer of alcoholic beverages must remit tax according to the following methods (Rule 12A-1.057):

If the dealer does not put the public on notice that the tax is included in the total charge, a dealer who sells packages must remit 6.35% of total receipts, and a dealer who sells mixed drinks must remit 6.59% of total receipts (Rule 12A-1.057);

If a dealer does put the public on notice that the tax is included in the total charge, a dealer who sells packages would divide total receipts by 1.0635 and subtract the quotient from the total receipts to figure the amount of tax to be remitted, and a dealer who sells mixed drinks would divide total receipts by 1.0659 and subtract the quotient from the total receipts to figure the amount of tax to be remitted (Rule 12A-1.057).

- **Communication services tax**

A separate tax applies to the provision of communication services. The tax is designed to simplify the previously complex structure of taxes on telecommunications by replacing various state and local taxes and fees with a single structure under which communications dealers pay a state communications services tax, a gross receipts tax, and any local communications taxes imposed.

Membership programs for streaming or downloading video and/or audio content are subject to communications services tax; see *Technical Assistance Advisement,* No. 14A19-006, Florida Department of Revenue, December 19, 2014, CCH FLORIDA TAX REPORTS, ¶ 206-006.

The combined gross receipts tax on communications services is 2.52%, comprised of the previous rate applied to communications services (2.37%) plus the additional rate of 0.15%. (Sec. 203.01). Direct-to-home satellite services are taxed at the rate of 10.8% of the sales price (Sec. 202.12). The combined rate for direct-to-home satellite services is 13.17%, exclusive of local surcharges. The combined rate for retail sales of communication services that is 9.17%, except for residential services, which are subject only to the gross receipts portion of the tax.

¶ 340   Local Taxes

Any county may impose a local option tourist development tax on transient leases or rentals at the rate of 1% or 2% of each whole and major fraction of each dollar of the total rental charged (Sec. 125.0104). However, the tax may not be levied in a county that adopts the convention development tax (discussed below). An additional 1% tax also may be levied if the 1% or 2% tax has been levied for at least three years prior to the imposition of the additional tax.

An additional 1% tax may be levied to pay the debt service on bonds issued to finance the construction, reconstruction, or renovation of a professional sports franchise facility or convention center, or the acquisition, construction, reconstruction, or renovation of a retained spring training franchise facility, and to pay planning and design costs incurred on such projects, and a further additional 1% tax may be levied to pay the debt service on bonds issued to finance the construction, reconstruction, or renovation of a facility for a new professional sports franchise, or the acquisition, construction, reconstruction, or renovation of a retained spring training franchise facility. A county with a high tourism impact, as certified by the Department of Revenue, may levy an additional 1% tax.

The 2% tourist development tax cap is waived for those counties that levy both a consolidated government convention development tax and a second additional local tourist development tax to finance professional sports franchise facilities. However, this change will not affect the validity of currently issued bonds.

An additional 2% tax may be levied on the sale of food, beverages, and alcohol in hotels and motels (Sec. 212.0306). An additional 1% tax may be levied on the sale of food, beverages, and alcohol in all other establishments that are licensed by Florida to sell alcoholic beverages for consumption on the premises. The tax does not apply to packaged alcoholic beverages sold for off-premises consumption. Establishments with gross annual revenues of $400,000 or less are exempt, as are licensed veterans' organizations, transactions that are exempt from the state sales tax, and sales in cities or towns imposing a municipal resort tax.

Counties that have imposed the tourism development tax may impose an additional tax of up to 1% of rentals or leases of living quarters or accommodations of six months or less (Sec. 125.0104(3)).

Tourist development taxation, registration and reporting requirements apply to taxable rental charges and room rates that are due on or after the effective date of the tax (Rule 12A-3.002). Tourist development taxes are imposed prior to the addition of Florida sales tax. They are also imposed prior to the addition of convention development taxes in counties that impose both taxes, excepting Miami-Dade, Duval and Volusia counties (Rule 12A-8.001, Rule 12A-9.001, Rule 12A-10.001).

- **Convention development tax**

The convention development tax on transient leases or rentals is levied at the rate of 2% in a county that is consolidated with a municipality (Sec. 212.0305(4)(a)), at the rate of 3% in a charter county (Sec. 212.0305(4)(b)), and at a maximum rate of 3% in a special taxing district that taxes tourist advertising within a county (Sec. 212.0305(4)(c)), within a county outside of the special taxing district (Sec. 212.0305(4)(d)), or within in a county outside of the special taxing district and northwest of State Road 415 (Sec. 212.0305(4)(e)). However, the convention development tax levied in a special taxing district may not exceed 2% without the approval of a super majority vote of the members of the governing body of the county.

The convention development tax has been imposed in Miami-Dade County at a rate of 3% (Bal Harbor and Surfside are exempt) (Rule 12A-8.002), in Duval County at a rate of 2% (Rule 12A-9.002), and in Volusia County at a rate of 3% (only Halifax Advertising Tax District and West Volusia Convention Development Tax District) (Rule 12A-10.002). Convention development taxes in these three counties apply before the addition of Florida sales tax and tourist development tax (Rule 12A-8.002, Rule 12A-9.002, Rule 12A-10.002).

The convention development tax applies to the amount of any payment made by any person to rent, lease, or use for a period of six months or less any living quarters or accommodations in a hotel, apartment hotel, motel, resort motel, apartment, apartment motel, rooming house, tourist or trailer camp, mobile home park, recreational vehicle park, condominium, or timeshare resort (Sec. 212.0305(4)(e)).

- **Communication services tax**

Charter counties and municipalities may levy a local communications services tax at the rate of up to 5.1% for counties and municipalities that do not levy permit fees and at the rate of up to 4.98% for counties and municipalities that do levy the fees, subject to certain add-ons (Sec. 202.19). Noncharter counties may levy the tax at a rate of up to 1.6%.

Taxing jurisdiction database: Local taxing jurisdictions are required to furnish to the Department of Revenue all information needed to maintain a database used to determine the taxing jurisdiction in which a service address is located (Sec. 202.22).

- **Discretionary sales surtaxes**

The following taxes are discretionary sales surtaxes: a charter county transit system surtax is authorized at the rate of 1% (Sec. 212.055(1)) (for a tax bracket chart, see ¶ 341); a local government infrastructure surtax is authorized at a rate of 0.5% or 1% (Sec. 212.055(2)); an indigent care surtax is authorized in counties of 50,000 population or less at a rate of 1.0% (Sec. 212.055(3)); a public hospital surtax is authorized at a rate of 0.5% (Sec. 212.055(5)), and a county may levy a surtax of up to 1% for emergency fire rescue services and facilities (Sec. 212.055(8)). A tourist impact tax is imposed in various counties. Surtaxes are imposed in some counties for various purposes. In general, a discretionary surtax applies only to the first $5,000 of the sales amount of any item of tangible personal property (Sec. 212.054(2)(b), Rule 12A-15.004).

¶340 Florida

The list of counties levying a surtax is subject to frequent revision (Rule 12A-15.001). An up-to-date listing of counties levying the surtax is available upon written request to the Bureau of Tax Information and Assistance, Florida Department of Revenue, Tallahassee, Florida 32399-0100 or by calling 1-800-872-9909 (Florida only) or (850) 488-6800.

The tax is levied on each dollar of rent (Rule 12A-3.006). Fractions of a dollar are rounded up if the amount is 51¢ or more.

If it is impractical to separately state Florida sales tax on each transaction because of the nature of business practices within the industry, concession stands in counties levying the surtax at the rate of 1% are required to remit tax at the rate of 7.51% of total taxable sales (Rule 12A-15.010). Taxable sales are derived by dividing total receipts by 1.075, and the difference between total receipts and taxable sales constitutes the tax due. The 7.51% rate recognizes the variations resulting from multiple sales transactions. In counties where the surtax rate is 0.5%, concession stand dealers are required to remit tax at the rate of 6.97%.

Amusement machines: The effective tax rate for amusement machines located in a county imposing a 1% surtax is 5% (Rule 12A-15.011(1)(c)). To compute sales tax due, operators of amusement machines should divide their total receipts from amusement machines by 1.050 to compute gross sales, which is then subtracted from total receipts to arrive at sales tax due.

The effective tax rate for amusement machines located in a county imposing a ½% surtax is 4.5%. To compute gross sales from which sales tax can be determined, operators of amusement machines should divide total receipts by 1.045.

Money inserted into a machine that dispenses tokens, slugs, coupons, or any other items used to operate entertainment or amusement machines are taxed in the same manner as amusement machines into which coins are placed directly. Thus, the effective tax rates on these machines are 5% (divisor of 1.050) in a county that imposes a 1% surtax and 4.5% (divisor of 1.045) in a county that imposes a ½% surtax.

Certain dealers of alcoholic beverages may include the tax in the total sales price if it is impractical to separately record the sales price and the tax. In such a case, the amount to be remitted as tax depends upon whether the dealer puts the public on notice that the tax is included in the sales price. In counties that levy the 1% surtax, alcoholic beverage dealers who include tax in the total price but who do not put the public on notice calculate the tax to be remitted as follows (Rule 12A-15.012):

(1) package goods dealers must remit 7.30% of their total receipts; and

(2) dealers in mixed drinks or a combination of mixed drinks and package goods in must remit 7.51% of their total receipts.

In counties levying the 0.5% surtax, alcoholic beverage dealers who include tax in the total price but who do not put the public on notice calculate the tax to be remitted as follows (Rule 12A-15.012):

(1) package goods dealers must remit 6.77% of their total receipts; and

(2) dealers of mixed drinks or a combination of mixed drinks and package goods must remit 6.97% of their total receipts.

In counties levying the 1% surtax, alcoholic beverage dealers who include the tax in the total price and put the public on notice calculate the tax to be remitted as follows (Rule 12A-15.012):

(1) package goods dealers divide total receipts by 1.073, and subtract the quotient from total receipts; and

(2) dealers of mixed drinks divide total receipts by 1.0751 and subtract the quotient from total receipts.

In counties levying the 0.5% surtax, alcoholic beverage dealers who include the tax in the total price and put the public on notice calculate the tax to be remitted as follows (Rule 12A-15.012):

    (1) package goods dealers divide total receipts by 1.0677, and subtract the quotient from total receipts; and

    (2) dealers of mixed drinks divide total receipts by 1.0697 and subtract the quotient from total receipts.

Multijurisdictional tourism, sports, and entertainment special districts: Multijurisdictional tourism, sports, and entertainment special districts, which are authorized in areas that are the site of a proposed or existing professional sports team, facility, or event reasonably anticipated to attract attendance of over 100,000, may levy a discretionary sales surtax on tangible personal property sold within the state by a dealer located in the special district and on admissions within the district, in order to develop and maintain related supporting improvements and infrastructure.

School capital outlay sales surtax: Florida school boards are authorized to levy a school capital outlay sales surtax of up to 0.5% with referendum approval (Sec. 212.055(7)). The surtax proceeds are to be used for fixed capital expenditures or fixed capital costs associated with the construction, reconstruction, or improvement of school facilities and campuses, and any related land acquisition, land improvement, design, and engineering costs, as well as costs for technology implementation. Neither the surtax proceeds or any interest accrued on the proceeds may be used for operational expenses. Any school board imposing the surtax is required to freeze noncapital local school property taxes for a period of at least three years.

Tax rate lookup: Local tax rates may be looked up by address at **http://dor.myflorida.com/dor/eservices/addlookup.html**. The following is a list of local sales and use taxes imposed by each county in Florida:

Local Sales Taxes and Current Rates as of March 1, 2017

COUNTY	AMOUNT OF TAX DUE ON	
	LIVING/SLEEPING ACCOMMODATIONS	OTHER TAXABLE TRANSACTIONS
11 ALACHUA	11.5%	6.5%
12 BAKER	10%	7%
13 BAY**	12%	7%
14 BRADFORD	11%	7%
15 BREVARD	12%	7%
16 BROWARD	11%	6%
17 CALHOUN	7.5%	7.5%
18 CHARLOTTE	12%	7%
19 CITRUS	11%	6%
20 CLAY	10%	7%
21 COLLIER	10%	6%
22 COLUMBIA	12%	7%
23 DADE**	13%	7%
24 DE SOTO	10.5%	7.5%
25 DIXIE	9%	7%
26 DUVAL	13%	7%
27 ESCAMBIA	11.5%	7.5%
28 FLAGLER	11%	7%
29 FRANKLIN	9%	7%
30 GADSDEN	9.5%	7.5%
31 GILCHRIST	9%	7%

COUNTY	AMOUNT OF TAX DUE ON	
	LIVING/SLEEPING ACCOMMODATIONS	OTHER TAXABLE TRANSACTIONS
32 GLADES	9%	7%
33 GULF	12%	7%
34 HAMILTON	10%	7%
35 HARDEE	9%	7%
36 HENDRY	10%	7%
37 HERNANDO	11.5%	6.5%
38 HIGHLANDS	9.5%	7.5%
39 HILLSBOROUGH	12%	7%
40 HOLMES	9%	7%
41 INDIAN RIVER	11%	7%
42 JACKSON	11.5%	7.5%
43 JEFFERSON	9%	7%
44 LAFAYETTE	7%	7%
45 LAKE	11%	7%
46 LEE	11%	6%
47 LEON	12.5%	7.5%
48 LEVY	9%	7%
49 LIBERTY	8%	8%
50 MADISON	10.5%	7.5%
51 MANATEE	12%	7%
52 MARION	11%	7%
53 MARTIN	11%	6%
54 MONROE	12.5%	7.5%
55 NASSAU**	11%	7%
56 OKALOOSA**	11%	6%
57 OKEECHOBEE	10%	7%
58 ORANGE	12.5%	6.5%
59 OSCEOLA	13.5%	7.5%
60 PALM BEACH	13%	7%
61 PASCO	9%	7%
62 PINELLAS	13%	7%
63 POLK	12%	7%
64 PUTNAM	11%	7%
65 ST. JOHNS	10.5%	6.5%
66 ST. LUCIE	11.5%	6.5%
67 SANTA ROSA	12%	7%
68 SARASOTA	12%	7%
69 SEMINOLE	12%	7%
70 SUMTER	9%	7%
71 SUWANNEE	10%	7%
72 TAYLOR	12%	7%
73 UNION	7%	7%
74 VOLUSIA**	12.5%	6.5%
75 WAKULLA	11%	7%
76 WALTON**	11%	7%
77 WASHINGTON	10%	7%

**

BAY — Local Option Tourist Development applies to Zip Codes 32401, 32404, 32405, 32407, 32408, 32410, and Bay's part of 32413.

DADE	Surfside and Bal Harbour are charged a 4% Municipal Resort Tax but are exempt from the Tourist Development and Convention Development Tax. Miami Beach is also charged a 4% Municipal Resort Tax and is exempt from the Tourist Development Tax; however, Miami Beach is not exempt from the Convention Development Tax.
NASSAU	Local Option Tourist Development applies to Amelia Island only.
OKALOOSA	Local Option Tourist Development Tax applies only to voting precincts 19, 20, 21, 22, 24, 27, 30, 33, 35, 38, 41, 42, and 44.
VOLUSIA	Living/Sleeping Accommodations only: Districts and Southeast Volusia Advertising District. The Convention Development tax applies to the Halifax and West Volusia Advertising Districts only. All areas outside these districts is 9.5%.
WALTON	Living/Sleeping Accommodations only: the 11% rate only applies to Zip Codes 32459, 32550, 32454, 32461, and Walton's part of 32413.

¶ 341   Bracket Schedule

Florida sales tax brackets can be obtained by downloading them from the Department of Revenue's website at **http://floridarevenue.com/Forms_library/current/dr2x.pdf**, faxing a forms request to the Department's distribution center at (850) 922-2208, calling the distribution center at (850) 488-8422, writing the distribution center at 168 Blountstown Highway, Tallahassee, Florida 32304, or visiting any local Department service center. A list of counties levying a local discretionary surtax can also be obtained by the same means.

The following brackets are to be used in the collection of tax on transactions taxable at the 6% rate:

¶ 342   Returns, Payments, and Due Dates

All dealers must make a return on or before the 20th day of the month to the Department of Revenue (Sec. 212.11(1)(b)). Returns are accepted as timely if postmarked on or before the 20th day of the month. If the 20th day falls on a Saturday, Sunday, or federal or state legal holiday, returns are accepted if postmarked on the next workday (Sec. 212.11(1)(e), Rule 12A-1.056(1)).

Dealers who paid more than $1,000 in Florida sales and use tax during the most recent state fiscal year (July 1—June 30) are required to pay tax and file returns on a monthly basis (*Tax Information Publication, No. 08A01-10*, Florida Department of Revenue, November 19, 2008, CCH FLORIDA TAX REPORTS, ¶ 205-278). If the amount reported over $1,000 was due to nonrecurring taxable business activities, the taxpayer may request permission to continue filing less frequently by sending a letter to the Department.

The Department of Revenue is authorized to require dealers to make returns and payments based on the amount of tax remitted in the preceding four calendars quarters, as follows: dealers who remitted $100 or less, annual reports and payments; dealers who remitted at least $100 but less than $500, semiannual reports and payments; dealers who remitted at least $500 but less than $1,000, quarterly reports and payments; dealers who remitted between $1,000 and $12,000, quarterly reports with monthly payments (Sec. 212.11(1)(c)).

Each dealer must file a return for each tax period even if no tax is due for that period (Sec. 212.11(1)(e)).

Annual report required from certain sellers: A seller of alcoholic beverages or tobacco products in Florida must file an information report designed to enforce the collection of sales and use tax. The annual report for the period from July 1 through June 30 must be filed with the Department of Revenue based on sales of those products to any retailer in the state. The report is due on July 1 and must be filed using the Department of Revenue's e-filing website, secure file transfer protocol, or electronic data interchange file with the department's e-filing provider unless the seller has problems arising from its computer capabilities. The report will be delinquent if not received by the department by September 30. (Sec. 212.133; *Tax Information Publication, No. 11A01-04,* Florida Department of Revenue, June 27, 2011, CCH FLORIDA TAX REPORTS, ¶ 205-655)

Voluntary payment: The Department of Revenue is authorized to enter into a contract with public or private vendors to develop and implement a voluntary system for sales and use tax collection and administration (Sec. 213.27(9)(a)).

• **Payment**

The full amount of the tax due, shown on the return, must accompany the return (Sec. 212.11, Sec. 212.14(2), Rule 12A-1.056(1)). Tokens may not be used to pay the tax (Sec. 212.18(2)). Failure to remit the full amount will cause the taxes to become delinquent. A return filed without payment is considered prima facie evidence of a dealer's intent to convert the money due the state (Sec. 212.14(3)).

Electronic funds transfers: Payment of taxes by electronic funds transfer (EFT) is required when the taxpayer is subject to sales and use tax and has paid the tax in the prior state fiscal year in an amount of $20,000 (Sec. 213.755). Dealers who file consolidated tax returns must pay tax and file tax returns electronically.

Taxpayers required to remit sales and use taxes by EFT are also required to file their returns electronically (Sec. 212.11(1)(f)). Electronic payments must be made on the last business day before the day the tax is due. Electronic returns must have an electronic date stamp on or before the due date. For taxpayers with two or more places of business who are filing a consolidated return, only one electronic initiation and payment is required.

To file and pay sales and use tax electronically, dealers should go to the department's website at **http://floridarevenue.com** and use the website to file and pay tax electronically or purchase software.

Estimated tax: Taxpayers with tax liability of more than $200,000 for the previous fiscal year must make payments of estimated sales and use tax, and returns must be filed, electronically (*Tax Information Publication, No. 10A01-14,* October 16, 2010, CCH FLORIDA TAX REPORTS, ¶ 205-580).

Use tax payment by consumers: Florida residents can file and pay use taxes online for Internet, catalog, and other out-of-state purchases. To file and pay online, taxpayers should use the link provided on the Web site of the Department of Revenue at **http://floridarevenue.com/taxes/Pages/consumer.aspx**.

School support organizations: In lieu of collecting sales and use tax from the purchaser, school support organizations may pay tax to their suppliers on the cost price of food, drink, and supplies necessary to serve such food and drink when the food, drink, and supplies are purchased for resale. "School support organization" is defined as an organization whose sole purpose is to raise funds to support extracurricular activities at public, parochial, or nonprofit schools that teach students in grades K through 12. (Sec. 212.08(7)(*ll*); *Tax Information Publication, No. 15A01-12,* Florida Department of Revenue, June 25, 2015, CCH FLORIDA TAX REPORTS, ¶ 206-056)

Collection allowance: The sales tax dealer's collection allowance is 2.5% of the first $1,200 of tax due for each reporting period, and is provided as compensation for recordkeeping and collection to taxpayers who timely file returns and pay taxes. The allowance is limited to those dealers who file and pay by electronic means (Sec. 212.12, F.S.). The same limitation applies on collection discounts for remitting the admissions tax (Sec. 212.04(5), F.S.). The allowance does not apply to the rental car surcharge (Sec. 212.0606, F.S.). Vendors may elect to forgo the allowance and instead direct that the amount be transferred into the Educational Enhancement Trust Fund (Sec. 212.12(1)(c), F.S.). For additional information, see *Tax Information Publication, No. 12A01-03,* Florida Department of Revenue, April 30, 2012, CCH FLORIDA TAX REPORTS, ¶ 205-738.

- **Uniform Sales Tax Administration Act**

Florida has enacted the Uniform Sales and Use Tax Administration Act, the product of the Streamlined Sales Tax Project (SSTP) (Sec. 213.256). The SSTP developed the Act and the related Streamlined Sales and Use Tax Agreement to simplify and modernize sales and use tax administration in order to substantially reduce the burden of tax compliance for all sellers and for all types of commerce. However, Florida has not conformed to all requirements of the Act.

Florida is one of the Streamlined Sales Tax Advisor states. For additional information on the uniform act, see the "Streamlined Sales Tax Project," discussion (listed in the Table of Contents).

¶ 343   Prepayment of Taxes

Florida has no provisions for the prepayment of sales and use taxes. However, estimated taxes must be paid by dealers in boats, motor vehicles, and aircraft; see **http://floridarevenue.com/Forms_library/current/dr300400.pdf** http://floridarevenue.com/Forms_library/current/dr300400.pdf.

Taxpayers with an estimated tax liability of more than $200,000 for the previous fiscal year must make payments and file returns electronically. See ¶ 342.

¶ 344   Vendor Registration

Persons who engage in business in Florida as retail dealers, charge admissions, lease or rent tangible personal property or living quarters, or sell taxable services must file an application (Form DR-1) with the Department of Revenue or with a county tax collector authorized to act as the Department's agent for the purposes of accepting dealer registration applications, for a separate dealer's certificate of registration, accompanied by a $5 registration fee, for each place of business (Sec. 212.18(3), Rule 12A-1.060(1)(a)). There is no requirement to pay an annual registration fee. No registration fee is required to conduct a mail order sales business.

Dealers who use independent sellers to sell merchandise may apply to the Florida Department of Revenue to obtain authorization to remit tax in lieu of having the independent seller register as a dealer and remit the tax (Rule 12A-1.0911(5)).

The applicant will be granted a separate Certificate of Registration (DR-11T) for each place of business (Sec. 212.18(3)(a), Rule 12A-1.060(1)(e)). Engaging in a business without first obtaining a Certificate of Registration or after the Certificate has been canceled is prohibited. In addition, failure or refusal to register as a dealer subjects the offender to an increased initial registration fee (Sec. 212.18(3)(a)).

A specific penalty of 100% of any unreported or any uncollected tax or fee applies to (1) any person who, after the Department's delivery of a written notice to the person's last known address specifically alerting the person of the requirement to register the person's business as a dealer, intentionally fails to register the business, or (2) any person who, after the Department's delivery of a written notice to the person's last known address specifically alerting the person of the requirement to collect tax on specific transactions, intentionally fails to collect that tax (Sec. 212.12(2)(d)). These penalties are in addition to any other penalties that may apply.

Any person or entity that conducts business in Florida and that contracts with other persons or entities to buy precious metals or jewelry through an Internet website, the U.S. mail, or telemarketing is required to register as a mail-in secondhand precious metals dealer. (*Tax Information Publication, No. 09A01-06*, Florida Department of Revenue, July 27, 2009, CCH FLORIDA TAX REPORTS, ¶ 205-378)

Secondhand dealers: Any person who is in the business of purchasing, consigning, or trading secondhand goods at a flea market must have a Certificate of Registration (DR-11S) issued for the flea market location, unless that person already has a business registered as a secondhand dealer in the same county as the flea market. Any person who purchases, consigns, or trades secondhand goods must register at least one address in that county. Effective July 1, 2016, any business purchasing secondhand goods through an automated kiosk is a secondhand dealer *(Tax Information Publication, No. 16A01-05,* Florida Department of Revenue, June 24, 2016, CCH Florida Tax Reports, ¶ 206-196).

An auction business that buys and sells estates, business inventory, surplus merchandise, or business liquidations is exempt from secondhand dealer registration requirements.

A person may not engage in the business as a secondary metals recycler at any location without registering with the department. The department can accept applications only from a fixed business address and may not accept an application that provides an address of a hotel room or motel room, a vehicle, or a post office box. For additional information, see *Tax Information Publication, No. 12A01-08,* Florida Department of Revenue, June 29, 2012, CCH Florida Tax Reports, ¶ 205-756.

Bond or security requirement: Individuals and entities seeking to obtain a dealer's certificate of registration may be required to post a cash deposit, bond, or other security (Sec. 212.14(4)).

• **Out-of-state companies responding to declared disasters or emergencies**

Out-of-state businesses operating in Florida solely to perform emergency-related work are not considered to have established a level of presence that would require the business to register, file, and remit state and local taxes or fees or be subject to any registration, licensing, or filing in the state, effective March 24, 2016. Activity conducted by such businesses during the disaster-related period must be disregarded with respect to any state or local tax on net or gross income or receipts, including any filing requirements for such taxes and specifically any filing required for a consolidated group. Taxes and registrations expressly subject to these provisions include: reemployment assistance tax; state or local professional or occupational licensing requirements or related fees; local business taxes; taxes on the operation of commercial vehicles; corporate income tax; and tangible personal property tax and use tax on certain equipment. (Sec. 213-055)

¶ 345   Sales or Use Tax Credits

Credits for tax paid in another state, tax paid in error, and job creation in an enterprise zone are discussed below.

• **Credit for tax paid in another state**

Credit is provided in Florida for a like tax paid in another state for the use, consumption, distribution, or storage of tangible personal property in Florida up to the amount of tax imposed in Florida (Sec. 212.06(7), Rule 12A-1.091(3)). The dealer must pay the Florida Department of Revenue the difference between the tax imposed by Florida and any lesser tax imposed in the other state.

Motor vehicles: A Department of Revenue publication provides information concerning the Florida sales tax credit for motor vehicles brought into Florida from another state in which a like tax was lawfully imposed and paid *(Tax Information Publication, No. 16A01-01R,* Florida Department of Revenue, February 26, 2016, CCH Florida Tax Reports, ¶ 206-161). The publication provides a state-by-state breakdown of (1) the rate of sales tax charged in other states; (2) whether Florida grants a credit for the other state's tax, and vice versa; and (3) the application of other states' taxes on sales of motor vehicles. The publication also contains information concerning the imposition of Florida use tax on motor vehicles exported to territories or foreign countries.

- **Credit for taxes paid in error**

A dealer who pays tax to the supplier on any purchase of tangible personal property that is later resold, may, within 36 months of the date of payment, take the amount paid as a credit against the tax to be remitted to the Department of Revenue. If a dealer purchases tangible personal property for resale and does not pay tax, but consumes the property purchases, the dealer is required to include the cost and pay tax on the amount (Rule 12A-1.013).

- **Credit or refund for bad debts**

Dealers can claim a credit or obtain a refund for any tax paid by on the unpaid balance due on worthless accounts within 12 months following the month in which the bad debt was charged off a federal income tax return. (Sec. 212.17(3); Rule 12A-1.012(3)) If accounts charged off are paid to the dealer in whole or in part, amounts paid must be included in the first return filed after the collection and the tax is paid.

Private-label credit card programs: A "private-label credit card" is defined as a charge card or credit card that carries, refers to, or is branded with the name or logo of a dealer and can be used for purchases from that dealer or for purchases from the dealer's affiliates or franchises (Sec. 212.17(4)(h)(3)). A dealer may claim a credit for or obtain a refund of tax remitted by the dealer on the unpaid balance of consumer accounts or receivables found to be worthless or uncollectible provided (Sec. 212.17(4)(a)):

— the accounts or receivables have been charged off as bad debt on the lender's books and records on or after January 1, 2014;

— a credit was not previously claimed and a refund was not previously allowed on any portion of the accounts or receivables; and

— the credit or refund is claimed within 12 months after the month in which the bad debt has been charged off by the lender for federal income tax purposes.

If the dealer or the lender subsequently collects all or part of the accounts or receivables for which a credit or refund has been granted, the dealer is required to include the taxable percentage of the amount collected in the first return filed after the collection and pay the tax on the portion of that amount for which a credit or refund was granted (Sec. 212.17(4)(b)). The credit or refund allowed includes all credit sale transaction amounts that are outstanding in the specific private-label credit card account or receivable at the time the account or receivable is charged off, regardless of the date on which the credit sale transaction actually occurred (Sec. 212.17(4)(c)).

- **Business incentive credits and refunds**

A number of exemptions, refunds, and job credits have been adopted to encourage development and employment in designated enterprise zones, high-crime urban areas, and rural areas within Florida, as discussed below. The Department of Economic Opportunity assists the governor in working with the Legislature, state agencies, business leaders, and economic development professionals to formulate and implement coherent and consistent policies and strategies designed to promote economic opportunities. The Division of Strategic Business Development administers most tax refund, tax credit, and grant programs.

Extension of enterprise zone incentives: Although the Florida Enterprise Zone Act ended on December 31, 2015, certain incentives are treated as if they did not expire, allowing businesses to apply for them for an additional three years, provided they meet the criteria. These provisions sunset December 31, 2018. (H.B. 33a, Laws 2015; *Tax Information Publication, No. 15ADM-04,* Florida Department of Revenue, September 8, 2015, CCH FLORIDA TAX REPORTS, ¶ 206-097)

Effective January 1, 2016, a business that entered into a contract with the Department of Economic Opportunity for a project between January 1, 2012, and July 1, 2015, and the contract is still active within the boundaries of an enterprise zone as they existed on May 1, 2015, may apply for the following incentives:

— the sales and use tax refund for building materials used in the rehabilitation of real property located in an enterprise zone;

— the sales and use tax refund for business property used in an enterprise zone;

— the sales and use tax exemption for electrical energy used in an enterprise zone; or

— the enterprise zone jobs credit against sales and use tax.

Credit for new employees: Eligible enterprise zone businesses may claim a credit against the sales tax for each new employee (Sec. 212.096). A "new employee" is defined as a person who either resides in an enterprise zone or, after June 30, 1998, who is a program participant in either the welfare transition program or the Job Training Partnership Act classroom training program, and who begins employment with an eligible business after July 1, 1995, and has not been previously employed within the preceding 12 months by the eligible business or a successor eligible business (Sec. 212.096).

The credit is allowed for up to 12 consecutive months (Sec. 212.096). Credits are not refundable, and unused credits may not be carried over to future tax periods.

Improved credit for new employees: A credit is allowed for an enterprise zone business that increases the total number of full-time jobs from the average of the previous 12 months.

The credit is computed as 20% of the actual monthly wages paid in Florida to each new employee hired when a new job has been created, unless the business is located in a rural enterprise zone, in which case the credit is 30% of actual monthly wages. If at least 20% of the business' employees are residents of an enterprise zone, the credit is calculated as 30% of the actual monthly wages paid to each new employee hired when a new job has been created, unless the business is located in a rural enterprise zone, in which case the credit is 45% of the actual monthly wages paid for a period of up to 24 consecutive months.

A rural enterprise zone is an enterprise zone that is nominated by: (1) a county having a population of 75,000 or fewer or a county with a population of 100,000 or fewer that is contiguous to a county with a population of 75,000 or less; (2) a municipality in such a county; or (3) such a county and one or more municipalities.

Credit for purchase of building materials: The purchase of building materials that are used in the rehabilitation of real property located in enterprise zones qualifies for a refund of previously paid taxes (Sec. 212.08(5)(g)). Only one refund is permitted for each parcel of real property. No refund will be granted unless the amount to be refunded exceeds $500. When at least 20% of the employees (excluding temporary and part-time employees) of the business are residents of an enterprise zone, the maximum refund will remain the lesser of 97% of the tax paid on the building materials used to rehabilitate the real property or $5,000. Otherwise the maximum refund will be the lesser of 97% of the tax paid on the building materials or $10,000. An application for refund must be submitted to the Department of Revenue within six months after the rehabilitation of the property is deemed to be substantially completed by the local building code inspector or by November 1 after the rehabilitated property is first subject to assessment.

Refund for sales and use tax on business property: Certain depreciable business property purchased by a business located in an enterprise zone is exempt from tax if the property is subsequently used in an enterprise zone (Sec. 212.08(5)(h)). The exemption may be asserted only by claiming a refund of previously paid taxes. The refund amount is the lesser of 97% of the state sales tax paid on the business property purchases or

$5,000. However, if at least 20% of the employees of the business are residents of an enterprise zone, the maximum refund is $10,000. In any event, no refund may be granted unless the amount to be refunded exceeds $100 in sales tax paid on purchases made within a 60-day time period, and local option taxes are not subject to the refund.

Urban high-crime area and rural area job credits: Eligible businesses are allowed a credit against their remitted sales and use tax for each qualified job they create in designated and ranked urban high-crime areas and rural areas (Sec. 212.097, Sec. 212.098). The credits range from $500 to $1,500 and are in addition to the $500 credit allowed for employees who are participating in the welfare transition program.

Qualified new businesses in the first tier with at least 10 qualified employees will be entitled to a credit of $1,500 per employee. New businesses in tier two must have at least 20 qualified employees and will be entitled to a credit of $1,000 for each. Tier three new businesses with at least 30 employees will qualify for a $500 credit for each of them. (Sec. 212.097(2))

Qualified existing businesses in the first tier are allowed a credit of $1,500 for each new employee beginning with the fifth employee. In a tier two business, the credit will be $1,000 per new employee beginning with the tenth new employee. The $500 credit for a tier three firm will be applied to each qualified new employee beginning with the 15th qualified new employee. An existing eligible business may not apply for the credit more than once in a 12-month period. (Sec. 212.097(3)(a))

Refunds for new jobs in target industry businesses: Qualified target industry businesses, after entering into tax refund agreements with the Office of Tourism, Trade, and Economic Development, are entitled to apply once each fiscal year for refunds from the Economic Development Incentives Account for sales and use taxes due and paid by them after entering into the agreements (Sec. 288.106). A "target industry business" is defined as a corporate headquarters business or any business that is engaged in certain target industries identified by the Department of Commerce in consultation with Enterprise Florida, Inc. Special consideration is given to businesses that export goods or services to international markets, businesses that replace domestic and international imports of goods or services, and to industries that facilitate the development of the state as a hub for domestic and global trade and logistics.

Qualified target industry businesses are entitled to refunds equal to $3,000 times the number of jobs specified in the tax refund agreement or equal to $6,000 times the number of jobs if the project is located in a rural county or an enterprise zone, plus an additional refund equal to $1,000 times the number of jobs specified in the tax refund agreement if such jobs pay an annual average wage of at least 150% of the average private-sector wage in the area or equal to $2,000 times the number of jobs if such jobs pay an annual average wage of at least 200% of the average private-sector wage in the area. The program is scheduled to expire on June 30, 2020.

A qualified target industry business is allowed sales and use tax refund payments, in addition to other payments authorized, equal to $1,000 multiplied by the number of jobs specified in the tax refund agreement if the local financial support is equal to that of the state's incentive award. In addition to the other tax refund payments authorized, a qualified target industry business is allowed a tax refund payment equal to $2,000 multiplied by the number of jobs specified in the tax refund agreement if the business (1) falls within one of the high-impact sectors; or (2) increases exports of its goods through a seaport or airport in Florida by at least 10% in value or tonnage in each of the years that the business receives a tax refund. (Sec. 288.106)

Brownfields: A bonus refund of sales and use tax, documentary stamp tax, corporate income tax, intangible personal property tax, emergency excise tax, insurance premium tax, or property tax, in an amount up to $2,500, is available to any qualified target industry business or other eligible business for each new Florida job created in a brownfield that is claimed on the business's annual tax refund claim (Sec. 288.107(2)).

Refunds for defense contractors and space flight businesses: Qualified applicants that (1) consolidate Department of Defense contracts, (2) obtain new Department of Defense production contracts, (3) convert defense production to non-defense production, or (4) contract for reuse of a defense-related facility are entitled to apply once each fiscal year to the Department of Commerce for a refund from the Economic Development Trust Fund for the sales and use tax due and paid by them, beginning with the applicant's first taxable year commencing after entering into a tax refund agreement (Sec. 288.1045(4)). Effective July 1, 2008, this refund program was extended to space flight business contractors. A "space flight business" is defined as the manufacturing, processing, or assembly of space flight technology products, facilities, propulsion systems, or space vehicles, satellites, or stations of any kind that possess the capability for space flight. The phrase includes vehicle launch activities, flight operations, ground control or ground support, and all administrative activities directly related to such activities. (Sec. 288.1045)

A qualified applicant is allowed tax refund payments equal to: (1) $3,000 times the number of jobs specified in the tax refund agreement; or (2) $6,000 times the number of jobs if the project is located in a rural county or an enterprise zone. In addition, a qualified applicant is allowed additional tax refund payments equal to: (1) $1,000 times the number of jobs specified in the tax refund agreement if such jobs pay an annual average wage of at least 150% of the average private sector wage in the area; or (2) $2,000 times the number of jobs if such jobs pay an annual average wage of at least 200% of the average private sector wage in the area. (Sec. 288.1045(2))

Jobs proposed under the application must pay at least 115% of the average annual wage in the area where the project is to be located. Applicants could not be certified as qualified after June 30, 2014 (Sec. 288.1045(7)).

Rural job tax credit recipients: A new or existing eligible business that receives a rural job tax credit is eligible for a tax refund of up to 50% of the amount of Florida sales tax on purchases of electricity paid by the business during the one-year period after the date the credit is received. The total amount of tax refunds approved for all eligible businesses may not exceed $600,000 during any calendar year. The Department of Revenue may adopt rules to administer this provision. (Sec. 212.098(12))

Energy Economic Zone Pilot Program: The program encourages the generation of renewable electricity and promotes green manufacturing. The Department of Community Affairs selected two areas in 2010, the city of Miami Beach and Sarasota County, to participate in the pilot project. Beginning July 1, 2012, all incentives and benefits currently included in the enterprise zone program are available to the two designated energy economic zones. A local governing authority may exempt certain developments in an energy economic zone from regulations relating to a development of regional impact. Incentives in the enterprise zone program include the enterprise zone jobs tax credit available against corporate income, sales and use, and property taxes, and the community contributions tax credit available against corporate income and insurance premiums taxes. (Sec. 377.809)

• Entertainment industry incentives

The entertainment industry financial incentive program provides a credit against corporate income taxes, sales and use taxes, or a combination of the two against qualified expenditures for a production. A "production" is defined as a theatrical or direct-to-video motion picture; a made-for-television motion picture; visual effects or digital animation sequences produced in conjunction with a motion picture; a commercial; a music video; an industrial or educational film; an infomercial; a documentary; a television pilot; a presentation for a television pilot; a television series, including a drama, reality show, comedy, soap opera, telenovela, game show, awards show, or miniseries; or a digital media project by the entertainment industry. Tax credits awarded may not be claimed against such liabilities for any tax period beginning before

July 1, 2011, regardless of when the credits are applied for or awarded. (Sec. 288.1254; *Tax Information Publication, No. 10A01-08*, June 29, 2010, CCH Florida Tax Reports, ¶ 205-522)

The tax credit program is repealed effective July 1, 2015, with certain exceptions.

- **Community contributions credits**

Through June 30, 2018, a community contribution tax credit is available to taxpayers who make donations to eligible sponsors, such as a sponsor of a community action program or a sponsor of a nonprofit community-based development organization aimed at low-income housing or entrepreneurial development (Sec. 212.08(5)(p); *Tax Information Publication, No. 15ADM-03,* Florida Department of Revenue, June 25, 2015, CCH Florida Tax Reports, ¶ 206-053).

The credit is available as a sales and use tax refund (or as a credit against corporate income or insurance premium tax) to taxpayers who make contributions to eligible sponsors for use in projects that are designed to (Sec. 212.08(5)(p)(2.b)):

(1) construct, improve, or substantially rehabilitate housing that is affordable to low-income households or very-low-income households;

(2) provide housing opportunities for persons with special needs;

(3) provide commercial, industrial, or public resources and facilities; or

(4) improve entrepreneurial and job-development opportunities for low-income persons.

The credit is computed as 50% of the taxpayer's annual community contribution and may be carried over for up to a three-year period without regard to any time limitation that would otherwise apply. However, the annual tax credit for all approved community contributions made by a taxpayer may not exceed $200,000 in any one year and the total amount of credits for all approved programs is limited.

The total amount of tax credits that may be granted is $21.4 million for the 2017-2018 fiscal year.

- **Scholarship funding**

A credit is available for 100% of an eligible contribution made to an eligible nonprofit scholarship-funding organization against any sales and use tax imposed by Florida and due from a direct pay permit holder as a result of the direct pay permit held. Unused credits may be carried forward for up to five years. (Sec. 212.1831, F.S.; Rule 12ER10-04) The credit is capped at $698,852,539 for the 2017-2018 fiscal year.

¶ 346   Deficiency Assessments

If a taxpayer fails to make records available for inspection, to register as a dealer, or to make a report and pay tax, makes a grossly incorrect report, or makes a report that is fraudulent, the Department of Revenue must make an assessment for the taxable period from an estimate based upon the best information then available to it (Sec. 212.12(5)(B), Sec. 212.12(7), Sec. 212.14(1)). The Department will collect the taxes, interest, and penalties due based on the assessment, which is considered *prima facie* correct. The burden to show that the assessment is incorrect is on the taxpayer.

Collection fee: The Department of Revenue must collect an administrative collection processing fee to offset payment processing and administrative costs incurred by the state due to late payment of a collection event. A "collection event" occurs when a taxpayer fails to timely file a complete return, pay the full amount of tax reported on a return, or timely pay the full amount due resulting from an audit after all appeal rights have expired. The fee is equal to 10% of the total amount of tax, penalty, and interest which remains unpaid after 90 days, or $10 for each collection event, whichever is greater.

The department will collect the fee within 90 days following the initial notification of the collection event. If the taxpayer demonstrates that the failure to pay was due to extraordinary circumstances, the department may waive or reduce the fee. (Sec. 213.24; *Tax Information Publication, No. 09ADM-02*, Florida Department of Revenue, June 11, 2009, CCH FLORIDA TAX REPORTS, ¶ 205-343)

¶ 347   Audit Procedures

The Department of Revenue is empowered to audit and examine the accounts, books, or records of all people subject to revenue laws (Sec. 212.12(5)(a), Sec. 212.13(1), Sec. 212.34). The Department may, as a result of the audit, credit any overpayment of tax and assess any underpayment of tax. No administrative finding of fact is necessary prior to the assessment of a deficiency. At the conclusion of an audit, the Department will issue a Notice of Intent to Make Audit Changes, which results in the issuance of an assessment after 30 days if the taxpayer does not request a conference (Rule 12A-1.056(1)).

The Department must send written notification informing the taxpayer of an audit at least 60 days prior to the date an auditor is scheduled to begin the audit (Sec. 212.13(5)(a), Rule 12A-1.093). The Department is not required to give 60-day prior notification if the taxpayer requests an emergency audit or in the case of a distress or jeopardy situation.

Dealers must keep the records required by the Department of Revenue (Sec. 212.12(6)(a), Sec. 212.13, Sec. 212.35, Rule 12A-1.093(2)). Books and records must be available for examination at reasonable hours (Sec. 212.13). The Department is authorized to issue subpoenas or subpoenas duces tecum compelling the attendance and testimony of witnesses and the production of books, records, written materials, and electronically recorded information (Sec. 212.14(7)).

If the records of the dealer are adequate, but voluminous, the Department may use a sample of the records to project the amount of taxable sales or purchases to total sales or purchases (Sec. 212.12(b)(c)).

For information on dealing with audit results, see GT-800004, Florida Department of Revenue, July 2015, CCH FLORIDA TAX REPORTS, ¶ 206-071.

Voluntary disclosure program: Voluntary disclosure is the process of reporting and paying previously unpaid or underpaid tax liabilities without being penalized. For frequently asked questions about the program and contact information, see *GT-800053*, Florida Department of Revenue, July 2015, CCH FLORIDA TAX REPORTS, ¶ 206-072.

• Communication services tax

An audit of a dealer of communications services performed by the Department will include a determination of the dealer's compliance with the jurisdictional location of its customers' service addresses and a determination of whether the rate collected for the local tax is correct (Sec. 202.37).

¶ 348   Statute of Limitations

The Department of Revenue may determine and assess the amount of any tax, penalty, or interest that is due (1) within three years after the date the tax is due, the return is due, or the return is filed, whichever is later, (2) within six years after the date a taxpayer either makes a substantial underpayment of tax or files a substantially incorrect return, (3) at any time while the right to a refund or credit of the tax is available to the taxpayer, (4) at any time after the taxpayer has failed to make any required payment of the tax, has failed to file a required return, or has filed a grossly false or fraudulent return, or (5) in any case in which there has been an erroneous refund of tax, within five years after making such refund, or at any time if it appears that any part of the refund was induced by fraud or the misrepresentation of a material fact (Sec. 95.091, Rule 12A-1.093(7)(a)). The Department of Revenue has the power to determine and assess taxes, penalties, and interest only with respect to those taxes that the Department is authorized to administer (Sec. 95.091(3)(a)1).

The above limitations will be tolled for a period of two years if the Department has issued a notice of intent to conduct an audit or investigation of the taxpayer's account within the applicable period of time. The Department must commence an audit within 120 days after issuing such notice, unless the taxpayer requests a delay (Sec. 95.091(3)(b)). If the taxpayer does not request a delay and the Department does not begin the audit within 120 days, the tolling period terminates.

If administrative or judicial proceedings for review of the assessment or collection start within a period of limitation, the running of the period is tolled during the pendency of the proceeding (Sec. 95.091, Sec. 213.21(1)). The running of the period of limitations on assessment is also tolled if a taxpayer assistance order from the Taxpayers' Rights Advocate is requested.

The statutory limitations may be extended by written agreement between the taxpayer and the Department of Revenue before the expiration of the time period (Sec. 213.23, Rule 12-16.001—Rule 12-16.005). Subsequent agreements may extend the time period when made before the expiration of the period previously agreed upon.

¶ 349   Application for Refund

Applications for refunds must be filed within three years after the date on which the tax was paid (Sec. 215.26(2)). See ¶ 345 concerning refunds for tax incentive programs.

Form DR-26S must be used to apply for a refund (Rules 12-26.003 and 12-26.004).

Refunds on exempt transactions: In order to obtain a refund of sales taxes paid with respect to an incentive program, a taxpayer must hold an unrevoked refund permit issued before the purchase for which a refund is sought (Sec. 212.095(2)). To procure a permit, the taxpayer must file an application stating an intent to file an application for refund for the current calendar year. Other information must also be furnished if the Department so requests.

When a sale is made to a person who claims to be entitled to a refund, the seller must make out a sales invoice containing (1) the name and business address of the purchaser, (2) a description of the item or services sold, (3) the date on which the purchase was made, (4) the price and amount of tax paid, (5) the name and place of business of the seller at which the sale was made, and (6) the refund permit number of the purchaser (Sec. 212.095(3)(a)). Only a registered or authorized dealer may execute a sales invoice.

The sales invoice must be retained by the purchaser for attachment to the application for refund (Sec. 212.095(3)(b)). Proof of payment of tax must also be attached.

The application must be filed with the Department no later than 30 days immediately following the quarter for which the refund is claimed (Sec. 212.095(4)(a)). A claim filed after 30 days must be accompanied by a justified excuse for late filing. In such case, the late filing may be accepted through 60 days following the quarter. Only refunds of $5 or more in any quarter are authorized unless the application is made upon forms prescribed by the Department. Claims for refund are filed and paid for each calendar quarter. A fee of $2 is deducted for each claim (Sec. 212.095(4)(b)).

Assignment of right to refund: A dealer may give a customer an assignment of rights to a refund of Florida sales tax so that the customer may seek a refund directly from the Department of Revenue. The department does not have the authority to require a dealer to refund tax directly to a customer. The department may issue a refund to the dealer or the dealer's assigns. A dealer who receives a refund request from a customer may either refund the tax directly to the customer through a direct refund or a credit or the dealer can provide the customer with an assignment of right so that the customer can seek the refund from the department. The dealer should maintain documentary proof, such as an invoice or cancelled check, that the tax was paid by the customer to the dealer, as well as any other documentation necessary to substantiate the customer's right to the refund. (*Technical Assistance Advisement, No. 10A-048,* Florida Department of Revenue, November 17, 2010, released January 2011, CCH FLORIDA TAX REPORTS, ¶ 205-598)

• **Communication services tax**

Any amount of communication services tax paid by a purchaser in excess of the amount due will be refunded regardless of whether the dealer files a written claim for refund (Sec. 202.23). The Department may, however, require the dealer to file a statement affirming that the dealer made the overpayment. The refund must be made within three years. If any refund exceeds the amount due the dealer, no penalties or interest will apply if the dealer reimburses the Department within 60 days of receiving notice of the error.

¶ 350   GEORGIA

¶ 351   Scope of Tax

Source.—Statutory references are to Chapter 8, Title 48, of the Georgia Code, as amended to date. Details are reported in the CCH GEORGIA STATE TAX REPORTS starting at ¶ 60-000.

Georgia sales and use taxes are imposed on the retail purchase, retail sale, rental, storage, use, or consumption of tangible personal property and certain services (Sec. 48-8-30(a)). These taxes are intended to cover all such purchases, uses, and services as provided in the law to the extent permitted under the federal and state Constitutions, with due regard being paid to the specific exemptions permitted by the sales and use tax provisions (Sec. 48-8-1). "Tangible personal property" is personal property that can be seen, weighed, measured, felt, or touched or that is in any other manner perceptible to the senses, and includes electricity, water, gas, steam, and prewritten computer software (Sec. 48-8-2(37)).

The sales and use taxes are in addition to all other taxes (Sec. 48-8-30(i)).

• **Use tax**

"Use tax" is imposed on the use, consumption, distribution, and storage of tangible personal property within the state (Sec. 48-8-2(13)). The use, consumption, distribution, or storage for use or consumption in Georgia of tangible personal property is equivalent to a sale at retail (Sec. 48-8-34(b)).

The owner or user of any tangible personal property that is purchased at retail outside Georgia is considered to be a dealer and is liable for a tax on the cost price of the property upon the first instance of use, consumption, distribution, or storage of the property in Georgia (Sec. 48-8-30(c)). A person who leases or rents tangible personal property outside of Georgia is considered to be a dealer when the property is first used within the state and is liable for a tax on the rental charge paid to the lessor (Sec. 48-8-30(e)).

The use of property by a person who acquires the property from another person where both persons have 100% common ownership of the property is exempt from tax if the sales or use tax was previously paid or credit was allowed for taxes paid to another state (Sec. 48-8-3(42)).

• **Services**

A person who has purchased or received any service within Georgia, the purchase of which is a "retail sale," is subject to tax on the gross charge or charges made for the purchase (Sec. 48-8-30(f)). This tax must be paid by the purchaser or recipient of the service to the service provider. However, a sale of services is not taxable to the service provider if it is not taxable to the purchaser of the service.

• **Incidence of tax**

The sales and use taxes are imposed on both the purchaser or lessee, the retail vendor or lessor, or the purchaser and provider of taxable services, but the measure of tax is different (Sec. 48-8-30(b), (c.1), (d), (e.1), and (f)). The tax on the purchaser is imposed on the sales price while the tax on the retail vendor is the greater of the tax based on the vendor's gross sales or the amount of taxes collected from the purchaser. No retail sale, lease, or rental is taxable to the retailer, dealer, or lessor that is not taxable to the purchaser at retail or to the person to whom the property is leased or rented.

Absorption of tax: As a general rule, a retailer cannot advertise or represent to the public that it will absorb all or any part of sales and use tax or that the purchaser is relieved from paying all or any part of the tax (Sec. 48-8-36). Effective July 1, 2012, two exceptions to this rule are:

(1) when the retailer states in the advertisement that the retailer will remit any part of the tax not paid by the purchaser, and

(2) when the retailer gives the purchaser written evidence that the retailer will be liable for and pay any tax the purchaser was relieved from paying.

If a retailer does in fact advertise that any part of the tax not paid by the purchaser will be remitted on the purchaser's behalf by the retailer, the retailer is solely liable for and must pay that part of the tax (Sec. 48-8-36).

Drop shipments: When a Georgia dealer sells to an out-of-state company and drop ships to a Georgia company, the Georgia dealer is required to collect tax or obtain a Certificate of Exemption or multistate jurisdiction exemption certificate from the out-of-state company.

A Georgia dealer is not required to collect Georgia sales and use taxes in the case of a third-party drop shipment if the product is being purchased for resale. In such a case, the purchaser must provide the seller with sufficient documentation that the product is being purchased for purposes of resale. The Uniform Sales & Use Tax Certificate—Multijurisdiction or an exemption certificate from the purchaser's state bearing their resale registration number, is considered sufficient documentation that the transaction is not a retail sale. However, such documentation is not sufficient proof if:

(1) the purchaser is a real property contractor,

(2) the exemption certificate is not accepted in good faith or is improperly completed,

(3) the purchaser's normal course of business is not that of a seller of the products being purchased as indicated on the exemption certificate,

(4) the transaction documents do not show that delivery was made to a person other than the purchaser,

(5) the purchaser has nexus with Georgia and is required to be registered, or

(6) the seller and purchaser are affiliated entities or persons in any way, for any purpose, or the seller performs any services in Georgia that are related to the sale, regardless of whether these services are performed under a separate agreement on the purchaser's behalf.

(*Georgia Sales and Use Tax Policy Statement for Third-Party Drop Shipment Transactions,* Georgia Department of Revenue, revised December 4, 2008, CCH GEORGIA TAX REPORTS, ¶ 200-708)

Online travel companies and hotel occupancy taxes: The Georgia Supreme Court affirmed a trial court judgment appealed by both parties in an action filed by the city of Atlanta against online travel companies (OTCs) seeking payment of hotel occupancy taxes. The OTCs calculated the local hotel occupancy tax based on the wholesale room rate. The city's action alleged that the tax should be calculated on the retail room rate charged to customers. Though no Georgia state or local governing authority required the OTCs to collect the tax, customers paid the Atlanta tax to the OTCs at issue under the OTCs' business model through a line item of "taxes and fees" and paid tax to no other entity.

The supreme court agreed with the trial court that the "rent" for occupying a hotel room in the city, and upon which the tax is based, is the room rate that the customer pays because the ordinance and enabling statute impose the tax on the customer occupying the room. More specifically, the statute and ordinance do not tax any transaction between nonoccupants such as an OTC and a hotel. The supreme court also upheld the injunction requiring the OTCs that voluntarily collect and remit the tax to do so on the retail rate (and to maintain records to this end) because the injunction reflected the voluntary nature of the tax collection. (*City of Atlanta v. Hotels.com,* Georgia Supreme Court, Nos. S11A0508, S11X0509, S11A0510, and S11X0512, May 16, 2011, CCH GEORGIA TAX REPORTS, ¶ 200-765)

¶351 **Georgia**

- **Nexus**

Every "retailer" or "dealer" doing business in Georgia and making sales of tangible personal property for use, consumption, distribution, or storage in Georgia, not otherwise exempted, must collect sales or use tax from the purchaser (Sec. 48-8-30(b)(1)). A "retailer" means every person making sales at retail or for distribution, use, consumption, or storage for use or consumption in Georgia (Sec. 48-8-2(32)).

Under Sec. 48-8-65(b)(2), a person or business outside Georgia engages in an activity within Georgia giving rise to a tax liability when the person or business:

(1) is a "dealer,"

(2) performs or carries on any employment, trade, business, profession, or any other act or activity for financial gain or profit within Georgia, such as, for example, the rental of real or personal property located in Georgia or the sale, exchange, or other disposition of tangible or intangible property having a situs in Georgia; or

(3) operates personally or through partners, employees, agents, or otherwise in Georgia so as to incur any liability or obligation with respect to the payment or collection of Georgia sales and use taxes.

A "dealer" is defined at Sec. 48-8-2(8), and, effective October 1, 2012, includes any person who:

— maintains or utilizes an office, distribution center, salesroom or sales office, warehouse, service enterprise, or any other place of business, whether owned by that person or any other person, other than a common carrier acting in its capacity as such, and.

— makes sales of tangible personal property or services that are subject to sales and use tax if any other person (other than a common carrier acting in its capacity as such) who has a substantial nexus in Georgia:

(1) delivers, installs, assembles, or performs maintenance services for the person's customers within the state;

(2) facilitates the person's delivery of property to customers in Georgia by allowing the person's customers to pick up property sold by the person at an office, distribution facility, warehouse, storage place, or similar place of business maintained by the person in Georgia; or

(3) conducts any other activities in Georgia that are significantly associated with the person's ability to establish and maintain a market in the state for the person's sales.

The presumption that such a person qualifies as a dealer in Georgia can be rebutted by showing that the person does not have a physical presence in the state and that any in-state activities conducted on its behalf are not significantly associated with the person's ability to establish and maintain a market in the state.

Affiliate nexus: With certain exceptions, a "dealer" includes an affiliate that sells at retail, offers for sale at retail in Georgia, or engages in the regular or systematic solicitation of a consumer market in Georgia through a related dealer located in Georgia. (See Sec. 48-8-2(8)(J), Code)

Effective October 1, 2012, it is rebuttably presumed that a "dealer" is one who makes sales of tangible personal property or services that are subject to sales and use tax if a "related member" (other than a common carrier acting in its capacity as such) that has substantial nexus in Georgia (1) sells a similar line of products as the person and does so under the same or a similar business name; or (2) uses trademarks, service marks, or trade names in Georgia that are the same or substantially similar to those used by the person. (Sec. 48-8-2(8)(K), Code)

"Click-through" nexus: Effective July 18, 2012, the definition of "dealer " was expanded to include a rebuttable presumption that any person who enters into an agreement with one or more persons who are Georgia residents under which the resident(s), for a commission or other consideration, based on completed sales, directly or indirectly refers potential customers (whether by a link on an Internet website, an in-person oral presentation, telemarketing, or otherwise) to the person, if the cumulative gross receipts from sales by the person to customers in Georgia who are referred to the person by all residents with such an agreement with the person exceed $50,000 during the preceding 12 months. (Sec. 48-8-2(8)(M), Code)

Trade show exclusion: As of October 1, 2012, a "dealer" for sales and use tax purposes expressly excludes a person whose only activity in Georgia is to engage in "convention and trade show activity" as described in IRC Sec. 513(d)(3)(A), so long as these activities are the dealer's sole physical presence in Georgia and the dealer (including any of its representatives, agents, salespersons, canvassers, independent contractors, or solicitors) (1) does not engage in the convention or trade show activities for more than five days (in whole or in part) in Georgia during any 12-month period; and (2) did not derive more than $100,000 of net income from these activities in the state during the prior calendar year. (Sec. 48-8-2(8), Code)

- **Streamlined Act status**

Georgia became a full member of the Governing Board of the Streamlined Sales and Use Tax Agreement, effective August 1, 2011, after enacting the necessary legislation (Sec. 48-8-160 *et seq.*). As a full member state, Georgia can vote on amendments to or interpretations of the Agreement and can vote to determine whether a petitioning state is in compliance with the Agreement. Georgia is also eligible as a full member state to have a representative serve on the SST Compliance Review and Interpretations Committee (CRIC). For additional information on Georgia's compliance with the SST Agreement, see ¶ 357.

The full text of the Agreement and Georgia's taxability matrix can be found on the SST Governing Board's Web site at **http://www.streamlinedsalestax.org/**.

¶ 352   Tax Base

Tax imposed on purchasers is based on the "sales price" of each purchase (Sec. 48-8-30(b) and (c.1)). On the first instance of use, consumption, distribution, or storage in Georgia of property purchased at retail out of state, tax is imposed on the owner or user on the basis of the cost price of the property (Sec. 48-8-30(c)). In the event of a lease or rental, the tax is imposed upon the gross "lease or rental" charge (Sec. 48-8-30(d) and (e.1)). The tax on the purchase of services is based on the gross charge made for the purchase (Sec. 48-8-30(f)).

In conformity with the SST Agreement, the definition of "sales price" lists the following items as not to be deducted from the sales price:

(1) the seller's cost of the property;

(2) the cost of materials used, labor, or service cost, interest, losses, all of the seller's transportation costs, all taxes imposed on the seller, and any other expense of the seller;

(3) charges by the seller for any services necessary to complete the sale; and

(4) delivery charges (except separately stated postage charges for delivery of direct mail; see Sec. 48-8-2(10)).

References to installation charges are removed from this list. Further, now expressly excluded from the definition of "sales price" is "credit for any trade-in." No longer expressly excluded from the definition of "sales price" are separately stated charges imposed by a seller for services necessary to complete a sale. (Sec. 48-8-2(34)(A))

"Cost price" means the actual cost of tangible personal property without deductions for the cost of materials used, labor costs, service costs, transportation charges, or other expenses of any kind (Sec. 48-8-2(2)).

The sales and use taxes are imposed on both the purchaser or lessee, the retail vendor or lessor, or the purchaser and provider of taxable services, but the measure of tax is different (Sec. 48-8-30). The tax on the purchaser is imposed on the sales price while the tax on the retail vendor is the greater of the tax based on the vendor's gross sales or the amount of taxes collected from the purchaser.

Taxability matrix: Georgia's taxability matrix is available on the SST Governing Board's website at **http://www.streamlinedsalestax.org/otm**.

¶ 353   List of Exemptions, Exceptions, and Exclusions

Unless otherwise indicated, the statutory exemptions listed below apply to both sales and use taxes; those applicable only to the use tax are listed separately. Items that are excluded from the sales or use tax base are treated at ¶ 352, "Tax Base." For information on the documentation required for each exemption, see *Georgia Sales and Use Tax Exemptions*, June 1, 2014, CCH GEORGIA TAX REPORTS, ¶ 200-912.

Sales tax holidays: Georgia does not have a permanent sales tax holiday, but has designated weekends on August 1-2, 2014 and on July 30-August 1, 2015, during which sales tax does not apply to purchases of (Sec. 48-8-3(75)):

(1) clothing and footwear with a sales price of $100 or less per article or pair, excluding accessories;

(2) single purchases for noncommercial use of $1,000 or less of computers, computer components, and prewritten computer software; and

(3) noncommercial purchases of general school supplies priced at up to $20 per item, including school supplies, school art supplies, school computer supplies, and school instructional materials.

In addition, energy-efficient (Energy Star) and water-efficient (WaterSense) products with a sales price of $1,500 or less are exempt on October 3-5, 2014 and on October 2-4, 2015. Eligible products include Energy Star-designated dishwashers, clothes washers, air conditioners, ceiling fans, fluorescent light bulbs, dehumidifiers, programmable thermostats, refrigerators, doors, and windows. (Sec. 48-8-3(82))

Additional information on tax holidays is available in Reg. Sec. 560-12-2-.110.

• **Sales and use tax exemptions, exceptions, and exclusions**

Admissions to major sporting events (exp. 12/31/2022)	Sec. 48-8-3[97]
Advertising inserts or supplements, printed	Sec. 48-8-3(61)
Agricultural commodities not sold as finished product	Sec. 48-8-5
Agricultural commodities commissions, sales to	Sec. 48-8-3(6.3)
Agricultural producers, sales to	Sec. 48-8-3.3(b)
Aircraft engine remanufacturing	Sec. 48-8-3(34.2)
Aircraft parts	Sec. 48-8-3(86)
Airlines, purchases of food and nonalcoholic beverages	Sec. 48-8-3(81)
Art sales to exempt organizations for use by museums	Sec. 48-8-3(14)

Bibles and other religious materials (exemption enjoined; see *Budlong v. Graham,* U.S. District Court for the Northern District of Georgia, 1:05-CV-2910-RWS, May 16, 2007, CCH GEORGIA TAX REPORTS, ¶ 200-556) . . . . Sec. 48-8-3(15(A), (16) (held unconstitutional 2/6/06))

Biomass material . . . . Sec. 48-8-3(83)

Blood banks . . . . Sec. 48-8-3(46)

Business reorganizations . . . . Sec. 48-8-3(21)

Cargo containers . . . . Sec. 48-8-3(39.1)

Child services organizations . . . . Sec. 48-8-3(41)

Clean room equipment . . . . Sec. 48-8-3(60)

Coin-operated amusement devices . . . . Sec. 48-8-3(43)

Coins, currency, or bullion . . . . Sec. 48-8-3(66)

Computer equipment, large sales . . . . Sec. 48-8-3(68)

Computer software, prewritten, delivered electronically or by load and leave . . . . Sec. 48-8-3(91)

Construction, alternative fuel facilities . . . . Sec. 48-8-3(34.4)

Construction, government property used and consumed . . . . Sec. 48-8-63(g)(1)

Construction materials, projects of regional significance (exp. 6/30/2019) . . . . Sec. 48-8-3(93)

Crab bait . . . . Sec. 48-8-3(48)

Daughters of the American Revolution, sales to . . . . Sec. 48-8-2(7.2)

Electricity used in manufacturing . . . . Sec. 48-8-3(90); Sec. 48-8-3.2

Eyeglasses and contact lenses (prescription) . . . . Sec. 48-8-3(47)

Food and food ingredients consumed in private schools . . . . Sec. 48-8-3(13)

Food and food ingredients (except drugs) donated for hunger relief (exp. 6/30/2021) . . . . Sec. 48-8-3(57.2)

Food and food ingredients (except drugs) donated for disaster relief (exp. 6/30/2020) . . . . Sec. 48-8-3(57.3)

Food and food ingredients sold to a qualified food bank (exp. 6/30/2021) . . . . Sec. 48-8-3(57.1)

Food stamp purchases . . . . Sec. 48-8-3(53)

Foreign educational or cultural institute . . . . Sec. 48-8-3(11)

Fuel for commercial fishing vessels . . . . Sec. 48-8-3(65)

Fuel for jet aircraft operated by qualifying air carriers at major airports . . . . Sec. 48-8-3(33.1)

Fuel for plant nursery structures . . . . Sec. 48-8-3(76)

Fuel for ships . . . . Sec. 48-8-3(17)

Funeral merchandise purchased from Crime Victims' Fund . . . . Sec. 48-8-3(63)

Georgia Aviation Authority . . . . Sec. 6-5-3

Georgia Medical Center Authority . . . . Sec. 20-15-6

Girl Scout cookies . . . . Sec. 48-8-3(59)

Government, sales to . . . . Sec. 48-8-3(1)

Grass sod sold by the producer . . . . Sec. 48-8-3(62)

Hearing aids . . . . Sec. 48-8-3(52)

Private school meals	Sec. 48-8-3(13)
Professional services	Sec. 48-8-3(22)
Property purchased by nonresidents moving into state	Sec. 48-8-3(19)
Public school transactions	Sec. 48-8-3(39)
Public transit authority sales	Sec. 48-8-3(4)
Public utility systems	Sec. 48-8-3(2)
Religious institutions, certain sales by	Sec. 48-8-3(15)(B), Sec. 48-8-3(15.1)
Religious publications (exemption enjoined; see *Budlong v. Graham,* U.S. District Court for the Northern District of Georgia, 1:05-CV-2910-RWS, May 16, 2007, CCH GEORGIA TAX REPORTS, ¶ 200-556)	Sec. 48-8-3(15(A), (16) (held unconstitutional 2/6/06))
Repair services	Sec. 48-8-3(23)
Resales	Sec. 48-8-2(6)(A), Sec. 48-8-38, Sec. 48-8-40
Rock Eagle 4-H Center	Sec. 48-8-3(38)
School events	Sec. 48-8-3(39)
School lunches	Sec. 48-8-3(12), (13)
State, county, or local government purchases	Sec. 48-8-3(1)
Supplies for ships	Sec. 48-8-3(17)
Transportation equipment for use in interstate commerce	Sec. 48-8-3(32), Sec. 48-8-3(33)
Transportation fares when for-hire master license is applicable (exp. 6/30/17)	Sec. 48-8-3(25)
Transportation of tangible personal property	Sec. 48-8-3(18)
U.S. government transactions	Sec. 48-8-3(1), Sec. 48-8-3(2), Sec. 48-8-63(f)
University system of Georgia	Sec. 48-8-3(8)
Urban transit	Sec. 48-8-3(5)
Water	Sec. 48-8-3(20)
Water conservation equipment	Sec. 48-8-3(36.1)
Wheelchairs	Sec. 48-8-3(72)

• Use tax exemptions

Farmer's use of self-produced agricultural products	Sec. 48-8-4

¶ 354   Rate of Tax

The state sales and use tax rate is 4% of the tax base (Sec. 48-8-30(b), (c), (c1), (d), (e), (e1), and (f), Code).

Motor fuels: Joint sales and use taxes levied on sales of motor fuels are 1% of the retail sales price of the motor fuel that is not more than $3.00 per gallon (Sec. 48-8-82, Code). The same holds true for county special purpose local option sales taxes, county sales and use taxes for education purposes, and water and sewer projects and costs taxes (Sec. 48-8-110.1, Code). Sales of motor fuel for highway use are exempt from the 4% state sales and use tax (Sec. 48-8-3.1, Code).

¶354   Georgia

Motor vehicles: Motor vehicles purchased on or after March 1, 2013, and titled in Georgia are exempt from sales and use tax and the annual *ad valorem* property tax, also known as the "birthday tax." These taxes are replaced by a one-time tax called the title *ad valorem* tax (TAVT) that is imposed at the rate of 6.5% on the fair market value of the vehicle at the time the vehicle is titled. Non-titled vehicles such as trailers and other non-motorized vehicles remain subject to ad valorem tax.

See also *Informational Bulletin,* Georgia Department of Revenue, March 6, 2013, CCH GEORGIA TAX REPORTS, ¶ 200-846 and *Informational Bulletin,* Georgia Department of Revenue, March 5, 2013, CCH GEORGIA TAX REPORTS, ¶ 200-849.

Consumer fireworks: A 5% excise tax is imposed on the sale within the state of consumer fireworks, as defined. The excise tax is paid by the seller and is due and payable in the same way as the state sales and use tax. (Sec. 25-10-1, Code; *Fireworks Excise Tax FAQs,* Georgia Department of Revenue, June 26, 2015, CCH GEORGIA TAX REPORTS, ¶ 200-993)

Hotel fees: Innkeepers in Georgia must charge a fee of $5.00 per night to a customer for each calendar day that a room, lodging, or accommodation is rented or leased. This fee does not apply with respect to extended stay rentals. The fee is to be collected by the innkeeper when the customer pays for the rental or lease, and the innkeeper must remit the fee on a monthly basis to the Georgia Department of Revenue. (Sec. 48-13-50.3(b), Code; see also *State Hotel-Motel Fee FAQ,* Georgia Department of Revenue, February 2016, CCH GEORGIA TAX REPORTS, ¶ 201-035)

¶ 355 Local Taxes

The joint county and municipal sales and use tax, the homestead option sales and use tax, the special county sales and use tax (Secs. 48-8-82, 48-8-110, Code), and the educational local option sales and use tax (Sec. 48-8-141, Code) are imposed at the rate of 1%. Beginning March 1, 2017, the Metropolitan Atlanta Rapid Transit Authority (MARTA) tax is imposed at the rate of 1.5% (previously, 1%) through June 30, 2057, and thereafter at the rate of 0.5% (Metropolitan Atlanta Rapid Transit Authority Act, Sec. 25).

Transportation: Only one transportation special purpose local option sales tax (T-SPLOST) can be imposed within a regional special district at one time (Sec. 48-8-245(c)(1)). The tax remains in effect for 10 years and is imposed at a rate of 1% (Sec. 48-8-241). The 12 special districts created for purposes of imposing the tax correspond with the boundaries of Georgia's 12 existing regional commissions, as set out in Sec. 50-8-4(f).

However, with voter consent, a special district mass transportation sales and use tax of up to 1% may be imposed on or after July 1, 2016, by a county that is not located within a special district that levies a T-SPLOST, that is a mass transportation regional system participant, and in which there is currently being levied and collected (1) a county special purpose local option sales tax; (2) a tax levied pursuant to a local constitutional amendment for purposes of a metropolitan area system of public transportation; or (3) a joint county and municipal sales and use tax. Such a county that is not a mass transportation regional system participant can levy the tax on or after July 1, 2017. (Sec. 48-8-261, Code)

Lodging taxes: Counties and municipalities are authorized to impose a tourism tax on charges for lodging and accommodations (Sec. 48-13-51, Code). The rate is generally limited to 3%, although certain counties and cities are authorized rates up to 8%, which is the tax rate in Atlanta.

Telecommunications: Georgia has adopted the provisions of the federal Mobile Telecommunications Sourcing Act (P.L. 106-252), under which wireless telecommunications are sourced to the customer's primary place of use, which is the residential or primary business address of the customer and which must be located in the service provider's licensed service area (Sec. 46-5-134, Code). The jurisdiction in which the primary place of use is located is the only jurisdiction that may tax telecommunications services, regardless of the customer's location when an actual call is placed or received.

Counties and municipalities that operate a 911 public safety answering point, and that meet certain conditions, can impose the prepaid wireless 911 fee by ordinance or resolution (Sec. 46-5-134.2(b)(1)). The Georgia Department of Revenue administers the prepaid wireless 911 fee.

Local tax rates: Charts of combined current and historical state and local tax rates by county are available at **http://dor.georgia.gov/sales-tax-rates-current-historical-and-upcoming**.

¶ 356   Bracket Schedule

In conformity with the SST Agreement, tax computation must be carried to the third decimal place and the tax rounded to a whole cent using a method that rounds up to the next cent when the third decimal place is greater than four. (Sec. 48-8-31).

¶ 357   Returns, Payments, and Due Dates

Sales and use tax returns are filed on a calendar month basis during the first six months from the date of registration (Reg. Sec. 560-12-1-.22). Thereafter, dealers may be permitted to file sales and use tax returns on a quarterly, annual, or special period basis as specified below. The dealer must request permission in writing and receive written approval by the Commissioner or a designee.

Returns are due on the 20th of the month following the end of the payment period (Sec. 48-8-49(a)).

Quarterly filing: Dealers whose sales and use tax liability for a consecutive six-month period has averaged less than $200 per month may be permitted to file returns and make payments on a quarterly basis for the three-month periods ending on the last days of March, June, September, and December (Reg. Sec. 560-12-1-.22).

Annual filing: Dealers whose sales and use tax liability for a consecutive six-month period has averaged less than $50 per month may be permitted to file returns and make payments on an annual, calendar year basis (Reg. Sec. 560-12-1-.22).

Special period filing: Dealers may be permitted to file returns on a special period other than monthly with the approval of the Commissioner. Dealers permitted to file on a special period basis must submit annually by November 1 to the Department the specific reporting periods for the next calender year (Reg. Sec. 560-12-1-.22).

Filing status changes: If a dealer's tax liability exceeds the limitations established for quarterly or annual filing, or if the Commissioner should determine that a loss of revenue might result from permitting such dealer to file on a quarterly or annual basis, a dealer may be required to return to a monthly or quarterly filing basis (Reg. Sec. 560-12-1-.22). Failure to file a quarterly, annual, or special period report on time or to remit the taxes due with the return is grounds for returning the dealer to a monthly or quarterly filing basis.

The Commissioner will provide all necessary forms (ST-3) for filing returns and instructions (Sec. 48-8-58(b), Reg. Sec. 560-12-3-.04). Amended returns are filed on Form ST3AR (Reg. Sec. 560-12-3-.06). Failure of a dealer to secure the forms does not relieve the dealer from the timely payment of the tax (Sec. 48-8-58(b)).

A dealer must include on its return the dealer's certificate of registration number, the registration numbers for each sales location or affiliated entity of the dealer, and the dealer's master number (provided such a number has been assigned by the Department of Revenue) (Sec. 48-8-50). In general, an "affiliated entity" is an entity that the dealer owns, is owned by, or is otherwise related to the dealer by common ownership or control (Sec. 48-8-50).

¶356   Georgia

• Payment

The Georgia Tax Center (GTC) has replaced the former e-File and e-Pay systems for reporting and paying sales and use taxes. Information on registration for the GTC is available at **https://gtc.dor.ga.gov/_/**.

The amount of tax shown on a return must be remitted with the return (Sec. 48-2-30, Sec. 48-2-38). Unless payment by electronic funds transfer is required, payment may be made in cash, check, or postal, bank, or express money orders (Sec. 48-2-31, Sec. 48-2-32). Upon request, the Commissioner will give a receipt for sums collected (Sec. 48-2-33).

Electronic filing and payment: Dealers required to pay by EFT must also file electronically. Electronic funds transfer is required when the liability in connection with any return, report, or other document pertaining to sales tax, use tax, personal income tax withholding, or motor fuel distributor tax exceeds $500. (Sec. 48-2-32(2.1); Reg. Sec. 560-3-2-.26, Reg. Sec. 560-3-2-.27)

Any Georgia taxpayer that is required to file a return electronically but fails to do so will be deemed to have failed to make the required filing, In addition to applicable penalties, the failure to make the required filing will result in the forfeiture of the compensation of dealers for reporting and paying tax because such compensation is allowed only if the return is timely filed. A taxpayer may be granted a waiver of this electronic filing requirement in cases of undue hardship. Further, no penalty will be assessed if the failure was due to reasonable cause and not due to gross or willful neglect or disregard of the laws and regulations. (Sec. 48-2-44.1)

Estimated tax: If a dealer's tax liability in the preceding calendar year was greater than $60,000 (excluding local sales taxes), the dealer must file a return and remit to the state revenue commissioner at least 50% of the estimated tax liability for the taxable period on or before the 20th day of the period (Sec. 48-8-49(b)(2)).

Vendor's compensation: Dealers filing timely returns and payments are entitled to retain a percentage of the tax as vendor's compensation (Sec. 48-8-50). The amount that may be retained is equal to 3% of the first $3000 of sales and use taxes collected for each location, and 0.5% of the remainder, except that in the case of sales and use taxes on sales of motor fuel, the dealer may retain 3% of the total, without limitation. See also ¶ 358.

• Direct payment

When the State Revenue Commissioner deems it impractical or inequitable for a taxpayer to pay sales and use tax separately due to the operation of his or her business, the taxpayer may be given a direct payment permit (Reg. Sec. 560-12-1-.16.) The direct payment permit will be issued only upon written application. In such cases, the taxpayer reports and pays tax directly to the Georgia Department of Revenue on all taxable purchases of property or services. The taxpayer furnishes each seller of tangible personal property or taxable services with a photographic copy of the permit or Certificate of Exemption bearing the registration number. The placement of such registration number on the taxpayer's purchase orders is sufficient to relieve sellers or dealers from collecting the sales or use tax due. (Reg. Sec. 560-12-1-.16)

Expiration: All direct payment authorization permits, letters, and certificates issued before October 1, 2016, expired on December 31, 2016, and cannot be used to make purchases after that date. Direct payment permits issued from October 1, 2016, forward are effective January 1, 2017, or the date of issuance, whichever is later. Direct payment permit applications are available through the Georgia Tax Center (GTC) website, **https://gtc.dor.ga.gov/_/**.

Beginning January 1, 2017, direct payment permit holders, for the privilege of using the permit, waive interest on refunds of taxes remitted on purchases made using the permit (Reg. Sec. 560-12-1-.16).

- **Payment or return date falling on holiday or weekend**

If the date prescribed for filing a return or paying tax is on a Saturday, Sunday or legal holiday, the return or payment may be made on the next day that is not a Saturday, Sunday or legal holiday (Sec. 48-2-39, Reg. Sec. 560-12-1-.22(6)).

Return and remittance dates are specified at **http://dor.georgia.gov/documents/20162017-sales-and-use-tax-timely-remittance-schedule**.

- **Uniform Sales Tax Administration Act**

Georgia became a full member of the Governing Board of the Streamlined Sales Tax Agreement on August 1, 2011. The Georgia Department of Revenue has released an informational bulletin detailing the conformity of its administrative policy to the Agreement, summarized as follows (*Informational Bulletin SUT 2010-10-13*, Georgia Department of Revenue, revised December 3, 2010):

Rate changes.—When there is a state-level sales or use tax rate or base change, the department will make a reasonable effort to provide as much advance notice to sellers as possible, limit the effective date to the first day of a calendar quarter, and notify sellers of changes in the tax base made by the Legislature or changes made to sales and use tax rules and regulations by the department. The department will treat the education local option sales tax (LOST) consistently with other local sales and use taxes by limiting the effective date for rate changes to the first day of a calendar quarter after a minimum of 60 days' notice.

Exemptions.—Sellers must use the standard form adopted by the SST Governing Board for claiming an exemption electronically. In addition, the department does not require a Model 4 seller to submit simplified electronic return part 2 information when that seller has no legal obligation to register in Georgia.

Telecommunications.—tax applies to local telephone services, which includes charges for local exchange telephone services, mobile wireless telephone services ("cellular telephone services"), and guaranteed charges for semi-public coinbox telephone services. Tax applies to vertical services, but does not apply to private communication services. The bulletin also contains telecommunications sourcing definitions such as "air-to-ground radiotelephone service" and "call-by-call basis,"

Other items.—The bulletin also discusses privacy protection under Model 1, outlines uniform rules for the recovery of bad debts, and details the amnesty provided to sellers that registered with the SST Centralized Registration System before the state joined the Agreement.

Numerous sales and use tax definitions and other changes have been enacted into law to conform to the SST Agreement (H.B. 1221, Laws 2010). A selective summary includes the following:

Important definitions:

Sales price.—The definition of "gross sales" is removed from the general sales and use tax definition statute. References to "gross sales" in the statute that imposes sales and use tax are replaced with "sales price," which is synonymous with "purchase price" (see ¶ 352);

Retail sale.—The definition of "retail sale" or "sale at retail" means any sale, lease, or rental for any purpose other than resale, sublease, or subrent. The definition is also amended to include the sale of alcoholic beverages when made to a purchaser for purposes other than resale, and charges applied to sales of telephone service that are made for local exchange telephone service (excluding coin operated telephone service) (Sec. 48-8-2(31));

Model 1 seller.—a seller registered under the Agreement that has selected a certified service provider (CSP) as its agent to perform all the seller's sales and use tax functions, other than the seller's obligation to remit tax on its own purchases;

Model 2 seller.—a seller registered under the Agreement that has selected a certified automated system to perform part of its sales and use tax functions, but retains the responsibility for remitting the tax;

Model 3 seller.—a seller registered under the Agreement that has (1) sales in at least five member states, (2) total annual sales revenue of at least $500 million, (3) a proprietary system that calculates the amount of tax due each jurisdiction, and (4) entered into a performance agreement with the member states establishing a tax performance standard for the seller. In this context, a seller includes an affiliated group of sellers utilizing the same proprietary system;

Model 4 seller.—a seller that is not a "Model 1 seller," a "Model 2 seller," or a "Model 3 seller;"

Bundled transaction: A "bundled transaction" is the retail sale of at least two products, except for real property or services to real property, when the products are otherwise distinct and identifiable and are sold for one nonitemized price (Sec. 48-8-2(3)). The term expressly excludes the sale of any products for which the "sales price" varies (or is negotiable) based on the purchaser's selection of the products included in the transaction. If a price is attributable to products that are taxable and products that are nontaxable, the part of the price attributable to the nontaxable products may be subject to tax unless the provider can identify it from its books and records. If the price is attributable to products that are taxable at different tax rates, the total price can be treated as attributable to the products that are subject to tax at the highest tax rate, unless the provider can identify the products subject to tax at the lower rate.

Computer software; digital goods: Definitions related to computer software and digital goods are adopted to conform to the Agreement. "Prewritten computer software" is taxable as tangible personal property. An exemption from sales and use tax is provided for sales of prewritten computer software delivered electronically or by load and leave (Sec. 48-8-2(26); Sec. 48-8-3(91)).

Rate and boundary changes: If there are fewer than 30 days between the enactment of a sales tax rate change and the effective date of the change, a seller will be relieved of liability for failing to collect tax at the new rate if it collected tax at the immediately preceding rate and its failure to collect at the new rate does not continue beyond 30 days after the date of enactment of the new rate. However, this relief from liability does not apply if the state revenue commissioner determines that the seller fraudulently failed to collect at the new rate or fraudulently solicited purchasers based on the immediately preceding rate. For a sales tax rate increase for services covering a period starting before and ending after the statutory effective date, the new rate will apply to the first billing period starting on or after the effective date. For a sales tax rate decrease for services covering a period starting before and ending after the statutory effective date, the new rate will apply to bills rendered on or after the effective date. Local jurisdiction boundary changes, for purposes of sales and use tax only, are effective only on the first day of a calendar quarter after at least 60 days' notice to sellers.

Relief from liability: Sellers and certified service providers (CSPs) will not be liable for charging and collecting an incorrect amount of sales or use tax as a result of its reliance upon erroneous data provided by the state in the taxability matrix or on state and local tax rates, local boundaries, or taxing jurisdiction assignments. A purchaser will be relieved from penalties for failing to pay the correct amount of sales or use tax under the one of the following four circumstances: (1) its seller or CSP relied on erroneous data provided by the state on tax rates, boundaries, taxing jurisdiction assignments, or in the state's taxability matrix; (2) it holds a direct pay permit and relied on such erroneous data; (3) it relied on erroneous data provided in the state's taxability matrix; or (4) in using databases provided by the state, it relied on erroneous data on tax rates, boundaries, or taxing jurisdiction assignments.

General sourcing provisions: The legislation includes general destination-based sourcing provisions that should not be interpreted as imposing sales and use tax with respect to any tangible personal property or service that was not subject to the tax before January 1, 2011. The general sourcing provisions are as follows (Sec. 48-8-77):

(1) If a product is received by the purchaser at a business location of the seller, the sale is sourced to that business location.

(2) If a product is not received by the purchaser at a business location of the seller, the sale is sourced to the location where receipt by the purchaser or the purchaser's donee, as designated by the purchaser, occurs, including the location indicated by instructions known to the seller for delivery to the purchaser or donee.

(3) If the previous two categories do not apply, the sale is sourced to the location indicated by an address for the purchaser available from the seller's business records maintained in the ordinary course of business when using this address does not constitute bad faith.

(4) If the previous three categories do not apply, the sale is sourced to the location indicated by an address for the purchaser obtained during the consummation of the sale, including the address of a purchaser's payment instrument if no other address is available and when using this address does not constitute bad faith.

(5) If the previous four categories do not apply, including when the seller lacks sufficient information to apply these categories, the location is determined by the address from which the tangible personal property was shipped, the digital good or computer software delivered electronically was first available for transmission by the seller, or the service was provided, disregarding any location that merely provided the digital transfer of the product sold.

Specific sourcing provisions apply with respect to leases and rentals, telecommunications services, and direct mail.

Tax computation: The legislation requires that tax computation be carried to the third decimal place, and that the tax to be rounded to a whole cent using a method that rounds up to the next cent when the third decimal place is greater than four (see ¶ 356). The legislation removes the provision authorizing the state revenue commissioner to prepare brackets of prices for the collection of sales and use tax.

Local sale and use taxes: The prohibition against a county, municipality, school district, or other political subdivision in Georgia imposing, levying, or collecting a gross receipts tax, sales tax, use tax, or tax on amusement admissions or services is repealed. Provisions are also amended to state that when a joint county and municipal sales and use tax rate increases from 1% to 2%, or when this tax is newly imposed at a rate of 2%, the amount in excess of 1% does not apply to the sale of motor vehicles. This amendment removes language that the amount in excess of 1% also does not apply to the furnishing for value to the public of rooms, lodging, or accommodations that are subject to the excise tax on rooms, lodgings, and accommodations.

Additional information: For details governing leases and rentals, telecommunications sourcing, nexus, and other areas in the context of the Streamlined Sales and Use Tax (SST) Agreement, see Reg. Sec. 560-12-1-0.21-.38.

¶ 358   Prepayment of Taxes

If the estimated tax liability of a dealer for any taxable period exceeds $5,000, the dealer must file a return and remit to the Commissioner, on or before the 20th day of the period, at least 50% of the estimated tax liability (Sec. 48-8-49(b)). "Estimated tax liability" means a dealer's tax liability adjusted to account for subsequent changes in the state sales and use tax rate based on the dealer's average monthly payments for the last fiscal year. Payment of estimated tax is credited against the amount due on the dealer's return covering the preceding reporting period (Sec. 48-8-49(b)). Estimated tax payments are not required unless, during the prior fiscal year, the dealer's monthly payments exceeded $5,000 per month for at least three consecutive months. Local sales taxes are excluded in determining estimated tax liability.

Prepayments of local taxes on motor fuels: Prepayments of certain local sales and use taxes may be required of distributors of motor vehicle fuels. The prepaid local tax is computed by multiplying the applicable rate imposed by a jurisdiction by the statewide average retail sales price by motor fuel type as determined by the Oil Pricing Information Service, the Energy Information Agency of the United States Department of Energy, or a similar reliable published index, less local sales and use taxes and the state excise tax imposed on distributors (Sec. 48-8-2(5.2); Sec. 48-8-82; Sec. 48-8-110.1(c); *Sales Tax Bulletin: Prepaid Local Tax on Motor Fuel Sales,* Georgia Department of Revenue, November 30, 2016, CCH Georgia Tax Reports, ¶ 201-098; *Policy Bulletin MFT-2015-01,* Georgia Department of Revenue, June 19, 2015, CCH Georgia Tax Reports, ¶ 200-991).

A licensed distributor that purchases motor fuel on which prepaid tax has been imposed, and that resells the fuel to a wholly or partially tax-exempt governmental entity, is entitled to a credit or a refund (Sec. 48-8-30(j)).

¶ 359   **Vendor Registration**

Any person who desires to engage in or conduct business as a seller or dealer in Georgia must file with the Commissioner an application for a certificate of registration (Forms CRF 002, 004, and 005) for each place of business (Sec. 48-8-59, Reg. Sec. 560-12-1-.09, Reg. Sec. 560-12-3-.02). When the application is approved, the Commissioner must issue to the applicant a separate certificate of registration (Form ST-2) for each place of business in the state (Sec. 48-8-59, Reg. Sec. 560-12-1-.09, Reg. Sec. 560-12-3-.03). Each certificate must be conspicuously displayed at the place of business for which issued. A certificate is not transferable and may be used only at the place designated in the certificate.

Each person whose business extends into more than one county is required to secure only one certificate of registration (Sec. 48-8-59). The certificate covers all operations of the company throughout the state.

There is no fee for the original certificate, but a $1 fee is charged for the renewal or issuance of a suspended or revoked certificate (Sec. 48-8-59, Reg. Sec. 560-12-1-.09).

A dealer must apply for a new certificate and return the old one if it discontinues business, changes location from one county to another, or changes the type of business (Reg. Sec. 560-12-1-.09). If the trade name is changed or the business changes location within the same county, the old certificate of registration must be returned and a new one reflecting the changes will be issued.

Contractors: General or prime contractors entering into contracts with subcontractors in which the aggregate amount of any single project is equal to or greater than $250,000 must file an initial notice with the Commissioner of Revenue within 30 days on Form S&UT 214-1 that identifies each applicable subcontractor and the contract amount (Reg. Sec. 560-12-2-.26).

General or prime contractors entering into such contracts with nonresident subcontractors are required to withhold 2% of the payments due the subcontractor, unless the subcontractor filed an approved surety bond with the Revenue Commissioner. Failure to withhold renders the prime or general contractor liable for any tax owed by the nonresident subcontractor. (Sec. 48-8-63(e); Reg. Sec. 560-12-2-.26(6))

Disaster relief: Immunity may be granted for the corporate and personal income tax liability, sales and use tax liability, and miscellaneous tax liability of businesses and employees that enter Georgia to repair damage due to a disaster or emergency. To ensure that businesses and individuals focus on quick response to the needs of the state and its citizens during a declared state of disaster or emergency, the General Assembly may deem that the disaster or emergency relief activity for a reasonable period of time during and after the disaster or emergency period does not establish any state or local tax liability.

An out-of-state business whose presence is solely that of conducting operations within the state for purposes of performing work or services on infrastructure related to a declared state of disaster or emergency during the disaster or emergency period is not considered to have established a level of presence that requires the business to register, file, and remit state or local taxes. Out-of-state businesses and employees, however, will be required to pay transaction taxes and fees including, but not limited to, hotel taxes, car rental taxes or fees, motor fuel taxes, or sales and use taxes on materials or services subject to sales and use taxes in the state that the out-of-state business or employee purchases for use or consumption in the state during the disaster or emergency period, unless the taxes are otherwise exempted. (Sec. 48-2-100)

Vendors to the state: Any nongovernmental vendor, or its affiliates, bidding on a state agency contract that exceeds $100,000 per year is required to register with the state and to collect and remit Georgia sales and use tax on all retail sales occurring in Georgia (Sec. 50-5-82).

SST conformity: Georgia is a member of the Governing Board of the Streamlined Sales and Use Tax (SST) Agreement. Sellers seeking the benefits of the Agreement must register through the SST central registration system to collect Georgia sales and use taxes.

The central registration system may be accessed on the SST Governing Board's website at **https://www.sstregister.org/**.

¶ 360   Sales or Use Tax Credits

The use, consumption, distribution, or storage of tangible personal property in Georgia is not subject to tax if a similar tax has been paid in another state that grants credit for a like tax paid in Georgia (Sec. 48-8-42, Reg. Sec. 560-12-1-.32). When the other state's tax is less than Georgia's, the difference must be paid to Georgia. Credit will be allowed for tax paid to a nonreciprocating state up to the amount of the Georgia tax only with respect to the use in the other state of tangible personal property by a manufacturer or fabricator in fulfillment of a contract to furnish the property and perform services relative to the property in the other state when the property was manufactured or fabricated in Georgia exclusively for use by the manufacturer or fabricator in fulfillment of the contract. For additional information, see *Policy Statement SUT 2008-10-10*, Georgia Department of Revenue, October 10, 2008, CCH GEORGIA TAX REPORTS, ¶ 200-629.

No credit is allowed for tax levied by a political subdivision of a state (Reg. Sec. 560-12-1-.32).

Credit is also allowed to dealers for the tax on amounts refunded to purchasers on returned merchandise.

Business Incentive refunds: see ¶ 364.

¶ 361   Deficiency Assessments

If a dealer fails to make a return and pay the required tax, or makes a grossly incorrect return or a return that is false or fraudulent, the Commissioner will assess and collect the tax, interest, and penalty, as accrued, based on the Commissioner's estimates for the taxable period of retail sales of the dealer, gross proceeds from rentals or leases of tangible personal property by the dealer, and the cost price of all articles of tangible personal property imported by the dealer for use, consumption, distribution, or storage for any use or consumption in Georgia (Sec. 48-2-48, Sec. 48-8-51(b)). The assessments are considered *prima facie* correct and the dealer has the burden to show otherwise.

Notices of assessment for errors made in reporting taxes are made on Forms 51A and 53A (Reg. Sec. 560-12-3-.20, Reg. Sec. 560-12-3-.21).

If any return is not filed, the Commissioner may make the return, which is deemed correct and sufficient for all legal purposes (Sec. 48-2-37).

No invoice or invoice inaccurate: When a dealer has imported tangible personal property and fails to produce an invoice showing the cost price of each article that is subject to tax or if the invoice does not reflect the true or actual cost price, the Commissioner will assess and collect the tax with interest and penalties on the true cost price (Sec. 48-8-52(b)). The assessment is considered *prima facie* correct and the dealer must prove otherwise.

Incorrect report of rentals: If the Commissioner believes the consideration reported from a lease or rental of tangible personal property does not represent the true or actual consideration, the Commissioner may fix the true or actual consideration and assess and collect the tax (Sec. 48-8-52(c)).

¶ 362   Audit Procedures

Dealers are required to keep proper records for a period of three years, and these records may be examined by the Commissioner (Sec. 48-8-52, Reg. Sec. 560-12-1-.15). Also, a dealer may be required to appear before the Commissioner and produce the books, records, and papers of the business (Sec. 48-8-55).

¶ 363   Statute of Limitations

Sales and use taxes must be assessed within three years after the return is filed (Sec. 48-2-49, Sec. 48-8-64). An early return is deemed filed on the last day prescribed for the filing of the return (Sec. 48-2-49). An assessment may be made any time if a false or fraudulent return is filed with the intent to evade tax or if no return is filed.

The taxpayer and the Commissioner may agree, before the time for assessment expires, to extend the time in which an assessment may be made (Sec. 48-2-49). Additional extensions may be agreed upon. The extension agreements are executed on Form ST-W1 (Reg. Sec. 560-12-3-.56).

If a claim for refund is filed within the last six months of the three-year period within which the Department may assess the tax, the period of limitation for assessment is extended for a period of six months beginning on the day on which the claim for the refund is filed (Sec. 48-2-49).

¶ 364   Application for Refund

A taxpayer may file a claim for refund of erroneously or illegally assessed and collected taxes within three years after the date the taxes were paid to the commissioner (Sec. 48-2-35(b)). Alternatively, the taxpayer may claim a refund from a dealer who has remitted the taxes to the state (Sec. 48-2-35.1). If a person files a refund claim with the commissioner initially, the person must provide the Department of Revenue with a notarized form prescribed by the commissioner and executed by the dealer stating that the dealer has not sought or will not seek a refund or credit of the taxes at issue, that the dealer will provide the person with any information or documentation necessary for the claim, and that the dealer has remitted the taxes to the state. If a person files a refund claim with the commissioner after unsuccessfully seeking a refund from the dealer, the person must provide the commissioner with a letter or other requested information indicating that the dealer refused to refund the taxes or did not act on the person's written refund request within 90 days. Upon the Commissioner's acceptance of such a letter or information, the dealer is deemed to have assigned all rights to the refund to the person.

Effective July 1, 2016, any taxpayer required to pay taxes electronically must file any claims for refund electronically through the Department's Georgia Tax Center.

A refund generally includes interest from the date the tax was paid (Sec. 48-2-35(a)). However, if a taxpayer does not obtain and use a Georgia sales and use tax exemption certificate or determination letter prior to purchasing tangible personal property, any refund on that purchase does not include interest (Sec. 48-2-35.1). When the taxpayer and the Commissioner agree to an extension of time in which an assessment may be made, the Commissioner may agree to similarly extend the period within which a claim for refund may be filed (Sec. 48-2-49(d)).

The taxpayer may request a conference or hearing before the Commissioner by written request in the claim for refund (Sec. 48-2-35(b)). The request is granted if the claim conforms to the law.

The Commissioner may set off any other unpaid state taxes against any refund allowed to the taxpayer (Sec. 48-2-35(c)).

A taxpayer whose refund claim is denied, or whose claim is not decided within one year from the date the claim was filed, may bring an action in the Georgia Tax Tribunal (Sec. 48-2-35(c)(4)). Such an action may not be maintained as a class action on behalf of similarly situated taxpayers (Sec. 48-2-35(c)(5)). Taxpayers can obtain the tax tribunal petition and view the explanation on the department's website at **http:// dor.georgia.gov/georgia-tax-tribunal** or at **https://gataxtribunal.georgia.gov/ documents**.

Refunds to customers: The Georgia Court of Appeals has ruled that Georgia law does not create a cause of action for customers to sue dealers for refunds of overcollected sales tax. The court noted that under Secs. 48-2-35.1(d) and 48-2-35, a taxpayer can (1) "seek a refund" of sales tax from a dealer, (2) file an administrative claim for a sales tax refund with the state revenue commissioner either initially or after unsuccessfully seeking a refund from the dealer, or (3) file a lawsuit against the Georgia Department of Revenue if the administrative claim against the state revenue commissioner fails. The appellate court found that the Legislature could have, but did not, include lawsuits against dealers among the other remedies under the law it provided for recovering allegedly overcollected sales tax. As a result, the appellate court found that the trial court erred in ruling that the plaintiffs could bring a direct cause of action for a sales tax refund against the power company.

The court also noted that Sec. 48-8-72, which requires written notice before a cause of action against a dealer for overcollected sales tax can accrue, was enacted to conform to the Streamlined Sales and Use Tax (SST) Agreement and merely contemplates, but does not expressly create, a cause of action against dealers. Instead, the legislative intent behind this provision was not to create a cause of action against sellers for overcollected sales taxes. The court also pointed out that Georgia law specifically states that no cause of action will accrue by virtue of the state being a member of the SST Agreement. Finally, because Georgia law allows consumers to initially seek a refund of overcollected sales taxes from a dealer, the Agreement required the state to adopt the written notice provision. (*Georgia Power Company v. Cazier,* Georgia Court of Appeals, No. A12A2440, March 29, 2013, CCH GEORGIA TAX REPORTS, ¶ 200-855)

Expedited refunds: Taxpayers may apply to the Revenue Commissioner for expedited payment of sales and use tax refund claims. A taxpayer must file a bond as part of the application. Approved refunds will be issued within 30 days of the date of the posting of the bond. Any assessment of taxes, interest, penalties, fees, or costs related to the payment of a refund claim will be made within three years of the refund payment date. Penalties apply in the case of frivolous claims. (Sec. 48-2-35.1)

Motor fuel credit card purchases by government agencies: A credit card issuer may obtain a refund for sales and use taxes paid on sales of motor fuel for highway use to a qualified governmental tax-exempt entity charged to a card held issued to such an entity when the card issuer bills the entity net of the applicable taxes. To claim the refund, a credit card issuer must be registered under IRC Sec. 4101 as a credit card issuer, establish that it has not collected the tax from the governmental entity, show that it repaid the tax to the dealer in full, and obtain the dealer's written consent to the allowance of the refund or otherwise make arrangements that directly or indirectly provide the dealer with reimbursement of the tax. (Sec. 48-9-10.1)

Business incentive refunds: A sales and use tax refund may be claimed from the incremental sales and use tax imposed on the sales generated by an approved company at a tourism attraction project (Sec. 48-8-270 *et seq.*). A "tourism attraction" is a cultural or historical site; a recreation or entertainment facility; a convention hotel and conference center; an automobile race track with other tourism amenities; a golf course facility with other tourism amenities; marinas and water parks with lodging and restaurant facilities designed to attract tourists to the state; or a Georgia crafts and products center (Sec. 48-8-271(5)). The term does not include any facility primarily devoted to the retail sale of goods, or to shopping centers, restaurants, movie theaters, or any recreational facility that does not serve as a likely destination where nonresidents would stay overnight in commercial lodging at the tourism attraction. "Incremental sales and use tax" means the state and local sales and use taxes (other than the sales tax for educational purposes) generated by the tourism attraction project above the amount of the sales and use taxes generated by the previous use of the property on which the project is located.

Tourism development projects must have "approved costs" of over $1 million and be open to the public at least 100 days per year (including the first year of operation). Moreover, for each year following the third year of operation, at least 25% of the visitors to the attraction must be from out-of-state (Sec. 48-8-274(d)). For new tourism attractions, "approved costs" includes items such as the costs of acquiring real property or rights in real property, costs for construction materials and equipment installed at the project and all labor costs in connection with the construction, and the cost of contract bonds. (See Sec. 48-8-271(3)(A)) For existing tourism attractions, "approved costs" includes the same items as for new tourism attractions, except that the items must relate to the expansion (and not the renovation) of the existing attraction. (See Sec. 48-8-271(3)(B))

The total sales and use tax refund allowed to an approved company over the 10-year term of the agreement is the lesser of the total amount of the incremental sales and use tax liability of the approved company or 25% of the approved costs for the tourism attraction project (Sec. 48-8-273(e)). The incremental sales and use tax refund accrues over the term of the agreement in an annual amount equal to the lesser of the incremental sales and use tax liability of the approved company for that year or 2.5% of the approved costs.

Applications for tourism attraction projects are filed with Georgia Department of Consumer Affairs. To claim the refund, an approved company must file a refund form with the Department of Revenue by March 31 of each year of the agreement to recover the incremental sales and use tax refund collected by the approved company and remitted to the department during the preceding calendar year (Sec. 48-8-274(a)-(c)). No sales and use tax refund will be granted to any approved project that is simultaneously receiving any other state tax incentive.

¶ 366   Scope of Tax

Source.—Statutory references are to Chapters 237 and 238, Hawaii Revised Statutes, as amended to date. Details are reported in the CCH HAWAII STATE TAX REPORTS starting at ¶ 60-000.

Hawaii's sales tax is a broad based general excise or privilege tax on all business and other activities conducted within the state (HRS Sec. 237-13). The tax applies not only to sales of goods and services but to "virtually every economic activity" not otherwise exempt (Rule 18-237-1). The general excise tax (GET) is imposed on gross income, gross proceeds of sales, or values of products in the distribution chain at varying rates. Businesses are not required to collect the general excise tax from their customers but they can visibly pass on the tax to their customers. A ruling discusses how the general excise tax differs from a sales tax, the maximum rates that businesses can charge customers; customer notification requirements; wholesale and retail sales; sales to exempt organizations; purchases by nonresidents; and other matters (*Tax Facts 37-1,* Hawaii Department of Taxation, March 2015, CCH HAWAII TAX REPORTS, ¶ 200-987).

Hawaii's complementary use tax is imposed on tangible personal property imported by a taxpayer in Hawaii whether owned, purchased from an unlicensed seller, or however acquired for use in the state. Use tax is also imposed on the value of services that are performed by an unlicensed seller at a point outside Hawaii and imported or purchased for use in Hawaii. (HRS Sec. 238-2).

Transient accommodations: A transient accommodations tax is imposed on the gross rental or gross rental proceeds from furnishing transient accommodations (*i.e.,* a room, apartment, suite, timeshare unit, or the like that will be occupied by a person for less than 180 consecutive days) (HRS Sec. 237D-1; HRS Sec. 237D-2; *Tax Facts 96-2,* Hawaii Department of Taxation, March 2016, CCH HAWAII TAX REPORTS, ¶ 201-003).

Special provisions and tax rates apply to resort time share rentals; see ¶ 369 and *Tax Facts 98-4,* Hawaii Department of Taxation, April 2016, CCH HAWAII TAX REPORTS, ¶ 201-002.

• **Incidence of tax**

The incidence of the general excise tax is on the seller, service provider, or person conducting business and activities in the state (HRS Sec. 237-13). Any "visible pass on" of the tax to the consumer or purchaser is a matter of contractual agreement (*General Excise Tax Memorandum No. 4,* Department of Taxation, February 1, 1987).

The incidence of the use tax is on the consumer or purchaser; however, the seller is normally required to collect and remit the use tax to the state (HRS Sec. 238-6).

Transient accommodations: Transient accommodations furnished through arrangements made by a travel agency or tour packager at noncommissioned negotiated contract rates are taxable to the provider of the services and the travel agency or tour packager on their portion of the proceeds (HRS Sec. 237-18(g)).

Online travel companies: The Hawaii Supreme Court held in a consolidated case that several online travel companies (OTCs) such as Travelocity, Expedia, Hotels.com, Hotwire, Orbitz, and Priceline were subject to general excise tax (GET) and failure-to-file penalties on their respective portions of gross income from sales of hotel room accommodations in Hawaii, but the OTCs were not subject to transient accommodations tax (TAT).

General excise tax.—The court found that the OTCs' transactions that involved selling Hawaii hotel room accommodations to transients over the Internet, as they were authorized to do through contracts with the hotels, were subject to the GET because the OTCs received their income by selling to transients the right to occupy hotel rooms located in Hawaii and the transients were Hawaii consumers when they purchased a Hawaii hotel room accommodation from an OTC. In addition, the OTCs actively solicited customers for the Hawaii hotel rooms and actively solicited Hawaii hotels to contractually provide the right to sell the right of hotel room occupancy on their websites. Even though the agreement between an OTC and a transient may have taken place outside Hawaii, such agreement was entered into with the intent that performance would occur entirely in Hawaii, and the occupancy rights that the OTCs sold were wholly and only consumable in Hawaii. Furthermore, the OTCs constructively benefitted from the state's services such as roads and access to police, fire, and lifeguard protection services. Therefore, there were sufficient business and other activities in Hawaii to impose the GET on the gross income resulting from the OTC transactions.

The court determined that the GET apportioning provision, which divides income between a hotel operator and a travel agency or tour packager, applied to the OTC transactions because:

(1) the OTCs operated as travel agencies;

(2) in the OTC transactions, the gross income was divided between the transient accommodations operator and the OTC; and

(3) the OTC transactions supplied transient accommodations at noncommissioned negotiated rates.

Transient accommodations tax.—The court determined that the OTCs were not subject to the TAT, because they were not "operators" for purposes of the TAT. In the part of the TAT definition relevant to OTCs, an "operator" is a person who is "engaging or continuing in any service business which involves the actual furnishing of transient accommodation." Since the court found the term "actual" in the statutory definition was ambiguous, it examined the legislative intent of the TAT and found that the TAT was imposed only on a single operator, not multiple operators. Therefore, since only the hotels providing the transient accommodations were the operators, the OTCs were not subject to the TAT. (*Travelocity.com, L.P. v. Hawaii Director of Taxation,* Hawaii Supreme Court, No. SCAP-13-0002896, March 17, 2015, CCH Hawaii Tax Reports, ¶ 200-988; motion for reconsideration denied April 2, 2015; see also *Announcement No. 2016-06,* Hawaii Department of Taxation, July 15, 2016, CCH Hawaii Tax Reports, ¶ 201-009)

• **Use tax**

The use tax is an excise tax levied on the use of tangible personal property in the state that is imported or purchased from an unlicensed seller for use in the state (HRS Sec. 238-2). Use tax liability accrues when the property is acquired by the importer or purchaser and becomes subject to the state's taxing jurisdiction.

Use tax does not apply to any property that has been subjected to general excise tax (HRS Sec. 238-3(b)). The same property may be subjected to use tax only once (HRS Sec. 238-3(c)). Use tax is imposed in addition to other state taxes, except as specifically provided by law or by a court of competent jurisdiction (HRS Sec. 238-3(d)).

The following are exempt from taxation because they are excluded from the definition of a taxable "use" (HRS Sec. 238-1):

(1) property brought into the state for temporary use without intent to keep it in the state permanently;

(2) use of property acquired by gift;

(3) the receipt of articles that are returned after temporary trial or without trial; and

(4) the use or retention of household goods, personal effects, and private automobiles imported into the state for nonbusiness use. However, it is presumed that an article acquired less than three months before it was imported into the state was acquired for use in Hawaii.

¶366   **Hawaii**

A Tax Information Release clarifies that an out-of-state licensed seller that is a manufacturer-retailer may deduct from its use tax base the difference between the landed value of the taxpayer's own property and what would comprise the tax base of a similarly situated in-state licensed seller that is a manufacturer-retailer. (*Tax Information Release No. 2009-04*, Hawaii Department of Taxation, September 14, 2009, CCH HAWAII TAX REPORTS, ¶ 200-763)

• **Nexus**

Hawaii requires persons engaging in business and other activities in Hawaii to collect and remit general excise or use tax (HRS Sec. 237-13; HRS Sec. 238-2). "Business" includes all activities (personal, professional, or corporate) engaged in or caused to be engaged in with the object of gain or economic benefit, either direct or indirect, excluding casual sales. The term "engaging," when used to refer to engaging or continuing in business, also includes the exercise of corporate or franchise powers (HRS Sec. 237-2; HRS Sec. 238-1).

• **Streamlined Act status**

Hawaii has enacted the Uniform (Simplified) Sales and Use Tax Administration Act, the product of the Streamlined Sales Tax Project (SSTP) (HRS Sec. 255D-1 *et seq.*). As a result, Hawaii is one of the Advisor states.

SST conformity legislation is pending in 2015 (S.B. 259, as introduced in the Hawaii House of Representatives on January 23, 2015).

¶ 367	Tax Base

General excise tax is based upon "gross income" or "gross proceeds of sale" (HRS Sec. 237-3). "Gross income" is the gross receipts (cash or accrued) received for personal services or derived from trade, business, commerce, or sales. "Gross income" includes the value proceeding or accruing from the sale of tangible personal property or services and all actual or accrued receipts from the investment of a business's capital, including interest, discount, rentals, royalties, fees, or other emoluments (without deductions for cost of property sold, cost of materials used, labor cost, taxes, royalties, interest, discount paid, or any other expense).

"Gross proceeds of sale" is the value actually proceeding from the sale of tangible personal property (without deductions for the cost of property sold or expenses of any kind) (HRS Sec. 237-3).

Transient accommodations: "Gross rental" or "gross rental proceeds," on which the tax is based, include the gross receipts, cash or accrued, that are received as compensation for furnishing transient accommodations. Any general excise tax or transient accommodations tax amounts that are passed on and collected are not included in gross rental or gross rental proceeds. (HRS Sec. 237D-1) The tax is imposed in addition to any other state taxes (HRS Sec. 237D-15). Special provisions apply to resort time share rentals; see ¶ 369 and *Tax Facts 98-4,* Hawaii Department of Taxation, April 2016, CCH HAWAII TAX REPORTS, ¶ 201-002.

Imported goods and services: For transactions involving imported property, services, or contracting that are subject to Hawaii general excise (sales) tax and also subject to sales and use tax in another state, taxpayers may offset against the general excise (sales) tax the amount of taxes paid to the other state or its political subdivisions (HRS Sec. 237-22). The offset amount may not exceed the amount of Hawaii general excise (sales) tax imposed. The offset must first be applied against Hawaii use tax, and any remaining amount may be applied against general excise (sales) tax.

Prepaid calling services: Gross income and gross proceeds from prepaid telephone calling services, and the recharge of such services, are subject to general excise tax as sales of tangible personal property (HRS Sec. 237-[50]). "Prepaid telephone calling service" means the advance purchase of manually or electronically dialed telephone calls originated by using an access number or authorization code. Distinctions between retail and wholesale transactions apply for tax purposes. General excise taxation of prepaid telephone calling services applies in lieu of taxation under Hawaii public service company tax law.

- **Use tax**

For use tax purposes, the basis of property is (Rule 18-238-2):

(1) the purchase price if the purchase and sale are consummated in Hawaii, and

(2) the value of the property if the purchase and sale are consummated outside Hawaii or if there is no purchase price.

"Price" is the total amount for which tangible personal property is purchased, valued in money, less cash, trade, and quantity discounts (Rule 18-238-2). "Value" is the fair and reasonable cash value at the time the tax accrues, including freight, insurance, and handling charges, less cash, trade, and quantity discounts. "Consummated" is the point in time when title passes or when the buyer takes possession.

¶ 368   List of Exemptions, Exceptions, and Exclusions

Unless otherwise indicated, the statutory exemptions, exceptions, and exclusions listed below apply to both sales and use taxes; those applicable only to the use tax are listed separately. Items that are excluded from the sales or use tax base are treated at ¶ 367, "Tax Base."

- **Sales and use tax exemptions, exceptions, and exclusions**

Administration of employee benefit plan by nonprofit organizations	HRS Sec. 237-24.3(5)
Agricultural and horticultural organizations (sales tax)	HRS Sec. 237-23(a)(5)
Agricultural commodities, transportation	HRS Sec. 237-24.3(1)
Agricultural products sold to purchaser for processing out of state	HRS Sec. 237-13(2)(D)
Air pollution control facilities	HRS Sec. 237-27.5
Air transportation services	HRS Sec. 237-18(f)
Aircraft or aircraft engine rental or lease payments	HRS Sec. 237-24.3(12)
Aircraft repair shop	HRS Sec. 237-24.9
Alcoholic beverages sold to carriers for out-of-state consumption	HRS Sec. 237-24.3(2)(A)
Alimony and similar payments	HRS Sec. 237-24(7)
Beverage container deposits	HRS Sec. 237-24.75(1)
Banks and financial corporations subject to the bank tax	HRS Sec. 237-24.8
Blind, deaf, and totally disabled persons (up to $2,000)	HRS Sec. 237-24(13)
Building and loan associations subject to the bank tax	HRS Sec. 237-24.8
Business and civic leagues	HRS Sec. 237-23(a)(5)
Call centers	HRS Sec. 237-29.8
Carriers, sales for out-of-state consumption to	HRS Sec. 237-24.3(2)
Carriers, sales in foreign trade zones to	HRS Sec. 212-8
Casual sales	HRS Sec. 237-1, HRS Sec. 237-2
Cemetery associations	HRS Sec. 237-23(a)(9)

• **Exemptions, exceptions, and exclusions applicable only to the use tax**

Containers and packages used in manufactured products sold at wholesale	HRS Sec. 238-2(1)
Contracting services imported by a licensed contractor	HRS Sec. 238-1, HRS Sec. 238-2.3
Feed imported for sale at wholesale	HRS Sec. 238-4
Gifts	HRS Sec. 238-1(2)
Household goods and other personal effects imported for nonbusiness use	HRS Sec. 238-1(5)
Manufacturing materials used in products taxed at wholesale rate . .	HRS Sec. 238-2(1)
Ocean going vehicles	HRS Sec. 238-1(7)
Out-of-state vendors	HRS Sec. 238-2
Personal property imported for nonbusiness use	HRS Sec. 238-1(5)
Property previously subject to general excise tax	HRS Sec. 238-3(b)
Property temporarily used in Hawaii	HRS Sec. 238-1(1)
Resales (wholesale)	HRS Sec. 238-2(1)
Ships' stores for vessels	HRS Sec. 238-1(4)
Tools, parts, and materials imported from out of state for construction of aircraft repair shop	HRS Sec. 238-1(8)
Trial use property	HRS Sec. 238-1(3)
Use of aircraft and vessels subjected to general excise tax	HRS Sec. 238-3(f)
Use of vessels constructed with state funds prior to July 1, 1969	HRS Sec. 238-3(h)

¶ 369   **Rate of Tax**

Hawaii general excise tax rates are 4%, 0.5%, and 0.15%. The 4% rate is generally the retail rate, and the 0.5% rate is generally the wholesale, intermediary, or manufacturer's rate. The 0.15% rate is imposed only on insurance producers.

• **Tax rate of 4%**

The following are taxed at the 4% general excise tax rate:

Amusements, including theaters, opera houses, moving picture shows, dance halls, radio broadcasting stations, and skating rinks (HRS Sec. 237-13(4));

Business, trade, activity, occupation, or calling not specifically enumerated in the taxation statute (HRS Sec. 237-13(10), Rule 18-237-13-06.05);

Contractors (HRS Sec. 237-13(3), HRS Sec. 237-16);

Professions (HRS Sec. 237-13(6));

Real estate brokers and salespersons (HRS Sec. 237-18(e));

Rentals of tangible personal property at retail (HRS Sec. 237-16);

Retail sales of tangible personal property for consumption or use by the purchaser (HRS Sec. 237-16);

Sales representatives or purchasing agents (HRS Sec. 237-13(5));

Service businesses (except wholesale service businesses) (HRS Sec. 237-13(6)).

• **Tax rate of 0.5%**

The following are taxed at the 0.5% general excise tax rate:

Aquaculture (seeds, cuttings, packaging, etc.) (HRS Sec. 237-4(a)(6),(7));

Blind, deaf, or totally disabled individuals or corporations owned by them (nonexempt gross income) (HRS Sec. 237-17, HRS Sec. 237-24(13));

Electricity (generated) sold to a public utility company for resale to the public (HRS Sec. 237-13.5);

Electricity produced from geothermal resources (HRS Sec. 182-16);

Geothermal resources (HRS Sec. 182-16);

Manufacturers (HRS Sec. 237-13(1));

Producers (HRS Sec. 237-13(2));

Sellers in the business of selling tangible personal property (HRS Sec. 237-13(2));

Service wholesalers or intermediaries (HRS Sec. 237-13(6));

Services performed for manufacturers on manufactured, milled, or processed products (HRS Sec. 237-18(c));

Services performed for sugar cane planters (HRS Sec. 237-18(d));

Sugar benefit payments received by sugar producers (HRS Sec. 237-13(8));

Technicians supplying physicians or dentists with medical or dental supplies (HRS 237-15)

Wholesalers (HRS Sec. 237-13(2));

Goods or services furnished by a dealer to a purchaser of tangible personal property in order to fulfill a warranty obligation of the manufacturer (HRS Sec. 237-4(a)(10)).

- **Tax rate of 0.15%**

Insurance producers are taxed at the 0.15% general excise tax rate (HRS Sec. 237-13(7)).

- **Rental motor vehicle, tour vehicle, and car-sharing vehicle surcharges**

There is a surcharge of $3 per day levied on the lessor of rental motor vehicles (HRS Sec. 251-2(a)). There is also a rental motor vehicle customer facility charge of $4.50 per day on rentals and leases of vehicles by concessions where customers pick up and return rental vehicles at a state airport facility (HRS Sec. 251-2(a)).

A tour vehicle surcharge of $65 is imposed for each tour vehicle with more than 25 passenger seats that is used or partially used during the month. The surcharge is $15 for each eight-to-25 passenger tour vehicle used or partially used during the month (HRS Sec. 251-2(b)(1)).

Car-sharing organizations are subject to a car-sharing vehicle surcharge tax of 25 cents per half hour, or any portion of a half hour, that a rental motor vehicle is rented or leased by the organization. However, for each rental of six hours or more, the tax will be assessed in the same manner as the rental motor vehicle surcharge and the tour vehicle surcharge taxes are assessed. (HRS Sec. 251-16)

Car-sharing organizations are required to register with the Director of Taxation and make a one-time payment of $20. A registered car-sharing organization must be subject to at least one of the vehicle surcharge taxes. (HRS Sec. 251-16)

For purposes of the surcharge tax, "car-sharing organization" means a rental motor vehicle lessor that operates a membership program in which (HRS Sec. 251-1)

(1) self-service access to a fleet of vehicles is provided, with or without requiring a reservation, exclusively to members of the organization who have paid a membership fee;

(2) members are charged a usage rate, either hourly or by the minute, for each use of a vehicle;

(3) members are not required to enter into a separate written agreement with the organization each time the member reserves and uses a vehicle; and

(4) the average paid use period for all vehicles provided by the organization during any taxable period is six hours or less.

The rental motor vehicle, tour vehicle, and car-sharing vehicle surcharge taxes may be visibly passed on to the vehicle lessees (HRS Sec. 437D-8.4).

• **Use tax**

The use tax rate is generally 4% (HRS Sec. 238-2, Rule 18-238-2). However, the following are subject to use tax at a rate of 0.5%:

Nonexempt purchases of licensed retailers and other persons importing for purposes of resale (HRS Sec. 238-2(2)(A));

Manufacturers importing or purchasing nonexempt material or commodities to be incorporated into finished or saleable products that will be sold at retail in Hawaii (HRS Sec. 238-2(2)(B));

Contractors importing or purchasing material or commodities that are incorporated into a finished work or project where it will remain in a form perceptible to the senses (HRS Sec. 238-2(1)(C));

Persons engaged in a service business or furnishing transient accommodations are subject to transient accommodations tax (see below) if the import or purchase of tangible personal property would have qualified as a sale at wholesale if the seller had been subject to sales tax (HRS Sec. 238-2(2)(D)).

Publishers of magazines or similar printed materials containing advertisements, if the publisher is a purchaser or importer licensed under the general excise (sales) tax law, Ch. 237, and is under contract with the advertisers to distribute a minimum number of magazines to the public, regardless of whether there is a charge to the recipients of the magazines (HRS Sec. 238-2(2)(E)); and

Services performed by an unlicensed seller at a point outside Hawaii and imported or purchased for use in Hawaii, if the importer or purchaser is general-excise-tax licensed in Hawaii and is (a) engaged in a service business or calling in which the imported or purchased services become identifiable elements, excluding overhead, of the services rendered, and the gross income of the importer or purchaser is subject to general excise tax on services at the 4% rate, (b) a manufacturer importing or purchasing services that become identifiable elements, excluding overhead, of a finished or saleable product (including the container or package in which the product is contained) and the finished or saleable product is to be sold in a manner that results in a further tax on the activity of the manufacturer as a retailer, or (c) a contractor importing or purchasing services that become identifiable elements, excluding overhead, of the finished work or project required under the contract and the gross proceeds derived by the contractor are subject to contractor's general excise tax (HRS Sec. 238-2.3).

• **Multiple rates**

A business that is subject to two or more tax rates must segregate items of gross income, gross proceeds of sales, or value of products. Failure to segregate items taxable at different rates subjects the aggregate to tax at the highest applicable rate (HRS Sec. 237-14).

¶369   Hawaii

• Transient accommodations tax

The transient accommodations tax rate is 9.25% (HRS Sec. 237D-2(a)).

Resort time share rentals: Beginning January 1, 2017, the 8.25% rate is increased to 9.25% of the fair market rental value (HRS Sec. 237D-2(c)). For January 1, 2016, to December 31, 2016, the previous rate of 7.25% of the fair market rental value was increased to 8.25% of the fair market rental value.

"Fair market rental value" means one-half of gross daily maintenance fees, including resort fees, that are paid by the owner and are attributable to the time share unit located in Hawaii. Amounts paid for optional goods and services, such as food and beverage services or beach chair or umbrella rentals, are excluded from the definition of "fair market rental value." (HRS Sec. 237D-2(c))

¶ 370 Local Taxes

Hawaii counties were authorized to adopt an ordinance before July 1, 2016, to impose a local general excise and use tax surcharge of up to 0.5% to fund a mass transit system.

Honolulu County has imposed a local 0.5% general excise and use tax surcharge to fund its mass transit system. The surcharge applies to all gross proceeds and income subject to the general excise tax, except gross proceeds or income taxable at the 0.5% and 0.15% rates, which are generally applicable to wholesalers, manufacturers, and insurance producers. Exemptions from the general excise tax also apply to the surcharge. The use tax surcharge applies to the value of property and services subject to use tax. The provision imposing the surcharge is scheduled to be repealed on December 31, 2027 (Act 240 (H.B. 134), Laws 2015; Ordinance 05-27 (Bill 40), Honolulu Ordinances 2005).

The maximum rate of the state general excise tax and county surcharge tax that sellers may pass on to customers is 4.712%. This rate is equal to the 4% general excise tax rate plus the 0.5% county surcharge tax rate, divided by 95.5%. For purposes of calculating the tax rate that sellers may pass on to customers, the tax rate on Oahu is divided by 95.5% because the tax is levied on the seller's gross receipts, and "gross receipts" are defined to include any tax that the business passes on to the customer. Thus, gross receipts of a seller on Oahu consist of two parts: (1) the tax, which is 4.5% of gross receipts and (2) the price, which is 95.5% of gross receipts. Furthermore, a seller on Oahu has the option of passing on no tax to the customer, passing on the state and local taxes at the rate of 4.5%, or passing on the state and local taxes at the optimum rate of 4.712% (*Announcement No. 2006-15,* Hawaii Department of Taxation, September 8, 2006, CCH HAWAII TAX REPORTS, ¶ 200-664).

¶ 371 Bracket Schedule

Hawaii law does not provide bracket schedules.

¶ 372 Returns, Payments, and Due Dates

The general excise and use tax return is due monthly; in the case of taxpayers whose annual tax liability does not exceed the following specified amounts, returns may be filed quarterly (no more than $4,000) or semiannually (no more than $2,000) with the consent of the Department of Taxation (HRS Sec. 237-30, HRS Sec. 237D-6, HRS Sec. 251-4, Rule 18-237-30(b)). In addition, an annual reconciliation return is required (HRS Sec. 237-33, Rule 18-237-33-01(a)).

A return must be signed by the person required to make the return or by a duly authorized agent (HRS Sec. 231-15, Rule 18-237-33-01(b)). A corporation's return may be made by any officer of the corporation, and a partnership's return may be made by any of the partners (HRS Sec. 231-15.6, Rule 18-237-33-01(b)).

If the due date for any document or remittance required by law falls on a Saturday, Sunday, or legal holiday, the document or remittance is not due until the next succeeding day that is not a Saturday, Sunday, or legal holiday (HRS Sec. 231-21).

All applications, returns, and payments must be filed or transmitted to the office of the taxation district in which the taxable privilege was exercised (HRS Sec. 237-34(a), Rule 18-237-30(g)). If tax is owed to more than one taxation district, returns must be transmitted to the first taxation district.

Due dates: Monthly, quarterly, and semiannual general excise tax returns, use tax returns, and transient accommodations tax returns are due on the 20th day of the month following the end of the applicable reporting period (HRS Sec. 238-5; HRS Sec. 237-30; HRS Sec. 238-13).

Oahu surcharge: The county surcharge tax, which is imposed on the island of Oahu must be reported on the same forms as taxpayers use to report the Hawaii general excise tax. Forms are available on the Hawaii Department of Taxation's Web site at **http://tax.hawaii.gov**.

Persons who do business on more than one island must separate their transactions by the taxing districts of Oahu, Maui, Kauai, and Hawaii so the transaction amounts can be correctly reported on the general excise tax returns. A worksheet (Form G-75) in the general excise tax booklet instructions will aid taxpayers in segregating their sales by district and completing the Schedule of Assignment of Taxes by District (*County Surcharge—Frequently Asked Questions,* Hawaii Department of Taxation, October 13, 2006).

Transient accommodations: The operator or plan manager of a transient accommodation must, no later than the 20th day of the month following the month in which the tax accrues, file a return and send in a payment (HRS Sec. 237D-6). If annual tax liability does not exceed $4,000, quarterly returns can be filed on or before April 20, July 20, October 20 and January 20, and semiannual returns may be filed on or before July 20 and January 20 if the tax liability does not exceed $2,000.

Each operator or plan manager must file a yearly return, which is due no later than April 20 (or the 20th day of the fourth month following the close of the taxable year) (HRS Sec. 237D-7). The return must show a summary of the operator's liability for the past tax year and include any remaining tax that may be owed.

Effective for all periods ending on March 31, 2016, and after, a travel agent or tour packager that divides income with a transient accommodations operator must report its share of the gross income on Line 13, Transient Accommodations Rentals. Transient accommodations operators must continue to report their share of the gross income on Line 13. (*Tax Information Release No. 2016-01,* Hawaii Department of Taxation, March 14, 2016, CCH HAWAII TAX REPORTS, ¶ 200-998)

Electronic filing and payment: Businesses may e-file their general excise/use tax and transient accommodations tax returns, for free, on the Department's Web site at **https://tax.hawaii.gov/eservices/business/**, and may pay those taxes by electronic funds transfer by completing Form EFT-1, Authorization for Electronic Funds Transfer, and mailing it to the Department. They may also pay online using an electronic check or credit card (Rules 18-231-9.4-01 through 18-231-9.4-09).

A taxpayer who is approved for automated clearing house (ACH) debit payments may use this option to make Hawaii general excise and use tax, personal income tax withholding, transient accommodations tax, and rental motor vehicle tax payments for annual returns. Questions regarding the ACH debit payment option may be directed to the Hawaii Department of Taxation's electronic processing unit at 808-587-1740 or **Tax.Efile@hawaii.gov**.

Motor vehicles: An owner of a motor vehicle that is purchased out-of-state and subsequently brought into Hawaii must provide, with the application for Hawaii motor vehicle registration, proof that Hawaii use tax has been paid (HRS 286-41). A Hawaii motor vehicle registration certificate cannot be issued without proof of payment of the use tax. Certification is made on Form G-27.

• **Tax system modernization**

The Department of Taxation's tax system modernization program is a collection of projects scheduled to be completed by 2020. According to the department, almost every technical system that the department uses will be upgraded or replaced to provide better taxpayer service and improved enforcement of tax laws. New online features will be available each year and operational processes will improve over time, resulting in faster processing and better customer service. In addition, the department will have new tools to help protect against fraud and identify when businesses and individuals are not properly filing returns and paying taxes. The release regarding the tax system modernization program is available on the department's website at **http://tax.hawaii.gov/geninfo/a2_b2_9tsm**.

¶ 373   **Prepayment of Taxes**

Hawaii makes no special provision regarding the prepayment of taxes.

¶ 374   **Vendor Registration**

Any person subject to general excise tax must obtain a license as a condition precedent to engaging or continuing in business (HRS Sec. 237-9). The Basic Business Application and related forms and instructions are available for download at **http://tax.hawaii.gov/forms/a1_b2_1geuse/**.

Tax benefits: Persons conducting business in Hawaii are not entitled to receive general excise tax benefits unless they (1) obtain a Hawaii business license and (2) file an annual general excise tax reconciliation tax return within 12 months of the due date prescribed for the return. For purposes of this provision, "general excise tax benefit" means any tax exemption, exclusion of a taxable amount, reduction from the measure of tax imposed, tax deduction, tax credit, lower rate of tax, segregation or division of taxable amounts between multiple taxpayers involved in the same transaction, or income splitting allowed under the general excise tax laws. The Director of Taxation may require any taxpayer to furnish information to determine the validity of any general excise tax benefit and may waive the denial of the general excise tax benefit if the failure to comply is due to reasonable cause and not to the taxpayer's willful neglect. (HRS Sec. 237-9.3; *Tax Information Release No. 2010-05*, Hawaii Department of Taxation, July 29, 2010, CCH HAWAII TAX REPORTS, ¶ 200-820)

The Director of Taxation is required to give written notice to nonprofit organizations that their general excise tax benefits may be denied for failure to obtain a license and timely file a reconciliation tax return (HRS Sec. 237-9.3(d); *Announcement No. 2012-09,* Hawaii Department of Taxation, August 15, 2012, CCH HAWAII TAX REPORTS, ¶ 200-921).

Tax clearance requirement: Any local or out-of-state business and nonprofit organization that plans to sell goods or services to or to contract with the state must first obtain federal and state tax clearance certificates, which confirm that the business or organization has filed all its tax returns and paid its taxes as of the date the certificate is issued. Without a tax clearance certificate, a business cannot enter into or bid on state or county contracts. The certificates can be applied for online (see below).

Online registration: Hawaii Business Express is a one-stop online business registration service that allows businesses to apply to the Hawaii Department of Taxation for Hawaii general excise (sales) tax licenses and personal income tax withholding numbers through Hawaii's official Internet portal, **https://portal.ehawaii.gov/home/online-services/hawaii-business-express/**. The service also allows businesses to file articles of business registration and register trade names with the Hawaii Department of

Consumer Affairs, to apply for tax clearance certificates, and to obtain unemployment insurance identification numbers. Hawaii Business Express also provides a live, online customer service to help answer user questions immediately.

Transient accommodations: Any person operating a transient accommodation must register with the Director of Taxation the name and address of each place of business within the state that is subject to the tax. The operator will receive a certificate of registration from the Director upon payment of a one-time fee of $5 for each registration for transient accommodations consisting of one to five units; $15 for each registration for transient accommodations consisting of six or more units; and $15 for each resort time share vacation plan within Hawaii. (HRS Sec. 237D-4(a)) A penalty is imposed if the taxpayer failed to timely provide the information before April 1, 2013 (*Announcement No. 2012-13,* Hawaii Department of Taxation, October 31, 2012, CCH Hawaii Tax Reports, ¶ 200-929).

Operators of transient accommodations were required to designate a local contact residing on the same island where the transient accommodation is located by December 31, 2015 (Uncodified Sec. 2(a), Act 326 (H.B. 2078), Laws 2012). The local contact must be an individual or company that has a contract with the transient accommodation's operator to provide certain services (Uncodified Sec. 2(h), Act 326 (H.B. 2078), Laws 2012 *Announcement No. 2014-03*, Hawaii Department of Taxation, April 3, 2014, CCH Hawaii Tax Reports, ¶ 200-980).

Network marketers: Persons engaged in network marketing, multi-level marketing, and similar businesses are authorized to obtain a vendor's license to become a Hawaii general excise and use tax collection agent on behalf of their direct marketers. The tax agent's direct sellers will then be deemed to be licensed for the business activity conducted directly through the marketing arrangement (HRS Sec. 237-9(d)).

Inactive status: A taxpayer that temporarily discontinues its business activity may request in writing that its license be placed on inactive status (Rule 18-231-3-14). A taxpayer who has temporarily ceased to do business or who has determined that no tax is owed for a particular tax period must still file an appropriate periodic return unless inactive status has been granted (Rule 18-237-30(h)).

• **License cancellation and revocation**

Cancellation: A taxpayer who goes out of business or who transfers ownership of a business must notify the district tax office to which the taxpayer reports by canceling its license not more than 10 days after the transfer of ownership or cessation of business activity (Rule 18-231-14.16(b)). A "transfer of ownership" means that the business is conducted by a different person or company. The conversion of a sole proprietorship to a partnership or corporation is considered a transfer of ownership.

A "Notice of Cancellation" (Form GEW-TA-RV-1) must be filed to cancel a general excise tax license. In addition, the licensee must return the license to the Department with the notice.

Revocation: The Director has the authority to revoke any license that has been abandoned (Rule 18-231-14.17). A license is deemed abandoned if the licensee has failed to file both periodic and annual returns for at least five years, excluding any periods in which the Department permitted the license to be placed on inactive status. The Director may also revoke a license if the Department is presented with adequate evidence that a licensee is deceased, has been dissolved, or has otherwise ceased to exist (Rule 18-231-14.18).

• **Use tax registration**

A seller who is not otherwise required to collect use tax may voluntarily register for authority to collect such tax (Rule 18-238-6).

¶374   Hawaii

¶ 375   Sales or Use Tax Credits

Use tax credits are allowed in many instances for sales taxes paid other states or counties. Taxpayers liable for use tax may receive credit for sales and use taxes paid to other states on the same transaction or property, up to the amount of use tax owed to Hawaii (HRS Sec. 238-3(i)).

If excess tax is paid, taxpayers may elect a credit against later taxes instead of a refund (HRS Sec. 237-37, HRS Sec. 238-7). However, no overpayment credit will be made unless the original payment of the tax resulted from the law being interpreted or applied to the taxpayer differently than to taxpayers in general (HRS Sec. 231-23(a)(1)(C), HRS Sec. 237-37, HRS Sec. 238-7).

• **Interest**

Interest on a credit is allowed from the later of the first calendar day after the return's due date, the first month following the month the return is received, or the date of payment, until the date the credit is taken (HRS Sec. 231-23(d)(4)).

¶ 376   Deficiency Assessments

If a return is erroneous or deficient, the Department of Taxation will correct the error or assess the proper amount of tax owed (HRS Sec. 237-36, HRS Sec. 238-7, HRS Sec. 238-13). If the Department proposes to assess any additional gross income or gross proceeds of sale, the taxpayer must be notified and will have 30 days to confer with the Department. After the expiration of the 30 days, the Department will assess any additional tax and notify the taxpayer. The taxpayer will have 20 days to pay the tax. However, no preliminary notice is required if the additional tax is calculated by the Department from gross income listed on the taxpayer's return.

"Whipsaw" assessments: The Hawaii Department of Taxation has issued a sales and use tax announcement discussing "whipsaw" assessments, which occur when (1) the department is forced to treat both sides of a transaction consistently where the facts or application of law to those facts are in dispute, (2) assess only one of two taxpayers based on one view of the facts or law, and (3) allow the statute of limitations on assessment against the other taxpayer to expire before the department can change its position to conform to a judicial ruling against it on its initial position. Such situations may occur when two or more persons involved in a sale of services or contracting are each claiming that the other is responsible for paying the sales or use tax on the services or contracting imported into Hawaii. The department points out that the "whipsaw" in this context may occur as a result of competing legal theories or disagreement as to the facts and circumstances surrounding the transaction.

To prevent such a whipsaw effect, the department must issue assessments to both taxpayers on inconsistent theories to toll the statute of limitations until the matter is resolved by the courts. The department's position is that the proper test for sourcing a sale of services or contracting is the "used or consumed" test, as opposed to an alternative test based upon the "place of performance." Although only one sourcing test should logically succeed, if the department does not assess both persons for the full amount of tax owed, for jurisdictional or procedural reasons, either or both taxpayers may prevail against the department, thereby denying the department the ability to collect the full amount of tax owed as a result of the sale. Therefore, when the facts or application of law to those facts are in dispute with regard to services or contracting, the department intends to assess all persons party to the transaction in order to protect the statute of limitations until the dispute is resolved by the courts. However, the department intends to collect 100% of the proper tax only once, whether it is all from one of the taxpayers or a combination of taxpayers. (*Announcement 2009-34*, Hawaii Department of Taxation, December 17, 2009, CCH HAWAII TAX REPORTS, ¶ 200-781)

• Failure to file a return

If a person fails, neglects, or refuses to make a return, the Department of Taxation may assess the tax on the basis of available information (HRS Sec. 237-38). The assessment is presumed to be correct unless it is appealed, and the burden of proving otherwise is upon the person assessed.

• Evidence of assessment

Notices and records of assessments and lists or other records of payments and unpaid amounts are *prima facie* evidence of the assessment of the property or the person assessed, the amount due and unpaid, the delinquency in payment, and compliance with the requirements of law (HRS Sec. 231-20).

¶ 377   Audit Procedures

The Department of Taxation or the Multistate Tax Commission may examine all account books, bank books, bank statements, records, vouchers, taxpayer's copies of federal tax returns, and any and all other documents relevant to a taxpayer's general excise or use tax liability (HRS Sec. 237-39, HRS Sec. 238-7, HRS. Sec. 238-13). The person by or for whom the return was made or whose tax is being assessed (or any employee) may be summoned and required to testify under oath; the production of books and records may be required; and testimony may be taken regarding the taxpayer's gross income or gross proceeds of sales for the audit period.

Returns may be audited on the basis of information received from the Internal Revenue Service, by random selection, or by examining claims for credit or refund of previously paid taxes (*Tax Information Release No. 89-2,* Department of Taxation, May 8, 1989). The auditor's duty is to determine the taxpayer's correct tax liability by examining the taxpayer's books and records and by interviewing witnesses.

The Department of Taxation has issued guidelines for audits. See, for example, *Tax Audit Guideline No. 2009-02*, Hawaii Department of Taxation, October 26, 2009, CCH HAWAII TAX REPORTS, ¶ 200-773, concerning the definition and treatment of items "substantially omitted."

¶ 378   Statute of Limitations

General excise and use taxes must be assessed or levied by the later of three years after the return was filed or the due date for the filing of the return, except that if a person has "substantially omitted" an item on a return, the statute of limitations is extended to six years (HRS Sec. 237-40(a), HRS Sec. 238-7). Court proceedings for the collection of tax may not be initiated after the limitations period unless the assessment was made before the limitations period expired. The statute of limitations for assessments may be extended by written agreement between the Department of Taxation and the taxpayer, provided the agreement is executed prior to the expiration of the limitations period (HRS Sec. 237-40(c)). The running of the statute of limitations is suspended for the period during which the Director of Taxation is prohibited from making an assessment because of bankruptcy and for 60 days thereafter (HRS Sec. 231-3.5).

False or fraudulent returns: General excise and use taxes may be assessed at any time if a taxpayer files a false or fraudulent return with intent to evade tax or fails to file the annual return (HRS Sec. 237-40(b)). However, before an assessment may be made after the normal three-year period, in the case of a return claimed to be false or fraudulent with intent to evade tax, a determination as to the claim must first be made by a circuit court judge.

Amended returns: The statutory period for the assessment of any deficiency or the determination of any refund attributable to a return reporting certain adjustments to gross income or gross proceeds of sale will not expire before the expiration of one year from the date on which the Department is notified by the taxpayer or the Internal Revenue Service, whichever is earlier, of such a return (HRS Sec. 237-33.5). Before the expiration of the one-year period, the Department and the taxpayer may agree in writing to an extension, and the period agreed upon may be further extended by subsequent written agreements.

- **Recordkeeping**

All books and records pertaining to general excise and use tax liability must be kept for a period of three years (HRS Sec. 237-41, HRS Sec. 238-9, HRS Sec. 238-13).

¶ 379   Application for Refund

Excess payments of general excise and use taxes may be refunded to the taxpayer upon application or applied to subsequent tax liability as an overpayment credit (HRS Sec. 231-23(a)(2), HRS Sec. 237-37, HRS Sec. 238-7, HRS Sec. 238-13).

Refunds must be issued within 90 days of the due date of the tax return or the date the tax return is filed, whichever is later, if the amount of tax paid with the return exceeds the amount determined to be the correct amount of tax due and the taxpayer requests a refund. (HRS Sec. 231-23(d)(1)) If the overpayment of tax results or arises from the filing of an amended return, the amount overpaid must be refunded within 90 days from the due date of the original return or the date the overpayment is discovered, whichever is later. (HRS Sec. 231-23(d)(2))

Refunds will be allowed if the original assessment contained clerical errors, transposed figures, typographical errors, and errors in calculation or if there was an illegal or erroneous assessment (HRS Sec. 231-23(a)(2)). Refunds will not be allowed unless the original payment of the tax was due to the law being interpreted or applied to the taxpayer differently than other taxpayers.

A request for credit or refund that is made by filing an amended return after an assessment is made will be denied because the law provides that either an appeal must be filed within 30 days after a notice of assessment was mailed or the assessment must be paid (*Tax Information Release No. 94-3,* Department of Taxation, May 24, 1994).

Refunds are paid on a "refund voucher" form that details each transaction. If the person entitled to a refund is delinquent in the payment of any tax, the amount of delinquent taxes may be withheld from the refund (HRS Sec. 231-23(c)(1)).

Refund appeals: Taxpayers may file an appeal with a district board of review or the Hawaii Tax Appeal Court at any time after 180 days from the date that a claim was filed if the Department has not given notice of a denial of the claim. Further, taxpayers may appeal the Department's denial of a refund claim to a board of review or the Tax Appeal Court within 30 days after notice of the denial of the claim. Refund or credit claims must be filed within the applicable statutory period of limitation (HRS 232-16, HRS 235-114, HRS 238-8).

¶ 380   IDAHO

¶ 381   Scope of Tax

Source.—Statutory references are to Title 63 of the Idaho Code, as amended to date. Details are reported in the CCH IDAHO STATE TAX REPORTS starting at ¶ 60-000.

The sales tax is an excise tax imposed on each sale at retail (IC Sec. 63-3619, Rule 35.01.02.068.01). The use tax is an excise tax imposed on the privilege of storing, using, or consuming within the state tangible personal property that was acquired for storage, use, or other consumption in the state (IC Sec. 63-3621(a), Rule 35.01.02.072.01). Use tax applies when property is purchased outside of Idaho or from a retailer not subject to the State Tax Commission's jurisdiction and is used, stored, or consumed in Idaho (Rule 35.01.02.072.06).

Use tax does not apply when property is purchased from an Idaho retailer and sales tax is paid to the retailer (IC Sec. 63-3621(c), Rule 35.01.02.072.05).

Cloud computing: "[R]emotely accessed computer software" is excluded from the definition of tangible personal property, and is therefore not subject to sales or use tax (IC Sec. 63-3616(b)). The exclusion applies to the right to use computer software that is not a custom computer program or where the software is accessed over the Internet, over private or public networks, or through wireless media, where the user has only the right to use or access the software by means of a license, lease, subscription, service, or other agreement. Notwithstanding the foregoing exclusions, "tangible personal property" includes computer software that constitutes digital music, digital books, digital videos and digital games when the purchaser has a permanent right to use such software, regardless of the method of delivery or access. If the right to use digital music, digital books, digital videos, or digital games is conditioned upon continued payment from the purchaser (*e.g.,* a paid subscription), it is not a permanent right of use. (IC Sec. 63-3616(b)).

• **Services**

The sales tax does not apply to sales of services except for the following (IC Sec. 63-3612(2)(a), IC Sec. 63-3612(2)(b), IC Sec. 63-3612(2)(d)—IC Sec. 63-3612(2)(h), IC Sec. 63-3612(2)(i), Rule 35.01.02.011.02):

(1) Producing, fabricating, or printing property to the special order of the customer;

(2) Producing, fabricating, processing, printing, or imprinting property for a consideration for consumers who furnish the materials used;

(3) Furnishing, preparing, or serving food, meals, and drinks for a consideration;

(4) Admission charges and charges to use property or facilities for recreation;

(5) Providing hotel, campground, and trailer court accommodations;

(6) Leasing or renting tangible personal property; and

(7) Intrastate transportation for hire by air of freight or passengers except as part of a flight by a certified air carrier or an air ambulance service.

Incidental services: When a sale of tangible personal property includes incidental services, the tax applies to the total amount charged, including fees for any incidental services other than separately stated transportation and installation fees (Rule 35.01.02.011.02).

• **Incidence of tax**

The sales tax is imposed on the consumer although the retailer is responsible for collecting the tax (IC Sec. 63-3619(b), Rule 35.01.02.068.02, Rule 35.01.02.068.07). Persons storing, using, or consuming tangible personal property in the state are liable for the use tax (IC Sec. 63-3621(a)), but a retailer engaged in business in the state is responsible for collecting the tax from the purchaser (IC Sec. 63-3621(b)).

Military personnel: A web page that provides Idaho tax information for military personnel can be found at **http://tax.idaho.gov/i-1011.cfm**.

• **Nexus**

A retailer engaged in business in Idaho is any retailer who: (1) engages in recurring solicitation of purchases from Idaho residents or otherwise purposefully directs its business activities at Idaho residents; and (2) has sufficient contact with Idaho, in accordance with the constitution of the United States, to allow Idaho to require the seller to collect and remit use tax on sales of tangible personal property or services made to customers in Idaho (IC Sec. 63-3611). The term includes any of the following:

(1) Any retailer maintaining, occupying or using, permanently or temporarily, directly or indirectly, or through a subsidiary or agent, by whatever name called, an office, place of distribution, sales or sample room or place, warehouse or storage place, or other place of business or maintaining a stock of goods;

(2) Any retailer having any representative, agent, salesman, canvasser or solicitor operating in Idaho under the authority of the retailer or its subsidiary for the purpose of selling, delivering, installing or the taking of orders for any tangible personal property;

(3) Any retailer, with respect to a lease or rental, deriving rentals from a lease or rental of tangible personal property situated in Idaho;

(4) Any retailer engaging in any activity in connection with servicing or installing tangible personal property in Idaho;

(5) Any retailer with substantial nexus in Idaho within the meaning of IC Sec. 63-3615A; and

(6) Any retailer having a franchisee or licensee operating under its trade name if the franchisee or licensee is required to collect the tax.

Substantial nexus: A retailer has substantial nexus with Idaho if both of the following apply (IC Sec. 63-3615A):

(a) The retailer and an in-state business maintaining one or more locations within Idaho are related parties; and

(b) The retailer and the in-state business use an identical or substantially similar name, trade name, trademark or goodwill to develop, promote or maintain sales, or the in-state business provides services to, or that inure to the benefit of, the out-of-state business related to developing, promoting or maintaining the in-state market.

Two entities are related parties if they meet any one of the following tests:

— both entities are component members of the same controlled group of corporations under IRC Sec. 1563;

— one entity is a related taxpayer to the other entity under IRC Sec. 267;

— one entity is a corporation and the other entity and any party, for which IRC Sec. 318 requires an attribution of ownership of stock from that party to the entity, own directly, indirectly, beneficially, or constructively at least 50% of the value of the outstanding stock of the corporation; or

— one or both entities is a limited liability company, partnership, estate or trust, none of which is treated as a corporation for federal income tax purposes, and such entity(s) and its members, partners or beneficiaries own in the aggregate directly, indirectly, beneficially, or constructively at least 50% of the profits, capital, stock or value of the other entity or both entities.

The provisions of IC Sec. 63-3615A do not apply to a retailer that had sales in Idaho in the previous year of less than $100,000.

¶381 Idaho

Cellular phones: A retailer is not considered to have stored, used, or consumed wireless telecommunications equipment by virtue of giving, selling, or otherwise transferring such equipment at a discount as an inducement to a consumer to commence or continue a contract for telecommunications service (IC Sec. 63-3621(a)).

• Streamlined Act status

Idaho became a participating state in the Streamlined Sales Tax Project (SSTP) as the result of Executive Order No. 2005-09, signed by the Governor on July 29, 2005. Idaho would have to enact legislation to implement the Agreement in order to join the State and Local Advisory Council, which advises the Governing board on the administration of the Agreement. The Idaho Legislature has failed to pass authorizing legislation that was introduced during the last several sessions.

¶ 382   **Tax Base**

Sales tax is imposed on the sales price of property sold at retail (IC Sec. 63-3619). The use tax base is the fair market value of the property at the time of first use in Idaho, and a recent sales price is presumptive evidence of such value unless the property is wireless telecommunications equipment, in which case a recent sales price is conclusive evidence of the property's value (IC Sec. 63-3621, Rule 35.01.02.072.01).

"Sales price" is the total amount for which property, including services rendered as a part of the sale, is sold, rented, or leased, valued in money, whether paid in money or otherwise, without any deduction for (1) the cost of property sold, (2) the cost of materials, labor, or service, losses, or any other expense, (3) transportation costs prior to sale, and (4) the face value of manufacturer's discount coupons (IC Sec. 63-3613(a)(1)—(4), Rule 35.01.02.043.01).

When the sale of property includes incidental services (except separately stated transportation and installation charges), the measure of tax is the total amount charged (Rule 35.01.02.011.02).

"Sales price" does not include the following (IC Sec. 63-3613(b)(1)—(10), Rule 35.01.02.043.02):

(1) retailer discounts allowed and taken, but only to the extent they represent price adjustments and not cash discounts for prompt payment;

(2) amounts allowed for trade-ins;

(3) amounts charged for returned property if refunded in cash or credit, but not if the customer is required to purchase other property at a greater price than the amount charged for the returned property;

(4) labor or service charges for installing or applying sold property;

(5) any tax imposed by the United States, except manufacturers' or importers' excise tax;

(6) finance charges, carrying charges, service charges, time-price differential, or interest;

(7) separately stated delivery and handling charges incurred after the sale;

(8) manufacturers' rebates when used as a down payment on a motor vehicle;

(9) fees imposed on an outfitter by a government entity; and

(10) discounts and other reductions on telecommunications equipment used in a marketing campaign.

Leases: Sales and use tax does not apply to a charge for personal property tax that is added to the rent paid for a lease of tangible personal property. The exemption applies if (1) the lessor separately states the charge for property tax to the lessee, (2) the amount charged to the lessee is not more than the property tax actually paid by the lessor, and (3) the lease agreement is for an initial period of one year or longer (IC Sec. 63-3622UU).

¶ 383   List of Exemptions, Exceptions, and Exclusions

Unless otherwise indicated, the statutory exemptions, exceptions, and exclusions listed below apply to both sales and use taxes; those applicable only to the use tax are listed separately. Items that are excluded from the sales or use tax base are treated at ¶ 382, "Tax Base."

- **Sales and use tax exemptions, exceptions, and exclusions**

Advertising space in a newspaper or magazine	IC Sec. 63-3616(c)
Aerial passenger tramway	IC Sec. 63-3622Y
Air ambulance services	IC Sec. 63-3612(2)(i)
Air carrier's receipts from regularly scheduled flight	IC Sec. 63-3612(2)(i)
Aircraft and parts used as a common carrier for hire	IC Sec. 63-3622GG
Aircraft (fixed wing) and parts used under government contract for wildfire activity	IC Sec. 63-3622GG
Aircraft parts, installed in a nonresident's private aircraft	IC Sec. 63-3621(GG)
Aircraft, personally owned, brought in by new residents	IC Sec. 63-3621(*l*)
Ammunition and wildlife purchased for use in a hunting or fishing operation	IC Sec. 63-3622D(2)
Amusement devices	IC Sec. 63-3623B
Bullion	IC Sec. 63-3622V
Canal company purchases	IC Sec. 63-3622O(1)(a), IC Sec. 63-3622O(1)(d)
Church meals	IC Sec. 63-3622J
Clean room environment	IC Sec. 63-3622NN
"Cloud" computing software	IC Sec. 63-3616(b)
Coal, petroleum, oil and gas used to produce heat	IC Sec. 63-3622G
Commemorative silver medallions	IC Sec. 63-3622PP
Computer software (custom)	IC Sec. 63-3616(b)(ii)
Computer software accessed over the Internet or by wireless media	IC Sec. 63-3616(b)(iii)
Contact lenses, prescription	IC Sec. 63-3622N
Containers	IC Sec. 63-3622E
Contractor's use of property when property entitled to production exemption	IC Sec. 63-3615(b)
Dental prostheses and orthodontic appliances	IC Sec. 63-3622N(a)
Durable medical equipment and supplies, as specified	IC Sec. 63-3622N
Discounts on telecommunications service	IC Sec. 63-3613(b)(10)
Educational institution purchases	IC Sec. 63-3622O(1)(a), IC Sec. 63-3622O(2)(a)
Electricity delivered to consumers	IC Sec. 63-3622F
Eyeglasses, prescription	IC Sec. 63-3622N
Fabricating property	IC Sec. 63-3622D(a)(1), IC Sec. 63-3622D(f)(2)
Farming operation chemicals and catalysts	IC Sec. 63-3622D(a)(3)
Farming operation property	IC Sec. 63-3622D(a)(2)
Farming operation safety equipment and supplies	IC Sec. 63-3622D(a)(4)
Food banks and soup kitchens	IC Sec. 63-3622O(1)(c), IC Sec. 63-3622O(2)(f)

Food (prepared) or beverages provided to restaurant or deli employees without charge	IC Sec. 63-3621(p)
Food processing or manufacturing chemicals and equipment	IC Sec. 63-3622D(a)(3)
Food stamp and WIC purchases	IC Sec. 63-3622EE, IC Sec. 63-3622FF
Forest protective association purchases	IC Sec. 63-3622O(2)(e)
4-H sales of animals at a fair or western Idaho spring lamb sale	IC Sec. 63-3622K(b)(7)
Fuel used in logging trucks	IC Sec. 63-3622JJ
Funeral property	IC Sec. 63-3622U
FFA sales of animals at a fair or western Idaho spring lamb sale	IC Sec. 63-3622K(b)(7)
Gas delivered to consumers	IC Sec. 63-3622F
Glider kits	IC Sec. 63-3622R(d)
Government entities	IC Sec. 63-3622O
Gratuities or tips for meal service	IC Sec. 63-3613(f)
Health-related entity purchases	IC Sec. 63-3622O(2)(a), IC Sec. 63-3622O(2)(c)
Idaho Digital Learning Academy, purchases by	IC Sec. 63-3622O(2)(a); IC Sec. 63-36504(2)
Idaho Foodbank Warehouse, Inc.	IC Sec. 63-3622O(2)(f)
Idaho national engineering and environmental laboratory	IC Sec. 63-3622BB
Interstate transactions	IC Sec. 63-3622A
Irrigation equipment	IC Sec. 63-3622W
Land and water use fees imposed on outfitters	IC Sec. 63-3613(b)(9)
Liquor sold by state liquor dispensary	IC Sec. 63-3622M
Literature published and sold by exempt entity	IC Sec. 63-3622I
Livestock sold at public livestock markets	IC Sec. 63-3622MM
Lodging for 30 consecutive days	IC Sec. 63-3612(2)(g)
Logging property	IC Sec. 63-3605A, IC Sec. 63-3622JJ
Machinery and equipment used to generate electricity by alternative methods (*e.g.,* solar, wind, geothermal, biomass, etc.) (rebate)	IC Sec. 63-3622QQ
Manufactured homes (new) (55% exempt) (park model RVs excluded, eff. 7/1/2017)	IC Sec. 63-3606, IC Sec. 63-3613(c)
Manufactured homes (used)	IC Sec. 63-3622R(b)
Manufacturing property	IC Sec. 63-3622D
Meals for the aging	IC Sec. 63-3622J
Meals sold under federal school lunch program	IC Sec. 63-3622J
Media measurement services	IC Sec. 63-3622LL
Medical equipment	IC Sec. 63-3622N
Military: household goods, vehicles, aircraft acquired in another state and used by military personnel and spouses temporarily assigned to Idaho	IC Sec. 63-3621(l)
Mining property	IC Sec. 63-3605B, IC Sec. 63-3622D(c)
Modular buildings (55% exempt)	IC Sec. 63-3606A, IC Sec. 63-3613(c)

¶383   Idaho

Vehicles or personally owned aircraft brought in by new residents . . IC Sec. 63-3621(*l*)

Vessels and certain vehicles sold to nonresidents for use outside Idaho . . . . IC Sec. 63-3622R

Water delivered to consumers . . . . IC Sec. 63-3622F

Wildlife (birds, fish, etc.) and their food, purchased for use in a taxable hunting or fishing business . . . . IC Sec. 63-3622D(1)

Wood used to produce heat . . . . IC Sec. 63-3622G

- **Exemptions, exceptions, and exclusions applicable only to the use tax**

Beverages and food, donations to individuals or registered nonprofit entities . . . . IC Sec. 63-3621(o)

Beverages and food, free tasting of . . . . IC Sec. 63-3621(n)

Household goods, vehicles, aircraft acquired in another state and used by military personnel and spouses temporarily assigned to Idaho . . . . IC Sec. 63-3621(l)

Property stored in Idaho and subsequently transported out of state for use thereafter . . . . IC Sec. 63-3615(c)

Use of tangible personal property incorporated into real property and donated to a nonprofit organization . . . . IC Sec. 63-3621(m)(1)

Use of tangible personal property incorporated into real property and donated to the state or its subdivisions . . . . IC Sec. 63-3621(m)(2), IC Sec. 63-3621(m)(3)

¶ 384   Rate of Tax

The Idaho sales and use tax rate is 6% (IC Sec. 63-3619, IC Sec. 63-3621).

Prepaid wireless fee: A 2.5% prepaid wireless E911 fee is imposed on the sales price of each purchase of prepaid wireless telecommunications service in Idaho from a seller for any purpose other than resale. A "prepaid wireless telecommunications service" is defined as a service that allows a caller to dial 911, must be paid for in advance, and is sold in predetermined units or dollars. (IC Sec. 31-4813(2)(a))

For fee purposes, a retail transaction is considered to have occurred in Idaho if (IC Sec. 31-4813(2)(c)):

    (1) the transaction is effected in person by the customer at a seller's location in Idaho;

    (2) the prepaid wireless telecommunications service is delivered to the subscriber at an Idaho address provided to the retailer;

    (3) the retailer's business records indicate that the subscriber's address is in Idaho;

    (4) the subscriber gives an Idaho address during the consummation of the sale; or

    (5) the subscriber's mobile telephone number is associated with an Idaho location.

Prepaid wireless E911 fees collected by sellers must be remitted to the State Tax Commission at the same times and in the same manner as the sales tax (IC Sec. 31-4813(3)(a)). The seller may deduct and retain 3% of the fees collected from consumers (IC Sec. 31-4813(3)(b)). The fee is subject to the sales tax provisions regarding audit and appeal procedures; collection, enforcement, penalties, and interest; and the statute of limitations and refunds (IC Sec. 31-4813(3)(c)).

¶ 385   Local Taxes

Idaho voters may authorize their county government to collect a local sales and use tax on all sales that are subject to Idaho sales and use tax. The tax must be approved by at least 66⅔% of the voters and may not exceed 10 years (IC Secs. 63-2601—63-2605). Also, the tax rate may not be greater than 0.5% of the sales price of the item subject to tax. The purpose of the tax is limited to county property tax relief and debt retirement for expansion of detention facilities. A county may contract with the Idaho State Tax Commission for the collection and administration of the tax.

Resort local taxes: See **http://tax.idaho.gov/i-1117.cfm**.

Mobile telecommunications: Idaho has conformed to the federal Mobile Telecommunications Sourcing Act (P.L. 106-252). Charges for wireless telecommunications are sourced to the customer's "place of primary use," which means the residential or primary business address of the customer within the licensed service area of the home service provider (IC Sec. 56-904). The jurisdiction in which the place of primary use is located is the only jurisdiction that may tax the communications services, regardless of the customer's location when a call is placed or received.

¶ 386   Bracket Schedule

The tax on each whole dollar is 6¢ plus an amount for each additional fractional dollar. The State Tax Commission provides schedules for collection of the 6% sales tax at **http://tax.idaho.gov/pubs/EIS00130_08-31-2006.pdf**(IC Sec. 63-3619(c), Rule 35.01.02.068.04). The tax is calculated on the entire amount of a consumer's purchases and not separately on each item. Any amount collected under the brackets that is in excess of the retailer's liability may be kept by the retailer as compensation for collecting the tax.

¶ 387   Returns, Payments, and Due Dates

Sales and use tax returns are required to be filed by every seller, by every retailer engaged in business in Idaho, and by every person who purchases tangible personal property that is subject to use tax and who has not paid use tax to a retailer required to collect the tax (IC Sec. 63-3623(d)). The returns are generally filed monthly on or before the 20th day of the month following the sale (IC Sec. 63-3623(c), Rule 35.01.02.105.02, Rule 35.01.02.105.09) and must be accompanied by the tax due (IC Sec. 63-3623(a), IC Sec. 63-3623(g), Rule 35.01.02.105.02, Rule 35.01.02.105.06, Rule 35.01.02.105.07). In some cases, returns may be filed quarterly, semiannually, or annually.

A return must be on the proper form as prescribed by the State Tax Commission and contain sufficient information to compute a tax liability (Rule 35.01.02.105.03). It must contain the total sales, nontaxable sales, taxable sales, items subject to tax, and tax due (IC Sec. 63-3623(e), IC Sec. 63-3623(f), Rule 35.01.02.105.06). Taxes previously paid by retailers on amounts represented by worthless accounts may be credited on a subsequent payment of tax or, if no tax is due, refunded (IC Sec. 63-3613(d); see also *Decision No. 24529,* Idaho State Tax Commission, August 14, 2012, CCH IDAHO TAX REPORTS, ¶ 400-699). The deduction is not limited to bad debts written off for income tax purposes.

Every person responsible for paying Idaho sales and use tax on behalf of a taxpayer as an officer, member, or employee of the taxpayer is personally liable for paying the tax, plus penalties and interest, if this person fails to carry out his or her duty (IC Sec. 63-3627). A district judge may issue a writ of mandate requiring a person to file a return in the event a return is not filed within 60 days of the due date (IC Sec. 63-3030A, IC Sec. 63-3635).

Payment methods: Payment may be made using credit cardsor e-checks, which are an electronic version of a paper check, for online payments of corporate income, personal income, withholding, franchise, sales and use, cigarette, tobacco, motor fuel, motor vehicle, severance, insurance, and utility taxes. A convenience fee is charged in the amount of 3% of any credit card payment and $5 for an e-check payment. To pay with an e-check or credit card, taxpayers should go to the "Electronic Payments" page on the State Tax Commission's Web site (**http://tax.idaho.gov/**) and click on "Debit Card/ Credit Card or E-Check." See also "Electronic filing and payment," below.

An administrative rule specifies what constitutes unacceptable tax payment methods (checks and drafts previously dishonored, from foreign institutions, or that result in processing fees) (Rule 35.02.01.131).

• Quarterly, semiannual, and annual returns

The State Tax Commission may require the filing of returns other than on a monthly basis to ensure payment or to facilitate collection (IC Sec. 63-3623(h)). Retailers or persons who owe $500 or less per quarter and have a satisfactory record of timely filing and payment may request permission to file quarterly or semiannually (Rule 35.01.02.105.02). Persons who have seasonal activities, such as Christmas tree sales or repeating fair booths, may request permission to file annually (Rule 35.01.02.105.02).

The returns are due on or before the 20th day of the month following the last day of the reporting period (Rule 35.01.02.105.09).

• Electronic filing and payment

The State Tax Commission is authorized to establish rules or procedures for the filing of tax returns and other documents via electronic transmission (IC Sec. 63-113). "Electronic transmission" means the use of a telecommunication or computer network to transfer information in an optical, electronic, magnetic, or other machine sensible form, including documents submitted by facsimile transmission and the use of third party value added networks. Documents filed electronically are deemed received on the date the document arrives at the State Tax Commission or at a third party value added network under contract with the State Tax Commission to receive the return or document.

To be considered valid, an electronically transmitted tax return or report must (1) be filed in a format prescribed by the State Tax Commission and be sufficiently free of errors to identify the filer and the tax type and to calculate the amounts due, (2) contain the taxpayer's name, address, and identifying number, (3) be signed by the taxpayer or other individual effecting the signature or verification, and (4) include sufficient information to permit the mathematical verification of any tax liability (IC Sec. 63-113).

Internet filing and payment: All taxes, interest, penalties or fees payable together with taxes and all other fees and amounts payable to the state must be paid by electronic funds transfer whenever the amount paid or payable is $100,000 or more (IC Sec. 67-2026). Internet applications allow businesses to report and pay Idaho sales and use tax online at the Idaho State Tax Commission website (**https:// idahotap.gentax.com/TAP/_/**).

Free Internet applications allow users to access past e-filings for up to one year, print receipts containing filing information, file zero returns, make adjustments, and file on behalf of multiple companies. Since most businesses usually file their sales and use tax and personal income tax withholding at the same time, the online services are linked to each other. Online payment options are also included in the e-filing services. Tax payments may be made electronically using Visa, MasterCard, or ACH debit or ACH credit systems through a secure payment server. Businesses that prefer paying with a paper check may still do so by printing a voucher off of the Internet applications to send with their payment.

• Filing date falling on weekend or holiday

If the due date for filing a return is a Saturday, Sunday, or holiday, the return is due on the next day that is not a Saturday, Sunday, or holiday (Rule 35.01.02.105.09).

- **Contractors**

Information on the application of Idaho sales and use tax to contractors (*i.e.,* persons who build, improve, repair, or alter real property) is available at **http://tax.idaho.gov/i-1013.cfm**.

- **Short-term rentals**

Airbnb, a peer-to-peer online marketplace and homestay network that enables people to list or rent short-term lodging in residential properties, has entered into an agreement with the Idaho State Tax Commission to collect and remit Idaho sales tax, travel and convention tax, and the Greater Boise Auditorium District tax (for rentals located within the District) for its hosts with Idaho listings. These taxes apply to sales for temporary lodging (30 days or less) in Idaho made through the Airbnb platform. Hosts will no longer be responsible for collecting these taxes and will not be able to opt-out of collection by Airbnb. Any booking a host has through Airbnb before December 1, 2016, will need to be reported to the Idaho State Tax Commission. Any other local sales tax will need to be collected and remitted by the host. Also, hosts who book their homes through websites other than Airbnb must still collect and remit taxes on those listings. (*Airbnb Voluntary Collection Agreement,* Idaho State Tax Commission, November 2016, CCH Idaho Tax Reports, ¶ 400-808; see also ¶ 389)

¶ 388   **Prepayment of Taxes**

Idaho has no sales and use tax provision regarding prepayment of taxes.

¶ 389   **Vendor Registration**

Before conducting business within the state, a retailer engaged in business in Idaho must file with the State Tax Commission an application for a seller's permit (IC Sec. 63-3620(a), Rule 35.01.02.070).

A permit is valid only for the person in whose name it is issued (IC Sec. 63-3620(a)). The permit or a copy thereof must be conspicuously displayed at each place where the person to whom it was issued conducts business.

A permit holder must notify the State Tax Commission if the ownership of a business has changed or if the business is terminated (Rule 35.01.02.070).

Initial permits are issued without charge (IC Sec. 63-3520(a), Rule 35.01.02.070). A $10 fee is imposed for the issuance or renewal of a permit that has been previously suspended or revoked for the first time and $25 after each successive revocation.

Additional information on the registration is available at **http://tax.idaho.gov/i-1159.cfm#sub1**

Short-term rentals: Homeowners who provide temporary lodging for a fee must charge tax on the accommodations. Idaho's 6% sales tax and the 2% state travel and convention tax apply to any sleeping accommodations rented for stays of 30 days or less. This includes the rental of a home, vacation home, cabin, lodge, condominium, townhouse, room in a private residence, or any other structure. Some Idaho resort cities and auditorium districts may also add a local sales tax on sleeping accommodations. See, '(for example, *Decision Nos. 1-328-246-784, 0-231-911-424, 0-941-912-064,* Idaho State Tax Commission, March 25, 2016, CCH Idaho Tax Reports, ¶ 400-799)

Registration to collect and remit the state sales, travel and convention, and Greater Boise Auditorium District taxes, is available at the Tax Commission's Idaho Business Registration Info webpage at **https://tax.idaho.gov/i-1159.cfm**. More information is available at **https://tax.idaho.gov/i-1013.cfm**.

- **Use tax registration**

Every retailer engaged in business in the state or maintaining a place of business in the state must register with the State Tax Commission and give the name and address of all agents operating in the state, the location of all places of business in the state, and such other information as the State Tax Commission may require (IC Sec. 63-3621(d)). This obligation is not imposed, however, on retailers that collect and remit the sales tax (IC Sec. 63-3621(c)).

- **Temporary seller's and wholesaler's permits**

The Idaho State Tax Commission is authorized to issue temporary seller's permits and wholesaler's permits (IC Sec. 63-3620). A maximum of three temporary permits may be issued to an applicant in one calendar year and each permit is valid only for the period of time shown on the face of the permit. Wholesalers who are not retailers but who purchase tangible personal property for resale may apply for a wholesaler's permit. Wholesaler's permits are valid for a period of no more than 12 consecutive months but may be renewed by the Commission upon request.

- **Promoters' obligations**

Operators or promoters of promoter-sponsored events must, before renting or leasing space to a retailer conducting business on the operator's or promoter's premises, obtain written evidence either (1) that the retailer holds a valid Idaho seller's permit for Idaho sales tax purposes or will apply for one, or (2) that the retailer will not be selling items taxable in Idaho or that he or she is not required to hold an Idaho seller's permit. Promoters may be appointed to issue temporary seller's permits to event participants and may receive a credit or refund of income or franchise tax of $1 for each permit issued (IC Sec. 63-3620C).

For additional information, see *Publication No. 643,* Idaho State Tax Commission, October 24, 2014, available at **http://tax.idaho.gov/pubs/ EBR00643_10-24-2014.pdf**.

¶ 390   Sales or Use Tax Credits

Idaho use tax is not imposed on property that has been subjected to a general retail sales or use tax by another state in an amount equal to or greater than the amount of Idaho tax, but is imposed to the extent that the amount of Idaho tax exceeds the amount of tax paid to the other state (IC Sec. 63-3621(l), Rule 35.01.02.072.07).

A purchaser required to file a return who has paid tax with regard to property purchased for resale and any purchaser required to file a use tax return who has paid tax with regard to property exempt from or not subject to tax must apply for credit of the tax paid against the tax due on the returns (IC Sec. 63-3626(a)). Any remaining balance may be refunded to the taxpayer if the taxpayer files a claim within three years after the payment was made.

Taxes paid on worthless accounts may be credited or refunded (see ¶ 387).

Incentives: For a discussion on rebates allowed for taxes paid on (1) certain electricity generation equipment, or (2) construction of a qualified new plant or building facility or small employer headquarters in Idaho, see ¶ 394.

¶ 391   Deficiency Assessments

The State Tax Commission examines a return as soon as practicable after it is filed to determine the correct amount of tax (IC Sec. 63-3040, IC Sec. 63-3635). The State Tax Commission may assert a deficiency if it is not satisfied with a return (IC Sec. 63-3629(b)). "Deficiency" is defined in the law (IC Sec. 63-3044, IC Sec. 63-3629(c)).

If a person fails to make a return, the State Tax Commission will estimate the amount of tax due (IC Sec. 63-3629(b)). Written notice of a deficiency determination must be given to the taxpayer (IC Sec. 63-3629(c), Rule 35.01.02.121.01) and must be accompanied by an explanation of the specific reason for the determination and an explanation of the taxpayer's right to appeal (IC Sec. 63-3629(c), IC Sec. 63-3045).

An assessment is made by recording in the State Tax Commission's office the liability of the taxpayer along with an identification of the taxpayer, the character of the liability assessed, the taxable period, if applicable, and the amount of the assessment (IC Sec. 63-3635, IC Sec. 63-3044). No tax collection activities may be commenced until the assessment has been made. However, the State Tax Commission may file a judicial action to require the taxpayer to file a return or to enjoin the taxpayer from violating a statutory or regulatory provision or may file an action for other injunctive or declaratory relief without first imposing a tax assessment. Upon a taxpayer's request, the State Tax Commission must furnish the taxpayer with a copy of the assessment record.

Transient equipment: The State Tax Commission may assess use tax on the basis of the fair rental value of property if the State Tax Commission determines that a taxpayer intended a use for the property that would have qualified the property as transient equipment when the property first became subject to use tax (IC Sec. 63-3621A).

Purchasers: The State Tax Commission may issue a notice of deficiency determination to a purchaser upon determining that a retail sale claimed to be exempt is not exempt and that the purchaser failed to pay the sales or use tax on the property or service purchased (IC Sec. 63-3624(h)).

¶ 392   Audit Procedures

The State Tax Commission employs auditors to examine taxpayers' books, papers, records, and equipment (IC Sec. 63-3042, IC Sec. 63-3624(B), IC Sec. 63-3624(e), Rule 35.01.02.111.05). A taxpayer must maintain every record that is necessary to a determination of its correct tax liability. Records kept out of state must be brought to Idaho if the State Tax Commission so requests or an auditor must be permitted to visit the place where the records are kept (IC Sec. 63-3042, IC Sec. 63-3624(f)). The State Tax Commission may also summon any person to appear before it and to produce books, papers, records, or other information, and may require the person to give testimony relevant to the inquiry (IC Sec. 63-3042, Rule 35.01.02.111.06). The State Tax Commission is not required to impose a tax assessment before conducting audits and investigations or making inquiries relating to matters within its jurisdiction (IC Sec. 63-3044, IC Sec. 63-3635).

The State Tax Commission may require the filing of reports by persons having information relating to sales subject to use tax (IC Sec. 63-3624(g)).

A person who refuses to comply with a summons or to permit the examination of records may be ordered by a district court to obey the State Tax Commission's demands and requests, and a refusal is treated as contempt of court (IC Sec. 63-3043).

For additional information on the audit process, see *Audits - Your Rights and Responsibilities* (Publication 230), Idaho State Tax Commission, November 27, 2013, CCH IDAHO TAX REPORTS, ¶ 400-755, also available at **http://tax.idaho.gov/pubs/EBR00230_11-27-2013.pdf**.

Voluntary disclosure: Information about the voluntary disclosure agreement program is posted at **http://tax.idaho.gov/i-1115.cfm**.

¶ 393   Statute of Limitations

Taxes must be assessed within three years of the due date of the return or the date the return was filed, whichever is later (IC Sec. 63-3633(a)). If the taxes are assessed within such period, they may be collected by levy or court proceeding within six years after the tax is assessed.

The period of limitations is suspended for the period during which the State Tax Commission is prohibited from making an assessment or collecting the tax and for 30 days thereafter (IC Sec. 63-3633(a)).

False or fraudulent returns: There is no statute of limitations if a false or fraudulent return is filed with the intent to evade tax or if there is a willful attempt to defeat or evade tax (IC Sec. 63-3633(b), IC Sec. 63-3633(d)).

Use tax returns: Taxes may be assessed within seven years of the time a use tax return should have been filed by the responsible person (IC Sec. 63-3633(c)). However, this seven-year limitations period does not apply if there is a false or fraudulent act with the intent to evade tax or if a retailer, seller, or responsible person has collected taxes and has failed to pay the taxes to the state.

• **Extension of limitations period**

The taxpayer and the State Tax Commission may agree in writing, before the expiration of the original statute of limitations, to extend the time within which an assessment may be made (IC Sec. 63-3633(e)). Subsequent extensions may be agreed upon before the prior extension period expires.

¶ 394   **Application for Refund**

Taxes that have been paid more than once or that have been erroneously collected or computed may be credited by the State Tax Commission on any amount due and payable from that person and the balance refunded (IC Sec. 63-3626(a), Rule 35.01.02.117.07). Taxes need not have been paid under protest in order to subsequently be able to claim a refund.

A refund claim must be made in writing and must include a detailed statement of the reason the claimant believes a refund is due (Rule 35.01.02.117.06). Form TCR (Sales Tax Refund Claim) is available for use in making a refund claim.

Purchasers should request a refund from the vendor to whom the excess tax was paid (Rule 35.01.02.117.01). If the purchaser can provide evidence that the vendor refused to refund the tax, the purchaser may file a refund claim directly with the State Tax Commission.

A retailer claiming a refund must state under oath that any amount refunded to the retailer has been or will be refunded by the retailer to the purchaser or that the refunded tax was never collected from a purchaser (Rule 35.01.02.117.06).

A claimant who files a sales or use tax return may claim a refund in the form of a credit against sales or use taxes due (Rule 35.01.02.117.07). The return on which the credit is claimed must be accompanied by a written refund claim.

A claim for refund may not be filed for taxes that have been asserted by a notice of deficiency determination (Rule 35.01.02.117.10).

• **Statute of limitations**

No credit or refund is allowed unless a claim is filed within three years from the time payment was made (IC Sec. 63-3626(b), Rule 35.01.02.117.09). If a deficiency or jeopardy determination is made, a refund claim must be filed within three years from the time payment was made or the date the deficiency was assessed.

• **Rebates for construction of corporate headquarters and new buildings**

Effective through December 31, 2020, a qualifying taxpayer may claim a rebate of 25% of Idaho sales and use taxes that the taxpayer or its contractors paid in regard to any property constructed, located, or installed within a project site containing new plant and building facilities in Idaho, To qualify for the rebate, a taxpayer must (1) invest at least $500,000 in new plant at the project site, (2) create at least 10 new jobs having a starting salary that exceeds a minimum amount set by statute, and (3) maintain a ratio of new employees to investment that exceeds one employee for each $50,000 of investment in new plant (IC Sec. 63-4408).

Rebate claims: A claim for rebate must be filed on or before the last day of the third calendar year following the year in which the sales or use taxes are paid. A rebate is subject to recapture if (1) the tax incentive criteria are not met at the project site during the project period, (2) the property is not used, stored, or consumed within the project site for a period of 60 consecutive months after the property was placed in service, or (3) the employment requirement is not maintained for 60 consecutive months from the date the project period ends (IC Sec. 63-4408).

- **Rebate for media productions**

A rebate is allowed for sales or use taxes paid on tangible personal property that is used directly by a media production company in media production if a minimum of $200,000 is spent on qualifying media production expenditures in Idaho within a consecutive 36-month period. The rebate is effective from July 1, 2006, until July 1, 2016 (IC Sec. 63-3622TT).

"Media production" is the production of programs through a variety of techniques and media including live action camera work, animation, computer-generated imagery or other recorded work during the process of preproduction, production, and post-production, that are intended to be exhibited in theaters, licensed for exhibition on television or cable stations or networks, licensed for or produced for sale or rental to home or commercial viewing markets, or a future viewing or listening medium (IC Sec. 63-3622TT). Media production projects include feature films, videos, television series or movies, industrials and education programs or shows, video or computer games, and documentaries, but shall not include news and athletic event programming, political advertisements, family or personal productions, filming of live staged events to which tickets are sold or any material of an indecent or obscene nature.

Application: The Department of Commerce and Labor will determine a company's eligibility to receive a rebate and may charge an application fee not in excess of $500. To receive a rebate, the media production company must apply to the State Tax Commission. If a rebate is not paid within 60 days from the date the Commission receives a qualified application, the amount owed to the taxpayer will accrue interest. Recapture applies if the tax incentive criteria are not met at the project site during the project period or if the media production company does not otherwise qualify for a rebate (IC Sec. 63-3622TT).

- **Rebate for retail developer's highway improvement expenses**

A qualified developer of a retail commercial complex whose stores sell tangible personal property or taxable services may claim a rebate of 60% of the Idaho sales or use tax taxes collected on purchases at the site as reimbursement for expenses incurred by the developer for the installation of approved transportation improvements (IC Sec. 63-3641). The rebate program represents a method of financing public transportation infrastructure projects by repaying construction costs incurred by the private sector.

To qualify for the rebate, the developer must build a complex that has a minimum cost of $4 million and must expend at least $8 million for the installation of a highway, highway interchange, and/or freeway interchange improvement.

Rebate claims: The developer claims a rebate by filing a refund request for taxes collected by stores in the complex. Stores in the complex must report their sales to the State Tax Commission separately from other stores in the state. No interest will be paid on the refunds, and all refunds will be paid from a newly created Demonstration Pilot Project Fund. Refund requests must be filed within two years of the developer's last expenditure on the transportation improvement. Total aggregate refunds may not exceed $35 million dollars or the amount expended, whichever is less. The developer will be ineligible for a rebate after recouping its costs of funding the transportation infrastructure project (IC Sec. 63-3641).

¶ 395   ILLINOIS

¶ 396   Scope of Tax

Source.—Statutory references are to the retailers' occupation tax (ROT), the use tax (UT), the service occupations tax (SOT), and the service use tax (SUT), which are codified as Title 35 of the Illinois Compiled Statutes, as amended to date. Details are reported in the CCH ILLINOIS STATE TAX REPORTS starting at ¶ 60-000.

The Illinois sales and use taxes are contained in four separate acts: the retailers' occupation tax (ROT Sec. 14 [35 ILCS 120/14]), the use tax (UT Sec. 1 [35 ILCS 105/1]), the service occupation tax (SOT Sec. 1 [35 ILCS 115/1]), and the service use tax (SUT Sec. 1 [35 ILCS 110/1]). Some of the provisions in the four acts are similar, and many of the provisions of the retailers' occupation tax are incorporated by reference into the other three taxes (UT Sec. 12 [35 ILCS 105/12], SUT Sec. 12 [35 ILCS 110/12], SOT Sec. 12 [35 ILCS 115/12]). Also, retailers' occupation tax regulations not incompatible with the use tax and service occupation tax are incorporated by reference into the use and service occupation tax regulations, and service occupation tax regulations not incompatible with the service use tax are incorporated by reference into the service use tax regulations (86 Ill. Adm. Code Sec. 150.1201, 86 Ill. Adm. Code Sec. 150.1201, 86 Ill. Adm. Code Sec. 150.1320, 86 Ill. Adm. Code Sec. 160.145).

• **Retailers' occupation tax**

The retailer's occupation tax (ROT) is imposed on persons engaged in the business of selling tangible personal property at retail (ROT Sec. 2 [35 ILCS 120/2], 86 Ill. Adm. Code Sec. 130.101). A person who holds itself out as making retail sales or who habitually makes such sales is considered to be a retailer (UT Sec. 2 [35 ILCS 105/2], ROT Sec. 1 [35 ILCS 120/1], 86 Ill. Adm. Code Sec. 130.115). The tax is measured by the "gross receipts" received from such sales (86 Ill. Adm. Code Sec. 130.101).

ROT is not imposed on intangible personal property or real property (86 Ill. Adm. Code Sec. 130.120(a) and (b), 86 Ill. Adm. Code Sec. 130.505).

Digital downloads: The redemption of digital codes used to acquire downloaded digital content is not subject to Illinois sales and use tax. The longstanding policy of the Illinois Department of Revenue treats digitized content delivered solely by electronic means as a transaction that does not involve the transfer of tangible personal property and is therefore not subject to Illinois sales and use tax. As *General Information Letter ST 01-0157-GIL,* September 25, 2001, clearly states, information or data delivered electronically via the Internet does not constitute the transfer of tangible personal property but rather the transfer of an intangible not subject to ROT. Accordingly, the sale of a digital code delivered by electronic means should not be subject to ROT, because the object of the transaction, the electronically delivered music or video recordings, is an intangible. Similarly, the redemption of a digital code printed on a tangible medium should not alter the applicability of Illinois sales and use tax when otherwise non-taxable transfers of digitized content are sold. (*General Information Letter ST 07-0066-GIL,* Illinois Department of Revenue, June 18, 2007).

Software: Canned software is considered to be tangible personal property regardless of the form in which it is transferred or transmitted, including tape, disc, card, electronic means or other media (86 Ill. Adm. Code 130.1935(a)). Custom software is generally not taxable (*General Information Letter ST 12-0022-GIL,* Illinois Department of Revenue, April 27, 2012, CCH ILLINOIS TAX REPORTS, ¶ 402-490).

A reseller of software will not be liable for sales tax, where a license agreement exists between the original seller of the software and the customer, provided that the reseller maintains a copy of the signed license agreement in its records and other criteria concerning the license transaction are met (*General Information Letter ST 13-0032-GIL,* Illinois Department of Revenue, June 19, 2013, CCH ILLINOIS TAX REPORTS, ¶ 402-689).

Software license agreements that authorize the transfer of the software without permission of the licensor are subject to sales and use tax. A software license must meet numerous requirements to constitute a nontaxable retail sale, including that the license agreement be in writing and restrictions on the duplication and transferring of the software. (*General Information Letter ST 14-0034-GIL,* Illinois Department of Revenue, July 29, 2014, CCH ILLINOIS TAX REPORTS, ¶ 402-835)

Software maintenance: In general, computer software maintenance agreements are treated the same as maintenance agreements for other types of tangible personal property. If the charges for the agreements are included in the property's selling price, those charges are subject to tax. Further, no tax is incurred on the maintenance services or parts when repair or servicing is performed. An example of an agreement included in the selling price of property is a manufacturer's warranty that is provided without additional cost to a purchaser of a new item. Sales of maintenance agreements sold separately from property are not taxable. However, when maintenance or repair services or parts are provided under separately sold agreements, the service providers will incur use tax on their cost price of property transferred to customers incident to the completion of the maintenance service. (*General Information Letter ST 13-0027-GIL,* Illinois Department of Revenue, May 28, 2013, CCH ILLINOIS TAX REPORTS, ¶ 402-674).

Cloud computing: Certain cloud computing services used through a customer's existing telecommunications, Internet, or network connections were not telecommunications services subject to the Illinois telecommunications excise tax. The cloud-based applications and services provided by the company are services that support a customer's telecommunication equipment, including its voice, video, messaging, presence, audio, web conferencing and mobile capabilities. (*General Information Letter ST 13-0074-GIL,* Illinois Department of Revenue, November 26, 2013, released February 2014, CCH ILLINOIS TAX REPORTS, ¶ 402-764).

• **Medical marijuana**

Illinois imposes a 7% tax on the privilege of cultivating medical cannabis. The privilege tax is paid by a cultivation center, not a dispensing organization or a qualifying patient, and is imposed in addition to all other Illinois state and local occupation and privilege taxes. Persons subject to the tax must apply to the Department of Revenue for a certificate of registration. (410 ILCS 130/200; 86 Ill. Adm. Code Sec. 429.105 *et seq.*)

• **Use tax**

The use tax (UT) complements the ROT and is imposed on the privilege of using in Illinois tangible personal property purchased anywhere at retail from a retailer (UT Sec. 3 [35 ILCS 105/3], 86 Ill. Adm. Code Sec. 150.101, 86 Ill. Adm. Code Sec. 150.125). Use tax is not imposed if the seller of the property would not be subject to ROT despite all elements of the sale occurring in Illinois (UT Sec. 3-65 [35 ILCS 105/3-65], 86 Ill. Adm. Code Sec. 150.101, 86 Ill. Adm. Code Sec. 150.301). Use tax is collected from purchasers by retailers maintaining a place of business in Illinois or by retailers authorized to collect the tax. The purpose of the tax is to prevent Illinois residents from avoiding ROT by making purchases in another state and to protect Illinois merchants against the diversion of business to out-of-state retailers (*Commonwealth Edison Co. et al. v. Department of Revenue et al.* (1989, Ill App Ct) 535 NE2d 30).

Construction contractors: The Department of Revenue has stated the following general principles concerning the tax obligations of out-of-state contractors (ST 12-0019-GIL, March 30, 2012, CCH ILLINOIS TAX REPORTS, ¶ 402-069).

"In Illinois, construction contractors are deemed end users of tangible personal property purchased for incorporation into real property. As end users of such tangible personal property, these contractors incur Use Tax liability for such purchases based upon their cost price of the tangible personal property. See 86 Ill. Adm. Code 130.1940 and 86 Ill. Adm. Code 130.2075. Therefore, any tangible personal property that a construction contractor purchases that will be permanently affixed to or incorporated into real property in this State will be subject to Use Tax. If such contractors did not pay the Use Tax liability to their suppliers, those contractors must self assess their Use Tax liability and pay it directly to the Department. If the contractors have already paid a tax in another state regarding the purchase or use of such property, they will be entitled to a credit against their Illinois Use Tax liability to the extent that they have paid tax that was properly due to another state. See 86 Ill. Adm. Code 150.310."

"It is important to note that since construction contractors are the end users of the materials that they permanently affix to real estate, their customers incur no Use Tax liability and the construction contractors have no legal authority to collect the Use Tax from their customers. However, many construction contractors pass on the amount of their Use Tax liabilities to customers in the form of higher prices or by including provisions in their contracts that require customers to "reimburse" the construction contractor for his or her tax liability. Please note that this reimbursement cannot be billed to a customer as "sales tax," but can be listed on a bill as a reimbursement of tax. The choice of whether a construction contractor requires a tax reimbursement from the customer or merely raises his or her price is a business decision on the construction contractor's part."

"If subcontractors are utilized and are acting as construction contractors, the transaction between the general contractors and the subcontractors is not a taxable transaction. The subcontractors incur Use Tax liability on any tangible personal property that they purchase for incorporation into real estate. If, however, general contractors make purchases of tangible personal property and then contract to have subcontractors install that tangible personal property, the general contractors incur Use Tax liability on that tangible personal property."

State contractors: No person may enter into a contract with a state agency unless the person and all of its affiliates collect and remit Illinois use tax on all sales of tangible personal property into the state of Illinois regardless of whether the person or affiliate is a retailer maintaining a place of business within Illinois (30 ILCS 500/50-12). Every bid and contract must contain a certification that the bidder or contractor is in compliance with the use tax collection and remittance requirement and that the bidder or contractor acknowledges that the contracting state agency may void the contract if the certification is false.

• **Service occupation tax**

The service occupation tax (SOT) is imposed on persons engaged in the business of making sales of services, *i.e.,* servicemen or service providers (SOT Sec. 1 [35 ILCS 115/1], SUT Sec. 2 [35 ILCS 110/2], SOT Sec. 2 [35 ILCS 115/2], SOT Sec. 3 [35 ILCS 115/3], 86 Ill. Adm. Code Sec. 140.101, 86 Ill. Adm. Code Sec. 140.120, 86 Ill. Adm. Code Sec. 140.201(f)). Tax is not imposed on the service itself, but is instead based on the selling price of tangible personal property transferred incident to the service. SOT is not imposed on the selling price of property that is subject to ROT or UT (86 Ill. Adm. Code Sec. 140.125(f)).

The SOT is not imposed on sales of intangible personal property or real property (86 Ill. Adm. Code Sec. 140.125(a) and (b)).

• **Service use tax**

The service use tax (SUT) is imposed on the privilege of using in Illinois real or tangible personal property received as an incident to a purchase of service from a service provider (SUT Sec. 1 [35 ILCS 110/1], SUT Sec. 3 [35 ILCS 110/3], 86 Ill. Adm. Code Sec. 160.101). The SUT complements the SOT and is not imposed on the use of the property in Illinois if the service provider is not subject to SOT on the transfer of the property despite all elements of the sale of service occurring in Illinois (SUT Sec. 3-55 [35 ILCS 110/3-55]). SUT is collected from purchasers by service providers required or authorized to collect the tax.

- **Incidence of tax**

The legal incidence of the ROT falls on the seller, which generally reimburses itself by collecting UT from its customer (86 Ill. Adm. Code Sec. 130.101(d)). A purchaser is liable for the UT and is required to pay UT to the seller or directly to the state in certain instances (86 Ill. Adm. Code Sec. 150.130).

A service provider who transfers property as an incident to a sale of service is liable for the SOT on the property transferred, and generally reimburses itself by collecting SUT from the purchaser (SOT Sec. 3-40 [35 ILCS 115/3-40]). A purchaser is liable for the SUT and is required to pay the SUT to the service provider or directly to the state in certain instances (86 Ill. Adm. Code Sec. 160.101(g)).

Drop shipments: A general information letter discusses the treatment of drop shipments and certificates of resale for sales tax purposes (*General Information Letter ST 13-0062-GIL,* Illinois Department of Revenue, October 22, 2013, CCH Illinois Tax Reports, ¶ 402-742).

- **Retailer v. service provider tests**

A case law standard has been developed to determine whether a business is a service subject to SOT or a retail occupation subject to ROT. The test, first applied in 1971 (*Spagat v. Mahin* (1971, SCt) 50 Ill2d 183, 277 NE2d 834), provides that if the article sold has no value to the purchaser except as a result of services rendered by the vendor and the transfer of the article to the purchaser is an actual and necessary part of the service rendered, then the vendor is engaged in the business of rendering service and not in the business of selling at retail. If the article sold is the substance of the transaction and the service rendered is merely incidental to, and an inseparable part of, the transfer to the purchaser of the article sold, then the vendor is engaged in the business of selling at retail.

Other factors developed in case law consider (1) the ratio between the bare cost of materials and the ultimate sales price, (2) the buyer's motive for selecting the particular seller, and (3) whether the item at issue is a unique or special-order item or a standard-stock item (*J.H. Walters & Co. v. Department of Revenue* (1969, SCt) 44 Ill2d 95, 254 NE2d 485). To aid taxpayers, the Department has issued regulations detailing the correct characterization for many occupations.

- **Nexus**

Illinois requires that any "retailer" or "retailer maintaining a place of business" in Illinois engaged in making a "sale at retail" collect use tax. A "retailer" is a person that is engaged or habitually engages in selling tangible personal property at retail. A "sale at retail" means the transfer of ownership or title to tangible personal property to a purchaser for the purpose of use, not resale, for consideration.

"Click-through" nexus: Beginning July 1, 2011, the nexus statute was amended to provide that a retailer is considered a "retailer maintaining a place of business" in Illinois for use tax purposes if (UT Sec. 2 [35 ILCS 105/2]; *Informational Bulletin, FY 2011-14,* Illinois Department of Revenue, June 2011, CCH Illinois State Tax Reports, ¶ 402-361):

> — the retailer has a contract with a person located in Illinois under which the person, for a commission or other consideration based upon the sale of tangible personal property by the retailer, directly or indirectly refers potential customers to the retailer by a link on the person's Internet website; or

> — the retailer has a contract with a person located in Illinois under which the retailer sells the same or a substantially similar line of products as the person located in Illinois and does so using an identical or substantially similar name, trade name, or trademark as the person located in Illinois, and the retailer provides a commission or other consideration to the person located in Illinois based upon the sale of tangible personal property by the retailer.

¶396 Illinois

Under each type of contract described above, a retailer is considered an Illinois retailer only if the cumulative gross receipts from sales of tangible personal property under the contract exceeded $10,000 during the preceding four quarterly periods ending on the last day of March, June, September, and December (UT Sec. 2 [35 ILCS 105/2]). Similar changes were made to the definition of a "serviceman maintaining a place of business" in Illinois for purposes of the sale of a service under the service use tax. (SUT Sec. 2 [35 ILCS 110/2])

Click-through nexus law invalidated: The Illinois Supreme Court held that the definition provisions in P.A. 96-1544 (H.B. 3659), Laws 2011, the sales tax click-through nexus law, are void and unenforceable because they impose a discriminatory tax on electronic commerce under the meaning of the federal Internet Tax Freedom Act. The click-through nexus law is discriminatory because it imposes a use tax collection obligation on out-of-state retailers who maintain clickable links on websites while it does not impose a similar obligation on similar types of advertising, such as promotional codes, made available by out-of-state retailers through newspapers or other printed publications or over-the-air broadcasting. In addition, no other Illinois law imposes a similar obligation on other out-of-state retailers. The court did not address the question of whether the click-through nexus law violated the Commerce Clause of the U.S. Constitution. (*Performance Marketing Ass'n, Inc. v. Hamer,* Illinois Supreme Court, No. 114496, October 18, 2013, CCH Illinois Tax Reports, ¶ 402-719).

For additional information on nexus issues, see *General Information Letter ST 15-0019-GIL,* Illinois Department of Revenue, March 18, 2015, released April 2015, CCH Illinois Tax Reports, ¶ 402-944.

- **Use of promotional codes**

A retailer is presumed to be maintaining a place of business in Illinois for use tax and service tax nexus purposes if that retailer has a contract with an Illinois person under which the person, for a commission or other consideration based on the sale of property by the retailer, directly or indirectly refers potential customers to the retailer by providing a promotional code or other mechanism that allows the retailer to track purchases referred by such persons. Examples of a mechanism that allows the tracking of purchases include the use of a link on the person's website, codes distributed through hand delivery or by mail, or codes distributed through radio or other broadcast media. The presumption can be rebutted by submitting proof that the referrals or other activities pursued in Illinois by such persons did not create nexus pursuant to the U.S. Constitution. (35 ILCS 105/2(1.1); 35 ILCS 110/2(1.1); *Informational Bulletin FY 2015-07,* Illinois Department of Revenue, December 2014, CCH Illinois Tax Reports, ¶ 402-896)

- **Sourcing**

Effective August 26, 2014, Illinois enacted rules for determining a seller's location for sales tax, use tax, service occupation tax, service use tax and local sales tax purposes (35 ILCS 120/2-12). The sourcing rules do not apply to retailers with respect to any activity not described in the rules.

Over-the-counter transactions will be deemed to occur at the retailer's same place of business where the buyer is present and pays for the property if the retailer regularly stocks the property or similar property for sale at the retailer's place of business, the buyer had no prior commitment to the retailer, and either (35 ILCS 120/2-12(1)):

(1) the buyer takes possession of the property at the same place of business, or

(2) the retailer delivers or arranges for the property to be delivered to the buyer.

Remote sales: Sales of property where the purchase is made and paid for over the phone, in writing or via the Internet will be deemed to occur at the retailer's same place of business if the retailer regularly stocks the property or similar property for sale at the retailer's place of business, the buyer had no prior commitment to the retailer, and the buyer takes possession of the property at the retailer's place of business. (35 ILCS 120/2-12(2))

Vending machine sales: A retailer's vending machine sales will be deemed to occur at the location of the vending machine when the sale is made, if (35 ILCS 120/2-12(3)):

> (1) the vending machine is operated by coin, currency, credit card, token, coupon or similar device;

> (2) the food, beverage or other property is contained in, and dispensed from, the vending machine; and

> (3) the buyer takes possession of the item immediately.

Mineral extraction: A producer of coal or other mineral mined in Illinois will be deemed to be engaged in the business of selling at the place where the coal or other mineral mined is extracted from the earth. "Extracted from the earth" means the location at which the coal or other mineral is extracted from the mouth of the mine. A "mineral" includes not only coal, but also oil, sand, stone taken from a quarry, gravel and any other thing commonly regarded as a mineral and extracted from the earth. (35 ILCS 120/2-12(4))

Leases: A retailer selling tangible personal property to a nominal lessee or bailee pursuant to a lease with a dollar or other nominal option to purchase is engaged in the business of selling at the location where the property is first delivered to the lessee or bailee for its intended use. (P.A. 99-126 (S.B. 1548), Laws 2015)

• Streamlined Act status

Illinois has enacted the Uniform (Simplified) Sales and Use Tax Act, and is one of the Streamlined Sales Tax Advisor States. For additional information, see ¶ 402.

¶ 397   **Tax Base**

The ROT (retailers' occupation tax) is based on "gross receipts" from retail sales of tangible personal property (ROT Sec. 2-10 [35 ILCS 120/2-10], 86 Ill. Adm. Code Sec. 130.101(a)).

"Gross receipts" means the total selling price or amount of retail sales (ROT Sec. 1 [35 ILCS 120/1], 86 Ill. Adm. Code Sec. 130.401). Payments from charge and time sales are included in gross receipts only when received. Receipts from the assignment of accounts receivable to a wholly owned subsidiary are likewise not included in basis until the purchaser makes payment. Amounts received as down payments are included in gross receipts (86 Ill. Adm. Code Sec. 130.430).

"Selling price" or the "amount of sale" is defined as the consideration for a sale valued in money, including cash, credits, property, and services (ROT Sec. 1 [35 ILCS 120/1], 86 Ill. Adm. Code Sec. 130.425). The selling price is determined without deduction for the cost of the property sold, the cost of materials used, the labor or service cost, the freight or transportation costs, salesmen's commissions, interest paid by the seller, or any other expenses (ROT Sec. 1 [35 ILCS 120/1], 86 Ill. Adm. Code Sec. 130.410). However, the selling price does not include value given for traded-in property of "like kind and character."

Internet access: Charges for Internet access that do not include charges for the line or other transmission charges or charges for canned computer software or other tangible personal property are generally not subject to Illinois retailers' occupation (sales) tax, Illinois use tax, or Illinois telecommunications tax.

A single monthly fee charged for a package of items including Internet access, e-mail, electronic newsletters, templates for creating websites, and other structures that customers can use to enter data onto an Internet format are generally not subject to telecommunications tax. Furthermore, unless charges are made for canned computer software or other tangible personal property, the charges would also be exempt from retailers' occupation (sales) tax and use tax (*General Information Letter ST 99-0026-GIL,* Illinois Department of Revenue, January 8, 1999).

Prepaid calling arrangements: Prepaid telephone calling arrangements are subject to Illinois retailers' occupation (sales), service occupation (sales), use, and service use tax as tangible personal property, regardless of the form the arrangements may be embodied or transmitted (UT Sec. 3 [35 ILCS 105/3], SUT Sec. 3 [35 ILCS 110/3], SOT Sec. 3 [35 ILCS 115/3], ROT Sec. 2 [35 ILCS 120/2]; *General Information Letter ST 13-0009-GIL,* Illinois Department of Revenue, February 5, 2013, CCH ILLINOIS STATE TAX REPORTS, ¶ 402-639).

Gratuities or tips: Mandatory gratuity charges that are separately stated on a dinner bill are not subject to Illinois sales tax if the gratuities are turned over as tips to employees. The gratuities are taxable if the meal vendor retains them, even if the vendor uses the gratuities as wages. (*General Information Letter ST 11-0058-GIL,* Illinois Department of Revenue, July 19, 2011, CCH ILLINOIS STATE TAX REPORTS, ¶ 402-383)

"Deal of the Day" vouchers: Deal-of the-Day vouchers are subject to sales tax on redemption by the voucher purchaser, not at the time of sale by the voucher retailer. The purchaser is buying the right to redeem the voucher, which is a nontaxable sale of an intangible (*General Information Letter ST 12-0009-GIL,* Illinois Department of Revenue, February 28, 2012, CCH ILLINOIS STATE TAX REPORTS, ¶ 402-456). The general information letter also provides examples for determining the taxability of a transaction. The letter notes that the department is preparing a bulletin to explain the treatment of websites that sell Deal-of-the-Day vouchers.

Delivery: Transportation and delivery charges are taxable when there is an "inseparable link" between the sale of property and its (86 Ill. Adm. Code Sec.130.410; 86 Ill. Adm. Code Sec.130.410). The rules determine whether an "inseparable link" exists and provide methods for determining the tax when the items sold are taxed at different rate, with numerous examples. See also *General Information Letter ST 16-0065-GIL,* Illinois Department of Revenue, December 15, 2016, CCH ILLINOIS STATE TAX REPORTS, ¶ 403-193.

• **UT**

The use tax is generally imposed on the selling price of tangible personal property purchased at retail and used in Illinois (UT Sec. 3-10 [35 ILCS 105/3-10]). If property used or consumed is a by-product or waste product that has been refined, manufactured, or produced from property purchased at retail, the use tax basis is the lower of (1) the fair market value, if any, of the by-product or waste product or (2) the selling price of the purchased property. "Fair market value" is the price at which property would change hands between a willing buyer and a willing seller and is established either by Illinois sales by the taxpayer of the by-product or waste product, or, if there are no such sales, comparable Illinois sales or purchases of property of like kind and character. "Selling price" has the same meaning as provided under the ROT; see above (UT Sec. 2 [35 ILCS 105/2], UT Sec. 2b [35 ILCS 105/2b], 86 Ill. Adm. Code Sec. 150.135, 86 Ill. Adm. Code Sec. 150.201(e), 86 Ill. Adm. Code Sec. 150.1101).

• **SOT and SUT**

The service occupation and service use taxes imposed on service providers are generally based on the "selling price" of tangible personal property transferred incidental to services (SUT Sec. 3-10 [35 ILCS 110/3-10], SOT Sec. 3-10 [35 ILCS 115/3-10], 86 Ill. Adm. Code Sec. 140.101(b)). However, certain service providers may choose to have the taxes imposed on the basis of cost price. "Selling price" is the consideration for a sale valued in money including cash, credits, and service, without deduction for the service providers cost of the property sold, cost of materials used, labor or service cost, or any other expense, but not including interest or finance charges separately stated or charges added to prices by sellers by reason of the seller's duty to collect the SUT from the purchaser (SUT Sec. 2 [35 ILCS 110/2], 86 Ill. Adm. Code Sec. 140.201(h), 86 Ill. Adm. Code Sec. 160.105(e)).

For purposes of computing the SOT and SUT, the selling price can in no event be less than the cost price of the property to the service provider (SUT Sec. 3-10 [35 ILCS 110/3-10], SOT Sec. 3-10 [35 ILCS 115/3-10], 86 Ill. Adm. Code Sec. 140.101(e)). "Cost price" is the consideration paid by a service provider for the purchase of tangible personal property from a supplier, without deduction of the supplier's cost of the property sold or any other expense of the supplier (SUT Sec. 2 [35 ILCS 110/2], SOT Sec. 2 [35 ILCS 115/2], 86 Ill. Adm. Code Sec. 140.201(a), 86 Ill. Adm. Code Sec. 140.301(a)).

The SOT and SUT are based on 50% of the service provider's entire billing to the service customer in the event the selling price of each item of property transferred incident to a sale of service is not shown as a separate and distinct item on the service provider's billing (SOT Sec. 3-10 [35 ILCS 115/3-10], SUT Sec. 3d [35 ILCS 110/3d], 86 Ill. Adm. Code Sec. 140.101(e)).

Elections available to service providers: At the election of any registered service provider made for each fiscal year, sales of service in which the aggregate annual cost price of tangible personal property transferred incident to the sales of service is less than 35% of the aggregate annual total gross receipts from all sales of service (75% in the case of service providers transferring prescription drugs or providers engaged in graphic arts production), the SOT and SUT will be based on the service provider's cost price of the tangible personal property transferred incident to the sale of those services (SUT Sec. 3-10 [35 ILCS 110/3-10], SOT Sec. 3-10 [35 ILCS 115/3-10]).

¶ 398   List of Exemptions, Exceptions, and Exclusions

Unless otherwise indicated, the statutory exemptions, exceptions, and exclusions listed below apply to the ROT, SOT, UT, and SUT; those applicable only to a specific tax are listed separately. Items that are excluded from the tax base are treated at ¶ 397, "Tax Base."

Agricultural machinery and equipment	35 [ILCS]105/3-5(11)
Aircraft maintenance facility machinery and equipment	35 [ILCS]120/1m, 35 [ILCS]120/1n
Aircraft parts, components, materials, etc.	35 [ILCS]110/3-5, 35 [ILCS]115/3-5
Aircraft support center	35 [ILCS]120/1o
Biodiesel fuel	35 [ILCS]105/3-10, 35 [ILCS]110/3-10, 35 [ILCS]115/3-10, 35 [ILCS]120/2-10
Building materials for use in River Edge Redevelopment Zone projects	35 [ILCS] 105/12, 35 [ILCS]110/12, 35 [ILCS]115/12, 35 [ILCS]120/2-54
Building materials for use in the South Suburban Airport project	35 [ILCS]120/1s
Bullion	35 [ILCS]105/3-20, 35 [ILCS]110/3-20, 35 [ILCS]115/3-20, 35 [ILCS]120/2-20
Computer software (custom)	35 [ILCS]105/3-25, 35 [ILCS]110/3-25, 35 [ILCS]115/3-25, 35 [ILCS]120/2-25

Farm machinery and equipment . . . . 35 [ILCS]105/3-5(11),
35 [ILCS]110/3-5(7),
35 [ILCS]115/3-5(7),
35 [ILCS]120/2-5(2)

Feminine hygiene devices (tampons, menstrual pads, and menstrual
cups) . . . . 35 [ILCS]105/3-5,
35 [ILCS]110/3-5,
35 [ILCS]115/3-5,
35 [ILCS]120/2-5

Food (reduced rate) . . . . 35 [ILCS]105/3-10,
35 [ILCS]110/3-10,
35 [ILCS]115/3-10,
35 [ILCS]120/2-10

Food for public assistance patients in long-term care (exp. 6/30/2016)
. . . . 35 [ILCS]105/3-10,
35 [ILCS]110/3-10,
35 [ILCS]115/3-10,
35 [ILCS]120/2-10

Fuel for international flights transporting cargo . . . . 35 [ILCS]105/3-5(12),
35 [ILCS]110/3-5(8),
35 [ILCS]115/3-5(8),
35 [ILCS]120/2-5(22)

Game and game birds, transactions that occur in a "game breeding
and hunting preserve area" . . . . 35 [ILCS] 105/3-5(26),
35 [ILCS]110/3-5(19),
35 [ILCS]115/3-5(20),
35 [ILCS] 120/2-5(32)

Gasohol . . . . 35 [ILCS]105/3-10,
35 [ILCS]110/3-10,
35 [ILCS]115/3-10,
35 [ILCS]120/2-10

Government, property purchased for lease to . . . . 35 [ILCS]105/3-5(23),
35 [ILCS]110/3-5(16),
35 [ILCS]115/3-5(17),
35 [ILCS]120/2-5(29)

High impact business, property for manufacturing, generating . . . . . 20 [ILCS]655/5.5

High impact service facility machinery and equipment . . . . 35 [ILCS]105/12,
35 [ILCS]110/12,
35 [ILCS]115/12,
35 [ILCS]120/1i,
35 [ILCS]120/1j

Horses, breeding or racing . . . . 35 [ILCS]105/3-5,
35 [ILCS]110/3-5,
35 [ILCS]115/3-5,
35 [ILCS]120/2-5

Hospitals, purchases or uses by . . . . 35 [ILCS]105/3-8,
35 [ILCS]110/3-8,
35 [ILCS]115/3-8,
35 [ILCS]120/2-9

Hospitals, computers and communication equipment purchased for lease to	35 [ILCS]105/3-5(22), 35 [ILCS]110/3-5(15), 35 [ILCS]115/3-5(16), 35 [ILCS]120/2-5(28)
Illinois transactions	35 [ILCS]105/3-5(4), 35 [ILCS]110/2, 35 [ILCS]115/2, 35 [ILCS]120/1g, 35 [ILCS]120/2-5(11)
Interstate transactions	35 [ILCS]115/3-45, 35 [ILCS]120/2-60
Legal tender	35 [ILCS]105/3-5(8), 35 [ILCS]110/3-5(4), 35 [ILCS]115/3-5(4), 35 [ILCS]120/2-5
Manufacturing machinery and equipment	35 [ILCS]105/3-50, 35 [ILCS]110/2, 35 [ILCS]115/2, 35 [ILCS]120/2-45
Mining machinery and equipment	35 [ILCS]105/3-5, 35 [ILCS]110/3-5, 35 [ILCS]115/3-5, 35 [ILCS]120/2-5
Motor vehicles over 8,000 lbs.	35 [ILCS] 105/3-5(33), 35 [ILCS]110/2(4a-5), 35 [ILCS]115/2(d-1.1), 35 [ILCS] 120/2-5(12-5)
Natural gas, electricity, and water delivered by pipes or wires	35 [ILCS]105/3, 35 [ILCS]110/2, 35 [ILCS]115/2, 35 [ILCS]120/2
Newsprint and ink	35 [ILCS]105/2, 35 [ILCS]110/2, 35 [ILCS]120/1
Nonprofit music or dramatic arts organization purchases	35 [ILCS]105/3-5(3), 35 [ILCS]110/3-5(3), 35 [ILCS]115/3-5(3), 35 [ILCS]120/2-5(9)
Nonprofit organization for elderly recreation	35 [ILCS]105/3-5(4), 35 [ILCS]110/2, 35 [ILCS]115/2, 35 [ILCS]120/1g, 35 [ILCS]120/1h, 35 [ILCS]120/2-5(11)
Nonprofit organization operated as service enterprise for elderly	35 [ILCS]105/3-5(1), 35 [ILCS]110/3-5(1), 35 [ILCS]115/3-5(1), 35 [ILCS]120/2-5(10)
Photoprocessing machinery and equipment	35 [ILCS]105/3-5(15), 35 [ILCS]110/3-5(11), 35 [ILCS]115/3-5(11), 35 [ILCS]120/2-5(20)

• Exemptions from ROT and UT

Breeding livestock .... 35 [ILCS]105/3-35,
35 [ILCS]110/3-35,
35 [ILCS]115/3-35,
35 [ILCS]120/2-35

Bulk vending machine sales .... 35 [ILCS]105/2,
35 [ILCS]120/1

Farm chemicals .... 35 [ILCS]105/3-35,
35 [ILCS]120/2-5(1)

Fuel for river vessels .... 35 [ILCS]120/2-5(24)

Isolated or occasional sales .... 35 [ILCS]105/2,
35 [ILCS]120/1

Meals for elderly .... 35 [ILCS] 105/2,
35 [ILCS]120/1

Motor vehicle sales to nonresidents .... 35 [ILCS]105/3-55(h),
35 [ILCS]120/2-5(25),
Notice ST-58: Reciprocal/
Non-Reciprocal Vehicle
Tax Rate Chart, January
2016, CCH Illinois Tax
Reports, ¶ 403-084

Newspapers and magazines .... 35 [ILCS]105/2,
35 [ILCS]110/2,
35 [ILCS]120/1

• Exemptions from SOT and SUT

Maintenance agreements, transfers pursuant to .... 35 [ILCS]105/3-65,
35 [ILCS]105/3-75,
35 [ILCS]110/3-55,
35 [ILCS]115/2,
35 [ILCS]120/2-55

• Exemptions from UT and SUT

Demonstration use of property .... 35 [ILCS]105/2,
35 [ILCS]110/2

Fuel for locomotives .... 35 [ILCS]105/3-55,
35 [ILCS]110/3-45

Manufacturing machinery and equipment .... 35 [ILCS] 105/3-85,
35 ILCS 110/3-70

Property acquired outside Illinois by nonresident .... 35 [ILCS]105/3-70

Property taxed in another state .... 35 [ILCS]105/3-55(d),
35 [ILCS]110/3-45(e)

Property used out of state by relocating business .... 35 [ILCS]105/3-70,
35 [ILCS]110/3-60

• Exemptions from ROT

Construction: building materials for public-private partnership
transportation projects .... 35 [ILCS]120/1r

Motor vehicles used for renting (one year or less) .... 35 [ILCS]120/2-5(5)

• Exemptions from UT

Nursing home residents, purchases of food and certain medical items
for use by .... 35 [ILCS]105/3-5(30)

¶ 399   **Rate of Tax**

The retailers' occupation tax, use tax, service occupation tax, and service use tax are generally imposed at the rate of 6.25% (UT Sec. 3-10 [35 ILCS 105/3-10], SUT Sec. 3-10 [35 ILCS 110/3-10], SOT Sec. 3-10 [35 ILCS 115/3-10], ROT Sec. 2-10 [35 ILCS 120/2-10], 86 Ill. Adm. Code Sec. 130.101(b), 86 Ill. Adm. Code Sec. 140.101(b), 86 Ill. Adm. Code Sec. 150.105, 86 Ill. Adm. Code Sec. 160.101(c)). A regulation details the methods used for calculating tax on sales of items subject to different tax rates (86 Ill. Adm. Code Sec. 150.525).

- **Food, medicine, and medical equipment**

Food for human consumption is taxable either at the full (high) state rate of 6.25% or at a reduced (low) state rate of 1%, plus any applicable local tax. Generally, food for human consumption that is to be consumed off the premises where sold, except for alcoholic beverages, soft drinks, candy, and food prepared for immediate consumption, is subject to retailer's occupation tax (sales) (ROT), service occupation tax (SOT), use tax (UT), and service use tax (SUT) at the low state rate. The high state rate of tax applies to food prepared for immediate consumption (such as hot food), and to soft drinks, candy, and alcoholic beverages. (UT Sec. 3-10 [35 ILCS 105/3-10], SUT Sec. 3-10 [35 ILCS 110/3-10], SOT Sec. 3-10 [35 ILCS 115/3-10], ROT Sec. 2-10 [35 ILCS 120/2-10], 86 Ill. Adm. Code Sec. 130.310(a), 86 Ill. Adm. Code Sec. 140.101(c), 86 Ill. Adm. Code Sec. 140.126).

Medicines, drugs, and medical appliances for human use and insulin, urine testing materials, syringes, and needles used by diabetics are also taxed at the rate of 1% (see, however, the use tax exemption above). Effective August 19, 2016, the 1% tax is imposed on sales of prescribed cancer treatment devices that are classified as Class III medical devices by the U.S. Food and Drug Administration (FDA), as well as any accessories and components related to those devices. Modifications to a motor vehicle for the purpose of rendering it usable by a disabled person are subject to the 1% sales and use tax rate (UT Sec. 3-10 [35 ILCS 105/3-10], SUT Sec. 3-10 [35 ILCS 110/3-10], SOT Sec. 3-10 [35 ILCS 115/3-10], ROT Sec. 2-10 [35 ILCS 120/2-10]).

The service occupation tax and the service use tax are imposed at the rate of 1% on food prepared for immediate consumption and transferred incident to a sale of service by an entity licensed under the Hospital Licensing Act, the Nursing Home Care Act, the Specialized Mental Health Rehabilitation Act, or the Child Care Act (SUT Sec. 3-10 [35 ILCS 110/3-10], SOT Sec. 3-10 [35 ILCS 115/3-10]).

The following two-part test determines whether food is taxed at the high rate as "food prepared for immediate consumption" or the low rate as "food prepared for consumption off the premises where sold" (86 Ill. Adm. Code 130.310; see also *General Information Letter ST 11-0109-GIL*, Illinois Department of Revenue, December 29, 2011, CCH Illinois Tax Reports, ¶ 402-441):

— If the retailer provides seating or facilities for on-premises consumption of food, all food sales by that retailer are presumed to be taxable at the high rate. However, this presumption can be rebutted if the retailer demonstrates that (1) the area for on-premises consumption is physically separated or otherwise distinguishable from the area where food not for immediate consumption is sold and (2) the retailer has a separate means of recording and accounting for receipts from sales of both high and low rate foods.

— If the retailer does not provide seating or facilities for on-premises consumption of food, then the low rate of tax will be applied to all food items except for food prepared for immediate consumption by the retailer and soft drinks, candy, and alcoholic beverages. In order for the low rate of tax to apply, a retailer that sells both high and low rate foods must separately record and account for receipts from both types of food sales.

Candy, soft drinks, and grooming products: Candy, grooming and hygiene products, and certain soft drinks are not eligible for the 1% reduced state rate allowed for qualifying food, medicines, and drugs and instead these products are subject to the full 6.25% state rate for purposes of Illinois retailers' occupation (sales) tax, service occupation tax, use tax, and service use tax. Details are in *Informational Bulletin FY 2010-01*, Illinois Department of Revenue, July 2009, CCH ILLINOIS TAX REPORTS, ¶ 401-995.

- **Motor fuel**

For current rates, see **http://www.revenue.state.il.us/TaxRates/ MotorFuel.htm**.

For prepayment rates, see ¶ 403.

- **Illinois hotel operators' occupation tax**

The Illinois hotel operators' occupation tax is imposed at a rate of 5% of 94% of the gross rental receipts, plus an additional tax of 1% of 94% of gross rental receipts (Hotel Operators' Occupation Tax Act, Sec. 3 [35 ILCS 145/3]).

The hotel tax is imposed on persons engaged in the business of renting, leasing, or letting rooms in a hotel. A hotel operator is liable for the hotel operators' occupation tax on rental receipts even if the hotel tax is not reimbursed by room occupants. A hotel operator may reimburse itself for its hotel tax liability by collecting a reimbursement charge from room occupants. (*General Information Letter ST 12-0020-GIL*, Illinois Department of Revenue, April 2, 2012, CCH ILLINOIS TAX REPORTS, ¶ 402-488; *General Information Letter ST 13-0028-GIL,* Illinois Department of Revenue, May 28, 2013, CCH ILLINOIS TAX REPORTS, ¶ 402-675).

- **Illinois automobile renting occupation and use tax**

A 5% tax is imposed on persons or companies engaged in the business of renting automobiles in Illinois when the rental is for a period of a year or less (Automobile Renting Occupation and Use Tax Act, Sec. 2 [35 ILCS 155/2], Automobile Renting Occupation and Use Tax Act, Sec. 3 [35 ILCS 155/3]). A 5% tax is also imposed on the privilege of using in the state an automobile that is rented from an auto rental business for a period of a year or less (Automobile Renting Occupation and Use Tax Act, Sec. 2 [35 ILCS 155/2], Automobile Renting Occupation and Use Tax Act, Sec. 4 [35 ILCS 155/4]).

- **Prepaid wireless E911 surcharge**

Statewide surcharge: Illinois imposes a statewide surcharge on, with certain exceptions, customers of telecommunications carriers and wireless carriers. Each carrier generally will impose a monthly surcharge of $0.87 for each network connection and for each qualifying commercial mobile radio service (CMRS) connection. State and local taxes will not apply to the surcharges, and the surcharges must be stated as separate items on subscriber bills. (50 ILCS 750/20); see also Publication-113, *Retailer's Overview of Sales and Use Tax and Prepaid Wireless E911 Surcharge,* Illinois Department of Revenue, September 2015, CCH ILLINOIS TAX REPORTS, ¶ 402-997

Local wireless surcharge: A local wireless surcharge imposed by a governmental unit or emergency telephone system board must not exceed $2.50 per commercial mobile radio service connection or in-service telephone number billed on a monthly basis. The surcharge is imposed based on the municipality or county encompassing the customer's place of primary use as defined in the Mobile Telecommunications Sourcing Conformity Act. (50 ILCS 750/15.3a)

A municipality with a population over 500,000 on June 29, 2015, can impose and collect a local monthly wireless surcharge not to exceed the highest monthly surcharge imposed as of January 1, 2014, by any other county or municipality. Beginning July 1, 2017, the amount of surcharge a municipality with a population over 500,000 may impose is limited to $2.50.

Emergency telephone system surcharge: A municipality with a population over 500,000 may continue to impose a $2.50 per network connection monthly surcharge until July 1, 2017. Any local non-wireless charge imposed by a municipality with a population of 500,000 or fewer may no longer be imposed after 2015. The Emergency Telephone Safety Act is repealed as of July 1, 2017.

Prepaid wireless 911 surcharge: The prepaid wireless 911 surcharge on retail transactions was increased to 3% from 1.5% on October 1, 2015. The reduction of the surcharge for municipalities having a population over 500,000 from 9% to 7% applies beginning July 1, 2017. The surcharge is not imposed on the provider or consumer of the federally funded Lifeline service where the consumer does not pay the provider for the service. (50 ILCS 753/15)

For additional information, see (*Publication 113, Retailer's Overview of Sales and Use Tax and Prepaid Wireless E911 Surcharge,* Illinois Department of Revenue, October 2011, CCH ILLINOIS TAX REPORTS, ¶ 402-422).

• Medical marijuana

Illinois imposes a 7% tax on the sales price per ounce on the privilege of cultivating medical cannabis. The privilege tax is paid by a cultivation center, not a dispensing organization or a qualifying patient, and is imposed in addition to all other Illinois state and local occupation and privilege taxes. Persons subject to the tax must apply to the Department of Revenue for a certificate of registration. (410 ILCS 130/200)

• Determination of tax rate when rate changes

The applicable tax rate is that rate in effect at the time tangible personal property is delivered, unless receipts were received by the seller before the rate change and tax paid on those receipts at the rate in effect at that time (86 Ill. Adm. Code Sec. 130.101(a)(1), 86 Ill. Adm. Code Sec. 150.115(a)).

Construction contracts: Property delivered to a construction contractor after the effective date of a rate increase for use in performing a binding construction contract entered into before the effective date of the rate increase is taxed at the rate in effect before the increase, provided the contractor is legally unable to shift the burden of the rate increase to the customer (86 Ill. Adm. Code Sec. 130.101(a)(2), 86 Ill. Adm. Code Sec. 150.115(b)).

¶ 400   Local Taxes

Home rule municipalities and counties that impose retailers' occupation taxes, service occupation taxes, and use taxes may do so only in 0.25% increments (Home Rule County ROT Law, Sec. 5-1006 [55 ILCS 5/5-1006], Home Rule County SOT Law, Sec. 5-1007 [55 ILCS 5/5-1007], Home Rule County UT Law, Sec. 5-1008 [55 ILCS 5/5-1008], Home Rule Municipal ROT Act, Sec. 8-11-1 [65 ILCS 5/8-11-1], Home Rule Municipal SOT Act, Sec. 8-11-5 [65 ILCS 5/8-11-5], Home Rule Municipal UT Act, Sec. 8-11-6 [65 ILCS 5/8-11-6]).

For specific rates imposed by home rule cities, non-home rule cities, and counties in Illinois, refer to the Tax Rate Finder website below.

Local sourcing: See *ST15-0001-GIL* Department of Revenue, January 7, 2015, CCH ILLINOIS TAX REPORTS, ¶ 402-923.

Cook County tax rate: The Cook County sales and use tax rate is 1.75%. The Cook County tax on titled property is 0.75%.

A Cook County tax on the use of non-titled personal property was prohibited by the Illinois County Code provision that no home rule county could impose a use tax based on the selling or purchase price of tangible personal property. A trial court's grant of injunctive relief in favor of two taxpayers and against enforcement of the tax ordinance was affirmed. (*Reed Smith LLP v. Ali,* Appellate Court of Illinois, First District, Nos. 1-13-2646, 1-13-2654, 1-13-3350, 1-13-3352, August 4, 2014, CCH ILLINOIS TAX REPORTS, ¶ 402-831).

County public safety or transportation tax: The county board of any county may impose a local retailers' occupation (sales) tax and service occupation use tax to provide revenue for public safety or transportation purposes, subject to approval by the voters (55 ILCS 5/5-1006.5).

Neither the county public safety and transportation taxes nor the home rule sales taxes apply to sales of qualifying food, drugs, and medical appliances, nor do they apply to items that must be titled or registered by an agency of the state government. For specific rates imposed by home rule cities and counties in Illinois, see "Local tax rates," below.

School facility tax: The county board of any county (except Cook County) may impose an Illinois retailers' and service occupation (sales) tax to be used exclusively for school facility purposes (55 ILCS 5/5-1006.7). The tax must be approved by the voters, may only be imposed in one-quarter percent increments, and may not exceed 1%. If adopted, the school facility occupation tax would be imposed upon all persons engaged in selling tangible personal property at retail in the county, other than personal property titled or registered with an Illinois state agency, and upon all persons engaged in selling services who transfer tangible personal property within the county as an incident to a sale of a service. Sellers may reimburse themselves for their tax liability by separately stating the tax as an additional charge.

A school facility occupation tax may not be imposed on food for human consumption that is to be consumed off the premises where it is sold, other than alcoholic beverages, soft drinks, and food that has been prepared for immediate consumption. The tax also may not be imposed on prescription and non-prescription medicines, drugs, medical appliances and insulin, urine testing materials, syringes and needles used by diabetics (55 ILCS 5/5-1006.7). The tax would be administered, collected, and enforced by the Department of Revenue.

Public facility tax: A county may impose a special retailers' occupation (sales) tax to provide revenue for public facility purposes. The term "public facilities purposes" includes the acquisition, development, construction, reconstruction, rehabilitation, improvement, financing, architectural planning, and installation of capital facilities consisting of buildings, structures, and durable equipment and for the acquisition and improvement of real property and interest in real property required, or expected to be required, in connection with the public facilities, for use by the county for the furnishing of governmental services to its citizens, including but not limited to museums and nursing homes. A ballot proposition submitted to the voters for approval of such a tax must contain specified language and information. (P.A. 95-1002 (S.B. 1290), Laws 2008)

STAR bond districts: Municipalities and counties are authorized to issue sales tax and revenue (STAR) bonds to promote new development of land that has been determined to be a blighted area. Local governments may pass ordinances imposing new retailers' occupation and service occupation taxes in the districts to pay off the STAR bonds. If additional sales taxes are imposed in a STAR bond district, both a STAR bond retailers' occupation tax and a STAR bond service occupation tax must be imposed. A municipality may impose the two taxes only within the portion of the STAR bond district that is located within the municipality's boundaries. The STAR bond retailers' occupation tax and the STAR bond service occupation tax may not exceed 1%, respectively, and may be imposed only in 0.25% increments on an annual basis. (50 ILCS 470/31)

Home rule municipalities with populations over one million (Chicago) may impose a soft drink retailers' occupation tax. The tax is based on gross receipts, and rates must be in increments of ¼% up to a maximum rate of 3% (Home Rule Municipal UT Act, Sec. 8-11-6b [65 ILCS 5/8-11-6b]). A fountain soft drink tax is imposed on persons selling fountain soft drinks at retail in the municipality. The tax cannot exceed 9% of the cost price of the drinks (Home Rule Municipal UT Act, Sec. 8-11-6b [65 ILCS 5/8-11-6b]).

A *Metro East Mass Transit District* may impose retailers' occupation tax, service occupation tax, and use tax at the rate of 0.25% (Local Mass Transit District Act, Sec. 5.01(b), (c), and (d) [70 ILCS 3610/5.01]).

The *Regional Transportation Authority (RTA)* retailers' occupation tax is imposed in Cook County at the following rates (Regional Transportation Authority Act, Sec. 4.03(e) [70 ILCS 3615/4.03]): (1) 1.25% on sales of food for off-premises consumption (except alcohol, soft drinks, and food prepared for immediate consumption), prescription and nonprescription medicines, drugs, medical appliances and insulin, urine testing materials, and syringes and needles used by diabetics; and (2) 1% on other taxable sales. In DuPage, Kane, Lake, McHenry, and Will counties, the tax is imposed at the rate of 0.75% on all taxable sales. The RTA service occupation tax is imposed at the same rates as listed above for the retailers' occupation tax, except that in Cook County it is also imposed on food prepared for immediate consumption and transferred incident to a sale of service by an entity licensed under the Hospital Licensing Act or the Nursing Home Care Act (Regional Transportation Authority Act, Sec. 4.03(f) [70 ILCS 3615/4.03]). The RTA use tax is imposed at the rate of 1% in Cook County and 0.25% in DuPage, Kane, Lake, McHenry, and Will counties (Regional Transportation Authority Act, Sec. 4.03(g) [70 ILCS 3615/4.03]).

The *Metropolitan Pier and Exposition Authority* imposes several local taxes. The rate of the food and beverage tax imposed by the Metropolitan Pier and Exposition Authority is 1% on the gross receipts from sales of food, alcoholic beverages, and soft drinks (Metropolitan Pier and Exposition Authority Act, Sec. 13 [70 ILCS 210/13]). The Authority imposes an occupation tax of 2.5% on the gross receipts of hotel operators in Chicago (Metropolitan Pier and Exposition Authority Act, Sec. 13 [70 ILCS 210/13]). The automobile renting occupation tax and the automobile renting use tax are imposed by the Metropolitan Pier and Exposition Authority at the rate of 6% (Metropolitan Pier and Exposition Authority Act, Sec. 13 [70 ILCS 210/13]).

The Authority imposes an occupation tax on airport transit operators at the following rates (Metropolitan Pier and Exposition Authority Act, Sec. 13 [70 ILCS 210/13]):

> Two dollars per taxi or livery vehicle departure with passengers for hire from commercial service airports (those receiving scheduled passenger service and enplaning more than 100,000 passengers a year) in the metropolitan area;

> For each departure with passengers for hire from a commercial service airport in the metropolitan area in a bus or van operated by a person other than a person described below: $9 per vehicle with a capacity of 1-12 passengers; $18 per vehicle with a capacity of 13-24 passengers; and $27 per vehicle with a capacity of over 24 passengers;

> For each departure with passengers for hire from a commercial service airport in the metropolitan area in a bus or van operated by a person regulated under federal or state law, operating scheduled service from the airport, and charging fares on a per passenger basis: $1 per passenger for hire in each vehicle.

Parking taxes: Home rule municipalities with a population of more than two million (Chicago) and home rule counties may impose sales and use tax on the use, for consideration, of parking lots, garages or other parking facilities, effective March 8, 2013. (65 ILCS 5/8-11-6a; 55 ILCS 5/5-1009)

County water commission tax: A tax may be imposed by a county at the rate of 0.25% (only DuPage County has elected to impose the tax) (Water Commission Act, Sec. 4(b), (c), and (d) [70 ILCS 3720/4]).

Local hotel taxes: The U.S. District Court for the Northern District of Illinois held that a 7% hotel tax imposed by the village of Rosemont, Illinois, on the full room rental fees charged by online travel companies (OTCs) is a valid use tax, and it does not violate the dormant Commerce Clause of the U.S. Constitution. Rosemont customers paid a room rental fee that included (1) the amounts that the hotels charged the OTCs, and (2) the OTCs' markup on the hotels' charges. The court held that the OTCs' facilitation of travel-related services was incidental to the rental of hotel rooms, and that the hotel tax was a use tax. Illlinois law establishes that a tax on hotel room rentals is a use tax, not an impermissible sales (occupation) tax. Services generally are not subject to sales tax. The OTCs had nexus with Illinois because (1) the tax was levied for the right to use a hotel room in Illinois, (2) the tax was paid by the person who used the room, and (3) the OTCs entered into contracts with hotels in Illinois for the right to market, facilitate, and book reservations and they profit from such reservations. The tax was fairly apportioned because it is imposed on a use that can occur in only one place. The tax does not discriminate against interstate commerce, as it is applied at the same rate to every hotel reservation in Rosemont. Finally, the tax is related to Illinois services because the renting person has the advantage of the state's police and fire protection, for example, while staying in Illinois. (*The Village of Rosemont v. Priceline.com, Inc.,* U.S. District Court, N.D. Illinois, No. 09 C 4438, October 14, 2011; CCH ILLINOIS TAX REPORTS, ¶ 402-417).

For discussion of tax liabilities under various local ordinances, see *Village of Bedford Park v. Expedia, Inc.,* U.S. District Court, N.D. Illinois, No. 13 C 5633, June 20, 2016, CCH ILLINOIS TAX REPORTS, ¶ 403-109.

Chicago: The city of Chicago imposes a 4% surcharge on sales of hotel accommodations at "vacation rentals" and "shared housing units" and in addition to the 4.5% gross rental or leasing charge on "shared housing units." (Chicago Ordinance O2016-5111, Chicago City Council, June 24, 2016)

Non-home-rule municipal taxes: Non-home-rule municipalities are authorized to impose local sales taxes up to 1.0% in increments of 0.25% (65 ILCS 5/8-11-1.1).

Sourcing of telecommunications charges: Illinois conforms to the federal Mobile Telecommunications Sourcing Act (Act), P.L. 106-252 (P.A. 92-0474 (H.B. 843), Laws 2001). All charges for mobile telecommunications services are considered to be provided by the customer's home service provider and sourced to the customer's place of primary use. All such charges are subject to sales tax based on the customer's place of primary use.

The service provider will be held harmless for an error in assigning wireless services to a jurisdiction if it utilizes an electronic database provided by the state or a designated entity, or, if the state has not provided or designated a database, if it utilizes a database that makes assignments based on a nine-digit zip code.

Calculation of tax: Retailers subject to any local tax may use the bracket schedules at ¶ 401 or may multiply the transaction amount by the combined rate of tax and round up to the nearest unit (86 Ill. Adm. Code Sec. 150.405).

Information on calculating tax for items taxable at different rates is available at **http://tax.illinois.gov/LegalInformation/regs/part150/150-525.pdf**.

- **Local tax rates**

The Illinois Department of Revenue publishes an online Tax Rate Finder for obtaining local tax rates. The Tax Rate Finder is available at **https://mytax.illinois.gov/_/**.

¶ 401   Bracket Schedule

The Department of Revenue may prescribe bracket schedules for use by retailers in collecting use tax from users (UT Sec. 3-45 [35 ILCS 105/3-45]). Retailers must publicly display the tax collection schedule (86 Ill. Adm. Code Sec. 150.520). Suppliers collecting tax from service providers must use the bracket schedule (86 Ill. Adm. Code Sec. 140.1020).

The Department has issued the following bracket schedules (86 Ill. Adm. Code Sec. 150):

6.25% Tax Rate

Sale			Tax	Sale			Tax
$0.00	to	$0.07	No tax	.56	to	.71	4¢
.08	to	.23	1¢	.72	to	.87	5¢
.24	to	.39	2¢	.88	to	1.03	6¢
.40	to	.55	3¢	and so forth.			

6.5% Tax Rate

Sale			Tax	Sale			Tax
$0.00	to	$0.07	No tax	.54	to	.69	4¢
.08	to	.23	1¢	.70	to	.84	5¢
.24	to	.38	2¢	.85	to	.99	6¢
.39	to	.53	3¢	1.00	to	1.15	7¢
				and so forth.			

6.75% Tax Rate

Sale			Tax	Sale			Tax
$0.00	to	$0.07	No tax	.52	to	.66	4¢
.08	to	.22	1¢	.67	to	.81	5¢
.23	to	.37	2¢	.82	to	.96	6¢
.38	to	.51	3¢	.97	to	1.11	7¢
				and so forth.			

7% Tax Rate

Sale			Tax	Sale			Tax
$0.00	to	$0.07	No tax	.50	to	.64	4¢
.08	to	.21	1¢	.65	to	.78	5¢
.22	to	.35	2¢	.79	to	.92	6¢
.36	to	.49	3¢	.93	to	1.07	7¢
				and so forth.			

7.125% Tax Rate

Sale			Tax	Sale			Tax
$0.00	to	$0.07	No tax	.50	to	.63	4¢
.08	to	.21	1¢	.64	to	.77	5¢
.22	to	.35	2¢	.78	to	.91	6¢
.36	to	.49	3¢	.92	to	1.05	7¢
				and so forth.			

7.25% Tax Rate

Sale			Tax	Sale			Tax
$0.00	to	$0.06	No tax	.49	to	.62	4¢
.07	to	.20	1¢	.63	to	.75	5¢
.21	to	.34	2¢	.76	to	.89	6¢
.35	to	.48	3¢	.90	to	1.03	7¢
				and so forth.			

7.5% Tax Rate

Sale			Tax	Sale			Tax
$0.00	to	$0.06	No tax	.60	to	.73	5¢
.07	to	.19	1¢	.74	to	.86	6¢
.20	to	.33	2¢	.87	to	.99	7¢
.34	to	.46	3¢	1.00	to	1.13	8¢
.47	to	.59	4¢	and so forth.			

7.75% Tax Rate

Sale			Tax	Sale			Tax
$0.00	to	$0.06	. . . .	No tax	.59	to	.70	. . . .	5¢
.07	to	.19	. . . .	1¢	.71	to	.83	. . . .	6¢
.20	to	.32	. . . .	2¢	.84	to	.96	. . . .	7¢
.33	to	.45	. . . .	3¢	.97	to	1.09	. . . .	8¢
.46	to	.58	. . . .	4¢	and so forth.			

8% Tax Rate

Sale			Tax	Sale			Tax
$0.00	to	$0.06	. . . .	No tax	.57	to	.68	. . . .	5¢
.07	to	.18	. . . .	1¢	.69	to	.81	. . . .	6¢
.19	to	.31	. . . .	2¢	.82	to	.93	. . . .	7¢
.32	to	.43	. . . .	3¢	.94	to	1.06	. . . .	8¢
.44	to	.56	. . . .	4¢	and so forth.			

8.25% Tax Rate

Sale			Tax	Sale			Tax
$0.00	to	$0.06	. . . .	No tax	.55	to	.66	. . . .	5¢
.07	to	.18	. . . .	1¢	.67	to	.78	. . . .	6¢
.19	to	.30	. . . .	2¢	.79	to	.90	. . . .	7¢
.31	to	.42	. . . .	3¢	.91	to	1.03	. . . .	8¢
.43	to	.54	. . . .	4¢	and so forth.			

8.5% Tax Rate

Sale			Tax	Sale			Tax
$0.00	to	$0.05	. . . .	No tax	.53	to	.64	. . . .	5¢
.06	to	.17	. . . .	1¢	.65	to	.76	. . . .	6¢
.18	to	.29	. . . .	2¢	.77	to	.88	. . . .	7¢
.30	to	.41	. . . .	3¢	.89	to	.99	. . . .	8¢
.42	to	.52	. . . .	4¢	1.00	to	1.11	. . . .	9¢
				and so forth.			

8.75% Tax Rate

Sale			Tax	Sale			Tax
$0.00	to	$0.05	. . . .	No tax	.52	to	.62	. . . .	5¢
.06	to	.17	. . . .	1¢	.63	to	.74	. . . .	6¢
.18	to	.28	. . . .	2¢	.75	to	.85	. . . .	7¢
.29	to	.39	. . . .	3¢	.86	to	.97	. . . .	8¢
.40	to	.51	. . . .	4¢	.98	to	1.08	. . . .	9¢
				and so forth.			

9% Tax Rate

Sale			Tax	Sale			Tax
$0.00	to	$0.05	. . . .	No tax	.50	to	.61	. . . .	5¢
.06	to	.16	. . . .	1¢	.62	to	.72	. . . .	6¢
.17	to	.27	. . . .	2¢	.73	to	.83	. . . .	7¢
.28	to	.38	. . . .	3¢	.84	to	.94	. . . .	8¢
.39	to	.49	. . . .	4¢	.95	to	1.05	. . . .	9¢
				and so forth.			

9.25% Tax Rate

Sale				Tax	Sale			Tax
$0.00	to	$0.05	....	No tax	.49	to	.59	5¢
.06	to	.16	....	1¢	.60	to	.70	6¢
.17	to	.27	....	2¢	.71	to	.81	7¢
.28	to	.37	....	3¢	.82	to	.91	8¢
.38	to	.48	....	4¢	.92	to	1.02	9¢

and so forth.

9.5% Tax Rate

Sale				Tax	Sale			Tax
$0.00	to	$0.05	....	No tax	.58	to	.68	6¢
.06	to	.15	....	1¢	.69	to	.78	7¢
.16	to	.26	....	2¢	.79	to	.89	8¢
.27	to	.36	....	3¢	.90	to	.99	9¢
.37	to	.47	....	4¢	1.00	to	1.10	10¢
.48	to	.57	....	5¢	and so forth.			

9.75% Tax Rate

Sale				Tax	Sale			Tax
$0.00	to	$0.05	....	No tax	.57	to	.66	6¢
.06	to	.15	....	1¢	.67	to	.76	7¢
.16	to	.25	....	2¢	.77	to	.87	8¢
.26	to	.35	....	3¢	.88	to	.97	9¢
.36	to	.46	....	4¢	.98	to	1.07	10¢
.47	to	.56	....	5¢	and so forth.			

In addition to the schedules listed above, the bracket table issued by the Department contains schedules for tax rates from 0.125% through 6.125% and from 10% through 12% (86 Ill. Adm. Code Sec. 150).

¶ 402   Returns, Payments, and Due Dates

Persons engaged in the business of selling tangible personal property at retail and service providers must generally file returns with the Department of Revenue on or before the 20th day of each calendar month covering the preceding calendar month (UT Sec. 9 [35 ILCS 105/9], SUT Sec. 9 [35 ILCS 110/9], SOT Sec. 9 [35 ILCS 115/9], ROT Sec. 3 [35 ILCS 120/3], 86 Ill. Adm. Code Sec. 130.501, 86 Ill. Adm. Code Sec. 140.401, 86 Ill. Adm. Code Sec. 150.901(a), 86 Ill. Adm. Code Sec. 160.135). However, the Department may require or authorize quarterly returns or annual returns for taxpayers with low average monthly liabilities and may require concessionaires at flea markets, art shows, and fairs to file daily reports and make daily payments of tax.

Annual exemption information reports: Each contractor or other entity that holds an enterprise zone building materials exemption certificate, a river edge building materials exemption certificate, an EDGE act exemption certificate, or a high impact business exemption certificate must annually report to the department the value of the tax benefits. (20 ILCS 605/605-320; 20 ILCS 655/8.1; *Information Bulletin FY 2014-11,* Illinois Department of Revenue, March 2014)

• Electronic filing

The Department of Revenue is authorized to institute the electronic filing of returns and other documents (Civil Administrative Code, Sec. 39c-1a [20 ILCS 2505/39c-1a]), and any return or document may be filed by facsimile transmission (fax) (Civil Administrative Code, Sec. 39c-1b [20 ILCS 2505/39c-1b]).

MyTax Illinois: MyTax Illinois is a free online account management system on the DOR Website (**https://mytax.illinois.gov/_/**) where taxpayers can register a new business, file returns, make payments, and manage their tax accounts.

• **Payment of tax**

Payment of ROT, SOT, UT, and SUT is generally made at the time the return is filed (UT Sec. 9 [35 ILCS 105/9], SUT Sec. 9 [35 ILCS 110/9], SOT Sec. 9 [35 ILCS 115/9], ROT Sec. 3 [35 ILCS 120/3], 86 Ill. Adm. Code Sec. 130.535). More frequent payments are required if a taxpayer's average monthly tax liability exceeds specified amounts. In addition, as discussed below, certain taxpayers must make their payments by electronic funds transfer.

Individual use tax reporting: In lieu of filing monthly use tax returns, individuals may elect to report their use tax liability on their standard individual income tax return if their annual individual use tax liability does not exceed $600. If an individual chooses to report use tax owed on the income tax return, the use tax may be (1) treated as being due at the same time as the income tax obligation, (2) assessed, collected, and deposited in the same manner as income taxes, and (3) treated as an income tax liability for all purposes. (35 ILCS 105/10; see also *PIO-36, Illinois Use Tax for Individual Taxpayers,* Illinois Department of Revenue April 1, 2012, CCH Illinois Tax Reports, ¶ 402-478).

Electronic funds transfer: Taxpayers with an annual tax liability of $20,000 or more and retailers of alcohol must make all payments by electronic funds transfer (UT Sec. 9 [35 ILCS 105/9], SUT Sec. 9 [35 ILCS 110/9], SOT Sec. 9 [35 ILCS 115/9], ROT Sec. 3 [35 ILCS 120/3]; *Informational Bulletin FY 2011-01*, Illinois Department of Revenue, July 2010, CCH Illinois Tax Reports, ¶ 402-169). Before August 1 of each year, the Department will notify all taxpayers required to make payments by electronic funds transfer. Such taxpayers must make electronic funds transfer payments for a minimum of one year, beginning on October 1. Any taxpayer not required to make payments by electronic funds transfer may make such payments with the permission of the Department.

• **Bad debts**

Effective July 1, 2015, a retailer is not liable for Illinois sales tax due and payable if the tax has become a bad debt and the following three conditions are met (35 ILCS 120/6d(a)):

(1) the tax is represented by amounts that are found to be worthless or uncollectible;

(2) the tax has been charged off as bad debt on the retailer's books and records; and

(3) the tax has been claimed on the retailer's federal income tax return as a bad debt deduction.

Credit cards: Separate rules apply for credit card purchases. When taxes were paid with a credit card purchase, for example, a deduction is available only for debts written off on or after January 1, 2016. If a retailer deducts a bad debt but later collects the tax due, the retailer must include the tax in the retailer's next return and remit the tax. The Department of Revenue will issue rules for taking a bad sales tax debt deduction. (35 ILCS 120/6d(b))

• **Uniform Sales Tax Administration Act**

Illinois has enacted the Uniform Sales and Use Tax Administration Act, the product of the Streamlined Sales Tax Project (SSTP), along with modifications recommended by the National Conference of State Legislators (NCSL). The SSTP developed the Act and the related Streamlined Sales and Use Tax Agreement to simplify and modernize sales and use tax administration in order to substantially reduce the burden of tax compliance for all sellers and for all types of commerce.

Illinois is not a member of the Agreement because, although it has enacted legislation authorizing it to enter into the Agreement (35 ILCS 171/5), it has not yet enacted the changes to its laws necessary to comply with the Agreement's requirements. However, as one of the SST Advisor States, it will, for a period of time, continue to have input through its representation on the State and Local Advisory Council, which advises the Board on matters pertaining to the administration of the Agreement. For additional information on the uniform act and the Agreement, see "Streamlined Sales Tax Project," in the Table of Contents.

¶ 403   Prepayment of Taxes

A retail seller of motor fuel who is not a licensed distributor or supplier must prepay part of the ROT to its distributor, supplier, or other reseller (if registered) (ROT Sec. 2d [35 ILCS 120/2d], 86 Ill. Adm. Code Sec. 130.551). The prepayment rates are subject to change every six months.

For the period between January 1, 2017, and June 30, 2017, the per gallon rates for the Illinois prepaid sales tax on gasohol and biodiesel blends (1%—10%) wereunchanged at 10 cents and and on other motor fuels were reduced from 13 cents to 12 cents. Current and historical prepayment rates are published on the Department of Revenue's website at **http://www.revenue.state.il.us/TaxRates/PrepaidSalesTax.htm**.

¶ 404   Vendor Registration

A person making retail sales of property or maintaining a place of business in the state must obtain a certificate of registration from the Department of Revenue (UT Sec. 6 [35 ILCS 105/6], SUT Sec. 6 [35 ILCS 110/6], SOT Sec. 6 [35 ILCS 115/6], ROT Sec. 2a [35 ILCS 120/2a], 86 Ill. Adm. Code Sec. 130.701, 86 Ill. Adm. Code Sec. 140.105, 86 Ill. Adm. Code Sec. 140.601, 86 Ill. Adm. Code Sec. 160.130). An applicant for a certificate must furnish a bond or an irrevocable bank letter of credit not to exceed the lesser of three times the applicant's average monthly tax liability or $50,000.

A certificate must be conspicuously displayed at the person's principal place of business in the state (UT Sec. 6 [35 ILCS 105/6], SUT Sec. 6 [35 ILCS 110/6], SOT Sec. 6 [35 ILCS 115/6], ROT Sec. 2a [35 ILCS 120/2a], 86 Ill. Adm. Code Sec. 130.725). Sub-certificates of registration bearing the same registration number as the certificate to which it relates are issued for display in a person's other places of business in the state (ROT Sec. 2a [35 ILCS 120/2a], 86 Ill. Adm. Code Sec. 130.715), including each truck, wagon, or other vehicle from which a person conducts business (86 Ill. Adm. Code Sec. 130.740).

The Illinois Department of Revenue publishes an overview of the sales and use tax for retailers. The publication can be found on the DOR's website at **http://www.revenue.state.il.us/Publications/Pubs/Pub-113.pdf**.

MyTax Illinois: MyTax Illinois is a free online account management system on the DOR Website (**https://mytax.illinois.gov/_/**) where taxpayers can register a new business, file returns, make payments, and manage their tax accounts.

Out-of-state retailers: For registration and collection responsibilities, see 86 Ill. Adm. Code Sec. 160.130 and 86 Ill. Adm. Code Sec. 150.805; see also *General Information Letter ST 13-0069-GIL,* Illinois Department of Revenue, November 26, 2013, CCH ILLINOIS TAX REPORTS, ¶ 402-760.

Out-of-state wineries that intend to sell wine directly to Illinois residents must complete an Application For State Of Illinois Winery Shipper's License. A licensee that is not required to register to collect and remit Illinois sales tax must register to collect and remit Illinois use tax for all gallons of wine sold by the licensee and shipped to persons in Illinois. (*General Information Letter ST 13-0025-GIL,* Illinois Department of Revenue, May 28, 2013, CCH ILLINOIS TAX REPORTS, ¶ 402-672).

Retailers with vending machines: A retailer must obtain an additional sub-certificate of registration for each vending machine added to its business. The retailer must report the number of sub-certificates requested and the total number of vending machines the retailer currently uses to make sales. (35 ILCS 120/2a)

Users: A user who is only occasionally liable to pay use tax or service use tax directly to the Department and not on a frequently occurring basis and who is not required to file returns as a retailer or service provider does not have to register with the Department (UT Sec. 10 [35 ILCS 105/10], SUT Sec. 10 [35 ILCS 110/10], 86 Ill. Adm. Code Sec. 150.701(b)). However, if the user has a frequently recurring direct use or service use tax liability to the Department, it must obtain a certificate of registration.

¶ 405   Sales or Use Tax Credits

The use in Illinois of property acquired outside the state (in such a way that there is no ROT or SOT liability) is not subject to use or service use taxes to the extent that a tax has been paid to another state on the sale or use of the property (UT Sec. 3-55(d) [35 ILCS 105/3-55], SUT Sec. 3-45(e) [35 ILCS 110/3-45], 86 Ill. Adm. Code Sec. 150.310(3), 86 Ill. Adm. Code Sec. 160.110(2)).

• Overpayment of tax

A taxpayer may request a credit memorandum for excess tax payments within 30 days of the date of payment (UT Sec. 9 [35 ILCS 105/9], ROT Sec. 3 [35 ILCS 120/3]). If no request is made, the taxpayer may credit the excess payment against tax liability subsequently to be remitted.

• Manufacturer's purchase credit

Purchases of manufacturing machinery and equipment that qualify for the use tax exemptions under UT Sec. 3-5(18) and SUT Sec. 2 are eligible for a nontransferable credit against use or service use tax. The credit includes purchases of graphic arts machinery and equipment that qualify for the use tax exemptions under UT Sec. 3-5(6) and SUT Sec. 3-5(5) (35 ILCS 105/3-85, 35 ILCS 110/3-70).

The amount of the credit equals 50% of the tax that would have been incurred on the purchase of the exempt manufacturing machinery and equipment if the manufacturing machinery and equipment exemption had not been applicable (35 ILCS 105/3-85; 35 ILCS 110/3-70; 86 Ill. Adm. Code 130.331).

• Other credits

Retailers, suppliers, servicepersons, and other taxpayers are allowed to claim a credit or refund for the sales or use tax paid on sales of building materials to a "High Impact Business."

A retailer who is required to pay ROT or UT on gross receipts from retail sales may, without filing a formal claim, take credit against the ROT or UT liability to the extent to which the retailer has paid ROT or UT in error to its supplier of the same property bought for resale and not first used before resale (UT Sec. 19 [35 ILCS 105/19], ROT Sec. 6a [35 ILCS 120/6a]). Penalties and interest are not charged on the amount of such credit. If the credit is allowed to the retailer, the supplier may not refund any tax to the retailer and file a claim for credit or refund.

A credit memorandum is issued to a retailer of motor fuel in an amount equal to the excess of the taxpayer's liability for the month that the return is filed (ROT Sec. 3 [35 ILCS 120/3]).

¶ 406   Deficiency Assessments

All returns are examined by the Department of Revenue and corrected if necessary (ROT Sec. 4 [35 ILCS 120/4]). If the Department determines that the tax is greater than that stated in the return, it will issue to the taxpayer a deficiency assessment or notice of tax liability for the amount of tax claimed to be due together with a 20% penalty (ROT Sec. 4 [35 ILCS 120/4], 86 Ill. Adm. Code Sec. 130.901(a)). An additional penalty is imposed if the deficiency is due to negligence (20%) or fraud (50%).

If the correction of a return results in an amount of tax that is understated on the taxpayer's return due to a mathematical error, the Department will notify the taxpayer that the amount of tax in excess of that shown on the return is due and has been assessed (ROT Sec. 4 [35 ILCS 120/4]). The notice of additional tax due will not be considered a notice of tax liability and the taxpayer will not have a right to protest. The term "mathematical error" means arithmetic errors or incorrect computations on the return or supporting schedules. No notice of additional tax due will be issued on and after each July 1 and January 1 covering gross receipts received during any month or period of time more than three years prior to the July 1 or January 1 when the notice was issued.

A deficiency assessment may also be issued to a taxpayer who files a return but does not pay the tax admitted to be due, and such a notice is *prima facie* evidence of the correctness of the amount of tax due.

The Department will also determine the amount of tax due from a person who fails to file a return, which amount is *prima facie* correct (ROT Sec. 5 [35 ILCS 120/5], 86 Ill. Adm. Code Sec. 130.901(e)). A deficiency assessment will then be issued to the taxpayer together with a 30% penalty. No penalty is imposed, however, if the failure to file is not intentional or fraudulent and has not occurred within the last two years.

¶ 407   **Audit Procedures**

The Department may hold investigations and hearings in order to administer and enforce the sales and use tax law (UT Sec. 11 [35 ILCS 105/11], SUT Sec. 11 [35 ILCS 110/11], SOT Sec. 11 [35 ILCS 115/11], ROT Sec. 8 [35 ILCS 120/8]). Books, papers, records, or memoranda bearing upon the sale and use of tangible personal property or services may be examined at such investigations or hearings, and persons having knowledge of a business may be required to attend. The attendance of witnesses and the production of records may be compelled by the issuing of subpoenas or by an attachment for contempt by any circuit court (ROT Sec. 10 [35 ILCS 120/10]). No person may be excused from testifying or producing records upon the ground that by doing so, the person will be incriminated or subjected to a criminal penalty, and no natural person will be prosecuted or subjected to a criminal penalty regarding any transaction about which the person testifies or produces evidence (ROT Sec. 9 [35 ILCS 120/9]).

When the Department finds that a taxpayer lacks documentary evidence to support a claim of exemption, it may notify the taxpayer in writing to produce such evidence within 60 days of the notice (ROT Sec. 7 [35 ILCS 120/7], 86 Ill. Adm. Code Sec. 130.801(f)). A transaction is conclusively presumed to be taxable if such evidence is not so produced.

See also *Illinois Audit Information,* Illinois Department of Revenue, October 2013, CCH Illinois Tax Reports, ¶ 402-754).

¶ 408   **Statute of Limitations**

As discussed below, a three-year limitations period generally applies to the issuance of a notice of tax liability. If a person files a fraudulent return or fails to file a return, however, a special statute of limitations applies to the assessment of tax.

Notice of tax liability: No notice of ROT liability can be issued on and after each January 1 and July 1 covering gross receipts received during any month or period of time more than three years before such January 1 and July 1, respectively (ROT Sec. 4 [35 ILCS 120/4], ROT Sec. 5 [35 ILCS 120/5], 86 Ill. Adm. Code Sec. 130.815). However, if a return is not filed at the required time, a notice of tax liability may be issued not later than three years after the time the return is filed. The limitations period for the SOT, UT, and SUT is the same, but starts to run from the date the tax is due instead of when gross receipts are received (UT Sec. 12 [35 ILCS 105/12], SUT Sec. 12 [35 ILCS 110/12], SOT Sec. 12 [35 ILCS 115/12], 86 Ill. Adm. Code Sec. 140.801, 86 Ill. Adm. Code Sec. 150.1001).

The taxpayer and Department may agree, before the time for issuing a notice of tax liability expires, to extend the time in which such a notice may be issued (ROT Sec. 4 [35 ILCS 120/4]). Additional extensions may be agreed upon. The limitations period is tolled if the Department has issued a notice of tax liability, even if the return was not corrected or the tax due determined before the issuance of the notice (ROT Sec. 4 [35 ILCS 120/4], ROT Sec. 5 [35 ILCS 120/5], 86 Ill. Adm. Code Sec. 130.815).

The three-year statute of limitations is suspended for the time that an Illinois resident taxpayer is out of the state (ROT Sec. 4 [35 ILCS 120/4], ROT Sec. 5 [35 ILCS 120/5], 86 Ill. Adm. Code Sec. 130.815). The statute is also suspended during periods that a court order restrains issuance of the notice of tax liability.

Fraudulent return or failure to file: If a taxpayer files a false or fraudulent return with the intent to evade tax, the tax may be assessed at any time (35 ILCS Sec. 735/3-10). Tax may also be assessed at any time if a taxpayer fails to file a return required by law. If the taxpayer shows that there was reasonable cause for the failure to file, however, the period will be limited to not more than six years after the original due date of each return that was required to be filed. The limitations on assessment will not apply if the Department has, within the six-year period of limitation, notified a person that a return is required by law from that person.

In the case of a failure to file a use tax or service use tax return, no notice of tax liability will be issued on and after each July 1 and January 1 covering tax due with that return during any month or period more than six months before that July 1 or January 1 (UT Sec. 12 [35 ILCS 105/12], SUT Sec. 12 [35 ILCS 110/12]).

If a taxpayer fails to file a return required by law but voluntarily discloses the failure to the Department, the tax may be assessed no more than four years after the original due date of each return that was required to be filed (86 Ill. Adm. Code Sec. 210.126).

The limitations discussed above will be tolled during any time period in which the order of any court has the effect of enjoining or restraining the Department from making an assessment.

Collection action: The Department may sue the taxpayer to recover taxes, including interest and penalties. If the taxpayer died or became legally disabled, the suit may be filed against the taxpayer's estate. The suit may not be instituted more than six years after (1) the date court proceedings have terminated, (2) the time for instituting a taxpayer suit has expired without suit being filed, or (3) the filing date for the return in cases in which the return constitutes the basis for the suit. (35 ILCS 120/5)

Specific information on penalties and interest may be found in *Publication-103, Penalties and Interest for Illinois Taxes,* Illinois Department of Revenue, September 2014, CCH ILLINOIS TAX REPORTS, ¶ 402-852.

Criminal prosecution: A criminal prosecution may be commenced at any time within three years of the commission of an offense (UT Sec. 14 [35 ILCS 105/14], SUT Sec. 15 [35 ILCS 110/15], SOT Sec. 15 [35 ILCS 115/15], ROT Sec. 13 [35 ILCS 120/13]).

¶ 409　　　　　　　　　　**Application for Refund**

Retailers (ROT Sec. 6 [35 ILCS 120/6], 86 Ill. Adm. Code Sec. 130.1501), service providers (SUT Sec. 17 [35 ILCS 110/17], SOT Sec. 17 [35 ILCS 115/17], 86 Ill. Adm. Code Sec. 140.1401), suppliers (SOT Sec. 17 [35 ILCS 115/17]), and purchasers (SUT Sec. 17 [35 ILCS 110/17], UT Sec. 19 [35 ILCS 105/19], 86 Ill. Adm. Code Sec. 150.1401, 86 Ill. Adm. Code Sec. 160.150) who pay sales and use tax, penalty, or interest erroneously, whether through a mistake of fact or error in law, may file a claim for credit or refund. The Department, if requested by the taxpayer, normally issues a credit memorandum or refund to the person who made the erroneous payment.

A claim for refund or credit filed on or after January 1 and July 1 is not valid unless the erroneous payment was made within three years prior to January 1 and July 1 of the year of the claim (ROT Sec. 6 [35 ILCS 120/6], UT Sec. 21 [35 ILCS 105/21], SUT Sec.

19 [35 ILCS 110/19], SOT Sec. 19 [35 ILCS 115/19]). If the taxpayer and the Department agree to extend the period of limitations to issue a notice of tax liability, the claim may be filed at any time prior to the end of the agreed upon extension period.

Refund or credit claims are made on forms furnished by the Department (SUT Sec. 17 [35 ILCS 110/17], SOT Sec. 17 [35 ILCS 115/17], UT Sec. 19 [35 ILCS 105/19], ROT Sec. 6a [35 ILCS 120/6a]). A claim is considered filed on the date it is received by the Department. The Department examines the claim and issues a tentative determination as soon as practicable after a credit or refund claim is filed (UT Sec. 20 [35 ILCS 105/20], SUT Sec. 18 [35 ILCS 110/18], SOT Sec. 18 [35 ILCS 115/18], ROT Sec. 6b [35 ILCS 120/6b]). If it determines that a refund or credit memorandum should issue, the Department may first apply the amount against any tax, penalty, or interest due under the Retailers' Occupation, Use Tax, Service Occupation, or Service Use Tax Acts, as well as under other local taxes (ROT Sec. 6 [35 ILCS 120/6], UT Sec. 22 [35 ILCS 105/22], SUT Sec. 20 [35 ILCS 110/20], SOT Sec. 20 [35 ILCS 115/20]).

Payment of refunds: taxpayers due a refund on Illinois taxes can opt for a debit card rather than a paper check if they file using the DOR's WebFile site at **http:\\www.tax.illinois.gov**. Taxpayers who already have checking or savings accounts and those who opt to use a different tax filing system will find that direct deposit is still quicker and might be more a more convenient way to access refund money, according to the DOR. (*Release,* Illinois Department of Revenue, February 14, 2013)

¶ 410 INDIANA

¶ 411 Scope of Tax

Source.—Statutory references are to Title 6, Article 2.5, of the Indiana Code, as amended to date. Details are reported in the CCH INDIANA STATE TAX REPORTS starting at ¶ 60-000.

The Indiana sales tax is imposed on "retail transactions" made in Indiana (IC 6-2.5-2-1, 45 IAC 2.2-1-1, 45 IAC 2.2-2-1). Persons acquiring property in retail transactions are liable for the sales tax and are required to pay the tax to the retail merchant, who must collect the tax as an agent for the state.

The sales tax is imposed on tangible personal property and/or taxable services acquired in a retail transaction for which a total combined charge or selling price is calculated (IC 6-2.5-1-1).

The use tax is a complementary tax that does not apply in situations in which the Indiana sales tax has been paid or in which the transaction is wholly or partially exempt from the sales tax and the property is being used, stored, or consumed for the purpose for which it was exempted (IC 6-2.5-3-4(a), 45 IAC 2.2-3-14).

Gasoline use tax: Indiana imposes a gasoline use tax to be paid by qualified distributors, refiners, or terminal operators (IC 6-2.5-3.5-19). The gasoline use tax is considered equivalent to the state sales tax that otherwise would be collected by a retail merchant in a retail sale and replaces a retail merchant's obligation to collect sales tax on the sale of gasoline. The 7% sales tax on gasoline is repealed, effective July 1, 2014 (IC 6-2.5-7-3(a)). Provisions concerning sales taxes on special fuels and kerosene remain effective. For additional information, see *Information Bulletin No. 83,* Indiana Department of Revenue, June 2014, CCH INDIANA TAX REPORTS, ¶ 402-103. See also ¶ 414 and ¶ 417.

Special fuels: For application of sales tax to special fuels sold through stationary metered pumps, see *Information Bulletin No. 15,* Indiana Department of Revenue, August 2014, CCH INDIANA TAX REPORTS, ¶ 402-129.

Digitized products: In conformity with the Streamlined Sales Tax Agreement, sales and use tax is imposed on "products transferred electronically" only if the products meet the definition of specified digital products, ancillary services, prewritten computer software, or telecommunication services. (*Commissioner's Directive No. 41,* Indiana Department of Revenue, December 2014, CCH INDIANA TAX REPORTS, ¶ 402-203). Before publication of this directive, sales and use tax was imposed on electronically transferred products based on whether they were taxable in their tangible forms. The change in tax treatment is effective on publication of the directive and will not apply retroactively. The sale of a digital code that may be used to obtain a product transferred electronically is taxed in the same manner as the product transferred electronically (IC 6-2.5-4-16.4).

Guidance discussing sales, leases, or the use of computer hardware, computer software and digital goods is found in (*Information Bulletin No. 8,* Indiana Department of Revenue, December 2016, CCH INDIANA TAX REPORTS, ¶ 402-517).

• **Taxability of services**

Services that are specifically deemed by statute to be taxable as retail transactions include the following (IC 6-2.5-4-3—IC 6-2.5-4-5; IC 6-2.5-4-10; IC 6-2.5-4-11):

— the softening and conditioning of water;

— the renting or furnishing of certain rooms, lodgings, or other accommodations for a period of less than 30 days;

— the furnishing or selling of electrical energy, natural or artificial gas, water, steam, or steam heat;

— the furnishing of intrastate telecommunications service, or local or intra-state cable television service, and satellite television, cable radio, or satellite radio services that terminate in Indiana; and

— the renting or leasing of tangible personal property to another person.

A unitary transaction subject to tax includes otherwise nontaxable services that are furnished together with items of tangible personal property under a single order or agreement and for which a total combined charge is calculated. Generally, services that are separately listed on a bill are not subject to tax.

Warranties and maintenance contracts: Sales of optional maintenance contracts that meet the definition of bundled transactions are subject to sales tax at the time of sale. Conversely, the sales of optional warranty contracts where delivery of tangible personal property is uncertain are not subject to sales tax. However, any parts or products transferred under an optional warranty contract are subject to use tax at the time of delivery. (*Information Bulletin No. 2,* Indiana Department of Revenue, March, 2013, CCH INDIANA TAX REPORTS, ¶ 401-952)

Sales of computer software maintenance contracts are generally subject to sales tax pursuant to IC 6-2.5-4-17. See *Information Bulletin No. 8,* Indiana Department of Revenue, November 2011, CCH INDIANA TAX REPORTS, ¶ 401-773).

Internet access: Indiana state and local governments may not tax Internet access or the use of Internet access, effective April 23, 2015 (IC 6-10-1-5). A prohibited "tax" includes any gross retail tax, sales tax or use tax, any charge for the purpose of generating government revenues, or any charge that is not a fee imposed for a specific privilege, service or benefit. Existing utility fees, communications fees and telecommunications fees are not considered a tax on Internet access with certain exceptions (IC 6-10-1-3(b)).

"Internet access" includes (IC 6-10-1-2):

— the purchase, use, or sale of communications services, including telecommunications, by an Internet access provider to the extent that the communications services are purchased, used, or sold to provide Internet access or to otherwise enable users to access content, information, or other services offered over the Internet;

— services that are incidental to providing Internet access, furnished to users as part of access, including a home page, electronic mail and instant messaging, video clips, and personal electronic storage capacity; and

— a home page, electronic mail and instant messaging, video clips, and personal electronic storage capacity that are provided independently or that are not packaged with Internet access.

It does not include voice, audio, or video programming, or certain other products and services that use Internet protocol or any successor protocol and for which there is a charge, regardless of whether the charge is separately stated or aggregated with the charges for excepted services.

The federal Internet Tax Freedom Act (ITFA), enacted in 1998 and extended multiple times, is now permanent.

• **Incidence of tax**

The consumer is liable for payment of the sales tax. The incidence of the use tax is also on the consumer or user. However, the seller is required to collect both the sales and use taxes as agent for the state and is personally liable for remittance of the tax, except that the consumer or user must pay the use tax directly to the Department of Revenue when the seller is not engaged in business in Indiana or does not have permission from the Department to collect the tax.

¶411   Indiana

- **Persons liable for sales tax**

Liability for the sales tax extends to the following persons and entities: individuals, assignees, receivers, commissioners, fiduciaries, trustees, executors, administrators, institutions, national and other banks, consignees, firms, partnerships, joint ventures, pools, syndicates, bureaus, associations, cooperative associations, societies, clubs, fraternities and sororities, lodges, corporations, Indiana political subdivisions engaged in private or proprietary activities, estates, trusts, or any groups or combinations acting as a unit (IC 6-2.5-1-3). The statutory definition of "person" also specifically includes limited liability companies.

Retail merchants who do not have a fixed place of business must list their residence as their place of business for registration purposes.

Prepaid calling arrangements: For purposes of the Indiana sales and use tax on telecommunications, a person is a retail merchant when the person sells: (1) a prepaid calling service or prepaid wireless calling service at retail; (2) a prepaid calling service authorization number or prepaid wireless calling service authorization number at retail; (3) the reauthorization of a prepaid calling service or prepaid wireless calling service; or (4) the reauthorization of a prepaid calling service authorization number or prepaid wireless calling service authorization number. (IC 6-2.5-4-6).

Mobile telecommunications: Indiana has conformed to the federal Mobile Telecommunications Sourcing Act (IC 6-8.1-15-1 *et seq.*). All charges for mobile telecommunications services are considered to be provided by the customer's home service provider and sourced to the customer's place of primary use. All such charges are subject to sales tax based on the customer's place of primary use.

- **Use tax applicability**

The use tax is imposed on the storage, use, or consumption of tangible personal property in Indiana that was acquired in a retail transaction, regardless of the location of the transaction or the retail merchant making the transaction (IC 6-2.5-3-2, *Information Bulletin No. 31,* Department of Revenue, January 31, 1986). Indiana residents are required to pay use tax on catalogue, mail-order, or online purchases if sales tax was not collected by the vendor. Use tax is not imposed if Indiana sales tax has been collected at the point of purchase or the property is exempt from the sales tax (IC 6-2.5-3-4(a), 45 IAC 2.2-3-4, 45 IAC 2.2-3-13).

All purchases of tangible personal property delivered to the purchaser for storage (except temporary storage), use, or consumption in Indiana are subject to the use tax (45 IAC 2.2-3-20).

Self-manufactured goods: Use tax is imposed on a person who (1) manufactures, fabricates, or assembles tangible personal property from materials either within or outside Indiana, and (2) uses, stores, distributes, or consumes tangible personal property in Indiana (IC 6-2.5-3-2(d)).

Use tax payment/collection: The person who uses, stores, or consumes the tangible personal property acquired in a retail transaction is personally liable for the use tax and must pay the tax to the retail merchant from whom the property was acquired if the merchant is doing business in Indiana or is authorized by the Department of Revenue to collect the use tax. In all other cases, the person must pay the tax directly to the Department of Revenue (IC 6-2.5-3-6). "Person" includes an individual retail merchant or an employee, officer, or member of a corporate or partnership retail merchant who is personally liable for use tax.

Contracting with state agencies: Out-of-state businesses that do business with the state of Indiana must register as retail merchants and collect and remit Indiana sales and use tax (IC 6-2.5-4.14).

Also, an Indiana state agency may not purchase property or services from any person or business that is delinquent in the payment of Indiana sales and use tax. However, if a statement is issued from the Department of Revenue indicating that the delinquent tax has been satisfied or released, property or services may be purchased.

Temporary storage: Property stored for use outside Indiana is excluded from use tax for not more than 180 days (IC 6-2.5-3-1(b), (d)).

• Nexus

Indiana requires any retail merchant engaged in business in Indiana to collect and remit gross retail (sales) or use tax (IC 6-2.5-2-1; 45 IAC 2.2-2-2; IC 6-2.5-3-2). A "retail merchant engaged in business in Indiana" includes any retail merchant who makes retail transactions in which a person acquires personal property or services for use, storage, or consumption in Indiana and who (IC 6-2.5-3-1):

(1) maintains an office, place of distribution, sales or sample location, warehouse, storage place, or other place of business that is located in Indiana and that the merchant maintains, occupies, or uses, either permanently or temporarily, directly or indirectly, either by the retail merchant or through a representative, agent, or subsidiary;

(2) maintains a representative, agent, salesperson, canvasser, or solicitor who, while operating in Indiana under the authority, and on behalf, of the retail merchant or a subsidiary sells, delivers, installs, repairs, assembles, sets up, accepts returns of, bills, invoices, or takes orders for sales of tangible personal property or services to be used, stored, or consumed in Indiana;

(3) is otherwise required to register as a retail merchant under IC 6-2.5-8-1; or

(4) may be required by the state to collect tax to the extent allowed under the Constitution of the United States and federal law.

An out-of-state vendor is not engaged in business in Indiana when its only activity is the following (*Information Bulletin No. 37,* Indiana Department of Revenue, May 2016, CCH INDIANA TAX REPORTS, ¶ 402-386):

— owning Indiana realty for investment;

— being "qualified" to do business in Indiana;

— purchasing goods in Indiana;

— conducting credit investigations;

— delivering goods by common carrier; or

— is closely related to another person that maintains a place of business in Indiana.

Printing: Tangible or intangible property owned or leased by a person who has contracted with a commercial printer and located at the premises of the commercial printer, is not considered to create an office or other place of business used by the person. Also, a commercial printer is not considered a representative, agent, salesman, canvasser, or solicitor for the person. (IC 6-2.5-3-1)

• Streamlined Act status

Indiana is a full member of the Streamlined Sales and Use Tax Agreement with a seat on the Governing Board. It has enacted all of the provisions necessary to comply with the Agreement's requirements and these provisions currently are in effect (IC 6-2.5-11-5; *Commissioner's Directive No. 21,* July 2014, CCH INDIANA TAX REPORTS, ¶ 402-123).

As a full member, Indiana may vote on amendments to or interpretations of the Agreement, and sellers registering under the SST system must collect and remit tax on sales into the state. See also ¶ 417.

¶411   Indiana

Taxability matrix: A chart of the taxable status of various items is accessible on the website of the SSTP at **http://www.streamlinedsalestax.org/**. A seller or certified service provider that acquires a taxability matrix from the Indiana Department of Revenue is relieved from liability for sales and use tax collection errors that result from reliance on the matrix (IC 6-2.5-11-10).

¶ 412   Tax Base

Both the sales tax (IC 6-2.5-2-2) and the use tax (IC 6-2.5-3-2) are measured by the gross retail income received by a retail merchant in a retail unitary transaction.

• "Unitary transaction" and "retail unitary transaction" defined

A "unitary transaction" includes all items of personal property and services that are furnished under a single order or agreement and for which a total combined charge or price is calculated (IC 6-2.5-1-1, 45 IAC 2.2-1-1). As it applies to the furnishing of public utility commodities or services, a "unitary transaction" means the public utility commodities and services that are invoiced in a single bill or statement.

A "retail unitary transaction" means a unitary transaction that is also a retail transaction (IC 6-2.5-1-2).

• "Gross retail income" defined

"Gross retail income" means the total gross receipts, of any kind or character, received in a retail transaction, excluding (IC 6-2.5-1-5) the following:

(1) the value of tangible personal property received in a like kind exchange in a retail transaction; and

(2) the receipts received in a retail transaction that constitute interest, finance charges, or insurance premiums on either a promissory note or an installment sales contract.

A public utility's or power subsidiary's gross retail income includes all gross retail income received, including any minimum charge, flat charge, membership fee, or any other form of a charge or billing.

Gross retail income received from selling at retail is taxable only to the extent that the income represents (1) the price of the property transferred, without the rendition of any service; and (2) any charges, except for charges relating to food serving or delivering, made for preparation, fabrication, alteration, modification, finishing, completion, delivery, or other service performed to the property transferred before its transfer and that are separately stated on the transferor's records (IC 6-2.5-4-1(e), IC 6-2.5-4-1(g), 45 IAC 2.2-4-1).

Separately stated installation charges are specifically excluded from gross receipts subject to tax (IC 6-2.5-1-5(b)(6)). Delivery charges, however, are taxable and include, but are not limited to, charges by the seller for transportation, shipping, postage, handling, crating, and packing (IC 6-2.5-1-5(a)(4)).

¶ 413   List of Exemptions, Exceptions, and Exclusions

Unless otherwise indicated, the statutory exemptions listed below apply to both sales and use taxes; those applicable only to the use tax are listed separately. Items that are excluded from the sales or use tax base are discussed under "Tax Base" at ¶ 412.

• Sales and use tax exemptions, exceptions, and exclusions

Accommodations purchased by Indiana state government agencies .	IC 6-2.5-5-16
Agricultural production	IC 6-2.5-5-1
	IC 6-2.5-5-2
	IC 6-2.5-5-4
Aircraft brought into Indiana for repairs, completion work, etc.	IC 6-2.5-5-42

¶ 414   Rate of Tax

The Indiana gross retail (sales) and use tax rate is 7% (IC 6-2.5-2-2). The auto rental excise tax rate is 4% (IC 6-6-9-7).

Motor vehicles: Effective July 1, 2014, the sales tax rate on a motor vehicle that a purchaser intends to transport to a destination outside Indiana within 30 days after delivery and title or register the vehicle for use in another state or country is the rate of that state or country. The seller and the purchaser must certify the state or country in which the motor vehicle will be used in an affidavit, the form of which will be prescribed by the Department of Revenue. (IC 6-2.5-2-3)

Prepaid wireless charge: An enhanced prepaid wireless charge of $1.00 is imposed on each retail transaction involving the purchase of prepaid wireless telecommunications service (IC 36-8-16.6-11; *Commissioner's Directive No. 39,* Indiana Department of Revenue, November 2016, CCH INDIANA TAX REPORTS, ¶ 402-496). "Prepaid wireless telecommunications service" means a prepaid wireless calling service that permits a user of the service to reach emergency services by dialing the digits 911 (IC 36-8-16.6-7). The federal government and any agencies of the federal government are exempt from this charge, as are certain eligible telecommunications carriers (IC 36-8-16.6-11).

• **Gasoline use tax**

Determination of tax rate and notice: Before the 22nd day of each month, the department must (IC 6-2.5-3.5-15):

     — determine the gasoline use tax rate to be used during the following month; and

     — provide a notice of the gasoline tax rate to be used during the following month, the source of the data used to determine the gasoline use tax rate, and the statewide average retail price per gallon.

The gasoline use tax rate is published monthly by the department in Departmental Notice No. 2, available on the department's website at **http://www.in.gov/dor/files/dn02.pdf**.

¶ 415   Local Taxes

Counties are not authorized to levy a general sales or use tax, however certain other specific taxes are allowed as noted below.

• **County auto rental excise tax**

Marion County: A supplemental auto rental excise tax is imposed on the rental of passenger motor vehicles and trucks in Marion county for periods of less than 30 days. The tax equals 6% of the gross retail income received by the retail merchant for the rental (IC 6-6-9.7-7).

• **County admissions tax**

Counties are authorized to impose an admissions tax for the privilege of attending an event in that county. After June 30 and before January 1 of the following year, a city council may impose, by ordinance, a youth sports complex admissions tax at a rate of 5%. The tax would not apply to an event sponsored by an educational institution, a religious organization, a political organization, or an event for which tickets are sold on a per vehicle basis as opposed to a per person basis.

Marion County: A county that contains a consolidated first class city is authorized to adopt an ordinance imposing a county admissions tax for the privilege of attending any event before January 1, 2041. After December 31, 2040, the tax may be imposed on any professional sporting event held in a facility financed by specified bonds or notes (IC 6-9-13-1). The rate of tax is 6% of the admission price (IC 6-9-13-2). After January 1, 2013, and before March 1, 2013, the city council may, by ordinance, increase the county admissions tax from 6% to 10%.

Hendricks County: A county with a population of more than 100,000 but less than 105,000 is authorized to adopt an ordinance imposing a $1 county admissions tax on the price of admission to an amusement park (IC 6-9-28-1—IC 6-9-28-3).

The person who pays the price for admission is liable for the tax (IC 6-9-13-3, IC 6-9-28-4). The person collecting the price of admission is required to collect the tax at the same time, whether the price paid is for a single admission, season tickets, or any other admission arrangement.

• **City admissions taxes**

An entertainment facility admissions tax may be adopted by any fiscal body of an Indiana city for the privilege of attending outdoor entertainment events that have a minimum capacity of at least 10,000 patrons (IC 6-9-34-1). The amount of tax is 50¢ for each paid admission.

The tickets to the event must be offered for sale to the public by a box office facility or an authorized agent of the facility in order for the tax to apply. The entertainment facility admission tax does not apply to events sponsored by educational institutions, or religious, charitable or political organizations. In addition, the tax does not apply to events where tickets are not sold on a per-person basis.

• **Motorsports race day admissions fees**

Effective July 1, 2013, Indiana legislation provides for creation of a "motorsports investment district" that will finance improvements at a qualified motorsports facility through certain tax incentives as well as the imposition of a fee on each person charged for admission to the motorsports facility on a race day in the amount of: 6% on any admissions charge of at least $150; 3% on any admissions charge of at least $100; and 2% on any admissions charge of less than $100. (IC 6-8-14)

"Race day" means a day on which a race is conducted in which a competitor may earn points toward a series championship. The person who collects the price for admission must collect the admissions fee. The person must collect the fee, as agent of the state, at the same time the price for admission is paid regardless of whether the price paid is for a single admission, for season tickets, or for any other admission arrangement. The fee collections are remitted to the Department of Revenue. The fees collected during a particular month must be remitted before the 15th day of the following month. A return prescribed by the department must be filed at the time fees are remitted.

- **County and city food and beverage tax**

Counties that meet specified population requirements may impose a food and beverage tax (IC 6-9-12-1—IC 6-9-12-9, IC 6-9-20-1—IC 6-9-20-9, IC 6-9-21-1—IC 6-9-21-6, IC 6-9-23-1—IC 6-9-23-8, IC 6-9-25-1—IC 6-9-25-10, IC 6-9-26-1—IC 6-9-26-16). In addition, municipalities in a county that meet specified population requirements may impose a food and beverage tax (IC 6-9-24-1—IC 6-9-24-9). The tax equals 1% (2% in Marion County and the Historic Hotels district of Orange County) of the gross retail income received by a merchant from a transaction, not including any state sales tax imposed. Towns that meet specified population requirements are also authorized to impose a 1% food and beverage tax (IC 6-9-27-1—IC 6-9-27-10).

Taxable transactions include transactions in which food or beverage is:

— served by a retail merchant off his premises;

— food sold in a heated state or heated by a retail merchant;

— two or more food ingredients mixed or combined by the seller for sale as a single item (other than food that is only cut, repackaged, or pasteurized by the seller, and eggs, fish, meat, poultry, and foods containing these raw animal foods requiring cooking by the consumer as recommended by the federal Food and Drug Administration, in chapter 3, subpart 3-401.11 of its food code, so as to prevent food borne illnesses); or

— food sold with eating utensils provided by the seller, including plates (not including a container or packaging used to transport the food), knives, forks, spoons, glasses, cups, napkins, or straws.

The local food and beverage tax does not apply to transactions that are exempt from the state sales tax.

Streamlined changes: To conform to the Streamlined Sales and Use Tax Agreement (see ¶ 417), the county and municipal food and beverage taxes have been amended to include as taxable: (1) food sold in a heated state or heated by the retailer; (2) certain food ingredients mixed or combined by the retailer; and (3) food sold with utensils provided by the retailer.

Counties and cities that impose a food and beverage tax are listed in *Commissioner's Directive #30,* available at **http://www.in.gov/dor/reference/files/cd30.pdf**.

- **County innkeepers' tax**

Counties are authorized to levy an innkeepers' tax on persons engaged in the business of renting or furnishing lodgings for periods of less than 30 days. For some counties, the tax rate is specifically set, while in other counties the rate levied may range up to a specified maximum. Counties may adopt ordinances requiring monthly returns and payment to the county treasurer; if such ordinance is not adopted, the tax is paid quarterly to the Department of State Revenue in the same manner as the state sales tax.

Counties that are not required to impose an innkeepers' tax under a specified statutory provision are authorized to levy such tax under the uniform county innkeepers' tax provisions (IC 6-9-18-1). However, a county that has imposed a tax under these uniform provisions is prohibited from imposing an innkeepers' tax under specific provisions. The tax rate under the uniform provisions may not exceed the rate of 5% and is in addition to the state sales tax.

¶415 Indiana

The uniform provisions authorize a county to impose a tax on a person engaged in the business of renting or furnishing, for periods of less than 30 days, rooms, lodgings, or accommodations in a hotel, motel, boat motel, inn, tourist cabin, college or university memorial union, or college or university residence hall or dormitory (IC 6-9-18-3). The tax may not apply to a student renting lodgings in a college or university residence hall while the student participates in studies for which credit is received.

An individual taxpayer or an employee, officer, or member of a corporation or partnership taxpayer is personally liable for payment of the county innkeeper's tax, plus any penalties and interest (IC 6-9-29-2).

A chart of counties that impose an innkeepers' tax is available at **http://www.in.gov/dor/3469.htm**.

¶ 416   Bracket Schedule

The sales and use taxes are measured by the gross retail income received by a merchant in a retail unitary transaction (see ¶ 412) and are imposed as follows (IC 6-2.5-2-2, IC 6-2.5-3-3, 45 IAC 2.2-2-3):

Unitary transactions in the amount of 1¢ to 7¢ are not subject to sales tax. (IC 6-2.5-2-2, 45 IAC 2.2-2-4, *Information Bulletin No. 33,* Department of Revenue, July 2014, CCH INDIANA TAX REPORTS, ¶ 402-114). A "unitary transaction" includes all items of property and/or services, whether or not such services would otherwise be taxable, furnished pursuant to a single order or agreement and for which a total combined charge or selling price is computed for payment. Items of 1¢ to 7¢ purchased or paid for at one time are not exempt if the total sale or sales are more than 7¢.

On a retail unitary transaction in which the gross retail income received is $1.07 or more, the tax is 7% of the gross retail income (IC 6-2.5-2-2). If the tax results in a fraction of one-half cent or more, the amount of the tax must be rounded off to the next additional cent (IC 6-2.5-2-2; 45 IAC 2.2-2-5).

Bracket schedules have been eliminated (IC 6-2.5-2-2). Tax is computed at 7% of the purchase price, carried to the third decimal place and rounded down to a whole cent if the third decimal is four or less, and rounded up to the next whole cent if the third decimal is greater than four (IC 6-2.5-2-2; 45 IAC 2.2-2-5).

¶ 417   Returns, Payments, and Due Dates

In general, persons liable for collecting the sales or use tax must file a monthly return with the Department of Revenue and pay the tax collected during the month (IC 6-2.5-6-1(a), 45 IAC 2.2-6-1). The return and payment are due not later than 30 days after the end of the reporting month for persons whose average monthly liability, as determined by the Department for the preceding calendar year, does not exceed $1,000. If the person's liability exceeds $1,000, the return and payment are due no later than 20 days after the end of the reporting month. Monthly returns for admissions tax are required before the 15th day of the month following the month in which the tax was collected (IC 6-9-13-4, IC 6-9-28-5). The tax must be remitted at the same time.

A person who has voluntarily registered as a seller under the Streamlined Sales Tax Agreement, but who is not a Model 1, 2, or 3 seller, whose liability for collections of gross retail and use taxes for the preceding calendar year does not exceed $1,000 is not required to file a monthly gross retail and use tax return (IC 6-2.5-6-1(i)).

The Department of Revenue may permit retail merchants to report and pay tax on a quarterly basis, provided that the merchant's average monthly liability in the previous calendar year did not exceed $75 (IC 6-2.5-6-1(d)). Annual reporting is allowed for merchants with average monthly liability of $10 or less, and semi-annual reporting for merchants with average monthly liability of $25 or less. Whenever the Department authorizes a retail merchant to report and pay gross retail (sales) and use taxes on other than a monthly basis, the return and payment is due by the last day of the month after the end of the authorized period.

When registering, the seller may select one of three methods of remittance of taxes to Indiana. Under Model 1, a seller selects a certified service provider (CSP) as an agent to perform all sales and use tax functions, except the seller's obligation to remit tax on its own purchases. Under Model 2, a seller selects a certified automated system (CAS) to use to calculate the amount of tax due on a transaction. Under Model 3, a seller with total annual sales revenue of at least $500 million utilizes its own proprietary automated sales tax system that has been certified as a CAS (*Commissioner's Directive No. 27,* Indiana Department of Revenue, August 2011, CCH INDIANA TAX REPORTS, ¶ 401-697).

Collection allowance: To compensate a retail merchant for collecting and remitting the sales and use taxes, a collection allowance may be deducted from the amount of taxes otherwise required to be remitted (IC 6-2.5-7-5(b); IC 6-2.5-6-10; 45 IAC 2.2-6-14). The sales tax collection allowance for retail merchants is 0.73% if the total sales tax collected was less than $60,000; 0.53% if the total sales tax collected was between $60,000 and $600,000; and 0.26% if the total sales tax collected was more than $600,000. (*Departmental Notice No. 27,* Indiana Department of Revenue, August 2014, CCH INDIANA TAX REPORTS, ¶ 402-140)

Forms of payment: A person may make a tax payment in cash, by bank draft, by check, by cashier's check, by money order, by electronic fund transfer (if approved by the Department), or by credit card, debit card, charge card, or a similar method (IC 6-8.1-8-1). Some payments must be made electronically (see below).

Gasoline use tax: A qualified distributor, a refiner, or a terminal operator that sells gasoline for delivery to a retail merchant located in Indiana must remit to the department the gasoline use tax for each gallon of gasoline sold based on the tax rate determined by the department, regardless of the amount of gasoline use tax that has actually been collected IC 6-2.5-3.5-16. The taxpayer may also deduct and retain a collection allowance and take the home energy assistance deduction, if applicable. A purchaser of gasoline at retail from a metered pump is not liable to Indiana for the amount of the payment.

Collection of tax: At the time of "purchase or shipment" of gasoline from a refiner or terminal operator to a distributor that is not a qualified distributor, the refiner or terminal operator must collect gasoline use tax from the distributor. At the time of purchase or shipment of gasoline from a qualified distributor to a retail merchant, the qualified distributor must collect gasoline use tax from the retail merchant. If gasoline is delivered to a retail merchant for resale and the tax has not been paid, the refiner, terminal operator or qualified distributor making the delivery must pay the tax to the department. If a purchase or shipment of gasoline is made to a distributor, other than a qualified distributor, outside Indiana for shipment into and subsequent sale or use by the distributor in Indiana, the distributor will pay tax directly to the department. If a purchase or shipment is made within Indiana for shipment and subsequent sale outside Indiana, the purchase or shipment is exempt from the gasoline use tax payment requirements. If a sale of gasoline is exempt from gasoline use tax, the person that pays the tax to the retail merchant may file a claim for refund. A "purchase or shipment" is an exchange transaction between refiners, terminal operators, or a refiner and a terminal operator, or a delivery by pipeline, ship or barge to a refiner or terminal operator. (IC 6-2.5-3.5-19)

Reimbursement of tax payments: A purchaser or recipient of gasoline from a distributor will pay the distributor an amount equal to the gasoline use tax paid by the distributor. The distributor must separately state the amount of tax paid on the invoice the distributor issues to its purchaser or recipient. However, a distributor that is a retail merchant, pays the gasoline use tax, and then sells gasoline that is exempt from use tax may not require the exempt purchaser to pay the gasoline use tax. Such a distributor may file a claim for refund. (IC 6-2.5-3.5-21; (IC 6-2.5-3.5-25))

Display of price: A retail merchant must display on the metered pump the total price per unit of the gasoline. A retail merchant may not advertise the gasoline at a price that is different from the price that it is required to display on the metered pump. (IC 6-2.5-3.5-24)

- **Electronic fund transfer payments**

When a person's estimated monthly sales and use tax liability for the current year or the preceding year exceeds $5,000, the person is required to pay the monthly taxes due by electronic fund transfer (EFT) or by delivering in person or by overnight courier a cashier's check, certified check, or money order to the Department of Revenue (IC 6-2.5-6-1(g)). The transfer or payment must be made on or before the due date. A payment made by EFT is considered made on the date that the taxpayer issued the payment order for the EFT. Business taxes may be filed and paid through INtax at **https://www.intax.in.gov/login**.

If payment is made by electronic funds transfer, a merchant is not required to file a monthly return, but instead must file a quarterly return within 20 days after the end of each calendar quarter (IC 6-2.5-6-1(h); IC 6-2.5-6-1(g)).

Gasoline use tax: The tax must be remitted semi-monthly through the Department of Revenue's online tax filing system. In addition, a refiner, terminal operator and qualified distributor must file an electronic report covering the taxes owed and the gallons of gasoline sold or received during the preceding month. (IC 6-2.5-3.5-20)

- **Electronic filing of returns**

The Commissioner of Revenue may permit the filing of any return or document by electronic data submission (IC 6-8.1-6-7).

All retail merchants and withholding agents are required to file and remit sales and use taxes through INtax, the Department of Revenue's online tax filing program. INtax allows businesses to (1) confirm that their filings and payments are received in a timely manner, (2) view their tax payment histories, and (3) schedule automatic debits from their banking accounts. Enrollment and other information on INtax is available on the Department's Web site at **https://www.intax.in.gov/login**.

Retail merchants remitting sales tax through electronic funds transfer (EFT) must file a monthly return when the remittance is due. The monthly return replaces the requirement to file a quarterly recap. (*Information Bulletin No. 77*, Indiana Department of Revenue, May 2012, CCH INDIANA TAX REPORTS, ¶ 401-850)

Electronic document delivery: The provision under which the commissioner permits the filing of any return or document electronically applies to a taxpayer required to report and remit sales taxes electronically. If the taxpayer provides written consent, the department may use a secure electronic delivery service to provide the taxpayer with any documents that would otherwise require mail delivery. A "secure electronic delivery service" is a service that: uses security procedures to provide, send, deliver, or otherwise communicate electronic records using security methods such as passwords, encryption and matching electronic addresses to U.S. postal addresses; or operates subject to the requirements of the federal Electronic Signatures in Global and National Commerce Act. (IC 6-8.1-3-11)

- **Uniform Sales Tax Administration Act**

Indiana has enacted the Uniform Sales and Use Tax Administration Act, the product of the Streamlined Sales Tax Project (SSTP). Indiana also has enacted legislation conforming its sales and use tax laws to provisions of the Streamlined Sales and Use Tax Agreement. For details of the most recent conforming amendments, see *Commissioner's Directive No. 21,* July 2014, CCH INDIANA TAX REPORTS, ¶ 402-123.

Bad debts: A "bad debt" is as defined in IRC Sec. 166, except it does not include: (1) financing charges or interest; (2) state or local sales or use taxes on the purchase price; (3) uncollectible amounts on property that remains in the possession of a seller until the full purchase price is paid; (4) expenses incurred in attempting to collect any debt; or (5) repossessed property (IC 6-2.5-6-9). A seller's certified service provider may make a deduction or claim a refund for bad debt on behalf of the seller if the certified service provider credits or refunds the full amount of the bad debt deduction or refund to the seller. A bad debt may be allocated among the states that are members of the Agreement if a seller's books and records support that allocation.

A retail merchant's right to a bad debt deduction against sales tax liability is not assignable to an individual or entity that is not part of the same affiliated group as the assignor (IC 6-2.5-6-9(c)).

Sourcing: Sales are sourced generally to the destination of the product sold, with a default to origin-based sourcing in the absence of that information (IC 6-2.5-13-1). Special sourcing rules apply to sales of vehicles, transportation equipment, and telecommunications. Retail sales in which a florist (1) takes an order from a purchaser, and (2) transmits the order by telegraph, telephone, or other means of communication to another florist for delivery are sourced to the location of the florist that originally took the order from the purchaser (IC 6-2.5-13-1(h)).

Local taxes: The county and municipal food and beverage taxes include as taxable: (1) food sold in a heated state or heated by the retailer; (2) certain food ingredients mixed or combined by the retailer; and (3) food sold with utensils provided by the retailer.

Regulations: For additional information, see Rules 45 IAC 2.2-1-1 through 45 IAC 2.2-6-12. See also "Streamlined Sales Tax Project," listed in the Table of Contents.

¶ 418   Prepayment of Taxes

Prior to July 1, 2014, any unqualified distributor purchasing or receiving gasoline from a refiner or terminal operator had to prepay a portion of the sales tax at the time of the purchase or shipment (former IC 6-2.5-7-9). This requirement was, repealed effective July 1, 2014, when the gasoline use tax became effective (see ¶ 411, ¶ 414, and ¶ 417).

¶ 419   Vendor Registration

Retail merchants are required to obtain a registered retail merchant's certificate before they can make retail transactions in Indiana (IC 6-2.5-8-1, 45 IAC 2.2-8-1). Even merchants who make retail transactions that are only subject to the use tax must obtain a certificate (IC 6-2.5-8-1, 45 IAC 2.2-8-4).

A registered retail merchant's Indiana sales and use tax certificate is valid for two years after the date the certificate is originally issued or renewed. If the retail merchant has filed all returns and remitted all taxes as required, the Department will renew the certificate within 30 days after the expiration date, at no cost to the retail merchant. (IC 6-2.5-8-1).

Entities that are closely related to out-of-state businesses that engage in taxable activities in Indiana must register as retail merchants in Indiana, and, when applicable, collect Indiana sales and use taxes (IC 6-2.5-8-10). "Closely related" means that the entities: (1) use an identical or substantially similar name, trademark, or good will to develop, promote, or maintain sales; (2) pay for each other's services in whole or in part contingent on the volume or value of sales; or (3) share a common business plan or substantially coordinate their business plans and at least one is a corporation with a certain level of stock ownership. New businesses that register are required to electronically file and pay these taxes using INtax (see ¶ 417).

Manufacturers and wholesalers may register with the Department as purchasers of property in exempt transactions by applying in the same manner and paying the same fee as retail merchants (IC 6-2.5-8-3, 45 IAC 2.2-8-6, *Information Bulletin No. 52,* Department of Revenue, January 2012). The Department may issue a manufacturer's or wholesaler's certificate for each place of business (IC 6-2.5-8-3, 45 IAC 2.2-8-7).

Revocation of certificate: The Department of Revenue may revoke a retail merchant's certificate if the retailer fails to file a return or remit tax. The department can revoke a certificate before a criminal adjudication or without a criminal charge being filed. (IC 6-2.5-8-7)

Call center contractors: An out-of-state company that has contracted with an Indiana call center operator for a telephone service is not required to register as a retail merchant or collect or remit Indiana sales or use tax, if that company's sole contact with Indiana is the call center contract (IC 6-2.5-8-12). A "telephone service" includes soliciting orders by telephone, accepting orders by telephone, and making and receiving any other telephone calls. The call center is not considered a place of business for purposes of Indiana sales and use tax, even if property owned by the out-of-state company is located at the call center, as long as the property is not held for sale or shipment in response to an order received by the call center. In addition, the call center operator is not an agent of the out-of-state company for purposes of Indiana sales and use tax.

Online registration: Business owners can complete the Business Tax Application (BT-1) online at the Indiana Department of Revenue's website (**http://www.in.gov/ dor/4337.htm**) to initiate Indiana sales tax, personal income tax withholding, county innkeepers tax, food and beverage tax, motor vehicle rental excise tax, out-of-state use tax, prepaid gasoline sales tax, and private employment agency taxes, for new businesses. The BT-1 cannot be used to update current information for existing businesses, unless new locations or new tax types are being added.

Gasoline wholesalers' permits: A distributor, refiner or terminal operator may receive gasoline within Indiana without paying the gasoline use tax if the person holds an uncancelled permit to collect payments of gasoline use tax from purchasers and recipients of gasoline. To obtain a permit, an application must be filed with the department. An audited and current financial statement and a $100 license fee must be submitted with the application. The department may require a permit applicant to file a bond as well. A permit is not assignable and is valid only for the person in whose name it is issued. The department may refuse to issue a permit under various conditions. (IC 6-2.5-3.5-17)

Delinquent merchants: If the Department of Revenue has notified a retail merchant that it will not renew the merchant's registered retail merchant's certificate due to delinquent sales and use taxes, and the merchant pays the taxes due before the certificate expires, the department will renew the certificate for one year. In addition, a wholesaler, retailer, dealer or other permit of any type may not be issued, renewed or transferred if the applicant is seeking a renewal or transfer and is at least 30 days delinquent in remitting sales taxes. (IC 6-2.5-8-1(h))

- **SST registrants**

To register under the SST Agreement, sellers must go to **https:// www.sstregister.org**. Sellers can also update previously submitted registration information at this website. The information provided will be sent to all of the full member states and to associate members for which the seller chooses to collect.

When a seller registers under the Agreement, it must select the certified technology model it will be using (or it must select "Other" if it will not be using one of the certified models). The models are the following:

—Certified Service Provider (CSP), an agent certified under the Agreement to perform all the seller's sales and use tax functions.

—Certified Automated System (CAS), software certified under the Agreement to calculate the appropriate tax (for which the seller retains responsibility for remitting).

—Certified System (CS), a proprietary automated sales tax system certified under the Agreement.

A purchaser's seller, a certified service provider, or a purchaser with a direct pay permit will not be held liable for penalties for failure to pay the correct amount of tax due if the error was caused by the Department providing erroneous data in tax rates, boundaries, taxing jurisdiction assignments, or the taxability matrix. Relief is limited to tax and interest attributable to the Department's erroneous classification in the taxability matrix of terms: (1) included as taxable or exempt; (2) included in the sales price; (3) excluded from the sales price; (4) included in a definition; or (5) excluded from a definition (IC 6-2.5-11-11(a)).

The Indiana Department of Revenue has issued a bulletin clarifying when the department may assess sales tax on retail sales made by a seller registered under the Streamlined Sales and Use Tax (SST) Agreement based on the seller's failure to timely file a sales tax return, if the seller is not legally required to register with Indiana. (*Information Bulletin No. 80*, Indiana Department of Revenue, November 2014, CCH INDIANA TAX REPORTS, ¶ 402-180)

¶ 420   **Sales or Use Tax Credits**

A person who has paid any sales, purchase, or use tax to any other state, territory, or possession of the United States is entitled to a credit against the Indiana use tax equal to the amount paid on the same item of tangible personal property (IC 6-2.5-3-5, 45 IAC 2.2-3-16). This credit does not, however, apply to the use tax paid on vehicles, aircraft, or watercraft registered or licensed by Indiana (IC 6-2.5-3-5, 45 IAC 2.2-3-17).

An information bulletin states that the credit does not apply to any sales tax paid to a foreign country (*Information Bulletin No. 31,* Department of Revenue, January 31, 1986). The bulletin also provides that an excise or use tax paid to another state or jurisdiction may not be applied against the Indiana use tax if such tax is unique to the product being used or sold.

Venture capital investment credit: Taxpayers may claim a credit against state tax liability, including liability for Indiana gross retail (sales) and use tax, for 20% of the qualified investment capital provided to a qualified Indiana business, as certified by the Indiana Department of Commerce, in the taxable year (IC 6-3.1-24-1 *et seq.*). Qualified investment capital may be either debt or equity capital. The total amount of credits that may be granted in a calendar year cannot exceed $10 million and the total amount of credits available for each qualified Indiana business is the lesser of 20% of the amount qualified investment capital provided to the business or $500,000.

To receive the credit, the taxpayer must claim the credit on its return in the manner prescribed by the Department of Revenue, including proof of entitlement required by the Department. If the total amount of available credits is claimed in a calendar year, credits are awarded in the chronological order in which the returns claiming the credits were filed. If a pass-through entity is entitled to the credit and the entity does not have state tax liability, the credit may be claimed by a shareholder, partner, or member of the entity in proportion to ownership percentage. Unused credit may be carried forward to subsequent taxable years until exhausted. The credit may not be carried back or refunded. Credits may not be claimed for providing qualified investment capital after 2016.

Riverboat building credit: A taxpayer liable for the gross income or sales and use tax may be entitled to a credit against its total tax liability in an amount equal to 15% of the qualified investment costs incurred during the tax year to build or refurbish a riverboat in Indiana (IC 6-3.1-17-1—IC 6-3.1-17-9).

• Multiple credits

Taxpayers may not use more than one of the following tax credits against Indiana corporate or personal income tax, sales and use tax, insurance premiums tax, and financial institutions tax: the military base investment cost credit, the enterprise zone investment cost credit, the industrial recovery tax credit, the military base recovery tax credit, the capital investment tax credit, the community revitalization enhancement district tax credit, the venture capital investment tax credit, and the Hoosier business investment tax credit (IC 6-3.1-1-3). Taxpayers who are granted more than one tax credit for the same project (1) must elect to apply only one of the credits, (2) are not permitted to change the credit selected in subsequent years, and (3) are not allowed to elect a subsequent credit for the same investment in following years if they use all of the credits that they were awarded (*Commissioner's Directive No. 29,* Indiana Department of Revenue, October 2014, CCH INDIANA TAX REPORTS, ¶ 402-163).

¶ 421   Deficiency Assessments

Indiana has uniform general administrative provisions for so-called "listed taxes," which include the sales (gross retail) and use tax (IC 6-8.1-1-1 *et seq.*). If a general administrative provision conflicts with a specific sales and use tax provision, the specific provision controls (IC 6-8.1-1-6). Both the general and specific administrative provisions applicable to sales and use taxes are discussed in the following paragraphs.

There are no sales and use tax provisions relating specifically to deficiency assessments. A general provision authorizes the Department of Revenue to issue a deficiency assessment including interest and penalties if a person has filed a tax return without including full payment of the tax or if the Department finds that tax is owed after a protest hearing (IC 6-8.1-1-1).

• Issuance of deficiency assessments

If a taxpayer fails to file a required return within 30 days of a demand notice, the Department of Revenue may prepare a tax return for the taxpayer. The return may consist of an actual return, an audit report, or notice of the tax due (IC 6-8.1-6-1, 45 IAC 15-11-3).

¶ 422   Audit Procedures

The Department of Revenue may audit any returns and investigate any matters relating to the sales and use taxes or other "listed taxes" (IC 6-8.1-3-12). The Department may enforce its audit and investigatory powers by petitioning for a court order.

The Department may make a proposed assessment if it believes that a person has not reported the correct amount of tax due (IC 6-8.1-5-1, 45 IAC 15-5-1). The notice of proposed assessment is prima facie evidence that the Department's claim is valid (IC 6-8.1-5-1, 45 IAC 15-5-3). The assessed person has the burden of proving that the claim is wrong.

¶ 423   Statute of Limitations

The general statute of limitations provisions under the Tax Administration Act apply to the sales and use taxes.

General rule: Tax may be assessed three years after the latest of (1) the date the return is filed, (2) the due date of the return, or (3) the end of the calendar year that contains the taxable period for which the return is filed (IC 6-8.1-5-2, 45 IAC 15-5-7, *Tax Policy Directive No. 1,* Department of Revenue, September, 2010, CCH INDIANA TAX REPORTS, ¶ 401-591).

The statute of limitations for claiming refunds is three years from the later of the due date of the return or the date the tax is paid. The department can make assessments related to erroneous refunds within two years after issuing a refund or within five years after issuing a refund if the refund was induced by fraud or misrepresentation.

No limitation: If a person files a fraudulent, unsigned, or substantially blank return or fails to file any return, no statute of limitations exists.

¶ 424   Application for Refund

In order to obtain a refund, a taxpayer must file a claim with the Department of Revenue within three years after the due date of the return or the date of payment, whichever is later (IC 6-8.1-9-1). For purposes of a refund claim, the due date for a sales or use tax return is deemed to be the end of the calendar year containing the taxable period for which the return is filed.

A claim for a sales and use tax refund must be filed on a Claim for Refund (Form GA-110L). The claim must set forth (1) the amount of refund claimed; (2) a sufficiently detailed explanation of the claim so that the Department may determine its correctness; (3) the tax period for which the overpayment is claimed; and (4) the year and date the overpayment was made (45 IAC 15-9-2(d)). Taxpayers who submit a refund claim with proper documentation, an explanation of the claimed refund, and authorized signature can expect a refund to be issued within 90 days without interest. If the taxpayer fails to meet the above criteria, the Department will send the taxpayer a letter explaining what steps need to be taken to correct the error. Additionally, the process does not extend the three year statute of limitations on the refund. See *Commissioner's Directive No. 13,* October 2015, CCH INDIANA TAX REPORTS, ¶ 402-311.

A sales (gross retail) and use tax statute provides that a person is entitled to a refund from the Department of Revenue when a retail merchant has erroneously or illegally collected the tax from a purchaser, has remitted the collected tax to the Department, and has not refunded the tax to the purchaser (IC 6-2.5-6-13). A retail merchant is not entitled to a refund unless the retail merchant refunds those taxes to the person from whom they were collected (IC 6-2.5-6-14.1).

Local taxes: The Indiana Tax Court did not have subject matter jurisdiction over a refund request for local innkeeper's tax because the court only has jurisdiction over appeals from final determinations made by the Department of Revenue. A casino paid tax to a county treasurer, then sought a refund from the Indiana Department of Revenue, which was denied because the tax was collected by the county. The county did not respond to the casino's request for a refund, and the casino then appealed to the Tax Court. In accordance with state law, the local ordinance did not provide for the making of refunds. The court said that the Legislature giving tax collection responsibility, but not the ability to make tax refunds, for purposes of the innkeeper's tax, did not produce an absurd result. (*Blue Chip Casino, LLC v. La Porte County Treasurer,* Indiana Tax Court, No. 49T101008-TA-37, March 16, 2015, CCH INDIANA TAX REPORTS, ¶ 402-225)

¶ 426   Scope of Tax

Source.—Statutory references are to Chapters 422 and 423 of the Code of Iowa, as amended to date. Details are reported in the CCH IOWA STATE TAX REPORTS starting at ¶ 60-000.

The Iowa sales tax is a broadly imposed general tax levied on the gross receipts from sales at retail of tangible personal property or on its lease or rental and on the furnishing of enumerated services (Sec. 422.43). The use tax on use of tangible personal property or enumerated services in the state is a complementary tax and does not apply in situations in which the sales tax is collected (Sec. 423.2, Sec. 423.4(1)).

Digitized products: A sale of tangible personal property does not occur if the substance of the transaction is delivered to the purchaser digitally, electronically, or utilizing cable, or by radio waves, microwaves, satellites, or fiber optics (Sec. 423.3(66)).

Prepaid phone servicess: Sales of prepaid calling services that use an authorization code and prepaid wireless calling services are taxable (Sec. 423.2(1)(a)(3)).

- **Incidence of sales tax**

Although the sales tax is generally imposed on a seller's gross receipts (Sec. 422.43), shifting of the tax to the purchaser is mandatory (Sec. 422.49). Sales tax must be separately stated, and the tax becomes a debt from the purchaser to the seller (Sec. 422.48, Rule 701—14.1(422)).

- **Services subject to tax**

In general, gross receipts from "services" are subject to tax (Sec. 422.43(10)). "Services" is defined as all acts or services rendered, furnished, or performed for a valuable consideration by any person engaged in business of providing certain enumerated services. A person is "engaged in the business of" providing a service if the person offers the service to the public or others for a consideration, regardless of whether the service is offered continuously, part time, seasonally, or for short periods (Rule 701—26.1(422)).

Gross receipts from the following activities are subject to tax:

— Selling tickets or admissions to places of amusement, fairs, and athletic events; operating games of skill, games of chance, raffles, bingo games, and amusement devices; and selling private club membership fees (Sec. 422.43(1) and (2));

— Providing gas, electricity, water, heat, pay television, or communication service (Sec. 422.43(1));

— Providing engraving, photography, retouching, printing, or binding services (Sec. 422.43(4));

— Providing vulcanizing, recapping, and retreading services (Sec. 422.43(5));

— Selling optional service or warranty contracts (Sec. 422.43(6));

— Providing transient lodging accommodations (Sec. 422.43(7));

— Providing solid waste collection and disposal services (Sec. 422.43(13)); and

— Providing mobile telecommunications services (Sec. 422.43(17)).

The Iowa Department of Revenue provides guidance regarding the applicability of sales and use taxes to various services. A list of taxable services is provided, and topics discussed include construction, employee services, exempt entities, purchases for resale, services for resale, restoring tangible property, and casual sales (*Publication 78-524, Iowa Sales and Use Tax: Taxable Services*, Iowa Department of Revenue, June 22, 2009, CCH IOWA TAX REPORTS, ¶ 201-265).

• **Use tax**

The use tax complements the sales tax. Consequently, a transaction that would be subject to Iowa sales tax if it were consummated in Iowa is subject to use tax if it takes place outside the state for use in Iowa (Rule 701—31.1(423)).

A use tax is imposed upon the use in Iowa of tangible personal property purchased for use in the state. Persons using the property in Iowa are liable for the tax until it is paid to the county treasurer, the Department of Transportation, a retailer, or the Department of Revenue and Finance (Sec. 423.2, Rule 701—31.2(423)). Evidence that tangible personal property was sold by any person for delivery in Iowa is prima facie evidence that the property was sold for use in Iowa (Sec. 423.5).

A use tax is also imposed upon the use in Iowa of specified services. The tax applies if the services are rendered, furnished, or performed in Iowa or if the product or result of the service is used in Iowa. Every person using the services or the products of the services in Iowa is liable for the tax until it is paid either to an Iowa use tax permit holder or to the Department of Revenue and Finance (Sec. 423.2, Rule 701—31.1(423), Rule 701—32.1(423)).

• **Nexus**

Every retailer maintaining a place of business in Iowa and making sales of tangible personal property for use in Iowa, not otherwise exempted, must collect sales or use tax from the purchaser (Sec. 423.29; Rule 701-30.1(423), IAC). "Retailer maintaining a place of business in this state" includes any retailer having or maintaining within the state, directly or by a subsidiary, an office, distribution house, sales house, warehouse, or other place of business, regardless of whether the place of business is located in the state permanently or temporarily; or, or any representative operating within this state under the authority of the retailer or its subsidiary, permanently or temporarily (Sec. 423.1(48)(a)).

Presumptions: A retailer is presumed to be maintaining a place of business in Iowa if any person with substantial nexus in the state, other than a person acting as a common carrier, does any of the following (Sec. 423.1(48)(b)(1)):

— sells a similar line of products as the retailer and does so under the same or similar business name;

— maintains an office, distribution facility, warehouse, storage place, or similar place of business in Iowa to facilitate the delivery of property or services sold by the retailer to the retailer's customers;

— uses trademarks, service marks, or trade names in the state that are the same or substantially similar to those used by the retailer;

— delivers, installs, assembles, or performs maintenance services for the retailer's customers;

— facilitates the retailer's delivery of property to customers in Iowa by allowing the retailer's customers to take delivery of property sold by the retailer at an office, distribution facility, warehouse, storage place, or similar place of business maintained by the person in the state; or

— conducts any other activities in Iowa that are significantly associated with the retailer's ability to establish and maintain a market in the state for the retailer's sales.

The presumption may be rebutted by a showing of proof that the person's activities in Iowa are not significantly associated with the retailer's ability to establish or maintain a market in Iowa for the retailer's sales (Sec. 423.1(48)(b)(2)).

— an office, distribution house, sales house, warehouse, or other place of business, regardless of whether the place of business is located in the state permanently or temporarily; or

— any representative operating within the state under the authority of the retailer or its subsidiary, permanently or temporarily.

• **Streamlined Act status**

Iowa is a full member of the Agreement with a seat on the Governing Board. It has enacted all of the provisions necessary to comply with the Agreement's requirements and these provisions currently are in effect (Sec. 423.1—Sec. 423.57). As a full member, it may vote on amendments to or interpretations of the Agreement, and sellers registering under the SST system must collect and remit tax on sales into the state. For additional information, see ¶ 432.

Taxability matrix: A chart of the taxable status of various items and services is accessible on the SST website at **www.streamlinedsalestax.org**.

¶ 427   Tax Base

Retail sales tax is computed upon the gross receipts from retail sales of tangible personal property, leases or rentals of such property, and the furnishing of various services (Sec. 422.43), less cash discounts and trade-ins (Sec. 422.42(3)).

For use tax purposes, "purchase price" is the total amount for which tangible personal property is sold (valued in money) regardless of how it is paid, excluding cash discounts or trade-ins (Sec. 423.1(3), Rule 701—30.2(423)).

"Value of services" means the price to the user exclusive of any tax directly imposed by the federal government or Iowa sales tax laws (Sec. 422.42(15)).

"Gross taxable services" is the total amount received in money, credits, property, or other consideration (valued in money) from services rendered, furnished, or performed in Iowa. Taxable services do not include services used to process tangible personal property that is used in retail sales and services (Sec. 422.42(6)).

For Streamlined Sales and Use Tax (SST) Agreement conformity purposes, the following are excluded from the "sales price" (Sec. 423.1(51)):

— any state or local tax on a retail sale that is imposed on the seller if the statute, rule, or local ordinance provides that the seller may, but is not required to, collect such tax from the consumer and if the tax is separately stated on the invoice, bill of sale, or similar document given to the purchaser; and

— any tribal tax on a retail sale that is imposed on the seller if the tribal law imposing the tax provides that the seller may, but is not required to, collect such tax from the consumer and if the tax is separately stated on any document given to the purchaser.

Bundling: Tax is imposed on the sales price from sales of bundled transactions (Sec. 423.2(8)(a)). The definition of "sales price" no longer includes a deduction for the value of exempt personal property given to the purchaser when taxable and exempt personal property have been bundled together and sold by the seller as a single product or piece of merchandise (Sec. 423.1(47)(a)).

¶ 428   List of Exemptions, Exceptions, and Exclusions

Unless otherwise indicated, the statutory exemptions, exceptions, and exclusions listed below apply to both sales and use taxes; those applicable only to the sales tax or only to the use tax are listed separately. Some items that are excluded from the sales or use tax base are treated at ¶ 427, "Tax Base."

Sales tax holiday: Sales of articles of clothing and footwear costing less than $100 are exempt during a period each year beginning at 12:01 a.m. on the first Friday in August and ending at midnight on the following Saturday. The exemption does not apply to special athletic clothing or footwear; accessories, including jewelry, handbags, luggage, umbrellas, wallets, and watches; clothing for animals; and the rental of clothing or footwear. There is an exemption for jogging suits and tennis shoes, however, because these items are worn outside athletics (Sec. 422.45(59)). An administrative rule contains a nonexclusive list of merchandise eligible for exemption during the two-day period in August (Rule 701—20.12(7)).

• **Sales and use tax exemptions, exceptions, and exclusions**

Admissions to events held by elementary and secondary institutions .	Sec. 423.2(3)
Advertising material sent out-of-state	Sec. 423.3(42)
Agricultural aerial spraying	Sec. 423.3(7)
Agricultural breeding livestock and domesticated fowl	Sec. 423.3(3)
Agricultural drainage tile	Sec. 423.3(5)
Agricultural irrigation equipment	Sec. 423.3(12)
Agricultural limestone for commercial agricultural production	Sec. 423.3(5)
Agricultural—diesel fuel trailers, seed tenders, ATVs, and UTVs	Sec. 423.3(8)
Agricultural—Livestock ear tags sold by certain organizations	Sec. 423.3(30)
Aircraft, interstate	Sec. 423.3(74)
Aircraft used for rental or lease	Sec. 423.3(77)
Argon and other similar gases used in manufacturing	Sec. 423.3(51)
Automated teller machines	Sec. 423.3(83)
Baling wire and binder twine for agricultural, livestock, or dairy production	Sec. 423.3(15)
Casual sales	Sec. 423.3(39)
Charitable activities	Sec. 423.3(78)
Clothing and footwear (annual $100 per item exemption eff. the first Friday and Saturday in August)	Sec. 422.45(59)
Coins, currency, and bullion	Sec. 423.3(91)
Communication services sold to other states	Sec. 423.3(36)
Community health centers, federal	Sec. 422.45(22)(a)
Community mental health centers	Sec. 422.45(22)(a)
Computers in specified uses; parts and supplies	Sec. 423.3(47), (92)
Construction equipment, leased or rented	Sec. 423D.3
Construction materials used in exempt projects	Sec. 423.3(37), (86), (91)
County fair authorities	Sec. 423.3(23)
County or city sales or services	Sec. 423.3(32)
County's purchases from federal government	Sec. 423.3(31)
Data center businesses	Sec. 423.3(95)
Detective and security services	Sec. 423.2(6)(a)
Design of new industrial machinery or equipment	Sec. 423.3(47)
Digitized products	Sec. 423.3(66)
Domesticated fowl	Sec. 423.3(3)
Drugs	Sec. 423.3(59)
Disaster or emergency responders from out-of-state	Sec. 423.33, Sec. 423.58
Educational activities	Sec. 423.3(17), (21), (78)
Electricity provided to governmental units	Sec. 423.3(32)

Telecommunications, central office and transmission equipment . . .	Sec. 423.3(47A), Sec. 423.3(70)
Transportation services	Sec. 423.3(60), (70)
Utilities sold to other states.	Sec. 423.3(36)
Utilities used in agricultural production	Sec. 423.3(10)
Utilities used in processing	Sec. 423.3(49)
Vehicles used in recycling or waste reprocessing	Sec. 423.3(46)
Vessels, services performed on	Sec. 423.3(86)
Vessels used on rivers, fuel.	Sec. 423.3(72)
Washers and dryers (self-pay)	Sec. 423.2(6)(a)
Water used in agricultural production	Sec. 423.3(10)
Web search portal property	Sec. 423.3(92)
Wind energy conversion property	Sec. 423.3(54)
Wood chips, sawdust, and other bedding material used in agricultural production	Sec. 423.3(9)
Youth athletic groups.	Sec. 423.3(78)

- **Exemptions from sales tax only**

Motor vehicles	Sec. 423.28

- **Exemptions from use tax only**

Aircraft used in interstate air carrier operation	Sec. 423.3(74)
Aircraft used for rental or lease	Sec. 423.3(77)
Tangible personal property used in the construction or repair of any ship, barge, or waterborne vessel	Sec. 423.4(13)
Vehicles replaced in inventory by a dealer	Sec. 423.6(25)
Vehicles transferred from a business entity to a corporation	Sec. 423.6(10)

¶ 429   Rate of Tax

The Iowa state sales and use tax rate is 6%. Beginning January 1, 2030, the rate is scheduled to decrease from 6% to 5%. (Sec. 423.2; Sec. 423.5).

Some sales and services are currently taxed at 5%:

(1) the state rate for hotel and motel lodging (the local hotel/motel tax, if any, will also apply);

(2) certain construction equipment sold to contractors (self-propelled building equipment, pile drivers, motorized scaffolding, attachments customarily drawn or attached to them, and replacement parts); and

(3) the short-term auto rental tax.

An increase or decrease in the retail sales tax rate may take effect only on January 1 or July 1, but not sooner than 90 days after its enactment (Sec. 422B.9(1)(a)).

If a person has paid sales, use, or occupation tax to another state at a rate lower than the Iowa sales or use tax rate, Iowa use tax is owed on the difference between the Iowa rate and the other state's rate (Sec. 423.25, Rule 701—30.7(423)). If the other state's rate is higher, no Iowa use tax is owed.

Rate changes: A seller is relieved of liability for failure to collect sales or use taxes at a new rate under all of the following conditions (Sec. 423.46):

— the department fails to provide for at least 30 days between the enactment of the statute that provides for a rate change and the effective date of such rate change;

— the seller continues to collect sales or use taxes at the rate in effect immediately prior to the rate change;

— the erroneous collection described above (seller continues to collect at the rate in effect immediately prior to a rate change) does not continue for more than 30 days after the effective date of the rate change.

This relief is inapplicable if a seller fraudulently fails to collect tax at the new rate or if a seller has solicited purchasers on the basis of the rate in effect immediately prior to the rate change.

• Lodging tax

Lodging is not subject to the 6% state sales tax, but the sales price for the rental of any lodging in Iowa is subject to a 5% state-level excise tax (Sec. 423A.3). The tax is collected by the lessor from the user of that lodging. The lessor must add the tax to the sales price of the lodging, and when collected the state-level tax must be separately stated from the sales price of the lodging and any local hotel/motel tax imposed. Rental of lodging by the same person for more than 31 consecutive days is exempt, as is the rental of sleeping rooms in dormitories and in memorial unions at all universities and colleges located in Iowa (Sec. 423A.5). Lodging is not subject to the local option sales tax (LOST) under any circumstances.

• Construction equipment

A 5% excise tax is imposed on the sales price or purchase price of all construction equipment sold or used in the state of Iowa (Sec. 423D.2). Leases or rentals of construction equipment are exempt (Sec. 423D.3). This tax is collected and paid over to the department by any retailer, retailer maintaining a place of business in this state, or user who would be responsible for collection and payment of the tax if it were a sales or use tax imposed under chapter 423.

• Motor vehicle and aircraft rentals and leases

A 5% automobile rental excise tax is imposed (Sec. 422C.3). A 6% excise tax is imposed on the rental for 60 days or less of motor vehicles that are registered for a gross weight of thirteen tons or less, or the rental of aircraft for a period of 60 days or less (Sec. 423.2).

• Manufactured housing, mobile homes, and modular homes

Manufactured housing and mobile homes are subject to use tax at the rate of 5% on 20% of the purchase price. Modular homes are subject to the 6% state sales tax, plus local option tax if applicable, on 60% of their purchase price (Sec. 423.3(64)). Use tax imposed on the use of manufactured housing is required to be paid by the owner to the licensed manufactured home retailer. A certificate of title will not be issued until the tax has been paid.

¶ 430   Local Taxes

A local option sales and service tax (LOST) of up to 1% may be imposed by counties on the same basis as state sales and service tax; a city may not impose a local option tax except under special circumstances (Sec. 422B.1.(2), Sec. 422B.8, Rule 701—107.2(422B)). A local option sales tax applies only to those incorporated and unincorporated areas in which a majority favor its imposition. All cities contiguous to each other are treated as one incorporated area, and a majority of those voting in the contiguous cities must favor the imposition of a local option tax.

Sourcing of telecommunications charges: Iowa has conformed to the federal Mobile Telecommunications Sourcing Act (Act), P.L. 106-252. All charges for mobile telecommunications services are considered to be provided by the customer's home service provider and sourced to the customer's place of primary use (Sec. 422.43(17)). All such charges are subject to sales tax based on the customer's place of primary use.

The service provider will be held harmless for an error in assigning wireless services to a jurisdiction if it utilizes an electronic database provided by the state or a designated entity, or, if the state has not provided or designated a database, if it utilizes a database that makes assignments based on a nine-digit zip code.

- **Local option hotel and motel tax**

Iowa cities and counties are allowed to impose a local option hotel and motel tax of up to 7% (Sec. 423A.4). The tax must be approved by voters and must be imposed in full percentage point increments.

The tax is imposed on the gross receipts from the renting of sleeping rooms, apartments, or sleeping quarters in a hotel, motel, inn, public lodging house, rooming house, mobile home, tourist court, or any other place where sleeping accommodations are furnished to transient guests for rent (Sec. 423A.2). Gross receipts include the entire cost directly or indirectly related to the renting of the room, but does not include charges for other items in relation to the renting of the room (including food, telephone, laundry, or recreational facility use) if the other charges are separately stated.

The tax does not apply to the following: (1) rooms rented for more than 31 consecutive days; (2) rooms rented in dormitories and memorial unions at all universities and colleges in the state; (3) contracts made directly with the federal government; and (4) renting rooms to guests of a religious institution on exempt real property owned by the religious institution, to provide a place for a religious retreat or function (Sec. 423A.5).

Retailers are prohibited from assuming or absorbing the tax, although they may advertise and charge a lump-sum price that "includes tax" without separately stating the charge for the tax (Sec. 423A.6).

- **Local tax rates**

Local sales tax rates may be looked up by address or ZIP code on the website of the Iowa Department of Revenue at **https://www.idr.iowa.gov/salestaxlookup**. Local sales tax rate charts listing current sales tax rates for Iowa counties and cities may be found at **https://tax.iowa.gov/iowa-local-option-tax-information**.

¶ 431 **Bracket Schedule**

In computing the tax to be collected as the result of any transaction, the tax computation must be carried to the third decimal place. Whenever the third decimal place is greater than four, the tax must be rounded up to the next whole cent; whenever the third decimal place is four or less, the tax must be rounded downward to a whole cent. Sellers may elect to compute the tax due on transactions on an item or invoice basis (Sec. 423.14(1)(b)).

Rate charts for 6% and 7% transactions are available at **https://tax.iowa.gov/sites/files/idr/forms1/79106.pdf**.

¶ 432 **Returns, Payments, and Due Dates**

Retailers with permits who are liable for payment of retail sales tax must make, sign, and file returns for the preceding calendar quarter by the last day of the month following the end of each quarter (Sec. 423.31(1)). Returns must be signed by the retailer or an authorized agent and certified to be correct (Sec. 423.31(1)). Unless otherwise provided, payment of retail sales tax must accompany the return (Sec. 423.31(1), Sec. 423.31(4)). A parent corporation and its affiliated corporations that make retail sales of taxable property or services may apply to the Director of Revenue and Finance for approval to make deposits and file consolidated sales tax returns for the affiliated group (Sec. 423.31(5)).

Duty to collect local tax: A person required to collect Iowa state sales tax is not required to collect local sales and services tax on transactions involving items delivered or services provided within the area where the local sales and services tax is imposed unless the person has a physical presence in that local taxing area (Sec. 422B.8).

• Electronic filing and payment

Businesses that are registered to collect Iowa sales or use tax must use the eFile & Pay system, which allows taxpayers to file their return information by telephone or via the Internet. Paper returns are no longer available. Tax payments may be remitted electronically through eFile & Pay. Alternatively, qualifying taxpayers who receive preprinted payment vouchers in the mail may remit payment by paper check.

Consolidated filers must use the Internet eFile & Pay application, not the phone system. Also, when using the Internet application, users must complete the local option portion of the return (*E-list Notice,* Iowa Department of Revenue, October 13, 2005).

Sellers not registered under the SST Agreement but who are otherwise registered in Iowa are required to file sales tax returns but are allowed to file a simplified electronic return (Sec. 423.49(4)(d)).

The eFile & Pay system may be accessed on the Department of Revenue's website at **https://tax.iowa.gov/efile-pay**.

• Quarterly returns

Retailers who collect between $120 and $6,000 in annual state sales tax must file on a quarterly basis (Rule 701—12.13(2)).

• Annual returns

If a retailer's annual sales or use tax liability or a consumer's annual use tax liability will not exceed $120 a year, the Director of Revenue and Finance may allow the retailer or consumer to file a return and pay the sales tax owed on a calendar year basis. The return and payment are due by January 31 following the end of the calendar year (Sec. 423.32(2), Sec. 423.13, Rule 701—12.1(422), Rule 701—12.13(422), Rule 701—30.3(423), Rule 701—30.4(423)).

• Monthly deposits

Sales tax: A retailer who collects more than $6,000 but not more than $60,000 in annual sales tax must make a monthly deposit with the Department of Revenue and Finance of all the money collected or at least ⅓ of the tax paid for the previous quarter. Monthly deposits are due on or before the 20th day of the following month, together with the "retailers monthly tax deposit" form. A deposit is not due for the third month of the calendar quarter but the total quarterly amount, less the two previous monthly deposits, is due with the quarterly report on the last day of the month following the end of the quarter. The same provisions apply to retailers who collect more than $50 but not more than $500 of retail sales tax in one month (Sec. 423.32(1)).

Any sales tax permit holder whose average monthly collection of sales tax is more than $25 but less than $50 has the option of making monthly remittances (Sec. 422.52(1)).

Use tax: A retailer who collects or owes more than $1,500 in use tax in one month must deposit the amount collected or owed together with a monthly deposit form by the 20th day of the month following the month of collection. No deposit form is due for the third month of the calendar quarter, but the total quarterly amount, less amounts paid during the two preceding months, is due with the quarterly report on the last day of the month following the end of the calendar quarter (Sec. 423.13, Rule 701—30.4(423)).

- **Semimonthly deposits**

Retailers who collect more than $60,000 in retail sales tax in a year must deposit the amount collected, or not less than ⅙th of the tax paid to the Department of Revenue and Finance for each semimonthly period during the preceding quarter. The first "retailers semimonthly tax deposit" form covers the period from the 1st through the 15th of the month, and the deposit is due by the 25th. The second semimonthly deposit form covers the period from the 16th through the end of the month, and the deposit is due by the 10th of the following month. No deposit is required for the last semimonthly period of the calendar quarter, but the total quarterly amount, less the amount deposited for the five previous semimonthly periods, is due with the quarterly report on the last day of the month following the month of collection (Rule 701—12.1(422), Rule 701—12.13(422)).

- **Seasonal returns**

Seasonal retailers with gross receipts during only one calendar quarter may be allowed to file and remit sales or use tax for a specific quarter or on an annual basis (Rule 701—12.1(422), Rule 701—12.3(422), Rule 701—30.4(423)).

- **Consolidated returns**

A parent corporation and its affiliated corporations that make retail sales of tangible personal property or taxable enumerated services may apply to the Director of Revenue and Finance for approval to make deposits and file a consolidated sales tax return for the consolidated group (Sec. 423.31(5)). An application for consolidation must be filed within 90 days prior to the beginning of the tax period for which the right to file a consolidated return is sought and must be signed by an officer of the parent corporation (Rule 701—13.4(422)).

- **Final return**

A retailer must file a final return and pay all tax owed by the end of the month following the month during which a business is sold. Any unpaid tax must be paid before title to personal property is transferred to the purchaser. Unpaid tax becomes delinquent one month after the sale (Rule 701—12.6(422, 423)).

- **Consumer's use tax return**

A person who purchases tangible personal property or services subject to use tax from out-of-state sources for use in Iowa is liable for payment of use tax. A consumer's quarterly use tax return must be filed to report and remit use tax on taxable property and services purchased for use in Iowa during the period of the return. No return is due if the seller collected use tax on the purchase (Rule 701—30.3(423)). The provisions for annual and seasonal returns apply to consumer's use tax returns. For additional information, see **https://tax.iowa.gov/consumers-use**.

- **Due dates**

If a sales and use tax due date falls on a Saturday, Sunday, legal holiday, or a legal banking holiday in Iowa, the payment, including any related payment voucher information is due on the next succeeding business day. Additionally, if the federal reserve bank is closed on the due date, preventing a person from being able to make an automated payment, the payment must be accepted as timely if made on the next day the federal reserve bank is open. (Sec. 423.50)

- **Extension of time for filing**

A 30-day extension of time to file a sales tax return may be granted by the Director of Revenue and Finance if necessity is shown. The extension must be requested by the original due date and will be granted only if 90% of the estimated tax due is paid by the 20th day of the month following the end of the quarter (Rule 701—12.12(422)).

A 30-day extension of time to file a use tax return may be granted by the Director if necessity is shown. The request must be signed by the retailer or an agent and received before the due date of the return (Rule 701—30.12(422)).

• Itinerant vendors

Persons who are not regularly engaged in selling at retail and have no fixed place of business, but who are temporarily engaged in selling from trucks, portable roadside stands, and concessions at state, county, district, or local fairs, must report and remit sales tax on a nonpermit basis (Sec. 423.36(6), Rule 701—12.4(422)).

• Streamlined Sales and Use Tax Agreement

Iowa is a member of the Governing Board of the Streamlined Sales Tax Project (SSTP).

Iowa sales and use tax law was rewritten by repealing the sales and use tax provisions in Iowa Code Chapters 422 and 423 and enacting a new Chapter 423 (H.F. 683, Laws 2003). The legislation allows Iowa to require remote sellers who compete with in-state retailers and do not currently collect Iowa sales and use taxes to collect and remit those taxes. In addition, the legislation organizes and simplifies existing sales and use tax provisions and establishes procedures for Iowa's entry into the Agreement.

The statutes incorporate certain requirements under the Agreement including: uniform tax rates, uniform standards for sourcing transactions, uniform definitions, centralized and electronic registration of sellers, no change in a seller's nexus status as a result of registration, monetary allowances for registering retailers, consumer privacy provisions, and a provision stating that the Agreement binds and benefits only its member states. Additionally, sales and use tax exemption provisions are consolidated. Previously, the exemptions were located throughout the Iowa Code and in Session Laws (Secs. 423.3, 423.6, 423.11).

Bad debts: A deduction for bad debts is allowed to sellers (Sec. 423.21). "Bad debt" is as defined in IRC Sec. 166, except it does not include: (1) financing charges or interest, (2) sales or use taxes on the purchase price, (3) uncollectable amounts on property that remains in the possession of a seller until the full purchase price is paid, (4) expenses incurred in attempting to collect any debt, or (5) repossessed property. A bad debt deduction may be claimed on the return for the period during which the bad debt is written off as uncollectable in the seller's books and records and is eligible to be deducted for federal income tax purposes.

Sourcing transactions: Sourcing rules establish which state is allowed to tax transactions that have connections to more than one state. There are general sourcing rules and sourcing rules applicable to specific types of transactions, such as sales of certain vehicles, direct mail, transportation equipment, and telecommunication services (Sec. 423.15). Generally, sales are sourced to the destination of the product sold, with a default to origin-based sourcing in the absence of that information.

Reliance on taxability matrix: A purchaser, a purchaser's seller or certified service provider, or a purchaser holding a direct pay permit who relies on erroneous data contained in the state's taxability matrix or erroneous data provided by the state with regard to tax rates, boundaries, or taxing jurisdiction assignments is relieved of liability for state sales or use tax, any local option sales tax, penalties and interest, as specified.

Direct mail provisions: "Direct mail" is printed material delivered or distributed by U.S. mail or other delivery service to a mass audience or to addressees on a mailing list provided by the purchaser or at the direction of the purchaser when the cost of the items is not billed directly to the recipients. Direct mail includes tangible personal property supplied directly or indirectly by the purchaser to the direct mail seller for inclusion in the package containing the printed material. Direct mail does not include multiple items of printed material delivered to a single address. (Sec. 423.1(14)) The term "direct mail" excludes the development of billing information or the provision of a data processing service that is more than incidental. "Advertising and promotional direct mail" is defined as direct mail that serves the primary purpose of attracting public attention to a product, person, business, or organization or an attempt to sell, popularize, or secure financial support for a product, person, business, or organization (Sec. 423.1(0A)). Additionally, the term "other direct mail" is defined as all direct mail that is not advertising and promotional direct mail even if advertising and promotional direct mail is included in the same mailing (Sec. 423.1(33A)).

A purchaser of advertising and promotional direct mail may provide the seller with one of the following: (1) a direct pay permit; (2) an agreement certificate of exemption claiming to be direct mail (or a similar document approved by the Department of Revenue); or (3) information showing the jurisdiction to which the advertising and promotional direct mail is to be delivered to the recipient. If the purchaser provides the seller a permit, a certificate of exemption, or an approved written statement, then in the absence of bad faith, the seller is relieved of the obligation to collect, pay, or remit tax on a transaction involving advertising and promotional direct mail to which the permit, certificate, or approved written statement applies. The purchaser must source the sale to the jurisdiction in which the advertising and promotional direct mail is to be delivered to the recipient and must report and pay any tax due accordingly. (Sec. 432.19)

¶ 433 Prepayment of Taxes

Iowa has no provisions regarding the prepayment of sales and use taxes.

¶ 434 Vendor Registration

Resident and nonresident persons who intend to engage in or conduct business as retailers at permanent locations in Iowa must apply for a permit on a prescribed form. Permits are not required for temporary locations, but sales tax must be collected and remitted. However, a retailer conducting a seasonal business must obtain a regular permit (Sec. 423.36(6), Rule 701—12.3(422)).

SST provisions: The statutory responsibilities and rights of sellers registered under the Streamlined Sales and Use Tax Agreement cannot be construed to relieve a seller of the obligation to register in Iowa if required to do so, and to collect and remit sales or use taxes for at least 36 months, and to meet any other requirements necessary for statutory amnesty for registered sellers, as provided. (Sec. 423.48(4); Sec. 423.54)

A model 2, model 3, or model 4 seller that makes no sales sourced to Iowa in the preceding 12 months may elect to be registered in Iowa as a seller that anticipates making no sales sourced in the state (Sec. 423.48(3)(d)). A seller making such an election is not relieved of the obligation to collect and remit sales or use taxes on sales sourced to Iowa.

Sales to the state: Any person making taxable sales of tangible personal property or furnishing services to any state agency must have a permit to collect sales or use tax prior to the sale (Sec. 423.13A). A state agency may not purchase tangible personal property or services from any person unless that person has a valid, unexpired permit and is in compliance with all other requirements imposed upon retailers, including, but not limited to, collection, remittance, and filing requirements (Sec. 423.36(1A)).

• Application for permit

Permits must be applied for on a prescribed form, including the name that will be used to transact business, the location of the place of business, the date the applicant will begin selling at retail, and any other information that the Director of Revenue and Finance may require. The application must be signed by an authorized person (Sec. 423.36(1), Rule 701—13.2(422)). A permit may be denied to an applicant who is substantially delinquent in paying any tax, penalty, or interest (Sec. 423.36(2)).

A separate permit must be obtained for each place of business at which taxable sales will occur. A permit remains valid if a business relocates within the state, provided that the ownership remains the same. The permit must be conspicuously displayed at the place of business for which it was issued (Sec. 423.36(3), Rule 701—13.10(422), Rule 701—13.11(422), Rule 701—13.12(422)).

Permits are valid until revoked by the Department of Revenue and Finance (Sec. 423.36(4)). A permit must be canceled when a business is sold; the purchaser must apply for a new permit (Rule 701—13.3(422)).

Permit requirements also apply to persons rendering, furnishing, or performing taxable services. A person who holds a retail sales tax permit need not obtain a separate permit to render services (Sec. 423.36(7)).

- **Reinstatement of canceled or revoked permits**

A previously canceled permit may be reinstated upon receipt of clearance for previous tax returns (Rule 701—13.6(422)).

A revoked sales tax permit may be reinstated or a new permit issued after all delinquent sales tax liabilities are paid, all returns are filed, and a bond is posted, provided no taxable sales were made during the revocation period (Rule 701—13.7(422)).

- **Certificate of registration**

Out-of-state retailers that maintain a place of business in Iowa must apply to the Department of Revenue and Finance for a certificate of registration to collect use tax (Sec. 423.30). The registration number must appear on the bill or invoice of purchases intended for use in Iowa and the use tax must be billed separately (Rule 701—29.1(423)).

The certificate of registration must be canceled when the holder discontinues selling tangible personal property for use in Iowa (Rule 701—29.2(423)).

Registration under Streamlined Agreement: By registering under the Agreement (see ¶ 432), a seller agrees to collect and remit sales and use taxes for all of its taxable Iowa sales (Sec. 423.48). Registration under the agreement and the collection of Iowa sales and use taxes may not be used as factors in determining whether the seller has nexus with Iowa for any tax. The seller is not required to pay registration fees or other charges. A written signature from the seller is not required, and the seller may register by way of an agent.

- **State contractors**

Retailers contracting with a state agency must certify that the retailer and its affiliates are registered to collect Iowa sales and use taxes (Sec. 423.2).

- **Out-of-state businesses responding to disasters or emergencies**

Certain tax exemptions are available for out-of-state businesses and nonresident employees performing critical disaster relief work in Iowa during a state emergency declared by the governor or a presidential declaration of a major disaster, generally effective April 21, 2016. A disaster response period begins 10 calendar days before the declared emergency and extends for a period of 60 days after the end of the disaster or emergency. (Sec. 29C.24):

Sales and use tax provisions: A sales and use tax exemption and an equipment tax exemption are enacted for tangible personal property or equipment purchased outside Iowa and brought into the state to aid in disaster relief during a disaster response period, as long as the property or equipment does not remain in Iowa after the disaster response period has ended. Additionally, qualified out-of-state disaster relief companies are not required to obtain a sales or use tax permit, collect and remit sales and use tax, or make and file applicable sales or use tax returns. (Secs. 423.33, Sec. 423.58, Sec. 423D.3)

¶434　Iowa

Registration and income tax provisions: An out-of-state business that conducts operations within Iowa in response to a declared state disaster or emergency is not considered to have established a level of presence that would subject that business to any state or local registration, license, or similar authorization as a condition of doing business or engaging in an occupation in Iowa. An out-of-state employee will not be considered to have established residency or a presence in the state that would require that person to file and pay income taxes or to be subjected to tax withholding or to file and pay any other state or local tax or fee during the disaster response period. Further, a business will not be required to file income taxes or to withhold and remit income tax from out-of-state employees. An out-of-state business will also not need to be included in a consolidated return and will not increase the amount of net income that the out-of-state business allocates and apportions to Iowa. The income and withholding exemptions are applicable to taxable years beginning on or after January 1, 2016. (Secs. 422.8, 422.13, 422.16, 422.33, 422.36, 422.37)

Property tax provisions: A property tax exemption is enacted as well for property of an out-of-state business that conducts operations within Iowa solely for the purpose of performing disaster or emergency-related work during a disaster response period. (Sec. 427.1(41))

¶ 435 Sales or Use Tax Credits

A credit is granted for comparable sales or use taxes paid to other states up to the amount of the Iowa liability (Sec. 423.25).

• Incentive refunds

For information on business incentive refunds, see ¶ 439.

¶ 436 Deficiency Assessments

A designated agent, auditor, clerk, or employee of the Department of Revenue and Finance may examine returns and make audits to learn whether any additional tax is due or to ascertain the amount of tax owed when no return is filed. The amount specified in a notice of assessment may be paid and contested by filing a claim for refund. However, no payment is required until the notice of assessment is issued (Rule 701—11.6(422, 423)).

Notice of assessment: If a sales or use tax return is not filed or if an incorrect or insufficient return is not remedied within 20 days after notice of adjustment from the Department of Revenue and Finance, the Department may estimate the tax that is owed from available information. A notice of assessment signed by the Director of Revenue and Finance will be mailed to the responsible taxpayer. The notice will fix the tax unless the taxpayer requests a hearing within 60 days after receipt or unless the taxpayer contests the determination by paying the tax, interest, and penalty and timely filing a claim for refund. Proceedings to collect the tax will not be commenced if a protest is filed within 60 days after the date of the assessment notice, unless the Department believes that the delay caused by appeal will result in an irrevocable loss of tax owed to the state. After the hearing, the Director must give the taxpayer a notice of decision (Sec. 423.37(2), Sec. 423.16, Rule 701—11.6(422, 423)).

Supplemental assessments and refund adjustments: Supplemental assessments and refund adjustments may be made at any time during the limitations period. If an adjustment is appealed and resolved, both the Department of Revenue and Finance and the taxpayer are precluded from making a supplemental assessment or refund adjustment for that tax period involving the issue appealed, unless there is fraud, misrepresentation, or a mathematical or clerical error (Rule 701—11.6(422, 423)).

¶ 437   **Audit Procedures**

The Department is authorized to determine the amount of tax due in the event that a taxpayer fails to file a return or fails to correct the return within 20 days of receiving notice that a filed return is incorrect or insufficient (Sec. 422.54, Sec. 422.70). The Department may make the determination on the basis of such information as the Department may be able to obtain, including sampling and, if necessary, may estimate the tax on the basis of external indices such as number of employees, rentals paid, stock on hand, and other factors.

The Department may examine a taxpayer's books, records, tax returns, and other documents for purposes of verifying the correctness of a return or estimating tax liability (Rule 701—11.4(422, 423), Rule 701—11.5(422, 423)). If a taxpayer fails or refuses to produce requested records, the Department is authorized to subpoena the taxpayer or other witnesses to produce the records.

The Department must inform the taxpayer when an examination has been completed and the amount of tax liability due upon completion of the audit (Rule 701—11.5(422, 423)).

¶ 438   **Statute of Limitations**

The limitations period for the issuance of sales and use tax deficiency assessments is three years (Sec. 423.37(1)). However, if a false or fraudulent return is made with intent to evade tax or if no return is filed, no limitations period applies (Sec. 423.37, Rule 701—11.2(422, 423)). Prosecution for evasion of use tax must be commenced within six years after commission of the offense (Sec. 423.40(6)).

The same limitations period also applies to the appeal period for revision of assessment of tax, interest, and penalties or notices from the Department of Revenue and Finance denying changes in filing methods, and refund claims or portions of refund claims (Sec. 421.10).

Extension of limitations period: The limitations period may be extended if the taxpayer signs a prescribed waiver agreement form (Sec. 422.54(3), Sec. 423.37(3), Rule 701—11.2(422,423)). The agreement must stipulate the period of extension and the tax period to which the extension applies and provide that a claim for refund may be filed by the taxpayer at any time during the period of extension.

• **Assessment after audit**

After books and records are examined by the Department of Revenue and Finance to verify a return or refund claim or to conduct an audit, an assessment must be issued within one year after the examination. If no assessment is issued within one year, the period for which the books and records were examined becomes closed. The one year limitation period does not extend the deficiency assessment limitation period (Rule 701—11.2(422, 423)).

• **Claim for refund or credit**

A refund or credit claim must be filed within three years after the tax payment becomes due (Sec. 423.47).

• **Penalties**

Prosecution for knowingly selling without a permit, selling after revocation of a permit, tax evasion, or any fraudulent practice must be commenced within six years after commission of the offense (Sec. 423.40(2)(b)).

¶ 439   **Application for Refund**

A refund or credit claim involving a payment that is made for a quarterly reporting period must be filed within three years after the tax payment becomes due (Sec. 423.47). Any refund must be certified by the Director of Revenue and Finance (Sec. 423.47).

Business incentive programs: Refunds pertaining to incentive tax programs may have shorter refund deadlines, typically six months or one year. The Department of Economic Development should be consulted.

• High Quality Job Creation Program refund

A business eligible for the High Quality Job Creation Program is entitled to a refund of sales and use taxes paid for goods and services relating to the construction or equipping of a facility of the eligible business (Sec. 15.331A; Sec. 331C). To receive tax incentives under the program, a business must meet several requirements. If the qualifying investment is $10 million or more, then the community must approve the start-up, location, or expansion of the business. Retail or service businesses are not eligible for tax incentives under the program. Additionally, a business that has closed or substantially reduced its operation in one area of the state and relocated substantially the same operation in the community is not eligible for incentives (Sec. 15.329(1)).

Effective July 1, 2014, the program is amended to allow businesses locating a project at a "brownfield site" or a "grayfield site" to receive tax incentives or project completion assistance for jobs that will pay less than 120% of the qualifying wage threshold. A business at a grayfield site must pay at least 100% of the qualifying wage threshold for jobs created or retained by the project and a business at a brownfield site must pay at least 90% of the qualifying wage threshold for jobs created or retained by the project.

Refund application: An eligible business must file a refund claim with the Department of Revenue within one year after project completion. Prior to final settlement, a contractor or subcontractor must file with the eligible business a statement of the amount of the sales of goods or services rendered upon which sales or use tax has been paid prior to project completion (Sec. 15.331A).

• Workforce housing program refund

The workforce housing tax incentive program allows a business to claim sales and use tax refunds and 10% income tax credits for qualifying new investments directly related to the acquisition, repair, rehabilitation, or redevelopment of a housing project, including costs that are directly related to new construction of dwelling units, if the new construction occurs in a distressed workforce housing community. (Sec. 15.352 *et seq.*; Sec. 15.355)

A housing project must include at least four or more single-family dwelling units, or one or more multiple dwelling unit buildings each containing three or more individual dwelling units, or two or more dwelling units located in the upper story of an existing multi-use building. Further, the project must consist of any of following (Sec. 15.353(1)(b)):

— rehabilitation, repair, or redevelopment at a brownfield or grayfield site that results in new dwelling units;

— the rehabilitation, repair, or redevelopment of dilapidated dwelling units;

— the rehabilitation, repair, or redevelopment of dwelling units located in the upper story of an existing multi-use building; or

— the new construction, rehabilitation, repair, or redevelopment of dwelling units in a distressed workforce housing community.

A housing business may claim a refund for sales and use taxes paid that are directly related to such a housing project (Sec. 15.355(2)). The refund is applicable to purchases of gas, electricity, water, or sewer utility services, goods, wares, or merchandise, or on services rendered, furnished, or performed to or for a contractor or subcontractor and used in the fulfillment of a written contract relating to the construction or equipping of a facility that is part of a project of the eligible business (Sec. 15.331A).

Tax incentives under the program will be issued on a first-come, first-served basis until the maximum amount of tax incentives allocated is reached.

• Information technology facility refund

The owner of an information technology facility located in Iowa on July 1, 2007, may make an annual application for up to five consecutive years to the Department of Economic Development for refund of the state sales or use tax paid on the sales price of all sales of fuel used in creating heat, power, and steam for processing or generating electrical current or from the sale of electricity consumed by computers, machinery or other equipment for operation of the technology facility. Among other requirements, the facility must be primarily engaged in providing computer-related services; the capital expenditures for computers, machinery and other equipment used in the operation of the facility must equal at least $1 million dollars; and the facility must be certified as meeting the Leadership in Energy and Environmental Design (LEED) green building standards (Sec. 423.4(8)).

The refund also is available to data center businesses that within the first three years of operation invest between $1 million and $10 million for a newly constructed building or at least $5 million for a rehabilitated building (Sec. 423.4(8)).

Refund applicants must use forms furnished by the Department and must separately list the amounts of sales and use tax paid during the reporting period. In addition, refund applicants may request when the refund begins but they may start only on the first day of a month and proceed for a continuous 12-month period. Applicants must file refund claims within three months after the end of each refund year.

• Refunds for renewable energy or wind energy production

A person in possession of a wind energy production tax credit certificate (Ch. 476B) or a renewable energy tax credit certificate (Ch. 476C) may apply for refund of the amount of sales or use tax imposed and paid upon purchases made by the applicant (Sec. 423.4(4)). The refunds may only be claimed on forms furnished by the Department of Revenue and filed by January 31 after the end of the calendar year in which the tax credit certificate is to be applied.

• Biodiesel production sales tax credit

From January 1, 2012, until January 1, 2025, a qualifying producer may apply for a refund of the amount of the sales tax imposed and paid upon purchases made by the producer (Sec. 423.4(9)). The refund is made on a quarterly basis at the rate of two cents per gallon for calendar years 2014 through 2024.

A biodiesel producer is not eligible to receive a refund on more than 25 million gallons of biodiesel produced each calendar year at each facility where the producer manufactures biodiesel. For corporate and personal income tax purposes, a subtraction adjustment is allowed for the amount of any biodiesel production refund, to the extent included in federal taxable income or adjusted gross income. (Sec. 423.4)

• Racetrack and raceway rebates

Iowa has established a pilot project sales tax rebate program to gauge the feasibility of using such an approach to assist large capital projects that have the potential to increase tourism into the state (H.F. 840, Laws 2005). The owner or operator of a specific automobile racetrack facility and entertainment complex in Iowa may apply to the Department of Revenue for a rebate of Iowa sales tax collected by retailers upon sales of merchandise or services to purchasers at the facility. The rebate is capped at 5% of the sales price of the tangible personal property or services furnished to purchasers at the automobile racetrack facility. The rebate program will apply to transactions on which sales tax is collected for the years 2006 through 2015, and the total rebate amount is limited to $12.5 million. However, the rebate program will cease if there is a change of control of the racetrack facility or if the facility is sold or transferred. Local-option sales taxes are not subject to the rebate (Sec. 423.4(5); Rule 701—235.1(423)).

A similar rebate is available to the owner or operator of a specific raceway facility from 2015 through 2024 (Sec. 423.4(11)).

• Rebates at the "field of dreams"

Iowa will offer rebates of sales tax collected at a specifically described baseball and softball complex with construction costs of at least $10 million completed after July 1, 2016. The rebate will remain in effect until 30 days after a total of $5 million in sales tax has been rebated. (Sec. 15F.207)

• Denial of refund

If a refund claim is denied, a protest must be filed with the Department within 30 days after the date of denial (Rule 701—12.9(422)).

¶ 440   KANSAS

¶ 441   Scope of Tax

Source.—Statutory references are to Title 79 of the Kansas Statutes Annotated, as amended to date. Details are reported in the CCH KANSAS STATE TAX REPORTS starting at ¶ 60-000.

Sales tax is imposed upon the privilege of engaging in the business of selling tangible personal property at retail or furnishing taxable services (Sec. 79-3603). Taxable services are listed below. The compensating (use) tax supplements the sales tax and is levied upon people who exercise the privilege of using, storing, or consuming in Kansas any article of tangible personal property that has not been subjected to sales or use tax by any state (Sec. 79-3703, Reg. 92-20-1).

• Incidence of tax

The sales tax is imposed upon the consumer or user and paid to the retailer, who is responsible for collecting and remitting the tax (Sec. 79-3604).

Each retail sale is presumed to be taxable (Reg. 92-19-61). Either the amount of tax on a sale must be separately stated on the invoice or billing, or the invoice or billing must bear the statement, "All applicable sales tax is included" (Sec. 79-3648, Reg. 92-19-61). If this requirement is not met, it will be presumed that the tax was not collected by the retailer.

The incidence of the use tax is upon the consumer (Sec. 79-3703). The use tax is also a debt from the purchaser to the retailer (Sec. 79-3705a).

• Taxable services

Gross receipts from the following are subject to sales tax:

Admissions to any amusement, entertainment, or recreation service, including state, county, district, and local fairs (Sec. 79-3603(e)); fees and charges by clubs and businesses for participation in recreational activities (Sec. 79-3603(m)); and dues charged by clubs and businesses for the use of recreational or entertainment facilities (Sec. 79-3603(n));

Certain gas, water, electricity, and heat services (Sec. 79-3603(c) and (u));

Coin-operated devices that dispense or provide tangible personal property, amusement, or other services (excluding laundry services) (Sec. 79-3603(f));

Dry cleaning, pressing, dyeing, and laundry services (excluding coin-operated laundry services) (Sec. 79-3603(i));

Hotel room rental services (Sec. 79-3603(g));

Installation or application services for tangible personal property that is not held for sale in the regular course of business after installation or application, regardless of whether it remains tangible personal property or becomes a part of real estate (excepting installation and application services performed in connection with certain "original construction") (Sec. 79-3603(p));

Interstate and intrastate telephone or telegraph services (subject to certain exceptions) (Sec. 79-3603(b));

Meals or drinks furnished at places where meals or drinks are regularly sold to the public (Sec. 79-3603(d));

Radio and television subscription services, such as cable and community antennae (Sec. 79-3603(k));

Repair, service, alteration, or maintenance of tangible personal property (except computer software) not held for sale in the regular course of business, including fees or charges made under service or maintenance agreements (Sec. 79-3603(q) and (r));

Tangible personal property rental or leasing services (Sec. 79-3603(h));

Telephone answering services, including mobile phone, beeper, and other similar services (Sec. 79-3603(t)); Also, gross receipts from the sale or recharge of a prepaid calling service (phone card) or prepaid authorization number, as discussed at ¶ 442 (Sec. 79-3603(b), (u));

Washing and waxing services for vehicles (Sec. 79-3603(j)).

Software maintenance: Mandatory computer software maintenance agreements that are sold with prewritten software are taxable as part of the taxable software sale. Separately stated charges for technical support services are included in the taxable charges. Charges for optional maintenance agreements sold with prewritten software, sold after the sale of the software, or that are sold by a different vendor are characterized as 50% for taxable software in a bundled transaction where the taxable and nontaxable products are not separately stated on the invoice to the customer. Charges for upgrades and enhancements for canned software are subject to tax, regardless of whether the charges are separately stated. However, sales of mandatory or optional maintenance agreements for custom software are not subject to tax. (*Revenue Ruling 19-2009-01*, Kansas Department of Revenue, June 2, 2009, CCH KANSAS TAX REPORTS, ¶ 201-223)

• Use tax

The compensating (use) tax supplements the sales tax and is levied upon people who exercise the privilege of using, storing, or consuming any article of tangible personal property in Kansas that has not been subjected to sales or use tax by any state (Sec. 79-3703, Reg. 92-20-1). All property purchased or leased in or out of Kansas and subsequently used, stored, or consumed in the state is subject to use tax if the same property or transaction would have been subject to Kansas sales tax had the transaction been wholly within the state.

Liability: Use tax is paid by the consumer or user to the retailer who has a duty to collect the tax (Sec. 79-3705a, Reg. 92-20-2a, Reg. 92-20-5). Use tax is a debt owed to the retailer by the consumer or user until paid; it is added to the purchase price and recovered in the same manner as other debts. If use tax is not collected or collectible by the retailer, the Kansas consumer must file a return and pay the tax.

• Nexus

A retailer doing business in Kansas is required to collect compensating use tax (and give the purchaser a receipt showing the tax) when the retailer sells tangible personal property for use, storage, or consumption in Kansas, even if the sale occurs outside of Kansas (Sec. 79-3705c; Sec. 79-3705d; Sec. 79-3705e). An out-of-state retailer will be considered to be doing business in Kansas (and thus required to register and collect and remit compensating use tax) when engaged in business in Kansas under, but not limited to, any of the following circumstances (Reg. 92-20-7(a)):

— it maintains directly, indirectly, or through a subsidiary, an office, distribution house, sales house, warehouse or other place of business;

— it has an agent, salesperson, or solicitor operating within the state under its authority or its subsidiary's authority, regardless of whether the agent, salesperson or solicitor is located in Kansas permanently or temporarily, or whether the retailer or subsidiary is qualified to do business within Kansas; or

— it solicits orders within Kansas through catalogues or other advertising media.

¶441   Kansas

Click-through nexus: A retailer is presumed to be doing business in Kansas if the retailer enters into an agreement with one or more Kansas residents under which the resident, for a commission or other consideration, directly or indirectly refers potential customers, whether by a link or an Internet website, by telemarketing, by an in-person oral presentation, or otherwise, to the retailer, if the cumulative gross receipts from sales by the retailer to customers in Kansas who are referred to the retailer by all residents with this type of an agreement with the retailer is more than $10,000 during the preceding 12 months (Sec. 79-3702(h)(2)(B); Sec. 79-3702(h)(2)(C)). However, this presumption can be rebutted by submitting proof that the Kansas residents with whom the retailer has an agreement did not engage in any activity within the state significantly associated with the retailer's ability to establish or maintain the retailer's market in the state during the preceding 12 months. The proof submitted may consist of sworn written statements provided and obtained in good faith from all of the residents with whom the retailer has an agreement stating that they did not engage in any solicitation in the state on behalf of the retailer during the preceding year (Sec. 79-3702(h)(2)(D)). "Preceding 12 months," as used above, includes the 12 months beginning prior to the effective date of this specific change in law creating click-through nexus (Sec. 79-3702(h)(2)(C)). Also, with respect to the effective date for the change in the law, the date when a retailer and a resident enter into the type of agreement described above is not relevant. (Sec. 79-3702(h)(2)(C))

Affiliate nexus: There is a rebuttable presumption that a retailer is doing business in Kansas if an affiliated person of the retailer with a physical presence (such as a warehouse), or employees or agents in Kansas, has sufficient nexus with Kansas constitutionally to require the person to collect and remit sales and use taxes on taxable retail sales of tangible personal property or services (Sec. 79-3702(h)(2)(A); Sec. 79-3702(h)(2)(B)). The above presumption can be rebutted by showing that the activities of the affiliated person in Kansas are not significantly associated with the retailer's ability to establish or maintain a market in Kansas for the retailer's sales (Sec. 79-3702(h)(2)(D)). "Affiliated person" is defined as any person that is a member of the same "controlled group of corporations" (defined in IRC Sec. 1563(a) as the retailer, or any other entity that, regardless of how it is organized, bears the same ownership relationship to the retailer as a corporation that is a member of the same controlled group of corporations). (Sec. 79-3702(h)(2)(D)(3)(j))

The rebuttal presumption that a retailer is doing business in Kansas also applies if any person (other than a common carrier acting in its capacity as such) who has sufficient nexus with Kansas constitutionally to require the person to collect and remit sales and use taxes on taxable retail sales does any of the following (Sec. 79-3702(h)(2)(A)):

— uses trademarks, service marks, or trade names in Kansas that are the same or substantially similar to those used by the retailer;

— delivers, installs, assembles, or performs maintenance services for the retailer's customers within Kansas;

— facilitates the retailer's delivery of property to customers in Kansas by allowing the retailer's customers to pick up property sold by the retailer at an office, distribution facility, warehouse, storage place, or similar place of business maintained by the person in Kansas; or

— conducts any other activities in the state that are significantly associated with the retailer's ability to establish and maintain a market in the state for the retailer's sales.

Additional information: for more information on click-through nexus and affiliate nexus, see *Notice 13-05,* Kansas Department of Revenue, May 10, 2013, CCH KANSAS TAX REPORTS, ¶ 201-617.

• **Streamlined Act status**

Kansas is a full member of the Agreement with a seat on the Governing Board. It has enacted all of the provisions necessary to comply with the Agreement's requirements and these provisions currently are in effect (Sec. 79-3665). As a full member, it may vote on amendments to or interpretations of the Agreement, and sellers registering under the SST system must collect and remit tax on sales into the state.

For additional information, see ¶ 447.

Taxability matrix: A chart of the taxable status of various items is accessible at **http://www.streamlinedsalestax.org/**.

¶ 442   Tax Base

Sales tax is imposed on the gross receipts from sales and services (Sec. 79-3603). "Gross receipts" means the total selling price or the amount received in money, credits, property, or other consideration valued in money from retail sales (Sec. 79-3602(h)). Any discounts allowed and credited by the retailer are excluded from the selling price (Reg. 92-19-46(b)).

Use tax is imposed on the consideration paid for an article of tangible personal property (Sec. 79-3703). "Purchase price" means the consideration paid by a person to a seller for an article of tangible personal property (Sec. 79-3702(a)).

Prepaid calling cards: Gross receipts received from the sale or recharge of a prepaid calling service (phone card) or prepaid authorization number are subject to sales tax. However, "gross receipts" does not include purchases of telephone, telegraph, or telecommunications services using a prepaid telephone calling card or prepaid authorization number. "Prepaid calling service" means the right to exclusively make telephone calls, paid for in advance, with the prepaid value measured in minutes or other time units, that enables the origination of calls using an access number or authorization code or both, whether manually or electronically dialed. (Sec. 79-3603(b),(u); Sec. 79-3673)

Cloud computing: A Kansas Department of Revenue opinion letter discusses the application of retailers' sales tax to charges imposed by an application service provider (ASP) on subscribers for "software as a service" (SaaS) for the use of software hosted on the ASP's remote servers. Specifically at issue was the taxability of charges for hosted software billed to Kansas physicians who accessed the out-of-state software via the Internet. No software was downloaded or delivered to the customer and no title to the software passed to the customers in this cloud computing model. The department referred the taxpayer to *Information Guide No. EDU-71R*, Kansas Department of Revenue, July 23, 2010 (CCH KANSAS TAX REPORTS, ¶ 201-326), which states that charges imposed by an ASP for using software on a remote server are not considered charges for a lease and are not subject to sales tax. Further, the department pointed out that Kansas law applies sales tax to only those services expressly described under Kansas law as subject to sales tax. The department also stated that charges for hosted software services are not subject to sales tax under Kansas law as sales of prewritten computer software because the software installed on the server (whether the server is in-state or out-of-state) is not delivered to the subscribers or installed on the subscribers' computers. (*Opinion Letter No. O-2012-001*, Kansas Department of Revenue, February 6, 2012, CCH KANSAS TAX REPORTS, ¶ 201-481)

Electronic cigarettes: Electronic cigarettes, including the consumable material for them, are subject to sales tax (Sec. 79-3606(a)). "Electronic cigarette" is defined as a battery-powered device, regardless of whether shaped like a cigarette, that can provide inhaled doses of nicotine by delivering a vaporized solution by means of cartridges or other chemical delivery systems (Sec. 79-3301(ff)).

¶442 Kansas

¶ 443   List of Exemptions, Exceptions, and Exclusions

Unless otherwise indicated, the statutory exemptions, exceptions, and exclusions listed below apply to both sales and use taxes. Items that are excluded from the sales or use tax base are treated at ¶ 442, "Tax Base."

Exemption certificates: When a seller obtains an exemption certificate, the certificate must claim an exemption that was authorized under Kansas law on the date of the transaction in the jurisdiction where the transaction is legally sourced, must be able to apply to the item being purchased, and must be reasonable for the purchaser's type of business. If the seller obtains an exemption certificate or equivalent relevant data, the seller is relieved of any liability for the tax on the transaction unless it is discovered by audit that the seller knew or had reason to know when the information was provided that the information was materially false or that the seller was knowingly evading taxes. (Sec. 79-3609(a); see also *Information Guide No. KS-1520*, Kansas Department of Revenue, November 2015, CCH KANSAS TAX REPORTS, ¶ 201-829)

- **Sales and use exemptions, exceptions, and exclusions**

Admissions to certain events sponsored by nonprofit organizations	Sec. 79-3606(m), Sec. 79-3606(rr)
Advertising services	Sec. 79-3606(nn)
Agricultural aids	Sec. 79-3606(t)
Agricultural fencing destroyed by wildfires (repair or replacement) (temporary for 2017 and 2018)	Sec. 79-3606d
Agricultural use of utilities	Sec. 79-3606(w)
Aircraft repair services and parts	Sec. 79-3606(g)
Alcoholic beverages subject to excise tax	Sec. 79-3606(a)
All American Beef Battalion, Inc., purchases by	Sec. 79-3606(eeee)
Aquatic plants and animals	Sec. 79-3606(o)
Armed Forces	Sec. 48-201
Bingo cards, faces, and instant tickets	Sec. 79-3603(v)
Broadcast services	Sec. 79-3606(nn)
Broadcasting machinery and equipment	Sec. 79-3606(zz)
Component parts	Sec. 79-3606(m)
Construction and materials used in an enterprise zone	Sec. 79-3606(cc)
Construction and materials used in nonprofit educational institution	Sec. 79-3606(d)
Construction and materials used in political subdivision	Sec. 79-3606(d)
Construction and materials used in residential construction	Sec. 79-3606(c)
Construction, certain original construction and repairs	Sec. 79-3603(p)
Containers not returned	Sec. 79-3602(*l*)
Contractors for exempt organizations	Sec. 79-3603(p)
Custom computer software and maintenance services	Sec. 79-3603(s)
Dietary supplements (prescription)	Sec. 79-3606(jjj)
Disaster recovery	Sec. 79-3606e; Sec. 79-3606f
Disposable supplies	Sec. 79-3602(*l*)
Domestic violence shelters, purchases by	Sec. 79-3606(hhh)
Drill bits used in the production of oil and natural gas	Sec. 79-3606(pp)
Drugs	Sec. 79-3606(p)
Easter Seals, Inc., purchases by	Sec. 79-3606(dddd)

¶443 Kansas

Professional services	Sec. 79-3602(k)
Property and services purchased by a port authority or its contractor	Sec. 79-3606(z)
Property consumed in irrigation of crops	Sec. 79-3602(m), Sec. 79-3606(n)
Property consumed in production	Sec. 79-3602(m), Sec. 79-3606(n)
Property purchased by railroad or public utility and used in interstate commerce	Sec. 79-3606(f), Sec. 79-3704(a)
Prosthetic appliances	Sec. 79-3606(r)
Public broadcasting stations	Sec. 79-3606(ss)
Railroad rolling stock repairs	Sec. 79-3606(y)
Religious organizations, nonprofit	Sec. 79-3606(aaa)
Resales	Sec. 79-3602(e)
Resales, machinery and equipment used in Kansas	Sec. 79-3606(kk), Sec. 79-3606(kk)(2), Sec. 79-3606(kk)(3)
Residential and nonprofit institutions use of utilities	Sec. 79-3606(w), Sec. 79-3606(x)
Schools	Sec. 79-3606(c)
Seeds and seedlings	Sec. 79-3606(mm)
Services, separately stated, to modify computer software for single end user	Sec. 79-3603(s)
Shelter Living, Inc., purchases by	Sec. 79-3606(ffff)
Textbook rentals	Sec. 79-3606(h)
Tires	Sec. 79-3606(a)
Tobacco products (except cigarettes) subject to nonrefundable excise tax	Sec. 79-3606(a)
Utilities consumed in production or manufacturing of tangible personal property, crop irrigation, or providing services	Sec. 79-3602(m)(B)
Utilities, residential and nonprofit institutions	Sec. 79-3606(w), Sec. 79-3606(x)
Utilities used in severing oil	Sec. 79-3606(w)
Vehicles or aircraft sold to nonresidents	Sec. 79-3606(k)
Volunteer fire departments	Sec. 79-3606(uu)

¶ 444   Rate of Tax

Effective July 1, 2015, the state retailers' sales and compensating use tax rate was increased from 6.15% to 6.5%. On July 1, 2013, the rate was decreased to 6.15% from the previous rate of 6.3%. (Sec. 79-3603; Sec. 79-3703).

If any article of tangible personal property was subjected to sales or use tax by another state at a lower rate, use tax is applied at the difference between the other rate and the Kansas rate (Sec. 79-3705).

Rental car tax: An additional tax of 3.5% is imposed on the rental or lease of motor vehicles owned by a car rental company and rented for a period of 28 days or less (Sec. 79-5117).

Professional sports admissions: The Kansas Athletic Commission is authorized to impose a tax, not exceeding 5%, against the gross receipts of each regulated sports contest held in Kansas (Sec. 74-50,186(c)). However, any tax collected against the gross receipts of a regulated sports contest will be exempt from Kansas sales tax. A "regulated sport" means professional boxing, sparring, professional kickboxing, professional mixed martial arts, and professional full contact karate (Sec. 74-50,182(m)).

Environmental surcharge: The business of laundering and drycleaning garments and other household fabrics is subject to an environmental surcharge (Sec. 65-34,150). The rate of tax is 2.5% of the gross receipts received from drycleaning or laundering services. The surcharge is imposed on the same tax base as the Kansas retailers' sales tax and is in addition to all other state and local sales or excise taxes. Receipts from coin-operated machines and certain commercial laundry services are exempt from the surcharge. For additional information, see *Information Guide: Dry Cleaning and Laundry Services Self-Audit Fact Sheet,* Kansas Department of Revenue, September 10, 2012, CCH KANSAS TAX REPORTS, ¶ 201-565.

Prepaid wireless 911 fee: A fee is imposed on all purchases of prepaid wireless phones and prepaid calling cards for cellular phones at a rate of 1.06% per retail transaction. The fee also applies to purchases involving "recharging" these items with additional minutes. Customers pay the fee to the retailer at the time of sale and are not required to file additional paperwork. Retailers must remit the fee electronically to the Kansas Department of Revenue at the same filing frequency as they remit sales tax. (Sec. 12-5372)

• Redevelopment districts

Within certain redevelopment districts an additional sales and use tax rate of 2% is collected until the earlier of (1) the date that bonds issued have been paid in full, (2) the date that refinance of the redevelopment project has been paid in full, or (3) the date of the final schedule maturity of the first series of bonds issued to finance the project (Sec. 79-3603, Sec. 79-3703).

• SST conforming provisions

State sales tax rate changes must take effect on the first day of a calendar quarter (Sec. 79-3666). Whenever there are fewer than 30 days between the effective date of a retailers' sales tax or compensating use tax rate change and the date that the rate change takes effect, a seller is relieved from liability for failing to collect tax at the new rate if it instead collected tax at the immediately proceeding rate, and if its failure to collect at the newly changed rate does not continue beyond 30 days after the effective date of the rate change. This relief from liability does not apply if the seller acted fraudulently in collecting tax at the previous rate.

Services: A state or local sales tax rate increase relating to services is applied to the first billing period starting on or after the effective date of the increase. A state or local sales tax rate decrease relating to services is applied to bills rendered on or after the effective date of the decrease (Sec. 79-3678).

¶ 445   Local Taxes

Kansas cities and counties are authorized by statute to impose sales taxes at various specific rates, subject to voter approval (Sec. 12-187, Sec. 12-188, Sec. 12-189). Cities are allowed to impose a city tax at a rate of up to 2% for general purposes and up to 1% for special purposes, so the maximum city tax rate may not exceed 3%. A grandfather clause provides that city retailers' sales taxes imposed as of July 1, 2006, pursuant to home rule authority may remain in effect until they are repealed (Sec. 12-187(d)).

Public improvement: A public improvement district may levy a Kansas property tax or impose a local Kansas sales tax at a rate of up to 0.5%, or both, for a period of up to 10 years. A public improvement district may be created by agreement between three or more counties not located in a metropolitan area for the purpose of constructing, operating, and maintaining public infrastructure improvements (Sec. 12-17,152).

Transportation development: Any municipality may impose a transportation development district sales tax for purposes of financing a project in the district. The tax is administered in the same manner as the countywide and city retailers' sales taxes. The taxes may be imposed in any increment of 0.10% or 0.25%, but may not exceed 1%, within a transportation development district in order to finance a project. A transportation development district sales tax can expire after a sufficient amount of the tax has been received to pay the cost of the project (Sec. 12-17,145).

Community improvement: Under the Community Investment District Act, a city or county can create a community improvement district for the purpose of financing infrastructure projects within the district. A city or county can impose a community improvement district sales tax in any increment of 0.10% or 0.25%, but cannot exceed 2%. (Sec. 74-50,115(f)(2))

Vehicles: Every city and county that imposes a sales tax must also impose a use tax for the privilege of using or storing a vehicle within a city or county (Sec. 12-198). The use tax rate is equal to the sales tax rate imposed in the city and county where the vehicle is registered.

Mobile telecommunications: Kansas conforms to the federal Mobile Telecommunications Sourcing Act (P.L. 106-252) (Sec. 79-3603(t)). Pursuant to federal law, charges for mobile telecommunications services are taxable only in the state and locality encompassing the street address where the customer resides or maintains its primary business address. Any other state or locality is prohibited from taxing the services, regardless of where the services originate, terminate, or pass through. These provisions do not apply to prepaid telephone calling services or air-ground service.

Lodging: A county with a population of more than 300,000 or a city located in whole or in part in such a county is authorized to impose a transient guest tax of up to 2%, subject to voter approval. The tax is levied on the gross rental receipts collected by a lodging business or accommodations broker from transient guests. "Transient guest" means a person who occupies a room in a hotel, motel or tourist court for not more than 28 consecutive days. (Sec. 12-1693; Sec. 12-1692; Sec. 12-1696)

Kansas counties and cities are authorized to impose an additional transient guest tax of up to 2%. The tax is levied on the gross rental receipts collected by a hotel, motel, or tourist court, exclusive of any charges for incidental services or facilities. As for imposition of the additional transient guest tax, a county cannot levy a guest tax within the boundaries of one of its cities if the city is levying a transient guest tax of its own. Also, a city cannot levy a guest tax if the county where it is located is presently imposing a countywide guest tax. (Sec. 12-1697; Sec. 12-1699)

• Current local sales tax rates

For more information and a list of current local rates, see *Information Guide No. KS-1700*, which is available on the website of the Kansas Department of Revenue at **http://www.ksrevenue.org/salesratechanges.html**.

¶ 446   **Bracket Schedule**

Tax computation must be carried to the third decimal place and must be rounded up to the nearest whole cent when the third decimal place is greater than four. The rounding rule may be applied to the aggregated state and local sales taxes (Sec. 79-3676).

Sellers may elect to compute the tax for a transaction on an item or invoice basis (Sec. 79-3676(b), K.S.A.).

¶446   Kansas

Bracket cards are published on the Kansas Department of Revenue's website at **www.ksrevenue.org**. Search for "bracket cards."

¶ 447   **Returns, Payments, and Due Dates**

Retailers must file sales (Sec. 79-3607) and use (Sec. 79-3706(a)) tax returns upon prescribed forms at the intervals discussed below. A retailer's previous year's tax liability will be used to determine filing requirements. If a retailer has no previous tax history, the Director of Taxation may use estimates to determine filing requirements. Any retailer's filing schedule may be modified when it becomes apparent that the original determination was inaccurate.

Electronic filing and payment: Electronic filing is required for retailers' sales and compensating use taxes. See *New Filing Requirements for Your Retailers' Sales, Compensating Use, and Withholding Tax,* Department of Revenue, May 21, 2010, CCH KANSAS TAX REPORTS, ¶ 201-299 and *Frequently Asked Questions Regarding the New Filing Requirements for Your Retailers' Sales, Compensating Use, and Withholding Tax*, Kansas Department of Revenue, June 2010.

A taxpayer whose total sales tax liability exceeds $45,000 in any calendar year must remit tax payments by electronic funds transfer (EFT) by the due date (Sec. 75-5151) Payment is made through the online WebTax system or the telephone TeleFile system by ACH debit or ACH credit by the due date. Credit card payments through third-party vendors are also accepted. See **http://www.ksrevenue.org/eservices.html**.

Vendor discounts: A discount rate is extended to some neighboring state retailers who collect and remit the Kansas Retailers' Compensating Use Tax. The discount rates for retailers in Colorado is 0%; Nebraska (3%), Missouri (3%) and Oklahoma (1%), with their total discount limited to $2,500.

- **15-day payments**

Retailers whose total sales (Sec. 79-3607) or use (Sec. 79-3706(a)) tax liability exceeds $32,000 in any calendar year must pay sales tax for the first 15 days of the month by the 25th of that month, accompanied by the return for the previous month. A retailer may satisfy the requirement of paying the tax owed for the first 15-day period by paying 90% of the liability for that period by the 25th of that month or by paying 50% of the liability for the same month of the previous year. The payment for the second 15-day period of each month must be paid when filing the return for that month.

- **Monthly returns**

If a retailer's sales (Sec. 79-3607) or use (Sec. 79-3706(a)) tax liability for any calendar year exceeds $3,200, monthly returns must be filed by the 25th of the following month, regardless of the accounting method used (Reg. 92-19-74, Reg. 92-20-6, Rev. Rul. 19-78-5).

- **Quarterly returns**

If sales (Sec. 79-3607) or use (Sec. 79-3706(a)) tax liability does not exceed $3,200 for a calendar year, retailers must file quarterly returns by the 25th day of the month following each quarter.

- **Annual returns**

Retailers must file annual returns by January 25 of the following year if not more than $80 of sales (Sec. 79-3607) or use (Sec. 79-3706(a)) tax is owed.

- **Extensions**

The Director of Taxation may extend the time to file a sales or use tax return for any period up to 60 days upon written request before the return and remittance are delinquent. The request for extension must state the reason for the request, give a date when the return and remittance will be filed, and be signed by the applicant. If an extension is approved, the taxpayer is liable for the tax and interest at 1.5% per month from the original due date until paid (Sec. 79-3607; Sec. 79-3706(a); Reg. 92-19-5). Permanent extensions are also available (Reg. 92-19-33).

• **Uniform Sales and Use Tax Administration Act**

Kansas has enacted the Uniform (Simplified) Sales and Use Tax Administration Act, the product of the Streamlined Sales Tax Project (SSTP) Kansas also has enacted legislation conforming its sales and use tax laws to provisions of the Streamlined Sales and Use Tax Agreement. Kansas provisions include the following:

Returns: A model 1, 2, or 3 seller is required to file its returns electronically. A seller that is registered under the Agreement and is not otherwise required to collect state or local sales or use tax and that does not use one of the technology models for remittance must file returns as follows (Sec. 79-3607(b)):

— anytime within one year of the month of initial registration;

— on an annual basis thereafter; and

— following any month in which the seller has accumulated Kansas state and local sales tax funds of $1,600 or more.

Bad debts: A retailer is eligible to claim a bad debt allowance if it was the original seller of the taxable goods or services, if it charged and remitted the retailers' sales or use tax on a sale that can be claimed as a worthless debt deduction under IRC Sec. 166, and if it has written off the bad debt as worthless or uncollectible in its books and records. Once a retailer sells, factors, assigns, or otherwise transfers an account receivable, installment contract, or other similar debt instrument for a discount of any kind that authorizes a third party to collect customer payments, the retailer is ineligible to claim a bad debt allowance, credit, or refund for bad debts arising under the instrument that was sold or transferred at a discount. (Reg. 92-19-3b)

Definitions: Numerous definitions have been added to the sales and use tax laws, while some existing definitions have been amended or repealed.

Returned goods: See Reg. 92-19-49b. Repossessions are governed by Reg. 92-19-3c.

Sourcing rules: Sales will be sourced generally to the destination of the product sold, with a default to origin-based sourcing in the absence of that information. Special sourcing rules apply to sales of vehicles, transportation equipment, and telecommunications. Special rules apply to the sourcing of direct mail (Sec. 79-3672(a)(2), (3)).

Leases and rentals of tangible personal property involving periodic payments are generally sourced under destination-based sourcing rules for the first lease payment and are sourced to the primary property location for subsequent lease payments. Leases with only one lease payment are generally sourced under the destination-based sourcing rules. These sourcing rules may not apply to leases and rentals of motor vehicles, trailers, semitrailers, and aircraft that do not qualify as transportation equipment (*Private Letter Ruling No. P-2006-010,* Kansas Department of Revenue, revised October 25, 2006, CCH KANSAS TAX REPORTS, ¶ 201-016).

For additional information, see the discussion of the "Streamlined Sales Tax Project," listed in the Table of Contents.

¶ 448   **Prepayment of Taxes**

Kansas has no provisions for the prepayment of sales or use taxes.

¶ 449   **Vendor Registration**

It is unlawful to engage in the retail selling of tangible personal property or to furnish taxable services without a registration certificate from the Director of Taxation (Sec. 79-3608). Any sales tax, penalty, or interest owed at the time of application must be paid before the certificate is issued. Utilities subject to sales tax are not required to register but must comply with all other provisions.

A separate registration certificate is required for each place of business and must be displayed there (Sec. 79-3608).

An unregistered vendor who does not pay sales or use tax may not use Kansas courts to enforce contractual obligations arising from the retail sale of taxable tangible personal property, things, or services (Sec. 79-3631).

Registration guidance, An information guide, Kansas Business Tax Application and Instructions discusses how to register for state business taxes including sales and use taxes, withholding tax, corporate income tax, privilege tax, tire excise tax, and cigarette and tobacco tax. The publication contains the business tax application and instructions and also discusses various permits, licenses, and surcharges. *(Information Guide No. KS-1216*, Kansas Department of Revenue, December 2015, CCH KANSAS TAX REPORTS, ¶ 201-827)

SSTP registration: Sellers may register through an agent. The appointment of the agent must be in writing and be submitted to the Director (Sec. 79-3608(a), K.S.A.).

By registering under the Agreement, the seller agrees to collect and remit sales and use taxes for all taxable sales into Kansas as well as the other member states, including member states joining after the seller's registration. Withdrawal or revocation of Kansas from the Agreement will not relieve a seller of its responsibility to remit taxes previously or subsequently collected on behalf of Kansas (Sec. 79-3679(b), K.S.A.). A seller registering under the Agreement is considered registered in Kansas and may not be required to pay any registration fees or other charges to register in Kansas if the seller has no legal requirement to register (Sec. 79-3608(c), K.S.A.). A written signature from the seller registering under the Agreement is not required. An agent may register a seller and a seller may cancel its registration under the system at any time under. Cancellation does not relieve the seller of its liability for remitting to Kansas any taxes collected (Sec. 79-3608(c), K.S.A.).

Government contractors: Sales tax registration is required of any person (or an "affiliated person" of the retailer) who sells or leases tangible personal property to the state, a state department, a state agency, or an agent of any of such governmental entity. Registering as a retailer will be a prerequisite to these sales and leases, and the registrants will be obligated to collect and remit sales or use tax on all taxable sales of tangible personal property to Kansas customers. "Affiliated person" is defined as any person that is a member of the same "controlled group of corporations" (defined in IRC Sec. 1563(a) as the retailer, or any other entity that, regardless of how it is organized, bears the same ownership relationship to the retailer as a corporation that is a member of the same controlled group of corporations). (Uncodified Sec. 9(a), S.B. 83, Laws 2013)

Contracts relieving tax collection requirements: Absent specific approval by a majority vote of each chamber of the Kansas Legislature, any ruling, contract, or agreement between a retailer and Kansas's executive branch, a state agency, or state department relieving the retailer of the sales and use tax collection requirement is null and void, despite the presence of a warehouse, distribution center, or fulfillment center in Kansas that is owned or operated by the retailer or an affiliated person of the retailer. This holds true whether the ruling, contract, or agreement is written, verbal, express, or implied. (Uncodified Sec. 9(b), S.B. 83, Laws 2013)

- **Out-of-state businesses responding to declared disasters or emergencies**

The Disaster Utilities Response Act (S.B. 109, Laws 2015) provides that an out-of-state business that conducts operations within Kansas for purposes of performing work or services related to a declared state disaster or emergency during the disaster response period are not required to register, file, or remit state or local corporate and personal income taxes, occupational license fees, sales and use taxes, or property taxes on equipment used during the disaster response period. "Disaster response period" means a period that begins 10 days prior to the first day of a declared state disaster or emergency and that extends for a period of 60 calendar days after the end of the declared disaster or emergency period, or any longer period authorized by the governor.

In addition, out-of-state employees are not considered to have established residency in the state that would require the employee or the employee's employer to file and pay state income taxes. However, out-of-state businesses and employees are required to pay transaction taxes and fees including, but not limited to, fuel taxes or sales or use taxes on tangible personal property, materials or services, consumed or used in the state subject to sales or use taxes, hotel taxes, car rental taxes or fees that the out-of-state business or employee purchases for use or consumption in the state during the disaster response period, unless otherwise exempted. (S.B. 109, Laws 2015)

For purposes of any state or local tax on or measured by, in whole or in part, net or gross income or receipts, all disaster- or emergency-related work of the out-of-state business that is conducted in Kansas will be disregarded with respect to any filing requirements for such tax, including the filing required for a unitary or combined group of which the out-of-state business may be a part. For the purpose of apportioning income, revenue or receipts, the performance by an out-of-state business of any work may not be sourced to or may not otherwise impact or increase the amount of income, revenue or receipts apportioned to Kansas.

Out-of-state businesses and employees that remain in the state after the disaster response period are subject to the state's normal standards for residency or doing business in the state and are responsible for tax requirements or obligations and registration, licensing, or filing requirements.

Upon request of the Kansas Department of Revenue, the out-of-state business or its affiliate that enters the state is required to provide a written statement that the business is in the state for disaster-or emergency-related purposes. An annual record of all declared state disasters and emergencies is to be maintained by the department, and the agency is authorized to promulgate any necessary rules and regulations to implement the Act. (S.B. 109, Laws 2015; *Notice 15-12,* Kansas Department of Revenue, July 1, 2015, CCH KANSAS TAX REPORTS, ¶ 201-794)

¶ 450 **Sales or Use Tax Credits**

Use tax credits are allowed in many instances for sales taxes paid other states or counties.

• **Allowable credits**

Taxpayers may take credit for a trade-in allowance.

No claim for a credit will be allowed unless the consumer or user had initially paid sales tax directly to the Department of Revenue (Reg. 92-19-49). Credits may not be used until the Director of Taxation has approved the claim and sent written confirmation to the retailer. The written confirmation must be attached to the tax return and may be used only to offset taxes owed. The balance of a credit may be carried forward until it is fully used. Interest will not be paid on credits.

Taxpayers may also take credit for the selling price of property returned by the purchaser when the full sale price, including sales tax, is refunded in cash or by credit (Sec. 79-3602(h)). Retailers may not receive credit for repossessed property returned to their stock if only the amount of cash actually received from the sale of such property was previously included in gross receipts (Reg. 92-19-49b).

¶450 Kansas

- **Limitations period**

No refund or credit will be allowed after one year from the due date of the return for the reporting period unless the taxpayer files the claim before the end of such period (*Notice 09-07,* Kansas Department of Revenue, October 13, 2009, CCH KANSAS TAX REPORTS, ¶ 201-261).

- **Excise tax**

Privileges taxes imposed by other states that do not attach to the selling price of tangible personal property by law are not allowed as credits against Kansas use tax (Reg. 92-20-15).

¶ 451   Deficiency Assessments

The Director of Revenue may examine a taxpayer's return and issue a notice of deficiency assessment for any additional taxes owed (Sec. 79-3610). A deficiency assessment may be based upon generally recognized and reliable sampling techniques. A taxpayer may request a hearing regarding any additional tax liability, including whether the use of a sampling technique reflects actual liability. The request for a hearing must be made within 60 days after the mailing of the notice of deficiency assessment. A final determination of tax owed will be made after a hearing.

¶ 452   Audit Procedures

The Director of Taxation or any designated officer or employee may conduct investigations and hearings to ascertain the correctness of any return or to determine the amount of tax due from any person engaged in the business of selling tangible personal property at retail or furnishing taxable services (Sec. 79-3611). All books, papers, records, or memoranda bearing upon taxable sales may be examined, and any person with knowledge of such sales may be required to attend and give testimony. The Director is authorized to administer oaths.

Hearings are not bound by the technical rules of evidence. Informality in a proceeding or the taking of testimony will not invalidate an order or decision made by the Director (Sec. 79-3611).

Audits may be based upon generally recognized sampling techniques in lieu of a complete examination even if the person being audited has complete records of transactions and does not consent to the use of sampling (Sec. 79-3610, Reg. 92-19-44). However, the portion of an audit based upon any sampling technique that is not generally recognized must be dismissed and a new audit performed.

Taxpayers must provide reasonably sufficient work space, lighting, and working conditions for Department of Revenue agents conducting sales or use tax audits (Reg. 92-19-45).

- **Audit rights**

The Department of Revenue must promulgate rules and directives under which a sales and use taxpayer will be provided with (1) a copy of all work papers compiled as a result of an audit, (2) a personal or telephonic conference with the Department after the completion of audit field work, and (3) a consideration of the taxpayer's convenience in the scheduling of an audit (Sec. 79-3652).

- **Managed audit agreements**

The Director of Taxation may enter into a managed audit agreement with a taxpayer who is willing and able to comply with Kansas tax laws to determine the amount of the taxpayer's liability (Sec. 79-3660). A managed audit agreement consists of an audit plan developed by the taxpayer and the Director under which the taxpayer agrees to review selected sales and purchase records to determine its sales and use tax liability (Sec. 79-3662). The Director agrees to accept the taxpayer's deficiency determination but will review the results of the taxpayer's determination in order to issue the final determination of tax liability. Once the managed audit is completed, interest on the tax liability will be calculated at 50% of the rate that would otherwise be imposed (Sec. 79-3664).

¶ 453   Statute of Limitations

Sales tax must be assessed within three years after a return was filed (Sec. 79-3609, Reg. 92-19-63). In the case of a false or fraudulent return with intent to evade payment of tax, the limitations period is two years from the discovery of the fraud. Except in cases of fraud, no assessment may be made for any period more than three years preceding the date a retailer registered with the state.

If a person required to file a sales tax return fails to do so, sales tax may be assessed at any time (Reg. 92-19-63). A levy or other proceeding to collect tax, penalty, and interest may also be commenced at any time.

• Refunds

No refund or credit will be allowed after one year from the due date of the return for the reporting period unless the taxpayer files the claim before the end of such period (*Information Guide No. KS-1220,* Kansas Department of Revenue, February 2015, CCH Kansas Tax Reports, ¶ 201-767).

¶ 454   Application for Refund

A "sales tax refund fund" of up to $100,000 is maintained by the Director of Taxation from sales tax collections and held for payment of sales tax refunds (Sec. 79-3620(b)). Also, a "compensating tax refund fund" of up to $10,000 is authorized (Sec. 79-3710).

• Application

In general, refund claims must be filed within three years from the date the tax payment was due (Sec. 79-3609; Reg. 92-19-49). Written claims must be supported by proof that the tax was actually paid.

Retailers' claims: Any retailer who reported and remitted sales tax that was not owed, was remitted in error, or was an overpayment may apply to the Kansas Department of Revenue for a refund. A refund claim is treated as an application to adjust or amend the return. A refund claim must be accompanied by an amended return for each period for which a refund is claimed (Sec. 79-3693(b); Reg. 92-19-49c(b)).

Purchasers' claims: A request for refund of retailers' sales tax may be filed directly by a purchaser if the purchaser provides a notarized statement to the Department of Revenue from the retailer stating that (1) the retailer will not claim a refund on the same tax included in the purchaser's request, (2) the retailer agrees to provide any information or documentation possessed by the retailer to the purchaser that is needed to submit the request for refund, (3) the retailer has remitted the tax for which the refund is requested, and (4) the retailer has not taken or will not take any credit on the tax for which the refund is requested (Sec. 79-3650).

¶ 456   Scope of Tax

Source.—Statutory references are to Chapter 139 of the Kentucky Revised Statutes, as amended to date. Details are reported in the CCH KENTUCKY STATE TAX REPORTS starting at ¶ 60-000.

The Kentucky sales tax is a general privilege tax levied on the gross receipts from sales at retail of tangible personal property or digital property or its lease or rental, and on the furnishing of specified services (KRS Sec. 139.090, KRS Sec. 139.200). The use tax on storage, use, or other consumption of tangible personal property or digital property in the state is a complementary tax and does not apply in situations in which the sales tax is collected (KRS Sec. 139.190, KRS Sec. 139.310).

"Tangible personal property" is defined as personal property that may be seen, weighed, measured, felt, or touched, or which is in any other manner perceptible to the senses. The definition includes natural, artificial, and mixed gas, electricity, water, steam, and prewritten computer software. (KRS Sec. 139.010(30))

Prepaid calling arrangements: Prepaid telephone calling services are subject to sales and use tax (KRS Sec. 139.200(2)(d)).

• Incidence of tax

Although the sales tax is generally imposed on a retailer's gross receipts (KRS Sec. 139.200), shifting of the tax to the purchaser is mandatory (KRS Sec. 139.210). Sales tax must be separately stated and the tax becomes a debt from the retailer to the commonwealth.

The incidence of the use tax is on the purchaser or consumer (KRS Sec. 139.330). The liability remains a debt to the state until paid except when the tax has been paid to a retailer doing business in the state who has furnished a receipt confirming payment.

• Services subject to tax

The services that are made specifically subject to the sales tax are the rental of transient accommodations, the furnishing of sewer services, intrastate and interstate telephone and telegraph services, and the sale of admissions (KRS Sec. 139.200). Tax also applies to the distribution, transmission, or transportation services for natural gas that is for storage, use, or other consumption in Kentucky (KRS Sec. 139.200(2)(f)). However, services furnished for natural gas classified for residential use or to a seller or reseller of natural gas are excluded from tax.

Use tax: The use tax is imposed on tangible personal property purchased for storage, use, or consumption in Kentucky; this tax complements the sales tax and is not levied when the sales tax is imposed (KRS Sec. 139.190, KRS Sec.139.310). It is specifically imposed on equipment brought into the state for use in construction (KRS Sec. 139.320). The use tax operates to protect Kentucky merchants from discrimination arising from Kentucky's inability to impose its sales tax on sales made outside the commonwealth to Kentucky residents by merchants of other states. The use tax is also imposed on property that has been purchased tax free for resale and is later consumed, rather than resold, by the purchaser.

• Responsibility for collecting tax

The sales tax, which is to be separately stated, is collected by the retailer from the purchaser unless the purchaser holds a direct pay authorization (KRS Sec. 139.210, 103 KAR 31:030). The taxes, held in trust for the commonwealth, are a debt of the retailer to the commonwealth.

Retailers who have sufficient contacts with Kentucky to constitute "nexus" with the commonwealth are required to collect the use tax from purchasers to be remitted to the

Department of Revenue (KRS Sec. 139.340). The tax remains a liability of the purchaser, however, until paid, unless the purchaser has a receipt showing payment of the tax to the retailer (KRS Sec. 139.330).

Charitable auctions: The definition of a "retailer" under Kentucky's sales and use tax laws excludes any person making sales at a charitable auction for a qualifying entity if (1) the qualifying entity is sponsoring the auction; (2) the purchaser of tangible personal property at the auction directly pays the qualifying entity for the property; and (3) the qualifying entity is responsible for the collection, control, and disbursement of the auction proceeds. If these three conditions are met, the qualifying entity sponsoring the auction is considered the retailer for purposes of the sales made at the auction. For these purposes, a "qualifying entity" is defined as a resident church, school, civic club, or any other nonprofit charitable, religious, or educational organization. (KRS 139.010(17)(c))

Sourcing: For purposes of a retailer's obligation to pay or to collect and remit sales and use taxes, the following sourcing rules apply to retail sales other than those related to communications services, florist wire services, or advertising and promotional direct mail and other direct mail (KRS Sec. 139.105(1)):

(1) If the purchaser receives tangible personal property, digital property, or a service at a business location of the retailer, the sale is sourced to that business location.

(2) If a purchaser or purchaser's donee receives tangible personal property, digital property, or a service at a location specified by the purchaser, the sale is sourced to that location.

(3) If a retailer does not know the address where the tangible personal property, digital property, or service is received, the sale is sourced to the first of the following addresses that is known to the retailer:

(a) the purchaser's address;

(b) the purchaser's billing address;

(c) the address of the purchaser's payment instrument; or

(d) the address from which the tangible personal property was shipped, from which the computer software delivered electronically or the digital property transferred electronically was first available for transmission by the retailer, or from which the service was provided, disregarding any location that merely provided the actual digital transfer of the product sold.

The above sourcing rules do not affect the obligation of a purchaser to remit use tax.

Direct mail sourcing: A purchaser of direct mail that is not a holder of a direct payment permit must provide to a retailer at the time of the transaction a direct mail form, or information that indicates the locations of the recipients to which the direct mail is delivered (KRS Sec. 139.777).

"Direct mail" is now defined as printed material delivered or distributed by U.S. mail or another delivery service to a mass audience or to addressees on a mailing list provided by the purchaser (or at the purchaser's direction) when the cost of the items is not billed directly to the recipient. "Other direct mail" is defined as any direct mail that is not "advertising and promotional direct mail," regardless of whether "advertising and promotional direct mail" is included in the same mailing.

If the purchaser provides the retailer information showing the jurisdictions to which advertising and promotional direct mail or other direct mail is delivered to recipients, the retailer must source the sale and collect the tax according to this delivery information. Absent bad faith, the retailer is relieved of any further obligation to collect the tax on any transaction where the retailer has collected the tax based on the delivery

¶456 Kentucky

information provided by the purchaser. If the purchaser of advertising and promotional direct mail does not provide the retailer with a direct pay permit, a completed SST exemption certificate, or other delivery information or authorized written statement as described above, the retailer must source the sale to the address from where the mail was shipped. If a purchaser of other direct mail does not provide the retailer with a direct pay permit, a completed SST exemption certificate, or other written statement authorized or accepted by the department, the retailer must source the sale to the location indicated by an address for the purchaser that is available from the retailer's business records maintained in the ordinary course of the retailer's business when use of this address does not amount to bad faith. If both advertising and promotional direct mail and other direct mail are combined in a single mailing, the sale must be sourced as "other direct mail."

Commercial printers and mailers engaged in business in Kentucky are not required to collect use tax on sales of printing, advertising and promotional direct mail, or other direct mail printed outside Kentucky and delivered outside Kentucky to the U.S. Postal Service for mass mailing to third-party Kentucky residents who are not purchasers of the mail if the commercial printers or mailers (1) maintain records related to those sales to assist the department in the collection of use tax, and (2) file sales and use tax reports if requested to do so by the department. If a commercial printer or mailer meets these two criteria, the purchaser of the printing or mail is solely responsible for reporting and paying use tax. (KRS Sec. 139.365)

Remote seller notice requirements: Out-of-state retailers not required to collect Kentucky use tax who expect less than $100,000 in gross sales to Kentucky residents and businesses in a calendar year must provide notice in their retail catalogs and on their retail Internet Web sites, online auction Web sites, and invoices and similar documents that purchasers of nonexempt tangible personal property or digital property for storage, use, or other consumption in Kentucky must report and pay use tax directly to the Kentucky Department of Revenue (KRS Sec. 139.450(2)(a)).

The use tax notice must be readily visible (KRS Sec. 139.450(2)(b)). Retailers are prohibited from stating or implying on their Web sites or in their catalogs that there is no Kentucky tax due on purchases made from the retailer, and specific wording is required (KRS Sec. 139.450(2)(c)),

It is sufficient if the retailer provides a prominent reference to a supplemental page or electronic link that contains the required use tax notification language. The referring language must state "See important Kentucky sales and use tax information regarding tax you may owe directly to the Commonwealth of Kentucky." A retailer can provide a consolidated notice to customers meeting the above notice requirements if the retailer is required to provide a similar use tax notification for another state. (KRS Sec. 139.450(5), (6))

Drop shipments: When all the parties are located in the state, the retailer furnishes a resale certificate to the primary seller, rendering the first sale a nontaxable transaction. The retailer then collects sales tax on behalf of the state on the secondary sale to its customer. However, different considerations arise when one or more of the parties is from outside the Commonwealth. A purchasing retailer who is not registered in Kentucky can submit a resale certificate (Form 51A1105) in a drop ship transaction if the retailer makes a notation on the face of the certificate to the effect that it is a nonresident purchaser who is not required to register in Kentucky. (103 KAR 31:111(3)) Further, instead of issuing the Kentucky resale certificate or a Streamlined Sales Tax Certificate of Exemption (Form 51A260), out-of-state entities can issue the Multistate Tax Commission's Uniform Sales and Use Tax Certificate-Multijurisdiction. The secondary sale by the retailer to its Kentucky customer is an exempt interstate sale as the retailer lacks nexus with Kentucky.

- **Nexus**

Out-of-state retailers that are engaged in business in Kentucky are required to collect from the purchaser use tax on sales of tangible personal property for storage, use, or other consumption in Kentucky (KRS Sec. 139.340; KRS Sec. 139.310). "Engaged in business in the state" includes any of the following (KRS Sec. 139.340(2)):

— having an office, distribution place, warehouse, or other place of business;

— having any agent operating in Kentucky under the authority of the retailer;

— the continuous solicitation of orders from residents in which the solicitation utilizes financial, telecommunication, or advertising systems within Kentucky;

— the lease of tangible personal property situated in Kentucky;

— the continuous solicitation of orders from residents if the retailer benefits from an agent or representative operating in the state under the authority of the retailer to repair or service tangible personal property sold by the retailer; or

— any retailer located outside Kentucky that uses a representative in Kentucky, either full-time or part-time, if the representative performs any activities that help establish or maintain a marketplace for the retailer, including receiving or exchanging returned merchandise.

Direct mail: A commercial printer or mailer engaged in business in Kentucky is not required to collect use tax on sales of printing or direct mail advertising materials that are both printed out of state and delivered out of state to the U.S. Postal Service for mass mailing to third-party Kentucky residents who are not purchasers of the advertising materials. The commercial printers or mailers must maintain records relating to such sales to assist in the collection of the use tax owed and file reports upon request. If the commercial printer or mailer complies with these requirements, the purchaser of the printing or direct mail advertising will have sole responsibility for payment of the use tax (KRS Sec. 139.340).

- **Streamlined Act status**

Kentucky is a full member of the Streamlined Sales Tax Agreement with a seat on the Governing Board. It has enacted all of the provisions necessary to comply with the Agreement's requirements and these provisions currently are in effect (KRS Sec. 139.780—KRS Sec. 139.795). As a full member, it may vote on amendments to or interpretations of the Agreement, and sellers registering under the SST system must collect and remit tax on sales into the state. For additional information, see ¶ 462.

Taxability matrix: A chart of the taxable status of various items is accessible under "Online Taxability Matrix" on the SST website at **www.streamlinedsalestax.org/apps/**.

¶ 457   Tax Base

Generally included in the tax base are all the costs of the property sold, including delivery charges prior to sale. The basis of the sales tax is gross receipts from retail sales. The basis of the use tax is sales price, which is defined identically to gross receipts (KRS Sec. 139.130).

- **Basis definitions**

The term "gross receipts" means the total amount of the sale, lease, or rental price as the case may be, of "retail sales" valued in money, whether or not received in money (KRS Sec. 139.050). The term "sales price" for use tax purposes is a gross amount without any deductions for the cost of the property sold, materials, labor, and transportation costs (KRS Sec. 139.130(1)). The sales price includes the cost of any services that are part of the sale, and the amount of any credit given to the purchaser by the seller (KRS Sec. 139.130(2)).

¶ 458   List of Exemptions, Exceptions, and Exclusions

Unless otherwise indicated, the statutory exemptions, exceptions, and exclusions listed below apply to both sales and use taxes. Items that are excluded from the sales or use tax base are treated at ¶ 457, "Tax Base."

- **Sales and use tax exemptions, exceptions, and exclusions**

Admissions to nonprofit charitable and educational institutions functions	KRS Sec. 139.495
Agricultural fuel	KRS Sec. 139.480(16)
Aircraft equipment, fuel, and parts used in interstate commerce	KRS Sec. 139.480(19)
Alcohol production with Kentucky coal	KRS Sec. 139.480(18)
Animal feed	KRS Sec. 139.480(9)
Aquatic organisms	KRS Sec. 139.480(28)
Baling twine and baling wire	KRS Sec. 139.480(27)
Blast furnaces (eff. 7/1/2018)	KRS Sec. 139.480(21)
Buffalo	KRS Sec. 139.48028
Catalogs or newspaper inserts sold out-of-state	KRS Sec. 139.470[14]
Cervids and cervid farming	KRS Sec. 139.480(28)
Charter buses	KRS Sec. 139.470(16), KRS Sec. 139.480(32)
Churches	KRS Sec. 139.495(1)
Coal for manufacturing electricity	KRS Sec. 139.480(2)
Constitutionally exempt property	KRS Sec. 139.470(1)
Containers sold empty to retailers for filling	KRS Sec. 139.470(2)(a)
County fair admissions (first $50,000)	KRS Sec. 139.470(24)
Credit unions	KRS Sec. 290.115
Embryos and semen used in livestock reproduction	KRS Sec. 139.480(25)
Enterprise incentives	KRS Sec. 154.20-200
Farm chemicals	KRS Sec. 139.480(8)
Farm facilities used for raising chickens or livestock	KRS Sec. 139.480(15)
Farm machinery	KRS Sec. 139.480(11)
Farm work stock used in farming	KRS Sec. 139.480(6)
Film rentals by theaters	KRS Sec. 139.484
Fluidized bed energy production facilities	KRS Sec. 139.480(20)
Food and food ingredients	KRS Sec. 139.485
Food purchased with food stamps	KRS Sec. 139.480(22)
Food sold to students in school cafeterias or lunchrooms	KRS Sec. 139.495(2)
Fuels used in manufacturing exceeding 3% of costs	KRS Sec. 139.480(3)
Gasoline subject to motor vehicle excise tax	KRS Sec. 139.050(3)(e), KRS Sec. 139.500
Government purchases	KRS Sec. 139.470(1), KRS Sec. 139.470(7)
Grain storage and processing	KRS Sec. 139.480(14)
Historical site operation and restoration	KRS Sec. 139.482(2)(b)
Historical sites, admission to	KRS Sec. 139.482(2)(a)

Horses, breeding fees and certain sales	KRS Sec. 139.531(2), KRS Sec. 139.531(3)
Industrial machinery	KRS Sec. 139.470(11), KRS Sec. 139.486
Industrial processing tools, supplies, and materials	KRS Sec. 139.470(11)
Livestock producing food for human consumption	KRS Sec. 139.480(4)
Llamas and alpacas	KRS Sec. 139.480(26)
Machinery delivered to manufacturer for use out of state	KRS Sec. 139.487
Machinery for new and expanded industry	KRS Sec. 139.170, KRS Sec. 139.480(10)
Mail order and telemarketing sales shipped out of state by common carrier	KRS Sec. 139.470(5)
Manufacturing or industrial processing	KRS Sec. 139.470(11)
Medical equipment and supplies; prescribed drugs	KRS Sec. 139.472
Mining and extraction	KRS Sec. 139.470(11), KRS Sec. 139.486
Motion picture production company	KRS Sec. 139.5381(2)
Motion pictures made in Kentucky	KRS Sec. 139.538
Motor vehicles	KRS Sec. 138.450(5), KRS Sec. 139.050(3)(f)
Motor vehicles and trailers sold to nonresidents	KRS Sec. 139.470(21)
New and expanded industry, machinery	KRS Sec. 139.170, KRS Sec. 139.480(11)
Newspaper inserts or catalogs sold out-of-state	KRS Sec. 139.4701214
Nonprofit educational institution sales	KRS Sec. 139.480(18)
Nonprofit institutions	KRS Sec. 139.495(1)
Occasional sales (first $1,000) by individuals or nonprofit organizations	KRS Sec. 139.496
Out-of-state nonprofit organizations, sales to	KRS Sec. 139.470(10)
Packaging (containers)	KRS Sec. 139.470(2)
Pollution control facilities and equipment	KRS Sec. 139.480(12)
Poultry used for breeding or egg production	KRS Sec. 139.480(5)
Prescribed medicines, equipment, and supplies	KRS Sec. 139.472
Property delivered out of state by common carrier	KRS Sec. 139.470(5)
Prosthetic devices and physical aids	KRS Sec. 139.472
Public school purchases	KRS Sec. 139.497
Railroad equipment, fuel, and parts used in interstate commerce . . .	KRS Sec. 139.480(1)
Ratite birds and eggs	KRS Sec. 139.480(24)
Recycling machinery and equipment	KRS Sec. 139.480(23)
Retail fixtures, metal, for use outside Kentucky	KRS Sec. 139.470(15)
Returnable containers	KRS Sec. 139.470(2)(b)
School tax rate increases annexed to residential telephone bills	KRS Sec. 139.470(9)
Schools, sales by	KRS Sec. 139.495(4)
Seeds and fertilizer for food for human consumption	KRS Sec. 139.480(7)
State and local purchases for public purposes	KRS Sec. 139.470(7)

¶458   **Kentucky**

Textbook and course material sales	KRS Sec. 139.480(18), KRS Sec. 139.495(3)
Tobacco buydowns	KRS Sec. 139.470(17)
Tombstones and grave markers	KRS Sec. 139.480(13)
United States government purchases	KRS Sec. 139.470(1)
Uranium for use outside the state	KRS Sec. 139.470(16)
Utility services, residential	KRS Sec. 139.470(8)
Vending machine bulk sales	KRS Sec. 139.470(6)
Vessels and maritime supplies used in commerce	KRS Sec. 139.483
Water sold for agricultural use	KRS Sec. 139.480(30)
Water use fees paid to Kentucky River Authority	KRS Sec. 139.470(12)
Youth programs, nonprofit educational	KRS Sec. 139.497

Use tax—charitable exemption: The Kentucky Court of Appeals has ruled that Sec. 170, Ky. Const., exempts an institution of purely public charity from the use tax imposed under KRS Sec. 139.310. Previously, the exemption provided by Sec. 170 was held to be limited to the property tax. (*Interstate Gas Supply, Inc. v. Finance and Administration Cabinet,* Kentucky Court of Appeals, No. 2013-CA-001766-MR, February 26, 2016, CCH Kentucky Tax Reports, ¶ 203-142)

¶ 459   Rate of Tax

The sales and use taxes are imposed generally at the rate of 6% (KRS Sec. 139.200, KRS Sec. 139.310, KRS Sec. 139.320).

Gross receipts derived from transactions based on fixed-price contracts, leases, or rental agreements entered into on or before March 9, 1990, are subject to tax at the rate of 5% (KRS Sec. 139.471).

Transient room tax: A transient room tax is imposed at the rate of 1% of the rent for every occupancy of any suite, room, rooms, or cabins. The tax applies to occupancy charges by all persons, companies, corporations, groups, or organizations doing business as motor courts, motels, hotels, inns, tourist camps or similar accommodations businesses. The tax does not apply to the rental or lease of any room or set of rooms that are equipped with a kitchen, in an apartment building, and that are usually leased as a dwelling for a period of 30 days or more by an individual or business that regularly holds itself out as exclusively providing apartments (KRS 142.400).

Telecommunications tax: An excise tax of 3% is imposed on the retail purchase of cable service, satellite broadcast and wireless cable service provided to a person whose primary use is in Kentucky, regardless of where or to whom those services are billed or paid (KRS Sec. 136.604; KRS Sec. 236.606). The tax is collected from consumers of those services. An exemption is provided for governmental agencies and eligible nonprofit educational, charitable, and religious institutions (KRS Sec. 136.608).

Motor vehicles: A motor vehicle usage tax equal to 6% of the retail price is imposed upon the use of all motor vehicles in Kentucky at the time of first titling or registration or upon the transfer of title or registration of any motor vehicle previously titled or registered in Kentucky. The usage tax is collected by the county clerk and remitted to the Department of Revenue. (KRS Sec. 138.460) A sales tax exemption is allowed for the sales price of any motor vehicle upon which any applicable vehicle usage tax has been paid (¶ 458). A trade-in allowance is available for new motor vehicles, dealer demonstrator vehicles, previous model year motor vehicles, and U-Drive-It motor vehicles that have been transferred within 180 days of being registered as a U-Drive-It and that have less than 5,000 miles (KRS 138-460(2)). Members of the U.S. Armed Forces on duty in Kentucky are exempt (KRS Sec. 138.470(4)).

Rate changes: If the department does not provide a seller with at least 30 days' notice from the enactment of a sales and use tax rate change to the effective date of the rate change, the seller will be relieved of liability for failing to collect tax at the new rate if the seller collected tax at the immediately preceding rate and if the seller's failure to collect tax at the new rate does not continue beyond 30 days following the date of the new rate's enactment. However, this relief does not apply if the department establishes that a seller fraudulently failed to collect tax at the new rate or solicited purchasers based on the immediately preceding rate.

¶ 460   Local Taxes

The Kentucky Constitution provides that the Kentucky General Assembly may enact legislation authorizing cities and towns to impose taxation for municipal purposes (Ky Const. Sec. 181). No authorization for local sales and use tax laws has been enacted. However, transient room taxes, payable as license taxes rather than sales taxes, are authorized for counties and cities at various rates.

An urban-county government is authorized to levy a transient room tax at a rate of 6% and an additional tax of up to 2.5% for the purpose of funding the renovation, expansion, or improvement of a convention center on or after July 15, 2016. The additional tax can remain in effect for the duration of the project and repayment of all related debt. (KRS Sec. 153.450)

Kentucky has conformed to the provisions of the federal Mobile Telecommunications Sourcing Act (P.L. 106-252), which provides that charges for telecommunications services are sourced to the service address of the customer (KRS Sec. 139.100).

¶ 461   Bracket Schedule

Kentucky does not utilize bracket schedules. Tax must be computed by applying the 6% rate to the sales price carried to the third decimal place and rounded to the nearest cent by eliminating any fraction less than one-half of one cent ($0.005) and increasing any fraction of one-half of one cent ($0.005) or higher to the next higher cent.

¶ 462   Returns, Payments, and Due Dates

Tax returns are due monthly (KRS Sec. 139.540) on the 20th day of any given month for the immediately preceding month (KRS Sec. 139.550, KRS Sec. 139.580). The return must contain, among other things, a statement of aggregate gross receipts for purposes of the sales tax and a statement of the aggregate total sales price for the use tax, as well as the amount of taxes owed for the period covered by the return (KRS Sec. 139.560).

For taxpayers who have a relatively high dollar value in monthly sales, where the average monthly tax liability exceeds $10,000, taxes for the period beginning on the 16th day of the preceding month and ending on the 15th day of the current month must be reported and remitted by the 25th day of the current month (103 KAR 25:131).

• Electronic funds transfer

The Department of Revenue may require any person who is required to collect or remit taxes and fees, and any person who acts on a taxpayer's behalf to remit those taxes and fees, to remit them by electronic fund transfer (KRS Sec. 131.155). Payment by electronic fund transfer may be required if (1) the average payment per reporting period is $10,000 or more for each tax or fee required to be collected or remitted, (2) the payment for each tax or fee required to be collected or remitted is made on behalf of 100 or more taxpayers, or (3) the aggregate of the funds to be remitted on behalf of others is $10,000 or more for each tax or fee required to be collected or remitted. The Department of Revenue may waive the requirement if a qualifying taxpayer is unable to remit funds electronically.

Any Kentucky state agency may accept electronic payments through means such as credit cards, debit cards, electronic checks, and automated clearing house (ACH) debits (KRS Sec. 45.345). Agencies are allowed to collect convenience fees from users for reimbursement of any fees charged by transaction providers.

Electronic filing: Taxpayers holding a valid sales and use tax permit may file Kentucky sales and use tax returns electronically at **http://onestop.ky.gov**. Special software is not required to use this filing option.

- **Direct payment**

In circumstances where normal tax collection procedures will be difficult to follow, the Department of Revenue may allow certain taxpayers to purchase taxable property, excluding energy and energy-producing fuels, without paying their vendors sales and use taxes (103 KAR 31:030(1)). The purchaser would then pay the taxes directly. The Department of Revenue typically allows direct payment for purchasers engaged in the business of manufacturing, transportation, distribution, mining, quarrying, compounding, and processing. An applicant for a permit (a "DP number")must have been engaged in business in Kentucky in excess of 24 months and have purchased tangible personal property of at least $10 million for use in Kentucky in the preceding calendar year. An applicant agrees to directly report and pay to the Department of Revenue the sales and use taxes that would have been remitted by the applicant's retailer had the direct pay permit not been used. Returns and payments may be made quarterly, instead of monthly, upon approval of the Department of Revenue.

The Department of Revenue may revoke or suspend any permit granted to the taxpayer if the taxpayer fails to comply with any of the provisions of the Kentucky sales and use tax laws (KRS Sec. 139.760).

- **Uniform Sales Tax Administration Act**

Kentucky has enacted the Uniform Sales and Use Tax Administration Act as well as legislation conforming its sales and use tax laws to provisions of the Streamlined Sales and Use Tax Agreement (SSUTA). Highlights include:

Digital property: The term "digital property" is defined as any of the following transferred electronically: digital audio works, digital books, finished artwork, digital photographs, periodicals, newspapers, magazines, video greeting cards, audio greeting cards, video games, electronic games, or any digital code related to such property (KRS Sec. 139.010(8)(a)) The term does not include digital audio-visual works or satellite radio programming (KRS Sec. 139.010(8)(b)).

Bundled transactions: If taxable goods are bundled with services and are sold as a single package for one price, the tax on the transaction generally is required to be computed on the entire amount. Excluded from the definition of "bundled transaction" is the retail sale of both a digital property and a service when the digital property is essential to the use of the service and provided exclusively in connection with the service, and when the true object of the transaction is the service.

Exemption certificates: A retailer that accepts an exemption certificate or resale certificate in good faith with respect to a transaction is relieved of the burden of proving the transaction is exempt from tax. However, a retailer may be found liable if it fraudulently fails to collect the tax or if it solicits a purchaser to improperly claim an exemption.

Bad debts: A refundable deduction for bad debt is available. "Bad debt" is as defined in IRC Sec. 166, except it does not include: (1) a financing charge; (2) interest; (3) sales or use tax on the purchase price; (4) an uncollectible amount on property that remains in the possession of a retailer until the full purchase price is paid; (5) an expense incurred in attempting to collect any debt; or (6) repossessed property.

Sourcing rules: Sales will be sourced generally to the destination of the product sold, with a default to origin-based sourcing in the absence of that information. See also ¶ 456.

Reliance on DOR data: Purchasers, purchaser's sellers, or certified service providers (CSPs) are relieved from civil penalties and interest for failing to pay the correct amount of tax based on reliance on erroneous data provided by the Department of Revenue (KRS Sec. 139.795(7)).

For additional information on the uniform act, see "Streamlined Sales Tax Project," listed in the Table of Contents.

Additional information: The Kentucky Department of Revenue has issued information for participants in the SSUTA. Information is provided on issues such as the filing of simplified electronic returns and the handling and acceptance of payments. In addition, personnel contact information is provided with respect to certified service provider (CSP) certification and sales and use tax issues. (*State Information for Streamlined Sales Tax Participants,* Kentucky Department of Revenue, August 28, 2015, CCH KENTUCKY TAX REPORTS, ¶ 203-128)

¶ 463   Prepayment of Taxes

Kentucky sales and use tax law has no specific provisions requiring prepayment of taxes except for energy direct pay authorizations.

¶ 464   Vendor Registration

Any Kentucky taxpayer who is either presently engaged in or wants to engage in business within Kentucky must file an application for a retail sales and use tax permit with the Kentucky Department of Revenue for each place of business in the form prescribed by the Department of Revenue (KRS Sec. 139.240, Revenue Circular 10C030). Permits are valid only for the taxpayer named on the permit, and are not transferable. Permits must be displayed conspicuously at the taxpayer's place of business (KRS Sec. 139.250). Online registration is available at **https://sut-sst.ky.gov/ KrcIfile/home.aspx**.

Every retailer, whether located within or outside of Kentucky, who is engaged in business in Kentucky, as defined in KRS Sec. 139.340(2), must register the names of Kentucky agents and the addresses of sales outlets with the Department of Revenue (KRS Sec. 139.390).

State contractors: The Kentucky Model Procurement Code is amended to provide that the Commonwealth cannot contract to acquire goods or services from a person or entity unless the person and the person's affiliates have registered with the Department of Revenue to collect and remit sales and use taxes. The registration requirement does not apply if the person or affiliate does not make sales to customers within the Commonwealth. The requirement does extend to foreign persons, even if the foreign person or affiliate is not otherwise legally required to collect and remit sales and use taxes. (KRS Sec. 45A.067)

¶ 465   Sales or Use Tax Credits and Incentives

Generally, retailers are not entitled to a refund or credit of the sales or use taxes paid that have been collected from a purchaser, unless the collected amount is refunded to the purchaser by the retailer (KRS Sec. 139.770(3)). Similarly, no purchaser will be entitled to a use tax credit or refund unless he or she reimburses the vendor for any sales tax that the vendor paid with respect to the property (KRS Sec. 139.690).

A use tax credit is granted for comparable sales tax paid to another state equal to or greater than the amount of the Kentucky liability provided that the other state grants credit for sales tax paid in Kentucky (KRS Sec. 139.510). If the sales tax paid in another state is not equal to or greater than the Kentucky liability, a taxpayer must pay the difference to Kentucky.

- **Vendor compensation**

Taxpayers that pay the tax on time may deduct from each return 1.75% of the first $1,000 of taxes due, and 1.5% of the taxes due in excess of $1,000 (KRS Sec. 139.570). Reimbursement is limited to $50 per taxpayer per reporting period (KRS Sec. 139.570).

- **Communications service credits**

A refundable credit against sales and use tax is available to any business whose communications service exceeds 5% of the business's Kentucky gross receipts during the preceding calendar year (KRS Sec.139.[991]). The credit is equal to the sales tax paid on the difference by which the communications service purchased by the business exceeds 5% of the business's gross receipts. If a business owns directly or indirectly 50% or more of another business, the credit must be computed on a combined basis and any intercompany Kentucky gross receipts must be excluded. An application for the refund must be filed with the Kentucky Department of Revenue by June 1 each year.

Also, a credit is available to any communications service provider or purchaser that has paid a tax in another state on the same communications service, to the extent of the amount of tax legally paid to the other state.

- **Enterprise incentives**

Kentucky has authorized sales and use tax exemptions for businesses establishing a new facility or expanding an existing facility in a designated preference zone under the Kentucky Enterprise Initiative Act (KRS Sec. 154.20-200 through KRS Sec. 154.20-216). The program allows eligible companies that establish a new facility or expand an existing facility to receive sales and use tax refunds for purchases of building materials, including research and development equipment purchases. Eligible companies include only business entities primarily engaged in manufacturing, service or technology, or operating or developing a tourism attraction. Any company whose primary purpose is retail sales is not an eligible company. An eligible company is required to make a minimum investment of $100,000 in a project located in a preference zone, or to invest $500,000 in a project that is not located in a preference zone.

- **Air carriers**

Certificated air carriers engaged in the transportation of persons or property for hire may take a credit for sales and use taxes paid in excess of $1 million annually on purchases of aircraft fuel (including jet fuel) (KRS Sec. 144.132(2)). Carriers must pay the first $1 million dollars of sales and use taxes directly to the Department of Revenue.

Effective 90 days after the adjournment of the 2017 legislative session, the credit is extended to include purchases of aircraft fuel by certificated air carriers that contract with one or more other certificated air carriers for the transportation of persons, property or mail (KRS Sec. 144.132(3))

- **Tourism development projects**

An approved company may receive a sales tax incentive based on sales generated by or arising at a tourism development project, a tourism attraction project, an entertainment destination center, or a lodging facility project. Incentives are generally available over 10 years (20 years for a lodging facility project). A "tourism development project" is a theme restaurant destination attraction project, an entertainment destination center project, a lodging facility project, or a tourism attraction project. Eligible costs include, but are not limited to, construction labor costs, the cost of acquiring real property, and the costs of architectural and engineering services. The expansion of a tourism development project is considered a new stand-alone project. (KRS Sec. 139.536; KRS Sec. 148.851(13)). The refund may rise to 50% of approved costs under certain circumstances (KRS Sec. 139.536(4)).

Retail sales facilities are not included, other than an entertainment destination center, a Kentucky crafts and products center, or a tourism attraction where the sale of goods is incidental to the project. Finally, recreational facilities are not included when nonresidents of Kentucky are not likely to lodge overnight near them (KRS Sec. 154.29-010). A theme restaurant destination attraction must have seating capacity of 450 guests and offer live musical or theatrical entertainment during peak business hours, and food and nonalcoholic drink options that constitute a minimum of 50% of total gross sales receipts (KRS Sec. 148.851).

Tourism attraction projects: A "tourism attraction project" is a cultural or historical site, a recreational facility, an entertainment facility, an area of natural phenomenon or scenic beauty, or a Kentucky crafts and products center (KRS Sec. 143.851(18)). To qualify for incentives for a tourism attraction project, total eligible costs must be more than $1 million ($500,000 in an enhanced incentive county; $5 million for a theme restaurant), the project must be open to the public at least 100 days (300 days for a theme restaurant) in any given year, and the project must attract at least 25% of its visitors from outside Kentucky in any year following the third year of operation. Additional requirements apply.

Entertainment destination center: To qualify for the incentive as an "entertainment destination center" project, total eligible costs must be more than $5 million, the facility must be at least 200,000 square feet and adjacent or complementary to an existing tourism attraction project or major convention facility, and the incentives must be dedicated to a public infrastructure purpose related to the project. In addition, the project must be open to the public at least 100 days per year, it must have at least one major theme restaurant and at least three additional entertainment venues, and meet other requirements. If an approved company is an entertainment destination center that has dedicated at least $30 million of the incentives to a public infrastructure purpose, the project agreement may be extended up to two additional years if the company agrees to reinvest in the original project 100% of any incentives received during the extension that were outstanding at the end of the agreement's original term. (KRS Sec. 148.853(2)(b))

Lodging facility projects: To qualify for the incentive as a lodging facility project, eligible costs must be more than $5 million. However, eligible costs must be more than $6 million if the facility is an integral part of a major convention or sports facility. In addition, eligible costs must be more than $10 million if the facility has at least 500 guest rooms. (Sec. 148.851(10))

Legacy expansion projects: Inducements" in the form of sales tax refunds are available for companies that operate, or intend to operate, a tourism attraction project, and that had an existing project that was approved prior to June 26, 2009. To qualify, an eligible company must invest at least $30 million in the expansion of the previously approved project, include a facility with a permanent seating capacity of at least 65,000 where premier events will be held, and present at least one new premier event annually at the project site. A "premier event" is a sports event that is nationally broadcast and in the premier series or top sanctioned level of similar types of events staged nationally. Approved companies are eligible to recover up to 25% of the approved costs of a legacy expansion project and all amounts outstanding under the agreement with the authority for the original project. The initial term of an agreement for a legacy expansion project is 10 years. Each year of the agreement term, an approved company will be eligible to recover 1/10 of the total approved incentives. (KRS Sec. 148.853(2)(e))

Rebates to government: A governmental entity may be granted a sales tax rebate of up to 100% of the state sales tax generated by the sale of admissions to a public facility and the sale of tangible personal property at the facility. A "public facility" is a building owned and operated by a governmental entity that is a multipurpose facility open to the general public for performances and programs relating to arts, sports, and entertainment, and that includes from 500 to 8,000 seats. It does not include a university, college, school gymnasium, or school auditorium. (KRS Sec. 139.533(1), (2))

- **Economic development projects**

Incentives are available for the acquisition or construction of a new facility or the expansion or rehabilitation of an existing facility, and the installation and equipping of the facility by an eligible company at a specific site in Kentucky to be used in a service or technology, manufacturing, or tourism attraction activity conducted by the company (KRS Sec. 154.31-010(6)). An eligible company must invest at least $500,000 in an economic development project, including the cost of land and excluding labor costs (KRS Sec. 154.31-020(2)). An additional $50,000 must be invested in electronic processing equipment installed as part of the economic development project if qualification is sought for the sales and use tax incentive for electronic processing equipment. Eligible companies are legal entities that are primarily engaged in manufacturing or service or technology activities, or in operating or developing a tourism attraction. Companies primarily engaged in retail sales are not eligible. (KRS Sec. 154.31-010(8)) The maximum sales and use tax incentive available to an approved company is the total amount of sales and use tax paid on purchases made on building and construction materials, research and development equipment, and electronic processing equipment.

Technology projects: Companies classified under the 2007 NAICS industry codes 511210 (software publishers), 518210 (data processing, hosting, and related services), 519130 (Internet publishing, broadcasting, and web search portal business), or 541511 (custom computer programming services) may qualify for a refund of up to 100% of Kentucky sales and use tax paid, reduced by the amount of permitted vendor compensation on the purchase of a communications system or computer system (or a combination of both) (KRS Sec. 139.534(1)(e)). Eligible companies must apply to the Kentucky Department of Revenue for preliminary approval before making the technology purchase. Once preliminary approval is given, the company must purchase the qualifying system on or after July 1, 2010, and must spend at least $100 million on the system, excluding tax. A qualifying system must be installed at a single location in Kentucky within 18 months of preliminary approval. To receive a full refund, an approved company must file a request for the sales and use tax refund within 60 days of the completed installation of the system. Refund requests filed after 180 days will be denied entirely. (KRS Sec. 139.534(3), (4))

Signature projects: Signature projects are those deemed to have a significant impact on the Commonwealth, and generally require the investment of at least $200,000, although the authority may, upon application, reduce the minimum capital investment from $200 million to as low as $150 million for existing agreements executed prior to January 1, 2008. (KRS Sec. 154.30-050(2)(a)(1)(b), KRS Sec. 154.30-050 (8)). The sales or use tax paid on the purchase of tangible personal property used in the construction of a portion of a signature project that does not relate to approved public infrastructure costs or approved signature project costs may be refunded to the agency (KRS 139.515; 103 KAR 31:180). Refunds are calculated based on the actual percentage of total expenditures made for tangible personal property used in constructing the project. Requests for refund must be filed within 60 days after the completion of each fiscal year.

- **Refund for certain nonprofit organizations**

A refund equal to 25% of the tax collected by a nonprofit institution on the sale of donated goods is allowed if the refund is used exclusively for capital construction costs of other retail locations in Kentucky and if the institution (KRS 139.495(5)):

— routinely sells such items;

— provides job training and employment to disadvantaged and disabled individuals;

— spends at least 75% of its annual revenue on job training, job placement, and related community services;

— submits a refund application within 60 days after the new retail location opens for business; and

— provides records of capital construction costs for the new retail location and any other information requested.

• **Alternative fuel, gasification, and renewable energy facility credits**

Under the Incentives for Energy Independence Act, companies that construct, retrofit, or upgrade alternative fuel, gasification, or renewable energy facilities in Kentucky may qualify for sales and use and other tax credits if the following minimum capital investments are made (KRS 139.517):

— $100 million for facilities that use coal as fuel;

— $50 million for a carbon dioxide transmission pipeline;

— $25 million for facilities that use biomass resources as fuel, including agricultural crops, trees, plants, or animal by-products; and

— $1 million for facilities that utilize renewable energy resources such as wind power, solar power, and hydropower.

Qualifying alternative fuel, gasification, or renewable energy facilities may claim sales and use tax credits equal to 100% of the sales and use taxes paid for the purchase of tangible personal property used to construct, retrofit, or upgrade the facility, including materials, machinery, and equipment, but excluding vendor compensation (KRS 139.517(2)). The sales and use tax credit expires upon the completion of the construction, retrofit, or upgrade of the facility, or five years from the date on which the eligible company begins incurring recoverable costs, whichever is earlier.

The sales tax incentive also applies to alternative fuel facilities newly constructed on or after August 1, 2010 (or retrofitted or upgraded on or after that date) if the facility then produces for sale alternative transportation fuels using natural gas or natural gas liquids as the primary feedstock. In addition, such a facility must have a minimum $1 million capital investment. A maximum of five such projects involving such an alternative fuel facility located in Kentucky may be approved. (KRS Sec. 154.27-020(4)(d); KRS Sec. 139.517(1)(b))

An approved company seeking a refund must file a request for incentives within 60 days following the end of the calendar year in which the activation date occurs. The request shall include all documentation relating to the payment of the sales and use tax. In subsequent years, the approved company must file a request for incentives within 60 days following the end of each calendar year (KRS 139.517(4)(b)).

• **Refunds for purchases of energy-efficiency machinery or equipment**

Kentucky-based manufacturers that purchase new or replacement machinery or equipment that reduces the consumption of energy or energy-producing fuels by at least 15% within a 12-month period, while maintaining or increasing the number of units of production for that same period, may apply for a refund of sales or use tax paid on the purchase. The refund does not apply to building improvements, such as windows or lighting, or to repair, replacement, and spare parts. Interest is not allowed on any refund (KRS 139.518; 103 KAR 31:200).

The manufacturer must file an application for preapproval with the Department of Revenue prior to purchasing the new or replacement machinery or equipment (KRS 139.518(4)). The preapplication must include a description of the new or replacement machinery or equipment; documentation of the amount of energy or energy-producing fuels consumed in the 12 month period prior to the application for preapproval; and any other information the department may request. To claim the refunds, the manufacturer must file an application for incentives that includes (1) documentation of the achievement of the required energy-efficiency standards within 18 months from the time the machinery or equipment was placed in service; and (2) verification that the Kentucky sales and use tax was paid on the purchase of the new or replacement machinery or equipment. The burden of proof that the purchase of the machinery or equipment resulted in a decrease in the consumption of energy or energy-producing fuels shall be upon the applicant (KRS 139.518(7)).

¶ 466   Deficiency Assessments

The Kentucky Department of Revenue has the authority to examine and audit any sales and use tax return (KRS Sec. 139.620). If the Cabinet determines that tax is owing, a deficiency assessment will be issued. In general, any deficiency assessment must be issued within four years after the date the return was filed. See ¶ 468 for a discussion of the statute of limitations on assessment of sales and use taxes.

¶ 467   Audit Procedures

The Department of Revenue is authorized to audit and examine returns and other records of the taxpayer in order to determine the correct amount of tax (KRS Sec. 131.130). In carrying out this function, the Cabinet may summon taxpayers and witnesses and require the production of books and documents.

¶ 468   Statute of Limitations

The general limitations period for sales and use tax within which the state must provide notice of assessment is four years from the date that the return was filed (KRS Sec. 139.620). Generally, refund claims must be made within four years of the date prescribed by law for filing a return, including any extensions, or the date the money was paid, whichever is later (KRS Sec. 139.770, KRS Sec. 134.580).

There are exceptions to this four-year statute of limitations for the taxpayer's failure to file any return, for a fraudulent return, and for a 25% underpayment of taxes owed (KRS Sec. 139.620(1)). If the taxpayer fails to file a return or commits fraud with respect to information provided to the Department of Revenue, taxes, penalties, and interest may be assessed at any time.

Notwithstanding the above statute of limitations, the taxpayer and the Kentucky Department of Revenue may mutually agree in writing to extend the statutory period. Such an extension also extends the taxpayer's time period during which to apply for a refund (Revenue Policy 51P420).

¶ 469   Application for Refund

Sales and use tax refunds and credit claims are governed by KRS Sec. 134.580 (KRS Sec. 139.770(1), KRS Sec. 134.580). Generally, a claim for refund or credit must be made by the taxpayer within four years of the date prescribed by law for the filing of a return, including any extensions of time for filing, or the date the money was paid, whichever is later (KRS Sec. 134.580). A claim for refund must be in the form prescribed by the Department of Revenue and must contain such information as the Cabinet may require (KRS Sec. 139.770(2)).

Retailers are not entitled to a refund or credit of the sales or use taxes paid that have been collected from a purchaser, unless the collected amount is refunded to the purchaser by the retailer (KRS Sec. 139.770(3)). Similarly, no purchaser will be entitled to a use tax credit or refund unless he or she reimburses the vendor for any sales tax that the vendor paid with respect to the property (KRS Sec. 139.690).

Class action refunds are prohibited (KRS Sec. 134.580).

See ¶ 465 for discussion of incentive tax credits and incentive refunds.

Source.—Statutory references are to Chapter 2, Title 47, Sub-title II, of the Louisiana Revised Statutes, as amended to date. Details are reported in the CCH LOUISIANA STATE TAX REPORTS starting at ¶ 60-000.

The Louisiana sales tax is a general tax levied on retail sales of tangible personal property or on its lease or rental and on the furnishing of specified services (Sec. 47:302, Reg. 4401, LAC). The tax has been deemed to be an excise tax. The use tax on consumption, use, distribution, or storage of tangible personal property in the state is a complementary tax and does not apply in situations where the sales tax is collected. The sales or use tax is in addition to other taxes.

Digital products: Any consideration paid for electronic receipt or access to data, information, materials, media, or other form of communications that are converted to readable, viewable, or usable form by browsers or software installed on mobile hardware or system hardware located in Louisiana is subject to sales, use, or lease tax (*Revenue Ruling No. 10-001*, Louisiana Department of Revenue, March 23, 2010, CCH LOUISIANA TAX REPORTS, ¶ 202-314).

Computer software: All computer software that is not included as part of a custom program is subject to state and local sales and use taxes (Sec. 47:301(16)(h), (22), and (23), La R.S.; Sec. 47:305.52). Custom computer software is excluded from the definition of "tangible personal property" for state sales and use taxes and local sales and use taxes imposed by jurisdictions that elect to exempt custom software by ordinance.

• **Services subject to tax**

Specified services are subject to the sales tax and only those services specified in the law are taxable (Sec. 47:301(14), Reg. 4301(14), LAC). Thus, the Louisiana sales tax is a limited tax on services in addition to being a general tax on retail sales of tangible property. Taxable services include lodging and associated storage and parking, admissions, printing, cleaning, cold storage, repair, and telecommunications.

Hotel tax: For purposes of the state sales and use tax imposed on hotels that furnish occupancy to transient guests, the definition of a "hotel" has been expanded to mean and include an establishment with any number of (formerly, six or more) sleeping rooms, cottages, or cabins and to include a residential location, including a house, apartment, condominium, camp, cabin, or other building structure used as a residence (Sec. 47:301(6)(a)). However, a hotel does not include any establishment or person leasing apartments or single family dwellings on a month-to-month basis. Also, a dealer shall not include persons leasing apartments or single family dwellings on a month-to-month basis (Sec. 47:301(4)(f)(iii)).

Automobile rentals: Effective April 1, 2016, tax is imposed on gross proceeds derived from the lease or rental of an automobile pursuant to an automobile rental contract, less any sales and use tax included in such contract (Sec. 47:551). A similar tax expired in 2012.

An automobile rental contract is an agreement for the rental of an automobile without a driver and designated to carry less than nine passengers for a period of not more than 29 calendar days. Rental agreements for a period of more than 29 calendar days are not subject to the tax, unless the actual period of the rental agreement is less than 29 days as a result of the exercise of a cancellation clause. (Sec. 47:551(A))

Prepaid calling arrangements: Any sale of a prepaid calling service or prepaid wireless calling service is taxable as a sale of tangible personal property (Sec. 47:301(16)(d)). Prepaid calling services and prepaid wireless calling services are subject to tax if the sale takes place in Louisiana. If a customer physically purchases a prepaid calling service or prepaid wireless calling service at the vendor's place of business, the sale is deemed to take place at the vendor's place of business. If a customer does not physically purchase a service at a vendor's place of business, the sale of a prepaid calling service or prepaid wireless calling service is deemed to take place at the first of the following locations that applies to the sale:

— the customer's shipping address, if the sale involves a shipment;

— the customer's billing address;

— any other address of the customer that is known by the vendor; or

— the address of the vendor or, alternatively in the case of a prepaid wireless calling service, the location associated with the mobile telephone number.

• **Use tax**

The use tax is imposed on the use, consumption, distribution, or the storage for use or consumption of tangible personal property in the state; this tax complements the sales tax and is not levied when the sales tax is imposed (Sec. 47:301(19), Sec. 47:302(A)(2), Reg. 4301(17), LAC). The use tax operates to protect Louisiana merchants from discrimination arising from the state's inability to impose its sales tax on sales made outside the state to Louisiana residents by merchants of other states.

• **Responsibility for tax collection**

Sales taxes are collected by the dealer from the purchaser or consumer, except for motor vehicles, for which the Vehicle Commissioner acts as collecting agent, and leases of property for offshore use (Sec. 47:303, Sec. 47:304). Although "dealer" is defined broadly by statute to include manufacturers, retailers, lessors, and service providers, as well as lessees, consumers, and recipients of taxable services (Sec. 47:301(4), Reg. 4307, LAC), Sec. 47:304 places the primary burden of operation of the sales tax system upon the seller of merchandise, the performer of taxable services, and the renter or lessor of property and requires these persons to collect the tax from the purchaser, user, consumer, or lessee (Reg. 4311, LAC). Lessees of railroad rolling stock used for freight or passenger service are specifically classified as dealers and responsible for collecting and paying the tax (Sec. 47:301(4)(k)). In addition, a person leasing property to a customer for offshore use is not considered a dealer for purposes of collecting the tax due on leases (Sec. 47:301(4)(d)(ii)). Instead, customers leasing such property are required to remit the tax themselves.

• **Nexus**

Louisiana requires any retailer engaging in business in a taxing jurisdiction to collect and remit sales or use tax. "Business" includes any activity engaged in by any person, or caused to be engaged in by him with the object of gain, benefit, or advantage, either direct or indirect. The term "business" shall not be construed to include the occasional and isolated sales by a person who does not hold himself out as engaged in business. (Sec. 47:301(1))

"Engaging in business in a taxing jurisdiction" means and includes any of the following methods of transacting business (Sec. 47:301(4)(h)):

— maintaining directly, indirectly, or through a subsidiary, an office, distribution house, sales house, warehouse, or other place of business or by having an agent, salesman, or solicitor operating within a taxing jurisdiction under the authority of the seller or its subsidiary irrespective of whether such place of business, agent, salesman, or solicitor is located in such taxing jurisdiction permanently or temporarily or whether such seller or subsidiary is qualified to do business in such taxing jurisdiction, or any person who makes deliveries of tangible personal property into a taxing jurisdiction other than by a common or contract carrier.

¶471 Louisiana

The provisions for establishing a person as a dealer for sales and use tax purposes may not be used in determining whether the person is liable for payment of Louisiana income and franchise taxes (Sec. 47:302(V)(3)).

- **Click-through nexus**

The definition of a "dealer" for tax collection purposes is expanded to include any person soliciting business through an independent contractor or other representative pursuant to an agreement with a Louisiana resident or business under which the resident or business, for a commission, referral fee, or other consideration, directly or indirectly, refers potential customers to the seller, whether by link on an Internet website, an in-person oral presentation, telemarketing, or otherwise. If the cumulative gross receipts from sales of tangible personal property to customers in Louisiana who are referred to the person through such an agreement exceeds $50,000 during the preceding 12 months, the presumption regarding the status of that person as a dealer may be rebutted if the person can demonstrate that he cannot reasonably be expected to have gross receipts in excess of $50,000 for the succeeding 12 months. (Sec. 47:302(V)(1)(a))

- **Affiliate nexus**

The law also expands the definition of a "dealer" to include any person who (Sec. 47:302(V)(1)(b)):

(1) Sells the same or a substantially similar line of products as a Louisiana retailer under the same or substantially similar business name, using the same trademarks, service marks, or trade names that are the same or substantially similar to those used by the Louisiana retailer.

(2) Solicits business and develops and maintains a market in Louisiana through an agent, salesman, independent contractor, solicitor, or other representative pursuant to an agreement with a Louisiana resident or business, under which the affiliated agent, for a commission, referral fee, or other consideration, engages in activities in Louisiana that benefits the person's development or maintenance of a market for its goods or services in the state. Such activities of the affiliated agent include referral of potential customers to the person, either directly or indirectly, whether by link on an Internet website or otherwise.

Substantial ownership interest: In addition, a person is presumed to be a dealer if it holds a substantial ownership interest, directly or through a subsidiary, in a retailer maintaining sales locations in Louisiana, or is owned, in whole or in substantial part, by a retailer maintaining sales locations in Louisiana or by a parent or subsidiary thereof. "Substantial ownership interest" means affiliated persons with respect to each other where one of such persons has an ownership interest of more than five percent, whether direct or indirect, in the other, or where an ownership interest of more than five percent, whether direct or indirect, is held in each of such persons by another person or by a group of other persons which are affiliated persons with respect to each other. (Sec. 47:302(V)(4)(c))

Federal preemption: If the U.S. Congress enacts legislation authorizing states to require a remote seller to collect sales and use taxes on taxable transactions, the federal law will preempt the provisions of the Louisiana law. (Sec. 2, Act 22 (H.B. 30), Laws 2016, First Extraordinary Session)

- **Remote retailer notices**

Effective July 1, 2017, remote retailers must begin notifying Louisiana purchasers, at the time of sale, that (Sec. 47:309.1):

(1) a purchase is subject to Louisiana use tax unless it is specifically exempt and

(2) there is no specific exemption for purchases made over the Internet, by catalog, or by other remote means.

The sale notice must also include a statement that Louisiana law requires that use tax liability be paid annually on the individual income tax return or through other means as may be required by administrative rule. (Sec. 47:309.1(C)(1))

A "remote retailer" is a retailer that purposefully avails itself of the benefits of an economic market in Louisiana or who has any other minimum contacts with the state and who (Sec. 47:309.1(B)(2)):

(1) is not required by law to register as a dealer or to collect Louisiana sales or use tax;

(2) makes retail sales of tangible personal property or taxable services in Louisiana and the cumulative annual gross receipts of the retailer and its affiliates from those Louisiana sales exceed $50,000 per calendar year; and

(3) does not collect and remit Louisiana sales and use tax on retail sales inLouisiana.

By January 31st of each year, a remote retailer must send to each Louisiana purchaser a notice containing the total amount paid by the purchaser to the retailer for property or taxable services in the preceding calendar year. The annual notice must list the dates and amounts of purchases if available, state whether the property or service is exempt from tax if known by the retailer, disclose the name of the retailer, and state that Louisiana use tax may be due. (Sec. 47:309.1(B)(2))

The notification must be sent by first class mail, certified mail, or electronically at the purchaser's choice and shall not be included with any other shipment or mailing from the retailer. Further, the envelope containing the annual notice shall include the words "IMPORTANT TAX DOCUMENT ENCLOSED". (Sec. 47:309.1(C)(2))

Also, by March 1st of each year, a remote retailer must file with the Department of Revenue an annual statement for each Louisiana purchaser that includes the total amount paid by the purchaser to that retailer for property or taxable services in the preceding calendar year. The statement must not contain detail as to the specific property or services purchased. The secretary may require the electronic filing of statements by a remote retailer who had sales in Louisiana in excess of $100,000 in the preceding calendar year. (Sec. 47:309.1(D))

- **Streamlined Act status**

Louisiana is an Advisor state to the Streamlined Sales Tax Project (SSTP). Louisiana has enacted the Uniform (Simplified) Sales and Use Tax Act and has enacted legislation authorizing it to enter into the Agreement (Sec. 47:335.2), but has not yet enacted all of the changes to its laws necessary to comply with the Agreement's requirements. However, it will continue to have input through its representation on the State and Local Advisory Council, which advises the Board on matters pertaining to the administration of the Agreement. For additional information, see ¶ 477.

¶ 472   **Tax Base**

The tax base differs depending upon whether the tax imposed is that on sales, on use, or on rental activities (Sec. 47:302). "Gross sales" is the basis for sales tax, whereas "cost price" is used for use tax and "gross proceeds" is used for rental transactions.

- **Basis definitions**

Gross sales: "Gross sales," the basis of the sales tax, is the sum total of all retail sales with only these specified deductions: trade-ins and returns (Sec. 47:301(5), Reg. 4301(5), LAC).

Cost price: "Cost price," the basis of the use tax, is the lower of cost or market value (Sec. 47:301(3), Reg. 4301(3), LAC). The only deduction permitted is the cost of installation, if separately stated. The statute has been held unconstitutional in including out of state labor and transportation charges in the basis of tax.

Gross proceeds: "Gross proceeds," the basis of the tax on rental transactions, are the amounts received by a rental business or paid by a renter for the use of tangible personal property (Sec. 47:302(B)). In the case of a monthly or longer term lease, the tax is imposed on the monthly payments or other schedule of payments (Reg. 4303, LAC).

¶ 473   List of Exemptions, Exceptions, and Exclusions

CAUTION: Exemptions temporarily limited: Louisiana has enacted an exclusive list of over 30 transactions that will be the only allowable exemptions and exclusions from Louisiana state sales and use tax for the period April 1, 2016, through July 1, 2018 (Act 25 (H.B. 61), Laws 2016, First Extraordinary Session). For additional information, see *Publications R-1002 and R-1002A,* Louisiana Department of Revenue, March 29, 2016, available on the Department of Revenue's website at **http://www.rev.state.la.us/NewsAndPublications/Publications**. This list of exemptions supersedes and controls over any conflicting provision during this period (Sec. 47:302[X]):

(1) Food for home consumption, as defined in Sec. 47:305(D)(1)(n) through (r) on January 1, 2003, as provided in Article VII, Section 2.2 of the Constitution of Louisiana;

(2) Natural gas, as provided in Article VII, Section 2.2 of the Constitution of Louisiana;

(3) Electricity, as provided in Article VII, Section 2.2 of the Constitution of Louisiana;

(4) Water, as provided in Article VII, Section 2.2 of the Constitution of Louisiana;

(5) Prescription drugs, as provided in Article VII, Section 2.2 of the Constitution of Louisiana;

(6) Gasoline and other motor fuels subject to the state excise tax on fuel;

(7) Sales to the United States government and its agencies, as provided in R.S. 47:301(10)(g);

(8) Sales of raw agricultural products, as provided in Sec. 47:301(10)(e) and 305(A)(3);

(9) Lease or rentals of railroad rolling stock as provided in Sec. 47:301(4)(k), piggyback trailers as provided in Sec. 47:305.45, and certain trucks and trailers in interstate commerce as provided in Sec. 47:305.50(A) and (B);

(10) Tangible personal property for resale as provided in Sec. 47:301(10)(a)(i);

(11) Feed and feed additives for animals held for business purposes as provided in Sec. 47:305(A)(4);

(12) Farm products produced and used by farmers as provided in Sec. 47:305(B);

(13) Sales of fertilizers and containers to farmers as provided in Sec. 47:305(D)(1)(f);

(14) Sales of seeds for planting crops as provided in Sec. 47:305.3;

(15) Sales of pesticides for agricultural purposes as provided in Sec. 47:305.8;

(16) Purchases, use, and lease of manufacturing machinery and equipment as provided in Sec. 47:301(3)(i)(i), (13)(k) and (28)(a);

(17) Sales of materials for further processing as provided in Sec. 47:301(10)(c)(i)(aa);

(18) Sale of 50-ton vessels and new component parts and sales of certain materials and services to vessels operating in interstate commerce as provided in Sec. 47:305.1 (A) and (B);

(19) Louisiana Tax Free Shopping Program for international visitors as provided in Sec. 51:1301;

(20) Sales of farm equipment used in poultry production as provided in Sec. 47:301(13)(c);

(21) Sales of pharmaceuticals administered to livestock for agricultural purposes as provided in Sec. 47:301(16)(f);

(22) Sales of livestock, poultry and other farm products and sales at public livestock auctions as provided in Sec. 47:305(A)(1) and (2);

(23) Materials used in the production of crawfish and catfish as provided in Sec. 47:305(A)(5) and (6);

(24) First $50,000 of farm equipment purchases as provided in Sec. 47:305.25;

(25) Fuel used on the farm as provided in Sec. 47:305.37;

(26) Taxation of electrical cooperatives as provided in Sec. 12:425;

(27) Overhaul of naval vessels as provided in Sec. 47:301(7)(c) and (14)(h);

(28) Purchases by state and local governments as provided in Sec. 47:301(8)(c);

(29) Transactions in interstate commerce and tangible personal property imported into this state, or produced or manufactured in this state, for export as provided in Sec. 47:305(E);

(30) Parish councils on aging in Sec. 47:305.66;

(31) Articles traded in on purchases of tangible personal property as provided in Sec. 47:301(13)(a);

(32) A factory built home as provided in Sec. 47:301(16)(g).

A release provides three separate lists of transactions thatare exempt and excluded from the Louisiana state sales taxes imposed by Sec. 47:301 (2%), Sec. 47:321 (1%), and Sec. 47:331 (0.97%), beginning April 1, 2016 (*Revenue Information Bulletin No. 16-012,* Louisiana Department of Revenue, March 23, 2016, CCH LOUISIANA TAX REPORTS, ¶ 202-697).

Another release lists 65 exemptions and exclusions that continue to be in effect for purposes of the additional 1% state sales tax. The sales tax exclusion for manufacturing machinery and equipment was not in effect from April 1, 2016, through June 30, 2016. (*Revenue Information Bulletin 16-013,* Louisiana Department of Revenue, March 24, 2016)

Also, under previous legislation, the Louisiana Legislature suspended all exemptions for business utilities from the sales tax levied on sales of steam, water, electric power or energy, and natural gas (including propane), effective from July 1, 2015, through the 60th day after final adjournment of the 2016 Regular Session of the Legislature. (H.C.R. 8, Laws 2015; *Revenue Information Bulletin No. 15-016,* Louisiana Department of Revenue, June 29, 2015, CCH LOUISIANA TAX REPORTS, ¶ 202-636)

A lawsuit has been filed alleging that HCR No. 8 was not passed in conformity with constitutional procedural requirements (*Louisiana Chemical Association v. State of Louisiana et al.,* Louisiana District Court, 19th Judicial District, Dkt. No. 640501, Section 24). Pending the outcome of the lawsuit, taxpayers should pay sales taxes as they become due. (*Statement of Acquiescence No. 15-001,* Louisiana Department of Revenue, August 13, 2015, CCH LOUISIANA TAX REPORTS, ¶ 202-655)

¶473   **Louisiana**

Except as otherwise indicated above, the statutory exemptions, exceptions, and exclusions listed below apply to both the sales and use taxes; those applicable only to the use tax or only to the lease tax are listed separately. Some items are not exempt at the time of sale, but may qualify for a refund (see ¶ 484).

Contracts of exemption: To encourage the establishment of new, and the retention of current, manufacturing entities, headquarters, or warehousing or distribution centers in Louisiana, state corporation franchise, corporation income, sales and use, and any other taxes imposed by the state on such businesses may be reduced, after all other tax incentives have been applied, to the levels imposed by competing states. The reduction is implemented through a contract of exemption from taxation between the state Board of Commerce and Industry and the taxpaying establishment or headquarters. Property taxes and local sales and use taxes may not be affected by these exemption contracts (Secs. 47:3201—47:3204).

For additional incentives based on contract exemptions, see ¶ 484.

Foreign travellers: Through July 1, 2017, individuals traveling in the United States for a three-month period or less with a foreign passport and/or a current U.S. visitor's visa and an international transportation ticket may apply for a refund of sales tax paid on qualifying items purchased from retailers participating in the Louisiana Tax Free Shopping (LTFS) Program. For additional information, see ¶ 484.

Hurricane victims: Purchases made with a voucher from the American Red Cross are not subject to Louisiana state or local sales tax. Any amount of a purchase that exceeds the value of the voucher, however, is subject to sales tax. The Red Cross is considered to be a federal agency and purchases by government agencies of the United States, Louisiana, or political subdivisions of Louisiana are exempt from state and local sales tax. Examples of exempt agencies include the Federal Emergency Management Agency (FEMA), any branch of the U.S. military, and state and local police and emergency agencies (*Release* and *Telephone Interview,* Louisiana Department of Revenue, September 9, 2005).

Annual consumer sales tax holidays: Sales tax is inapplicable to the first $2,500 of the sales or cost price of any consumer purchases of tangible personal property that occur on the first consecutive Friday and Saturday of August each year. "Consumer purchases" are defined as purchases of items of tangible personal property other than vehicles subject to license and title and do not include the purchase of meals furnished for consumption on the premises where purchased, including "to-go" orders. The holiday is applicable to the sales tax levied by the state and its political subdivisions whose boundaries are coterminous with those of the state (Sec. 47:305.54).

Purchases of most items of tangible personal property during the 2016 and 2017 general sales tax holiday weekends are subject to 3% state sales tax. Beginning July 1, 2018, eligible purchases will again be exempted fully from the state sales tax.

Annual tax holiday for hurricane preparedness: Sales and use taxes are inapplicable to the first $1,500 of the sales price of purchases of hurricane-preparedness items or supplies that occur during the last weekend in May of each year beginning at 12:01 a.m. on Saturday and ending at 11:59 p.m. on Sunday. "Hurricane-preparedness items or supplies" include: portable self-powered light sources; portable self-powered radios, two-way radios or weatherband radios; tarpaulins or other flexible waterproof sheeting; ground anchor systems or tie-down kits; gas or diesel fuel tanks; packages of AAA-cell, AA-cell, C-cell, D-cell, 6-volt or 9-volt batteries excluding automobile and boat batteries; cell phone batteries and chargers, non-electric food storage coolers; portable generators used to provide light or communications or preserve food in the event of a power outage; storm shutter devices; carbon monoxide detectors; and blue ice products. The holiday is inapplicable to hurricane-preparedness items or supplies sold at any airport, public lodging establishment or hotel, convenience store or entertainment complex (Sec. 47:305.58.).

The annual tax holiday for hurricane preparedness was cancelled in 2016. Purchases of the specified items during the 2017 and 2018 hurricane preparedness sales tax holiday are subject to 3% state sales tax. Beginning July 1, 2018, specified hurricane preparedness items will again be exempted fully from the state sales tax.

Annual tax holiday for sales of firearms, ammunition, and hunting supplies: Sales and use taxes levied by the state and its political subdivisions are inapplicable to the sales price or cost price of any consumer purchases of firearms, ammunition, and hunting supplies that occur each calendar year on the first consecutive Friday through Sunday of September. "Hunting supplies" are defined as any tangible personal property for the use of hunting, including but not limited to archery, off-road vehicles, vessels such as ATVs, airboats, and pirogues, accessories, animal feed, apparel, shoes, bags, float tubes, binoculars, tools, firearm and archery cases, firearm and archery accessories, range finders, knives, decoys, treestands, blinds, chairs, optics, hearing protection and enhancements, holsters, belts, slings, and miscellaneous gear. "Firearms" are defined as shotguns, rifles, pistols, revolvers, or other handguns. (Sec. 47:305.62)

During the first weekend in September in 2016 and 2017, purchases of eligible items are subject to 3% state sales tax. Beginning July 1, 2018, eligible purchases will again be exempted fully from the state sales tax.

Renewal of exemption certificates: A Louisiana sales tax exemption certificate granted to a holder of a direct payment number, a dealer for sales of property or services for resale, or a manufacturer for purchases of manufacturing machinery and equipment will be renewed by the Department of Revenue without the taxpayer having to reapply for the certificate unless the department determines that the taxpayer no longer qualifies for the exemption. (Sec. 47:13)

Official exemption tables: The Louisiana Department of Revenue publishes a sales tax exemption table showing the exemption/exclusion or tax rate for various transactions from 2003 to the present. The table includes legislative changes enacted through the 2014 Regular Session. (*Publication R-1002, Table of Sales Tax Rates for Exemptions,* Louisiana Department of Revenue, August 2015, available on the DOR's website at **http://www.rev.state.la.us/NewsAndPublications/Publications**).

The Department of Revenue also has issued a 26-page chart showing the state sales tax rate or exemption status for over 200 types of transactions for three time periods: (1) April 1, 2016, to June 30, 2016, (2) July 1, 2016, to June 30, 2018, and (3) July 1, 2018, to March 31, 2019. See *Publication R-1002A,* Louisiana Department of Revenue, March 24, 2016, available on the Department of Revenue's website at **http://revenue.louisiana.gov/Publications/R%201002A.pdf**.

- **Sales and use tax exemptions, exceptions, and exclusions**

Admissions, nonprofit events	Sec. 47:305.13, Sec. 47:305.14, *Revenue Information Bulletin 16-020,* April 7, 2016
Advertising services	Sec. 47:302(D)
Agricultural products	Sec. 47:305(A)(1) Sec. 47:305.[62]
Aircraft, antique	Sec. 47:6001(A), Sec. 47:6001(B)
Aircraft, exported	Sec. 47:301(10)(m)
Aircraft used as demonstrators	Sec. 47:305(D)(1)(i)
Airlines, commuter	Sec. 47:301(7)(d), Sec. 47:301(10)(k)

¶473 Louisiana

Firefighting equipment	Sec. 47:301(10)(o)
First use outside state, sales	Sec. 47:305.10
Fishermen, commercial	Sec. 47:305.20, Sec. 47:306(B)(1)(d)(ii) Sec. 47:305.20(G) Sec. 47:337.10(N)
Food banks	Sec. 47:301(10)(j)
Food for home preparation	Art. VII, Sec. 2.2, La Const.; Reg. 4401(F)(H)
Food for school meals	Sec. 47:301(10)(dd)
Food stamp purchases	Sec. 47:305.46
Foreign shoppers (refund) (expires 7/1/17)	Sec. 51:1302
Fruits	Sec. 47:305(D)(1)(n)— Sec. 47:305(D)(1)(r)
Fuel, farm	Sec. 47:305.37
Fuel or gas, including but not limited to butane and propanel	Sec. 47:301(10(x))
Fuel, utilities	Sec. 47:305.39
Funeral directing services	Sec. 47:301(10(s))
Gasoline, gasohol	Sec. 47:305(D)(1)(a) Sec. 47:711
Girls State of Louisiana	Sec. 47:301(7)(g), Sec. 47:301(10)(r), Sec. 47:301(18)(f)
Glasses, prescription	Sec. 47:305(D)(1)(k)
Government, federal, purchases by	Sec. 47:301(10)(g)
Government, state and local, purchases by	Sec. 47:301(8)(c)
Hospitals, free	Sec. 47:301(7)(e), Sec. 47:301(10)(p), Sec. 47:301(18)(c), Sec. 47:301(21)
Hospitals, meals	Sec. 47:305(D)(2)
Housing (temporary) for homeless persons	Sec. 47:301(6)(c)
Human tissue	Sec. 33:2717, Sec. 47:301(10)(d)
Immovable property	Sec. 47:301(16)(q)
Industrial exemptions	Sec. 47:3201— Sec. 47:3204
Installation charges	Sec. 47:301(13)(a)
Insulin	Sec. 47:305.2
Interstate commerce, repairs to property	Sec. 47:301(14)(g)
Interstate commerce, transactions (see also *Revenue Information Bulletin No. 16-034,* Louisiana Department of Revenue, July 14, 2016, CCH Louisiana Tax Reports, ¶ 202-734)	Sec. 47:305(E)
Interstate commerce, certain vehicles used in	Sec. 47:305.50
Interstate telecommunications	Sec. 47:301(14)(i)(iii)(cc)
Isolated sales	Sec. 47:301(10)(c)

¶473   Louisiana

Pelletized paper waste	Sec. 47:301(10)(n)
Performing arts presentations	Sec. 47:305.42
Pesticides, agricultural	Sec. 47:305.8
Pollution control and cleanup equipment	Sec. 47:301(10)(*l*)
Poultry	Sec. 47:305(A)(1)
Printing, raw materials	Sec. 47:305.44
Professional services and work products	Sec. 47:301(14), Sec. 47:301(16)(d)
Property rented or leased to accredited colleges	Sec. 47:301(8)(b)
Prosthetic devices	Sec. 47:305(D)(1)(k)
Public trusts, bulk purchase of materials	Sec. 38:2212.3
Racehorses, claim races	Sec. 47:305(A)(2)
Radiation therapy treatment centers	Sec. 47:305[62]
Railroads, rolling stock, and container cars	Sec. 47:305.45, Sec. 47:305.50
Raw agricultural commodities	Sec. 47:301(10)(e), Sec. 47:305(A)(3)
Raw materials for further processing	Sec. 47:301(10)(c)
Religious camps or retreats	Sec. 47:301(6)(b)
Religious literature	Sec. 47:301(8)(d)
Religious organization newspapers	Sec. 47:305.14
Renal dialysis equipment	Sec. 47:305(G)
Resale sales	Sec. 47:301(10)
Residential utilities	Art. VII, Sec. 2.2, La Const.
Restorative materials, dental	Sec. 47:305(D)(1)(t)
Research and development parks (university)	Sec. 47:3389
Retirement centers, nonprofit	Sec. 47:305.33
Rooming houses, meals	Sec. 47:305(D)(2)
Services, as specified	Sec. 47:301(14)
School athletic events, admissions	Sec. 47:301(14)(b)
School buses	Sec. 47:301(10)(i)
Schools, meals	Sec. 47:305(D)(2)
Schools, parochial and private	Sec. 47:301(10)(q)
Seed, crops	Sec. 47:305.3
Sheltered workshops, sales	Sec. 47:305.38
Ships and ships' supplies (built in Louisiana)	Sec. 47:305.1(A)
Ships, barges in interstate commerce, materials purchased	Sec. 47:305.1(B)
Soft drinks	Sec. 47:305(D)(1)(n)— Sec. 47:305(D)(1)(r)
Special fuel	Sec. 47:711
Steam	Sec. 47:305(D)(1)(b)
Steelworks, utilities used in	Sec. 47:305.51
Storm shutter devices	Sec. 47:301(10)(ee) and (18)(o)

Superdome admissions	Sec. 39:467
Telecommunications services	Sec. 47:321(C), *Revenue Information Bulletin 16-022,* April 7, 2016
Telephone directories	Sec. 47:301(8)(t)
Thrift shops located on military installations	Sec. 47:305.14(A)(4)
Toledo Bend dam project	Sec. 47:305.5
Trade-ins	Sec. 47:301(13), Sec. 47:305(C)(2)
U.S. Navy, contract services	Sec. 47:301(7)(c), Sec. 47:301(14)(h)
U.S. Navy, equipment leased	Sec. 47:301(7)(c)
Vegetables	Sec. 47:305(D)(1)(n)— Sec. 47:305(D)(1)(r)
Vehicles (off-road) purchased by out-of-state buyers	Sec. 47:305.56
Vehicles purchased for leasing	Sec. 47:305.36
Vehicles used in interstate commerce	Sec. 47:305.50
Vending machine sales	Sec. 47:301(10)(b)
Water, as utility	Sec. 47:305(D)(1)(c)
Watercraft (new) used as demonstrators	Sec. 47:305(D)(1)(i), (H) Sec. 47:321(H)
Waterfowl, nonprofit organization sales	Sec. 47:305.43
Wheelchairs and wheelchair lifts	Sec. 47:305(D)(1)(k)
Wireless telephones sold with service	Sec. 47:301(10)(v)
Youth organizations, food sales	Sec. 47:301(10)(h)

• Exemptions, exceptions, and exclusions applicable only to the use tax

Agricultural products consumed by farmers and their families	Sec. 47:305(B)
Board roads providing access to oil field operators	Sec. 47:301(3)(c)
Cars (certain) of active duty military personnel	Sec. 47:305.48
Items on which Louisiana sales tax has been collected	Sec. 47:301(19), Sec. 47:302(A)(2)

• Exemptions, exceptions, and exclusions applicable only to the lease tax

Automobile rentals for specified purposes	Sec. 47:551(A)
Copyrighted broadcast material	Sec. 47:305(F)
Equipment, for re-rental, used for oil, gas, sulphur, or mineral wells .	Sec. 47:301(7)(b)
Film rental by theaters	Sec. 47:305.9
Freight cars, certain per-diem charges	Sec. 47:305.45
Helicopters used for mineral production	Sec. 47:302.1
Motor vehicles leased or rented to vehicle dealers or manufacturers and provided for use by their customers at no charge	Sec. 47:301(7)(h)
Property used in performance of contract with U.S. Navy	Sec. 47:301(7)(c)
Renal dialysis equipment	Sec. 47:305(G)
Private or parochial schools	Sec. 47:301(7)(f)

¶473 **Louisiana**

Vehicle rentals of less than 30 days . . . . Sec. 47:551(C)

Vessels leased for offshore mineral production . . . . Sec. 47:305.19

• Partial sales tax exemptions

Effective July 1, 2016, the following transactions are exempt from the sales taxes imposed by Sec. 47:302 (2% rate) and Sec. 321.1 (new additional 1% rate) (Sec. 47:302(AA); Sec. 47:321.1(F)(66)):

(1) Sales of room rentals by a camp or retreat facility owned by a nonprofit organization;

(2) Sales of room rentals by a homeless shelter;

(3) Sales, leases, and rentals of tangible personal property and sales of services necessary to operate free hospitals;

(4) Sales, leases, or rentals of tangible personal property to Boys State of Louisiana, Inc. and Girls State of Louisiana, Inc.;

(5) Sales by nonprofit entities that sell donated goods;

(6) Isolated or occasional sales of tangible personal property by a person not engaged in such business;

(7) Sales of human tissue transplants;

(8) Sales of food items by a youth-serving organization chartered by the U.S. Congress;

(9) Sales and donations of tangible personal property by food banks;

(10) Sales or purchases of fire-fighting equipment by volunteer fire departments;

(11) Sales to, and leases, rentals, and use of educational materials and equipment used for classroom instruction by parochial and private elementary and secondary schools that comply with the court order from the *Dodd Brumfield* decision and IRC Sec. 501(c)(3);

(12) Sales by parochial and private elementary and secondary schools that comply with the court order from the *Dodd Brumfield* decision and IRC Sec. 501(c)(3);

(13) Certain admissions to athletic and entertainment events held for or by an elementary or secondary school and membership fees or dues of nonprofit, civic associations;

(14) Sales or use of materials used directly in the collection of blood;

(15) Sales or use of apheresis kits and leukoreduction filters;

(16) Sales or use of orthotic devices, prosthetic devices, hearing aids, eyeglasses, contact lenses, and wheelchairs prescribed by physicians, optometrists, or licensed chiropractors used exclusively by the patient for personal use;

(17) Sales or use of ostomy, colostomy, and ileostomy devices and equipment;

(18) Sales or use of adaptive driving equipment and motor vehicle modifications prescribed for personal use;

(19) Sales of meals by educational institutions, medical facilities, mental institutions, and occasional meals furnished by educational, religious, or medical organizations;

(20) Purchase or rental of kidney dialysis machines, parts, materials, and supplies for home use under a physician's prescription;

(21) Sales of admissions to entertainment events by Little Theater organizations;

(22) Sales of admissions to musical performances sponsored by nonprofit organizations;

(23) Sales of admissions to entertainment events sponsored by domestic non-profit charitable, religious, and educational organizations;

(24) Sales of admissions, parking fees, and sales of tangible personal property at events sponsored by domestic, civic, educational, historical, charitable, fraternal, or religious nonprofit organizations;

(25) Sales of admissions and parking fees at fairs and festivals sponsored by nonprofit organizations;

(26) Purchases of fishing vessels, supplies, fuels, lubricants, and repairs for the vessels of licensed commercial fishermen;

(27) Sales of butane, propane, or other liquified petroleum gases for private, residential consumption;

(28) Sales and purchases by certain organizations that provide training for blind persons.

Note: The following transactions were already exempt from the additional 1% sales tax imposed by Sec. 321.1: (3), (5), (6), (7), (8), (9), (14), and (15).

¶ 474   Rate of Tax

From April 1, 2016, through June 30, 2018, the total Louisiana state sales and use tax rate is 5%, which consists of a permanent 4% rate and a temporary 1% additional tax (Sec. 47:321). The 4% rate is comprised of:

(1) a base rate of 2% (Sec. 47:302);

(2) an additional rate of 0.97% (Sec. 47:331(c));

(3) a 0.03% rate imposed by the Louisiana Tourism Promotion District (Sec. 51:1286); and

(4) a 1% rate imposed by the Louisiana Recovery District (Sec. 39:2006) or the tax that replaced the recovery district tax upon its expiration.

The Louisiana Tourism Promotion District and the Louisiana Recovery District are special taxing districts whose boundaries are coterminous with the state (Sec. 39:2002, Sec. 51:1282). Effective one day after its expiration (October 1, 1996), the 1% tax imposed by the Louisiana Recovery District was replaced by a new additional 1% state sales and use tax. This additional 1% tax does not apply to the furnishing of telecommunications services for compensation (Sec. 47:321).

Temporary additional tax: Another additional state sales and use tax rate of 1% is imposed on sales and leases of tangible personal property and sales of certain services for the period beginning April 1, 2016, through June 30, 2018 (27 months) (Sec. 321.1(A)). However, the temporary additional tax expires on July 1, 2016, for manufacturing equipment and machinery. Construction contracts entered into and reduced to writing prior to or within 90 days of the April 1, 2016, effective date of the 1% Louisiana state sales and use tax rate increase are not subject to the 1% additional levy; see *Revenue Information Bulletin No. 16-016,* Louisiana Department of Revenue, April 19, 2016, CCH Louisiana Tax Reports, ¶ 202-716.

There are 65 items that are exempt or excluded from this temporary additional tax, including food for home consumption, prescription drugs, gasoline and other motor fuels, and materials for further processing (Sec. 321.1(F)). The transactions that are exempt from the 1% additional tax do not completely match the transactions that are exempt from the current 4% tax. For additional information, see *Publication R-1002A,* Louisiana Department of Revenue, March 29, 2016, available on the Department of Revenue's website at **http://revenue.louisiana.gov/Publications/ R-1002A%203-29-16.pdf**.

Automobile rentals: Effective April 1, 2016, a 3% tax (2.5% state, 0.5% local) is imposed on gross proceeds derived from the lease or rental of an automobile pursuant to an automobile rental contract, less any sales and use tax included in the contract (Sec. 47:551).

Telecommunications: Interstate telecommunications services that either originate or terminate in Louisiana and that are charged to a Louisiana service address are subject to a "prepaid 911 charge" (Sec. 47:301(14)(i)). The rate is 4%, effective October 1, 2016 (previously, 2%) (Sec. 47:302, Sec. 47:331(c)). See ¶ 475 for sourcing of telecommunications charges. See also *Revenue Information Bulletin 16-022,* Louisiana Department of Revenue, April 7, 2016.

Machinery and equipment: The purchase, lease, or rental of certain manufacturing, agriculture, and logging machinery and equipment is 100% excluded from Louisiana sales and use tax for all periods beginning on or after July 1, 2009 (Sec. 47:301(3)(i), (13)(k) and (28)). For guidance on the scope of the exclusion, see *Revenue Information Bulletin No. 09-016,* Louisiana Department of Revenue, June 23, 2009, CCH LOUISIANA TAX REPORTS, ¶ 202-230.

• Suspension of exemptions

Aside from the temporary limitation on exemptions discussed at ¶ 473, Louisiana suspended numerous statutory exemptions as a temporary fundraising measure from July 1, 2002, through June 30, 2009; the suspension of the exemptions against the 1% component of the tax has been extended permanently (Secs. 47:302(Q), 47:321(H), and 47:331(O)(1)).

The following exemptions are subject to the 1% component of the tax (*Revenue Information Bulletin No. 09-014,* Louisiana Department of Revenue, June 23, 2009, CCH LOUISIANA TAX REOPRTS, ¶ 202-228):

— purchases by pari-mutuel racetracks (Sec. 4:168);

— purchases by off-track betting facilities (Sec. 4:227);

— purchases by nonprofit electrical cooperatives (Sec. 12:425);

— purchases by the Louisiana Insurance Guaranty Association (Sec. 22:1389);

— sales of feed and feed additives for animals used for business purposes (Sec. 47:305(A)(4),);

— sales of materials, supplies, equipment, fuel, and bait used in the production and harvesting of crawfish (Sec. 47:305(A)(5));

— sales of materials, supplies, equipment, fuel, and bait and related items other than vessels used in the production and harvesting of catfish (Sec. 47:305(A)(6));

— energy sources used to fuel the generation of electric power for resale or used by an industrial manufacturing plant for self-consumption or cogeneration (Sec. 47:305(D)(1));

— all energy sources when used for boiler fuel except refinery gas (Sec. 47:305(D)(1));

— new automobiles, trucks, and aircraft removed from inventory for use as demonstrators (Sec. 47:305(D)(1));

— sales of adaptive driving equipment and motor vehicle modifications that are prescribed by physicians, licensed chiropractors, or driver rehabilitation specialists licensed by the state (Sec. 47:305(D)(1));

— sales of meals to the staff and students of educational institutions, to the staff and patients of hospitals, to the staff, inmates, and patients of mental institutions, and to boarders of rooming houses and occasional meals furnished by educational, religious, or medical organizations in facilities not open to outsiders or the general public (Sec. 47:305(D)(2));

— amounts paid by radio and television broadcasters for the rights to broadcast film, video, and tape (Sec. 47:305(F));

— sales of admission tickets by Little Theater organizations (Sec. 47:305.6);

— sales of tickets to musical performances of nonprofit musical organizations (Sec. 47:305.7);

— rentals of motion picture films to commercial theaters (Sec. 47:305.9);

— sales of admissions to entertainment events sponsored by domestic nonprofit charitable, religious, and educational organizations (Sec. 47:305.13);

— sales of outside gate admissions to grounds and parking fees at fairs and festivals sponsored by recognized nonprofit organizations chartered under the state of Louisiana (Sec. 47:305.18);

— leases of vessels for use offshore for the production of oil, gas, sulphur, and other minerals or for the providing of services to those engaged in such production (Sec. 47:305.19);

— the first $50,000 of the sales price of farm implements used for agricultural purposes in the production of food and fiber (other than rubber tired farm tractors, cane harvesters, cane loaders, cotton pickers, combines, haybalers, and attachments and to those implements, including clippers, cultivators, discs, plows, spreaders, and sprayers; such equipment continues to be fully exempt from the sales tax on the first $50,000 of their sales prices) (the 1% tax is due on the first $50,000 of the sales prices of farm implements other than those listed because of the continued partial suspension of the exemption provided by Sec. 47:305.25(A)(5)) (Sec. 47:305.25(A)(4));

— sales of on-the-farm facilities used to dry or store grain or any materials sued to construct such on the farm facilities (Sec. 47:305.25(A)(5));

— vehicles furnished by a dealer in new vehicles when withdrawn from inventory and furnished to a secondary school, college, or public school board on a free loan basis for exclusive use in a driver education program accredited by the Louisiana Department of Education (Sec. 47:305.26);

— purchases of materials for the construction and operation of nonprofit retirement centers (Sec. 47:305.33);

— leases of motor vehicles, trailers, or semi-trailers, as defined, that will be stored, used, or consumed in Louisiana exclusively for lease or rental (Sec. 47:305.36);

— purchases, sales, and rentals of tangible personal property by Ducks Unlimited and Bass Life Associates (Sec. 47:305.41);

— tickets to dance, drama, or performing arts performance sponsored by domestic nonprofit organizations (Sec. 47:305.42);

— purchases and sales made by nonprofit organizations dedicated exclusively to the conservation of migratory North American waterfowl and wetland habitat of the conservation of fish (Sec. 47:305.43(A));

— purchases of certain materials for use in commercial printing processes (Sec. 47:305.44);

— the sale or use of pharmaceutical samples approved by the U.S. Food and Drug Administration that are manufactured in the state or imported into the state for distribution without charge to physicians, dentists, clinics, or hospitals (Sec. 47:305.47);

— catalogs distributed in the state free or charge (Sec. 47:305.49);

¶474 Louisiana

— materials used in the restoration, renovation, or rehabilitation of existing structures or in new housing construction in certain designated areas (Sec. 47:315.2; Sec. 40:582.1—Sec. 40:582.7; Sec. 47:1515; Sec. 33:2718.3); and

— antique airplanes held by private collectors and not being used for commercial purposes (Sec. 47:6001).

¶ 475   Local Taxes

Many cities, towns, and parishes in Louisiana levy a sales and use tax in addition to the 4% tax levied by the state. The taxes are administered by the respective cities and parishes. The state sales tax on motor vehicles is collected by the Department of Revenue and Taxation, and by agreement, the Department also collects the city and parish tax on motor vehicles, with the exception of Tallulah, which specifically exempts motor vehicles from its tax.

With voter approval, the New Orleans Redevelopment Authority is authorized to levy sales and use taxes at a rate not to exceed 1% in the aggregate (as well as ad valorem property taxes) (Sec. 33:4720.56).

Sourcing of telecommunications charges: Louisiana has conformed to the federal Mobile Telecommunications Sourcing Act (Act), P.L. 106-252. All charges for mobile telecommunications services are considered to be provided by the customer's home service provider and sourced to the customer's place of primary use (Sec. 47:301(14)). All such charges are subject to sales tax based on the customer's place of primary use.

The service provider will be held harmless for an error in assigning wireless services to a jurisdiction if it utilizes an electronic database provided by the state or a designated entity, or, if the state has not provided or designated a database, if it utilizes a database that makes assignments based on a nine-digit zip code.

Local exemption for resale of services: A Louisiana local sales and use tax exemption is applicable to services for resale. A local collector is required to accept a resale certificate issued by the Louisiana Department of Revenue that exempts the service for resale from local sales and use taxation provided the taxpayer includes the parish of its principal place of business and local sales tax account number on the state certificate. However, in the case of an intra-parish transaction from dealer to dealer, the local tax collector may require that the local exemption certificate be used in lieu of the state certificate. The department is required to accommodate the inclusion of such information on its resale certificate for such purposes. (Sec. 47:301(10)(a)(ii), La R.S.)

• **Uniform Local Sales Tax Code**

The Uniform Local Sales Tax Code (UTC) was enacted effective July 1, 2003, to consolidate various provisions applicable to Louisiana local sales and use taxes and to require local sales taxes to be administered and collected in conformity with its provisions (Sec. 47:337.1 *et seq.*). The UTC applies in the assessment, collection, administration, and enforcement of the sales and use tax of any local taxing authority. Other provisions of law or local ordinance control, however, with respect to local sales and use tax rates, effective dates, purposes, and certain exclusions and exemptions.

The UTC provides for the creation and implementation of a uniform electronic local return and remittance system and creates the Uniform Electronic Local Return and Remittance Advisory Committee. It is the duty of the Louisiana Department of Revenue, with the advice of the Advisory Committee, to design, implement, and operate the system and the required postings of information on the Internet and to provide the staff and equipment necessary to receive and transmit to local collectors the electronic returns and funds. Local collectors must provide staff, equipment, and information necessary for the receipt and transmission of electronic returns and funds. The system and the posting of tax rates and optional exemptions will be established, managed, and supervised by the Department of Revenue.

The electronic system must include a method for allowing a taxpayer to file a sales tax return, at no charge to the taxpayer or any tax authority, that is uniform for each taxing authority except for those provisions for which the local ordinances retain control. The electronic system also must: (1) include a web page through which a secured electronic local sales tax return may be filed; (2) allow for the remittance of any tax, penalty, interest, or other amounts due; and (3) provide for the transmission to, and retrieval of, the data and funds of local collectors.

A taxpayer may rely on the information on the system and such reliance is an absolute defense against any claim for a taxing authority's sales and use tax (Sec. 47:337.23).

• **Local tax rates**

Local sales tax rate information for cities, towns, and parishes is available on the website of the Louisiana Association of Tax Administrators at **http://www.laota.com**. On the "For Taxpayers" tab, click "Parish Map," then click on the specific parish for rate information.

A City to Parish Index is also available on the same website under the "For Taxpayers" tab.

¶ 476   **Bracket Schedule**

Bracket schedules for purposes of collecting the correct amount of tax are available from the Department of Revenue at **http://revenue.louisiana.gov/ TaxForms/1083(8_11).pdf**

¶ 477   **Returns, Payments, and Due Dates**

Returns, on prescribed forms, are generally due monthly by the 20th of the month and are to include payment of the taxes for the previous calendar month period (Sec. 47:306). Although the forms are generally mailed to the dealer, failure of the taxpayer to receive them does not relieve the dealer of the responsibility of timely payment and filing (Reg. 4351, LAC). For purposes of remitting the tax, dealers are deemed to be agents of the state.

Taxpayers whose monthly tax liability averages less than $500 must file returns and pay taxes on a quarterly basis (Sec. 47:306, Reg. 4351, LAC). Quarterly returns are due on the 20th day of the month following the taxable quarter. However, a dealer may elect to file returns and pay taxes on a monthly basis with the Secretary's approval.

Unless otherwise specifically provided, when the due date of any report or return prescribed under the laws administered by the Department of Revenue and Taxation falls on a Saturday, Sunday, or legal holiday (*i.e.,* any legal holiday observed by the state of Louisiana or the U.S. Postal Service), the report or return will be considered timely if it is filed on the next business day (Reg. 4903, LAC).

Local use tax returns: A taxpayer may elect to file a separate local use tax return with the parish tax collector or central collection commission and remit all local taxes due. If a dealer has withheld and remitted tax for a specific purchase from a taxpayer who subsequently files a paid local use tax return, the taxpayer may file an annual use tax refund request with the Department of Revenue in a manner to be determined by the Department, which may include electronic filing. (Sec. 47:302(W)).

Extensions: The Secretary of Revenue and Taxation, for good cause, may extend for up to 30 days the time for making returns (Sec. 47:306(A)(4); Reg. Sec. 4351, LAC). The secretary may, for good cause shown, extend the time by which a licensed vehicle dealer may remit Louisiana sales and use taxes for up to 90 days (Sec. 47:306(E); Sec. 47:337.18(D)).

No taxable sales: In months in which there are no taxable sales or amounts, the return should be marked "no taxable sales or amounts." Otherwise, if no return is filed, a computer-generated assessment will be sent from the Department (Reg. 4351, LAC).

Irregular sales tax number: Dealers who register as having occasional taxable sales or amounts are assigned an irregular sales tax number that permits the dealer to file returns only for months in which there are taxable sales (Reg. 4351, LAC). The assignment of a use tax number to contractors permits the same filing procedure as does an irregular sales tax number. Irregular returns are due on the 20th day of the month following the month in which the tax becomes effective.

Vendor compensation: Dealers, manufacturers, wholesalers, jobbers, and suppliers may receive vendor's compensation for collecting and remitting tax in the amount of 0.935% of the sales tax due, but only if the payment is timely filed with the Secretary of the Department of Revenue (Sec. 47:306(A)(3)(a)).

Applicable to all taxable transactions occurring on or after April 1, 2016, the amount of dealer compensation is capped at $1,500 per month ($18,000 per year) for a dealer who operates one or more business locations within the state. The compensation is only allowed on the original 4% state sales tax. Any additional sales tax levied by the state will not be used in calculating a vendor's compensation payment. (Sec. 47:306(A)(3)(a); see also *Revenue Information Bulletin 16-015,* Louisiana Department of Revenue, April 1, 2016, CCH LOUISIAN TAX REPORTS, ¶ 202-701)

Online filing and payment: Electronic filing and payment is available at **http://www.rev.state.la.us/EServices/LouisianaFileOnline**.

• **Electronic funds transfer**

The Department of Revenue and Taxation is authorized to require payment by electronic funds transfer when the tax due in connection with the filing of any return, report, or other document exceeds $5,000 (Sec. 47:1519; *2017 Electronic Funds Transfer Guidelines,* Louisiana Department of Revenue, **http://revenue.louisiana.gov/Publications/20201(1_17).pdf**). These thresholds also apply whenever a taxpayer's average monthly filing amount exceeds the threshold or, if a company files personal income tax withholding returns and payments on behalf of other taxpayers, whenever its average total payment for all tax returns filed in the preceding 12 months exceeds the threshold.

In lieu of payment by electronic funds transfer, a taxpayer may make full payment in investable funds delivered in person or by courier to the Department on or before the close of business on the date that payment is due (Sec. 47:1519).

Funds transferred electronically must be received by the Department on or before the date required by law, and taxpayers must make a separate transfer for each return (Sec. 47:1519, Reg. 4910, LAC).

If any taxpayer fails to comply with the electronic funds transfer requirements, the taxpayer's payment will be considered delinquent, and the taxpayer will be subject to penalties and interest (Sec. 47:1519).

Online filing and payment: Electronic filing and payment is available at **http://www.rev.state.la.us/EServices/LouisianaFileOnline**.

Local taxes: Parish E-File (**http://parishe-file.com**) is a free public service provided by the Department to businesses in Louisiana and those headquartered out of state. There are no fees associated with its use. Taxpayers may file and remit sales and use taxes in multiple parishes at one time. In addition to state sales and use tax forms, business owners and tax practitioners can access sales and use tax returns for all 64 Louisiana parishes. The Parish E-File Web site provides secure registration for business proprietors and tax practitioners. Registration requires: (1) an e-mail address; (2) a bank account number and routing number; and (3) sales tax account numbers for all returns.

Beginning January 1, 2015, the collector for any Louisiana taxing authority may require the electronic filing and remittance of local sales and use tax by taxpayers who are required by the Department of Revenue to electronically file or remit state sales and use tax. However, if a taxpayer can show cause that the electronic filing of a return and remittance would create an undue hardship on the taxpayer, the local collector may exempt the taxpayer from the requirements. (Sec. 47:337.23(K)(1))

Failure of a taxpayer to comply with the electronic filing requirements will result in assessment of a penalty of $100 or 5% of the tax owed on the return, whichever is greater. However, the total penalty per return may not exceed $5,000. The penalty may be waived in whole or in part if the local collector determines that the failure to comply was reasonable and attributable, not to negligence, but to a cause that is submitted to the collector in writing. (Sec. 47:337.23(K)(2))

• Uniform Sales and Use Tax Administration Act

Louisiana has enacted the Uniform Sales and Use Tax Administration Act, the product of the Streamlined Sales Tax Project (SSTP), but it has not yet enacted the changes to its laws necessary to comply with the requirements of the Streamlined Sales and Use Tax Agreement. The SSTP developed the Act and the related Agreement to simplify and modernize sales and use tax administration in order to substantially reduce the burden of tax compliance for all sellers and for all types of commerce. For additional information on the uniform act, see "Streamlined Sales Tax Project," listed in the Table of Contents.

• Uniform Local Sales Tax Code

The Uniform Local Sales Tax Code (UTC) consolidates various provisions applicable to Louisiana local sales and use taxes and requires local sales taxes to be administered and collected in conformity with its provisions. For additional information, see ¶ 475.

• Direct payment permits

Taxpayers who have met the following requirements may secure a direct payment number that enables them to purchase materials without payment of tax to the vendor (Sec. 47:303.1):

(1) the taxpayer is engaged primarily in manufacturing at a facility within the state tangible personal property for resale;

(2) the taxpayer has paid all taxes due in a timely manner;

(3) the taxpayer has an annual average of $5 million of taxable purchases or leases for three calendar years prior to application and for each subsequent three-year period; and

(4) the taxpayer maintains adequate procedures and records for timely reporting and payment of state and political subdivision taxes.

Holders of direct payment numbers remit sales and use taxes for which they are liable directly to the Department. If the taxpayer meets the qualifications above and obtains written approval from the local agency or agencies charged with collection of the sales and use taxes imposed by the political subdivisions in the parish or parishes where the taxpayer has a manufacturing establishment or facility, the Department will issue a direct payment number to the taxpayer. If the taxpayer meets the qualifications, but written approval is denied or withheld by the local agency or agencies described above, the Department will issue the taxpayer a direct payment number applicable only for purposes of the state sales and use tax. Additionally, taxpayers who have entered into a tax exemption contract with the Department of Economic Development are issued a direct payment number that may be held for term of the contract. Taxpayers with a direct payment number issued in connection with a tax exemption contract are not responsible for the remittance of use taxes when filing monthly tax returns and when the purchases are exempt pursuant to the annual tax exemption contract contact. (Sec. 47:303.1(B)(3))

¶477 Louisiana

¶ 478   Prepayment of Taxes

There is no prepayment requirement.

¶ 479   Vendor Registration

Vendor registration is informally authorized in Louisiana, not specifically being a part of the law or related regulations. Business persons who qualify as a "dealer" under the definition found at Sec. 47:301(4), are asked to contact the Application Central Registration Unit within the Department of Revenue and Taxation. They will then be furnished an application form and directions as needed for completing registration. Once registered, dealers will be sent appropriate return forms.

Online travel companies: Hotel dealers who use online forums to facilitate or transact business and are required to collect state sales and use tax for furnishing occupancy at a residential location (Sec. 47:306.4). The definition of a "hotel" includes a residential location, such as a house, apartment, condominium, camp, cabin, or other building structure used as a residence, that furnishes occupancy to transient guests (Sec. 47:301(6)(a); *Revenue Information Bulletin No. 16-036,* Louisiana Department of Revenue, July 19, 2016, CCH Louisiana Tax Reports, ¶ 202-740).

• **Import permits**

Persons who import property other than by common carrier must obtain a permit for the transportation that is used (Sec. 47:313). If the tax has not been paid, the failure to obtain a permit may be construed as an attempt to evade payment of the tax and the means of transportation may be subject to forfeiture and sale.

¶ 480   Sales or Use Tax Credits

A credit may be granted for comparable taxes paid to other states provided that the other state grants a similar credit (Sec. 47:303; Sec. 47:337.86). The credit may not be greater than the Louisiana sales or use tax liability would be for the property.

Homestead waiver credit: Homeowners who elect to waive their real property homestead exemption are entitled to a credit against Louisiana sales and use tax. The amount of the credit is equal to the lesser of the total local sales and use taxes paid by the homeowner or the amount of extra property tax the homeowner paid because of the waiver of the homestead exemption. The waiver must be filed by July 30 of each year and is applicable for the calendar year in which the waiver is filed (Sec. 47:315.4, Sec. 47:1711).

SAVE credits (repealed): For tax years beginning on or after January 1, 2015, until its repeal, effective March 14, 2016, the Board of Regents conducted a Student Assessment for a Valuable Education (SAVE) Credit Program for each student enrolling at a public institution of higher education. Each student assessed was granted a SAVE credit against individual income, sales and use, gasoline, and special fuels taxes equal to the individual amount of a SAVE assessment. The SAVE credit was a transferable, nonrefundable credit against the tax liability of a student or the student's parent or legal guardian. (Sec. 47:6039; *Revenue Information Bulletin No. 16-017,* Louisiana Department of Revenue, April 1, 2016, CCH Louisiana Tax Reports, ¶ 202-703)

Rebates and refunds: See ¶ 484.

¶ 481   Deficiency Assessments

The Secretary of Revenue and Taxation is authorized to perform an audit or determine the tax due by estimate or otherwise when a taxpayer fails to file a return or the return does not correctly compute the tax (Sec. 47:1562). After determining the tax, penalty or interest due, the Secretary sends a deficiency notice informing the taxpayer that the amount determined will be assessed after 15 calendar days from the date of notice.

Self-assessment: When the taxpayer has filed a return and computed the tax, that tax, together with penalties and interest, is considered assessed and is entered by the Secretary in the official records (Sec. 47:1568). When payment has not been enclosed, a notice is sent to the taxpayer allowing 10 calendar days from the date of the notice before the assessment is collectible by distraint and sale.

Voluntary disclosure agreements: A "voluntary disclosure agreement" is a contractual agreement between a qualified applicant and the secretary of the DOR wherein the applicant agrees to pay the tax and interest due on an undisclosed liability, and the secretary agrees to remit or waive payment of penalties in whole or in part. A rule provides definitions of terms, sets forth the conditions under which an applicant may qualify for a voluntary disclosure agreement, outlines the process for entering into a voluntary disclosure agreement with the DOR, and specifies the requirements that must be complied with in order for the DOR to remit or waive payment of the whole or any part of the penalties under a valid voluntary disclosure agreement (LAC 61:III.2103).

¶ 482   Audit Procedures

The Secretary of Revenue and Taxation is expressly authorized to conduct audits (Sec. 47:1541, Sec. 47:1562). In addition, the Secretary is authorized to examine records and property (Sec. 47:1542), conduct hearings (Sec. 47:1544), take oaths (Sec. 47:1513), issue subpoenas (Sec. 47:1545), and compel testimony (Sec. 47:1547). Under the sales and use tax statutes, the Secretary is specifically authorized to examine the records of transportation companies (Sec. 47:311).

Sampling: The Department of Revenue and taxpayers may enter into binding agreements to use sampling procedures to project audit findings (Sec. 47:1541; *Revenue Information Bulletin No. 12-010*, Louisiana Department of Revenue, January 4, 2012, CCH Louisiana Tax Reports, ¶ 202-420). Sampling audit methods are appropriate if (1) the taxpayer's records are so detailed, complex, or voluminous that an audit of all detailed records would be unreasonable or impractical; (2) the taxpayer's records are inadequate or insufficient to the extent that a competent audit of the period in question is not otherwise possible; and (3) the cost to the taxpayer or the state for an audit of all detailed records would be unreasonable in relation to the benefits derived, and sampling procedures are expected to produce a reasonable result. The sampling procedures must conform to generally recognized sampling techniques. The Secretary must notify the taxpayer in writing of the sampling procedure intended to be used, including, but not limited to, how the tax will be computed, the population to be sampled, and the type of tax for which the tax liability will be established.

Audit protests: The Audit Protest Bureau (APB) is responsible for the audit protest process after a proposed assessment of tax is issued but before the issuance of a formal assessment or a suit is filed by LDR or the taxpayer. The APB is an independent unit within the LDR, reporting directly to the secretary. For additional information, see *Revenue Information Bulletin No. 10-013*, Louisiana Department of Revenue, June 29, 2010, CCH Louisiana Tax Reports, ¶ 202-329.

• Managed audits

A "managed audit" is a review and analysis of invoices, checks, accounting records, or other documents or information to determine the correct amount of tax. A managed audit may be limited to certain categories of liability. A managed audit allows certain businesses to conduct a type of self-audit where most of the audit functions are performed primarily by the taxpayer with guidance and verification provided by Department of Revenue employees.

The Secretary may enter into such an agreement with the taxpayer that specifies the period to be audited and the procedures to be followed. The decision to authorize a managed audit rests solely with the secretary, who, before entering into an agreement, may consider the taxpayer's history of compliance, the taxpayer's ability to pay any expected liability, the time and resources the taxpayer has to dedicate to the audit, and the availability of the taxpayer's records.

The secretary may not assess a penalty and may abate all or a part of the interest that would have accrued on any amount due identified during the managed audit unless fraud or willful evasion of tax is discovered. The taxpayer also is entitled to a refund of any overpayment disclosed by the managed audit. (*Revenue Information Bulletin No. 12-010*, Louisiana Department of Revenue, January 4, 2012, CCH LOUISIANA TAX REPORTS, ¶ 202-420)

¶ 483   **Statute of Limitations**

The limitation period for assessment of all state and local taxes, except property taxes, is set by the Louisiana Constitution at three years from the 31st day of December in the year the taxes were due (La. Const. Sec. 19, Art. 19). This period is called the "prescription" period in Louisiana. The same period is applicable to requests for refunds by taxpayers (Sec. 47:1623).

• **Suspension of limitation period**

The period of limitations is suspended by any of the following events (Sec. 47:1580):

    (1) The issuance of a tax assessment by the Secretary;

    (2) The filing of a summary proceeding in court;

    (3) The filing of a pleading, by the taxpayer or by the Secretary, with the Board of Tax Appeals or any state or federal court;

    (4) The filing of a false or fraudulent return;

    (5) The willful failure to file a return with intent to defraud; or

    (6) Written agreement between the taxpayer and the Secretary.

In effect, there is no limitation on the assessment of taxes in cases of fraud or willful failure to file returns to avoid taxes.

¶ 484   **Application for Refund**

When merchandise is returned to the dealer or a service charge is refunded to a customer on which tax has already been remitted, the dealer applies for a refund by filing an amended return (Sec. 47:315(A)). The form is obtained from the Department to ensure correct identification and account information (Reg. 4369, LAC). If the tax has not yet been remitted and a refund is made to the customer, the dealer may deduct the tax in his or her current return.

Specific refund or rebate provisions: Refunds or contractual rebates may be claimed under specific circumstances, as follows: bad debts (Sec. 47:315(B)); natural disasters (Sec. 47:315.1); construction of low-income housing (Sec. 47:315.2); construction of certain enterprise zone businesses (Sec. 51:1787; Sec. 51:2456); the Quality Jobs Program (Sec. 51:2453); the Competitive Projects Payroll Incentive Program (Sec. 51:3111); procurement processing companies (Sec. 47:6301) (see below); foreign shoppers (see below) (Sec. 51:1302); personal property covered by Medicare (Sec. 47:315.3); waiver of homestead exemption (Sec. 47:315.4); sales of items donated to charitable institutions (Sec. 47:315.5); and transit-oriented developments (Sec. 51:1787(C)).

Rebate requests for the Enterprise Zone and Quality Jobs incentive programs must be submitted electronically.

For projects for which advance notification is filed on or after April 1, 2016, the total amount of Louisiana corporate and personal income tax credits and sales tax rebates available to taxpayers who invest in projects located in an enterprise zone may not exceed $100,000 per net new job created (Sec. 51:1787(A)(1)(c)(i); see also *Revenue Information Bulletin 16-018,* Louisiana Department of Revenue, April 1, 2016, CCH LOUISIANA TAX REPORTS, ¶ 202-702).

Projects with a North American Industry Classification System (NAICS) Code of 44, 45, or 72 (which includes retailers, restaurants, and hotels) are generally ineligible for enterprise zone refunds if the contract was not entered into before July 1, 2015 (Sec. 51:1787(B)(3)(b)).

Electronic filing: For taxable years beginning on and after January 1, 2016, electronic filing is required for all schedules and invoices if a refund claim for an overpayment of sales tax is $25,000 or more or if the claim for refund is made by a tax preparer on behalf of the taxpayer, regardless of the amount of the refund. The taxpayer may be exempt from this requirement if the taxpayer can prove that the electronic filing of a schedule or invoice would create an undue hardship. Also, the requirement does not apply to the Louisiana Tax Free Shopping Program or to cases of a bad debt. (Sec. 47:1520.2; *Revenue Information Bulletin No. 16-040,* Louisiana Department of Revenue, July 19, 2016, CCH LOUISIANA TAX REPORTS, ¶ 202-741)

Tax-free shopping: The Louisiana Tax Free Shopping Program, which provides an exemption through July 1, 2017, in the form of a refund on most retail purchases made by international visitors to the state, has opened refund centers in Baton Rouge, Kenner, Lafayette, Metairie, New Orleans, and Shreveport.

In order to be eligible for the program, a visitor must be travelling on a foreign passport with a current U.S. tourist visa and stay in the country for less than 90 days (Sec. 51:1302). The sales tax refund is provided on tangible items purchased at tax-free stores and permanently removed from the United States. There is no refund for sales taxes paid for personal services, such as hotels, restaurants, entertainment, and transportation. When making a purchase, an international visitor must display his or her foreign passport or current official picture identification and pay the purchase price including the sales tax. The visitor is given a voucher along with a sales receipt or invoice. The refund is paid is U.S. currency up to $500, and checks are issued on refunds over $500. Refunds can also be obtained by mail.

• Rebates for procurement processing companies

Under the Procurement Processing Company (PPC) Rebate Program, the Secretary of the Louisiana Department of Economic Development (LDED) is authorized to contract with PPCs that will generate sales of items subject to sales and use taxes by recruiting purchasing companies to Louisiana. The contract will provide an incentive to the PPC that will be paid in the form of a rebate of a portion of the state sales and use taxes collected on new taxable sales by a purchasing company that is managed by a PPC. (Sec. 47:6301 *et seq.*)

The LDED is required to certify the amount of new taxable sales involved and determine the amount of tax rebate to be paid to the PPCs from the sales taxes generated by the operations of the PPCs in the state. Rebate payments will be based upon the amount of "new taxable sales," which are sales of taxable goods and services that would not have occurred in Louisiana but for the operation in the state of a PPC (Sec. 47:6301(A)(3)). The term does not include any sales or purchases of services or property upon which such sales and use tax would have been due if the PPC was not operating in Louisiana.

"Procurement processing company" is defined as a company engaged in managing the activities of unrelated purchasing companies (Sec. 47:6301(A)(4)). "Purchasing company" is defined as a company engaged in the activity of selling property and services to affiliated entities (Sec. 47:6301(A)(5)).

¶484 Louisiana

¶ 486   Scope of Tax

Source.—Statutory references are to Title 36, Maine Revised Statutes Annotated, as amended to date. Details are reported in the CCH MAINE STATE TAX REPORTS starting at ¶ 60-000.

The sales tax is imposed on all sales of tangible personal property, products transferred electronically, and taxable services sold at retail in Maine (Sec. 1811, Tit. 36, M.R.S.A.). Separate rates are specifically provided for liquor sales; rentals of living quarters in hotels, rooming houses, and tourist or trailer camps; rentals of automobiles for periods of less than one year; and sales of prepared food and alcoholic beverages in establishments licensed for on-premises consumption of liquor. The tax is collected by the retailer from the consumer (Sec. 1753, Tit. 36, M.R.S.A.).

The use tax is imposed on the storage, use or other consumption of tangible personal property or a service the sale of which would have been subject to Maine sales tax (Sec. 1861, Tit. 36, M.R.S.A.).

A Maine resident or business does not escape tax by making out-of-state purchases. Use tax is computed on the purchase price of an item. Common taxable items are office supplies and equipment, computer hardware, software and supplies, janitorial supplies, fax machines and supplies, photocopiers and supplies, and books. Also, if a taxpayer has an inventory of items for sale and the taxpayer removes goods from this inventory for the taxpayer's own use, use tax applies. Use tax, in this case, is based on the cost of the item to the taxpayer when the taxpayer purchased the item.

Products transferred electronically: Maine sales tax applies at the general rate to "products transferred electronically,". A "product transferred electronically" is sold in Maine if (Sec. 1811, Tit. 36, M.R.S.A.):

— the product is delivered electronically to a purchaser located in Maine;

— the product is received by the purchaser at the seller's location in Maine;

— a Maine billing address is provided by the purchaser in connection with the transaction; or

— a Maine billing address is indicated in the seller's business records.

A "product transferred electronically" is a digital product transferred to a purchaser electronically, the sale of which in nondigital physical form would be subject to tax as a sale of tangible personal property (Sec. 1752(9-E), Tit. 36, M.R.S.A.).

Sales outside the state: Sales of tangible personal property delivered by the seller to a location outside Maine or to the U.S. Postal Service, a common carrier, or a contract carrier hired by the seller for delivery to a location outside Maine are not subject to sales and use tax regardless of whether the property is purchased F.O.B. shipping point or other point in the state and regardless of whether passage of title occurs in the state (Sec. 1760(82), Tit. 36, M.R.S.A.).

Auctions: Auction sales of privately held wine are subject to Maine sales and use tax, effective October 15, 2015. If an auction permit holder fails to collect, report and remit taxes, the holder may be refused additional auction permits. (Sec. 1209, Tit. 36, M.R.S.A.)

Additional information about taxability of auction sales and auctioneers is available in *Sales and Use Tax Instructional Bulletin No. 15,* Maine Revenue Services, January 25, 2017, CCH MAINE TAX REPORTS, ¶ 200-858.

Marijuana: Maine voters passed a statewide referendum that legalizes sales of recreational marijuana for adults over the age of 21 and places a sales tax of 10% on retail sales of marijuana and marijuana products (Question 1 (Ballot Initiative), passed by Maine voters, November 8, 2016). However, legal retail sales of recreational marijuana and the taxation of such sales have been delayed until February 1, 2018 (L.D. 88 (H.P. 66), Laws 2017).

A sales and use tax bulletin covers sales of medical marijuana and related products. Topics include sales of medical marijuana, commercial agricultural production, manufacturing, purchases, and reporting and payment of tax. *(Sales and Use Tax Instructional Bulletin No. 60,* Maine Revenue Services, August 1, 2016, CCH MAINE TAX REPORTS, ¶ 200-844)

- **Gross receipts tax**

A tax is imposed on the gross receipts of persons engaged in the business of providing nursing home patient care (Sec. 2821, Tit. 36, M.R.S.A., Sec. 2822, Tit. 36, M.R.S.A.). All charges made by the business upon or with respect to receipt of care by patients are subject to the tax.

The tax is also imposed on the gross receipts of sales of prepared food by businesses that are licensed for on-premises consumption of liquor.

The gross receipts tax is imposed in lieu of sales and use tax but is administered in the same manner as the sales and use tax (Sec. 2823, Tit. 36, M.R.S.A., Sec. 2824, Tit. 36, M.R.S.A.).

- **Taxable services**

The following are taxable services under the sales and use tax provisions (Sec. 1752(17-B), Tit. 36, M.R.S.A.):

— rental of living quarters in any hotel, rooming house, tourist or trailer camp;

— rental or lease of an automobile or a camper trailer or motor home, as defined;

— rental or lease of a pickup truck or van with a gross vehicle weight of less than 26,000 pounds from a person primarily engaged in the business of renting automobiles;

— prepaid calling services;

— transmission or distribution of electricity;

— the sale of an extended service contract on an automobile that entitles the purchaser to specific benefits in the service of the automobile for a specific duration.

For information on extended warranties, service contracts, and maintenance agreements, see *Sales and Use Tax Instructional Bulletin No. 53,* Maine Revenue Services, October 9, 2013, CCH MAINE TAX REPORTS, ¶ 200-723.

Service provider tax: A service provider tax is imposed on the providers of certain services; specifically: (Sec. 2552, Tit. 36, M.R.S.A.; *Sales and Use Tax Instructional Bulletin No. 55,* Maine Revenue Services, June 16, 2014, CCH MAINE TAX REPORTS, ¶ 200-760)

— fabrication services;

— rental of video media and video equipment;

— rental of furniture, audio media and audio equipment pursuant to a rental-purchase agreement;

— telecommunications services and ancillary services;

— the installation, maintenance, or repair of telecommunications equipment;

— private nonmedical institution services;

— community support, day habilitation, home support, and residential training services to persons with specified mental conditions; and

— satellite radio services, but not extended cable and satellite television services (eff. January 1, 2016).

For exemptions from the service provider tax, see ¶ 488.

Unlike the sales tax, the service provider tax is imposed on the service provider, not the consumer. The law does allow the provider to pass the tax on to the consumer, but only if it is separately stated and identified as a "service provider tax."

• **Responsibility for tax**

Although the liability for, or incidence of, the sales tax is declared to be on the consumer, the retailer is liable to the state for payment of the tax (Sec. 1753, Tit. 36, M.R.S.A.). The retailer is required to add the amount of the tax to the sales price and may recover the amount of the tax from the consumer in an action at law (Sec. 1812, Tit. 36, M.R.S.A.). If Maine sales tax is not separately stated, a retailer must include a statement on a sales slip or invoice to the purchaser that the price paid includes Maine sales tax (Sec. 1753, Tit. 36, M.R.S.A.).

Retailers are not permitted to advertise or state to the public or to any consumer (whether directly or indirectly) that the tax is not considered an element of the selling price or that the tax will be refunded (Sec. 1761, Tit. 36, M.R.S.A.).

Every person storing, using or otherwise consuming tangible personal property or services in Maine is liable for the use tax until he or she has paid the tax or received a receipt from a registered seller showing that the seller has collected the sales or use tax (Sec. 1861, Tit. 36, M.R.S.A.).

Taxpayers are required to declare use tax liability on their income tax returns (Sec. 1861-A, Tit. 36, M.R.S.A.). See ¶ 492 for additional reporting requirements.

A retailer withdrawing tangible personal property purchased for resale from inventory for the retailer's own use becomes liable for the use tax at the time of withdrawal (Sec. 1861, Tit. 36, M.R.S.A.).

• **Nexus**

Maine requires any retailer doing business in Maine to collect and remit sales or use tax. Maine does not define the term "doing business," but requires sellers of tangible personal property or taxable services to register with the Maine State Tax Assessor when they have a substantial physical presence in Maine sufficient to satisfy the requirements of the Due Process and Commerce Clauses of the U.S. Constitution. (Sec. 1754-B(1)(G), Tit. 36, M.R.S.A.)

Every agent, representative, salesperson, solicitor, or distributor that has a substantial physical presence in Maine sufficient to satisfy the requirements of the Due Process and Commerce Clauses of the U.S. Constitution is required to register as a seller in Maine if the person (Sec. 1754-B(1)(E), Tit. 36, M.R.S.A.):

    — makes retail sales in Maine on behalf of a principal that is outside Maine; and

    — receives compensation by reason of sales made outside Maine by a principal for use, storage, or other consumption in Maine.

The following activities do not constitute a substantial physical presence in Maine (Sec. 1754-B(1)(G), Tit. 36, M.R.S.A.):

    — solicitation of business in Maine through catalogs, flyers, telephone, or electronic media when delivery of goods is effected by the U.S. mail or an interstate third-party carrier;

    — attending trade shows, seminars, or conventions in Maine;

    — holding a meeting of a corporate board of directors or shareholders, or holding a company retreat or recreational event in Maine;

— maintaining a bank account or banking relationship in Maine; or

— using a vendor in Maine for printing.

Affiliate nexus: There is a rebuttable presumption that a seller is engaged in business in Maine if an affiliated person has a substantial physical presence in Maine (Sec. 1754-B(1-A), Tit. 36, M.R.S.A.). A seller is presumed to be engaged in business in Maine if any person (other than a person acting in its capacity as a common carrier) has a substantial physical presence in Maine and (Sec. 1754-B(1-A)(B), Tit. 36, M.R.S.A.):

— sells a similar line of products as the seller and does so under a business name that is the same or similar to that of the seller;

— maintains an office, distribution facility, warehouse, or storage place or similar place of business in Maine to facilitate the delivery of property or services sold by the seller;

— uses trademarks, service marks, or trade names in Maine that are the same or substantially similar to those used by the seller;

— facilitates the seller's delivery of property to customers in Maine by allowing the customers to pick up the property at an office, distribution facility, warehouse, storage place, or similar place of business maintained by the person in Maine; or

— conducts any activities in Maine that are significantly associated with the seller's ability to establish and maintain a market in Maine.

A seller may rebut the presumption by demonstrating that the person's activities in Maine are not significantly associated with the seller's ability to establish or maintain a market in Maine. An "affiliated person" is a person that is a member of the same controlled group of corporations as the seller or any other entity that bears the same ownership relationship to the seller as a corporation that is a member of the same controlled group of corporations. "Controlled group of corporations" has the same meaning as in IRC Sec. 1563(a).

Click-through nexus: There is a rebuttable presumption that a seller engaged in business in Maine if the seller enters into an agreement with a person, under which the person, while in Maine, directly or indirectly refers potential customers to the seller in exchange for a commission or consideration. The referral of customers may be by a link on an Internet website, telemarketing, an in-person presentation, or otherwise. The presumption applies only if the cumulative gross receipts from retail sales by the seller to customers in Maine referred by all persons with this type of an agreement are in excess of $10,000 during the preceding 12 months. (Sec. 1754-B(1-A)(C), Tit. 36, M.R.S.A.)

A seller may rebut the presumption by submitting proof that the person with whom the seller has an agreement did not engage in any activity within Maine that was significantly associated with the seller's ability to establish or maintain the seller's market in Maine during the preceding 12 months.

• **Streamlined Act status**

Maine has enacted the Uniform (Simplified) Sales and Use Tax Act (see ¶ 492).

Maine has enacted legislation authorizing it to enter into the Streamlined Sales and Use Tax Agreement (36 M.R.S.A. Sec. 7124), but has not enacted the changes to its laws necessary to comply with the Agreement's requirements. However, Maine will continue to have input as an Advisor State.

¶ 487   **Tax Base**

The sales tax is imposed on the value of all tangible personal property and taxable services sold at retail in the state, with value being measured by the sales price (except as otherwise provided) (Sec. 1811, Tit. 36, M.R.S.A.). Similarly, the use tax is imposed on purchases at retail when the sales tax is not paid at the time of purchase, the tax being determined by applying the tax rate to the sales price of purchases for use or consumption in the state (Sec. 1861, Tit. 36, M.R.S.A.).

- **"Sale price" defined**

"Sale price" is defined as the total amount of a retail sale valued in money, whether received in money or otherwise (Sec. 1752(14), Tit. 36, M.R.S.A.). Consequently, tax applies to cash sales, to credit sales and to transactions when the sale price is paid in part or in whole by barter, rendition of services, or any other valuable consideration. The term specifically includes (Sec. 1752(14), Tit. 36, M.R.S.A.).

(1) Charges for services that are a part of a retail sale such as assembly, alteration, and fabrication charges;

(2) All receipts, cash, credits, and property of any kind or nature and any amount for which credit is allowed by a seller to a purchaser, without any deduction on account of the cost of the property sold, the cost of materials used, labor or service cost, interest paid, losses, or any other expenses;

(3) Any charge, deposit, fee or premium imposed by Maine.

The term does not include the following (Sec. 1752(14), Tit. 36, M.R.S.A.):

(1) Discounts allowed and taken on sales;

(2) Allowances in cash or by credit made upon the return of merchandise or with respect to fabrication services pursuant to warranty;

(3) The price of property returned or fabrication services rejected by customers when the full price is refunded either in cash or by credit;

(4) The price received for labor or services used in installing, applying, or repairing the property sold or fabricated, if separately charged or stated;

(5) Any amount charged or collected, in lieu of a gratuity or tip, as a specifically stated service charge, when that amount is to be disbursed by a hotel, motel, restaurant, or other eating establishment to its employees as wages;

(6) The amount of any federal tax imposed with respect to retail sales, whether imposed upon the retailer or consumer, except any manufacturers', importers', alcohol, or tobacco excise tax;

(7) Transportation charges for shipments made directly to the purchaser, provided the charges are separately stated and the transportation occurs by common or contract carrier or U.S. mail;

(8) The new car arbitration account fee imposed by Sec.1169(11), Tit. 10, M.R.S.A.;

(9) The recycling assistance fee imposed by Sec. 4832(1), Tit. 36, M.R.S.A. or the motor vehicle oil change premium imposed by Sec. 1020, Tit. 10, M.R.S.A.;

(10) The lead acid battery deposit imposed by Sec.1604(2-B), Tit. 38, M.R.S.A.; and

(11) Any amount charged or collected by a person engaged in the rental of living quarters as a forfeited room deposit or cancellation fee if the prospective occupant of the living quarters cancels the reservation on or before the scheduled date of arrival.

- **"Retail sale" defined**

A "retail sale" is any sale of tangible personal property or a taxable service in the ordinary course of business (Sec. 1752.11, Tit. 38, M.R.S.A.). It includes:

— Conditional sales, installment lease sales and any other transfer of tangible personal property when the title is retained as security for the payment of the purchase price and is intended to be transferred later;

— Sale of products for internal human consumption to a person for resale through vending machines when sold to a person more than 50% of whose gross receipts from the retail sale of tangible personal property are derived from sales through vending machines. The tax must be paid by the retailer to the State;

— A sale in the ordinary course of business by a retailer to a purchaser who is not engaged in selling that kind of tangible personal property or taxable service in the ordinary course of repeated and successive transactions of like character; and

— The sale or liquidation of a business or the sale of substantially all of the assets of a business, to the extent that the seller purchased the assets of the business for resale, lease or rental in the ordinary course of business, except when:

(a) the sale is to an affiliated entity and the transferee, or ultimate transferee in a series of transactions among affiliated entities, purchases the assets for resale, lease or rental in the ordinary course of business; or

(b) the sale is to a person that purchases the assets for resale, lease or rental in the ordinary course of business or that purchases the assets for transfer to an affiliate, directly or through a series of transactions among affiliated entities, for resale, lease or rental by the affiliate in the ordinary course of business.

A "retail sale" does not include any casual sale, a sale for resale, or certain other enumerated transactions (Sec. 1752.11(B), Tit. 38, M.R.S.A.).

¶ 488   List of Exemptions, Exceptions, and Exclusions

Unless otherwise indicated, the statutory exemptions listed below apply to both sales and use taxes; exemptions applicable to the use tax only are listed separately. Items that are excluded from the sales or use tax base are treated at ¶ 487, "Tax Base."

• **Sales and use exemptions, exceptions, and exclusions**

Advertising or promotional materials	Sec. 1760(83), Tit. 36, M.S.R.A.
Agricultural, aquacultural, and silvicultural products	Sec. 1760(7), Tit. 36, M.R.S.A.
Agricultural and aquacultural fuel	Sec. 2013(2), (3), Tit. 36, M.R.S.A.
Aircraft	Secs. 1760(45), (88), Tit. 36, M.R.S.A.
Aircraft fuel	Sec. 1760(8), Tit. 36, M.R.S.A.
Aircraft and aircraft repair or replacement parts	Sec. 1760(23-C), (45), (76), (88-A) Tit. 36, M.R.S.A.
All-terrain vehicles (ATVs) or snowmobiles sold to individual nonresidents unless the seller is a Maine retailer	Sec. 1760(25-C), Tit. 36, M.R.S.A.
Air pollution control facilities	Sec. 1760(30), Tit. 36, M.R.S.A.
Ambulance corps. and fire departments (nonprofit)	Sec. 1760(26), Tit. 36, M.R.S.A.
Animal shelters	Sec. 1760(60), Tit. 36, M.R.S.A.
Automobiles and parts for use as rentals for less than one year	Sec. 1752(B)(3), Tit. 36, M.R.S.A.

Boarding care facilities	Sec. 1760(16), Tit. 36, M.R.S.A.
Bait sold to commercial fishermen	Sec. 1760(7), Tit. 36, M.R.S.A.
Boats sold to nonresidents	Sec. 1760(25), Tit. 36, M.R.S.A.
Broadcasting equipment	Sec. 1760(31), Tit. 36, M.R.S.A.
Camps, nonprofit	Sec. 1760(17), Tit. 36, M.R.S.A.
Carryout bags, single-use	Sec. 1752(14), Tit. 36, M.R.S.A.
Casual sales	Sec. 1752(17-B), Tit. 36, M.R.S.A.
Charitable organizations fulfilling the wishes of children with life-threatening diseases	Sec.1760(63), Tit. 36, M.R.S.A.
Child advocacy organizations, child abuse councils	Sec. 1760(49), Tit. 36, M.S.R.A.
Church-affiliated residential homes	Sec.1760(44), Tit. 36, M.R.S.A.
Churches	Sec. 1760(16), Tit. 36, M.R.S.A.
Coal, oil, and wood for residential use	Sec. 1760(9), Tit. 36, M.R.S.A.
Coin-operated vending machines	Sec. 1760(34), Tit. 36, M.R.S.A.
Community action agencies	Sec.1760(49), Tit. 36, M.R.S.A.
Community mental health facilities	Sec.1760(28), Tit. 36, M.R.S.A.
Community mental retardation facilities	Sec.1760(28), Tit. 36, M.R.S.A.
Construction contracts with tax-exempt organization or government agency	Sec. 1760(61), Tit. 36, M.R.S.A.
Custom computer software programs	Sec. 1752(1-E), Tit. 36, M.R.S.A., Sec. 1752(17), Tit. 36, M.R.S.A.
Day-care centers	Sec. 1760(43), Tit. 36, M.R.S.A.
Dental health centers	Sec. 1760(16), Tit. 36, M.R.S.A.
Diabetic supplies	Sec. 1760(33), Tit. 36, M.R.S.A.
Educational television or radio stations	Sec. 1760(16), Tit. 36, M.R.S.A.

Electricity, gas, and water for residential use	Sec. 1760(9-B), Tit. 36, M.R.S.A., Sec. 1760(9-C), Tit. 36, M.R.S.A., Sec. 1760(39), Tit. 36, M.R.S.A.
Electricity sold to net energy billing customers	Sec. 1760(80), Tit. 36, M.S.R.A.
Electricity used in commercial farming, fishing, aquaculture	Sec. 2013(2), (3) Tit. 36, M.R.S.A.
Emergency services by out-of-state providers during declared disaster or emergency	Sec. 9901, Tit. 10, M.R.S.A.
Emergency shelter and feeding organizations	Sec. 1760(47), Tit. 36, M.R.S.A., Sec. 1760(47-A), Tit. 36, M.R.S.A.
Employee meals or lodging credited against wages	Sec. 1760(75), Tit. 36, M.R.S.A.
Eye banks	Sec. 1760(77), Tit. 36, M.R.S.A.
Federal government transactions	Sec. 1760(2), Tit. 36, M.R.S.A.
Feed for farm animals	Sec. 1760(7), Tit. 36, M.R.S.A.
Fertilizers	Sec. 1760(7), Tit. 36, M.R.S.A.
Financial institutions exempt under federal law	Sec. 1760(1), Tit. 36, M.R.S.A.
Free publications and components	Sec. 1760(14-A), Tit. 36, M.R.S.A.
Food stamp purchases	Sec. 1760(54), Tit. 36, M.R.S.A.
Fuel and electricity used at a manufacturing facility	Sec. 1760(9-D), Tit. 36, M.R.S.A.
Fuel for burning blueberry fields	Sec. 1760(9-A), Tit. 36, M.R.S.A.
Fuel for agricultural and aquacultural use	Sec. 2013(2), (3), Tit. 36, M.R.S.A.
Fuel oil or coal used in manufacturing	Sec. 1760(9-G), Tit. 36, M.R.S.A.
Funeral services	Sec. 1760(24), Tit. 36, M.R.S.A.
Grocery staples	Sec. 1752(3-B), Tit. 36, M.R.S.A., Sec. 1760(3), Tit. 36, M.R.S.A.
Hay and organic bedding material for farm animals	Sec. 1760(78), Tit. 36, M.R.S.A.

Historical societies	Sec. 1760(42), Tit. 36, M.R.S.A.
Home health agencies	Sec. 1760(16), Tit. 36, M.R.S.A.
Home heating oil and kerosene	Sec. 1760(9), Tit. 36, M.R.S.A.
Hospices, nonprofit	Sec. 1760(55), Tit. 36, M.R.S.A.
Hospitals	Sec. 1760(16), Tit. 36, M.R.S.A.
Housing development organizations, nonprofit	Sec. 1760(72), Tit. 36, M.R.S.A.
Insecticides and fungicides	Sec. 1760(7), Tit. 36, M.R.S.A.
Interstate transactions	Sec. 1760(41), Tit. 36, M.R.S.A.
Interstate transmissions	Sec. 1752(18-D), Tit. 36, M.R.S.A.
Jet or turbojet aircraft fuel	Sec. 1760(8), Tit. 36, M.R.S.A.
Leases not deemed to be in lieu of purchase	Sec. 1752(13), Tit. 36, M.R.S.A.
Libraries (public) (sales to and by) and library support organizations (sales by)	Sec. 1760(50), Tit. 36, M.R.S.A.
Machinery and equipment used in broadcasting	Sec. 1760(31), Tit. 36, M.R.S.A.
Machinery and equipment used in farming, fishing, aquaculture, wood harvesting	Sec. 2013(2), (3) Tit. 36, M.R.S.A.
Machinery and equipment used for manufacturing and research . . .	Sec. 1760(31), Tit. 36, M.R.S.A., Sec. 1760(32), Tit. 36, M.R.S.A.
Maine Science and Technology Commission	Sec. 1760(68), Tit. 36, M.R.S.A.
Meals served by youth camps, by schools to college employees, by retirement facilities to residents, or to hospital patients and the elderly	Sec. 1760(6), Tit. 36, M.R.S.A.
Medical supplies and equipment for nonprofit charitable organizations	Sec. 1760(16), (62), Tit. 36, M.R.S.A.
Mental health facilities	Sec. 1760(28), Tit. 36, M.R.S.A.
Mobile and modular homes	Sec. 1760(40), Tit. 36, M.R.S.A.
Monasteries and convents	Sec. 1760(65), Tit. 36, M.R.S.A.

Property consumed in manufacturing	Sec. 1760(74), Tit. 36, M.R.S.A.
Property purchased outside the state	Sec. 1760(45), Tit. 36, M.R.S.A.
Property sales delivered out of state	Sec. 1760(80)[81], Tit. 36, M.R.S.A.
Property temporarily stored in state	Sec. 1752(16), Tit. 36, M.R.S.A.
Prescription drugs; prosthetic and orthotic devices	Sec. 1760(5), Tit. 36, M.R.S.A.
Prosthetic devices	Sec. 1760(5-A), Tit. 36, M.R.S.A.
Publications distributed without charge, and components	Sec. 1760(14-A), Tit. 36, M.R.S.A.
Railroad track materials	Sec. 1760(52), Tit. 36, M.R.S.A.
Regional planning commissions	Sec. 1760(37), Tit. 36, M.R.S.A.
Rental charges for continuous residence	Sec. 1760(20), Tit. 36, M.R.S.A.
Rental charges for state institutions and hospitals	Sec. 1760(18), Tit. 36, M.R.S.A.
Rental charges for student living quarters	Sec. 1760(19), Tit. 36, M.R.S.A.
Rentals and sales for rental of videotapes, video equipment, and home video games	Sec. 1752(11-B), Tit. 36, M.R.S.A.
Rentals of automobiles on a long-term basis	Sec. 1752(11)(B)(5), Tit. 36, M.R.S.A.
Resales	Sec. 1752(11), Tit. 36, M.R.S.A.
Research corporations	Sec. 1760(16), Tit. 36, M.R.S.A.
Residential electricity, gas, and water	Sec. 1760(9-B), Tit. 36, M.R.S.A., Sec. 1760(9-C), Tit. 36, M.R.S.A., Sec. 1760(39), Tit. 36, M.R.S.A.
Residential facilities for medical patients and their families	Sec. 1760(46), Tit. 36, M.R.S.A.
Returnable containers	Sec. 1760(12), Tit. 36, M.R.S.A.
Rural community health centers	Sec. 1760(16), Tit. 36, M.R.S.A.
Schools and school-sponsored organizations	Sec. 1760(16), Tit. 36, M.R.S.A., Sec.1760(64), Tit. 36, M.R.S.A.

• Exemptions, exceptions, and exclusions to use tax only

Merchandise donated by a retailer from inventory to a tax-exempt donee	Sec. 1864, Tit. 36, M.R.S.A.
Returned merchandise donated to charity	Sec. 1863, Tit. 36, M.R.S.A.
Sales or use tax previously paid in other jurisdictions	Sec. 1862, Tit. 36, M.R.S.A.

• Exemptions, exceptions, and exclusions from service provider tax

Air ambulance services	Sec. 2557(5), Tit. 36, M.R.S.A.
Boarding care facilities	Sec. 2557(3), Tit. 36, M.R.S.A.
Casual sales	Sec. 2557, Tit. 36, M.R.S.A. Sec. 1752(1) Tit. 36, M.R.S.A. Sec. 1764 Tit. 36, M.R.S.A.
Centers for Innovation, sales to	Sec. 2557(29), Tit. 36, M.R.S.A.
Charitable organizations fulfilling the wishes of children with life-threatening diseases	Sec. 2557(21), Tit. 36, M.R.S.A.
Child abuse and advocacy organizations	Sec. 2557(13), Tit. 36, M.R.S.A.
Church affiliated residential homes	Sec. 2557(10), Tit. 36, M.R.S.A.
Churches	Sec. 2557(3), Tit. 36, M.R.S.A.
Community action agencies	Sec. 2557(13), Tit. 36, M.R.S.A.
Community mental health facilities	Sec. 2557(6), Tit. 36, M.R.S.A.
Community mental retardation facilities	Sec. 2557(6), Tit. 36, M.R.S.A.
Construction contracts with exempt organizations	Sec. 2557(31), Tit. 36, M.R.S.A.
Day-care centers	Sec. 2557(9), Tit. 36, M.R.S.A.
Dental health centers	Sec. 2557(3), Tit. 36, M.R.S.A.
Educational television or radio stations	Sec. 2557(3), Tit. 36, M.R.S.A.
Emergency shelter and feeding organizations	Sec. 2557(12), Tit. 36, M.R.S.A.
Eye banks	Sec. 2557(28), Tit. 36, M.R.S.A.

Sales for resale	Sec. 2557(30), Tit. 36, M.R.S.A.
Schools and school-sponsored organizations	Sec. 2557(3), Tit. 36, M.R.S.A.
Services for hearing-impaired individuals	Sec. 2557(25), Tit. 36, M.R.S.A.
State and local government transactions	Sec. 2557(2), Tit. 36, M.R.S.A.
State-chartered credit unions	Sec. 2557(26), Tit. 36, M.R.S.A.
Support systems for single-parent families	Sec. 2557(25), Tit. 36, M.R.S.A.
Telecomunications services, international and interstate	Sec. 2557(33), (34), Tit. 36, M.R.S.A.
Veterans' medical support organizations, sales to	Sec. 1760(37), Tit. 36, M.R.S.A.
Veterans' Memorial Cemetery Associations	Sec. 2557(15), Tit. 36, M.R.S.A.
Vietnam veteran registries	Sec. 2557(24), Tit. 36, M.R.S.A.
Volunteer ambulance corps and fire departments	Sec. 2557(5), Tit. 36, M.R.S.A.
Volunteer search and rescue organizations	Sec. 2557(16), Tit. 36, M.R.S.A.
Youth organizations, nonprofit	Sec. 2557(18), Tit. 36, M.R.S.A.

¶ 489   Rate of Tax

As of January 1, 2016, the sales or use tax is imposed at the following rates (Sec. 1811, Tit. 36, M.R.S.A., Sec. 1861, Tit. 36, M.R.S.A.):

8% on liquor sold in licensed establishments;

9% on lodging, *i.e.,* rentals of living quarters in any hotel, rooming house or tourist or trailer camp;

8% on the value of prepared food; and

10% on rentals or leases of automobiles (less than 10,000 lbs.), pickup trucks or vans (less than 26,000 lbs.) for less than one year;

5.5% on rentals of automobiles for one year or more. The value of the rental or lease of an automobile for one year or more is:

    — the total monthly lease payment multiplied by the number of payments in the lease or rental, plus

    — the amount of equity involved in any trade-in and the value of any cash down payment.

The rate on all other tangible personal property and taxable services is 5.5%.

Previous tax increases: Effective from October 1, 2013, to December 31, 2015, Maine's general sales tax rate was increased from 5% to 5.5%, the hotel room tax rate was increased from 7% to 8%, the tax on prepared food was increased from 7% to 8%, and the tax on liquor sold in licensed establishments was increased from 7% to 8%.

Marijuana: Legal retail sales of recreational marijuana (cannabis) and the corresponding 10% tax on such sales are delayed until February 1, 2018 (L.D. 88 (H.P. 66), Laws 2017).

• Service provider tax

A tax on service providers is imposed at the rate of 6% (5% before January 1, 2016) of the value of certain services (Sec. 2552, Tit. 36, M.R.S.A.). A provider of services may pass the service provider tax onto its customer if the tax is separately stated on the customer's bill as a "service provider tax."

The tax does not apply to sales to certain governmental entities and a variety of nonprofit and advocacy institutions. For a list of services subject to the tax, see ¶ 486. For exemptions, see ¶ 488.

• Fuel and electricity used at manufacturing facilities

Ninety-five percent of the sale price of fuel and electricity purchased for use at a manufacturing facility is exempt from sales tax. The remaining 5% of the purchase price is taxable at 6%, for an effective tax rate of 0.3% (Sec. 1760(9-D), Tit. 36, M.R.S.A., *General Information Bulletin No. 82,* Bureau of Taxation, July 1, 1993).

A similar exemption applies with respect to 95% of the sales price of fabrication services for the production of fuel for use at a manufacturing facility (Sec. 2557, Tit. 36, M.R.S.A.).

• Recycling assistance fee

A recycling assistance fee of $1 is imposed, in addition to the sales or use tax, on retail sales of new tires and new lead-acid batteries (Sec. 4832(1), Tit. 36, M.R.S.A.).

• Prepaid wireless fee

Effective January 1, 2017, the state prepaid wireless telecommunications service E911 fee is $1.16 (previously, $1.01) per retail transaction. (Sec. 7104-C(1), Tit. 35-A, M.R.S.A.)

A seller of prepaid wireless telecommunications services must collect the prepaid wireless fee from the prepaid wireless consumer for each retail transaction occurring in Maine and separately state it on the customer's bill. The prepaid wireless fee is the liability of the consumer, except that the seller is liable to remit all prepaid wireless fees that it collects from consumers, including all such charges that the seller is deemed to collect when the amount of the prepaid wireless fee has not been separately stated on an invoice, receipt or similar document provided to the consumer by the seller. (Sec. 7104-C, Tit. 35-A, M.R.S.A.)

The amount of the prepaid wireless fee that is collected by a seller may not be included in the base for measuring any tax, fee, surcharge or other charge imposed by Maine, any political subdivision of Maine or any intergovernmental agency. Prepaid wireless fees collected by sellers must be remitted to the State Tax Assessor at the times and in the manner provided for the remittance of sales and use tax. The assessor must establish registration and payment procedures that substantially coincide with sales and use tax registration and payment procedures. (Sec. 7104-C, Tit. 35-A, M.R.S.A.)

A seller who is not a prepaid wireless telecommunications service provider may deduct and retain 3% of the prepaid wireless fee that is collected by the seller from a consumer (Sec. 7104-C(2)(G), Tit. 35-A, M.R.S.A.).

• Bulk motor oil premium

A premium is imposed on the first sale or distribution in Maine of bulk motor vehicle oil (Sec. 1020(6), Tit. 10, M.R.S.A.). For gasoline engine bulk motor vehicle oils, the premium is $1.10 per gallon. For diesel engine bulk motor vehicle oils the premium is 35¢ per gallon. In addition, a 35¢ per gallon bulk motor vehicle oil premium will apply with respect to prepackaged motor vehicle oil. Bulk motor vehicle oil premiums must be paid to the Maine State Tax Assessor and are reported on line 14A of the sales tax return (Form ST-7). The premium is scheduled to remain in effect until at least June 30, 2018, but no later than December 31, 2030.

¶ 490   Local Taxes

No local sales or use taxes are imposed in Maine.

Maine conforms to the federal Mobile Telecommunications Sourcing Act (P.L. 106-252), under which wireless telecommunications services are sourced to the customer's "primary place of use," which is the residential or primary business address of the customer and must be located in the service provider's licensed service area. The jurisdiction in which the primary place of use is located is the only jurisdiction that may tax the communications services, regardless of the customer's location when an actual call is placed or received.

¶ 491   Bracket Schedule

Bracket collection schedules are available at **http://www.maine.gov/revenue/ salesuse/tax%20rate%20schedules10012013.pdf**.

Amount of Sale Price   *Amount of Tax*

If the tax rate is 5.5%	
$0.00 to $0.09, inclusive	No tax
$0.10 to $0.18, inclusive	1 cent
$0.19 to $0.36, inclusive	2 cents
$0.37 to $0.54, inclusive	3 cents
$0.55 to $0.72, inclusive	4 cents
$0.73 to $0.90, inclusive	5 cents
$0.91 to $1.09, inclusive	6 cents
$1.10 to $1.27, inclusive	7 cents
$1.28 to $1.45, inclusive	8 cents
$1.46 to $1.63, inclusive	9 cents
$1.64 to $1.81, inclusive	10 cents
$1.82 to $2.00, inclusive	11 cents
If the tax rate is 7%	
$0.01 to $0.07, inclusive	No tax
$0.08 to $0.21, inclusive	1 cent
$0.22 to $0.35, inclusive	2 cents
$0.36 to $0.49, inclusive	3 cents
$0.50 to $0.64, inclusive	4 cents
$0.65 to $0.78, inclusive	5 cents
$0.79 to $0.92, inclusive	6 cents
$0.93 to $1.00, inclusive	7 cents
If the tax rate is 8%	
$0.01 to $0.06, inclusive	No tax
$0.07 to $0.13, inclusive	1 cent
$0.14 to $0.25, inclusive	2 cents
$0.26 to $0.38, inclusive	3 cents
$0.39 to $0.50, inclusive	4 cents
$0.51 to $0.63, inclusive	5 cents
$0.64 to $0.75, inclusive	6 cents
$0.76 to $0.88, inclusive	7 cents
$0.89 to $1.00, inclusive	8 cents

Amount of Sale Price		*Amount of Tax*
	If the tax rate is 10%	
$0.01 to $0.10, inclusive	. . . .	No tax
$0.11 to $0.20, inclusive	. . . .	2 cents
$0.21 to $0.40, inclusive	. . . .	4 cents
$0.41 to $0.60, inclusive	. . . .	6 cents
$0.61 to $0.80, inclusive	. . . .	8 cents
$0.81 to $1.00, inclusive	. . . .	10 cents

When the sale price exceeds $1, the tax to be added to the price is the scheduled amount for each whole dollar plus the scheduled amount for each fractional part of $1.

When several items are purchased together and at the same time, the tax must be computed on the total amount of the several items, except that purchases taxed at different rates must be separately totaled (Sec. 1812(2), Tit. 36, M.R.S.A.).

When the tax to be paid includes a fraction of one cent, the fraction is not required to be paid if it is less than one-half cent. A full cent must be paid if the fraction is one-half cent or more (*Sales/Excise Tax Division General Information Bulletin No. 88,* Maine Revenue Services, September 1, 1988).

¶ 492   Returns, Payments, and Due Dates

In general, every retailer must file a sales tax return on or before the 15th day of the month following the calendar month in which the taxable transactions occurred (Sec. 1951-A, Tit. 36, M.R.S.A.). The State Tax Assessor may, however, permit the filing of returns on a seasonal, annual or other basis. In practice, payment accompanies the report. Registered retailers must file the report whether or not any tax is due. Persons who are not required to be registered as sellers, however, need not file reports for periods in which no tax is due.

Use tax: Every person subject to the use tax must file similar monthly reports and pay the tax or furnish a receipt for the tax from a registered retailer (Sec. 1951-A, Tit. 36, M.R.S.A.).

Individual income taxpayers are required to declare their use tax liability for the period covered by their income tax returns (Sec. 1861-A, Tit. 36, M.R.S.A.). Alternatively, they may elect to report an amount that is 0.04% of their Maine adjusted gross income. However, taxpayers using this method must add use tax on any items with a purchase price over $1,000.

Individuals must report their use tax liability on any single item with a purchase price of more than $5,000 on or before the 15th of the month following the purchase (Sec. 1861-A, Tit. 36, M.R.S.A.).

Consolidated filing: Retailers who make sales at more than one business location may file a consolidated return that includes a schedule showing a breakdown of taxable sales made at each location (Rule 304).

• **Quarterly reporting**

A registrant whose total tax liability normally is less than $100 per month may, at the discretion of the State Tax Assessor, be permitted to file four quarterly reports each year in lieu of monthly reports (Rule 304).

• **Semiannual reporting**

A registrant whose total tax liability normally is less than $50 per month may be permitted to file two semiannual reports each year in lieu of monthly reports (Rule 304 (18-125 CMR 304)).

• Annual reporting

A registrant whose total tax liability normally is less than $25 per month may, at the discretion of the State Tax Assessor, be permitted to file one annual report each year in lieu of monthly reports (Rule 304 (18-125 CMR 304)).

Nursing home businesses: No later than January 30 each year, nursing home businesses must provide to persons paying for the nursing home care statements showing the total gross receipts tax arising with respect to such payments (Sec. 2825, Tit. 36, M.R.S.A.).

Casual rentals: An individual taxpayer whose only sales tax collection obligation is the collection of sales tax on casual rentals of living quarters, and whose sales tax liability with respect to the rentals during the period of the individual's income tax return is expected to be less than $2,000, may report and pay the sales tax on his or her Maine individual income tax return for that year instead of filing reports with the State Tax Assessor on or before the 15th day of each month. If the taxpayer's actual liability for the year is $2,000 or more, the taxpayer must file the reports on or before the 15th day of each month during the following year (Sec. 1951-A(3), Tit. 36, M.R.S.A.).

• Electronic filing and payment

Sales, use, and service provider taxpayers must file their returns electronically. Taxpayers without computer or Internet access can satisfy the electronic filing requirement by filing by telephone via the TeleFile system. Payment by electronic funds transfer or paper check is accepted using either filing system. (Rule 104.03 (18-125 CMR 104.03))

Payment: For 2013, a taxpayer with a combined tax liability of $14,000 or more was required to remit all Maine tax payments electronically. For 2014, the threshold is reduced to $12,000, and for 2015 and thereafter, $10,000 (Rule 102 (18-125 CMR 102)).

Internet filing: Taxpayers can register to file a Maine Sales, Use and Service Provider Tax Internet Return at **http://www.maine.gov/revenue/netfile/ gateway2.htm**.

• Uniform Sales Tax Administration Act

Maine enacted the Uniform Sales and Use Tax Administration Act, the product of the Streamlined Sales Tax Project (SSTP), effective March 1, 2002. The SSTP developed the Act and the related Streamlined Sales and Use Tax Agreement to simplify and modernize sales and use tax administration in order to substantially reduce the burden of tax compliance for all sellers and for all types of commerce. For additional information on the uniform act, see "Streamlined Sales Tax Project," listed in the Table of Contents.

¶ 493   Prepayment of Taxes

Maine does not require prepayment of sales or use taxes.

¶ 494   Vendor Registration

Every agent, representative, salesperson, solicitor, or distributor that has a substantial physical presence in Maine sufficient to satisfy the requirements of the Due Process and Commerce Clauses of the U.S. Constitution is required to register with the State Tax Assessor as a seller in Maine if the person (Sec. 1754-B(1)(E), Tit. 36, M.R.S.A.; *Sales and Use Tax Instructional Bulletin No. 43,* Maine Revenue Services, October 9, 2013, CCH MAINE TAX REPORTS, ¶ 200-740):

— makes retail sales in Maine on behalf of a principal that is outside Maine; and

— receives compensation by reason of sales made outside Maine by a principal for use, storage, or other consumption in Maine.

The following persons must register as retailers and collect and remit sales taxes (Sec. 1754-B(1)(D), Tit. 36, M.R.S.A.):

(1) Sellers of tangible personal property or taxable services, at retail or otherwise, that maintain an office, manufacturing facility, distribution facility, warehouse or storage facility, sales or sample room or other place of business in Maine;

(2) Sellers of tangible personal property or taxable services that do not maintain a place of business in Maine but make retail sales or solicit orders for retail sales through one or more salespeople within the state;

(3) Lessors engaged in leasing tangible personal property located in Maine that do not maintain a place of business in the state but make retail sales to purchasers from the state;

(4) Consignees, agents or salespeople who make retail sales in Maine of tangible personal property or taxable services on behalf of a principal located outside the state and not holding a valid registration certificate;

(5) Agents, representatives, salespersons, solicitors or distributors who receive compensation for sales of tangible personal property or taxable services made outside the state by a principal but for use, storage or other consumption in Maine;

(6) Persons who manage, operate, or collect or receive rents from a hotel, rooming house or tourist or trailer camp in Maine; and

(7) Sellers of tangible personal property or taxable services that have a substantial physical presence in Maine sufficient to satisfy the requirements of the Due Process and Commerce Clauses of the U.S. Constitution.

Each application for a registration certificate must contain a statement of the type(s) of tangible personal property that the applicant intends to purchase for resale and the type(s) of taxable services that the applicant intends to sell (Sec. 1754-B(2), Tit. 36, M.R.S.A.). Each retailer registered for sales and use tax purposes must inform the State Tax Assessor in writing of any changes to the type(s) of tangible personal property that it purchases for resale or the type(s) or types of taxable services that it sells.

On November 1 of each year, the State Tax Assessor will review the returns filed by each registered retailer, unless the retailer has a resale certificate expiring after December 31 of that year. If the retailer reports $3,000 or more in gross sales during the 12 months preceding the assessor's review, the assessor will issue a resale certificate to the retailer effective for five calendar years. If a registered retailer fails to meet the $3,000 threshold, the retailer is not entitled to renewal unless certain conditions are met. (Sec. 1754-B(20C), Tit. 36 M.R.S.A.)

Electronic registration: New businesses may register with the state for income tax withholding, sales and use tax, and service provider tax through the official state Web site at **https://www.maine.gov/cgi-bin/online/suwtaxreg/index**. There is no fee to use the online registration service.

• **Out-of-state wine shippers**

Maine permits the direct shipment of wine from outside the state and requires persons holding a wine direct shipper license to register with the Maine State Tax Assessor to collect and remit sales and use taxes (Sec. 1403-A, Tit. 36, M.R.S.A.). In this context, a "direct shipper" is a farm winery or other winery that holds a federal basic wine manufacturing permit, that has obtained a wine direct shipper license from the state, and that is located inside or outside the state. To receive a certificate of approval, a direct shipper of wine located outside Maine must comply with the state's sales and use tax laws, including the sales and use tax registration requirements. Shipments must be made to a recipient for personal use and not for resale. (Sec. 1403-A(9), Tit. 36, M.R.S.A.).

• Transient vendors

In the case of vendors selling from vehicles, each vehicle will be deemed a place of business requiring a registration certificate (Sec. 1754, Tit. 36, M.R.S.A.).

Certain lessors of retail space: A person who rents or leases space to more than four persons at one location for less than 12 months to use for retail sales must register with the State Tax Assessor for sales and use tax purposes. Also, such a person may not rent or lease space to another person without verifying that the person is the holder of a valid registration certificate. Each person required to register must maintain a list that includes (1) the names, addresses and sales tax registration certificate numbers of those persons who have rented or leased space at that location for the purpose of making retail sales, and (2) the dates on which those rentals or leases occurred. (Sec. 1754-A, Tit. 36, M.R.S.A.)

• Revocation of registration certificates

The assessor may revoke a registration certificate if (Sec. 1757, Tit. 36, M.R.S.A.)

— a registrant has failed to file a bond or deposit within 15 days after receipt of notice,

— there is good cause for revoking the certificate, or

— a registrant has failed to file a return within 15 days after the due date.

If a registrant fails to pay taxes due, the registrant will receive notification from the assessor that the registration certificate has been suspended from the date of notice of the suspension until the delinquent tax is paid or a required bond or deposit is filed with the assessor or it is determined by an appropriate court that revocation is not warranted (Sec. 1757, Tit. 36, M.R.S.A.).

¶ 495   Sales or Use Tax Credits

Maine provides various sales and use tax credits. Some of those credits are discussed below.

• Taxes paid in other jurisdictions

The use tax provisions do not apply with respect to the use, storage or consumption in Maine of purchases outside the state, where the purchaser has paid a sales or use tax equal to or greater than the amount imposed by Maine in another taxing jurisdiction (Sec. 1862, Tit. 36, M.R.S.A.). Proof of payment of the tax must be made in accordance with the rules made by the State Tax Assessor. If the amount of tax paid in another taxing jurisdiction is not equal to or greater than the amount of tax imposed by Maine, then the purchaser must pay the difference (to the extent of the amount imposed by Chs. 211 to 225) to the State Tax Assessor.

• Tax paid on hotel room rental by person in continuous residence

Rentals by persons residing continuously for 28-days or more at any one hotel, rooming house, tourist or trailer camp are tax-exempt (Sec. 1760(20), Tit. 36, M.R.S.A.). Consequently, the tax paid by the purchaser during the initial 28-day period must be refunded by the retailer, and the retailer is entitled to a corresponding credit on the tax paid by the purchaser and reported and paid to the state by the retailer. The credit is to be taken by the retailer on the report covering the month in which the refund was made to the tenant (Sec. 1760(20), Tit. 36, M.R.S.A.).

• Nursing home care

A resident individual or a resident trust acting on behalf of a resident individual is allowed a refundable credit equal to 80% of the gross receipts tax arising from all payments made for nursing home care in the preceding calendar year (Sec. 5219-I, Tit. 36, M.R.S.A.).

• **Overpayment of tax**

When, upon written application by a taxpayer or during the course of an audit, the State Tax Assessor determines that any tax had been paid more than once or has been erroneously or illegally collected or computed, the amount collected in excess of that legally due, with interest at the specified rate, is to be credited on any taxes then due from taxpayer and the balance refunded (Sec. 2011, Tit. 36, M.R.S.A.). Unless the taxpayer specifically requests a cash refund, the State Tax Assessor may credit the refund amount to the taxpayer's sales and use tax account. In such cases, however, no further interest accrues from the date of the election to credit the refund amount.

• **Property purchased for resale**

A retailer may claim a credit if the retailer has paid sales tax on tangible personal property purchased for resale at retail (Sec. 1811-B, Tit. 36, M.R.S.A.). The credit may be claimed only on the return that corresponds to the period in which the tax was paid. The credit may not be claimed if the item has been withdrawn from inventory by the retailer for the retailer's own use. A retailer may carry forward the credit or obtain a refund if the retailer's sales and use tax liability for the tax period in question is less than the credit being claimed.

• **Pine Tree Development Zone reimbursements**

A reimbursement is allowed for sales and use taxes paid on the sale or use of tangible personal property that is physically incorporated in, and becomes a permanent part of, real property owned by or sold to a qualified Pine Tree Development Zone business and that is used directly and primarily by that business in one or more qualified business activities (Sec. 2016(2), Tit. 36, M.R.S.A.).

Reimbursement claims: A claim for reimbursement must be filed by the contractor or subcontractor within three years from the date on which the tangible personal property was incorporated into real property. The claim must be submitted on a form prescribed by the State Tax Assessor and must be accompanied by a statement from a Zone business certifying, under penalties of perjury, that tax was paid by the claimant on personal property that has been placed in use directly and primarily in a qualified business activity. All records pertaining to the certification and to the transactions in question must be retained for at least six years by the contractor or subcontractor, the Zone business, and the person, if any, that sold the real property in question to that business. The Assessor will pay the approved amounts to each qualifying applicant within 30 days after receipt of a properly completed claim (Sec. 2016(2), Tit. 36, M.R.S.A.).

Reimbursements are limited to taxes paid in connection with sales of tangible personal property that occur within 10 years from the date the Zone business receiving the property is certified, or by December 31, 2018, whichever occurs first (Sec. 2016(2), Tit. 36, M.R.S.A.).

¶ 496   Deficiency Assessments

The sales and use taxes are self-assessing, in that the taxpayer makes a return to the State Tax Assessor and pays the amount of tax shown on the return. If no sales tax return is filed, or the Commissioner determines that the full amount of tax has not been assessed, the tax may be assessed with interest to the last date prescribed for payment of tax (Sec. 186, Tit. 36, M.R.S.A.). Interest accrues automatically.

• **False or fraudulent returns**

In the case of a false or fraudulent return filed with intent to evade a tax, or of a failure to file a return, the State Tax Assessor may make an assessment at any time, determining the tax due based upon the best information available (Sec. 141(2), Tit. 36, M.R.S.A.). In any proceeding for the collection of tax for the period involved, that estimate will constitute *prima facie* evidence of the tax liability.

Use of electronic devices or software: The possession, purchase, ownership, manufacturing, sale, installation or transfer of a device or software intended to falsify the sales records, such as transaction reports on a point-of-sale electronic cash register, to avoid sales tax is a crime. The illegal devices and software are known as automated sales suppression devices and phantom-ware. "Transaction report" means a report that includes, but is not limited to, sales, sales tax collected and other data that is printed on cash register tape at the end of the day or a shift or any other report from an electronic cash register. Subscribers can view the text of the legislation. (Sec. 909, Tit. 17-A, M.R.S.A.)

Appeals conferences: Taxpayers have 20 days after filing a statement of appeal to request that the appeals office hold an appeals conference to receive additional information or to hear arguments regarding the assessment or determination (Sec. 151-D(10)(A), Tit. 36, M.R.S.A.). Previously, the request for an appeals conference had to be included in the statement of appeal.

¶ 497 Audit Procedures

The State Tax Assessor and agents acting under his or her authority have power to extensively examine witnesses and records for assessment purposes (Sec. 112(2), Tit. 36, M.R.S.A.).

• Examination of witnesses and records

The State Tax Assessor may examine under oath any person whose testimony is deemed necessary to determine the amount of tax due (Sec. 112(3), Tit. 36, M.R.S.A.). Any justice of the Superior Court may compel the attendance of witnesses and the giving of testimony before the State Tax Assessor in the same manner, to the same extent and subject to the same penalties as if the testimony was being heard before the Superior Court.

The State Tax Assessor may examine or investigate the place of business, books, documents, and any relevant personal property of any person believed to be liable for sales and use taxes (Sec. 112(4), Tit. 36, M.R.S.A.).

¶ 498 Statute of Limitations

In general, the State Tax Assessor must make a deficiency assessment within three years from the latter of the date a return was filed and the due date for the return (Sec. 141(1), Tit. 36, M.R.S.A.). However, the assessment period is extended to six years from the date a return was filed if the tax liability shown on the return is less than one-half the liability determined to be due and the additional liability is attributable to unreported information that was required to be reported on the return (Sec. 141(2), Tit. 36, M.R.S.A.). There is no assessment limitation period with respect to time periods for which a fraudulent return or no return was filed.

Delinquent taxes, including taxes owed by taxpayers filing for protection under the U.S. Bankruptcy Code, may be collected by levy within 10 years from the time the assessment of the tax becomes final or before the expiration of the agreed-upon collection period (Sec. 176-A, Tit. 36, M.R.S.A.). Any levy action ordered by the assessor prior to the expiration of the 10-year collection period continues for six months from the date such levy is first made or until the liability is satisfied or becomes unenforceable, whichever occurs first. The running of the 10-year period for collection of tax is stayed during the time that a consensual payment plan between the taxpayer and the assessor is in effect. However, when a taxpayer institutes a federal bankruptcy proceeding, the assessor's right to collect any tax due by levy continues until six years after the date of discharge or dismissal of the proceeding.

¶ 499   **Application for Refund**

If any tax has been assessed at an excessive amount because of departmental clerical error or illegal computation and collection, the State Tax Assessor may credit the amount on taxes due from the taxpayer and refund the balance of the overpayment, provided that a written petition stating the grounds for which the refund is claimed is filed with the State Tax Assessor or the overpayment is discovered on audit within three years of the date of the overpayment (Sec. 2011, Tit. 36, M.R.S.A.).

A taxpayer may request a credit or refund of any Maine tax that is administered by the State Tax Assessor within three years from the date the return was filed, or three years previously, two years from the date the tax was paid, whichever period expires later (Sec. 144, Tit. 36, M.R.S.A.).

• **Interest on refunds**

In general, interest, at a rate determined annually by the State Tax Assessor, will be paid from the date the return listing the overpayment was filed, or the payment was made, whichever is later, on any balance refunded (Sec. 186, Tit. 36, M.R.S.A., Sec. 2011, Tit. 36, M.R.S.A.).

No interest may be paid, however, with respect to refunds of sales tax on depreciable machinery and equipment purchases (Sec. 2011, Tit. 36, M.R.S.A.). In cases of excessive or erroneous collections, the State Tax Assessor will pay interest only upon proof that interest was included in the repayment by the retailer to the person from whom the tax was originally collected (Sec. 1814(3), Tit. 36, M.R.S.A.).

• **Refund of tax paid on hotel room rental by person in continuous residence**

Rentals by persons residing continuously for 28 days or more at any one hotel, rooming house, tourist or trailer camp are tax-exempt (Sec. 1760(20), Tit. 36, M.R.S.A.). Consequently, the tax paid by the purchaser during the initial 28-day period must be refunded by the retailer. The retailer is entitled to a corresponding credit.

• **Refund on inventory goods removed from state**

A business that operates both inside and outside Maine may request a sales tax refund on property that was placed in inventory in Maine and later withdrawn from inventory for:

    — use at a fixed location of the business in another taxing jurisdiction;

    — fabrication, attachment or incorporation into other property for use at a fixed location of business in another taxing jurisdiction; or

    — incorporation into real property in another taxing jurisdiction.

A refund will not be available if the property was used for any other purpose prior to withdrawal. The business must maintain inventory records that make it possible to trace to the acquisition and disposition of such property. A refund is not available if the taxing jurisdiction to which the supplies and equipment are removed levies a sales or use tax. (Sec. 2012, Tit. 36, M.R.S.A.)

• **Rental vehicle excise tax reimbursement**

A sales and use tax refund may be claimed based on the portion of the excise tax paid on automobiles rented for less than one year if the registration is surrendered before it expires (Sec. 2015(1), Tit. 36, M.R.S.A.). Refund claims made be made annually, on or before each September 1, for registrations surrendered during the most recently completed period from July 1 to June 30.

• **Commercial production machinery and equipment; electricity**

Persons not holding exemption certificate cards that purchase qualifying depreciable machinery and equipment or electricity for use in commercial agricultural production, commercial aquaculture, commercial wood harvesting, or commercial fishing may apply for a refund of sales and use tax paid with respect to such qualifying property (Sec. 2013(2), Tit. 36, M.R.S.A.). Purchases of electricity or of fuel for a commercial fishing vessel must be prorated if the taxpayer used the electricity or fuel in both qualifying and nonqualifying activities.

- **Material used in fish passage facilities**

Taxes on the sale or use of materials used in the construction of fish passage facilities in new, reconstructed or redeveloped dams are refundable if the facilities are built pursuant to plans and specifications approved by the Department of Inland Fisheries and Wildlife or the Department of Marine Resources (Sec. 2014, Tit. 36, M.R.S.A.).

- **Communications machinery and equipment used in underserved area**

A reimbursement of sales tax is allowed for taxes paid on machinery and equipment purchased for use by a person to develop an advanced communications technology infrastructure in a qualifying ConnectME zone. "Advanced communications technology infrastructure" means any communications technology infrastructure or infrastructure improvement that expands the deployment of, or improves the quality of, broadband availability and wireless service coverage. A "qualifying ConnectME zone" is a geographical area that is eligible for tax reimbursement as an unserved or underserved area, as determined by the ConnectME Authority (Sec. 2017, Tit. 36, M.R.S.A.; Rule 324 (18-125 CMR 124)).

A claim for reimbursement must be filed on an approved form with the state tax assessor within three years of the date on which the machinery and equipment was purchased. The reimbursement claim must include a statement from the Authority certifying that the machinery and equipment is being used primarily to develop an advanced communications technology infrastructure in a qualifying ConnectME zone. The total amount of reimbursements in any fiscal year may not exceed $500,000 (Sec. 2017(3) and (4), Tit. 36, M.R.S.A.).

¶ 500   MARYLAND

¶ 501   Scope of Tax

Source.—Statutory references are to Titles 11 and 13 of the Tax General Article of the Maryland Code, as amended to date, except as otherwise indicated. Details are reported in the CCH MARYLAND STATE TAX REPORTS starting at ¶ 60-000.

The Maryland sales and use tax is imposed on every retail sale and on the use in Maryland of tangible personal property (unless specifically exempt by law) and on every retail sale and use in Maryland of a taxable service (Sec. 11-102(a), Tax General Art.). A "sale for use" is also subject to tax (Sec. 11-502(a), Tax General Art.).

The Maryland sales and use tax is a general tax on all retail sales or use of tangible personal property in the state. For sales and use tax purposes, "sale" includes lease, rental, and royalty or license transactions. A constitutional or statutory exclusion must exist for sales of tangible personal property to be exempt from tax. On the other hand, since only "taxable service" is subject to tax, services not specifically subject to tax by statute are exempt.

If a person pays the sales or use tax when the retail sale is made, the person is not required to pay the tax again upon using the tangible personal property or taxable service in the state (Sec. 11-221(b), Tax General Art.).

• **Use tax**

"Use" means an exercise of a right or power to use, consume, possess, or store tangible personal property or a taxable service, including (1) tangible personal property acquired for use or resale in the form of real estate by a builder, contractor, or landowner; or (2) unless specifically exempted, facilities, tools, tooling, machinery, or equipment (including dies, molds, and patterns) even if the buyer intends to transfer title to the property before or after use (Sec. 11-101(n), Tax General Art.).

• **"Taxable service"**

The following services are defined as taxable (Sec. 11-101(m), Tax General Art.):

— fabrication, printing, or production of tangible personal property by special order;

— commercial cleaning or laundering of textiles for a buyer engaged in a business that requires these recurring services;

— cleaning of a commercial or industrial building;

— cellular telephone or other mobile telecommunications service;

— "900," "976," "915," and other "900"-type telecommunications service;

— custom calling service provided in connection with basic telephone service;

— telephone answering services;

— pay per view television service;

— credit reporting and security services (including detective, guard and armored car services and security systems services);

— a transportation service for the transmission, distribution, or delivery of taxable electricity or natural gas;

— a prepaid telephone calling arrangement.

"Corkage" charges: Maryland sales and use tax applies to a charge by a restaurant, club, or hotel with a class B or C license for the privilege of consuming wine that is not purchased from or provided by the license holder (Sec. 11-101(m)(13), Tax General Art.).

• **Legal incidence of tax**

Subject to certain exceptions, the buyer must pay the sales or use tax to the vendor; the vendor is required to collect the tax as trustee for the state (Sec. 11-403(b), Tax General Art.).

Absorption of tax: A vendor may assume or absorb all or any part of the sales and use tax imposed on a retail sale or use and pay that sales and use tax on behalf of the buyer (Sec. 11-402, Tax General Art.). A vendor who makes a sale subject to the sales and use tax is obligated to pay the tax that the vendor collects for that sale or that the vendor assumes or absorbs for that sale with the return that covers the period in which the vendor makes that sale.

Service providers deemed consumers: In certain cases, when a person purchases materials or supplies in connection with providing a service to another person, the service provider is considered the consumer of the purchased items and is liable for the sales and use tax to the vendors. The following are "deemed consumers" for sales and use tax purposes:

(1) construction contractors are considered the ultimate consumers/users of all materials incorporated or used in the performance of their contracts (Reg. 03.06.01.19(A));

(2) persons offering sports facilities to the public are considered the consumers of all materials and supplies purchased to operate the facilities (Reg. 03.06.01.20);

(3) persons providing certain services are considered the consumers of the materials and supplies used in rendering such services, including materials and supplies that may pass on to clients or customers as part of the services rendered.

Drop shipments: When all the parties are located in the state, the retailer furnishes a resale certificate to the primary seller, rendering the first sale a nontaxable transaction. The retailer then collects sales tax on behalf of the state on the secondary sale to its customer. However, different considerations arise when one or more of the parties are not within the state.

If the seller and the consumer are both in Maryland, and the retailer is an unregistered out-of-state dealer, the seller may either (Reg. Sec. 03.06.01.14):

— require the retailer to register as a Maryland vendor and furnish a resale certificate or

— collect the tax from the retailer based upon the wholesale price paid.

Online travel companies (OTCs): For the sale or use of an accommodation facilitated by an "accommodations intermediary," such as an OTC, the taxable price is the full amount of the consideration paid by a buyer for the sale or use of an accommodation, but not including any tax remitted to a taxing authority. (Sec. 11-101(a)(2), Tax General Art.)

• **Nexus**

"Vendor" includes, for an out-of-state vendor, a salesman, representative, peddler, or canvasser whom the Comptroller, for the efficient administration of this title, elects to treat as an agent jointly responsible with the dealer, distributor, employer, or supervisor (Sec. 11-101, Tax General Art.):

(1) under whom the agent operates; or

(2) from whom the agent obtains the tangible personal property or taxable service for sale.

The term "engage in the business of an out-of-state vendor" means to sell or deliver tangible personal property or a taxable service in Maryland. The term includes (Sec. 11-701(b), Tax General Art.):

¶501   **Maryland**

— permanently or temporarily maintaining, occupying, or using any office, sales, or sample room, or distribution, storage, warehouse, or other place for the sale of tangible personal property or a taxable service directly or indirectly through an agent or subsidiary;

— having an agent, canvasser, representative, salesman, or solicitor operating in the state for the purpose of delivering, selling or taking orders for tangible personal property or a taxable service; or

— entering the state on a regular basis to provide service or repair for tangible personal property.

Disaster-related work by out-of-state contractors: See ¶ 509.

• Streamlined Act status

Maryland has enacted the Uniform (Simplified) Sales and Use Tax Act.

Maryland is an Advisor State to the Streamlined Sales Tax Project (SSTP). It has enacted legislation authorizing it to enter into the Streamlined Sales and Use Tax Agreement (Sec. 11-106, Gen. Tax Art.), but has not yet enacted the changes to its laws necessary to comply with the Agreement's requirements. For additional information, see ¶ 507.

¶ 502   **Tax Base**

The sales and use tax is computed on either (1) the taxable price of each separate sale, (2) the combined taxable price of all retail sales on the same occasion by the same vendor to the same buyer, or (3) 95.25% of the gross receipts from retail sales of tangible personal property made through vending machines or other self-service machines (Sec. 11-301, Tax General Art.).

Combined sales: A vendor must compute the tax on the total taxable price of all sales to a buyer in the same licensed business location on the same business day, whether or not at different counters or departments, without regard to the individual taxable prices of the separate items, except when it is impractical to do so (Reg. 03.06.01.02). In the latter case, the buyer may, nevertheless, demonstrate prior sales on the same day and request a combination of all taxable prices.

• "Taxable price" defined

"Taxable price" means the value in money of the consideration that is paid, delivered, payable, or deliverable by a buyer to a vendor in the consummation and complete performance of a sale, without deduction for any expense or cost. The consideration may take the form of money, rights, property, promises, or anything else of value, or by exchange or barter (Reg. 03.06.01.08(A), Reg. 03.06.01.08(B)).

Generally, the cost of labor or service rendered, any material used, or any property sold may not be deducted, regardless of how any contract, invoice, or other evidence of the transaction is stated or computed (Sec. 11-101(*l*), Tax General Art., Reg. 03.06.01.08(A), Reg. 03.06.01.08(B)).

Communications services: The taxable price of communications services does not include the price of any nontaxable services made in connection with a taxable service (Sec. 11-101(*l*), Tax General Art.). Charges do not need to be separately stated for nontaxable services to be excluded as long as the vendor keeps adequate records to reasonably identify those charges that were subject to tax and those that were not subject to tax.

• Items not excludable

The following items are part of the "taxable price" even if separately stated on the invoice and, thus, may not be deducted before the computation of the tax (Reg. 03.06.01.08(B)):

(1) Any charge based on the amount or frequency of purchase (such as a small order charge), the method of billing (such as a split billing), or the nature of the item sold (such as a slow-moving charge);

(2) Any commission or other form of compensation for the services of an agent, factor, consultant, broker, or similar person;

(3) Any charges for mandatory warranties, maintenance, service agreements, or insurance coverage;

(4) Any portion of the price described as a "donation" when the donation is in fact required by the vendor as a condition of the sale;

(5) The assumption of any liabilities of the vendor;

(6) The performance of any personal or other services for or on behalf of the vendor;

(7) All services necessary to complete a sale, such as assembly, fabrication, alteration, lubrication, engraving, monogramming, cleaning, customization, and dealer preparation;

(8) Prompt payment discounts and manufacturers' rebates.

• "Gross receipts" defined

"Gross receipts" as a basis for determination of the tax is applicable only to retail sales of tangible personal property through vending machines. Unlike ordinary transactions where the tax base is "taxable price," the deductions or exclusions under Sec. 11-101(*l*)(3), Tax General Art., are not applicable to "gross receipts." Moreover, operators of vending machines may not collect the tax from buyers as separately stated items (Sec. 11-405, Tax General Art.).

¶ 503   List of Exemptions, Exceptions, and Exclusions

Unless otherwise indicated, the statutory exemptions, exceptions, and exclusions listed below apply to both sales and use taxes. Items that are excluded from the sales or use tax base are treated at ¶ 502, "Tax Base."

Energy Star sales tax holiday: The weekend that consists of the Saturday immediately preceding the third Monday in February through the third Monday in February each year is a tax-free weekend during which sales and use tax will not apply to the sale of any Energy Star product or solar water heater. "Energy Star product" is defined as an air conditioner, clothes washer or dryer, furnace, heat pump, standard size refrigerator, compact fluorescent light bulb, LED light bulb (through 6/30/2017), dehumidifier, boiler, or programmable thermostat that has been designated as meeting or exceeding the applicable Energy Star efficiency requirements developed by the U.S. Environmental Protection Agency and the U.S. Department of Energy.

Back-to-School sales tax holiday: The seven-day period from the second Sunday in August through the following Saturday is a tax-free period for back-to-school shopping in Maryland during which sales and use tax does not apply to the sale of any item of clothing or footwear, excluding accessory items, with a taxable price of $100 or less.

• Sales and use exemptions, exceptions, and exclusions

Admission fees, when sold by a person whose gross receipts from the sale are subject to the admissions and amusement tax	Sec. 11-101(j), Tax General Art., Sec. 11-221(a)(1), Tax General Art.
Advertising: literature and advertising newspaper supplements for distribution out of state	Sec. 11-215(d), Tax General Art.

Domestic or residential rate schedule of electricity, steam, or gas . . . Sec. 11-207(a),
Tax General Art.

Drugs and medical supplies sold to or by physicians and hospitals . . Sec. 11-211(a),
Tax General Art.

Electricity: generating equipment . . . . Sec. 11-101(d),
Tax General Art.,
Sec. 11-101(j),
Tax General Art.

Electricity, steam, gas used in residential condominium, retirement
community . . . . Sec. 11-207(a),
Tax General Art.

Electricity: used to operate machinery or equipment . . . . Sec. 11-210(a),
Tax General Art.

Electricity (residential) generated by wind or solar equipment . . . . . Sec. 11-207(a)(5),
Tax General Art.

Energy-efficient appliances . . . . Sec. 11-226,
Tax General Art.

Film production activities . . . . Sec. 11-226,
Tax General Art.,
Sec. 4-501,
Art. 83A, MD Code

Energy-related equipment (geothermal or solar) . . . . Sec. 11-230,
Tax General Art.,

Flags, state and federal . . . . Sec. 11-205,
Tax General Art.

Food: snack food sold through vending machines . . . . Sec. 11-206(g),
Tax General Art.,
Sec. 11-206(h),
Tax General Art.

Food: sold at less than $1.00; purchased with food stamps; sold in
vehicles in interstate commerce; sold for off-premises
consumption, including food sold by a vendor who provides no
facilities for on-premises consumption . . . . Sec. 11-206(b),
Tax General Art.,
Sec. 11-206(c),
Tax General Art.,
Sec. 11-206(e),
Tax General Art.,
Sec. 11-206(g),
Tax General Art.,
Sec. 11-206(h),
Tax General Art.

Food: sold at or by certain exempt organizations . . . . Sec. 11-206(d),
Tax General Art.

Food: tips and cover charges in food establishments . . . . Sec. 11-101(j),
Tax General Art.

Fuel: diesel fuel used for mining reclamation . . . . Sec. 11-212(2),
Tax General Art.

Fuel: farm equipment or agricultural purposes . . . . Sec. 11-201(a),
Tax General Art.

Fuel: for use in commercial fishing vessels . . . .   Sec. 11-218(3),
Tax General Art.

Fuel: motor fuel subject to motor fuel or motor carrier tax . . . .   Sec. 11-221(a),
Tax General Art.

Fuel (coal, firewood, heating oil, propane or LP gas) used in residential
    property . . . .   Sec. 11-207(a),
Tax General Art.

Geothermal or solar energy equipment . . . .   Sec. 11-230,
Tax General Art.,

Gift and thrift shops, hospital, volunteer staff . . . .   Sec. 11-204(b)(3),
Tax General Art.

Government transactions: sales of U.S or state government documents
    . . . .   Sec. 11-215(d),
Tax General Art.

Government transactions: sales to Maryland and the federal
    government; sales of testing equipment for the Department of
    Defense . . . .   Sec. 11-101(c),
Tax General Art.,
Sec. 11-220(a),
Tax General Art.,
Sec. 11-222,
Tax General Art.

Health and physical aids . . . .   Sec. 11-211(b),
Tax General Art.,
Sec. 11-211(c),
Tax General Art.

Insurance services . . . .   Sec. 11-219(a),
Tax General Art.

Interstate transactions, including cargo handling equipment used in
    international marine terminals and films or video tape used in
    TV broadcasting to areas outside the state . . . .   Sec. 11-208(a), Tax
General Art.,
Sec. 11-208(b),
Tax General Art.

Lodging provided at corporate facilities . . . .   Sec. 11-231,
Tax General Art.,
Sec. 20-404,
Local Govt. Art.

Machinery, equipment, fuel, and utilities used to manufacture Energy
    Star windows and doors . . . .   Sec. 11-210(e),
Tax General Art.

Machinery, equipment, tools, and spare parts: computer hardware if
    capitalized and used in production or research and development
    . . . .   Sec. 11-217,
Tax General Art.

Machinery, equipment, tools, and spare parts: used in mining . . . . .   Sec. 11-217,
Tax General Art.

Machinery, equipment, tools, and spare parts: used in printing . . . . .   Sec. 11-215,
Tax General Art.

Machinery, equipment, tools, and spare parts: used in production or research and development if the buyer is obligated to transfer title after use to the person for whom the buyer manufactures goods or performs work . . . .   Sec. 11-101(f), Tax General Art.

Machinery, equipment, tools, and spare parts: used in publishing and broadcasting . . . .   Sec. 11-101(j), Tax General Art.

Magazine sales by schools and parent-teacher associations . . . .   Sec. 11-204(b)(5), Tax General Art.

Mail order: catalogs for distribution out of state . . . .   Sec. 11-215(d), Tax General Art.

Mail order: computerized mailing lists for distribution out of state . .   Sec. 11-215(d), Tax General Art.

Mail order: direct mail advertising literature for distribution out of state . . . .   Sec. 11-215(d), Tax General Art.

Manufacturing: items used or incorporated in a production activity or consumed directly and predominantly in manufacturing and utilities and fuel consumed directly in manufacturing . . . . . .   Sec. 11-101(e), Tax General Art., Sec. 11-101(l), Tax General Art.

Maryland Vending Program for the Blind . . . .   Sec. 11-204(b)(4), Tax General Art.

Medical and dental: sales of drugs and medical supplies to or by physicians and hospitals; health and physical aids; and patients' medical records . . . .   Sec. 11-211(a), Tax General Art.

Mental hospital gift shops . . . .   Sec. 11-204(b)(2), Tax General Art.

Mining: fabrication, processing, or service of wood products by a sawmill for use in mining and diesel fuel used for mining reclamation . . . .   Sec. 11-212, Tax General Art.

Mobile homes, except for the first sale . . . .   Sec. 11-213, Tax General Art.

Modular buildings (40% exemption) . . . .   Sec. 11-104, Tax General Art.

Motion pictures, motion picture trailers, or movie advertising posters: rentals . . . .   Sec. 11-221(a), Tax General Art.

Motor vehicles: buses used in public transportation system . . . .   Sec. 11-223(1), Tax General Art.

Motor vehicles: farm vehicles used in farming . . . .   Sec. 11-201(a)(6), Tax General Art.

Motor vehicles: leases of at least one year . . . .   Sec. 11-221(a), Tax General Art.

Motor vehicles: sales, other than house or office trailers, that will be registered in another state . . . .   Sec. 11-208(c), Tax General Art.

Motor vehicles: subject to the motor vehicle excise tax	Sec. 11-221(a), Tax General Art.
Motor vehicles: used principally in interstate or foreign commerce . .	Sec. 11-208(c), Tax General Art.
Newspapers	Sec. 11-215(c), Tax General Art.
Nonprofit charitable, educational, or religious organizations, including the American Red Cross	Sec. 11-204(a)(3), (6) Tax General Art.
Nonresident property	Sec. 11-214, Tax General Art.
Occasional sales of less than $1,000 not made through an auctioneer or dealer	Sec. 11-209(a), Tax General Art.
Packaging and shipping: shipping materials sold with other tangible personal property; containers used to transport farm products	Sec. 11-201(a), Tax General Art., Sec. 11-202, Tax General Art.
Parent-teacher associations	Sec. 11-204(a)(6), Tax General Art.
Pellet stoves (multifuel)	Sec. 11-226(c), Tax General Art.
Personal or professional services	Sec. 11-219(a), Tax General Art.
Pollution control equipment	Sec. 11-210(b), Tax General Art.
Precious metal bullion or coins	Sec. 11-214.1, Tax General Art.
Printing: printing of tangible personal property, or sales of printed material, for resale or incorporation into a product for sale; sales of photographic materials used in printing; sales of nonphotographic materials to printers of tangible personal property for sale; sales to or use by printers of printing equipment	Sec. 11-215, Tax General Art.
Religious organizations and churches	Sec. 11-204(b)(1), Tax General Art.
Rentals and leases: by the Maryland Port Authority of machinery and equipment	Sec. 11-208(a), Tax General Art.
Rentals and leases: motion pictures, trailers, or movie advertising posters	Sec. 11-221(a), Tax General Art.
Resales: tangible personal property for resale or for use or incorporation in other property to be produced for sale	Sec. 11-101(d), Tax General Art., Sec. 11-101(l), Tax General Art., Sec. 11-210(c), Tax General Art.

Research and development: machinery, equipment, tools, and spare parts (including computer hardware) used in, items to be consumed, mutilated, or tested to destruction in, and items to become a component part of, a product produced through research and development . . . . Sec. 11-217, Tax General Art.

School-related organizations, sales by . . . . Sec. 11-206(b)(6), Tax General Art.

Seafood prepared for off-premises consumption . . . . Sec. 11-206(f), Tax General Art.

Senior citizens' organizations . . . . Sec. 11-204(a)(4), Tax General Art.

Snack food sold for off-premises consumption or through vending machines . . . . Sec. 11-206(g), Tax General Art.

Snowmaking, electricity and fuel for equipment . . . . Sec. 11-229, Tax General Art.

Solar or geothermal energy equipment . . . . Sec. 11-230, Tax General Art.,

Storage: temporary storage in Maryland of property bought out of state for use in another state . . . . Sec. 11-216(a), Tax General Art.

Tobacco cessation products . . . . Sec. 11-211(b)(18), Tax General Art.

Transportation services . . . . Sec. 11-223, Tax General Art.

Vending machines, bulk sales for 75¢ or less . . . . Sec. 11-201.1, Tax General Art.

Vending machines, sales of snack food, milk, fruit, vegetables . . . . . Sec. 11-206(g), Tax General Art., Sec. 11-206(h), Tax General Art.

Veterans' organizations . . . . Sec. 11-204(a)(8), Tax General Art.

Vessels: sales subject to the excise tax . . . . Sec. 11-221(a), Tax General Art.

Volunteer fire companies, ambulance companies, and rescue squads . . Sec. 11-204(a)(5), Tax General Art.

Water delivered through conduits or pipes . . . . Sec. 11-224, Tax General Art.

Wind energy equipment . . . . Sec. 11-230, Tax General Art.,

Wood products: fabrication, processing, or service of wood products by a sawmill for use in farming or mining . . . . Sec. 11-201(a), Tax General Art., Sec. 11-212(1), Tax General Art.

Wood products: wood, wood bark, refuse derived fuel for heating equipment . . . . Sec. 11-207(b), Tax General Art.

¶503 Maryland

¶ 504   Rate of Tax

The basic sales and use tax rate is 6¢ for each dollar, plus 1¢ for each 17¢ or fraction thereof in excess of exact dollars. This rate is reflected as a bracket schedule applied to the "taxable price" (see ¶ 506). "Taxable price" is defined and discussed under "Tax Base" at ¶ 502.

- **Special rates**

Alcoholic beverages: The sales and use tax rate applicable to sales of alcoholic beverages is 9% (Sec. 11-104(g), Tax General Art.).

The general sales and use tax rate, rather than the rate applicable to alcoholic beverages, applies to a separately stated charge, made in connection with a sale of alcoholic beverages, for any labor or service rendered, material used, or property sold. The general rate also applies to a mandatory gratuity or service charge for serving food or beverages to a group of more than 10 individuals. (Sec. 11-104(g)(2), Tax General Art.)

Vending machines: The sales and use tax is computed on (1) the taxable price of each separate sale; (2) the combined taxable price of all retail sales on the same occasion by the same vendor to the same buyer if a combined sale is made; or (3) 94.5% (previously, 95.25%) of the gross receipts from the retail sales if retail sales of tangible personal property or a taxable service are made through vending or other self-service machines (Sec. 11-104(b), Tax General Art.). However, tax does not apply to sales from bulk vending machines for 25¢ or less (Sec. 11-201.1, Tax General Art.).

Admissions and amusement tax: A state admissions and amusement tax is imposed at a rate of 30% of the net proceeds derived from any charge for the operation of an electronic bingo machine permitted under a commercial bingo license or an electronic tip jar machine authorized as specified (Sec. 4-102(d), Tax General Art; Sec. 4-105(a-1), Tax General Art.). If proceeds are also subject to local admissions and amusement tax, the state rate cannot exceed a rate that, when combined with the local rate, exceeds 35%. Local admissions and amusement tax rates applicable to electronic bingo machine and tip jar proceeds cannot exceed the local rate imposed as of January 1, 2009.

Dyed diesel fuel: Dyed diesel fuel sold by a marina is subject to sales and use tax at a rate of 6%, applied to 94.5% of gross receipts. A marina must pay sales and use tax on dyed diesel fuel sales and may not collect the tax from the buyer as a separately stated item. A "marina" is a person who maintains a place of business where motor fuel is sold primarily to vessels. (Sec. 11-410, Tax General Art.)

Short-term vehicle rentals: The tax rate for short-term vehicle rental agreements with a taxable price of $2 or more is, for a rental truck, 8¢ for each exact dollar and 2¢ for each 25¢ or part of 25¢ over an exact dollar. Effective July 1, 2013, the short-term vehicle rental tax applies to rentals of motorcycles for a period of 180 days or less. The rate for a passenger car, motorcycle, or multipurpose passenger vehicle is 23¢ for each exact multiple of $2 and:

If the excess over an exact multiple of $2 is:	Tax:
1¢ to 9¢	1¢
9¢ to 18¢	2¢
18¢ to 27¢	3¢
27¢ to 35¢	4¢
35¢ to 44¢	5¢
44¢ to 53¢	6¢
53¢ to 61¢	7¢
61¢ to 70¢	8¢
70¢ to 79¢	9¢
79¢ to 87¢	10¢

If the excess over an exact multiple of $2 is:	Tax:
87¢ to 96¢	11¢
96¢ to $1.05	12¢
$1.05 to $1.14	13¢
$1.14 to $1.22	14¢
$1.22 to $1.31	15¢
$1.31 to $1.40	16¢
$1.40 to $1.48	17¢
$1.48 to $1.57	18¢
$1.57 to $1.66	19¢
$1.66 to $1.74	20¢
$1.74 to $1.83	21¢
$1.83 to $1.92	22¢
$1.92 to $2.00	23¢

(Sec. 11-104(c), Tax General Art.).

Long-term vehicle rentals: Sales and use tax does not apply to a vehicle lease for a period of at least one year (Sec. 11-221(a)(5), Tax General Art.).

Mobile homes; modular homes: The tax rate applies to 60% of the taxable price of the first sale of mobile homes (Sec. 11-104(d) and (f), Tax General Art.).

Electricity: For electricity not distributed by a public service company, a special Maryland use tax on electricity is imposed at the rate of .062 cents per kilowatt hour (Sec. 11-01A-01—Sec. 11-01A-06, Tax General Art.). However, the special use tax does not apply to (1) electricity used for residential purposes, (2) electricity used only for emergency back-up generation, and (3) on-site generated electricity (Reg. 03.06.01.34).

E-911 prepaid wireless fee: Purchases of prepaid wireless telecommunications service in Maryland are subject to a prepaid wireless E-911 fee of 60 cents per retail transaction. The fee is not subject to sales and use tax (Sec. 1-313, Public Safety Art.). "Prepaid wireless telecommunications service" means a commercial mobile radio service that:

— allows a consumer to dial 911 to access the 911 system;

— must be paid for in advance; and

— is sold in predetermined units that decline with use in a known amount.

The fee must be collected by the seller on each retail transaction in the state. A retail transaction occurs in the state if: the sale or recharge takes place at the seller's place of business located in the state; the consumer's shipping address is in the state; or no item is shipped, but the consumer's billing address, or the location associated with the consumer's mobile telephone number, is in the state. A seller must report and remit the fee in the same manner as sales and use tax. On or after January 1, 2014, a seller may deduct and retain 3% of fees collected. (Sec. 1-313, Public Safety Art.).

¶ 505   Local Taxes

A county, municipal corporation, special taxing district, or other political subdivision of the state may not impose any retail sales or use tax other than a tax on the sale of fuels, utilities, space rentals, or controlled dangerous substances, unless authorized by statute (Sec. 11-102(b), Tax General Art.). A code county may impose a sales or use tax on food and beverages authorized by Article 25B, Sec. 13H of the Code.

Counties, municipal corporations, and the Maryland Stadium Authority are authorized to impose a tax on admissions (Sec. 4-102, Tax General Art.). The tax may be collected on gross receipts from admissions or amusement charges, and on admissions at reduced charge or no charge if there is a charge for other admissions. Taxable admissions charges include separate charges for admission to a place or charges for use of a game or recreational facility, as well as charges for refreshments, merchandise or services sold in connection with entertainment at a nightclub or other hall (Sec. 4-101(b), Tax General Art.). The taxable price, for sales tax purposes, does not include the separately-stated admissions and amusement charge (Sec. 11-101(j)(3)(i)(6)(D), Tax General Art.). If gross receipts subject to the admissions and amusement tax are also subject to the sales and use tax, a county or municipal corporation may not set a rate that, when combined with the sales and use tax, exceeds 11% of the gross receipts. Local rates of admissions and amusement taxes are available at **http:// taxes.marylandtaxes.com/Business_Taxes/Business_Tax_Types/Admis sions_and_Amusement_Tax/Tax_Information/Tax_Rates/.**

Prince George's County is required to impose and collect a tax on telecommunications at a rate of not less than 5% (Sec. 9-606, Political Subdivisions Art.).

Heavy equipment rentals: Maryland imposes a 2% tax on gross receipts from short-term rentals (365 days or less) of heavy equipment by a person whose principal business is the short-term lease or rental of heavy equipment (Sec. 9-609, Political Subdivisions Art.). The rental business must collect the tax from rental customers and remit the tax to the county and the municipal corporation on a quarterly basis. If the business is located in a municipal corporation, the tax must be remitted to the county and the municipal corporation in proportion to the personal property tax rates of the county and the municipal corporation. The tax does not apply to rentals by a business located in a jurisdiction that does not impose a personal property tax. Such heavy equipment property is not subject to Maryland's personal property tax.

A rental business must submit to the county and the municipal corporation a statement of property that is subject to the gross receipts tax and exempt from property tax. By February 28, the county or the municipal corporation will provide a statement to each taxpayer that includes the gross receipts tax remitted during the previous calendar year, the property tax that would have been due, and the gross receipts tax shortage or surplus. If the gross receipts tax paid is less than the property tax that would have been paid, the statement will include a bill for the shortage. (Sec. 9-609, Political Subdivisions Art.)

Hotel taxes: Counties are authorized to impose a local hotel rental tax at various specified rates (Sec. 20-402, Local Govt. Art.; Sec. 20-403, Local Govt. Art.). In addition, a municipal corporation may impose a hotel rental tax on a transient charge paid to a hotel (Sec. 20-432, Local Govt. Art.). The tax may not exceed 2% and it may not be imposed if (1) the hotel has 10 or fewer sleeping rooms; or (2) the municipal corporation is located within a county that either distributes at least 50% of total hotel tax revenues to promote tourism within the county or does not impose a tax on transient charges paid to a hotel. "Transient charge" is defined as a hotel charge for sleeping accommodations for a period not exceeding four consecutive months. The term does not include any hotel charge for services or for accommodations other than sleeping accommodations.

If a county is authorized to impose a tax on transient charges paid to hotels, the county may impose a hotel rental tax within the municipal corporation that is lower than the rate imposed outside the municipality (Sec. 20-436, Local Govt. Art.).

Rates may not exceed 3% in Cecil County, 4% in Talbot County, and 5% in Calvert, Carroll, Charles, Dorchester, Frederick, St. Mary's, and Sommerset counties. The maximum rate is 6% in Garrett and Wicomico counties. (Sec. 20-405(b), Local Govt. Art. 24) Code counties (except Allegany County) that have adopted home rule (Caroline, Kent, Queen Anne's, and Worcester) may impose a hotel rental tax of up to 3%, or up to 5% with the unanimous consent of the county commissioners. Allegany County may set a hotel rental tax rate of up to 3%, or up to 8% with the unanimous consent of the county commissioners. The rate for Washington county is 6% (Sec. 20-405(d), Local Govt. Art.).

Baltimore County levies a room tax of 8% (Sec. 11-4-402, Baltimore County Code).

¶ 506   **Bracket Schedule**

The amount of tax at the 6% rate is calculated as follows (Sec. 11-104(a), Tax General Art.):

Taxable Price	Tax
If taxable price is less than $1	
20¢	1¢
21¢ to less than 34¢	2¢
34¢ to less than 51¢	3¢
51¢ to less than 67¢	4¢
67¢ to less than 84¢	5¢
84¢ to less than $1.00	6¢
If taxable price is $1 or more	
For each exact dollar	6¢
For that part of a dollar in excess of an exact dollar	
At least 1¢ but less than 17¢	1¢
17¢ to less than 34¢	2¢
34¢ to less than 51¢	3¢
51¢ to less than 67¢	4¢
67¢ to less than 84¢	5¢
84¢ to less than the next exact dollar	6¢

A 6% rate schedule is available for taxable sales up to $100; go to **http://taxes.marylandtaxes.com/Business_Taxes/Business_Tax_Types/Sales_and_Use_Tax/Tax_Information/Tax_Rates/Tax_rate_chart.pdf.**

Minimum taxable levels: The sales and use tax does not apply to sales of less than 20¢ or to sales of food for less than $1.

Treatment of "breakage": Rate charts issued by the Maryland Taxpayer Service Section are generally used in determining the tax on a sale. Such charts are based on even multiples of 17 cents, with the tax on a fractional multiple being rounded up to the next cent. Because of this rounding, the amount collected will almost always be more than a flat 6% of taxable sales. Vendors are required to report the exact amount collected. Any "breakage" (the difference between the actual collection and the calculated amount) cannot be retained by vendors and must be remitted to the state (*Sales & Use Tax Tip # 8,* Comptroller of the Treasury, January 1990).

¶ 507   **Returns, Payments, and Due Dates**

Vendors are required to complete, under oath, and file a sales and use tax return with the Comptroller on or before the 20th day of the month following the month in which a vendor made a retail sale or sale for use, made a purchase under a direct payment permit, made a sale under a prepayment authorization or through a vending machine, or as required by regulation (Sec. 11-502(a), Tax General Art., Reg. 03.06.03.03). Taxpayers registered with the Comptroller must file returns in accordance with their filing schedules, even if no taxes are due.

Taxpayers must use the precoded forms issued by the Retail Sales Tax Division; internally generated returns are not acceptable. However, the failure to receive a return from the Comptroller does not alter the obligation to file on time (Reg. 03.06.03.03).

The sales and use tax returns must state, for the period covered, the gross proceeds of the business, the taxable price of sales on which the tax is computed, and the tax due. For a vendor making sales for use, the return must state the total value of the tangible personal property or taxable service and the tax due (Sec. 11-502(b), Tax General Art.).

In addition, if the Comptroller determines from a taxpayer's application for a sales tax license, previous reporting history, or through audit that a taxpayer is expected to remit less than $100 per month in taxes, the taxpayer may be assigned a filing or reporting basis that is less frequent than monthly or a different due date. A vendor who does not normally make taxable sales in each calendar month may be assigned a seasonal or other irregular filing basis (Reg. 03.06.03.03) but must notify the Comptroller if there is reason to believe that future tax obligations will average more than $100 per month, and file a supplemental return for any month in which taxes exceed $100.

- **Returns of buyers**

Buyers are required to complete, under oath, and file a sales and use tax return if they fail to pay the sales and use tax to vendors at the time tax collection is required or if they are required by regulation to file a tax return (Sec. 11-501(a), Tax General Art., Reg. 03.06.03.03).

Buyer's tax returns must be filed on or before the 20th day of the month that follows the month in which the purchase or use was made or on other dates that the Comptroller may specify by regulation. Taxpayers registered with the Comptroller must file returns in accordance with their filing schedules even if no taxes are due. The tax return must state the total value of the tangible personal property or taxable service and the sales and use tax due.

- **Payment of tax**

Taxes must be paid at the time of filing the returns; if an extension of the time for filing is granted, the time for payment is unaffected by such extension (Sec. 11-601, Tax General Art.).

Electronic filing: The Comptroller may require the payment of unpaid sales and use tax of $10,000 or more in connection with a tax return, report, or other document required to be filed in funds that are immediately available to the state on the date the payment is due (Sec. 13-104(a), Tax General Art., Sec. 13-105, Tax General Art.). Information on bFile, the electronic filing and payment system, is available at **https://interactive.marylandtaxes.com/Business/bFile/OSC/SelectApp.aspx**.

Direct payment: The Maryland Comptroller of the Treasury is permitted to enter into agreements allowing vendors with Maryland sales and use tax liability to compute the tax for purchases during a specific period using a predetermined agreed-upon effective rate (Sec. 11-407, Tax General Art.). Additionally, the Comptroller is authorized to issue direct payment permits to vendors subject to an effective rate agreement. Permit holders must file tax reports and make payments of all taxes due on or before the 21st day of the month succeeding the month in which the tax becomes due.

Vendors who make sales to holders of a direct payment permit must maintain records of the amount and description of each sale and the identity of the permit holder (Reg. 03.06.01.31(A)).

- **Uniform Sales Tax Administration Act**

Maryland has enacted the Uniform Sales and Use Tax Administration Act, the product of the Streamlined Sales Tax Project (SSTP), along with modifications recommended by the National Conference of State Legislators (NCSL). The SSTP developed the Act and the related Streamlined Sales and Use Tax Agreement to simplify and modernize sales and use tax administration in order to substantially reduce the burden of tax compliance for all sellers and for all types of commerce.

Maryland also has enacted legislation that "acknowledges" the Streamlined Sales and Use Tax Agreement (Ch. 311 (H.B. 559), Laws 2003). No substantive changes to state law were made as a result of the enactment of the bill. In order to become a member of the SST Governing Board, a state's laws, regulations, and policies must be substantially compliant with each of the Agreement's requirements.

Maryland's Comptroller is required to propose legislation and regulations to bring Maryland law into compliance with the Agreement within 90 days of the enactment of federal legislation authorizing member states of the Agreement to require remote sellers to collect and remit sales and use tax (Ch. 513 (H.B. 694), Laws 2004).

For additional information on the uniform acts, see "Streamlined Sales Tax Project," listed in the Table of Contents.

¶ 508   **Prepayment of Taxes**

If the nature of a vendor's business makes collection of the sales and use tax impracticable, the vendor may, upon approval of the Comptroller, prepay the tax (Sec. 11-406, Tax General Art.). However, the vendor may not collect the sales and use tax from buyers as a separately stated item.

¶ 509   **Vendor Registration**

Persons must be licensed by the Comptroller before they can engage in business in the state as a retail vendor or as an out-of-state vendor (Sec. 11-701(d), Tax General Art., Sec. 11-702, Tax General Art., Sec. 11-712, Tax General Art.).

• Application and approval of license

Applicants for a vendor's license must submit an application to the Comptroller for each place of business or for each vehicle in the state where the applicant sells tangible personal property or a taxable service, or for each vehicle from which sales are made (Sec. 11-703, Tax General Art., Sec. 11-704, Tax General Art.). If the applicant has no fixed place of business and does not sell from a vehicle, the license application must be submitted for the place designated as the address to which notices are mailed.

Special license for out-of-state vendors: The Comptroller may issue a special license to out-of-state vendors who are not required to be licensed but who are making taxable sales to Maryland residents and would like to collect the tax as a convenience for its Maryland customers. Such license may be issued by submitting to the Comptroller the required form (Sec. 11-707, Tax General Art.).

The license must be displayed in each place of business in Maryland (Sec. 11-708, Tax General Art.) and, generally, may not be transferred (Sec. 11-709, Tax General Art.).

• Disaster-related work performed by out-of-state contractors

An out-of-state business that performs disaster or emergency related work in Maryland during a disaster period does not establish a level of presence that would require the business or its out-of-state employees to be subject to state or local licensing or registration requirements, state or county income taxes, income tax withholding with respect to out-of-state employees, unemployment insurance contributions, personal property tax, or any requirement to collect sales and use tax (Sec. 14-219(b)(5), Pub. Safety Art.). "Disaster period" means a period that begins 10 days before the first day and ends 60 days after the last day of a declared state disaster or emergency (Sec. 14-219(a)(4), Pub. Safety Art.).

An "out-of-state business" is a business entity that (1) had no registrations, nexus, or tax filings in Maryland prior to the declared state disaster or emergency and (2) is requested by a registered business or the state or a local government to perform disaster or emergency related work during a disaster period. The term includes a business entity that is affiliated with a business in the state solely through common ownership (Sec. 14-219(a)(6), Pub. Safety Art.). "Disaster or emergency related work" means repairing, renovating, installing, building, rendering services, or other business activities that relate to infrastructure that was damaged, impaired or destroyed by the declared disaster or emergency (Sec. 14-219(a)(3), Pub. Safety Art.).

A business must provide to the Comptroller a statement that the business is in the state solely for purposes of performing disaster or emergency related work. (Sec. 14-219(d), Pub. Safety Art.)

¶ 510   Sales or Use Tax Credits

There is no system for crediting sales and use taxes paid to other states. However, since the law does not tax the use of property or service purchased in another state when the buyer has already paid a sales or use tax in that state before bringing the property or service into Maryland, the arrangement has the same effect as a credit against the taxpayer's Maryland use tax liability (Sec. 11-221(c), Tax General Art.). If the tax paid to the other state is less than the Maryland sales and use tax, a proration formula applies.

Returned goods: If a vendor refunds the tax to a buyer in connection with the return of merchandise previously purchased, the amount of tax refunded may be credited against the vendor's tax liability.

Collection expense credit: A person who timely files a sales and use tax return is allowed a credit for collection expense equal to 1.2% of the first $6,000 of the gross amount of sales and use tax due to the Comptroller with each return, and 0.9% of the gross amount of sales and use tax payable in excess of $6,000. The credit does not apply to any sales and use tax that a vendor is required to pay for any taxable purchases or uses made by the vendor (Sec. 11-105, Tax General Art.).

The credit may not exceed $500 for each return, and the total maximum credit a vendor who files or is eligible to file a consolidated return, as provided, is allowed for all returns filed for any period is likewise limited to $500 (Sec. 11-105(b)(2)(C), Tax General Art.).

¶ 511   Deficiency Assessments

A deficiency assessment may result (1) from an examination or audit of a taxpayer's filed return, (2) if a person fails to file a tax return, or (3) if a person fails to keep records or to obtain a resale certificate (Sec. 13-407, Tax General Art.). The Comptroller must mail a notice of assessment to the person against whom the assessment is made (Sec. 13-410, Tax General Art.). Such assessments are prima facie correct (Sec. 13-411, Tax General Art.).

Assessment when tax return filed: If the Comptroller examines or audits a tax return and determines that the tax due exceeds the amount shown on the return, the Comptroller will assess a deficiency (Sec. 13-401, Tax General Art.).

Assessment when no tax return filed: If a person who did not file a return fails to file after notice and demand, the Comptroller may compute and assess the tax by using the best information available (Sec. 13-402, Tax General Art.).

Assessment when records not kept or resale certificate not obtained: When persons fail to keep required records, the Comptroller may compute and assess the tax by use of a survey of the business, a survey of other persons engaged in a similar business, or by other means (Sec. 13-407, Tax General Art.). In addition, when persons fail to obtain proper resale certificates, the Comptroller may assess the sales and use tax on the sale, and such assessment will be considered final.

¶ 512   Audit Procedures

The Comptroller may examine or audit a filed return (Sec. 13-301, Tax General Art.) and examine records or other relevant data, conduct an investigation, hold a hearing, administer oaths, take testimony and other evidence, and subpoena persons or relevant documents (Sec. 13-302(a), Tax General Art.). If a person fails to comply with these discovery procedures, the Comptroller may compel enforcement by petition with a circuit court (Sec. 13-302(b), Tax General Art.).

If the Comptroller determines that the taxpayer's records are so detailed, complex, or voluminous that an audit of all detailed records would be unreasonable or impractical, the Comptroller may compute the sales and use tax by using scientific random sampling techniques (Sec. 13-302(a-1), Tax General Art.).

¶ 513   **Statute of Limitations**

Maryland has different statutes of limitation for tax assessment, tax collection suits, and tax refund claims.

• Time limit for recovery of taxes

An action to recover sales and use taxes may not be brought after four years from the date on which the tax is due (Sec. 13-1102(a), Tax General Art.); however, there is no time limit for assessment in the event of fraud or gross negligence (Sec. 13-1102(b), Tax General Art.). An underpayment of 25% or more of the sales and use tax is prima facie evidence of gross negligence.

• Time limit for collection of taxes

Sales and use tax may not be collected after seven years from the date the tax is due (Sec. 13-1103(a), Tax General Art.). If a tax assessment was made within the four-year recovery period, the seven-year time limit for collection starts from the date of the assessment (Sec. 13-1103(c), Tax General Art.). If the Comptroller fails to collect a tax and a receiver or trustee is appointed within the seven-year period, the period for collecting the tax extends for two years from the date the receiver or trustee is appointed (Sec. 13-1103(b), Tax General Art.).

• Time for filing claims for refund

A claim for refund of sales and use tax may not be filed after four years from the date the tax was paid (Sec. 13-1104(g), Tax General Art.).

¶ 514   **Application for Refund**

A claim for refund may be made for (1) an erroneous tax, penalty, or interest overpayment; (2) an erroneous, illegal, or wrongful assessment; (3) payment of tax on a sale that became exempt because the property was for use in another state; (4) a tax refunded to a buyer on a canceled or rescinded sale; (5) a tax paid on a canceled or rescinded sale for which the vendor refuses to give a refund to the customer; or (6) a tax paid on a cash sale or sale for use that is not a retail sale, where the taxable price is under $500 (Sec. 13-901(g), Tax General Art.).

Item resold without being used: If any portion of a property is resold without having first been used by the buyer, the buyer may apply for a refund of the taxes attributable to the resold portion (Reg. 03.06.01.07(A)).

Effect of amount of claim: For claims not exceeding $250, a licensed taxpayer may request a refund by deducting the amount from the total tax due with any return (Reg. 03.06.03.05(B)). For claims in excess of $250 or in excess of the amount to be reported on a return, a claim for refund must be filed.

¶ 516   Scope of Tax

Source.—Statutory references are to Chapters 64G, 64H, 64I, and 62C of the General Laws, as amended to date. Details are reported in the CCH Massachusetts State Tax Reports starting at ¶ 60-000.

The sales tax is imposed on a vendor's gross receipts from sales at retail in Massachusetts of tangible personal property and of certain services performed in the state (Sec. 2, Ch. 64H, G.L.). The use tax complements the sales tax and is imposed on the storage, use, or other consumption in the state of tangible personal property or certain services purchased from any vendor for storage, use, or other consumption in the state (Sec. 2, Ch. 64I, G.L.). The use tax does not apply to transactions that have been subject to the sales tax (Sec. 7(a), Ch. 64I, G.L.).

• **Incidence of tax**

Although the sales tax is imposed on a vendor's gross receipts, and the vendor is responsible for remitting the sales tax to the state (except in the case of sales of motor vehicles and trailers) (Sec. 2, Ch. 64H, G.L.), the vendor must add the tax to the sales price charged the purchaser (Sec. 3(a), Ch. 64H, G.L.). The tax constitutes a debt from the purchaser to the vendor and is recoverable at law in the same manner as other debts.

The liability for the use tax is imposed on the person storing, using, or otherwise consuming a taxable property or service in the state (Sec. 3, Ch. 64I, G.L.). However, if the property or service is purchased from a vendor engaged in business in the state, the vendor is responsible for collecting the use tax from the purchaser and remitting the tax to the state (Sec. 4, Ch. 64I, G.L.).

Out-of-state retailers: In *Town Fair Tire Centers, Inc. v. Commissioner of Revenue,* 454 Mass. 601 (2009), CCH Massachusetts Tax Reports, ¶ 401-256, the court held that a tire seller was not required to collect Massachusetts use tax on tire sales made in New Hampshire to Massachusetts residents because there was no evidence that the tires were actually used in Massachusetts. Thus, absent evidence of actual storage or use in Massachusetts, the commissioner will not assess use tax against an out-of-state registered vendor on sales to a Massachusetts resident where the resident purchases and takes possession of the property outside Massachusetts. *Town Fair Tire* does not change or overrule *Circuit City Stores, Inc. v. Commissioner of Revenue,* 439 Mass. 629 (2003), CCH Massachusetts Tax Reports, ¶ 401-846. When a sale is consummated in Massachusetts, the seller must collect tax, even if the item is picked up at an out-of-state location. Moreover, *Town Fair Tire* does not change the statutory rule that tangible personal property sold for delivery in Massachusetts is presumed to be sold for storage, use, or consumption in the Massachusetts, regardless of whether the seller delivers the property or arranges delivery by common carrier or otherwise. If an out-of-state vendor has not collected tax on the sale, the purchaser using the property in Massachusetts owes use tax. (*Technical Information Release 10-2,* Massachusetts Department of Revenue, February 11, 2010, CCH Massachusetts Tax Reports, ¶ 401-277)

Prepaid calling arrangements: Prepaid calling arrangements are taxed at the point of sale instead of being taxed upon use. The statutory definition of "Sale at retail" includes both the sale and recharge of such arrangements (Sec. 1, Ch. 64H, G.L.).

Absorption of tax: A vendor is no longer prohibited from advertising to the public that tax will be assumed or absorbed by the vendor (former Sec. 23, Ch. 64H, G.L.), However, a similar use tax provision remains in effect (Sec. 24, Ch. 64I, G.L.). A vendor may offer a discount equal to the amount of applicable tax and may advertise the discount as a "store sponsored sales tax holiday" or use similar language (*Technical Information Release 10-11,* Department of Revenue, August 9, 2010, CCH Massachusetts Tax Reports, ¶ 401-306).

Marijuana: Effective December 15, 2016, a marijuana excise tax applies to the sale of marijuana or marijuana products by a marijuana retailer, to anyone other than a marijuana establishment. The excise tax is levied in addition to state sales tax. (Sec. 1, Ch. 64N, G.L.)

In addition, any city or town may impose a local sales tax on the sale or transfer of marijuana or marijuana products by a marijuana retailer operating within the city or town, to anyone other than a marijuana establishment. (Sec. 3, Ch. 64N, G.L.)

For tax rates, see ¶ 519 and ¶ 520.

• **Taxability of services**

Although the sales and use tax law refers to services as being taxable (Sec. 2, Ch. 64H, G.L., Sec. 2, Ch. 64I, G.L.), the term "services" by definition is limited to telecommunications services (Sec. 1, Ch. 64H, G.L.). However, certain producing, fabricating, processing, printing, imprinting, and information services are taxable by reason of their inclusion in the definition of "sale" and "selling," and the sale of gas, electricity, and steam is generally taxable because those substances are considered to be "tangible personal property."

Internet access: Massachusetts currently does not tax Internet access charges, but it does tax telecommunications services. The federal Internet Tax Freedom Act prohibits Massachusetts from taxing telecommunications services purchased by Internet service providers to provide Internet access (*Technical Information Release 05-8,* Massachusetts Department of Revenue, July 14, 2005, CCH MASSACHUSETTS TAX REPORTS, ¶ 350-382).

Services connected with a sale: A service transaction is subject to sales tax if a transfer of tangible personal property occurs, the value of the property is not inconsequential in relation to the total charge, and the charge for the property is not separately stated on the bill to the customer (Reg. 830 CMR 64H.1.1(2)). The service provider must collect sales tax from the customer based on the total amount charged.

Satellite broadcasting: An excise tax is imposed on the gross revenues of a provider from the sale of direct broadcast satellite service to a customer in Massachusetts. The tax is passed on to customers as a separately stated item on their bills. The release discusses the definition of "gross revenues." (*Technical Information Release 09-14,* Massachusetts Department of Revenue, July 28, 2009, CCH MASSACHUSETTS TAX REPORTS, ¶ 401-254)

The constitutionality of the tax was upheld in *DIRECTV v. Massachusetts Department of Revenue,* Massachusetts Supreme Judicial Court, No. SJC-11658, February 18, 2015, CCH MASSACHUSETTS TAX REPORTS, ¶ 401-536. A petition for Certiorari was denied November 2, 2015, by the U.S. Supreme Court (*DIRECTV, LLC v. Massachusetts Department of Revenue,* U.S. Supreme Court, Dkt. 14-1499).

• **Nexus**

Massachusetts vendors are responsible for collecting the sales tax from their purchasers (Sec. 2, Ch. 64H, G.L.; Sec. 3(a), Ch. 64H, G.L.). Vendors "engaged in business in the commonwealth" are responsible for collecting tax (Sec. 4, Ch. 64I, G.L.). The phrase "engaged in business in the commonwealth" includes the following:

— having a business location in the commonwealth;

— regularly or systematically soliciting orders for the sale of services to be performed within the commonwealth or for the sale of tangible personal property for delivery to destinations in the commonwealth;

— otherwise exploiting the retail sales market in the commonwealth through any means, including, but not limited to

(a) in-state salespersons, solicitors, or representatives,

(b) catalogs or other solicitation materials sent through the mails or otherwise,

¶516   Massachusetts

(c) billboards,

(d) advertising or solicitations in newspapers, magazines, radio or television broadcasts, computer networks, or any other communications medium; and

(e) regularly engaging in the delivery of property or the performance of services in the commonwealth.

Massachusetts' nexus provision was amended to enable the state to collect sales and use taxes from foreign vendors that do not maintain a business location in the state but exploit the state's retail sales market through the use of catalogs and other solicitation materials sent through the mails or through media advertising (Sec. 1, Ch. 64H, G.L.). The Department of Revenue has stated that the definition of "engaged in business in the commonwealth" will be enforced to the extent allowed under constitutional limitations (*Technical Information Release No. 96-8,* October 16 1996, CCH MASSACHUSETTS TAX REPORTS, ¶ 350-199). A person is considered to have a business location in the commonwealth if that person (Sec. 1, Ch. 64H, G.L.):

— owns or leases Massachusetts real property;

— has one or more employees located in Massachusetts (an employee is considered so located if the employee's service is performed entirely within the state or if the service is performed both in and out of the state, the employee commences his or her activities at, and returns to, a place in the state);

— regularly maintains a stock of tangible personal property in Massachusetts for sale in the ordinary course of business (for this purpose, property on consignment held and offered for sale by a consignee on its own account is not considered stock maintained by the consignor); or

— regularly leases out tangible personal property for use in Massachusetts (provided that a person having a business location in the state solely by reason of this provision is considered to have an in-state business location only with respect to such leased property).

• **Streamlined Act status**

Massachusetts has enacted the Uniform (Simplified) Sales and Use Tax Administration Act, the product of the Streamlined Sales Tax Project (SSTP) (Ch. 4 (S.B. 1949), Laws 2003). Massachusetts is an Advisor State to the SSTP because it has not yet enacted the changes to its laws necessary to comply with the Streamlined Sales and Use Tax Agreement's requirements. However, it will continue to have input through its representation on the State and Local Advisory Council, which advises the Board on matters pertaining to the administration of the Agreement. For additional information on the uniform act, see "Streamlined Sales Tax Project," listed in the Table of Contents.

¶ 517   **Tax Base**

The sales tax is imposed on a vendor's gross receipts from sales at retail of tangible personal property and services (Sec. 2, Ch. 64H, G.L.). The use tax is imposed on the purchase price of property and services purchased for storage, use, or other consumption in the state (Sec. 2, Ch. 64I, G.L.).

The term "gross receipts" is defined as the total sales price received by vendors as a consideration for retail sales (Sec. 1, Ch. 64H, G.L.). The term "sales price" is defined as the total amount paid by a purchaser to a vendor as consideration for a retail sale, valued in money or otherwise.

In determining the sales price, no deduction is allowed for the cost of property sold, the cost of materials used, labor or service costs, interest charges, losses, or other expenses, or of transportation costs incurred prior to the sale of the property. In addition, any amount paid for any services that are a part of the sale and any amount for which credit is given to the purchaser by the vendor must be included in the sales price. However, credit given for trade-ins of motor vehicles, including snowmobiles and recreational vehicles, may be deducted from the sales price (Sec. 24, Ch. 64H, G.L.).

The following items are not included in the sales price: (1) cash discounts allowed and taken on sales; (2) amounts charged for property returned within a specified period by a purchaser to a vendor upon a rescission of a sales contract when the entire amount charged (less handling costs) is returned to the purchaser; (3) amounts charged for labor or services rendered in installing or applying the property sold; (4) the sales tax itself; (5) separately stated charges for transportation occurring after the property is sold; and (6) the federal manufacturers' excise tax on motor vehicles.

Coupons and rebates: A manufacturer's coupon or manufacturer's rebate that is used to reduce the price paid by a retail customer at the point of sale is treated as a cash discount and excluded from the sales price. However, a rebate taken after the sale does not decrease the sales price (Reg. 830 CMR 64H.1.4).

Computer software: Standardized computer software transferred by electronic, telephonic, or similar means is subject to sales and use tax as a transfer of tangible personal property (Sec. 1, Ch. 64H, G.L.).

Charges for cloud computing products sold by a taxpayer are not subject to sales and use tax when the products are used with the customer's own software, or open-source software available for free on the Internet, because there is no sale of prewritten software. Cloud computing products that include software licensed by the taxpayer are subject to tax as services that are part of the sales price of prewritten software, whether or not there is a separately stated charge for the software or a sublicense of the software to the customer. See *Letter Ruling 12-8,* Department of Revenue, July 16, 2012, CCH MASSACHUSETTS TAX REPORTS, ¶ 401-404.

Similarly, sales of remote data backup and restoration services are not taxable, because the object of the transaction is to acquire remote data storage (*Letter Ruling 12-11,* Department of Revenue, September 25, 2012, CCH MASSACHUSETTS TAX REPORTS, ¶ 401-412).

On the other hand, a taxpayer's sales of virtual computing offerings, including remote access, remote support, and online conferencing, are taxable because the customer is purchasing the right to use the taxpayer's computer software (*Letter Ruling 12-10,* Department of Revenue, September 25, 2012, CCH MASSACHUSETTS TAX REPORTS, ¶ 401-417; see also *Letter Ruling 12-13,* Department of Revenue, November 9, 2012, CCH MASSACHUSETTS TAX REPORTS, ¶ 401-425).

Service charges: A separately stated gratuity, service charge, or tip that is distributed by a vendor to service employees, wait staff employees, or service bartenders is not included in the definition of the "sales price" of a taxable item (Sec. 1, Ch. 64H, G.L.; Reg. 830 CMR 64H.6.5).

Bundled transactions: When a cellular telephone or other wireless communications device is sold in a bundled transaction that includes taxable telecommunications services, the taxable sales price of the phone or device is the higher of the price paid by the retail customer or the wholesale cost of the phone or device. The rule is the same whether the vendor is an independent retailer, including a franchisee of a telecommunications carrier, or a telecommunications carrier. See *Directive 11-2,* Massachusetts Department of Revenue, April 27, 2011, CCH MASSACHUSETTS TAX REPORTS, ¶ 401-353.

¶ 518   **List of Exemptions, Exceptions, and Exclusions**

Unless otherwise indicated, the statutory exemptions, exceptions, and exclusions listed below apply to both sales and use taxes; those applicable only to the sales tax or only to the use tax are listed separately. Items that are excluded from the sales or use tax base are treated at ¶ 517, "Tax Base."

¶518   Massachusetts

Sales tax holiday: Two-day sales tax holidays were in effect in August of most recent years, including 2015. The holidays did not apply to sales of telecommunications, tobacco products, gas, steam, electricity, motor vehicles, motorboats, meals, or any single item with a price in excess of $2,500.

Medical marijuana: The sales tax exemption for medicine on prescription in Sec. 6(*l*), 64H, G.L. applies to sales of marijuana and products containing marijuana to a qualifying patient or the patient's personal caregiver pursuant to a written certification by a licensed physician (*Directive 15-1,* Massachusetts Department of Revenue, June 19, 2015, CCH MASSACHUSETTS TAX REPORTS, ¶ 401-546).

- **Sales and use tax exemptions, exceptions, and exclusions**

Admissions charges by food and beverage facilities	Sec. 1, Ch. 64H, G.L.
Advertising services	Sec. 1, Ch. 64H, G.L.
Agricultural production, items used in connection with	Sec. 1(r), Ch. 64H, G.L., Sec. 1(s), Ch. 64H, G.L.
Aircraft	Sec. 6(uu) and (vv), Ch. 64H, G.L.
Aircraft fuel	Sec. 6(j), Ch. 64H, G.L.
Alcoholic beverages sold for off-premises consumption	Sec. 6(g), Ch. 64H, G.L.
Animal feed	Sec. 6(p), Ch. 64H, G.L.
Animals, fur-bearing	Sec. 6(p), Ch. 64H, G.L.
Animals produced for research or testing	Sec. 6(p), Ch. 64H, G.L.
Baby oil	Sec. 6(*l*), Ch. 64H, G.L.
Blood and blood plasma	Sec. 6(*l*), Ch. 64H, G.L.
Books, religious	Sec. 6(m), Ch. 64H, G.L.
Books, school	Sec. 6(m), Ch. 64H, G.L.
Breast pumps	Sec. 6(*l*), Ch. 64H, G.L.
Buses	Sec. 6(aa), Ch. 64H, G.L.
Cast metal production, items used in	Sec. 6(ee), Ch. 64H, G.L.
Casual and isolated sales	Sec. 6(c), Ch. 64H, G.L.
Clothing	Sec. 6(k), Ch. 64H, G.L.
Coins, bullion, and legal tender	Sec. 6(*ll*), Ch. 64H, G.L.
Colostomy and ileostomy supplies	Sec. 6(z), Ch. 64H, G.L.
Commercial fishing, items used in connection with	Sec. 6(r), Ch. 64H, G.L.
Concrete mixing units	Sec. 6(y), Ch. 64H, G.L.
Construction materials, contracts with exempt entities	Sec. 6(f), Ch. 64H, G.L.
Containers	Sec. 6(q), Ch. 64H, G.L.
Data processing services	Sec. 1, Ch. 64H, G.L.
Dental equipment and supplies	Sec. 6(*l*), Ch. 64H, G.L.
Direct mail promotional items	Sec. 6(ff), Ch. 64H, G.L.
Eyeglasses, prescription	Sec. 6(*l*), Ch. 64H, G.L.
Federally exempt (IRC Sec. 501(c)(3)) organizations	Sec. 6(e), Ch. 64H, G.L.
Fertilizer	Sec. 6(p), Ch. 64H, G.L.
Flags, American	Sec. 6(w), Ch. 64H, G.L.
Food products	Sec. 6(h), Ch. 64H, G.L.
Food stamps, purchases with	Sec. 6(kk), Ch. 64H, G.L.

Funeral items	Sec. 6(n), Ch. 64H, G.L.
Government entities, sales to	Sec. 6(d), Ch. 64H, G.L.
Gun safes and trigger lock devices	Sec. 6(rr), Ch. 64H, G.L.
Industrial manufacturing plants, items used by	Sec. 6(i), Ch. 64H, G.L., Sec. 6(r), Ch. 64H, G.L.
Information services	Sec. 1, Ch. 64H, G.L.
Ingredient or component parts of property to be sold	Sec. 6(r), Ch. 64H, G.L.
Insulin and insulin needles and syringes	Sec. 6(*l*), Ch. 64H, G.L.
Insurance policies and service transactions	Sec. 1, Ch. 64H, G.L.
Life sciences companies, purchases of tangible personal property by	Sec. 6(xx), Ch. 64H, G.L.
Livestock and poultry	Sec. 6(p), Ch. 64H, G.L.
Machinery and power used in an industrial manufacturing plant	Sec. 6(s), Ch. 64H, G.L.
Manufacturing corporations, items used in research and development by	Sec. 6(r), Ch. 64H, G.L., Sec. 6(s), Ch. 64H, G.L.
Meals, exempt	Sec. 6(cc), Ch. 64H, G.L.
Medical equipment	Sec. 6(*l*), Ch. 64H, G.L.
Medicine, prescription	Sec. 6(*l*), Ch. 64H, G.L.
Motion pictures	Sec. 6(m), Ch. 64H, G.L.
Motion pictures production companies (exp. 1/1/2023)	Sec. 6(ww), Ch. 64H, G.L.
Motor fuels	Sec. 6(g), Ch. 64H, G.L.
Motor vehicles sold to disabled persons, disabled veterans	Sec. 6(u), Ch. 64H, G.L.
Newspapers, items used in publishing	Sec. 6(r), Ch. 64H, G.L., Sec. 6(s), Ch. 64H, G.L.
Oxygen	Sec. 6(*l*), Ch. 64H, G.L.
Photocopies by nonprofit libraries	Sec. 1, Ch. 64H, G.L.
Plants producing food for human consumption	Sec. 6(p), Ch. 64H, G.L.
Printed material delivered out of state	Sec. 6(ff), Ch. 64H, G.L.
Printing equipment and materials, prepress	Sec. 6(gg), Ch. 64H, G.L., Sec. 6(ss), Ch. 64H, G.L.
Prosthetic devices and equipment	Sec. 6(*l*), Ch. 64H, G.L.
Publications, exempt organizations	Sec. 6(m), Ch. 64H, G.L.
Railroad fuel	Sec. 6(j), Ch. 64H, G.L.
Resale, property purchased for	Sec. 8(a), Ch. 64H, G.L.
Research and development corporations, items used by	Sec. 6(r), Ch. 64H, G.L., Sec. 6(s), Ch. 64H, G.L.
Scientific equipment, donated	Sec. 6(jj), Ch. 64H, G.L.
Services, in general	Sec. 1, Ch. 64H, G.L.
Services, professional or personal	Sec. 1, Ch. 64H, G.L.
Services, repair and installation	Sec. 1, Ch. 64H, G.L.
Services, transportation	Sec. 1, Ch. 64H, G.L.
Solar, wind-powered, and heat pump systems, residential energy equipment	Sec. 6(dd), Ch. 64H, G.L.

¶518 Massachusetts

Telephone service, residential . . . . Sec. 6(i), Ch. 64H, G.L.

Transportation charges . . . . Sec. 1, Ch. 64H, G.L.,
Directive 04-5

Utilities, items used in furnishing . . . . Sec. 6(i), Ch. 64H, G.L.

Utilities, purchases by small businesses . . . . Sec. 6(qq), Ch. 64H, G.L.

Utilities, residential use . . . . Sec. 6(j), Ch. 64H, G.L.

Vending machines, sales of food . . . . Sec. 6(h), Ch. 64H, G.L.

Vending machines, sales under 10¢ . . . . Sec. 6(t), Ch. 64H, G.L.

Vessels and barges . . . . Sec. 6(o), Ch. 64H, G.L.

Water . . . . Sec. 6(i), Ch. 64H, G.L.

- **Exemptions, exceptions, and exclusions applicable only to the sales tax**

Amusement and sporting event tickets . . . . Sec. 1, Ch. 64H, G.L.

Casual sales, motor vehicles, trailers, airplanes, and boats . . . . Sec. 6(c), Ch. 64H, G.L.

- **Exemptions, exceptions, and exclusions applicable only to the use tax**

Items subject to Massachusetts sales tax . . . . Sec. 2, Ch. 64H, G.L.

Items subject to sales or use tax in other states . . . . Sec. 7(c), Ch. 64I, G.L.

¶ 519   Rate of Tax

The Massachusetts sales and use tax rate is 6.25% (Sec. 2, Ch. 64H, G.L., Sec. 2, Ch. 64I, G.L.).

Satellite broadcasting: Direct broadcast satellite service is subject to a 5% excise tax (Sec. 2, Ch. 64M, G.L.). Direct broadcast satellite service providers must collect the tax from subscribers (Sec. 3, Ch. 64M, G.L.). Returns must be filed monthly by the 20th of the month (Sec. 16(l), Ch. 62C, G.L.). Direct broadcast satellite service providers must register with the state (Sec. 4, Ch. 64M, G.L.; Sec. 67, Ch. 62C, G.L.).

- **Room occupancy tax**

An excise tax is levied on the transfer of occupancy of one or more rooms in a bed and breakfast establishment, hotel, lodging house, or motel by an operator, if the total amount of rent charged is not less than $15 per day (Sec. 3, Ch. 64G, G.L.).

The tax does not apply if the occupancy is for more than 90 consecutive days (Sec. 1(g), Ch. 64G, G.L.). When a hotel operator and an occupant agree in advance in writing that a room occupancy will exceed 90 days, the operator is not required to collect tax on the occupancy. If the occupancy terminates prior to 90 days, the operator must retroactively collect tax. If the length of a room rental is not agreed to in advance, the operator must collect and remit tax on the occupancy. After the passage of the 90th day, the operator must return or credit any tax collected to the occupant. The operator may recover any tax paid by taking a credit against tax owed on future returns or by filing an application for abatement with the Department on Form CA-6 (*Technical Information Release 07-2,* Massachusetts Department of Revenue, January 26, 2007, CCH MASSACHU-SETTS TAX REPORTS, ¶ 401-049; see also *Lowney v. Commissioner of Revenue,* Massachusetts Appeals Court, No. 05-P-1353, November 9, 2006, CCH MASSACHUSETTS TAX REPORTS, ¶ 401-035).

The tax is based on the total amount of rent charged for each occupancy (Sec. 3, Ch. 64G, G.L.). "Rent" is the consideration received without any deduction whatsoever (Sec. 1(j), Ch. 64G, G.L.).

Operators subject to the tax can pass the tax along to their customers in the form of a separately stated charge (Sec. 4, Ch. 64G, G.L., Sec. 5. Ch. 64G, G.L.).

The room occupancy excise tax is imposed at a rate of 5% plus a surtax of 14% of the tax imposed for a total tax of 5.7% (Sec. 3, Ch. 64G, G.L., Sec. 22, Ch. 546, Laws 1969, Reg. 830 CMR 64F.6.1(3)).

Exemptions: Exempted from tax are the following accommodations (Sec. 2, Ch. 64G, G.L.):

— rooms at federal, state, or municipal institutions.

— rooms at religious, charitable, educational, or philanthropic institutions.

— privately owned and operated convalescent homes or homes for the elderly, infirm, indigent, or chronically ill.

— religious or charitable homes for the aged, infirm, indigent, or chronically ill.

— summer camps for the young (18 and under) or for developmentally disabled individuals.

— a bed and breakfast home (one where three or fewer rooms are let) (Sec. 1(b), Ch. 64G, G.L.).

In addition, there is a room occupancy excise tax exemption for employees of the United States military traveling on official military orders (Sec. 12, Ch. 64G, G.L.; *TIR No. 98-1*, January 21, 1998).

Licensing requirements: No person is allowed to operate a bed and breakfast establishment, hotel, lodging house or motel without a certificate of registration (Sec. 6, Ch. 64G, G.L.).

• **Marijuana taxes**

Effective December 15, 2016, a marijuana excise tax applies to the sale of marijuana or marijuana products by a marijuana retailer, to anyone other than a marijuana establishment, at a rate of 3.75% of the total sales price received by the marijuana retailer. The excise tax is levied in addition to state sales tax. (Sec. 1, Ch. 64N, G.L.)

Local option sales taxes on marijuana are authorized, see ¶ 520, below.

¶ 520   **Local Taxes**

No general local sales and use taxes are authorized (Sec. 2, Ch. 64H, G.L., Sec. 4, Ch. 64H, G.L., Sec. 5, Ch. 64I, G.L., *TIR No. 1987-11*, September 29, 1987).

• **Tax and surcharges for Boston convention center financing**

A convention center financing fee of 2.75% is levied upon the transfer of occupancy of hotel, motel, or other lodging rooms in Boston, Cambridge, Springfield, and Worcester to fund the construction and renovation of convention and exhibition facilities in Massachusetts (Sec. 9, Ch. 152, Laws 1997, Reg. 830 CMR 64F.6.1(6)).

A 5% convention center financing (CCF) surcharge is imposed on the price of tickets for any water-based sightseeing, tourist venue, or entertainment cruise or tour, or for any land-based sightseeing, tourist venue, or trolley tour, originating or located in Massachusetts and conducted partly or wholly within the city of Boston. The surcharge does not apply to children's tickets costing $6 or less or to for tours or cruises sold to an organized school or youth group and accompanying adults. There are two other surcharges relating to parking. (*Technical Information Release 05-1*, Department of Revenue, January 25, 2005, CCH MASSACHUSETTS TAX REPORTS, ¶ 350-373)

• **Local lodgings and meals taxes**

Lodgings tax: Cities and towns are authorized to impose local room occupancy excise taxes. Occupancies that are exempt from the state room occupancy excise tax are also exempt from local taxes. The maximum local rate that may be imposed is 6% of the total amount of rent for each hotel, motel, or lodging house room that rents for $15 per day or more. In Boston, the maximum rate is 6.5%. Operators are required to remit the local tax to the Commissioner at the same time and in the same manner as the state room occupancy tax. (Sec. 3A, Ch. 64G, G.L.; Reg. 830 CMR 64G.3A.1; Reg. 830 CMR 62C.16.1)

An additional convention center financing fee of 2.75% is levied upon the transfer of room occupancy by any operator of a hotel, motel or other lodging room in Boston, Cambridge, Chicopee, Springfield, West Springfield, and Worcester to fund the construction and renovation of convention and exhibition facilities in Massachusetts (Reg. 830 CMR 62C.16.1(6)).

Meals tax: Cities and towns are authorized to impose a 0.75% local meals tax on sales of restaurant meals (Sec. 2, Ch. 64L, G.L.). Vendors must remit the tax to the Department of Revenue at the same time and in the same manner as state sales tax. A release explains registration and reporting requirements and sourcing rules applicable to restaurants, caterers, restaurant delivery companies, and transient vendors *(Technical Information Release 09-13*, Massachusetts Department of Revenue, July 23, 2009, CCH MASSACHUSETTS TAX REPORTS, ¶ 401-251).

Cities and towns imposing taxes: A list of municipalities that impose the local option taxes on sales of meals and/or lodging is available from the MDOR at **https://dlsgateway.dor.state.ma.us/DLSReports/ DLSReportViewer.aspx?ReportName=RoomsMealsLocalOptionsAdoptedRates &ReportTitle=Meals%20and%20Rooms%20Adoption%20and%20Rates**.

- **Local marijuana taxes**

In addition to the statewide taxes on marijuana retailers, any city or town may impose a local sales tax on the sale or transfer of marijuana or marijuana products by a marijuana retailer operating within the city or town, to anyone other than a marijuana establishment, at a rate not greater than 2% of the total sales price received by the marijuana retailer (Sec. 3, Ch. 64N, G.L.).

¶ 521   **Bracket Schedule**

Tax must be computed to the third decimal place and rounded to the nearest whole cent, rounding up whenever the third decimal place is greater than four *(Technical Information Release 09-11*, Massachusetts Department of Revenue, July 22, 2009, CCH MASSACHUSETTS TAX REPORTS, ¶ 401-250).

¶ 522   **Returns, Payments, and Due Dates**

Vendors who have made any sales that are subject to sales or use tax and purchasers who are required to pay the use tax must file returns on a monthly, quarterly, or annual basis (Sec. 16(h) and (i), Ch. 62C, G.L., Reg. 830 CMR 62C.16.2). A return must be filed within 20 days after the end of the period covered by the return. In general, taxes are due and payable at the time the return is required to be filed, determined without regard to any filing extensions (Sec. 32(a), Ch. 62C, G.L., Sec. 2, Ch. 64H, G.L., Sec. 2, Ch. 64I, G.L.).

Deemed filing and payment dates: Returns that are filed and tax payments that are made before their due dates are deemed to be filed and paid on the due dates, determined without regard to filing extensions or any election to pay the tax in installments (Sec. 79(a), Ch. 62C, G.L.).

The postmark date made by the U.S. Postal Service will be deemed the date of payment for a sales or use tax payment that is received after the due date if the payment was (1) mailed in the U.S. on or before the second day prior to the due date, (2) properly addressed to the office where the payment was required to be made, and (3) sent by first-class mail, postage prepaid (Sec. 33A, Ch. 62C, G.L.).

If the due date for filing a return or making a tax payment falls on a Saturday, Sunday, or legal holiday, the filing or payment may be made on the next succeeding business day.

• Filing periods

Although the law generally requires sales and use tax returns to be filed on a monthly basis, it also gives the Commissioner the discretion to adopt other filing periods (Sec. 16(h) and (i), Ch. 62C, G.L.). The Commissioner has exercised this discretion by adopting regulations that require certain taxpayers to file quarterly or annual returns in lieu of monthly returns, as discussed below.

Materialmen: A materialman is required to file a sales and use tax return each month (Sec. 16(h), Ch. 62C, G.L.). A "materialman" is a person who is primarily engaged in the retail sale of building material, tools, and equipment to building contractors for the improvement of real property and who is authorized by law to file a mechanics lien upon real property for improvements related to the property (Sec. 1, Ch. 62C, G.L.). Each return must be filed within 50 days after the expiration of the period covered by the return.

• Electronic filing and payment

Taxpayers that remit wage withholding, sales and use tax, and other transactional taxes must file all returns and documents for these taxes by electronic means and pay by electronic funds transfer (EFT) if the combined liability for the three categories of taxes for the preceding calendar year is $5,000 or more (*TIR No. 16-9,* November 1, 2016, CCH MASSACHUSETTS TAX REPORTS, ¶ 401-599). Any filing entity may voluntarily file electronically, even where the total annual amount remitted falls below the threshold. A filing entity must register for participation in the electronic filing program, whether its participation is mandatory or voluntary.

MassTaxConnect is available for business taxpayers to file returns or submit payments online for the various types of business taxes. A TIR discusses: (1) the process for filing amended returns for business taxes where the DOR would process such returns through an automated process; (2) the process for submitting an abatement application for a tax or penalty that was assessed by the DOR for business taxes; (3) the process by which the Commissioner may treat an amended return for a business tax as an application for abatement; and (4) the regulatory changes related to the new processes implemented in conjunction with MassTaxConnect. According to the DOR, MassTaxConnect will be extended to all other tax types, including personal income taxes and fiduciary income taxes, by the end of 2017. (*Technical Information Release 15-13,* Massachusetts Department of Revenue, November 17, 2015, CCH MASSACHUSETTS TAX REPORTS, ¶ 401-563)

• Individual use tax liability

An individual who owes Massachusetts use taxes on purchases of tangible personal property is required to pay that tax liability annually either by entering the liability on the taxpayer's personal income tax return or by filing a separate use tax return. A taxpayer who elects to report use taxes on a personal income tax return must enter either (1) the estimated liability based on the taxpayer's Massachusetts adjusted gross income (AGI) as described below or (2) the exact amount of the liability based upon actual taxable purchases for the calendar year (Sec. 4A(a), Ch. 64I, G.L.).

The following is the amount of a taxpayer's estimated use tax liability for items having a total purchase price of less than $1,000:

— (1) $0 if AGI is $0 to $25,000;

— (2) $15 if AGI is $25,001 to $40,000;

— (3) $25 if AGI is $40,001 to $60,000;

— (4) $35 if AGI is $60,001 to $80,000;

— (5) $45 if AGI is $80,001 to $100,000; and

— (6) AGI multiplied by 0.0005 if AGI is above $100,000.

For each purchased item with a sales price of $1,000 or greater, the actual use tax liability for each purchase must be added to the amount of the estimated liability derived from the table above (Sec. 4A(b), Ch. 64I, G.L.).

• **Uniform Sales and Use Tax Administration Act**

Massachusetts has enacted the Uniform (Simplified) Sales and Use Tax Administration Act, the product of the Streamlined Sales Tax Project (SSTP) (Ch. 4 (S.B. 1949), Laws 2003) but it has not yet enacted the changes to its laws necessary to comply with the Agreement's requirements. See also ¶ 516.

¶ 523   Prepayment of Taxes

The Commissioner has the authority to require taxpayers to file quarterly returns and to make estimated payments of tax accruing for each tax period within the quarter prior to the filing of the quarterly return (Sec. 45A, Ch. 62C, G.L.).

A nonresident contractor that enters into a contract of more than $20,000 pursuant to which tangible personal property will be consumed or used in the state must deposit with the Commissioner an amount equal to 6.25% of the total amount to be paid under the contract or furnish the Commissioner with a guarantee bond in that amount to secure payment of the sales or use tax due on the property.

Detailed information for nonresident contractors, including how to register with the Department and how to obtain a bond and file it with the Department, is contained on the Department's website at **www.dor.state.ma.us/business/** (search for "OSC").

Prepayment on tobacco products: Every person selling tobacco products (cigarettes, cigars, smoking tobacco, and smokeless tobacco) to others for resale in Massachusetts must prepay the sales tax on such products. The sales tax will be calculated on each sale by multiplying the sales tax rate by the price at which such person sells the tobacco products at wholesale. The amount of the sales tax must be separately stated on the customer invoice or other record. The prepayment requirement does not apply to manufacturers and unclassified acquirers to the extent they distribute tobacco products through a licensed wholesaler or unclassified acquirer. A retailer of tobacco products may claim a credit in the amount of the prepayment against the total amount of sales tax that would normally be due by the retailer for that period. (Sec. 3A, Ch. 64H, G.L.; *Technical Information Release 08-13*, Massachusetts Department of Revenue, September 18, 2008, CCH MASSACHUSETTS TAX REPORTS, ¶ 401-193)

¶ 524   Vendor Registration

A vendor doing business within the Commonwealth must obtain a registration for each place of business (Sec. 7, Ch. 64H, G.L., Sec. 9, Ch. 64I, G.L.). A "vendor" is any person selling taxable tangible personal property or services (Sec. 1, Ch. 64H, G.L.).

Certificates of registration are issued by the Commissioner upon applications submitted by vendors accompanied by the requisite fee (Sec. 67, Ch. 62C, G.L.). Certificates may be issued for specified terms of not less than three years and are subject to renewal without the payment of an additional fee. The certificates are not assignable; however, a vendor that moves its business to a new location may obtain, without payment of a fee, a certificate for the new location that is valid for the balance of the unexpired term of the certificate for the old location.

A business filing entity must register using MassTaxConnect for either mandatory or voluntary participation. The registration procedure can be found at **https://mtc.dor.state.ma.us/mtc/_/**.

Display of certificates: Certificates of registration must be displayed conspicuously in the manner the Commissioner prescribes (Sec. 67, Ch. 62C, G.L.). A regulation discusses the proper manner for displaying certificates for places of business having no cash register, one cash register, or multiple cash registers; nonpublic places of business; vending machines; merchandising devices such as carts, stands, and trucks; and out-of-state vendors (Reg. 830 CMR 62C.67.1). A vendor that does not properly display the certificate may have the certificate suspended or revoked.

¶ 525   Sales or Use Tax Credits

A credit for taxes paid to another state on interstate telecommunications services is provided. The credit may not, however, exceed the tax imposed by Massachusetts (Sec. 1, Ch. 64H, G.L.).

Unlike most states, Massachusetts does not allow vendors a credit or deduction as compensation for collecting and remitting sales and use taxes.

Bad debts: Vendors may recover tax paid on accounts that are later determined to be worthless by filing a claim for reimbursement on an annual basis (Sec. 33, Ch. 64H, G.L.; Sec. 34, Ch. 64I, G.L.) An account is considered "worthless" when it is written off as uncollectible for federal income tax purposes pursuant to IRC Sec. 166 (*Technical Information Release 00-3,* February 2000, CCH Massachusetts Tax Reports, ¶ 350-258). In order to claim reimbursement on worthless accounts, the claimant (*Technical Information Release 07-3,* February 2007, CCH Massachusetts Tax Reports, ¶ 401-054):

— must be a "vendor" within the meaning of the statute;

— must have been the original vendor or the particular good or service; and

— must have collected and remitted the tax sought to be reimbursed.

A retailer was not entitled to reimbursement of Massachusetts sales tax paid on uncollectible credit sales because the tax at issue was paid by a bank and not the retailer. The purchases were made with a private label credit card issued by the bank pursuant to an agreement with the retailer. Credit was extended to purchasers by the bank, and the bank paid the retailer the full sales price, including sales tax, of each transaction. The purpose of the bad debt statute is to reimburse vendors who financed unrecovered sales tax. In this case, sales tax was financed by the bank. The retailer has not been harmed by the purchasers' defaults because it merely remitted sales tax it received from the bank. Although the statute does not explicitly condition relief on a vendor advancing credit, because the vendor is the only identified "actor" in the statute, the common sense interpretation is that it is the vendor who must extend credit to the purchaser. (*Sears, Roebuck & Co. v. Commissioner of Revenue,* Massachusetts Appellate Tax Board, Nos. C293755, C294129, C299055, C305010, C293636, C298514, C298936, C305046, January 11, 2012, CCH Massachusetts Tax Reports, ¶ 401-384).

¶ 526   Deficiency Assessments

Sales and use taxes are deemed to be assessed at the lesser of the amount shown as the tax due on a return (or any amendment, correction, or supplement to a return) or the amount properly due, and at the time the return is actually filed or required to be filed, whichever occurs later (Sec. 26(b), Ch. 62C, G.L., Reg. 830 CMR 62C.26.1(3)). The Commissioner may then assess any additional amount of tax (including interest and penalties) that is determined to be owed (Sec. 26(a), Ch. 62C, G.L., Reg. 830 CMR 62C.26.1(4)).

• Notice of assessment

The Commissioner must provide the taxpayer with a written notice of a deficiency assessment stating the amount of the assessment, the amount of any balance due, and the date when the assessment is required to be paid (Sec. 31, Ch. 62C, G.L.). The notice must include a clear and accurate calculation of the accrual of penalties and interest assessed and must display the interest rates, periods, and the taxes and penalties upon which the assessed amounts are calculated (Sec. 32(d), Ch. 62C, G.L.). A taxpayer's failure to receive the notice, however, does not affect the validity of the assessment (Sec. 31, Ch. 62C, G.L., Reg. 830 CMR 62C.26.1(6)(h)).

The assessment occurs on the earlier of the date of the notice of assessment or the date the Commissioner enters the amount of the assessment on the Department of Revenue's instruction to bill (Reg. 830 CMR 62C.26.1(6)(f)).

Abatement; amended returns: Procedures for how a business taxpayer may apply for an abatement of business tax types, including sales and use taxes, corporate excise taxes, withholding taxes, certain fuel taxes, cigarette taxes, as well as a number of other taxes, are described in Reg. 830 CMR 62C.37.1. Effective November 30, 2015, the abatement application procedure outlined by the regulation will apply only to abatement applications seeking:

    (1) to abate a tax or penalty that has been assessed by the Department, rather than an amount self-assessed by the taxpayer;

    (2) to appeal a responsible person determination; or

    (3) to reduce an assessed tax or penalty on an amended return, to the extent that the amended return is treated by the commissioner as an application for abatement.

Filers of business tax types may no longer file an abatement application to amend a return and, except as specified, an amended return is not a form approved by the commissioner to seek abatement of tax. A TIR explains:

    (1) the processes for filing amended returns and applications for abatement after December 5, 2016, that apply to all taxpayers, and

    (2) how a taxpayer's rights remain protected under the new processes, including the consent process for extending the time to act on an amended return treated as an application for abatement

(*Technical Information Release 16-13,* Massachusetts Department of Revenue, December 2, 2016; **http://www.mass.gov/dor/businesses/help-and-resources/legal-library/tirs/tirs-by-years/2016-releases/tir-16-13.html**)

• **Voluntary disclosure program**

The Massachusetts Department of Revenue has announced a pilot voluntary disclosure program so that business taxpayers may settle uncertain tax issues and have related penalties waived. The program covers a variety of Massachusetts that are open for assessment, including the sales tax and the broadcast satellite services tax. Taxpayers with a potential uncertain tax liability of at least $100,000 are eligible to participate in the program, however, any tax issues under audit (pending or current) are not eligible. Uncertain tax issues arise when case law provides no clear guidance and the department has not issued any written guidance. In general, an "uncertain tax issue" is one in which taxpayers would be required to maintain a reserve in accordance with ASC 740: Accounting for Uncertainty in Income Taxes (formerly FIN 48).

A taxpayer or authorized representative may begin the process by submitting an anonymous letter that requests participation in the program and describes the uncertain tax issues, including why the issue is uncertain, the approximate amount in dispute, and the applicable tax periods. If accepted by the department, the taxpayer has 45 days to write to the department and let the department know its identity and if it wants to proceed. The taxpayer must provide the department with specified information and documentation.

When the taxpayer and the Department have agreed to settlement terms, they each must sign a written settlement agreement reflecting the terms agreed upon. Once a settlement agreement has been signed, the matter in question may not be reopened absent fraud, omission of a material fact, misrepresentation of a material fact, or mutual mistake relating to a material fact.

If an agreement cannot be reached, the voluntary disclosure case will be closed, and the department may use the information provided to audit the taxpayer's tax returns. (AP 637: *Voluntary Disclosure Program for the Settlement of Uncertain Tax Issues,* Massachusetts Department of Revenue, March 2016, CCH MASSACHUSETTS TAX REPORTS, ¶ 401-577) (MA ¶ 526)

¶ 527   Audit Procedures

The Commissioner and the Commissioner's duly authorized representatives may inspect returns (Sec. 20, Ch. 62C, G.L.) and examine a taxpayer's books, papers, records, and other data for purposes of verifying the taxpayer's returns (Sec. 24, Ch. 62C, G.L.). Records must be kept at convenient locations accessible to the Commissioner and must be available for inspection at any reasonable time (Sec. 25, Ch. 62C, G.L., Reg. 830 CMR 62C.25.1(4)). However, taxpayers may not be subjected to unnecessary inspections, examinations, or investigations of their records, and only one inspection of a taxpayer's general books of account for a particular tax may be made for any taxable period unless the taxpayer requests otherwise or the Commissioner notifies the taxpayer in writing that an additional inspection is necessary (Reg. 830 CMR 62C.25.1(4)).

Joint examination of returns: The Commissioner is authorized to participate jointly with officials of the U.S. government and of other states in the examination, verification, assessment, audit, or other activity to determine the proper tax liability due on any Massachusetts tax return or on a federal or other state's return for a tax that is similar to a tax imposed by Massachusetts (Sec. 23, Ch. 62C, G.L., Reg. 830 CMR 62C.23.1(4)).

Early mediation: The Early Mediation Program expands the range of options for resolving tax disputes of $250,000 or more and, in appropriate cases, offers an expedited process. The program is administered jointly by the Audit Division, the Legal Division, and the Office of Appeals. Use of the program in any particular case is optional for both the department and the taxpayer. Early mediation does not eliminate or replace existing administrative appeal options, including the taxpayer's opportunity to request a pre-assessment conference, a post-assessment abatement hearing, and/or settlement consideration with the Office of Appeals if the case is not resolved through the early mediation process.

The program is a collaborative dispute resolution process, designed to resolve all issues in a disputed matter. The mediator's recommendation is not binding on either party. The mediator will make a recommendation only after he or she feels that the parties have made substantial and diligent efforts to settle the matter (or a particular issue) on their own. (*Administrative Procedure 635,* Massachusetts Department of Revenue, December 27, 2012)

¶ 528   Statute of Limitations

A deficiency assessment must be made within three years after the pertinent return was due or filed, whichever is later (Sec. 26(b), Ch. 62C, G.L.). In the case of a failure to file a return, or a fraudulent return filed with intent to evade a tax, the Commissioner may make an assessment at any time, without giving notice of the intention to assess, determining the tax due according to the Commissioner's best information and belief (Sec. 26(d), Ch. 62C, G.L.). Before the expiration of the time prescribed for the assessment of the tax, the Commissioner and the taxpayer may consent in writing to extend the time for the assessment (Sec. 27, Ch. 62C, G.L.).

The taxpayer may confer with the Commissioner within 30 days after the date of the notice of intention to assess (Sec. 26(b), Ch. 62C, G.L.). Upon the expiration of the 30-day period, the assessment is made and the taxpayer is again notified. For additional details, see Reg. 830 CMR 62C.26.1.

¶ 529   Application for Refund

Refunds may be made upon the Commissioner's determination that taxes have been overpaid or upon a taxpayer's application for abatement. The Commissioner is authorized to establish procedures for making refunds or abatements of tax by the electronic transfer of funds (Sec. 78, Ch. 62C, G.L.). See also ¶ 526, above.

Applications for refunds must be filed within three years from the date the return was filed, or two years from the date the tax was assessed or deemed assessed, or one year from the date the tax was paid, whichever is later. A denied refund cannot be (1) credited to other tax periods; (2) used to offset other liabilities, such as child support; or (3) designated as a contribution (TIR 04-3, April 8, 2004).

• **Overpayment of tax**

The Commissioner, upon determining that an overpayment of the full amount of any tax, including interest and penalties, has been made, may deduct the overpaid amount from any other taxes due from the taxpayer and refund the balance (Sec. 36, Ch. 62C, G.L., Reg. 830 CMR 62C.26.1(5)). If the balance is more than $10, the Commissioner must refund it to the taxpayer (Reg. 830 CMR 62C.26.1(17)(c)). If the balance is $10 or less, the Commissioner has the discretion to refund the balance unless the taxpayer applies for the refund. Interest generally will not be paid on an overpayment of a Massachusetts tax that is refunded within 90 days (formerly, 45 days) after the last day prescribed for filing the return, determined without regard to any extension of time for filing the return.

Applications for refunds: If a taxpayer has been informed that the Commissioner has made an overpayment determination involving an amount of $10 or less, the taxpayer may apply for the refund by sending to the Department of Revenue a letter containing the taxpayer's name, Social Security or tax identification number, and the tax period in which the overpayment was made (Reg. 830 CMR 62C.26.1(17)(c)). If a taxpayer has not been informed that the Commissioner has made an overpayment determination, the taxpayer may apply for a refund by filing an amended return before the return's due date or by filing an amended return and an application for abatement after the return's due date.

¶ 530   MICHIGAN

¶ 531   Scope of Tax

Source.—Statutory references are to Ch. 205 of the Michigan Compiled Laws, as amended to date. Details are reported in the CCH MICHIGAN STATE TAX REPORTS starting at ¶ 60-000.

The Michigan sales tax is imposed on persons engaged in the business of making sales at retail (Sec. 205.52(1)). The term "sale at retail" is defined to include all sales of tangible personal property (unless exempt) transferred for consideration in the ordinary course of business for a purpose other than resale (Sec. 205.51(1)(b)). The sale of digital goods, including e-books, podcasts, electronic music, and telephone ringtones, are not subject to sales tax. The sale of services is not taxable unless the service is specifically made subject to tax.

The use tax applies to tangible personal property purchased outside Michigan, but stored, used, or consumed in Michigan (Sec. 205.93(1)). It is imposed on the privilege of using, storing, or consuming tangible personal property in Michigan (Sec. 205.93(1)). The use tax also applies to certain telecommunication services, the service of providing lodging, transmisson and distribution of electricity, and certain laundry and cleaning services (Sec. 205.93a). The use tax is a complementary tax and does not apply in situations in which the Michigan sales tax has been paid (Sec. 205.94(a)).

The Department of Treasury considers several factors to determine whether property is tangible personal property, subject to sales and/or use taxes, or has lost its character as personal property and has become a fixture through its affixation to real estate (RAB 2016-4, Michigan Department of Treasury, February 2016, CCH MICHIGAN TAX REPORTS, ¶ 402-048).

Cloud computing: The Michigan Court of Claims has held that a taxpayer's purchases of cloud computing services were not subject to the use tax because transactions involving the remote access to a third-party provider's technology infrastructure are properly characterized as nontaxable services and not the sale of prewritten software. (*Auto-owners Insurance Company v. Department of Treasury,* Michigan Court of Claims, March 20, 2014, CCH MICHIGAN TAX REPORTS, ¶ 401-882; but see *Notice to Taxpayers Regarding Auto-Owners Insurance Company v. Department of Treasury,* Michigan Department of Treasury, January 6, 2016, CCH MICHIGAN TAX REPORTS, ¶ 402-042)

Marijuana: The Michigan Department of Treasury has provided guidance on the application of the Medical Marihuana Facilities Licensing Act to marijuana growers, processors, secure transporters, dispensaries, and safety compliance facilities. The Act authorizes the licensing of such entities by the Department of Licensing and Regulatory Affairs and requires an initial application fee and an annual regulatory assessment. A 3% excise tax will be imposed on the gross retail income of licensed medical marijuana dispensaries. It is expected that retail sales of medical marijuana will be subject to the 6% state sales tax. Applications for a license may not be made until 360 days after the December 20, 2016, effective date of the legislation. (*Treasury Update,* volume 2, issue 1, Michigan Department of Treasury, November 30, 2016)

• **Use tax**

The use tax applies to the use, storage, or consumption in Michigan of tangible personal property (Sec. 205.93(1)). It complements the sales tax by protecting Michigan merchants from discrimination arising from the inability of the state to impose a sales tax on sales made outside Michigan to Michigan residents by out-of-state merchants. Generally, "tangible personal property" includes computer software offered for general use to the public (Sec. 205.92(k)), but does not include software originally designed for the exclusive use and special needs of a purchaser. Moreover, "tangible personal property" does not include commercial advertising elements (Sec. 205.92(*l*)).

The use tax is not imposed if the sales tax has already been imposed (Sec. 205.94(a)).

Presumptions: Tangible personal property purchased outside the state and used solely for personal, nonbusiness purposes is presumed exempt from the tax if the property was purchased by a person who was a nonresident at the time of purchase and was brought into the state more than 90 days after the date of purchase or if the property was purchased by a person who was a resident at the time of purchase and was brought into the state more than 360 days after the purchase date (Sec. 205.93). It is also presumed that tangible personal property that has been purchased is subject to the use tax if the property was brought into the state within 90 days of the purchase date and is considered as acquired for storage, use, or consumption in the state; see *Podmajersky v. Department of Treasury,* Michigan Court of Appeals, No. 310996, August 13, 2013, CCH MICHIGAN TAX REPORTS, ¶ 401-812.

Exempt-use property converted to taxable use: A person who acquires tangible personal property or services for any exempt use and who subsequently converts the property or service to a taxable use is liable for the Michigan use tax for all tax years that are open under the statute of limitations provided in Sec. 205.27a. If property or services are converted from an exempt use to a taxable use, the use tax is imposed without regard to any subsequent exempt use (Sec. 205.97(2)).

• **Responsibility for tax**

The sales tax is levied upon all persons engaged in the business of making sales at retail (Sec. 205.52(1)), but the retailer can add to the sales price the amount of any sales tax (Sec. 205.73).

The use tax is imposed on the privilege of using, storing, or consuming tangible personal property in Michigan (Sec. 205.93(1), Sec. 205.97). Because the use tax usually falls on sales made outside the state, responsibility for its payment lies with the consumer (Sec. 205.93(1), *LR 95-1,* Department of Treasury). Out-of-state sellers are required to register with the Michigan Department of Treasury and collect the use tax from Michigan customers (Sec. 205.95), but constitutional considerations (Sec. 1, Art. IX, Mich. Const.) limit the ability of Michigan to force out-of-state vendors to register and collect use taxes.

Although remittance of the sales and use tax is normally the responsibility of the vendor, the burden is transferred to the consumer in the following instances:

     — A Michigan consumer who fails to pay the use tax to the seller becomes liable for the tax and must pay it directly to the state (Sec. 205.96, M.C.L.);

     — A person who converts tangible personal property or service originally exempt from use tax to property or service subject to tax becomes liable for remittance of the use tax, without regard to any subsequent exempt use (Sec. 205.97, M.C.L.);

     — A lessor of tangible personal property must pay either sales tax on the purchase price of the property or use tax on the total rentals charged each month. The rule gives the lessor the option to choose which method to use (R205.132, Mich. Admin. Code; see also *RAB 2015-25,* Michigan Department of Treasury, December 2, 2015, CCH MICHIGAN TAX REPORTS, ¶ 402-025).

• **Nexus**

Michigan has added affiliate and click-through nexus provisions to the sales and use tax laws, effective October 1, 2015. Guidance on these provisions is available in *RAB 2015-22,* Michigan Department of Treasury, November 3, 2015, CCH MICHIGAN TAX REPORTS, ¶ 402-018.

Affiliate nexus: The legislation provides that a seller is presumed to be engaged in business in Michigan if it or any other person, including an affiliated person, other than a common carrier, engages in the following activities (Sec. 205.52b; Sec. 205.95a):

— sells a similar line of products as the seller under the same or a similar business name;

— uses its employees, agents, independent contractors, or representatives to promote sales by the seller in Michigan;

— maintains an office, distribution facility, warehouse, storage place, or similar place of business in Michigan to facilitate the delivery of tangible personal property sold by the seller to customers in the state;

— uses, with the seller's knowledge or consent, trademarks, service marks, or trade names in the state that are the same or substantially similar to those used by the seller;

— delivers, installs, assembles, or performs maintenance or repair services for the seller's customers in Michigan;

— facilitates the seller's delivery of property to customers by allowing the seller's customers in Michigan to pick up tangible personal property sold by the seller at an office, distribution facility, warehouse, storage place, or similar place of business maintained by the person in Michigan;

— shares management, business systems, business practices, or employees with the seller, or, in the case of an affiliated person, engages in intercompany transactions related to the activities occurring with the seller to establish or maintain the seller's market in Michigan; or

— conducts any other activities in Michigan that are significantly associated with the seller's ability to establish and maintain a market in Michigan.

The presumption may be rebutted by demonstrating that activities of the other person or affiliated person were not significantly associated with the seller's ability to establish or maintain a market in Michigan. (Sec. 205.52b; Sec. 205.95a)

Click-through nexus: The legislation also provides that a seller is presumed to be engaged in business in Michigan if the seller enters into an agreement with one or more residents under which the resident, for a commission or other consideration, directly or indirectly, refers potential customers to the seller by a link on an Internet website, in-person oral presentation, or otherwise. The presumption requires that the cumulative gross receipts from sales by the seller to customers in Michigan who are referred to the seller must be greater than $10,000 during the immediately preceding 12 months and that the seller's total cumulative gross receipts from sales to customers in Michigan must be greater than $50,000 during the immediately preceding 12 months.

The presumption may be rebutted by demonstrating that the persons with whom the seller had agreements did not engage in activities that were significantly associated with the seller's ability to establish or maintain a market in Michigan. The presumption would be considered rebutted by evidence of the following:

(1) written agreements prohibiting all residents with an agreement with the seller from engaging in solicitation in Michigan on behalf of the seller and

(2) written statements from all residents with an agreement with the seller stating that the residents did not engage in any solicitation activities on behalf of the seller during the immediately preceding 12 months.

An agreement where a seller purchases advertisements from a person in Michigan to be delivered via television, radio, print, the Internet, or any other medium is not an agreement that would lead to a presumption of nexus unless the revenue paid to the persons is commissions that are based on completed sales.

Traditional nexus: An out-of-state seller is also subject to Michigan's use tax collection responsibility when it engages in any of the following activities (*RAB 1999-1,* Michigan Department of Treasury, May 1999):

— It has one or more employees resident or temporarily present in Michigan engaging in any activity other than those presumed not to create nexus as described below (an employee temporarily present in Michigan for two days will create nexus);

— It owns, rents, leases, maintains, or has the right to use and uses tangible personal or real property that is permanently or temporarily physically located in Michigan;

— Its employees own, rent, lease, use, or maintain an office or other place of business in Michigan;

— It has goods delivered to Michigan in vehicles the out-of-state seller owns, rents, leases, uses, or maintains or has goods delivered by a related party acting as a representative of the out-of-state seller;

— Its agents, representatives, independent contractors, brokers or others, acting on its behalf, own, rent, lease, use, or maintain an office or other place of business in Michigan, and this property is used in the representation of the out-of-state seller in Michigan;

— Its agents, representatives, independent contractors, brokers or others acting on behalf of the out-of-state seller, are regularly and systematically present in Michigan conducting activities to establish or maintain the market for the out-of-state seller whether or not these individuals or organizations reside in Michigan. Activities that establish or maintain the market for the out-of-state seller include, but are not limited to, the following:

(a) soliciting sales;

(b) making repairs or providing maintenance or service to property sold or to be sold;

(c) collecting current or delinquent accounts, through assignment or otherwise, related to sales of tangible personal property or services;

(d) delivering property sold to customers;

(e) installing or supervising installation at or after shipment or delivery;

(f) conducting training for employees, agents, representatives, independent contractors, brokers or others acting on the out-of-state seller's behalf, or for customers or potential customers;

(g) providing customers any kind of technical assistance or service including, but not limited to, engineering assistance, design service, quality control, product inspections, or similar services;

(h) investigating, handling, or otherwise assisting in resolving customer complaints;

(i) providing consulting services; or

(j) soliciting, negotiating, or entering into franchising, licensing, or similar agreements.

• Streamlined Act status

Michigan is a full member of the Streamlined Sales and Use Tax Agreement with a seat on the Governing Board. It has enacted all of the provisions necessary to comply with the Agreement's requirements and these provisions currently are in effect (Sec. 205.171.—Sec. 205.191; Sec. 205.801—Sec. 205.833). As a full member, it may vote on amendments to or interpretations of the Agreement, and sellers registering under the SST system must collect and remit tax on sales into the state. For additional information, see ¶ 537.

¶531 Michigan

Taxability matrix: A chart of the taxable status of various items is accessible on the website of the Streamlined Sales Tax Project at **www.streamlinedsalestax.org**.

¶ 532   Tax Base

The basis of the sales tax is the gross proceeds from retail sales (Sec. 205.52). The basis of the use tax is price (Sec. 205.93).

• "Gross proceeds" defined

The statute defines "gross proceeds" as the amount received in money, credits, subsidies, property or other money's worth in consideration of a sale at retail in Michigan, without deduction for the cost of property sold, the cost of material used, the cost of labor or service purchased, an amount paid for interest or a discount, or other expenses (Sec. 205.51(1)(i)). No deduction is allowed for losses.

• "Price" defined

The statute defines "price" as the aggregate value in money of anything paid or delivered, or promised to be paid or delivered, by a consumer to a seller in the consummation and complete performance of the transaction by which tangible personal property or services were purchased or rented for storage, use, or other consumption in Michigan (Sec. 205.92(f)). No deduction is allowed for the cost of the property sold, cost of materials used, labor or service, interest or discount paid, or any other expense.

Trade-in value: The agreed-upon value of a motor vehicle or recreational vehicle used as part payment of the purchase price of a new or used motor vehicle or a new or used recreational vehicle is excluded from the tax base for purposes of Michigan sales tax. The agreed-upon value of the trade-in vehicle must be separately stated on the invoice or other similar document given to the purchaser. Beginning December 15, 2013, the maximum trade-in value is limited to $2,000. Beginning January 1, 2015, and each January thereafter, the allowable trade-in value increases by $500 unless Section 105D of the Social Welfare Act is repealed. Beginning January 1 of the year in which the trade-in value exceeds $14,000, there will no longer be a limit on the agreed-upon value of the trade-in vehicle. (Sec. 205.92(f)(xii))

A credit for the agreed-upon value of a titled watercraft used as part payment of the purchase price of a new or used watercraft is excluded from the tax base so long as the agreed-upon value is separately stated on the invoice or bill of sale. (Sec. 205.92(f)(xi))

Effective December 15, 2013, the exclusion is expanded to apply to vehicles purchased from out-of-state dealers. Previously, the trade-in credit only applied to vehicle purchases from in-state licensed dealers. Also, leases and rentals of motor vehicles, RVs, and watercraft are excluded from the application of the trade-in credit. (Sec. 205.51; Sec. 205.92)

• Sourcing rules

In conformity with the Streamlined Sales and Use Tax Agreement, sales are sourced generally to the destination of the product sold, with a default to origin-based sourcing in the absence of that information (Secs. 205.69, 205.110). Special sourcing rules apply to sales of vehicles, transportation equipment, and telecommunications, as well as to rental and lease transactions.

Direct mail: Michigan legislation effective September 6, 2016, clarifies how a seller or purchaser of advertising and promotional direct mail collects, pays, or remits sales tax or use tax and the sourcing of other direct mail in order to conform with the Streamlined Sales and Use Tax Agreement by enacting new provisions that (Sec. 205.21a):

— require a seller to source the sale of advertising and promotional direct mail to the jurisdictions to which the mail was to be delivered to recipients, and pay the applicable tax, if the purchaser provided that information;

— require the purchaser to source the sale of advertising and promotional direct mail to the jurisdictions to which it was to be delivered, and pay the applicable tax, if the purchaser provided the seller with a direct payment authorization or exemption form from the Department of Treasury;

— require a sale of advertising and promotional direct mail to be sourced as provided under the General Sales Tax Act and the Use Tax Act (Acts) if the purchaser did not provide information about the delivery jurisdictions or provide a direct payment authorization or an exemption form;

— require the purchaser to source the sale of other direct mail and pay the applicable tax, if the purchaser provided the seller with a direct payment authorization or exemption form;

— require a sale of other direct mail to be sourced as provided in the Acts, if the purchaser did not provide a direct payment authorization or exemption form;

— relieve the seller of any obligation to collect, pay, or remit the applicable tax in situations in which the purchaser was required to pay the tax and source the sale; and

— describe the circumstances under which the provisions apply.

¶ 533 List of Exemptions, Exceptions, and Exclusions

Unless otherwise indicated, the statutory exemptions, exceptions, and exclusions listed below apply to both sales and use taxes; those applicable only to the sales tax or only to the use tax are listed separately. Items that are excluded from the sales or use tax base are treated at ¶ 532, "Tax Base."

Exemption certificates: A seller that receives a properly completed certificate of exemption is not liable for sales or use tax on a transaction, even if it was improperly claimed by the purchaser. For additional information, see *Revenue Administrative Bulletin 2016-14,* Michigan Department of Treasury, June 30, 2016, CCH MICHIGAN TAX REPORTS, ¶ 402-099.

• Sales and use tax exemptions, exceptions, and exclusions

Advertising supplements	Sec. 205.54a(1)(f), Sec. 205.94(1)(l)
Agricultural equipment	Sec. 205.54a, Sec. 205.94
Agricultural processing	Sec. 205.54a(1)(e), Sec. 205.94(1)(f)
Aircraft, aircraft parts	Sec. 205.54x, Sec. 205.94(1)(u), Sec. 205.94(1)(v), Sec. 205.94(1)(w), Sec. 205.94(1)(y), Sec. 205.94k
Ambulance equipment	Sec. 205.54a(1)(h), Sec. 205.94(1)(r)
American Red Cross	Sec. 205.54(7), Sec. 205.94(1)(g)
Automobile demonstrators	Sec. 205.51(1)(b), Sec. 205.94(c)

¶533 Michigan

Prosthetic devices	Sec. 205.54a(1)(h), Sec. 205.94(1)(p)
Railroad equipment	Sec. 205.54m, Sec. 205.94*l*
Repair and maintenance service charges	Sec. 205.55a
Resales	Sec. 205.51(1)(b), Sec. 205.67, Sec. 205.94(1)(c), Sec. 205.104
Returnable beverage container deposits	Sec. 205.54g(1)(b), Sec. 205.94d
Rolling stock used in interstate commerce	Sec. 205.54(r), Sec. 205.94(k) *RAB 2016-2,* January 8, 2016, CCH MICHIGAN TAX REPORTS, ¶ 402-044
Rooms and lodging	Sec. 205.92(f), Sec. 205.93a(b)
Sales to United States government and its agencies	Sec. 205.54(7), Sec. 205.94(1)(g)
Telecommunication transmission equipment	Sec. 205.54v, Sec. 205.94q
Textbooks	Sec. 205.54a(1)(k)
Tips, separately stated	Sec. 205.51(1)(i)
Vessels, interstate commerce	Sec. 205.54a(1)(d), Sec. 205.94(1)(j)
Water, bulk sales	Sec. 205.51(1)(d), Sec. 205.94(1)(q)

• Exemptions, exceptions, and exclusions applicable only to the sales tax

Bullion and investment coins	Sec. 205.54(s), Sec. 205.94(u)
Fundraising sales (limited exemption)	Sec. 205.54o(1), Sec. 205.54o(2)
Occasional sales	Sec. 205.51(1)(g)
School meals	Sec. 205.54a(1)(c)
Tangible personal property sold to central city business engaged in high-technology activity	Sec. 205.54*l*
Vehicle core charges (eff. 3/29/2017)	Sec. 205.51,
Vending machines, certain unsorted sales	Sec. 205.54g(4)
Vending machines, commissions paid nonprofit organizations (limited exemption)	Sec. 205.54f
Vending machines, sealed beverages sold from	Sec. 205.54g(4)
Veterans' organizations, certain fundraising by	Sec. 205.54o(3)

• Exemptions, exceptions, and exclusions applicable only to the use tax

Automobile transfers; intracorporate, estate, or intrafamily	Sec. 205.93(3)
Improvements affixed to real property in another state	Sec. 205.94z

¶ 534　　　　　　　　　Rate of Tax

The sales and use tax rates are set at 6% (Sec. 205.52(1), Sec. 205.93(1)). The sales tax is based on the gross proceeds of sales, and the use tax is based on the selling price of the item used, stored, or consumed or the selling price of the services used or consumed.

• Reduced tax rate applicable to certain residential fuels

The sale or consumption for residential use of electricity, natural gas, or home heating fuel is subject to sales or use tax at the rate of 4%.

• Airport parking tax

An excise tax is assessed on parking facilities located within five miles of the Detroit Metro Airport at the rate of 27% of the amount collected (Sec. 207.371—Sec. 207.375). The airport parking tax is repealed on the date that all bonds issued under the act are retired.

• Diesel fuel use tax

The Use Tax Act's definition of "price" imposes a diesel fuel use tax on interstate motor carriers that is collected under the International Fuel Tax Agreement (Sec. 205.92(f)). Interstate motor carriers are entitled to a credit in the amount of 6% of the price of diesel fuel purchased in Michigan and used in a qualified commercial motor vehicle.

• State and local components added to Michigan use tax

The Michigan use tax includes both a state share tax levied by the state and a local community stabilization share tax levied by the local community stabilization authority. The local community stabilization share tax replaced the metropolitan areas component tax. (Sec. 205.92c; Sec. 205.93)

The rate of the local community stabilization share tax is the rate calculated by the Department of Treasury sufficient to generate certain specified dollar amounts for FY 2015-16 through FY 2027-28. For each subsequent fiscal year, the local community stabilization share tax rate is the rate calculated by the department sufficient to generate the amount distributed in the preceding year adjusted by an industrial and commercial personal property growth factor set by the department. The total combined rate of the tax levied by the state and the authority may not exceed 6%. (Sec. 205.93)

¶ 535　　　　　　　　　Local Taxes

The Michigan Constitution allows local government units to levy taxes that are authorized by law or charter (Sec. 31, Art. IX, Mich. Const.). Currently, no general local sales and use taxes are imposed in Michigan.

Michigan conforms to the federal Mobile Telecommunications Sourcing Act (P.L. 106-252) under which mobile telecommunications are sourced to the customer's "primary place of use."

- **City utility users tax**

The governing body of a city of one million or more may adopt a uniform ordinance to levy a tax on utilities users at a rate of tax in increments of ¼ of 1%, but not to exceed 5% (Sec. 141.1151—Sec. 141.1177).

Rate reduction: If the total revenue generated by the utility user tax for a fiscal year exceeds $45 million by 5% or more, the tax rate for the following fiscal year must be reduced by ¼ of 1% for each full 5% collected in excess of $45 million unless the excess amount is dedicated and used exclusively to hire and retain additional police officers.

"Public utility services" are defined by the ordinance to mean the providing, performing, or rendering of public service of a telephone, electric, steam, or gas nature, the rates or other charges for which are subject to regulation by state public utility regulatory bodies, federal public utility or regulatory bodies or both, and the rendering of public service of an electric or gas nature by a government-owned facility.

Renaissance zone legislation: Public utility services provided in designated renaissance zones to persons or corporations are exempt from the city utility users tax.

- **County lodging taxes**

A county with a population of less than 600,000 that contains a city of over 40,000 (Kent County meets these qualifications) may impose an excise tax on persons engaged in the business of providing rooms to transient guests (persons staying less than 30 days) for dwelling, lodging, or sleeping purposes. Hospitals and nursing homes are exempt. The rate may not exceed 5% of the total charge for accommodations, excluding food and beverages (Sec. 141.861, Sec. 141.862).

The county lodging tax is imposed in addition to other charges, fees, or taxes (Sec. 141.866).

- **County sports and convention facilities excise tax**

Subject to voter approval, certain cities and counties are authorized to impose excise taxes on food service establishments, rental cars, and accommodations to help finance professional sports, entertainment, or convention facilities or a professional baseball stadium (Sec. 207.752(1)). The rate of tax may not exceed 1% of gross receipts from the sale of food and beverages or charges for accommodations and 2% of gross receipts from car rentals (Sec. 207.752(2)). The enabling legislation also imposes certain restrictions and requirements on leasing contracts and local ordinances (Sec. 201.757), permits local officials to enter into agreement with the Department of Treasury to administer and collect the tax (Sec. 201.754), and provides that the tax is in addition to any other taxes, charges, or fees (Sec. 201.755).

- **Convention and tourism marketing tax**

Convention and tourism bureaus in counties with a population of over 1.5 million and designated contiguous counties may assess owners of transient facilities with 35 or more rooms up to 2% of room charges on stays of less than 30 consecutive days. Hospitals and nursing homes are exempt. Room charges do not include food, beverages, telephone service, or state sales or use tax (Sec. 141.882, Sec. 141.883).

- **Community convention or tourism marketing tax**

Convention or tourist bureaus in counties with populations of less than 650,000 or in certain cities, villages, or townships within a county of less than 650,000 or a combination of both, may assess owners of transient facilities with 10 or more rooms up to 5% of room charges. Room charges do not include food, beverages, telephone service, or state sales or use tax (Sec. 141.872, Sec. 141.873). An owner of a building or combination of buildings with less than 10 rooms may agree in writing to be subject to the assessment (Sec. 141.879). College or school dormitories, hospitals, nursing homes, and facilities operated by organizations exempt from federal taxation are exempt (Sec. 141.872(m)).

Permissive 4% tax: Under certain circumstances, convention or tourist bureaus in counties with populations of less than 650,000 are authorized to impose a community convention or tourism marketing tax of 4% rather than the 2% tax otherwise permitted (Sec. 141.873). The tax is assessed against owners of transient facilities of 10 or more rooms, but may be passed on to guests if the assessment is disclosed on a bill. Among other matters, the 4% tax must be approved by owners representing not less than 80% of the rooms available for rent in an assessment district, and the entire fee collected must be paid to a nonprofit tourism promotion organization that receives funding from a contiguous county's 5% excise tax on accommodations.

¶ 536   Bracket Schedule

Sellers must compute the sales or use tax due by carrying the computation to the third decimal place and rounding to a whole cent using a method that rounds up to the next cent whenever the third decimal place is greater than four (Sec. 205.73).

Although the sales tax is levied on the gross proceeds of retail sales, sellers are allowed to reimburse themselves by adding the tax to the amount of sale (Sec. 205.73).

Retailers are not allowed to advertise or hold out to the public that the tax is not considered an element in the price charged the consumer (Sec. 205.73). If reimbursement is collected in an amount greater than necessary to pay the tax, the extra amount must be remitted to the Department of Treasury. No person other than the state may be enriched or gain any benefit from the collection or payment of the tax.

¶ 537   Returns, Payments, and Due Dates

Every person liable for the sales tax must file a sales tax return (Sec. 205.56(1)). A use tax return must be filed by (1) a seller who collects use tax from a purchaser, and (2) a person who uses, stores, or consumes tangible personal property subject to the use tax if the use tax was not paid to the seller (Sec. 205.96(1)).

Aviation fuel sales: Beginning April 1, 2016, and each following calendar quarter, every taxpayer making retail sales of aviation fuel must file an informational report with the Michigan Department of Treasury that shows the following for the immediately preceding calendar quarter:

— the entire amount of the taxpayer's taxable retail sales of aviation fuel;

— the gross proceeds of the taxpayer's business from taxable retail sales of aviation fuel;

— the amount of tax for which the taxpayer is liable from retail sales of aviation fuel; and

— the number of taxable gallons of aviation fuel sold at each airport by the taxpayer and the gross proceeds from those sales.

The report must be filed by the last day of the month that immediately follows the end of a calendar quarter. (Sec. 205.56c; Sec. 205.96c)

• **Return and tax payment due dates**

Generally, on or before the 20th day of each month, a taxpayer must file a return and remit the tax due for the preceding month (Sec. 205.56(1), Sec. 205.96(1)). As discussed below, certain taxpayers must make payment by electronic funds transfer. When necessary to ensure payment of the tax or to provide more efficient administration, the State Treasurer is authorized to require filing and payment for other than monthly periods (Sec. 205.56(4), Sec. 205.96(3)).

Sales and use taxes accrue to the state on the last day of each calendar month (Sec. 205.56(3), Sec. 205.96(5)).

• Electronic funds transfers (EFT)

Payment requirements for large retailers: A retailer or other business with sales and use tax liabilities of $720,000 or more in the prior calendar year must remit by EFT, by the 20th of the month, an amount equal to 75% of its liability in the immediately preceding month or 75% of its liability for the same month in the immediately preceding year, whichever is less. Also due will be a reconciliation payment equal to the difference between the tax liability determined for the previous month and the amount of tax previously paid for that month. (Sec. 205.56(2), M.C.L.; Sec. 205.96(2), M.C.L.)

Sellers are subject to a similar electronic funds transfer provision under the Use Tax Act (Sec. 205.96(3)).

A large retailer described above may deduct from its monthly sales or use tax payment to the Department of Treasury 0.50% of the tax due at a rate of 4%, with no cap on the amount of the deduction (Sec. 205.54(3), Sec. 205.94f(3)).

Payment methods: All remittances of taxes must be made to the department payable to the state of Michigan by bank draft, check, cashier's check, certified check, money order, cash, or electronic funds transfer. The department may accept major credit cards and debit cards for payment but may add a processing fee that may not exceed the charges that the state incurs because of the use of the credit or debit card. A remittance other than cash or electronic funds transfer is not treated as a final discharge of liability for the tax until the instrument remitted has been honored. (Sec. 205.19(1))

Michigan Treasury Online: An online portal called "Michigan Treasury Online" allows business taxpayers to make changes to their registration account information. Through the portal, businesses may register for taxes, file returns and make payments, update addresses, discontinue a tax, register a representative to discuss tax issues with the department, and take steps to close or sell a business. The service is accessible from a link at **http://www.michigan.gov/treasury**.

• Uniform Sales Tax Administration Act

Michigan has enacted the Uniform Sales and Use Tax Administration Act and legislation conforming Michigan law to the Streamlined Sales and Use Tax Agreement was enacted effective September 1, 2004. The legislation was enacted in four linked bills (Act 172 (H.B. 5502), Act 173 (H.B. 5503), Act 174 (H.B. 5504), and Act 175 (H.B. 5505), Laws 2004).

H.B. 5505, Laws 2004, designated the "Streamlined Sales and Use Tax Revenue Equalization Act," is intended to retain certain exemptions eliminated from the general sales and use taxes by the conformity provisions in H.B. 5502 and H.B. 5503. Specifically, H.B. 5505 imposes taxes and creates credits relating to interstate motor carriers, certain motor vehicles, and aircraft, effective September 1, 2004. Additional conformity legislation was enacted in 2008 (H.B. 5555 and H.B. 5556, Laws 2008) and 2009 (Act 138 (H.B. 4906), Laws 2009).

Rounding rule: See ¶ 536.

Exemptions: The exemptions formerly allowed for the sale of diesel fuel to an interstate motor carrier and for the storage, registration, or transfer of certain vehicles or aircraft are eliminated. Rather than an exemption, a seller must collect tax on the transaction and the taxpayer may then claim a credit for the amount of tax paid. See ¶ 540.

Other exemption provisions, including those for food, drugs, and medical equipment, have been amended to conform to the SST Agreement.

Bad debts: See ¶ 540.

Definitions: Numerous definitions have been added to the sales and use tax laws and some existing definitions are amended or repealed to conform to the SST Agreement.

Sourcing rules: See ¶ 532.

A certified service provider or seller who uses a certified automated system pursuant to the Streamlined Sales and Use Tax Agreement will be notified by the Michigan Department of Treasury if it has misclassified an item or transaction in regards to its sales and use taxability. The seller or certified service provider must revise the classification within 10 days of notification. If the seller or service provider fails to do so, it will be liable for collecting the correct amount of tax. (Sec. 205.825)

For additional information on the uniform act, see "Streamlined Sales Tax Project," listed in the Table of Contents.

¶ 538   Prepayment of Taxes

Any wholesaler or retailer purchasing or receiving gasoline or diesel fuel from a refiner, pipeline terminal operator, or marine terminal operator must prepay a portion of the sales tax due on such gasoline or diesel fuel at the time of the purchase or shipment (Sec. 205.56a(1)).

The prepayment requirement also applies to a gasoline or diesel fuel importer (not a refiner or terminal operator) whose first sale in Michigan is to a refiner or terminal operator (*LR 85-12,* Department of Treasury). Transfers or exchanges of gasoline or diesel to other refiners or sales for immediate export are not subject to sales tax and are, thus, not subject to the prepayment requirement (*LR 87-15,* Department of Treasury). Prepayment is not required on retail sales to the final consumers (*LR 87-15,* Department of Treasury).

Prepayment rate: The Department of Treasury announces the prepayment rate monthly in a Revenue Administration Bulletin (RAB). Current and historical rates are available on the Department of Treasury's website at **https://www.michigan.gov/ taxes/0,4676,7-238-43519_43529-154427--,00.html**. Scroll down to the heading "FAQs for General Sales and Use Tax."

Interstate shipments of fuel: Beginning April 1, 2016, for a purchase or shipment of fuel in Michigan from a refiner, pipeline terminal operator, or a marine terminal operator, an exception to the requirement for prepayment of sales tax is enacted for an exporter or supplier for immediate export out of state. An exception to the prepayment requirement is also authorized for an out-of-state purchase or receipt of fuel for subsequent shipment into Michigan when the purchaser is a refiner or terminal operator and the purchase of fuel is part of a bulk transfer. (Sec. 205.56a(3); *Notice,* Michigan Department of Treasury, March 23, 2016, CCH MICHIGAN TAX REPORTS, ¶ 402-068)

• **Due dates for remittance**

Retailers and distributors who make tax prepayments directly to the Department and others who receive prepayments must remit all prepayments received between the 1st and 15th of each month to the Department before the 25th of the month (Sec. 205.56a(5)). Prepayments received between the 15th and the end of the month must be remitted before the 10th of the next month.

¶ 539   Vendor Registration

The General Sales Tax Act requires every person engaged in the business of selling tangible personal property at retail to obtain a sales tax license before engaging in business (Sec. 205.53(1)). There is no fee for the license. The Department of Treasury may deny a license to an applicant that it considers an agent or representative of a principal required to be licensed (Rule R205.1).

Michigan Treasury Online: Beginning in 2015, a new online portal called "Michigan Treasury Online" allows business taxpayers to register for taxes. The service is accessible from a link at **http://www.michigan.gov/treasury**.

• **Use tax registration**

The Use Tax Act requires certain persons to register their business activities (Sec. 205.95(a), Rule R205.26). Registration carries with it the obligation to file tax returns on preidentified forms furnished by the Department of Treasury and collect the use tax from the consumer.

A business holding a sales tax license need not have a separate use tax registration (*LR 88-33,* Department of Treasury). For instance, an out-of-state retailer with no nexus in Michigan cannot be required to collect Michigan use tax (*LR 87-25,* Department of Treasury). However, some out-of-state sellers voluntarily register to collect use tax to relieve their customers of this burden.

Persons required to register: See "Affiliate nexus" and "Click-through nexus" at ¶ 531.

¶ 540   **Sales or Use Tax Credits**

Use tax credits are allowed in many instances for sales taxes paid to other states or counties.

A credit in the form of a prompt payment discount is given for collection of the tax.

• **Fuel credits**

An interstate motor carrier is entitled to a use tax credit of 6% of the price of diesel fuel purchased in Michigan and used in a qualified commercial motor vehicle (Sec. 205.94).

Prepaid tax on gasoline: Credits against the sales tax may be claimed for prepaid sales tax on gasoline (see ¶ 538) (Sec. 205.56a(3)).

The refund that may be claimed for tax paid on gasoline that is subsequently used in tax-exempt agricultural production is also in the nature of a credit.

• **Property taxed in another state**

Michigan *exempts* from use tax property on which sales or use tax equal to or in excess of that imposed by Michigan has been paid to another state or local government, provided the other state or local government extends a reciprocal exemption to Michigan (Sec. 205.94(1)(e)). If the tax paid was less than what Michigan would have imposed, the difference is paid to Michigan.

However, under the Multistate Tax Compact as adopted by Michigan (Sec. 205.581), each purchaser liable for use tax on tangible personal property is entitled to a *credit* for the amount of sales or use taxes paid to another state and/or political subdivision of such state with respect to the same property. Where tax liability is incurred in two states on the same property, the Multistate Tax Commission recommends that the state where tax liability was first incurred allow the credit as against the state where the tax was first paid.

A Letter Ruling (*LR 73-7,* Department of Treasury) cites the Use Tax Act exempting provision in making the following distinction: If the tangible personal property is delivered to the purchaser in the state of sale, the sales tax paid would be *credited* in Michigan; but if the property is shipped directly to the customer in Michigan, the customer is liable for use tax on the basis of the purchase price. (The Letter Ruling is silent as to the applicability of the MTC provision in this case.)

• **Charitable auction refund or credit**

See the discussion at ¶ 544.

• Returned merchandise

A seller may claim a credit for sales tax paid on tax-paid goods that are subsequently returned by customers for full refund or credit (Sec. 205.51(1)(b)). However, no credit may be claimed as a result of repossessions (Rule R205.16).

• Bad debts

A bad debt deduction may be claimed by a taxpayer on the return for the period during which the bad debt is written off as uncollectable in the taxpayer's books and records and is eligible to be deducted for federal income tax purposes under IRC Sec. 166, with certain adjustments (Sec. 204.54i). A taxpayer who is not required to file federal income tax returns may deduct a bad debt on a return filed for the period in which the bad debt is written off as uncollectable in the taxpayer's books and records and would be eligible for a bad debt deduction for federal income tax purposes if the taxpayer were required to file a federal income tax return (Sec. 204.54i; Sec. 205.99a; see also *RAB 2015-27,* Michigan Department of Treasury, December 2, 2015, CCH MICHIGAN TAX REPORTS, ¶ 402-026).

The Michigan bad debt deduction statute does not permit a deduction for sales tax paid on property that is repossessed (*Daimler Chrysler Services of North America v. Department of Treasury,* Michigan Court of Appeals, No. 288347, January 21, 2010, CCH MICHIGAN TAX REPORTS, ¶ 401-478).

Finance companies: The U.S. Supreme Court denied the request of a motor vehicle financing company to decide whether a retroactive change in a Michigan sales tax refund statute for bad debts satisfied due process when applied to deny refunds for the preceding five-year period. In *DaimlerChrysler Services North America LLC v. Dep't of Treasury,* 723 N.W.2d 569 (2006), CCH MICHIGAN TAX REPORTS, ¶ 401-245, the Michigan Court of Appeals held that a motor vehicle financing company was a "taxpayer" entitled to refunds of sales tax paid and remitted by dealerships on installment sales when the purchasers subsequently defaulted on their obligation to repay the amount financed, including the sales tax previously remitted. In response, the Michigan Legislature retroactively amended the bad debt sales tax statute to overturn the effect of the decision. The taxpayer in the current case filed a refund action asserting that the amendments violated the Due Process Clause of the U.S. Constitution because they imposed an indefinite period of retroactivity and were applied to a five-year period in the taxpayer's case. However, the Court of Appeals affirmed the dismissal of the taxpayer's action for the reasons stated in the contemporaneously argued case of *GMAC, LLC v. Dep't of Treasury,* 781 N.W.2d 310 (Mich. Ct. of App. 2009), CCH MICHIGAN TAX REPORTS, ¶ 401-460. In *GMAC,* the court held that a seven-year retroactive application of the amendments did not violate due process or the requirement that such legislation be limited to a modest period of retroactivity. The Michigan Supreme Court denied review. *Ford Motor Credit Co. v. Dep't of Treasury,* 486 Mich. 962, 782 N.W.2d 771, January 12, 2010, CCH MICHIGAN TAX REPORTS, ¶ 401-474; U.S. Supreme Court, Dkt. 10-481, petition for certiorari denied January 18, 2011. See also, on this topic, *Home Depot USA, Inc. v. Department of Treasury,* Michigan Court of Appeals, No. 301341, May 24, 2012, CCH MICHIGAN TAX REPORTS, ¶ 401-679, leave to appeal denied, Michigan Supreme Court, Dkt. No. 145412, October 22, 2012.

Claimant election: If a taxpayer who reported the tax and a lender execute and maintain a written election designating which party may claim the deduction, a claimant is entitled to a deduction or refund of the tax related to a sale at retail that was previously reported and paid if all of the following conditions are met (Sec. 205.54i(3); Sec. 205.99a(3)):

— no deduction or refund was previously claimed or allowed on any portion of the account receivable; and

— the account receivable has been found worthless and written off by the taxpayer that made the sale or by the lender on or after September 30, 2009.

¶540 Michigan

A "lender" is (1) any person who holds or has held an account receivable which that person purchased directly from a taxpayer who reported the tax; (2) any person who holds or has held an account receivable pursuant to that person's contact directly with the taxpayer who reported the tax; or (3) the issuer of the private label credit card. The term "lender" does not include the issuer of a credit card or instrument that can be used to make purchases from a person other than the vendor whose name or logo appears on the card or instrument, or that vendor's affiliates.

¶ 541   Deficiency Assessments

The Department of Treasury may make a deficiency assessment for the sales or use tax in the following situations (Sec. 205.67, Sec. 205.104):

— if a taxpayer fails to file a return;

— if a taxpayer fails to maintain or preserve proper records as required;

— if there is reason to believe that records or returns are inaccurate or incomplete and that additional taxes are due.

The Department may also issue an assessment against a seller required to collect the use tax who fails to do so (Sec. 205.99).

Injunction unavailable: Proceedings for the assessment of tax may not be enjoined under Michigan law (Sec. 205.28(1)(b)). A federal statute also prohibits federal district courts from issuing injunctions when there is a "plain, speedy, and efficient remedy" in state courts (28 U.S.C. § 1341).

• Assessment based on taxpayer's records

The Commissioner of Revenue is authorized to examine the taxpayer's records and use them as a basis for assessing taxes in cases when the taxpayer fails or refuses to make a return, or there is reason to believe that the return is inaccurate (Sec. 205.21).

• Offers in compromise

Michigan makes available an offer-in-compromise program (Sec. 205.28(23a)). To be eligible under the program, there must be a doubt as to liability, doubt as to collectibility, or the taxpayer must have been granted a related tax compromise under the federal offer-in-compromise program. Other features of the Michigan program include:

— a required payment of $100 or 20% of the offer made (whichever is greater) at the time an offer is submitted;

— a prohibition against levying against property to collect a tax liability while a compromise is pending;

— publication of a public report on a granted offer-in-compromise;

— an independent administrative review process;

— revocation of compromise under certain conditions, such as an intent to mislead in obtaining a compromise or a failure to meet terms of a compromise; and

— offer rejections that are final and not subject to appeal.

For additional information, see *Guidelines for Offer in Compromise Program,* Michigan Department of Treasury, December 16, 2014, CCH MICHIGAN TAX REPORTS, ¶ 401-952.

¶ 542   Audit Procedures

Although sales and use taxes are, generally, self-assessed, several procedures are provided to ensure compliance with the law and to facilitate assessment in case of noncompliance.

Sampling: The Department utilizes the electronic statistical sampling, manual random sampling, and judgmental block sampling methods. When electronic records are available, the Department uses its statistical sampling software to apply sampling procedures. A review of all electronic records may be conducted if the auditor determines it would be more efficient. Manual random sampling will be used when electronic records are unavailable. If this method is deemed ineffective, a detailed review of records may be made with supervisory approval. When it is determined to be cost effective, the auditor may use judgment block sampling, which requires basing a conclusion on a non-random selection from a population. (*Internal Policy Directive 2009-2*, Michigan Department of Treasury, June 22, 2009, CCH Michigan Tax Reports, ¶ 401-431)

Indirect audit procedures: Effective April 10, 2014, if a taxpayer fails to file a sales and use tax return or fails to maintain sufficient records, or the Michigan Department of Treasury believes that records or returns are inaccurate, the department may base an assessment on an indirect audit procedure (Sec. 205.68, MCL). An "indirect audit procedure" includes the following elements:

(1) review of the taxpayer's books and records, including the use of an indirect method to test their accuracy;

(2) evaluation of both the credibility of the evidence and the reasonableness of the conclusion before a determination of tax liability;

(3) use of any reasonable method to reconstruct income, deductions, or expenses, including the use of third-party records; and

(4) investigation of all reasonable evidence submitted by the taxpayer refuting the computation.

If a taxpayer has filed all required returns and has maintained sufficient records, the department must not base a tax deficiency determination or assessment on an indirect audit procedure unless it has a documented reason to believe that the records and returns are inaccurate or incomplete. (Sec. 205.68, MCL)

• Recordkeeping

If a person fails or refuses to make a return, or if there is reason to believe that a return is inaccurate, the Department of Treasury may obtain information on which to base an assessment of tax (Sec. 205.21). The Department, by its duly authorized agents, may examine the books, records, and papers and audit the accounts of a person or any other records pertaining to the deficient tax.

A person may not be excused from testifying or from producing any records requested by the Department merely because such testimony or evidence may incriminate the person or subject him to a criminal penalty (Sec. 205.3(a)). However, the person shall be exempt from criminal prosecution for the transaction about which he or she testified, unless the person commits perjury during the trial.

A taxpayer must keep accurate and complete records for the proper determination of tax liability (Sec. 205.28(3)). For sales and use tax purposes, such records include records of inventory, purchases, receipts, sales, and tax-exempt sales (Sec. 205.67, Sec. 205.104). In the absence of such records, the Department may make an assessment on the basis of any information that is, or may become, available (Sec. 205.67, Sec. 205.104). Such an assessment is presumed to be correct, and the burden is on the taxpayer to refute its correctness.

¶ 543   **Statute of Limitations**

The uniform tax provisions on statutes of limitations are applicable to sales and use taxes (Sec. 205.20). The statutes of limitations are as follows:

¶543 Michigan

General rule: Four years from the due date or actual filing date of the return, whichever is later, for assessments (Sec. 205.27a(2)), and six years for collection of a final assessment (Sec. 600.5813, *RAB 93-15,* Department of Treasury).

Failure to file: A person who has failed to file a return is liable for all taxes due for the entire period for which the person would be subject to the taxes (Sec. 205.27a(2)).

Concealment of tax liability: A person who fraudulently conceals all or part of a tax liability may be assessed up to two years after the discovery of the fraud (Sec. 205.27a(2)). The assessment will include penalties and interest computed from the date the tax liability originally accrued.

Suspension of statute of limitations: The running of the statute of limitations is suspended for the following periods (Sec. 205.27a(3)):

— the period pending a final determination of tax, including audit, conference, hearing, and litigation of liability for a tax, and for one year after that period;

— a period that the taxpayer and the Commissioner have consented to in writing;

— the one-year period for completion of audit fieldwork and the nine-month period for issuance of a final assessment, or pending the completion of an appeal of a final assessment; and

— a period of 90 days after a decision and order from an informal conference, or a court order that finally resolves an appeal of a decision of the department in a case in which a final assessment was not issued prior to appeal.

The suspension applies only to those items that were the subject of the audit, conference, hearing, or litigation (Sec. 205.27a(4); see also *RAB 2015-26*, Michigan Department of Treasury, December 2, 2015, CCH MICHIGAN TAX REPORTS, ¶ 402-027).

¶ 544   Application for Refund

Refunds of sales and use tax overpayments are governed by uniform tax provisions that generally apply to all taxes (Sec. 205.20). Pursuant to these provisions, the Department of Treasury may refund or credit the following (Sec. 205.30(1)):

— any overpayment of taxes; or

— any taxes, together with penalties and interest, that are erroneously or unjustly assessed, excessive in amount, or wrongfully collected.

Procedure: A taxpayer claiming a refund or credit must file a petition for refund with the Department (Sec. 205.30(2)). A tax return filed that reflects an overpayment or credits in excess of the tax liability by itself constitutes a claim for refund.

Statute of limitations: Refunds must generally be filed within four years from the date for the filing of the original return (Sec. 205.27a(2), *LR 88-82,* Commissioner of Revenue), except that a claim for refund based on the laws or Constitution of the United States or the Michigan Constitution of 1963 must be filed within 90 days after the date set for filing a return (Sec. 205.27a(6)).

The period to claim a refund is extended when a taxpayer obtains an extension of time to file the original return or if the refund claim period is extended by statute, for example, if the refund is pending final determination of a federal tax liability (*RAB 93-14,* Department of Treasury).

A taxpayer is not entitled to a refund once the time to challenge the assessment has expired (*RAB 94-1,* Department of Treasury). This prevents circumvention of the statutory limits for challenging an assessment, decision, or order by resort to the refund procedures.

• **Charitable auction refund or credit**

A nonprofit organization that sells an item at a charitable auction is allowed to claim a Michigan sales tax refund of 6% of the gross proceeds of the auctioned item in excess of the fair market value of that auctioned item. Alternatively, the nonprofit organization may choose to apply a credit to reduce its sales tax liability. The nonprofit organization may not seek a credit or refund for any portion of a qualified sale of an auctioned item for which sales tax was collected from the purchaser, unless the tax collected was refunded to the purchaser. In addition, the nonprofit organization must retain in its records certification of the fair market value supplied by the donor of an auctioned item on a form prescribed by the Department of Treasury (Sec. 205.184).

¶ 546   Scope of Tax

Source.—Statutory references are to Chapter 297A of the Minnesota Statutes, as amended to date. Details are reported in the CCH MINNESOTA STATE TAX REPORTS starting at ¶ 60-000.

The Minnesota sales tax is a general tax levied on the gross receipts from sales at retail of tangible personal property or on its lease or rental, and on the furnishing of specified services (Sec. 297A.61(4), Sec. 297A.62, Rule 8130.0110, Rule 8130.2300). The use tax on consumption, use, distribution, or storage of tangible personal property in the state is a complementary tax and does not apply in situations in which the sales tax is collected (Sec. 297A.63(1), Rule 8130.3800).

Digital products: Sales and use tax applies to the furnishing for a consideration of specified digital products or other digital products or granting the right for a consideration to use specified digital products and other digital products on a temporary or permanent basis, regardless of whether the purchaser is required to make continued payments for such right. Specified digital products include digital audio works, digital audiovisual works, and digital books transferred electronically to a customer. Other digital products include greeting cards and online video or electronic games transferred electronically. Digital textbooks prescribed to enrolled students in conjunction with a course of study in a school, college, university, or private career school are exempt. (Sec. 297A.61(3)(*l*); *Sales Tax Fact Sheet No. 177,* Minnesota Department of Revenue, January 2014, CCH MINNESOTA TAX REPORTS, ¶ 203-938)

A sale of specified digital products or other digital products to an end user with or without rights of permanent use, and regardless of whether rights of use are conditioned upon payment by the purchaser, is a retail sale (Sec. 297A.61(4)(o)). However, when a digital code has been purchased that relates to specified digital products or other digital products, the subsequent receipt of or access to the related specified digital products or other digital products is not a retail sale.

Digital presentations: An exemption is available for certain interactive live or prerecorded presentations such as lectures, seminars, workshops, or courses that are accessed electronically as digital audio works or digital audiovisual works. (Sec. 297A.67(33))

Repair and maintenance: Charges for repairing and maintaining electronic and precision equipment are taxable if the charge is deductible as a business expense under the federal Internal Revenue Code (Sec. 297A.61(3)(m)(1)). Charges for repairing and maintaining commercial and industrial machinery are also taxable (Sec. 297A.61(3)(m)(2)). See also *Revenue Notice No. 16-03,* March 7, 2016, CCH MINNESOTA TAX REPORTS, ¶ 204-137.

For nformation regarding the tax treatment of labor for installation, fabrication, construction, and repair services, see (*Sales Tax Fact Sheet No. 152,* Minnesota Department of Revenue, August 2016, CCH MINNESOTA TAX REPORTS, ¶ 204-159)

Industry fact sheets: Fact sheets for the sales and use taxation of various industries are available at **http://www.revenue.state.mn.us/businesses/sut/Pages/Industry-Guides.aspx**

• **Incidence of tax**

Although the sales tax is generally imposed on a seller's gross receipts (Sec. 297A.62), shifting of the tax to the purchaser is mandatory. Sales tax must be separately stated, and the tax becomes a debt from the purchaser to the seller (Sec. 297A.77).

The incidence of the use tax is on the purchaser or consumer (Sec. 297A.63). The use tax is also a debt from the purchaser to the seller (Sec. 297A.77(4)).

Drop shipment sales: A seller engaged in drop shipping may claim a resale exemption based on an exemption certificate provided by its customer or reseller or based on any other acceptable information available to the seller that provides evidence of qualification for a resale exemption, regardless of whether the customer or reseller is registered to collect and remit sales and use tax in Minnesota. (Sec. 297A.665(b)(3)).

• **Services subject to tax**

Specified services are subject to the sales or use tax (Sec. 297A.61—Sec. 297A.135). Taxable services include fabrication of tangible personal property from materials furnished by the customer; preparation of meals; entertainment admissions and membership fees; computer software; lodging; utilities; telecommunications; installation; parking; cleaning; detective and security; pet care; lawn care; prepaid calling services; and nonprescription massage services (Sec. 297A.61(3)(g)).

Internet service: Tax on Internet access service is barred under the federal Internet Tax Freedom Act (ITFA), which is now permanent; see *Revenue Notice No. 16-02*, Minnesota Department of Revenue, February 29, 2016, CCH MINNESOTA TAX REPORTS, ¶ 204-135.

VoIP service: Voice over Internet Protocol (VoIP) services are subject to sales and use tax as telecommunications services. A VoIP service does not qualify as an exempt information service because it uses computer processing applications solely for the management, control, or operation of a telecommunications system or the management of a telecommunications service. (*Modification of Revenue Notice No. 05-03*, Minnesota Department of Revenue, April 13, 2009, CCH MINNESOTA TAX REPORTS, ¶ 203-452)

Pay television services: Taxable services include pay television services. Pay television service includes point-to-multipoint distribution direct-to-home satellite service or any similar or comparable method of service. Pay television service also includes all programming services, including subscriptions, digital video recorders, pay-per-view, and music services. (Sec. 297A.61(3)(i))

Ticket resales: Resellers of admission tickets are required to charge tax on the total amount for which the ticket is resold (Sec. 297A.68(43)). "Ticket reseller" means a person who purchases admission tickets to a sporting event, theater, musical performance, or place of public entertainment or amusement of any kind; resells admission tickets to such events; and is registered to collect sales and use tax.

A ticket reseller who did not purchase its tickets exempt for resale may either claim a refund (if it paid tax on the purchase of the original ticket) or pass on to the ticket purchaser an amount equal to the sales tax paid on the original ticket sale, after calculating the tax based on the sales price of the ticket. The credited amount that can be passed on to the purchaser is limited to the lesser of (1) the tax paid at the time of the original ticket sales, or (2) the tax charged by the reseller. However, if the sales tax was not paid on the original ticket sale, then the reseller must charge the sales tax on the full price of the ticket resold, and is not allowed to pass on any credit. (Sec. 297A.68(43))

Warehousing and storage: The service of warehousing or storage of tangible personal property is taxable, effective for sales and purchases made after March 31, 2014, except that storage of agricultural products, refrigerated storage, and storage of electronic data are not taxable. In addition, self storage and the storage of motor vehicles, recreational vehicles, and boats are not taxable if the charge for storage is not deductible as a business expense under the Internal Revenue Code. (Sec. 297A.61(3)(m)(3))

Motor vehicle repair: A sale of motor vehicle repair paint and materials by a motor vehicle repair or body shop business is a retail sale, and sales tax is imposed on the gross receipts from the sale. The motor vehicle repair or body shop that purchases motor vehicle repair paint and motor vehicle repair materials for resale must either (1) separately state each item of paint and each item of materials, and the sales price of each, on the invoice to the purchaser or (2) calculate the sales price of the paint and materials using a specified method that estimates the amount and monetary value of the paint and materials. (Sec. 297A.61(4)(n))

- **Use tax**

The use tax is imposed on the use, storage, distribution, or consumption in Minnesota of tangible personal property or taxable services (Sec. 297A.63, Rule 8130.3800). In addition, the use tax is specifically imposed on persons who use, store, distribute, or consume in Minnesota tangible personal property that has been manufactured, fabricated, or assembled within or without the state.

The use tax is intended to complement the sales tax, and applies to the following situations (Rule 8130.0110):

— out-of-state purchases of property to be used in state in transactions that otherwise would have been taxable if they had occurred in state;

— purchases for resale or other nontaxable use of property that is subsequently used by the purchaser for a taxable purpose; and

— purchases of property from a Minnesota vendor when no sales tax was paid on the purchases.

A *de minimis* exemption exists for purchases totaling less than $770 per year (Sec. 297A.67(21)).

- **Nexus**

Minnesota law requires retailers who maintain a place of business in the state to collect and remit sales or use taxes on sales in Minnesota or to destinations in Minnesota (Sec. 297A.66(2)). The "destination of a sale" is the location to which the retailer makes delivery to the purchaser of the property by any means of delivery, including the U.S. Postal Service or a common or contract carrier (Sec. 297A.66(1)). "Maintaining a place of business in the state" means having an office, place of distribution, sales or sample room or place, warehouse or other place of business or any agent operating in the state under the authority of the retailer, whether temporarily or permanently. The place of business may be maintained directly or through a subsidiary or an affiliate. (Sec. 297A.66(1))

Affiliate nexus: A "retailer maintaining a place of business in this state" includes an affiliate of a retailer and affiliated entities. An entity is an affiliate of a retailer if the entity uses the retailer's facilities or employees in Minnesota to advertise, promote, or facilitate the establishment or maintenance of a market for sales of items by the retailer in Minnesota or to provide services to the retailer's purchasers in Minnesota, and the retailer and the entity are related parties (Sec. 298A.66(1), Sec. 298A.66(4)).

The state may not use a seller's registration under the Streamlined Agreement as a factor in determining whether the seller has nexus with Minnesota for any tax at any time (Sec. 297A.66(5)).

Systematic solicitation: Out-of-state retailers who do not maintain a place of business in the state are nevertheless required to collect and remit sales and use tax if they systematically solicit sales from potential customers in Minnesota. Such solicitation includes distribution of catalogs; advertisements sent by mail, displayed on billboards, published in newspapers, journals, national or regional publications, broadcast on radio or television stations located in Minnesota; or solicitations by communication systems such as telegram, telephone, computer database or cable (Sec. 297A.66(3)). Systematic solicitation is presumed to occur if either (Sec. 297A.66(3)):

(a) 100 or more sales are made to Minnesota destinations within 12 consecutive months, or

(b) 10 or more sales totalling more than $100,000 are made to Minnesota destinations within 12 consecutive months.

Accommodations intermediary services: Services provided by an online lodging seller or other accommodations intermediary in connection with lodging and related services provided by a hotel, rooming house, resort, campground, motel, or trailer camp are subject to tax (Sec. 297A.61(3)(g)). Accommodations intermediaries are required to collect sales tax and remit it to the Commissioner of Revenue for services provided in connection with or for lodging located in Minnesota. An "accommodations intermediary" is any person or entity, other than an accommodations provider, that facilitates the sale of lodging and that charges a room charge to a customer (Sec. 297A.61(47)). "Facilitates the sale" includes brokering, coordinating, or in any way arranging for the purchase of or the right to use accommodations by a customer. "Furnishes" includes the sale of use or possession, or the sale of the right to use or possess (Sec. 297A.61(48)).

• Click-through nexus

A retailer is presumed to have a solicitor in Minnesota if it enters into an agreement with a resident under which the resident, for a commission or other consideration, directly or indirectly refers potential customers, whether by a link on an Internet website or otherwise, to the seller (Sec. 297A.66(4a)). A "solicitor" is a person, whether an independent contractor or other representative, who directly or indirectly solicits business for the retailer.

This provision applies only if the total of gross receipts from sales to customers located in Minnesota who were referred to the retailer by all residents with this type of agreement with the retailer is at least $10,000 in the 12-month period ending on the last day of the most recent calendar quarter before the calendar quarter in which the sale is made. "Gross receipts" means receipts from sales to customers located in Minnesota who were referred to the retailer by all residents with this type of agreement. The term "resident" includes an individual who is a Minnesota resident or a business that owns tangible personal property located in Minnesota or has one or more employees providing services for the business in Minnesota. (Sec. 297A.66(4a))

The presumption above may be rebutted by proof that the resident with whom the seller has an agreement did not engage in any solicitation in Minnesota on behalf of the retailer that would satisfy the nexus requirement of the U.S. Constitution during the 12-month period in question. (Sec. 297A.66(4a)(c))

• Streamlined Act status

Minnesota is a full member of the Streamlined Sales and Use Tax Agreement with a seat on the Governing Board. It has enacted all of the provisions necessary to comply with the Agreement's requirements and these provisions currently are in effect (Sec. 297A.995). As a full member, it may vote on amendments to or interpretations of the Agreement, and sellers registering under the SST system must collect and remit tax on sales into the state. For details, see ¶ 552.

Taxability matrix: A chart of the taxable status of various items is accessible on the website of the Streamlined Sales Tax Project at **http://www.streamlinedsalestax.org**.

¶ 547   Tax Base

The basis of the sales tax is gross receipts from sales at retail (Sec. 297A.62). The basis of the use tax is "purchase price," which has the same definition as "sales price"(Sec. 297A.61(28), Sec. 297A.63).

• Basis definitions

"Gross receipts" is the total amount received, in money or otherwise, for all sales at retail as measured by the sales price and may be reported on the cash or the accrual accounting method (Sec. 297A.61(8), Rule 8130.1800).

¶547   Minnesota

"Sales price" is the total amount of consideration, including cash, credit, property, and services, for which personal property or services are sold, leased, or rented, valued in money, whether received in money or otherwise, without any deduction for the following Sec. 297A.61(7):

— the seller's cost of the property sold;

— the cost of materials used, labor or service cost, interest, losses, all costs of transportation to the seller, all taxes imposed on the seller, and any other expenses of the seller;

— charges by the seller for any services necessary to complete the sale, other than delivery and installation charges;

— delivery charges;

— installation charges; and

— the value of exempt property given to the purchaser when taxable and exempt personal property have been bundled together and sold by the seller as a single product or piece of merchandise.

Sales price does not include the following:

— discounts, including cash, terms, or coupons that are not reimbursed by a third party and that are allowed by the seller and taken by a purchaser on a sale;

— interest, financing, and carrying charges from credit extended on the sale of personal property or services, if the amount is separately stated on the invoice, bill of sale, or similar document given to the purchaser; and

— any taxes legally imposed directly on the consumer that are separately stated on the invoice, bill of sale, or similar document given to the purchaser.

Installation: Charges for installation services are taxable if the installation charges would be subject to sales tax when the installation is provided by the seller of the item being installed (Sec. 297A.61(3)).

• Sourcing

The following sourcing rules apply regardless of the characterization of a product as tangible personal property, a digital good, or a service (Sec. 297A.668).

Sales are sourced generally to the destination of the product sold, with a default to origin-based sourcing in the absence of that information. Special sourcing rules apply to sales of transportation equipment and telecommunications. The following general sourcing rules apply (Sec. 297A.668):

— when the product is received by the purchaser at a business location of the seller, the sale is sourced to that business location;

— when the product is not received by the purchaser at a business location of the seller, the sale is sourced to the location where receipt by the purchaser, or the purchaser's designated donee, occurs;

— if neither of the above apply, the sale is sourced to the location indicated by an address for the purchaser that is available from the business records of the seller that are maintained in the ordinary course of the seller's business when use of this address does not constitute bad faith;

— if none of the above apply, the sale is sourced to the location indicated by an address for the purchaser obtained during the consummation of the sale, including the address of a purchaser's payment instrument, if no other address is available, when use of this address does not constitute bad faith;

— if none of the other rules apply, including the circumstance in which the seller is without sufficient information to apply the previous rules, then the location will be determined by the address from which tangible personal property was shipped, from which the digital good or the computer software delivered electronically was first available for transmission by the seller, or from which the service was provided (Sec. 297A.668(2)).

Special sourcing rules apply to sales of transportation equipment and telecommunications.

Florist sales: Florist sales are sourced as follows (Sec. 297A.668(9)(a)):

— When a Minnesota retailer takes a florist sales order directly from a customer, regardless of whether the customer is physically present in Minnesota when placing the order, and delivers the items to the customer or a third person either within or outside Minnesota, and regardless of the delivery method, the florist sale is sourced according to general destination sourcing rules.

— When one retailer transmits a florist sales order to another retailer of florist sales through a floral network service or floral delivery association, whether by telephone, telegraph, Internet, or other means of communication, the florist sale is sourced to the location of the retailer who originally takes the order from the customer and accepts payment.

For purposes of these sourcing provisions, "florist sales" means sales at retail of flowers, wreaths, floral bouquets, potted plants, hospital baskets, funeral designs, seeds, nursery seedling stock, trees, shrubs, plants, sod, soil, bulbs, sand, rock, and all other floral or nursery products (Sec. 297A.668(9)(b)).

Direct mail: Separate sourcing provisions apply for advertising and promotional direct mail and for other direct mail. "Advertising and promotional direct mail" means printed material that is direct mail, the primary purpose of which is to attract public attention to a product, person, business, or organization or to attempt to sell, popularize, or secure financial support for a person, business, organization, or product. "Other direct mail" means printed material that is direct mail, but is not advertising and promotional direct mail, regardless of whether advertising and promotional direct mail is included in the same mailing. (Sec. 297A.668(7))

If a purchaser of advertising and promotional direct mail or other direct mail provides an exemption certificate, the seller is generally relieved of all obligations to collect and remit the tax on any transaction to which the certificate applies, the purchaser sources the sale to the jurisdictions where the mail is to be delivered to recipients, and the purchaser reports and pays the tax. If a purchaser of advertising and promotional direct mail provides the seller with the jurisdictional delivery information, the seller must source the sale to the jurisdictions where the mail is delivered to recipients and must collect and remit the tax. Otherwise, the sale is sourced to the address from which the tangible personal property was shipped or from which the service was provided. If a purchaser of other direct mail does not provide an exemption certificate, the sale is sourced to the purchaser's address. (Sec. 297A.668(7))

¶ 548   **List of Exemptions, Exceptions, and Exclusions**

Unless otherwise indicated, the statutory exemptions listed below apply to both sales and use taxes. Items that are excluded from the sales or use tax base are treated at ¶ 547, "Tax Base."

¶548   Minnesota

• Sales and use tax exemptions, exceptions, and exclusions

¶548 Minnesota

Motor vehicles, leased-to-own from a charitable organization . . . . . . Sec. 297B.03(14)

Motor vehicles subject to motor vehicle excise tax . . . . Sec. 297A.67(26)

Motor vehicles, purchase or lease by political subdivisions . . . . Sec. 297A.70(2), (3)

Natural gas for residential use . . . . Sec. 297A.67(15)

Natural gas vehicle fuel . . . . Sec. 297A.68(20)

Newspapers . . . . Sec. 297A.68(10)

Newspapers, advertising . . . . Sec. 297A.68(10)

Nonprofit organizations . . . . Sec. 297A.70(4), (10), (13), (14)

Nonresident property brought into state . . . . Sec. 297A.67(22)

Nursing homes and boarding care homes, nonprofit and certified . . . Sec. 297A.70(18)

Occasional sales . . . . Sec. 297.67(23), Sec. 297A.68(25)

Occasional sales of farm equipment . . . . Sec. 297A.68(25)

Packaging materials . . . . Sec. 297A.68(2)

Packing materials, household moves out of state . . . . Sec. 297A.68(16)

Patent, trademark, and copyright documents . . . . Sec. 297A.68(33)

Personal property and services sold to qualified Greater Minnesota businesses . . . . Sec. 297A.68(49)

Petroleum products for certain day care transportation and mobile medical units . . . . Sec. 296A.07(4)(2) and (4)

Pollution control equipment, steel reprocessors . . . . Sec. 297A.68(8)

Prizes, games at fairs, etc. . . . . Sec. 297A.68(29)

Production, materials consumed . . . . Sec. 297A.68(2)

Prosthetic devices . . . . Sec. 297A.67(7)

Public safety radio communication systems . . . . Sec. 297A.70(8)

Real property rental, 30 or more days . . . . Sec. 297A.61(3)(b)(2)

Religious orders and affiliated institutions of higher education . . . . . Sec. 297A.70(9a)

Resales . . . . Sec. 297A.61(4)

Sacramental wine . . . . Sec. 297A.70(9)

Satellite broadcasting facilities . . . . Sec. 297A.71(9)

Schools . . . . Sec. 297A.70(2), (11)

Schools and colleges, instructional materials . . . . Sec. 297A.67(13a)

Schools and colleges, meals . . . . Sec. 297A.67(5)

Schools and colleges, textbooks . . . . Sec. 297A.67(13)

Seeds . . . . Sec. 297A.69(2)

Services performed by off-duty, licensed peace officers . . . . Sec. 297A.61(3)(g)(5)

Ships, parts and materials for interstate use . . . . Sec. 297A.68(17)

Ski machinery . . . . Sec. 297A.68(34)

Ski passes, cross country . . . . Sec. 297A.67(9)

Snowmobile fuel . . . . Sec. 297A.68(19)

Snow production, electricity . . . . Sec. 297A.68(21)

Solar energy systems . . . . Sec. 297A.67(29)

Solid waste processing . . . . Sec. 297A.68(24)

State lottery, communications services	Sec. 297A.61(24)
Student organizations, fundraising events	Sec. 297A.70(11)
Superbowl tickets	Sec. 297A.68(9)
Taconite (and other ores and metals) production, materials consumed	Sec. 297A.68(4)
Telemarketers, communication services	Sec. 297A.68(26)
Television commercials and production	Sec. 297A.68(30)
Textbooks (including digital books used in a school or college)	Sec. 297A.67(13)
Tickets, out-of-state events	Sec. 297A.69(32)
Tires, farm	Sec. 297A.69(5)
Tools, dies, jigs, and similar items	Sec. 297A.68(6)
Towns, sales to	Sec. 297A.70(a)(7); Sec. 297A.70(b)(5), (d)
Transit system fuel	Sec. 297A.68(19)
United States, sales to	Sec. 297A.70(2)
Veterinary services	Sec. 297A.61(3)
Waste processing equipment	Sec. 297A.68(24), Sec. 297A.68(84)
Waste tire cogeneration facilities	Sec. 297A.68(24)
Water, residential use	Sec. 297A.67(15)
Water used for fire protection	Sec. 297A.70(3)
Wholesale sales	Sec. 297A.61(4)
YMCA, YWCA, and JCC memberships, fees	Sec. 297A.70(12)

¶ 549   Rate of Tax

The general rate of sales and use tax is 6.875%. The rate is scheduled to revert to 6.5% on July 1, 2034. (Sec. 297A.62(1), Sec. 297A.63(1)). Any reference to the general sales tax rate includes both the 6.5% general tax and the 0.375% additional tax (Sec. 297A.62(4)).

Some rates are different from the general rate. The tax rate on sales of intoxicating liquor (beer, wine, and other alcoholic beverages) is 9% (a 6.5% sales and use tax and a 2.5% liquor gross receipts tax) (Sec. 297A.62(2)). Near-beer products such as O'Doul's and Sharps are subject to the 6.5% sales and use tax. The sale of 3.2% malt liquor is taxed at 9% when the sale is made at an on- or off-sale municipal liquor store or at an establishment that is licensed to sell intoxicating liquor.

Motor vehicle sales and leases: Sales of motor vehicles are subject to sales tax at a rate of 6.5%. Leases of motor vehicles are taxed at 6.875%. (Sec. 297A.62(1) and (1a); Sec. 297B.02(1))

Motor vehicle rentals: A tax of 9.2% of the sales price and a fee of 5% of the sales price are imposed on the lease or rental in Minnesota of a passenger automobile, passenger van, or pickup truck for not more than 28 days. The 5% fee is imposed to compensate the lessor for registering the vehicles. The tax and fee apply regardless of whether the vehicle is licensed in the state (Sec. 297A.64). The rental motor vehicle tax and fee are not imposed when a lease or rental of a vehicle is exempt from sales tax.

Leased personal property: For leases of tangible personal property, except leases of motor vehicles (discussed above), each lease payment is a separate sale. Therefore, the 6.875% rate applies to all lease payments until the rate changes.

Manufactured homes, modular homes, and park trailers: Although tax is imposed on manufactured or modular homes used for residential purposes and new or used park trailers at the rate of 6.875%, the operative rate is less because the tax is imposed on only 65% of the dealer's cost for the home (Sec. 297A.62(3)). Thus, the tax rate is effectively 4.6%. Sales are sourced to the site where the housing is first set up or installed (Sec. 297A.668(8)).

Waste collection: Waste management services in the seven-county metropolitan area are not subject to sales tax but are subject to the solid waste management tax at the general rate plus a fee of $6.66 per ton or $2 per cubic yard for facilities measuring waste by volume.

Cigarettes: Sales of cigarettes are exempt from the general sales tax (Sec. 297A.67(32)). However, cigarettes are subject to a cigarette sales tax that is imposed upon the sale of cigarettes by distributors to retailers and cigarette subjobbers. The tax is equal to 6.5% of the weighted average retail price expressed in cents per pack rounded to the nearest one-tenth of a cent. The weighted average retail price is determined annually by the Commissioner, with new rates published by May 1, and effective for sales on or after August 1 (Sec. 297F.25).

Beginning January 1, 2017, the Minnesota cigarette sales tax rate was increased from 54.3 cents per pack of 20 cigarettes to 55 cents per pack.

Prepaid wireless service fees: There is a prepaid wireless E911 fee (currently, 95 cents per retail transaction) and a prepaid wireless Telecommunications Access Minnesota (TAM) fee (currently 5 cents per month for each customer access line). The fees must be increased or reduced proportionately to fluctuations in the E911 and TAM fees that apply to other customers (Sec. 403.161(1)). The fees are not imposed on a minimal amount of prepaid wireless telecommunications service (either 10 minutes or less or $5 or less) that is sold with a prepaid wireless device and is charged a single nonitemized price. (*Sales Tax Fact Sheet No. 179,* Minnesota Department of Revenue, May 2016, CCH MINNESOTA TAX REPORTS, ¶ 204-146)

¶ 550   Local Taxes

For certain local taxes administered by the Department of Revenue, such as lodging, entertainment, admissions, or food and beverage taxes, the municipality must adopt the state's sales and use tax definitions in the statutes or, for terms not defined in statutes or rules, the definitions must be consistent with the department's position as to the extent of the tax base (Sec. 645.025). A local government must receive voter approval of the imposition of a local sales tax at a general election before requesting legislative authorization for the local tax (Sec. 297A.99(3)).

Rate changes: If there are not at least 30 days between the enactment of a new tax rate and the effective date of the new rate, then for up to 30 days sellers and certified service providers (CSPs) are relieved of liability for failing to collect tax at the new rate. The seller or CSP must continue to impose and collect the tax at the rate that immediately precedes the new rate. The relief is not available if the seller or CSP fraudulently fails to collect tax at the new rate or if the seller solicits purchasers on the basis of the preceding rate. (Sec. 297A.995(10))

If there are not at least 30 days between the enactment of a new tax rate and the effective date of the new rate, then for up to 30 days a purchaser is relieved from liability for failing to pay tax at the new rate. The purchaser must pay the tax at the immediately preceding tax rate. The relief is not available if the purchaser fraudulently fails to pay the tax at the new rate. (Sec. 297A.995(10))

A transitional period is provided for retail sales of services that cover a billing period starting before and ending after the effective date of a rate change. For a rate increase, the new rate applies to the first billing period starting on or after the effective date. For a rate decrease, the new rate applies to bills rendered on or after the effective date. (Sec. 297A.63(3))

Local rates: Local tax information and rate charts for sales and use taxes and special taxes for Minnesota counties and cities is located on the Department of Revenue's website at **http://www.revenue.state.mn.us/businesses/sut/Pages/Local_Tax_Info.aspx.**

Limitations: In conformity with the Streamlined Sales and Use Tax Agreement (¶ 552), a political subdivision may not have more than one local sales tax rate or more than one local use tax rate. This limitation does not apply to sales or use taxes imposed on electricity, piped natural or artificial gas, or other heating fuels delivered by the seller, or the retail sale or transfer of motor vehicles, aircraft, watercraft, modular homes, manufactured homes, or mobile homes.

Effective dates: A political subdivision may only change its tax rate starting on the first day of a calendar quarter, and only after 90 days notice to the Commissioner of Revenue, and at least 60 days notice from the Commissioner to sellers prior to the change. Similar provisions apply to local boundary changes. Rate changes relating to catalog sales require 120 days notice to sellers.

Limited taxation of motor vehicles: Any political subdivision is prohibited from imposing a tax greater than $20 per vehicle on the sale, transfer, or use of a motor vehicle. If a local government is imposing a tax that exceeds this limit, a mechanism is provided for eliminating the tax over a four-year period through a 25% reduction per year.

Sourcing of telecommunications charges: Minnesota has conformed to the federal Mobile Telecommunications Sourcing Act (Act), P.L. 106-252. All charges for mobile telecommunications services are considered to be provided by the customer's home service provider and sourced to the customer's place of primary use (Sec. 297A.61(3)(i)). All such charges are subject to sales tax based on the customer's place of primary use.

- **Transportation taxes**

Metropolitan transportation area: The counties of Anoka, Carver, Dakota, Hennepin, Ramsey, Scott, and Washington (the metropolitan transportation area) may impose a 0.25% transportation sales and use tax and a $20-per-vehicle excise tax on retail sales of motor vehicles in the counties. In order to impose these taxes, a county would have to enter into a joint powers agreement with the other counties imposing the tax. (Sec. 297A.992)

Greater Minnesota: Counties outside the metropolitan transportation area may impose a transportation sales tax of up to 0.5% and a $20-per-vehicle excise tax on retail sales of motor vehicles. Two or more counties may enter into a joint powers agreement to impose the taxes. These taxes must be approved by a majority of voters in each of the affected counties (Sec. 297A.993).

¶ 551   Bracket Schedule

In computing sales or use tax to be collected or remitted as the result of a transaction, the tax computation must be carried to the third decimal place. In computing the tax "amounts of tax less than one-half of one cent must be disregarded and amounts of tax of one-half cent or more must be considered an additional cent" (Sec. 297A.76(1)). Additionally, when the seller is collecting or remitting both state and local taxes, this rounding rule shall be applied to the aggregated state and local taxes.

Sellers may elect to compute the tax due on a transaction on either an item basis or an invoice basis (*Revenue Notice No. 05-08,* Minnesota Department of Revenue, August 29, 2005, CCH MINNESOTA TAX REPORTS, ¶ 300-397).

Sales tax rate schedules for various tax rates are available at **http://www.revenue.state.mn.us/businesses/sut/Pages/Rates_Effective_070109.aspx**.

¶ 552   **Returns, Payments, and Due Dates**

Returns are generally due monthly by the 20th of the month and are to include payment of the taxes for the previous calendar month period (Sec. 289A.18(4), Sec. 289A.20(4), Rule 8130.7300). The due date is extended to the following business day when the original date falls on a Saturday, Sunday, or holiday (Sec. 270.27). Date of a postmark stamp is deemed to be delivery or payment date (Sec. 270.271).

Accelerated June payments: Vendors who have a sales tax liability of at least $250,000 during a fiscal year ending June 30, and who are required to make an June accelerated payment, must remit 81.4% of their June liability by two business days before June 30. The remaining payment and return for June are due August 20 (or the next business day if August 20 falls on a weekend or holiday). (Sec. 289A.20(4)(b), Minn Stats; Sec. 270C.39, Minn Stats) In determining whether a June accelerated payment is required, a taxpayer should subtract the liquor tax, local taxes, and solid waste management taxes from the total amount of tax owed during the state's fiscal year.

Return requirement: The following persons are required to file sales and use tax returns: (1) any retailer located or maintaining a place of business in Minnesota; (2) any retailer holding a Minnesota sales and use tax permit; (3) any out-of-state retailer engaging in the regular or systematic soliciting of business in Minnesota; (4) purchasers of exempt goods who have made nonexempt uses of the property; (5) persons liable for the use tax; and (6) persons holding direct pay permits (Sec. 289A.11(3), Rule 8130.7900).

Minimum use tax liability: Persons making annual purchases of less than $18,500 that are subject to use tax may file an annual return. If purchases greater than $18,500 are made, the reporting period is considered ended at the end of the month the excess purchases occurred and a return must be filed for the preceding period (Sec. 289A.11(1)). Annual returns are due by April 15 for individuals and by February 5 for all businesses (Sec. 289A.18(4)). Individuals may pay Minnesota use tax over the Internet on the Minnesota Department of Revenue website at **https://www.mndor.state.mn.us/ur/jsp/Login.jsp**.

Electronic filing and payment: All sales and use tax (and most other business tax return information) must be filed electronically. Information on the E-Services system is available at **http://www.revenue.state.mn.us/eservices/Pages/eservices_help.aspx**. Instructional videos introducing taxpayers to the system are available on the DOR's website, **www.revenue.state.mn.us**.

A vendor that has a tax liability of $10,000 or more must remit by electronic means all liabilities on returns due for periods beginning in all subsequent calendar years (Sec. 289A.20(4)(c), Minn Stats).

Credit or debit card payment: A third-party payment service allows taxpayers to submit tax payments for multiple tax types with a credit or debit card. The service is operated by Value Payment Systems, through the website **http://www.payMNtax.com**. According to the DOR, the service includes features such as digital time stamps on transactions, email reminders for upcoming tax payments, and eventually the ability to schedule estimate payments in advance. There is a convenience fee imposed to use the new service.

Direct payment: Qualifying businesses may remit sales tax directly to the department, instead of paying tax to the seller at the time of purchase. The department grants direct pay authority to businesses that satisfy certain requirements and make a sufficient volume of taxable purchases to justify the expense of regular sales and use tax audits by the department. Generally, only large manufacturers satisfy the requirements. Direct pay authority cannot be used in place of other sales tax exemptions.

To qualify for direct pay authority, a business must be registered as a sales and use tax monthly filer and must purchase substantial amounts of tangible personal property, such as fuels, chemicals, component parts, or inventory, in circumstances where it is unclear if the items will be used for a taxable or exempt purpose. A release discusses how to apply for direct pay authority; businesses that regularly make purchases from a particular vendor; recordkeeping requirements; restrictions on direct pay authority; and other matters. The release is available on the department's website at **http:// www.revenue.state.mn.us/businesses/sut/Pages/Direct-Pay-Authorization.aspx.**

- **Other reporting periods**

Certain taxpayers may elect to file on a quarterly or an annual returns basis (Sec. 289A.20(4)). Reports are due by the 20th day of the month following the close of the authorized period, except that annual sales tax returns must be filed by February 5 following the close of the calendar year (Sec. 289A.18(4)).

Quarterly and annual returns are specifically authorized by law. A retailer that has an average monthly sales and use tax liability (including local taxes administered by the state) of $500 or less in any quarter of a calendar year and that has substantially complied with the tax laws during the preceding four calendar quarters may request authorization to file and pay taxes quarterly in subsequent quarters. The authorization will remain in effect as long as the retailer's quarterly returns show sales and use tax liabilities of less than $1,500 and the retailer continues to comply with state tax laws.

A retailer that has an average monthly sales and use tax liability (including local taxes administered by the state) of $100 or less during a calendar year and that has substantially complied with the tax laws during that period may request authorization to file and pay taxes annually in subsequent years. The authorization will remain in effect as long as the retailer's annual returns show sales and use tax liabilities of less than $1,200 and the retailer continues to comply with state tax laws. (Sec. 289A.18(4))

In addition, the Commissioner may grant quarterly or annual filing and payment authorization to retailers if the Commissioner determines that the retailers' future tax liabilities will be less than the monthly totals specified above.

- **Streamlined Sales and Use Tax Administration Act**

Minnesota has enacted the Uniform Sales and Use Tax Administration Act and is in compliance with the Streamlined Sales and Use Tax Agreement. A seller that registers under the Agreement, does not use one of the technology models, and does not have a legal requirement to register in Minnesota must file a return by February 5 of the year following the calendar year in which the seller registers, and must file subsequent returns by February 5 of each succeeding year (Sec. 289A.18(4)(g)). A return must also be filed by the 20th of the month following any month by which the seller has accumulated $1,000 or more in Minnesota state or local tax funds.

Bad debts: "Bad debt" is defined as in IRC Sec. 166, except it does not include: (1) financing charges or interest; (2) sales or use taxes on the purchase price; (3) uncollectible amounts on property that remains in the possession of a seller until the full purchase price is paid; (4) expenses incurred in attempting to collect any debt; or (5) repossessed property (Sec. 289A.40(2)).

A retailer's certified service provider (CSP) may claim a bad debt allowance on behalf of the retailer if the CSP credits or refunds the full amount of the bad debt deduction or refund to the retailer. A bad debt may be allocated among the states that are members of the Agreement if a retailer's books and records support that allocation (Sec. 289A.50(2)).

Multiple points of use (MPU): A business purchaser that has not received authorization to pay the tax directly to the Commissioner of Revenue may use an exemption certificate indicating multiple points of use (MPU) if (1) the purchaser knows at the time of its purchase of a digital good, computer software delivered electronically, or a service that the good or service will be concurrently available for use in more than one taxing jurisdiction; and (2) the purchaser delivers to the seller the exemption certificate indicating multiple points of use at the time of purchase (Sec. 297A.668(6a)).

Upon receipt of the fully completed MPU exemption certificate, the seller is relieved of the obligation to collect, pay, or remit the applicable tax, and the purchaser is obligated to collect, pay, or remit the applicable tax on a direct pay basis. A purchaser that has received authorization to pay the tax directly to the commissioner is not required to provide an MPU certificate. This provision was added to conform Minnesota law with the SST Agreement.

Sourcing rules: See ¶ 547.

For additional information on the uniform act, see "Streamlined Sales Tax Project," listed in the Table of Contents.

Tax data: With certain exceptions, sellers and certified service providers (CSPs) who charged and collected the incorrect amount of tax are relieved from liability to Minnesota if they used a certified automated system (CAS) that the state certified as accurate (Sec. 297A.995(10)). Purchasers are relieved from liability for additional tax, penalty, and interest resulting from having paid the incorrect amount of tax when the purchaser or the seller relied on erroneous data provided by the Department of Revenue regarding tax rates, boundaries, taxing jurisdiction assignments, and the taxability matrix (Sec. 297A.995(11)).

¶ 553   Prepayment of Taxes

Minnesota does not have sales and use tax provisions that require the prepayment of taxes.

¶ 554   Vendor Registration

Applications for vendor permits are filed with the Commissioner of Revenue (Sec. 297A.83(1), Rule 8130.2500). Retailers maintaining a place of business in Minnesota or out-of-state retailers systematically soliciting sales from Minnesota customers are required to get a permit (Sec. 297A.66(2), Sec. 297A.66(3), Rule 8130.4200). Out-of-state retailers may also voluntarily register and receive permits (Sec. 297A.83(6)). Permits are valid until revoked, but are not assignable and are valid only for the persons in whose name they have been issued and for the transaction of business at the places designated (Sec. 297A.84). Wholesalers that also sell to final users must obtain a permit.

The Commissioner has discretion not to issue permits to those who do not maintain a place of business in Minnesota (Sec. 297A.83(3)).

• **Flea markets, trade shows, etc.**

Operators of flea markets, craft shows, or similar events are required to verify in advance of leasing or renting space that the vendors who are participating in the event have valid sellers' permits or that the goods they will be selling are not taxable (Sec. 297A.87(2), Rule 8130.3600).

• **Mobile businesses**

An applicant who has no regular place of doing business and who moves from place to place attaches the permit to the cart, stand, truck, or other merchandising device (Sec. 297A.83(2)(b)).

¶ 555 Sales or Use Tax Credits

A credit is granted for comparable sales or use taxes paid to other states up to the amount of the Minnesota liability (Sec. 297A.80). The credit is not allowed, however, if the tax paid in the other state is subject to refund or was erroneously paid (Rule 8130.4400).

¶ 556 Deficiency Assessments

The Commissioner of Revenue is authorized to assess delinquent sales and use taxes upon available information provided that the taxpayer is notified in writing of the basis for the assessment (Sec. 270.10, Sec. 270.101(3)). The Commissioner may make any audit or examination that is considered necessary and use statistical or sampling techniques consistent with accepted accounting principles (Sec. 289A.35).

In addition, the Commissioner may require security to ensure collection of the tax (Sec. 297A.28).

Proof of exemption: If a seller claims that certain sales are exempt and does not provide the exemption certificate or other information to substantiate the exemption claim within 120 days after the commissioner requests substantiation, then the exemptions claimed by the seller that required substantiation are disallowed. (Sec. 297A.665(f)).

• **Order of assessment**

When the tax determined by the Commissioner differs from that reported on the return, an order of assessment is issued (Sec. 289A.37(1)). An "order of assessment" explains the basis of the assessment and notifies the taxpayer about appeal procedures. The order is final when issued, and the delinquent amount must be paid within 60 days unless an appeal is made. Erroneous refunds are considered tax underpayments.

¶ 557 Audit Procedures

The authority of the Department of Revenue for conducting audits is derived from the statutory duty of the Department to assess liability for taxes (Sec. 270.101(3)). Statutory authority is granted to the Commissioner to audit and to make any examinations necessary to determine the correct tax (Sec. 289A.35, Sec. 289A.36(1), Sec. 289A.36(2)). In addition, the Commissioner is authorized to enter into compromise agreements with taxpayers that are binding in the absence of fraud (Sec. 270.67).

¶ 558 Statute of Limitations

In general, taxes must be assessed within 3½ years after a return is filed (Sec. 289A.38). In the case of a fraudulent return or when no return is filed, the assessment may be made at any time. When 25% or more of the taxes are omitted on a return, assessment may be made within 6½ years after the due date or the filing date of the return, whichever is later.

Refunds: Claims for refund must be filed within 3½ years of the due date of the return or one year from payment of the tax, whichever is later (Sec. 289A.40). In the case of bad debts, claims must be filed within 3½ years from the date the bad debt was written off on the taxpayer's books or from the date the claimant's federal income tax return claiming the bad debt deduction was filed or was eligible to be filed, whichever is later (Sec. 289A.40(2)).

The assessment or the refund period may be extended with the mutual agreement of the taxpayer and Commissioner (Sec. 289A.42).

Purchaser refund claims filed directly with the Commissioner of Revenue must be filed within 3½ years from the 20th day of the month following the month of the invoice date for the purchase (Sec. 289A.38(15)).

Collection: The period of limitation for the collection of taxes is five years from the date of the assessment (Sec. 270.70). A lien created under the tax laws is enforceable for 10 years from the date of notice (Sec. 270.69(4)). Notice must be filed within five years from the date of assessment or final administrative or judicial determination. Liens may be renewed for an additional 10-year period.

¶ 559   Application for Refund

Taxpayers who have overpaid taxes may seek refund with a written application that contains the taxpayer's name, date, the tax period for which refund is sought, type of tax, amount of refund claimed, and grounds for refund (Sec. 289A.65(1), Sec. 289A.65(4)).

Sales tax is refundable to the vendor only to the extent that it is credited or returned to the purchaser by the vendor. A purchaser may apply directly, but no more than twice in a year, if the purchaser is registered and the refund amount requested exceeds $500.

If the Commissioner discovers an overpayment in the course of an audit, he or she is required to make a refund without the necessity of a request by the taxpayer.

Return by vendor: Within 60 days after receiving a sales or use tax refund, vendors must return to the Commissioner of Revenue any amount of the refund that has not been credited or refunded to the purchaser (Sec. 289A.50(2)(c)). If the commissioner determines that the vendor did not return a refund to a purchaser, the commissioner may assess the vendor for underpayment of sales tax and interest on the portion of the refund that was not refunded or credited to the purchaser (Sec. 289A.50(2)(d)). The assessment may be made within 3 ½ years after the commissioner refunds the tax and interest to the vendor. If part of the refund was induced by fraud or misrepresentation of a material fact, the assessment may be made at any time.

Interest: The rate of interest accruing on overpayments of tax is the same as the rate applicable to deficiencies (Sec. 270.76, Sec. 289A.56). Interest is paid from the date of payment to the date the refund is paid or credited, provided the refund claim includes a detailed schedule reflecting the tax periods covered in the claim. If the detailed claim is not included, interest is computed from the date the refund claim is filed.

• Exemptions available by refund

Certain transactions in which property is made exempt by statute are treated as regular sales, but taxpayers are entitled to refund of the tax paid (Sec. 297A.15(5)). The exempt materials to which this provision applies are materials used to construct access for the handicapped, materials purchased for the construction or expansion of manufacturing facilities in distressed counties, "capital equipment" and "replacement capital equipment" as defined by statute, enterprise information technology equipment, electricity, and computer software purchased by qualified data centers, and construction materials used in the construction or expansion of aerospace or defense-related manufacturing facilities (see ¶ 548). For capital equipment and replacement capital equipment, only two refund claims may be filed each year, but effective September 1, 2014, the exemption is available at the point of sale.

Interest accrues on the refund amount from the date the refund claim is filed with the Commissioner (Sec. 297A.75).

• Denial of refund claim

When a refund claim is denied by the Commissioner, the taxpayer has two alternative courses of relief: an administrative appeal; or action in the district court, which must be brought within 18 months of the date of the denial (Sec. 289A.50(7)).

¶ 560   MISSISSIPPI

¶ 561   Scope of Tax

Source.—Statutory references are to Title 27 of the Mississippi Code of 1972, as amended to date. Details are reported in the CCH MISSISSIPPI TAX REPORTS starting at ¶ 60-000.

The Mississippi General Sales Tax is, technically speaking, a privilege tax. It is levied on the privilege of engaging in business in Mississippi and measured by the gross proceeds of sales or gross income or values, as the case may be, that are derived from such business or occupation (Sec. 27-65-13). It is not a "pure" sales tax, which is levied on sales of tangible personal property at retail. Nevertheless, the tax closely resembles a sales tax when considered from the standpoint of the merchant.

Unlike the usual sales tax, there is no occasion to determine whether income accrues from the sale of tangible personal property or the rendering of service, inasmuch as it is taxable in either case. The question of determining whether a sale is made at wholesale or retail is pertinent only in determining the person on whom liability for the tax ultimately rests. The taxability of an item and the applicable rate of tax depend on the class in which the item falls (Sec. 27-65-5).

Digital products: Sales and use tax is imposed on selling, renting, or leasing specified digital products (Sec. 27-65-26). Taxable products include electronically transferred digital audio-visual works, digital audio works, and digital books. The tax is imposed when (1) the sale is to an end user, (2) the seller grants the right of permanent or less than permanent use of the products transferred electronically, or (3) the sale is conditioned or not conditioned upon continued payment. A sale of a digital code that allows the purchaser to obtain a specified digital product is taxed in the same manner as a sale of the specified digital product. A sale of specified digital product for resale in the regular course of business is considered a wholesale sale if the sale is made to a regular dealer of specified digital products and the dealer holds a sales tax permit and is located in Mississippi (Sec. 27-65-5).

Prepaid (debit) telephone cards: Any sale of a prepaid telephone calling card or prepaid authorization number, or both, is deemed a sale of tangible personal property (Sec. 27-65-19). If the sale of a prepaid telephone calling card or prepaid authorization number does not take place at the vendor's place of business, it is conclusively determined to take place at the customer's shipping address. The reauthorization of a prepaid telephone calling card or a prepaid authorization number is conclusively determined to take place at the customer's billing address.

- **Incidence of tax**

In general, every person engaging in Mississippi in the business of selling any tangible personal property or in rendering taxable services is subject to sales tax (Sec. 27-65-17, Sec. 27-65-23). Salesmen engaged in itinerant solicitation are specifically taxable.

The seller is obligated to collect the sales tax from the purchaser at the time of the sale, "insofar as practicable" (Sec. 27-65-31).

- **Taxable services**

Generally, sales tax is imposed on the following services (Sec. 27-65-23): air conditioning installation and repair; vehicle repair or service; billiards, pool, or domino parlors; bowling alleys; burglar and fire alarm systems or service; car washing services; computer software sales and service; custom creosoting or treating, custom planing, custom sawing; custom meat processing; electrical work and wiring and all repairs or installation of electrical equipment; elevator or escalator installation, repair, or servicing; film developing or photo finishing; foundries, machine or general repairing; furniture repair or upholstering; geophysical surveying services for the exploration, development, drilling, production, distribution, or testing of oil, gas, water, or other mineral resources; grading, excavating, ditching, dredging or landscaping; hotels, motels, tourist courts or camps, trailer parks; insulating services or repairs; jewelry or watch repairs; laundering, cleaning, pressing, or dying; marina services; mattress renovating; office and business machine repair; parking garages and lots; plumbing or pipe fitting; public storage warehouses (except certain temporary storage); refrigeration equipment repairs; radio or television installation, repair, or servicing; renting or leasing personal property used in Mississippi; shoe repair; storage lockers; telephone answering or paging services; termite or pest control services; tin and sheet metal shops; TV cable systems, subscription TV services, and other similar activities; vulcanizing, repair, or recapping of tires or tubes; welding; and woodworking or wood turning shops.

Tax is not imposed on most professional services. For a full description and list of taxable services, see Sec. 27-65-23.

• Use tax

The compensating (use) tax is an excise or privilege tax imposed on the privilege of using, storing, or consuming within the state any article of tangible personal property, regardless of the manner in which possession of the property was acquired (Sec. 27-67-5). The rate of tax is the same as the corresponding rate that is imposed by the sales tax, which, in turn, depends on the type of property or transaction in question.

The primary purpose of the Compensating (Use) Tax Law is to protect Mississippi against the unfair competition of importations into Mississippi, without the payment of a retail sales tax of goods, wares, or merchandise usually carried for sale in Mississippi.

• Responsibility for collecting tax

The seller must add the tax to the sales price or the gross income and, to the extent practicable, collect the tax from the purchaser at the time the sales price or gross income is collected (Sec. 27-65-31, Sec. 27-67-11(3)). The tax is a debt from the purchaser to the seller until paid and is collectable at law in the same manner as other debts; see *Nortrax South, Inc. v. Thornhill Forestry Service, Inc.,* Mississippi Court of Appeals, No. 2014-CA-01355-COA, February 16, 2016, CCH MISSISSIPPI TAX REPORTS, ¶ 200-809.

The tax must be stated separately from the sales price on the sales invoice and shown separately on the seller's records (Sec. 27-65-31, Sec. 27-67-11(3)). The purchaser pays the tax to the seller as trustee for and on account of the state, and the seller is required to collect the tax from the purchaser at the time the sales price or gross income is collected. There is a presumption that the seller collected the tax from the purchaser.

Sales tax permits: When a person or entity applies for a sales tax permit in Mississippi, the person or entity agrees to be subject to the jurisdiction of Mississippi and must collect and remit Mississippi sales and use tax, regardless of the person's or entity's presence in the state (Sec. 27-65-27).

Drop shipments: If a retailer has a valid Mississippi sales tax permit, the retailer should furnish a copy of the permit to the primary seller, rendering the first sale a nontaxable transaction. The retailer then collects sales tax on behalf of the state on the sale to its Mississippi customer. If the retailer is not registered to do business in Mississippi and the primary seller has nexus with Mississippi, the sale to the retailer is a taxable transaction by the primary seller, who is responsible for remitting the tax. An exception to the latter rule applies if (1) the Mississippi customer is a licensed dealer purchasing the item for resale, (2) the Mississippi customer has a direct pay permit, or (3) the Mississippi customer is an exempt entity. (Rule 35.IV.3.05)

¶561   **Mississippi**

• Nexus

Sales tax (privilege tax) or use tax is imposed on every person engaging or continuing in the business of selling any tangible personal property, maintaining a place of business, or doing business in Mississippi (Sec. 27-65-17; Sec. 27-67-11). "Business" means all activities or acts engaged in for benefit or advantage, either direct or indirect. Business includes activities engaged in by exempt organizations or political entities in competition with privately owned business. However, the term "business" does not include (Sec. 27-65-9):

(1) sales of prepaid student meal plans by public or private universities, colleges and community or junior colleges, and

(2) sales of prepared meals by any public or private school to students in Kindergarten through Grade 12.

Under sales tax statutory provisions, "doing business" includes (Sec. 27-65-9):

— any person owning personal property in Mississippi under a lease or rental agreement;

— any person installing personal property in Mississippi; and

— any person represented in Mississippi by salespeople who take orders to be filled from points outside the state for subsequent delivery of merchandise in equipment owned or leased by the seller, to customers located in Mississippi.

For use tax purposes, a person "doing business" or "maintaining a place of business" in Mississippi means a person (Sec. 27-65-3):

— having an office, distribution house, sales room or house, warehouse, any other place of business in Mississippi;

— owning personal property located in Mississippi used by another person; or

— installing personal property in Mississippi.

It also includes any person selling or taking orders for tangible personal property, either personally, by mail, or through an employee, representative, salesperson, commission agent, canvasser, solicitor, or independent contractor or by any other means, in Mississippi (Sec. 27-65-9).

A person who does not maintain a place of business in the state but who is represented by salespeople who solicit or accept orders for merchandise that is subsequently delivered in Mississippi must collect use tax (Rule 35.IV.3.05).

• Streamlined Act status

Mississippi has enacted the Uniform (Simplified) Sales and Use Tax Administration Act, the product of the Streamlined Sales Tax Project (SSTP) (Ch. 338 (S.B. 2089), Laws 2003).

Mississippi is an Advisor State to the SSTP and has enacted some, but not all, of the changes to its laws necessary to comply with the Streamlined Sales and Use Tax Agreement's requirements.

¶ 562   **Tax Base**

The sales tax is computed on gross income or gross proceeds of sales of the business, regardless of the fact that small unit sales may be within the bracket of one of the schedules that does not provide for the collection of the tax from the customer (Sec. 27-65-31).

The term, "gross proceeds of sale," means the value accruing from the full sale price of tangible personal property, including installation charges and carrying charges, without deduction for delivery charges, cost of property sold, or other expenses (Sec. 27-65-3(h)). In the case of a trade-in that is taken as part payment, gross proceeds of sale includes only the difference between the selling price and the amount allowed for a trade-in of property of the same kind.

"Gross proceeds of sale," includes consideration received by a seller from third parties if the consideration is directly related to a price reduction or discount, the seller has an obligation to pass the price reduction or discount through to the purchaser, and the amount of the consideration is fixed and determinable by the seller at the time of the sale. In addition, one of the following criteria must be met (Sec. 27-65-3(h)):

(1) The purchaser presents a third-party coupon, certificate, or other documentation to the seller to claim a price reduction or discount with the understanding that the third party will reimburse any seller to whom the coupon, certificate, or documentation is presented;

(2) The purchaser identified himself or herself to the seller as a member of a group or organization entitled to a price reduction or discount; or

(3) The price reduction or discount is identified as a third-party price reduction or discount on the invoice received by the purchaser or on a coupon, certificate, or other documentation presented by the purchaser.

Sourcing: Mississippi has conformed to the Streamlined Sales Tax (SST) Agreement with respect to definitions and sourcing rules for telecommunications services. Sourcing rules are provided for (1) telecommunications services sold on a call-by-call basis, (2) telecommunications services sold on a basis other than a call-by-call basis, (3) mobile telecommunications services other than air-to-ground radio telephone service and prepaid calling service, (4) post-paid calling services, (5) prepaid calling or prepaid wireless calling services, (6) private communication services, and (7) ancillary services (Sec. 27-65-19(1)(e)(v)).

¶ 563   List of Exemptions, Exceptions, and Exclusions

Unless otherwise indicated, the statutory exemptions, exceptions, and exclusions listed below apply to both sales and use taxes; those applicable only to the use tax are listed separately. Items that are excluded from the sales or use tax base are treated at ¶ 562, "Tax Base."

Material purchase certificate: A material purchase certificate (MPC) is a certificate obtained from the Tax Commissioner that entitles the holder to purchase materials and services that will become a component part of a structure to be erected or repaired without paying contractors' sales tax (Sec. 27-65-3(m)). A person who pays tax on a qualified purchase may, after obtaining an MPC for the project, take a credit for the sales tax paid on the purchase. Any penalties and interest owed by the taxpayer on a return or in an audit must be determined after taking this credit.

• **Sales tax holidays**

Clothing and footwear: Each year, the sales tax holiday begins on the last Friday in July and ends at midnight the following Saturday. During the sales tax holiday, customers do not have to pay Mississippi sales tax on purchases of eligible articles of clothing or footwear priced at less than $100. The following items do not qualify for the sales tax holiday: jewelry, handbags, luggage, umbrellas, wallets, watches, backpacks, briefcases, garment bags, skis, swim fins, roller blades, skates, and similar items and accessories. Cities may decide by resolution not to participate in the annual sales tax holiday. (Sec. 27-65-111(bb))

Firearms and ammunition: Retail sales of firearms, ammunition, and hunting supplies are exempt when sold during the annual tax-free Mississippi Second Amendment Weekend holiday, which begins at 12:01 a.m. on the last Friday in August and ends at 12:00 midnight on the following Sunday. "Hunting supplies" means tangible personal property used for hunting, including, and limited to, archery equipment, firearm and archery cases, firearm and archery accessories, hearing protection, holsters, belts, and slings. Hunting supplies does not include animals used for hunting. The exemption applies only if (1) title to and/or possession of an eligible item is transferred from a seller to a purchaser and/or (2) a purchaser orders and pays for an eligible item and the seller accepts the order for immediate shipment, even if delivery is made after the time period above, provided that the purchaser has not requested or caused the delay in shipment. (Sec. 27-65-111(ff))

- **Sales and use tax exemptions, exceptions, and exclusions**

Admissions to certain religious or charitable events	Sec. 27-65-22(3)(a), (n)
Admissions to certain sporting events sanctioned by Mississippi Athletic Commission	Sec. 27-65-22(3)
Aerospace facilities, construction materials and equipment	Sec. 27-65-101(1)(kk)
Agricultural cooperative associations	Sec. 27-65-103(b)
Agricultural landscaping services	Sec. 27-65-103(d)
Agricultural medicines, hormones, and nutrients	Sec. 27-65-103(e)
Agricultural products sold by producers of livestock, poultry, fish, honey bees or other products	Sec. 27-65-103(a), Sec. 27-65-103(b), Sec. 27-65-103(c)
Aircraft repair, parts	Sec. 27-65-101(1)(ee)
Art museums, nonprofit, gifts or sales	Sec. 27-65-111(q)
Automotive parts manufacturing (construction materials, equipment, repairs, and utiities)	Sec. 27-65-101(1)(gg)
Baling wire	Sec. 27-65-103(a)
Barges	Sec. 27-65-101(1)
Boats and trailers exported out-of-state within 48 hours	Sec. 27-65-101(1)(s)
Boys' Club	Sec. 27-65-111(f)
Broadband telecommunications equipment (exp. 6/30/2020)	Sec. 27-65-101(5)
Choctaw Indians, sales to	Sec. 27-65-105(d), Sec. 27-65-215
Churches (exempt under IRC Sec. 501(c)(3)), electricity, fuel, water, and utilities sold to	Sec. 27-65-19(1)(a)(ii)
Clean energy facilities, construction materials and equipment	Sec. 27-65-101(1)(ll)
Commercial fishing boats	Sec. 27-65-101(1)(d)
Commercial laundering, self-service	Sec. 27-65-101(1)(o)
Computer software sold over the Internet for first use outside Mississippi	Sec. 27-65-101(1)(ii)
Construction, approved business industries	Sec. 27-65-101(1)(v) Sec. 27-65-101(1)(ff), (gg), (kk)—(nn)
Construction, component parts	Sec. 27-65-3(m), Sec. 27-65-5(2), Sec. 27-65-21
Construction, headquarters facilities, component materials, machinery, and equipment (subject to job creation requirements)	Sec. 27-65-101(1)(r)
Construction, health care facilities	Sec. 27-65-101(1)(pp)
Construction, residential	Sec. 27-65-21(1)(b)(i)
Construction to repair damage caused by natural disaster	Sec. 27-65-21(1)(b)(iii)
Cotton bagging and ties	Sec. 27-65-103(a)

Milk products, equipment and supplies used (reduced tax rate)	Sec. 27-65-17, Sec. 27-65-19(c)
Mississippi Blood Services, sales of property or services to	Sec. 27-65-111(ee)
Mississippi Major Economic Impact Act businesses, sales to	Sec. 27-65-101(1)
Mississippi Technology Alliance, sales to	Sec. 27-65-111(y)
Motor fuels	Sec. 27-65-111(n)
Motor vehicles exported out-of-state within 48 hours	Sec. 27-65-101(s), Sec. 27-65-111(i)
Mules	Sec. 27-65-103(c)
Natural gas storage	Sec. 27-65-101(1)(t)
Newspapers	Sec. 27-65-111(b)
Nonprofit organizations	Sec. 27-65-111(e), (s), (z), (aa), (jj)-(rr)
Occasional or casual sales	Sec. 27-65-17
Oil pollution cleanup machinery and equipment	Sec. 27-65-101(1)(u)
Oil production facility (renewable crude from biomass); construction materials and equipment	Sec. 27-65-101(1)(nn)
Offshore drilling equipment	Sec. 27-65-101
Orphanages	Sec. 27-65-111(e)
Packaging and shipping materials	Sec. 27-65-5(3), Sec. 27-65-101(1)(a)
PGA host of golf tournament held in Mississippi, purchases of equipment and supplies	Sec. 27-65-101(1)(oo)
Pollution control equipment	Sec. 27-65-101(1)(w)
Poultry	Sec. 27-65-103(b)
Public storage facilities, storage of perishable goods	Sec. 27-65-101(1)(m)
Publishing	Sec. 27-65-111(b)
Railroad equipment	Sec. 27-65-101(1)(g), Sec. 27-65-101(1)(h), Sec. 27-65-107(a)
Raw materials	Sec. 27-65-101(1)(b), (jj)
Religious institutions	Sec. 27-65-111(e)
Resales	Sec. 27-65-107(d)
Restaurant meals, served to employees or donated to charity	Sec. 27-65-3(h)
Rolling stock	Sec. 27-65-101(1)(g), Sec. 27-65-101(1)(h), Sec. 27-65-107(a)
School fundraising sales	Sec. 27-65-111(cc)
Schools	Sec. 27-65-105(b), Sec. 27-65-111(g)
School buses	Sec. 27-65-105(i), Sec. 27-65-111(g)
Seeds	Sec. 27-65-103(a)
Semi-trailers, out-of-state sales	Sec. 27-65-101(1)(s)
Ship manufacturing and repair	Sec. 27-65-101(1)(i)
State or local government transactions	Sec. 27-65-105(a)
Stevedoring charges	Sec. 27-65-101

Technology intensive enterprises	Sec. 27-65-101(1)(gg)
Textbooks, sales to students	Sec. 27-65-105(c)
Transportation equipment and supplies	Sec. 27-65-101
Tourism: guided tours on navigable waters of Mississippi	Sec. 27-65-22(3)(m), Sec. 27-65-101(1)[rr]
Truck-tractors and semi-trailers for interstate use	Sec. 27-65-101(1)[rr]
Utilities for residential use	Sec. 27-65-19(2)
Utilities for specified manufacturing, producing, processing, and commercial fishing	Sec. 27-65-107(f), (g), and (h)
Vending machines, food and soft drinks sold under "full service sales" agreement	Sec. 27-65-111(m)
Vessel and barge repair	Sec. 27-65-101(1)(b), (i)
Vessels	Sec. 27-65-101(1)
WIC food sales to Choctaw Indians	Sec. 27-65-111(v)
YMCA, YWCA	Sec. 27-65-111(f)

• Exemptions, exceptions, and exclusions applicable only to the use tax

Jet aircraft engines for testing	Sec. 27-67-7(o)
Literature, tapes, or slides used by a church for religious purposes ..	Sec. 27-67-7(i)
Motion picture films, tapes, or records for exhibition by exhibitor paying sales tax on admissions income or by television or radio broadcasting station operator	Sec. 27-67-7(f)
Motor vehicles owned by new residents of Mississippi, under certain circumstances	Sec. 27-67-7(d)
Nonresidents' temporary use of property in state	Sec. 27-67-7(c)
Packaging material used to ship items for federal government	Sec. 27-67-6
Personal and household effects of persons who become new residents of Mississippi	Sec. 27-67-7(e)
Project subject to Mississippi sales tax	Sec. 27-67-7(a)
Property already subject to tax by other states	Sec. 27-67-7(a)
Rolling stock and component parts use	Sec. 27-67-7(h)

¶ 564   Rate of Tax

As a general rule, the rate of tax on services and on the sale of most items of tangible personal property is equal to 7% of the gross proceeds or value (Sec. 27-65-17, Sec. 27-65-19, Sec. 27-65-23). Alternative rates that are applied to specific transactions are discussed below.

• Agricultural, vehicular transactions

Retail and casual sales and rentals of automobiles and trucks with a gross weight of 10,000 lbs. or less are taxed at a rate of 5% of gross sales (Sec. 27-65-201(2); Rule 25).

The following transactions are taxed at the rate of 3% of gross sales (Sec. 27-65-17, Sec. 27-65-23, Sec. 27-65-201(2), Rule 25):

— retail sales of aircraft, automobiles, trucks (greater than 10,000.00 lbs.), truck-tractors, semitrailers, and manufactured or mobile homes (*Note:* sales of truck-tractors and semitrailers for interstate use are exempt; see ¶ 563);

— sales of materials and income from services for use in track and track structures to a railroad whose rates are set by the Interstate Commerce Commission or the Mississippi Public Service Commission;

A reduced tax rate of 3.5% is imposed on sales of materials used in the repair, renovation, addition to, expansion, and/or improvement of buildings and related facilities used by a dairy producer. "Dairy producer" is defined as any person engaged in the production of milk for commercial use. (Sec. 27-65-17(1)(m))

The following transactions are taxed at the rate of 1.5% of gross sales (Sec. 27-65-17, Sec. 27-65-23, Sec. 27-65-201(2), Rule 25):

— retail sales of farm tractors and parts and labor used to maintain and/or repair such tractors when made to farmers for agricultural purposes;

— retail sales of farm implements sold to farmers and used directly in the production of poultry, ratite, domesticated fish, livestock, livestock products, agricultural crops or ornamental plant crops or used for other agricultural purposes, and parts and labor used to maintain and/or repair such implements;

— sales to a professional logger of equipment used in logging, pulpwood, or tree-farming operations that is self propelled or mounted so that it is permanently attached to other equipment that is either self propelled or drawn by a self-propelled vehicle, and parts and labor used to maintain and/or repair such equipment.

• Mobile, modular, and manufactured homes

Retail sales of mobile homes, manufactured homes and factory-built components of modular homes, panelized homes and precut homes, and panel constructed homes consisting of structural insulated panels are taxed at the rate of 3%. (Sec. 27-65-17(1)(d) and (k)).

Sellers of modular homes, panelized homes and precut homes, and panel constructed homes consisting of structural insulated panels, must disclose to the buyers of such homes the amount of sales tax or use tax paid on the factory-built components of such homes (Sec. 27-65-17(1)(k)).

• Refineries

A tax rate of 1.5% is imposed on the gross proceeds of sales for manufacturing or processing machinery to be installed and/or used at a refinery in Mississippi without regard as to whether the machinery retains its identity as tangible personal property after installation. Also, a tax rate of 3.5% is imposed on 103.5% of the total contract price or compensation paid for the performance of a construction activity at or in regard to a refinery in Mississippi. (Sec. 27-65-24; Sec. 27-67-5)

• Additional surcharges

Private carriers: The retail sales of private carriers of passengers and light carriers of property (automobiles and light trucks) are taxed an additional 2% in addition to the already applicable 5% sales tax rate (Sec. 27-65-17(2)).

Motorcycles and ATVs: Motorcycle and all-terrain vehicle (ATV) retailers are required to collect a $50 trauma care fee on every retail sale of a new or used motorcycle or ATV in the state (Sec. 63-17-171). The fee also is imposed on new and not previously registered motorcycles and ATVs purchased in another state and brought into Mississippi.

This point-of-sale fee is in addition to the regular 7% sales tax collected on retail sales of motorcycles and ATVs. The fee itself is not subject to the sales tax. The purchaser may qualify for exemptions provided in the sales tax law, such as exemptions for exempt entities and the 48-hour drive out exemption. (Sec. 63-17-171; see also *Notice 72-14-09,* Mississippi Department of Revenue, October 3, 2014)

• Interstate telecommunications

There is a 7% telecommunications tax on (1) intrastate telecommunications services, (2) interstate telecommunications services, (3) international telecommunications services, (4) ancillary services, and (5) products delivered electronically, including software, music, games, reading materials, and ring tones. Sourcing rules are provided for (1) telecommunications services sold on a call-by-call basis, (2) telecommunications services sold on a basis other than a call-by-call basis, (3) mobile telecommunications services other than air-to-ground radio telephone service and prepaid calling service, (4) post-paid calling services, (5) prepaid calling or prepaid wireless calling services, (6) private communication services, and (7) ancillary services (Sec. 27-65-19(1)(e)(i); Rule 35.IV.06.02).

Mobile telecommunications: Mobile telecommunications service providers are subject to the 7% tax on gross income received on services from all intrastate and interstate transmission charges. Subject to the provisions of the federal Mobile Telecommunications Sourcing Act (4 U.S.C. 116(c)), the tax applies only to mobile telecommunications service charges that are deemed to be provided to a customer by a home service provider if the customer's place of primary use is located in Mississippi (Sec. 27-65-19).

• Manufacturing/utility transactions—Industrial rate

Certain manufacturing and utility transactions are taxed at the rate of 1.5% of gross sales or value (Sec. 27-65-17, Sec. 27-65-19, Sec. 27-65-24), as follows:

— sales of manufacturing machinery and machine parts when made to a manufacturer or custom processor for plant use in this state;

— sales of public utilities and certain fuels to a producer or processor for use directly in the production of poultry or poultry products, livestock or livestock products, or plants or food by commercial horticulturists; the processing of milk and milk products; the processing of poultry and livestock feed; the irrigation of farm crops; and the processing of domestic fish or marine aquaculture products;

— sales of machinery, machine parts, or equipment to an operator or lessee of any structure, facility, or land that is acquired or leased under the provisions of Title 59, Chapter 9, Mississippi Code of 1972 (pertaining to the expansion and development of ports and harbors in the state), for use exclusively and directly on such structure, facility, or land;

— sales of fuel (including electricity, current, power, steam, coal, natural gas, liquefied petroleum gas) to a manufacturer, custom processor, or public service company for industrial purposes, except that the tax imposed on such sales of natural gas may not exceed 10.5 cents per 1,000 cubic feet.

— purchases by scrap metal recyclers of manufacturing machinery, manufacturing machine parts, electricity, current, power, steam, coal, natural gas, liquefied petroleum gas or other fuel used exclusively and directly in the manufacturing process; see *Notice 72-13-005 (Scrap Metal Recyclers*, Mississippi Department of Revenue, June 26, 2013).

• Technology intensive enterprises

Sales to a technology intensive enterprise in a Tier Two or Tier One area of component materials used in the construction of a facility, or any addition or improvement thereto, and sales of machinery and equipment to be used in such building, addition, or improvement, are exempt from one-half of the sales taxes otherwise imposed on such transactions (Sec. 27-65-101(4)). Such sales in a Tier Three area are exempt (Sec. 27-65-101(1)(gg)). The sales of machinery and equipment must occur not later than three months after completion of construction of the facility, addition, or improvement.

Machinery and parts: Sales of machinery and machine parts to a technology intensive enterprise are taxed at the reduced tax rate of 1.5% if the machinery and machine parts will be used exclusively and directly within Mississippi for industrial purposes, including manufacturing or research and development activities (Sec. 27-65-17(1)). The reduced 1.5% tax rate also applies to electricity, current, power, steam, coal, natural gas, liquefied petroleum gas, or other fuel sold to or used by a qualified technology intensive enterprise (Sec. 27-65-19(1)).

To qualify for the reduced tax rate, a technology intensive enterprise must (1) meet the minimum criteria established by the Mississippi Development Authority, (2) employ at least 10 persons in full-time jobs, and (3) provide a basic health care plan to all employees at the facility. In addition, at least 10% of the workforce in the facility must be scientists, engineers, or computer specialists, and the average wage of all workers must be at least 150% of the state average annual wage. Finally, the enterprise must either manufacture plastics, chemicals, automobiles, aircraft, computers, or electronics, or be a research and development facility, a computer design or related facility, a software publishing facility, or other technology intensive facility or enterprise (Sec. 27-65-17(1)).

- **Oil recovery projects**

Tax is imposed at the rate of 1.5% on the sale of fuel and energy or naturally occurring carbon dioxide and anthropogenic carbon dioxide lawfully injected into the earth for use in agriculture or aquaculture or for either (1) use in an enhanced oil recovery project, including use for cycling, repressuring, or lifting of oil, or (2) permanent sequestration in a geological formation. (Sec. 27-65-19(1)(c); *Notice 72-13-005*, Mississippi Department of Revenue, June 25, 2013, CCH Mississippi Tax Reports, ¶ 200-727)

- **Data/information enterprises**

Sales to a data/information enterprise in a Tier Two or Tier One area of component materials used in the construction of a facility, or any addition or improvement thereon, and sales or leases of machinery and equipment to be used in such building, addition, or improvement, are exempt from one-half of the sales taxes normally imposed on such transactions (Sec. 27-65-101(3)). Such sales to a data/information enterprise in a Tier Three area are exempt from sales tax (Sec. 27-65-101(1)(ff)).

- **Electric power associations**

The following transactions are taxed at the rate of 1% of gross sales or value (Sec. 27-65-17, Sec. 27-65-23):

— sales of tangible personal property to electric power associations for use in the ordinary and necessary operation of the generating and distribution systems; and

— income from services that are performed for electric power associations in the ordinary and necessary operation of generating or distribution systems.

- **Admission to amusements**

Although gross income from admission charges by persons in the business of providing amusement activities is usually taxed at the rate of 7% (Sec. 27-65-22(1)), alternative rates that are applied to specific transactions are discussed below.

Sales of admission to publicly-owned enclosed coliseums and auditoriums (except admissions to certain exempt sports events), livestock facilities, agriculture facilities, or other facilities constructed, renovated, or expanded with funds from a specified grant program are taxed at 3% of gross income (Sec. 27-65-22(1)).

The operator of the place of amusement and the person conducting the amusement may be jointly liable for the payment of the tax imposed, based on the actual charge of admission (Sec. 27-65-22(2)).

• **Salesmen's tax**

A tax is levied on persons engaged in the itinerant solicitation and taking of orders for merchandise over regular routes and at regular intervals for subsequent delivery to retailers or consumers within Mississippi. The rate is 3% of the gross amount of orders taken, when delivery is made to consumers located in Mississippi and when the merchandise is for consumption by such customers (Sec. 27-67-505). The rate for sales made to retailers is 0.125% of the total amount of orders.

• **Special rules**

Contractors: Persons in the business of performing a contract for a consideration, or any similar activity involving real property or the drilling or redrilling of oil wells, are assessed a tax of 3.5% of the total contract price or compensation received, when such compensation exceeds $10,000; however, a special rate of 1.5% is applied to that part of the total contract price or compensation that represents the sale of manufacturing or processing machinery to a manufacturer or processor (Sec. 27-65-21). The tax is imposed on the prime contractor (as defined by regulation) (Rule 41) and must be paid by it. Excluded from the tax are (1) contracts for construction of a residence (excluding apartments, condominiums, hotels, hospitals, nursing homes, and other commercial buildings), (2) contracts in excess of $100 million, and (3) contracts at cost to restore, repair, or replace utility systems damaged or destroyed by a natural disaster (Sec. 27-65-21(1)(b)).

When a person who is engaged in a service business taxable under Sec. 27-65-23 also qualifies as a contractor and contracts with the owner of any project to perform any services for an amount in excess of $10,000, the person will be subject to tax at the contractor's rate, rather than at the rate imposed by Sec. 27-65-23 (Sec. 27-65-21).

The 3.5% tax rate also applies to sales and construction activities pertaining to permanently-moored floating structures and cruise vessels (Sec. 27-65-18).

Car rentals: In addition to the regular sales tax that is imposed on service businesses by Sec. 27-65-23, there is an additional tax, at the rate of 6%, on the gross proceeds of persons engaged in the business of renting motor vehicles under agreements with terms of not more than 30 days (Sec. 27-65-231(1)).

Vending machines: Wholesale sales of food and drink for human consumption, when made to full service vending machine operators, are taxed at the rate of 8% of gross sales or value (Sec. 27-65-17).

Beverages: Wholesale and retail sales of beer and other alcoholic beverages are taxed at the rate of 7% (Sec. 27-65-17, Sec. 27-65-25).

¶ 565   Local Taxes

The imposition of a sales tax by a municipality or levee district is not authorized by the general sales tax law (Sec. 27-65-73).

• **Tourism taxes**

Various counties and cities are authorized by the state legislature to impose a sales tax on restaurants, hotels, motels, and other specified businesses within their jurisdictions. These taxes may have names such as tourist promotion taxes and tourism and convention taxes. Such a tax is not effective until the governing authority of the city or county adopts a levying resolution. Local tax offices should be consulted to determine the type of tax and the current rates.

Local tax rates for cities and counties are available at **http://www.taxrates.com/ state-rates/mississippi/**.

¶565   **Mississippi**

• **Jackson special infrastructure tax**

The City of Jackson imposes a special infrastructure tax at the rate of 1% that applies to:

— all sales of tangible personal property taxed at 7% or higher made from a business location in the City of Jackson, regardless of the point of delivery in Mississippi;

— all commercial utilities not currently exempt from sales tax; and

— all taxable services subject to the 7% rate performed at a location in Jackson, even if the service provider is not physically located in Jackson.

Services performed outside the city limits of Jackson by a service provider physically located in Jackson are not subject to the tax. (Sec. 27-65-241)

¶ 566   **Bracket Schedule**

The Commissioner is authorized to promulgate rules or regulations for the maintenance of brackets or schedules by which the applicable tax will be collected from the purchaser (Sec. 27-65-31, Rule 64).

The tax is due on the gross proceeds of sales or gross income regardless of the fact that small unit sales may not amount to enough to collect a tax or may be within a bracket of the schedule that does not provide for the collection of the computed liability.

Sales through vending machines are considered to have the tax included in the unit price of the merchandise. The tax thus collected may be excluded from total vending machine receipts to determine the base on which the tax liability is computed.

The following schedule provides for the collection of the tax at the rate of 7% from the purchaser on sales taxable under Sec. 27-65-17, Sec. 27-65-19, Sec. 27-65-22, Sec. 27-65-23, and Sec. 27-65-25 of the Sales Tax Law and under Sec. 27-67-05 of the Use Tax Law.

7% Tax Rate

Sale		Tax
.00 to .07	. . . .	.00
.08 to .21	. . . .	.01
.22 to .35	. . . .	.02
.36 to .49	. . . .	.03
.50 to .64	. . . .	.04
.65 to .78	. . . .	.05
.79 to .92	. . . .	.06
and so forth.		

¶ 567   **Returns, Payments, and Due Dates**

In general, monthly sales tax returns must be filed by the 20th of the month following the period covered (Sec. 27-65-33, Rule 11). Quarterly sales tax returns must be filed by the 20th of the month following the end of the quarter. Returns that are filed on a four-week accounting period (*i.e.*, 13 returns per year) must be filed by the 20th of the month following the period covered. Returns and payments placed in the mail must be postmarked by the due date in order to be timely filed, except that when the due date falls on a weekend or holiday, returns and payments placed in the mail must be postmarked by the first working day following the due date to be considered timely filed (Sec. 27-65-33).

Collection allowance: See ¶ 570.

Accelerated payments in June: A taxpayer with an average monthly sales tax or use tax liability of at least $50,000 for the preceding taxable year must, make payments by

June 25 each year that are equal to 75% of (1) the taxpayer's estimated sales tax or use tax liability for June of the current calendar year or (2) the taxpayer's sales tax or use tax liability for June of the preceding calendar year. For purposes of calculating a taxpayer's estimated sales tax liability for the month of June of the current calendar year, the taxpayer does not have to include taxes due on credit sales for which the taxpayer has not received payment before June 20 (Sec. 27-65-33, Sec. 27-67-17).

Quarterly returns: If the monthly sales tax liability does not exceed $100, a quarterly return and remittance may be made by the 20th of the month following the end of the quarter for which the tax is due (Sec. 27-65-33). If the liability exceeds $100, the taxpayer may apply to the Commissioner for permission to file quarterly returns. Such permission will generally be granted, provided the taxpayer executes a surety bond for double the amount of tax paid by the taxpayer for any previous three-month period within the past calendar year (Sec. 27-65-33(e), Rule 54). The bond must be conditioned on the prompt payment of all taxes accruing for each quarterly return.

Electronic funds transfers: The Commissioner may require payment of amounts of $20,000 or more in "immediately available funds," either by wire transfers through the Federal Reserve System or any other means established by the Commissioner (Sec. 27-3-81). In a Revenue Rule, the Commissioner announced implementation of an electronic filing program for payment of Mississippi taxes and the filing of returns. The Commissioner will send written notification to those taxpayers or agents who are required to file their tax returns and related documents electronically and make payments electronically. Taxpayers filing by Electronic Data Interchange will be notified within 180 days prior to any due date, and taxpayers filing by other electronic means will be notified within 90 days of any due date.

The department's online filing system is accessed through the Taxpayer Access Point (TAP). Information about TAP, including instructional videos, can be accessed at **https://tap.dor.ms.gov/_/**.

• **Use tax**

Persons who are subject to use tax must remit to the Commissioner the tax due for the month by the 20th day of the next succeeding month (Sec. 27-67-17). A return must be filed when tax is remitted. The return must detail the purchase price or value of the item in question and such other information as the Commissioner may deem necessary for the determination of the proper amount of tax.

¶ 568   **Prepayment of Taxes**

In general, taxpayers who maintain no permanent place of business and taxpayers who are in the business of making retail sales of mobile homes may be required to prepay the tax (Sec. 27-65-27). In lieu of prepayment, the taxpayer may file a cash or surety bond (Sec. 27-65-27, Rule 54).

Contractors: For contracts exceeding $75,000, the taxes accrue before work is begun (Rule 54). The prepayment of the contractors' tax and any use tax due is a condition precedent to the commencement of work (Sec. 27-65-21, Rule 41). In lieu of prepayment, the contractor may file a surety bond in an amount sufficient to guarantee the payment of all taxes.

¶ 569   **Vendor Registration**

Any person who engages in a business or activity that is subject to sales tax is required to apply to the Commissioner for a permit to engage in the activity (Sec. 27-65-27).

The applicant must agree to pay the applicable tax to the state and to keep adequate records as required by law.

Once issued, a permit remains in force as long as the person to whom it is issued continues in the same business at the same location, or until revoked for cause by the Commissioner.

A taxpayer that fails to obtain a sales tax permit before engaging in business in Mississippi must pay the retail rate on all purchases of tangible personal property and/or service in the state, even if the property and/or service is purchased for resale. Upon obtaining a sales tax permit, a previously unregistered taxpayer must file a return and report and pay sales taxes and applicable penalties and interest for all tax periods during which the person engaged in business in the state without a sales tax permit. On the return and in any audit, a credit will be allowed for sales taxes paid on a purchase that would have constituted a wholesale sale if the taxpayer had a sales tax permit at the time of purchase. Penalties and interest will be determined after the taking of the above credit. (Sec. 27-65-3(e))

- **Use tax**

Every person who renders services in this state or who sells tangible personal property for use, storage, or consumption in this state is required to register with the Commissioner and to furnish any information relating to the business activity, as the Commissioner may require (Sec. 27-67-9).

- **Disaster or emergency assistance by out-of-state businesses**

The "Facilitating Business Rapid Response to State Declared Disasters Act of 2015," effective March 30, 2015, provides that an out-of-state business that conducts operations within Mississippi for purposes of performing work or services related to a declared state disaster or emergency during the disaster response period will not be considered to have established a level of presence that would require that business to register, file, or remit state or local corporate and personal income, privilege license, property, or sales and use taxes. Such eligible businesses or their out-of-state employees may not be subject to any state or local business licensing or registration requirements or state and local taxes or fees, including property tax on equipment brought into the state temporarily for use during a disaster response period. (S.B. 2762, Laws 2015)

For purposes of any state or local tax on or measured by net or gross income or receipts, all activity of the out-of-state business that is conducted in Mississippi will be disregarded with respect to any tax filing requirement, including the filing required for a unitary or combined group of which the out-of-state business may be a part. For the purpose of apportioning income, revenue or receipts, the performance of any work in accordance with the Act may not be sourced to or may not otherwise impact or increase the amount of income, revenue or receipts apportioned to the state. Further, any out-of-state employee will not be considered to have established residency or a presence in the state that would require that person or his or her employer to file and pay income taxes, be subjected to tax withholdings or to file and pay any other state or local tax or fee during the disaster response period.

Out-of-state businesses and out-of-state employees are required to pay transaction taxes and fees, including fuel taxes or sales and use taxes on materials or services consumed or used in the state subject to tax, hotel taxes, and car rental taxes on purchases for use or consumption in the state during the disaster response period, unless otherwise exempted. Any out-of-state business or out-of-state employee that remains in Mississippi after the end of the disaster response period will become subject to the state's normal standards for establishing presence, residency or doing business in the state and will therefore become responsible for any business or employee tax requirements that ensue. A "disaster response period" is defined in the law as a period that begins 10 days prior to the first day of the governor's proclamation or the President's declaration, whichever occurs first, and that extends 60 calendar days after the declared state disaster or emergency, or any longer period authorized by the governor. However, in no event may the disaster response period exceed 120 days. (S.B. 2762, Laws 2015)

¶ 570   Sales or Use Tax Credits and Incentives

Use tax credits are allowed in many instances for sales taxes paid other states or counties. The general use tax offset given by Mississippi for sales tax paid in other states is discussed below.

Collection allowance: A 2% credit in the form of a prompt payment discount is given for collection of the tax, with a maximum of $50 per month or $600 per calendar year for each business location (Sec. 27-65-33(1)).

• **Tax paid to other states**

Persons using business property in this state that has been used by them in other states are entitled to a credit for sales and use tax that was paid to other states (Sec. 27-67-7(a)). The amount of the credit is equal to the aggregate of all such state rates multiplied by the value of the property at the time of importation into Mississippi.

Persons using business property in Mississippi that was acquired from another person who used it in other states are entitled to a credit equal to the applicable rate in the state of last prior use multiplied by the value of the property at the time of importation into Mississippi (Sec. 27-67-7(a)). However, the credit for use tax paid to another state does not apply to personal property that was only stored or warehoused in such other state and first used in Mississippi.

Motor vehicles: Credit for sales or use tax paid to another state does not apply on the purchase price or value of trailers, boats, travel trailers, motorcycles, all-terrain cycles, automobiles, trucks, truck-tractors, and semitrailers that are imported and first used in Mississippi (Sec. 27-67-7(a)).

Beer: Wholesale sales of beer are subject to tax, and the retailer is entitled to a credit for the amount of tax paid to the wholesaler on the retail tax return covering the subsequent sales of the same property (Sec. 27-65-17). Adequate invoices and records substantiating the credit must be maintained.

Interstate telecommunications: A credit is available for sales taxes paid in another state on the gross income from interstate telecommunications services if the business proves that the tax was actually due and paid and only to the extent that the rate of sales tax imposed by the other state does not exceed the Mississippi rate (see ¶ 564).

• **Incentive payments**

Family-oriented projects: Incentive payments based upon Mississippi sales tax revenue are allowed for up to 35% of the original indebtedness, project capital cost, or both, that is incurred by persons, corporations, or other entities to locate family-oriented enterprise projects such as campgrounds and theme parks in Mississippi (Sec. 57-30-1). The incentive payments, made by the Mississippi Development Authority to approved participants on a semiannual basis in January and July, are based on the amount of sales tax revenue collected from a project.

Tourism-related projects: Eligible persons, corporations, or other entities that make capital expenditures to locate a tourism project in Mississippi are authorized to receive tourism sales tax incentive payments (rebates) for an amount not to exceed 30% of the approved project costs incurred by the participant. Eighty percent of the sales tax revenues collected from the operation of the tourism project will be deposited into a Tourism Sales Tax Incentive Fund, from which incentive payments will be paid to approved participants semiannually, in January and July (Sec. 57-26-1).

A tourism project includes any of the following: (1) a theme park, water park, entertainment park, or outdoor adventure park, a cultural or historical educational center or museum, a motor speedway, an entertainment center or complex, a convention center, a professional sports facility, a spa, a natural phenomenon or scenic landscape attraction, or a marina open to the public that has a minimum private investment of $10 million; (2) a hotel with a minimum private investment of $40 million in land, buildings, architecture, engineering, fixtures, equipment, furnishings, amenities, and other related soft costs as well as a minimum private investment of $150,000 per guest room; (3) a public golf course with a minimum private investment of $10 million; (4) a full-service hotel with a minimum private investment of $15 million in land, buildings, architecture, engineering, fixtures, equipment, furnishings, amenities, and other related soft costs, a minimum private investment of $200,000 per guest room or suite, a minimum of 25 guest rooms or suites, and guest amenities such as restaurants and spas; (5) a tourism attraction located within an entertainment district that is open to the public, has seating accommodations for at least 40 persons, is open at least five days per week from at least 6:00 p.m. until midnight, serves food and beverages, and provides live entertainment at least three nights per week, and (6) a cultural retail attraction, which is a project that combines destination shopping with cultural or historical interpretive elements specific to Mississippi. Also, certain retail activities in connection with a resort development are eligible. (Sec. 57-26-1)

A person, corporation, or other entity desiring to participate in the tourism project sales tax incentive program must submit an application, plans for a proposed tourism project, and a $5,000 application fee to the Mississippi Development Authority (MDAS). The MDA may not issue a certificate designating an entity as an approved participant in the Tourism Project Sales Tax Incentive Program after July 1, 2014, for tourism projects that are cultural retail attractions, or from and after July 1, 2016, for other tourism projects. (Sec. 57-26-5)

¶ 571 Deficiency Assessments

The Commissioner is authorized to make assessments of unpaid taxes, damages, and interest from any information that is available (Sec. 27-65-37, Sec. 27-65-35). Such determinations are presumed to be correct, and the burden is on the taxpayer to establish any inaccuracy. No injunction may be awarded by any court or judge to restrain the collection of sales or use taxes (Sec. 27-65-71).

¶ 572 Audit Procedures

The Commissioner is authorized to audit the records and returns of a taxpayer in order to determine whether any taxes are due and unpaid (Sec. 27-65-37). A taxpayer's records may be sampled for audit purposes at the discretion of the Commissioner and any assessment resulting from such a sampling will be considered prima facie correct (Sec. 27-65-43). For additional information on audit procedures, see *Form 15-001: Information Concerning Audit Procedures and Appeal Process,* Mississippi Department of Revenue, which can be accessed under "Publications" at **http://www.dor.ms.gov.**

Voluntary disclosure: Voluntary disclosure is the process of reporting previously unpaid tax liabilities. The program is designed to promote compliance and to benefit taxpayers who discover a past filing obligation and liability that have not been discharged. For details, see Voluntary Disclosure Agreement (VDA) Program, *Revenue Technical Bulletin TB 71-500-09-1,* Mississippi Department of Revenue, March 1, 2017, CCH Mississippi Tax Reports, ¶ 200-842, also available at **http://www.dor.ms.gov/Business/Documents/Voluntary%20Disclosure.pdf**

• **Out-of-state taxpayer**

The Commissioner is authorized to audit, examine, or inspect the books, records, invoices, papers, memoranda, or other data of any taxpayer that is liable for Mississippi sales tax. If a taxpayer that is doing business in Mississippi maintains its principal place of business outside the state, the audit, examination, or inspection may be made outside the state to the same extent as could be made within Mississippi (Sec. 27-3-63, Sec. 27-3-65).

¶ 573   Statute of Limitations

With respect to a tax return that was timely filed, the amount of taxes that is due must be determined and assessed within 36 months from the date the return was filed, and no suit or other proceedings for the collection of any taxes may be commenced after the expiration of 36 months from the date such return was filed (Sec. 27-65-42).

However, when an audit of the return has been initiated, and the taxpayer notified thereof by certified mail, within the 36-month examination period, the determination of the correct tax liability may be made after the expiration of the examination period (Sec. 27-65-42).

In the case of a false or fraudulent return that was filed with the intent to evade tax, or in the case of no return having been filed, the amount of tax due may be determined, assessed, and collected, and suit or proceedings for the collection of the tax may be begun, at any time after the tax becomes due (Sec. 27-65-42).

Claim for refund: A taxpayer may apply to the Commissioner for a revision of the tax liability at any time within 36 months from the date of the assessment or the date the return was filed (Sec. 27-65-42). No credit or refund will be allowed with respect to claims filed after the expiration of that time period.

¶ 574   Application for Refund

The Commissioner may allow the taxpayer to take credit for an overpayment on a subsequent return or have the taxpayer file for a refund (Sec. 27-65-53).

If an audit reveals that a taxpayer has overpaid the tax due with respect to a discontinued business or, with respect to a continuing business, that the amount of the overpayment exceeds the estimated liability for the next 12 months, such amount will be refunded to the taxpayer (Sec. 27-65-53). The state auditor may issue a warrant to the state treasurer in favor of the taxpayer for the amount of tax that was erroneously paid.

Appeals: Taxpayers aggrieved by an assessment of tax, the denial of a refund claim, or the denial of a waiver of a tag penalty, have 60 days from the date of the action to file an appeal with the board of review. After the board of review renders its decision, a taxpayer aggrieved by it has 60 days from the date of the board's order to request a hearing before the Board of Tax Appeals. After a decision by the State Tax Commission, a taxpayer has 60 days in which to seek judicial review of the Commission's order by filing a petition in the chancery court.

¶ 575   MISSOURI

¶ 576   Scope of Tax

Source.—Statutory references are to Chapter 144 of the Revised Statutes of Missouri, as amended to date. Details are reported in the CCH MISSOURI STATE TAX REPORTS starting at ¶ 60-000.

The Missouri sales tax is imposed on sellers for the privilege of engaging in the business of selling tangible personal property or rendering certain taxable services at retail in the state (Sec. 144.020.1, Sec. 144.021). Sales tax is not imposed on sales of realty (12 CSR 10-3.330). Tax is also imposed on admission charges, rentals, and leases (Sec. 144.020.1(2), Sec. 144.020(8)).

The sales tax is in addition to all other taxes (Sec. 144.050).

Sales of services: Taxable services include only the following (Sec. 144.020.1(3)— Sec. 144.020.1(7), Sec. 144.021):

— furnishing electricity, water, or gas to domestic, commercial or industrial users agricultural uses are excluded (*Norwin G. Heimos Greenhouse, Inc. v. Director of Revenue,* Mo SCt, No. 68265, February 17, 1987; CCH MISSOURI TAX REPORTS, ¶ 201-041; 12 CSR 10-108.300);

— providing telecommunications services;

— the furnishing of rooms, meals, and drinks by a hotel, motel, tavern, inn, restaurant, eating house, drug store, dining car, tourist cabin, tourist camp, or other place that regularly provides such services; and

— transporting passengers in intrastate commerce.

Computer software: Generally, the sale of canned computer software programs is taxable as the sale of tangible personal property. The sale of customized software programs is treated as the sale of a nontaxable service if the true object of the transaction is providing technical professional service. Also, the sale of software as a service (SaaS) is not subject to tax. (12 CSR 10-109.050(1); see also *Letter Ruling No. LR 7615,* Missouri Department of Revenue, August 21, 2015, CCH MISSOURI TAX REPORTS, ¶ 204-008).

A Missouri Administrative Hearing Commission (AHC) decision held that an out-of-state corporation's sale of canned computer software to a customer through a load-and-leave delivery method was not subject to Missouri use tax because the software was not tangible personal property; rather, it was intangible (*FileNet Corp. v. Director of Revenue,* Administrative Hearing Commission (Missouri), No. 07-0146 RS, August 20, 2010, CCH MISSOURI TAX REPORTS, ¶ 203-347).

A taxpayer's sales of software applications through Internet downloads were not subject to Missouri sales tax because the software was delivered solely over the Internet (*Letter Ruling No. LR6144,* Missouri Department of Revenue, March 5, 2010, CCH MISSOURI TAX REPORTS, ¶ 203-283; see also *Letter Ruling No. LR 7074,* Missouri Department of Revenue, March 29, 2012, CCH MISSOURI TAX REPORTS, ¶ 203-602).

Nicotine and vapor products: Sales of alternative nicotine products and vapor products (e-cigarettes) are subject to state and local sales tax, but cannot be otherwise taxed or regulated as tobacco products (Sec. 407.296(3)).

• **Use tax**

The compensating use tax is imposed for the privilege of storing, using or consuming tangible personal property in the state, but not until the property has come to rest in the state or is commingled with the general mass of property in the state (Sec. 144.610.1). Storage does not include property that is temporarily kept or retained in Missouri for subsequent use outside the state and the term "use" does not include the temporary storage of property in Missouri for subsequent use outside the state (Sec. 144.605).

Use tax is not imposed on receipts that were subject to sales tax or on sales that would be exempt from the sales tax if made in Missouri (Sec. 144.615(2), Sec. 144.615(3)).

• **Incidence of tax**

Sellers are subject to and are primarily responsible for collecting and remitting sales tax (Sec. 144.021, Sec. 144.080.1). However, purchasers must pay the amount of sales tax to the sellers (Sec. 144.060).

Liability for use tax is imposed on persons storing, using, or consuming tangible personal property in the state (Sec. 144.610.2, 12 CSR 10-4.010(2), 12 CSR 10-4.127(2)). However, the burden of collecting use tax is imposed on vendors (Sec. 144.635, 12 CSR 10-4.127(1)).

Online travel companies: The Missouri Supreme Court dismissed a hotel and tourism tax case, holding that online travel companies that facilitated the booking of hotel and motel rooms over the Internet were not required to collect taxes on the marked-up room rate charged to customers. (*St. Louis County v. Prestige Travel, Inc.,* Supreme Court of Missouri, No. SC91228, June 28, 2011, CCH MISSOURI TAX REPORTS, ¶ 203-453)

Deal-of-the-day vouchers: The amount included in gross receipts when a purchase is made with a voucher sold by a third party, such as Groupon, depends on the nature of the voucher. If the voucher offers a specific dollar value that may be used toward the purchase of unspecified products or services, the face value of the voucher must be included in gross receipts even if the amount paid for the voucher is less than the face value. However, if the voucher offers a specific product or service for the price paid for the voucher, the price paid must be included in gross receipts. In this case, customers pay $29 for one month of unlimited yoga classes, not for a voucher worth $29 for anything the taxpayer may sell. Thus, the taxpayer must include $29 in gross receipts subject to tax. (*Letter Ruling No. LR 7156,* Missouri Department of Revenue, October 1, 2012, CCH MISSOURI TAX REPORTS, ¶ 203-664)

Gift certificates: A radio station's sales of gift certificates to individuals to purchase goods and services at various community businesses are not subject to sales or use tax, because the taxpayer is selling gift certificates, which are not tangible personal property or an enumerated taxable service. The sales of goods and taxable services by the community businesses in exchange for the gift certificates are subject to sales tax. Sales tax is imposed on the face value of the gift certificates. (*Letter Ruling No. LR 7171,* Missouri Department of Revenue, November 7, 2012, CCH MISSOURI TAX REPORTS, ¶ 203-676)

Drop shipments: When all the parties are located in the state, the retailer furnishes a resale certificate to the primary seller, rendering the first sale a nontaxable transaction. The retailer then collects sales tax on behalf of the state on the secondary sale to its customer. However, different considerations arise when one or more of the parties are not within the state.

Missouri exempts the primary sale, that to an out-of-state retailer by a Missouri manufacturer who drop ships the product to the retailer's customer. The secondary sale by the retailer to its Missouri customer is an exempt interstate sale when the retailer lacks any Missouri nexus. When that is the case, the customer is subject to use tax because no sales tax has been paid. (Sec. 144.610; see also *Letter Ruling No. LR10139,* Missouri Department of Revenue, December 17, 1997, CCH MISSOURI TAX REPORTS, ¶ 300-580)

¶576 Missouri

- **Nexus**

Missouri requires every retailer engaged in business in Missouri and selling tangible personal property for use or consumption and not for resale to collect and remit sales and use tax upon every retail sale in Missouri (Sec. 144.010; Sec. 144.020). Effective August 28, 2013, the term "engaging in business" in Missouri includes any activity that falls within the terms "engaging in business in this state" and "maintains a place of business in this state" as they are defined in the use tax law. (Sec. 144.010) "Engaged in business activities in the state" includes (Sec. 144.605(2)):

— maintaining or having a franchisee or licensee operating under the seller's trade name in Missouri if the franchisee or licensee is required to collect sales tax; or

— soliciting sales or taking orders by sales agents or traveling representatives.

A vendor is presumed to "engage in business activities within this state" if any person, other than a common carrier acting in its capacity as such, that has substantial nexus with Missouri: (Sec. 144.605(2)):

— sells a similar line of products as the vendor and does so under the same or similar business name;

— maintains an office, distribution facility, warehouse, or storage place, or similar place of business in Missouri to facilitate the delivery of property or services sold by the vendor to the vendor's customers;

— delivers, installs, assembles, or performs maintenance services for the vendor's customers within the state;

— facilitates the vendor's delivery of property to customers in the state by allowing the vendor's customers to pick up property sold by the vendor at an office, distribution facility, warehouse, storage place, or similar place of business maintained by the person in the state; or

— conducts any other activities in the state that are significantly associated with the vendor's ability to establish and maintain a market in the state for the sales.

This presumption may be rebutted by demonstrating that the person's activities in the state are not significantly associated with the vendor's ability to establish and maintain a market in the state for sales (Sec. 144.605(2)).

The term "maintains a place of business in this state" includes maintaining, occupying, or using, permanently or temporarily, directly or indirectly, by whatever name called, an office, place of distribution, sales or sample room or place, warehouse or storage place, or other place of business in this state, whether owned or operated by the vendor or by any other person other than a common carrier acting in its capacity as such. (Sec. 144.605(3))

Click-through nexus: A vendor is presumed to be engaging in business activities within the state if the vendor enters into an agreement with a resident of Missouri under which the resident, for a commission or other consideration, refers customers to the vendor, whether by a link on a website, an in-person presentation, telemarketing or otherwise, and the vendor's cumulative gross receipts from sales to all Missouri customers referred by residents with such an agreement exceed $10,000 in the preceding 12 months. (Sec. 144.605(2))

This presumption may be rebutted by showing that the Missouri resident did not engage in activity within Missouri that was significantly associated with the vendor's market in Missouri in the preceding 12 months. Such proof may consist of sworn written statements from all of the residents with whom the vendor has an agreement stating that they did not engage in any solicitation in the state on behalf of the vendor during the preceding year, provided that such statements were provided and obtained in good faith. (Sec. 144.605(2))

Out-of-state vendors: Out-of-state vendors with sufficient contact with Missouri must register and collect sales or use taxes; see ¶ 584. The extent of the contact with the state and the nature of business of the vendor will determine what tax the vendor is subject to (12 CSR 10-4.085). The Department of Revenue has established criteria to be used, but not exclusively, in determining if an out-of-state vendor is subject to the sales tax. A vendor must pay or collect sales tax if within Missouri it directly or by any agent or representative :

— has or utilizes an office, distribution house, sales house, warehouse, service enterprise, or other place of business;

— maintains a stock of goods;

— regularly solicits orders unless the activity in the state consists solely of advertising or of solicitation by direct mail;

— regularly engages in the delivery of property in the state other than by common carrier or U.S. mail; or

— regularly engages in any activity in connection with the leasing or servicing of property in the state.

If an out-of-state vendor is not subject to the sales tax, it will be subject to the use tax. Generally, an out-of-state vendor must register with the Department of Revenue, and collect and remit use tax when the vendor has sufficient nexus with Missouri. Sufficient nexus exists when the vendor has a physical presence in Missouri. Physical presence means (12 CSR 10-114.100):

(1) owning or leasing real or tangible personal property within the state; or

(2) having employees, agents, representatives, independent contractors, brokers or others that reside in, or regularly and systematically enter into Missouri on behalf of the vendor.

However, a vendor does NOT have sufficient nexus if the only contact with Missouri is delivery of goods by common carrier or mail, advertising in the state through media, or occasionally attending trade shows at which no orders for goods are taken and no sales are made (12 CSR 10-114.100).

Out-of-state vendors who solicit sales in Missouri by television broadcast or other advertising media are subject to Missouri use tax on sales of goods delivered to the purchaser in Missouri, if one of the following conditions is met (12 CSR 10-4.085(3)):

— the out-of-state vendor has an office, distribution house, sales house, warehouse, service enterprise or other place of business in Missouri; or

— the out-of-state vendor makes the sales through local television stations, cable companies or other advertising media agents for the out-of-state vendor.

An out-of-state vendor does not have sufficient nexus if the only contact with the state is delivery of goods by common carrier or mail, advertising in the state through media, or occasionally attending trade shows at which no orders for goods are taken and no sales are made (12 CSR 10-114.100(3)(B)). Likewise, occasional deliveries into the state by the vendor's delivery vehicles with no other contacts do not constitute physical presence to establish sufficient nexus (12 CSR 10-114.100(3)(C)).

Once sufficient nexus has been established, the out-of-state vendor is liable for use tax on all sales of tangible personal property made in Missouri, whether or not the sales activity related to the property or activity would be sufficient in and of itself to establish physical presence (12 CSR 10-114.100(3)(D)). Once nexus has been established, it will continue for a reasonable period of time after the vendor no longer has a physical presence in the state. The Department will presume that the vendor has nexus with the state for any sales to Missouri customers made during at least one reporting period after the vendor no longer has physical presence in the state. A vendor registered with the Department to collect tax will continue to have nexus until the vendor withdraws its registration (12 CSR 10-114.100(3)(E)).

Agreements to exempt collection requirement: Agreements between the executive branch and any person that exempt the person from the collection of sales and use taxes will be void unless approved by both chambers of the General Assembly (Sec. 144.030(3)).

Trade shows: For purposes of collecting use tax in Missouri against an out-of-state business, occasionally (14 days or less) attending a trade show in Missouri as a consumer or participating as an exhibitor at a trade show in Missouri, but neither taking orders nor making sales, does not create nexus. If orders are taken or sales are made, nexus would be established. (12 CSR 10-114.100(3)(B))

• **Streamlined Act status**

Missouri has enacted the Uniform (Simplified) Sales and Use Tax Administration Act, the product of the Streamlined Sales Tax Project (SSTP).

Missouri is an Advisor State to the SSTP because, although it has enacted legislation authorizing it to enter into the Streamlined Sales and Use Tax Agreement (Secs. 144.1000—144.1015), it has not yet enacted the changes to its laws necessary to comply with the Agreement's requirements. However, it will continue to have input through its representation on the State and Local Advisory Council, which advises the Governing Board on matters pertaining to the administration of the Agreement.

¶ 577   Tax Base

The tax base for the sales tax is the purchase price paid or charged; if the sale involves the exchange of property, the tax base is the consideration paid or charged plus the fair market value of the exchanged property (Sec. 144.020.1(1), 12 CSR 10-3.136, 12 CSR 10-4.035). Sellers are required to report to the Director of Revenue their "gross receipts" and remit tax due on the gross receipts (Sec. 144.080.1, Sec. 144.100.1, Sec, 144.100.2). The tax base for the use tax is the sales price (Sec. 144.610.1(1)). Sales tax may apply to the same property when there are distinct transactions, such as the purchase of bowling shoes by a bowling business and the rental of the shoes to customers (12 CSR 10-3.179).

"Gross receipts" means the total amount of the sales price of sales at retail plus services that are a part of the sales, but does not include the sales price of returned property and charges incident to the extension of credit (Sec. 144.010.1(3)). Also included in "gross receipts" are taxes collected by the seller in excess of the amount that the law authorizes as reimbursement (12 CSR 10-3.210) and the fair market value of property received as consideration (12 CSR 10-3.122). Furthermore, in transactions not at arm's length in which the consideration received is less than the fair market value of the item sold or leased, "gross receipts" includes the fair market value of the item sold or leased or service performed (12 CSR 10-3.138).

"Sales price" is the money value of consideration paid or given by a purchaser to a vendor for tangible personal property including any services that are part of the sale, any amount for which credit is given, without deduction for the cost of property sold, cost of materials, labor or service cost, losses, or any other expenses (Sec. 144.605(8)). "Sales price" does not include cash discounts, amounts charged for property returned by customers, amounts charged for labor or services rendered in installing sold property, and charges incident to the extension of credit.

Sales taxes received by a vendor are not includable in "gross receipts" if the tax is separately charged or stated (Sec. 144.285.5, 12 CSR 10-3.210, 12 CSR 10-3.464, 12 CSR 10-3.498).

Any charges, fees, or assessments added by vendors to the sale price of sales at retail are includable as taxable gross receipts (12 CSR 10-3.890). This includes charges, fees, or assessments for community or area betterment, tourism, or marketing programs. However, such a charge, fee, or assessment that is collected by the vendor only at the specific direction of a customer is not considered a part of taxable gross receipts if it is separately billed and accounted for by the vendors and the proceeds are forwarded to the program-sponsoring organization.

"Telecommunications services" means the transmission of information by wire, radio, optical cable, coaxial cable, electronic impulses, or other similar means. It does not include any of the following services, if the services are separately stated either on the customer's bill or on the seller's records: (1) access to the Internet or to interactive computer services or electronic publishing services, although the telecommunications services used to provide such access remain taxable; (2) answering services and paging services; (3) private mobile radio services other than two-way commercial mobile radio services, meaning that services such as wireless telephone services, personal communications services, and enhanced specialized mobile radio services remain subject to tax; and (4) cable or satellite television or music services (Sec. 144.010(13)).

• **Trade-ins**

When an article is taken in trade as a credit or part-payment on the purchase price of the article being sold, sales and use taxes are computed only on that portion of the purchase price that exceeds the actual allowance made for the article traded in or exchanged, provided that there is a bill of sale or other record showing the actual allowance made for the article traded in or exchanged (Sec. 144.025). Also, the article being traded in either must have had sales or use tax paid on it at the time of purchase, or must have been exempt from the tax. If the trade-in or exchange allowance plus any applicable rebate exceeds the purchase price, no sales or use tax is owed.

Grain or livestock raised by a taxpayer may be used as an trade-in allowance when purchasing a motor vehicle or trailer for agricultural use (Sec. 144.025.5).

¶ 578   List of Exemptions, Exceptions, and Exclusions

Unless otherwise indicated, the statutory exemptions, exceptions, and exclusions listed below apply to both sales and use taxes; those applicable only to the use tax are listed separately. Items that are excluded from the sales or use tax base are treated at ¶ 577, "Tax Base."

Sales tax holiday: No tax is collected on purchases of specified clothing, personal computers, computer software, and school supplies during the annual three-day tax holiday beginning at 12:01 AM on the second Friday in August and ending at midnight on the following Sunday (Sec. 144.049). Retail sales of the following are exempt:

— any article of clothing with a taxable value of $100 or less;

— school supplies, but not to exceed $50 per purchase;

— computer software with a taxable value of $350 or less;

— graphing calculators, up to $150; and

— personal computers or computer peripheral devices, up to $1,500.

Apple iPads have been held to qualify for the sales tax holiday exemption as personal computers, but electronic book readers that download off the Internet are not personal computers because they are not akin to laptop, desktop, or tower computer systems and are not used to perform the functions traditionally associated with personal computers (*Letter Ruling No. LR6870*, Missouri Department of Revenue, July 29, 2011, CCH Missouri Tax Reports, ¶ 203-490)

Green tax holiday: A "Show Me Green" sales tax holiday is held annually. During the seven-day period beginning on April 19 and ending April 25 of each year, all retail sales of Energy Star certified new appliances of up to $1,500 per appliance are exempt from state sales tax. Energy Star-certified appliances include clothes washers and dryers, water heaters, trash compactors, dishwashers, conventional ovens, ranges, stoves, air conditioners, furnaces, refrigerators, and freezers that are approved by both the U.S. Environmental Protection Agency and the U.S. Department of Energy as eligible to display the Energy Star label. (Sec. 144.526)

A political subdivision may allow the sales tax holiday to apply to its local sales taxes by enacting an ordinance to that effect. The sales tax holiday may not apply to any retailer when less than 2% of the retailer's merchandise offered for sale qualifies for the sales tax holiday. (Sec. 144.526)

Revenue-sharing agreements: A political subdivision may enter into a revenue-sharing agreement with private entities providing goods or services for place of amusement, entertainment or recreation, games, or athletic events. However, revenues retained by such private entities will not qualify for the sales tax exemption for amounts paid for admission or fees for places of amusement, entertainment or recreation, games, or athletic events that are owned or operated by a political subdivision. (Sec. 144.030(2)(18))

- **Sales and use tax exemptions, exceptions, and exclusions**

Admission charges to places operated by political subdivisions	Sec. 144.010.1(1), Sec. 144.030.2(17), Sec. 144.030.2(21)
Advertising	Sec. 144.034
Agricultural machinery and equipment	Sec. 144.030.2(22)
Aircraft and aircraft parts	Sec. 144.030.2(21), Sec. 144.030.2(41), Sec. 144.030.2[43], Sec. 144.043
Ambulatory aids	Sec. 144.030.2(18)
Amusement devices (coin-operated) and parts	Sec. 144.518
Animals for feeding or breeding purposes, and captive wildlife	Sec. 144.030.2(7), Sec. 144.030.2(22)
Anodes	Sec. 144.030.2(13)
Aviation jet fuel (exp. 12/31/2023)	Sec. 144.809
Barges	Sec. 144.030.2(30)
Batteries	Sec. 144.046
Bingo supplies	Sec. 313.085(1)
Boat rentals	Sec. 144.020.1(8)
Broadcasting (equipment, machinery, and utilities used or consumed in)	Sec. 144.054.3

Fertilizer	Sec. 144.030.2(1)
Film rentals	Sec. 144.030.2(9)
Food stamp purchases	Sec. 144.037, Sec. 144.038
Fuel for ships	Sec. 144.030.2(26)
Fuel to dry crops	Sec. 144.030.2(22)
Fuel used in manufacturing gas, steam, electricity, or in furnishing water	Sec. 144.030.2(1)
Gases and electricity used in steelmaking	Sec. 144.036
Government contracts	Sec. 144.030.2(6)
Grain	Sec. 144.030.2(1)
Grain bins	Sec. 144.030.2(34)
Hearing aids	Sec. 144.030.2(18)
Home heating oil	Sec. 144.030.2(23)
Hotel or motel operator purchases of nonreusable items furnished to guests	Sec. 144.011.1(11)
Initiation fees, fraternal organizations	Sec. 144.011.1(13)(a)
Initiation fees, military posts	Sec. 144.011.1(13)(b)
Instructional classes	Sec. 144.010.1(12)(a) Sec. 144.018.2 Sec. 144.020.1(2)
Insulin	Sec. 144.030.2(18)
Internet access	Sec. 144.030.2(45)
Interstate commerce	Sec. 144.030.1, Sec. 144.610, Sec. 144.615(1)
Interstate compact agency	Sec. 144.030.2(27)
Isolated or occasional sales	Sec. 144.010.1(2)
Leases and rentals, tax paid when property purchased	Sec. 144.020.1(8)
Laundries (materials, machinery, and energy used by)	Sec. 144.054.5
Light aircraft and equipment	Sec. 144.043
Limestone	Sec. 144.030.2(1)
Liquidation sales	Sec. 144.010.1(2), Sec. 144.011.1(2), Sec. 144.011.1(7), Sec. 144.011.1(8)
Livestock	Sec. 144.010.1(4), Sec. 144.030.2(29)
Lottery tickets or prizes	Sec. 313.321
Lubricants for farm machinery	Sec. 144.030.2(22)
Machinery, manufacturing, and mining	Sec. 144.030.2(5)
Machinery, pumping	Sec. 144.030.2(10)
Manufactured housing (see also ¶ 579)	Sec. 144.010.2, Sec. 144.011.1(12), Sec. 700.010.5
Manufacturing (energy, equipment, and materials used or consumed in)	Sec. 144.054.2

Research and development (energy, equipment, and materials used or consumed in) . . . .   Sec. 144.054.2

Research and development (property and utilities used in agriculture/ biotechnology, pharmaceuticals, plant genomics) . . . .   Sec. 144.030.2(33)

Reusable containers . . . .   Sec. 144.011.1(9)

Rural water district purchases . . . .   Sec. 144.030.2(16)

Schools, private . . . .   Sec. 144.030.2(22)

Schools, public . . . .   Sec. 144.030.2(19), Sec. 144.030.2(20)

Seeds . . . .   Sec. 144.030.2(1)

Senior citizen handicraft sales . . . .   Sec. 144.030.2(24)

Shooting ranges . . . .   Sec. 144.030.2(41)

Special fuel. . . . .   Sec. 144.030.2(1)

State and local government purchases . . . .   Sec. 144.030.1

State eleemosynary and penal institutions . . . .   Sec. 144.030.2(20)

State relief agencies . . . .   Sec. 144.030.2(20)

State senator or representative . . . .   Sec. 144.039

Steelmaking, raw materials used . . . .   Sec. 144.030.2(2)

Textbooks, college . . . .   Sec. 144.517

Ticket sales by certain nonprofit and scientific associations . . . .   Sec. 144.030.2(21), (39)

Utilities for domestic use . . . .   Sec. 144.030.2(23)

Vending machines and parts . . . .   Sec. 144.518

Vending machines on premises of religious or charitable organizations and public schools . . . .   Sec. 144.012

Vessels, documented (in-lieu tax; see ¶ 579) . . . .   Sec. 306.016

- **Exemptions, exceptions, and exclusions applicable only to the use tax**

Items stored in Missouri for less than 12 months for use out of state .   Sec. 144.610.1, Sec. 144.615(3)

Receipts from the sale of property subject to the sales tax . . . .   Sec. 144.615(2), Sec. 144.615(3)

Sales that would be exempt from sales tax if made in Missouri . . . . .   Sec. 144.615(2), Sec. 144.615(3)

¶ 579   **Rate of Tax**

The Missouri sales tax and the use tax are imposed at the rate of 4.225% and consist of a general sales and use tax of 4% (Sec. 144.020.1(1), Sec. 144.610.1), a wildlife conservation tax of 0.125% (Sec. 43, Art. IV, Mo. Const.), and a soil and water conservation and park tax of 0.10% (Sec. 47, Art. IV, Mo. Const.). The 0.10% tax for soil and water conservation and parks ends in 2016.

In addition to being subject to state sales and use taxes, retail sales may also be subject to city and county sales taxes; see ¶ 580 for a further discussion of local taxes.

- **Retail sales of food**

The tax rate on all retail sales of food is 1.225% (Sec. 144.014). The term "food" includes only those products and types of food for which food stamps may be redeemed pursuant to the federal Food Stamp Program, including food dispensed through vending machines. All other sales of food are taxed at the full state rate plus any applicable local tax.

With the exception of vending machine sales, the term "food" does not include food or drink sold for consumption on or off the premises by a restaurant, delicatessen, cafe, or other eating establishment that derives more than 80% of its total gross receipts from food sales (Sec. 144.014).

Mandatory gratuities reported as tip income and withheld from wages are excluded from tax (Sec. 144.020.1(6)).

• Vending machine sales

Sales of tangible personal property, other than photocopies and tobacco products, through vending machines are subject to tax based on 135% of the net invoice price of the tangible personal property. The applicable tax rate is the rate in effect at the location of the vending machine. Sales of photocopies and tobacco products are subject to tax on their retail sales price. Purchases of machines or parts for machines used in a commercial vending machine business are exempt from tax if tax is paid on the gross receipts derived from the use of the machines (Sec. 144.518; 12 CSR 10-103.400).

Purchases of tangible personal property, except cigarettes, cigars, and other tobacco products, to be sold in a vending machine are exempt as sales for resale (Sec. 144.012).

• Motor vehicles, trailers, boats, and outboard motors

Effective July 5, 2013, the state and local use taxes on the storage, use, or consumption of motor vehicles, trailers, boats, and outboard motors ware repealed and replaced with a sales tax to be collected for the titling of such property (Sec. 144.069).

The rate of tax associated with titling such property is the sum of the state and local sales tax rates in effect at the address of the owner of the property (Sec. 144.069).

All local taxing jurisdictions that have not previously approved a local use tax must put to a vote of the people whether to discontinue collecting sales tax on the titling of motor vehicles, trailers, boats, and outboard motors purchased from a source other than a licensed Missouri dealer. If a taxing jurisdiction does not hold such a vote on or before the general election in November, 2016, the taxing jurisdiction must cease collecting the sales tax. Taxing jurisdictions may at any time hold a vote to repeal the tax. Language repealing the tax must be put to a vote of the people if 15% of the registered voters in a taxing jurisdiction sign a petition requesting such a vote.

• Manufactured and modular homes

Transfers of manufactured homes are not "retail sales" and are, therefore, not subject to sales and use taxes unless the transfer (Sec. 144.011(1)(12)):

> (1) involves the delivery of a "Manufacturer's Statement of Origin" to a person other than a manufactured home dealer for purposes of allowing that person to obtain a title to the home from the Department of Revenue or agency of another state;

> (2) involves the delivery of a "Repossessed Title" to a Missouri resident if sales tax was not paid on the transfer in (1) above; or

> (3) is the first transfer occurring after December 31, 1985, if sales tax was not paid on any pre-1986 transfer of the same home.

If the transfer of a manufactured home meets the criteria for taxation, only 60% of the purchase price of a new manufactured home is taxable, and the other 40% is exempt from sales tax. This is because 40% of the sale of a new manufactured home is considered to be a sale of a service and 60% is considered the sale of tangible personal property. Dealers selling new manufactured homes must collect and remit the tax on 60% of the retail sales price and provide to the buyers signed receipts confirming the payment of tax. (Sec. 144.044; 12 CSR 10-103.370)

Sales of used manufactured homes are exempt (Sec. 144.044(4)).

¶579　**Missouri**

- **Change in tax rate**

Sales and use taxes are calculated at the tax rate in effect on the date of sale (12 CSR 10-3.131, 12 CSR 10-4.624). Cash or charge sales made after the effective date of a rate change are subject to the new rate. Charge sales made before the effective date of a rate change are subject to the old rate.

- **In-lieu tax on documented vessels**

A boat or vessel documented by the U.S. Coast Guard or other federal government agency is not subject to state or local sales or use tax, but instead must pay an in-lieu watercraft tax (Sec. 306.016). The tax rates range from $500 for watercraft with a purchase price of less than $15,000 to $10,500 for watercraft with a purchase price of $650,001 to $750,000, with an additional $1,500 fee added for each $100,000 increment above a purchase price of $750,000.

¶ 580   **Local Taxes**

Cities, counties, and certain special districts are authorized to levy a variety of sales taxes and various rates. Upon voter approval, any county or municipality may impose a local use tax at a rate equal to the rate of the local sales tax in effect in that county or municipality.

Regional taxes: The governing body of any county within the Kansas and Missouri Regional Investment District may, subject to authorization by a majority of its electors, levy and collect a county sales tax to support the district. The sales tax may be imposed at a rate of up to 0.50% for up to 15 years, and may be renewed by the voters of that county prior to its expiration. The sales tax is to be administered, enforced, and collected in the same manner as other countywide sales taxes (Sec. 70-535).

Transportation: A transportation development district may impose a sales tax in increments of 0.125% up to a maximum of 1%, upon voter approval. The tax may be applied to all retail sales in the district except: (1) the sale or use of motor vehicles, trailers, boats or outboard motors; (2) sales of electricity or electrical current, water and gas, natural or artificial, or (3) sales of service to telephone subscribers, either local or long distance (Sec. 238.235).

Mobile telecommunications: Missouri has adopted the provisions of the federal Mobile Telecommunications Sourcing Act (4 USC 116-126) (Sec. 32-087(12)(3)). Wireless telecommunications services are sourced to the customer's "primary place of use," which is the residential or primary business address of the customer and which must be located in the service provider's licensed service area. The jurisdiction in which the primary place of use is located is the only jurisdiction that may tax the communications services, regardless of the customer's location when an actual call is placed or received.

- **Local rate chart**

Tables of local sales and use tax rates are available on the website of the Department of Revenue at **http://dor.mo.gov/business/sales/rates/**.

¶ 581   **Bracket Schedule**

The Director of Revenue is authorized to establish brackets showing the amount of tax that is to be collected by sellers on taxable sales (Sec. 144.285.1). When statements covering taxable purchases are rendered on a monthly or other periodic basis, a seller has the option of collecting tax either by applying the tax rate to the total amount of the purchases, rounded to the nearest whole cent, or by using the brackets established by the Director of Revenue (Sec. 144.285.2). Vendors also have the option of determining the amount of tax by applying the tax rate on each taxable purchase, rounded to the nearest whole cent (Sec. 144.285.4).

The bracket schedules below have been established by the Director.

4.225% State Rate

Sale	Tax
$0.00 to $0.11	No tax
.12 to .35	1¢
.36 to .59	2¢
.60 to .82	3¢
.83 to 1.06	4¢
and so forth.	

4.850% State and Local Rate

Sale	Tax
$0.00 to $0.10	No tax
.11 to .30	1¢
.31 to .51	2¢
.52 to .72	3¢
.73 to .92	4¢
.93 to 1.13	5¢
and so forth.	

4.975% State and Local Rate

Sale	Tax
$0.00 to $0.10	No tax
.11 to .30	1¢
.31 to .50	2¢
.51 to .70	3¢
.71 to .90	4¢
.91 to 1.10	5¢
and so forth.	

5.100% State and Local Rate

Sale	Tax
$0.00 to $0.09	No tax
.10 to .29	1¢
.30 to .49	2¢
.50 to .68	3¢
.69 to .88	4¢
.89 to 1.07	5¢
and so forth.	

5.225% State and Local Rate

Sale	Tax
$0.00 to $0.09	No tax
.10 to .28	1¢
.29 to .47	2¢
.48 to .66	3¢
.67 to .86	4¢
.87 to 1.05	5¢
and so forth.	

4.600% State and Local Rate

Sale	Tax
$0.00 to $0.10	No tax
.11 to .32	1¢
.33 to .54	2¢
.55 to .76	3¢
.77 to .97	4¢
.98 to 1.19	5¢
and so forth.	

5.725% State and Local Rate

Sale	Tax
$0.00 to $0.08	No tax
.09 to .26	1¢
.27 to .43	2¢
.44 to .61	3¢
.62 to .78	4¢
.79 to .96	5¢
.97 to 1.13	6¢
and so forth.	

5.850% State and Local Rate

Sale	Tax
$0.00 to $0.08	No tax
.09 to .25	1¢
.26 to .42	2¢
.43 to .59	3¢
.60 to .76	4¢
.77 to .94	5¢
.95 to 1.11	6¢
and so forth.	

5.975% State and Local Rate

Sale	Tax
$0.00 to $0.08	No tax
.09 to .25	1¢
.26 to .41	2¢
.42 to .58	3¢
.59 to .75	4¢
.76 to .92	5¢
.93 to 1.08	6¢
and so forth.	

6.100% State and Local Rate

Sale	Tax
$0.00 to $0.08	No tax
.09 to .24	1¢
.25 to .40	2¢
.41 to .57	3¢
.58 to .73	4¢
.74 to .90	5¢
.91 to 1.06	6¢
and so forth.	

4.725% State and Local Rate

Sale	Tax
$0.00 to $0.10	No tax
.11 to .31	1¢
.32 to .52	2¢
.53 to .74	3¢
.75 to .95	4¢
.96 to 1.16	5¢
and so forth.	

6.475% State and Local Rate

Sale	Tax
$0.00 to $0.07	No tax
.08 to .23	1¢
.24 to .38	2¢
.39 to .54	3¢
.55 to .69	4¢
.70 to .84	5¢
.85 to 1.00	6¢
and so forth.	

6.600% State and Local Rate

Sale	Tax
$0.00 to $0.07	No tax
.08 to .22	1¢
.23 to .37	2¢
.38 to .53	3¢
.54 to .68	4¢
.69 to .83	5¢
.84 to .98	6¢
.99 to 1.13	7¢
and so forth.	

6.725% State and Local Rate

Sale	Tax
$0.00 to $0.07	No tax
.08 to .22	1¢
.23 to .37	2¢
.38 to .52	3¢
.53 to .66	4¢
.67 to .81	5¢
.82 to .96	6¢
.97 to 1.11	7¢
and so forth.	

6.850% State and Local Rate

Sale	Tax
$0.00 to $0.07	No tax
.08 to .21	1¢
.22 to .36	2¢
.37 to .51	3¢
.52 to .65	4¢
.66 to .80	5¢
.81 to .94	6¢
.95 to 1.09	7¢
and so forth.	

¶581   **Missouri**

5.475% State and Local Rate	
Sale	Tax
$0.00 to $0.09	No tax
.10 to .27	1¢
.28 to .45	2¢
.46 to .63	3¢
.64 to .82	4¢
.83 to 1.00	5¢
and so forth.	

6.225% State and Local Rate	
Sale	Tax
$0.00 to $0.08	No tax
.09 to .24	1¢
.25 to .40	2¢
.41 to .56	3¢
.57 to .72	4¢
.73 to .88	5¢
.89 to 1.04	6¢
and so forth.	

6.975% State and Local Rate	
Sale	Tax
$0.00 to $0.07	No tax
.08 to .21	1¢
.22 to .35	2¢
.36 to .50	3¢
.51 to .64	4¢
.65 to .78	5¢
.79 to .93	6¢
.94 to 1.07	7¢
and so forth.	

5.600% State and Local Rate	
Sale	Tax
$0.00 to $0.08	No tax
.09 to .26	1¢
.27 to .44	2¢
.45 to .62	3¢
.63 to .80	4¢
.81 to .98	5¢
.99 to 1.16	6¢
and so forth.	

6.350% State and Local Rate	
Sale	Tax
$0.00 to $0.07	No tax
.08 to .23	1¢
.24 to .39	2¢
.40 to .55	3¢
.56 to .70	4¢
.71 to .86	5¢
.87 to 1.02	6¢
and so forth.	

7.225% State and Local Rate	
Sale	Tax
$0.00 to $0.06	No tax
.07 to .20	1¢
.21 to .34	2¢
.35 to .48	3¢
.49 to .62	4¢
.63 to .76	5¢
.77 to .89	6¢
.90 to 1.03	7¢
and so forth.	

7.725% State and Local Rate	
Sale	Tax
$0.00 to $0.06	No tax
.07 to .19	1¢
.20 to .32	2¢
.33 to .45	3¢
.46 to .58	4¢
.59 to .71	5¢
.72 to .84	6¢
.85 to .97	7¢
.98 to 1.10	8¢
and so forth.	

¶ 582   Returns, Payments, and Due Dates

Sellers and vendors file quarterly returns with the Director of Revenue on or before the last day of the month following each calendar quarter, showing the gross receipts (sales tax) or sales price (use tax) and accompanied by the tax due (Sec. 144.080.1, Sec. 144.100, Sec. 144.655.1, 12 CSR 10-3.452). However, if the tax is greater than $500 in a calendar month, it must be paid to the Director by the 20th day of the following month and, for use tax, is a credit against the use tax liability shown on the return (Sec. 144.080.2, Sec. 144.655.2, 12 CSR 10-3.460, 12 CSR 10-4.600). Sellers and vendors whose tax liability is less than $100 in a calendar quarter may file annual returns for the calendar year on or before January 31 of the following year (Sec. 144.080.3, Sec. 144.655.3, 12 CSR 10-3.462, 12 CSR 10-4.610).

A seller whose state sales tax liability (exclusive of local taxes) in each of at least six months during the prior 12 months was $15,000 or more must remit payment on a quarter-monthly basis (Sec. 144.081, 12 CSR 10-3.626).

The Director may require returns and payment for monthly or annual periods instead of calendar quarters, in which case payment must be made on or before the last day of the month following the collection period (Sec. 144.090).

A business with a sales tax license is required to file a return, and a business subject to use tax must file a combined use/sales tax return, even if there were no sales during the period covered by the return (12 CSR 10-3.454, 12 CSR 10-4.185).

A vendor unable to file a return by the due date may estimate the amount due for the first two months of a quarter and file an estimated return (12 CSR 10-4.170).

Electronic filing and payment: The Missouri Department of Revenue is authorized to allow the electronic filing, issuance, or renewal of tax records, reports, returns, and other related documents (Sec. 32.080). Information about online filing and payment is available on the Missouri DOR's website at **http://dor.mo.gov/online.php**.

By January 1, 2015, the Missouri Department of Revenuehad to begin to develop a process by which all departmental tax forms and documents that are generally provided to the public are available in an electronic format online. Furthermore, by that same date, the department must also begin to develop a process by which any tax records, reports, returns, and other documents that the public must submit to the department may be electronically submitted. Eventually, the payment of all related amounts and fees must also be capable of electronic submission. This paperless service must be fully developed and implemented by January 1, 2021. (Sec. 32.029)

• Collection discount

A seller or vendor may deduct and retain 2% of the amount of a timely remittance made to the Director of Revenue (Sec. 144.140, Sec. 144.710, 12 CSR 10-3.496, 12 CSR 10-4.305). A business that has a direct payment agreement with the Department may also take the discount (Sec. 144.190.4). The discount is not allowed for payments made within any period of extension. If a seller's check is returned unpaid from a bank, the discount may not be taken (12 CSR 10-4.190).

• Use tax returns filed by purchasers

A person who stores, uses, or consumes tangible personal property in the state and who did not pay use tax to the vendor when the purchase was made generally must file a quarterly return with the Director of Revenue on or before the last day of the month following the calendar quarter, accompanied by any use tax due (Sec. 144.655.4). The Director may require annual filing instead of quarterly filing, or, at the taxpayer's request, may allow monthly filing. However, a use tax return is not required to be filed if the calendar year aggregate of purchases on which taxes were not paid does not exceed $2,000 (Sec. 144.655.5).

• Timeliness of return or payment

A return or payment delivered by U.S. mail to the Director of Revenue after the date in which it was required to be filed is considered to be timely filed if the postmark date is on or before the time prescribed for filing and if the document is deposited in the mail with proper postage and is properly addressed (12 CSR 10-3.506). For use tax, the postmark date is prima facie evidence of the date of filing (12 CSR 10-4.310).

If the deadline falls on a Saturday, Sunday, or legal holiday, the filing or payment is timely if made on the next succeeding business day (12 CSR 10-3.506, 12 CSR 10-4.160).

• Internet installment payments

Taxpayers that have received a delinquent notice from the state can establish an installment agreement through the Department's secure website (**http://dor.mo.gov/cacs/**). Business taxpayers will use their sales tax license number and PIN. Taxpayers can select a number of payment options, including the number or dollar amount of payments and type of payment (credit card, electronic funds transfer, or check/money order). After setting up the payment plan, taxpayers will receive a letter stating the terms of their agreement with the Department as well as a reminder letter each time a payment is due or scheduled to be paid by an electronic funds transfer or credit card.

¶582   Missouri

- **Uniform Sales and Use Tax Act**

Missouri has enacted the Uniform (Simplified) Sales and Use Tax Administration Act, the product of the Streamlined Sales Tax Project (SSTP) (H.B. 1150, Laws 2002). However, it has not yet enacted legislation to comply with the Streamlined Sales and Use Tax Agreement. For additional information on the Act and Agreement, see "Streamlined Sales Tax Project," listed in the Table of Contents.

¶ 583   Prepayment of Taxes

Although the law states that sellers and vendors are to report their gross receipts and pay tax on that amount (Sec. 144.100.2; Sec. 144.021; Sec. 144.655), they may report sales on an accrual basis. A taxpayer using the accrual basis of accounting reports the gross receipts from its sales in the period in which the transaction is completed, rather than the period in which the payment is actually received (12 CSR 10-103.560; 12 CSR 10-4.628). When the taxpayer and the purchaser enter into an installment agreement and the taxpayer uses the accrual basis of accounting, the taxpayer reports the sale price in gross receipts when the revenue is recognized pursuant to generally accepted accounting principles (12 CSR 10-103.560).

¶ 584   Vendor Registration

A seller, including an itinerant or temporary business, responsible for collecting sales tax must obtain a retail sales license from the Director of Revenue before making retail sales (Sec. 144.083, Sec. 144.087.1, 12 CSR 10-3.468). A city or county occupation license or state license required for conducting the business will not be issued before a retail sales license is secured. The retail sales license is valid until revoked or surrendered. Revocation may occur after ten days' notice only if the licensee is in default in the payment of sales tax or personal income withholding taxes for a period of 60 days. Failure to pay within ten days of a default notice results in the issuance of a revocation order that makes the retail sales license null and void (12 CSR 10-3.466). A license will not be reissued until the taxpayer completes a new application, posts bond, files all returns due, and pays all delinquencies. If a retail sales license is revoked, any city or county occupation license or state license is null and void (Sec. 144.083.2).

Consumer cooperatives that purchase goods in quantity and maintain an inventory must have a retail license (12 CSR 10-3.470).

Vendors who sell tangible personal property for storage, use, or consumption in the state must register with the Director of Revenue and give the names and addresses of agents operating in the state and the location of distribution or sales houses, offices, and other places of business in the state (Sec. 144.650, 12 CSR 10-4.070). Contractors purchasing property from out-of-state vendors for use, storage, or consumption in Missouri must register with the Department of Revenue (12 CSR 10-4.075).

Motor vehicle dealers: A motor vehicle dealer may apply to the Director of Revenue to collect the sales tax required on all motor vehicles sold by the dealer. If authorized, the dealer must file a return and remit to the Department of Revenue the tax collected, less a 2% timely filing deduction. Motor vehicle dealers receiving authority to collect and remit sales taxes on motor vehicles are subject to all provisions under the sales tax law and must file a monthly sales tax report. (Sec. 144.060; Sec. 144.070.8)

State contracts: Missouri state agencies may not enter into contracts with any vendor that makes taxable sales in Missouri but fails to collect the sales or use tax due on such transactions (Sec. 34.040.6). This provision also applies to "affiliates of a vendor", which are defined as any person or entity controlled by or under common control with the vendor.

Agreements between the executive branch and any person that exempt the person from the collection of sales and use taxes will be void unless approved by both chambers of the General Assembly (Sec. 144.030(3)).

Disaster assistance: The Facilitating Business Rapid Response to State Declared Disasters Act (Sec. 190.270, *et seq.*) provides that an out-of-state business that is responding to a declared state disaster or emergency or any of its out-of-state employees are not subject to Missouri use tax on equipment used or consumed if the equipment does not remain in the state after the disaster period, unless the out-of-state business or employee remains in Missouri after the conclusion of the disaster period. Also, such a business its out-of-state employees are not subject to Missouri income tax and withholding registration, filing, and remittance requirements, unless the out-of-state business or an out-of-state employee remains in Missouri after the conclusion of the disaster period.

An out-of-state business includes a business that is affiliated with a registered business solely through common ownership if that entity does not have any registrations, tax filings, or nexus in the state before the declared disaster or emergency. A prior registration as an out-of-state business for a declared disaster or emergency must not be considered a registration in Missouri.

• Compliance

By using "data warehousing," the Department of Revenue matches data from a number of outside sources to the Department's internal data to identify businesses and individuals that are either not properly registered, not filing, or not correctly reporting their tax liabilities. The data warehouse, known as the Tax Compliance System, is used for analyzing data to detect noncompliance in all major tax areas, including sales and use tax. Both resident and nonresident individuals and companies will be identified. Once identified, taxpayers that are believed to be not in compliance are contacted, the proper tax liability is determined, and the taxpayer is required to pay the amounts owed along with statutory penalties and interest (*News Release,* Missouri Department of Revenue, August 10, 2005).

¶ 585   Sales or Use Tax Credits

Use tax is not imposed on property that has been subjected to tax by another state except to the extent the use tax imposed in Missouri exceeds the tax imposed in the other state (Sec. 144.615(5), 12 CSR 10-4.100). Insurance proceeds received from the theft or casualty of a motor vehicle, trailer, boat, or outboard motor are allowed as a credit against the purchase price of replacement property (Sec. 144.027.1).

Trades: Property taken in trade is also allowed as a credit against the purchase price (Sec. 144.025.1). When a person trades tangible personal property to a motor vehicle dealer for a motor vehicle or trailer, tax is due on the difference between the price of the motor vehicle or trailer purchased and the amount allowed for the trade-in. If the amount allowed for the trade-in is greater than the purchase price of the motor vehicle or trailer, no tax is due. When a manufacturer's rebate is offered, the tax due is based on the purchase price of the motor vehicle or trailer less the rebate. A trade-in allowance applies only to transactions between a purchaser and a motor vehicle dealer (12 CSR 10-103.350(3)(D)). See also ¶ 577.

• Bad debts

A rule explains when a seller may claim a Missouri sales or use tax credit or refund for tax paid on a sale that has become a bad debt (12 CSR 10-115.100). A seller may file for a credit or refund within the three-year statute of limitations for sales that were reported using the accrual or gross sales method and that have been written off as bad debts for state or federal income tax purposes. Under the accrual or gross sales method, a seller reports a sale and remits the tax at the time of the sale, but the receipts are not received from the buyer until a later date. The three-year limitations period is calculated from the due date of the return or the date the tax was paid, whichever is later. If a bad debt credit or refund is allowed and the debt is later collected, that amount must be reported on the next return as a taxable sale.

The Missouri Supreme Court held that two retailers that sold merchandise that was bought with private label credit cards (PLCC) were not entitled to a Missouri sales tax refund on bad debts that were written off for federal income tax purposes by the PLCC issuer banks. The retailers were legally obligated to remit the tax and eligible to apply for a refund, but only if they suffered a bad debt loss. (*Circuit City Stores, Inc. v. Director of Revenue,* Missouri Supreme Court, Nos. SC93687 and SC93711, July 29, 2014, CCH MISSOURI TAX REPORTS, ¶ 203-904)

¶ 586   Deficiency Assessments

An additional sales or use tax assessment may be made by the Director of Revenue when a return and payment are deemed to be unsatisfactory (Sec. 144.210.2, Sec. 144.210.3, Sec. 144.670, Sec. 144.715). Notice of the assessment must be given to the taxpayer by certified or registered mail at the taxpayer's last known address. The additional assessment may be based on facts contained in the return or on any information in the Director's possession. However, the Director may only base an additional assessment upon a taxpayer's use tax liability if the taxpayer fails to file a return, the Director is of the opinion when examining the accuracy of a taxpayer's return that the taxpayer's books and records are incomplete or illegible, or the taxpayer denies the Director access to books and records when the Director seeks to examine the accuracy of a taxpayer's return.

The timely payment discount is not allowed in calculating an assessment, and interest and penalties are added (12 CSR 10-3.556).

A billing is not an assessment, but is notice that if it is not paid, an assessment will be made (12 CSR 10-3.542).

- **Failure to file return**

Except in cases of fraud or evasion, if a person neglects or refuses to make a return and pay tax, the Director may make an estimate based on information in his or her possession of the gross receipts of the person during the delinquent period and may make an assessment against the person on the basis of the estimated amount (Sec. 144.250.4). The delinquent taxpayer must be given written notice of the assessment by certified or registered mail at the taxpayer's last known address (Sec. 144.250.5).

- **Payment of assessment**

Any sales or use tax assessment is due and payable 60 days after the notice of assessment is mailed to the taxpayer, unless a petition for review is filed with the Administrative Hearing Commission (Sec. 144.230, Sec. 144.720).

¶ 587   Audit Procedures

Books and records, including federal and state income tax returns, required to be kept by taxpayers are subject to inspection by the Director of Revenue during business hours (Sec. 144.320, Sec. 144.640, 12 CSR 10-3.578). A company with a location in Missouri that keeps its records outside the state must, upon request, make available at the Missouri location records pertaining to the Missouri location (12 CSR 10-3.572). The Director may hold investigations and hearings to ascertain the correctness of a return or to determine the amount of tax due, and may examine any books, papers, or records, and compel the attendance of persons with knowledge of relevant facts (Sec. 144.330, Sec. 144.645). A person testifying or producing records under oath at an investigation is immune from prosecution or criminal penalty relating to transactions upon which the person testifies or produces evidence (Sec. 144.340).

- **Exemption certificates**

Sellers must have in their possession and available for inspection all exemption certificates for the period of an audit at the commencement of the audit (12 CSR 10-3.538). However, in appropriate cases, the Department may permit deductions even though exemption certificates were secured after the audit started (12 CSR 10-3.538, 12 CSR 10-4.145).

¶ 588   **Statute of Limitations**

Generally, a notice of additional sales or use tax assessment must be mailed to the taxpayer within three years after the return was filed or required to be filed (Sec. 144.220.3, Sec. 144.720, 12 CSR 10-4.150, 12 CSR 10-4.320). Before the three-year period expires, the Director and a taxpayer may agree in writing to extend the period (Sec. 144.746). An assessment may be made at any time if the taxpayer refuses or neglects to file a return or files a fraudulent return (Sec. 144.220.1).

An Administrative Hearing Commission or court order that stays or suspends the assessment or collection of taxes tolls the statute of limitations (Sec. 136.255).

¶ 589   **Application for Refund**

Taxes, penalties, and interest paid more than once, erroneously or illegally collected or computed, or unconstitutionally imposed or collected must be credited against any taxes due from the person legally obligated to remit the tax, and the balance together with interest must be refunded, provided duplicate copies of a claim for refund are filed within three years from the date of overpayment (Sec. 144.190.2, Sec. 144.696). No refund is to be allowed for any amount of tax paid by a seller that is based upon charges incident to credit card discounts (Sec. 144.100.4).

Before the end of the three-year period for claiming a refund, the taxpayer may make a written agreement with the Director of Revenue to extend the period (Sec. 144.746). Taxes incorrectly computed because of clerical error or mistake on the part of the Director of Revenue are credited against taxes due and the balance is refunded to the person legally obligated to remit the tax (Sec. 144.190.1, Sec. 144.695, Sec. 144.696).

A claim for refund must be in writing under oath and state the specific grounds for the claim (Sec. 144.190.3, Sec. 144.696). Forms are available from the Department of Revenue (12 CSR 10-3.518, 12 CSR 10-4.260). The Director may bring an action against a person who has been erroneously credited or to whom an erroneous refund is made. Funds are set aside by the General Assembly from which refunds are made (Sec. 144.200, Sec. 144.695).

Serial claims: A person legally obligated to remit sales and use tax who has received a refund for a specific issue and subsequently submits a refund claim on the same issue for a tax period beginning on or after the date the original refund check was issued may not receive a refund for the subsequent claim (Sec. 144.90.6). This prohibition does not apply, however, if the additional refund claim is filed due to any of the following: (1) receipt of additional information or an exemption certificate from the purchaser; (2) a decision by a court of competent jurisdiction or the Administrative Hearing Commission; or (3) changes in regulations or policy by the Department of Revenue.

¶ 590   MONTANA

¶ 591   General Sales and Use Taxes Not Imposed

There are no general sales or use taxes imposed by the state of Montana or by local jurisdictions. However, there is a 4% statewide lodging facility use tax (Sec. 15-65-111, MCA), and a limited sales tax may be imposed by resort communities (Sec. 7-6-1502, MCA).

There is also a 3% sales and use tax on accommodations and campgrounds in Montana (Sec. 15-68-102, MCA). This tax is paid in addition to the lodging facility use tax.

Rental vehicles: There is a 4% sales and use tax on the base charge for rental vehicles (Sec. 15-68-102, MCA).

- **Online travel companies**

A Montana appeals court held that charges made by online travel companies (OTCs) for accommodations are not subject to the lodging facility use tax, but are subject to sales tax, and the rental vehicle charges by OTCs are subject to sales tax. Fees charged by the owner or operator of a facility for use of the facility for lodging are subject to a lodging facility use tax.

The court held that the OTCs were not owners or operators for purposes of the tax, because they do not possess, run, control, manage, or direct the functioning of a hotel or rental agency. Sales tax is imposed on a purchaser and must be collected by the seller and is applied to the sales price. As fees received for services rendered, the amount of the charges the OTCs retained as compensation is subject to sales tax. Also, sales tax is imposed on the base charge for rental vehicles. The court found that "base rental charge" and "sales price" are synonyms for sales tax statutory purposes. (*Montana Department of Revenue v. Priceline.com, Inc.,* Montana Supreme Court, No. DA 14-0260, August 12, 2015, CCH Montana Tax Reports, ¶ 401-269)

¶ 606   Scope of Tax

Source.—Statutory references are to Chapters 77 and 81 of the Revised Statutes of Nebraska, as amended to date. Details are reported in the CCH NEBRASKA STATE TAX REPORTS starting at ¶ 60-000.

The sales tax is imposed on gross receipts from retail sales of tangible personal property in Nebraska; the gross receipts of every person engaged as a public utility, a county or community antenna or satellite television service operator, or as a retailer of intellectual or entertainment properties; the gross receipts of any person involved in connecting and installing telephone communication, telegraph, or community antenna or satellite television service; the gross receipts from sales of admissions in Nebraska; and the gross receipts from sales of certain warranties, guarantees, service agreements, or maintenance agreements (Sec. 77-2703(1), Reg. 1-001.01). The sales tax is imposed on the transaction and not on the property sold (Reg. 1-001.02).

The use tax complements the sales tax and is imposed on the storage, use, or other consumption in Nebraska of tangible personal property purchased, leased, or rented from any retailer and on any transaction subject to sales tax when the sales tax has not been paid (Sec. 77-2703(2), Reg. 1-002). Use tax is not imposed on the gross receipts required to be included in the measure of the sales tax on which sales tax has been paid (Sec. 77-2704.29, Reg. 1-002.04A). In addition, no use tax is imposed on the storage, use, or consumption of property acquired outside the state that would be exempt from sales and use tax if acquired in Nebraska or that is used directly in the repair and maintenance of certain transportation equipment (Sec. 77-2704.30, Reg. 1-002.04B, Reg. 1-002.04D).

Digital goods: In conformity with the Streamlined Sales and Use Tax Agreement, retail sales of digital audio works, digital audiovisual works, digital codes, and digital books delivered electronically are subject to tax if the products are taxable when delivered on tangible storage media. (Sec. 77-2701.16(9); Sec. 77-2703; see also *Revenue Ruling 01-11-3,* Nebraska Department of Revenue, August 4, 2011, CCH NEBRASKA TAX REPORTS, ¶ 201-012)

Prepaid telephone calling arrangements: Gross receipts from furnishing telephone communications service do not include the gross income attributable to services rendered using a prepaid telephone calling arrangement (Sec. 77-2702.07(2)(a)). However, the sale of prepaid telephone calling arrangements and the recharge of these arrangements are taxable retail sales (Sec. 77-2701.16(8)).

• **Taxable services**

Services are not generally taxable. However, the following specified service transactions are subject to sales tax: telephone services (including prepaid telephone calling arrangements) and telegraph, gas, electricity, sewer and water services; installations of telephone, telegraph, or community or county antenna television services; sales made by community antenna television service operators, sales of admissions, and sales of certain warranties, service, and maintenance agreements (Sec. 77-2702.07(2), Sec. 77-2702.13(1)(g)). Satellite service operators and satellite service are subject to the same sales and use tax treatment as community antenna television service operators.

The following services are also taxable (Sec. 77-2702.07):

— building cleaning and maintenance, pest control, and security;

— motor vehicle washing, waxing, towing, and painting;

— computer software training;

— installing and applying tangible personal property if the sale of the property is subject to tax;

— repair or maintenance services performed on items subject to sales tax, except motor vehicles;

— services provided by recreational vehicle parks;

— animal specialty services, except for veterinary services and certain services performed on livestock;

— detective services.

Bundled services and property: Tangible personal property used incidentally by service providers in the provision of services is not purchased for resale and is subject to sales tax. Further, the total charge for the services and transferred tangible personal property is considered one transaction even if the two elements are contracted for separately. The following factors are used to determine whether the principal object of the transaction is a transfer of tangible personal property or performance of a service: (1) the object of the buyer; (2) the seller's type of business; (3) whether the tangible personal property was provided as a retail enterprise with a profit-making motive; (4) whether the property could be sold without the service; (5) the extent that the services contributed to the value of the property transferred; and (6) any other relevant factors. If the performance of services is the principal object of the transaction, any tangible personal property transferred is incidental to the services. (*Revenue Ruling 01-08-6*, Nebraska Department of Revenue, October 31, 2008, CCH NEBRASKA TAX REPORTS, ¶ 200-906)

Net metering of electricity: Sales tax is imposed on the gross amount of electricity sold by a local distribution utility to a customer-generator because this sale is a single taxable transaction separate from any sale of excess electricity by the customer-generator to the local distribution utility. As a separately defined transaction, the sale cannot be considered as a trade-in. The sale of excess electricity by the customer-generator to the local distribution utility qualifies as a sale for resale because the local distribution utility purchases the electricity to sell to other customers and sells electricity in the regular course of its business. (*Revenue Ruling 01-10-3*, Nebraska Department of Revenue, August 4, 2010, CCH NEBRASKA TAX REPORTS, ¶ 200-979)

Computer software and services: The gross receipts from the transfer of computer software is taxable, no matter the method of delivery. Services provided by a consultant that are part of the transfer of computer software to the customer are also taxable. In addition, the following software goods and services are taxable:

— service or maintenance contracts;

— software installation and delivery (including the provision of software patches or security updates);

— access codes for specific video games;

— security services; and

— software training if the training is provided in Nebraska by the software retailer. Training provided by the retailer via the Internet is also taxable as long as the person receiving the training is located in Nebraska.

Website development is taxable if the website is transferred on a tangible storage medium to the customer. Cloud computing services are generally not taxable. For additional details, see (*Information Guide 6-511-2011*, Nebraska Sales and Use Tax Guide for Computer Software, Nebraska Department of Revenue, revised January 22, 2014, **http://www.revenue.nebraska.gov/info/6-511.pdf**)

Internet access charges are not taxable (*General Information Letter 1-14-2*, Nebraska Department of Revenue, August 22, 2014, CCH NEBRASKA TAX REPORTS, ¶ 201-196).

Warranties, guarantees, and service and maintenance agreements: The sale of a maintenance agreement is taxable if the property covered by the agreement is taxable.

¶606 Nebraska

The charge remains taxable whether it is included in the sales price of the property, invoiced separately, or purchased at a later date. Charges for maintenance agreements to maintain computer software that include updates, enhancements, modifications, or free or reduced-price upgrades are taxable. Sales of home warranties and maintenance agreements are taxable if they are sold for a nonitemized price and cover both tangible personal property and buildings and fixtures. Tax on a motor vehicle maintenance agreement must be paid to the county treasurer when the vehicle is registered. If it is purchased at a later date, tax is due at the time the agreement is sold. Both mandatory and optional agreements are taxable.

The following maintenance agreements and charges are exempt:

— agreements covering only real estate, fixtures, or structures;

— agreements covering agricultural machinery and equipment used in commercial agriculture;

— agreements covering exempt durable medical equipment, mobility-enhancing equipment, and prosthetic devices;

— charges for help desk or technical support services for software that are provided separately from a maintenance agreement, so long as no updates or enhancements are provided;

— reimbursement received by a dealer from a vehicle manufacturer when the dealer provides a loaner vehicle to a customer when repairs are performed under a maintenance agreement; and

— agreements covering exempt manufacturing machinery and equipment.

For a maintenance agreement covering tangible personal property that does not provide full coverage of parts and repair labor, any amount charged to the customer is taxable. (*Information Guide 6-516-2013,* Nebraska Sales and Use Tax Guide for Warranties, Guarantees, Service, and Maintenance Agreements, Nebraska Department of Revenue, October, 2014, **http://www.revenue.nebraska.gov/info/6-516.pdf**)

• **Incidence of tax**

The sales tax is imposed on the consumer, although the retailer is required to collect the tax (Sec. 77-2703(1)(a), Reg. 1-001.03). The tax required to be collected is a debt owed by the retailer to the state.

The use tax is imposed on the person storing, using, or otherwise consuming in Nebraska tangible personal property purchased from a retailer (Sec. 77-2703(2)(a)), although retailers engaged in business in the state must collect the tax (Sec. 77-2703(2)(b)).

Drop shipments: When all the parties are located in the state, the retailer furnishes a resale certificate to the primary seller, rendering the first sale a nontaxable transaction. The retailer then collects sales tax on behalf of the state on the secondary sale to its customer. However, different considerations arise when one or more of the parties are not within the state. A Nebraska manufacturer (primary seller) who makes a sale to an out-of-state retailer not doing business in Nebraska and who then delivers the product to the retailer's Nebraska customer is required to collect sales tax from the retailer unless a resale certificate is submitted. (Sec. 77-2701.32; Sec. 77-2701.34; Reg. 1-006)

Nebraska does not, like most states, collapse the three-party, two-sale drop shipment situation into a single taxable event. In addition to holding the primary seller taxable on the sale to an out-of-state retailer, the state also requires the ultimate consumer to pay use tax on the basis of the retail price paid. (Reg. 1-006)

• **Nexus**

Every retailer engaged in business in Nebraska who sells, leases, or rents tangible personal property for storage, use, or other consumption in the state must collect the tax due from the purchaser (Sec. 77-2703(2)(b)). "Business" means any activity engaged in by any person with the object of gain, benefit, or advantage (Sec. 77-2701.07).

"Engaged in business in the state" means any of the following (Sec. 77-2701.13; Reg. 1-004.02):

— maintaining, occupying, or using, permanently or temporarily, directly or indirectly, or through a subsidiary or agent, an office, place of distribution, sales or sample room or place, warehouse, storage place, or other place of business in the state;

— having any representative, agent, salesperson, canvasser, or solicitor operating in the state under the authority of the retailer or its subsidiary for the purpose of selling, delivering, or taking orders for any tangible personal property;

— deriving rentals from a lease of tangible personal property in the state by any retailer;

— soliciting retail sales of tangible personal property from Nebraska residents on a continuous, regular, or systematic basis by means of advertising that is broadcast or relayed from a transmitter within the state or distributed from a location within the state;

— soliciting orders from residents of the state for tangible personal property by mail, if the solicitations are continuous, regular, seasonal, or systematic and if the retailer benefits from any banking, financing, debt collection, or marketing activities occurring in the state or benefits from the location in the state of authorized installation, servicing, or repair facilities;

— being owned or controlled by the same interests that own or control any retailer engaged in business in the same or similar line of business in the state; or

— maintaining or having a franchisee or licensee operating under the retailer's trade name in Nebraska if the franchisee or licensee is required to collect the tax.

• Streamlined Act status

Nebraska has enacted the Uniform Sales and Use Tax Administration Act, the product of the Streamlined Sales Tax Project. Nebraska is a full member of the Streamlined Sales and Use Tax Agreement with a seat on the Governing Board. It has enacted all of the provisions necessary to comply with the Agreement's requirements and these provisions currently are in effect (Sec. 77-2712.03). As a full member, it may vote on amendments to or interpretations of the Agreement, and sellers registering under the SST system must collect and remit tax on sales into the state. For additional information, see ¶ 612.

Taxability matrix: Nebraska maintains a chart of the sales and use tax treatment of various items that may be found at **www.streamlinedsalestax.org**.

Border states compact: The Nebraska Department of Revenue publishes a guide on the Midwest Border States Compact explaining the sales and use tax responsibilities of out-of-state vendors doing business in Nebraska. The Midwest Border States Compact is a group of states working together to increase compliance by informing consumers about use tax and seeking voluntary registration from out-of-state businesses. Besides Nebraska, the group is composed of Illinois, Iowa, Kansas, Minnesota, Missouri, North Dakota, and South Dakota. The guide provides examples of activities that create nexus and explains the process of applying for a license in another state. The guide can be viewed on the department's Web site at **http://www.revenue.ne.gov/ info/7-227.pdf**.

¶606 Nebraska

¶ 607   Tax Base

The sales tax is imposed on gross receipts (Sec. 77-2703(1), Reg. 1-001.01, Reg. 1-006.06) and the use tax is imposed on the sales, lease, or rental price (Sec. 77-2703(2), Reg. 1-002.07, Reg. 1-018.01).

- **"Gross receipts" defined**

"Gross receipts" mean the total amount of the sale, lease, or rental price of the retail sales of retailers valued in money whether received in money or otherwise, without deduction for:

(1) the cost of property sold,

(2) the cost of materials used, labor or service cost, interest paid, losses, or any other expense,

(3) transportation costs prior to sale,

(4) any excise or property tax levied against the property except as otherwise provided in the law, and

(5) charges for warranties, guarantees, or maintenance agreements.

However, a deduction may be taken for the cost of property sold if the retailer has purchased the property for some purpose other than resale, has reimbursed the vendor for tax that the vendor is required to pay to the state or has paid use tax with respect to the property, and has resold the property before making any use of it other than retention, demonstration, or display while holding it for sale in the regular course of business. (Sec. 77-2702.07(1), Reg. 1-007.01)

- **Sales price**

"Sales price" means the total amount for which property is sold valued in money whether paid in money or otherwise, without any deduction for (1) the cost of the property sold, (2) the cost of materials, labor or service costs, interest paid, losses, or any other expense, (3) transportation costs, (4) the cost of computer software contained on the property, and (5) the cost of any license, franchise, or lease for the use of computer software or entertainment properties such as videotapes or movie films (Sec. 77-2702.17(1)). "Sales price" also includes any services that are a part of the sale and any amount for which credit is given to the purchaser by the seller.

When merchandise is purchased with silver coins having an actual value in excess of their face amount, the sales tax is imposed on the fair market value of the merchandise (Ruling No. 1-80-1).

- **"Rental price" or "lease price" defined**

"Rental price" or "lease price" means the total amount for which property is rented or leased, with rent or lease payments set at a fair market value valued in money whether paid in money or otherwise, without deduction for:

(1) the cost of the property,

(2) the cost of material, labor or service cost, interest, losses, or any other expense, and

(3) transportation costs.

"Rental price" or "lease price" also includes services that are a part of the lease or rental and any amount for which credit is given to the lessee by the lessor or renter. (Sec. 77-2702.12)

- **Sourcing**

In conformity with the Streamlined Sales and Use Tax Agreement (¶ 612), sales are sourced generally to the destination of the product sold, with a default to origin-based sourcing in the absence of that information. Special sourcing rules apply to sales of vehicles, transportation equipment, and telecommunications. The following general sourcing rules apply:

— when the property is received by the purchaser at a business location of the retailer, the sale is sourced to that business location;

— when the property is not received by the purchaser at a business location of the retailer, the sale is sourced to the location where receipt by the purchaser, or the purchaser's designated donee, occurs;

— if neither of the above apply, the sale is sourced to the location indicated by an address or other information for the purchaser that is available from the business records of the retailer that are maintained in the ordinary course of the retailer's business when use of this address does not constitute bad faith;

— if none of the above apply, the sale is sourced to the location indicated by an address for the purchaser obtained during the consummation of the sale, including the address of a purchaser's payment instrument, if no other address is available, when use of this address does not constitute bad faith;

— if none of the other rules apply, including the circumstance in which the retailer is without sufficient information to apply the previous rules, then the location will be determined by the address from which tangible personal property was shipped, from which the digital good or the computer software delivered electronically was first available for transmission by the retailer, or from which the service was provided.

Leases and rentals of motor vehicles: The sales and use tax on lease and rental payments of motor vehicles is sourced to the primary property location associated with each lease payment (*Information Guide 3-373-1998,* Nebraska Sales Tax on Leased Vehicles, Nebraska Department of Revenue, October, 2014, **http://www.revenue.nebraska.gov/info/6-373.pdf**).

Direct mail: The sourcing of "advertising and promotional direct mail" is distinguished from the sourcing of "other direct mail" (Sec. 77-2703.03). "Advertising and promotional direct mail" means direct mail that has the primary purpose of attracting attention to a product, person, business, or organization or attempting to sell or secure financial support for a product, person, business, or organization (Sec. 77-2703.03(2)). In the circumstance where the purchaser fails to provide a direct pay permit or a list of jurisdictions for delivery, "other direct mail" will be sourced to the purchaser's address (Sec. 77-2703.03(3)). The default sourcing option for "advertising and promotional direct mail" will remain the shipping point.

U.S. postage charges for the delivery of direct mail are exempt from Nebraska sales and use taxes if they are separately stated on the invoice or bill of sale. The exemption applies to all types of direct mail, whether deemed advertising and promotional direct mail or other direct mail. (Sec. 77-2701.11; *Revenue Ruling 01-14-1,* Nebraska Department of Revenue, May 5, 2014, CCH NEBRASKA TAX REPORTS, ¶ 201-163)

¶ 608   List of Exemptions, Exceptions, and Exclusions

Unless otherwise indicated, the statutory exemptions, exceptions, and exclusions listed below apply to both sales and use taxes. Items that are excluded from the sales or use tax base are treated at ¶ 607, "Tax Base." A chart of sales tax exemptions may be viewed on the department's website at **http://www.revenue.nebraska.gov/question/exempt_sales_chart.html**

Conformity to Streamlined Agreement: Nebraska has conformed its definitions to those in the Streamlined Sales and Use Tax Agreement (see ¶ 612). Numerous previously nonconforming definitions have been amended to conform to the Agreement. For example, the exemption for "food and food products" has been amended to exempt "food and food ingredients."

- **Sales and use exemptions, exceptions, and exclusions**

Admissions charged by nonprofit organizations conducting school and/or certain sports events	Sec. 77-2704.10(6)-(8)
Admissions and memberships to nonprofit zoos and aquariums	Sec. 77-2701.04(3)
Advertising supplements distributed with newspapers	Sec. 77-2704.07
Agricultural chemicals, machinery, and equipment	Sec. 77-2704.36, Sec. 77-2704.37
Agricultural machinery, repair or replacement parts for	Sec. 77-2704.64
Aircraft delivered in state to nonresident	Sec. 77-2704.26
Aircraft fuel	Sec. 77-2704.03
Airport authorities, purchases by	Sec. 77-2704.15
Animal life whose products constitute food	Sec. 77-2702.13(2)(b)
Aquariums (nonprofit), purchases by	Sec. 77-2701.04(3)
Automobile museums (historic)	Sec. 77-2704.65
Biomass energy projects (C-BED)	Sec. 77-2704.57
Bullion and currency	Sec. 77-2704.66
Carrier engaged in multistate operations	Sec. 77-2706(6)
Cement manufacturing supplies	Sec. 77-2702.13(2)(a)
Chemicals for agriculture	Sec. 77-2702.13(2)(b)
Child-caring or child placement agency	Sec. 77-2704.12(1), Sec. 77-2704.12(2)
Church meals	Sec. 77-2704.10(2)
Coin-operated machine laundry and cleaning receipts	Sec. 77-2704.14
Common and contract carrier motor vehicles, watercraft, and aircraft	Sec. 77-2702.13(2)(f)
Construction services and building materials by a housing agency . .	Sec. 77-2704.15
Construction labor	Sec. 77-2704.55(1)
Containers	Sec. 77-2702.13(2)(c)
Contractor appointed as purchasing agent by exempt organization . .	Sec. 77-2704.12(3)
Court reporter transcripts	Sec. 77-2704.58
Customized molds, dies, and patterns	Sec. 77-2704.40
Data center property for use outside Nebraska	Sec. 77-2704.62
Diesel and compressed fuels	Sec. 77-2704.05
Direct mail postage	Sec. 77-2701.11
Energy for hospitals	Sec. 77-2704.13(2)
Energy for irrigation or farming	Sec. 77-2704.13(1)
Energy for manufacturing, processing, or refining	Sec. 77-2704.13(2)
Energy to produce electricity	Sec. 77-2704.13(2)
Energy to produce vehicle fuel by compression of natural gas	Sec. 77-2704.13(2)
Feed for animal life	Sec. 77-2704.41
Food and food ingredients	Sec. 77-2704.24
Fuels for irrigation or farming	Sec. 77-2704.13(1)
Fuels for manufacturing, processing, or refining	Sec. 77-2704.13(2)
Game birds	Sec. 77-2704.46
Government, purchases or lease-purchases of property by	Sec. 77-2704.15(1)

¶ 609   Rate of Tax

The Nebraska sales and use tax rate is 5.5% (Sec. 77-2701.02, Sec. 77-2703, Reg. 1-002.07).

The Tax Commissioner meets with representatives of the legislature within 10 days after July 15 and November 15 of each year to determine whether the sales and use tax rate should be changed (Sec. 77-2715.01). If it is determined that the rate must be changed, the representatives must petition the Governor to call a special session of the legislature to make the necessary rate change.

Sales tax is imposed at the rate in effect at the time the gross receipts are realized under the retailer's accounting method (Sec. 77-2703(1), Reg. 1-016), and use tax is imposed at the rate in effect when a person's liability for the tax becomes certain under its accounting method (Sec. 77-2703(2)(a), Reg. 1-016). Cash basis retailers collect and report tax at the rate in effect at the time cash payments are received, even though the payments are in satisfaction of an obligation predating a rate change. An accrual basis taxpayer collects and reports tax at the rate existing at the time the sale is recorded.

Prepaid wireless surcharge: Each seller of prepaid wireless telecommunications services must collect from the consumer on each retail transaction, a prepaid wireless surcharge. The seller must disclose the amount of the surcharge on an invoice, receipt, or other similar document. The amount of the surcharge is not included in the base for measuring any tax, surcharge, or fee charged by the state or a political subdivision of the state. The Department of Revenue will determine the surcharge on an annual basis, effective January 1. (Sec. 86-903)

The rate of the surcharge is 1% from January 1, 2017 to December 31, 2017, unchanged from the previous year.

• Lodging tax

In addition to the sales and use tax, Nebraska imposes a lodging tax at the rate of 1% upon the total consideration charged for hotel room occupancy (Sec. 81-1253); *Information Guide 8-364-1980, Nebraska Lodging Tax* (Rev. 2015), Nebraska Department of Revenue, **http://www.revenue.nebraska.gov/info/5-141.pdf**.

¶ 610   Local Taxes

An incorporated municipality may impose a sales and use tax at a rate of 0.5%, 1%, 1.5%, 1.75%, or 2% (Sec. 77-27,142). Hovever, a city of the metropolitan class (*i.e.*, Omaha) may not impose a local sales tax above 1.5%.

Counties may impose a hotel occupancy sales tax at a rate not exceeding 2% of the total charged for occupancy in a hotel (Sec. 81-1254).

Mobile telecommunications: Nebraska conforms to the provisions of the federal Mobile Telecommunications Sourcing Act (P.L. 106-252), effective for billing periods ending on or after August 1, 2002 (Sec. 13-326(2)(b), Sec. 77-2702.07(2)(a), and Sec. 77-27,147(2)). Mobile telecommunications services are sourced to the customer's "place of primary of use," which is the residential or primary business address of the customer and must be located within the service area of the home service provider.

Municipal counties: One or more counties and at least one municipality in each county may create a local governing body, called a municipal county, that has the authority to levy a local Nebraska sales and use tax and property tax. Subject to voter approval, a municipal county may impose a sales and use tax of 0.5%, 1.0%, or 1.5% on transactions within the county that are subject to state sales and use tax (Sec. 13-2813).

• Local tax rates

The Nebraska Department of Revenue maintains a local sales tax rate finder on its website at **http://www.revenue.nebraska.gov/ratefinder.html**. Rates may be looked up by address or ZIP code.

¶ 611   Bracket Schedule

Computation of sales or use tax must be carried to the third decimal place and rounded down to a whole cent whenever the third decimal place is four or less and rounded up to a whole cent whenever the third decimal place is greater than four (Sec. 77-3,117(3)). Retailers may compute tax on any transaction on either an item or invoice basis.

The Tax Commissioner has the duty to prescribe bracket schedules for the use of retailers in collecting tax from consumers (Sec. 77-2703(1)(d), Reg. 1-011). Sales tax rate cards for any county or city in Nebraska are available for printing at **http://www.dort.mo.gov/tax/business/sales/taxcards/**.

Even though retail sales may be made without the imposition of tax, *e.g.,* sales of less than 10¢, the receipts from such sales are still includible in the tax base upon which the retailer must compute and remit the tax (Reg. 1-011.03). Tax is computed on the combined total of all items purchased, rather than on each separate item.

When more than one item is purchased, the tax may be computed on the total amount of the combined taxable purchases or on the individual items. However, when the tax is allowed to be included in the amount of the purchase, the tax is computed on each item separately, rather than on the total of all purchases (Reg. 1-011.04).

¶ 612   **Returns, Payments, and Due Dates**

Returns must be filed by every retailer liable for collection of sales tax, every retailer engaged in business in Nebraska, and every person whose purchase of personal property is subject to use tax but who has not paid the use tax to a retailer required to collect the tax (Sec. 77-2708(1)(b)(ii)).

Returns generally are due on the 20th day of the succeeding month (Sec. 77-2708(1)(b)(i)). Returns must be accompanied by the tax due (Sec. 77-2708(1)(a), Sec. 77-2708(1)(b)(i), Sec. 77-2708(1)(c)). Annual returns are required if the yearly tax liability is less than $900, and quarterly returns are required if a taxpayer's yearly tax liability is between $900 and $3,000. Seasonal retailers whose yearly tax liability is $900 or more may be granted special permission to file annual returns. The Commissioner may require a particular taxpayer to file returns and pay tax for periods other than monthly periods.

A return must be signed by the person required to file the return or by the person's authorized agent (Sec. 77-2708(1)(b)(iii), Reg. 1-010.04).

Collection allowance: Vendors and other taxpayers may deduct and withhold 2.5% of the first $3,000 of taxes remitted each month as reimbursement for the cost of collecting the tax. (Sec. 77-2703(2)(d) and Sec. 77-2708(1)(d)).

Individual use tax returns: If sales tax is not collected by the seller on any taxable sale, the purchaser must remit the use tax directly to the state. Examples of sales that may require the remittance of use tax are the purchase of digital goods, and of items via the Internet, the home shopping channel, or by mail order without the payment of sales tax. Individual use tax can be reported on Form 1040N or Nebraska and Local Individual Use Tax Return, Form 3.

• **Electronic funds transfer (EFT)**

Electronic filing of returns and payment by electronic fund transfer are required for any taxpayer whose payments of any tax for the prior year exceeded a specified amount (Sec. 77-1784). The EFT threshold was reduced from $9,000 to $8,000 in July 2014, to $7,000 in July 2015, to $6,000 in July 2016, and is scheduled to be reduced to $5,000 in July 2017 (Sec. 77-1784). The Commissioner may allow annual, semiannual, or quarterly returns for any retailer making monthly remittances or payment of taxes by EFT (Sec. 77-2708(1)(b)(i)). If the difference between the amount paid and the amount due, as reconciled at least once a year, is more than 10% of the amount paid, a penalty of 50% of the unpaid amount is imposed.

The Tax Commissioner may accept electronically filed applications and other documents required to be filed with the Tax Commissioner (Sec. 77-1784). The Tax Commissioner may establish criteria for electronic filings and may refuse to accept electronic filings or payments that do not satisfy the criteria or that are made before the criteria are established.

Electronic payment methods: The U.S. Bank is the data collection service for Nebraska taxpayers scheduling ACH (Automated Clearing House) debit tax payments to the Nebraska Department of Revenue. Two methods of entering payment information are available. The first method is similar to an electronic check where all financial information must be entered for each transaction. In the second method, called the "registered method," information is stored on behalf of the taxpayer. Retrieval is based upon the Nebraska State ID number and password. A web-based filing system is available at **http://www.revenue.nebraska.gov/electron/bus_e-pay.html**. An identical password must be used for all payments being made for all tax programs that have the same Nebraska identification number. Any changes to banking or other information must be made by the taxpayer when scheduling a payment.

Additional information on EFT and e-filing requirements can be found at **http://www.revenue.state.ne.us/electron/mandate_info.html**.

- **Direct payment permits**

The Tax Commissioner may issue direct payment permits authorizing certain taxpayers to pay state and local sales and use taxes directly to the state in lieu of paying the taxes to the seller. The permits may be issued to any person who annually purchases at least $3 million of taxable property, excluding purchases for which a resale certificate could be used and purchases of motor vehicles. (Sec. 77-2705.01; *Direct Payment Permits,* Nebraska Department of Revenue, January 9, 2014, **http://www.revenue.nebraska.gov/info/direct_pay.html**)

Managed compliance agreement: The Tax Commissioner may enter into a managed compliance agreement with a holder of a direct payment permit if the holder makes monthly sales or use tax payments by electronic funds transfer. The agreement establishes a percentage of purchases that are presumed to be taxable. If the difference between the amount of taxes paid under the agreement and the estimated actual tax liability of the taxpayer is within agreed-upon limits for a tax period, no additional tax payment will be required and no refund will be allowed. However, if the difference is not within agreed-upon limits, the difference must be remitted or refunded with interest. The amount of taxes paid must be between 95% and 105% of the taxpayer's estimated actual tax liability. The percentage of purchases that are presumed taxable will be adjusted as necessary to result in substantially all of the taxpayer's tax liability being paid each year (Sec. 77-2705.05).

- **Uniform Sales and Use Tax Administration Act**

Nebraska has enacted the Uniform Sales and Use Tax Administration Act, the product of the Streamlined Sales Tax Project (SSTP), and has conformed its laws to the related Streamlined Sales and Use Tax Agreement to simplify and modernize sales and use tax administration in order to substantially reduce the burden of tax compliance for all sellers and for all types of commerce. For complete information, see **http://www.revenue.nebraska.gov/streamline/streamline.html**

Bad debts: "Bad debt" is as defined in IRC Sec. 166, except it does not include: (1) financing charges or interest, (2) sales or use taxes charged on the purchase price, (3) uncollectable amounts on property that remains in the possession of a seller until the full purchase price is paid, (4) expenses incurred in attempting to collect any debt, or (5) repossessed property (Sec. 77-2708(j)). If the taxpayer subsequently collects a debt, in whole or in part, for which a deduction had been claimed, the tax on the amount collected must be reported and claimed on the return filed for the period in which the collection was made.

¶ 613   **Prepayment of Taxes**

There are no sales and use tax provisions concerning prepayment of taxes.

¶ 614   **Vendor Registration**

All retailers selling, leasing, or renting tangible personal property for storage, use, or other consumption in Nebraska must register with the Tax Commissioner (Sec. 77-2705(1)). Information that must be furnished includes the name and address of all agents operating in the state, the name and address of any officer, director, partner, limited liability company (LLC) member, employee (other than an employee whose duties are purely ministerial in nature), and any person with a substantial interest in the retailer, who is or who will be responsible for the collection or remittance of the sales tax; the location of all distribution or sales houses, offices or other places of business in the state, other information required by the Commissioner, and if the retailer is an individual, the retailer's social security number.

Any person desiring to engage in or to conduct business as a seller in Nebraska must apply for a permit for each place of business (Sec. 77-2705(3), Reg. 1-004). An application for a permit must be made on a form prescribed by the Commissioner, must set forth the name and location of the business, must provide other information as required by the Commissioner, and must be signed by the an owner and include his or her social security number if the owner is a natural person (Sec. 77-2705(4)). In the case of a corporation, the application must be signed by an executive officer or some person authorized by the corporation to sign tax-related applications. There is no application fee.

An applicant will be issued a separate permit for each place of business (Sec. 77-2705(5), Reg. 1-004). A permit is not assignable and is valid only for the person in whose name it is issued and only for transacting business at the designated place.

Online registration: To register under the Streamlined Sales and Use Tax Agreement, sellers must go to **https://www.sstregister.org**. Sellers can also update previously submitted registration information at this website. The information provided will be sent to all of the full member states and to associate members for which the seller chooses to collect.

Contractors: Before performing any construction work in Nebraska, a contractor is required to be registered on the Contractor Registration Database at **http://dol.nebraska.gov/conreg**.

• Out-of-state disaster responders

The Facilitating Business Rapid Response to State Declared Disasters Act provides that an out-of-state business assisting in repairing, renovating, installing, or building infrastructure related to a declared state disaster or emergency is not subject to registration with the Secretary of State or withholding or income tax registration, filing, or remitting requirements. A declared state disaster or emergency is "a disaster or emergency event for which a Governor's state of emergency proclamation has been issued or that the President of the United States has declared to be a major disaster or emergency." (Uncodified L.B. 913, Laws 2016)

An out-of-state business or its out-of-state employees providing assistance in Nebraska related to a declared disaster or emergency during a disaster period also is not subject to sales, use, or *ad valorem* taxes on equipment brought into the state temporarily for use or consumption during the disaster period if such equipment does not remain in the state after the disaster period. (Uncodified L.B. 913, Laws 2016)

¶ 615 **Sales or Use Tax Credits**

Nebraska use tax is not imposed on property that has been subjected to a sales or use tax by another state at a rate equal to or greater than the Nebraska rate if the other state grants a reciprocal exclusion or exemption to similar transactions in Nebraska, but use tax is imposed to the extent that Nebraska's rate exceeds the other state's rate (Sec. 77-2704.31, Reg. 1-002.04C, Reg. 1-071). The credit is first applied against the use tax due the state, and secondly to the use tax due a subdivision.

Other credits are provided to contractors appointed as purchasing agents who incorporate tax-paid inventory items into a project (Sec. 77-2704.12(3)) and to taxpayers qualifying under the Employment Expansion and Investment Incentive Act and the Employment and Investment Growth Act (Sec. 77-27,188, Sec. 77-4104).

Refunds for pollution control facilities, generation of electricity from renewable energy resources, and redevelopment or tourism development projects are discussed at ¶ 619.

The Nebraska Advantage Act, the Nebraska Advantage Rural Development Act, and similar programs provide various tax incentives based on the amount of a taxpayer's investment, hiring and wages paid in the state (Sec. 77-27, 187; Sec. 77-5701; *Revenue Ruling 29-14-1,* Nebraska Department of Revenue, October 24, 2014, CCH NEBRASKA TAX REPORTS, ¶ 201-1942). The incentives include a total or partial refund of sales and use taxes, as well as a refundable credit against corporate or personal income tax or personal income tax withholding, and a personal property tax exemption for qualifying personal property (Sec. 77-5725).

The deduction of local option sales tax refunds made pursuant to the Employment and Investment Growth Act or the Nebraska Advantage Act from sales taxes remitted to municipalities is delayed for one year after the refund is made to the taxpayer (Sec. 27-77, 144).

- **Research and development credit**

A business firm that makes expenditures in research and experimental activities (as defined in IRC Sec. 174) may claim a credit of 3% of the amount the business firm spends on research and experimental activities in the state in the tax year in excess of the base amount. The base amount is the average amount expended in research and experimental activities by the business firm in the state in the two tax years immediately preceding the first tax year in which the credit is claimed. The credit may be claimed for five consecutive tax years. (Sec. 77-5803).

The credit may be used to obtain a refund of sales and use taxes paid before the end of the tax year for which the credit was allowed, but the amount refunded cannot exceed the amount of the sales and use taxes paid by the taxpayer on the qualifying expenditures (Sec. 77-5804).

¶ 616   Deficiency Assessments

The Tax Commissioner may make deficiency determinations when not satisfied with the amount of tax shown due on returns or when no returns are filed (Sec. 77-2709(1), Sec. 77-2709(2)). A penalty equal to the greater of 10% of the deficiency or $25 is added to each deficiency determination, except that the penalty is increased to the greater of 25% of the deficiency or $50 if there is fraud or intent to evade tax (Sec. 77-2709(1), Sec. 77-2709(2), Sec. 77-2709(4)). The Commissioner may offset overpayments for one period against underpayments for other periods when making a determination. Interest is also imposed on the amount of the deficiency (Sec. 77-2709(3)).

Taxpayers generally have 60 days from the date of postmark of a Notice of Deficiency Determination to file a petition for redetermination. (Reg. 33-003.01(C); See *Information Guide 7-149-1979, How to Protest a Notice of Deficiency Determination,* Nebraska Department of Revenue, May 12, 2014, **http://www.revenue.nebraska.gov/info/7-149.pdf**)

A flowchart on the refund, protest, and appeals process can be viewed on the department's website at **http://www.revenue.nebraska.gov/info/appeal_flowchart.pdf**.

¶ 617   Audit Procedures

The Tax Commissioner may examine the books, papers, records, and equipment of any person selling tangible personal property and any person liable for use tax to verify the accuracy of any return or to determine the amount required to be paid (Sec. 77-2711(4), Reg. 1-008.06). In such an examination, an inquiry will be made regarding the accuracy of the reporting of city sales and use taxes and the accuracy of the allocation of the tax due among the various cities and villages. A taxpayer may keep its books and records outside the state, but must make them available to the Commissioner at all times (Sec. 77-2711(5)).

For use tax purposes, the Commissioner may also require the filing of reports by any person who has information relating to taxable sales of property (Sec. 77-2711(6), Reg. 1-008.05).

Municipal audits: Upon written request to the Tax Commissioner, a municipality that has imposed a local option sales tax may certify an employee to inspect confidential tax records of businesses with a sales tax permit for locations within the boundaries of that municipality. The information must be viewed at the premises of the Department of Revenue. The employee certified for such an inspection may not disclose any information obtained during the review. If a disclosure occurs, the employee will be subject to a Class I misdemeanor. (Sec. 77-2711(14))

¶ 618   Statute of Limitations

A notice of a deficiency determination must be personally served or mailed within three years after the last day of the calendar month following the period for which the amount is proposed to be determined or three years after the return is filed, whichever period expires later (Sec. 77-2709(5)(c)). If a return is not filed, a notice of determination must be mailed or personally served within five years after the last day of the calendar month following the period for which the amount is proposed to be determined.

A determination may be made for a discontinued business at any time thereafter within the period of limitations, without regard to whether the determination is issued before the due date of the liability (Sec. 77-2709(6)).

• **Prosecutions**

Prosecution must be instituted within three years after an offense is committed (Sec. 77-2713(6)). When the offense is the failure to act before a certain date, a prosecution must be commenced no later than three years after that date. Venue is proper in any county where the person or corporation to whose liability the proceeding relates resides or has a place of business or in any county in which the criminal act is committed.

¶ 619   Application for Refund

The Tax Commissioner may credit an overpayment of tax against any amount then due and payable from the taxpayer and refund the balance (Sec. 77-2708(2)(a)). However, no refund is allowed unless a claim is filed on a form prescribed by the Commissioner within three years from the required filing date following the close of the period for which the overpayment was made, within six months after any determination becomes final, or within six months from the date of overpayment with respect to such determinations, whichever expires later (Sec. 77-2708(2)(b)). Failure to timely file a claim constitutes a waiver of any demand against the state on account of overpayment. No refund of less than $2 will be made (Sec. 77-2708(2)(c)).

A flowchart on the refund, protest, and appeals process can be viewed on the department's website at **http://www.revenue.nebraska.gov/info/ appeal_flowchart.pdf**.

Air or water pollution control facilities: The owner of an air or water pollution control facility may apply to the Tax Commissioner for a refund of sales and use tax that it or a contractor has paid on the purchase of tangible personal property incorporated into the facility (Sec. 77-27,150). Before an applicant applies for a refund, the Department of Environmental Quality must find that the facility is designed and operated primarily for control, capture, abatement, or removal of industrial or agricultural waste from air or water and is suitable, adequate, and meets the standards and regulations adopted pursuant to the Environmental Protection Act (Sec. 77-27,151).

An application for refund must be filed within three years of the date of payment of the sales and use tax. The law and regulations state what information is required to be included in the application (Reg. 1-084.04). If a refund claimant desires a hearing, a request must be made when the claim is filed or before the Tax Commissioner takes action on the claim.

Generation of electricity in a renewable electric generation facility: A sales and use tax refund or income tax credit may be claimed by an electrical generating facility located in Nebraska that is first placed into service on or after July 14, 2006, with a rated production of one megawatt or greater and that utilizes eligible renewable resources as its fuel source (Sec. 77-27,235). Eligible renewable resources are wind, moving water, solar, geothermal, fuel cell, methane gas, or photovoltaic technology.

The amount of the renewable energy tax credit or refund is calculated as follows (Sec. 77-27,235(1)):

— For electricity generated on or after July 14, 2006 and before January 1, 2010 the credit was equal to .075 cent for each kilowatt-hour of electricity generated by a new zero-emission facility;

— For electricity generated on or after January 1, 2010 and before January 1, 2013, the credit was equal to .05 cent for each kilowatt-hour of electricity generated by a new zero-emission facility; or

— For electricity generated on or after January 1, 2013 and before January 1, 2018, the credit is equal to .025 cent for each kilowatt-hour of electricity generated by a new zero-emission facility.

The credit or refund may be earned for production of electricity for ten years after the date that the facility is placed in operation beginning on or after June 12, 2006 (Sec. 77-27,235(2)).

A claim to use the credit to obtain a refund of the state sales and use taxes paid, either directly or indirectly, by the producer may be filed quarterly for electricity generated during the previous quarter by the 20th day of the month following the end of the calendar quarter. The amount refunded may not exceed the amount of the state sales and use taxes paid during the quarter (Sec. 77-27,235(3)).

Redevelopment or tourism development projects: The Nebraska Advantage Transformational Tourism and Redevelopment Act, provides incentives for development projects (Sec. 77-1031). The program, which requires approval by municipal voters, permits proceeds from the local option sales tax to be used for redevelopment or tourism development projects in the local area. A taxpayer who meets the requirements in the project agreement will be entitled to a refund of local option sales tax up to a rate of 1.5% for purchases on which the tax is levied within the project boundaries during each year of the "entitlement period". The entitlement period means the year during which the required investment and increases in employment are met and each year thereafter until the end of the ninth year following the year of the application. The four investment tiers for a tourism development project range from investments of $10 million up to $50 million. The investment tiers for a redevelopment project involve an investment of at least $7.5 million or $10 million. If a taxpayer fails to meet the project requirements by the end of the fourth year after the application was submitted or throughout the entitlement period, the municipality may recapture some or all of the incentives provided to the taxpayer. (Sec. 77-1031)

Other refund opportunities: For credits that may be claimed as refunds, see also ¶ 615.

¶ 620   NEVADA

¶ 621   Scope of Tax

Source.—Statutory references are to Chapters 372 and 374 of the Nevada Revised Statutes, as amended to date. Details are reported in the CCH NEVADA STATE TAX REPORTS starting at ¶ 60-000.

The Nevada sales tax is a general tax levied on the gross receipts from sales at retail of tangible personal property or on its lease or rental and on the furnishing of specified services (Sec. 372.060, Sec. 372.105). The use tax on consumption, use, or storage of tangible personal property in the state is a complementary tax and does not apply in situations in which the sales tax is collected (Sec. 372.345).

• Services subject to tax

Because the tax is related to sales or use of tangible personal property, receipts from services are generally not subject to tax. However, when services are rendered to fabricate tangible personal property from materials furnished by the customer, such services are considered taxable sales (Sec. 372.060(3), Sec. 374.060).

• Use tax

The use tax is imposed on the use, storage, or consumption in Nevada of tangible personal property; this tax complements the sales tax and is not levied when the sales tax is imposed (Sec. 372.190, Sec. 374.195). The use tax is also imposed on property that has been purchased tax free for resale and is later consumed, rather than resold, by the purchaser.

A user becomes and remains liable for the use tax unless the user has paid the tax to the retailer and obtained a receipt (Sec. 372.190, Sec. 374.195). Out-of-state retailers may register under the use tax law, which is for the purpose of facilitating collection directly from the retailer.

• Responsibility for sales and use tax collection

The sales tax is collected by the retailer from the consumer "insofar as it can be done" (Sec. 372.110, Sec. 374.115).

Retailers who have sufficient contacts with Nevada to constitute nexus with the state are required to collect the use tax from purchasers to be remitted to the Department of Taxation (Sec. 372.195, Sec. 374.200). The tax remains a liability of the purchaser, however, until paid, unless the purchaser has a receipt showing payment of the tax to the retailer (Sec. 372.190, Sec. 374.195).

Drop shipments: When all the parties are located in the state, the retailer furnishes a resale certificate to the primary seller, rendering the first sale a nontaxable transaction. The retailer then collects sales tax on behalf of the state on the secondary sale to its customer. A third party drop shipper may accept in good faith an out-of-state resale certificate, or a Streamlined Sales Tax Resale Certificate from a retailer in state or out-of-state who is selling to the end user in Nevada. (Sec. 372.155(2); Sec. 372.225(2))

• Nexus

Sales and use tax applies to every retailer whose activities satisfy the U.S. Constitution's Commerce Clause nexus standard (Sec. 372.724).

Effective July 1, 2015, a rebuttable presumption is created for Nevada sales and use tax purposes that a retailer is required to impose, collect and remit sales and use taxes if the retailer is (Sec. 372.7243; Sec. 374.7243):

(1) part of a controlled group of business entities that has a component member that has physical presence in Nevada; and

(2) the component member engages in certain activities in Nevada that relate to the ability of the retailer to make retail sales to residents of Nevada.

Those activities are when a component member:

— sells a similar line of products or services as the retailer and does so under a business name that is the same or similar to that of the retailer;

— maintains an office, distribution facility, warehouse or storage place or similar place of business in Nevada to facilitate the delivery of tangible personal property sold by the retailer to the retailer's customers;

— uses trademarks, service marks or trade names in Nevada that are the same or substantially similar to those used by the retailer;

— delivers, installs, assembles or performs maintenance services for the retailer's customers within Nevada;

— facilitates the retailer's delivery of tangible personal property to customers in Nevada by allowing the retailer's customers to pick up tangible personal property sold by the retailer at an office, distribution facility, warehouse, storage place or similar place of business maintained by the component member in Nevada; or

— conducts any other activities in Nevada that are significantly associated with the retailer's ability to establish and maintain a market in Nevada for the retailer's products or services.

A retailer may rebut this presumption by providing proof that the component member with physical presence in Nevada did not engage in any activity in Nevada that was significantly associated with the retailer's ability to establish or maintain a market in Nevada for the retailer's products or services.

The law also creates a rebuttable presumption, effective October 1, 2015, that a retailer is required to impose, collect and remit sales and use taxes if:

(1) the retailer enters into an agreement with a resident of Nevada under which the resident receives certain consideration for referring potential customers to the retailer through a link on the resident's Internet website or otherwise; and

(2) the cumulative gross receipts from sales by the retailer to customers in Nevada through all such referrals exceeds $10,000 during the preceding four quarterly periods ending on the last day of March, June, September and December.

This presumption may be rebutted by providing proof that each resident with whom the retailer has an agreement did not engage in any activity that was significantly associated with the retailer's ability to establish or maintain a market in Nevada for the retailer's products or services during the preceding four quarterly periods. (Sec. 372.7243; Sec. 374.7243)

• Streamlined Act status

Nevada is a full member of the Streamlined Sales and Use Tax Agreement with a seat on the Governing Board, effective April 1, 2008. It has enacted all of the provisions necessary to comply with the Agreement's requirements (Secs. 360B.010—360B.375). For details, see ¶ 627.

As a full member, Nevada may vote on amendments to or interpretations of the Agreement, and sellers registering under the SST system must collect and remit tax on sales into the state.

Taxability matrix: A chart of the taxable status of various items is accessible on the website of the Streamlined Sales Tax Project at **www.streamlinedsalestax.org**.

¶621 Nevada

¶ 622   Tax Base

The sales tax is based on the gross receipts of the retailer (Sec. 372.105, Sec. 374.110, Sec. 377.040).

The use tax is based upon the sales price of the article purchased (Sec. 372.185, Sec. 374.190).

• **"Gross receipts" defined**

"Gross receipts," the basis for the sales tax, means the total amount of the sale, lease, or rental price of the retail sales of retailers, whether received in money or otherwise, without any deduction of the following (Sec. 372.025, Sec. 374.030):

— the cost of the property sold, except under the situation described below;

— the cost of the materials used, labor or service rendered, interest paid, losses or any other expense; or

— the cost of transportation of the property prior to its sale to the buyer.

Note that the term used in the tax return form is "total sales," which is equivalent to the term "gross receipts" in the sales tax statute.

The cost of the property sold may be deducted if the retailer bought property for its own use, paid the tax at the time of purchase, and later resold the property without any intervening use. The cost of the property may be deducted from gross receipts to avoid a double imposition of the tax (Sec. 372.025, Sec. 374.030). Additional regulatory conditions are prescribed in Reg. 372.780.

If the retailer takes the deduction, no refund or credit will be allowed to the retailer's vendor with respect to the sale of the property (Sec. 372.025, Sec. 374.030).

The "total amount of the sale, lease, or rental price" includes all of the following (Sec. 372.025(2)):

— any services that are a part of the sale;

— all receipts, cash, credits, and property of any kind; and

— any amount for which credit is allowed by the seller to the purchaser.

• **"Sales price" defined**

"Sales price," the basis for the use tax, means the total amount for which tangible property is sold, valued in money, whether paid in money or otherwise, without any deduction of the following (Sec. 372.065(1), Sec. 374.070(1)):

— the cost of the property sold;

— the cost of materials used, labor or service rendered, interest charged, losses, or any other expenses; or

— the cost of transportation of the property (delivery charges) prior to its purchase.

The "total amount for which property is sold" includes all of the following (Sec. 372.065(2), Sec. 374.070(2)):

— any services that are a part of the sale; and

— any amount for which credit is given to the purchaser by the seller.

Discounts and coupons: "Sales price" includes consideration received by a seller from a third party if:

— the seller actually receives consideration from a person other than the purchaser and the consideration is directly related to a price reduction or discount on the sale;

— the seller has an obligation to pass the price reduction or discount through to the purchaser;

— the amount of the consideration attributable to the sale is fixed and determinable by the seller at the time of the sale of the item to the purchaser; and

— any of the following criteria are satisfied:

(1) the purchaser presents a coupon, certificate or other documentation to the seller to claim a price reduction or discount, and the coupon, certificate or other documentation is authorized, distributed or granted by a third party with the understanding that the third party will reimburse any seller to whom the coupon, certificate or other documentation is presented;

(2) the purchaser identifies himself to the seller as a member of a group or organization entitled to a price reduction or discount. For the purposes of this subparagraph, a preferred customer card that is available to any patron does not constitute membership in such a group; or

(3) the price reduction or discount is identified as a third-party price reduction or discount on the invoice received by the purchaser or on the coupon, certificate or other documentation presented by the purchaser.

Any invoice, billing, or other document given to a purchaser that indicated that the sales price for which tangible personal property is sold may state separately any amount received by the seller for any transportation, shipping or postage charges for the delivery of the property to a location designated by the purchaser and must state separately any amount received by the seller for: (1) any installation charges for the property; (2) any credit for any exempt trade-in; (3) any interest, financing and carrying charges from credit extended on the sale; and (4) any taxes legally imposed directly on the consumer. (Sec. 360B.290)

• **Exclusions from definition of gross receipts or sales price**

The following are excluded from "gross receipts" or "sales price" (Sec. 372.025(3), Sec. 372.065(3), Sec. 374.030(3), Sec. 374.070(3)):

— cash discounts allowed and taken on sales;

— sales prices refunded, either in cash or credit, due to sales returns;

— the price received, or, in the case of use tax, the amount charged, for labor or services used in installing or applying the property sold;

— the amount of any tax, other than manufacturers' or importers' excise tax, levied by the United States on retail sales, whether imposed upon the retailer or consumer; and

— the amount of any allowance against the selling price given by a retailer for the value of a used vehicle that is taken in trade on the purchase of another vehicle.

• **Sourcing rules**

In conformity with the Streamlined Agreement (¶ 627), retail sales are sourced generally to the destination of the product sold, with a default to origin-based sourcing in the absence of that information. Special rules apply to leases and rentals. The following general sourcing rules apply:

— if the property is received by the purchaser at a business location of the seller, the sale is sourced to that place of business;

— if the property is not received by the purchaser at a business location of the seller, the sale is sourced to a location indicated to the seller in instructions provided by the purchaser for delivery to the purchaser or to the purchaser's donee. If no instructions are provided, the sale is sourced to the location where the purchaser or the purchaser's donee receives the property;

— if the circumstances above do not apply, the sale is sourced to the address of the purchaser in the seller's business records maintained in the ordinary course of the seller's business, unless use of that address would constitute bad faith;

— if none of the above apply, the sale is sourced to the address of the purchaser obtained during the consummation of the sale, including, if no other address is available, the address of the purchaser's payment instrument, unless use of that address would constitute bad faith;

— if none of the other rules apply, the sale is sourced to the address from which the property was shipped or, if it was delivered electronically, at the address from which it was first available for transmission by the seller.

Direct mail: Effective July 1, 2015, Nevada sales and use tax laws were amended to comply with the Streamlined Sales and Use Tax Agreement regarding direct mail. The amended law removes the distinction between a seller who maintains a place of business in Nevada and one who does not maintain a place of business in Nevada by requiring the purchaser to report and pay any applicable sales or use taxes. The seller is relieved of any obligation to collect, pay or remit sales or use tax applicable to the transaction, assuming there is no bad faith. (Sec. 360B.281(b))

¶ 623 List of Exemptions, Exceptions, and Exclusions

Unless otherwise indicated, the statutory exemptions listed below apply to both the sales and use tax. Items that are excluded from the sales or use tax base are treated at ¶ 622, "Tax Base."

- **Sales and use tax exemptions, exceptions, and exclusions**

Agriculture	Sec. 372.280, Sec. 372.281, Sec. 372.2871
Artworks for sale or public display	Sec. 374.055, Sec. 374.085, Sec. 374.291
Broadcast transmissions	Sec. 372.734, Sec. 374.739
Cigarettes subject to excise tax	Sec. 370.165, Sec. 370.350
College textbooks	Sec. 372. 287, Sec. 374.292
Common carriers	Sec. 372.330, Sec. 374.335
Companies locating to or expanding in Nevada (partial abatements; see also ¶ 630)	Sec. 374.357
Containers	Sec. 372.290, Sec. 374.295
Contractors for exempt entities	Sec. 372.340, Sec. 374.345
Farm animals for human consumption	Sec. 372.280(1), Sec. 372.280(2)
Farm machinery sold out of state	Sec. 374.7273
Food for human consumption	Sec. 372.284, Sec. 374.289
Fertilizer for food crops	Sec. 372.280(4)
Government transactions	Sec. 372.325, Sec. 372.327, Sec. 374.330, Sec. 374.331

Public school transactions	Sec. 372.325,
	Sec. 372.327,
	Sec. 374.330,
	Sec. 374.331
Resales	Sec. 372.050,
	Sec. 372.155,
	Sec. 372.225,
	Sec. 374.055,
	Sec. 374.160,
	Sec. 374.165,
	Sec. 374.230,
	Sec. 374.235
School meals and food	Sec. 372.285,
	Sec. 374.290
Seeds and plants for human consumption	Sec. 372.280(3)
Textbooks, college	Sec. 372.287,
	Sec. 374.292
Utilities	Sec. 372.295,
	Sec. 374.300

¶ 624 Rate of Tax

Nevada sales and use taxes are imposed on a statewide basis at the rate of 6.85%, the components of which are (1) a 2% state rate under the general Sales and Use Tax Act (Sec. 372.105, Sec. 372.185), (2) a 2.6% state rate under the Local School Support Tax Law (Sec. 374.110, Sec. 374.190), and (3) a 2.25% state-mandated local rate under the City-County Relief Tax Law (Sec. 377.040). The 6.85% rate is increased by local taxes in certain counties, as discussed at ¶ 625.

• Transitional rules—Prior contracts

There are several codified provisions exempting transactions entered into prior to the adoption of the sales and use laws or prior to changes in the tax rates (Sec. 372.305, Sec. 372.310, Sec. 374.310, Sec. 374.315).

• Special tax rate

A tax rate of 10% is applicable to sales of the drugs amygdalin and procaine hydrochloride under a special statute (Sec. 585.497).

¶ 625 Local Taxes

The Department is required to post on its Web site the rates of Nevada sales and use taxes and the rates for each local government and Indian reservation or Indian colony within the state. Additionally, the Department must post a matrix for determining the taxability of products in Nevada and any change in the taxability of a product must be listed in the matrix (see ¶ 621). If a registered seller or CSP fails to collect the correct amount of any sales or use tax as a result of reasonable reliance on the information posted on the Department's Web site, the Department must waive any liability of the registered seller or CSP for the amount of sales or use tax uncollected as a result of that reliance, and any penalties and interest on that amount. Additionally, if a purchaser fails to pay the correct amount of any sales or use tax as a result of reasonable reliance on the information posted on the Department's Web site, liability will be waived for the amount of sales or use tax which the purchaser failed to pay as a result of that reliance, and any penalties and interest on that amount will be waived, as well (Sec. 360B.250).

The following chart shows the combined state and local sales and use tax rates imposed by Nevada counties as of April 1, 2017:

Jurisdiction	Local Rate	Jurisdiction	Local Rate
Carson	7.60%	Lincoln	7.100%
Churchill	7.60%	Lyon	7.100%
Clark	8.25%*	Mineral	6.850%
Douglas	7.100%	Nye	7.600%
Elko	7.100%	Pershing	7.100%
Esmeralda	6.850%	Storey	7.60%
Eureka	6.850%	Washoe	8.265%
Humboldt	6.850%	White Pine	7.725%
Lander	7.100%		

New taxes and rate changes: A new local sales or use tax or a rate change for an existing local sales or use tax becomes effective on the first day of the first calendar quarter that begins at least 120 days after the effective date of the ordinance.

Boundary changes: If the boundary of a local government that has imposed a sales or use tax is changed, any rate change resulting from the boundary change becomes effective on the first day of the first calendar quarter that begins at least 60 days after the effective date of the boundary change.

• **Tax for infrastructure**

The board of commissioners of any county may impose a tax for infrastructure (Sec. 377B.100). The tax may be imposed at a rate not to exceed.125% for counties in which the population is 100,000 or more but less than 700,000 or .25% in other counties (Sec. 377B.110).

• **School facilities tax**

Additional tax is imposed on retailers within a county in which (1) the board of county commissioners has not imposed the tax for infrastructure at the maximum rate, (2) the board of trustees of the county's school district has applied for a grant from the state fund to assist school districts in financing capital improvements, and (3) the state board of examiners has approved the application by the board of trustees (Sec. 6, Ch. 596, Laws 1999). Collection of tax must begin on the first day of the first calendar quarter that begins at least 30 days after the application is approved (Sec. 7, Ch. 596, Laws 1999). Money collected must be used for the cost of extraordinary maintenance, extraordinary repair, and extraordinary improvement of school facilities within the county. The rate of tax is the difference between the maximum rate that may be imposed as a tax for infrastructure and the rate imposed by the county. The additional tax may not exceed.125% of the gross receipts from a retailer from the sale of tangible personal property sold at retail or stored, used, or otherwise consumed in the county.

• **Smaller counties' facilities tax**

The board of a county whose population is less than 100,000 (counties other than Clark and Washoe) are authorized to enact an ordinance to impose a local sales and use tax at the rate of not more than 0.25% to acquire, develop, construct, equip, operate, maintain, improve and manage libraries, parks, recreational programs and facilities, and facilities and services for senior citizens, and to preserve and protect agriculture, or for any combination of these purposes. The levy of such a tax may not exceed 30 years. Prior to enactment, the board must submit the ordinance for approval by the registered voters of the county (Ch. 371 (S.B. 170), Laws 2005).

• **Local lodging tax**

Counties with a population of 700,000 or more (Clark County), and incorporated cities within those counties (Las Vegas), must impose a 2% tax on the gross receipts from the rental of transient lodging. The tax is imposed on all persons in the business of providing lodging. Counties with a population of less than 700,000, and incorporated cities within those counties, must impose a 1% tax (Sec. 244.3352, Sec. 268.096).

The taxes are levied on gross receipts, and operators can pass the taxes along to their paying guests. Gross receipts subject to taxation, however, do not include either the county or city tax collected from guests under the mandatory lodging tax programs (Sec. 244.3352, Sec. 268.096).

A county (and its incorporated cities) whose population is 100,000 or more but less than 700,000 is prohibited from imposing a new lodging tax or increasing the rate of an existing one. A county (and its incorporated cities) whose population is 700,000 or more (Clark County) may impose a new lodging tax or increase the rate of an existing one pursuant to the provisions of the optional or mandatory lodging tax program (Sec. 244.3359).

An additional room tax is imposed on the gross receipts from the rental of transient lodging in counties with a population of 300,000 or more (currently, Clark (Las Vegas) and Washoe (Reno). Counties) must impose the additional 3% tax. However, if the sum of the rates of all other taxes existing on July 31, 2008, and imposed by Nevada or any unit of local government on the gross receipts from the rental of transient lodging in any area of the county exceeds 10%, the new tax must be imposed at a rate equal to the difference between 13% and the sum of the rates of the existing taxes. If the sum of the rates of the existing taxes in any area of the county was at least 13% already, no new additional tax will be imposed in that area. (Initiative Petition No. 1, Laws 2009)

Temporary tax: The Department of Taxation may take over the management of a local government that is experiencing a severe financial emergency. If the Department determines that available revenue is not sufficient to pay for required debt service and operating expenses, it may impose temporary taxes for up to five years. Among the taxes that may be imposed is an additional tax on transient lodging at a rate not to exceed 1% of the gross receipts from the rental of transient lodging within the boundaries of the local government (Sec. 354.705).

Optional county lodging tax: Subject to voter approval, a county or transportation district can impose a 1% tax on gross receipts from the rental of transient lodging (Sec. 244.3351). The county tax may be imposed throughout the county, including the incorporated cities.

A city located in a county whose population is 100,000 or more but less than 700,000 is prohibited from imposing a new lodging tax or increasing the rate of an existing one, except that a city that has created a taxing district to defray the cost of additional police protection may impose a tax of not more than 1% of the gross receipts from the rental of transient lodging within that district. The proceeds of the tax must be used to fund railroad grade separation projects. A city located in a county whose population is 700,000 or more cannot impose a new lodging tax or increase the rate of an existing one unless it does so under the provisions of the additional city lodging tax program (Sec. 268.0968).

Additional city lodging tax: The governing body of any incorporated city having a population of at least 200,000 persons is authorized to create a district to finance the costs of improving a central business district (not necessarily contiguous with the city) and to impose, in addition to any existing occupancy tax, a tax on persons engaged in the business of providing transient lodging in the district, not to exceed 2% of the gross receipts from the rental of such lodging. Any such tax will be collected locally (Sec. 268.803, Sec. 268.804).

Transient lodgings: The definition of "transient lodgings" varies and is specified in the local enacting ordinances. In 1997 the legislature directed counties (Sec. 244.33565) and cities (Sec. 268.0195) to adopt ordinances defining the term "transient lodging" and provided that the definition may include vacation trailer parks, campgrounds and parks for recreational vehicles.

¶ 626   Bracket Schedule

In determining the amount of taxes due, the amount due must be computed to the third decimal place and rounded to a whole cent using a method that rounds up to the next cent if the numeral in the third decimal place is greater than 4. A retailer may compute the amount due on a transaction on the basis of each item involved in the transaction or a single invoice for the entire transaction (Sec. 360.489).

Bracket or rate schedules are prescribed by the Department of Taxation. The bracket schedules (Reg. 372.760) are set up to include all the taxes listed at ¶ 624, including the local taxes. Additional bracket schedules are available online at **http:// tax.nv.gov/Publications/Sales_and_Use_Tax_Publications/**.

6.5% Tax Rate

Sale	Tax
$0.01 to $0.07	No tax
.08 to .23	1¢
.24 to .38	2¢
.39 to .53	3¢
.54 to .69	4¢
.70 to .84	5¢
.85 to .99	6¢
1.00 to 1.15	7¢
and so forth.	

7% Tax Rate

Sale	Tax
$0.01 to $0.07	No tax
.08 to .21	1¢
.22 to .35	2¢
.36 to .49	3¢
.50 to .64	4¢
.65 to .78	5¢
.79 to .92	6¢
.93 to 1.07	7¢
and so forth.	

7.25% Tax Rate

Sale	Tax
$0.01 to $0.06	No tax
.07 to .20	1¢
.21 to .34	2¢
.35 to .48	3¢
.49 to .62	4¢
.63 to .75	5¢
.76 to .89	6¢
.90 to 1.03	7¢
and so forth.	

6.85% Tax Rate

Sale	Tax
$0.01 to $0.07	No tax
.08 to .21	1¢
.22 to .36	2¢
.37 to .51	3¢
.52 to .65	4¢
.66 to .80	5¢
.81 to .94	6¢
.95 to 1.09	7¢
and so forth.	

Unless a retailer uses the alternative procedure described in the following paragraph that allows him or her to incorporate the sales tax into the sales price, the retailer must compute the combined state and local sales taxes upon gross receipts by using the bracket schedule if the gross receipts are not more than the highest amount shown on the bracket card (see above). If the gross receipts are more than that amount, the retailer must compute the tax to the nearest cent at the applicable rate (Reg. 372.760).

All-inclusive pricing: A retailer may include the tax in the sales price of an item provided the public is notified by a sign posted by the retailer that is visible to all customers and states that the sales tax is included in the sales price. In the absence of such a notification, the total amount charged to the customer is deemed to be the price of the item (Reg. 372.760).

¶ 627   Returns, Payments, and Due Dates

The Department of Taxation prescribes a combined sales and use tax return that incorporates all sales and use taxes levied by state, county, and city jurisdictions (Sec. 372.365, Sec. 374.370). Included are the state sales and use tax, the local school support tax, and the city-county relief tax. In addition, the mass transit, road construction, tourism, or flood control levies by certain counties are reported and collected via the same return.

The returns must be signed by the taxpayer or the taxpayer's agent, but need not be verified by oath (Sec. 372.360, Sec. 374.365).

When an account goes out of business, the retailer must notify the Tax Commission by marking the last return it files as a "final return."

- **Taxpayers required to file returns**

Sales tax: Every retailer must file a return for sales tax purposes (Sec. 374.370, Sec. 372.360).

Use tax: The following are required to file a return for use tax purposes: (1) every retailer maintaining a place of business in Nevada and (2) every person purchasing tangible personal property, the storage, use, or other consumption of which is subject to use tax, who has not paid the use tax to a retailer (Sec. 374.370, Sec. 372.360).

- **Information returns**

The Department of Taxation may require the filing of reports by any person or class of persons who possesses information relating to sales of tangible personal property, the storage, use, or consumption of which is subject to tax (Sec. 372.745, Sec. 374.750). The report must set forth the names and addresses of the purchaser, the sales price of the property, the date of sale, and such other information as the Department may require.

- **Payment of tax**

Remittance of the sales and use tax must be made to the Department of Taxation at the same time as the filing of the return (Sec. 372.375, Sec. 374.380). Such payments are deposited by the Department with the State Treasury to the credit of the sales and use tax account of the general fund, but the local school support taxes are subsequently transferred to the various county school district funds (Sec. 372.780, Sec. 374.785). The sales and use tax account in the general fund may be used for the payment of sales or use tax refunds (Sec. 372.785).

Electronic payment: Nevada allows online registration, filing, and payment by electronic funds transfer (EFT) of money for taxes, fees, interest, penalties, or other charges (Nevada uncodified regulations, LCB File No. R062-05). To register, file, or pay online, a taxpayer, its security administrator or authorized user must go to the Department's website at **https://www.nevadatax.nv.gov/#**.

Electronic returns must be completed and submitted with payment no later than midnight Pacific Time on the return due date. Online payment may be submitted only by automated clearinghouse (ACH) debit. If a return is submitted electronically but payment is mailed, a copy of the printout of the electronic return confirmation page must be submitted with the payment, which must be postmarked by the return due date. A zero-return must be submitted in the event that no taxes are due for the reporting period (Nevada uncodified regulations, Sec. 23, LCB No. R062-05).

The Nevada Department of Taxation accepts ACH credits as a method of payment for taxes.

Deferred payments: A person may apply to the Office of Economic Development for a five-year deferment of the payment of the sales or use taxes on the sale of eligible property for a sales price of $1 million or more for use by the person in a business in Nevada (Sec. 372.397, Sec. 374.402). In order to qualify for the deferment, the person must meet the eligibility requirements for a partial abatement of sales and use taxes (see ¶ 630), the purchase must be consistent with the State Plan for Economic Development, and the Office must determine that:

(1) deferment is a significant factor in the decision of the person to locate or expand its business in Nevada, and

(2) the eligible property will be retained at the location of the person's business in Nevada for at least five years after the date the Office certifies the deferment.

If the Office certifies a person's eligibility for a deferment, payment of the total amount of tax due on the sale of the eligible property must be deferred without interest for the 60-month period beginning on the date that the Office makes that certification. However, installment payments of the tax will begin after one year. (Sec. 372.397(4), Sec. 374.402(4))

• **Due dates**

Taxpayers whose taxable sales do not exceed $10,000 per month must file a return and pay the tax on a quarterly basis, on or before the last day of the month next succeeding the end of the calendar quarter (Sec. 372.355, Sec. 372.380, Sec. 374.360, Sec. 374.385).

Taxpayers with monthly taxable sales of more than $10,000 must file a return and pay the tax on a monthly basis, on or before the last day of the month next succeeding the month being reported (Sec. 372.360).

The Department of Taxation may require the filing of returns and payment of taxes for periods other than calendar months or quarters if it deems this action necessary in order to ensure payment or collection of the tax (Sec. 372.380, Sec. 374.360). Taxpayers whose taxable sales have not exceeded $1,500 during a calendar year may file an annual return (Sec. 372.380). The annual return is due no later than January 31 of the next year. A taxpayer's written request to be considered for annual reporting must be received by the Department no later than September 30 of the year preceding the year for which the request is intended. However, requests for annual filing cannot be considered until the taxpayer has reported four quarterly (or 12 monthly) returns to the Department. Once the taxpayer's account has been reviewed and verified, the Department will update the taxpayer's reporting period to annually and send notification of the change to the taxpayer.

Taxpayers are required to file returns even if no tax is due.

If sales or use tax is due and payable on a day on which a Federal Reserve Bank is closed and, as a result of that closure, the taxpayer is not able to remit the tax electronically as required, the tax may be paid on the next succeeding day on which the Federal Reserve Bank is open. Additionally, if any sales or use tax is due on a Saturday, Sunday or legal holiday, the return may be filed on the next succeeding business day. (Sec. 360B.300)

• **Uniform Sales Tax Administration Act**

Nevada has enacted the Uniform Sales and Use Tax Administration Act, as well as legislation conforming its sales and use tax laws to provisions of the Streamlined Sales and Use Tax Agreement. For detailed information, see the Department of Revenue's website at **http://tax.nv.gov/FAQs/SST**.

Definitions: Numerous definitions have been added or amended to conform with the Agreement.

Taxability matrix: See ¶ 621.

Sourcing rules: See ¶ 622.

Certified software: The Department of Revenue will review software for certified service providers (CSP) and certify automated software systems that adequately classify different transactions. Liability will be waived by the Department on the amount of uncollected sales or use tax, and the resulting penalties and interest on that amount, that is uncollected due to a reliance on a faulty certified automated system. However, the waiver will not apply if the Department notifies the registered seller or CSP that an item or transaction is being incorrectly classified by the certified automated system, and the system is not corrected within 10 days of receipt of the notice.

Rate postings: The Department is required to post on its website (**http:// tax..nv.gov**) the rates of Nevada sales and use taxes and the rates for each local government and Indian reservation or Indian colony within the state. If a registered seller or CSP fails to collect the correct amount of any sales or use tax as a result of reasonable reliance on the information posted on the Department's website, the Department must waive any liability of the registered seller or CSP for the amount of sales or use tax uncollected as a result of that reliance, and any penalties and interest on that amount. Additionally, if a purchaser fails to pay the correct amount of any sales or use tax as a result of reasonable reliance on the information posted on the Department's website, liability will be waived for the amount of sales or use tax which the purchaser failed to pay as a result of that reliance, and any penalties and interest on that amount will be waived, as well.

Resale certificates: The person who makes the sale must receive a certificate to the effect that the property is purchased for resale from the purchaser. Additionally, the certificate must include that the purchaser:

— is engaged in the business of selling tangible personal property;

— is registered pursuant to the Agreement or holds a permit; and

— at the time of purchasing the property, intends to sell it in the regular course of business or is unable to ascertain at the time of purchase whether the property will be sold or will be used for some other purpose.

Direct pay permits: Any purchaser who obtains a direct pay permit must determine the amount of sales and use taxes that are due and payable to an Indian reservation or Indian colony in Nevada upon the purchase of tangible personal property from such a seller, and report and pay those taxes to the appropriate authority. Previously, the direct pay permit provisions only applied to Nevada and local governments within Nevada.

Bad debts: A retailer is authorized to deduct bad debt from its taxable sales (Sec. 372.368). The amount that may be deducted is the amount that may be deducted under IRC Sec. 166 minus:

— finance charges or interest;

— sales or use tax charged on the sales price;

— uncollectible amounts on property that remains in the possession of the seller until the full purchase price is paid;

— expenses incurred in attempting to collect bad debt; and

— the value of any repossessed property.

If a retailer subsequently collects a debt, in whole or in part, for which the retailer claimed a bad debt deduction, the tax must be reported on the return that covers the period in which the debt was collected.

The right of a retailer to claim a deduction or refund under the Nevada Sales and Use Tax Act is not affected by the assignment of a debt by the retailer to an entity that is part of an affiliated group that includes the retailer, the writing off by the entity of the debt as a bad debt, and the eligibility of the entity to deduct the bad debt under the federal law.

The right of a retailer to claim a bad debt deduction or refund is not affected by the assignment of a debt by the retailer to an entity that is part of an affiliated group that includes the retailer, the writing off by the entity of the debt as a bad debt, or the eligibility of the entity to deduct the bad debt under the federal law (Sec. 372.368(10)).

New taxes, rate changes, boundary changes: See ¶ 625.

Exemptions: See ¶ 623.

Exemption certificates: A retailer is liable for the payment of sales tax if the purchaser improperly claimed an exemption and the retailer: (1) fraudulently failed to collect the tax; (2) solicited a purchaser to participate in an unlawful claim of an exemption; or (3) accepted a certificate of exemption from a purchaser who claimed an entity-based exemption and the item was received by the purchaser at the seller's location, and the department posted on its website a certificate of exemption that clearly and affirmatively indicated that the claimed exemption was not available. An "entity-based exemption" is defined as an exemption based on who purchases the product or who sells the product and that is not available to all. (Sec. 372.347(5))

For additional information on the uniform act and the SST Agreement, see "Streamlined Sales Tax Project," listed in the Table of Contents.

¶ 628　　　　　　　　　　Prepayment of Taxes

Nevada has no provision for the prepayment of sales or use taxes.

¶ 629　　　　　　　　　　Vendor Registration

Every person desiring to conduct business as a seller within Nevada must file with the Department of Taxation an application for a permit for each place of business (Sec. 372.125, Sec. 374.130). Registration may be accomplished online at the Nevada Department of Taxation's website at **https://www.nevadatax.nv.gov/#**. The taxpayer must submit a completed online Nevada Business Registration and confirm that the information given is correct and that the signatory is authorized to act on behalf of the business (Nevada uncodified regulations, Sec. 21, LCB No. R062-05).

A permit must be conspicuously displayed at all times at the place of business for which it is issued. A permit is valid only for the person in whose name it is issued and for the transaction of business at the place designated on it. A permit is not assignable (Sec. 372.135, Sec. 374.140).

Transient vendors can be required to obtain the standard seller's permit described above, but the Department may, if given sufficient advance notice, issue a temporary permit to sellers at one-time events such as craft fairs. Since sellers can include wholesalers, a wholesaler may be required to have a permit if the wholesaler sells taxable property at retail (Sec. 372.070).

Information to be provided with permit: When the Department grants a permit for a seller's place of business it must also provide the applicant with a full, written explanation of the applicant's liability for the collection and payment of Nevada sales and use (Sec. 372.135) and local school support (Sec. 374.140) taxes. The explanation must include the procedures for the collection and payment of taxes that specifically apply to the type of business conducted by the applicant, including an explanation of the circumstances under which a service provided by the applicant is taxable, the procedures for administering exemptions, and the circumstances under which charges for freight are taxable.

• SST conforming provisons

When registering under the Agreement, a seller may select a model for remittance.

(1) A model 1 seller elects to use a certified service provider as its agent to perform all the functions of the seller relating to sales and use taxes, other than the obligation of the seller to remit the taxes on its own purchases.

(2) A model 2 seller elects to use a certified automated system to calculate the amount of sales or use taxes due on its sales transactions.

(3) A model 3 seller, under such conditions as the Department deems appropriate in accordance with the Agreement, elects to use its own proprietary automated system to calculate the amount of sales or use taxes due on its sales transactions.

The Department will allow model 1, 2, and 3 sellers to submit tax returns in a simplified format that does not include any more data fields than are permitted in accordance with the Agreement (Sec. 360B.200). The Department will require sellers registered under the Agreement to file only one tax return for each taxing period for all sales and use taxes collected on behalf of the state and each local government in the state. Only one tax remittance is required with each return, except the Department may require additional remittances if a seller collected more than $30,000 in Nevada state and local sales and use taxes during the preceding calendar year. (Sec. 360B.200)

A seller registered under the Agreement who does not maintain a place of business in the state and is not a model 1, 2, or 3 seller may file returns at a frequency that does not exceed once per year unless the seller accumulates more than $1,000 in the collection of sales and use taxes on behalf of the state and the local governments in the state (Sec. 360B.200).

A seller that does not use certified service providers as an agent may elect to be registered in one or more states as a seller that anticipates making no sales into the state or states if the seller has not had sales into the state or states for the preceding 12 months. This election does not relieve the seller of its agreement to collect taxes on all sales into the states or its liability for remitting to the proper states any taxes collected.

• **Security deposit**

The Department may require any person subject to sales and use taxes to deposit security in the following cases:

(1) When the security is deemed necessary to ensure compliance with the Sales and Use Tax Act (Sec. 372.510; Sec. 374.515);

(2) When a person served notice of a jeopardy determination petitions for redetermination (Sec. 360.416);

(3) When a person obtains a permit to collect sales tax (NAC 372.825).

Amount of security: A security deposit of at least $100 is mandatory for persons who obtain a permit to collect sales tax. The amount of the security deposit is determined by computing the taxpayer's average monthly taxable sales and multiplying the taxable Nevada sales by the applicable county sales tax rate where the business is located (Supplemental Information Instructions for Form APP-01.01).

The amount of security may not exceed two times the estimated average tax due quarterly for quarterly payers, or three times the estimated average tax due monthly for monthly payers, but not less than $50. After three years of perfect report, the taxpayer may apply for a waiver of the security deposit.

If a sales tax return is filed late, the security required is recalculated on the basis of the current month's sales (Sec. 372.510).

¶ 630   **Sales or Use Tax Credits**

In determining the amount of use tax that is due from a taxpayer, the department will allow a credit in an amount equal to sales tax paid for the same purchase of tangible personal property to a state or local government outside Nevada (Reg. 372.055).

Collection allowance: A credit against the tax in the form of a 0.5% collection allowance is given for collection of the sales tax, but not the use tax (Sec. 372.370, Sec. 374.375). Certain alcohol tax, cigarette tax, and sales and use tax collection allowances for retailers were temporarily reduced to 0.25%, effective January 1, 2009. The reduction is scheduled to expire on June 30, 2009. (S.B. 2 a, Laws 2008 (Special Session)).

Returned goods: The sales tax on returned goods is credited by excluding from the tax base the sales price of the returned goods. The excluded amount includes the sales tax previously collected (Reg. 372.090).

Tax previously paid: A credit (in lieu of refund) may also be obtained for use tax paid on an item on which sales tax has previously been paid by the vendor (Sec. 372.630(2), Sec. 374.635(2)).

- **Economic development zone credit**

A credit (in lieu of a refund) to recover the local school support tax may be obtained by qualified businesses within a specially benefited zone (Sec. 374.643). The credit is equal to the amount of tax paid for all tangible personal property purchased in the conduct of its business for the period stated in the agreement with the city or county, but not to exceed five years. To be entitled to the credit (or refund), the city or county that designated the specially benefited zone must have adopted an ordinance authorizing such claims.

- **Abatements for new or expanding businesses**

People who maintain a business or intend to locate a business in Nevada may apply to the Commission on Economic Development for an abatement from tax on gross receipts from the sale, storage, use, or other consumption of eligible machinery or equipment used by the business (Sec. 374.357). A person who intends to locate or expand a business in Nevada may apply to the Commission on Economic Development for a partial abatement of local school support tax for up to two years.

Abatements also are available for businesses that are or will be located in a foreign trade zone (Sec. 361.0687(4)), and businesses in an historically underutilized business zone, a redevelopment area, an area eligible for a community development block grant, or an enterprise community (Sec. 274.310).

- **Abatements for renewable energy generation**

Partial abatements of local sales and use taxes are available to certain facilities for the generation of process heat from solar renewable energy, wholesale facilities for the generation of electricity from renewable energy, facilities for the generation of electricity from geothermal resources, or facilities for the transmission of electricity produced from renewable energy or geothermal resources (Sec. 701A.360; NAC 701A.2—36). A partial abatement of the local sales and use tax will be for three years from the date of approval of the application. The abatement will be equal to that portion of the combined rate of all the local sales and use tax payable by the facility each year that exceeds 0.6%.

The Department of Taxation will issue to the facility a certification that will clearly state that the purchaser is only required to pay sales and use tax at a rate of 2.6% (Sec. 701A.360). The abatement will be equal to that portion of the combined rate of all the local sales and use tax payable by the facility each year that exceeds 0.25%. The Department of Taxation will issue to the facility a certification that will clearly state that the purchaser is only required to pay sales and use tax at a rate of 2.25% (Sec. 701A.370). The abatements will cease to be effective June 30, 2049.

- **Abatements for data centers**

Effective January 1, 2016, a partial abatement of property taxes and local sales and use taxes is available to a data center that locates or expands within the state and meets certain qualifications. Partial abatements may be sought for periods of up to 10 years, or for periods over 10 years but not more than 20 years. Any such abatement of the local sales and use taxes may not include, for fiscal year 2015-2016, an abatement of the local school support tax. The amount of the abatement may not exceed 75% of the amount of personal property taxes payable by a data center for eligible equipment and machinery located in the data center. If the Office of Economic Development approves a partial abatement for a data center, the Office may grant the same partial abatement to certain businesses that colocate with the data center. (Sec. 374.356)

Applicants seeking a partial abatement for a period of not more than 10 years, must meet the following requirements (Sec. 360.754):

— the data center will, not later than the date that is five years after the date on which the abatement becomes effective, have 10 or more full-time resident employees and will continue to employ 10 or more full-time resident employees until at least the date that is 10 years after the date on which the abatement becomes effective;

— not later than the date that is five years after the date on which the abatement becomes effective, the data center and/or colocated businesses must make a cumulative capital investment of at least $25 million in capital assets that will be used or located at the data center;

— the data center must pay to its employees at least 100% of the average statewide hourly wage, in addition to minimum health care benefits and insurance that must be provided; and

— at least 50% of the employees engaged or anticipated to be engaged in the construction of the data center are residents of Nevada, unless satisfactory proof is provided that there is an insufficient number of state residents available and qualified for such employment.

For applicants seeking a partial abatement for a period of 10 years, but not more than 20 years, the following requirements must be met (Sec. 360.754):

— the data center will, not later than the date that is five years after the date on which the abatement becomes effective, have 50 or more full-time resident employees and will continue to employ 50 or more full-time resident employees until at least the date that is 20 years after the date on which the abatement becomes effective;

— not later than the date that is five years after the date on which the abatement becomes effective, the data center and/or colocated businesses must make a cumulative capital investment of at least $100 million in capital assets that will be used or located at the data center;

— the data center must pay to its employees at least 100% of the average statewide hourly wage, in addition to minimum health care benefits and insurance that must be provided; and

— at least 50% of the employees engaged or anticipated to be engaged in the construction of the data center are residents of Nevada, unless satisfactory proof is provided that there is an insufficient number of state residents available and qualified for such employment.

The Office of Economic Development may not approve any application for a partial abatement submitted that is received on or after January 1, 2036.

¶ 631   Deficiency Assessments

A deficiency assessment may be made by the Department of Taxation (1) if it is not satisfied with the return filed or the amount of tax required to be paid, or (2) if any person subject to tax fails to make a return.

If a return made or any amount paid is not satisfactory to the Department, the Department may compute the amount required to be paid on the basis of the return filed, any information that it has or that may come into its possession, or a reasonable estimate of the amount (Sec. 360.300).

If a person fails to make a return, the Department shall make an estimate of the amount of gross receipts or the amount of the total sales price, on the basis of any information that it has or that may come into its possession (Sec. 360.300).

The collection of sales and use tax may not be prevented by injunction, writ of mandate, or any other legal or equitable process issued against the state or any officer of the state (Sec. 372.670, Sec. 374.675).

• Deficiency determinations

Taxes become delinquent if not paid by the due dates specified by law. Penalties applicable to delinquent payments commence from the due date.

The Department must give a person against whom a determination has been made prompt written notice of the estimate, determination, and penalty, either personally or by mail. If service by mail, the service is complete at the time of deposit with the U.S. Postal Service. The service of notice tolls any limitation for the determination of a further deficiency (Sec. 360.350).

All determinations made by the Department become final after 30 days if the taxpayer does not file a petition for redetermination, or 30 days after service of notice of the final order or decision on such petition (Sec. 360.360, Sec. 360.390).

• Discontinuance of business

When a business is discontinued, a determination may be made at any time within the time limits authorized for making assessments as to liability arising out of that business, regardless of whether the determination is issued before the due date of the liability, which is apparently the due date for filing the return and paying the tax (Sec. 360.300). Thus, estimated assessments may be issued before the return is actually due. This power would be useful if earlier returns had not been filed, and the last return for the discontinued business is not yet due.

¶ 632 Audit Procedures

The Department of Taxation may examine the books, papers, records, and equipment of any person selling tangible personal property and any person liable for the use tax (Sec. 372.740, Sec. 374.745). The character of the business may also be investigated in order to verify the accuracy of any return made or to determine any amount to be paid if no return was filed.

The Department may authorize any person, in writing, to perform the examination function. It may also delegate authority to its representatives to conduct hearings, adopt regulations, or perform any other duties (Sec. 372.730, Sec. 374.735).

The Department may employ accountants, auditors, investigators, assistants, and clerks for the efficient administration of the sales and use tax (Sec. 372.730, Sec. 374.735).

Any person selling or using tangible personal property in the state who is required to obtain a seller's permit or file a sales or use tax return and who keeps records outside the state must reimburse the Department of Taxation for the cost of any employees sent out of state to examine the records (Sec. 372.740). The cost will consist of the allowance paid to state officers and employees while travelling outside Nevada plus the actual expenses incurred during the examination.

¶ 633 Statute of Limitations

Nevada has specific time limits for the assessment of taxes, for actions to collect taxes, and for claims for refund of taxes. There is also a time period limitation for prosecution of criminal actions.

• Time limit for assessment

A notice of tax deficiency must be served within three years after the last day of the calendar month following the period to which the deficiency relates, or within three years after the return is filed, whichever expires later (Sec. 360.355).

In the case of failure to make a return, or of a claim for an additional amount pursuant to a redetermination, the time limit for filing notice is eight years after the calendar month following the period for which the assessment is proposed to be determined.

The right to assess in cases of fraud or intent to evade the tax is without a time limit.

The time may be extended by mutual written agreement made before the expiration of the time prescribed or agreed upon. The periods may be expressly waived by the taxpayer.

• **Time limit for collection**

The Department of Taxation may bring suit to collect a delinquent tax, together with penalties and interest, within four years after the tax becomes due, or after the tax becomes delinquent, or within five years after the last recording of the abstract of the judgment or the certificate of delinquency (Sec. 360.510).

• **Time limit for refunds or credits**

A claim for refund or credit must be filed with the Department of Taxation within three years from the last day of the month following the close of the period for which the overpayment was made (Sec. 372.635, Sec. 374.640).

When the claim for refund or credit arises from a recomputation of the tax by the Department of Taxation or an assessment by reason of failing to file a return, the claim must be made within six months from the date of overpayment or after the determinations become final, whichever period expires later (Sec. 372.635, Sec. 374.640), unless the credit relates to a period for which a waiver has been made.

Failure to file a claim within the time limits described above constitutes a waiver of any demand against the state on account of overpayment (Sec. 372.650, Sec. 374.655).

A suit against the Department of Taxation in connection with a disallowed claim must be made within 90 days after the mailing of the Department's action on the claim (Sec. 372.680, Sec. 374.685). Failure to bring timely suit constitutes a waiver of any demand against the state on account of alleged overpayments.

• **Time limit for criminal prosecutions**

Any prosecution for violation of any penal provisions of the Sales and Use Tax Act must be instituted within three years of the commission of the offense (Sec. 372.770, Sec. 374.775).

¶ 634   Application for Refund

A refund or credit may result either from an action by the Department of Taxation to refund an excess collection or from a claim filed by a taxpayer against the Department of Taxation.

• **Refund or credit of excess collections**

If the Department of Taxation determines that a tax, penalty, or interest (1) has been paid more than once, or (2) has been erroneously or illegally collected or computed, the Department certifies such excess collection to the State Board of Examiners (Sec. 372.630, Sec. 374.635(1)). If the State Board of Examiners approves, the excess is credited against any other such tax or fee then due from the taxpayer or other person before any portion of the overpayment may be refunded.

Any overpayment of use tax by a purchaser is credited or refunded by the state to the purchaser (Sec. 372.630(2), Sec. 374.635(2)). However, no credit or refund of use tax may be allowed unless the person who paid the tax reimburses the vendor for the amount of the sales tax paid by the vendor (Sec. 372.640, Sec. 374.645).

• **Claim for credit or refund**

A claim for refund or credit must be brought by the person who paid the amount that is the subject of the claim; an assignee of such person has no standing to claim for the refund (Sec. 372.700, Sec. 374.705). This provision, however, is not intended to apply to involuntary assignments arising by operation of law, such as trustees in bankruptcy and executors or administrators of estates (*Letter to CCH,* Department of Taxation, September 7, 1990).

The filing of such a claim is a prerequisite for a court to assume jurisdiction if the claimant decides to file suit in connection with a denied claim (Sec. 372.675, Sec. 374.680).

The claim must be filed within the three-year statutory period, unless the credit relates to a period for which the statute of limitations has been waived. The claim must be in writing and must state the specific grounds upon which the claim is founded (Sec. 372.645, Sec. 374.650).

¶ 635   NEW HAMPSHIRE

¶ 636   General State Tax Not Imposed

Neither the state of New Hampshire nor any of its political subdivisions imposes any form of general sales or consumption tax based upon the sale of tangible personal property. However, the state does impose a limited sales tax at the rate of 9% applicable to meals; the transient occupancy of hotel rooms and similar quarters; and gross receipts from the rental of motor vehicles (RSA 78-A:6). For further details on that tax, see the discussion at ¶ 60-150 of the CCH NEW HAMPSHIRE TAX REPORTS.

¶ 651   Scope of Tax

Source.—Statutory references are to Title 54, Chapter 32B of the Revised Statutes, as amended to date. Details are reported in the CCH NEW JERSEY STATE TAX REPORTS starting at ¶ 60-000.

Sales and use taxes are imposed under the Sales and Use Tax Act (Sec. 54:32B-1) on receipts from retail sales of tangible personal property or digital property (Sec. 54:32B-3(a)); sales of enumerated services (Sec. 54:32B-3(b)); the use of tangible personal property or digital property and services (Sec. 54:32B-6); occupancies of hotel and motel rooms (Sec. 54:32B-3(d)); food and beverages sold by restaurants and caterers (Sec. 54:32B-3(c)); admission and cabaret charges (Sec. 54:32B-3(e)); and telecommunications services (Sec. 54:32B-3(f)). The tax is collected by the seller from the customer when collecting the price, service charge, amusement charge or rent to which it applies (Sec. 54:32B-12(a)).

The tax on sales of tangible personal property is general, applying to all such property unless specifically exempted. The tax on services is selective, applying only to services as enumerated. Services rendered for a person within New Jersey, but actually performed outside the state, are taxable if performed on property that is subject to use tax or will be subject to use tax when it is received by or comes into possession or control of such person in New Jersey (Sec. 54:32B-2(y)).

Digital products: The sales and use taxes apply to the following property:

— magazines and periodicals, whether or not accessed by electronic means; however, the exemption is retained for newspapers, magazines and periodicals sold by subscription, and membership periodicals (Sec. 54:32B-8.5(a));

— a specified digital product, which is defined as an electronically transferred digital audio-visual work, digital audio work, or digital book (Sec. 54:32B-2(zz)).

To maintain New Jersey's tax treatment of digital property within the parameters of the SST Agreement, 2011 legislation made certain ancillary changes (Sec. 54:32B-2). Specifically, the law:

(1) revises the definition of "retail sale" to clarify that sales of specified digital products are only taxable to end-users;

(2) specifies that a digital code that provides a purchaser the right to obtain the product is treated as a specified digital product for tax purposes;

(3) stipulates that specified digital products are subject to tax regardless of whether the sale of the product is for permanent or less-than-permanent use and regardless of whether continued payment is required;

(4) provides an exemption for video programming services, including video-on-demand television services, and for broadcasting services, including content to provide such services; and

(5) provides an exemption for specified digital products that are accessed but not delivered electronically.

Prewritten software delivered electronically is taxable as tangible personal property (Sec. 54:32B-2(g); *Technical Bulletin TB-51R,* New Jersey Division of Taxation, July 5, 2011, CCH NEW JERSEY STATE TAX REPORTS, ¶ 401-578). Nevertheless, receipts from sales of prewritten software delivered electronically and used directly and exclusively in the conduct of the purchaser's business, trade, or occupation are exempt from tax (Sec. 54:32B-8.56(15)).

Since prewritten computer software is defined as tangible personal property, servicing, installing, or maintaining software is subject to tax, whether the software is serviced, installed, or maintained at the purchaser's location or from or at a seller or service provider's remote location (Reg. 18:24-25.6).

Software as a service (cloud computing): A taxpayer's charges for software as a service are not subject to New Jersey sales or use tax so long as the software is only accessed by the user and there is no transfer or delivery of the software to the user. The taxpayer provides software that is provided as a service, in which a user pays a monthly fee in exchange for use of a web application hosted on the taxpayer's computer systems. (*LR: 2012-4-SUT,* New Jersey Division of Taxation, June 22, 2012, CCH NEW JERSEY STATE TAX REPORTS, ¶ 401-651; *Technical Bulletin TB-72,* New Jersey Division of Taxation, July 3, 2013, CCH NEW JERSEY STATE TAX REPORTS, ¶ 401-742)

Fuel surcharges: The retail sale of motor fuels is exempt from sales tax. Thus, when purchased by the seller of services or property, gasoline is not subject to sales tax. However, a separately stated fuel surcharge is an expense that a seller incurs in order to perform a service or sell a product. The taxability of a fuel surcharge follows the taxability of the service provided or the product sold. Thus, if the transaction is for a service or product that is not subject to sales tax, then the fuel surcharge is also not subject to tax. On the other hand, if the transaction is for a service or product that is subject to sales tax, then the fuel surcharge is subject to tax. (*Notice,* New Jersey Division of Taxation, August 7, 2008)

Leases and rentals: A publication explains how and when sales and use tax is imposed on lease and rental transactions in New Jersey (*Bulletin S&U-12,* New Jersey Division of Taxation, March 2016, CCH NEW JERSEY STATE TAX REPORTS, ¶ 401-947; also available at **http://www.state.nj.us/treasury/taxation/pdf/pubs/sales/su12.pdf**)

• **Taxable services**

Taxable services include the following:

— processing and printing services (Sec. 54:32B-3(b)(1));

— installation and maintenance services (Sec. 54:32B-3(b)(2));

— real estate maintenance or repair (Sec. 54:32B-3(b)(4));

— storage and safe deposit rentals (Sec. 54:32B-3(b)(3));

— advertising services (Sec. 54:32B-3(b)(5)); and

— telecommunications services (Sec. 54:32B-3(f)).

— the furnishing of space for storage of tangible personal property, by a person engaged in the business of furnishing space for such storage (Sec. 54:32B-3(b)(3));

— tanning services, including the application of a temporary tan provided by any means (Sec. 54:32B-3(b)(8));

— massage, bodywork, or somatic services, except such services provided pursuant to a doctor's prescription (Sec. 54:32B-3(b)(9));

— tattooing, including all permanent body art and permanent cosmetic make-up applications (except as prescribed in connection with breast reconstructive surgery) (Sec. 54:32B-3(b)(10));

— investigative and security services (Sec. 54:32B-3(b)(11));

— information services (Sec. 54:32B-3(b)(12); *Publication ANJ-29,* New Jersey Division of Taxation, August 20, 2013,);

— transportation services originating in New Jersey and provided by a limousine operator, except such services provided in connection with funeral services (Former Sec. 54:32B-3(b)-8.11; repealed, effective May 1, 2017);

— initiation fees, membership fees or dues for access to or use of the property or facilities of a health and fitness, athletic, sporting or shopping club or organization, except for memberships in a club or organization whose members are predominantly age 18 or under (Sec. 54:32B-2);

— receipts from parking, storing or garaging a motor vehicle, excluding charges for residential parking; employee parking provided by an employer or at a facility owned or operated by the employer (Sec. 54:32B-3(b)(i));

— municipal parking taxes (Sec. 54:32B-3(b)(i)).

Wages, salaries and other compensation paid by an employer to an employee for rendering services otherwise taxable are not subject to tax (Sec. 54:32B-3(b)(6)).

Cosmetic medical procedures: Before July 1, 2014, a gross receipts tax was imposed on the purchase of certain cosmetic medical procedures (Former Sec. 54:32E-1).

- **Transactions subject to use tax**

The use tax is imposed, unless the property or service has already been subject to the sales tax, on the use of property or services within New Jersey (Sec. 54:32B-6).

The use tax is imposed on the following (Sec. 54:32B-6):

— use of tangible personal property purchased at retail;

— use of tangible personal property manufactured, processed, or assembled by the user, if items of the same kind are offered for sale by the user in the regular course of business, or if items of the same kind are not offered for sale by the user in the regular course of business and are used as such or incorporated into a structure, building, or real property. The mere storage, keeping, retention or withdrawal from storage of such property, however, without actual use, is not a taxable use; and

— use of tangible personal property, however acquired, when not acquired for resale, upon which taxable production, processing, fabricating or imprinting services have been performed or with respect to which taxable installation, maintenance or repair services have been performed.

For additional information, see *Publication ANJ-7,* New Jersey Division of Taxation, March 2017, CCH New Jersey Tax Reports, ¶ 402-057.

- **Responsibility for tax**

Sales tax is collected by sellers from their customers (Sec. 54:32B-12(a)). The sellers are personally liable for the tax collected or required to be collected (Sec. 54:32B-14). If a customer fails to pay a tax to the seller, the customer must pay the tax directly to the state.

Use tax: Any person required to collect tax under the Sales and Use Tax Act must file a certificate of registration with the Division of Taxation (Sec. 54:32B-15), and is required to file returns (Sec. 54:32B-17) and pay taxes (Sec. 54:32B-18). See also ¶ 656 and ¶ 659.

State contractors: Businesses that have entered into contracts with the state of New Jersey are required to collect use tax on sales of tangible personal property delivered into the state (Sec. 52:32-44).

- **Business purchases**

The New Jersey Division of Taxation publishes a bulletin that provides information on the sales and use tax treatment of business purchases of various goods and services. It explains when a business owner is required to pay sales tax on a purchase, when a sales tax exemption certificate may be used, and when use tax is due. (*Bulletin S&U-9,* New Jersey Division of Taxation, March 2016, CCH New Jersey State Tax Reports, ¶ 401-943)

• **Nexus**

New Jersey requires any seller doing business in New Jersey to collect and remit sales or use tax. New Jersey does not define the term "doing business."

A "seller" includes (Sec. 54:32B-2):

— a person maintaining a place of business in New Jersey and making taxable sales of tangible personal property, specified digital products, or services to persons within New Jersey;

— a person who solicits business either by employees, independent contractors, agents or other representatives or by distribution of catalogs or other advertising matter and by reason thereof makes taxable sales to persons within New Jersey; and

— any other person making taxable sales to persons within New Jersey of tangible personal property, specified digital products, or services.

Trade shows: An out-of-state business creates nexus for purposes of collecting use tax in New Jersey by participating as an exhibitor at a trade show and taking orders at a trade show in New Jersey. An out-of-state business does not establish nexus with New Jersey if it attends a trade show in New Jersey as a consumer. (*CCH Sales and Use Tax Nexus Survey,* New Jersey Division of Taxation, September 23, 2010, CCH New Jersey Tax Reports, ¶ 401-531)

Click-through nexus: Beginning July 1, 2014, an out-of-state seller, who makes taxable sales of tangible personal property, specified digital products, or services, is soliciting business in New Jersey through in-state representatives if that seller meets the following conditions (Sec. 54:32B-2):

(1) the seller enters into an agreement with a New Jersey independent contractor or other representative (in-state representative) to refer potential customers via a link on a website, or otherwise, to that out-of-State seller in exchange for consideration based on completed sales; and

(2) the seller has sales from these referrals to customers in New Jersey in excess of $10,000 for the prior four quarterly periods ending on the last day of March, June, September, and December.

An out-of-State seller that meets both conditions above is presumed to be soliciting business and has nexus with New Jersey. The out-of-state seller must register with New Jersey for sales tax purposes (see ¶ 659) and collect and remit sales tax on all sales delivered into New Jersey unless the presumption can be rebutted.

An out-of-state seller that is presumed to be soliciting business in New Jersey through in-state representatives may rebut that presumption by establishing that the only in-state activity of the in-state representative(s) on its behalf is placing a link on the in-state representatives' website(s) to the out-of-state seller's website for compensation; and, certifying that none of the in-state representative(s) engage in any solicitation activity in the state targeted at potential New Jersey customers on behalf of the out-of-state seller. (Sec. 54:32B-2; *Technical Bulletin B-76,* New Jersey Division of Taxation, December 12, 2014, CCH New Jersey Tax Reports, ¶ 401-848; *Technical Bulletin TB-78,* New Jersey Division of Taxation, July 30, 2015, CCH New Jersey Tax Reports, ¶ 401-893)

An out-of-State seller will successfully rebut the presumption of soliciting business in New Jersey by meeting both of the following conditions:

(1) *Prohibition language.*—the agreement between the out-of-state seller and the in-state representative provides that the in-State representative is prohibited from engaging in any solicitation activities in New Jersey that refer potential customers to the seller including, but not limited to: distributing flyers, coupons,

newsletters and other printed promotional materials, or electronic equivalents, verbal solicitation, initiating phone calls, and sending e-mails; and

(2) *Proof of compliance.*—the: the out-of-state seller must annually obtain from the in-state representative(s) a signed certification stating that the in-state representative did not engage in any prohibited solicitation activities in New Jersey on behalf of the out-of-state seller at any time during the prior four quarterly periods.

The certification may be submitted in either hard-copy or electronic format and must contain the name, address, and signature of the in-state representative. The certification must also contain a statement that the certification and any information submitted with it are subject to verification and audit by the division. The out-of-state seller will be considered to have satisfied the second condition if it receives signed certifications from its in-state representatives and accepts the certifications in good faith. The out-of-state seller must retain copies of the certifications and must make the copies available at the division's request. (*Technical Bulletin B-76,* New Jersey Division of Taxation, December 12, 2014, CCH NEW JERSEY TAX REPORTS, ¶ 401-848)

• **Streamlined Act status**

New Jersey is a full member of the Streamlined Sales and Use Tax Agreement with a seat on the Governing Board. It has enacted all of the provisions necessary to comply with the Agreement's requirements and these provisions currently are in effect (54:32B-44, *et seq.*). As a full member, New Jersey may vote on amendments to or interpretations of the Agreement, and sellers registering under the SST system must collect and remit tax on sales into the state. For additional details, see ¶ 654.

Taxability matrix: A chart of the taxable status of various items is accessible on the website of the Streamlined Sales Tax Project at **http://www.streamlinedsalestax.org**.

¶ 652	Tax Base

The New Jersey sales tax is based on receipts, as defined by statute (Sec. 54:32B-3). The use tax is generally based on the consideration given or contracted to be given for the property or for the use of the property (Sec. 54:32B-6).

• **"Receipt" defined**

"Receipt" means the amount of the sales price and the charge for any taxable service, whether received in money or other consideration, including any amount for which credit is allowed, without deduction for expenses or early payment discounts (Sec. 54:32B-2(d), Reg. 18:24-1.4(a), Reg. 18:24-1.4(c), Reg. 18:24-1.4(d)). However, credit for property of the same kind (that is not tangible personal property purchased for lease) accepted in part payment and for resale is excluded.

Prepaid telephone calling arrangements: Sales and use taxes are imposed on receipts from the retail sale or recharge of prepaid telephone calling arrangements (Sec. 54:32B-2(ll); Sec. 54:32B-3.4(d)).

Virtual currency: The New Jersey Division of Taxation has issued guidance concerning the treatment of virtual currency, such as bitcoin and other cryptocurrencies for purposes of corporation business, gross income (personal), and sales and use taxes. When a customer uses convertible virtual currency to pay for property, the sale is treated as a barter transaction. As a result, if a seller uses convertible virtual currency as consideration for goods or services, sales tax is due based on the amount allowed in exchange for the virtual currency. If the customer that provides convertible virtual currency in the trade receives property that is subject to tax, the customer owes tax based on the market value of the virtual currency at the time of the transaction, converted to U.S. dollars. (*Technical Advisory Memorandum TAM-2015-1(R),* New Jersey Division of Taxation, July 28, 2015, CCH NEW JERSEY TAX REPORTS, ¶ 401-891)

- **Basis of use tax**

The use tax is imposed on the consideration given or contracted to be given for property or for the use of property (Sec. 54:32B-6).

The tax base for the use of tangible personal property upon which taxable services (such as processing, printing, installation, maintenance, or repair) were performed includes the consideration for any tangible personal property transferred in conjunction with the service, but excludes transportation costs if separately stated in the written contract, if any, and on the bill rendered to the purchaser (Sec. 54:32B-6).

The basis of tax of tangible personal property purchased by a New Jersey resident outside the state for use outside the state that subsequently becomes subject to use tax is the purchase price, except that when the property is used outside the state for more than six months, it is taxed on the basis of its current market value, and if property is brought into the state and used in the performance of a contract for a period of less than six months, the tax may be based on the fair rental value of the property for the period of use in New Jersey (Sec. 54:32B-7(b)).

- **Sourcing of sales**

Sales are sourced generally to the destination of the product sold, with a default to origin-based sourcing in the absence of that information. The following general sourcing rules apply (Sec. 54:32B-3.1(a)):

(1) when the product is received by the purchaser at a business location of the seller, the sale is sourced to that business location;

(2) when the product is not received by the purchaser at a business location of the seller, the sale is sourced to the location where the purchaser or his donee receives the product;

(3) if neither of the above applies, the sale is sourced to the location indicated by an address for the purchaser that is available from the business records of the seller that are maintained in the ordinary course of the seller's business when use of this address does not constitute bad faith;

(4) if none of the above apply, the sale is sourced to the location indicated by an address for the purchaser obtained during the consummation of the sale, including the address of a purchaser's payment instrument, if no other address is available, when use of this address does not constitute bad faith;

(5) If none of the other rules apply, or if the seller is without sufficient information to apply the previous rules, then the location will be determined by the address from which tangible personal property was shipped, from which the digital good or the computer software delivered electronically was first available for transmission by the seller, or from which the service was provided.

Separate sourcing rules apply to sales of prewritten computer software (see Reg. 18:24-25.7), leases and rentals, and telecommunications (Sec. 54:32B-3.1(b) and (c)).

¶ 653   List of Exemptions, Exceptions, and Exclusions

Unless otherwise indicated, the statutory exemptions, exceptions, and exclusions listed below apply to both sales and use taxes; those applicable only to the use tax are listed separately. Items that are excluded from the sales or use tax base are treated at ¶ 652, "Tax Base."

• Sales and use tax exemptions, exceptions, and exclusions

Admission charges	Sec. 54:32B-2(o), Sec. 54:32B-2(r), Sec. 54:32B-3(e)(1), Sec. 54:32B-3(h)
Advertising and advertising services	Sec. 54:32B-3(b)(5), Sec. 54:32B-8.30, Sec. 54:32B-8.39
Agricultural property	Sec. 54:32B-8.16
Aircraft	Sec. 54:32B-8.35
Boats and vessels (50% exemption; $20,000 maximum tax)	Sec. 54:32B-4.2
Bibles or similar sacred scripture (the Division of Taxation is currently taxing these sales)	Sec. 54:32B-8.25
Buses and repair and replacement parts to regulated carriers and to school bus operators for public passenger transportation	Sec. 54:32B-8.28
Casual sales	Sec. 54:32B-8.6
Catalysts	Sec. 54:32B-8.20
Cleaning and laundry services	Sec. 54:32B-3(b)(2), Sec. 54:32B-3(b)(4)
Clothing and footwear (except furs, accessories, sport or recreational equipment, or protective equipment)	Sec. 54:32B-8.4
Commercial ships engaged in interstate commerce, commercial fishing boats, and government-owned boats	Sec. 54:32B-8.6, Sec. 54:32B-8.12, Sec. 54:32B-13(b)
Computer software, prewritten and used in business	Sec. 54:32B-8.56(15)
Construction materials used in fulfilling government contracts or contracts with nonprofit organizations	Sec. 54:32B-8.22, Sec. 54:32B-9(a)
Drugs for human use	Sec. 54:32B-8.1
Electricity	Sec. 54:32B-8.13, Sec. 54:32B-8.46
Energy devices or systems and cogeneration facilities	Sec. 54:32B-8.13(d), Sec. 54:32B-8.33
Energy devices or systems and cogeneration facilities	Sec. 54:32B-8.13(d), Sec. 54:32B-8.33
Energy sold to or by postconsumer material manufacturers (refund; exp. 12/31/2017)	Sec. 54:32B-8.47, Sec. 48:2-21.34
Eyeglasses	Sec. 54:32B-8.1
Ferryboats	Sec. 54:32B-8.12
Films, records, and tapes	Sec. 54:32B-8.18
Firearm vaults and trigger locks	Sec. 54:32B-8.50, Sec. 54:32B-8.51
Flags	Sec. 54:32B-8.26
Florists and nurseries	Sec. 54:32B-8.16
Food and food ingredients	Sec. 54:32B-8.2
Food stamp purchases	Sec. 54:32B-2(d)

Fuel	Sec. 54:32B-8.7
Funeral items	Sec. 54:32B-8.17
Fur garments: laundering, dry cleaning, tailoring, etc.	Reg. 18:24-6.8
Garbage removal and sewer services	Sec. 54:32B-3(b)(4)
Gas	Sec. 54:32B-8.7
Gold and silver	Sec. 54:32B-8.32
Government transactions	Sec. 54:32B-9(a)
Hotel rental to a permanent resident, when the rent is not more than $2 per day, and by nonprofit organizations	Sec. 54:32B-2(m), Sec. 54:32B-3(d)
Installation of property resulting in capital improvements	Sec. 54:32B-3(b)(2)
Insurance transactions	Sec. 54:32B-2(e)(4)(A)
Interstate sales	Sec. 54:32B-8.10
Limousines, repairs, parts sold to licensed operators	Sec. 54:32B-8.52
Manufacturing, processing, assembling, or refining equipment	Sec. 54:32B-8.13(a)
Meals to elderly and disabled persons	Sec. 54:32B-3(c)
Medical equipment (durable)	Sec. 54:32B-8.1
Medicine and medical supplies	Sec. 54:32B-8.1
Mobile homes except first sale	Sec. 54:4-1.7
Motor fuels	Sec. 54:32B-8.8
Motor vehicles, zero-emission	Sec. 54:32B-8.55
Newspapers, magazines, and periodicals	Sec. 54:32B-8.5, Sec. 54:32B-11(5)
Nonprofit organizations	Sec. 54:32B-9(b), Sec. 54:32B-9(c), Sec. 54:32B-9(e)
Nonresident purchase of a motor vehicle, aircraft, or boat	Sec. 54:32B-10(a)
Packaging supplies	Sec. 54:32B-8.15
Paper products	Sec. 54:32B-8.44
Pollution control (effluent) equipment	Sec. 54:32B-8.36
Printing production equipment	Sec. 54:32B-8.29
Production, film or video	Sec. 54:32B-8.49
Professional or personal transactions	Sec. 54:32B-2(e)(4)(A)
Prosthetic devices and equipment	Sec. 54:32B-8.1
Railroad rolling stock	Sec. 54:32B-8.27
Recycling equipment (refund)	Sec. 54:32B-8.36
Relocating businesses	Sec. 34:1B-187
Rental transactions between related persons	Sec. 54:32B-8.53
Renting and servicing trucks, tractors, trailers, semi-trailers, and commercial motor vehicles	Sec. 54:32B-3(b)(2), Sec. 54:32B-8.43
Repair of a residential heating system unit serving no more than three families living independently of each other	Sec. 54:32B-3(b)(4)
Resales	Sec. 54:32B-2(e)(1), Sec. 54:32B-8.17, Sec. 54:32B-12(b)

¶653   New Jersey

Research and development property	Sec. 54:32B-8.14
Sale-leaseback transactions	Sec. 54:32B-8.57
School textbooks	Sec. 54:32B-8.21
Shoe repairing and shining	Sec. 54:32B-3(b)(2)
Software, prewritten, delivered electronically	Sec. 54:32B-8.56
Steam	Sec. 54:32B-8.13
Tangible personal property delivered to the purchaser outside of New Jersey for use outside New Jersey	Sec. 54:32B-8.10
Tattooing and cosmetic services provided pursuant to a doctor's prescription in conjunction with reconstructive breast surgery	Sec. 54:32B-3(b)(10)
Tangible personal property purchased for lease	Sec. 54:32B-8.40
Telecommunications equipment	Sec. 54:32B-8.13(c)
Telephone and telegraph equipment sold to a service provider	Sec. 54:32B-8.13(c)
Transportation of persons or property	Sec. 54:32B-8.11
Urban Enterprise Zones, sales to qualified businesses	Sec. 52:27H-79
Utilities—Sales of equipment for use in the production of gas, electricity, refrigeration, steam, or water	Sec. 54:32B-8.7
Vending machine sales of 25¢ or less	Sec. 54:32B-8.9
Veterans' organizations	Sec. 54:32B-9(b), (f)
Veterans' homes concession stands	Sec. 54:32B-8.54
Water	Sec. 54:32B-8.7

• Exemptions, exceptions, and exclusions applicable only to the use tax

Boats and vessels (use by a resident purchaser within New Jersey for up to 30 days)	Sec. 54:32B-6.1
Paper used in publication of newspapers and periodicals	Sec. 54:32B-8.5
Property converted into, or that becomes a component part of, a product produced for sale or for market sampling	Sec. 54:32B-11(4)
Property or services already subjected to sales tax	Sec. 54:32B-6
Property or services that would be exempt from sales tax if sold in New Jersey	Sec. 54:32B-11(3)
Property purchased by a nonresident	Sec. 54:32B-11(2)
Property used before July 1, 1966, the effective date of the Sales and Use Tax Act	Sec. 54:32B-11(1)
Property used in performing services when the property becomes a physical component part of the serviced property or when the property is later transferred to the purchaser of the service . .	Sec. 54:32B-2(e)(1)
Storage, keeping, retention, or withdrawal from storage of tangible personal property by the person who manufactured, processed, or assembled the property	Sec. 54:32B-6
Use of property or services upon which a sales or use tax has been paid to another state that allows a corresponding exemption with respect to property or services upon which the sales or use tax was paid to New Jersey, except to the extent the rate in New Jersey exceeds the rate in the other state	Sec. 54:32B-11(6)

¶ 654 **Rate of Tax**

The New Jersey sales and use tax rate was reduced from 7% to 6.875% on January 1, 2017, and is further reduced to 6.625% on January 1, 2018. Transitional provisions apply for taxing sales transactions that stretch across the tax rate change dates. (Sec. 54:32B-3; Sec. 54:32B-5; Sec. 54:32B-6).

Businesses located in Salem County are authorized to collect the tax at one-half the current rate on sales of tangible personal property or digital property, with certain exceptions (Sec. 54:32B-8.45) (see ¶ 655).

Urban Enterprise Zones: New Jersey has established Urban Enterprise Zones and UEZ-impacted business districts in which sales and use tax on certain items may be charged at 50% of the regular rate on sales of merchandise qualified for the reduced rate (Sec. 52:27H-80). For more information, see **http://www.state.nj.us/treasury/taxation/uezrefundsofsales.shtml**.

Occupancy tax: A statewide hotel and motel occupancy tax is imposed. The tax rate is 5% of the rent paid by hotel and motel guests, but is reduced in certain localities (see ¶ 655). The state occupancy tax is in addition to the state sales tax (Sec. 54:32D-1). The combined rates of these taxes plus state and local sales and use taxes must not exceed 14%.

A bulletin explains the application of the sales and use tax to the sale of hotel occupancies and related goods, services, and fees. It also explains other taxes that may apply to the sale of hotel occupancies. Charges for occupancies of a room or rooms in a hotel in New Jersey are subject to sales tax, the state occupancy fee, and, if applicable, the municipal occupancy tax. Sales tax does not apply to charges for the rental of real property, such as house rentals or commercial leases. (*Bulletin S&U-13,* New Jersey Division of Taxation, July 2016, CCH NEW JERSEY TAX REPORTS, ¶ 401-974)

Motor vehicle rentals: Rentals and leases of motor vehicles are subject to sales and use tax. A $5 per day domestic security fee is imposed on rentals from a location within New Jersey for a period of not more than 28 days (Reg. 18:40-1.3). The fee is not included in the receipts subject to sales tax (*Technical Bulletin TB-47 (R2),* July 21, 2006, CCH NEW JERSEY TAX REPORTS, ¶ 401-190).

Tire fee: A fee of $1.50 is imposed on the purchaser of a new motor vehicle tire if the purchase is subject to New Jersey sales tax. The fee also is imposed on new tires that are component parts of a purchased or leased motor vehicle. The fee must be collected from the purchaser by the seller, and generally must be stated separately on any bill, invoice, receipt, or similar document. However, the fee will not be considered part of the receipt for purposes of determining sales tax (Sec. 54:32F-1).

• **Transitional provisions**

The Division of Taxation may not hold a seller liable for failure to collect tax due at a new tax rate, if the director provides less than 30 days between the date a change in rate is enacted and the date that change takes effect. However, the director is not required to provide relief in instances where the seller collected the tax at a rate other than the immediately preceding tax rate and in instances where the seller's failure to collect tax at the new rate extends more than 30 days after the date the new rate is enacted. Moreover, the director is not required to provide relief if a seller fraudulently failed to collect tax at the new rate or solicits purchasers using the immediately preceding tax rate. (Sec. 54:32B-5)

¶ 655 **Local Taxes**

Any city of the fourth class is authorized to enact an ordinance levying a tax on retail sales (Sec. 40:48-8.15). Atlantic City imposes a luxury tax at the rate of 9%, except that the sale of alcoholic beverages is taxed at the rate of 3% (Reg. 18:25-1.5).

Maximum combined rate for sales in Atlantic City: The maximum combined rate of tax for sales that are subject to both the state sales and use tax and the Atlantic City luxury tax is 13% (Sec. 54:32B-8.19). The state occupancy tax is imposed at the rate of 1%. Alcoholic beverages sold by the drink in Atlantic City are taxed at a combined rate consisting of a 3% local luxury tax and the rate of the state sales tax. Charges for prepared food are subject only to the state's sales tax.

Salem County reduced rate: Businesses in Salem County collect the state sales tax at one-half the state rate on tangible personal property other than the following: motor vehicles; alcoholic beverages; cigarettes; catalogue or mail-order sales; sales of services (*e.g.,* maintenance and repairs); prepared food, meals, and beverages; telephone and electronically communicated sales; sales made from locations outside of the county; and charges for room occupancy, admissions, and amusements (Sec. 54:32B-8.45).

Sports and entertainment districts: Any eligible municipality may establish a sports and entertainment district within the municipality and impose sales taxes to finance development of sports and entertainment facilities. An eligible municipality that establishes a sports and entertainment district may impose a 2% tax on any of the following to pay for project costs of the facility for a period of not more than 30 years: (1) sales within the district of taxable tangible personal property; (2) sales within the district of taxable food and drink; (3) charges for hotel rooms occupied within the district; or (4) admission charge to a place of amusement within the district. (Secs. 34:1B-190—Sec. 34:1B-206)

Eligible Municipalities are also authorized to impose an additional charge of 2%, collected from hotels situated within the district (Sec. 34:1B-194).

Admissions surcharges: An eligible municipality may a impose surcharge of up to 5% of the admission charge to major places of amusement that seat at least 10,000 patrons, but excluding motion picture theaters, amusement parks, and places of amusement owned by, or located on property owned by, the state or an independent state authority (Sec. 40:48G-1). The city of Newark imposes a 1.375% admissions surcharge on events at the Prudential Center.

Parking surcharges: A surcharge of 7% may be imposed on fees for the parking, garaging, or storing of motor vehicles, except for parking in a garage that is part of a solely residential premises. Qualified municipalities include the cities of Camden, Passaic, Paterson, and Trenton. (Sec. 40:48C-1.5; Sec. 40:48C-1.6)

Also, municipalities are authorized to impose a 7% special event parking tax surcharge on fees for the parking, garaging, or storing of motor vehicles for events held in the municipality during weekday evenings (beginning at 6:00 p.m. or later), and held at any time on Saturdays, Sundays, and holidays. Special events include, but are not limited to, spectator sporting events, trade shows, expositions, concerts, and other public events. (Sec. 40:48C-6(b))

Mobile telecommunications: New Jersey has adopted the provisions and definitions of the federal Mobile Telecommunications Sourcing Act (P.L. 106-252) (Sec. 54:32B-2, Sec. 54:32B-3, Sec. 54:32B-6). Mobile telecommunications services are sourced to the customer's "place of primary of use," which means the residential or primary business address of the customer, and must be located within the service area of the home service provider in accordance with 4 U.S.C. Sec. 124 (part of the federal Mobile Telecommunication Sourcing Act).

Rate changes: The effective date of any sales and use tax rate changes will be the first day of the calendar quarter following the expiration of one full calendar quarter immediately following enactment of the rate change (Sec. 54:32B-28.1(a)).

- **Occupancy taxes**

    Municipalities are authorized to impose a hotel/motel occupancy tax at a rate of up to 3% (Sec. 54:32D-1).

Newark: Newark imposes a 6% hotel use or occupancy tax, and the state occupancy tax is reduced to 1%. For any calendar year, hotel owners must pay the real property tax (ad valorem taxes, payment in lieu of taxes, or payment of annual service charges) or the hotel use or occupancy tax, whichever is greater (Sec. 40:48E-5).

Cape May County: Contiguous municipalities within a county of the sixth class (Cape May County) may, by ordinance, establish tourism improvement development districts which may levy a sales and use tax on "predominantly tourism related retail receipts" at a rate not to exceed 2% (Sec. 40:54D). Wildwood, Wildwood Crest, and North Wildwood impose the tax at the rate of 2%.

A 1.85% tourism assessment is imposed on the rent for any occupancy of a room in a hotel, motel, or other transient accommodation in Cape May County. The tourism assessment is in addition to the 2% tourism tax currently imposed. Thus, room rentals in Wildwood, Wildwood Crest, and North Wildwood are subject to a total rate that includes the New Jersey sales tax rate, the 2% tourism tax, and the 1.85% tourism assessment. The state occupancy tax in these areas is 3.15%.

¶ 656   Bracket Schedule

Tax is calculated to the third decimal place (Sec. 54:32B-4). One-half cent or higher is rounded up to the next cent; less than one-half cent is dropped in order to round the result down. Sellers may compute the tax due on a transaction on either an item or an invoice basis.

Alternatively, the 6.875% tax may be collected according to the following bracket collection schedule (Sec. 54:32B-4):

Sales price	Tax
1¢ to 7¢	No Tax
8¢ to 21¢	1¢
22¢ to 36¢	2¢
37¢ to 50¢	3¢
51¢ to 65¢	4¢
66¢ to 79¢	5¢
80¢ to 94¢	6¢
95¢ to $1.09	7¢

In addition to a tax of 6.875¢ on each full dollar, a tax is collected on each part of a dollar in excess of a full dollar in accordance with the above formula.

An expanded version of the above schedule is available at **http://www.state.nj.us/treasury/taxation/pdf/other_forms/sales/st75.pdf**.

¶ 657   Returns, Payments, and Due Dates

The Director of the Division of Taxation is expressly authorized to prescribe and classify due dates for tax payments and filing of returns (Sec. 54:32B-17). A regulation requires sellers required to collect taxes to file quarterly tax returns, accompanied by tax payments, with the Director of the Division of Taxation on or before the 20th day of the month (Reg. 18:24-11.2). However, monthly remittances of tax must be made to the Director by those sellers whose tax liability exceeds $500 for the first or second month of a quarterly filing following the quarter covered by the return. If less than $30,000 in New Jersey sales and use taxes was collected by the seller during the preceding calendar year, a monthly remittance is not required, regardless of the amount of tax due for that particular month.

Customers who fail to pay tax to the seller are required to pay the tax directly to the Director and it is the duty of the customer to file a return with the Director within 20 days (Sec. 54:32B-14(b)).

- **Payment due with return**

All of the taxes for the period for which a return is required to be filed, or for such lesser interval as is designated by the Director, must be paid when the return is due, or on the date set by the Director for the lesser interval, regardless of whether a return is filed (Sec. 54:32B-18).

- **Electronic filing and payment**

All taxpayers must file their sales and use tax quarterly returns and monthly remittance statements electronically, either online or by phone through the NJ Sales and Use Tax EZ File Systems, and submit payments electronically by electronic check (e-check), electronic funds transfer (EFT), or credit card. A taxpayer must make sales and use tax payments by electronic funds transfer if the taxpayer had a prior year liability of $30,000 or more (Sec. 54:48-4.1). Information about EZ File is available at **http://www.state.nj.us/treasury/taxation/suezfilefaq.shtml**.

Taxpayers that sell, store, deliver, transport, or generate natural gas or electricity are required to remit sales and use tax, corporation business (income) tax, transitional energy facility tax, and uniform transitional utility taxes and assessments by EFT regardless of the amount of their prior year liability (Sec. 54:48-4.1; Reg. 18:2-3.4).

- **Uniform Sales Tax Administration Act**

New Jersey has enacted the Uniform Sales and Use Tax Administration Act and is a member of the related Streamlined Sales and Use Tax Agreement (SSUTA). The Division of Taxation has adopted a chapter of administrative and procedural rules to conform to the SSUTA (Regs. 18:24B-1.1, *et seq.*).

Sourcing: See ¶ 652.

Direct mail provisions: Sales in which promotional materials are delivered individually to potential customers via direct means are known by many different names including direct marketing, direct mail, direct mail advertising, telemarketing, mail order and door-to-door selling among others. In addition, such sales are often made using mailing lists and other marketing techniques such as leaflets, brochures, letters, catalogs, or print ads that are mailed or distributed directly to current and potential customers. The common feature in these types of sales is that the ads or promotional materials are delivered directly to the customer and are designed to induce the customer to make a purchase.

A purchaser of direct mail that is not a holder of a direct payment permit must provide to a seller at the time of the transaction a direct mail form or information that indicates the locations of the recipients to which the direct mail is delivered. If the purchaser of direct mail does not have a direct pay permit and does not provide the seller with either a direct mail form or delivery information, the seller will collect the tax as if the taxable location is the address from which tangible personal property was shipped, from which the digital good or the computer software delivered electronically was first available for transmission by the seller, or from which the service was provided. (Sec. 54:32B-3.3).

Registration and remittance under SST: See ¶ 659; see also *Bulletin S&U-5*, New Jersey Division of Taxation, March 2015, CCH New Jersey Tax Reports, ¶ 401-872.

Bad debts: A bad debt deduction may be claimed on the return for the period during which the bad debt is written off as uncollectable in the taxpayer's books and records and is eligible to be deducted for federal income tax purposes. A taxpayer who is not required to file federal income tax returns may deduct a bad debt on a return filed for the period in which the bad debt is written off as uncollectable in the taxpayer's books and records and would be eligible for a bad debt deduction for federal income tax purposes if the taxpayer was required to file a federal income tax return (Sec. 54:32B-12.1(d)).

There is not a separate line on the sales and use tax return for bad debts. Instead, a taxpayer should include the amount on the "Deductions" line of the quarterly sales tax return for the period in which the bad debt is written off as uncollectible (*Notice,* New Jersey Division of Taxation, October 18, 2005).

A seller's certified service provider may claim a credit or refund for a bad debt on behalf of the seller if the certified service provider credits or refunds the full amount of the bad debt deduction or refund to the seller (Sec. 54:32B-12.1(g)).

Reliance on erroneous data: A seller or certified service provider is not liable for having charged and collected an incorrect amount of sales or use tax resulting from their reliance on erroneous data provided by the Director of Revenue or in the taxability matrix provided for under the Agreement (Sec. 54:32B-14(g), (i)).

• Bulk sales

When a person required to collect tax makes a sale, transfer, or assignment in bulk of some or all of the person's business assets, the purchaser must notify the Director by registered mail at least 10 days before taking possession of the assets of the sale and of the price, terms, and conditions, and whether the seller owes any tax. The Director must respond within 10 days of receiving the notice and notify the purchaser, transferee, or assignee that a possible claim for state taxes exists and include the amount of the state's claim. If the purchaser fails to give notice, the purchaser is personally liable for the taxes ordinarily due from the seller. Whenever the Director informs the purchaser that a possible tax claim against the seller exists, a first priority tax lien attaches to the purchase monies to be paid by the purchaser to the seller. To avoid personal liability for the seller's unpaid taxes, the purchaser must withhold from the purchase monies sufficient amounts to pay such taxes (Sec. 54:32B-22).

¶ 658   Prepayment of Taxes

Prepayment of the tax is required before certain property may be registered.

Boats: No registration certificate for any boat or other vessel, for which registration is required, will issue without proof that the tax was paid or that no tax is due (Sec. 54:32B-13(b)).

Motor vehicles; mobile homes: New motor vehicle registration certificates will not be issued unless the registrant proves either that the tax on the vehicle has been paid or that no tax is due (Reg. 18:24-7.3). In addition, no certificate of ownership for a manufactured or mobile home, whether new or used, will be issued in the absence of proof that any tax due has been paid or that no tax is due (Reg. 18:24-7.19).

¶ 659   Vendor Registration

All persons required to collect the sales tax and those who purchase tangible personal property for resale or lease must register with the Director of the Division of Taxation at least 15 business days before commencing business or opening a new place of business in New Jersey (Sec. 54:32B-15). This requirement applies whether or not a person has a regular place of business in state. Within five days of registration, the Director will issue, without charge to the registrant, a certificate of authority along with duplicates for each additional place of business.

The central registration system may be accessed on the Division's Web site at: **http://www.state.nj.us/treasury/taxation/streamregpro.shtml** or go directly to **http://www.streamlinedsalestax.org**.

Registration and remittance under SST: A seller that registers to pay or collect and remit sales or use tax in accordance with the terms of the Streamlined Sales and Use Tax Agreement may select one of the following methods of remittance or other method allowed by state law to remit the taxes collected (Sec. 54:32B-15):

Model One: A seller that selects a certified service provider as an agent to perform all the seller's sales or use tax functions, other than the seller's obligation to remit tax on its own purchases;

Model Two: A seller that selects a certified automated system to use which calculates the amount of tax due on a transaction; or

Model Three: A seller that uses its own proprietary automated sales tax system that has been certified as a certified automated system.

Model sellers and certified service providers are allowed monetary allowances in accordance with the terms of the Agreement.

• Optional registration

Persons not otherwise required to collect any sales or use tax, and who sell property or services subject to the use tax, may elect to file a registration certificate with the Director (Sec. 54:32B-15). The Director may issue a certificate of authority authorizing collection of use tax.

In addition, the Director may issue direct-payment permits in situations in which a purchaser of property or services is unable to determine how the items will be used.

¶ 660 Sales or Use Tax Credits

If a retail sales or use tax equal to or greater than the amount of the New Jersey tax is paid to another state or jurisdiction without any right to a refund or credit, the property that is the subject of the tax is not subject to the New Jersey use tax when imported for use or consumption in New Jersey (Sec. 54:32B-11(6)). If the New Jersey tax rate is higher than the tax rate of the other state or jurisdiction, the new Jersey tax is imposed on the difference. No exemption is allowed for property or services on which a tax has been paid to another state or jurisdiction, unless the other state or jurisdiction allows a corresponding exemption when a sales or use tax is paid to New Jersey.

¶ 661 Deficiency Assessments

The State Uniform Procedure Law governs all collection procedures when it is not in conflict with the sales and use tax provisions (Sec. 54:32B-28, Reg. 18:24-2.2).

Sales and use taxes are self-assessing, in that they are based upon receipts from sales and collected by the seller or another person authorized to collect taxes. However, if no sales tax return is filed, or if the return is incorrect or insufficient, the Director is authorized to compute the correct amount of tax due on the basis of any available information and issue a tax assessment (Sec. 54:32B-19, Sec. 54:49-6). This information may be based on estimates derived from external evidence such as stock on hand, purchase invoices, rental paid, number of rooms, location, scale of rents or charges, comparable rents or charges, and number of employees. Notice of the determination of taxes due is given to the seller or other person liable for the collection of tax.

Cigarette sales: New Jersey has enacted legislation to facilitate the collection of cigarette and sales and use taxes on retail sales of cigarettes shipped from outside the state and regulates those sales. The measure requires that all retail cigarette sales in New Jersey be made "face-to-face" unless the seller has (1) complied with the federal Jenkins Act, 15 U.S.C. Sec. 375, which requires anyone selling cigarettes to a buyer in another state to report the sale to the state tobacco tax administrator for the buyer's state; (2) verified payment of, paid, or collected all applicable state taxes, including the cigarette tax (currently $2.40 per pack) and the sales and use tax (currently 6% of the retail price); (3) verified that the purchaser is 18 years of age or older; and (4) received payment for the sale from the purchaser by a credit or debit card that has been issued in the purchaser's name or by check. Sellers taking an order for a non-face-to-face sale may request that purchaser's provide their e-mail addresses (Sec. 54:40A-47 *et seq.*).

¶ 662 Audit Procedures

The Director has the power to assess and determine the taxes due (Sec. 54:32B-24(6)) using any information available to him, whether from the seller's place of business or from any other source, when he deems that the return(s) filed are incorrect or insufficient (Sec. 54:32B-19, Reg. 18:2-2.15). Records will be deemed incorrect or insufficient if the accounting system used does not provide adequate internal control procedures that assure the accuracy and completeness of the transactions recorded and the records themselves are not maintained according to regulatory requirements.

Records must be available for inspection or examination at any time upon demand by the Director and must be preserved for four years (Sec. 54:32B-16).

The New Jersey Division of Taxation's audit procedure manual provides an overview of the procedures and guidelines available to the Division for completing all types of audits. Among other topics, the manual details audit preparations and procedures, confidentiality, and discussions of audits with respect to specific tax types. The manual can be accessed on the Division's website at **http://www.state.nj.us/treasury/taxation/pdf/njmap.pdf**. (New Jersey Manual of Audit Procedures, New Jersey Division of Taxation, March 1, 2017)

Exemption certificates: In an audit situation, if the seller either has not obtained an exemption certificate or has obtained an incomplete exemption certificate, the seller has at least 120 days after the division's request for substantiation of the claimed exemption to either:

(1) obtain a fully completed exemption certificate from the purchaser, taken in good faith, which, in an audit situation, means that the seller obtain a certificate claiming an exemption that: (a) was statutorily available on the date of the transaction, (b) could be applicable to the item being purchased, and (c) is reasonable for the purchaser's type of business; or

(2) obtain other information establishing that the transaction was not subject to the tax.

If the seller obtains this information, the seller is relieved of any liability for the tax on the transaction unless it is discovered through the audit process that the seller had knowledge or had reason to know at the time such information was provided that the information relating to the exemption claimed was materially false or the seller otherwise knowingly participated in activity intended to purposefully evade the tax that is properly due on the transaction. The burden is on the division to establish that the seller had knowledge or had reason to know at the time the information was provided that the information was materially false. (*Technical Bulletin TB-66*, New Jersey Division of Taxation, September 26, 2011, CCH NEW JERSEY TAX REPORTS, ¶ 401-598)

• **Voluntary disclosure**

Taxpayers who realize they have a tax filing obligation or their business activity creates nexus for state tax purposes may come forward and file the appropriate tax returns, registration materials, and pay outstanding tax obligations. By participating, the taxpayer will be eligible for the terms that are offered under the program, including anonymity pending an agreement and relief from late filing and late payment penalties. The general look-back period is four years (three prior years and the current year).

To be eligible for the program, there must have been no previous contact with the taxpayer by the Division or any of its agents, taxpayers must not be registered for the taxes they wish to come forward regarding, the taxpayer must not be currently under any criminal investigation, and the taxpayer must be willing to pay outstanding tax liabilities and file the prior year returns within a reasonable period.

For additional information, see *Voluntary Disclosure Program*, New Jersey Division of Taxation, August 20, 2010, CCH NEW JERSEY TAX REPORTS, ¶ 401-523.

¶ 663   Statute of Limitations

An assessment of additional tax may not be made more than four years from the date the return was filed, except an assessment may be made at any time when a willfully false or fraudulent return is filed with the intent to evade tax or when no return is filed (Sec. 54:32B-27, Sec. 54:49-6).

A return filed before the last day prescribed by law or by applicable regulations will be considered as filed on the last day (Sec. 54:49-6).

¶ 664   Application for Refund

The Director will refund or credit any tax, penalty, or interest erroneously or illegally collected or paid if the taxpayer files for a refund within four years of payment (Sec. 54:32B-20). A customer who has actually paid the tax may file for a refund, and a person who is required to collect the tax may also qualify, provided that the person (1) has collected the tax and paid it to the director, (2) files the application within four years after receiving payment from the customer, and (3) satisfactorily establishes that the refund amount applied for has been repaid to the customer. The claim for refund must be under oath in such form as the Director may prescribe (Sec. 54:49-14). No claim for refund is permitted to be filed with respect to tax paid, after protest has been filed with the Director or after proceedings on appeal have started, until the protest or appeal has been finally determined. Each taxpayer must file a separate refund claim (Sec. 54:49-14). A claim on behalf of a class is not permitted. For additional information, see Reg. 18:2-5.8.

Discriminatory tax: If a tax is declared to be discriminatory in a final judicial decision from which all appeals have been exhausted, the Director may, within the Director's sole discretion, refund or credit only the discriminatory portion of the tax (Sec. 54:49-14).

• Refund for equipment used for recycling or effluent treatment

Receipts from sales of equipment used exclusively to recycle solid waste or treat effluent from a primary wastewater treatment facility are exempt. However, tax is first collected and will be refunded by the Division of Taxation to the purchaser who files a claim for refund within three years of the date of purchase, accompanied by a determination of environmental benefit issued by the Department of Environmental Protection (Sec. 54:32B-8.36).

• Refund for energy sales to or by manufacturers of postconsumer materials

Receipts from the sale or use of energy utility service to or by a postconsumer material manufacturing facility for use or consumption directly and primarily in the production of tangible personal property, other than energy, are exempt from sales and use tax and the transitional energy facility assessment (TEFA) unit rate surcharge for a period of seven years (Sec. 54:32B-8.60). Owners of eligible postconsumer material manufacturing facilities must continue to pay the taxes as the price of energy and utility service is collected, but the manufacturing facility owner then may file for quarterly refunds of the sales and use tax and TEFA surcharge allowable under the exemption. Claims must be filed within 30 days of the close of the calendar quarter in which the sale or use was made or rendered. If the owner of a postconsumer material manufacturing facility relocates the facility to a location outside New Jersey during the exemption period, the owner of the facility will be required to pay the amount of tax for which an exemption was allowed and refunded. (Sec. 54:32B-8.60)

• Refund for materials used to construct an off-track wagering facility

A one-time rebate of sales and use tax is available for the purchase of certain materials and supplies used for the construction of certain off-track wagering facilities. Specifically, the amount of rebate is equal to the sales and use tax collected from the retail sale or use of construction materials and construction supplies used by (1) a contractor of a person who is, as of January 1, 2012, a lessee of a racetrack owned by the New Jersey Sports and Exposition Authority, or (2) a contractor of a joint venture entered into between or among two persons who are lessees, or their affiliates, of the New Jersey Sports and Exposition Authority for the construction of an off-track wagering facility licensed by the New Jersey Racing Commission. (Uncodified Ch. 40 (S.B. 2078), Laws 2012)

¶ 665   NEW MEXICO

¶ 666   Scope of Tax

Source.—Statutory references are to sections of the New Mexico Statutes Annotated, as amended to date. Details are reported in the CCH NEW MEXICO TAX REPORTS starting at ¶ 60-000.

The gross receipts tax is a general excise tax imposed on persons for the privilege of engaging in business in the state (Sec. 7-9-4).

A tax referred to as the "governmental gross receipts tax" is imposed on every agency, institution, instrumentality, and political subdivision of the state, excepting however any entity licensed by the Department of Health that is principally engaged in providing health care services and any school district, for the privilege of engaging in certain activities (Sec. 7-9-4.3).

The compensating (use) tax is imposed on persons for the privilege of using tangible property in the state that was (1) manufactured by the person, (2) acquired inside or outside of New Mexico as the result of a transaction with a person outside New Mexico that would have been subject to the gross receipts tax if the property had been acquired from a person with nexus with New Mexico, or (3) acquired in a transaction that was not initially subject to the compensating tax or gross receipts tax but which should have been subject to tax because of the buyer's subsequent use of the property (Sec. 7-9-7). The compensating use tax is also imposed on persons for the privilege of using services rendered in the state in a transaction not initially subject to the gross receipts tax but which should have been subject to gross receipts tax because of the buyer's subsequent use of the services.

Sales on tribal land: The New Mexico Taxation and Revenue Department ruled that a food retailer who operates a food establishment on tribal land could treat 90% of the gross receipts from sales on that tribal land as being attributable to sales to a member of the tribe, nation or pueblo and, therefore, as receipts exempt from gross receipts tax. Sales of tangible personal property to Indian tribes or tribe members are not taxable. According to 2010 federal census data, approximately 96% of the residents on the tribal land are Native American. (*Ruling No. 406-13-1,* New Mexico Taxation and Revenue Department, August 5, 2013, CCH NEW MEXICO TAX REPORTS, ¶ 401-542)

Prepaid calling cards: The sale or recharge of these calling cards is the sale of a license to use the telecommunications system and subject to the gross receipts tax (Reg. 3.2.1.16(G)).

• **Services**

Services performed in New Mexico are subject to the gross receipts tax (Sec. 7-9-3(F), 3 NMAC 2.1.18.1). In addition, receipts from selling a service performed outside the state, the product of which is initially used in the state, are included in the definition of gross receipts. Nonetheless, such receipts generally are exempt from the gross receipts tax (Sec. 7-9-13.1).

Lodging: The receipts of hotels, motels, and similar facilities from guests or occupants are taxable; they are not receipts from leasing real property (Sec. 7-9-53; 3 NMAC 2.211.8; 3 NMAC 2.211.14). Such receipts do not include amounts paid as a municipal lodgers or room tax.

The U.S. District Court for the District of New Mexico held that the marked-up rates charged to customers by online travel companies (OTCs) were not subject to a local lodger's tax ordinance because the OTCs were not vendors under the ordinance. (*City of Gallup, New Mexico v. Hotels.com, L.P.,* U.S. District Court, District of New Mexico, No. 07-CV-644, March 1, 2010, CCH NEW MEXICO TAX REPORTS, ¶ 401-497)

Cloud computing: The New Mexico Taxation and Revenue Department has issued a ruling discussing the application of sales tax to several transactions involving access to web-based services. An out-of-state company's receipts from providing access to customers in New Mexico to computing resources, using either open source operating system software or third-party operating system software, were receipts from providing a license to use, which is subject to gross receipts tax. However, receipts from providing storage capacity for data on a server located outside New Mexico were not taxable gross receipts. The company's data transfer fees for uploading data, downloading data, or moving data within the company's network as part of the customer's use of the company's web-based services were exempt because the receipts were from services performed outside New Mexico. (*Ruling No. 401-13-3,* New Mexico Taxation and Revenue Department, July 19, 2013, CCH NEW MEXICO TAX REPORTS, ¶ 401-526) See also *Ruling No. 401-13-2,* New Mexico Taxation and Revenue Department, June 26, 2013, CCH NEW MEXICO TAX REPORTS, ¶ 401-524.

• **Incidence of tax**

The gross receipts tax is imposed on persons engaging in business in the state, that is, the sellers or lessors of property and the sellers of services (Sec. 7-9-3.3, 3 NMAC 2.6.9). These persons are solely liable for the tax and are not acting merely as tax collectors for the state (3 NMAC 2.4.8).

The compensating tax is imposed on the user of tangible property or services rendered in the state (Sec. 7-9-7), but a seller with sufficient nexus with New Mexico has a duty to collect the compensating tax from the buyer and remit it to the state (Sec. 7-9-10). The user of the property is liable for the tax, but is discharged if the tax was paid to the seller (Sec. 7-9-9).

Assumption of tax liability by another: With the approval of the secretary of the Taxation and Revenue Department, a person may assume the gross receipts tax liability or governmental gross receipts tax liability of another person in some circumstances. The secretary may approve a person's request to assume liability if the person agrees to assume the rights and responsibilities as taxpayer under the Tax Administration Act under one or more of three types of agreements (Sec. 1, Ch. 87 (H.B. 315), Laws 2013):

(1) an agreement to collect and pay taxes for persons in a business relationship,

(2) an agreement to collect and pay taxes for a direct sales company, and

(3) a manufacturer's agreement to pay gross receipts tax or governmental gross receipts tax on behalf of a utility company.

To enter into an agreement to assume tax liability, a person must complete a form prescribed by the secretary and provide any additional required information or documentation. An agreement is effective for the period of time specified in the agreement. Failure of a person to fulfill all the requirements of an agreement may result in the department revoking the agreement.

A person approved by the secretary to pay the gross receipts tax or governmental gross receipts tax is deemed to be the taxpayer with respect to that tax and with respect to all rights and responsibilities related to that tax. However, the person will not be entitled to take any credit against the tax for which the person has assumed liability. In addition, the person may not claim a refund of tax on the basis that the person is not statutorily liable to pay the tax.

The department will relieve from liability and hold harmless from tax assumed by another person under agreement a taxpayer that would otherwise be liable for the tax. The provisions of this legislation apply to gross receipts tax or governmental gross receipts tax received in tax periods beginning on or after May 1, 2013. (Ch. 87 (H.B. 315), Laws 2013)

¶666   New Mexico

• Nexus

The gross receipts tax is a general excise tax imposed on persons for the privilege of engaging in business in the state (Sec. 7-9-4). "Engaging in business in the state" means carrying on or causing to be carried on any activity with the purpose of direct or indirect benefit (Sec. 7-9-3.3). Such activities include the selling or leasing of property or the performance of services in the state (Sec. 7-9-3).

A seller not subject to gross receipts tax on sales must collect the compensating tax from the buyer and pay the tax to the state if the seller attempts to exploit New Mexico's markets by carrying on an activity in New Mexico, including (Sec. 7-9-10):

— maintaining an office or other place of business;

— soliciting orders through employees or independent contractors;

— soliciting orders through advertisements in New Mexico newspapers, magazines, or radio or television stations;

— soliciting orders through programs broadcast by New Mexico radio or television stations or transmitted by cable systems;

— canvassing;

— demonstrating;

— collecting money; or

— warehousing or storing merchandise, or delivering or distributing products as a consequence of an advertising or other sales program.

However, the term "activity" does not include (Sec. 7-9-10):

— having a website as a third-party provider on a computer physically located in New Mexico but owned by another nonaffiliated person; or

— using a nonaffiliated third-party call center to accept and process telephone or electronic orders of tangible personal property or licenses primarily from non-New Mexico buyers, which orders are forwarded to a location outside New Mexico.

Remote sales: An out-of-state limited partnership that sold computers and related products to individual in-state consumers using the mail, telephone, and Internet was subject to the state's gross receipts tax. While the partnership contended that the sales occurred where the titles transferred, and thus argued that the computers and related products were sold out-of-state and not in New Mexico, the Court concluded that the partnership was in fact selling this property in the state because, among other reasons, that was where the property was ultimately used or located. Although the partnership itself lacked a physical presence in New Mexico, the presence of the service provider, to which nearly three-quarters of the partnership's New Mexico customers subscribed, resulting in approximately 1,300 service calls and installation visits, established the requisite substantial nexus. (*Dell Catalog Sales L.P. v. New Mexico Taxation and Revenue Department,* New Mexico Court of Appeals, No. 26,843, June 3, 2008, petition for certiorari denied, U.S. Sup. Ct., March 23, 2009; CCH New Mexico Tax Reports, ¶ 401-200)

An out-of-state company that sold property that was drop shipped to customers in New Mexico was not liable for New Mexico gross receipts tax, because it did not have nexus with New Mexico, even though it had gross receipts from selling property in New Mexico. Under the taxpayer's sales agreement with its customers, the transfer of title, ownership and risk of loss from the taxpayer to its customers outside the taxpayer's home state occurred when the taxpayer received a purchase order from the customer, and the customer received the property from the taxpayer. Before the property was received by the customer, however, it was briefly owned by the taxpayer, although the taxpayer did not take physical possession of the property. Such brief ownership of the property by the taxpayer, without having physical possession of the property, was not sufficient ownership of property in New Mexico to establish nexus. Thus, the taxpayer was not liable for gross receipts tax. In addition, the taxpayer was not liable for compensating tax on its drop shipment sales because they were sales of property in New Mexico rather than sales made outside New Mexico. The vendor was selling tangible personal property rather than using it in New Mexico. (*Ruling No. 401-09-5*, December 3, 2009, CCH NEW MEXICO TAX REPORTS, ¶ 401-258)

- **Online retailers**

The New Mexico Supreme Court has held that an out-of-state Internet book retailer had substantial nexus with New Mexico, and New Mexico may impose gross receipts tax on the Internet book retailer's sales to New Mexico residents without violating the federal Commerce Clause. U.S. Supreme Court case law analyzing the federal Commerce Clause holds that substantial nexus exists when activities performed in a state on behalf of an out-of-state retailer are significantly associated with the out-of-state retailer's ability to establish and maintain a market for its sales in that state. In this case, a book-selling subsidiary of the Internet book retailer performed activities in New Mexico for the Internet book retailer's benefit. The court determined that substantial nexus existed between the Internet book retailer and New Mexico because the corporation: (1) promoted the Internet book retailer through sales of gift cards that bore the Internet book retailer's name and were redeemable at the Internet book retailer's website; (2) had a policy of sharing customers' email addresses with the Internet book retailer; (3) implicitly endorsed the Internet book retailer through the companies' shared loyalty program and the affiliated corporation's book return policy; and (4) used logos and trademarks in New Mexico that the Internet book retailer also used.

During the audit period, the parent company of the Internet book retailer and the corporation had an ownership interest of between 40% and 100% in the Internet book retailer and a 100% interest in the corporation. The court noted that the shared ownership of the Internet book retailer and the affiliated corporation was not related to the substantial nexus inquiry. The case law governing the treatment of nexus did not require the in-state actor to have any particular relationship with the out-of-state retailer. The issue was whether the in-state actor engaged in activities on behalf of the out-of-state retailer. (*New Mexico Taxation and Revenue Department v. Barnesandnoble.com, LLC*, New Mexico Supreme Court, No. 33,627, June 3, 2013, CCH NEW MEXICO TAX REPORTS, ¶ 401-501)

- **Streamlined Act status**

New Mexico is an Advisor State to the Streamlined Sales Tax Project (SSTP). It has enacted legislation authorizing it to enter into the Streamlined Sales and Use Tax Agreement (Ch. 225 (H.B. 575), Laws 2005), but has not yet enacted the changes to its laws necessary to comply with the Agreement's requirements. However, it will have input through its representation on the State and Local Advisory Council, which advises the Governing Board on matters pertaining to the administration of the Agreement.

The New Mexico Attorney General has opined that granting amnesty to a seller under the SST Agreement for New Mexico gross receipts taxes owed on sales during the period the seller was not registered in New Mexico would violate the New Mexico Constitution. Amnesty would constitute a subsidy to the seller's business and violate Article IX's Anti-Donation Clause. (*Opinion No. 12-01*, January 9, 2012, CCH NEW MEXICO TAX REPORTS, ¶ 401-403)

¶ 667   **Tax Base**

The gross receipts tax is an excise tax on the gross receipts of persons engaging in business in New Mexico (Sec. 7-9-3.5). Certain items are statutorily excluded from the definition of "gross receipts" (Sec. 7-9-3.5). It is not considered to be engaging in business to maintain a website on a nonowned computer in New Mexico, to use a nonaffiliated third-party call center to accept and process telephone or electronic orders of tangible personal property or licenses primarily from non-New Mexico buyers if the orders are forwarded to a location outside New Mexico for filling, or to provide services to non-New Mexico customers (Sec. 7-9-3(E)).

The governmental gross receipts tax is an excise tax on the gross receipts of New Mexico state agencies, institutions, instrumentalities, and political subdivisions (Sec. 7-9-4.1).

The compensating (use) tax is an excise tax based on the value of the tangible property manufactured or acquired or services rendered (Sec. 7-9-4.1).

- **Gross receipts**

"Gross receipts" defined: "Gross receipts" means the total amount of money or the value of other consideration received from the following (Sec. 7-9-3(F)):

— selling property in the state;

— leasing property employed in the state;

— selling services performed outside the state, the product of which is initially used in the state;

— performing services in the state; and

— consignment sales.

When the money or other consideration received does not represent the value of the property or service exchanged, "gross receipts" means the reasonable value of the property or service (Sec. 7-9-3(F), 3 NMAC 2.1.14.3, 3 NMAC 2.1.14.4).

Intangible property: A 2005 case held that the gross receipts tax does not apply to the royalties received by an out-of-state intangible holding company attributable to the use of its licensed trademarks in New Mexico. The New Mexico Legislature intended that the granting of a license to use property be treated as a sale and be taxed where the sale occurred, which was outside of New Mexico (all activity related to the license agreement took place in Michigan). The fact that the trademarks were used in New Mexico did not change the result. The Legislature also intended to exempt out-of-state grants of licenses to use intangibles in New Mexico from compensating tax by amending the definition of property subject to compensating tax to exclude intangible property (*Kmart Corp. v. New Mexico Department of Taxation and Revenue,* New Mexico Supreme Court, No. 27,269, December 29, 2005, CCH NEW MEXICO TAX REPORTS, ¶ 401-115).

Remote sales: An out-of-state limited partnership that sold computers and related products to individual in-state consumers using the mail, telephone, and Internet was subject to the state's gross receipts tax. While the partnership contended that the sales occurred where the titles transferred, and thus argued that the computers and related products were sold out-of-state and not in New Mexico, the Court concluded that the partnership was in fact selling this property in the state because, among other reasons, that was where the property was ultimately used or located. Although the partnership itself lacked a physical presence in New Mexico, the presence of the service provider, to which nearly three-quarters of the partnership's New Mexico customers subscribed, resulting in approximately 1,300 service calls and installation visits, established the requisite substantial nexus. (*Dell Catalog Sales L.P. v. New Mexico Taxation and Revenue Department,* New Mexico Court of Appeals, No. 26,843, June 3, 2008, petition for certiorari denied, U.S. Sup. Ct., March 23, 2009; CCH NEW MEXICO TAX REPORTS, ¶ 401-200)

An out-of-state company that sold property that was drop shipped to customers in New Mexico was not liable for New Mexico gross receipts tax, because it did not have nexus with New Mexico, even though it had gross receipts from selling property in New Mexico. Under the taxpayer's sales agreement with its customers, the transfer of title, ownership and risk of loss from the taxpayer to its customers outside the taxpayer's home state occurred when the taxpayer received a purchase order from the customer, and the customer received the property from the taxpayer. Before the property was received by the customer, however, it was briefly owned by the taxpayer, although the taxpayer did not take physical possession of the property. Such brief ownership of the property by the taxpayer, without having physical possession of the property, was not sufficient ownership of property in New Mexico to establish nexus. Thus, the taxpayer was not liable for gross receipts tax. In addition, the taxpayer was not liable for compensating tax on its drop shipment sales because they were sales of property in New Mexico rather than sales made outside New Mexico. The vendor was selling tangible personal property rather than using it in New Mexico. (*Ruling No. 401-09-5*, December 3, 2009, CCH NEW MEXICO TAX REPORTS, ¶ 401-258)

- **Compensating tax—Value of property**

The value of the tangible property is the adjusted basis of the property for federal income tax purposes determined as of the date of the property's acquisition, its introduction into the state, or its conversion to use, whichever is later (Sec. 7-9-7). If no adjusted basis for the property is established, a reasonable value of the property will be used.

The compensating tax on services is calculated on the value of the services at the time they were rendered (Sec. 7-9-7).

¶ 668   List of Exemptions, Exceptions, Deductions, and Exclusions

The statutory exemptions and deductions below are listed separately by gross receipts tax and by compensating tax. Items that are excluded from the gross receipts or compensating tax base are discussed at ¶ 667, "Tax Base."

Tax holiday: A gross receipts tax holiday is established for the first weekend of August (Friday through Sunday) each year. Deductible purchases include articles of clothing or footwear that cost less than $100 (except athletic or protective gear); desktop, laptop, tablet, or notebook computers or e-readers that have computing functions whose sales price does not exceed $1,000, and any associated monitor, speaker, printer, keyboard, microphone, or mouse whose price does not exceed $500; and school supplies under $30, not including watches, radios, compact disc players, headphones, sporting equipment, portable or desktop telephones, copiers, office equipment, furniture, or fixtures (Sec. 7-9-95).

- **Gross receipts tax exemptions**

Agricultural products and services	Sec. 7-9-18
Alternative fuel	Sec. 7-9-26
Bail bonds	Sec. 7-9-24
Boats	Sec. 7-9-22.1
Directed energy and satellites programs, sales by DOD contractors	Sec. 7-9-41.3
Dividends and interest	Sec. 7-9-25
Disabled street vendor, sales by	Sec. 7-9-41.3
Dues and registration fees of organizations	Sec. 7-9-39
Enterprise zones; tax incentives	Secs. 5-9-1—5-9-15
Feed for livestock	Sec. 7-9-19
Food stamp purchases	Sec. 7-9-18.1
Foreign nations' receipts (if required by U.S. treaty)	Sec. 7-9-13A(4)
Gasoline, ethanol, and special fuel	Sec. 7-9-26
Government transactions	Sec. 7-9-13
Health care services entity licensed by Dept. of Health	Sec. 7-9-4.3

• List of compensating tax exemptions

• List of deductions from gross receipts tax

- **List of deductions from compensating tax**

¶ 669   **Rate of Tax**

The gross receipts tax (Sec. 7-9-4) and the compensating (use) tax for tangible personal property (Sec. 7-9-7) are imposed at the rate of 5.125%. The compensating (use) tax rate for services is 5%.

The governmental gross receipts tax (Sec. 7-9-4.1) is imposed at the rate of 5%.

Interstate telecommunications services: The rate of tax on interstate telecommunications gross receipts is 4.25% (Sec. 7-9C-3). Such services for Internet access are exempt (Sec. 7-9C-7).

Leased vehicle gross receipts tax and surcharge: A 5% excise tax is imposed on gross receipts from the business of leasing vehicles used in New Mexico (Sec. 7-14A-3). Also, a surcharge is imposed on leases of vehicles at the rate of $2 per day for each vehicle leased (Sec. 7-14A-3.1(B)).

The lease of a temporary replacement vehicle is exempt from the leased vehicle surcharge if the lessee signs a statement that the temporary replacement vehicle is to be used as a replacement for another vehicle that is being repaired, serviced or replaced. The exemption applies to a dealer or repair facility that leases a car on behalf of the client.

¶ 670   Local Taxes

The levy of local gross receipts taxes is authorized by New Mexico statutes (Sec. 3-18-2, Sec. 7-19D-9, Sec. 7-20E-9); those taxes are in addition to the state gross receipts tax. Cities and counties in the state impose local gross receipts or sales taxes at different rates. The increments in which the taxes may be imposed are limited by statute, as are the maximum rates, which are as follows:

County gross receipts tax: 0.4375%
County infrastructure gross receipts tax: 0.125%
County capital outlay gross receipts tax: 0.25%
County environmental services gross receipts tax 0.125%
County fire protection excise tax .... 0.25% or 0.125%
County health care gross receipts tax 0.0625%
Special county hospital gross receipts tax 0.125%
Local hospital gross receipts tax: 0.125%
County hospital emergency gross receipts tax 0.25%
County correctional facility gross receipts tax 0.125%
County emergency gross receipts tax 0.375%
County hold harmless gross receipts tax 0.375%
County education gross receipts tax 0.5%
Countywide/county area emergency communications and emergency medical and behavioral health services tax 0.25%
County regional transit gross receipts tax 0.50%
County quality of life gross receipts tax 0.25%
County regional spaceport gross receipts tax 0.50%
County water and sanitation gross receipts tax 0.25%
Municipal gross receipts tax 1.25%
Municipal infrastructure gross receipts tax 0.25%
Municipal environmental services gross receipts tax 0.0625%
Municipal capital outlay gross receipts tax 0.25%
Municipal regional transport gross receipts tax 0.50%
Municipal quality of life gross receipts tax 0.25%
Municipal regional spaceport gross receipts tax 0.50%
Municipal higher education facilities gross receipts tax 0.25%
Municipal hold harmless gross receipts tax 0.375%
Federal water project gross receipts tax 0.25%

Minor league baseball stadium surcharge: A municipality located in a class A county with more than 200,000 population may impose a stadium surcharge of 5% or more on tickets, parking, and all other products or services sold at or related to a minor league baseball stadium (Sec. 3-65-4).

Sourcing of telecommunications charges: New Mexico has conformed to the federal Mobile Telecommunications Sourcing Act, P.L. 106-252. All charges for mobile telecommunications services are considered to be provided by the customer's home service provider and sourced to the customer's place of primary use (H.B. 299, Laws 2002). All such charges are subject to sales tax based on the customer's place of primary use.

The service provider will be held harmless for an error in assigning wireless services to a jurisdiction if it utilizes an electronic database provided by the state or a designated entity, or, if the state has not provided or designated a database, if it utilizes a database that makes assignments based on a nine-digit zip code.

Municipal and county hold harmless gross receipts taxes: Both municipalities and counties may pass ordinances imposing a hold harmless gross receipts tax not to exceed ⅜% of the gross receipts of any person engaging in business in the municipality or county, respectively, for the privilege of engaging in such business. Both municipalities and counties may impose the tax in increments of ⅛%. Such a tax is not subject to referendum. The revenue for such a tax may be dedicated to a specific purpose or area of government services, including but not limited to police protection, fire protection, public transportation or street repair and maintenance. (Sec. 7-19D-18; Sec. 7-20E-28)

- **Combined state, municipal, and county tax rate chart**

A Gross Receipts Tax Rate Schedule of local rates, updated in January and June each year, is available on the Department's website at **http://tax.newmexico.gov/ gross-receipts-tax-historic-rates.aspx**.

¶ 671   Bracket Schedule

New Mexico has no bracket schedules for the gross receipts or compensating taxes.

¶ 672   Returns, Payments, and Due Dates

Taxpayers who are registered for gross receipts or compensating tax purposes must file a return with the Revenue Division, Taxation and Revenue Department, for each reporting period whether or not any tax is due (3 NMAC 2.11.15). Returns must be made on Form CRS-1, "Combined Report Form." However, a person engaged solely in exempt transactions is not required to file a return (Sec. 7-9-5).

Electronic filing: Gross receipts and compensating taxes, local options gross receipts taxes, leased vehicle gross receipts taxes, interstate telecommunication gross receipts taxes, and withholding taxes that are due at the same time as gross receipts taxes must be filed electronically if the taxpayer is required to file monthly. (3 NMAC 1.4.10; 3 NMAC 1.4.18; see also *FYI-108,* Electronic Filing Mandate, New Mexico Taxation and Revenue Department, April 28, 2016, CCH NEW MEXICO TAX REPORTS, ¶ 401-705)

- **Due dates**

Returns must be filed on or before the 25th day of the month following the month in which the taxable event took place (Sec. 7-1-13, Sec. 7-9-11, 3 NMAC 1.4.8). Payment of gross receipts and compensating taxes must precede or accompany the return (Sec. 7-1-13, 3 NMAC 1.4.10.2).

Semiannual or quarterly filing: The Department may allow a taxpayer to report on a six-month or quarterly basis, instead of monthly, if the taxpayer's anticipated tax liability is less than $200 per month; a surety bond may be required (Sec. 7-1-15, 3 NMAC 1.4.11.2). A taxpayer granted such authority must file a return and pay the tax on or before the 25th day of the month following the close of the six-month or quarterly period (3 NMAC 2.11.13).

• Methods of payment

Special payment provisions, which ensure that tax funds are immediately available to the state, apply to taxpayers whose average tax payments during the preceding calendar year were $25,000 or more for certain taxes, including gross receipts and compensating (sales and use) taxes, local option gross receipts taxes, interstate tele-communications gross receipts taxes, and the leased vehicle gross receipts tax (Sec. 7-1-13.1). Such taxpayers must employ one (or more) of the following methods to pay their taxes or become subject to penalties and interest: (1) electronic payments; (2) U.S. currency; or (3) checks. Checks drawn on and payable at a New Mexico financial institution must be received by the Department at least one banking day prior to the payment due date; checks drawn on and payable at a non-New Mexico financial institution must be received at least two banking days prior to the payment due date. For additional information, see *FYI-401, Special Payment Methods*, New Mexico Taxa-tion and Revenue Department, September 2012, CCH NEW MEXICO TAX REPORTS, ¶ 401-445.

Credit card payment: The Taxation and Revenue Department is authorized to accept payment of taxes by credit card (Sec. 7-1-13.2). If the Department must pay a charge to accept payment by credit card, the amount of the charge will be added to the amount due.

• Estimated reporting agreements

Taxpayers may enter into agreements with the Department to report gross receipts (sales) and compensating (use) tax liability on an estimated basis (Sec. 7-1-10). An agreement may not be for a period of longer than four years. An estimated reporting agreement must include: (1) the specific receipts, deductions, or values to be reported on an estimated basis and the methodology to be used in making the estimates, (2) the period during which the agreement is in effect, (3) procedures for terminating the agreement prior to its expiration, and (4) a declaration that all statements made by the taxpayer in the application and agreement are true. No penalty may be imposed for tax due in excess of the amount paid under an approved estimated reporting agreement.

¶ 673   **Prepayment of Taxes**

There are no specific provisions in the gross receipts and compensating tax statutes regarding the prepayment of taxes.

¶ 674   **Vendor Registration**

A statute provides for the registration and identification of taxpayers (Sec. 7-1-12). Form RP-31, "Application for Registration," is used for that purpose.

Persons doing business with the state must be registered for payment of the gross receipts tax under the Gross Receipts Tax Registration Act, Sec. 7-10-1 *et seq.*

Exempt taxpayers: Persons conducting only activities that are exempt from the gross receipts and compensating taxes do not have to register to file returns for those taxes (Sec. 7-9-5, 3 NMAC 2.12.8). Examples of persons not having to register are provided by regulation (3 NMAC 2.5.8). If some of a person's business transactions are taxable and some are exempt, the person must register and file returns, but need not include the gross receipts or value of exempt property.

Exempt buyers: Exempt buyers and lessees must be registered in order to issue nontaxable transaction certificates (Sec. 7-9-43).

Construction contractors: Contractors not located in New Mexico must furnish security or a surety bond to the department for the gross receipts taxes due as a result of construction services performed in New Mexico. Specifically, such a bond must be furnished when the contractor (1) does not have a principal place of business in New Mexico, and (2) enters into a construction contract to be performed in New Mexico.

The surety bond must be in an amount equal to the gross receipts tax due based on the amount in the contract. The bond must be furnished when the contract is entered into by the parties. If the contract amount changes 10% or more, the contractor is required to increase or decrease the amount of the bond no later than 14 days after the contract change becomes effective. (*New Mexico Bulletin B-200.28,* New Mexico Taxation and Revenue Department, June 19, 2012, CCH NEW MEXICO TAX REPORTS, ¶ 401-437)

- **Out-of-state disaster responders**

Certain temporary corporate income, personal income, sales and property tax and registration exemptions are provided for out-of-state businesses and individuals who enter New Mexico to respond to declared disasters and perform work on critical infrastructure. An out-of-state business that conducts operations within New Mexico in response to a declared state disaster or emergency is not considered to have established a level of presence or nexus that would require that business to register, file or remit state or local taxes or fees, including gross receipts taxes or property tax on equipment brought into the state temporarily for use during the disaster response period and subsequently removed from New Mexico. Further, for purposes of the corporate income, personal income or sales taxes, all activity of the out-of-state business during the disaster response period conducted in New Mexico is disregarded with respect to any filing requirements. This includes the filing required for a unitary or combined group of which the out-of-state business may be a part. Finally, when apportioning income, revenue or receipts, the performance by an out-of-state business of any work during a disaster response period will not be sourced to or otherwise impact or increase the amount of income, revenue or receipts apportioned to New Mexico. (S.B. 19, Laws 2016)

The legislation allows compensation to be allocated to the taxpayers' state of residence if the activities, labor or services are performed in New Mexico for disaster or emergency related critical infrastructure work, in response to a declared state disaster or emergency. An out-of-state employee will not be considered to have established residency or a presence in the state that would require that person or that person's employer to file and pay income taxes or to be subjected to tax withholdings or to file and pay any other state or local tax or fee during the disaster response period. (S.B. 19, Laws 2016)

¶ 675   **Sales or Use Tax Credits**

Several types of credits are allowed against the New Mexico gross receipts and compensating (use) taxes and are discussed below. For additional details about the credits, see *FYI-106, Claiming Tax Credits for CRS Taxes and Business-Related Income,* New Mexico Taxation and Revenue Department, September 2012, CCH NEW MEXICO TAX REPORTS, ¶ 401-452.

- **Credit for out-of-state taxes**

Gross receipts tax: New Mexico allows a credit against the New Mexico gross receipts tax for sales taxes paid to another state or the state's political subdivision on services performed in the other state (Sec. 7-9-79.1). The amount of the credit is limited to the product of the New Mexico gross receipts tax rate multiplied by the amount of receipts subject to tax by both New Mexico and the other state or political subdivision.

Compensating (use) tax: If property is bought outside New Mexico for use in the state and a gross receipts, sales, compensating, or similar tax is paid on the sale or a compensating or use tax is paid on the use of the property subsequent to its acquisition by the person using the property in New Mexico, the amount of tax paid may be credited against the New Mexico compensating tax due on the property (Sec. 7-9-79).

The credit may not exceed the amount of compensating tax assessed on the property by New Mexico (3 NMAC 2.79.1.8). The credit may not be claimed as a refund if it exceeds the amount of the compensating tax, and it may not be used as a credit against the tax on other out-of-state purchases.

This credit is different from the exemption allowed for personal effects brought into New Mexico by a user who is establishing a residence in New Mexico or who is in the state only temporarily.

• Credit for taxes paid to certain Native American pueblos

A credit against state gross receipts taxes and local option gross receipts taxes is provided for Santa Ana Pueblo, Santa Clara Pueblo, Laguna Pueblo, Isleta, Sandia, and Nambe Pueblo gross receipts, sales, or similar taxes if such taxes have been levied by the pueblos on taxable transactions that occurred on land that is owned by or for the benefit of the pueblos and located within the exterior boundaries of the pueblos (Sec. 7-9-88, Sec. 7-9-88.1).

The amount of the credit is the lesser of 75% of the tax imposed by the pueblos on the receipts from a qualifying transaction or 75% of the total tax amount from the state gross income tax and local option gross receipts taxes that are imposed on the receipts from the same transaction. The credit is applied proportionately against the amount of the state gross receipts tax and local option gross receipts taxes and against the amount of distribution of those taxes.

A credit is also allowed for a portion of tax paid to the Navajo nation on receipts from selling coal (Sec. 7-9-88.2).

• Investment credit

An investment credit is allowed for qualified equipment used in manufacturing (Sec. 7-9A-5). The credit is in the amount of the compensating tax rate applied to the value of the qualified equipment and may be claimed by a taxpayer carrying on a manufacturing operation in the state. The credit is administered by the Taxation and Revenue Department (Sec. 7-9A-4).

Until July 1, 2020, to claim the credit, taxpayers are required to create one full-time equivalent (FTE) employee for every $500,000 in value of qualified equipment, up to $30 million; and one FTE employee for every $1 million in value of qualified equipment claimed over $30 million (Sec. 7-9A-7.1). After June 30, 2020, taxpayers must create one FTE employee for every $100,000 in value of qualified equipment claimed.

• Affordable housing credit

The New Mexico Mortgage Finance Authority may issue an investment voucher to a "person" that has invested in an "affordable housing project" approved by the Authority, or in a trust fund administered by the Authority (Sec. 7-9I-3(A)). The amount of the voucher may be applied as a credit against the holder's applicable New Mexico "modified combined tax" (*i.e.*, gross receipts tax, compensating tax, withholding tax, interstate telecommunications gross receipts tax, 911 emergency surcharge, and telecommunications relay service surcharge) (Sec. 7-9I-1). Effective July 1, 2015, counties and municipalities are no longer eligible for the credit.

The value of an approved voucher is equal to 50% of the amount of cash invested or the fair market value of the land, buildings, materials, or services invested by a person in the affordable housing project (Sec. 7-9I-3(A)). Unused credit may be carried forward for up to five years.

• Construction project credits

A construction contractor that sells a construction project may take a credit against the gross receipts tax due on the sale (3 NMAC 2.79.1.9). The credit is allowed for the compensating tax paid on construction services and on materials that became an ingredient or component part of the project (Sec. 7-9-79(B)). The credit may be applied only for the compensating tax itself, not to any penalties or interest arising from delinquent taxes.

• Technology jobs credit

A technology jobs tax credit against gross receipts and compensating tax or personal income tax withholding for qualified expenditures by technology-based businesses is available for qualifying expenses incurred.

Amount of credit: The basic credit is allowed at a rate equal to 4% of the amount of qualified expenditures made by a taxpayer for conducting qualified research at a qualified facility. Any amount of credit of approved basic credit not claimed may be claimed in subsequent reporting periods (Sec. 7-9F-5).

Definitions: For purposes of the credit, a qualified facility is a facility in New Mexico that is not operated by the taxpayer for any federal government agency or department. Qualified research is research undertaken to discover technological information to be applied in the development of a new or improved business component of the taxpayer relating to the business's substantive function, performance, reliability, or quality. Expenses in connection with improvements in style, taste, or cosmetic or seasonal design factors are not included (Sec. 7-9F-8).

Qualified expenditures include expenditures for depletable land and rent paid or incurred for land or improvements; the allowable amount paid or incurred to operate or maintain a facility, buildings, equipment, computer software, computer software upgrades; amounts paid to consultants and contractors performing work in New Mexico; and amounts paid for payroll, technical books, manuals, and test materials. Not included are expenditures on property owned by a municipality or county in connection with an industrial revenue bond project, property for which the taxpayer has received a capital equipment tax credit or investment tax credit, property that was owned by the taxpayer or an affiliate before July 1, 2000, or research and development expenditures that were reimbursed by a person not affiliated with the taxpayer (Sec. 7-9F-8).

Rural areas: The amount of the basic or additional credit for which a taxpayer is otherwise eligible is doubled if the qualified facility is in a rural area. A rural area is defined as any area of the state other than (1) a class A county, (2) a class B county that has a net taxable value for rate setting purposes for any property tax year of more that $3 billion, (3) the municipality of Rio Rancho, and (4) the area within three miles of the exterior boundaries of a class A county (Sec. 7-9F-3).

• Rural job tax credits

Employers approved for in-plant training assistance may apply to the New Mexico Taxation and Revenue Department to obtain a rural job tax credit that may be applied against their New Mexico personal income tax or their combined modified tax liability for each qualifying job the employer creates (Sec. 7-2E-1). For purposes of this credit "combined modified tax liability" means the total liability for the reporting period for New Mexico gross receipts (sales) tax, other than New Mexico local option gross receipts tax, and includes New Mexico compensating (use) tax, New Mexico personal income tax withholding, New Mexico 911 emergency surcharge, and New Mexico telecommunications relay service surcharge, minus the amount of any other credits applied against any or all of these taxes or surcharges.

The credit is equal to $1,000 per qualified job and may be claimed for four years in municipalities and areas of counties with populations of 15,000 or less (tier one area) and for two years in municipalities with a population over 15,000 (tier two area). The maximum credit amount with respect to each qualifying job is equal to $4,000 in wages paid in a tier one area or $2,000 in wages paid in a tier two area. The credit may be claimed for each qualifying job for a maximum of four qualifying periods for each qualifying job performed or based at a location in a tier one area or (2) two qualifying periods for each qualifying job performed or based at a location in a tier two area (Sec. 7-2E-1).

• **Laboratory partnership with small business credit**

National laboratories that assist small businesses through technology and expertise may claim a credit against New Mexico gross receipts (sales) tax for qualified expenditures made in rendering such assistance. Small business assistance relates to the transfer of technology, including software and manufacturing, mining, oil and gas, environmental, agricultural, information, and solar and other energy technologies, and also includes nontechnical assistance rendered in expanding the New Mexico base of suppliers, through training and mentoring, development of business systems, and other supplier development initiatives (Sec. 7-9E-5).

The credit that a national laboratory can claim against its gross receipts tax liability for assistance to each small business in Bernalillo County is $10,000 per year, and for those outside of Bernalillo County, $20,000 per year. The total amount of credits that can be claimed is $2.4 million per year. If more than one national lab claims the credit, those labs are required to coordinate their efforts (Sec. 7-9E-5).

• **Credit for creation of high-wage jobs**

A refundable credit may be claimed against New Mexico modified combined tax liability for each new high-wage economic-based job created by an eligible employer during a period beginning on or after July 1, 2004, and ending on July 1, 2020 (Sec. 7-9G-1). The term "modified combined tax liability" includes gross receipts (sales) and compensating (use) tax, interstate telecommunications gross receipts (sales) tax, and certain other surcharges, but specifically excludes any local gross receipts (sales) taxes. The credit is equal to 10% of the wages and benefits distributed to an eligible employee in a new high-wage economic-based job, but may not exceed $12,000 per employee. The credit may be claimed in the year in which the eligible job is created and each of the following three years.

To be eligible for the credit, the high-wage job must (1) have been created during the specified period; (2) be occupied for at least 48 weeks of a qualifying period; (3) for jobs created before July 1, 2015, pay at least $40,000 if the job is located in a municipality with 40,000 or more residents, or at least $28,000 if the job is located in a smaller area, and (4) for jobs created after July 1, 2015, and before July 1, 2020, pay at least $60,000 if the job is located in a municipality with 60,000 or more residents, or at least $40,000 if the job is located in a smaller area. In addition, a new high-wage job is eligible for the credit only if an employer's total number of employees with new high-wage jobs at a given location on the last day of the qualifying period exceeds the number of such jobs on the day the subject job was created (Sec. 7-9G-1).

• **Credit for receipts from selling a service for resale**

A gross receipts or governmental gross receipts tax credit may be claimed for receipts from selling a service for resale. The credit is equal to 10% of the receipts multiplied by either 3.775% if a taxpayer's business location is within a municipality or 5% if the business location is in an unincorporated area of a county. The credit is available only if the buyer resells the service in the ordinary course of business, the resale is not subject to gross receipts tax or governmental gross receipts tax, and the buyer delivers to the seller documentation in a form prescribed by the New Mexico Taxation and Revenue Department clarifying that the service is purchased for resale in the ordinary course of business. Credits do not apply to receipts from selling services to a governmental entity (Sec. 7-9-96; 3 NMAC 3.2.302.8).

¶675   New Mexico

• Credit to health care providers for unpaid services

A gross receipts tax credit may be claimed by a medical doctor or licensed osteopathic physician for 100% of the value of unpaid qualified health care services provided while on call to a hospital (Sec. 7-9-96.2).

"Qualified health care services" means medical care services provided by a licensed medical doctor or licensed osteopathic physician while on call to a hospital. The value of qualified services is the amount charged for the qualified health care services but may not exceed 130% of the reimbursement rate for the services under the Medicaid program. To qualify for the credit, medical services must remain unpaid after one year from the date of billing and the services must have been provided to a person without health insurance or whose health insurance would not cover the services and who was not eligible for Medicaid. The services must also not be reimbursable under a program established in the Indigent Hospital and County Health Care Act (Sec. 7-9-96.2; Sec. 7-9-96; 3 NMAC 3.2.302.8).

• Credit to hospitals

A gross receipts tax credit is available to licensed for-profit hospitals. The credit equals roughly 20% of the state gross receipts tax rate in fiscal year 2008; 40% in fiscal year 2009; 60% in fiscal year 2010; 80% in fiscal year 2011; and the entire state gross receipts tax rate in fiscal year 2012 and beyond (Sec. 7-9-96.1).

• Advanced energy credit for electricity generators

An advanced energy tax credit is available against gross receipts tax, compensating tax, or withholding tax. The credit may be claimed by a taxpayer who holds an interest in a new solar thermal electric generating facility or new or repowered coal electric generating facility that begins construction before December 31, 2015. To qualify for the credit, the solar or coal facility must meet specified emissions standards (Sec. 7-9G-2; 3 NMAC 3.13.8.2—3.13.8.13).

The amount of the advanced energy tax credit is up to 6% of the eligible generation plant costs of a qualified generating facility. The maximum credit claimed per generating facility is limited to $60 million. "Eligible generation plant costs" means expenditures for the development and construction of a qualified generating facility, including permitting; site characterization and assessment; engineering; design; carbon dioxide capture, treatment, compression, transportation and sequestration; site and equipment acquisition; and fuel supply development. (Sec. 7-9G-2)

To apply for the credit, an entity that holds an interest in a qualified electric generating facility must apply for a certificate from the New Mexico Environment Department (NMED). NMED is required to determine if the facility is eligible for the credit, issue a certificate stating whether or not the facility is eligible, and issue rules governing the credit. NMED will also issue a schedule of application fees not to exceed $150,000.

• Credits for alternative energy

Two credits are available that are directly related to alternative energy, as follows:

Biodiesel blending facility tax credit: A taxpayer who is a rack operator and who installs biodiesel blending equipment in property owned by the taxpayer for the purpose of establishing or expanding a facility to produce blended biodiesel fuel is eligible to claim a credit against gross receipts tax or compensating tax. The amount of the credit is 30% of the purchase cost of the equipment plus 30% of the cost of installing that equipment. The credit cannot exceed $50,000 with respect to equipment installed at any one facility (Sec. 7-9-79.2; 3 NMAC 13.21.8).

The Energy, Minerals and Natural Resources Department (EMNRD) is responsible for validating the credit and issuing a certificate of eligibility that includes the estimated amount of the credit. The aggregate amount of all credits validated by EMNRD cannot exceed $1 million. The credit may be carried forward for four years from the date of the certificate of eligibility.

Alternative energy product manufacturers tax credit: A credit is available against combined reporting taxes (gross receipts, compensating and withholding) for manufacturing alternative energy products (Sec. 7-9J-4(A)). An "alternative energy product" is an alternative energy vehicle, fuel cell system, renewable energy system or component of an alternative energy vehicle, fuel cell system or renewable energy system or components for integrated gasification combined cycle coal facilities, and equipment related to sequestration of carbon from integrated gasification combined cycle plants; or, beginning in taxable year 2011 and ending in taxable year 2019, a product extracted from or secreted by a single cell photosynthetic organism (Sec. 7-9J-2(A)).

The credit may be claimed by a taxpayer in an amount for which the taxpayer has been granted approval by the Taxation and Revenue Department and does not exceed 5% of the taxpayer's qualified expenditures. To be eligible, the taxpayer must show that they have hired an additional full time employee from the previous year for each $500,000 of qualified expenditures up to $30 million, and an additional full time job for each $1 million of qualified expenditures above $30 million. Any portion of the credit that remains unused at the end of the taxpayer's reporting period may be carried forward for five years. (Sec. 7-9J-4(A); 3 NMAC 13.7.14)

• **Research and development credit for small business (repealed)**

Until June 30, 2015, a taxpayer that is a qualified research and development small business was eligible for a credit in a reporting period in an amount equal to the sum of all gross receipts taxes or 50% of withholding taxes paid on behalf of employees and owners with no more than 5% ownership that are due to the state or payable by the taxpayer with respect to that business for that reporting period (Former Sec. 7-9H-3).

¶ 676 Deficiency Assessments

The Taxation and Revenue Department may assess a taxpayer who is liable for taxes (Sec. 7-1-17). Taxes due of less than $10 are not assessed, except for the $5 penalty for late-filed returns set forth at Sec. 7-1-69 (3 NMAC 1.6.9).

Tax assessments are effective when any of the following occurs (Sec. 7-1-17):

— a taxpayer's return shows a tax liability;

— a "notice of assessment of taxes" from the Department is mailed or delivered to a taxpayer (the notice must include the remedies available to the taxpayer (3 NMAC 1.6.11)); or

— a proper jeopardy assessment has been made.

¶ 677 Audit Procedures

In order to determine tax liability, collect taxes, and enforce tax laws, the Taxation and Revenue Department may audit taxpayer records and require persons to testify, as discussed below.

Taxpayer rights: see *FYI-400, Tax Audits and Protest Procedures (Your Rights as a Taxpayer),* New Mexico Taxation and Revenue Department, September 2013, CCH NEW MEXICO TAX REPORTS, ¶ 401-547.

• **Authority to audit**

To determine a person's tax liability or to enforce a tax law, the Department may examine records, books, information, or equipment; require a person to testify; and issue subpoenas and summonses (Sec. 7-1-4). If a person does not cooperate, the Department may ask a court to enforce the subpoena or summons. A taxpayer's records must be made available for inspection (Sec. 7-1-11).

If a taxpayer's records and books of account do not exist or are insufficient to determine the taxpayer's liability, the Department may use any reasonable method of estimating the tax liability, including, but not limited to, using information about similar persons, businesses or industries (Sec. 7-1-11).

- **Audits of nontaxable transactions**

When a seller claims a deduction from the gross receipts or compensating taxes, the transaction must be documented so that it can be verified upon audit (3 NMAC 2.43.1.10).

Evidence of exemption: If a seller cannot provide an nontaxable transaction certificate (NTTC) within 60 days from the date that a notice requiring possession of NTTCs is given to the seller by the Department of Taxation and Revenue, the Secretary of Taxation and Revenue may accept other evidence (1) prior to the issuance of an audit assessment, or (2) if the audit assessment is protested, prior to either the taxpayer's withdrawal of the protest or the formal hearing of the protest, provided, however, that the protest was acknowledged by the department prior to December 31, 2011. (Sec. 7-9-43)

- **Managed audit program**

A taxpayer may apply to the Taxation and Revenue Department to use the agency's procedures and guidelines to self-audit its compliance with gross receipts (sales), compensating (use), and local option gross receipts taxes (Sec. 7-1-11.1). A written agreement must be executed by the taxpayer and the Department that includes: (1) a declaration that all statements made by the taxpayer in the application and agreement are true; (2) a specification of the period to be audited; (3) the types of receipts or transactions to be audited; (4) the procedures to be used in conducting the audit; (5) the records to be reviewed; (6) the date of commencement of the audit; and (7) the date the results must be presented to the Department. The agreement must also contain a waiver by the taxpayer of limitations on assessments for the period to be audited.

Taxpayers found to have tax due as a result of a managed audit are not subject to penalty for failure to pay, and interest does not accrue on the amount of tax due if it is paid within 30 days of the date of the assessment resulting from the managed audit.

For additional information, see *FYI-404, Managed Audits for Taxpayers,* New Mexico Taxation and Revenue Department, September 2012, CCH NEW MEXICO TAX REPORTS, ¶ 401-446.

¶ 678   **Statute of Limitations**

Generally, no assessment of tax (or start of court proceedings without a prior assessment) may be made after three years from the end of the calendar year in which the tax payment was due (Sec. 7-1-18).

False or fraudulent return: If, however, a false or fraudulent return was made with intent to evade tax, assessment may be made within ten years from the end of the calendar year in which the tax was due (Sec. 7-1-18). "Tax" is defined by regulation (3 NMAC 1.1.16).

Failure to file: For failure to file a required return, assessment may be made within seven years from the end of the calendar year in which the tax was due (Sec. 7-1-18).

Understatement of tax: For understating in a return the amount of tax liability by more than 25%, assessment may be made within six years (Sec. 7-1-18).

- **Limitation on actions**

An action or proceeding to collect taxes or interest under an assessment or notice of assessment must be taken within the later of (1) ten years from the date of the assessment or notice or (2) with respect to undischarged amounts in a bankruptcy proceeding, one year after the later of the issuance of the final order or the date of the last scheduled payment (Sec. 7-1-19, 3 NMAC 1.1.17, 3 NMAC 1.10.15).

¶ 679   Application for Refund

Refunds may be claimed by taxpayers who believe that they have paid tax for which they are not liable, who have been denied any credit or rebate claimed, or who claim a prior right to property held under a levy (Sec. 7-1-26, 3 NMAC 1.9.8, 3 NMAC 2.43.1.12).

A taxpayer may dispute a tax liability or other administrative action against the taxpayer in one of two ways:

(1) file a written protest, containing the requisite information and within the specified time period, with the department without making a payment; or

(2) pay the disputed tax liability and then file a timely refund claim containing the requisite information.

(*FYI-402 Taxpayer Remedies,* New Mexico Taxation and Revenue Department, July 30, 2013, CCH NEW MEXICO TAX REPORTS, ¶ 401-528)

• **Refund claim procedures**

A claim for a refund must state in writing the nature of the complaint and the relief requested and contain other information needed to verify the claim's accuracy (Sec. 7-1-26, 3 NMAC 1.9.8). An information return is not a claim for refund (3 NMAC 1.9.8).

Time limit: Refund claims must be filed within the following time periods (Sec. 7-1-26):

— within three years of the end of the calendar year in which (1) the payment was due or an overpayment resulted from an assessment, whichever is later or (2) the property was levied upon;

— within one year of the date on which a tax assessment is made or a proceeding begun in court by the Department with respect to any period that is covered by a waiver of time limits signed by the taxpayer;

— within one year of the date of a tax assessment made against a taxpayer who has filed a false or fraudulent return, failed to file a return, or understated tax liability by more than 25%, when the assessment applies to a period ending at least three years prior to the beginning of the year in which the assessment is made (Note: the statute provides that the refund claim may not be made with respect to any period not covered by the assessment); or

— within one year of the date payment of tax was made if the payment was not made within three years of the end of the calendar year in which the original due date of the tax or date of the assessment occurred.

A taxpayer who timely pursues more than one of the remedies listed above is deemed to have elected the first remedy invoked (Sec. 7-1-26).

¶ 681   Scope of Tax

Source.—Statutory references are to Article 28 of the Tax Law, Chapter 60, Consolidated Laws, as amended to date. Details are reported in the CCH NEW YORK TAX REPORTS starting at ¶ 60-000.

Retail sales of tangible personal property are subject to the state sales tax (Sec. 1105(a), Tax Law). The state sales tax applies to sales, other than for resale, of gas, electricity, refrigeration and steam; of gas, electric, refrigeration and steam service; of telephony (including voice-over-Internet (VoIP)) and telegraphy; of telephone and telegraph service; and of telephone answering services (Sec. 1105(b), Tax Law). The tax is not imposed, however, upon interstate and international telephony and telegraphy and telephone and telegraph service, nor upon internet access services.

Digitized products: Sales of canned software over the Internet are considered to be taxable sales of tangible personal property (*Response to CCH Internet/Electronic Products Survey,* New York Department of Taxation and Finance, November 15, 1999). However, see *TSB-A-08(62)S,* November 24, 2008, CCH NEW YORK TAX REPORTS, ¶ 406-277, and *TSB-A-09(2)S,* January 21, 2009, CCH NEW YORK TAX REPORTS, ¶ 406-313. See also "Cloud computing," below.

Pictures (digital photographs), downloaded digital music, downloaded videos and, probably, electronic greeting cards are treated as nontaxable intangible property. See *TSB-A-08(22)S,* May 2, 2008, CCH NEW YORK TAX REPORTS, ¶ 406-055.

A taxpayer's sales of electronic books (e-books) were not subject to New York sales and use tax because the e-books are not tangible personal property and do not constitute information services (*TSB-A-11(20)S,* July 8, 2011, CCH NEW YORK TAX REPORTS, ¶ 407-317; see also *TSB-M-11(5)S,* April 7, 2011, CCH NEW YORK TAX REPORTS, ¶ 407-192).

An electronic news service or electronic periodical may qualify for exemption if certain criteria are met; see *TSB-M-14(4)S,* April 2014, CCH NEW YORK TAX REPORTS, ¶ 408-275. The exemption is limited to $2,981 from June 1, 2017, to May 31, 2018.

Modular homes: The definition of "tangible personal property" is excludes a modular home that is permanently affixed to real property. However, if the modular home is removed from the realty, then the home and its component parts would be tangible personal property whether sold as a whole or as parts. (Sec. 1101(b)(6), Tax Law). For additional information, see ¶ 684 and *TSB-M-09(19)S,* November 24, 2009, CCH NEW YORK TAX REPORTS, ¶ 406-602.

• **Taxable services**

The sales of the following services, other than for resale, are subject to the state sales tax:

— *information services:* the services of furnishing information by printed, mimeographed, multigraphed or other method of duplication (Sec. 1105(c)(1), Tax Law);

— *processing and printing services:* the services of producing, fabricating, processing, printing or imprinting tangible personal property for a party who provides the tangible personal property (not purchased for resale) upon which the services are performed (Sec. 1105(c)(2), Tax Law);

— *installation, repair and maintenance services performed upon tangible personal property:* storage and safe deposit rental; the services of installing tangible personal property (excluding a mobile home) or maintaining, servicing, or repairing tangible personal property (including a mobile home) are taxable; whether such services are performed directly or by coin-operated equipment and whether or not the tangible personal property is transferred in connection with such services (Sec. 1105(c)(3), Tax Law, Reg. Sec. 527.5(a)). The tax does not apply, however, to maintenance or repair services performed upon property held for sale in the regular course of business (Reg. Sec. 527.5(b)(2)). Certain other repair and installation services are also not subject to tax;.

— *service contracts and extended warranties:* sales of service contracts are considered to be sales of taxable repair and maintenance services; see *TB-ST-836,* June 5, 2015, CCH NEW YORK TAX REPORTS, ¶ 408-428;

— *real estate maintenance, service or repair:* the services of maintaining or repairing real property (Sec. 1105(c)(5), Tax Law; see also *TB-ST-129,* March 17, 2016, CCH NEW YORK TAX REPORTS, ¶ 408-696);

— *motor vehicle parking and garaging services:* the services of parking, garaging, or storage for motor vehicles by persons operating a garage, parking lot or other similar place of business (Sec. 1105(c)(6), Tax Law). The tax does not apply when the garage is part of premises occupied solely as a private one or two-family dwelling. Parking charges paid to a homeowner's association by its members are exempt from the New York parking tax, the Metropolitan Commuter Transportation District tax, and most local sales taxes. Beginning January 1, 2009, a vendor who sells or rents motor vehicles may not use an exempt use certificate when purchasing parking services (*TSB-M-08(4)S; TSB-M-08(4.1)S*).

— *interior decorating and designing services:* (Sec. 1105(c)(7), Tax Law);

— *protective and detective services:* (Sec. 1105(c)(8), Tax Law);

— *telephonic and telegraphic entertainment and information services:* the services of furnishing or providing an entertainment or information service by means of interstate or intrastate telephony, telegraphy, telephone or telegraph service (including those services provided through 800- or 900- telephone numbers, mass announcement and interactive information network services) (Sec. 1105(c)(9), Tax Law). Prepaid telephone calling services are also included. Tax applies to prepaid mobile calling services under the same rules that apply to prepaid telephone calling services;

— *transportation services:* Specified intrastate transportation services, defined to include the service of transporting, carrying or conveying a person or persons by livery service (Sec. 1101(b)(34), Tax Law; *TSB-M-09(7)S,* May 22, 2009, CCH NEW YORK TAX REPORTS, ¶ 406-400). Tax does not apply to transportation of people in connection with emergency services or funerals. Storage in transit is not taxable if certain conditions are met; see *TSB-M-14(16)S,* November 17, 2014, CCH NEW YORK TAX REPORTS, ¶ 408-271.

— *Cloud computing:* Cloud computing is a term used to describe the delivery of computing resources, including software applications, development tools, storage, and servers over the Internet. Rather than purchasing hardware or software, a consumer may purchase access to a cloud computing provider's hardware or software. Cloud computing offerings are generally divided into three categories:

— *Software as a service (SaaS),* in which a consumer purchases access to a software application that is owned, operated, and maintained by a SaaS provider, and located on a server that is owned or leased by the SaaS provider. The software is not transferred to the customer, and the customer does not have the right to download, copy, or modify the software. Sales tax authority on SaaS transactions is still evolving. Some states have taken the position that SaaS transactions are a sale of software, reasoning that using software by electronically accessing it is no different than downloading it. Other states have deemed it a service based on the fact that no software is transferred.

— *Platform as a service (PaaS),* in which, the provider sells access to a platform and software development tools that a consumer uses to create its own applications. A consumer deploys the applications it creates onto the provider's infrastructure. The consumer has control over its deployed applications but does not control the underlying infrastructure.

— *Infrastructure as a service (IaaS)*, in which providers sell access to storage, networks, equipment, and other computing resources that the provider operates and maintains. A consumer purchases the ability to store data or deploy and run software using the provider's equipment. The consumer does not manage or control the cloud infrastructure but has control over its applications and data.

New York has no specific authority on the taxability of any of the above categories. However, see *TSB-A-15(12)S,* March 17, 2015, released May 2015, CCH NEW YORK TAX REPORTS, ¶ 408-413 (reformatting electronic data and transferring the reformatted data to third parties is not a taxable service); *TSB-A-15(2)S,* April 14, 2015, CCH NEW YORK TAX REPORTS, ¶ 408-397 (a customer may use vendor's application programming interfaces (APIs), but providing a customer with computing power is not a taxable service); *TSB-A-13(22)S,* July 25, 2013, CCH NEW YORK TAX REPORTS, ¶ 407-895 (sales of access to forms via software stored on the taxpayer's website are taxable when accessed by a NY customer because the taxpayer's product is prewritten computer software); *TSB-A-09(44)S,* Sept. 24, 2009, CCH NEW YORK TAX REPORTS, ¶ 406-551 (discusses the sales and use tax treatment of various Internet advertising, set-up, support, and service fees relating to real estate listings, including application service provider (ASP) fees for website functionality that are considered receipts from the sale of prewritten computer software and are subject to tax); *TSB-A-09(25)S,* June 8, 2009, CCH NEW YORK TAX REPORTS, ¶ 406-432 (web based software applications developed by the taxpayer for use by homecare agencies to track patient care and employee time and attendance, and for billing purposes, are subject to sales tax); *TSB-A-09(15)S,* April 15, 2009, CCH NEW YORK TAX REPORTS, ¶ 406-377 (charges for online access to "loan origination and processing services," which, among other things, allowed customers to complete and print certain loan processing documents, constituted receipts from the sale of prewritten computer software); and *TSB-A-08(62)S,* Nov. 24, 2008, CCH NEW YORK TAX REPORTS, ¶ 406-277 (license to use software product that allowed a customer to upload and image to a website and manipulate the image to show various colors and views, constituted the sale of prewritten computer software).

- **Use tax**

The use of tangible personal property or taxable services within the state is taxable, unless the property or service has already been subject to the sales tax (Sec. 1110, Tax Law).

The state use tax is imposed on receipts from the following items or services:

— *use of tangible personal property purchased at retail in the state* (Sec. 1110, Tax Law);

— *use of tangible personal property manufactured, processed or assembled by the user:* the use of tangible personal property (other than computer software used by the author or other creator) manufactured, processed or assembled by the user, if items of the same kind are offered for sale by the user in the regular course of business, or items of the same kind are not offered for sale by the user in the regular course of business and the item is either used as such or incorporated into a structure, building or real property by a contractor, subcontractor or repairman in erecting structures or building on or otherwise making improvements to real property or maintaining, servicing or repairing real property (Sec. 1110, Tax Law);

— *use of information services, interior decorating and designing services, and protective and detective services:* information services by printed, mimeographed, multigraphed, or any other method of duplication (Sec. 1110, Tax Law), interior decorating and designing services and protective and detective services;

— *use of tangible personal property, however acquired* (but not for resale upon which certain taxable services are performed);

— *use of telephone answering services:* the tax is based upon the consideration given or contracted to be given for the service (including the consideration for any tangible personal property transferred in connection with the performance of the service) plus the cost of transportation of the property so transferred and of the tangible personal property upon which the service was performed, unless such cost is separately stated in the written contract and on the bill rendered to the purchaser (Sec. 1110, Tax Law);

— *use of certain computer software:* the use of any computer software written or otherwise created by a user who, in the regular course of business, offers software of a similar kind for sale as such or as a component part of other property (Sec. 1110, Tax Law; see also *TB-ST-128,* August 5, 2014, CCH NEW YORK TAX REPORTS, ¶ 408-177);

— *use of any prepaid telephone calling service* (Sec. 1110, Tax Law); and

— *use of gas or electricity* (Sec. 1110, Tax Law).

• **Responsibility for tax**

The collection of sales and use taxes is generally performed by "persons required to collect tax," which includes vendors of tangible personal property or services, recipients of amusement charges, operators of hotels and insurers licensed to issue physical or property damage liability insurance for motor vehicles registered in New York State (Sec. 1131(1), Tax Law, Sec. 341(f), Tax Law; *TB-ST-331,* May 9, 2012, CCH NEW YORK TAX REPORTS, ¶ 407-553).

Those persons required to collect tax must collect the tax from the customer when collecting the price, amusement charge or rent to which it applies. Such persons are personally liable for the tax imposed, collected or required to be collected (Sec. 1133(a), Tax Law), but the liability is transferred to the purchaser if the tax has not been paid to the person required to collect it (Sec. 1133(b), Tax Law).

Persons required to collect the tax may not advertise or suggest that the tax is not considered an element of the selling price. A vendor may not indicate that he or she will pay the tax, or that the tax will be refunded.

Drop shipments: For sales tax purposes, drop shipments consist of two transactions:

(1) the sale from the third-party seller to the primary seller; and

(2) the sale from the primary seller to the primary seller's customer.

When the primary seller is registered for New York sales tax purposes, and the third-party seller and the primary seller's customer are located in New York, the primary seller should furnish Form ST-120, Resale Certificate, to the third-party seller. The third-party seller then delivers the order to the primary seller's customer or to the seller's unaffiliated fulfillment services provider. The primary seller collects the sales tax from the customer, reports the sale and remits the sales tax to the department on the appropriate sales tax return. If the primary seller is a qualified out-of-state purchaser, he or she can also use Form ST-120 to make tax-exempt purchases of tangible personal property for resale. (*TB-ST-190,* New York Department of Taxation and Finance, August 5, 2014, CCH NEW YORK TAX REPORTS, ¶ 408-178)

Room remarketers: Room remarketers are required to collect state and local sales tax on hotel occupancies, with tax also due on the markup. New York City's locally-administered hotel room occupancy tax was changed to conform it to the methodology of the state tax in regard to room remarketers. A room remarketer is a person, such as an online travel agency (OTC), that reserves, arranges for, conveys, or furnishes

¶681   New York

occupancy, whether directly or indirectly, to an occupant for rent in an amount determined by the room remarketer. (Sec. 1101(c), Tax Law; Sec. 1119, Tax Law; *TSB-M-10(10)S;* and *TSB-M-10(18)S,* August 13, 2010, CCH NEW YORK TAX REPORTS, ¶ 406-930; *TSB-M-12(8)S,* July 26, 2012, CCH NEW YORK TAX REPORTS, ¶ 407-612)

When occupancy is provided for a single consideration with property, services, amusement charges, or any other items, whether or not such other items are taxable, the rent portion of the consideration for such transaction must be computed as follows: either the total consideration received by the room remarketer multiplied by a fraction, the numerator of which is the consideration payable for the occupancy by the room remarketer and the denominator of which is such consideration payable for the occupancy plus the consideration payable by the remarketer for the other items being sold, or by any other method as may be authorized by the Commissioner of Taxation and Finance. If the room remarketer fails to separately state the tax on the rent so computed on a sales slip, invoice, receipt, or other statement given to the occupant or fails to maintain records of the prices of all components of a transaction, the entire consideration must be treated as rent subject to tax.

In a case concerning a lawsuit brought by online travel companies against New York City, the New York Court of Appeals held that the taxpayers' facial constitutional challenge to the local law was without merit. The plain language of the enabling statute authorizes the city to impose a tax such as the Legislature has or would have the power and authority to impose on persons occupying hotel rooms in the city, and the city properly exercised this broad authority when it enacted the local law. In addition, the statute authorized a broad range of taxation. Pursuant to the statute, the city may tax a rent or charge, and it may collect the tax from a hotel owner or a person entitled to be paid the rent or charge. By its own terms, the local law applies only to fees required for occupancy. As such, the local law is not unconstitutional because the state Legislature granted the city the authority to impose a tax on hotel occupants, and the law taxes only payments for the occupancy of a hotel room. (*Expedia, Inc. v. City of New York Department of Finance,* New York Court of Appeals, No. 180, November 21, 2013, CCH NEW YORK TAX REPORTS, ¶ 407-974)

Purchases of hotel room occupancies by room remarketers: An exemption is provided for the purchase of hotel room occupancies by room remarketers when those purchases are made from hotels for later resale, applicable to rent paid for hotel occupancies on or after June 1, 2016 (Sec. 1115(kk), Tax Law; *TSB-M-16(2)S,* May 4, 2016, CCH NEW YORK TAX REPORTS, ¶ 408-734). A similar exemption applies in New York City (Sec. 11-2502(a)(4), NYC Admin. Code).

Prior to June 1, 2016, room remarketers could seek a credit or refund for the tax they paid to the hotel operators if the room remarketers satisfied certain conditions (Sec. 1105(e)(2), Tax Law).

- **Nexus**

The term "vendor" includes persons who solicit business within the State through employees, independent contractors, agents or other representatives and, by reason thereof, make sales to persons within the state of tangible personal property or services that are subject to sales tax. Accordingly, if a business located outside New York solicits sales of taxable tangible personal property or services through employees, salespersons, independent agents, or representatives located in New York, the business must register as a vendor and obtain a Certificate of Authority for New York sales tax purposes. The term "vendor" also includes certain exempt organizations which make sales of tangible personal property through a shop or store operated by the organization, or which sell food and drink in New York State. (Sec. 1101(b)(8), Tax Law; Reg. Sec. 526.10(a)(3))

Furthermore, the Commissioner may treat any salesman, representative, peddler or canvasser as the agent of the vendor, distributor, supervisor or employer under whom he or she operates or from whom he or she obtains tangible personal property or for whom he or she solicits business, and hold him or her jointly responsible with the principal, distributor, supervisor or employer for the collection and payment of tax (Sec. 1101(b)(8)(ii), Tax Law). Additionally, a person is deemed to be a vendor of telephonic or telegraphic entertainment or information services, liable for the tax, if he or she, an affiliate or agent bills the service.

Fulfillment companies: "Fulfillment services" are defined as accepting orders or responding to consumer correspondence or inquiries electronically or via mail, telephone, fax, or the Internet; billing and collection activities; or shipping of orders from inventory (Sec. 1101(b)(18), Tax Law). The definition of "vendor" excludes any person who purchases fulfillment services carried on in New York from a nonaffiliated person and a person that owns tangible personal property located on the premises of a nonaffiliated fulfillment services provider performing services for that person. The purchaser of the fulfillment services must not otherwise be a vendor. (Sec. 1101(b)(8), Tax Law)

Internet advertising: The term "vendor" does not include a person having its advertising stored on a server or other computer equipment located in New York or a person whose advertising is disseminated or displayed on the Internet by an individual or entity having nexus with New York (Sec. 12, Tax Law).

Remote sellers: Any person making taxable sales of tangible personal property or services is rebuttably presumed to be a vendor subject to New York sales and compensating use tax when the seller enters into an agreement with a New York resident to directly or indirectly refer customers to the seller, whether by a link on an Internet Web site or otherwise, for a commission or other consideration, and the agreement generates sales of over $10,000 in the prior four quarterly reporting periods. In such a situation, the seller is presumed to be soliciting business in New York through an independent contractor or other representative and will have to charge sales tax on all sales into the state. This presumption may be rebutted by proof that the resident did not engage in any solicitation activities in New York on behalf of the seller that would satisfy the nexus requirement of the U.S. Constitution during the previous four quarterly periods in question. (Sec. 1101(b)(8)(vi), Tax Law; *TSB-M-08(3)S; TSB-M-08(3.1)S; TSB-M-08(9)S*)

Taxpayer appellants Amazon.com and Overstock.com, both online retailers who sell their products solely through the Internet, failed to demonstrate that the statute that requires out-of-state Internet retailers with no physical presence in New York to collect New York sales and use taxes is facially unconstitutional under either the Commerce Clause or the Due Process Clause. (*Overstock.com, LLC v. New York State Department of Taxation and Finance,* Court of Appeals of the State of New York, Nos. 33 and 34, March 28, 2013, CCH NEW YORK TAX REPORTS, ¶ 407-797; *certiorari denied,* U.S. Supreme Court, Dkt. 13-252, December 2, 2013; *Amazon.com LLC v. New York State Department of Taxation and Finance,* U.S. Supreme Court, Dkt. 13-259, *certiorari denied,* December 2, 2013)

Affiliate nexus: An "affiliate" is considered to be an entity that directly, indirectly or constructively controls a vendor of enumerated services, is controlled by the vendor, or is under the control of a common parent along with the vendor (Sec. 1101(b)(8)(ii), Tax Law). However, the in-state activities of an affiliate in providing accounting or legal services or advice, or in directing the activities of a seller, including but not limited to, making decisions about (a) strategic planning, (b) marketing, (c) inventory, (d) staffing, (e) distribution, or (f) cash management, do not make the seller a vendor (Sec. 1101(b)(8)(i), Tax Law).

The definition of "vendor" provides that the presence of an affiliate in New York makes the remote affiliate a vendor in either of two circumstances:

(1) where the in-state affiliate uses in the state a trademark, service mark, or trade name that is the same or similar to that of the remote affiliate; or

(2) where the in-state affiliate engages in activities that help the remote affiliate develop or maintain a market for its goods or services in the state, to the extent that those activities are sufficient to give the state nexus over the remote affiliate under the nexus requirements of the U.S. Constitution.

(Sec. 1101(b)(8)(i)(l), Tax Law; *TSB-M-09(3)S,* May 6, 2009; CCH NEW YORK TAX REPORTS, ¶ 406-386; *TSB-M-10(12)S,* August 19, 2010, CCH NEW YORK TAX REPORTS, ¶ 406-941)

- **Streamlined Act status**

New York is an Advisor State to the Streamlined Sales Tax Project (SSTP). Although it has enacted legislation authorizing it to enter into the Streamlined Sales and Use Tax Agreement (Sec. 1173, Tax Law), it has not yet enacted the changes to its laws necessary to comply with the Agreement's requirements. However, it will continue to have input through its representation on the State and Local Advisory Council, which advises the Board on matters pertaining to the administration of the Agreement.

¶ 682	**Tax Base**

In general, the New York State sales and use taxes are imposed on receipts from every retail sale of taxable tangible personal property and specified services (Sec. 1105, Tax Law, Sec. 1110, Tax Law).

- **"Receipt" defined**

The term "receipt" is defined as the amount of the sales price of any item of property or the charge for any service subject to the sales or use tax, valued in money (whether received in money or otherwise) (Sec. 1101(b), Tax Law, Reg. Sec. 526.5(a)). Included in the taxable receipts are any amounts for which credit is allowed by the vendor to the purchaser, without any deduction for expenses or early payment discounts and any charges by the vendor to the purchaser for shipping or delivery (regardless of whether such charges are separately stated in the written contract or on the bill rendered to the purchaser and regardless of whether such shipping or delivery is provided by the vendor or by a third party). See also *TB-ST-838,* May 14, 2012, CCH NEW YORK TAX REPORTS, ¶ 407-557.

The taxable receipts do not include any credit for tangible personal property accepted in part payment and intended for resale.

¶ 683	List of Exemptions, Exceptions, and Exclusions

Unless otherwise indicated, the statutory exemptions, exceptions and exclusions listed below apply to both sales and use taxes; those applicable only to the use tax are listed separately. Items that are excluded from the sales or use tax base are treated at ¶ 682, "Tax Base."

The New York Department of Taxation and Finance has issued a sales and use tax bulletin as a quick reference guide for taxable and exempt property and services. The bulletin describes taxable property and services (including examples), exempt property and services (including examples), and exemption documents. See *TB-ST-740,* New York Department of Taxation and Finance, June 17, 2010, CCH NEW YORK TAX REPORTS, ¶ 406-848. The tax bulletin is also available on the department's website at **https:// www.tax.ny.gov/pubs_and_bulls/tg_bulletins/ sales_tax_bulletins_by_number.htm**.

• Sales and use tax exemptions, exceptions, and exclusions

Admissions for the benefit of: exempt religious, charitable, scientific, etc. organizations; organizations predominantly comprised of past or present members of the U.S. armed forces; organizations conducted solely for the purposes of maintaining symphony orchestras or operas and receiving substantial support from voluntary contributions; and voluntary fire or ambulance companies . . . . Sec. 1105(f)(1), Tax Law, Sec. 1116(b), Tax Law, Sec. 1116(d), Tax Law, Sec. 1116(d)(1), Tax Law, Sec. 1116(d)(3), Tax Law

Admissions to agricultural fairs; historical homes and gardens; and historic sites, houses, shrines and museums . . . . Sec. 1116(d), Tax Law

Admissions to amusement parks (75% exemption) . . . . Sec. 1122, Tax Law

Admissions to cabaret or roof garden to attend theatrical or musical performance . . . . Sec. 1123, Tax Law

Admissions to race tracks, boxing, sparring or wrestling matches, dramatic or musical arts performances, motion picture theaters or sporting facilities where the patron is a participant . . . . . . Sec. 1116(d), Tax Law

Advertisements . . . . Sec. 1105(c)(1), Tax Law, Sec. 1115(a), Tax Law, Sec. 1115(n), Tax Law

Advertising supplements . . . . Sec. 1115(a), Tax Law

Aircraft and aircraft maintenance . . . . Sec. 1115(a)(21), Sec. 1115(dd), Tax Law Sec. 1101(b)(iv), Tax Law

Aircraft, general aviation . . . . Sec. 1115(a)(21-a), Tax Law

Alcoholic beverage tasting . . . . Sec. 1115(a)(33), Tax Law, Sec. 1118(13), Tax Law

Alternative motor vehicle fuels (E85, CNG, natural gas for conversion to CNG, and hydrogen fuels) (exp. 9/1/2021) . . . . Sec. 1115(a)(42), Tax Law

Broadcasting, machinery, equipment, and certain services . . . . Sec. 1115(a)(38), Tax Law

Bulk vending machine sales of tangible property at 50¢ or less . . . . . Sec. 1115(a)(13-a), Tax Law

Cameras, movieolas, projectors and sound recorders used in movie, video or sound productions . . . . Sec. 1105(a), Tax Law, Sec. 1105(c)(2), Tax Law, Sec. 1105-B(a), Tax Law

Capital improvements to real property, construction materials used for . . . . Sec. 1115(a)(17), Tax Law

Cargo handling machinery, Port of New York . . . . Sec. 1115(a)(41), Tax Law

Cartons, containers and other packaging materials actually transferred to a customer in connection with the performance of certain taxable services . . . . Sec. 1115(19), Tax Law

Certain sales of tangible property at private residences	Sec. 1115(a)(18), Tax Law
Certain services performed upon property delivered outside New York State	Sec. 1119(a), Tax Law
Certain transfers between corporations and partnerships	Sec. 1101(b)(4)(iv), Tax Law
Clothing and footwear priced at less than $110	Sec. 1109(g), Tax Law; Sec. 1115(a)(30), Tax Law
Coin-operated car wash services	Sec. 1115(t), Tax Law
Coin-operated luggage cart sales	Sec. 1115(a)(13-b), Tax Law
Coin-operated photocopy machines charging 50¢ or less	Sec. 1115(a)(31), Tax Law
Coin-operated telephones charging 25¢ or less	Sec. 1115(e), Tax Law
Coins and precious metal bullion	Sec. 1115(a)(27), Tax Law
Commercial aircraft primarily engaged in intrastate, interstate or foreign commerce; machinery or equipment to be installed on such aircraft; property used by such aircraft for maintenance and repairs; and flight simulators purchased by commercial airlines	Sec. 1105(c)(3)(v), Tax Law, Sec. 1115(a)(21), Tax Law
Commercial fishing vessels: property used for such vessels	Sec. 1115(a)(24), Tax Law
Commercial vessels primarily engaged in interstate or foreign commerce; property used by such vessels for fuel, provisions, supplies, maintenance and repairs	Sec. 1115(a)(8), Tax Law
Composition, typography and progressive proofs used directly and predominantly in production	Sec. 1115(a)(12), Tax Law
Computer hardware used in designing software	Sec. 1115(a)(35), Tax Law
Computer software	Sec. 1101(b)(5), Tax Law, Sec. 1101(b)(6), Tax Law, Sec. 1101(b)(14), Tax Law, Sec. 1110(g), Tax Law, Sec. 1118(11), Tax Law
Construction material used for capital improvements to real property	Sec. 1115(a)(17), Tax Law
Construction materials used by contractor for exempt organizations .	Sec. 1115(a)(15), Tax Law, Sec. 1115(a)(16), Tax Law

Credit unions	Sec. 1768, Tit. 12, USC; see *TSB-M-06(4.1)S*, July 12, 2012
Distribution of property by a corporation to its stockholder as a liquidating dividend or by a partnership to its partners in whole or partial liquidation	Sec. 1101(b)(4)(iv), Tax Law
Drugs and medicines for human beings	Sec. 1115(a)(3), Tax Law
Dues and/or initiation fees paid to a social or athletic club not exceeding $10 per year	Sec. 1105(f)(2), Tax Law
Dues paid to fraternal societies operating under the lodge system or to college fraternities	Sec. 1105(f)(2), Tax Law
Electronic news services; electronic periodicals (limited exemption; see ¶ 681)	Sec. 1101(b)(37), Tax Law; Sec. 1101(b)(38), Tax Law
Eligible food purchased with food stamps	Sec. 1115(k), Tax Law
Emissions inspection equipment	Sec. 1115(a)(31), Tax Law
Energy produced by cogeneration by certain coop apartments	Sec. 1115(b)(iii), Tax Law
Farm production, certain services related to	Sec. 1105(c)(3)(vi), Tax Law
Fees for the services of advertising agencies or other persons acting in a representative capacity	Sec. 1105(c)(1), Tax Law
Feminine hygiene products	Sec. 1115(a)(3-a), Tax Law
Ferry boats and fuel, provisions, supplies, maintenance, and repairs	Sec. 1115(a)(43), Tax Law
Film production, materials and services	Sec. 1115(a)(39), Tax Law, Sec. 1115(bb), Tax Law
Flags of the United States and New York State	Sec. 1115(a)(11), Tax Law
Food and drink sold for off-premises consumption	Sec. 1105(d)(i), Tax Law
Food and drink sold through bulk vending machines at 50¢ or less	Sec. 1115(a)(13-a), Tax Law
Food and drink sold to airlines for in-flight consumption	Sec. 1105(d)(ii)(A), Tax Law
Food, beverages, dietary foods and health supplements sold for human consumption	Sec. 1115(a)(1), Tax Law, Sec. 1115(w), Tax Law
Footwear and clothing priced at less than $110	Sec. 1109(g), Tax Law; Sec. 1115(a)(30), Tax Law
Footwear and clothing (New York City)	Sec. 1107(b)(11), Tax Law; Sec. 1210(a)(1)(i)

Fuel, alternative for motor vehicles (E85, CNG, natural gas for conversion to CNG, and hydrogen fuels) (exp. 9/1/2021) . . .	Sec. 1115(a)(42), Tax Law
Fuel cell electricity generating systems equipment	Sec. 1115(kk), Tax Law
Fuel cell fuel (hydrogen or electricity) for fuel cell generating systems equipment	Sec. 1115(kk)(2), Tax Law
Fuel sold for use in airplanes	Sec. 1115(a)(9), Tax Law, Sec. 1115(j), Tax Law
Fuel sold for use in commercial and general aviation aircraft (local exemption; eff. 12/1/2017)	Sec. 1210(a)(4)(xiii), Tax Law
Fuel used by commercial fishing vessels	Sec. 1115(a)(24), Tax Law
Fuel used by commercial vessels engaged in interstate commerce . .	Sec. 1115(a)(8), Tax Law
Fuel, utilities used in farm production	Sec. 1115(c), Tax Law, Sec. 1115(j), Tax Law
Fuel, utilities used in horticultural and floricultural operations	Sec. 1115(c), Tax Law
Fuel, utilities used in manufacturing or processing	Sec. 1115(c), Tax Law
Fuel, utilities used in research and development	Sec. 1115(b)(ii), Tax Law
Furnishing personal or individual information that may not be substantially incorporated in reports furnished to other persons	Sec. 1105(c)(1), Tax Law
Gas and electricity used to provide gas or electric service	Sec. 1115(w), Tax Law
Gifts of tangible property	Sec. 1101(b)(5), Tax Law, Sec. 1101(b)(7), Tax Law, Sec. 1101(b)(12), Tax Law, Sec. 1105(a), Tax Law, Sec. 1110(a), Tax Law
Government organizations	Sec. 1116(a), Tax Law
Horse boarding, certain services related to	Sec. 1105(c)(3)(vi), Tax Law
Hotel occupancies by authorized representatives of posts or organizations comprised of past or present members of the U.S. Armed Forces	Sec. 1116(a)(5), Tax Law
Hotel occupancies by permanent residents	Sec. 1105(e), Tax Law
Hotel occupancies where the daily rental charge is $2 or less	Sec. 1105(e), Tax Law
Improving real property by a capital improvement	Sec. 1101(b)(9)(i), Tax Law, Sec. 1115(a)(17), Tax Law
Information services used by newspapers and radio and television broadcasters in the collection and dissemination of news . . .	Sec. 1105(c)(1), Tax Law, Sec. 1115(i)(C), Tax Law, Sec. 1119(c), Tax Law
Informational reports rendered to insurance companies on the risk desirability of applicants	Sec. 1105(c)(1), Tax Law

Installation, maintenance and repair services performed by a person not engaged in such business	Sec. 1105(c)(5), Tax Law, Sec. 1115(a)(18), Tax Law
Installation, maintenance and repair services performed on property installed on qualifying tractors, trailers or semitrailers for purposes of equipping, maintenance or repair	Sec. 1115(a)(26), Tax Law
Installation, maintenance and repair services performed on qualifying tractors, trailers or semi-trailers used in combination with a gross vehicle weight in excess of 26,000 pounds	Sec. 1115(a)(26), Tax Law
Installation of mobile home	Sec. 1105(c)(3), Tax Law
Installing, maintaining or repairing fishing vessels	Sec. 1105(c)(3)(vii), Tax Law
Installing, maintaining or repairing property used in farm production	Sec. 1115(a)(6), Tax Law
Installing, maintaining or repairing property used in gas or oil production	Sec. 1105(a)(3)(ix), Tax Law
Installing, maintaining or repairing property used in horticultural and floricultural operations	Sec. 1105(c)(3)(vi), Tax Law
Installing personal property that constitutes a capital improvement to real property	Sec. 1101(b)(9), Tax Law, Sec. 1115(a)(17), Tax Law
Insurance companies, nonprofit	Sec. 6707, Insurance Law
Interstate and international telephone and telegraph service	Sec. 1105(b), Tax Law
Interstate transactions	Sec. 1105(b), Tax Law, Sec. 1115(d), Tax Law, Sec. 1115(n), Tax Law, Sec. 1118(2), Tax Law, Sec. 1119(a), Tax Law
Internet access services	Sec. 1115(v), Tax Law
Internet data center	Sec. 1115(a)(37), Tax Law
Kero-jet fuel	Sec. 1115(j), Tax Law
Laundering, dry-cleaning, tailoring, weaving, pressing, shoe repairing and shoe shining services	Sec. 1105(c)(3)(ii), Tax Law
Lease entered into merely as security agreement	Sec. 1101(b)(5), Tax Law
Leases of real property	Sec. 1101(b)(5), Tax Law, Sec. 1111(i), Tax Law
Hotel occupancies purchased for resale by room remarketers	Sec. 1115(kk), Tax Law, Sec. 11-2502(a)(4), NYC Admin. Code
Machinery and equipment used for disposing of industrial waste as part of a process for preventing water or air pollution	Sec. 1115(a)(12), Tax Law

Machinery and equipment used in manufacturing or processing . . .	Sec. 1115(a)(12), Tax Law, Sec. 1210(a)(1), Tax Law
Machinery and equipment used in mining or extracting operations .	Sec. 1115(a)(12), Tax Law, Sec. 1210(a)(1), Tax Law
Machinery and equipment used to prepare food for sale	Sec. 1115(a)(12), Tax Law, Sec. 1115(c), Tax Law
Maintenance and repair services performed upon property held for sale in the regular course of business	Sec. 1105(c)(5), Tax Law
Manufactured or processed tangible property donated to an exempt organization	Sec. 1115(*l*), Tax Law
Medical equipment and supplies	Sec. 1115(g), Tax Law
Military decorations, service flags, prisoner of war flags, and blue star banners	Sec. 1115(a)(11-a), Tax Law Sec. 1115(a)(11-b), Tax Law
Military members' vehicles purchased out-of-state and registered in NY	Sec. 1115(a)(14-a), Tax Law
Milk crates	Sec. 1115(a)(19-A), Tax Law
Motor fuel, alternatives (E85, CNG, natural gas for conversion to CNG, and hydrogen fuels) (exp. 9/1/2021)	Sec. 1115(a)(42), Tax Law
Motor fuel and diesel motor fuel purchased by a religious, charitable, scientific, etc. organization for its own heating use and consumption	Sec. 1116(b)(5), Tax Law
Motor fuel and diesel motor fuel purchased by an exempt hospital for its own heating use and consumption	Sec. 1116(b)(5), Tax Law
Motor fuel and diesel motor fuel purchased by an exempt Native American nation or tribe	Sec. 1116(a)(6), Tax Law
Motor fuel and diesel motor fuel purchased by the United States, New York State, their agencies and instrumentalities for their own use or consumption	Sec. 1116(b)(5), Tax Law
Motor vehicle insurance damage award to nonresident claimant who is not the insured, whose vehicle is registered outside New York State, and who elects not to replace or repair the damaged vehicle within New York (withholding tax on transfers of motor vehicle insurance damage awards)	Sec. 1105(c)(1), Tax Law
Motor vehicle insurance damage awards to claimant who repaired or replaced the damaged vehicle and paid the sales or use tax due on the repair or replacement before receiving the voucher and stub from the insurer (withholding tax on transfers of motor vehicle insurance damage awards)	Sec. 1105(c)(1), Tax Law
Motor vehicle parking, garaging and storing services where the garage is part of premises occupied solely as a private one- or two-family dwelling	Sec. 1105(c)(6), Tax Law

Motor vehicles sold between close family members	Sec. 1115(a)(14), Tax Law
Motor vehicles sold to certain nonresidents	Sec. 1117(a), Tax Law, Sec. 1117(c), Tax Law
Natural gas used for personal residence consumption	Sec. 1115(a)(25), Tax Law
New mobile homes sold to a contractor	Sec. 1101(b)(4), Tax Law, Sec. 1101(b)(11), Tax Law
Newspapers and periodicals; paper used in publication of newspapers and periodicals	Sec. 1118(5), Tax Law
Nonprofit organizations	Sec. 1116(a), Tax Law
Occupancies in a hotel operated by a religious, charitable, scientific, etc. organization in furtherance of its nonprofit activities	Sec. 1116(c), Tax Law, Sec. 1116(g), Tax Law
Omnibus parts, equipment, lubricants, motor fuel and diesel motor fuel purchased and used in the operation of an omnibus (credit or refund)	Sec. 1115(a)(32), Tax Law, Sec. 1115(u), Tax Law, Sec. 1119(b), Tax Law
Parts, tools, supplies and services used in connection with manufacturing or processing operations	Sec. 1105-B(a), Tax Law
Parts, tools, supplies and services used in connection with mining and extracting operations	Sec. 1105-B(a), Tax Law
Passenger car rentals when leased for a minimum term of one year .	Sec. 1111(i)(B), Tax Law
Pipelines and drilling equipment	Sec. 1115(a)(12), Tax Law
Pollution control, machinery and equipment	Sec. 1115(a)(40), Tax Law
Precious metal bullion sold for investment	Sec. 1115(a)(27), Tax Law
Printer's purchases of tangible property which becomes a part of the property on which the services are performed or is later transferred to the customer in connection with the service . . .	Sec. 1105(c)(2), Tax Law
Printing services performed on tangible property furnished by the purchaser and delivered to the purchaser outside of New York State	Sec. 1115(d), Tax Law
Production services relating to mailing lists when mailed, shipped or otherwise distributed from New York to prospective customers located outside New York State	Sec. 1115(n)(2), Tax Law
Promotional material distributed out-of-state or shipped by common carrier from outside New York State	Sec. 1115(n), Tax Law
Property and services used to produce live public theatrical and musical performances	Sec. 1115(x), Tax Law
Property installed in tractors, trailers or semi-trailers for their equipping, maintenance or repair	Sec. 1115(a)(26), Tax Law
Prosthetic aids, hearing aids, eyeglasses and artificial devices	Sec. 1115(a)(4), Tax Law

Protective and detective services performed by a licensed port
watchman . . . . Sec. 1105(c)(8), Tax Law,
Sec. 1119(c), Tax Law

Rental or lease of trucks, trailers or tractor-trailer combinations to an
authorized carrier when operated by the owner of the vehicle or
the owner's employee . . . . Sec. 1115(a)(22),
Tax Law

Related-person sales of property or services in connection with Dodd-
Frank compliance . . . . Sec. 1115(jj),
Tax Law

Residential energy sources and services (reduced rate) . . . . Sec. 1105-A(a), Tax Law,
Sec. 1105-A(d), Tax Law,
Sec. 1210(a)(3)(i),
Tax Law

Sales and amusement charges by or to, as well as any use or
occupancy by: the United Nations or any international
organization of which the U.S. is a member; any religious,
charitable, scientific, etc. organization; any post of past or
present members of the U.S. armed forces; any not-for-profit
health maintenance organization; and any cooperative or
foreign corporation doing business in New York State pursuant
to the Rural Electric Cooperative Law . . . . Sec. 1116(a), Tax Law,
Sec. 1116(a)(3), Tax Law,
Sec. 1116(a)(4), Tax Law,
Sec. 1116(a)(5), Tax Law,
Sec. 1116(a)(7), Tax Law,
Sec. 1116(a)(8), Tax Law

Sales and amusement charges by or to certain Native American
nations or tribes; sales to individual Native American members
of an exempt nation or tribe . . . . Sec. 1116(a)(6), Tax Law,
Sec. 1116(b)(1), Tax Law

Sales and amusement charges by or to the United States, New York
State, their agencies or instrumentalities; uses and occupancies
by such governmental entities . . . . Sec. 1116(a)(1), Tax Law,
Sec. 1116(a)(2), Tax Law

Sales for resale . . . . Sec. 1101(b)(4), Tax Law,
Sec. 1105, Tax Law

Services and repairs performed upon exempt medical equipment . . . Sec. 1115(g), Tax Law

Services and repairs performed upon exempt prosthetic devices . . . . Sec. 1115(g), Tax Law

Services rendered by persons not engaged in a regular business . . . Sec. 1105(c)(3)(i),
Tax Law

Services rendered to commercial aircraft primarily engaged in
intrastate, interstate or foreign commerce; installing,
maintaining or repairing machinery and equipment on such
commercial aircraft; property used by such aircraft for
maintenance and repairs; and flight simulators purchased by
commercial airlines . . . . Sec. 1105(c)(3)(v),
Tax Law,
Sec. 1115(a)(21),
Tax Law

Services rendered to commercial vessels primarily engaged in interstate or foreign commerce; property used by such vessels for fuel, provisions, supplies, maintenance and repairs	Sec. 1105(c)(3)(iv), Tax Law, Sec. 1115(a)(8), Tax Law
Services rendered to railroad rolling stock primarily engaged in carrying freight in intrastate, interstate or foreign commerce .	Sec. 1105(c)(3)(viii), Tax Law
Services rendered upon property used directly and predominantly in the production for sale of tangible personal property by farming	Sec. 1105(c)(3)(vi), Tax Law, Sec. 1115(a)(6), Tax Law
Services rendered with respect to fishing vessels used directly and predominantly in the harvesting of fish for sale; property used by such vessels for fuel, provisions, supplies, maintenance and repairs	Sec. 1105(c)(3)(vii), Tax Law, Sec. 1115(a)(24), Tax Law
Services that consist of the practice of architecture or engineering and are performed by a licensed architect or engineer	Sec. 1105(c)(7), Tax Law
Settlement funds or grantor trusts set up to deal with claims from the Holocaust, World War II, and Nazi persecution	Sec. 13, Tax Law
Solar energy systems (commercial) equipment and installation	Sec. 1115(hh), Tax Law
Solar energy systems (residential) equipment and installation	Sec. 1115(ee), Tax Law
Shopping papers and materials used in connection with their publication	Sec. 1115(a)(20), Tax Law, Sec. 1115(i), Tax Law
Student meals	Sec. 1105(d)(ii)(B), Tax Law
Tangible property designed for use in some manner relating to domestic animals or poultry when sold by a licensed veterinarian	Sec. 1115(f), Tax Law, Sec. 1119(a), Tax Law
Tangible property incorporated into manufactured product	Sec. 1118(4), Tax Law
Tangible property purchased outside the state and used in New York State	Sec. 1110(e), Tax Law
Tangible property sold by funeral director	Sec. 1115(a)(7), Tax Law
Tangible property sold by railroad in reorganization to a profitable railroad	Sec. 1115(h), Tax Law
Tangible property used for nonprofit organizations	Sec. 1115(a)(15), Tax Law, Sec. 1115(a)(16), Tax Law, Sec. 1115(l), Tax Law
Tangible property used in constructing or rehabilitating industrial or commercial real property located in an economic development zone (credit or refund)	Sec. 1119(a), Tax Law
Tangible property used in farm production	Sec. 1115(a)(6), Tax Law

¶683　**New York**

Tangible property used in horticultural and floricultural operations . .	Sec. 1115(a)(6), Tax Law
Tangible property used in research and development	Sec. 1115(a)(10), Tax Law
Telephone and telegraph services used to collect and disseminate news	Sec. 1115(b)(i), Tax Law
Telecommunications machinery and equipment	Sec. 1115(a)(12-a), Tax Law
Textbooks, college	Sec. 1115(a)(34), Tax Law
Theatrical productions, live	Sec. 1115(x), Tax Law; Sec. 1123, Tax Law
Tractors, trailers and semi-trailers used in combinations having a gross vehicle weight in excess of 26,000 pounds	Sec. 1115(a)(26), Tax Law
Training services rendered to racehorses	Sec. 1115(m)(1), Tax Law
Transportation services provided by affiliated livery vehicles in NYC .	Sec. 1101(b)(34), Tax Law
Trash removal services rendered by or on behalf of a municipal corporation	Sec. 1116(e), Tax Law
Unenumerated services	Sec. 1105(c)(1), Tax Law
Used mobile homes	Sec. 1115(a)(23), Tax Law
Vending machine sales of bulk items sold at 50¢ or less	Sec. 1115(a)(13-a), Tax Law
Vending machine sales of certain food and beverage items sold at $1.50 or less	Sec. 1115(a)(1), Tax Law, Sec. 1115(a)(13), Tax Law
Vending machine sales of items sold at 10¢ or less	Sec. 1105(d)(i)(3), Tax Law
Vessels for local transit service (refund or credit)	Sec. 1119(b), Tax Law
Vessels: pending registration or used by the purchaser for up to 90 days	Sec. 1118(13), Tax Law
Vessels: sales, leases, or uses in excess of $230,000	Sec. 1115(jj), Tax Law
Vessels sold to nonresidents	Sec. 1117, Tax Law
Veterans' home gift shops, sales by	Sec. 1115(ff), Tax Law
Veterans' sales to benefit veterans' organizations ($2,500 limit)	Sec. 1115(a)(18-a), Tax Law
Veterinary services	Sec. 1115(f), Tax Law, Sec. 1119(a), Tax Law
Water and sewer line protection programs (residential)	Sec. 1115(ii), Tax Law
Water when delivered to the consumer through mains or pipes	Sec. 1115(a)(2), Tax Law
World Trade Center area (lease exemptions)	Sec. 1115, Tax Law; TSB-M-05(12)S

- **Exemptions, exceptions, and exclusions applicable only to the use tax**

Computer software not considered to be tangible personal property prior to September 1, 1991, and used by the purchaser, creator or copyright owner in New York State prior to that date	Sec. 1101(b)(6), Tax Law, Sec. 1101(b)(14), Tax Law
Foreign airlines—Spare parts, consumable technical supplies and maintenance and ground equipment for use exclusively in the operation or handling of aircraft and aircraft stores brought into New York State from a foreign country by a foreign airline hold a foreign air carrier permit	Sec. 1118(8), Tax Law
Motor vehicles purchased outside of New York State by a person while he or she was in U.S. military service	Sec. 1115(a)(14-a), Tax Law
Paper used in newspapers and periodical publications	Sec. 1118(5), Tax Law
Property and services exempt from sales tax	Sec. 1118(3), Tax Law
Property and services taxed by another jurisdiction	Sec. 1118(7), Tax Law
Property incorporated into produced articles	Sec. 1118(4), Tax Law
Property purchased while a nonresident of New York State	Sec. 1118(2), Tax Law
Racehorses—Use of racehorses purchased outside New York State and brought into the state for the purpose of entering a racing event on which pari-mutuel wagering is authorized by law . . .	Sec. 1118(9), Tax Law, Sec. 1118(10), Tax Law
Temporary construction of world's fair—Property used exclusively for the temporary construction or repair of any building or exhibit located entirely on land owned by New York City and leased by it to a corporation organized for the sole purpose of holding a world's fair	Sec. 1118(6), Tax Law
Uses prior to August 1, 1965	Sec. 1118(1), Tax Law

¶ 684   Rate of Tax

The New York State sales and use tax is imposed at the rate of 4% (Sec. 1105, Tax Law, Sec. 1110, Tax Law).

A special tax at the rate of 6% is imposed upon passenger car rentals (Sec. 1160, Tax Law), as well as hotel occupancies (Sec. 1104(a), Tax Law). An additional 5% sales and use tax is imposed on passenger car rentals within the Metropolitan Commuter Transportation District (Sec. 1166-A, Tax Law).

For a table of the combined state and city and county sales and use taxes in each locality, see ¶ 685.

- **Metropolitan commuter transportation district**

An additional New York State sales and compensating use tax rate of $\frac{3}{8}$% is imposed in the Metropolitan Commuter Transportation District (Sec. 1109(a), Tax Law), which district consists of New York City and the Counties of Dutchess, Nassau, Orange, Putnam, Rockland, Suffolk and Westchester (Reg. Sec. 530.1).

- **Residential energy sources and services**

There is currently no statewide sales and use tax imposed upon retail sales or uses of fuel oil, coal, propane (except when sold in containers of less than 100 pounds), natural gas, electricity or steam when used for residential purposes, or wood when used for residential heating purposes (Sec. 1105-A, Tax Law).

The state sales tax, however, is imposed upon (1) highway diesel motor fuel delivered at a filling station or into a repository equipped to dispense fuel into the fuel tank of a motor vehicle, and (2) non-highway diesel motor fuel, except when used exclusively for residential purposes and delivered into a storage tank that is not equipped with a hose or other apparatus for dispensing the fuel into the fuel tank of a motor vehicle and which tank is attached to the heating unit burning the fuel (Sec. 1105-A, Tax Law). For deliveries of fuel exceeding 4,500 gallons, a certificate signed by the purchaser and stating that the product will be used exclusively for residential purposes is required.

Residential solar energy equipment and installation services are exempt (Sec. 1115(ee), Tax Law).

Localities (except New York City) may adopt reduced rates on retail sales and uses of certain residential energy sources or may exempt such sales and uses (Sec. 1210(a)(3)(i), Tax Law). See also ¶ 685.

• Motor fuel

The sales tax on qualified motor fuel is capped at 8¢ per gallon (the rate that would be charged if gasoline were priced at $2 per gallon) outside the Metropolitan Commuter Transportation District (MCTD) and 8.75¢ per gallon within the MCTD. (Sec. 1111(m), Tax Law; *TSB-M-06(8)S,* CCH NEW YORK TAX REPORTS, ¶ 300-517).

"Qualified fuel" means motor fuel or highway diesel motor fuel that is (1) sold for use directly and exclusively in the engine of a motor vehicle; or (2) sold by a retail gas station (other than water-white kerosene sold exclusively for heating purposes in containers of no more than twenty gallons) (Sec. 1111(m)(7), Tax Law).

The Commissioner of Taxation and Finance is required to establish an average price (not including sales tax or fuel excise tax) on motor fuel and highway diesel fuel during each quarter. Counties and cities that have elected a cents-per-gallon method of tax must multiply the average price by the local sales tax rate. If the result of this computation is less than the locality's effective cents-per-gallon rate, localities must drop their cents-per-gallon rate to the lower rate, rounded to the nearest cent. The average price is also multiplied by the state percentage sales tax rate and the Metropolitan Commuter Transportation District (MCTD) percentage tax rate. If the result of this computation is a lower state or MCTD cents-per-gallon rate, the state or MCTD cents-per-gallon rate is also adjusted to the lower rate. The new rates would also take effect on the first day of the next succeeding sales tax quarter.

• Modular homes

Sixty percent of the charge for the sale of a new module home module is subject to sales tax. In addition, sales tax must be charged on 100% of the vendor's charge for shipping and delivery of the modules. The charges for the sale of modules, charges for shipping and delivery, and charges for installation of the modules at the building site must be reasonable and separately stated in order for the 60% rule to apply. If the installation of the modules at the building site will constitute a capital improvement, then charges for the installation would not be subject to sales or use taxes, provided the installation charges are reasonable and stated separately from all other charges. For additional information, see *TSB-M-09(19)S,* November 24, 2009, CCH NEW YORK TAX REPORTS, ¶ 406-602.

¶ 685   Local Taxes

Cities and counties in New York (except counties wholly within a city) (Sec. 1210, Tax Law), as well as certain school districts (Sec. 1211(a), Tax Law), are authorized, pursuant to Article 29, Tax Law, to impose local sales and use taxes. The local taxes are in addition to the state rate and the additional Metropolitan Commuter Transit District tax, where applicable.

Local taxes on motor fuels: Counties and cities, including New York City, are allowed to change their percentage rate sales tax to a cents-per-gallon method at a rate of cents per gallon equal to $2 or $3 (*TSB-M-06(8)S*).

• Imposition of local taxes

Local jurisdictions may adopt the entire state tax package, with exemptions provided for items used in the production of tangible personal property and sales of utilities or telephone central office equipment, station apparatus or comparable telegraph equipment used in receiving at destination or in initiating and switching telephone or telegraph communication or in receiving, amplifying, processing, transmitting, and retransmitting telephone and telegraph signals (Sec. 1210(a)(1), Tax Law). The credit or refund for tangible personal property used to rehabilitate property in an economic development zone is allowed only when specifically provided by a local jurisdiction.

In the alternative, local jurisdictions may adopt one or more of the taxes included in the entire state tax package, except that the sales and use taxes on tangible personal property and on services may only be adopted as part of the entire state tax package (Sec. 1210(b)(1), Tax Law). Local jurisdictions not adopting the entire state tax package may tax telephone answering services but only if they also impose the compensating use tax upon such services. The jurisdiction is determined by the location of the person or business for whom the telephone answering service is being provided, regardless of the location of the telephone answering service (*TSB-M-91(13)S*).

Upon either election, the provisions of the local tax must be uniform (Sec. 1210(a)(1), Tax Law, Sec. 1210(b)(1), Tax Law).

No transaction may be taxed by any county or by any city within such county, or by both, at an aggregate rate in excess of the highest rate set for that jurisdiction (Sec. 1223, Tax Law). When a transaction is taxed by both a county and a city, the rate of tax on the transaction imposed by the county or city is deemed to be reduced (or the entire tax eliminated) to the extent necessary to avoid exceeding the maximum tax rate.

Counties having one or more cities of less than one million have prior right to impose local sales taxes on the entire state tax package to the extent of one-half the maximum rate authorized (Sec. 1224(a), Tax Law). Each city in such a county has prior right to impose local sales taxes on the entire state tax package to the extent of one-half the maximum rate authorized (Sec. 1224(b)(2), Tax Law). When the entire state tax package is not adopted, each city in a county having one or more cities of less than one million has prior right to impose local sales taxes on sales of the following: utilities; food and drink sold by restaurants; hotel room occupancies; and admissions charges, social or athletic club dues, and roof garden or cabaret charges (Sec. 1224(b)(1), Tax Law).

• Residential energy sources

Local governments, including New York City, may exempt or impose reduced rates on retail sales and uses of certain residential energy sources (Sec. 1210(a)(3)(i), Tax Law). See "Combined state and local rates" below.

• Fuel and utilities used in manufacturing

The statewide exemption for fuel and utilities used or consumed in producing tangible personal property and utilities does not apply in New York City (Sec. 1107(b), Tax Law).

• Additional tax on sales of utility services for school district purposes

School districts that are coterminous with or partly or wholly within cities having a population of less than 125,000 may impose a tax on sales of utility services at a rate of up to 3%. The Newburgh Enlarged City School District and Peekskill City School District each impose a 3% sales tax on consumer utilities. Such taxes are in addition to the state, city and county taxes (Sec. 1212(a), Tax Law).

¶685   New York

- **Determining the rate of local tax to be collected**

The place of delivery is controlling for purposes of determining the applicable local tax rate (Sec. 1213, Tax Law).

Local sales tax jurisdictions are generally allowed to increase or decrease their local sales and use tax (sales tax) rate effective on March 1, June 1, September 1, or December 1 of each year. A bulletin describes how sales tax is applied when the sales tax rate in a locality changes (*TB-ST-895,* New York Department of Taxation and Finance, March 10, 2014, CCH NEW YORK TAX REPORTS, ¶ 408-044).

- **Mobile telecommunications**

New York has conformed to the provisions of the federal Mobile Telecommunications Sourcing Act (P.L. 106-252) for sales and use tax purposes (Sec. 1111(k), Tax Law, Sec. 1133(e), Tax Law). Wireless telecommunications services are sourced to the customer's "primary place of use," which is the residential or primary business address of the customer and which must be located in the service provider's licensed service area. The jurisdiction in which the primary place of use is located is the only jurisdiction that may tax the communications services, regardless of the customer's location when an actual call is placed or received (Sec. 1115(cc), Tax Law).

- **Combined state and local rates**

A table of combined state and local sales tax rates is available in *Publication 718, New York State and Local Sales Tax Rates by Community,* March 1, 2015, CCH NEW YORK TAX REPORTS, ¶ 65-905, also available at **http://www.tax.ny.gov/pdf/publications/sales/pub718.pdf.**

The effective dates of the rates are listed in *Publication 718A, Enactment and Effective Dates of Sales & Use Tax Rates,* October 2016, CCH NEW YORK TAX REPORTS, ¶ 65-907, also available at **http://www.tax.ny.gov/pdf/publications/sales/pub718a.pdf.**

Sales and use tax rates may be looked up by address at **http://www8.tax.ny.gov/JRLA/jrlaStart.**

- **Clothing and footwear**

For the local sales and use tax rates on clothing and footwear, see *Publication 718-C,* December 1, 2015, CCH NEW YORK TAX REPORTS, ¶ 65-908.

- **Motor fuels**

For the local sales and use tax rates on sales of qualified motor fuel, highway diesel motor fuel, and B20 biodiesel, see *Publication 718-F,* August 1, 2016, CCH NEW YORK TAX REPORTS, ¶ 65-921.

- **Residential and commercial energy sources and systems**

Those counties and cities that impose local sales and use taxes on residential energy sources are listed in *Publication 718-R,* September 1, 2015, CCH NEW YORK TAX REPORTS, ¶ 65-922.

Counties and cities that impose local sales and use taxes on the retail sale and installation of commercial solar energy systems equipment are listed in *Publication 718-CS,* March 1, 2015, CCH NEW YORK TAX REPORTS, ¶ 65-998.

Counties and cities that impose local sales and use taxes on the retail sale and installation of residential solar energy systems equipment are listed in *Publication 718-S,* March 1, 2015, CCH NEW YORK TAX REPORTS, ¶ 65-914.

• **State publications listing local rates**

All of the state publications listed above and many more can be found on the department's website at **https://www.tax.ny.gov/pubs_and_bulls/publications/ pub_numeric_list.htm**.

• **New York City**

Effective August 1, 2009, the New York City local sales and use tax rate was increased to 4.5%. As a result of this change, the combined state and local sales and use tax rate imposed in New York City is 8.875%. This rate includes the 4% state tax, the .375 % MCTD tax, and the 4.5% New York City sales tax (Sec. 1210, Tax Law).

New York City imposes its tax on selected services, including information services; processing and printing services; installation, repair and maintenance services performed upon tangible personal property; storage and safe deposit rental; real estate maintenance, and service or repair (Sec. 1212, Tax Law, Sec. 11-2002, NYC Adm. Code). The 4.5% NYC tax also is imposed on receipts from credit rating and reporting services and numerous personal services not subject to the state tax, such as barbering, beauty, weight control, hair restoration, and massage, through November 30, 2017 (Sec. 11-2002, NYC Adm. Code; Sec. 11-2040, NYC Adm. Code).

Hotel room occupancy tax: The base rate of the New York City hotel occupancy tax is determined in accordance with the following tax table (Sec. 11-2502(a), NYC Adm. Code):

— If the daily rent is $10 or more, but less than $20, the daily tax rate is $0.50;

— If the daily rent is $20 or more, but less than $30, the daily tax rate is $1.00;

— If the daily rent is $30 or more, but less than $40, the daily tax rate is $1.50;

— If the daily rent is $40 or more, the daily tax rate is $2.00.

An additional tax is imposed for every occupancy of each room in a hotel in New York City at the rate of 5.875% of the rent or charge per day for each such room, until November 30, 2019. Beginning December 1, 2019, the rate is reduced to 5%. (Sec. 11-2502(a), NYC Adm. Code)

¶ 686   Bracket Schedule

The amount of tax is computed by multiplying the amount of sale by the applicable tax rate and rounding the result to the nearest whole cent (Reg. Sec. 530.4). Amounts of ½ cent or more are rounded up to the next whole cent. If the sales tax computation results in a tax of five mills or less, no sales tax is due (Sec. 1132(b), Tax Law).

Separate bracket collection schedules that had been issued by the Department of Taxation and Finance have been discontinued.

¶ 687   Returns, Payments, and Due Dates

Every person who is required to register with the Commissioner of Taxation and Finance, or who voluntarily registers, is required to file returns (Sec. 1136(a), Tax Law). If more than one place of business is maintained, a single consolidated return for all places of business or a separate return for each place of business should be filed, depending on the election made on the Certificate of Registration.

All registered vendors that have no taxable activity during a reporting period can file using the Department's "No Sales Tax Due" Online Return. For any reporting period in which a vendor has collected sales tax, or needs to report use tax, the vendor cannot use Web filing and must file a paper return. Vendors can Web file late and final returns. However, there is a $50 penalty for late filing a sales tax return, even if no tax is due.

Annual filers can use the Department's fill-in version of Form ST-101, New York State and Local Annual Sales and Use Tax Return. The fill-in form can be used by filers of Form ST-101 and by filers of Form ST-102-A, New York State and Local Annual Sales and Use Tax Return for a Single Jurisdiction (*Important Notice N-07-7,* New York Department of Taxation and Finance, February 2007, CCH NEW YORK TAX REPORTS, ¶ 405-640).

Security for payment of tax: Any person who fails to collect, truthfully account for or pay over the sales tax, or file sales tax returns and whose financial condition is found to impair the ability to pay over tax may be required, upon notice from the commissioner, to collect such taxes and deposit them at least one time per week in a separate account in any banking institution in the state. The notice may require either that such account be held in trust for and payable to the commissioner or that such person authorize the commissioner to debit the account. Any person who fails to comply with such notice is required to file a bond. The commissioner may revoke or suspend any person's sales tax certificate of authority if the person fails to obtain such a bond or fails to comply with the notice issued by the commissioner. (Sec. 1137(e) Tax Law)

• Persons required to file monthly returns

Every person whose taxable receipts, amusement charges, rents, and purchases subject to use tax, total $300,000 or more in any quarter of the preceding four quarters, or a distributor of automotive fuel with sales of 100,000 gallons or more in any quarter of the preceding four quarters, must file a "part-quarterly" return each month (Sec. 1136(a), Tax Law). Persons required to file monthly may elect to file either a long-form or short-form part-quarterly return.

• Persons required to file quarterly returns

Persons with taxable receipts of $300,000 or less or distributors whose sales of automotive fuel total less than 100,000 gallons in every quarter of the preceding four quarters must file quarterly returns (Sec. 1136(a), Tax Law). If the Commissioner of Taxation and Finance deems it necessary to protect revenue, he or she may give notice to quarterly filers requiring such persons to file either short-form or long-form part-quarterly returns, in addition to filing a quarterly return.

• Persons required to file annual information returns

In addition to other required sales and use tax returns, motor vehicle insurers, franchisors, and alcoholic beverage wholesalers are required to file annual information returns providing specified information about their transactions. Licensed farm wineries, farm distilleries, and/or farm breweries are exempt from the annual information return filing requirements (Sec. 1136(i)(1)(C), Tax Law; *TSB-M-15(6)S,* New York Department of Taxation and Finance, December 15, 2015, CCH NEW YORK TAX REPORTS, ¶ 408-594).

Due date: Returns must be filed in electronic format on or before March 20 each year covering the four preceding sales tax quarters. (Sec. 1136(i)(2), Tax Law)

• Customers

If a customer fails to pay tax to the person required to collect the tax, the customer must file a return with the Commissioner and pay the tax (Sec. 1133(b), Tax Law).

Lines on the personal income tax forms and other appropriate tax forms instruct taxpayers to report unpaid state and local use taxes. In addition, the Commissioner must instruct taxpayers of their legal requirements to remit such use taxes when they make purchases outside New York, whether in person or by remote means, such as the Internet, mail-order, and catalog sales.

• Payment of tax

All sales and use tax required to be collected is due and payable to the Commissioner of Taxation and Finance on or before the date set for the filing of the return for the reporting period, without regard to whether a return is filed and whether the return filed is correct or complete. The tax is due and payable whether or not it has been collected by the vendor from the purchaser (Reg. Sec. 533.4(a)).

All money collected as tax, purportedly in accordance with a tax schedule, whether or not the receipts are subject to tax, must be remitted at the time a return is filed.

Tax collection on Native American reservations: The Commissioner is required to promulgate rules and regulations necessary to implement the collection of sales, excise, and use taxes on retail sale items, motor fuel, diesel motor fuel, and cigarette or other tobacco products, purchased by non-Native Americans, for personal consumption, on Native American reservations (Secs. 284-e, 301-a(1), 471-e, 1112, 1210(m)).

A proposed comprehensive agreement between the state of New York and the Oneida Nation of Indians that would require the Nation to adhere to minimum pricing standards for cigarettes and impose a Nation sales tax that equals or exceeds the state's and counties' sales, use, and occupancy taxes on cigarette sales to non-Indian customers.

Portions of the settlement will require New York state legislative approval, approvals by Madison County and Oneida County, the Department of the Interior, the New York State Attorney General, as well as judicial approval. The agreement is not effective until these approvals are secured.

• **Direct payment permits**

A direct payment permit allows eligible businesses that are unable to determine at the time of a purchase how otherwise taxable property or services will be used to pay sales tax directly to the department instead of paying tax to a seller. A direct payment permit is not the same as a sales tax exemption certificate. An exemption certificate allows a purchaser to make tax-free purchases that would otherwise be subject to sales tax. (*TB-ST-163*, June 24, 2013, CCH NEW YORK TAX REPORTS, ¶ 407-865)

Eligibility: To be eligible for a direct payment permit, a business must:

— be registered for sales tax purposes;

— maintain a place of business in New York;

— have filed all required returns and paid all taxes due on time for the four preceding sales tax quarters immediately prior to applying for a direct payment permit (an exception applies to a new vendor that has not yet filed returns); and

— be unable to determine at the time of a purchase how otherwise taxable property or services will be used.

Application process: A business must file Form AU-298, Application for a Direct Payment Permit, and attach a statement that describes: the specific reasons the direct payment permit is needed; the types of transactions for which the permit will be used; and how the business will account for any taxes due, including the types of records that will be kept. The department will issue a specifically numbered direct payment permit to approved applicants for use when making qualifying purchases.

Use of a direct payment permit: A direct payment permit may only be used by the business to which it has been issued; and when the business is unable to determine at the time of a purchase how otherwise taxable property or services will be used.

A business that has received a direct payment permit must provide a seller with a copy of the permit when first making a qualifying purchase of tangible personal property or services. The business remains liable for the taxes due, and its permit is subject to revocation.

Reports and payment: Once property or services that have been purchased under a direct payment permit are actually used, the permit holder must:

— determine whether or not that use is taxable;

— maintain records detailing all purchases and how and where they are used; and

— report and remit any taxes due with the sales tax return covering the period when the taxable use occurs.

The following rules should be used to compute and report taxes due:

— purchases originally made and delivered in a jurisdiction having a higher tax rate than the eventual jurisdiction of use are subject to tax and must be reported for the jurisdiction having the higher rate;

— purchases originally made and delivered in a jurisdiction having a lower tax rate than the eventual jurisdiction of use must be reported for the jurisdiction of delivery at the lower tax rate and are also subject to additional use tax for the jurisdiction with the higher rate; and

— purchases made in bulk and later used in jurisdictions having different tax rates are subject to tax based on the rate in the jurisdiction of use.

A business must return its direct payment permit to the department if it closes or suspends operations, or changes its business's name or legal form (e.g., a corporation reorganizes as an LLC). A business that changes its business's name or legal form must apply for a new Certificate of Authority and a new direct payment permit.

• Electronic filing and payment

The Department of Taxation and Finance is authorized to require electronic filing (e-file) and electronic payment (e-pay) of all tax documents (Sec. 29, Tax Law).

The Department requires most part-quarterly (monthly) and quarterly sales tax filers to Web File their sales tax returns and make the payments associated with those returns by electronic withdrawal from their bank accounts. The e-file mandate applies to sales tax filers who meet these conditions:

— don't have a tax preparer to prepare sale tax returns;

— use a computer to prepare, document, or calculate returns; and

— have broadband Internet access.

For additional information, see *TB-ST-275*, July 27, 2012, CCH New York Tax Reports, ¶ 407-618.

Segregated sales tax accounts: Vendors that failed to collect, truthfully account for, or pay over sales tax monies, or to file returns as required by law, are required to set up separate bank account into which only sales tax moneys are deposited at least weekly, and which the vendor authorizes the Department to debit that account. The segregated account provisions are set to expire December 31, 2016.

Return preparers: If a tax return preparer prepared at least one authorized tax document for more than 10 different taxpayers during calendar year 2012, then all tax documents prepared by that preparer must be filed electronically. Tax preparers remain subject to the mandate if they were subject to it in a previous year, even if they did not meet the threshold in calendar year 2012. Any return or report that includes one or more tax documents that cannot be filed electronically shall not be deemed to be an authorized tax document for purposes of this requirement. (Sec. 29, Tax Law).

• Due dates

Returns must be filed within 20 days after the end of the period being reported. Monthly returns are due by the 20th day of the following month (Sec. 1136(b), Tax Law). Quarterly returns are due on or before March 20, June 20, September 20 and December 20 for the three-month periods ending with the last day of February, May, August and November, respectively. The annual return covers the period from March 1st through the end of the following February.

The Commissioner of Taxation and Finance may permit or require returns to be made covering other periods and specify other due dates (Sec. 1136(c), Tax Law). Returns may be required for shorter periods than those prescribed and due on different dates if the Commissioner deems it necessary in order to insure the payment of taxes.

¶ 688 Prepayment of Taxes

Motor fuel distributors and cigarette agents must prepay sales tax on motor fuel imported into, and cigarettes possessed for sale or use in, New York.

• Motor fuel distributors

Every distributor of motor fuel is required to prepay the sales tax for each gallon of motor fuel which is imported or caused to be imported for use, distribution, storage or sale into the state (Sec. 1102(a)(1), Tax Law). The prepaid sales tax is imposed on the owner of the motor fuel being imported at the time the off-loading of the motor fuel is commenced at or into any terminal, facility or other land-sited repository (Reg. Sec. 561.3(a)(1)). If the party off-loading the motor fuel is not a registered distributor, the party owning the motor fuel after it is off-loaded is responsible for payment of the tax.

Prepaid tax is also imposed upon every gallon of motor fuel produced, refined, manufactured or compounded in the state (Sec. 1102(a)(2), Tax Law).

Prepayment rates vary by region (Sec. 1111(e), Tax Law). The first region consists of the localities included in the Metropolitan Commuter Transportation District (MCTD), excluding all localities included in the counties of Nassau and Suffolk, and the prepaid rate in this region is 17.50 cents. The second region consists of the localities included in the counties of Nassau and Suffolk, and the prepaid rate in this region is 21 cents. The third region consists of the area of the state outside the first two regions, and the prepaid rate in this region is 16 cents. (*TSB-M-14(6)S*, May 15, 2014, CCH NEW YORK TAX REPORTS, ¶ 408-092; *Important Notice N-14-6*, May 15, 2014, CCH NEW YORK TAX REPORTS, ¶ 408-093; *Important Notice N-14-7*, May 15, 2014, CCH NEW YORK TAX REPORTS, ¶ 408-094)

Alternative fuels: Until September 1, 2021, CNG and hydrogen fuels are exempt from the prepaid sales tax requirement (Sec. 1115(a)(42), Tax Law). In addition, E85 fuel is exempt from the prepaid tax provided it is delivered to and placed in a storage tank of a filling station to be dispensed directly into a motor vehicle for use in its operation (*TSB-M-06(10)S*). The exemption does not apply to sales of B20 (*TSB-M-16(3)M, TSB-M-16(4)S*, July 22, 2016, CCH NEW YORK TAX REPORTS, ¶ 408-793).

Effective December 1, 2017, sales of fuel for use in commercial and general aviation aircraft are exempt from local sales taxes and from the prepayment of sales tax on motor fuels (Sec. 1102(a)(1), Tax Law; Sec. 1210(a)(4)(xiii), Tax Law).

• Cigarette agents

Cigarette tax agents must prepay a portion of the sales tax on cigarettes possessed for sale or use in New York on which they are required to affix cigarette tax stamps (Sec. 1103, Tax Law; *TB-ST-685*, November 26, 2014, CCH NEW YORK TAX REPORTS, ¶ 408-286). The tax is to be paid at the same time and in the same manner as cigarette taxes imposed pursuant to Article 20, Tax Law.

For the period September 1, 2016, through August 31, 2017, the prepaid sales tax on cigarettes is 83 cents (previously, 82 cents) on packages of 20 cigarettes and $1.04 (previously, $1.02) on packages of 25 cigarettes (*Important Notice N-16-6*, July 2016, CCH NEW YORK TAX REPORTS, ¶ 408-803).

¶ 689 Vendor Registration

The following must register with the Commissioner of Taxation and Finance (Sec. 1134(a)(1), Tax Law):

— every person required to collect sales and use taxes commencing business or opening a new place of business;

— every person purchasing or selling tangible personal property for resale commencing business or opening a new place of business;

— every person selling automotive fuel including persons who are not distributors;

— every person previously described who takes possession of or pays for business assets under a bulk sale; and

— every person required to register whose certificate of authority has been revoked.

Upon registration, a certificate of authority to collect the tax together with duplicate certificates for additional places of business will be issued (Sec. 1134(a)(2), Tax Law). There is no registration fee.

Medical marijuana vendors: The sale of medical marijuana and sales of related products purchased to administer medical marijuana are exempt from sales tax. However, an organization registered to collect the excise tax on marijuana also must register as a vendor in order to issue and accept certain sales tax exemption certificates. A registered organization may also be able to use certain exemption forms related to farming, as discussed in the document. See *TSB-M-16(1)S,* New York Department of Taxation and Finance, January 7, 2016, CCH New York Tax Reports, ¶ 408-611.

- **Certificates of authority**

A certificate or duplicate must state the place of business to which it applies and be prominently displayed (Sec. 1134(a)(2), Tax Law). The certificates are nonassignable and nontransferable and must be surrendered to the Department immediately upon the registrant's ceasing to do business at the place named. The certificates are issued for a period of not less than three years, subject to renewal. Certificates for show vendors, temporary vendors and entertainment vendors, however may be issued for a specified term of less than three years (Sec. 1134(a)(2), Tax Law).

- **Contractors with state agencies**

Persons seeking to enter into contracts having a value in excess of $15,000 with state agencies or public authorities must certify that they, their affiliates, their subcontractors and the affiliates of their subcontractors have a valid certificate of authority (Sec. 5-a, Tax Law). This requirement arises if the total amount of such persons' sales delivered into New York State are in excess of $300,000, and with respect to any affiliates, subcontractors, or affiliates of subcontractors whose sales delivered into New York State exceeded $300,000. If the contract has a term of more than one year, the certification must be done annually. The certification must also be done before any contract is renewed. The certification is made on Form ST-220-TD.

The certification requirement is not applicable if the covered agency and the contract approver determine in writing that the contractor is the only person capable of performing the contract and the contract is necessary to (1) address an emergency; (2) ensure the provision of essential services; and/or (3) ensure the public health, safety and welfare.

For additional information, see *TB-ST-118,* New York Department of Taxation and Finance, June 12, 2013, CCH New York Tax Reports, ¶ 407-862.

- **Motor vehicle registration agents**

Certain persons can be authorized by the Tax Department to collect and remit sales tax from the purchaser of a motor vehicle even though the person collecting the tax did not sell the motor vehicle to the purchaser (Sec. 1142(13), Tax Law; *TSB-M-06(15)S*). Before the person can collect tax, the person must:

— have been certified by the Department of Motor Vehicles as a "Partner" to perform the functions of registering motor vehicles and accepting applications for certificates of title of motor vehicles;

— register with the Tax Department as a person required to collect sales tax; and

— agree to be subject to Tax Department and local taxing jurisdiction with respect to the functions of person required to collect sales tax.

¶ 690   Sales or Use Tax Credits

Subject to certain conditions and limitations, credits and refunds for state and local sales and use taxes are authorized for the following (Reg. Sec. 534.1(a)): (1) the purchase of tangible personal property used in a specified manner; (2) the purchase of tangible personal property or services used by specified omnibus carriers to provide local transit service; (3) the purchase of tangible personal property used in the performance of specified taxable services on a retail sale by a contractor; and (4) the purchase of tangible personal property by a contractor, subcontractor or repairman who was required to pay tax on the purchase if the property was sold at retail by the contractor, subcontractor or repairman.

• Credit for tax collected and paid over

Vendors are allowed a credit equal to 5% of the state portion of the sales and use tax collected and remitted. The maximum amount of the credit is $200 (Sec. 1137(f), Tax Law). Effective June 1, 2010, the credit, is no longer allowed for persons who:

— file or are required to file Form ST-809 (monthly sales tax return); or

— pay or are required to pay taxes by electronic funds transfer (i.e., PrompTax).

• Bad debts

When a receipt, amusement charge, or hotel rent has been ascertained to be uncollectible, either in whole or in part, the vendor may apply for a refund or credit of the tax paid within three years from the date on which the tax was payable (Reg. Sec. 534.7(b)). A refund or credit is not available for transactions financed by a third party or for a debt assigned to a third party.

• Property or services upon which tax is paid to other jurisdictions

Credit is allowed for use tax paid to out-of-state jurisdictions which allow a corresponding exemption (Sec. 1118(7)(a), Tax Law). When the tax imposed is at a higher rate than that imposed by the first taxing jurisdiction, tax must be collected to the extent of the difference in rates.

• Empire Zones

All Empire Zone designations expired on June 30, 2010. With the expiration of the Empire Zones designations, the sales tax refund or credit on certain building materials used in an Empire Zone has been discontinued. (*TSB-M-10(6)S,* June 30, 2010, CCH NEW YORK TAX REPORTS, ¶ 406-868)

The Excelsior Jobs Program, which replaced the Enterprise Zone Program, includes no sales and use tax benefits.

• Economic Transformation and Facility Redevelopment Program

Participants in the Economic Transformation and Facility Redevelopment Program, or their contractors, may claim a refund of state sales or use tax paid on tangible personal property that is used in constructing, expanding or rehabilitating industrial or commercial real property located in an ETA. The tangible personal property must become an "integral component part" of the real property in order to qualify for the refund. The refund is available for property purchased after the participant receives its certificate of eligibility and used before a certificate of occupancy is issued for the real property. The participant or contractor may only apply for a refund once per sales tax quarter and the amount may not be claimed as a credit on a sales tax return. The provisions are scheduled to expire on December 31, 2021. (Sec. 1119(f), Tax Law) For additional information, see *TSB-M-11(9)S*, June 10, 2011, CCH NEW YORK TAX REPORTS, ¶ 407-285.

- **Business Incubator and Innovation Hot Spot Support Program**

The Empire State Development Corporation (ESDC) may designate five "New York State innovation hot spots" in SFY 2013-14 and an additional five in SFY 2014-15. Entities designated as innovation hot spots must demonstrate an affiliation with and the support of at least one college, university, or independent research institution, and offer programs consistent with regional economic development strategies. In addition to a number of income tax benefits, qualified entities in innovation hot spots are eligible for a credit or refund of sales and use tax imposed on the retail sale of tangible personal property or services (Sec. 38(d), Tax Law; *TSB-M-14(1)C, (1)I, (2)S,* Taxpayer Guidance Division, New York Department of Taxation and Finance, March 7, 2014, CCH NEW YORK TAX REPORTS, ¶ 408-039).

- **START-UP NY Program**

The SUNY Tax-Free Areas to Revitalize and Transform Upstate (START-UP) New York program provides personal and corporate income tax, sales and use tax, property tax, and transfer tax incentives to promote business and job creation by transforming public higher education through tax-free communities in upstate New York and other strategically-designated locations. The program provides tax benefits to approved businesses that locate in vacant space or land of approved New York state public and private colleges and universities, approved strategic state assets, and New York state incubators affiliated with private universities or colleges that are designated as tax-free NY areas. The program is administered by Empire State Development (ESD). Approved businesses will be issued a certificate of eligibility by the sponsoring campus, university, or college. (Sec. 39, Tax Law; Sec. 430 *et seq.*, Tax Law; *TSB-M-13(7)S,* October 22, 2013, CCH NEW YORK TAX REPORTS, ¶ 407-949)

Applicability: The tax benefits apply to taxable years beginning on or after January 1, 2014, to sales tax quarters beginning on or after March 1, 2014, or to transactions occurring on or after January 1, 2014, whichever is applicable.

Qualifications: Among other requirements for eligibility, a business must be a new start-up company, an out-of-state company relocating to New York, or an expansion of an existing New York company. The business must also create and maintain net new jobs. Businesses will not be eligible if they compete with existing businesses that are not within the tax-free area, and certain types of businesses are specifically excluded (*e.g.,* restaurants, real estate management companies, and retail, wholesale, or personal service businesses).

Sales and use tax provisions: An approved business that is located in a tax-free NY area is eligible for a credit or refund of New York State and local sales and use taxes, including the 3/8% tax imposed by the state in the Metropolitan Commuter Transportation District (MCTD), imposed on the sale of tangible personal property, utility services, and services taxable under Tax Law Sec. 1105(c). The credit or refund does not apply to:

— the sales tax imposed under Tax Law Sec. 1105(d) on sales of food or drink at restaurants, taverns, or other establishments, or by caterers;

— the sales tax on rent for hotel occupancy imposed under Tax Law Sec. 1105(e);

— the sales tax on admission charges and dues imposed under Tax Law Sec. 1105(f); and

— the sales tax on transportation services imposed under Tax Law Sec. 1105(c)(10).

In addition, a credit or refund is available for certain purchases of tangible personal property by contractors, subcontractors, and repairmen that is used in constructing, improving, maintaining, servicing, or repairing real property of an approved business that is located in a tax-free NY area. The credit or refund is allowed for 120 consecutive months beginning with the month during which the business locates in the tax-free NY area. (*TSB-M-13(7)S,* October 22, 2013, CCH NEW YORK TAX REPORTS, ¶ 407-949)

Claims: A claim for credit or refund for the sales and use tax paid on eligible purchases must be made by filing Form AU-11, Application for Credit or Refund of Sales or Use Tax. Taxpayers may submit Form AU-11 electronically using Sales Tax Web File. An approved business may file a claim for credit or refund only once each sales tax quarter. No interest is payable on any credit allowed or refund made. (*TSB-M-13(7)S,* October 22, 2013, CCH NEW YORK TAX REPORTS, ¶ 407-949)

Penalties for fraud: In the case of a business that acts fraudulently in connection with the START-UP NY program, the business will be immediately terminated from the program; subject to applicable criminal penalties, including the felony crime of offering a false instrument for filing in the first degree; and required to pay back all tax benefits that the company and its employees have received. (*TSB-M-13(7)S,* October 22, 2013, CCH NEW YORK TAX REPORTS, ¶ 407-949)

¶ 691 Deficiency Assessments

The sales and use tax is self-assessed since the person required to collect the tax or the person required to pay the tax computes the tax and pays the tax at the time of filing returns. The Commissioner of Taxation and Finance, however, determines the tax if the return is incorrect or insufficient, or if no return is filed (Sec. 1138(a)(1), Tax Law). The Commissioner, or duly authorized agents or employees of the Commissioner, may inspect the records of the taxpayer and may, if necessary, estimate the tax on the basis of external indices.

A notice of the determination of the tax due will be mailed by registered or certified mail, to the person liable for the collection or payment of the tax (Sec. 1147(a)(1), Tax Law). The determination will finally and irrevocably fix the tax unless the person against whom it is assessed, within 90 days, applies to the Division of Tax Appeals for a hearing, or unless the Commissioner redetermines the tax (Sec. 1138(a)(1), Tax Law).

• **Determination of tax—Estimated assessments**

The Commissioner of Taxation and Finance may estimate tax due on the basis of external indices, such as stock on hand, purchases, rental paid, number of rooms, location, scale of rents or charges, comparable rents or charges, type of accommodations and service, number of employees or other factors (Sec. 1138(a)(1), Tax Law).

The Commissioner is authorized to determine the liability of any officer, director or employee of a corporation, member or employee of a partnership, or employee of an individual proprietorship who is under a duty to act for the corporation, partnership, or proprietorship in complying with tax law requirements (Sec. 1138(a)(3)(B), Tax Law). The Commissioner may determine the amount of the tax liability from such information as may be available. The Commissioner's determination finally and irrevocably fixes the tax and liability for the tax with respect to the officer, director, partner, or employee, unless the officer, director, partner, or employee applies to the Division of Tax Appeals for a hearing within 90 days after notice of the determination.

¶ 692 Audit Procedures

When the person required to collect the tax or the person required to pay the tax fails to file a return or files a return that is incorrect or insufficient, the Commissioner of Taxation and Finance determines the tax (Sec. 1138(a)(1), Tax Law). The Commissioner may make an assessment of the tax due after examining the taxpayer's books and records, or may estimate the tax due on the basis of external indices. For details, see *Publication 130-F,* New York Department of Taxation and Finance, July 2012.

• **Adequacy of records**

The Commissioner or duly authorized agents or employees may inspect the records of the taxpayer (Sec. 1135(e), Tax Law). Inspection may be at any time, upon demand. Records must be preserved for three years unless a shorter or longer period is prescribed by the Commissioner.

Records must include a true copy of each sales slip, invoice, receipt, statement or memorandum upon which the tax is required to be stated separately (Sec. 1135(a)(1), Tax Law). Indirect audit methods are used when the taxpayer's records are inadequate.

• **Additional powers of the Commissioner of Taxation and Finance**

The Commissioner may require any person required to collect the tax to keep detailed records of all receipts, amusement charges, dues or rents received, charged or accrued (Sec. 1142(5), Tax Law). Records of nontaxable transactions may also be required. The Commissioner may also require details of the nature, type, value and amount of all purchases, sales, services rendered, admissions, memberships, occupancies, names and addresses of customers and other facts relevant in determining the tax due.

The Commissioner or the Commissioner's employees or agents have the power to administer oaths and take affidavits in relation to the exercise of their powers (Sec. 1143(a), Tax Law). The Commissioner has the power to subpoena and require the attendance of witnesses and the production of books, papers and documents to secure pertinent information and to examine them, and to issue commissions for the examination of out-of-state witnesses who are unable to attend or are excused from attendance.

¶ 693 Statute of Limitations

The limitation periods for any proceeding or action taken by the state or the Commissioner of Taxation and Finance to levy, appraise, assess, determine or enforce the collection of any tax or penalty supersede any limitation periods set forth in the Civil Practice Law and Rules for the assessment of taxes (Sec. 1147(b), Tax Law).

No assessment of additional tax will be made after the expiration of more than three years from the date of the filing of a return (Sec. 1147(b), Tax Law).

When a taxpayer willfully files a false or fraudulent return with intent to evade tax, there is no limitation period on assessment. A purchaser who furnishes a vendor with a false or fraudulent certificate of resale or other exemption certificate or other document with the intent to evade the tax may be taxed at any time (Sec. 1147(b), Tax Law).

If no return has been filed, there are no time limitations on assessment (Sec. 1147(b), Tax Law).

A tax liability will not be enforceable and will be extinguished after 20 years from the first date a warrant could be filed by the department (Sec. 174-b, Tax Law).

• **Date of filing**

A return filed before the last day prescribed for the filing, or before the last day of any extension of time for filing, will be deemed to be filed on the last day (Sec. 1147(b), Tax Law).

• **Suspension of limitation period when notice appealed**

The period in which the Commissioner may make an assessment is suspended until the time for filing a petition contesting the notice of assessment has expired or when a petition is timely filed, until the decision of the Administrative Law Judge or Tax Appeals Tribunal becomes final (Sec. 1147(d), Tax Law).

¶ 694   **Application for Refund**

To claim a refund or credit for any tax, penalty or interest collected or paid, a person must file an application with the Commissioner of Taxation and Finance within three years after the tax payment due date (Sec. 1139(a), Tax Law). The application must be in a form prescribed by the Commissioner. No refund or credit of tax, penalty or interest erroneously, illegally or unconstitutionally collected or paid will be made until it is established that the tax has been repaid to the customer.

The Commissioner of Taxation and Finance is required to grant or deny an application for refund within six months after receiving it in a form that is able to be processed (Sec. 1139(b), Tax Law).

• **Application procedures**

When an application for credit has been filed, the applicant may immediately take the credit on the return which is due coincident with or immediately subsequent to the time the credit application is filed (Sec. 1119(a), Tax Law). Taking the credit on the sales and use tax return is deemed to be part of the credit application. The application for credit, or a copy of the application if filed earlier, must be attached to the return on which the credit is taken.

• **Timeliness of applications**

An application for a refund or credit must be filed with the Commissioner within the following time limitations (Sec. 1139(c), Tax Law):

— when the tax was paid by the applicant to a person required to collect tax, within three years after the date the tax was payable by the person who collected the tax (Sec. 1139(a), Tax Law);

— when the tax, penalty or interest was paid by the applicant directly to the Commissioner, within three years after the date the tax, interest or penalty was payable (Sec. 1139(a), Tax Law);

— when a taxpayer requests a refund of an overpayment of sales tax, the refund claim must be filed within three years from the time the return was filed or two years from the time the tax was paid, whichever is later. If no return was filed, the taxpayer must file the refund claim within two years from the time the tax was paid.

If a taxpayer has consented in writing to the extension of the period for assessment, the period for filing an application for credit or refund does not expire prior to six months after the expiration of the period within which the assessment may be made (Sec. 1147(c), Tax Law).

• **Repayment of tax to a customer**

Any person who erroneously, illegally, or unconstitutionally collected any tax from a customer and remitted the tax to the Commissioner must repay the tax to the customer before the Commissioner may issue a refund. An accurate record of the amount of tax repaid to each customer, the reason for repayment and proof of repayment must be kept and made available to the Commissioner upon request (Reg. Sec. 534.8).

Motor fuel sold to exempt entities: Credit card issuers and fuel distributors may apply for refunds or credits of state and local sales taxes, excise taxes, and petroleum business taxes, on motor fuel and diesel motor fuel sold to exempt government entities when certain criteria are met (*TSB-M-08(12)S*, November 5, 2008, CCH NEW YORK TAX REPORTS, ¶ 406-212).

Source.—Statutory references are to Chapter 105, Subchapter VIII, Articles 39, 40, and 42 of the North Carolina General Statutes, as amended to date. Details are reported in the CCH NORTH CAROLINA TAX REPORTS starting at ¶ 60-000.

The North Carolina sales tax is a general tax levied on the gross receipts from sales at retail of tangible personal property or on its lease or rental (Sec. 105-164.4, Reg. Sec. 17:07B.4401). Except for a limited number of specified services (see ¶ 697, Tax Base, below), the furnishing of services is generally not taxable. The use tax on consumption, use, or storage of tangible personal property in the state is a complementary tax and does not apply in situations in which the sales tax is collected (Sec. 105-164.6). The sales or use tax is in addition to other taxes (Sec. 105-164.2).

Digital products: Sales and use taxes apply to the following digital property delivered or accessed electronically: audio and audiovisual works, books, magazines, newspapers, newsletters, reports or other publications, and photographs or greeting cards (Sec. 105-164.4(a)(6b)). The tax is applicable regardless of whether the purchaser has a right to use the digital property permanently or to use it without making continued payments. Tax does not apply to a service that is taxed under another subdivision or to an information service. For additional information, see Important Notice: *Certain Digital Property Subject to Sales and Use Tax,* North Carolina Department of Revenue, December 9, 2009, CCH NORTH CAROLINA TAX REPORTS, ¶ 202-465.

Prepaid calling arrangements: The sale or recharge of prepaid telephone calling service is taxable at the general rate of tax and the tax applies regardless of whether tangible personal property, such as a card or a telephone, is transferred. The tax also applies to a service that is sold in conjunction with prepaid wireless calling service (Sec. 105-164.4(a)(4d)).

• **Use tax**

The use tax is imposed on the storage, use, or consumption in North Carolina of tangible personal property, including property that becomes part of a building or other structure in the state (Sec. 105-164.6). The use tax operates to protect North Carolina merchants from discrimination arising from the state's inability to impose its sales tax on sales made outside the state of North Carolina to North Carolina residents by merchants of other states. The use tax is also imposed on property that has been purchased tax free for resale and is later consumed, rather than resold, by the purchaser.

• **Responsibility for sales tax collection**

The sales tax, which is to be separately stated, is collected by the seller from the purchaser (Sec. 105-164.7). It is a debt from the purchaser to the seller recoverable by law. Every sale is presumed to be a taxable sale at retail (Sec. 105-164.28).

Real property contractors and retailer-contractors: A real property contractor is the consumer of tangible personal property that the real property contractor installs or applies for others and that becomes part of real property (Sec. 105-164.4H(a)). A "real property contractor" is defined as a person that contracts to perform construction, reconstruction, installation, repair, or any other service with respect to real property and to furnish tangible personal property to be installed or applied to real property in connection with the contract and the labor to install or apply the tangible personal property that becomes part of real property. The term includes a general contractor, subcontractor, or a builder (Sec. 105-164.3(33a)).

Beginning January 1, 2015, a "retailer-contractor" is defined as a person that acts as a retailer when it sells tangible personal property at retail and as a real property contractor when it performs real property contracts (Sec. 105-164.3(35a)). A retailer-contractor that purchases tangible personal property to be installed or affixed to real property may purchase items exempt from tax under a certificate of exemption, provided that the retailer-contractor also purchases inventory items from the seller for resale. When the tangible personal property is withdrawn from inventory and installed or affixed to real property, use tax must be accrued and paid on the retailer-contractor's purchase price of the tangible personal property. Tangible personal property that the retailer-contractor withdraws from inventory for use that does not become part of real property is also taxable. (Sec. 105-164.4H(b); see also *Important Notice,* North Carolina Department of Revenue, December 22, 2016, CCH NORTH CAROLINA TAX REPORTS, ¶ 202-756)

The North Carolina Department of Revenue provides guidance to assist taxpayers in determining whether a transaction is:

(1) a real property contract with respect to a capital improvement to real property;

(2) subject to sales and use tax as a retail sale of repair, maintenance, or installation services to real property; or

(3) exempt.

Examples of transactions are provided by category such as brickwork and masonry, central air conditioning, concrete and stonework, electrical work, flooring, landscaping, plumbing, and roofs. (*Important Notice: Additional Information Regarding Real Property Contracts and Retail Sales of Repair, Maintenance, and Installation Services to Real Property,* North Carolina Department of Revenue, March 17, 2017, CCH NORTH CAROLINA TAX REPORTS, ¶ 202-762)

• **Responsibility for use tax collection**

Retailers who have sufficient contacts with North Carolina to constitute nexus with the state are required to collect the use tax from purchasers and to remit the tax collected to the Secretary of Revenue (Sec. 105-164.7, Sec. 105-164.8). The tax remains a liability of the purchaser until paid, unless the purchaser has a receipt showing payment of the tax to the retailer (Sec. 105-164.6(d)).

Online retailers: There is a rebuttable presumption that an online retailer is soliciting business in the state, for sales and use tax purposes, if an in-state entity refers customers to the retailer by a link on a website in return for a commission or other consideration (Sec. 105-164.13(43a)). The presumption is applicable only if the cumulative gross receipts from sales by the retailer to North Carolina purchasers who are referred to the retailer by all residents with this type of agreement with the retailer are in excess of $10,000 during the preceding four quarterly periods. The presumption could be rebutted by proof that the resident with whom the retailer has an agreement did not engage in any solicitation in North Carolina on behalf of the seller that would satisfy the nexus requirement of the U.S. Constitution during the four quarterly periods in question. For additional information, see *Important Notice: Certain Digital Property Subject to Sales and Use Tax*, North Carolina Department of Revenue, December 9, 2009, CCH NORTH CAROLINA TAX REPORTS, ¶ 202-465.

• **Accommodations; Online travel companies**

Legislation effective June 1, 2014, provides that gross receipts derived from the rental of an accommodation (a hotel room, motel room, residence, cottage, or similar lodging facility) include the sales price of the rental of the accommodation. The sales price of the rental of an accommodation is determined as if the rental were a rental of tangible personal property.

The sales price of the rental of an accommodation marketed by a facilitator, such as an online travel company, includes charges designated as facilitation fees and any other charges necessary to complete the rental (Sec. 105-164.4F(b)). The facilitators are required to send the room provider the tax due on the sales price. (Sec. 105-164.4F(c))

Litigation: Multiple online travel companies (OTCs) that operate websites that allow consumers to select and pay the OTCs for hotel rooms are not subject to North Carolina local occupancy taxes imposed by Wake, Dare, Buncombe, and Mecklenburg counties, and further were not required to collect and remit that tax. According to the appellate court, the OTCs are neither operators nor retailers within the meaning of the state sales tax. Moreover, the OTCs' gross receipts are not subject to the North Carolina sales tax and, as such, the gross receipts the OTCs derive from the rentals are not subject to the room occupancy tax imposed by the counties. (*Wake County v. Hotels.com, LP,* North Carolina Court of Appeals, No. COA13-594, August 19, 2014, CCH NORTH CAROLINA TAX REPORTS, ¶ 202-633)

- **Nexus**

   "Engaged in business" is defined as any of the following (Sec. 105-164.3(9)):

   — maintaining, occupying, or using permanently or temporarily, directly or indirectly, or through a subsidiary or agent, by whatever name, any office, place of distribution, sales or sample room, warehouse or storage place, or other place of business for selling or delivering tangible personal property, digital property, or a service for storage, use, or consumption in North Carolina, or permanently or temporarily, directly or through a subsidiary, having any representative, agent, sales representative, or solicitor operating in North Carolina in the selling or delivering (it is irrelevant whether a corporate retailer, agent, or subsidiary engaged in business in North Carolina is legally domesticated or qualified to do business in the state);

   — maintaining in the state, either permanently or temporarily, directly or through a subsidiary, tangible personal property or digital property for the purpose of lease or rental;

   — making a remote sale, as provided; or

   — shipping wine directly to a North Carolina purchaser, as authorized.

Remote sales: A "remote sale" is defined as a sale of tangible personal property or digital property ordered by mail, telephone, via the Internet, or by another similar method, to a purchaser who is in North Carolina at the time the order is remitted, from a retailer who receives the order in another state and delivers the property or causes it to be delivered to a person in North Carolina. It is presumed that a resident of North Carolina who remits an order was in North Carolina at the time the order was remitted. (Sec. 105-164.3(33c))

A retailer who makes a remote sale is engaged in business in North Carolina and is subject to sales and use tax if at least one of the following conditions is met (Sec. 105-164.8(b)):

   — the retailer is a corporation engaged in business under the laws of North Carolina or a person domiciled in, a resident of, or a citizen of, North Carolina;

   — the retailer maintains retail establishments or offices in North Carolina, whether the remote sales subject to tax result from or are related in any other way to the activities of those establishments or offices;

   — the retailer solicits or transacts business in North Carolina by employees, independent contractors, agents, or other representatives, whether the remote sales subject to tax result from or are related in any other way to the solicitation or transaction of business;

   — the retailer, by purposefully or systematically exploiting the market provided by North Carolina by any media-assisted, media-facilitated, or media-solicited means, including direct mail advertising, distribution of catalogs, computer-assisted shopping, television, radio or other electronic media, telephone solicitation, magazine or newspaper advertisements, or other media, creates nexus with North Carolina (a nonresident retailer who purchases advertising to be delivered by television, radio, in print, on the Internet, or by any other medium is not considered to be engaged in business in North Carolina based solely on the purchase of the advertising);

— through compact or reciprocity with another jurisdiction of the United States, that jurisdiction uses its taxing power and its jurisdiction over the retailer in support of North Carolina's taxing power;

— the retailer consents, expressly or by implication, to the imposition of the tax; or

— the retailer is a holder of a wine shipper permit.

A retailer is presumed to be soliciting or transacting business by an independent contractor, agent, or other representative if the retailer enters into an agreement with a North Carolina resident who, for a commission or other consideration, directly or indirectly refers potential customers, whether by link on an Internet Web site or otherwise, to the retailer. The presumption applies only if the cumulative gross receipts from sales by the retailer to North Carolina purchasers who are referred to the retailer by all residents with this type of agreement with the retailer is in excess of $10,000 during the preceding four quarterly periods. The presumption may be rebutted by proof that the resident with whom the retailer has an agreement did not engage in any solicitation in North Carolina on behalf of the seller that would satisfy the nexus requirement of the U.S. Constitution during the four quarterly periods in question. (Sec. 105-164.8(b))

• **Streamlined Act status**

North Carolina is a full member of the Streamlined Sales and Use Tax Agreement with a seat on the Governing Board. It has enacted all of the provisions necessary to comply with the Agreement's requirements and these provisions currently are in effect). As a full member, it may vote on amendments to or interpretations of the Agreement, and sellers registering under the SST system must collect and remit tax on sales into the state. For additional information, see ¶ 702.

¶ 697   **Tax Base**

The sales tax is based on the merchant's gross retail sales of tangible personal property after deducting exempt receipts (Sec. 105-164.4).

Retail sales include all sales of tangible personal property for any use on the part of the purchaser other than for resale (Sec. 105-164.3(12), Sec. 105-164.3(13)). A sale includes any transfer of title or possession, or both (Sec. 105-164.3(15)). Gross sales means the sum total of proceeds from all retail sales, whether made in cash or through the extension of credit, and without allowance for cash discounts, cost of property sold, cost of materials used, labor or service costs, interest paid, or any other expenses (Sec. 105-164.3(6)).

Bundled transactions: For treatment of taxable and nontaxable transactions bundled for a single price, see *Directive No. SD-07-1,* North Carolina Department of Revenue, October 1, 2007, CCH North Carolina Tax Reports, ¶ 202-392.

Services: The North Carolina sales tax is imposed on a limited number of services. These taxable services are (Sec. 105-164.4, G.S.; *Sales and Use Tax Technical Bulletin* Sec. 1-1, North Carolina Department of Revenue, CCH North Carolina Tax Reports, ¶ 65-405):

— hotel and motel rentals;

— dry cleaning, laundry, and similar services;

— telecommunications;

— satellite services;

— cable service; and

— video programming service.

Certain computer software maintenance services are also taxable, depending upon whether the software is canned or custom, and whether the contract is mandatory or optional (Sec. 105-164.3(5c), (29a), and (37), G.S.; Sec. 105-164.13(43), (43a), and (43b), G.S).

Service and installation charges are included in the sales price (Sec. 105-164.3(37), G.S.).

Service contracts: See *Important Notice: Service Contracts,* North Carolina Department of Revenue, November 15, 2016, CCH NORTH CAROLINA TAX REPORTS, ¶ 202-752.

Repair, maintenance, and installation services: The general rate of tax applies to the sales price of the sales price of, or the gross receipts derived from, repair, maintenance, and installation services (Sec. 105-164.4(a)(15); see also Important Notice: *Repeal of Installation Charges Exemption,* North Carolina Department of Revenue, January 11, 2016, CCH NORTH CAROLINA TAX REPORTS, ¶ 202-696).

However, effective March 1, 2016, the following repair, maintenance, and installation services are exempt (Sec. 105-164.3(33d); *Directive No. SD-16-2,* North Carolina Department of Revenue, February 5, 2016, CCH NORTH CAROLINA TAX REPORTS, ¶ 202-705):

— such services provided for an item for which a service contract on the item is exempt;

— such services purchased for resale; and

— such services used to maintain or repair tangible personal property or a motor vehicle pursuant to a taxable service contract if the purchaser of the contract is not charged for the item.

See also *Directive No. SD-16-4,* North Carolina Department of Revenue, November 15, 2016, CCH NORTH CAROLINA TAX REPORTS, ¶ 202-751, and *Important Notice,* North Carolina Department of Revenue, December 22, 2016, CCH NORTH CAROLINA TAX REPORTS, ¶ 202-756.

Taxability matrix: A chart of the taxable status of various items is accessible on the state's website at **http://www.dornc.com/taxes/sales/streamlined.html** or under "Certificates of Compliance" on the website of the Streamlined Sales Tax Project at **http://www.streamlinedsalestax.org**.

- **Sourcing**

In conformity with the Streamlined Sales and Use Tax Agreement, sales are generally sourced to the place of delivery (Sec. 105-164.4B). When a seller of a product does not know the address where the product is received, the sale is sourced to the first address or location below that is known to the seller:

— (1) the business or home address of the purchaser;

— (2) the billing address of the purchaser or, if the product is a prepaid telephone calling service that authorizes the purchase of mobile telecommunications service, the location associated with the mobile telephone number;

— (3) the address from which tangible personal property was shipped or from which a service was provided.

Special provisions apply to sourcing of admissions to entertainment activities, leases and rentals, direct mail, and telecommunications services (Sec. 105-164B; Sec. 105-164.4C; Sec. 105-164.4E; Sec. 105-164.4F; Sec. 105-164.4G; Important Notice: *Adver-*

tising and Promotional Direct Mail and Other Direct Mail Sourcing, North Carolina Department of Revenue, November 2013, CCH NORTH CAROLINA TAX REPORTS, ¶ 202-589). See also Important Notice: *Sourcing for Certain Digital Property Subject to Sales and Use Tax*, North Carolina Department of Revenue, August 2013, CCH NORTH CAROLINA TAX REPORTS, ¶ 202-581.

¶ 698   List of Exemptions, Exceptions, and Exclusions

Unless otherwise indicated, the statutory exemptions, exceptions, and exclusions listed below apply to both sales and use taxes. Items that are excluded from the sales or use tax base are treated at ¶ 697, "Tax Base." Reduced tax rates apply to certain items and transactions; see ¶ 699, "Rate of Tax."

Annual sales tax holidays repealed: The annual back-to-school sales tax holiday and the Energy Star sales tax holiday are repealed effective July 1, 2014. (Ch 316 (H.B. 998), Laws 2013). (fromer Sec. 105-164.13C).

Qualifying farmers: Effective July 1, 2014, for purposes of the sales and use tax exemptions available to qualifying farmers, a "qualifying farmer" is defined as a person who has an annual gross income for the preceding taxable year of $10,000 or more from farming operations or who has an average annual gross income for the three preceding taxable years of $10,000 or more from farming operations. A qualifying farmer includes a dairy operator, poultry farmer, egg producer, livestock farmer, a farmer of crops, and a farmer of an aquatic species, as defined. A qualifying farmer may apply to the Secretary of Revenue for an exemption certificate number. The exemption certificate expires when a person fails to meet the income threshold for three consecutive taxable years or ceases to engage in farming operations. Exemptions available to a qualifying farmer are listed at Sec. 105-164.13E(a)(1)-(9).

A person who does not meet the definition of a "qualifying farmer" may apply to the North Carolina Department of Revenue for a conditional exemption certificate. A person with a conditional exemption certificate may purchase items exempt from sales and use tax to the same extent as a qualifying farmer. To receive a conditional exemption certificate, a person must certify that she or he intends to engage in farming operations and that the person will timely file state and federal income tax returns that reflect income and expenses incurred from farming operations during the taxable years to which the conditional exemption certificate applies. (Sec. 105-164.13E(b); *Important Notice: Qualifying Farmer and Conditional Farmer Exemption*, North Carolina Department of Revenue, June 25, 2014, CCH NORTH CAROLINA TAX REPORTS, ¶ 202-620)

- **Sales and use tax exemptions, exceptions, and exclusions**

Admissions to certain nonprofit entertainments and youth sports contests	Sec. 105-13(60)
Admissions to commercial agricultural fairs	Sec. 105-164.13(60)
Agricultural fuel and electricity, farm machinery, fertilizer, seeds, and other specified items sold to a farmer	Sec. 105-164.13E
Agricultural products sold in their original state	Sec. 105-164.13(4b)
Agricultural products sold to manufacturers for further processing	Sec. 105-164.13(4)
Aircraft parts, accessories, and lubricants sold to air carriers	Sec. 105-164.13(45), (45a)
Artwork sold to state agencies for state buildings	Sec. 105-164.13(29)
Audiovisual masters	Sec. 105-164.13(22a)
Aviation gasoline and jet fuel for commercial air carriers (exp. 1/1/2020)	Sec. 105-164.13(11b)
Baked goods sold by artisan bakeries	Sec. 105-164.13B
Blind merchants	Sec. 105-164.13(20)

Charitable meal sales	Sec. 105-164.13(31)
Cherokee Indian sales	Sec. 105-164.13(25)
Commercial fishing	Sec. 105-164.13(9)
Custom computer software; "load and leave" delivery	Sec. 105-164.13(43)
Customized motor vehicle transactions	Sec. 105-164.13(32)
Customized therapeutic, prosthetic, or artificial devices	Sec. 105-164.13(12)
Datacenter support equipment	Sec. 105-164.13(55a)
Delivery charges for direct mail	Sec. 105-164.13(33a)
Debit card (federal or state issued) purchases for emergency assistance	Sec. 105-164.13(58)
Department of Transportation sales	Sec. 105-164.13(40)
Diesel fuel for railroad companies for use in rolling stock	Sec. 105-164.13(11a)
Donated property and food	Sec. 105-164.13(42)
Eggs, chicks, and poults	Sec. 105-164.13(4a)
Electricity for use by an Internet data center	Sec. 105-164.13(55)
Electricity sold by municipality under contract with a federal agency .	Sec. 105-164.13(46)
Exports to foreign countries	Sec. 105-164.13(33)
Farm machinery	Sec. 105-164.13(1)b
Farmers, exemptions available to qualifying farmers	Sec. 105-164.13E(a)(1)-(9)
Fertilizer	Sec. 105-164.13(1)
Fish and seafood sold in their original state	Sec. 105-164.13(7)
Food and prepared food for use in a prepaid meal plan	Sec. 105-164.13(63)
Food (excluding prepared food, candy)	Sec. 105-164.13B
Food stamp program purchases	Sec. 105-164.13(38)
Forest and mine products sold in their original state	Sec. 105-164.13(3)
Fuel for commercial ocean-going vessels	Sec. 105-164.13(24)
Fuel sales to small power production facilities to generate electricity .	Sec. 105-164.13(8a)
Government transactions	Sec. 105-164.13(17)
Ice used to preserve agriculture, aquaculture, and commercial fishery products	Sec. 105-164.13(4b)
Installation, repair, and maintenance services, as specified	Sec. 105-164.3(33d)
Insurance companies, nonprofit, capital expenditures	Sec. 105-164.14(i)
Interior design services	Sec. 105-164.13(59)
Interstate carriers, fuel, lubricants, parts, and accessories	Sec. 105-164.14(a)
Insurance policies	Sec. 105-164.3(20)
Inventory donated to a nonprofit organization	Sec. 105-164.13(42)
Laundry and dry cleaning equipment, materials	Sec. 105-164.13(10)
Laundry, coin-, token-, or card-operated machines	Sec. 105-164.4(4)
Legend and nonlegend drugs donated to nonprofit organizations . . .	Sec. 105-164.13(42)
Livestock breeding facilities, equipment, and supplies	Sec. 105-164.13(4c)
Logging machinery	Sec. 105-164.13(4f)
Maintenance, repair, and installation services, as specified	Sec. 105-164.3(33d)
Ractured homes and modular homes (50% exemption)	Sec. 105-164.13(64), Sec. 105-467(a)(1)

Manufacturing and industrial exemptions	Sec. 105-164.13(5)-(10)
Medical equipment and supplies	Sec. 105-164.13(12)
Mobile classrooms sold to local boards of education or local boards of community college trustees	Sec. 105-164.13(41)
Motion picture leases and rentals	Sec. 105-164.13(21), Sec. 105-164.13(22)
Motor fuel on which a North Carolina excise tax has been paid	Sec. 105-164.13(11), Sec. 105-434, Sec. 105-435
Motor vehicle service contracts	105-164.4I(b)(1), 105-164.13(62a)
Motor vehicles	Sec. 105-164.13(32)
Natural gas, piped, that is subject to excise tax	Sec. 105-164.13(44)
Newspaper advertising supplements	Sec. 105-164.13(36)
Nonprofit organizations	Sec. 105-164.13(35)
Nonprofit sales for the state of North Carolina	Sec. 105-164.13(34)
Occasional rental of private residence	Sec. 105-164.4(a)(3)
Packaging, shipping, and delivery materials	Sec. 105-164.13(23)
Prescription medicines and insulin	Sec. 105-164.13(13)
Products of forests and waters in their original state	Sec. 105-164.13(3), Sec. 105-164.13(7)
Property delivered by common carrier outside North Carolina	Sec. 105-164.13(33a)
Property sold to manufacturers as a component of other property	Sec. 105-164.13(8)
Prosthetic and orthopedic devices	Sec. 105-164.13(12)
Public school book purchases	Sec. 105-164.13(14)
Recycling facility (major), lubricants and certain supplies	Sec. 105-164.13(10a)
Religious organizations food	Sec. 105-164.13(31a)
Repair, maintenance, and installation services, as specified	Sec. 105-164.3(33d)
Repossessed articles	Sec. 105-164.13(16)
Resales	Sec. 105-164.3(13), Sec. 105-164.13(42)
Sales by manufacturers to merchants or other manufacturers	Sec. 105-164.13(5)
Sales to North Carolina state agencies	Sec. 105-164.13(52)
School events, admissions to	Sec. 105-13(60)
School meals	Sec. 105-164.13(26)
Securities sold by financial institutions	Sec. 105-164.3(20)
Seeds	Sec. 105-164.13(1)a
Service contracts	Sec. 105-164.4I(b)
Supplemental food program purchases	Sec. 105-164.13(38)
Surveyor, certain sales to	Sec. 105-164.13(53)
Telephone service, public coin-operated	Sec. 105-164.4(a)(4a)
Tobacco barns or rackss	Sec. 105-164.13E
Vending machine one-cent sales	Sec. 105-164.13(30)
Veterinarian prescription drug sales	Sec. 105-164.13(13)
Wood chippers	Sec. 105-164.13(4g)

¶ 699   **Rate of Tax**

The state general sales and use tax rate is 4.75% (Sec. 105-164.4; Sec. 105-164.6(b)). Examples of items taxed at the general rate include admissions to entertainment activities, rentals of rooms to transients, the operation of a dry cleaning business, the sale of articles at a flea market, and tangible personal property purchased inside or outside North Carolina that becomes part of a structure in North Carolina (Sec. 105-164.4).

Service contracts: Effective January 1, 2014, the general rate of tax of 4.75% applies to the sales price of a service contract (Sec. 105-164.4(11)). See also ¶ 697 and ¶ 708.

- **SST conformity**

North Carolina has conformed to the rate requirements contained in the Streamlined Sales and Use Tax Agreement. Consequently, reduced or increased sales and use tax rates imposed on certain items and activities have been repealed and the items are made either subject to the general rate of tax, subject to a privilege tax, or exempt from tax. For exemptions, see ¶ 698.

> *Fuel:* Sales of fuel, other than electricity, for farm operations and laundries are exempt (Sec. 105-164.13(1)). The tax applies to pressing and dry-cleaning establishments for electricity and gas that is used for laundering, pressing and cleaning services (Sec. 105-164.4(a)(1f)c).

> *Manufactured and modular homes:* Applicable to sales made on or after September 1, 2014, a sales and use tax exemption applies to 50% of the sales price of a modular home or a manufactured home, including all accessories attached when delivered to the purchaser. (Sec. 105-164.13(64); Sec. 105-467(a)(1))

> A "modular home" is a factory-built structure that (1) is designed to be used as a dwelling, (2) is manufactured in accordance with the specifications for modular homes under the North Carolina State Residential Building Code, and (3) bears a seal or label issued by the Department of Insurance (Sec. 105-164.3). The sale of a modular home to a modular home builder is considered a retail sale, and a person who sells a modular home at retail is allowed a credit for sales or use tax paid to another state on tangible personal property incorporated in the home. Moreover, the retail sale of a modular home occurs when a modular home manufacturer sells a modular home to a modular home builder or directly to the end user of such a home (Sec. 105-164.4(a)(8)).

- **Combined general rate**

The combined general rate is the sum of the state's general rate of tax plus the sum of the rates of the local sales and use taxes (see ¶ 700) imposed in each locality. The following items sold at retail are specifically taxable at the combined general rate (Sec. 105-164.4(a)(1a)), G.S.:

> *Aircraft; certified jet engines; aviation gasoline and jet fuel:* There is a maximum tax of $2,500 on aircraft with on a maximum takeoff weight of more than 9,000 pounds but not in excess of 15,000 pounds (Sec. 105-164.4(a)(1a), *Sales Tax Rate Increase for Aircraft*, North Carolina Department of Revenue, September 30, 2015, CCH NORTH CAROLINA TAX REPORTS, ¶ 202-681). See ¶ 698 for the exemption for aviation gasoline and jet fuel sold to commercial air carriers.

> *Manufactured homes and modular homes:* The retail sale of a modular home occurs when a modular home manufacturer sells a modular home to a modular homebuilder or directly to the end user of the modular home. Subject to a 50% the exemption; see above.

Liquor: Spirituous liquor other than mixed beverages (Sec. 105-164.4(a)(7)).

Repair, maintenance, and installation services: Specified services are exempt; see ¶ 698;

Satellite and cable services: Video programming services, such as direct-to-home satellite services or cable services, are taxed at the combined general rate (Sec. 105-164.4(a)(6)). The combined general rate also applies to satellite digital audio services (Sirius and XM) (Sec. 105-164.4(a)(6)(a));

Telecommunications: The combined general rate applies to the gross receipts derived from providing toll or private telecommunications services that both originate and terminate within North Carolina and that are not otherwise subject to a privilege tax (Sec. 105-164.4(a)(4c)). Voice mail is taxable as a telecommunications service;

- **Privilege tax on appliances**

A $3 privilege tax imposed on the sale of "white goods" (*i.e.,* refrigerators, ranges, water heaters, freezers, unit air-conditioners, washing machines, dishwashers, clothes dryers, and other similar domestic and commercial large appliances) (Sec. 105-187.20(2), Sec. 105-187.21).

- **Privilege tax on certain research and development companies**

A 1% privilege tax is imposed on research and development companies in the physical, engineering, or life sciences fields that are classified under NAICS Code 54171 and that purchase equipment, attachments, or repair parts for equipment that meets certain requirements. The maximum tax that may be imposed is capped at $80 (Sec. 105-164.4(1d); Reg. Sec. 17:07B.0201).

- **Privilege tax on mill machinery and parts**

Mill machinery and mill machinery parts and accessories are exempt from sales and use tax but are subject to a privilege tax at the rate of 1% of the purchase price of the item purchased, with a maximum tax of $80 per article (Sec. 105-187.51; Sec. 17:07D.0101).

- **Privilege tax on recycling**

Recycling equipment (cranes, structural steel crane support systems, foundations related to the cranes and support systems, port and dock facilities, rail equipment, and material handling equipment) is exempt from sales and use tax but subject to a privilege tax at the rate of 1% of the sales price of the item purchased, with a maximum tax of $80 per article (Sec. 105-187.51B).

Applicable to purchases made on or after July 1, 2016, the tax applies to a person who gathers and obtains ferrous metals, nonferrous metals, and items that have served their original economic purpose, who converts them by processes, including sorting, cutting, classifying, cleaning, baling, wrapping, shredding, or shearing, into a new or different product for sale consisting of prepared grades for the purchase of equipment, or an attachment or repair part for the equipment, that meets certain requirements. (Sec. 105-187.51B(a)(7); *Important Notice: Certain Recyclers,* North Carolina Department of Revenue, August 11, 2016, CCH NORTH CAROLINA TAX REPORTS, ¶ 202-738)

- **Privilege tax on data centers**

Prior to July 1, 2015, a privilege tax was imposed on an eligible data center (other than "Internet data center" as defined in Sec. 105-164.3(8e)), that purchases machinery or equipment to be located and used at the data center that is capitalized for tax purposes under the IRC and is used for specified purposes. The tax was imposed at a 1% rate on the sales price of the eligible equipment and machinery with a maximum tax of $80 per article. The privilege tax expired for sales occurring on or after July 1, 2015 (Sec. 105-187.51C).

¶699   North Carolina

The exemption provided in Sec. 105-164.13(55) for "sales of electricity for use at an eligible Internet datacenter and eligible business property to be located and used at an eligible Internet datacenter" remains in effect.

- **Privilege tax on software publishers**

A 1% privilege tax (maximum $80 per article) is imposed on a software publishing company that is included in the industry group 5112 of NAICS and purchases equipment or an attachment or repair part for equipment that meets all of the following requirements (Sec. 105-187.51B):

— the item is capitalized by the company for tax purposes under the IRC;

— the item is used by the company in the research and development of tangible personal property; and

— the item would be considered mill machinery if it were purchased by a manufacturing industry or plant and used in the research and development of tangible personal property manufactured by the industry or plant.

- **Privilege tax on machinery refurbishers**

A privilege tax is imposed on an industrial machinery refurbishing company that is included in industry group 811310 of NAICS and that purchases equipment or an attachment or repair part for equipment that meets all of the following requirements (Sec. 105-187.51B):

— it is capitalized by the company for tax purposes;

— it is used by the company in repairing or refurbishing tangible personal property; and

— it would be considered mill machinery, as provided, if it were purchased by a manufacturing industry or plant and used by the industry or plant to manufacture tangible personal property.

The tax is imposed at 1% of the sales price of the equipment or other tangible personal property. The maximum tax is $80.00 per article.

- **Privilege tax on ports facilities**

A privilege tax is imposed on companies located at a ports facility for waterborne commerce that purchase specialized equipment to be used at the facility to unload or process bulk cargo to make it suitable for delivery to and use by manufacturing facilities. Such purchases are subject to the privilege tax at the rate of 1% of the sales price of the equipment or other tangible personal property purchased, with a cap of $80 per article. (Sec. 105-187.51B(a)(5))

Applicable retroactively to purchases made on or after July 1, 2013, the tax is expanded to apply to parts, accessories, or attachments used to maintain, repair, replace, upgrade, improve, or otherwise modify machinery and equipment that is used at the facility to unload or to facilitate the unloading or processing of bulk cargo to make it suitable for delivery to and use by manufacturing facilities. (*Important Notice: Certain Purchases for Use at a Ports Facility,* North Carolina Department of Revenue, July 15, 2016, CCH North Carolina Tax Reports, ¶ 202-732)

- **Privilege tax on precious metals extraction companies**

Effective July 1, 2016, the 1% privilege tax applies to a company primarily engaged in processing tangible personal property for the purpose of extracting precious metals, to determine the value for potential purchase for the purchase of equipment, or an attachment or repair part for the equipment, that meets certain requirements.

"Precious metal" is defined as gold, silver, platinum, or palladium, but excluding coins, medals, medallions, tokens, numismatic items, art ingots, or art bars. (Sec. 105-187.51B(a)(6))

• **Privilege tax on fabrication of metal work**

Effective July 1, 2016, the 1% privilege tax is imposed on certain purchases by a company that is engaged in the fabrication of metal work, has annual gross receipts, including the gross receipts of all related persons from the fabrication of metal work of at least $8 million, and purchases equipment, or an attachment or repair part for equipment. (Sec. 105-187.51B(a)(8))

The purchased equipment must be capitalized by the company for tax purposes under the Internal Revenue Code and used by the company at the establishment in the fabrication or manufacture of metal products or used by the company to create equipment for the fabrication or manufacture of metal products. *(Important Notice: Certain Metal Work Fabrication Companies,* North Carolina Department of Revenue, July 25, 2016, CCH NORTH CAROLINA TAX REPORTS, ¶ 202-734)

• **Privilege tax on large manufacturing and distribution facilities**

A privilege tax is imposed on large manufacturing and distribution facilities that purchase mill machinery, distribution machinery, or parts and accessories for such machinery, or distribution machinery for storage, use, or consumption within North Carolina. The privilege tax on such purchases by large manufacturing and distribution facilities is imposed at a rate of 1% with a cap of $80 per article. These provisions expire for sales that occur on or after July 1, 2018. (Sec. 105-187.51D)

• **Highway use tax**

In addition to other taxes, a highway use tax is imposed at the rate of 3% of the retail value of a motor vehicle for which a certificate of title is issued (Sec. 105-187.3). However, a retailer may elect to base the tax on the gross receipts of the lease or rental of the vehicle. Under this election, the rate of tax is 8% of gross receipts from a short-term lease (less than 365 continuous days), and 3% of gross receipts from a long-term lease (365 continuous days or more) (Sec. 105-187.5(a)).

Maximum tax: A maximum tax of $250 (formerly, $150) applies when a certificate of title is issued for a motor vehicle that, at the time of applying for a certificate of title, is and has been titled in the name of the owner of the motor vehicle in another state for at least 90 days prior to the date of application for a certificate of title in North Carolina (Sec. 105-187.6(c)).

Effective January 1, 2016, the maximum highway use tax is $2,000 for each certificate of title issued for a Class A or Class B motor vehicle that is a commercial motor vehicle (formerly, $1,000) and for each certificate of title issued for a recreational vehicle (formerly $1,500) (Sec. 105-187.3(a)).

¶ 700   Local Taxes

The combined general rate in each locality is the sum of the state general rate (see ¶ 699) and the local rate for that locality. The combined state and local tax rate as of January 1, 2017, is:

  7% in Alexander, Anson, Ashe, Buncombe, Cabarrus, Catawba, Cherokee, Cumberland, Davidson, Duplin, Edgecombe, Greene, Halifax, Harnett, Haywood, Hertford, Jackson, Lee, Martin, Montgomery, New Hanover, Onslow, Pitt, Randolph, Robeson, Rowan, Sampson, Surry, and Wilkes Counties;

  7.25% in Mecklenburg County and effective April 1, 2017, Wake County;

  7.50% in Durham and Orange Counties; and

  6.75% in all other counties.

(*Form E-505,* North Carolina Department of Revenue, revised January 20, 2016, CCH NORTH CAROLINA TAX REPORTS, ¶ 202-684; *Important Notice: Wake County Transit Sales and Use Tax,* North Carolina Department of Revenue, January 20, 2017, CCH NORTH CAROLINA TAX REPORTS, ¶ 202-759)

Mobile telecommunications: North Carolina has adopted the provisions of the federal Mobile Telecommunications Sourcing Act (P.L. 106-252) (Sec. 105-164.3(21), Sec. 105-164.4C). Wireless telecommunications services are sourced to the customer's primary place of use, which is the residential or primary business address of the customer and which must be located in the service provider's licensed service area.

Vehicle rental tax: A county that is authorized to impose an additional 0.5% North Carolina sales and use tax for public transportation is considered a regional public transportation authority that is authorized to levy a vehicle rental tax (Sec. 30, Ch. 162 (H.B. 1963), Laws 2006). Currently, the authority to levy the 0.5% public transportation local sales and use tax is applicable to Mecklenburg County. The vehicle rental tax may not exceed 5% of the gross proceeds of a short-term vehicle rental (Sec. 105-551). Other regional public transportation authorities, consisting of two or more counties, are also authorized to levy a vehicle rental tax of up to 5% (Sec. 105-550; Sec. 105-551). North Carolina currently has two such authorities: one in the Triad (Winston, Greensboro, High Point, or Forsyth and Guilford Counties) and one in the Triangle (Raleigh, Durham, Chapel Hill, or Durham, Wake, and Orange Counties).

A county may by resolution impose a tax at the rate of 1.2%, and a city may by resolution impose a tax at the rate of 0.8%, on the gross receipts from the short-term lease or rental of heavy equipment by a person whose principal business is the short-term lease or rental of heavy equipment at retail. "Heavy equipment" is defined as earthmoving, construction, or industrial equipment that is mobile, weighs at least 1,500 pounds, and is: (1) a self-propelled vehicle that is not designed to be driven on a highway; or (2) industrial lift equipment, industrial material handling equipment, industrial electrical generation equipment, or a similar piece of industrial equipment. The term includes an attachment for heavy equipment, regardless of the weight of the attachment. (Sec. 153A-156.1; Sec. 160A-215.2)

Beach nourishment: The board of commissioners of counties in North Carolina may, by resolution, levy an additional 1% local sales and use tax for beach nourishment (Sec. 105-528). A board that intends to adopt a resolution to levy such a tax must first provide at least 10 days notice of its intent, and must then hold a public hearing. A tax levied under this act as well as a county's authorization to levy such a tax expires eight years after the effective date of its levy (Sec. 105-530).

- **Tax jurisdiction databases**

Databases that provide information on taxing jurisdiction boundaries are available at **http://www.dornc.com/taxes/sales/boundary_database.html.** A seller that relies on information provided in such databases is not liable for underpayments of tax attributable to erroneous information provided in those databases (Sec. 105-164.42L).

- **Local tax rates**

Local sales and use tax rates for each county in North Carolina can be found on the Department of Revenue's website at **http://www.dornc.com/taxes/sales/taxrates.html**.

Local tax rates are also available at **http://www.dornc.com/downloads/gen562bycity.pdf**

Occupancy tax rates are set by local governments and are subject to change at any time. Please contact the county and/or municipality for their current rates.

¶701   Bracket Schedule

Tax computation must be carried to the third decimal place and rounded up for tax that is one-half cent or more, and rounded down for tax that is less than one-half cent (Sales and Use Tax Technical Bulletin 1-5). Sellers may compute the tax due on an item or invoice basis.

Reproduced below are retail tax calculation tables compiled by the Department of Revenue for use in collecting the tax due. Use of the tables does not relieve a retailer of liability for the applicable rate of tax due on the retailer's gross receipts or net taxable sales (Sec. 105-164.10).

3% Tax Rate

Sale	Tax
$0.00 to $0.16	No tax
.17 to .49	1¢
.50 to .83	2¢
.84 to 1.16	3¢
and so forth.	

6% Tax Rate

Sale	Tax
$0.00 to $0.08	No tax
.09 to .24	1¢
.25 to .41	2¢
.42 to .58	3¢
.59 to .74	4¢
.75 to .91	5¢
.92 to 1.08	6¢
and so forth.	

7% Tax Rate

Sale	Tax
$0.00 to $0.07	No tax
.08 to .21	1¢
.22 to .35	2¢
.36 to .49	3¢
.50 to .64	4¢
.65 to .78	5¢
.79 to .92	6¢
.93 to 1.07	7¢
and so forth.	

4% Tax Rate

Sale	Tax
$0.00 to $0.12	No tax
.13 to .37	1¢
.38 to .62	2¢
.63 to .87	3¢
.88 to 1.12	4¢
and so forth.	

6.5% Tax Rate

Sale	Tax
$0.00 to $0.07	No tax
.08 to .23	1¢
.24 to .38	2¢
.39 to .63	3¢
.64 to .69	4¢
.70 to .84	5¢
.85 to .99	6¢
and so forth.	

7.5% Tax Rate

Sale	Tax
$0.00 to $0.06	No tax
.07 to .19	1¢
.20 to .33	2¢
.34 to .46	3¢
.47 to .59	4¢
.60 to .73	5¢
.74 to .86	6¢
.87 to .99	7¢
and so forth.	

¶702　Returns, Payments, and Due Dates

It is the taxpayer's responsibility to obtain whatever forms are needed from the Secretary of Revenue (Sec. 105-164.15). The return, when filed, must be complete and accurate to prevent its rejection (Sec. 105-164.16(a)). In the event that a taxpayer makes a grossly incorrect or fraudulent return, the Secretary may estimate and assess the correct tax along with interest and penalties (Sec. 105-164.32).

Every person engaged in the business of selling tangible personal property at retail or making purchases subject to the use tax must file a report for each reporting period showing gross sales and/or receipts and an itemization of all exempt sales or receipts that are not included in the computation of tax due (Reg. Sec. 17:07B.0104). Reports for periods in which no sales are made should be marked "no sales."

Due dates: Taxpayers who are consistently liable for more than $100 but less than $10,000 a month in state and local sales and use taxes must file a return and pay the tax due by the 20th of each month (Sec. 105-164.16(b1)).

Taxpayers who are consistently liable for at least $10,000 per month in taxes must prepay the tax (see ¶ 703) and must file a return on a monthly basis (Sec. 105-164.16(b2)).

Taxpayers required to report on a quarterly basis must file their returns by the last day of the month following the end of the quarter. A seller whose state and local tax collections are less than $1,000 in a calendar year cannot be required to remit tax more often than annually. Taxpayers that are consistently liable for less than $100 in taxes per month may file their returns on a quarterly basis after seeking approval from the Secretary of Revenue (Sec. 105-164.16).

The annual reporting period ends on December 31 and the return must be filed by the due date of the individual's income tax return. Taxpayers may also obtain permission to file estimated returns if exact figures cannot be obtained within these filing deadlines. Special rules apply to reporting utility service sales (Sec. 105-164.16(c), Sec. 105-164.20, Sec. 105-164.21A).

The Secretary will prescribe where taxes are to be paid and whether taxes must be paid in cash, by check, by electronic funds transfer, or by another method (Sec. 105-241(a)).

Accrual basis of reporting: Certain retailers of are required to report and remit sales tax on an accrual basis of accounting, as follows:

— a retailer who sells electricity, piped natural gas, or telecommunications service.

— a retailer who derives gross receipts from a prepaid meal plan, notwithstanding that the retailer may report tax on the cash basis for other sales at retail and that the revenue has not been recognized for accounting purposes; and

— a retailer who sells or derives gross receipts from a service contract.

(Important Notice: *Basis of Sales and Use Tax Reporting,* North Carolina Department of Revenue, May 4, 2015, CCH NORTH CAROLINA TAX REPORTS, ¶ 202-666)

Electronic funds transfer: Taxpayers are required to pay sales and use taxes by electronic funds transfer (EFT) if the taxpayer paid $240,000 or more in sales and use taxes during a during a selected 12-month period (Sec. 105-241(b), Reg. Sec. 17:01C.0504). Taxpayers are notified by the Department of Revenue if they are required to pay be EFT. Once required to pay a tax by EFT, a taxpayer must continue to do so until notified by the Department that the requirement has been suspended. Taxpayers who voluntarily wish to pay sales and use taxes electronically must be consistently liable for at least $20,000 a month and be paying sales and use taxes semi-monthly.

• **Direct payment permits**

A general direct pay permit authorizes its holder to purchase any tangible personal property, digital property, or service without paying tax to the seller. Such a permit also authorizes the seller to not collect any tax on a sale to the permit holder. A person who purchases an item under a direct pay permit is liable for use tax due on the purchase. The tax is payable when the property is placed in use or the service is received. A direct pay permit does not apply to taxes on sales of electricity or the gross receipts derived from rentals of accommodations, as specified. (Sec. 105-164.27A(a); Reg. Sec. 17:07B.5301)

A person who purchases an item for storage, use, or consumption in North Carolina whose tax status cannot be determined at the time of the purchase because of one of the reasons listed below, may apply to the Secretary for a general direct pay permit:

— the place of business where the item will be used stored, used, or consumed is not known at the time of the purchase and a different tax consequence applies depending on where the item is used; or

— the manner in which the item will be used stored, used, or consumed is not known at the time of the purchase and one or more of the potential uses is taxable but others are not taxable.

Businesses, such as manufacturers, that purchase tangible personal property that could be either subject to tax or exempt are eligible for a direct pay permit. Multistate taxpayers that use the same type property in various locations inside and outside North Carolina are also eligible. A taxpayer's annual purchases of tangible personal property should exceed $5 million to obtain a permit. Retail and wholesale businesses with locations only in North Carolina whose exempt purchases are for resale purposes are not eligible for a direct pay permit.

Jet engines: A person that purchases a qualified jet engine may apply to the Secretary of Revenue for a direct pay permit (Sec. 105-164.27A(a2)). The maximum use tax on a qualified jet engine is $2,500 for a person that purchases a qualified jet engine under a direct pay permit; otherwise, no maximum tax is applicable. (Important Notice: *Qualified Jet Engine,* North Carolina Department of Revenue, October 6, 2015, CCH NORTH CAROLINA TAX REPORTS, ¶ 202-682)

- **Bad debt deduction**

Accounts of purchasers representing taxable sales on which North Carolina sales and use tax has been paid that are found to be worthless and that are charged off for income tax purposes may be deducted from gross retail sales as worthless accounts or bad debts (Sec. 105-164.13(15)). The amount of any deduction taken for bad debts can not include accrued interest. If a deduction is taken for a bad debt that is subsequently collected in whole or in part, the tax on the amount collected must be reported and paid on the return for the period in which the collection occurs. A taxpayer must claim the deduction for a bad debt within three years of charging off the debt for income tax purposes (*Directive No. SD-03-2,* Department of Revenue, October 15, 2003).

Third party lenders: A taxpayer failed to qualify for a bad debt deduction for accounts held and charged off as worthless by third-party banks, for North Carolina sales and use tax purposes, because of its decision to contract with those banks to extend credit to its customers. The taxpayer offered its customers the option of using private label credit cards to purchase merchandise but did not extend financing of its own. Under the agreements between the taxpayer and the third-party banks, the banks were the sole and exclusive owners of the credit card accounts. Although the statutory bad debt deduction would have been applicable to accounts between the taxpayer and its customers, the deduction is inapplicable to accounts held by a third party. In addition, the taxpayer failed to charge off the accounts on its federal income tax returns, but the third-party banks claimed a bad debt deduction for the uncollectible receivables related to the accounts on their federal income tax returns. (*Final Agency Decision 09 REV 4211,* North Carolina Department of Revenue, January 13, 2011, CCH NORTH CAROLINA TAX REPORTS, ¶ 202-490; see also *Home Depot U.S.A., Inc. v. North Carolina Department of Revenue,* North Carolina Superior Court, No. 11 CVS 2261, November 6, 2015, CCH NORTH CAROLINA TAX REPORTS, ¶ 202-687)

- **Uniform Sales Tax Administration Act**

North Carolina has enacted the Uniform Sales and Use Tax Administration Act, the product of the Streamlined Sales Tax Project (SSTP) (Sec. 105-164.42A). The SSTP developed the Act and the related Streamlined Sales and Use Tax Agreement to simplify and modernize sales and use tax administration in order to substantially reduce the burden of tax compliance for all sellers and for all types of commerce.

Taxability matrix: See ¶ 697.

Vendor registration: See ¶ 704.

Sourcing: See ¶ 697.

For additional information on North Carolina's implementation of the SST Agreement, see *North Carolina Information For Streamlined Sales Tax Participants,* North Carolina Department of Revenue, July 1, 2012, CCH NORTH CAROLINA TAX REPORTS, ¶ 202-548. See also **http://www.dornc.com/taxes/sales/streamlined.html**.

For additional information on the uniform act, see "Streamlined Sales Tax Project," listed in the Table of Contents.

¶ 703   **Prepayment of Taxes**

A taxpayer consistently liable for at least $20,000 a month in state and local sales and use taxes must make a monthly prepayment of the next month's tax liability. The prepayment is due when the monthly return is due (the 20th day of the month following the calendar month covered by the return) (Sec. 105-164.16(b2), G.S.). Taxpayers exempt from the prepayment requirements are still subject to the monthly reporting and payment requirements.

For taxpayers who pay online via the North Carolina Department of Revenue website, the E-500 Sales and Use Online Filing and Payments system at **http://www.dor.state.nc.us/electronic/business.html**, requires two separate payments, one payment for the current period and one payment for the prepayment for the next period. Both payments can be made with one login to the E-File system. This payment option is unavailable for Form E-500J. The prepayment must equal at least 65% of any of the following: (1) the amount of tax due for the current month; (2) the amount of tax due for the same month in the preceding year; or (3) the average monthly amount of tax due in the preceding calendar year. A taxpayer will not be subject to interest or penalties for the underpayment of a prepayment if one of the above three calculation methods is used. In addition, a taxpayer is not required to use the same method for calculating the amount of the prepayment each month.

¶ 704   **Vendor Registration**

Persons engaged in businesses subject to the sales and use tax must register and secure a certificate of registration from the Secretary of Revenue (Sec. 105-164.4(c)). There is no application fee. A retailer whose business extends into more than one county is required to secure only one certificate to cover all operations of the business throughout the state (Sec. 105-164.29(b)). Certificates are not assignable. The certificate is valid until it becomes void or is revoked for failure to comply with sales and use tax provisions (Sec. 105-164.4(c)) or other violations (Sec. 105-164.29(d)).

There is no fee to apply for a certificate of registration in North Carolina, and the department does not contract this service out to third parties.

• **SST registration**

To register under the Streamlined Sales and Use Tax Agreement (SST), sellers must go to **https://www.sstregister.org**. Sellers can also update previously submitted registration information at this website. The information provided will be sent to all of the full member states and to associate members for which the seller chooses to collect.

When a seller registers under the Agreement, it must select the certified technology model it will be using (or it must select "Other" if it will not be using one of the certified models). The models are the following:

Model One: Certified Service Provider (CSP), an agent certified under the Agreement to perform all the seller's sales and use tax functions;

Model Two: Certified Automated System (CAS), software certified under the Agreement to calculate the appropriate tax (for which the seller retains responsibility for remitting);

Model Three: Certified System (CS), a proprietary automated sales tax system certified under the Agreement.

¶ 705   **Sales and Use Tax Credits**

Credits are allowed for sales or use taxes due and paid to another state (Sec. 105-164.6(c)). A credit for taxes paid on products that have been returned to the retailer is allowed (Reg. Sec. 17:07B.3003), and worthless accounts that have been charged off may be deducted from gross sales (Sec. 105-164.13(15)).

¶ 706   **Deficiency Assessments**

After discovering that tax is due from a taxpayer, the Secretary must notify the taxpayer in writing of the kind and amount of tax due and of the Secretary's intent to assess the taxpayer for the tax (Sec. 105-241.1(a)). The notice must describe the basis for the proposed assessment and identify the amounts of any tax, interest, additions to tax, and penalties included in the proposed assessment. The notice must also advise the taxpayer that the proposed assessment will become final unless the taxpayer makes a timely request for a hearing. The Secretary must base a proposed assessment on the best information available, and a proposed assessment is presumed to be correct.

Final assessment: If a taxpayer does not apply for a hearing, the proposed assessment becomes final without further notice (Sec. 105-241.1(d)). If a taxpayer applies for a hearing, however, the proposed assessment becomes final when the taxpayer is notified of the Secretary's decision made after the hearing. An assessment that is final is immediately due and collectible.

Except in the case of a jeopardy assessment, the Secretary may not assess a taxpayer for a tax until the notice required by Sec. 105-241.1(a), has been given and one of the following has occurred:

— the time for applying for a hearing has expired;

— the Secretary and the taxpayer have agreed upon a settlement; or

— the taxpayer has filed a timely application for a hearing, and the Secretary, after conducting the hearing, has given the taxpayer written notice of the decision.

¶ 707   **Audit Procedures**

North Carolina sales and use tax laws contain no special provisions detailing audit procedures other than the authority to examine taxpayer records and make additional assessments. The DOR may not employ an agent who is compensated in whole or in part by the state for services rendered on a contingent basis or any other basis related to the amount of tax, interest, or penalty assessed against or collected from the person (Sec. 105-243.1(a1)).

Taxpayer conversations: The Department (DOR) must document advice given to a taxpayer in a conversation with that taxpayer when the taxpayer gives the DOR the taxpayer's identifying information, asks the Secretary about the application of a tax to the taxpayer in specific circumstances, and requests that the Secretary document the advice in the taxpayer's records. This provision is applicable to a conversation that is conducted by telephone or in person, is between a taxpayer and an employee of the DOR, and occurs at an office of the DOR if the conversation is in person. This provision is inapplicable to a conversation that occurs at a presentation, conference, or other forum. (Sec. 105-258.2(b))

Similar provisions apply to conversations between the DOR and a person requesting advice about whether registration as a retailer or wholesaler is required (Sec. 105-258.2(c)).

Voluntary disclosure: The Department of Revenue's Voluntary Disclosure Program allows taxpayers who have not filed returns or paid any taxes and who have not yet been contacted by the Department, to contact the Department anonymously about settling any unpaid tax liability owed to the Department. For details, see **http:// www.dornc.com/practitioner/voluntary.html**.

Interest waivers: For statewide taxes, except motor fuel taxes, the Secretary of Revenue may reduce or waive interest on taxes imposed prior to or during a period in which a taxpayer has declared bankruptcy (Sec. 105-237(a)).

¶ 708   **Statute of Limitations**

As a general rule, the Secretary of Revenue has three years after the date that the taxpayer's return was filed or was required to be filed, whichever is later, during which to assess additional taxes (Sec. 105-241.1(e)). Assessments may be made at any time when (1) no certificate application was ever filed; (2) no return was ever filed; (3) there has been a fraudulent application, return, or attempt to evade tax. The taxpayer may sign a written waiver extending the period of limitations.

Effective May 11, 2016, the statute of limitations for assessing a responsible person for unpaid taxes of a business entity provides that the period of limitations expires the later of:

    (1) one year after the expiration of the period of limitations for assessing the business entity; or

    (2) one year after a tax becomes collectible from the business entity.

(Important Notice: Responsible Person Liability Statute of Limitations Amended, North Carolina Department of Revenue, May 23, 2016, CCH NORTH CAROLINA TAX REPORTS, ¶ 202-717)

¶ 709   **Application for Refund**

If the Secretary determines that a seller overcollected North Carolina sales tax on a transaction, the secretary is required to take one of the following actions (Sec. 105-164.11(a)):

    — if the secretary determines that the seller overcollected tax on a transaction, the secretary may allow a refund of the tax (the secretary may allow a refund only if the seller gives the purchaser credit for or a refund of the overcollected tax, and the secretary shall not refund the overcollected tax to the seller if the seller has elected to offset a use tax liability on a related transaction as outlined below);

    — if the secretary determines that a seller who overcollected sales tax on a transaction is instead liable for a use tax on a related transaction, the secretary may allow the seller to offset the use tax liability with the overcollected sales tax (the secretary shall not allow an offset if the seller has elected to receive a refund of the overcollected tax as outlined above, and the decision by a seller to receive an offset of tax liability rather than a refund of the overcollected tax does not affect the liability of the seller to the purchaser for the overcollected tax); or

    — if neither of the above provisions apply, the secretary will retain the total amount collected on the transaction.

The DOR must refund an overpayment anytime it discovers an overpayment was made in error as long as the discovery is made within the statute of limitations period (Sec. 105-241.7). A taxpayer may request a refund by filing an amended return reflecting the overpayment or filing a refund claim. A claim for refund must identify the taxpayer, the type and amount of tax overpaid, the filing period to which the overpayment applies, and the basis for the claim. The taxpayer's statement of the basis of the claim does not limit the taxpayer from changing the basis at a later date.

Within six months from the time the refund claim is filed, the DOR must (1) send the taxpayer the full amount of the refund requested; (2) send the taxpayer an adjusted amount; (3) deny the refund and send the taxpayer a notice of proposed denial; or (4) send the taxpayer a letter requesting additional information. If a taxpayer does not respond to a request for additional information, the DOR may deny the refund and send the taxpayer a notice of proposed denial. If a taxpayer provides the requested information, the DOR must respond within the later of (1) the remainder of the six-month period; (2) 30 days after receiving the information, or (3) a time period mutually agreed upon by the taxpayer and the DOR. A taxpayer may treat the DOR's failure to timely respond to the refund request as outlined above as a proposed denial of the refund request. A notice of proposed denial must state the basis for the denial, although the basis may be changed at a later date. (Sec. 105-241.7)

Procedure for refund of overpayment: If a taxpayer claims that a tax payment was excessive or incorrect, the taxpayer may apply to the Secretary for a refund of the overpayment (Sec. 105-266.1(a)). The refund application must be made within three years after the date set by statute for the filing of the return or within six months after the date of the payment, whichever is later (Sec. 105-266.1(a), Sec. 105-266(c)). The Secretary is prohibited from refunding an overpayment before the taxpayer has filed the final return for the tax period (Sec. 105-266(a)).

• Specific refunds

The Secretary is specifically authorized to refund sales and use taxes paid to certain interstate carriers, nonprofit organizations, state and local governmental entities, motorsports teams, and other entities, as follows (Sec. 105-164.14):

Motorsports: Until January 1, 2020, a professional motorsports racing team is allowed a refund of 50% of the sales and use tax paid on tangible personal property, other than tires or accessories, that comprises any part of a professional motor racing vehicle (Sec. 105-164.14A(a)(4)). The refund also applies to aviation fuel used to travel to and from motorsports events by members of such a team or a motorsports sanctioning body (Sec. 105-164.14A(a)(5)).

Until January 1, 2020, a sales and use tax exemption is enacted for the sale of an engine provided with an operator to a professional motorsports racing team or a related member of a team for use in competition in a sanctioned race series (Sec. 105-164.13(65)).

For additional information, see Important Notice: *Certain Motorsports Exemptions and Refunds,* North Carolina Department of Revenue, December 22, 2015, CCH NORTH CAROLINA TAX REPORTS, ¶ 202-693.

Railroad intermodal facility: Until 2038, the owner or lessee of an eligible railroad intermodal facility is allowed a refund of sales and use tax paid on building materials, building supplies, fixtures, and equipment that become a part of the real property of the facility. Liability incurred indirectly by the owner or lessee of the facility for sales and use taxes on these items is considered tax paid by the owner or lessee. (Sec. 105-164.14A(a)(7))

Major recycling facilities: Owners of major recycling facilities are allowed a refund of sales and use taxes paid such facilities on building materials, building supplies, fixtures, and equipment that become part of the real property of the recycling facility. (Sec. 105-164.14A(a)(2))

Utilities: A utility company is allowed a refund of part of the sales and use taxes paid on the purchase of railway cars and locomotives and accessories for a railway car or locomotive the utility company operates (Sec. 105-164.14(a2)).

Nonprofit entities; hospitals; government entities: A nonprofit entity is allowed a semiannual refund of sales and use taxes paid on direct purchases of tangible personal property and services for use in carrying on the work of the nonprofit entity. Sales and use tax liability indirectly incurred by a nonprofit entity through reimbursement to an authorized person of the entity for the purchase of tangible personal property and services for use in carrying on the work of the nonprofit entity is considered a direct purchase by the entity. Sales and use tax liability indirectly incurred by a nonprofit entity on building materials, supplies, fixtures, and equipment that become a part of or annexed to any building or structure that is owned or leased by the nonprofit entity and is being erected, altered, or repaired for use by the nonprofit entity for carrying on its nonprofit activities is considered a sales or use tax liability incurred on direct purchases by the nonprofit entity. The refund does not apply to purchases of electricity, telecommunications service, ancillary service, piped natural gas, video programming, or a prepaid meal plan. Certain hospitals, as defined, and other organizations may claim a refund for taxes paid on purchases of over-the-counter drugs. (Sec. 105-164.14(b))

Specified government entities are allowed refunds of tax paid on certain purchases of tangible personal property and services (Sec. 105-164.14(c), (e)).

A request for a refund must be in writing and must include any information and documentation required by the Secretary. A request for a refund for the first six months of a calendar year is due the following October 15; a request for a refund for the second six months of a calendar year is due the following April 15. (Sec. 105-164.14(b))

Refund of local taxes to school administrative units: A local school administrative unit and a joint agency created by interlocal agreement among such units, as specified, to jointly purchase food service-related materials, supplies, and equipment on their behalf is allowed an annual refund of sales and use taxes paid on direct purchases of tangible personal property and services other than electricity and telecommunications service. Sales and use taxes indirectly incurred by an entity on building materials, supplies, fixtures, and equipment that become a part of or annexed to any building or structure owned or leased by the entity that is being erected, altered, or repaired for use by the entity is considered to be a liability eligible for refund (Sec. 105-467).

Service contracts: A retailer is allowed a refund of sales tax remitted on a rescinded sale or cancelled service (Sec. 105-164.11A). A sale is rescinded when the purchaser returns an item to the retailer and receives a refund, in whole or in part, of the sales price paid, including a refund of the pro rata amount of the sales tax based on the taxable amount of the sales price refunded. A service is cancelled when the service is terminated and the purchaser receives a refund, in whole or in part, of the sales price paid, including a refund of the *pro rata* amount of the sales tax paid based on the taxable amount of the sales price refunded. A retailer entitled to a refund may reduce taxable receipts by the taxable amount of the refund for the period in which the refund occurs or may request a refund of an overpayment, as specified, provided the tax has been refunded to the purchaser. When a service contract is cancelled and a purchaser receives a refund, in whole or in part, of the sales price paid for the service contract, the purchaser may receive a refund of the *pro rata* amount of the sales tax paid based on the taxable amount of the sales price refunded. (Sec. 105-164.11A; see also Important Notice: *Service Contracts,* North Carolina Department of Revenue, September 26, 2014, CCH NORTH CAROLINA TAX REPORTS, ¶ 202-639)

¶ 711   Scope of Tax

Source.—Statutory references are to Chapters 40-57.3, 57-39.2 and 57-40.2 of the North Dakota Century Code, as amended to date. Details are reported in the CCH NORTH DAKOTA TAX REPORTS starting at ¶ 60-000.

In general, sales tax is levied on retail sales, including leases and rentals, of tangible personal property consisting of goods, wares, or merchandise, and specified services. A special sales tax is levied on manufactured homes used for residential or business purposes and on retail sales of farm machinery, farm machinery repair parts, and irrigation equipment used exclusively for agricultural purposes (Sec. 57-39.2-01(7), Sec. 57-39.2-02.1). The sales tax is imposed upon purchasers; however, it is measured by a retailer's gross receipts, and retailers are responsible for collecting and remitting the tax to the state (Sec. 57-39.2-02.1, Sec. 57-39.2-08.2, Sec. 57-39.2-12).

Hotel/motel accommodations: Retail sales, leases, and rentals of hotel, motel, and tourist court accommodations are taxable (Sec. 57-39.2-02.1). However, rentals for 30 or more consecutive days or one month are exempt (Sec. 57-39.2-04).

Digital products: Sales of items delivered electronically, including specified digital products, are exempt from sales and use tax. "Specified digital products" means digital audio-visual works, digital audio works (including ringtones), and digital books. Definitions for these digital products that conform to the Streamlined Sales and Use Tax (SST) Agreement have been adopted. The exemption does not include prewritten computer software, which is taxable. (Sec. 57-39.2-04; Sec. 57-40.2-04)

• Incidence of use tax

The use tax is imposed upon the storage, use, or consumption in the state of tangible personal property purchased at retail (Sec. 57-40.2-02.1, Sec. 57-40.2-06). The use tax is imposed on the consumer (Sec. 57-39.2-02.1, Sec. 57-40.2-13), but the retailer is responsible for collecting and remitting the tax (Sec. 57-40.2-07), unless the retailer has no nexus with the state. The severance of sand, gravel, or coal from the land is a taxable use (Sec. 57-40.2-01(9)).

Purchasers may obtain permits to pay sales or use taxes directly to the Tax Commissioner (Sec. 57-39.2-14.1; see ¶ 717). Retailers are prohibited from reimbursing purchasers or absorbing sales or use tax (Sec. 57-39.2-09, Sec. 57-40.2-08).

Manufactured homes: Effective for taxable events occurring after June 30, 2013, a manufactured home removed from North Dakota for installation in another state is not stored, used, or consumed in North Dakota (Sec. 57-40.2-02.1(2)).

• Nexus

Every retailer engaged in business in North Dakota and making sales of tangible personal property for use in North Dakota, not otherwise exempted, must collect sales or use tax from the purchaser (Sec. 57-39.2-14; Sec. 57-40.2-07(1)). A "retailer maintaining a place of business" in North Dakota includes any retailer (Sec. 57-40.2-01):

— having or maintaining, directly or by subsidiary, an office, distribution house, sales house, warehouse, or other place of business in North Dakota;

— having any agent operating in North Dakota under the authority of the retailer or the subsidiary; and

— engaged in regular or systematic solicitation of sales of tangible personal property in North Dakota by the distribution of catalogs, periodicals, advertising flyers, or other advertising by print, radio, television, mail, telegraphy, telephone, computer database, cable, optic, microwave, or other communication system for the purpose of effecting retail sales of tangible personal property.

• Streamlined Act status

North Dakota is a full member of the Streamlined Sales and Use Tax Agreement with a seat on the Governing Board. It has enacted all of the provisions necessary to comply with the Agreement's requirements and these provisions currently are in effect (Sec. 57-39.4-01). As a full member, it may vote on amendments to or interpretations of the Agreement, and sellers registering under the SST system must collect and remit tax on sales into the state. For details, see ¶ 717.

Taxability matrix: A chart of the taxable status of various items is accessible on the website of the Streamlined Sales Tax Project at **http://www.streamlinedsalestax.org**.

¶712   Tax Base

The sales tax base is the gross receipts of retailers from all retail sales, but the tax is imposed on the purchaser and is added to the purchase price (Sec. 57-39.2-01(3), Sec. 57-39.2-02.1, Sec. 57-39.2-08.2). "Gross receipts" is the total amount of sales made by retailers valued in money. A "retail sale" includes the leasing or renting of tangible personal property; the sale of steam, gas, and communication service (both one-way and two-way) to retail users; the sale of vulcanizing, recapping and retreading services for tires; mail order sales; the sale of hotel, motel, or tourist court accommodations; admissions to entertainment or athletic events; and sales of magazines and other periodicals (Sec. 57-39.2-01(7)).

Manufactured homes: The basis of sales tax on manufactured homes (formerly, mobile homes; see Sec. 57-40.2-02.1 for definition) is (1) gross receipts from all sales at retail of manufactured homes used for residential or business purposes, or (2) the dealer's cost of purchasing a manufactured home sold in conjunction with installation in North Dakota if the tax on gross receipts from retail sales has not previously been paid. (Sec. 57-39.2-02.2).

• Use tax

Use tax is computed upon the fair market value of tangible personal property at the time it was brought into North Dakota for storage, use, or consumption, whether or not it was purchased at retail (Sec. 57-40.2-02.1).

"Purchased at retail" includes completion of fabricating, compounding, or manufacturing of tangible personal property by a person for storage, use, or consumption by that person; the leasing or renting of tangible personal property if its sale, storage, use, or consumption was not previously subjected to North Dakota sales or use tax; the purchase of magazines or other periodicals (excluding newspapers, magazines, or periodicals furnished free to members by nonprofit organizations); the severance of sand or gravel from the soil; the purchase, lease, or rental of tangible personal property from any bank for storage, use, or consumption; and the purchase of an item of tangible personal property by a purchaser who rents or leases it to a person under a finance leasing agreement whereby the property is substantially consumed, if the purchaser elects to treat it as a retail purchase (Sec. 57-40.2-01(5)).

• Sourcing rules

Retail sales must be sourced as follows (Sec. 57-39.2-29; Sec. 57-39.4-11(1)):

— when the product is received by the purchaser at a business location of the seller, the sale is sourced to that business location;

— when the product is not received by the purchaser at a business location of the seller, the sale is sourced to the location where receipt by the purchaser, or the purchaser's designated donee, occurs, including the location indicated by instructions for delivery to the purchaser or donee;

— if neither of the above apply, the sale is sourced to the location indicated by an address for the purchaser that is available from the business records of the seller that are maintained in the ordinary course of the seller's business when use of this address does not constitute bad faith;

— if none of the above apply, the sale is sourced to the location indicated by an address for the purchaser obtained during the consummation of the sale, including the address of a purchaser's payment instrument, if no other address is available, when use of this address does not constitute bad faith;

— if none of the other rules apply, including the circumstance in which the seller is without sufficient information to apply the previous rules, then the location will be determined by the address from which tangible personal property was shipped, from which the digital good or the computer software delivered electronically was first available for transmission by the seller, or from which the service was provided. Any location that merely provided the digital transfer of the product sold is disregarded.

Direct mail: There are separate sourcing provisions for advertising and promotional direct mail and for other direct mail. If a purchaser of advertising and promotional direct mail provides the seller with the jurisdictional delivery information, the seller must source the sale to the jurisdictions where the mail is delivered to recipients and must collect and remit the tax. If a purchaser of advertising or promotional direct mail does not provide a direct pay permit, SST exemption certificate, statement, or jurisdictional delivery information, the sale is sourced to the address from which the tangible personal property was shipped or from which the service was provided. If a purchaser of other direct mail does not provide a direct pay permit or SST exemption certificate, the sale is sourced to the purchaser's address. (Sec. 57-39.2-29, Sec. 57-39.4-14)

Other sourcing rules: Special sourcing rules apply to leases and rentals (Sec. 57-39.4-11(2)) and telecommunications (Sec. 57-39.2-29, Sec. 57-39.4-15).

¶ 713   List of Exemptions, Exceptions, and Exclusions

Unless otherwise indicated, the statutory exemptions, exceptions, and exclusions listed below apply to both sales and use taxes; those applicable only to the use tax are listed separately. Items that are excluded from the sales or use tax base are treated at ¶ 712, "Tax Base."

- **Sales and use tax exemptions, exceptions, and exclusions**

Admissions to educational, religious, and charitable activities	Sec. 57-39.2-04(4)
Agricultural byproducts for the manufacturing or generation of steam or electricity	Sec. 57-39.2-04(34), Sec. 57-40.2-04(15)
Agricultural commodity processing facility	Sec. 57-39.2-04.4
Air carrier transportation property	Sec. 57-39.2-04(38), Sec. 57-40.2-04(21)
Aircraft subject to aircraft excise tax	Sec. 57-39.2-04(37)
All-terrain vehicles	Sec. 57-39.2-04(13), Sec. 57-40.2-04(3), Sec. 57-40.3-01(2), Sec. 57-40.3-02
Ambulances, air ambulances	Sec. 57-40.3-04(16), Sec. 57-40.5-03(6)
Artificial body parts	Sec. 57-39.2-04(26)(b), Sec. 57-40.2-04(12)(b)
Bibles, hymnals, textbooks, and prayerbooks	Sec. 57-39.2-04(25), Sec. 57-40.2-04(11)
Biodiesel or green diesel equipment	Sec. 57-39.2-04(51)

Bladder dysfunction supplies	Sec. 57-39.2-04 (26) (j)
Canadian residents (refund of sales tax)	Sec. 57-39.2-28
Carbon dioxide for enhanced oil or gas recovery	Sec. 57-39.2-04 (49), Sec. 57-40.2-04 (24)
Charitable activities held in a public facility, $10,000 of receipts from	Sec. 57-39.2-04 (4)
Church suppers and bazaars	Sec. 57-39.2-04 (40)
Coal mining machinery for a new mine	Sec. 57-39.2-04.8
Coal that is exempt from coal severance tax (see Secs. 57-61-01.1 and 57-61-01.4), and beneficiated coal	Sec. 57-39.2-1, Sec. 57-40.2-04 (22), (41)
Coinoperated amusement and entertainment machines, gross receipts from	Sec. 57-39.2-04 (56)
Coins, bullion, and currencies	Sec. 57-39.2-04 (31), Sec. 57-40.2-04 (16)
Computer equipment sold to primary sector business	Sec. 57-39.2-04.3 (3)
Construction materials: fertilizer or chemical processing facility	Sec. 57-39.2-[33]
Construction materials: new or expanded liquefied natural gas (LNG) facility	Sec. 57-40.2-03.3 (4) (e))
Crutches	Sec. 57-39.2-04 (26) (e), Sec. 57-40.2-04 (12) (e)
Dentures	Sec. 57-39.2-04 (26) (c), Sec. 57-40.2-04 (12) (c)
Diabetic supplies	Sec. 57-39.2-04 (36)
Digital products	Sec. 57-39.2-04 (26) (c) [54], Sec. 57-40.2-04 (12) (c) [25]
Educational activities held in a public facility, $10,000 of receipts from	Sec. 57-39.2-04 (4)
Electrical generation and production equipment	Sec. 57-39.2-04.2, Sec. 57-40.2-04.2
Electricity	Sec. 57-39.2-04 (27), Sec. 57-40.2-04 (13)
Electronic gaming equipment	Sec. 57-39.2-04 (42), Sec. 57-40.2-04 (24)
Eyeglasses (prescription)	Sec. 57-39.2-04 (26) (d), Sec. 57-40.2-04 (12) (d)
Fairs	Sec. 57-39.2-04 (4)
Farm machinery or irrigation equipment (used), rental of	Sec. 57-39.5-01 (4), Sec. 57-39.5-02
Farm machinery or irrigation equipment and parts (used)	Sec. 57-39.2-04 (45), Sec. 57-40.2-02.1
Federal corporations transactions	Sec. 57-39.2-04 (1), Sec. 57-39.2-04 (6), Sec. 57-40.2-04 (15)
Federal government transactions	Sec. 57-39.2-04 (1), Sec. 57-39.2-04 (6), Sec. 57-40.2-04 (15)

Fertilizer for commercial use	Sec. 57-39.2-04(8), Sec. 57-40.2-04(9)
Flight simulators	Sec. 57-39.2-04(39), Sec. 57-40.2-04(22)
Food and food products	Sec. 57-39.2-04.1, Sec. 57-40.2-04.1
Fuels subject to special tax	Sec. 57-39.2-04(10), Sec. 57-40.2-04(4)
Fuels used for heating purposes	Sec. 57-39.2-04(53)
Gaming tickets	Sec. 57-39.2-04(10)
Gas processing facilities, construction or expansion	Sec. 57-39.2-04.2, Sec. 57-40.2-04.5
Government transactions	Sec. 57-39.2-04(1), Sec. 57-39.2-04(6), Sec. 57-40.2-04(15)
Handicapped persons' prosthetic devices	Sec. 57-39.2-04(26)(a) and (b), Sec. 57-40.2-04(12)(a) and (b)
Hospitals and other medical facilities	Sec. 57-39.2-04(17), Sec. 57-39.2-04(24)
Hotel and motel accommodations for thirty or more consecutive days	Sec. 57-39.2-04(22)
Hydrogen and hydrogen equipment	Sec. 57-39.2-04(50)
Insecticides, fungicides, herbicides, and other agricultural chemicals and supplies	Sec. 57-39.2-04(8), Sec. 57-40.2-04(9)
Insulin	Sec. 57-39.2-04(36)
Internet access services (eff. 7/1/2017)	Sec. 57-39.2-01(21), (22), (23)
Insurance premiums	Sec. 57-39.2-04(10), Sec. 57-40.2-04(4)
Interstate commerce sales	Sec. 57-39.2-04(1)
Irrigation equipment repair parts	Sec. 57-39.2-04(45)
Liquefied natural gas (LNG), sales of from qualified facility	Sec. 57-39.2-04(58)
Livestock and poultry feed	Sec. 57-39.2-04(11), Sec. 57-40.2-04(15)
Lodging for thirty or more consecutive days	Sec. 57-39.2-04(22)
Lottery tickets (North Dakota state lottery only)	Sec. 57-39.2-04(47)
Magazines and periodicals of a nonprofit organization	Sec. 57-39.2-01(9)
Manufacturing equipment for new or expanded plant or recycling facility	Sec. 57-39.2-04.3, Sec. 57-40.2-04(15)
Materials installed out of state when state has no sales tax	Sec. 57-39.2-04(12)
Medical supplies	Sec. 57-39.2-04(24), Sec. 57-39.2-04(26), Sec. 57-40.2-04(12)
Manufactured homes on which sales tax previously paid	Sec. 57-39.2-04(35), Sec. 57-40.2-04(19)

¶713　**North Dakota**

Shut-in meals	Sec. 57-39.2-04(29)
Snowmobiles	Sec. 57-39.2-04(13), Sec. 57-40.2-04(3), Sec. 57-40.3-01(2), Sec. 57-40.3-02
State government	Sec. 57-39.2-04(1), Sec. 57-39.2-04(6), Sec. 57-40.2-04(15)
Steam for processing agricultural products	Sec. 57-39.2-02.1(b)
Student meals	Sec. 57-39.2-04(23)
Telecommunications equipment sold to primary sector business	Sec. 57-39.2-04.3(3)
Telecommunications infrastructure, equipment for	S.B. 2142, Laws 2013; Sec. 57-39-2-01
Textbooks	Sec. 57-39.2-04(5)
Transportation services (common carrier)	Sec. 57-39.2-04(2)
Water	Sec. 57-39.2-04(33), Sec. 57-40.2-04(18)
Wheelchairs	Sec. 57-39.2-04(26)(e), Sec. 57-40.2-04(12)(e)

- **Exemptions, exceptions, and exclusions applicable only to the use tax**

Construction: machinery, equipment, and other tangible personal property used to construct an agricultural commodity processing facility (refund)	Sec. 57-39.2-04.3, Sec. 57-39.2-04.4
Donations by retailers to exempt organizations	Sec. 57-40.2-04(20)
Drop-shipment sales	Sec. 57-40.2-06
Lease or rental of property on which tax was previously paid	Sec. 57-40.2-04(14)
Medical equipment purchased by hospital and installed by a contractor	Sec. 57-40.2-03.3
Railway cars and locomotives used in interstate commerce	Sec. 57-40.2-04(5)
Temporary use of personal property in North Dakota	Sec. 57-40.2-04(2)
Transactions subjected to sales tax	Sec. 57-40.2-04(1)

¶714   Rate of Tax

The general sales and use tax rate is 5% (Sec. 57-39.2-02.1, Sec. 57-40.2-02.1).

- **Reduced rates**

A reduced sales tax rate of 3% is imposed on the gross receipts from sales and on the storage, use, and consumption in North Dakota of manufactured homes, new farm machinery, new irrigation equipment used exclusively for agricultural purposes, and aircraft used exclusively for aerial application of agricultural materials (Sec. 57-40.5-02).

The tax rate imposed on retail sales of natural gas is 1% (Sec. 57-39.2-03.6; Sec. 57-40.2-02.1). Natural gas and fuels used for heating purposes are exempt (Sec. 57-39.2-04(53)).

- **Rate changes**

The effective date of a rate change is the first day of a calendar quarter (Sec. 57-39.4-05). The effective date of a rate change for services covering a period starting before and ending after the statutory effective date is as follows (Sec. 57-39.4-30):

— for a rate increase, the new rate applies to the first billing period starting on or after the effective date; and

— for a rate decrease, the new rate applies to bills rendered on or after the effective date.

If an unconditional contract for the sale of tangible personal property is entered into before the effective date of a sales and use tax rate change, goods delivered before the effective date are subject to the prior rate (Rule Sec. 81-04.1-01-09.1). Goods delivered after the effective date are subject to the new tax rate. If a contract provides for a specific time when title passes, the rate in effect on that day applies. For lease agreements entered into before the date of a rate change, the lease or rental payment is taxed at the rate in effect on the date the payment is due.

• Alcohol and tobacco

The sales (Sec. 57-39.2-03.2) and use (Sec. 57-40.2-03.2) tax on retail sales of alcoholic beverages and tobacco products is 7%.

• Motor vehicles and aircraft

An excise tax on motor vehicles is imposed at the rate of 5% (Sec. 57-40.3-02). Beginning July 1, 2015, a motor vehicle is exempt from the motor vehicle excise tax if it is donated to a qualified North Dakota nonprofit organization that has an established program with the primary purpose of receiving donations of motor vehicles that it then donates to qualifying individuals with a demonstrated need of a motor vehicle necessary to the individual's effort to become a self-sufficient member of the work force (Sec. 57-40.3-04). Transfers of motor vehicles by way of gift between a husband and wife, parent and child, grandparent and grandchild, or brothers and sisters are also exempt (Sec. 57-40.3-04).

The excise tax on aircraft is also imposed at the rate of 5% (Sec. 57-40.5-02). However, aircraft and helicopters designed or modified for exclusive use as agricultural aircraft in the aerial application of agricultural chemicals, insecticides, fungicides, growth regulators, pesticides, dusts, fertilizer, and other agricultural materials are subject to tax at the rate of 3%.

Surcharge on vehicle rentals: Motor vehicles under 10,000 lbs. that are rented for less than 30 days are subject to the 5% state sales tax and a 3% rental surcharge (Sec. 57-39.2-03). Such vehicle rentals are exempt from local taxes (Sec. 57-39.2-04(13)).

• Bingo cards

A 3% bingo cards excise tax is imposed instead of sales tax on gross proceeds from retail sales of bingo cards to final users (Sec. 53-06.1-12).

• Prepaid wireless 911 emergency fee

A prepaid wireless emergency 911 fee of 2% is imposed on the gross receipts of sellers from all sales at retail of prepaid wireless services in North Dakota. The prepaid wireless emergency 911 fee is the liability of the consumer and not of the seller or any provider, except that the seller will be liable to remit all prepaid wireless emergency 911 fees collected from the consumer. The seller may file the prepaid emergency 911 fee return and pay the fees due monthly at the same time that North Dakota sales and use tax is due. (Sec. 57-40.6-02)

¶715   Local Taxes

Home rule counties are authorized to impose a sales tax (Sec. 11-09.1-05). Home rule cities are authorized to levy sales and use taxes (Sec. 40-05.1-06). Home rule counties and cities must enter into collection agreements with the Tax Commissioner (Sec. 57-01-02.1). In addition to sales and use taxes, cities are also authorized to impose local taxes on lodging accommodations, restaurant meals, and on-sale beverages (Sec. 40-57.3-01; Sec. 40-57.3-01.1).

¶715   North Dakota

Local taxing jurisdictions may have different tax bases and rates for fuel used to power motor vehicles, aircraft, locomotives, or watercraft; electricity, piped or natural gas, or other fuels delivered by the seller (Sec. 57-39.4-03). Home rule counties and cities are allowed to have tax treatments and tax rates that are different from the state treatment and rates for sales of fuel used to power motor vehicles, aircraft, locomotives, or watercraft, and all fuels delivered by the seller. If federal law prohibits the imposition of local tax on a product that is subject to state tax, the state may impose an additional tax rate on the product, provided that the rate achieves tax parity for similar products (Sec. 57-39.4-09).

Contractors' limited exemption: The following jurisdictions provide for a limited exemption when a Contractor's Certificate is used: Alexander, Anamoose, Aneta, Bismarck, Bottineau, Burleigh County, Cooperstown, Devils Lake, Dickinson, Drake, Drayton, Dunseith, Edgeley, Enderlin, Fairmount, Fargo, Forman, Fort Ransom, Gackle, Garrison, Glenburn, Glen Ullin, Grenora, Gwinner, Halliday, Hankinson, Hannaford, Hettinger County, Lakota, LaMoure, Leonard, Lidgerwood, Lisbon, Mandan, Max, McVille, Mohall, Morton County, New Salem, Northwood, Page, Ray, Rolla, St. John, Streeter, Surrey, Underwood, Ward County, Washburn, Williston, Wimbledon, Woodworth and Wyndmere (*Guideline, Local Option Taxes By Location*, North Dakota Office of State Tax Commissioner; January 1, 2017)

Sourcing of mobile telecommunications charges: North Dakota has conformed to the federal Mobile Telecommunications Sourcing Act (Act), P.L. 106-252. All charges for mobile telecommunications services are considered to be provided by the customer's home service provider and sourced to the customer's place of primary use (Sec. 57-34.1-04). All such charges are subject to sales tax based on the customer's place of primary use.

The service provider will be held harmless for an error in assigning wireless services to a jurisdiction if it utilizes an electronic database provided by the state or a designated entity, or, if the state has not provided or designated a database, if it utilizes a database that makes assignments based on a nine-digit zip code.

- **Motor vehicle rentals**

Any city may impose a local motor vehicle rental tax at a rate of up to 1% on motor vehicle rentals for periods of fewer than 30 days (Sec. 40-57.3-01.2). The tax is imposed on gross receipts of retailers who are in the primary business of renting motor vehicles for fewer than 30 days. The vehicle must be delivered to the renter at an airport or delivered to a renter who was picked up by the retailer at an airport. Such a tax would be imposed in addition to the state sales tax on motor vehicle rentals.

- **City lodging taxes**

Governing bodies of any city may impose a city tax up to 2% of the gross receipts of leases or rentals of hotel, motel, or tourist court accommodations within the city for periods less than 30 consecutive calendar days or one month. The tax is in addition to the state sales tax on rental accommodations, and taxpayers must add the city lodging taxes to the sales, lease, or rental price and must collect the tax from the consumer. A retailer may not advertise or hold out or state to the public or to any consumer, directly or indirectly, that the city lodging taxes or any part of such taxes imposed will be assumed, absorbed, or refunded by the taxpayer. City lodging taxes are not subject to the Streamlined Sales and Use Tax Act as adopted in North Dakota.

With the exception of home rule cities, collection and administration of the tax are in the hands of the State Tax Commission (Sec. 40-57.3-01). Home rule cities have the option of collecting the lodging tax themselves or contracting with the State Tax Commission for collection of the tax (Sec. 40-57.3-04).

Locally-administered taxes: Fargo, Grand Forks, Minot, Valley City, and West Fargo impose a local lodging tax, however, their taxes are administered locally.

• City lodging and restaurant taxes

In addition to the basic city lodging tax, a city may impose a city lodging and restaurant tax at a rate not to exceed 1%. The tax is imposed on the gross receipts of leases or rentals of hotel, motel, or tourist court accommodations for periods less than 30 consecutive calendar days or one month and upon the gross receipts of restaurant sales of prepared food and beverages, except alcoholic beverages sold for off-premises consumption. The tax is in addition to state and local sales tax on such items. (Sec. 40-57.3-01.1).

• Local tax rates

City sales and use taxes: Local option sales and use tax rates and lodging and restaurant tax rates imposed by North Dakota cities are listed in chart form at **http://www.nd.gov/tax/data/upfiles/media/local-option-taxes_1.pdf?20170222090400**. Updates are posted at least 60 days prior to the start of each quarter at **www.nd.gov/tax/salesanduse**. Local sales and use taxes are subject to maximum dollar amount limitations. The limitations for each city are listed in the chart under Maximum Local Option Tax Due.

All sales that are exempt from state sales and use taxes are also exempt from local taxes. Additional exemptions applicable to each city's sales and use tax are listed in the chart.

A local tax rate lookup tool for any location or address in North Dakota is available at **https://apps.nd.gov/tax/tap/_/**.

Standing Rock Sioux Tribe: Cannon Ball, Fort Yates, Porcupine, Selfridge and Solen are located on Standing Rock Sioux Reservation in Sioux County. They do not have local city taxes, but are subject to the 0.25% tribal local tax. All taxable transactions within Sioux County are subject to one state-level (state or tribe) 5%, 7%, or 3% tax and an additional 0.25% tribal local tax.

¶716   Bracket Schedule

A retailer must determine the amount of tax charged by applying the applicable tax rate to each taxable item or to the total purchase, carried to the third decimal place. Amounts of tax less than one-half cent must be disregarded and amounts of tax of one-half cent or more must be considered an additional cent of tax. When a local sales tax applies, the determination of tax charged to and received from each customer are applied to the aggregated state and local taxes (Sec. 57-39.2-08.2).

¶717   Returns, Payments, and Due Dates

Returns for the preceding calendar quarter must be filed by the last day of the month following the end of the quarter on forms prescribed by the Commissioner (Sec. 57-39.2-11, Sec. 57-40.2-13). The return must be signed by the retailer or a duly authorized agent under penalty of perjury. The Tax Commissioner may prescribe alternative methods for signing, subscribing, or verifying a return filed by electronic means, including telecommunications, that shall have the same validity and consequence as the actual signature and written declaration for a paper return.

Payment of sales tax for the preceding period accompanies the return (Sec. 57-39.2-12(1), Sec. 57-39.2-12(2), Sec. 57-40.2-07(4), Sec. 57-40.2-07(6)). Sales and use tax is payable in quarterly installments due by the last day of the month following each calendar quarter. If taxable sales for the preceding calendar year were $333,000 or more, sales and use tax is payable monthly by the last day of the following month, except that tax collected during May in odd-numbered years is payable by June 22.

If a business is sold or discontinued, a final sales tax return must be filed within 15 days. Payment of the tax is due immediately prior to the sale and becomes delinquent and subject to penalties 15 days after the sale (Sec. 59-39.2-12(1), Sec. 57-40.2-07(4), Rule Sec. 81-04.1-01-06).

Direct payment: The Tax Commissioner may issue a direct payment permit authorizing the holder to pay sales and use tax directly to the Commissioner and not to the retailer (Sec. 57-39.2-14.1). The retailer is relieved of any liability or obligation to collect sales or use tax if the permit holder provides a direct payment certificate in the form prescribed by the Commissioner. The application for a direct payment permit is a letter stating the applicant's name, address, and sales and use tax account number; a description of the business, accounting system, and volume of purchases; and justification for adopting the direct payment method (Rule 81-04.1-01-05).

SST registrants: Streamlined Sales and Use Tax (SST) registrants who have voluntarily registered to collect North Dakota sales and use tax, and who have not contracted with a certified service provider (CSP), must file an annual sales tax return at the end of each calendar year. These taxpayers must also file an annual return each time they have collected $1,000 of state and local tax. The annual return period ending December 31 includes the time period since the last return was filed. Voluntary registrants who have not contracted with a CSP must file the December 31 return even if they made no sales in North Dakota or collected no tax during the reporting period. The return is due January 31 of the following year.

Internet filing: Taxpayers may register online for North Dakota's NDTAP program, which allows taxpayers to file sales tax returns and pay sales tax via the Internet, at **https://apps.nd.gov/tax/tap/_/**.

Retailers who are required to file monthly sales and use tax returns must file the returns electronically (Sec. 57-39.2-12).

Collection allowance: A retailer that pays tax when due may deduct 1.5% of the sales and use tax owed as reimbursement for administrative expenses (Secs. 57-39.2-12.1, 57-40.2-07.1). Reimbursement for businesses filing on a monthly basis may not exceed an aggregate of $110 (previously, $90.75) per return for taxable periods beginning after June 30, 2013. The Tax Commissioner may allow a retailer who fails to timely file a return or pay the tax due to deduct and retain the retailer compensation, provided good cause is shown (Secs. 57-39.2-12.1(5), 57-40.2-07.1(5)).

Certified service providers (CSPs) may deduct and retain a monetary allowance for taxes collected and remitted on behalf of remote sellers who are registered to collect tax in North Dakota. Remote sellers who are registered to collect the tax and use a certified automated system (CAS) may deduct and retain a monetary allowance. "Remote seller" means a retailer that does not have an adequate physical presence to establish nexus in North Dakota for sales and use tax purposes (Secs. 57-39.2-12.1, 57-40.2-07.1).

- **Uniform Sales Tax Administration Act**

North Dakota enacted the Uniform Sales and Use Tax Administration Act and legislation conforming its sales and use tax laws to provisions of the Streamlined Sales and Use Tax Agreement, effective October 1, 2005 (Ch. 582 (S.B. 2050), Laws 2005; Ch. 581 (S.B. 2359), Laws 2005).

The Agreement establishes performance standards for multistate sellers and standards for certification of a certified service provider (CSP), an agent certified by the states to perform all of a seller's sales and use tax functions, and a certified automated system (CAS), software certified by the states to calculate the tax imposed, determine the amount to remit, and maintain a record of the transaction.

Sourcing: North Dakota uses destination-based sourcing for general retail sales. See ¶ 712.

Registration: See ¶ 719.

Returns: Only a single tax return need be filed for each tax period, including all jurisdictions in the state in which a seller is taxable. A simplified electronic return (SER) may be filed under certain circumstances (57-39.4-19).

For additional information on the uniform act and agreement, see "Streamlined Sales Tax Project," listed in the Table of Contents.

¶718   Prepayment of Taxes

There are no statutory provisions for prepayment of sales and use tax.

¶719   Vendor Registration

Retailers may not transact business in North Dakota without a permit issued by the Tax Commissioner (Sec. 57-39.2-14, Sec. 57-40.2-07(1)). Persons with nexus in North Dakota who make taxable sales in North Dakota or who make sales destined for North Dakota are subject to permit requirements (Rule Sec. 81-04.1-01-03.1).

New businesses may register at **http://www.nd.gov/businessreg/**.

• Permit requirements

A permit must be issued for each separate place of business in North Dakota and must be conspicuously displayed (Sec. 57-39.2-14, Sec. 57-40.2-07(1)). A permit may not be assigned and is valid only for the person in whose name it is issued and for transaction of business at the place designated in the permit.

When a retail business is sold, the holder of the sales tax permit must notify the Tax Commissioner immediately and surrender the permit for cancellation (Rule Sec. 81-04.1-01-06). A new permit must be applied for by the purchaser of a business, if a business changes from one type of ownership to another, and if one or more partners enter or leave a partnership.

Permits are effective until revoked by the Commissioner (Sec. 57-39.2-14).

Special event requirements: The promoter or organizer of a special event that has 10 or more sellers must provide a list of the sellers to the North Dakota State Tax Commissioner. The list is due within 20 days following the event. A promoter or organizer of an event organized for the exclusive benefit of a nonprofit organization does not have to submit a list of sellers (Sec. 57-39.2-10.1).

"Special event" means an entertainment, amusement, recreation, or marketing event that occurs at a single location on a recurring or irregular basis and where sales, displays, or promotional activities occur. Special events include auto shows, boat shows, gun shows, sport shows, knife shows, home shows, craft shows, flea markets, carnivals, circuses, bazaars, fairs, and art or other merchandise displays or exhibits.

• SST registration

To register under the Streamlined Sales and Use Tax Agreement (SST), sellers must go to **https://www.sstregister.org**. Sellers can also update previously submitted registration information at this website. The information provided will be sent to all of the full member states and to associate members for which the seller chooses to collect.

When a seller registers under the Agreement, it must select the certified technology model it will be using (or it must select "Other" if it will not be using one of the certified models). The models are the following:

Model One: Certified Service Provider (CSP), an agent certified under the Agreement to perform all the seller's sales and use tax functions;

Model Two: Certified Automated System (CAS), software certified under the Agreement to calculate the appropriate tax (for which the seller retains responsibility for remitting);

Model Three: Certified System (CS), a proprietary automated sales tax system certified under the Agreement.

¶718   North Dakota

A model two, model three, or model four seller may elect to be registered in one or more states as a seller that anticipates making no sales into the state or states if it has not had sales into the state or states for the preceding 12 months. This election does not relieve the seller of its agreement to collect taxes on all sales into the states or its liability for remitting to the proper states any taxes collected. A seller is not relieved of any legal obligation it may have under a state's laws to register in that state. A seller is also not relieved of its obligation to collect and remit taxes for at least 36 months in a state and meet all other requirements for amnesty under the SST Agreement in order to be eligible for amnesty in the state. (Sec. 57-39.4-04)

Whenever a new state joins the SST Agreement, model one sellers will automatically be registered in the new state. Model two, three, and four sellers will also be automatically registered in the new state, but they may register as a seller that anticipates making no sales into the new state. Upon registration, the SST Governing Board will provide information regarding simplified electronic returns and remittances in any member state. A member state may provide information on tax return filing options in the state. (Sec. 57-39.4-04)

¶720 Sales or Use Tax Credits

Effective July 1, 2017, retailers that collect excess sales or use taxes from a customer and then properly refund such excess taxes to the customer are required to file an amended return for the period the excess tax was collected and then file a claim for refund (Sec. 57-39.2-27, Sec. 57-40.2-17). Previously, such retailers had to deduct the refunded taxes as a credit on their next return.

Use tax credits are allowed in many instances for sales taxes paid other states or counties.

¶721 Deficiency Assessments

If an incorrect or insufficient return is filed, the Tax Commissioner may estimate the amount of tax that is due on the basis of external factors, such as the number of employees, rentals paid, and stock on hand. The person liable for the tax must be given a notice of determination (Sec. 57-39.2-15).

Settlement: Effective August 1, 2015, the North Dakota Tax Commissioner may accept, for legal settlement purposes, a reduced amount of any tax administered and collected by the Commissioner if information is received from the taxpayer that the tax, as assessed, exceeds the actual amount due and the assessed tax is final and nonreviewable. However, if the Commissioner receives information that the tax was under assessed, the additional amount of tax that is determined to be due may be assessed by the Commissioner, even though the assessment made is final and nonreviewable. (Sec. 57-01-11)

¶722 Audit Procedures

The Commissioner may investigate or examine a taxpayer's books, records, memoranda, computer printouts, accounts, vouchers, corporate or committee minutes, and any other pertinent documents; tangible personal property, equipment, and computer systems; and business facilities, plants, and shops (Sec. 57-39.2-21, Rule Sec. 81-01.1-01-03). All items and places must be made available to the Tax Commissioner upon request.

The Commissioner may require the taxpayer to be present to answer questions, provide testimony, and submit proof of material or information being examined. The Tax Commissioner's examination or investigation may extend to any person with access to information that may be relevant to a taxpayer's audit (Rule Sec. 81-01.1-01-03).

Exemptions: Sellers are allowed 120 days after a request for substantiation of an exemption to obtain a fully completed exemption certificate or other information establishing the exemption). An exemption certificate must claim an exemption that was statutorily available on the date of the transaction in the jurisdiction where the transaction is sourced, that could be applicable to the item being purchased, and that is reasonable for the purchaser's type of business. If a seller obtains an exemption certificate or other exemption information, the seller must be relieved of any liability unless the seller knew the information was false or the seller intended to evade the tax. (Sec. 57-39.4-18)

Contract auditing: With certain safeguards, the State Tax Commissioner can authorize others to audit taxpayers on its behalf (Sec. 57-39.4-02).

¶ 723   Statute of Limitations

A notice of determination resulting from an incorrect or insufficient return must be given within three years after the date the return was due or filed, whichever is later (Sec. 57-39.2-15). If the tax due exceeds the amount paid by 25% or more, the notice of tax due must be given within six years after the date the return was due or filed, whichever is later. If a taxpayer fails to file a return, the notice of determination may be given up to six years after the date the return was due. If a return contains fraudulent information or if failure to file a return is caused by fraudulent intent or willful attempt to evade payment of the tax, no limitations period applies. The determination of tax due becomes final and irrevocable unless the taxpayer files a written protest within 30 days after the notice of determination is given.

Extension of assessment period: The assessment period may be extended by written agreement between the Tax Commissioner and the taxpayer (Sec. 57-39.2-15.1). The extension may be further extended by subsequent written agreements prior to the expiration of the period previously agreed upon. However, no additional extension may be made for more than one year from the date of the extension agreement. If the taxpayer agrees to an extension of time for assessment of tax, the time for refund claims is similarly extended.

¶ 724   Application for Refund

Effective July 1, 2017, a taxpayer must file a claim for refund with the Tax Commissioner within three years after the due date of the return or the date the return was filed, whichever is later. For purposes of this provision, "taxpayer" means a person who is required under sales or use tax laws to file a return and who has remitted the tax for which a refund is claimed. (Sec. 57-39.2-[new]; S.B. 2129, Laws 2017)

Previously, a person who made an erroneous payment had to present a claim for refund or credit to the commissioner not later than three years after the due date of the return for the period for which the erroneous payment was made or one year after the erroneous payment was made, whichever was later (former Sec. 57-39.2-2.24).

The Tax Commissioner must approve the payment of any refund (Sec. 57-39.2-25(1)). Interest of 10% accrues on overpayment of tax beginning 60 days after the later of the due date of the return, the date the return was filed, or the date the tax was fully paid, until the date of the refund.

The Tax Commissioner must notify a taxpayer if a claim for refund or credit is disallowed (Sec. 57-39.2-25(2)). The Tax Commissioner's decision is final and irrevocable unless the taxpayer files a written protest within 30 days after the date of the notice.

¶ 726   Scope of Tax

Source.—Statutory references are to Chapters 5739 and 5741 of the Ohio Revised Code, as amended to date. Details are reported in the CCH OHIO TAX REPORTS starting at ¶ 60-000.

The Ohio sales tax applies to all retail sales, unless otherwise exempt (Sec. 5739.02). "Sale" and "selling" are defined to include all sales of tangible personal property (unless exempt) and the sale of certain specified services (Sec. 5739.01(B)(1)).

The use tax applies to tangible personal property stored, used, or consumed in Ohio, including self-produced property, unless otherwise exempt (Sec. 5741.02(E)). It also applies to taxable services when the benefit of the service is realized in Ohio. The use tax is a complementary tax and does not apply in situations where the Ohio sales tax has been collected and paid (Sec. 5741.02(C)(1)).

Digital products and services: The sale of digital products transferred electronically, such as downloaded books, music, or ideos, is exempt. However, digital products that fall within definitions of "electronic information services" or "electronic publishing" are taxable when sold for use in a business (Sec. 5739.01(B)(3)(e); Sec. 5739.01(Y)(1)(c); Sec. 5739.01(LLL); OAC 5703-9-46(B); see also *Sales and Use Tax Information Release ST 1999-04,* Ohio Department of Taxation, September 23, 2016, CCH OHIO TAX REPORTS, ¶ 404-538).

Electronically transferred digital audiovisual works, digital audio works, or digital books provided for permanent or less than permanent use are taxable, regardless of whether or not continued payment is required (Sec. 5739.01(B)(12)). "Specified digital product" means an electronically transferred digital audiovisual work, digital audio work, or digital book. "Digital audiovisual work" means a series of related images that, when shown in succession, impart an impression of motion, together with accompanying sounds, if any. "Digital audio work" means a work that results from the fixation of a series of musical, spoken, or other sounds, including digitized sound files that are downloaded onto a device and that may be used to alert the customer with respect to a communication. "Digital book" means a work that is generally recognized in the ordinary and usual sense as a book. These definitions apply to transactions on or after January 1, 2014. (Sec. 5739.01(QQQ))

Cloud computing: A taxpayer's provision to its customers of hosted software applications via access to the taxpayer's computer hardware in order to support customers' telecommunications equipment was subject to Ohio sales tax because the service constituted automatic data processing. The cloud-based service qualified as automatic data processing because the taxpayer was providing its customers with access to computer equipment to process data. However, the service is sourced to Ohio only if the benefit of the service is received in Ohio (*i.e.,* the customer is located in Ohio and accesses the service from a location in Ohio). Furthermore, the charges for hosting services were also taxable because they were part of the price of the automatic data processing service. The software and hardware used to provide the cloud-based service were not subject Ohio use tax because they were located outside of Ohio. (*Opinion of the Tax Commissioner, No. 14-0001,* Ohio Department of Taxation, February 4, 2014, CCH OHIO TAX REPORTS, ¶ 404-196)

- **Incidence of tax**

The incidence of both the sales and use taxes is on the purchasers or consumers, but sellers or sellers are required to collect and remit such taxes to the state. There is, however, a separate excise tax on retailers to ensure that sellers or sellers collect and remit the consumers' taxes (Sec. 5739.10).

If a seller collects the tax and fails to remit it, the seller is personally responsible for the money. If the seller fails to collect the tax, the Tax Commissioner can collect the tax from either the seller or the consumer on the basis of any information in his possession. Both seller and consumer are personally liable for uncollected tax (Sec. 5739.13).

Use tax: Responsibility for payment of the use tax lies with the consumer, and this responsibility is not extinguished until the tax has been paid to the state or to a seller (Sec. 5741.02(B)).

Drop shipments: When all the parties are located in the state, the retailer typically furnishes a resale certificate to the primary seller, rendering the first sale a nontaxable transaction. The retailer then collects sales tax on behalf of the state on the secondary sale to its customer. However, different considerations arise when one or more of the parties are not within the state. (*Sales and Use Tax Information Release ST 1989-01,* Ohio Department of Taxation, November 1989, CCH OHIO TAX REPORTS, ¶ 403-363)

Ohio exempts the sale of the primary (or initial) Ohio seller to an out-of-state retailer provided that the purchaser furnishes a resale exemption certificate from its state. The secondary sale is also exempt when it is made by an out-of-state retailer who lacks Ohio nexus. In this situation, the ultimate consumer is liable for use tax because sales tax has not previously been paid. (Sec. 5741.02(B))

• **Services subject to sales tax**

The following services are subject to sales tax (Sec. 5739.01(B)(2)—(B)(5); Sec. 5739.01(B)(11)):

— furnishing of lodging by a hotel to transient guests;

— repairing or installing tangible personal property (other than property the sale of which would be exempt or, with respect to installation services, property incorporated into a public utility service system);

— washing, cleaning, waxing, polishing, or painting motor vehicles;

— laundry and dry cleaning services;

— automatic data processing, computer services, or electronic information services provided to businesses when the object of the transaction is such services;

— telecommunications services sold by a telephone company;

— satellite broadcasting services;

— landscaping and lawn care services; snow removal services;

— private investigation and security services;

— building maintenance and janitorial services (except certain cleaning; see *Sales Tax Information Release ST 2002-04,* Ohio Department of Taxation, September 14, 2015, CCH OHIO TAX REPORTS, ¶ 404-363);

— employment and employment placement services;

— exterminating services;

— personal care services, such as skin care, the application of cosmetics, manicuring, pedicuring, hair removal, tattooing, body piercing, tanning, and massage;

— motor vehicle towing services;

— certain intrastate motor vehicle and aircraft passenger services;

— physical fitness facility and recreation or sports club services;

— storage services;

— printing and photographic services;

— certain production and fabrication services;

— health care services provided or arranged by a Medicaid health-insuring corporation for Medicaid enrollees residing in Ohio under the corporation's contract with the state.

Bundled telecommunications and cable services: If telecommunications services, mobile telecommunications services, or cable television services are sold bundled in a transaction with other distinct services for a single price that is not itemized, the entire price is taxable, unless the seller can reasonably identify the nontaxable portion using its books and records kept in the regular course of business (Sec. 5739.01(H)(1)(b)(4)). Upon a consumer's request, the seller must disclose the selling price for the taxable services included in the selling price for the taxable and nontaxable services billed on an aggregated basis.

Professional employer organizations (PEOs): Shared employees whose services are subject to sales tax are considered the employees of the client employer for purposes of collecting and levying sales tax on the services performed by the shared employee. A client employer or PEO will not be relieved of any sales tax liability with respect to its goods or services. (Sec. 4125.041)

• Use tax

The use tax complements the sales tax, protecting Ohio merchants from discrimination arising from the inability of the state to impose a sales tax on sales made to Ohio residents by merchants of other states (Sec. 5741.02). It applies to the storage, use, or other consumption in Ohio of tangible personal property or the receipt of benefit in Ohio arising from the purchase of any taxable service.

The use tax is not imposed if the sales tax has already been imposed and paid (Sec. 5741.02(C)(1)) or if the sales tax does not apply (Sec. 5741.02(C)(2)). However, if property or services originally exempt as purchases for resale are subsequently stored, used, or consumed in a taxable manner, they are subject to tax (Sec. 5741.02(D)).

• Nexus

Ohio has no statutory definition of "engaged in the business of selling tangible personal property in this state." However, it does specifically define "nexus" and "substantial nexus" in the context of a taxpayer's level of business activity in the state. "Nexus with the state" means that a seller engages in continuous and widespread solicitation of purchases from Ohio residents or otherwise purposefully directs its business activities at Ohio residents (Sec. 5741.01(H)).

Substantial nexus: "Substantial nexus with the state" means that a seller has sufficient contact with Ohio, in accordance with the U.S. Constitution's Commerce Clause, to allow Ohio to require the seller to collect and remit use tax on sales of tangible personal property or services made to consumers in Ohio (Sec. 5741.01(I)(1)). Specifically, effective July 1, 2015, substantial nexus is presumed to exist if a seller does any of the following (Sec. 5741.01(I)(2)):

— Uses an office, distribution facility, warehouse, storage facility, or similar place of business within Ohio, whether operated by the seller or any other person, other than a common carrier acting in its capacity as a common carrier (Sec. 5741.01(I)(2)(a));

— Regularly uses employees, agents, representatives, solicitors, installers, repairers, salespersons, or other persons in Ohio for the purpose of conducting the business of the seller or either to engage in a business with the same or a similar industry classification as the seller selling a similar product or line of products as the seller, or to use trademarks, service marks, or trade names in Ohio that are the same or substantially similar to those used by the seller (Sec. 5741.01(I)(2)(b));

— Uses any person, other than a common carrier acting in its capacity as a common carrier, in Ohio for any of the following purposes (Sec. 5741.01(I)(2)(c)):

(i) Receiving or processing orders of the seller's goods or services;

(ii) Using that person's employees or facilities in Ohio to advertise, promote, or facilitate sales by the seller to customers;

(iii) Delivering, installing, assembling, or performing maintenance services for the seller's customers;

(iv) Facilitating the seller's delivery of tangible personal property to customers in Ohio by allowing the seller's customers to pick up property sold by the seller at an office, distribution facility, warehouse, storage facility, or similar place of business.

— Makes regular deliveries of tangible personal property into Ohio by means other than common carrier (Sec. 5741.01(I)(2)(d));

— Has an affiliated person that has substantial nexus with Ohio (Sec. 5741.01(I)(2)(e));

— Owns tangible personal property that is rented or leased to a consumer in Ohio, or offers tangible personal property, on approval, to consumers in Ohio (Sec. 5741.01(I)(2)(f));

— Enters into an agreement with one or more residents of Ohio under which the resident, for a commission or other consideration, directly or indirectly refers potential customers to the seller, whether by a link on a web site, an in-person oral presentation, telemarketing, or otherwise, provided the cumulative gross receipts from sales to consumers referred to the seller by all such residents exceeded ten thousand dollars during the preceding twelve months (Sec. 5741.01(I)(2)(g)). This provision is commonly known as "click-through nexus."

After July 1, 2015, the following criteria no longer form the basis for a presumption of substantial nexus: (1) a seller's registration to do business in Ohio and (2) any other contact with Ohio that forms the basis of substantial nexus as permitted under the U.S. Constitution's Commerce Clause.

Rebuttal of presumption: The presumption may be rebutted by demonstrating that the persons with whom the seller had agreements did not engage in activities that were significantly associated with the seller's ability to establish or maintain a market in Ohio (Sec. 5741.01(I)(4)). The presumption of substantial nexus for other specified activities performed by the seller or an affiliated person may also be rebutted if it can be shown that those activities did nothing to establish or maintain a market for the seller in Ohio (Sec. 5741.01(I)(3)).

An "affiliated person" is any person that is a member of the same controlled group of corporations as the seller or any other person that, notwithstanding the form of organization, bears the same ownership relationship to the seller as a corporation that is a member of the same controlled group of corporations (Sec. 5741.01(I)(6)(a)).

The Ohio Department of Taxation has updated an information release explaining the nexus standards that are applied to determine whether an out-of-state seller is required to collect and remit Ohio use tax from its customers in Ohio (*Use Tax Information Release ST 2001-01*, Ohio Department of Taxation, August 11, 2016, CCH OHIO TAX REPORTS, ¶ 404-523).

• **Streamlined Act status**

Ohio is a full member of the Streamlined Sales and Use Tax Agreement (SSUTA). As a full member, it may vote on amendments to or interpretations of the Agreement, and sellers registering under the SST system must collect and remit tax on sales into the state. For additional information on Ohio's implementation of the SSUTA, see ¶ 727 and ¶ 732.

A taxability matrix of the taxable status of various items is accessible on the website of the Streamlined Sales Tax Project at **http://www.streamlinedsalestax.org**.

¶ 727   Tax Base

Ohio sales and use taxes are generally based on "price" as defined by the statute. Other provisions govern what other amounts are considered to be part of the "price," and therefore subject to the tax.

• **"Price" defined**

The term "price" means the aggregate value in money of anything paid or delivered, or promised to be paid or delivered, in the complete performance of a retail sale (Sec. 5739.01(H)(1)), or in a transaction by which tangible personal property is purchased or a service provided for storage, use, or other consumption or benefit in Ohio (Sec. 5741.01(G)).

The price is the amount charged before any deductions on account of the cost of the property sold, the cost of materials used, labor or service costs, interest or discount paid or allowed after the sale is consummated, delivery charges, installation charges, or exempt property bundled with taxable property. Price does not include the tax unless the seller establishes to the Tax Commissioner's satisfaction that the tax has been added to the price. Price also does not include unreimbursed discounts or coupons, or separately stated interest or taxes (Sec. 5739.01(H)(1)(b), Sec. 5741.01(G)).

Mandatory service charges that include gratuities for waiters or others are included in the tax base.

• **Sourcing of sales**

Ohio conforms with the sourcing provisions of the SST Agreement. All sales must be sourced as follows:

— if the consumer or the consumer's donee receives tangible personal property or service at a seller's place of business, the sale must be sourced to that place of business (Sec. 5739.033(C)(1));

— if the tangible personal property or service is not received at the seller's place of business, the sale must be sourced to the location known to the seller where the consumer, or the consumer's donee, receives the tangible personal property, including any location indicated by instructions for delivery to the consumer or donee (Sec. 5739.033(C)(2));

— if neither of these standards is met, the sale is sourced to the location indicated by the consumer's address as available from the seller's business records, provided the address is not used in bad faith (Sec. 5739.033(C)(3));

— in the event these standards are not met, the sale must be sourced to the location indicated by an address for the consumer obtained by the seller during the consummation of the sale, including the address associated with the consumer's payment instrument, and provided that the use of this address does not constitute bad faith (Sec. 5739.033(C)(4));

— if none of the above described circumstances are met, including in a situation in which the seller does not have sufficient information to apply them, the sale will be sourced to the address from which tangible personal property was shipped or the service provided (Sec. 5739.033(C)(5)). In making this determination, however, any location serving merely to provide the electronic transfer of the property sold or the service provided is disregarded (Sec. 5739.033(C)(6)).

Additional sourcing rules apply for direct payment permit holders (Sec. 5739.031(C)), lodging (Sec. 5739.033(E)), leases and rentals (Sec. 5739.033(G)), transportation (Sec. 5739.033(F)), and titled motor vehicles, watercraft, and outboard motors (Sec. 5741.05(A)). Sourcing of direct mail is explained in *Sales Tax Information Release ST 2013-01*, Ohio Department of Taxation, August 16, 2013, CCH OHIO TAX REPORTS, ¶ 404-139.

Consumer protection: Consumers are protected from additional sales tax liability when they remit sales tax to a seller in an amount invoiced by the seller on the basis of the location where the consumer receives tangible personal property or a digital good, or where the seller receives the order. (Sec. 5739.033(B)(2)).

Sourcing of mobile telecommunications charges: Ohio has conformed to the federal Mobile Telecommunications Sourcing Act (Act), P.L. 106-252. All charges for mobile telecommunications services are considered to be provided by the customer's home service provider and sourced to the customer's place of primary use (S.B. 143, Laws 2002). All such charges are subject to sales tax based on the customer's place of primary use.

The service provider will be held harmless for an error in assigning wireless services to a jurisdiction if it utilizes an electronic database provided by the state or a designated entity, or, if the state has not provided or designated a database, if it utilizes a database that makes assignments based on a nine-digit zip code.

¶728 List of Exemptions, Exceptions, and Exclusions

Unless otherwise indicated, the statutory exemptions, exceptions, and exclusions listed below apply to both sales and use taxes; those applicable only to the use tax are listed separately. Items that are excluded from the sales or use tax base are treated at ¶727, "Tax Base."

Tax holidays: A sales tax holiday for school supplies, instructional materials, and clothing took place from August 5, 2016, through August 7, 2016, only (S.B. 264, Laws 2016). During that weekend, an exemption applied to school supplies with a price of $20 or less, clothing with a price of $75 or less, and school instructional materials with a price of $20 or less. A similar sales tax holiday also took place in 2015.

• Sales and use tax exemptions, exceptions, and exclusions

Advertising	Sec. 5739.02(B)(37), Sec. 5739.01(Y)(2)(k)
Aircraft in fractional ownership, parts and services for	Sec. 5739.02(B)(45)
Aircraft, repair parts and maintenance services	Sec. 5739.02(B)(49)
Agriculture	Sec. 5739.01(E)(2), Sec. 5739.02(B)(17), Sec. 5739.02(B)(24), Sec. 5739.02(B)(30), Sec. 5739.02(B)(31), Sec. 5739.02(B)(36), Sec. 5739.02(B)(42)
Alternative fuel (local tax exemption)	Sec. 5735.40
Animal shelters	Sec. 5739.02(B)(12), Sec. 5739.02(B)(29)
Arts performances	Sec. 5739.02(B)(12)
Auction sales	Sec. 5739.01(L), Sec. 5739.02(B)(8)
Automatic data processing and computer services	Sec. 5739.01(Y)(1), Sec. 5739.01(Y)(2)
Bees	Sec. 5739.01(E)(2), Sec. 5739.02(B)(17), Sec. 5739.02(B)(38)
Bullion and coins for investment	Sec. 5739.02(B)(54) (eff. 01/01/2017)

Cable television services, interactive	Sec. 5739.01(AA)
Candy	Sec. 5739.02(B)(2), Sec. 5741.02(C)(2)
Casual sales	Sec. 5739.02(B)(8)
Charitable contributions via 900 numbers	Sec. 5739.01(FF)
Churches	Sec. 5739.02(B)(9), Sec. 5739.02(B)(12)
Coin-operated car wash sales	Sec. 5739.01(E)
Coin-operated refrigerated food vending machines	Sec. 5739.02(B)(37)(c)
Community centers	Sec. 5739.02(B)(12)
Computer data centers	Sec. 122.175
Computer equipment sold to individual licensed or certified to teach and use in elementary or secondary schools	Sec. 5739.02(B)(40)
Computer equipment leased and stored in Ohio for up to 90 days ...	Sec. 5741.02(c)(8)
Computer services	Sec. 5739.01(Y)(1), Sec. 5739.01(Y)(2)
Construction materials and services	Sec. 5739.02(B)(13)
Controlled circulation publications	Sec. 5739.02(B)(4)
Convention center, building materials	Sec. 5739.02(B)(13)
Crude oil production property and services	Sec. 5739.01(E)(2)
Dairy processing cleaning equipment and supplies	Sec. 5739.011(B)(13)
Dental services	Sec. 5739.01(C), Sec. 5739.01(D)(2)
Deposits on beverage containers or cases	Sec. 5739.01(H)(1)
Digital advertising services (eff. 10/12/2016)	Sec. 5739.01(Y)(2)(k)
Direct marketing items	Sec. 5739.02(B)(37)(b)
Direct selling entities, sales of equipment and software for warehouse use	Sec. 5739.02(B)(48)
Drugs prescribed for humans	Sec. 5739.02(B)(18)
Educational institutions, nonprofit	Sec. 5739.02(B)(12)
Egg handling and cleaning; transportation of eggs	Sec. 5739.02(B)(24)
Electricity providers, property and services sold to and used by	Sec. 5739.02(B)(43)
Electronic information service providers, equipment purchased by (25% refund; see ¶ 739)	Sec. 5739.071(A)
Electronic publishing	Sec. 5739.02(B)(42)(n)
Employer-provided meals	Sec. 5739.02(B)(5)
Energy converstion equipment	Sec. 5739.02(B)(40), Sec. 5727.01(O)
Energy conversion facilities	Sec. 5709.50
Farming property	Sec. 5739.01(E)(2), Sec. 5739.02(B)(17)
Fire protection vehicles and equipment	Sec. 5739.02(B)(20)
Fishing, commercial	Sec. 5739.01(E)(6), Sec. 5739.02(B)(42), Sec. 5741.02(C)(2)
Flight simulators, replacement parts, and services	Sec. 5739.02(B)(50)

Manufacturing	Sec. 5739.01 (E) (2), Sec. 5739.01 (E) (9), Sec. 5739.011
Meals, employees	Sec. 5739.02 (B) (5)
Meals, students	Sec. 5739.02 (B) (3)
Medical devices	Sec. 5739.02 (B) (19)
Medical services	Sec. 5739.01 (C), Sec. 5739.01 (D) (2)
Mining	Sec. 5739.01 (E) (2), Sec. 5741.02 (C) (2)
Motion pictures, copyrighted	Sec. 5739.01 (B) (5), Sec. 5741.01 (D)
Motor fuel subject to excise tax	Sec. 5739.02 (B) (6)
Motor vehicle emission inspection certificates, fees charged for	Sec. 5739.02 (B) (26)
Motor vehicles (not titled in state) sold to nonresidents	Sec. 5739.02 (B) (23)
Motor vehicles used primarily for highway transportation of property for hire	Sec. 5739.01 (Z), Sec. 5739.02 (B) (33)
Natural gas, property used or consumed directly in production of . . .	Sec. 5739.01 (E) (2)
Natural gas, providing services to those engaged in production of or exploration for	Sec. 5739.01 (E) (2)
Newspapers, including community newspapers	Sec. 5739.02 (B) (4)
Nonprofit organizations	Sec. 5739.02 (B) (9), Sec. 5739.02 (B) (12)
Nurserymen	Sec. 5739.01 (E) (2), Sec. 5739.02 (B) (17)
Occasional sales	Sec. 5739.02 (B) (8)
Optical services	Sec. 1785.01 (A)
Out-of-state, items used (certain purchases of)	Sec. 5739.02 (B) (21)
Oxygen and oxygen dispensing equipment	Sec. 5739.02 (B) (18)
Packaging	Sec. 5739.01 (E) (2), Sec. 5739.02 (B) (15)
Parent/teacher associations (PTA)	Sec. 5739.02 (B) (12)
Personal or professional services	Sec. 5739.01 (B) (5), Sec. 5739.01 (Y) (2)
Pollution control equipment	Sec. 5709.25
Portable grain bins	Sec. 5739.02 (B) (32)
Prepaid telephone calling card transactions, transfers of	Sec. 5739.01 (B) (8)
Printed matter, items used or consumed in producing and preparing for sale	Sec. 5739.01 (E) (8), Sec. 5739.01 (E) (14)
Professional sports teams, leases to by county	Sec. 5739.02 (B) (52)
Prosthetic devices for humans	Sec. 5739.02 (B) (19)
Public broadcasting	Sec. 5739.02 (B) (12)
Public utilities (natural gas, water, steam) delivered via wires, pipes, or conduits	Sec. 5739.02 (B) (7)

• Exemptions, exclusions, and exceptions applicable only to the use tax

Property or services exempt from the sales tax .... Sec. 5741.02(C)(2)

Property or services upon which taxes have been paid to another
jurisdiction, to the extent of the amount of tax actually paid to
the other jurisdiction .... Sec. 5741.02(C)(5)

Transient use of property purchased out-of-state by tourist, or
nonresident for nonbusiness use .... Sec. 5741.02(C)(4)

¶729   Rate of Tax

The permanent rate of the state sales and use taxes is 5.75% (Sec. 5739.02(A), Sec. 5741.02(A)).

• Privilege tax directly on seller

In addition to the sales tax, Ohio statutes subject sellers to an excise tax on the privilege of making sales. It is equal to the combined state and local sales tax rates, with a deduction for sales not covered by the sales tax, but, since a credit for any sales tax collected and paid to the Tax Commissioner is given against this excise tax, few sellers are affected (Sec. 5739.10).

• Wireless 911 chargees

Wireless surcharge: A wireless surcharge is imposed at the rate of 28 cents per month on each wireless telephone number of a wireless service subscriber with a billing address in Ohio. Wireless service providers and resellers of wireless service are required to collect the wireless 911 charge as a specific line item on each subscriber's monthly bill. Wireless lifeline service providers are exempt. The wireless 911 surcharge is exempt from state and local taxation. (Sec. 5507.42)

Wireless service providers or resellers of wireless service are required to remit the charges collected for the second preceding calendar month to the Tax Commissioner by the last day of the month. Providers or resellers may retain 2% of the amount of surcharges collected as a billing and collection fee. (Sec. 5507.46)

Prepaid wireless charge: The prepaid wireless charge is eliminated effective July 1, 2014, and replaced with a charge imposed at the rate of 0.5% of the sales price of the service. The seller of the prepaid wireless calling service must collect the charge at the time of sale and itemize the charge on the sales receipt or invoice. However, if a minimal amount of a prepaid wireless calling service is sold with a prepaid wireless calling device for a single, nonitemized price, the seller may choose not to collect the charge. "Minimal" means either ten minutes or less or five dollars or less. (Sec. 5507.42)

When a prepaid wireless calling service is sold with one or more other products or services at one nonitemized price, the charge is imposed on the entire price. However, if the amount of the prepaid calling service is disclosed as a dollar amount, the seller may choose to apply the charge only to the dollar amount. Also, if the seller can identify the portion of the nonitemized price that is attributable to the prepaid wireless calling service, from the seller's books and records, the seller may elect to apply the charge to that portion only. (Sec. 5507.42)

Sellers of prepaid wireless calling service must file a return and remit the full amount due by the 23rd day of each month. Payments must be made electronically and returns must be filed using the Ohio business gateway, Ohio telefile system, or other electronic means prescribed by the commissioner. A seller may retain 3% of the total charges as a collection fee. Sellers of prepaid wireless calling service are subject to sales tax requirements regarding audits, assessments, appeals, enforcement, liability, and penalties. (Sec. 5507.46; Sec. 5507.52)

The most significant local sales and use taxes are those levied by counties and transit districts. Counties can impose rates of up to 1.5% (Sec. 5739.021, Sec. 5739.026), and transit authorities can impose their own 1.5% rate (Sec. 5739.023). Any county or transit authority imposing a sales tax must also impose the corresponding use tax at the same rate (Sec. 5741.021—Sec. 5741.023).

Notification of local rate changes: The commissioner is required to notify all vendors and sellers when local sales tax rates change due to a modification of a county's jurisdictional boundaries or a transit authority's territory (Sec. 5739.04). The notification must be made within 30 days of the change, and the rate change will not apply to sales made by a vendor until the first day of a calendar quarter following the expiration of 60 days from the date of notice by the tax commissioner.

Also, vendors making sales from a printed catalog are not required to apply changes in local sales tax rates that differ from those in the catalog until the beginning of a calendar quarter following 120 days after the commissioner notifies all vendors of the rate change (Sec. 5739.021(B)(3)).

Impact facilities: A board of county commissioners of a county that levies a county sales and use tax may enter into an agreement before June 1, 2015, with a person that proposes to construct an impact facility in the county to provide payments to the person of up to 75% of the county sales and use tax collected by the person at the facility. (Sec. 333.02)

An "impact facility" is defined as meeting the following criteria (Sec. 333.01):

— it is used for the sale of tangible personal property or services;

— at least 10% of the facility's total square footage is dedicated to educational or exhibition activities;

— at least $30 million is invested in land, buildings, infrastructure, and equipment for the facility over a period of no more than two years;

— an annualized average of at least 150 new full-time-equivalent positions are created and maintained at the facility; and

— more than 50% of the visitors to the facility are reasonably anticipated to live at least 50 miles from the facility.

The agreement would last for a term of 10 years or until the person's qualifying investment has been realized through the payments, whichever occurs first. (Sec. 333.02)

• Sourcing rules

Sourcing is discussed at ¶ 727.

• Resort area tax

A municipality or township meeting certain requirements may declare itself to be a resort area and levy a tax of 0.5%, 1%, or 1.5% on the privilege of making sales or providing intrastate transportation of passengers or property primarily to or from the municipality or township by railroad, watercraft, or motor vehicle subject to regulation by the Public Utilities Commission (Sec. 5739.101; *Sales and Use Tax Information Release ST 2008-03*, Ohio Department of Taxation, April 29, 2016, CCH OHIO TAX REPORTS, ¶ 404-528).

• Lodging tax

The existence of a state levy does not prevent local governments from imposing their own tax on the furnishing of lodging by a hotel to transient guests (Sec. 5739.08). Counties and cites and townships, convention facilities authorities, and a lake facilities authority may levy an excise tax on the furnishing of lodging by a hotel to transient guests (Sec. 505.56; Sec. 505.57; Sec. 351.021; and Sec. 353.06).

The rate of local lodging tax generally cannot exceed 3% (Sec. 5739.02(C), Sec. 5739.024); however, a special lodging tax in support of a convention center may be increased to 7%. A tax in effect on March 13, 1999, may be increased by an additional 4% on each transaction. The statutes impose restrictions on the right of localities to impose the taxes and determine which local governments have priority.

Online travel companies: An Ohio district court decision holding that online travel companies (OTCs) were not liable for local occupancy taxes was upheld because the OTCs were not "vendors," "operators," or "hotels" within the meaning of the local ordinances and regulations. The municipalities, townships, and counties that filed the lawsuit claimed that the OTCs violated local tax laws by failing to pay a transient occupancy tax on the difference between the contractually agreed-upon wholesale room rate, charged by hotels to the OTCs, and a higher retail rate charged by the OTCs to the customers. However, the OTCs did not perform functions associated with owning or operating hotels and, therefore, did not fall within the scope of the occupancy tax laws. Furthermore, the language of the tax ordinances expressly applied to the cost of furnishing lodging, not to service or booking fees charged by the OTCs. (*City of Columbus v. Hotels.com,* U.S. Court of Appeals for the Sixth Circuit, No. 10-4531, September 10, 2012, CCH Ohio Tax Reports, ¶ 404-055)

- **Local and state tax rates**

The latest information on sales tax rates as well as rate changes planned in any of Ohio's 88 counties is available at **http://www.tax.ohio.gov/sales_and_use/ rate_changes.aspx**.

Information on local taxing jurisdictions and tax rates for all addresses and locations in the State of Ohio is available on The Finder at **http://www.tax.ohio.gov/ online_services/thefinder.aspx**.

¶ 731   **Bracket Schedule**

A seller must compute the tax due by multiplying the price by the aggregate rate of taxes in effect. The computation must be carried out to three decimal places and rounded to the nearest whole cent, rounding up if the number in the third decimal place is greater than four. A seller may compute the amount due on a transaction either on an item basis or an invoice basis (Sec. 5739.025).

The Department of Taxation has produced tax rate schedules to assist sellers and sellers in collecting the proper amount of tax. The schedule cards are available from any taxpayer service center or on the Department's website at **http://www.tax.ohio.gov/ sales_and_use/tax_rate_schedules.aspx**.

¶ 732   **Returns, Payments, and Due Dates**

Each person required to have a seller's license must file sales tax returns and pay the amount of taxes due to the Tax Commissioner (Sec. 5739.12, Sec. 5739.30). Use tax provisions are comparable, and sellers required or authorized to collect use taxes or consumers subject to use tax liability must file returns with the Tax Commissioner (Sec. 5741.12, Sec. 5741.22).

Registered sellers may file use tax returns on an annual basis. However, sellers that collect more than $1,000 in taxes in any one month must file a return for that month. Sellers that collect over $18,000 of tax at any point in a calendar year must begin filing returns on a monthly basis unless the seller can substantiate that its future tax collections will be less than $1,000 a month. Business consumers and holders of direct pay permits must file returns on a monthly basis unless their average monthly liability is less than $5,000, in which case they may file quarterly (OAC 5703-9-13).

Individual consumers must report use tax annually if their tax liability is less than $1,000 (OAC 5703-9-13). Individuals with a liability of more than $1,000 have the same filing requirements as business consumers. Extraordinary purchases or purchases of a motor vehicle or titled watercraft or outboard motor made by individuals must be reported separately.

Sales and use tax returns must be filed on a monthly basis for any seller or seller that elects to employ a CSP or that uses a certified automated system (OAC 5703-9-13).

Returns filed on a semiannual basis will be for the reporting periods January through June and July through December. Returns filed on a quarterly basis will be for the reporting periods January through March, April through June, July through September, and October through December. All returns must be filed on or before the 23rd day of the month following the end of the reporting period (OAC 5703-9-13).

• Direct payment

Upon application, the Tax Commissioner may issue a direct payment permit that authorizes a consumer to pay the sales tax directly to the state (relieving the seller or seller of responsibility for collecting the tax) if direct payment would improve compliance and make administration of the tax more efficient (Sec. 5739.031(A)). A manufacturer or other purchaser seeking a direct payment permit must file a permit application with the Tax Commissioner using Form ST-900, Application for Direct Payment Permit. For additional information, see *Sales and Use Tax Information Release ST 2003-01,* Ohio Department of Taxation, March 15, 2016, CCH OHIO TAX REPORTS, ¶ 404-466.

• Prearranged payment

A vendor may be authorized to report and pay sales tax on the basis of established percentages if the commission finds that it would improve compliance and increase the efficiency of the administration of the tax. A qualifying vendor must apply for prearranged authority and agree in writing to the terms and conditions as set forth by the Commissioner. The agreement will specify the percentage of total sales subject to tax and the effective rate of taxation, for each vendor's license covered by the authority. These percentages will be computed based on a test check of a representative sample of the vendor's business activity. Prearranged authority requires that the vendor continue collecting tax from the consumer on taxable sales and report the tax computed under the terms of the agreement. If required by the commissioner, the taxpayer must post a notice at the location where the product is offered for sale that the tax is included in the selling price. (Sec. 5739.05(C); Rule 5703-9-08(C))

The proportion of taxable sales is based solely on the terms of the agreement until the vendor or Commissioner believes that the business has changed to make the agreement no longer representative. Cancellation of a prearranged agreement is effective on the last day of the month in which the notice is received. (Sec. 5739.05(C))

• Prompt payment discount

If the sales or use tax return is filed and the tax paid before the due date, the seller is entitled to a discount of 0.75% of the amount shown to be due on the return. The discount is in consideration for prompt payment and for other services performed in the collection of the tax (Sec. 5739.12, Sec. 5741.12(A)).

A seller that uses a certified service provider (CSP) who receives an allowance for performing the seller's sales and use tax functions in Ohio is not entitled to retain the discount (Sec. 5739.12).

• Sales tax returns

The sales tax return provided by the Tax Commissioner is a combined return covering state, county, and transit district sales taxes. The form starts with gross sales, and then allows deductions for exempt sales and motor vehicle sales (which are paid under other provisions) to arrive at taxable sales. The next line, tax liability on reportable sales, requires that the taxpayer enter either the amount that should have been collected or the amount that was actually collected—whichever is greater. Any excess collection must be remitted. Deductions for credit balances and previously reported tax and the discount for prompt payment are then subtracted.

The sellers' monthly sales tax return is due on the 23rd day of the month for the tax collected during the preceding month (Sec. 5739.12). The return is considered filed when it is received by the Tax Commissioner.

• Use tax returns

Sellers required to register or authorized to collect use taxes must file Form UT-1018 (Sec. 5741.12(A)). Consumers are required to file form UT-1014 if the tax was not paid to the seller (Sec. 5741.12(B)). Consequently, the consumer's use tax return is used primarily to report purchases from out-of-state sellers who do not collect the Ohio use tax. The return is filed on or before the 23rd day of each month, unless the Commissioner determines that more frequent filings are necessary or authorizes less frequent filings.

• Electronic filing and payment

Any person required to have a seller's license is required to file sales and use tax returns and remit payments electronically using the Ohio business gateway, the Ohio telefile system or any other means set forth by the Tax Commissioner (see **http:// www.tax.ohio.gov/online_services/business_taxes_sales_filing.aspx**). Sellers may be excused from electronic filing by the Tax Commissioner for good cause. (Sec. 5739.12; Sec. 5739.122; Sec. 5741.12; Sec. 5741.121)

A consumer who is not required to be registered as a seller must remit tax electronically if the total amount of tax due in a calendar year is at least $75,000. If a consumer's tax payment for each of two consecutive years drops below $75,000, the consumer is relieved of the requirement to remit taxes by electronic funds transfer for the year that next follows the second of the consecutive years, and is relieved of that requirement for each succeeding year unless the tax payment in a subsequent year is at least $75,000. (Sec. 5741.121)

Accelerated payments: Any taxpayer who is required to remit sales or use tax by EFT must remit 75% of its anticipated tax liability for a month by the 23rd day of that month. By the 23rd day of the following month, the taxpayer must determine the actual tax liability for the preceding month, subtract the prepayment made in the previous month, and remit the balance owing (Sec. 5741.121(B); Sec. 5739.122(B)).

Additional charges: For failure to make a payment as required, the Tax Commissioner may impose an additional charge of up to 5% of the unpaid amount. If taxes required to be paid by EFT are remitted by some other means, the Commissioner may impose an additional charge not to exceed the lesser of (1) 5% of the amount of taxes required to be paid by EFT or (2) $5,000. However, the Commissioner may waive all or a portion of an additional charge (Sec. 5739.12, Sec. 5739.122).

• Sales of manufactured homes and mobile homes

The sale of a new manufactured or mobile home is not treated as the sale of a motor vehicle. A dealer in new motor vehicles that purchases a new manufactured home or new mobile home from a manufacturer, remanufacturer, distributor, or another dealer is not liable for sales and use tax at the time of purchase, but must pay the tax, based on the dealer's cost, at the time the vehicle is sold to a purchaser (other than another new motor vehicle dealer purchasing the home for resale) (Sec. 5739.0210(E)). The tax is due on the earlier of (1) the date that the vehicle is delivered to the purchaser, (2) the date the purchaser remits the full price for the vehicle, or (3) in the case of a dealer-financed transaction, the date the purchaser completely executes the financing for the new vehicle.

The dealer may not charge the tax to the purchaser of the new home, but may pass the tax through to the purchaser as part of the dealer's cost of the vehicle (Sec. 5739.0210(F)). The price on which the tax is based is the aggregate value in money of anything previously paid or delivered, or promised to be paid or delivered, by the new motor vehicle dealer for that dealer's previous purchase of the new vehicle from the manufacturer, remanufacturer, distributor, or other new motor vehicle dealer (Sec. 5739.0210(E)).

Used homes: Sales of used manufactured or mobile homes are exempt from sales and use tax, provided that transfer tax is paid on the sale (Sec. 5739.0210(C)).

• **Acceleration of tax on leases**

In the case of the lease of any (1) motor vehicle designed by the manufacturer to carry a load of not more than one ton, (2) watercraft, (3) outboard motor, (4) aircraft, or (5) business equipment (other than motor vehicles designed to carry loads in excess of one ton), the seller is required to calculate the sales or use tax due on the entire amount to be paid during the lease period, and to collect the tax due at the time the lease is consummated (Sec. 5739.01(H)(4), Sec. 5741.01(G)(6)).

• **Uniform Sales Tax Administration Act**

Ohio has enacted the Uniform Sales and Use Tax Administration Act and legislative changes designed to conform its laws to the requirements of the Streamlined Sales and Use Tax Agreement. For additional information, see "Streamlined Sales Tax Project" listed in the Table of Contents.

Sourcing: See ¶ 727.

Exemption certificates: A seller is relieved from sales and use tax liability, except in certain enumerated circumstances, if the seller obtains a fully completed exemption certificate from the consumer (Sec. 5741.02(E)(2)). In addition, when claiming an exemption for building and construction materials and services sold to a contractor for incorporation into real property, the contractor must obtain certification of the claimed exemption from the contractee, in addition to the exemption certificate provided by the contractor to the seller.

Bad debts: In reporting gross sales and net taxable sales, a seller or seller may exclude an amount equal to the sum of the seller's bad debts (Sec. 5739.121; Rule 5703-9-44). The definition of a "bad debt" is conformed to the Streamlined Sales and Use Tax Agreement.

¶ 733   **Prepayment of Taxes**

In situations in which collection of the sales tax would impose an unreasonable burden on the seller, the Tax Commissioner can authorize the seller to prepay the tax, if the seller plainly states to customers that the tax has been paid in advance (Sec. 5703.05, Sec. 5739.05, Rule 5703-9-08). This can be accomplished by the conspicuous placement on the premises of a sign stating that the tax was paid in advance (Rule 5703-9-08).

A similar provision allows prepayment of the use tax (Sec. 5741.06).

¶ 734   **Vendor Registration**

Anyone making taxable retail sales in Ohio must be licensed as a vendor (seller) for sales tax purposes and/or registered with the Tax Commissioner for use tax purposes. The Commissioner maintains listings of persons who are so licensed or registered (Sec. 5739.18, Sec. 5741.18). The following persons are specifically required to obtain transient vendor licenses: vending machine operators operating vending machines located on land owned by others; persons who sell at temporary exhibitions, shows, fairs, flea markets, and similar events; and persons who effectuate leases of motor vehicles, watercraft, outboard motors, and aircraft and leases of tangible personal property to be used primarily in business.

All vendors are required to display their vendor licenses prominently, in plain view, at all of their places of business (Sec. 5739.17(E)).

Registration information is provided at **http://www.tax.ohio.gov/business/ business_registration.aspx**.

• Vendor licensing

Anyone making retail sales subject to the sales tax must obtain a vendor's license for each fixed place of business from which taxable sales are made (Sec. 5739.17(A), Sec. 5739.31, Rule 5703-9-01). If a seller has no fixed place of business and sells from a vehicle, each vehicle intended to be used within a county constitutes a place of business for purposes of the licensing requirement.

Applications for vendor's licenses are made to the county auditor of each county where the applicant desires to engage in business (Sec. 5739.17(A)). An initial license fee is required for each fixed place of business in the county where retail sales will be consummated. All licenses must be renewed annually by February 1 (Sec. 5739.17(E)).

Business succession: A vendor's license terminates if the business is moved to a new location or the business is sold (Sec. 5739.17(A), Rule 5703-9-01). A license also terminates when the form of ownership of a business changes, as when a sole proprietorship or partnership is incorporated or a partnership or corporation is dissolved.

Cancellation: The Tax Commissioner is allowed to cancel a vendor's license if the vendor fails to notify the commissioner that the location of its fixed place of business has changed or that its business has closed and if ordinary mail sent to the address on the vendor's license is returned as undeliverable (Sec. 5739.17(B)).

• Use tax registration

Any seller of tangible personal property or services who has substantial nexus with Ohio must register with the Tax Commissioner and supply such information required by the Commissioner with respect to the seller's contacts with the state (Sec. 5741.17(A)). Sellers lacking substantial nexus with the state may voluntarily register with the Commissioner, and upon doing so, are entitled to the same benefits and are subject to the same duties and requirements as sellers required to be registered (Sec. 5741.17(B)).

• SST registration

To register under the Streamlined Sales and Use Tax Agreement (SST), sellers must go to **https://www.sstregister.org**. Sellers can also update previously submitted registration information at this website. The information provided will be sent to all of the full member states and to associate members for which the seller chooses to collect.

When a seller registers under the Agreement, it must select the certified technology model it will be using (or it must select "Other" if it will not be using one of the certified models). The models are the following:

Model One: Certified Service Provider (CSP), an agent certified under the Agreement to perform all the seller's sales and use tax functions;

Model Two: Certified Automated System (CAS), software certified under the Agreement to calculate the appropriate tax (for which the seller retains responsibility for remitting);

Model Three: Certified System (CS), a proprietary automated sales tax system certified under the Agreement.

Registration with a central registration system under the Streamlined Sales and Use Tax (SST) Agreement may not be used as the basis for establishing nexus with

Ohio for purposes of any state or local taxes (Sec. 5703.65). Provisions and guidelines for registering with a multistate central registration system for the collection of Ohio sales and use tax can be found at Rule 5703-9-50, Ohio Admin. Code.

¶ 735   Sales or Use Tax Credits

Use tax credits are allowed in many instances for sales taxes paid other states or counties.

¶ 736   Deficiency Assessments

If any vendor (seller) or consumer fails to collect or remit sales or use tax, or fails to pay the proper amount, the Tax Commissioner can use any information in his or her possession to make an assessment against that person for the tax (Sec. 5739.13, Sec. 5741.13).

The Commissioner may audit a sample of a seller's sales or a consumer's purchases for a representative period to determine the effective tax rate (the rate of tax that will result when the tax tables are applied to a particular seller's sales or consumer's purchases) in order to compute the assessment.

The Tax Commissioner is authorized to issue an assessment on any transaction for which sales or use tax was due and unpaid on the date the seller or consumer was informed by an agent of the Commissioner of an investigation or audit (Sec. 5739.13). If the seller or consumer remits any payment of the tax for the period covered by the assessment after the seller or consumer was informed of the investigation or audit, the payment will be credited against the assessment.

A tax assessment made against a seller does not discharge the purchaser's or consumer's liability to reimburse the seller for the tax applicable to the transaction, nor does making an assessment against a seller or consumer bar the Tax Commissioner from assessing the same tax against another person, or electing a different collection remedy, although no assessment can be issued if the tax has actually been paid by another.

If an assessment is not completely paid within 60 days, interest will be applied to the amount of tax due from the date of assessment to the date of full payment or the date it is certified to the attorney general for collection, whichever occurs earlier. If the assessment is referred to the attorney general for collection, interest shall bear upon the entire unpaid portion of the assessment from the date of certification to the date of full payment. (Sec. 5739.13(C))

¶ 737   Audit Procedures

Because Ohio sales and use taxes are collected under a bracket system designed to collect at least the percentage tax imposed by the state, plus local levies, the actual ratio that the amount of taxes collected will bear to total sales will vary.

When adequate records are not available to determine the effective rate that should be applied to a seller's total sales, the audit procedure is to conduct a "test check" of the business to establish an effective rate. A test check might also be conducted to establish the percentage of sales that are under 16¢ or otherwise exempt from the tax (Sec. 5739.05).

In assessing the excise tax imposed on sellers to the extent that they fail to collect and remit the sales and use taxes, the Commissioner is authorized to use test checks to determine the proportion that taxable retail sales bear to total sales. For purposes of the excise tax, sellers are not required to maintain records of individual sales of property under 16¢ or sales of food for human consumption off the premises, and so the test check provides the only basis of an assessment (Sec. 5739.10).

Test checks are also specifically authorized for use in determining the amount of tax a seller must pay in advance under a tax prepayment plan available where conditions are such that the maintenance of more detailed records would impose an unreasonable burden on the seller (Sec. 5739.05).

• **Voluntary disclosure**

Ohio Department of Taxation guidance explains the procedure for voluntary disclosure agreements for the payment of sales tax. If a taxpayer owes tax on purchases or failed to collect tax on its own sales, it must generally pay the tax and interest for the thirty-six months prior to making the voluntary disclosure request. When the department enters into a voluntary disclosure agreement, it:

(1) waives civil and criminal penalties (except for tax collected but not remitted);

(2) limits liabilities for sales and use tax to the voluntary disclosure period (except for tax collected but not remitted);

(3) keeps the company's identity from other parties; and

(4) allows the company to remain anonymous until the signed agreement is returned.

In order to request a voluntary disclosure, a taxpayer must complete a *Request for Sales and Use Tax Voluntary Disclosure,* Form ST VDA. Practitioners and taxpayers must report liability on a specific spreadsheet. The spreadsheet may be found on the department's website at **http://www.tax.ohio.gov/other/voluntary_disclosure/ sutvda.aspx**. (*Sales and Use Tax Voluntary Disclosure,* Ohio Department of Taxation, December 7, 2015, CCH Ohio Tax Reports, ¶ 404-400)

¶ 738   **Statute of Limitations**

No sales or use tax assessment can be issued against a seller, seller, or consumer more than four years after the later of either: (1) the return date for the period in which the sales or purchase was made, or (2) the date the return was actually filed (Sec. 5739.16, Sec. 5741.16).

A consumer that provides a fully completed exemption certificate may be assessed tax resulting from the denial of the claimed exemption within the later of four years after the return date for the period in which the sale or purchase was made, four years after the applicable return was filed, or one year after the date the certificate was provided (Sec. 5739.16).

The statute of limitations does not apply when a seller, seller, or consumer fails to file a return, when the seller or consumer and the Tax Commissioner waive the time limit in writing, or when the Tax Commissioner has substantial evidence of amounts of taxes collected by a seller from consumers on retail sales which were not returned to the state (Sec. 5739.16, Sec. 5741.16).

Further, no assessment can be issued against a seller or consumer for any sales tax imposed for any period during which there was in effect a tax rule under which collection or payment was not required. The Commissioner can still make an assessment if there is substantial evidence of amounts of taxes collected from consumers on retail sales which were not returned to the state (Sec. 739.16).

¶ 739   **Application for Refund**

The Ohio Tax Commissioner is required to notify taxpayers in a timely manner to resolve credit account balances (Sec. 5703.05(P)).

The commissioner must review taxpayer accounts not later than 60 days before the taxpayer may file a refund claim to determine if a taxpayer has a credit account balance and, if so, to notify the taxpayer. A "credit account balance" is the amount of any tax or fee that a taxpayer has overpaid, after accounting for accelerated payments, tax credits, and tax credit balances that may be carried forward. The review of taxpayer accounts is required regardless of whether or not the taxpayer has filed a refund application or an amended return. Upon discovering that a taxpayer has a credit account balance, the commissioner may either apply the amount as a credit in the taxpayer's next reporting period for that tax or fee, or issue a refund to the taxpayer. However, the commissioner must first deduct any certified tax debt before issuing a refund. (Sec. 5703.77)

The Tax Commissioner must refund to sellers any sales or use taxes that were illegally or erroneously paid or assessed (Sec. 5739.07, Sec. 5741.10).

When use tax is paid by the buyer or consumer directly to the State Treasurer, the refund is made directly to the buyer or consumer by the Treasurer (Sec. 5741.10).

• Application

Applications for refunds must be filed on forms provided by the Tax Commissioner within four years from the date of the illegal or erroneous payment of the tax unless the seller or consumer waives the time limitation for assessment by the Commissioner (Sec. 5739.07, Sec. 5741.10). Refunds are not available when the seller has been reimbursed by the consumer (Sec. 5739.07).

An application received after the last date of filing will be considered timely filed if postmarked no later than the last date of filing. If the postmark is affixed by a private postal meter (and the postmark is no later than the last day for filing), the postmark is illegible or there is no postmark, the application will be considered timely filed if it is delivered by the postal service no later than 7 days after the last day for filing (Sec. 5703.053).

• Refund directly to consumers

The Tax Commissioner may make refunds of illegally or erroneously paid sales tax to the consumer rather than the seller, but only if (1) the consumer paid the tax directly to the state and not through a seller, (2) the Tax Commissioner had not refunded the tax to the seller, and the seller has not refunded the tax to the consumer, or (3) the consumer has received a refund from a manufacturer or other person, other than the seller, of the full purchase price, but not the tax, paid to the seller in settlement of a complaint by the consumer about the property or service purchased (Sec. 5739.07).

An application for a refund must be filed with the Tax Commissioner within four years from the date of the illegal or erroneous payment of the tax unless the seller or consumer waives the time limitation.

• Incentive refund

Partial tax refund for electronic information service providers: The Tax Commissioner will refund 25% of the sales and use taxes paid by an electronic information service provider on purchases of the following (Sec. 5739.071(A)):

— computers, computer peripherals, software, telecommunications equipment, and similar tangible personal property primarily used to acquire, process, or store information for use by business customers or to transmit or disseminate information to such customers;

— services to install or repair such property; and

— agreements to repair or maintain such property.

The procedures and time limitations generally applicable to applying for sales and use tax refunds also apply to refunds authorized under this provision.

¶740   OKLAHOMA

¶741   Scope of Tax

Source.—Statutory references are to Title 68, Articles 13 and 14, of the Oklahoma Statutes, as amended to date. Details are reported in the CCH OKLAHOMA TAX REPORTS starting at ¶ 60-000.

The Oklahoma sales tax is an excise tax imposed on the sale of tangible personal property and services, not otherwise exempt, to the consumer (Sec. 1351). It is a general sales tax on the sale, lease, or rental of tangible personal property at retail in the state (Sec. 1354, subsec. A), and a limited sales tax imposed on the performance of certain taxable services (listed below) at retail to consumers or users in Oklahoma (Sec. 1354).

The use tax is a complementary tax and does not apply in situations in which the sales tax is collected (Sec. 1404(c)). It is imposed on the storage, use, or other consumption in Oklahoma of tangible personal property (Sec. 1402).

Digital products: Oklahoma also does not tax sales of digital products transferred electronically (Sec. 1354, subsec. A(4)(a)(9)). Prewritten computer software that is electronically delivered is not subject to sales tax (Sec. 1357).

- **Services subject to tax**

The sales tax is levied on the following types of services (Sec. 1354, subsec. A):

— natural or artificial gas, electricity, ice, steam, or other utility or public services, except water, sewage, and refuse collection;

— transportation for hire to persons by common;

— telephone or telegraph service;

— printing service, with some exceptions;

— lodging services;

— parking or storage services;

— certain computer services;

— prepared food and drink;

— advertising, unless exempt;

— use of health clubs or similar facilities, charges for using items for amusement or recreation, admission to and use of tennis, racquetball, or handball courts, or rental of amusement, sports, entertainment, or other equipment;

— admission to places of amusement or sports exhibitions;

— vending machine sales;

— rental or lease of tangible personal property;

— motion picture licensing, unless exempt; and

— flowers, plants, shrubs, trees, and floral items.

- **Use tax**

The use tax complements the sales tax, protecting Oklahoma merchants from discrimination arising from the inability of the state to impose the sales tax on out-of-state purchases by Oklahoma residents. It is imposed on the storage, use, or other consumption in Oklahoma of tangible personal property purchased or brought into Oklahoma (Sec. 1402). It is not imposed in situations in which the sales tax has already been applied by Oklahoma. A credit is given for taxes paid another state, if the other state extends the same credit to the Oklahoma sales tax (Sec. 1404(c)).

A letter ruling issued by the Oklahoma Tax Commission states that use tax applies when:

(1) tangible personal property is purchased outside Oklahoma by an Oklahoma or out-of-state purchaser,

(2) the property is bought into Oklahoma for use or consumption, and

(3) sales tax is not required to be paid to the other state.

In such a case, the purchaser would be required to report and pay use tax to the Commission. However, the purchaser would be required to pay Oklahoma use tax to the out-of-state vendor in this scenario if the out-of-state vendor is authorized or required by Oklahoma law to collect, report, or remit Oklahoma use tax.

If the property is not received by the purchaser at a business location of the vendor, the sale is sourced to the location where the purchaser or the purchaser's donee receives the item, including the location indicated by instructions for delivery to the purchaser or purchaser's donee, and regardless of whether the vendor or purchaser hires a common carrier for shipping. *(Letter Ruling 13-014,* Oklahoma Tax Commission, May 13, 2013; CCH OKLAHOMA TAX REPORTS, ¶ 201-118)

Drop shipments: When all the parties are located in the state, the retailer furnishes a resale certificate to the primary seller, rendering the first sale a nontaxable transaction. The retailer then collects sales tax on behalf of the state on the secondary sale to its customer. However, different considerations arise when one or more of the parties are not within the state. Although Oklahoma does not use the actual words "drop shipment" in its laws or regulations, several statutory and regulatory provisions apply.

Oklahoma exempts the primary sale (the sale to an out-of-state retailer by an Oklahoma manufacturer who drop ships the product to the retailer's customer) if the retailer furnishes a resale exemption from its state or similar evidence, such as a Multistate Tax Commission certificate, showing that the sale is a sale for resale. (Sec. 1357(3); Rule 710:65-13-200)

The secondary sale by the retailer to its Oklahoma customer may be an exempt interstate sale if the retailer lacks any Oklahoma nexus. When that is the case, the customer is subject to use tax because no sales tax has been paid (Sec. 1402; see also *Letter Ruling LR-LR-12-002,* March 12, 2012, CCH OKLAHOMA TAX REPORTS, ¶ 20131125471).

• **Nexus**

Oklahoma has taken an aggressive nexus position by adoption of a policy statement making clear its intent to include within the sales and use tax levies all sales and uses of tangible personal property occurring within the state through the "continuous, regular or systematic solicitation in the Oklahoma consumer market by out-of-state vendors" through mail order and catalog publications and through advertisements in newspapers or radio or television media operating within the state (Sec. 1354.1).

Effective November 1, 2016, under the Oklahoma Retail Protection Act of 2016, the definition of "maintaining a place of business in this state" is rebuttably presumed to include (Sec. 1352(13)):

(1) (a) utilizing or maintaining in Oklahoma (directly or by subsidiary) an office, distribution house, sales house, warehouse, or other physical place of business, whether owned or operated by the vendor or any other person (other than a common carrier acting in its capacity as such), or

(b) having agents operating in Oklahoma, whether the place of business or agent is within the state temporarily or permanently or whether the person or agent is authorized to do business in the state; and

(2) the presence of any person (other than a common carrier acting in its capacity as such) who has substantial nexus in Oklahoma and who:

(a) sells a similar line of products as the vendor under the same or a similar business name;

(b) uses trademarks, service marks, or trade names in Oklahoma that are the same or substantially similar to those used by the vendor;

(c) delivers, installs, assembles, or performs maintenance services for the vendor;

(d) facilitates the vendor's delivery of property to customers in the state by permitting the vendor's customers to pick up property sold by the vendor at an office, distribution facility, warehouse, storage place, or similar place of business maintained by the person in Oklahoma; or

(e) conducts any other activities in Oklahoma that are significantly associated with the vendor's ability to establish and maintain a market in the state for the vendor's sale.

The presumption is rebuttable by showing that the person's activities in Oklahoma are not significantly associated with the vendor's ability to establish and maintain a market in the state for the vendor's sales.

Prior law: Since November 1, 2016, the code no longer provides that a "retailer" includes making sales of tangible personal property to purchasers in Oklahoma by mail, telephone, the Internet, or other media who has contracted with an entity to provide and perform installation or maintenance services for the retailer's purchasers in Oklahoma. The use tax code was also amended to no longer state that the processing of orders electronically (including by facsimile, telephone, the Internet, or other electronic means) does not relieve a retailer of the duty to collect tax from the purchaser if the retailer is doing business in Oklahoma. (former Sec. 1401(9)(b))

Retailer compliance initiatives: Effective November 1, 2016, the state's out-of-state retailer use tax registration, collection, and remittance compliance initiatives are expanded to also apply with respect to sales tax. Under the initiative as amended, the Oklahoma Tax Commission will not seek payment of uncollected use taxes from an out-of-state retailer who registers to collect and remit applicable sales and use taxes on sales made to purchasers in Oklahoma prior to registration under the initiative, provided that the retailer was not registered in Oklahoma in the 12-month period preceding November 1, 2016.

Other changes concerning the compliance initiatives include the removal of provisions under former (Sec. 1402(C)):

(1) prohibiting an out-of-state retailer's registration to collect use tax under the initiative as a factor in determining nexus for other Oklahoma taxes,

(2) allowing out-of-state retailers registering under the initiative a vendor discount for timely reporting and remittance of use tax, and

(3) prohibiting the charging of a registration fee against an out-of-state retailer who voluntarily registers to collect and remit use tax under the initiative.

Annual use tax notice requirements: Out-of-state retailers who are not required to collect Oklahoma use tax and who make sales of tangible personal property delivered to Oklahoma customers for use in the state, must, by February 1st of each year, provide each of these customers a statement of the total sales made to them during the preceding calendar year. The statement must contain language substantially similar to: *"You may owe Oklahoma use tax on purchases you made from us during the previous tax year. The amount of tax you owe is based on the total sales price of [insert total sales price] that must be reported and paid when you file your Oklahoma income tax return unless you have already paid the tax."* For reasons of confidentiality, the statement cannot contain any other information that would indicate, imply, or identify the class, type, description, or name of the products sold. (Uncodified Sec. 4, Ch. 311 (H.B. 2531), Laws 2016)

• Streamlined Act status

Oklahoma is a full member of the Streamlined Sales and Use Tax Agreement with a seat on the Governing Board. It has enacted all of the provisions necessary to comply with the Agreement's requirements and these provisions currently are in effect (68 O.S. Sec. 1354.7). As a full member, it may vote on amendments to or interpretations of the Agreement, and sellers registering under the SST system must collect and remit tax on sales into the state. For additional information, see ¶ 747.

A chart of the taxable status of various items is accessible on the website of the Streamlined Sales Tax Project at **http://www.streamlinedsalestax.org**.

¶ 742 **Tax Base**

The Oklahoma sales tax is levied upon the "gross receipts" or "gross proceeds" of the sale of tangible personal property (unless exempt) and certain specified services (Sec. 1354).

"Gross receipts" and "gross proceeds" are defined as the total amount of consideration for a taxable sale, whether in money or otherwise (Sec. 1352(G), Rule 710:65-1-9).

"Gross receipts" and "gross proceeds" include (but are not limited to):

— cash paid;

— any amount for which payment is charged, deferred, or otherwise to be made in the future, regardless of the time or manner of;

— any amount for which credit or a discount is allowed by the vendor;

— any amount of deposit paid for transfer of possession; and

— any value of a trade-in or other property accepted by the vendor as consideration, except for certain trade-in parts.

• Use tax basis

The Oklahoma use tax is levied on the purchase price of taxable transactions (Sec. 1402).

The term "purchase price" means the consideration paid or given or contracted to be paid or given by any person to the seller of an article of tangible personal property for the article purchased (Sec. 1401(d)).

• Sourcing of sales

Sourcing rules are discussed at ¶ 745.

¶ 743 **List of Exemptions, Exceptions, and Exclusions**

Unless otherwise indicated, the statutory exemptions, exceptions, and exclusions listed below apply to both sales and use taxes; those applicable only to the sales tax or only to the use tax are listed separately. Items that are excluded from the sales or use tax base are treated at ¶ 742, "Tax Base."

Sales tax holiday: There is an annual three-day sales tax holiday for sales of certain clothing and footwear starting at 12:01 a.m. on the first Friday in August and ending at midnight on the following Sunday. Retailers may not charge state, county, or municipal sales tax during the annual holiday period (Sec. 1357.10(A); Rule 710:65-13-511(a)).

The holiday applies to the sale of any article of clothing or footwear that is designed to be worn on or about the human body and that has a sales price of less than $100. Items having a sales price of $100 or more are subject to sales tax. "Clothing" means all apparel for humans that is suitable for general use, and includes items such as household and shop aprons, baby receiving blankets, belts and suspenders, costumes, hats and caps, insoles for shoes, athletic and non-athletic uniforms, wedding apparel, and adult and children's diapers, including disposable diapers (Rule 710:65-13-511(c)).

The holiday does not apply to the rental of clothing or footwear, the sale of special clothing or footwear primarily designed for athletic or protective use, or the sale of accessories (Rule 710:65-13-511(b)). "Accessories" include items such as handbags, jewelry, luggage, umbrellas, wallets, watches, and similar items carried on or about the body (68 O.S. Sec. 1357.10(B); Rule 710:65-13-511(c)).

Tornado disaster relief: Oklahoma provides ongoing sales and use tax relief related to damage caused by tornadoes occurring within the state (Sec. 1362). Previously, such relief was enacted on an *ad hoc* basis after each such disaster. The legislation exempts the sales value of tangible personal property withdrawn from inventory and donated to assist persons affected by tornadoes for which a Presidential Major Disaster Declaration was issued and that occurred not only in calendar year 2013, but in any subsequent year (Sec. 1362). Similarly, the legislation permits the 1% collection discount allowed vendors for record-keeping and prompt payment if the delinquent filing of a sales tax report or in remittance of tax was due to a tornado for which a Presidential Major Disaster Declaration was issued (Sec. 1367.1(B)). The legislation also allows a credit with respect to the vehicle excise tax paid on or after January 1, 2012, on a vehicle that replaces a vehicle that was destroyed by a tornado for which a Presidential Major Disaster Declaration was issued (Sec. 2103.1).

- **Limitation on exemptions**

Taxpayers who receive incentive payments under the new Oklahoma 21st Century Quality Jobs Incentive Act may not claim the following sales and use tax exemptions (Sec. 3607):

— the exemption for sales of computers, data processing equipment, related peripherals and telephone, telegraph or telecommunications service and equipment for use in a qualified aircraft maintenance or manufacturing facility;

— the exemption for sales of tangible personal property consumed or incorporated in the construction or expansion of a qualified aircraft maintenance or manufacturing facility;

— the exemption for sales of tangible personal property purchased and used by licensed radio or television stations in broadcasting;

— the exemption for new and expanding computer services and data processing or research and development businesses.

- **Sales and use tax exemptions, exceptions, and exclusions**

Admissions: professional sporting events	Sec. 1356, subsecs. 53, 54
Admissions: annual womens' event	Sec. 1356, subsec. 60
Advertising	Sec. 1357, subsecs. 4, 5, 6
Agriculture-related exemptions	Sec. 1358
Aircraft maintenance facilities, repairs, and parts	Sec. 1357, subsecs. 16, 17, 20, 28
Aircraft with excise tax paid	Sec. 1355, subsecs. 4, 9
Animal feed and supplements	Sec. 1358, subsec. 4
Athletic events and admissions, sales by certain exempt organizations	Sec. 1356, subsecs. 8, 15, 44
Biomedical research foundations	Sec. 1357, subsec. 25
Blood banks	Sec. 1357, subsec. 23
Blue Star Mothers of America	Sec. 1356, subsec. 70
Boy Scouts	Sec. 1356, subsec. 9

Materials and supplies for use on international or interstate vessels .	Sec. 1357, subsec. 29
Meals delivered to the elderly and homebound	Sec. 1357, subsec. 13a, Sec. 1357, subsec. 13b
Medical sales reimbursed by Medicare or Medicaid	Sec. 1357, subsec. 6
Medicine	Sec. 353.1, Tit. 59, Sec. 1357, subsec. 7
Metal castings patterns	Sec. 1359, subsec. 11
Methanol and "M-85" with excise taxes paid	Sec. 1355, subsec. 1
Migrant health centers	Sec. 1356, subsec. 22
Motion picture or television production companies, certain sales to (See also ¶ 750)	Sec. 1357, subsec. 23
Motor fuel with motor fuel tax paid	Sec. 1355, subsec. 1
Motor vehicle leases with motor vehicle excise tax paid	Sec. 1355, subsec. 6
Motor vehicles with motor vehicle excise tax paid	Sec. 1355, subsec. 2
Museums	Sec. 1356, subsec. 25, Sec. 1356, subsec. 26
Natural gas for residential use	Sec. 1357, subsec. 8
Natural gas subject to gross production tax	Sec. 1355, subsec. 3
New and expanding business	Sec. 1359, subsec. 7
New and expanding businesses, computer services	Sec. 54003 Sec. 1357, subsec. 19
New and expanding businesses, research and development	Sec. 54003
Newspapers	Sec. 1354, subsec. 1(A)
Nonprofit organizations	Sec. 1356
Oil drums for recycling	Sec. 1357, subsec. 8
Oklahoma government	Sec. 1356, subsec. 1
Organizations that provide food for the needy	Sec. 1357, subsec. 13, 14
Packaging materials	Sec. 1359, subsec. 4, Sec. 1359, subsec. 10
Parent-Teacher Association sales	Sec. 1356, subsec. 13
Partnership transfers	Sec. 1360
Periodicals	Sec. 1354, subsec. A(1)
Pesticides	Sec. 1358, subsec. 5
Petroleum subject to gross production tax	Sec. 1355, subsec. 3
Pollution control and cleanup equipment	Sec. 1359, subsec. 6
Private schools	Sec. 1356, subsec. 12
Private scientific and educational libraries	Sec. 1356, subsec. 6, Sec. 1354, subsec. A(5)
Property purchased and used by radio or TV stations	Sec. 1359, subsec. 9
Prosthetic devices sold to an individual	Sec. 1357, subsec. 22
Public contracts	Sec. 1356, subsec. 10
Qualified federal facility	Sec. 1356, subsec. 3
Rail cars leased to haul coal for electricity plants	Sec. 1357, subsec. 27
Railroad track spikes	Sec. 1357, subsec. 19
Refuse service	Sec. 1354, subsec. A(2)
Religious organizations	Sec. 1356, subsec. 6

¶743   Oklahoma

YMCA/YWCA . . . . Sec. 1356, subsecs. 23, 63

Youth camps supported by churches . . . . Sec. 1356, subsec. 29

• Exemptions to sales tax only

Resale of motor fuel to "Group Five" vendor . . . . Sec. 1357, subsec. 3,
Sec. 1363, subsec. 5

• Exemptions to use tax only

Airline property . . . . Sec. 1404, subsec. 6

Nonresident's relocation of personal property . . . . Sec. 1404, subsec. 1

Nonresident's use of personal property . . . . Sec. 1404, subsec. 5

Property temporarily in Oklahoma for repairs . . . . Sec. 1402

Railroad property . . . . Sec. 1404, subsec. 8

Sales tax exemptions applied to use tax . . . . Sec. 1404, subsec. 4

Sales tax paid . . . . Sec. 1404, subsec. 3

Storage pending shipment . . . . Sec. 1402

Tax paid in another state . . . . Sec. 1404, subsec. 3

¶ 744   Rate of Tax

The sales tax (Sec. 1354) and use tax (Sec. 1402) are imposed at the rate of 4.5% of the gross receipt or gross proceeds (sales tax) or the purchase price of tangible personal property (use tax). This is also the rate levied on sales by out-of-state vendors to consumer-users in Oklahoma (Sec. 1354.2).

• Prepaid wireless fee

The prepaid wireless 911 fee is collected from consumers who purchase a prepaid wireless telecommunications service in a retail transaction that is not for resale (Sec. 2843.2). A "prepaid wireless telecommunications service" is a telecommunications wireless service other than a traditional calling card that provides the right to use mobile wireless services and other non-telecommunications services (including downloaded services), and that is paid for in advance and sold in predetermined units or dollars that decline in number with use in a known amount (Rule 710:95-17-3). The fee is imposed in the amount of 50 cents on each retail transaction but may be proportionately increased or decreased when there is a change in the amount of the 911 emergency wireless telephone fee (Sec. 2843.2(B), (G)).

¶ 745   Local Taxes

Any county or, effective November 1, 2014, transportation authority or regional economic development authority may levy a tax of up to 2% on the gross proceeds or gross receipts derived from sales or services in the county or district upon which the state sales tax is levied (Sec. 1370; Sec. 1370.7). Before the tax can be levied, it must be approved by a majority of the registered voters of the county or district voting at a special election. Special elections may be called by either the board of county commissioners or by an initiative petition signed by at least 5% of the registered voters in the county or district who were registered as of the date of the last general election. If the voters fail to approve the tax, no new election can be held until six months have passed.

Any tax levied by counties with 300,000 or fewer people must be designated for a particular purpose. Purposes can include, but are not limited to, economic development, general operations, capital improvements, county roads, or any other purpose necessary to promote safety, security, and general well-being.

When the tax is put to the voters, the county must state whether it is to be imposed for a limited period or for a period unlimited in duration.

¶744   Oklahoma

Administration of local taxes: In order to maintain conformity with the SST Agreement, the Oklahoma Tax Commission (OTC) must have authority to assess, to collect and to enforce any taxes, penalties, or interest. Therefore, the board of county commissioners or the governing body of any incorporated city or town must enter into a contract authorizing the OTC to assess, collect, and enforce sales tax levied by the locality and remit the taxes to the locality (Sec. 2702). However, the OTC may contract these enforcement activities back to the municipalities (Sec. 2702).

This provision was upheld as constitutional by the Oklahoma Supreme Court (*City of Tulsa v. State,* Oklahoma Supreme Court, No. 109559, May 15, 2012, CCH OKLAHOMA TAX REPORTS, ¶ 201-082)

Municipal taxes on annexed military installations: Effective November 1, 2014, a municipality's sales tax, use tax, and hotel occupancy tax ordinances apply to the part or whole of a military installation that is located on federal property annexed by the municipality on or after July 1, 1998 (Sec. 21-109(B)). However, application is limited to activities on the installation engaged in by the private sector involving:

(1) the sale of goods and services taxable under the Oklahoma Sales Tax Code;

(2) the storage, use, or other consumption of tangible property taxable under the Oklahoma Use Tax Code; and

(3) the occupancy of hotel or motel rooms for rent, whether or not received in money.

Otherwise, municipal revenue and taxation ordinances, and the licensing and regulatory authority of any municipality, do not apply to any military installation located on annexed federal property (Sec. 21-109(B)).

- **Counties with more than 300,000 people**

Counties with a population of more than 300,000 according to the latest federal decennial census can levy sales taxes for periods of up to three years upon approval of voters, as follows:

Qualified aircraft facilities: Taxes imposed under Sec. 1370.2, are not to exceed 1% and must be used solely for the purpose of development of qualified aircraft maintenance or manufacturing facilities or other specified airport improvements. Further, revenue from these taxes can only be used to finance 25% of the total cost of construction of the facilities.

Qualified manufacturing facilities: A sales tax not to exceed 1% may be imposed for the purposes of acquisition and development of qualified manufacturing facilities, related machinery and equipment, and any necessary infrastructure changes or improvements related to such facilities located within the county (Sec. 1370.2A). A "qualified manufacturing facility" is defined as a new or expanding manufacturing or production facility whose total cost of acquisition and construction exceeds $15 million and that will employ, within three years after completion of the facility, at least 1,000 new full-time-equivalent employees as certified by the Oklahoma Employment Security Commission.

Facilities for federal government use: Taxes imposed under Sec. 1370.4, may not exceed 1% and must be used to develop facilities for lease or conveyance to the federal government and any necessary infrastructure improvements directly related to such facilities located within the county. The tax may not be collected until an agreement to locate such a facility within the county has been reached.

- **Lodging taxes**

A county with a population of less than 200,000 is permitted to impose a local sales tax of up to 5% on lodging, subject to voter approval (Sec. 1370.9). The tax must be for a specific purpose and may be for a limited or unlimited period of time. The tax may not be imposed on campsites or for public lodging within the corporate limits of a municipality in the county that has levied the tax (Sec. 1370.9).

- **City or town sales and use tax**

Incorporated cities or towns are authorized to assess, levy, and collect sales and use taxes (Sec. 2701).

The tax must be approved by voters, and proposed taxing ordinances cannot be brought before voters more than three times in a calendar year or twice in any six-month period. The tax may be levied for a limited purpose or for general purposes. If levied for a limited purpose, funds must be put in a separate account.

Use tax: Municipalities levying a sales tax can also levy a use tax at the same rate (Sec. 1411). Credit must be given for payment of other municipal sales taxes.

- **Sourcing rules**

Sourcing rules are conformed with the Streamlined Sales and Use Tax Agreement (Sec. 1354.27). Retail sales, excluding leases and rentals, are sourced according to the following provisions:

　　— when a product is received by a purchaser at a business location of the seller, the sale is sourced to that business location;

　　— when the product is not received by a purchaser at a business location of the seller, the sale is sourced to the location where receipt by the purchaser or the purchaser's donee occurs, including the location indicated by instructions for delivery to the purchaser or donee, known to the seller;

　　— when the two circumstances above do not apply, the sale is sourced to the purchaser's address that is available from the seller's business records, when use of this address does not constitute bad faith;

　　— when the three circumstances above do not apply, the sale is sourced to the location of the purchaser's address obtained during consummation of the sale, including the address of a purchaser's payment instrument, if no other address is available, when use of this address does not constitute bad faith;

　　— when none of the other rules apply, including the circumstance in which the seller does not have sufficient information to apply the other rules, the sale is sourced to the address from which the tangible personal property was shipped, from which the digital good or the computer software delivered electronically was first available for transmission by the seller (disregarding any location that merely provided the digital transfer of the product sold), or from which the service was provided;

Florists: All sales by a florist are sourced to its business location (Rule 710:65-18-3).

Direct mail: Sourcing for "advertising and promotional direct mail" and "other direct mail" is detailed in Rule 710:65-18-6.

Telecommunications: Sourcing for telecommunications is detailed in Rule 710:65-19-330.

Mobile telecommunications: Oklahoma has conformed to the federal Mobile Telecommunications Sourcing Act (Act), P.L. 106-252. All charges for mobile telecommunications services are considered to be provided by the customer's home service provider and sourced to the customer's place of primary use (Sec. 55001 *et seq.*). All such charges are subject to sales tax based on the customer's place of primary use. The service provider will be held harmless for an error in assigning wireless services to a jurisdiction if it utilizes an electronic database provided by the state or a designated entity, or, if the state has not provided or designated a database, if it utilizes a database that makes assignments based on a nine-digit zip code.

¶745　Oklahoma

• **Local tax rates**

A local sales and use tax rate locator is available on the website of the Oklahoma Tax Commission at **https://www.ok.gov/tax/Businesses/Tax_Types/Business_Sales_Tax/Oklahoma_Sales_and_Use_Tax_Rate_Locator_System_/**. Rates may be searched by address or ZIP code, and are available in chart form for cities, municipalities, and ZIP codes.

Charts of current and historical local sales/use and lodging taxes is available at **https://www.ok.gov/tax/Businesses/Tax_Types/Business_Sales_Tax/Sales_Use_Lodging_Tax_Rate_Charts/**.

¶ 746   Bracket Schedule

In conformity with the Streamlined Sales and Use Tax Agreement (¶ 747), the tax must be rounded to a whole cent using a method that rounds up to the next cent whenever the third decimal place is greater than four (Sec. 1362(B)). The vendor or direct payment permit holder may elect to compute the tax due on transactions on an item or invoice basis.

For the convenience of the vendor or direct payment permit holder, the Oklahoma Tax Commission is authorized to establish a bracket system to be followed in collecting state or local sales taxes (Sec. 1362(C)). However, use of the bracket system does not relieve the vendor or direct payment permit holder from the obligation to remit the correct amount of tax (Sec. 1362(C)).

The following brackets were provided by the OTC.

5% Tax Rate		6% Tax Rate	
Sales Up To	Tax	Sales Up To	Tax
$0.09	0.00	$0.08	0.00
0.29	0.01	0.24	0.01
0.49	0.02	0.41	0.02
0.69	0.03	0.58	0.03
0.89	0.04	0.74	0.04
1.09	0.05	0.91	0.05
1.29	0.06	1.08	0.06
1.49	0.07	1.24	0.07
1.69	0.08	1.44	0.08
1.89	0.09	1.58	0.09
2.09	0.10	1.74	0.10
and so forth.		1.91	0.11
		and so forth.	

7% Tax Rate		10% Tax Rate	
Sales Up To	Tax	Sales Up To	Tax
$0.07	0.00	$0.04	0.00
0.21	0.01	0.14	0.01
0.35	0.02	0.24	0.02
0.49	0.03	0.34	0.03
0.64	0.04	0.44	0.04
0.78	0.05	0.54	0.05
0.92	0.06	0.64	0.06
1.07	0.07	0.74	0.07
1.21	0.08	0.84	0.08
1.35	0.09	0.94	0.09
1.49	0.10	1.04	0.10
1.64	0.11	1.14	0.11

7% Tax Rate

Sales Up To	Tax
1.78	0.12

and so forth.

10% Tax Rate

Sales Up To	Tax
1.24	0.12
1.34	0.13
1.44	0.14
1.54	0.15

and so forth.

8% Tax Rate

Sales Up To	Tax
$0.06	0.00
0.18	0.01
0.31	0.02
0.43	0.03
0.56	0.04
0.68	0.05
0.81	0.06
0.93	0.07
1.06	0.08
1.18	0.09
1.31	0.10
1.43	0.11
1.56	0.12
1.68	0.13

and so forth.

5.125% Tax Rate

Sales Up To	Tax
$0.09	0.00
0.29	0.01
0.48	0.02
0.68	0.03
0.87	0.04
1.07	0.05
1.26	0.06
1.46	0.07
1.65	0.08
1.85	0.09
2.04	0.10

and so forth.

9% Tax Rate

Sales Up To	Tax
$0.05	0.00
0.16	0.01
0.27	0.02
0.38	0.03
0.49	0.04
0.61	0.05
0.72	0.06
0.83	0.07
0.94	0.08
1.05	0.09
1.16	0.10
1.27	0.11
1.38	0.12
1.49	0.13
1.61	0.14

and so forth.

6.125% Tax Rate

Sales Up To	Tax
$0.08	0.00
0.24	0.01
0.40	0.02
0.57	0.03
0.73	0.04
0.89	0.05
1.06	0.06
1.22	0.07
1.38	0.08
1.55	0.09
1.71	0.10
1.87	0.11

and so forth.

7.125% Tax Rate

Sales Up To	Tax
$0.07	0.00
0.21	0.01
0.35	0.02
0.49	0.03
0.63	0.04
0.77	0.05
0.91	0.06

10.125% Tax Rate

Sales Up To	Tax
$0.04	0.00
0.14	0.01
0.24	0.02
0.34	0.03
0.44	0.04
0.54	0.05
0.64	0.06

¶746 Oklahoma

7.125% Tax Rate

Sales Up To	Tax
1.05	0.07
1.19	0.08
1.33	0.09
1.47	0.10
1.61	0.11
1.75	0.12

and so forth.

10.125% Tax Rate

Sales Up To	Tax
0.74	0.07
0.83	0.08
0.93	0.09
1.03	0.10
1.13	0.11
1.23	0.12
1.33	0.13
1.43	0.14
1.53	0.15

and so forth.

8.125% Tax Rate

Sales Up To	Tax
$0.06	0.00
0.18	0.01
0.30	0.02
0.43	0.03
0.55	0.04
0.67	0.05
0.79	0.06
0.92	0.07
1.04	0.08
1.16	0.09
1.29	0.10
1.41	0.11
1.53	0.12
1.66	0.13

and so forth.

5.25% Tax Rate

Sales Up To	Tax
$0.09	0.00
0.28	0.01
0.47	0.02
0.66	0.03
0.85	0.04
1.04	0.05
1.23	0.06
1.42	0.07
1.61	0.08
1.80	0.09
1.99	0.10

and so forth.

9.125% Tax Rate

Sales Up To	Tax
$0.05	0.00
0.16	0.01
0.27	0.02
0.38	0.03
0.49	0.04
0.69	0.05
0.71	0.06
0.82	0.07
0.93	0.08
1.04	0.09
1.15	0.10
1.26	0.11
1.36	0.12
1.47	0.13
1.58	0.14

and so forth.

6.25% Tax Rate

Sales Up To	Tax
$0.07	0.00
0.23	0.01
0.39	0.02
0.55	0.03
0.71	0.04
0.87	0.05
1.03	0.06
1.19	0.07
1.35	0.08
1.51	0.09
1.67	0.10
1.83	0.11

and so forth.

7.25% Tax Rate

Sales Up To	Tax
$0.06	0.00
0.20	0.01

10.25% Tax Rate

Sales Up To	Tax
$0.04	0.00
0.14	0.01

7.25% Tax Rate

Sales Up To		Tax
0.34	. . . .	0.02
0.48	. . . .	0.03
0.62	. . . .	0.04
0.75	. . . .	0.05
0.89	. . . .	0.06
1.03	. . . .	0.07
1.17	. . . .	0.08
1.31	. . . .	0.09
1.44	. . . .	0.10
1.58	. . . .	0.11
1.72	. . . .	0.12

and so forth.

10.25% Tax Rate

Sales Up To		Tax
0.24	. . . .	0.02
0.34	. . . .	0.03
0.43	. . . .	0.04
0.53	. . . .	0.05
0.63	. . . .	0.06
0.73	. . . .	0.07
0.82	. . . .	0.08
0.92	. . . .	0.09
1.02	. . . .	0.10
1.12	. . . .	0.11
1.21	. . . .	0.12
1.31	. . . .	0.13
1.41	. . . .	0.14
1.51	. . . .	0.15

and so forth.

8.25% Tax Rate

Sales Up To		Tax
$0.06	. . . .	0.00
0.18	. . . .	0.01
0.30	. . . .	0.02
0.42	. . . .	0.03
0.54	. . . .	0.04
0.66	. . . .	0.05
0.78	. . . .	0.06
0.90	. . . .	0.07
1.03	. . . .	0.08
1.15	. . . .	0.09
1.27	. . . .	0.10
1.39	. . . .	0.11
1.51	. . . .	0.12
1.63	. . . .	0.13

and so forth.

4.50% Tax Rate

Sales Up To		Tax
$0.11	. . . .	0.00
0.33	. . . .	0.01
0.55	. . . .	0.02
0.77	. . . .	0.03
0.99	. . . .	0.04
1.22	. . . .	0.05
1.44	. . . .	0.06
1.66	. . . .	0.07
1.88	. . . .	0.08
2.11	. . . .	0.09
2.33	. . . .	0.10

and so forth.

9.25% Tax Rate

Sales Up To		Tax
$0.05	. . . .	0.00
0.16	. . . .	0.01
0.27	. . . .	0.02
0.37	. . . .	0.03
0.48	. . . .	0.04
0.59	. . . .	0.05
0.70	. . . .	0.06
0.81	. . . .	0.07
0.91	. . . .	0.08
1.02	. . . .	0.09
1.13	. . . .	0.10
1.24	. . . .	0.11
1.35	. . . .	0.12
1.45	. . . .	0.13
1.56	. . . .	0.14

and so forth.

5.50% Tax Rate

Sales Up To		Tax
$0.09	. . . .	0.00
0.27	. . . .	0.01
0.45	. . . .	0.02
0.63	. . . .	0.03
0.81	. . . .	0.04
0.99	. . . .	0.05
1.18	. . . .	0.06
1.36	. . . .	0.07
1.54	. . . .	0.08
1.72	. . . .	0.09
1.90	. . . .	0.10
2.09	. . . .	0.11

and so forth.

¶746   **Oklahoma**

6.50% Tax Rate

Sales Up To	Tax
$0.07	0.00
0.23	0.01
0.38	0.02
0.53	0.03
0.69	0.04
0.84	0.05
0.99	0.06
1.15	0.07
1.30	0.08
1.46	0.09
1.61	0.10
1.76	0.11
1.92	0.12

and so forth.

9.50% Tax Rate

Sales Up To	Tax
$0.05	0.00
0.15	0.01
0.26	0.02
0.36	0.03
0.46	0.04
0.56	0.05
0.68	0.06
0.78	0.07
0.89	0.08
0.99	0.09
1.10	0.10
1.21	0.11
1.31	0.12
1.42	0.13
1.52	0.14
1.63	0.15

and so forth.

7.50% Tax Rate

Sales Up To	Tax
$0.06	0.00
0.19	0.01
0.33	0.02
0.46	0.03
0.59	0.04
0.73	0.05
0.86	0.06
0.99	0.07
1.13	0.08
1.26	0.09
1.39	0.10
1.53	0.11
1.66	0.12
1.79	0.13

and so forth.

10.50% Tax Rate

Sales Up To	Tax
$0.04	0.00
0.14	0.01
0.23	0.02
0.33	0.03
0.42	0.04
0.52	0.05
0.61	0.06
0.71	0.07
0.80	0.08
0.90	0.09
0.99	0.10
1.09	0.11
1.19	0.12
1.28	0.13
1.38	0.14
1.47	0.15
1.57	0.16

and so forth.

8.50% Tax Rate

Sales Up To	Tax
$0.05	0.00
0.17	0.01
0.29	0.02
0.41	0.03
0.52	0.04
0.64	0.05
0.76	0.06
0.88	0.07
0.99	0.08
1.11	0.09

5.55% Tax Rate

Sales Up To	Tax
$0.09	0.00
0.27	0.01
0.45	0.02
0.63	0.03
0.81	0.04
0.99	0.05
1.17	0.06
1.35	0.07
1.53	0.08
1.71	0.09

8.50% Tax Rate

Sales Up To	Tax
1.23	0.10
1.35	0.11
1.47	0.12
1.58	0.13
1.70	0.14

and so forth.

5.55% Tax Rate

Sales Up To	Tax
1.89	0.10
2.07	0.11

and so forth.

6.55% Tax Rate

Sales Up To	Tax
$0.07	0.00
0.22	0.01
0.38	0.02
0.53	0.03
0.68	0.04
0.83	0.05
0.99	0.06
1.14	0.07
1.29	0.08
1.45	0.09
1.60	0.10
1.75	0.11
1.90	0.12

and so forth.

9.55% Tax Rate

Sales Up To	Tax
$0.05	0.00
0.15	0.01
0.26	0.02
0.36	0.03
0.47	0.04
0.57	0.05
0.68	0.06
0.78	0.07
0.89	0.08
0.99	0.09
1.09	0.10
1.20	0.11
1.30	0.12
1.41	0.13
1.51	0.14
1.62	0.15

and so forth.

7.55% Tax Rate

Sales Up To	Tax
$0.06	0.00
0.19	0.01
0.33	0.02
0.46	0.03
0.59	0.04
0.72	0.05
0.86	0.06
0.99	0.07
1.12	0.08
1.25	0.09
1.39	0.10
1.52	0.11
1.65	0.12
1.78	0.13

and so forth.

10.55% Tax Rate

Sales Up To	Tax
$0.04	0.00
0.14	0.01
0.23	0.02
0.33	0.03
0.42	0.04
0.52	0.05
0.61	0.06
0.71	0.07
0.80	0.08
0.90	0.09
0.99	0.10
1.09	0.11
1.18	0.12
1.27	0.13
1.37	0.14
1.46	0.15
1.56	0.16

and so forth.

8.55% Tax Rate

Sales Up To	Tax
$0.05	0.00
0.17	0.01

5.75% Tax Rate

Sales Up To	Tax
$0.08	0.00
0.26	0.01

8.55% Tax Rate

Sales Up To		Tax
0.29	. . . .	0.02
0.40	. . . .	0.03
0.52	. . . .	0.04
0.64	. . . .	0.05
0.76	. . . .	0.06
0.87	. . . .	0.07
0.99	. . . .	0.08
1.11	. . . .	0.09
1.22	. . . .	0.10
1.34	. . . .	0.11
1.46	. . . .	0.12
1.57	. . . .	0.13
1.69	. . . .	0.14

and so forth.

5.75% Tax Rate

Sales Up To		Tax
0.43	. . . .	0.02
0.60	. . . .	0.03
0.78	. . . .	0.04
0.95	. . . .	0.05
1.13	. . . .	0.06
1.30	. . . .	0.07
1.47	. . . .	0.08
1.65	. . . .	0.09
1.82	. . . .	0.10
1.99	. . . .	0.11

and so forth.

6.75% Tax Rate

Sales Up To		Tax
$0.07	. . . .	0.00
0.22	. . . .	0.01
0.37	. . . .	0.02
0.51	. . . .	0.03
0.66	. . . .	0.04
0.81	. . . .	0.05
0.96	. . . .	0.06
1.11	. . . .	0.07
1.26	. . . .	0.08
1.40	. . . .	0.09
1.55	. . . .	0.10
1.70	. . . .	0.11
1.85	. . . .	0.12

and so forth.

9.75% Tax Rate

Sales Up To		Tax
$0.05	. . . .	0.00
0.15	. . . .	0.01
0.25	. . . .	0.02
0.35	. . . .	0.03
0.46	. . . .	0.04
0.56	. . . .	0.05
0.66	. . . .	0.06
0.76	. . . .	0.07
0.87	. . . .	0.08
0.97	. . . .	0.09
1.07	. . . .	0.10
1.17	. . . .	0.11
1.28	. . . .	0.12
1.38	. . . .	0.13
1.48	. . . .	0.14
1.58	. . . .	0.15

and so forth.

7.75% Tax Rate

Sales Up To		Tax
$0.06	. . . .	0.00
0.19	. . . .	0.01
0.32	. . . .	0.02
0.45	. . . .	0.03
0.58	. . . .	0.04
0.70	. . . .	0.05
0.83	. . . .	0.06
0.96	. . . .	0.07
1.09	. . . .	0.08
1.22	. . . .	0.09
1.35	. . . .	0.10
1.48	. . . .	0.11

10.75% Tax Rate

Sales Up To		Tax
$0.04	. . . .	0.00
0.13	. . . .	0.01
0.23	. . . .	0.02
0.32	. . . .	0.03
0.41	. . . .	0.04
0.51	. . . .	0.05
0.60	. . . .	0.06
0.69	. . . .	0.07
0.79	. . . .	0.08
0.88	. . . .	0.09
0.97	. . . .	0.10
1.06	. . . .	0.11

7.75% Tax Rate

Sales Up To	Tax
1.61	0.12
1.74	0.13

and so forth.

10.75% Tax Rate

Sales Up To	Tax
1.53	0.16
1.62	0.17
1.72	0.18
1.81	0.19
1.90	0.20

and so forth.

8.75% Tax Rate

Sales Up To	Tax
$0.05	0.00
0.17	0.01
0.28	0.02
0.39	0.03
0.51	0.04
0.62	0.05
0.74	0.06
0.85	0.07
0.97	0.08
1.08	0.09
1.19	0.10
1.31	0.11
1.42	0.12
1.54	0.13
1.65	0.14

and so forth.

¶747   Returns, Payments, and Due Dates

Sales tax returns (Sec. 1365) and use tax returns (Sec. 1405) for each calendar month are due on or before the 20th day of the next month. Returns are required for each monthly period whether taxable or nontaxable sales are made (Rule 710:65-3-7).

Vendors may be authorized to file semiannual returns if the tax liability for any one month does not exceed $50 (Sec. 1365(B), Rule 710:65-3-1).

Simplified electronic returns (SERs): SERs are an option for the reporting and remittance of sales and use tax for states like Oklahoma that are members of the Streamlined Sales and Use Tax (SST) Agreement. Sellers desiring to report sales and use tax using the SER to the states where they have sales normally register on the SST Governing Board's website at **http://www.streamlinedsalestax.org**, are assigned an SST identification (ID), and select a certified service provider (CSP) with whom they contract to transmit their SER to participating states. Alternatively, sellers can register with the SST Governing Board and elect to develop their own web service if they certify their web service with each participating state before any SER is transmitted.

Oklahoma permits sellers who have not registered on the SST Governing Board's website to use SERs by registering with Oklahoma, by completing a Business Tax Registration Application, and by being assigned a state ID. Such sellers can choose to contract with a CSP or develop their own web service to transmit their SER. A seller that indicates at the time of registration with the SST Agreement that it anticipates making no sales that would be sourced to Oklahoma is not required to file a sales tax return (until the month following the month in which the first sale occurs). (*Simplified Electronic Return,* Oklahoma Tax Commission, November 6, 2012, CCH OKLAHOMA TAX REPORTS, ¶ 201-088)

¶747   Oklahoma

- ## Electronic funds transfer (EFT)

Every taxpayer owing an average of $2,500 or more per month in sales taxes in the previous fiscal year must participate in the Tax Commission's EFT and electronic data interchange (Sec. 1365). Taxes collected the 1st through the 15th day of each month are due on the 20th day of the same month and taxes collected from the 16th through the end of the month are due on the 20th day of the following month.

Payments may be made online through the Taxpayer Access Point at **https:// oktap.tax.ok.gov/oktap/Web/_/**.

- ## Payment by credit or debit card

Payments required under any state tax law, including sales and use tax laws, may be made by a nationally recognized credit or debit card in addition to cash, money order, bank draft, check, and cashier's check (Sec. 218A.). If payment is made by credit or debit card, the Tax Commission may add an amount equal to the service charge collected by the credit card company. The Tax Commission determines which nationally recognized credit or debit cards will be accepted.

- ## Direct payment

Persons who make taxable purchases of at least $800,000 annually for use in Oklahoma enterprises, and who wish to remit the sales and use taxes due directly to the Oklahoma Tax Commission rather than to the vendor, may apply to the Commission for a direct payment permit. Permits are valid for three years. (Sec. 1364.1; Rule 710:65-9-10(a)) The purchases may not be made for resale and direct pay permit applicants must agree to give a resale certificate, rather than the direct payment permit, for any item purchased for resale (Rule 710:65-9-10(b)(1), (5)).

Effective July 1, 2013, direct pay permits may be issued to medical practitioners who make purchases of medical appliances, drugs for the treatment of human beings, medical devices, and other medical equipment when the cost of such items will be reimbursed by Medicare or Medicaid (Sec. 1364.1(B)(2)). "Practitioner" is defined in this context as a physician, osteopathic physician, surgeon, podiatrist, chiropractor, optometrist, pharmacist, psychologist, ophthalmologist, nurse practitioner, audiologist, or hearing aid dealer or fitter who is licensed by the state (Sec. 1357.6(B)).

To obtain a permit, one must file an application with the Tax Commission's Taxpayer Assistance Division that includes an agreement to accrue and remit all taxes due and to pay the taxes as required (Sec. 1364.1). Direct pay permit applicants must agree to make the payments to the state on or before the 20th day of the month following each monthly period in which the items become subject to tax by reason of their consumption in Oklahoma (Rule 710:65-9-10(b)(4)). Medical practitioners qualifying for a direct pay permit who owe an average of $500 or less per month may, instead of filing monthly reports, file quarterly reports and remit the taxes on or before the 20th day of the month following the calendar quarter (Sec. 1364.1(A)(1)(b)).

No sales or use tax is due from a direct pay permit holder on tangible personal property intended exclusively for use in states other than Oklahoma but that is stored in Oklahoma pending shipment to such other states or that is temporarily retained in Oklahoma for purposes of fabrication, repair, testing, alteration, maintenance, or other service (Sec. 1364.1(1)(a)).

- ## Uniform Sales Tax Administration Act

Oklahoma has enacted the Uniform Sales and Use Tax Administration Act and legislation to conform to the Streamlined Sales and Use Tax Agreement. For additional information on the uniform act, see "Streamlined Sales Tax Project," listed in the Table of Contents.

Sourcing of sales: See ¶ 745.

SST registration: See ¶ 749.

• **Vendor compensation**

If sales tax and use tax reports are timely filed and the taxes timely remitted, a collection discount of 1% may be claimed as a deduction by the seller, vendor, or out-of-state vendor or seller as remuneration for keeping records, filing returns, and remitting the tax (Sec. 1367.1; Sec. 1410.1(A)). No deduction is allowed if tax payments are remitted directly by the holder of a direct payment permit. The collection discount deduction may not exceed $3,300 per month per sales or use tax permit.

• **Consumer Compliance Initiative (use tax amnesty)**

The Oklahoma Tax Commission will waive penalties, interest, and collection fees for businesses that regularly make purchases of tangible personal property outside Oklahoma for their own use, storage, or consumption within Oklahoma. To qualify for relief, a consumer must:

(1) voluntarily file delinquent use tax returns and pay the related consumer use tax; and

(2) apply to the commission for an Oklahoma consumer use tax account in order to report and remit use taxes monthly.

The commission will refrain from assessing use tax for more than one year prior to the date that a consumer registers to pay consumer use tax. The rule outlines how to apply for a consumer use tax account (Rule 710:1-13-3).

The Initiative does not apply to use taxes already paid or remitted to the state, or to any matter for which a consumer has received notice of the commencement of an audit where the audit is not finally resolved (including any related administrative and judicial processes).

¶748   **Prepayment of Taxes**

Oklahoma has no provisions regarding prepayment of sales or use taxes.

¶749   **Vendor Registration**

All Group One and Group Three vendors must secure a permit to do business from the OTC prior to engaging in business (Sec. 1364, Rule 710:65-9-1). The permit is good for three years and is issued for a fee of $20.

Group One vendors are those who regularly and continuously engage in a business at an established place of business and make sales subject to the sales tax (Sec. 1363).

Group Three vendors are transient persons, firms, or corporations that make seasonal sales or make sales through peddlers, solicitors, or other salespersons without establishing places of business in Oklahoma.

Separate permits are necessary for each additional place of business (Sec. 1364.E), and permits are not assignable (Sec. 1364.F).

Group Two vendors, defined as those who occasionally make sales or become subject to the Sales Tax Act (Sec. 1363), do not require permits (Sec. 1364.K). Group Five motor fuel distributors receive limited permits.

Electronic filing required: New sales tax registrants who are required to report and remit sales tax must file their monthly sales tax report in compliance with the Commission's electronic funds transfer and electronic data interchange program on the 20th day of the month following the month in which the sale occurred. A taxpayer may be granted an exception to the electronic reporting requirement by applying to the Commission in writing for a determination that the taxpayer is unable to comply with the requirement.

The instructions for applying for an exemption to electronic filing are available in the Oklahoma Business Registration Packet at **http://www.tax.ok.gov/**. Guidelines used in determining whether a taxpayer is unable to report electronically are that the taxpayer lacks a computer or Internet access, the taxpayer does not use a tax preparer that has a computer or Internet access, and the taxpayer is unable to use the Telefile system (Rule 710:65-3-1).

- **Solicitation permit**

Persons desiring to engage in continuous, regular, or systematic solicitations through display of products by advertisement in newspapers or radio or television media in Oklahoma (defined as Group Four vendors by Sec. 1363) must secure a solicitation permit from the Tax Commission (Sec. 1354.4). The permit is good for three years and is issued for a fee of $20.

- **SST registration**

To register under the Streamlined Sales and Use Tax Agreement (SST), sellers must go to **https://www.sstregister.org**. Sellers can also update previously submitted registration information at this website. The information provided will be sent to all of the full member states and to associate members for which the seller chooses to collect.

When a seller registers under the Agreement, it must select the certified technology model it will be using. The models are the following:

Model One: Certified Service Provider (CSP), an agent certified under the Agreement to perform all the seller's sales and use tax functions;

Model Two: Certified Automated System (CAS), software certified under the Agreement to calculate the appropriate tax (for which the seller retains responsibility for remitting);

Model Three: Certified System (CS), a proprietary automated sales tax system certified under the Agreement.

Model Four: a seller that is registered under the SST Agreement and that is not a Model 1 Seller, Model 2 Seller, or Model 3 Seller.

- **Out-of-state companies responding to disasters or emergencies**

Out-of-state businesses that come to Oklahoma to perform work or services in response to a declared state disaster or emergency in Oklahoma are not considered to have established a level of presence that would require the business to register, file or remit state or local taxes (Sec. 55005(C)). Furthermore, the employees of the out-of-state business are exempt from any state licensing or registration requirements or filing and remitting Oklahoma personal income tax for work accrued during the disaster response period (Sec. 55005(D)). A "disaster response period" begins 10 days prior to a disaster being declared, and lasts 60 days after the declared state disaster (Sec. 55055(B)(4)). The following transaction taxes and fees, however, are not exempt for an out-of-state business or employee: fuel taxes, sales taxes, hotel taxes, or car rental taxes (Sec. 55005(E)).

For purposes of any state or local tax on, or measured by, net or gross income or receipts, all activity of the out-of-state business that is conducted in Oklahoma for such disaster work is disregarded with respect to any filing requirements for such tax, including the filing required for a unitary or combined group of which the out-of-state business may be a part. For purposes of apportioning income, revenue or receipts, the performance by an out-of-state business of such disaster work is not sourced to or does not otherwise impact or increase the amount of income, revenue or receipts apportioned to Oklahoma. (Sec. 55005(C)

¶ 750 Sales or Use Tax Credits

Use tax credits are allowed in many instances for sales taxes paid to other states or counties. Oklahoma law provides an exemption equal to any tax paid by the person using tangible personal property in Oklahoma under the laws of some other state (Sec. 1404(c); Rule 710:65-21-20(3)). In cases in which the sales tax is paid out of state, the Oklahoma use tax applies only to the extent that the other tax paid is lower than the Oklahoma use tax.

Incentives are given for the location or expansion of manufacturing or other business in the state.

Collection discount: see ¶ 747.

Sales tax relief for low-income persons: Resident individuals who have lived in Oklahoma during the entire tax year and whose gross household incomes for the year do not exceed $30,000 may file a claim for sales tax relief (Sec. 5011(A)). For an individual claiming one or more allowable personal exemptions other than the allowable personal exemption for that individual or the spouse of that individual, an individual with a physical disability constituting a substantial handicap to employment, or an individual who is 65 years of age or older at the close of the tax year, a claim for sales tax relief may be filed if the gross household income for the year does not exceed $50,000.

Residents of counties levying a local sales tax who have gross household incomes that do not exceed $12,000 per year can file a claim for sales tax relief (Sec. 1370.3). The credit is in the amount of $40 multiplied by the number of personal exemptions to which the taxpayer would be entitled under the Oklahoma Income Tax Act, not including the extra exemptions provided taxpayers who are blind or over 65 years of age.

• **Incentive rebates**

Film or television productions: The Oklahoma Film Enhancement Rebate Program, administered by the Office of the Oklahoma Film and Music Commission and the Oklahoma Tax Commission, was created under the state's Compete With Canada Film Act (Sec. 3624(A)). Under the program, a rebate of up to 35% of documented expenditures made in Oklahoma that are directly attributable to the production in Oklahoma of a film, television production, or television commercial, may be paid to the production company responsible for the production. "Film," "expenditure," and "production company" are defined in Sec. 3623 for purposes of the rebate program.

The amount of rebate paid to a production company will be increased by an additional 2% of documented expenditures if the company spends at least $20,000 for the use of music created by an Oklahoma resident that is recorded within the state, or for the cost of recording songs or music in the state for use in the production (Sec. 3624(B)). Eligibility criteria for payment of a rebate is set forth in Sec. 3624(D).

A production company is not eligible to receive both a rebate under this program and the sales tax exemption under Sec. 1357(23).

The Compete With Canada Film Act terminates effective July 1, 2024, and no claims will be paid under the Act after that date. (Sec. 3626).

¶ 751 Deficiency Assessments

If a taxpayer fails to file a report or return, the Tax Commission can determine the correct amount of the tax from any information in its possession or that it can obtain (Sec. 221(a), Rule 710:65-5-4). If the Tax Commission determines that additional tax is due it must give written notice of its proposed assessment to the taxpayer at the last known address. Assessments can be issued against legal entities as well as other persons who may be liable (Rule 710:65-5-5).

¶752 Audit Procedures

In the administration of any state tax, the Tax Commission can conduct an examination or investigation of the place of business, tangible personal property, and books, records, papers, accounts, and documents of any taxpayer (Sec. 206; Rule 710:65-5-1). If the books, records, and papers of a taxpayer are in the possession of someone other than the taxpayer, the Tax Commission may subpoena the production of the records.

The Commission can also require taxpayers to furnish any information deemed necessary to determine the amount of state tax liability (Sec. 248).

An auditor for the Commission can suggest a sample audit rather than a detailed audit, with the auditor selecting the periods to sample and applying the results to all the periods of the audit (Rule 710:65-5-2). The taxpayer must agree in writing to this arrangement.

Voluntary Disclosure Program: "Voluntary disclosure" generally arises when a taxpayer or a representative contacts the Commission prior to any initial contact by the Commission, the federal Internal Revenue Service, or an agent of these tax authorities concerning the filing of a return and/or the payment of a tax liability.

A major component of the program is to help resolve sales and use, withholding, and corporate income and franchise tax liabilities when nexus is the central issue. A program guide briefly explains: how to qualify for the program; the benefits of a voluntary disclosure, such as a limited look-back period and consideration for a specified interest and/or penalty waiver; how to apply, even anonymously, to the program using Form 892; the Commission's application review and approval process; the Commission's right to audit certain taxpayer documents for the designated voluntary disclosure period; and the taxpayer's right to confidentiality throughout the whole process. (*Voluntary Disclosure Agreement Guide,* Oklahoma Tax Commission, October 2014, CCH OKLAHOMA TAX REPORTS, ¶ 201-145, also available at **https://www.ok.gov/tax/documents/VDA%20Information%20Guide%20vs%203.pdf**)

¶753 Statute of Limitations

No assessment of any tax can be made after the expiration of three years from the date the return was required to be filed or the date the return was actually filed, whichever is later (Sec. 223(a), Sec. 223(b)).

Prior to expiration of this three-year limitations period, the Tax Commission and the taxpayer can consent in writing to extend the period.

• False or fraudulent return

In the case of either a false or a fraudulent report or return, or failure to file a report or return, the Tax Commission is authorized to compute, determine, and assess the estimated amount of tax due from any information in its possession without time limitation (Sec. 223(c)).

¶754 Application for Refund

Any taxpayer who has paid taxes through error of fact or computation or misinterpretation of law can file a verified claim for refund within three years from the date of payment (Sec. 227). The claim must specify the name of the taxpayer, the date the tax was paid, the tax period for which the tax was paid, the nature and kind of tax, the amount claimed as erroneously paid, and the grounds upon which a refund is sought. The Tax Commission may accept an amended sales tax return or report in lieu of a verified claim for refund if the amended return or report establishes a lesser tax liability than the return or report filed previously.

A regulation requires that copies of canceled checks also be provided by the claimant (Rule 710:65-11-1).

¶ 755   OREGON

¶ 756   **State Tax Not Imposed**

There are no sales or use taxes imposed by the state of Oregon. However, some local jurisdictions impose limited taxes on sales of food and/or transient lodging. For details, consult the CCH OREGON TAX REPORTS, beginning at ¶ 31-001.

¶ 770   PENNSYLVANIA

¶ 771   Scope of Tax

Source.—Statutory references are to the Pennsylvania Tax Reform Code of 1971, as amended to date. Details are reported in the CCH PENNSYLVANIA TAX REPORTS starting at ¶ 60-000.

The sales tax is an excise tax imposed on the sale at retail within Pennsylvania of tangible personal property and certain services (Sec. 202(a), Act of March 4, 1971, P.L. 6; Reg. Sec. 31.1). The use tax is an excise tax imposed on the use within the Commonwealth of tangible personal property and certain services purchased outside the Commonwealth and on taxable purchases within the Commonwealth upon which no sales tax has been paid (Sec. 202(b), Act of March 4, 1971, P.L. 6; Reg. Sec. 31.1, Reg. Sec. 31.7(a)). Use tax is not imposed if the sales tax has been paid (Sec. 202(b), Act of March 4, 1971, P.L. 6).

Digital products: Sales of digital property recorded and delivered on a tangible medium such as a computer diskette or a CD are taxable (Sec. 202, Act of March 4, 1971, P.L. 6, [72 P.S. §7202]; Policy Statement 60.19, Department of Revenue, CCH PENNSYLVANIA TAX REPORTS, ¶ 64-754a). In accordance with the holding in *Graham Packaging Co. v. Commonwealth of Pennsylvania,* Pennsylvania Commonwealth Court, No. 652 F.R. 2002, September 15, 2005, CCH PENNSYLVANIA TAX REPORTS, ¶ 203-456, the sale or use of all canned software is subject to sales and use tax regardless of the method of delivery.

Effective August 1, 2016, sales and use tax is imposed on downloaded videos; photographs; books; any otherwise taxable printed matter; applications (commonly known as apps); games; music; any other audio, including satellite radio service; canned software; and any other otherwise taxable tangible personal property electronically or digitally delivered, streamed, or accessed. These items are taxable as tangible personal property and are considered tangible personal property whether they are electronically or digitally delivered, streamed, or accessed and whether they are purchased singly, by subscription, or in any other manner, including maintenance, updates, and support. (Sec. 201(o)(4)(b), Act of March 4, 1971, P.L. 6)

Purchases of canned computer software licenses were subject to Pennsylvania sales and use tax because canned software is considered tangible personal property and the definition of "sale at retail" specifically includes a grant of a license to use tangible personal property. In concluding that canned software is tangible personal property, the court declined to adopt the "essence of the transaction" test as the Commonwealth Court did in *Graham Packaging.* Rather, the court found that factors listed in the Statutory Construction Act, particularly the former statute and legislative and administrative interpretations of the statute, supported the conclusion that the Legislature intended to tax canned software as tangible personal property. (*Dechert LLP v. Pennsylvania,* Pennsylvania Supreme Court, No. 12 MAP 2008, July 20, 2010, CCH PENNSYLVANIA TAX REPORTS, ¶ 204-027)

Cloud computing: Charges for the use of canned computer software that is hosted on a server and accessed electronically by a taxpayer's customers and employees (also known as "software as a service" or "SaaS") are subject to Pennsylvania sales and use tax if the user is located in Pennsylvania. Because computer software is tangible personal property, a charge for electronically accessing software is taxable. In accessing the software the user is exercising a license to use the software, as well as control or power over the software at the user's location. The taxpayer is required to collect tax from a customer when the user is located in Pennsylvania. Charges for remote software access are not subject to tax if the user is located outside Pennsylvania, even if the server that hosts the software is located in the state. (*Legal Letter Ruling No. SUT-12-001,* Pennsylvania Department of Revenue, May 31, 2012, CCH PENNSYLVANIA TAX REPORTS, ¶ 204-185)

• Medical marijuana tax

Pennsylvania imposes a 5% tax on the gross receipts of a grower/processor from the sale of medical marijuana to a dispensary, effective May 18, 2016. The tax is charged against and paid by the grower/processor and cannot be added as a separate charge or line item on any sales slip, invoice, receipt, or other statement or memorandum of the price paid by a dispensary, patient, or caregiver.

The tax is to be administered in the same manner as the state gross receipts tax, except that estimated tax payments under that law are not required. A grower/processor must make quarterly payments each calendar quarter; the tax is due and payable on the 20th day of January, April, July, and October for the preceding calendar quarter.

Medical marijuana is not subject to the state sales tax. Growers/processors must provide information as required by the Department of Revenue. (Act No. 2016-16 (S.B. 3), Laws 2016)

• Taxable services

The following services are subject to sales and use taxes (Sec. 201(k), Act of March 4, 1971, P.L. 6, Sec. 201(o), Act of March 4, 1971, P.L. 6; Reg. Sec. 31.1(4), Reg. Sec. 31.5):

— cleaning, inspecting, lubricating, polishing, washing, or waxing motor vehicles;

— applying or installing tangible personal property as a repair or replacement part of personal property other than clothing or shoes;

— altering, cleaning, dry-cleaning, dyeing, fitting, laundering, mending, pressing, or repairing tangible personal property other than clothing or shoes;

— the imprinting or printing of tangible personal property of others;

— labor or service charges by a vendor for delivering, installing, or applying tangible personal property sold by the vendor;

— lobbying services;

— adjustment, collection or credit reporting services;

— secretarial or editing services;

— disinfecting or pest control services, building maintenance or cleaning services;

— employment agency or help supply services (not including professional employer organization services; see *All Staffing, Inc. v. Pennsylvania*, Pennsylvania Commonwealth Court, No. 325 F.R. 2006, January 5, 2010, CCH PENNSYLVANIA TAX REPORTS, ¶ 203-970);

— lawn care service;

— self-storage service; and

— nonenhanced telecommunications services (including sales of prepaid calling arrangements).

The Department of Revenue has issued a list of various items that indicates whether the items are subject to sales and use tax (*Notice*, Pennsylvania Department of Revenue, December 26, 2009, CCH PENNSYLVANIA TAX REPORTS, ¶ 203-968).

The Department of Revenue bulletin classifies and defines various telecommunications services as enhanced or nonenhanced services for sales and use tax purposes. Enhanced telecommunications services, which are excluded from tax, include data processing, information retrieval, video on demand, video programming, and voice mail. Nonenhanced telecommunications services include broadband transmission, digital subscriber line (DSL), direct broadcast satellite, intranet transmission, integrated services digital network (ISDN), and plain old telephone service (POTS) splitter transmissions (*Sales Tax Bulletin 2005-03,* Pennsylvania Department of Revenue, September 30, 2005, CCH PENNSYLVANIA TAX REPORTS, ¶ 203-461).

The use of property upon which taxable services have been performed is deemed to be a use of the services by the person using the property (Sec. 201(o)(7), Act of March 4, 1971, P.L. 6).

• **Incidence of tax**

Sales and use taxes are collected by vendors from purchasers and paid over to the Commonwealth (Sec. 202(a), Act of March 4, 1971, P.L. 6, Sec. 237(b), Act of March 4, 1971, P.L. 6). If use tax is not paid to a vendor, the purchaser must pay it to the Commonwealth (Sec. 202(b), Act of March 4, 1971, P.L. 6; Reg. Sec. 31.7(a)).

"Vendor" means a person maintaining a place of business in Pennsylvania who sells or leases tangible personal property or renders services, the sale or use of which is subject to tax (Sec. 201(p), Act of March 4, 1971, P.L. 6).

• **Nexus**

Any seller maintaining a place of business in Pennsylvania must collect and remit sales or use tax. "Maintaining a place of business" includes (Sec. 201(b), Act of March 4, 1971, P.L. 6, [72 P.S. § 7201(b)]; Reg. Sec. 56.1):

(1) Having, maintaining, or using within Pennsylvania (either directly or through a subsidiary) an office, distribution house, sales house, warehouse, service enterprise, other place of business, or an agent or representative, regardless of whether the place of business, representative, or agent is located in Pennsylvania permanently or temporarily, or whether the person or subsidiary maintaining the place of business or agent is authorized to do business in the state;

(2) Engaging in any activity as a business within Pennsylvania (either directly or through a subsidiary, representative, or agent) in connection with the lease, sale or delivery of tangible personal property or the performance of services on tangible personal property for use, storage or consumption in connection with the sale or delivery for use of taxable services including, but not limited to, having, maintaining or using any office, distribution house, sales house, warehouse or other place of business, any stock of goods or any solicitor, canvasser, salesman, representative or agent under its authority, at its direction or with its permission, regardless of whether the person or subsidiary is authorized to do business in Pennsylvania; or

(3) Regularly or substantially soliciting orders within Pennsylvania in connection with the lease, sale or delivery of tangible personal property to or the performance of services on tangible personal property or in connection with the sale or delivery of taxable services for Pennsylvania residents by means of catalogs or other advertising, whether the orders are accepted within or without Pennsylvania.

(4) Entering the state to provide assembly, service, or repair of tangible personal property, either directly or through an agent.

(5) Delivering tangible personal property to locations within the state, if the delivery includes unpacking, positioning, placing, or assembling the property.

(6) Having any contact within the state that would allow the state to require a person to collect and remit tax under the U.S. Constitution; or

(7) Providing a customer's mobile telecommunications service if the service provider is the customer's home service provider under the Mobile Telecommunications Sourcing Act (discussed at ¶ 775).

"Click-through" nexus: The Department of Revenue has issued a bulletin addressing the sales tax collection responsibilities of retailers located outside Pennsylvania that have nexus with Pennsylvania, including retailers that have click-through nexus. The department notifies taxpayers of its intent to treat a remote seller as "maintaining a place of business" in Pennsylvania if the remote seller regularly solicits orders from Pennsylvania customers via the website of an entity or individual physically located in Pennsylvania, such as via click-through technology. The department reminds retailers having nexus with the state to collect sales tax on Internet, catalog and telephone sales. (*Sales and Use Tax Bulletin 2011-01*, Department of Revenue, December 1, 2011, CCH PENNSYLVANIA TAX REPORTS, ¶ 204-148)

• **Streamlined Act status**

Pennsylvania is not a member of the Streamlined Sales and Use Tax Agreement.

¶ 772   Tax Base

Tax is imposed on each separate sale at retail, computed and collected on the basis of the total amount of taxable items in the transaction (Reg. Sec. 31.2(3)). The tax base for the sales and use tax is generally the purchase price of tangible personal property and services (Sec. 202(a), Act of March 4, 1971, P.L. 6; Reg. Sec. 31.2) however, there are exceptions as discussed below. "Purchase price" is defined as the total value of anything paid, delivered, or promised to be paid and delivered in complete performance of a sale or purchase at retail, without deduction for the cost or value of the property sold, transportation, labor or service, interest or discount paid after consummation of the sale, commonwealth taxes, or any other expense (Sec. 201(g), Act of March 4, 1971, P.L. 6; Reg. Sec. 31.2(1), Reg. Sec. 33.1, Reg. Sec. 33.2). However, gratuities or separately stated deposit charges for returnable containers are excluded from the purchase price.

If there is a transfer or retention of possession or custody, whether it is a rental, lease, service, or otherwise, of tangible personal property, the full consideration paid or delivered is considered to be the purchase price even if it is designated as payment for processing, laundering service, maintenance, insurance, repairs, depreciation, or otherwise (Sec. 201(g)(4), Act of March 4, 1971, P.L. 6).

¶ 773   List of Exemptions, Exceptions, and Exclusions

Unless otherwise indicated, the statutory exemptions listed below apply to both sales and use taxes; those applicable only to the use tax are listed separately. Items that are excluded from the sales or use tax base are treated at ¶ 772, "Tax Base."

A detailed list of taxable and exempt property is included in the Retailers' Information Guide, published and updated periodically by the Pennsylvania Department of Revenue and available at **http://www.revenue.pa.gov/FormsandPublications/ FormsforBusinesses/Documents/Sales-Use%20Tax/rev-717.pdf**.

• **Sales and use tax exemptions, exceptions, and exclusions**

Advertising inserts	Sec. 204(30), Act of March 4, 1971, P.L. 6 [72 P.S. §7204]
Agricultural property	Sec. 201(k)(8), Act of March 4, 1971, P.L. 6 [72 P.S. §7201], Sec. 201(o)(4), Act of March 4, 1971, P.L. 6 [72 P.S. §7201], Sec. 204(62), Act of March 4, 1971, P.L. 6 [72 P.S. §7204(62)]
Air conditioning equipment, residential, repair of	Sec. 201(aa), Act of March 4, 1971, P.L. 6 [72 P.S. §7201(aa)]
Broadcasting equipment	Sec. 201(d)(12), Act of March 4, 1971, P.L. 6 [72 P.S. §7201], Sec. 201(k)(8), Act of March 4, 1971, P.L. 6 [72 P.S. §7201], Sec. 201(o)(4), Act of March 4, 1971, P.L. 6 [72 P.S. §7201]
Cable or video programming basic service	Sec. 201(*ll*), Act of March 4, 1971, P.L. 6 [72 P.S. §7201]
Caskets, burial vaults, and tombstones	Sec. 204(31), Act of March 4, 1971, P.L. 6 [72 P.S. §7204]
Charitable organizations	Sec. 204(10), Act of March 4, 1971, P.L. 6 [72 P.S. §7204]
Cleaning and laundering clothes	Sec. 201(k)(4), Act of March 4, 1971, P.L. 6 [72 P.S. §7201], Sec. 201(o)(4), Act of March 4, 1971, P.L. 6 [72 P.S. §7201]
Clothing and footwear; clothing patterns	Sec. 204(26), Act of March 4, 1971, P.L. 6 [72 P.S. §7204]
Coal	Sec. 204(18), Act of March 4, 1971, P.L. 6 [72 P.S. §7204]
Coin-operated self-service laundry equipment	Sec. 201(k)(4), Act of March 4, 1971, P.L. 6 [72 P.S. §7201], Sec. 201(o)(4), Act of March 4, 1971, P.L. 6 [72 P.S. §7201]

¶773 Pennsylvania

Firewood, fire pellets	Sec. 204(44), Act of March 4, 1971, P.L. 6 [72 P.S. §7204]
Fish feed	Sec. 204(39), Act of March 4, 1971, P.L. 6 [72 P.S. §7204]
Flags	Sec. 204(32), Act of March 4, 1971, P.L. 6 [72 P.S. §7204]
Food and beverages	Sec. 204(29), Act of March 4, 1971, P.L. 6 [72 P.S. §7204], Sec. 204(49), Act of March 4, 1971, P.L. 6 [72 P.S. §7204], Sec. 204(53), Act of March 4, 1971, P.L. 6 [72 P.S. §7204], Sec. 204(61), Act of March 4, 1971, P.L. 6 [72 P.S. §7204]
Food stamp purchases	Sec. 204(46), Act of March 4, 1971, P.L. 6 [72 P.S. §7204]
Fruit processing	Sec. 201(d), Act of March 4, 1971, P.L. 6 [72 P.S. §7201]
Fuel oil	Sec. 204(5), Act of March 4, 1971, P.L. 6 [72 P.S. §7204]
Gas	Sec. 204(5), Act of March 4, 1971, P.L. 6 [72 P.S. §7204]
Gasoline and motor fuels	Sec. 204(11), Act of March 4, 1971, P.L. 6 [72 P.S. §7204]
Government sales, official documents	Sec. 204(66), Act of March 4, 1971, P.L. 6 [72 P.S. §7204]
Helicopters and similar rotorcraft	Sec. 204(67), (68), Act of March 4, 1971, P.L. 6, [72 P.S. §7204]
Horses delivered out of state or for racing	Sec. 204(38), Act of March 4, 1971, P.L. 6 [72 P.S. §7204], Sec. 201(k)(8)(b), Act of March 4, 1971, P.L. 6 [72 P.S. §7201]

Horticulture and floriculture property	Sec. 201(k)(8)(b), Act of March 4, 1971, P.L. 6 [72 P.S. § 7201], Sec. 201(o)(4), Act of March 4, 1971, P.L. 6 [72 P.S. § 7201]
Interior office building cleaning services, costs of supplied employee	Sec. 201(aa), Act of March 4, 1971, P.L. 6 [72 P.S. § 7201], Sec. 204(51), Act of March 4, 1971, P.L. 6 [72 P.S. § 7204]
Internet access services	Sec. 201(rr)(3), Act of March 4, 1971, P.L. 6 [72 P.S. § 7201]
Interstate transactions	Sec. 201(o)(4)(A), Act of March 4, 1971, P.L. 6 [72 P.S. § 7201]
Isolated sales	Sec. 204(1), Act of March 4, 1971, P.L. 6 [72 P.S. § 7204]
Kerosene	Sec. 204(5), Act of March 4, 1971, P.L. 6 [72 P.S. § 7204]
Keystone Opportunity Expansion Zone (KOEZ) businesses	Sec. 511, Act of October 6, 1998, P.L. 705, No. 92, [73 P.S. § 820.511]
Keystone Opportunity Zone (KOZ) businesses	Sec. 204(57), Act of March 4, 1971, P.L. 6 [72 P.S. § 7204], Sec. 511, Act of October 6, 1998, P.L. 92 [73 P.S. § 820.511]
Labor charge for equipment leases	Sec. 201(g)(4), Act of March 4, 1971, P.L. 6 [72 P.S. § 7201]
Lawn care services	Sec. 201(k)(17), Act of March 4, 1971, P.L. 6 [72 P.S. § 7201], Sec. 201(o)(15), Act of March 4, 1971, P.L. 6 [72 P.S. § 7201]
Magazines	Sec. 204(50), Act of March 4, 1971, P.L. 6 [72 P.S. § 7204]
Mail order catalogs and direct mail advertising literature	Sec. 204(35), Act of March 4, 1971, P.L. 6 [72 P.S. § 7204]

Manufacturing, property used in	Sec. 201(c), Act of March 4, 1971, P.L. 6 [72 P.S. § 7201], Sec. 201(k)(8), Act of March 4, 1971, P.L. 6 [72 P.S. § 7201], Sec. 201(o)(4), Act of March 4, 1971, P.L. 6 [72 P.S. § 7201]
Medical marijuana (subject to a separate tax; see ¶ 771)	Act No. 2016-16 (S.B. 3), Laws 2016
Medicine and medical, dental, and optical supplies	Sec. 204(4), Act of March 4, 1971, P.L. 6 [72 P.S. § 7204], Sec. 204(17), Act of March 4, 1971, P.L. 6 [72 P.S. § 7204], Sec. 204(56), Act of March 4, 1971, P.L. 6 [72 P.S. § 7204]
Memorials, property used to construct	Sec. 204(45), Act of March 4, 1971, P.L. 6 [72 P.S. § 7204]
Mining property	Sec. 201(c)(3), Act of March 4, 1971, P.L. 6 [72 P.S. § 7201], Sec. 201(k)(8), Act of March 4, 1971, P.L. 6 [72 P.S. § 7201], Sec, 201(o)(4), Act of March 4, 1971, P.L. 6 [72 P.S. § 7201]
Motion picture film for commercial exhibition	Sec. 204(34), Act of March 4, 1971, P.L. 6 [72 P.S. § 7204]
Motor fuels	Sec. 204(11), Act of March 4, 1971, P.L. 6 [72 P.S. § 7204]
Newspapers	Sec. 204(30), Act of March 4, 1971, P.L. 6 [72 P.S. § 7204]
Nonprofit educational institution	Sec. 204(10), Act of March 4, 1971, P.L. 6 [72 P.S. § 7204]
Nonresidents' user of property in Pennsylvania	Sec. 201(j), Act of March 4, 1971, P.L. 6, Sec. 204(2), Act of March 4, 1971, P.L. 6 [72 P.S. § 7204], Sec. 204(3), Act of March 4, 1971, P.L. 6 [72 P.S. § 7204]

Packaging and wrapping charges for items to be resold	Sec. 204(13), Act of March 4, 1971, P.L. 6, [72 P.S. § 7204(13)]
Packaging and wrapping material	Sec. 204(13), Act of March 4, 1971, P.L. 6 [72 P.S. § 7204]
Philadelphia Economic Development District, sales to businesses in .	Act 226 (H.B. 1321), Laws 2004.
Printing, property used in	Sec. 201(c)(2), Act of March 4, 1971, P.L. 6 [72 P.S. § 7201]
Processing, property used in	Sec. 201(d), Act of March 4, 1971, P.L. 6 [72 P.S. § 7201], Sec. 201(k)(8), Act of March 4, 1971, P.L. 6 [72 P.S. § 7201], Sec. 201(o)(4), Act of March 4, 1971, P.L. 6 [72 P.S. § 7201]
Rail transportation equipment	Sec. 204(36), Act of March 4, 1971, P.L. 6 [72 P.S. § 7204]
Religious organization	Sec. 204(10), Act of March 4, 1971, P.L. 6 [72 P.S. § 7204]
Religious publications	Sec. 204(28), Act of March 4, 1971, P.L. 6 [72 P.S. § 7204]
Resales	Sec. 201(k)(8), Act of March 4, 1971, P.L. 6 [72 P.S. § 7201]
Research, property used in	Sec. 201(c)(5), Act of March 4, 1971, P.L. 6 [72 P.S. § 7201]
Ridesharing	Sec. 6, Act of Dec. 14, 1982, P.L. 279 [72 P.S. § 7202]
School buses	Sec. 204(43), Act of March 4, 1971, P.L. 6 [72 P.S. § 7204]
Sports program sales	Sec. 204(49), Act of March 4, 1971, P.L. 6 [72 P.S. § 7204]
State and local government transactions	Sec. 204(12), Act of March 4, 1971, P.L. 6 [72 P.S. § 7204]
Steam	Sec. 204(5), Act of March 4, 1971, P.L. 6 [72 P.S. § 7204]

¶773   **Pennsylvania**

Stenographic services	Sec. 201(y), Act of March 4, 1971, P.L. 6 [72 P.S. §7201]
Strategic Development Areas, sales to qualified businesses	Sec. 2931-C, Act of March 4, 1971, P.L. 6 [72 P.S. §7201]
Telephone services, basic local residential	Sec. 201(m), Act of March 4, 1971, P.L. 6 [72 P.S. §7201]
Textbooks	Sec. 204(33), Act of March 4, 1971, P.L. 6 [72 P.S. §7204]
Tourist promotion agency purchases	Sec. 204(41), Act of March 4, 1971, P.L. 6 [72 P.S. §7204]
Transfer of vehicles	Sec. 204(24), Act of March 4, 1971, P.L. 6 [72 P.S. §7204]
Trout	Sec. 204(42), Act of March 4, 1971, P.L. 6 [72 P.S. §7204]
Utility services and property	Sec. 201(k)(8), Act of March 4, 1971, P.L. 6 [72 P.S. §7201], Sec. 201(o)(4), Act of March 4, 1971, P.L. 6 [72 P.S. §7201]
Vessels and property used by vessels	Sec. 204(14)—Sec. 204(16), Act of March 4, 1971, P.L. 6 [72 P.S. §7204]
Veterans' organizations	Sec. 9303, Act of August 1, 1975, P.L. 92 [51 P.S. §8903]
Volunteer firefighters' organizations	Sec. 204(10), Act of March 4, 1971, P.L. 6 [72 P.S. §7204]
Water	Sec. 204(25), Act of March 4, 1971, P.L. 6 [72 P.S. §7204]

¶774   Rate of Tax

Sales and use taxes are imposed at the rate of 6% (Sec. 202, Act of March 4, 1971, P.L. 6 [72 P.S. §7202]; Reg. Sec. 31.2). The hotel occupancy tax is also imposed at the rate of 6% (Sec. 210, Act of March 4, 1971, P.L. 6 [72 P.S. §7210]).

Medical marijuana: Pennsylvania imposes a 5% tax on the gross receipts of a grower/processor from the sale of medical marijuana to a dispensary, effective May 18, 2016. The tax is charged against and paid by the grower/processor and cannot be added as a separate charge or line item on any sales slip, invoice, receipt, or other statement or memorandum of the price paid by a dispensary, patient, or caregiver.

Medical marijuana is not subject to the state sales tax. (Act No. 2016-16 (S.B. 3), Laws 2016)

¶ 775   Local Taxes

A 2% local sales and use tax is imposed in Philadelphia (Phila. Code Sec. 19-2701). An excise tax on hotel occupancies is imposed at the rate of 1%.

Philadelphia has an additional 6% hotel room rental tax on transients (Sec. 19-2402, Philadelphia Code) plus a 1% tourism and marketing tax on hotel room rentals (Sec. 19-2402.1, Philadelphia Code), and a 1.2% hospitality tax. (Sec. 19-2402.2, Philadelphia Code).

Allegheny County (Pittsburgh) imposes a 1% sales, use, and hotel occupancy tax upon each separate sale at retail of tangible personal property or services within the boundaries of the county (Sec. 3152-B, Act of July 28, 1953, P.L. 723; Secs. 1—3, Art. IV, Allegheny Co.; Ordinance No. 32066 of March 31, 1994). Allegheny County also imposes an additional 5% convention center tax on hotel, motel, and room rental charges.

All third through eighth class counties are authorized to impose a hotel occupancy tax of up to 3% of the consideration received by hotel operators for each temporary room rental (Sec. 1770.2, County Code Act of August 9, 1955, P.L. 323 [16 P.S. § 1770.2]).

Online travel companies: The Pennsylvania Supreme Court denied a petition for appeal in a case in which the Commonwealth Court held that an online travel company (OTC) was not liable for Philadelphia hotel tax on the difference between the room rates it contracted with hotels and the rates, including fees, it charged its customers for rooms, because the OTC was not an "operator" under the ordinance (*Philadelphia v. Philadelphia Tax Review Board,* Pennsylvania Supreme Court, No. 86 EAL 2012, August 15, 2012).

Mobile telecommunications: Pennsylvania conforms to the federal Mobile Telecommunications Sourcing Act (MTSA) (P.L. 106-252) (Sec. 203-A, Act of March 4, 1971, P.L. 6, [72 P.S. § 7203-A]). Wireless telecommunication services are sourced to the customer's "primary place of use," which is the residential or primary business address of the customer and must be located in the service provider's licensed service area. The jurisdiction in which the primary place of use is located is the only jurisdiction that may tax the communications services, regardless of the customer's location when a call is placed or received.

¶ 776   Bracket Schedule

The 6% Pennsylvania sales and use taxes are computed in accordance with the following bracket schedule (Sec. 203, Act of March 4, 1971, P.L. 6; Reg. Sec. 31.2):

Purchase price	Tax
10¢ or less	0
11¢ but less than 18¢	1¢
18¢ but less than 35¢	2¢
35¢ but less than 51¢	3¢
51¢ but less than 68¢	4¢
68¢ but less than 85¢	5¢
85¢ but less than $1.01	6¢

The tax on purchases in excess of $1 is 6% of each dollar plus the above bracket amounts on any fraction of a dollar.

A complete bracket schedule, including sales of up to $3000, is available at **http://www.revenue.pa.gov/FormsandPublications/FormsforBusinesses/Documents/Sales-Use%20Tax/rev-221.pdf**.

¶775 Pennsylvania

¶ *777* Returns, Payments, and Due Dates

A licensee must file monthly returns if its total tax reported for the third calendar quarter of the preceding year is $600 or more (Sec. 217(a), Act of March 4, 1971, P.L. 6 [72 P.S. § 7217]; Reg. Sec. 34.3(a)(3)). The returns are due by the 20th day of the following month.

Returns must be filed on forms prescribed by the Department of Revenue by all persons who are required to pay tax or collect and remit tax to the Department (Sec. 215, Act of March 4, 1971, P.L. 6 [72 P.S. § 7215], Sec. 216, Act of March 4, 1971, P.L. 6 [72 P.S. § 7216]). If monthly returns are not required, quarterly returns are filed by licensees on or before April 20, July 20, October 20, and January 20 for the preceding three months ending the last day of March, June, September, and December (Sec. 217(a), Act of March 4, 1971, P.L. 6 [72 P.S. § 7217(a)]; Reg. Sec. 34.3(a)(3)).

Electronic filing: Sales and use tax returns may be filed electronically (Sec. 3003.8, Act of March 4, 1971, P.L. 6, [72 P.S. § 10003.8]). Taxpayers can access the online system by going to **www.etides.state.pa.us** and following the steps for electronic signature/filer registration or enterprise registration.

Payment by credit or debit card: Businesses may use credit or debit cards to pay sales and use taxes. Payments can be made by phone or over the Internet to Official Payments Corp., the state's credit/debit card service provider. A convenience fee is charged by the service provider. Additional information about credit/debit card payments is available on the DOR's website at **www.doreservices.state.pa.us/Business-Tax/CreditCardBusinessTax.htm**.

- **Electronic funds transfer (EFT)**

Effective January 1, 2014, all tax payments of $1,000 or more (previously, $10,000), other than personal income tax payments made by individuals, must be made electronically, and electronic filing is required for returns or reports filed by a third-party tax preparer who submits more than 10 (previously, 50) returns or reports per year to the Department of Revenue. (Reg. Sec. 5.3). A separate transfer must be made for each payment.

A taxpayer who is not required to remit payments by EFT may do so after receiving approval from the Secretary of Revenue (Reg. Sec. 5.4).

Additional information is available at **https://www.doreservices.state.pa.us/BusinessTax/default.htm**.

- **Collection discount**

For sales and use tax returns due on or after August 1, 2016, the collection discount allowed to licensees as compensation for collecting and remitting the tax is the lesser of:

    — 1% of the amount of tax collected or

    — $25 per return for a monthly filer,

    — $75 per return for a quarterly filer, or

    — $150 per return for a semiannual filer.

Previously, the discount was a flat 1% of the amount of tax collected. (Sec. 227, Act of March 4, 1971, P.L. 6, [72 P.S. § 7227])

¶ *778* Prepayment of Taxes

The Department of Revenue may require or authorize certain categories of vendors selling property for resale to precollect from the purchaser the tax the purchaser will collect on the sale (Sec. 239, Act of March 4, 1971, P.L. 6 [72 P.S. § 7239]). A vendor cannot be required to precollect tax from a purchaser who purchases for resale more than $1,000 worth of property from the vendor per year. The purchaser who prepays the tax may, under Department regulations, be relieved of the duty to obtain a license if that duty arises only by reason of the sale of property with respect to which tax is prepaid. The vendor who has prepaid the tax may be reimbursed for the prepaid tax from the tax collected on the subsequent sale, and any remaining tax collected must be remitted with a return to the commonwealth.

A vendor prohibited by law or regulation from charging or collecting the purchase price before or at the time of delivery must prepay the tax, but is entitled to a credit or refund if the purchaser fails to pay the purchase price and tax and they are written off as uncollectible (Sec. 247, Act of March 4, 1971, P.L. 6 [72 P.S. § 7247]). Petitions for refund must be filed within 105 days of the close of the fiscal year in which the accounts were written off.

A sales and use tax licensee whose total sales and use tax liability for the third calendar quarter of the preceding year exceeds $25,000 is required to file by the 20th of each month a return that includes a prepayment in the amount of 50% of the licensee's total sales and use tax liability for the same month in the preceding calendar year. A licensee whose actual tax liability for the third calendar quarter of the preceding year equals or exceeds $25,000, but is less than $100,000, has the option of making prepayment in an amount equal to or greater than 50% of the licensee's actual tax liability for the current month (Sec. 217(a), Act of March 4, 1971, P.L. 6, [72 P.S. § 7217(a)(3)]). The return must also include tax due for the preceding month, less any amounts paid as a prepayment in the preceding month. (Sec. 202.2, Act of April 9, 1929 (P.L.343, No.176)[72 P.S. § 202.2])

The Department of Revenue may require taxpayers subject to the prepayment requirement to file returns and remit tax electronically. If a licensee fails to make a timely payment, or makes a payment of less than the required amount, the department may impose an additional penalty equal to 5% of the amount that was not timely paid. (Sec. 202.2, Act of April 9, 1929 (P.L.343, No.176)[72 P.S. § 202.2])

¶ 779   Vendor Registration

All persons maintaining a place of business in the Commonwealth and making taxable sales or leases of tangible personal property or services must apply for a license with the Department of Revenue before beginning business (Sec. 208, Act of March 4, 1971, P.L. 6 [72 P.S. § 7208]; Reg. Sec. 34.1(a), (e)). A person maintaining more than one place of business in the commonwealth is issued a license for the principal place of business. Copies of the license must be displayed at additional places of business. A license is valid for a period of five years.

Remote sellers: The Department of Revenue established September 1, 2012, as the deadline by which remote sellers with physical presence in Pennsylvania had to become licensed and begin collecting sales tax. Businesses with Pennsylvania nexus that did not register and begin collecting tax by that date will face "a variety of escalating enforcement options," including assessment, audit, lien, or referral to a collection agency or the Office of Attorney General. (*News Release*, Pennsylvania Department of Revenue, January 27, 2012)

Additional information is available at **https://www.doreservices.state.pa.us/ BusinessTax/default.htm**.

¶ 780   Sales or Use Tax Credits

Credit is allowed for taxes paid to another state on tangible personal property and services purchased for use in that state and later brought into the Commonwealth, provided the other state grants substantially similar credit to Pennsylvania residents (Sec. 206, Act of March 4, 1971, P.L. 6 [72 P.S. § 7206], Reg. Sec. 31.2(4), Reg. Sec. 31.7(b)).

• Taxes paid; purchases resold

When a licensee pays sales or use tax on a purchase and later sells or leases that item as a normal retail sale of inventory, a credit may be claimed on the licensee's return for the amount of tax previously paid (Reg. Sec. 58.11). This credit must be taken within three years from the date the tax was originally paid. The total amount of credit that can be taken on any one return may not exceed the total amount due for that period before the credit; any credit exceeding the tax due may be carried forward on later returns. If the total credit cannot be recovered within the three-year period, a timely petition for refund may be filed.

• Bad debts

Sales tax paid to the Department of Revenue on sales attributable to bad debts may be refunded. The procedures for petitions for refunds (72 P.S. § 9702) must be followed (Sec. 247.1, Act of March 4, 1971, P.L. 6 [72 P.S. § 7247.1]), and the three-year time limit for petitions for refunds applies (Sec. 3003.1, Act of March 4, 1971, P.L. 6 [72 P.S. § 10003.1]). No deduction or credit for bad debt may be taken on any return (Sec. 247.1, Act of March 4, 1971, P.L. 6 [72 P.S. § 7247.1]).

Partial payments must be prorated between the original purchase price and the sales tax due on the sale. If the transaction was comprised of both taxable and nontaxable components, any payments made to a vendor are to be allocated proportionally between the two. If the debt is subsequently collected, the vendor or affiliate must remit the proportional tax (Sec. 247.1, Act of March 4, 1971, P.L. 6 [72 P.S. § 7247.1]).

• Investment tax credit for production of qualified fuels

The Coal Waste Removal and Ultraclean Fuels Act entitles developers of new facilities for the production of one or more qualified fuels to an investment tax credit against Pennsylvania sales and use tax (Sec. 1803-A, Tax Reform Code of 1971 [72 P.S. § 8803-A]). Qualified fuels are those produced from nontraditional coal culm and silt feedstocks. The credit, which may not exceed 15% of the capital cost of a facility used to produce qualified fuels, is computed as a percentage of the federal basis of the qualifying property.

• Call center credit

A sales and use tax credit is available to call centers for gross receipts taxes paid by a telephone company on receipts derived from the sale of incoming and outgoing interstate telecommunications services to the call center (Sec. 206(b), Act of March 4, 1971, P.L. 6 [72 P.S. § 7206(b)]). A taxpayer must submit an application to the Department for gross receipts tax paid on the receipts derived from the sale of incoming and outgoing interstate telecommunications services incurred in the prior calendar year by February 15. The Department will notify the taxpayer of the amount of the applicant's credit by April 15 of the calendar year following the close of the calendar year during which the gross receipts tax was incurred.

• Data center refund

Beginning July 1, 2017, an owner, operator, or qualified tenant of a certified computer data center may apply to the Department of Revenue for a refund of sales or use tax paid on certain equipment that is used to outfit, operate, or benefit a computer data center and component parts, installations, refreshments, replacements, and upgrades to the equipment. The initial application must be filed by July 30, 2017, and subsequent applications must be filed by July 30 of the following years. The department will notify applicants of the amount of their tax refund by September 30, 2017, and by September 30 of the following years. (Sec. 2901-D, Act of March 4, 1971, P.L. 6; Sec. 2902-D(a), Act of March 4, 1971, P.L. 6; Sec. 2913-D, Act of March 4, 1971, P.L. 6)

To qualify for the refund, a data center owner or operator must apply to the Department of Revenue for certification. The application must include the name, address, and telephone number of the owner or operator; the address of the computer data center site; and anticipated investment or employee compensation information. The department may not certify any computer data center for the refund after December 31, 2029.

A computer data center must meet the requirements in either (1) or (2) below, after taking into account the combined investments made and annual compensation paid by the owner or operator of the computer data center or the qualified tenant:

(1) On or before the fourth anniversary of certification, the computer data center must create a minimum investment of:

(a) at least $25 million of new investment if the computer data center is located in a county with a population of 250,000 or fewer individuals or

(b) at least $50 million of new investment if the computer data center is located in a county with a population of more than 250,000 individuals.

(2) One or more taxpayers operating or occupying a computer data center, in the aggregate, must pay annual compensation of at least $1 million to employees at the certified computer data center site for each year of the certification after the fourth anniversary of certification.

¶781   Deficiency Assessments

The Department of Revenue must make inquiries, determinations, and assessments of sales and use tax (Sec. 230, Act of March 4, 1971, P.L. 6 [72 P.S. §7230]). If the tax remitted with a return is less than the tax due or collected as shown on the return, the Department will issue an assessment for the difference plus 3% of the difference, which must be paid within ten days after notice is mailed to the taxpayer (Sec. 231(a), Act of March 4, 1971, P.L. 6 [72 P.S. §7231]; Reg. Sec. 35.1(b)(1), Reg. Sec. 35.2(b)(2)). An additional 3% of the difference is added for each month the assessment remains unpaid, not to exceed 18% of the difference. If an addition to tax is imposed because of an understatement, no addition will be imposed on an underpayment (Sec. 266(b), Act of March 4, 1971, P.L. 6 [72 P.S. §7266]).

An estimated assessment may be made in the event no return is filed (Sec. 231(c), Act of March 4, 1971, P.L. 6 [72 P.S. §7231(c)]; Reg. Sec. 35.1(b)(3)). Tax must be paid within 30 days after notice of the assessment is mailed to the taxpayer. The Department may base an assessment upon effective rates by business classification, and such an assessment is prima facie correct unless the taxpayer establishes that such rate is based on a sample inapplicable to it (Sec. 231(d), Act of March 4, 1971, P.L. 6 [72 P.S. §7231(d)]; Reg. Sec. 35.1(b)(4)).

An assessment may be made at any time during the period of limitations even if one or more previous assessments have been made against the taxpayer for the same year (Sec. 258, Act of March 4, 1971, P.L. 6 [72 P.S. §7258]; Reg. Sec. 35.1(c)).

¶782   Audit Procedures

The Department of Revenue is authorized to examine the books, papers, and records of any taxpayer, including transient vendors, to verify the accuracy and completeness of a return or to determine the tax if no return is filed (Sec. 248.2, Act of March 4, 1971, P.L. 6 [72 P.S. §7248.2], Sec. 272, Act of March 4, 1971, P.L. 6 [72 P.S. §7272]; Reg. Sec. 35.1(c)). The Department may enter upon the premises of a taxpayer or a taxpayer's agent, representative, employee, accountant, or custodian. Taxpayers must give the Department or its agents the means, facilities, and opportunities to make inspections and examinations. The production of books may be compelled and persons may be examined under oath.

When an audit is performed, the auditor verifies the proper charging of tax on taxable transactions, the proper reporting and remittance of tax, and the proper payment of tax on taxable acquisitions (Reg. Sec. 35.1(a)). After the records, the nature of the business, and the type and frequency of sales have been reviewed, a determination is made whether to examine records for the entire audit period or whether to perform a block test audit or random sample procedure, or a combination of procedures. The reasons for selecting a block test period or random statistical sample procedure and the findings of the audit are discussed with the taxpayer, who may comment in writing.

The department may not enter into a contingent fee contract under which the contractor directly conducts a field audit. (Sec. 4, Act 71 (S.B. 591) Laws 2013)

¶783   **Statute of Limitations**

Sales and use tax must be assessed within the later of three years from the date the return is filed or the end of the year in which the liability arose (Sec. 258, Act of March 4, 1971, P.L. 6 [72 P.S. §7258]; Reg. Sec. 35.1(c)). However, tax may be assessed and collected at any time if no return is filed (Sec. 259, Act of March 4, 1971, P.L. 6 [72 P.S. §7259]; Reg. Sec. 35.1(c)) or if the taxpayer willfully files a false or fraudulent return with the intent to evade tax (Sec. 260, Act of March 4, 1971, P.L. 6 [72 P.S. §7260]; Reg. Sec. 35.1(c)).

¶784   **Application for Refund**

The Department of Revenue must refund all taxes, interest, and penalties to which the commonwealth is not rightfully entitled (Sec. 252, Act of March 4, 1971, P.L. 6 [72 P.S. §7252]). However, a refund is made only when the person who actually paid the tax files a petition for refund with the Department within three years of the payment of the tax or if the tax was paid as a result of an assessment, files a petition for reassessment within 90 days after the notice of assessment was mailed (72 P.S. §9702(a)). The petition must be accompanied by an affidavit stating that the facts contained therein are true.

Article XXVII of the Tax Reform Code, enacted by Act 119 of 2006 ((S.B. 1993), §28) governs the procedure for refunds and for petitions for reassessment of taxes assessed after 2007. A petition for refund must state the following (72 P.S. §9703):

— the tax type and tax periods included within the petition;

— the amount of tax that the taxpayer claims was overpaid;

— the basis of the taxpayer's claim for refund.

If tax is paid under a law that is later found by a court to have been erroneously interpreted or to be unconstitutional, a petition for refund may be filed before or after the final judgment but within three years of the date of the payment or pursuant to section 3003.1 (Sec. 253(d), Act of March 4, 1971, P.L. 6 [72 P.S. §7253(d)]).

Bad debts: See ¶780.

¶ 785   RHODE ISLAND

¶ 786   Scope of Tax

Source.—Statutory references are to Title 44 of the General Laws of 1956, as amended to date. Details are reported in the CCH RHODE ISLAND TAX REPORTS starting at ¶ 60-000. Rhode Island taxes are administered by the Department of Revenue, Division of Taxation (Sec. 44-1-1).

Rhode Island imposes a tax on sales and rentals of tangible personal property, other than sales for resale (Sec 44-18-18). Also subject to tax are the following categories of services, some of which also involve the transfer of tangible personal property (Sec. 44-18-7(16); Sec. 44-18-7.3):

— transportation services, including taxicab, limousine, charter bus, transit, and other ground transportation services;

— pet care services (except veterinary and laboratory testing services);

— producing, fabricating, processing, printing or imprinting tangible personal property for consumers who furnish the materials used;

— furnishing and distributing tangible personal property for a consideration by social or athletic clubs;

— preparing or serving meals, food and drinks (including related cover, minimum, or entertainment charges);

— transfers of possession of tangible personal property where the seller retains title as security for payment;

— furnishing gas, electricity, steam, refrigeration, or water; and

— providing telecommunications services.

The rental of living quarters in a hotel, rooming house, or tourist camp, constitutes a retail sale for Rhode Island sales tax purposes, and is therefore taxable (Sec. 44-18-18).

Sales and use tax also applies to sales of.

— prewritten software delivered electronically or by load and leave, including charges by the seller for any services (training, maintenance, consultation, etc.) necessary to complete the sale (Reg. SU 11-25);

— over-the-counter drugs; and

— medical marijuana.

Digital products; software:

"Specified digital products," which are electronically transferred digital audio-visual works, digital audio works, and digital books, are not considered prewritten computer software and are not subject to tax (Reg. SU 11-25).

• **Hotel tax**

The hotel tax is imposed on hotel operators, room resellers or resellers of travel packages, based on the total consideration for occupancy of any space. However, a house, condominium, or other residential dwelling is exempt from the statewide hotel tax if the dwelling is rented in its entirety. (Sec. 44-18-36.1; *Notice 2015-4,* Rhode Island Division of Taxation, July 2015, CCH RHODE ISLAND TAX REPORTS, ¶ 200-825; see also ¶ 789, ¶ 790, ¶ 794)

Room resellers: Effective July 1, 2015, a "room reseller" or "reseller" means any person, except a tour operator, having any right, permission, license, or other authority from or through a hotel to reserve or arrange the transfer of occupancy of accommodations, such that the occupant pays all or a portion of the rental and other fees to the room reseller or reseller. A room reseller or reseller includes, but is not limited to, sellers of travel packages.

Room resellers or resellers (also known as "online travel companies" or "OTCs") are required to register with and collect and pay sales and use taxes and hotel taxes, calculated on the amount of rental and other fees paid by the occupant to the room reseller, less the amount of any rental and other fees paid by the room reseller to the hotel. The hotel must collect and pay taxes on the amount of rental and other fees paid to the hotel by the room reseller and/or the occupant.

No assessment will be made by the Tax Administrator against a hotel because of an incorrect remittance of the taxes by a room reseller. Likewise, no assessment will be made against a room reseller because of an incorrect remittance of taxes by a hotel.

The amount of taxes collected by the hotel and/or room reseller from the occupant must be stated and charged separately from the rental and other fees and must be shown separately on all records. (Sec. 44-18-7.3(4)(i))

Travel packages: A "travel package" is a room(s) bundled with one or more other, separate components of travel, such as air transportation, car rental or similar items, which travel package is charged to the customer or occupant for a single price. When the room occupancy is bundled for a single consideration, with other property, services, amusement charges, or any other items, the separate sale of which would not otherwise be subject to sales and use tax, the entire single consideration is treated as the rental or other fees for room occupancy subject to sales and use tax. However, if the amount of the rental or other fees for room occupancy is stated separately from the price of other property, services, amusement charges, or other items, on any sales slip, invoice, receipt, or other statement given the occupant, and such rental and other fees are determined by the Tax Administrator to be reasonable in relation to the value of such other property, services, amusement charges or other items, only the separately stated rental and other fees are subject to sales and use tax. (Sec. 44-18-7.3(4)(ii))

Hosting platforms: A "hosting platform" is an electronic or operating system in which a person or entity provides a means through which an owner may offer a residential unit for tourist or transient use. This service is usually, though not necessarily, provided through an online or web-based system that generally allows an owner to advertise the residential unit through a hosted website and provides a means for a person or entity to arrange tourist or transient use in exchange for payment, whether the person or entity pays rent directly to the owner or to the hosting platform. (Sec. 43-63.1-2(5))

Hosting platforms that list short-term residential rentals located in Rhode Island must register for, charge, collect, and remit sales and hotel taxes (Sec. 42-63.1-2(5); *Notice 2015-15,* Rhode Island Division of Taxation, September 2015, CCH RHODE ISLAND TAX REPORTS, ¶ 200-835).

- **Use tax**

A compensating use tax is imposed upon the storage, use or other consumption in Rhode Island of tangible personal property (including a motor vehicle, boat, airplane or trailer) purchased from a retailer (Sec. 44-18-20(1); Reg. SU 11-114).

- **Streamlined Act status**

Rhode Island is a full member of the Governing Body of the Streamlined Sales Tax Project (SSTP) and has enacted the changes to its laws necessary to comply with the Streamlined Sales and Use Tax Agreement's requirements. For additional information, see ¶ 792.

Rhode Island's taxability matrix can be found at on the website of the STTP at **http://www.streamlinedsalestax.org**.

¶786   Rhode Island

Tax Base

The sales tax is based upon sales at retail (Sec. 44-18-18). It is measured by the gross receipts of the retailer from such sales. The term "retail sale" includes the rental of living quarters in a hotel, rooming house or tourist camp (Sec. 44-18-8), and such rental is based upon the total amount of charges for occupancy up to the first 30 consecutive calendar days of each rental period and excludes rental charges for living quarters for which the occupancy has a one-year written lease (Sec. 44-18-18).

The use tax is based on the storage, use or other consumption in Rhode Island of tangible personal property purchased from any retailer (Sec. 44-18-20). The use tax is imposed on motor vehicles, boats, airplanes, and trailers, regardless of whether such items were purchased from a licensed dealer. The tax is measured by the price of the property.

Prepaid telephone calling arrangements: The definition of taxable "sales" includes the transfer for consideration and the recharge of prepaid telephone calling card arrangements sourced to Rhode Island (Sec. 44-18-7(d)(12)). "Prepaid telephone calling card arrangements" include prepaid telephone calling cards or the prepaid right to exclusively purchase telecommunications services using an access number or an authorization code, or both, whether manually or electronically dialed. Telephone calls made with prepaid telephone cards are not subject to tax as telecommunications services (Sec. 44-18-7(d)(9)).

Suppression devices; phantom-ware: Any person who knowingly sells, purchases, installs, transfers or possesses an automated suppression device or phantom-ware is guilty of a felony and, upon conviction, will be subject to a fine not exceeding $50,000 or imprisonment not exceeding five years, or both. In addition, such person is liable to the state for all taxes, interest, and penalties due as a result of the person's use of an automated sales suppression device or phantom-ware and all profits associated with the person's sale of an automated sales suppression device or phantom-ware. (Sec. 44-19-42(b)-(d))

An automated sales suppression device or phantom-ware and any device containing such device or software will be deemed contraband and will be subject to seizure by the tax administrator or by a law enforcement officer when directed to do so by the tax administrator (Sec. 44-19-42(e)).

An "automated sales suppression device," also known as a "zapper," means a software program, carried on a memory stick or removable compact disc, accessed through an Internet link, or accessed through any other means, that falsifies transaction data, transaction reports, or any other electronic records of electronic cash registers and other point-of-sale systems. "Phantom-ware" means a hidden programming option, whether preinstalled or installed at a later time, embedded in the operating system of an electronic cash register or hardwired into the electronic cash register that can be used to create a virtual second till or may eliminate or manipulate transaction records. (Sec. 44-19-42(a))

- **"Gross receipts" defined**

"Gross receipts" are defined as the total amount of the sales price of the retail sales of retailers (Sec. 44-18-13).

- **"Sales price" defined**

"Sales price" is defined to mean the total amount (valued in money) for which tangible personal property is sold, leased or rented or for which public utility service is furnished (Sec. 44-18-12; Reg. SU 11-20). With respect to telecommunications service, however, taxpayers are allowed a credit or refund of sales tax paid to another state to which the tax is properly due for the identical service.

"Sales price" also includes the total amount charged for the rental of living quarters in any hotel, rooming house, or tourist camp (Sec. 44-18-12).

"Sales price" specifically includes the following (Sec. 44-18-12):

— services that are part of the sale;

— cash and property received; and

— credit given to the purchaser by the seller.

• Nexus

Persons who sell or deliver tangible personal property for storage, use or consumption in Rhode Island, or who engage in any activity related to such sales or delivery, are engaged in business in Rhode Island, and consequently required to collect tax (Sec. 44-18-23; Reg. SU 11-20) The conditions under which Rhode Island statutes provide that out-of-state vendors must collect tax are broad, as "engaging in business in Rhode Island" is defined to include the systematic exploitation of the Rhode Island market, even if the vendor has no property, employees or representatives in the state.

"Amazon" provision: Retailers engaged in business in Rhode Island are required to collect tax (Sec. 44-18-22). The definition of a "retailer" includes a so-called Amazon provision, which creates a rebuttable presumption that a seller is soliciting business in the state through an agent if the seller enters into an agreement with a state resident under which the resident, for a commission or other consideration, refers potential customers to the seller through a website link or otherwise. The presumption applies if the seller's cumulative gross receipts from sales to Rhode Island customers referred by residents with such an agreement exceed $5,000 during the four preceding quarterly periods ending on the last day of March, June, September, and December. The presumption can be rebutted by proof that the state resident did not engage in any solicitation on behalf of the seller that would satisfy the nexus requirements of the U.S. Constitution during the four quarterly periods in question. (*Notice,* Rhode Island Division of Taxation, July 2, 2009, CCH RHODE ISLAND TAX REPORTS, ¶ 200-739)

Contingent provisions on enactment of federal remote sales legislation: Effective upon passage of, and in accordance with, any federal law authorizing states to require sellers to collect tax on remote sales, sellers making remote sales in Rhode Island would be required to collect and remit tax on such sales (Sec. 44-18-15.2(2)(c)). "Remote sale" means a sale into the state on which the seller would not be legally required to collect and remit tax unless provided by federal law (Sec. 44-18-15.2(2)).

Upon the enactment of federal remote seller legislation, specified changes in rates and exemptions would take effect on the date that the state requires sellers to collect tax on remote sales. See ¶ 789.

• Sourcing rules

Retail sales are sourced according to the following rules (RI Gen. Laws Sec. 44-18.1-10; RI Gen. Laws Sec. 44-18.1-11):

— When the product is received by the purchaser at a business location of the seller, the sale is sourced to that business location;

— When the product is not received by the purchaser at a business location of the seller, the sale is sourced to the location where receipt by the purchaser, or the purchaser's designated donee, occurs;

— If neither of the above applies, the sale is sourced to the location indicated by an address for the purchaser that is available from the business records of the seller that are maintained in the ordinary course of the seller's business when use of this address does not constitute bad faith;

— If none of the above apply, the sale is sourced to the location indicated by an address for the purchaser obtained during the consummation of the sale, including the address of the purchaser's payment instrument, if no other address is available, when use of this address does not constitute bad faith;

— If none of the other rules apply, or if the seller is without sufficient information to apply the previous rules, then the location will be determined by the address from which tangible personal property was shipped, from which the digital good or the computer software delivered electronically was first available for transmission by the seller, or from which the service was provided.

Special provisions apply to leases and rentals and telecommunications. Sourcing for direct mail is discussed in Reg. SST 13-01.

¶ 788   List of Exemptions, Exceptions, and Exclusions

Unless otherwise indicated, the statutory exemptions, exceptions, and exclusions listed below apply to both sales and use taxes. Items that are excluded from the sales or use tax base are treated at ¶ 787, "Tax Base."

- **Sales and use tax exemptions, exceptions, and exclusions**

Agricultural products constituting food	Sec. 44-18-30(9), (62)
Air and water pollution control facilities	Sec. 44-18-30(15)
Aircraft and aircraft parts	Sec. 44-18-30(59)
Alcoholic beverages (excluding beer) sold by package liquor stores	Sec. 44-18-30(64)
Alternative fuel stations, construction costs	Sec. 44-18-30(53)
Alternative fuels	Sec. 44-18-30(52)
Artists, composers, and writers, works produced by RI residents	Sec. 44-18-30B
Blood	Sec. 44-18-30(60)
Boat manufacturers' promotional and product literature	Sec. 44-18-30(39)
Boats, new or used	Sec. 44-18-30(49)
Boats or vessels brought into the state for winter storage, repair, maintenance or sale	Sec. 44-18-30(47)
Boats purchased by nonresidents and not registered in state	Sec. 44-18-30(31)
Boats, trade-in value	Sec. 44-18-30(42)
Building materials used to reconstruct manufacturing facility following a disaster	Sec. 44-18-30(54)
Buses used at least 80% in interstate commerce	Sec. 44-18-40
Carrier access service	Sec. 44-18-30(46)
Cash discounts	Sec. 44-18-12(b)(1)
Clothing alterations charges	Sec. 44-18-12(b)(3)
Clothing and footwear (up to $250 per item)	Sec. 44-18-30(27)
Coffins, caskets, shrouds and other burial garments	Sec. 44-18-30(12)
Coins having numismatic or investment value	Sec. 44-18-30(44)
Commercial fishing vessels	Sec. 44-18-30(27)
Common carriers, sales for use outside state	Sec. 44-18-33
Compressed air	Sec. 44-18-30(34)
Computer software purchased for manufacturing purposes	Sec. 44-18-30(7)
Construction materials used to build farm structures	Sec. 44-18-30(45)
Containers with tax-exempt contents	Sec. 44-18-30(4)(B)
Demonstration boats	Sec. 44-18-26.1
Diesel retrofit technology	Sec. 44-18-30(63)

Utilities used for residential purposes . . . . Sec. 44-18-30(20),
Sec. 44-18-30(21),
Sec. 44-18-30(29)

Utilities used in manufacturing . . . . Sec. 44-18-30(7)

¶ 789   **Rate of Tax**

The sales and use tax rate is 7% (Sec. 44-18-18).

Upon enactment of any federal law that requires remote sellers to collect and remit taxes, the following changes would take effect on the date that the state requires sellers to collect tax on remote sales:

— the state sales and use tax rate would decrease from 7% to 6.5% (Sec. 44-18-18);

— the meals and beverage tax rate would increase from 1% to 1.5% (Sec. 44-18-18.1); and

— clothing would be fully exempt (currently the portion of an item's sales price that exceeds $250 is taxable) (Sec. 44-18-30(27)).

• **Hotel tax**

The hotel tax is imposed, in addition to any sales tax, at the rate of 5% of the total consideration charged for occupancy of any space (not exceeding 30 days) furnished by any hotel in Rhode Island (Sec. 44-18-36.1).

Room resellers: The hotel tax is imposed on room resellers or resellers of travel packages. However, a house, condominium, or other resident dwelling is exempt from the statewide hotel tax if the house, condominium, or other resident dwelling is rented in its entirety. (Sec. 44-18-36.1) See also ¶ 786.

• **Surcharge on rental vehicles**

The first 30 consecutive days of a motor vehicle rental are subject to a surcharge of 8% of gross receipts. The surcharge is computed prior to the assessment of any applicable sales taxes, but is subject to sales tax. (Sec. 31-34.1-2(a))

The rental company must remit 40% of the collected surcharge to the state, but may retain 60% as reimbursement for motor vehicle licensing fees, title fees, registration fees and transfer fees paid to the state of Rhode Island and excise taxes imposed upon the rental companies' motor vehicles during the prior calendar year (Sec. 31-34.1-2(b)).

• **Surcharge on medical marijuana**

A surcharge of 4.0% is imposed upon the net patient revenue received each month by every compassion center (Sec. 44-67-3). "Compassion centers" are certain registered nonprofit entities that acquire possess, cultivate, manufacture, deliver, transfer, transport, supply, or dispense marijuana or related supplies to registered qualifying patients and their designated caregivers (Sec. 44-67-2(2)). The monthly surcharge is due to the tax administrator no later than the 20th of the month following the month that the net patient revenue was received (Sec. 44-67-4).

¶ 790   **Local Taxes**

There is no statutory authority in Rhode Island for counties or municipalities to impose local general sales and use taxes.

Meals tax: A 1% local sales and use tax is imposed statewide on all meals and beverages sold in or from eating or drinking establishments, regardless of whether prepared at the establishment or consumed at the establishment's premises (Sec. 44-18-18.1; Reg. SU 04-147). Vending machine sales are exempt.

The retailer must collect the tax from the purchaser and remit the tax to the Division of Taxation, which must then distribute the collected taxes, penalties, and other amounts to the cities and towns where the meals were delivered. Retailers that sell prepared foods in bulk are considered eating establishments and are required to collect the tax.

Hotel tax: A 1% local hotel tax is imposed in addition to the 5% state hotel tax (Sec. 44-18-36.1; see also ¶ 786, ¶ 794).

Mobile telecommunications: The federal Mobile Telecommunications Sourcing Act (4 USC 116-126) has been adopted (Sec. 44-18-7(d)(9)). Mobile telecommunications services that are deemed to be provided by the customer's home service provider are subject to tax if the customer's place of primary use is in Rhode Island regardless of where the mobile telecommunications services originate, terminate, or pass through.

¶ 791   Bracket Schedule

Tax must be computed to the third decimal place and rounded to the nearest whole cent, rounding up whenever the third decimal place is greater than four. Tax may be computed on an item or invoice basis (Sec. 44-18.1-25).

The sales and use tax is collected according to the following bracket collection schedule (Sec. 44-18-19):

Amount of Sale	Amount of Tax
$0.01 to $0.07 inclusive	No tax
0.08 to 0.21 inclusive	1¢
0.22 to 0.35 inclusive	2¢
0.36 to 0.49 inclusive	3¢
0.50 to 0.64 inclusive	4¢
0.65 to 0.78 inclusive	5¢
0.79 to 0.92 inclusive	6¢
0.93 to 1.07 inclusive	7¢

When the amount of the sale is more than $1.07, the amount of the tax is collected at the rate of 7¢ on each full dollar.

¶ 792   Returns, Payments, and Due Dates

In general, sales or use tax returns are filed on a monthly basis, with such returns covering the month preceding the date in which the tax is due and payable (Sec. 44-19-10(a)). All sales tax permit holders must file an annual reconciliation by January 31. The reconciliation is a separate form that must be filed in addition to the return due in January.

Returns are due, usually with payments, on or before the 20th day of each month. Any information concerning gross receipts from rentals or leases of tangible personal property must be included in the returns.

For purposes of the use tax, returns are required from every retailer maintaining a place of business in Rhode Island and from every person purchasing tangible personal property subject to the use tax who has not paid the use tax to a retailer required to collect it. Purchasers should not pay the tax to a person who does not hold a seller's permit or a certificate of authority to collect tax (Reg. SU 95-114).

Consumers' use tax: Consumers who make purchases from out-of-state retailers that do not collect Rhode Island sales tax are required to report and pay the use tax due on such purchases on Schedule U of their personal income tax returns. A use tax lookup table with reference to a taxpayer's federal adjusted gross income is included on Schedule U as a "safe harbor" alternative to listing the actual amount of the taxpayer's use tax obligation. If a taxpayer uses the lookup table, the taxpayer must list on the return not only the result from the lookup table, but also the actual amount of each single purchase whose purchase price equals or exceeds $1,000. The AGI income ranges within the lookup table are adjusted annually for inflation. (Sec. 44-30-100)

- **Quarterly reports**

When a taxpayer's tax liability for six consecutive months has averaged less than $200 monthly, quarterly returns and remittances in lieu of monthly returns may be made on or before the last day of July, October, January, and April of each year for the preceding three calendar months, provided special authorization in writing is received from the Tax Administrator (Sec. 44-19-10(a)). Such authorization may be revoked if the taxpayer's liability exceeds $600 in taxes for any subsequent quarter.

- **Material suppliers**

A retailer that qualifies as a "materialman" for six consecutive months within the most recent 12-month period may elect to report sales on a cash basis as consideration is received, rather than on an accrual basis on the return for the period in which the transaction took place, provided that the materialman receives written approval of the tax administrator (Sec. 44-19-41).

A "materialman" is a retailer (1) engaged in the business primarily of selling lumber and building materials to contractors, subcontractors, or repairmen to be used in the construction, erection, altering, or repairing of buildings or other structures or in the making of improvements or preparation on land; (2) whose lumber and building material sales comprise at least 50% of total sales; and (3) who may file a mechanic's lien for such materials.

- **Electronic funds transfer**

A seller is required to remit payments electronically if the seller's average monthly sales and use tax liability in the previous calendar year was at least $200. A seller that fails to remit payments electronically is subject to a penalty of the lesser of $500 or 5% of the amount not remitted electronically, unless the failure was due to reasonable cause (Sec. 44-19-10.3; Reg. EFT 09-01).

A person engaged in commercial farming is not required to file Rhode Island sales and use tax returns electronically (Sec. 44-19-10.3(d)).

- **Uniform Sales Tax Administration Act**

Rhode Island has enacted the Uniform Sales and Use Tax Administration Act (SSUTA), the product of the Streamlined Sales Tax Project Sec. 44-59-1 *et seq.*) and has enacted the law changes necessary to comply with the SSUTA's requirements. The SSUTA was developed to simplify and modernize sales and use tax administration in order to substantially reduce the burden of tax compliance for all sellers and for all types of commerce.

Sourcing: See ¶ 787.

Centralized registration: See ¶ 794.

Bad debt deduction: See ¶ 795.

For additional information on the uniform act, see "Streamlined Sales Tax Project," listed in the Table of Contents, or go to the Project's website at **www.streamlinedsalestax.org**.

¶ 793   Prepayment of Taxes

Every licensed cigarette distributor and dealer must prepay the sales tax on cigarettes possessed for sale or use in Rhode Island upon which the distributor or dealer is required to affix cigarettes stamps (Sec. 44-19-10.1). A prepayment requirement also applies to little cigars at the rate of 40¢ per pack.

The tax must be computed annually by multiplying the minimum price of standard brands of cigarettes in effect as of each April 1 by the cigarette tax rate imposed. The tax must be prepaid at the time the distributor or dealer purchases the stamps from the tax administrator. However, the tax administrator may permit a licensed distributor or dealer to pay the tax within 30 days after the date of purchase if a sufficient bond has been filed with the tax administrator.

¶ 794   **Vendor Registration**

Prior to commencing business, every person subject to the sales tax, including operators of hotels, motels, boarding houses, and tourist camps, must file an application with the Tax Administrator for a permit for each place of business (Sec. 44-19-1(a), Reg. SU 87-21). The Tax Administrator is given specific authority to determine the form, contents and signatures of the application.

Upon receipt of the application and a $10 fee for each permit, the Tax Administrator issues (or renews) a separate permit for each place of business in Rhode Island (Sec. 44-19-1(a), Sec. 44-19-2). All permits expire on June 30 of each year and must be renewed annually on or before February 1st of each year. The permit is not assignable and is valid only for the person to whom it is issued and for the transaction of business at the place designated (Sec. 44-19-2). The permit must be conspicuously displayed at the place for which it is issued.

Centralized registration: Rhode Island participates in the Streamlined Sales Tax Agreement's centralized online registration system. Under the registration system (Sec. 44-18.1-4; Sec. 44-18.1-32):

— a seller registered under the Agreement is registered in each member state;

— the payment of registration fees or other charges is not required for a seller to register in a state in which the seller has no legal requirement to register;

— a written signature from the seller is not required;

— a certified service provider may register a seller under uniform procedures adopted by the member states;

— a seller may cancel its registration under the system at any time under uniform procedures adopted by the Agreement's Governing Board. Cancellation does not relieve the seller of its liability for remitting to the proper states any taxes collected.

A seller that registers to pay or collect and remit sales or use tax in accordance with the terms of the Agreement may select one of the following methods of remittance or other method allowed by state law to remit the taxes collected:

— *Model 1:* a model 1 seller that selects a certified service provider as an agent to perform all the seller's sales or use tax functions, other than the seller's obligation to remit tax on its own purchases;

— *Model 2:* a model 2 seller that selects a certified automated system to use that calculates the amount of tax due on a transaction; or

— *Model 3:* a model 3 seller that uses its own proprietary automated sales tax system that has been certified as a certified automated system.

Hotel tax: Operators of hotels and, effective July 1, 2015, room resellers and resellers are required to register with and collect and pay to the tax administrator the sales and use and hotel taxes (Sec. 44-18-7.3(4)(i); *Notice 2015-14,* Rhode Island Division of Taxation, September 2015, CCH RHODE ISLAND TAX REPORTS, ¶ 200-834; see also ¶ 786).

Short-term rentals.—Someone who rents out an entire house, an entire beach cottage, an entire condominium, an entire apartment, or other such accommodation, for a period of 30 days or less must register with the Division of Taxation for a sales tax permit and pay the required annual $10 fee; charge the 7% sales tax and 1% local hotel tax on the transaction; and send the tax collected to the division.

Someone who rents out a room for 30 days or less must register for a sales tax permit with the division and pay the required annual $10 fee; charge the 7% sales tax, the 5% statewide hotel tax, and the 1% local hotel tax on the transaction; and send the tax that is collected to the division. (Sec. 42-63.1-2; see also *Notice 2015-11,* Rhode Island Division of Taxation, July 15, 2015, CCH RHODE ISLAND TAX REPORTS, ¶ 200-831)

Also, hosting platforms that list short-term residential rentals located in Rhode Island must register for, charge, collect, and remit sales and hotels taxes (Sec. 42-63.1-2(5); *Notice 2015-15,* Rhode Island Division of Taxation, September 2015, CCH RHODE ISLAND TAX REPORTS, ¶ 200-835).

Transportation networks: Effective July 1, 2016, transportation network companies, such as Uber, are subject to sales and use tax,. "Transportation network companies" (TNC) are defined as entities that use a digital network to connect transportation network company riders to transportation network operators who provide prearranged rides. Any TNC operating in Rhode Island is a retailer that is required to file a business application and registration form, as well as obtain a permit to charge, collect, and remit Rhode Island sales and use tax. (Sec. 44-18-7.3(b)92(ii); *Notice 2016-02,* Rhode Island Division of Taxation, June 30, 2016, CCH RHODE ISLAND TAX REPORTS, ¶ 200-858)

- **Use tax**

Every retailer selling tangible personal property for storage, use, or other consumption in Rhode Island as well as every operator of a hotel, rooming house or tourist camp, must register with the Tax Administrator and give any required information, including the name and address of all agents operating in the state, the location of all distribution or sales houses or offices, or of any hotel, rooming house or tourist camp or other places of business in the state (Sec. 44-19-7; Reg. SU 11-20).

¶795 **Sales or Use Tax Credits**

Taxpayers, when computing the use tax due on an article brought into Rhode Island for use, storage or other consumption therein, may credit the amount of the sales or use tax that they were lawfully obligated to pay and did pay in another taxing jurisdiction (Sec. 44-18-30A, Reg. SU 87-29).

- **Telecommunications**

In general, "sales price" means the total amount (valued in money) for which tangible personal property is sold, leased or rented or for which public utility is furnished (Sec. 44-18-12(1)). With respect to telecommunications service, however, taxpayers are allowed a credit or refund of sales tax paid to another state to which the tax is properly due for the identical service.

- **Bad debts**

"Bad debt" is as defined in IRC Sec. 166, except it does not include: financing charges or interest; sales or use taxes charged on the purchase price; uncollectable amounts on property that remains in the possession of a seller until the full purchase price is paid; expenses incurred in attempting to collect any debt; or repossessed property (Sec. 44-18.1-21(B)).

Claim period: A bad debt deduction may be claimed on the return for the period during which the bad debt is written off as uncollectable in the taxpayer's books and records and is eligible to be deducted for federal income tax purposes. A taxpayer who is not required to file federal income tax returns may deduct a bad debt on a return filed for the period in which the bad debt is written off as uncollectable in the taxpayer's books and records and would be eligible for a bad debt deduction for federal income tax purposes if the taxpayer was required to file a federal income tax return (Sec. 44-18.1-21(C)).

Source.—Statutory references are to Chapter 36, Title 12, of the Code of Laws of South Carolina, as amended to date. Details are reported in the CCH SOUTH CAROLINA TAX REPORTS starting at ¶ 60-000.

Sales tax is imposed on persons engaged in the business of selling tangible personal property, whether new or used, at retail in South Carolina (Sec. 12-36-910(A)). The use tax is imposed on the storage, use, or consumption in South Carolina of tangible personal property purchased at retail for such purposes (Sec. 12-36-1310(A)). An Attorney General Opinion indicates that if the first use was intended to be outside the state, goods brought into South Carolina at a later date are not subject to use tax. The use tax and sales tax are complementary, in that use tax is not imposed on sales upon which the sales tax has been paid (Sec. 12-36-130(1)).

Sales and use taxes are in addition to all other taxes (Sec. 12-36-910(A)).

"Tangible personal property" is personal property that may be seen, weighed, measured, felt, touched, or that is perceptible to the senses. Specifically included in the definition are services and intangibles, including communications, laundry and related services, furnishing of accommodations, and sales of electricity. Stocks, notes, bonds, mortgages, and other evidences of debt are specifically excluded from the definition, as is the transmission of computer database information by a cooperative service when the database information has been assembled by and for the exclusive use of the members of the cooperative service (Sec. 12-36-60).

"Tangible personal property" includes houses severed from the land and resold. It also includes such intangibles as information when they are reduced to a tangible form, such as a report. The retailer may add the sales tax to the sales price, but the inability, impracticability, refusal, or failure to add the tax to the sales price and collect from the purchaser does not relieve the retailer of liability from the tax (Sec. 12-36-1940).

Communication services: Charges paid by a customer for streaming television programs, movies, music, and similar content are charges for communication services and are subject to sales and use taxes, whether they are paid for as part of a subscription service, per item, or per event. The streaming transmission of video or audio data over the Internet is no different than cable and satellite transmission of television, movies, music, and other similar content, and cloud-based services for processing and routing telephone calls, which are taxable communications services. Internet access charges and non-automated answering services are not taxable. A revenue ruling explains the application of South Carolina sales and use tax to communication services (*Revenue Ruling 17-2,* March 10, 2017, CCH SOUTH CAROLINA TAX REPORTS, ¶ 400-855).

Warranties; maintenance or service contracts: A sale or renewal of a warranty, maintenance, or similar service contract for tangible personal property is subject to sales and use tax, if purchased in conjunction with the sale of tangible personal property. The sale of a warranty, service, or maintenance contract for tangible personal property is exempt if purchased after the purchase of the tangible personal property (Sec. 12-36-90(1)(c)(iii); Sec. 12-36-910(B); Sec. 12-36-1310(B)(6); *Revenue Ruling 11-1,* South Carolina Department of Revenue, November 9, 2011; CCH SOUTH CAROLINA TAX REPORTS, ¶ 400-596). A sale or renewal of a warranty, maintenance, or similar service contract for tangible personal property is exempt if the sale or purchase of the tangible personal property covered by the contract is exempt or excluded from tax (Sec. 12-36-2120(69)).

Online travel companies: The South Carolina Supreme Court has determined that service and facilitation fees charged by an online travel company for providing hotel reservations in South Carolina were subject to the state sales tax because these fees qualified as gross proceeds derived from the furnishing of sleeping accommodations and the online travel company was an entity engaged in the business of furnishing accommodations. (*Travelscape LLC v. South Carolina Department of Revenue*, South Carolina Supreme Court, No. 26913, January 18, 2011, CCH SOUTH CAROLINA TAX REPORTS, ¶ 400-560)

Vacation rentals: A ruling addresses the taxability of accommodations where:

— the owner rents a home on a short term basis;

— the owner rents for 90 or more days consecutively to one person;

— the owner rents for short and long terms during the year;

— the owner rents his/her place of abode with five or fewer bedrooms on a short term basis; and

— the owner rents his/her place of abode with six or more bedrooms on a short term basis.

If a real estate agent, broker, listing service, or internet booking service rents the owner's home or rooms, then the agent or service is liable for sales tax on accommodations for any rentals made consisting of less than 90 consecutive days. (*Revenue Ruling 16-10,* South Carolina Department of Revenue, July 27, 2016, CCH SOUTH CAROLINA TAX REPORTS, ¶ 400-828)

Net metering of electricity: Under net metering, a public utility customer that generates more energy from a renewable energy facility, such as wind turbines or solar panels, than the customer uses, receives a credit from the public utility. The electric meter at the customer's premises records electricity in both directions, allowing the customer's excess energy produced from the renewable energy facility to be carried forward and used to offset the customer's future electricity use. When the customer "banks" the excess renewable energy, it retains ownership over the energy. Therefore, the customer's use of its own energy is not a sale from the public utility to the customer, nor is it consideration submitted by the customer for the utility's electricity. Consequently, the value assigned to the excess energy used to offset future usage is not subject to the sales and use tax or the electric power tax. (*Revenue Ruling 10-10,* South Carolina Department of Revenue, October 26, 2010, CCH SOUTH CAROLINA TAX REPORTS, ¶ 400-557)

• **Incidence of sales tax**

The sales tax is a vendor tax, imposed on persons engaged or continuing in South Carolina in the business of selling tangible personal property at retail (Sec. 12-36-2650).

Drop shipments: Because South Carolina retail sales, on which the sales tax is imposed, specifically do not include wholesale or intermediary sales, a South Carolina manufacturer or distributor who makes a sale to an out-of-state retailer is not subject to tax on this primary sale (Sec. 12-36-910; Sec. 12-36-110; Sec. 12-36-120). If the out-of-state retailer does not have South Carolina nexus and thus is not liable for collection of the tax, the use tax is owed by the ultimate consumer (Sec. 12-36-1330).

• **Incidence of use tax**

Liability for use tax is imposed on persons storing, using, or consuming in South Carolina tangible personal property purchased at retail. Such persons are relieved of liability if they obtain a receipt from a retailer maintaining a place of business in the state or who is authorized to collect use tax for the state (Sec. 12-36-1330(A)).

• **Nexus**

An out-of-state seller that makes retail sales of tangible personal property for storage, use, or other consumption in South Carolina must collect and remit use tax if the seller (Sec. 12-36-1340):

— maintains a place of business in South Carolina;

— qualifies to do business in South Carolina;

— solicits and receives purchases or orders by an agent or salesperson in South Carolina; or

— distributes catalogs, or other advertising matter, and, by reason of that distribution, receives and accepts orders from residents within South Carolina.

A retailer is maintaining a place of business in South Carolina if the retailer has or maintains within South Carolina, directly or by a subsidiary, an office, distribution house, sales house, warehouse, or other place of business, or any agent operating in South Carolina under the retailer's authority, regardless of whether the business or agent is permanently or temporarily located in South Carolina or whether the retailer or subsidiary is admitted to do business in South Carolina. (Sec. 12-36-80)

The Department of Revenue (DOR) has added the following activities that are capable of creating nexus in South Carolina for sales and use tax purposes (*Revenue Ruling 14-4,* South Carolina Department of Revenue, September 10, 2014, CCH SOUTH CAROLINA TAX REPORTS, ¶ 400-730):

— the business's sole activity in South Carolina is maintaining an inventory;

— the business's sole activity in South Carolina is maintaining or using a distribution facility (subject to the limited safe harbor statute);

— the business sells tangible personal property to South Carolina residents from outside the state and delivers merchandise to customers in returnable containers;

— the business sells tangible personal property at retail to businesses in South Carolina from outside the state and delivers the merchandise by the business's railcars or tractor-trailers and leaves the trailer or railcar with the customer for a specified number of days;

— the business sells tangible personal property to South Carolina residents from outside the state and provides in-state phones and kiosks that permit customers to access inventories and purchase from remote subsidiaries;

— the business's in-state representative maintains an in-home office in South Carolina;

— the business sells tangible personal property to South Carolina residents from outside the state and ships the product for distribution to a third-party distributor located in South Carolina;

— the business sells tangible personal property to South Carolina residents from outside the state, makes remote sales to state residents, and holds two or more one-day seminars in South Carolina;

— the business sells tangible personal property to South Carolina residents from outside the state, makes remote sales to state residents, holds two or more one-day seminars in South Carolina, and has employees visit the state five times during the year;

— the business sells gift cards in affiliated South Carolina stores;

— the business makes remote sales of "canned software" to state residents and sends a representative to customize it or to provide other information technology services;

— the business sells tangible personal property over the Internet and operates a website that is maintained on a server owned by the business and located in South Carolina; and

— the business sells tangible personal property to South Carolina residents from outside the state and is the single member in a single member LLC that is a disregarded entity operating in South Carolina.

The DOR also has identified the following activities as not creating nexus on behalf of a business:

— the business is an Internet-based retailer with an out-of-state office that enters into an agreement with a South Carolina website operator wherein the operator hosts advertisements directing consumers to the out-of-state retailer's website and is paid for each ad displayed;

— the business makes remote sales of digital content downloaded by South Carolina residents;

— the business maintains a bank account in South Carolina;

— the business is listed in the local phone books of South Carolina cities; and

— the business uses local phone numbers in South Carolina that are forwarded to its out-of-state headquarters.

See also ¶ 809, regarding out-of-state businesses providing disaster assistance in South Carolina.

Nexus-creating activities: The effect upon nexus of various activities conducted in South Carolina are discussed in *Revenue Ruling 07-3*, South Carolina Department of Revenue, September 25, 2007, CCH SOUTH CAROLINA TAX REPORTS, ¶ 300-244.

Distribution facilities safe harbor (expired): The ownership or use of a distribution facility was not considered evidence of a person's physical presence within South Carolina to impose nexus for sales and use tax purposes. A business was required to meet the following conditions in order to receive the exemption (Sec. 12-36-2691):

— place the distribution facility in service after December 31, 2010, and before January 1, 2013;

— make, or cause to be made through a third party, a capital investment of at least $125 million after December 31, 2010, and before December 31, 2013;

— create at least 2,000 full-time jobs, including a comprehensive health plan for those employees, after December 31, 2010, and before December 31, 2013; and

— after meeting the initial job requirements, maintain at least 1,500 full-time jobs until January 1, 2016.

The nexus safe harbor for distribution facilities expired January 1, 2016, or earlier if the business failed to meet the requirements noted above.

A retailer using the nexus safe harbor also was required to notify a purchaser in a confirmation email that the purchaser may owe use tax on the total sales price of the transaction and include a link within the email to the Department of Revenue's website. The statement within the confirmation email had to indicate that the purchaser may remit use tax to the department via its website or on the purchaser's income tax returns. Also, by February 1 of every year, the retailer was required to provide to each purchaser to whom goods were delivered in South Carolina a statement of the total sales made to the purchaser during the preceding calendar year. The retailer had to further notify the purchaser on invoices or other similar documents that use tax was imposed on its sales of tangible personal property stored, used, or consumed in South Carolina.

• **Streamlined Act status**

South Carolina has enacted the Uniform (Simplified) Sales and Use Tax Administration Act (see ¶ 807). However, South Carolina is not a member of the Streamlined Sales and Use Tax Agreement (SSUTA), because it has not yet enacted the changes to its laws necessary to comply with the Agreement's requirements. However, it will continue to have input through its representation on the State and Local Advisory Council, which advises the Board on matters pertaining to the administration of the SSUTA.

¶ 802   **Tax Base**

The tax base for the sales tax is the gross proceeds of sales (Sec. 12-36-910(A)); the tax base for the use tax is the sales price of the property, gross proceeds from certain services, or fair market value of property imported into the state (Sec. 12-36-1310(A)).

"Gross proceeds of sale" means the value proceeding or accruing from the sale, lease, or rental of tangible personal property and includes the following (Sec. 12-36-90(1)):

— proceeds from consignment sales;

— proceeds from the sale of tangible personal property (without deduction for the cost of the goods, materials, labor, service, or transportation, interest, losses, federal manufacturers or importers excise taxes, or any other expenses); and

— the fair market value of property withdrawn from inventory (except for certain exemptions).

The following are not included in "gross proceeds of sale" (Sec. 12-36-90(2)):

— cash discounts;

— sales price of returned property;

— trade-ins;

— federal taxes, except for manufacturer's or importer's excise taxes;

— motor vehicles operated with dealer or transporter license plates;

— charges attributable to the statutory cost of a government license or permit;

— fees imposed on the sale of motor oil, new tires, lead-acid batteries, and white goods, including the refundable deposit when a lead-acid battery core is not returned to a retailer;

— the sales price of property sold but charged off as a bad debt or uncollectible account; and

— interest, fees, or charges imposed for late payment of an electricity or natural gas bill.

"Sales price" means the total amount for which tangible personal property is sold, with no deduction for the cost of the property sold, cost of materials used, labor or service cost, interest, losses, or other expenses (Sec. 12-36-130). "Sales price" includes service and transportation costs that are a part of the sale and federal manufacturer's or importer's excise taxes. Cash discounts, amounts charged for returned property, trade-ins, bad debts, and federal taxes (except manufacturer's and importer's excise taxes) are excluded from "sales price."

Bundled telecommunications: When taxable and nontaxable telecommunications charges are combined in a bundled transaction, the portion of the price attributable to any nontaxable property or services is subject to tax, unless the provider can reasonably identify the nontaxable portion from its books and records kept in the ordinary course of business for purposes other than sales taxes (Sec. 12-36-910(B)(3)(b)). A "bundled transaction" is a transaction consisting of distinct and identifiable properties or services sold for one nonitemized price but treated differently for tax purposes.

Prepaid phone cards: Prepaid telephone calling cards sold in South Carolina may be subject to sales and use tax, depending on whether the purchased telephone service applies to land-based telephones or wireless telephones and devices. Land-based prepaid telephone calling cards are not taxable because the card itself is not being sold;

rather, the service sold is a future right to telephone service. This intangible right to future service is classified as an intangible evidence of debt and is not subject to sales tax. Alternatively, prepaid telephone calling cards enabling access for wireless telephones and devices are subject to sales tax at the time of retail purchase (*Revenue Ruling 04-4*, South Carolina Department of Revenue, March 25, 2004).

Unlike land-based calling cards, prepaid wireless calling arrangements are expressly subject to sales and use taxes (Sec. 12-36-910(B)(5); Sec. 12-36-1310(B)(3)).

¶ 803   List of Exemptions, Exceptions, and Exclusions

Unless otherwise indicated, the statutory exemptions listed below apply to both sales and use taxes; those applicable only to the use tax are listed separately. Items that are excluded from the sales or use tax base are treated at ¶ 802, "Tax Base."

Sales tax holidays: There is one permanent annual sales tax holiday in South Carolina, as follows:

Back-to-school holiday: Sales of clothing, school supplies, computers, and printers are exempt from state and local sales tax on sales made during the period beginning at 12:01 a.m. on the first Friday in August and ending at midnight the following Sunday (Sec. 12-36-2120(57)). The exemption does not apply to jewelry, cosmetics, eyeware, furniture or items placed on layaway or similar deferred payment and delivery plans, items that are rented, or any items sold or leased for use in a trade or business. It also does not apply to sales of mobile phones or portable devices whose primary function is to allow users to download or listen to music, view videos, or read books. However, portable devices that have computing functions and that allow users to access multiple software applications do qualify for exemption during the tax holiday so long as they do not allow users to make telephone calls.

Unlike similar tax-free periods in other states, the exemption is not limited by the price of the items.

For examples of taxable and exempt items, see *Information Letter 14-10*, South Carolina Department of Revenue, July 10, 2014, CCH SOUTH CAROLINA TAX REPORTS, ¶ 400-723.

• Sales and use tax exemptions, exceptions, and exclusions

Advertising, direct mail material and postage	Sec. 12-36-2120(49), Sec. 12-36-2120 [58]
Agricultural chemicals	Sec. 12-36-2120(6)
Agricultural packaging machinery	Sec. 12-36-2120(17)
Aircraft parts	Sec. 12-36-2120(52)
Amusement park rides, machinery, and equipment	Sec. 12-36-2120(73)
Aircraft fuel (manufacturer inceive)	Sec. 12-36-2120(9)
Asphalt products used out of state	Sec. 12-36-2120(37)
Audiovisual masters	Sec. 12-36-2120 [55]
Automatic teller machine transactions	Sec. 12-36-2120(11)
Building materials research and test facility, nonprofit	Sec. 12-36-2120(78)
Charitable hospitals, sales to	Sec. 12-36-2120(47)
Children's clothing sold to tax-exempt nonprofit organizations for distribution to the needy	Sec. 12-36-2120(82)
Clean-room clothing	Sec. 12-36-2120(54)
Clothing, footwear, school supplies, computers (annual 3-day exemption)	Sec. 12-36-2120(57)

College athletic tickets, rights to purchase (FY 2014-15-2016)	Sec. 106-7, H.B. 4701, Laws 2014, Sec. 109.7, H.B. 3701, Laws 2015
Computer equipment (manufacturer incenive)	Sec. 12-36-2120(65)
Concession sales at festivals, charitable organizations	Sec. 12-36-2120(39)
Construction, fabrication instate for contract out of state	Sec. 12-36-110(2)
Construction (manufacturing incentive)	Sec. 12-36-2120(67)
Construction materials, homes for the needy	Sec. 12-36-2120(81)
Containers and chassis sold to shipping lines	Sec. 12-36-2120(40)
Containers for agricultural products	Sec. 12-36-2120(7)
Containers used incident to sale and delivery of property	Sec. 12-36-2120(14)
Contractors, government	Sec. 12-36-2120(29)
Cooking oil used to prepare ready-to-eat food	Sec. 12-36-120
Database information, cooperative services	Sec. 12-36-60
Datacenters, computer equipment, software, and electricity used by .	Sec. 12-36-2120
Data processing	Sec. 12-36-910([C])
Dental prosthetic devices	Sec. 12-36-2120(28)
Depreciable business assets sold with business	Sec. 12-36-2120(42)
Drop shipments	Sec. 12-36-110, Sec. 12-36-120, Sec. 12-36-910
Durable medical equipment paid with Medicare/Medicaid funds (phased-out rate—see ¶ 804)	Sec. 12-36-2120(74)
Elderly persons (85 years and older), sales to (1% exemption; see ¶ 804)	Sec. 12-36-2620(2), Sec. 12-36-1740(2)
Electricity sold to radio and television stations	Sec. 12-36-2120(26)
Electricity used by manufacturers and miners	Sec. 12-36-2120(19)
Electricity used to irrigate crops	Sec. 12-36-2120(44)
Equipment, parts, and materials (manufacturing)	Sec. 12-36-120
Farm products sold by producer	Sec. 12-36-2120(6), (23)
Feed for poultry and livestock	Sec. 12-36-2120(4), Sec. 12-36-2120(5)
Food (unprepared) for home use or eligible for purchase with USDA food coupons	Sec. 12-36-2120(75)
Food prepared or packaged for the homeless or needy	Sec. 12-36-2120(10)
Food purchased by restaurants	Sec. 12-36-120
Footwear, clothing, school supplies, computers (annual 3-day exemption)	Sec. 12-36-2120(57)
Fuel (agricultural)	Sec. 12-36-2120(15), Sec. 12-36-2120(18), Sec. 12-36-2120(32)
Fuel (manufacturing and mining)	Sec. 12-36-2120(9)
Fuel (motor, subject to gasoline tax)	Sec. 12-36-2120(15)
Fuel (residential purposes)	Sec. 12-36-2120(33)
Fuel (ships)	Sec. 12-36-2120(13)

Fuel (transportation companies)	Sec. 12-36-2120(9)
Fuel cells and other hydrogen devices	Sec. 12-36-2120(71)
Gasoline	Sec. 12-36-2120(15)
Government transactions	Sec. 12-36-2120(2)
Hearing aids	Sec. 12-36-2120(38)
Heavy equipment rental fee	Sec. 12-31-60
Housing for livestock and poultry	Sec. 12-36-2120(45)
Injectable medications and biologics	Sec. 12-36-2120(80)
Interstate transactions	Sec. 12-36-2120(1), Sec. 12-36-2120(36)
Laundries, purchases of supplies and machinery	Sec. 12-36-2120(24)
Library book purchases	Sec. 12-36-2120(3)
Livestock	Sec. 12-36-2120(4), Sec. 12-36-2120(5)
Lodging	Sec. 12-36-70(1)
Lottery tickets	Sec. 12-36-2120(60)
Machinery (farm)	Sec. 12-36-2120(16)
Machinery (laundry)	Sec. 12-36-2120(24)
Machinery (manufacturing)	Sec. 12-36-2120(17), Sec. 12-36-2120(51)
Machinery (mining)	Sec. 12-36-2120(17)
Machinery (research and development)	Sec. 12-36-2120 [56]
Manufactured homes (partial or full exemption — see ¶ 804)	Sec. 12-36-2110(B)
Manufacturers' warranties, materials used in servicing	Sec. 12-36-90(1)(c)
Manufacturing, ingredients and component parts	Sec. 12-36-120
Materials and supplies used for painting, repair, or reconditioning of ships	Sec. 12-36-2120(13)
Meals for elderly	Sec. 12-36-2120(10)
Meals for school children	Sec. 12-36-2120(10)
Medical equipment (durable; paid with Medicare/Medicaid funds— see ¶ 804)	Sec. 12-36-2120(74)
Medicine, over-the-counter sales to free health clinics	Sec. 12-36-2120(63)
Medicine, prescription sales	Sec. 12-36-2120(28)
Missile assembly materials	Sec. 12-36-2120(22)
Modular homes (partial exemption — see ¶ 804)	Sec. 12-36-2120(34)
Monorail cars and parts	Sec. 12-36-2120(20)
Motion picture film sold or rented to or by theaters	Sec. 12-36-2120(35)
Motion picture production companies (partial rebate)	Secs. 12-62-30, 12-62-40, 12-62-60; Sec. 12-36-2120(43)
Motor fuel subject to gasoline tax; natural and liquefied petroleum gasses	Sec. 12-36-2120(15)
Motor vehicle extended service contracts	Sec. 12-36-2120(53)
Motor vehicles sold to nonresident military personnel	Sec. 12-36-2120(25)
Motor vehicles sold to nonresidents	Sec. 12-36-930

¶803   South Carolina

Motor vehicles with special license plates	Sec. 12-36-90(2)(e), Sec. 12-36-110(1)(c)(v)
Museums	Sec. 12-36-2130(2)
Native American tribal government purchases	Sec. 27-16-130
Newspapers and newsprint paper	Sec. 12-36-2120(8)
Nonprofit organizations, sales by	Sec. 12-36-2120(41)
Nursery products sold by producer	Sec. 12-36-2120(23)
Nursery stock	Sec. 12-36-2120(6)
Petroleum asphalt products used out of state	Sec. 12-36-2120(37)
Pollution prevention and control machinery	Sec. 12-36-2120(17)
Portable toilets, rental or lease (70% exemption)	Sec. 12-36-2120(62)
Postage costs associated with advertising material	Sec. 12-36-2120(49)
Prescription medicine and prosthetic devices	Sec. 12-36-2120(28)
Professional services	Sec. 12-36-110
Promotional maps, brochures, etc.	Sec. 12-36-140(C)(3)
Property shipped out of state to fulfill construction contracts	Sec. 12-36-110(2)
Prosthetic devices	Sec. 12-36-2120(28)
Railroad cars and locomotives	Sec. 12-36-2120(20)
Recycling facilities	Sec. 12-36-2120(17)
Recycling machines	Sec. 12-36-2120(17)
Religious organizations, sales by	Sec. 12-36-2120(41)
Resales	Sec. 12-36-120
Research district	Sec. 12-36-2120(72)
School meals	Sec. 12-36-2120(10)
Schools: textbooks or other learning media	Sec. 12-36-2120(3)
Seeds and seedlings	Sec. 12-36-2120(6)
Sheriff's sale, items sold at	Sec. 12-36-2120(68)
Ships, purchases of supplies and fuel	Sec. 12-36-2120(13)
Solid waste disposal bags	Sec. 12-36-2120(48)
State Department of General Services' sales to other state departments	Sec. 12-36-2120(30)
Sweetgrass baskets	Sec. 12-36-2120(64)
Technology-intensive facilities, electricity and computer equipment sales to	Sec. 12-36-2120(65), (66)
Telecommunications charges attributable to government fees	Sec. 12-36-90(2)(f)
Telegraph messages	Sec. 12-36-2120(11)
Telephone toll charges	Sec. 12-36-2120(11)
Television and radio stations, sales	Sec. 12-36-2120(26)
Vacation time-sharing interests	Sec. 12-36-2120(31)
Vessels and barges greater than 50 tons burden	Sec. 12-36-2120(21)
Veterinarians, sales of medicines to	Sec. 12-36-2120(6), Sec. 12-36-2120(28)
Viscosupplementation therapies (year-to-year exemption FY 2012 through FY 2016)	H.B. 4701, Laws 2014, H.B. 3701, Laws 2015

War memorials . . . . Sec. 12-36-2120(46)

Water . . . . Sec. 12-36-2120(12)

Water-processing equipment . . . . Sec. 12-36-2120(17)

Wholesale sales . . . . Sec. 12-36-120

Withdrawals from inventory by manufacturers . . . . Sec. 12-36-90(1)(c)

Wrapping paper . . . . Sec. 12-36-2120(14)

Zoological park purchases of plants and animals . . . . Sec. 12-36-2120(27)

• **Use tax exemptions, exceptions, or exclusions**

Private schools, tangible personal property sold to (year-to-year
    exemption from 1995 through 2016) . . . . H.B. 4701, Laws 2014,
                                            H.B. 3701, Laws 2015

Property of certain organizations operating museums . . . . Sec. 12-36-2130(2)

Property subject to sales tax and on which the sales tax has been paid .
. . . . Sec. 12-36-2130(1)

¶ 804   Rate of Tax

The South Carolina sales, use, and casual excise tax rate is 6%, with certain exceptions (Sec. 12-36-1110).

The sale or lease of the following items is subject to a tax rate of 5%, with a maximum tax of $300 (Sec. 12-36-1110; Sec. 12-36-2110; *Revenue Ruling 08-8,* June 30, 2008, CCH SOUTH CAROLINA TAX REPORTS, ¶ 400-416):

    — aircraft;

    — motor vehicles, including low-speed vehicles, motorcycles and recreational vehicles;

    — fire trucks and fire equipment (see *Revenue Ruling 08-10,* July 18, 2008, CCH SOUTH CAROLINA TAX REPORTS, ¶ 400-422);

    — boats (see *Revenue Ruling 08-7,* June 30, 2008, CCH SOUTH CAROLINA TAX REPORTS, ¶ 400-415);

    — certain horse trailers (see *Revenue Ruling 08-9,* July 18, 2008, CCH SOUTH CAROLINA TAX REPORTS, ¶ 400-421);

    — trailers pulled by a truck tractor; and

    — self-propelled light construction equipment with compatible attachments limited to a maximum of one hundred sixty net engine horsepower.

1% exclusion for the elderly: Individuals who are age 85 or older may claim a 1% exclusion from the state sales, use, casual excise, or transient accommodations tax rate on sales for personal use. Individuals must request the exclusion and present proof of age at the time of sale. The exclusion does not affect local rates. (Sec. 12-36-2620; Sec. 12-36-2630; Sec. 12-36-2640; see also *Revenue Ruling 16-9,* South Carolina Department of Revenue, July 27, 2016, CCH SOUTH CAROLINA TAX REPORTS, ¶ 400-827)

• **Transient accommodations**

Sales tax is imposed at the rate of 7% of the tax base on the rental or charges for transient accommodations (Sec. 12-36-920). This tax is composed of three segments: a 4% sales tax, a 1% sales tax, and a 2% local accommodations tax, which is credited to the state's political subdivisions (Sec. 12-36-2630). The 1% tax is not imposed on purchases for personal use by individuals who are age 85 or older (*Revenews No. 53,* Tax Commission, June 1990). The 7% tax is billed and paid as a single item, and the separate taxes are not itemized. See also *2013 Accommodations Tax Fact Sheet,* South Carolina Department of Revenue, October 18, 2013, CCH SOUTH CAROLINA TAX REPORTS, ¶ 400-693.

Guest charges for room service, laundering and dry cleaning services, in-room movies, telephone charges, and meeting room rentals are subject to sales tax at the lower regular sales tax rate and not at the higher rate imposed on the furnishing of accommodations. Charges for amenities, entertainment, special items in promotional tourist packages, and other guest services are not taxable as additional guest charges (Sec. 12-36-920(B)). Also, if they are separately stated on the bill and are optional, these charges are not subject to the 7% tax on accommodations (*Revenue Ruling 14-5,* South Carolina Department of Revenue, October 1, 2014, CCH SOUTH CAROLINA TAX REPORTS, ¶ 400-732).

Personal residences: The 7% sales tax on accommodations does not apply to gross proceeds from the rental of a personal residence for fewer than 15 total days in a taxable year if that income is also excluded from the taxpayer's gross income pursuant to IRC Sec. 280A(g). (Sec. 12-36-920(A)(2))

- **Admissions**

Sales and use taxes are not imposed on admissions. However, South Carolina imposes a 5% admissions tax on the price of paid admissions to places of amusement. The tax is added to the admissions price and paid by ticket purchasers. Persons operating places of amusement are responsible for collecting and remitting the tax. (Sec. 12-21-2420)

The tax does not apply to:

— any amount separately stated on the admission ticket that is collected for the purpose of repaying money borrowed to construct an athletic stadium or field at any accredited college or university;

— any amount included in an admission charge, whether separately stated or not, that is a fee or tax imposed by a political subdivision of South Carolina, or

— admissions to the state museum.

- **Casual excise tax**

The casual excise tax on motor vehicles, boats, motors, or airplanes is imposed at the rate of 6% (Sec. 12-36-1710).

The maximum tax on sales or rentals of motor vehicles, motorcycles, boats, trailers, recreational vehicles, and aircraft is $300 (Sec. 12-36-2110(A)).

- **Self-propelled construction equipment**

A maximum tax of $300 is imposed on each sale or lease of self-propelled light construction equipment (maximum 160 horsepower) with compatible attachments (Sec. 12-36-2110(A)(7)).

- **Heavy equipment rental surcharge**

Prior to 2017, persons in the business of renting heavy equipment to the public were subject to and had to collect a 3% surcharge on rental contracts for heavy equipment for periods of 31 days or less (Sec. 12-37-717).

Effective January 1, 2017, the surcharge on the rental of heavy equipment was discontinued and replaced by a 2.5% heavy equipment rental fee. The rental fee does not apply to the rental of heavy equipment property rented directly to the federal government, South Carolina, or any political subdivision of South Carolina. The rental fee is not subject to sales or use tax. Qualified heavy equipment property subject to the rental fee is exempt from personal property tax. ((H.B. 3891), Laws 2016, (Sec. 56-31-60, S.C. Code.))

• **Religious organization's purchases**

A $300 maximum tax is imposed on the purchase of a musical instrument or piece of office equipment by a religious organization (Sec. 12-36-2110(C)).

• **Manufactured and modular homes**

For manufactured homes, the tax is computed on 65% of the sales price, as reduced by any trade-in allowance, at the rate of 5% of the first $6,000 of the amount taxable plus 2% of the amount taxable that exceeds $6,000 (Sec. 12-36-2110(B)). The tax is limited to $300 for sales of manufactured homes that meet the energy efficiency standards of having storm or double pane glass windows, insulated or storm doors, and actual installed insulation values of R-11 for walls, R-19 for floors, and R-30 for ceilings. However, variations are allowed, and the exemption on tax due above $300 applies if the total heat loss does not exceed the using level of the three insulation standards. The special rules for modular and manufactured homes do not apply to portable classrooms, storage-type manufactured buildings, recreation vehicles, travel trailers, campers, manufactured condominium and motel units, and similar property (Reg. Sec. 117-178).

From July 1, 2009, to July 1, 2019, a manufactured home is exempt from sales tax if it meets the requirements of the U.S. Environmental Protection Agency and the U.S. Department of Energy's ENERGY STAR program, or has been designated as meeting these agencies' energy-saving efficiency requirements. (Sec. 12-36-2110(B))

Modular homes: Fifty percent of the gross proceeds of the sale of both on-frame and off-frame modular homes is exempt from sales and use tax (Sec. 12-36-2120(34)). The maximum sales tax is inapplicable to single-family modular homes. A "modular home" is defined as a manufactured single family dwelling (or an integral part) over 35 feet in length or over eight feet in width that is so constructed that it may be transported from one site to another, and temporarily or permanently affixed to real estate; made up of one or more components; and constructed with the same or similar electrical, plumbing, heating, and sanitary facilities as on-site constructed housing (Reg. Sec. 117-335).

• **Telephone service**

Sales and use tax applies to gross proceeds accruing or proceeding from the business of providing 900/976 telephone service. The rate of tax is 10% (Sec. 12-36-2645).

Wireless 911 charge: The Commercial Mobile Radio Service (CMRS) E911 monthly surcharge rate is $0.62 (*Rate Change Notification: E911 Monthly Surcharge,* South Carolina Department of Revenue, May 28, 2014). The surcharge is collected from CMRS subscribers and on each sale of prepaid wireless telecommunications service (*Important Notice,* South Carolina Department of Revenue, April 16, 2012, CCH SOUTH CAROLINA TAX REPORTS, ¶ 400-612).

• **Durable medical equipment**

The sales and use tax has been eliminated for retailers/providers that make sales after 2012 of durable medical equipment and related supplies that meet the following criteria:

— the equipment and related supplies are defined under federal and state Medicaid and Medicare laws;

— the purchase is paid directly by U.S. or South Carolina funds under the Medicaid or Medicare programs, where state or federal law or regulation authorizing the payment prohibits the payment of sales or use tax; and

— the durable medical equipment and related supplies are sold by a provider who holds a South Carolina retail sales tax license and whose principal place of business is located within South Carolina.

¶804   South Carolina

Sales that do not meet the above criteria are subject to the state sales tax rate of 6%. All sales, including sales of durable medical equipment and related supplies qualifying for the exemption, are subject to the general local option taxes collected by the Department of Revenue.

¶ 805   Local Taxes

A county may, upon referendum approval, levy a sales and use tax of up to 1% on the gross proceeds of sales under the Local Option Sales and Use Tax (LOST) (Sec. 4-10-20). However, the school boards of certain counties are authorized to impose a county-wide sales and use tax upon approval of the county electorate.

Capital projects taxes: A county governing body may impose a 1% sales and use tax for a specific purpose and for a limited amount of time to collect a limited amount of money in order to defray debt service on bonds issued to pay for authorized projects (Sec. 4-10-310; Sec. 4-10-470).

Transportation taxes: Counties are authorized to impose a sales and use tax of up to 1% within the county area for a single transportation-related project facility or for multiple transportation-related project facilities and for a specific period of time to collect a limited amount of money if they opt to utilize a tax rather than the imposition of tolls (Sec. 4-37-30). In order to implement the tax, the county must pass an ordinance, subject to referendum approval by the electorate of the county.

Hotel and meals taxes: A local governing body may impose a tax on transient accommodations, not to exceed 3% (Sec. 6-1-510). However, the tax may not exceed 1.5% within the boundaries of a municipality without the consent of the appropriate municipal governing body. In addition, a local governing body may impose a local hospitality tax not to exceed 2% of the charges for food and beverages (Sec. 6-1-720). However, the tax may not exceed 1% within the boundaries of a municipality without the consent of the appropriate municipal governing body.

Local taxes authorized on vehicles, boats, aircraft: A county may impose a sales and use tax in lieu of personal property taxes on private passenger motor vehicles, motorcycles, general aviation aircraft, boats, and boat motors. The imposition, or its subsequent rescission, is subject to local voter approval (Sec. 4-10-540; *Information Letter 07-1,* South Carolina Department of Revenue, January 8, 2007, CCH SOUTH CAROLINA TAX REPORTS, ¶ 340-250).

Education development: A county may impose a 1% local sales and use tax to pay for specific public school capital improvements in the county (Sec. 4-10-420). The tax must be approved by a majority of the voters at a referendum conducted in an even-numbered year and may not be imposed for more than 15 years (Sec. 4-10-425). The tax may be imposed in counties that have collected at least $7 million in state accommodations taxes in the most recent fiscal year and in other counties that meet specific criteria. Once a county meets the threshold, it thereafter remains eligible to impose this tax.

Tourism promotion: A municipality located in a county with state accommodations tax revenues of at least $14 million in a fiscal year may impose a local option sales tax at a rate no greater than 1% for purposes of tourism promotion. The application of this tax may continue for a period of 10 years and applies in addition to other local sales and use taxes. Tangible personal property subject to the maximum tax and unprepared food purchased with U.S. Department of Agriculture food coupons are exempt. (Sec. 4-10-920; Sec. 4-10-930; Sec. 4-10-940)

Sourcing of telecommunications charges: South Carolina has conformed to the federal Mobile Telecommunications Sourcing Act (Act), P.L. 106-252. All charges for mobile telecommunications services are considered to be provided by the customer's home service provider and sourced to the customer's place of primary use (Sec. 12-36-910(B)(3); Sec. 12-36-1910; Sec. 12-36-1920). All such charges are subject to sales tax based on the customer's place of primary use.

The service provider will be held harmless for an error in assigning wireless services to a jurisdiction if it utilizes an electronic database provided by the state or a designated entity, or, if the state has not provided or designated a database, if it utilizes a database that makes assignments based on a nine-digit zip code.

• **Local nexus**

A retailer that has Commerce Clause nexus with South Carolina and that purposefully avails itself of the benefits of the economic market of a county or that purposefully directs its efforts toward the residents of a county would have a minimal connection with that county sufficient to require it to remit that county's local sales and use tax on deliveries into the county, even if the retailer has no physical presence in that county.

Delivery: A retailer must remit a county's tax if the retailer ships property into the county using its own vehicles or using a contract carrier (*i.e.,* a carrier that works specifically for the retailer with respect to the delivery).

A retailer that uses a common carrier (*e.g.,* UPS) to ship property into a county must remit the county's tax only if the retailer is subject to that county's jurisdiction under the Due Process clause. For instance, a retailer would be subject to the county of delivery's jurisdiction if (1) the retailer or a subsidiary maintains an office, warehouse, distribution house, other place of business, or property of any kind in the county, (2) the retailer or a subsidiary has an agent, representative (including delivery personnel or independent contractor), salesman, or employee operating within the county, (3) the retailer advertises via advertising media (*e.g.,* newspapers, television, cable systems, or radio) located in the county, or (4) the retailer advertises via advertising media that is located outside the county of delivery but has coverage within that county (*Revenue Ruling 09-9,* June 16, 2009, CCH SOUTH CAROLINA TAX REPORTS, ¶ 400-488).

• **Local tax rate chart**

Local tax rate information is available on the website of the South Carolina Department of Revenue at **https://dor.sc.gov/tax/sales**.

¶ 806   **Bracket Schedule**

Computation schedules are available on the Department of Revenue's website at **https://dor.sc.gov/tax/sales**.

For purposes of the state sales tax on accommodations and the combined state sales and local tax for counties imposing a local sales tax, retailers may round tax of more than 50¢ to the next whole cent and round down tax of 50¢ or less (Sec. 12-36-940).

¶ 807   **Returns, Payments, and Due Dates**

Persons liable for sales and use tax must file returns with the Department on or before the 20th day of the month following the month in which the tax accrued, accompanied by the tax due (Sec. 12-36-2570). The return shows, by location, the gross proceeds of wholesale and retail sales, sales price of property, and any other information required by the Department. Returns are timely filed if mailed and postmarked on or before the due date. Returns may be filed every 28 days if permitted by the Department and they must be filed within 20 days following the period covered (Sec. 12-36-2570).

A business subject to sales tax on accommodations, with more than one place of business in the state, must separately report in its return the gross proceeds from business done within and without municipalities (Sec. 12-36-920(D)). Taxpayers who own or manage rental units in more than one county or municipality must separately report the gross proceeds from business done in each county or municipality.

The Department may require returns and payment for other than monthly periods (Sec. 12-36-2590).

Filing returns: For sales tax returns, taxpayers can use MyDORWAY (see **https://dor.sc.gov/mydorway**).

Report of use tax: Consumers may report use tax on their personal income tax returns.

Bad debts: Sales that are charged off as bad debts or uncollectible accounts for South Carolina corporate and personal income tax purposes are excluded from the definition of "gross proceeds of sales" and "sales price," and are therefore exempt from sales and use taxes (Sec. 12-36-90(2)(h), Sec. 12-36-130). A taxpayer who has paid the tax on the unpaid balance of such an account is eligible to claim a deduction on the taxpayer's sales or use tax return within one year of the month the debt was determined to be worthless. See also *Revenue Ruling 13-4,* South Carolina Department of Revenue, June 12, 2013, CCH SOUTH CAROLINA TAX REPORTS, ¶ 400-678.

Quarterly returns: Quarterly returns and remittance may be made on or before the 20th day of the month following the quarter for which the tax is due, provided the Department gives its authorization and the tax does not exceed $100 for any month (Sec. 12-36-2580).

Special reporting requirements: A business subject to tax on lodging rentals that has more than one place of business in the state must report separately in its return the total proceeds derived from business done inside and outside municipalities. A business that owns or manages rental units in more than one county or municipality must report separately in its return the gross proceeds from business done in each county or municipality. (Sec. 12-36-920(D))

Real estate agents, brokers, corporations, and listing services required to remit tax on lodging rentals must notify the South Carolina Department of Revenue if rental property, previously listed by them, is dropped from their listings. The notification may be sent to the department twice a year- once by July 31 for listings dropped from January through June, and by January 31, for listings dropped from July through December. (Sec. 12-36-920(C); *Information Letter 11-19,* South Carolina Department of Revenue, November 18, 2011, CCH SOUTH CAROLINA TAX REPORTS, ¶ 400-598)

- **Electronic filing and payment**

Taxpayers who file sales, use, accommodations, local option, and/or special local taxes and owe $15,000 or more per month in tax liability are mandated to file and pay electronically. For details, see MyDORWAY on the Department of Revenue's website at **https://dor.sc.gov/mydorway**.

- **Uniform Sales Tax Administration Act**

South Carolina has enacted the Uniform (Simplified) Sales and Use Tax Administration Act, the product of the Streamlined Sales Tax Project (SSTP) (Sec. 12-35-010 *et seq.*). South Carolina has not yet conformed its laws to the requirements of the Streamlined Sales and Use Tax Agreement.

For additional information, see "Streamlined Sales Tax Project," listed in the Table of Contents.

| ¶ 808 | Prepayment of Taxes |

There are no provisions regarding prepayment of taxes. Retailers must pay estimated taxes in certain cases.

| ¶ 809 | Vendor Registration |

A retailer must obtain a retail license for each permanent branch, establishment, or agency (Sec. 12-36-510(A), Reg. Sec. 117-145; see MyDORWAY at**https://dor.sc.gov/mydorway**). The cost for each license is $50, payable at the time of application. An artist or craftsman selling its own products at arts and craft shows must obtain a retail license, for use only for one location at a time, and pay a license tax of $20 upon application. Retailers operating a transient or temporary business must obtain a retail license, valid only for one location at a time, and pay a license tax of $50 at the time of application.

A "transient business" is a business that does not have a permanent retail location in the state (Sec. 12-36-510(A)). "Temporary business" is a business that makes retail sales not exceeding 30 consecutive days at one location.

The application for a license must show the name, address, and any other information required by the Department for each location (Sec. 12-36-540). A separate license is issued for each location. A license remains valid as long as the licensee continues in the same business, unless revoked (Sec. 12-36-550). Licenses are not transferable or assignable and must be conspicuously displayed.

Transfer of license: A retailer may have its license transferred from one location to another without incurring additional license tax liability upon written application to and approval of the Commission (Reg. Sec. 117-175.2). Only an abandonment and simultaneous move to a new location will qualify for the transfer.

Vending machine operators: A retail license must be obtained for each point from which the service for such machines or other property originates (Reg. Sec. 117-145).

Laundries: Each pickup and delivery point is a separate branch or establishment (Reg. Sec. 117-175.3).

Deceased retailer: The business of a deceased retailer may be operated by the personal representative for purposes only of administering the estate, provided a certified copy of Letters Testamentary is filed with the Department of Revenue and Taxation and the Department gives its approval (Reg. Sec. 117-175.1).

Exemptions from license requirements: The following do not need a license (Sec. 12-36-510(B)):

— persons selling at flea markets or yard sales not more than once per calendar quarter, unless done so as a regular business;

— organizations exempt from tax on concession sales at festivals;

— persons furnishing accommodations to transients for one week or less in any calendar quarter (except rental agencies or persons with more than one rental unit); and

— nonprofit and religious organizations whose sales are exempt.

Revocation of license: The Department may revoke the license of any person who fails, neglects, violates, or refuses to comply with a law or regulation (Sec. 12-54-90). The taxpayer must be given ten days written notice of the failure to comply. A new license will not be issued until all outstanding liabilities are satisfied.

Disaster or emergency assistance: An out-of-state business that performs work or services in South Carolina related to a declared state disaster or emergency is not considered to have established a level of presence that would require the business to register, file, and remit various state or local taxes or that would require the business or its out-of-state employees to be subject to any state licensing or registration requirements. The exemption includes all state or local business licensing or registration requirements or state and local taxes or fees including, but not limited to, unemployment insurance, state or local occupational licensing fees, sales and use tax, or property tax on equipment used or consumed during the disaster period, as well as South Carolina Public Service Commission and Secretary of State licensing and regulatory requirements. Out-of-state employees are not considered to have established residency or a presence in South Carolina that would require that person or that person's employer to file and pay income taxes or to be subjected to tax withholdings or to file and pay any other state or local tax or fee resulting from his/her performance of disaster- or emergency-related work within South Carolina related to a declared state

¶809   South Carolina

disaster or emergency during a disaster period. However, out-of-state businesses and employees are not exempt from transaction taxes and fees such as motor fuel taxes, sales and use taxes, accommodations taxes, or car rental taxes unless the taxes or fees are otherwise exempted during the disaster period. Out-of-state businesses or out-of-state employees that remain in South Carolina after the disaster period will be subject to South Carolina's normal standards for establishing presence, residency, or doing business in South Carolina and the resulting requirements. (Sec. 12-2-110; *Information Letter 15-15,* South Carolina Department of Revenue, October 15, 2015, CCH SOUTH CAROLINA TAX REPORTS, ¶ 400-790; *Information Letter 16-13,* South Carolina Department of Revenue, October 14, 2016, CCH SOUTH CAROLINA TAX REPORTS, ¶ 400-832)

• Closing or selling business

A retail license must be returned to the Department of Revenue and Taxation for cancellation when a business is closed or sold (Sec. 12-36-530). Failure to comply may result in the Department's refusal to issue a new retail license.

• Voluntary disclosure program

The Department of Revenue operates a voluntary disclosure procedure for taxpayers who have sufficient nexus with South Carolina and who have not registered with the Department to collect or remit taxes. A taxpayer may be deemed a voluntary filer if the taxpayer either registers to collect or remit taxes without having been contacted previously by the Department or responds to the Department's nexus questionnaire timely and completely upon receipt. A taxpayer may not file a claim for refund for the tax periods prior to the time of voluntary filing. However, a voluntary filer may claim a lack of nexus for periods after voluntary filing.

If a taxpayer qualifies as a voluntary filer the Department will:

— accept the filing of tax returns and payment of all required taxes for the three immediately preceding tax years, or the number of preceding tax years that nexus existed if less than three years;

— apply interest in accordance with the state's Code; and

— waive all penalties, except in the cases of material misrepresentation of facts or fraud.

For additional information, see *Revenue Procedure 09-2,* South Carolina Department of Revenue, March 9, 2009, CCH SOUTH CAROLINA TAX REPORTS, ¶ 400-468.

¶ 810   Sales or Use Tax Credits

The amount of state and local sales or use tax paid to another state on the purchase of tangible personal property in that state is allowed as a credit against any use tax imposed on that property in South Carolina (Sec. 12-36-1310(C)). If the South Carolina use tax is more than the tax imposed in the other state, the user must pay the difference to the Department of Revenue and Taxation (*Revenue Ruling 06-4,* South Carolina Department of Revenue, May 19, 2006, CCH SOUTH CAROLINA TAX REPORTS, ¶ 300-231).

Collection discount: A credit in the form of a prompt payment discount is given for collection of the Tax (Sec. 12-36-2610). The discount is generally 2%, but is 3% if the tax shown on the return is less than $100. A discount allowed to a taxpayer may not exceed $3,100 for taxpayers who file electronically (otherwise, $3,000) in any one state fiscal year. Out-of-state retailers, who cannot be required to register for sales and use tax, are allowed a discount of up to $10,000 in any one state fiscal year if they voluntarily register to collect and remit use tax on items of tangible personal property sold to customers in South Carolina. A taxpayer operating more than one business is limited to a single discount for all businesses (Reg. Sec. 117-174.221).

• **Incentive payments and rebates**

Incentives are available for motion picture productions, and production of electricity or methane gas from biomass resources. For details, see ¶ 814.

¶ 811   Deficiency Assessments

The Department of Revenue may estimate the tax liability of a person who fails to file a required return and may issue a proposed assessment of tax, penalties, and interest due (Sec. 12-60-430). Notice of the proposed assessment is sent to the person, explaining its basis and stating that an assessment will be made unless the taxpayer protests (Sec. 12-60-420). A deficiency assessment may not be made until 30 days after the proposed assessment is sent or, if the taxpayer files a timely written protest, until the taxpayer's appeal is finally decided (Sec. 12-60-440).

¶ 812   Audit Procedures

The Department of Revenue or authorized agent may examine the books, invoices, papers, records, memoranda, equipment, or licenses bearing on any matter required to be included on a return (Sec. 12-54-100). The examination may be delayed for 30 days if the taxpayer so requests.

The Department may summon a person who failed to file a timely return, delivered an erroneous return, or refused to allow an authorized agent of the Department to examine its books and records (Sec. 12-54-110). The Department may also summon a third-party record holder or any other person it deems necessary. A person summoned must produce the books and give testimony respecting any item on the return. Failure to obey the summons may result in the Department applying to a circuit judge for an attachment for contempt.

The Director or designees may administer an oath to a person or take the acknowledgment of a person with respect to any required return or report (Sec. 12-36-2670).

¶ 813   Statute of Limitations

Taxes must be assessed within 36 months from the date the return was filed or due to be filed, whichever is later (Sec. 12-54-85). However, taxes may be assessed and collected at any time when a fraudulent return is filed with the intent to evade tax. A determination and assessment may also be made after the 36-month limitation period if it is made within 180 days of receiving notice from the Internal Revenue Service of a final determination of an income adjustment made by the Internal Revenue Service. In addition, taxes may be assessed within six years (72 months) if there is a 20% understatement of the total taxes and fees required to be shown on the tax return or document. In determining whether gross proceeds of sales are understated, only retail sales are considered. A taxpayer may agree in writing to extend the period in which an assessment may be made.

¶ 814   Application for Refund

A taxpayer may seek a refund of any state tax by filing a written claim for refund with the Department of Revenue (Sec. 12-60-470). Claims for credit or refund must be filed within three years of the time the return was filed, including any extensions, or two years from the date of payment, whichever is later (Sec. 12-54-85). If no return was filed, a claim for a refund must be filed within two years from the date of payment. The appropriate division of the Department will decide what refund is due, if any, and give the taxpayer written notice of its decision as soon as practicable after a claim has been filed.

The Department may grant a refund of any amount it determines to have been erroneously or illegally collected, even if the taxpayer did not file a claim for refund (Sec. 12-60-470).

¶811   South Carolina

Assignment: A purchaser who has paid sales tax to a retailer for a transaction may claim a refund if the retailer who paid the sales tax to the state has assigned to the purchaser, in writing, the right to a refund of the sales tax paid (Sec. 12-60-470(C)(2)).

• Incentive payments and rebates

Rebate for motion picture productions: Motion picture production companies with production costs exceeding $1 million are eligible for a rebate of up to 30% of the cost of goods and services purchased within the state. The total amount of the rebate available to production companies is limited to the amount of funds allocated to the South Carolina Film Commission to fund the rebate (Sec. 12-62-60; *Revenue Ruling 08-12,* August 2, 2008, CCH SOUTH CAROLINA TAX REPORTS, ¶ 400-430).

Rebates are also available for up to 25% of the South Carolina payroll in connection with the production (Sec. 12-62-50(A)(1)).

Incentive payment for production from biomass resources: An incentive payment will be allowed for producing electricity or methane gas fuel from biomass resources after June 30, 2008, and before July 1, 2018, as follows (Sec. 12-63-20(B)):

— 1¢ per kilowatt-hour (kwh) for electricity produced from biomass resources in a facility not using biomass resources before June 30, 2008, or in facilities that produce at least 25% more electricity from biomass resources than the greatest three-year average before June 30, 2008;

— 9¢ per therm for methane gas fuel produced from biomass resources in a facility not using biomass resources before June 30, 2008, or in facilities that produce at least 25% more methane gas from biomass resources than the greatest three-year average before June 30, 2008.

The maximum incentive payment is $100,000 per year per taxpayer for five years. A biomass resource means wood, wood waste, agricultural waste, animal waste, sewage, landfill gas, and other organic materials. Total incentive payments may not exceed a specified amount for a fiscal year and must apply proportionately to all eligible claimants (Sec. 12-63-20(B)).

• Guide to incentive payments

The current edition of *South Carolina Tax Incentives for Economic Development* is available on the department's website at **https://dor.sc.gov/policy/index/policy-manuals**.

¶ 816   Scope of Tax

Source.—Statutory references are to Title 10, Chapters 10-45 and 10-46 of the South Dakota Codified Laws. Details are reported in the CCH SOUTH DAKOTA TAX REPORTS starting at ¶ 60-000.

The sales and service tax is imposed on the privilege of engaging in business as a retailer and applies to sales at retail in South Dakota of tangible personal property, consisting of goods, wares, or merchandise, to consumers or users (Sec. 10-45-2). The tax is also imposed on the gross receipts of any person from engaging or continuing in the practice of any business in which services are rendered; all services are taxable except those specifically exempted (Sec. 10-45-4).

The use tax is imposed on the privilege of using, storing, and consuming tangible personal property purchased for use in South Dakota as well as the use of taxable services in South Dakota (Sec. 10-46-2). The use tax extends to property originally purchased for use in another state but thereafter used, stored, or consumed in South Dakota (Sec. 10-46-3); however, property more than seven years old at the time it is brought into the state is exempt (Sec. 10-46-3). The age of the exempt property is determined by its date of manufacture, if documented, or by the date of purchase by the person bringing the property to South Dakota (Rule 64:06:03:23.01).

The use tax is not imposed on sales the gross receipts from which have been included in the measure of the sales tax (Sec. 10-46-6).

The sales tax is in addition to all other state or local occupation or privilege taxes (Sec. 10-45-21).

Contractors' excise taxes: Prime contractors engaged in realty improvement contracts are subject to the contractors' excise tax (Sec. 10-46A-1; Sec. 10-46A-1.1) or the alternate contractors' excise tax, both of, which are imposed at a special rate; see ¶ 819. For details of these taxes, see *Contractors' Excise*, South Dakota Department of Revenue, January 2017, CCH SOUTH DAKOTA TAX REPORTS, ¶ 201-160.

Services: While most states impose their sales and use taxes only on specified services, the South Dakota retail sales and service tax applies generally to all services performed in the state (Sec. 10-45-4; Sec. 10-46-2.1). Exemptions are provided only for certain specified services, such as health services (Sec. 10-45-12.1; Sec. 10-46-17.3). See ¶ 818.

Digital products: Sales and use tax applies to all sales, leases, or rentals of any product transferred electronically (Sec. 10-45-2.4; Sec. 10-45-1.16(2); 10-46-2.4). The tax will apply if:

— the sale is to an end user;

— the sale is to a person who is not an end user, unless otherwise exempted;

— the seller grants the right of permanent or less than permanent use of the products transferred electronically; or

— the sale is conditioned or not conditioned upon continued payment.

A "product transferred electronically" is defined as any product obtained by the purchaser by means other than tangible storage media (Sec. 10-45-1). A product transferred electronically does not include any intangible items such as a patent, stock, goodwill, trademark, franchise, or copyright. The term "end user" does not include any person who received by contract any product transferred electronically for further commercial broadcast, rebroadcast, transmission, retransmission, licensing, relicensing, distribution, redistribution, or exhibition of the product, in whole or in part, to another person.

The sale of a digital code that may be utilized to obtain a product transferred electronically must be taxed in the same manner as the product transferred electronically. A digital code is a code that permits a purchaser to obtain at a later date a product transferred electronically. (*Tax Facts—Internet,* South Dakota Department of Revenue, June 2013, CCH SOUTH DAKOTA TAX REPORTS, ¶ 201-045).

• Telecommunications services

Interstate, intrastate, and international telecommunication services that start or end in South Dakota and that are billed or charged to a South Dakota address are subject to sales tax (Sec. 10-45-6.1). However, the tax does not apply to (1) 800 or 800-type services, unless the service begins and ends in South Dakota, (2) any sale of a telecommunication service to a provider of telecommunication services, including access service, for use in providing any telecommunication service, or (3) any sale of interstate telecommunication service provided to a certified call center when the call center provides the telecommunications service provider with a valid exemption certificate.

The term "telecommunication service" is defined as the electronic transmission, conveyance, or routing of voice, data, audio, video, and any other information or signals to a point, or between or among points. The term includes the following services (Sec. 10-33A-2):

— 800 or 900 service;

— fixed or mobile wireless service;

— paging service;

— prepaid wired or wireless calling service;

— private communication service; and

— value-added non-voice data service.

Ancillary services: Tax is imposed upon the privilege of the use of any ancillary service. "Ancillary services" are defined as services that are associated with or incidental to the provision of telecommunications services, including detailed telecommunications billing, directory assistance, vertical services, and voice mail services. (Sec. 10-45-1.18; Sec. 10-46-1.3)

Bundled services: A sale of bundled telecommunications, ancillary services, Internet access, or audio or video programming services that includes both taxable and nontaxable services is subject to sales and use taxes in its entirety, unless the portion of the price attributable to the nontaxable services can be reasonably identified from the provider's books and records (Sec. 10-45-1.7).

Internet services: A publication explains how sales and use tax applies to Internet access and Internet related services. The publication discusses Internet access equipment, telecommunication services, wireless and portable Internet devices, web page development, advertising on web pages, web hosting services, products and services for resale, support services, Voice over Internet Protocol (VoIP), Internet sales, and Internet auction services (*Tax Facts—Internet,* South Dakota Department of Revenue, June 2013, CCH SOUTH DAKOTA TAX REPORTS, ¶ 201-045).

• Incidence of sales tax

The sales tax is imposed on the privilege of engaging in the business of a retailer (Sec. 10-45-2) but a retailer may add the tax to the price of the product or service sold (Sec. 10-45-22).

Controlled groups: Payments made by a member of a controlled group to another member that represent an allocation, reimbursement, or charge for services provided or rendered are exempt from tax (Sec. 10-45-20.1). However, receipts from the lease of tangible personal property between members of a controlled group, or between mem-

¶816   South Dakota

bers of a financial institution and a related corporation, are subject to sales and use tax, unless the sales or use tax has been paid on the property by the lessor (Sec. 10-45-20.1). A "controlled group" includes corporations or other entities eligible to file a consolidated federal income tax return, subchapter S corporations, limited liability companies, limited liability partnerships, general partnerships, or limited partnerships with at least 80% ownership.

Drop shipments: If all the parties are located in the state, the retailer furnishes an exemption certificate to the primary seller, rendering the first sale a nontaxable transaction. The exemption certificate may indicate the license number of the seller from the seller's state. The retailer then collects sales tax on behalf of the state on the secondary sale to its customer. The purchaser will be responsible for remitting use tax on the purchase if the retailer does not collect sales tax.

If a South Dakota manufacturer (primary seller) makes a sale to an out-of-state retailer not doing business in South Dakota and delivers the product to the retailer's South Dakota customer, the manufacturer must collect sales tax from the retailer based on the wholesale price if the retailer does not provide an exemption certificate. A resale exemption certificate may be accepted from retailers registered in any state. The customer is responsible for payment of use tax on the secondary transaction if the manufacturer does not collect sales tax from the retailer. (*Tax Facts - Drop Shipments,* South Dakota Department of Revenue, June 2013, **http://dor.sd.gov/Taxes/Business_Taxes/Publications/PDFs/Tax%20Facts/Drop%20Shipments.pdf**)

• **Nexus**

Every retailer engaged in business in South Dakota and making sales of tangible personal property for use, storage, or other consumption in South Dakota, not otherwise exempted, must collect sales or use tax (Sec. 10-46-2). For tax collection and reporting purposes, "retailer maintaining a place of business in the state" means a retailer having or maintaining within South Dakota, directly or by a subsidiary, an office, distribution house, sales house, warehouse, or other place of business, or any agent operating in the sate under the authority of the retailer or its subsidiary, regardless of whether the business or agent is permanently or temporarily located in the state or whether the retailer or subsidiary is admitted to do business in the state (Sec. 10-46-1(9)).

Affiliate nexus: A retailer is considered to be engaged in the business of selling tangible personal property, services, and products transferred electronically for use in South Dakota if either of the following is true (Sec. 10-45–2.5):

— (1)(a) the retailer holds a substantial interest in, or is owned by, a South Dakota retailer, and (b) the retailer sells the same or a substantially similar line of products under the same or similar business name as the related South Dakota retailer, or the in-state facility or in-state employee of the related retailer is used to advertise, promote, or facilitate sales by the retailer to a consumer; or

— (2) the retailer holds a substantial ownership interest in or is owned by a business that maintains a distribution house, sales house, warehouse, or similar place of business in South Dakota that delivers property sold by the retailer to consumers.

The electronic processing of orders does not relieve a retailer of responsibility for collecting tax from the purchaser if the retailer is doing business in South Dakota. There is a rebuttable presumption that any retailer that is part of a controlled group that has a component member that is a retailer engaged in business in South Dakota is also considered a retailer engaged in business in South Dakota (Sec. 10-45–2.8).

Notification requirements: Out-of-state retailers that are not registered to collect and remit sales and use tax, but sell tangible personal property, services, or products transferred electronically for use in South Dakota, are required to notify buyers that

South Dakota ¶816

they must pay and report South Dakota use tax on their purchases. The required notice must be readily visible on a page necessary to facilitate the applicable transaction and must contain the following information (Sec. 10–63–2; *Tax Facts—South Dakota Sales Tax Public Notice for Non-Collection Retailers*, South Dakota Department of Revenue and Regulation, April 2011, CCH SOUTH DAKOTA TAX REPORTS, ¶ 201-003):

— (1) the noncollecting retailer is not required to and does not collect South Dakota sales or use tax;

— (2) the purchase is subject to state use tax unless it is specifically exempt from taxation;

— (3) the purchase is not exempt merely because the purchase is made over the Internet, by catalog, or by other means;

— (4) the state requires each South Dakota purchaser to report any purchase that was not taxed and pay tax on the purchase, and the tax may be reported and paid on the South Dakota use tax form; and

— (5) the use tax form and corresponding instructions are available on the South Dakota Department of Revenue and Regulation website.

A *de minimis* retailer and a *de minimis* online auction website are exempt from the notice requirements (Sec. 10–63–8). A "de minimis retailer" is defined as any noncollecting retailer that made total gross sales in South Dakota in the prior calendar year of less than $100,000 and reasonably expects that South Dakota sales in the current calendar year will be less than $100,000 (Sec. 10–4–1.13). A "de minimis online auction website" is defined as any online auction website that facilitates total gross sales in South Dakota in the prior calendar year of less than $100,000 and reasonably expects South Dakota sales in the current calendar year to be less than $100,000 (Sec. 10–63–8).

• **Nexus expansion enjoined pending court decision**

South Dakota enacted sales and use tax collection requirements for remote sellers who meet certain sales thresholds (S.B. 106, Laws 2016). It provides that a retailer is presumed to be liable for the collection of sales and use tax in South Dakota, even if the seller does not have a physical presence in state, if the seller meets either of the following criteria in the previous or current calendar year:

(1) the seller's gross revenue from the sale of tangible personal property, any product transferred electronically, or services delivered into South Dakota exceeds $100,000; or

(2) the seller sold tangible personal property, any product transferred electronically, or services for delivery into South Dakota in 200 or more separate transactions.

The legislation provides for an expedited appeals process for any challenges to the constitutionality of the law.

Note: The legislation enacting this provision also provided for an automatic injunction if the law was challenged in court. A challenge invoking the injunction was filed on April 28, 2016. The injunction will be in effect throughout the court case. If the injunction is lifted or dissolved, the obligation to collect will begin from that day forward.

• **Streamlined Act status**

South Dakota is a full member of the Streamlined Sales and Use Tax Agreement with a seat on the Governing Board. It has enacted all of the provisions necessary to comply with the Agreement's requirements and these provisions currently are in effect (Sec. 10-45C-3). As a full member, it may vote on amendments to or interpretations of the Agreement, and sellers registering under the SST system must collect and remit tax on sales into the state. For additional information, see ¶ 822.

¶816   South Dakota

¶ 817   Tax Base

The tax base for the sales tax is the gross receipts from sales or services (Sec. 10-45-2, Sec. 10-45-4). "Gross receipts" is defined as the total amount or consideration, including cash, credit, property, and services, for which tangible personal property or services are sold, leased, or rented, valued in money, whether received in money or otherwise, without any deduction for (Sec. 10-45-1.14):

— the retailer's cost of the property or service sold;

— the cost of materials used, labor or service cost, interest, losses, all costs of transportation to the retailer, all taxes imposed on the retailer, and any other expense of the retailer; or

— charges by the retailer for any services necessary to complete the sale whether or not separately stated, including delivery charges.

Gross receipts do not include (Sec. 10-45-1.16):

— discounts, including cash, term, or coupons that are not reimbursed by a third party that are allowed by a retailer and taken by a purchaser on a sale;

— interest, financing, and carrying charges from credit extended on the sale of tangible personal property or services, if the amount is separately stated on the invoice, bill of sale, or similar document given to the purchaser; or

— any taxes imposed directly on the consumer, including retail sales and service tax, gross receipts tax on visitor-related businesses, municipal non-valorem tax or municipal gross receipts tax, that are separately stated on the invoice, bill of sale, or similar document given to the purchaser.

The tax base for the use tax is the purchase price of tangible personal property or the value of services (Sec. 10-46-2, Sec. 10-46-2.1). The tax base for the use tax on property not originally purchased for use in South Dakota but subsequently used, stored, or consumed in the state is the fair market value of the property at the time it is brought into South Dakota (Sec. 10-46-3). Sales tax is computed on taxable receipts even though such receipts include single sales on which no tax can be charged to a customer (Rule 64:06:01:50).

"Tangible personal property" is defined as personal property that can be seen, weighed, measured, felt, or touched, or that is in any other manner perceptible to the senses. The term includes electricity, water, gas, steam, and prewritten computer software (Sec. 10-45-1; Sec. 10-46-1(12)).

• **Sourcing rules**

A retailer must source sales of tangible personal property and services to the location where the tangible personal property or services are received (Sec. 10-45-108).

The general sourcing rules for determining a seller's obligation to collect and remit sales or use tax on a retail sale of a product are set forth below. These sourcing rules apply regardless of the characterization of a product as tangible personal property, a digital good, or a service. The sourcing rules do not apply to sales of watercraft, modular homes, manufactured homes, mobile homes, and certain motor vehicles, trailers, semitrailers, or aircraft.

A retail sale, excluding a lease or rental, of a product will be sourced as follows (Rule ARSD 64:06:01:63):

(1) If the product is received by the purchaser at a business location of the seller, the sale is sourced to that business location;

(2) If the product is not received by the purchaser at a business location of the seller, the sale is sourced to the location where received by the purchaser, or the purchaser's donee, if known by the seller;

(3) If neither of the above applies, the sale is sourced to the address for the purchaser in the business records of the seller that are maintained in the ordinary course of the seller's business, provided that the use of this address does not constitute bad faith;

(4) If none of the above applies, the sale is sourced to the location indicated by an address for the purchaser obtained during the consummation of the sale, including the address of a purchaser's payment instrument, if no other address is available, provided that use of this address does not constitute bad faith; and

(5) If none of the above sourcing rules applies, or if the seller is without sufficient information to apply any of the above rules, then the sale is sourced to the address (disregarding any location that merely provided the digital transfer of the product sold) from which: (a) tangible personal property was shipped, (b) a digital good was first available for transmission by the seller, or (c) a service was provided.

Separate sourcing rules apply to leases and rentals (Rule ARSD 64:06:01:64), products concurrently available for use in more than one jurisdiction (see ¶ 822), telecommunications (Rule ARSD 64:06:02:91), and transportation equipment (Rule ARSD 64:06:01:66).

- **Taxability matrix**

A matrix of the taxability in South Dakota of various goods and services is available at **http://www.streamlinedsalestax.org/**

¶ 818   List of Exemptions, Exceptions, and Exclusions

Unless otherwise indicated, the statutory exemptions listed below apply to both sales and use taxes; those applicable only to the use tax are listed separately. Items that are excluded from the sales or use tax base are treated at ¶ 817, "Tax Base."

Air transportation services: The South Dakota Department of Revenue issued a statement on their blog stating that effective June 9, 2014, all air transportation services are no longer subject to sales or use tax. The Department determined that the Federal Anti-Head Act of 1973 exempts gross receipts received for intrastate and interstate air transportation services from South Dakota sales tax.

Taxpayers remain responsible for sales or use tax on the sale of any taxable product or service. The release listed some businesses that may be affected by this change: aerial sightseeing services, air transportation services; air ambulance services, and any air transportation service in Federal Airways.

Air transportation services provided with other taxable services that are not separately stated are taxable. For example, sky diving lessons are taxable. If there is a single charge for the lessons and flight, the entire charge is taxable. However, if the charge for the lessons and flight are separately stated, the charge for the lessons are taxable and the charge for the flight is exempt. (*Blog,* South Dakota Department of Revenue, June 9, 2014)

- **Sales and use tax exemptions, exceptions, and exclusions**

Admissions to certain places of amusement	Sec. 10-45-13(1)
Advertising services	Sec. 10-45-12.1,
	Sec. 10-46-17.3
Agricultural services and equipment; maintenance services	Sec. 10-45-1(1),
	Sec. 10-45-3.4,
	Sec. 10-45-12.1,
	Sec. 10-45-93,
	Sec. 10-46-17.3,
	Sec. 10-46-17.6,

¶818 **South Dakota**

Storage or warehousing of farm products	Sec. 10-45-12.1, Sec. 10-46-17.3
Television broadcasting	Sec. 10-45-12.1, Sec. 10-46-17.3
Trading stamps	Sec. 10-45-12.1, Sec. 10-46-17.3
Transportation services	Sec. 10-45-12.1, Sec. 10-46-17.3
Vessels	Sec. 10-45-62, Sec. 10-46-51
Warranty services	Sec. 10-45-11.1, Sec. 10-46-17.3
Water	Sec. 10-45-19.3
Wrapping materials	Sec. 10-45-14.4, Sec. 10-46-9.3
Youth associations' activities	Sec. 10-45-13(5), Sec. 10-45-13(9), Sec. 10-45-13(10)

- **Exemptions, exceptions and exclusions applicable only to the use tax**

Farm equipment that is at least 7 years old when brought to South Dakota	Sec. 10-46E-3
Materials for signs manufactured for installation outside South Dakota	Sec. 10-46-5.4
Nonresidents' personal effects	Sec. 10-46-8

¶ 819   **Rate of Tax**

Effective June 1, 2016, the sales and use taxes are imposed at the rate of 4.5% (previously, 4%) of the tax base, which is defined at ¶ 817 (Sec. 10-45-2, Sec. 10-45-5, Sec. 10-45-5.3, Sec. 10-45-6, Sec. 10-45-6.1, Sec. 10-45-6.2, Sec. 10-45-8, Sec. 10-45-71, Sec. 10-46-2.1, Sec. 10-46-2.2, Sec. 10-46-58, Sec. 10-46-69, Sec. 10-46-69.1, Sec. 10-46-69.2, Sec. 10-46E-1, Sec. 10-46-58.1).

The new tax rate applies to:

(1) the sale, lease, or rental of tangible personal property, products transferred electronically, and services;

(2) the excise tax on the purchase of farm machinery;

(3) the amusement device tax; and

(4) special jurisdiction tax rates on Indian Country where there is a tax collection agreement.

sonal sales and use tax (tourism tax)

visitor-related business is subject to an additional 1.5% tax on its gross receipts d during the months of June, July, August, and September (Sec. 10-45D-2). A elated business includes any lodging establishment, campground, motor vehicle visitor attraction, recreational service, recreation equipment rental, spectator any other visitor-intensive business. For additional information, see *Tax Facts -* *Tax,* South Dakota Dept. of Revenue, June 2016, CCH SOUTH DAKOTA TAX ¶ 201-140.

• **Telecommunications sales tax**

A 4% tax is imposed on interstate, intrastate, or international telecommunications that start or end in South Dakota and that are billed or charged to a South Dakota address (Sec. 10-45-6.1).

Mobile telecommunications: A 4% tax also is imposed on the gross receipts or privilege of use of "mobile telecommunications services," as defined in U.S.C. Sec. 124(7), that originate and terminate in the same state and are billed to a customer with a place of primary use in South Dakota (Sec. 10-45-6.2). See ¶ 820 for sourcing of telecommunications charges.

• **Contractors' excise taxes**

The realty improvement contractors' excise tax is imposed at the special rate of 2% of the tax base, defined at ¶ 817 (Sec. 10-46A-1). The alternate realty improvement contractors' excise tax, which applies to realty improvements performed for utility companies, also is imposed at the rate of 2% (Sec. 10-46B-1 *et seq.*). Effective July 1, 2014, the contractor's 1% excise tax on new or expanded renewable power production facilities was repealed (former Sec. 10-46C-1 *et seq.*).

Rate increases: No tax increase may apply to materials incorporated in construction work pursuant to construction contract bids or contracts entered into on or before the effective date of a rate increase (Sec. 10-45-2.2, Sec. 10-46-5.2, Sec. 10-46A-14, Sec. 10-46B-12).

• **Amusement excise tax**

An excise tax of 4% is imposed on gross receipts from mechanical or electron amusement devices (Sec. 10-58-1).

• **Motor vehicle excise tax**

A motor vehicle excise tax of 3% is imposed in lieu of sales and use taxes on sa motor vehicles (Sec. 32-5B-1).

Beginning July 1, 2015, a 4.5% South Dakota gross receipts tax is imposed rental of motorcycles in lieu of the excise tax on motor vehicles (Sec. 32-5B-20) is in addition to any applicable sales or use taxes imposed on the rental of a ve

• **Farm equipment excise tax**

A 4% state excise tax is imposed on gross receipts from the sale and machinery, attachment units, and irrigation equipment used exclusively fo purposes (Sec. 10-46E-1). The storage, use, or consumption of farm ma subject to the tax (Sec. 10-46E-3). Imposition of the state excise ta transactions exempt from state and municipal sales and use tax. T reported on the sales tax return (*Tax Facts #110*, South Dakota Depar and Regulation, March 2006, CCH SOUTH DAKOTA TAX REPORTS, ¶ 200-

The use, storage, or consumption of farm machinery, att irrigation equipment used exclusively for agricultural purposes tha years old at the time it is brought into South Dakota by the perso property for use in another state is exempt (Sec. 10-46E-3).

¶ 820   **Local Taxes**

Municipalities may impose a sales and use tax at a ra 10-52-2). The municipal tax rate applies to gross receipts fro 64:06:03:41.01). The highest rate of a municipal sales tax ar vending machines that sell multiple items that are taxed vendor maintains records and inventories documenting ac

¶820   **South Dakota**

• *Sea

A
receive
visitor-
rental,
event, o
Tourism
REPORTS,

U.S. Maste

- **SSTP conformity**

Changes for South Dakota municipal sales and use tax resulting from the adoption of the Streamlined Sales and Use Tax Agreement (see ¶ 816) include one general municipal sales and use tax rate for each city for all taxable sales of items or services, the taxation of food at a city's general municipal tax rate, the elimination of all exemptions for construction materials delivered to a construction company truck for use outside city limits, new sales tax rates for some cities, new municipal tax reporting codes for many cities, and the reporting of municipal gross receipts tax under a separate code from the municipal sales tax.

When a new tax rate is enacted and becomes effective 30 or fewer days from the date of enactment retailers will have a 30-day grace period from liability for failure to collect or report sales and use tax. To qualify for relief from liability during the grace period, a retailer must collect and report sales and use tax at the immediately preceding rate and its failure to collect or report at the new rate cannot extend beyond 30 days from the enactment date of the new rate. (Sec. 10–45–111)

Sourcing: See ¶ 817.

- **Contractors' excise taxes**

A municipality is authorized to impose a realty improvement contractors' excise tax or alternate tax at a rate not exceeding ½ of 1% (Sec. 10-46A-11, Sec. 10-46B-9).

- **Tribal taxes**

Four Indian Tribes have comprehensive tax agreements with the State of South Dakota. They are the Cheyenne River Sioux Tribe; the Oglala Sioux Tribe (Pine Ridge Reservation); the Rosebud Sioux Tribe; and the the Standing Rock Sioux Tribe. The Sisseton-Wahpeton Oyate Tribe has a limited tax collection agreement that includes contractors' excise tax and use tax. All businesses, including those owned by tribal members, are responsible for collecting and remitting tax.

Indian country controlled by a Tribe that is part of a tax collection agreement is considered a Special Jurisdiction. All tax due in each Special Jurisdiction is reported on the state tax return using the code assigned to that Special Jurisdiction. The tax remitted is then distributed between the State and Tribal Governments based on the tax collection agreements. (*Tax Facts—Tribal—Special Jurisdiction,* June 2016, CCH SOUTH DAKOTA TAX REPORTS, ¶ 201-105)

The tribes impose a 4% tribal sales and use tax, a 3% farm machinery (agricultural and irrigation) tax, and a 2% contractor's excise tax. The tribal tax is not in addition to the state tax. However, some cities located on a reservation do have a municipal tax rate that is paid in addition to the reservation tax.

- **Mobile telecommunications**

South Dakota has adopted legislation conformed to the federal Mobile Telecommunications Sourcing Act (Act), P.L. 106-252. All charges for mobile telecommunications services are considered to be provided by the customer's home service provider and sourced to the customer's place of primary use (Sec. 10-45-6.2; Rule 64:06:02.92). All such charges are subject to sales tax based on the customer's place of primary use.

The service provider will be held harmless for an error in assigning wireless services to a jurisdiction if it utilizes an electronic database provided by the state or a designated entity, or, if the state has not provided or designated a database, if it utilizes a database that makes assignments based on a nine-digit zip code.

- **Local tax rates**

A local sales tax rate locator is available on the website of the Department of Revenue and Regulation at **http://arcgis.sd.gov/server/drr/taxmatch/**. Rates for municipal and tribal taxes are available by jurisdiction, address, or ZIP code.

Local sales tax rate charts are available on the department's website at **http:// dor.sd.gov/Taxes/Business_Taxes/Publications/Municipal_Tax.aspx**.

¶ 821 **Bracket Schedule**

In computing the tax, the tax amount must be carried to the third decimal place (Sec. 10-45-1.4). Amounts of tax less than one-half of one cent are disregarded and amounts of tax of one-half cent or more are considered an additional cent. A seller may choose to compute the tax due on an item or invoice basis (Rule 64:06:01:50).

The following bracket schedules have been issued by the Department of Revenue and Regulation for purposes of collecting the tax (Sec. 10-45-23, Rule 64:06:01:39.01):

3% Tax Rate

Sale	Tax
$0.01 to $0.16	No tax
.17 to .49	1¢
.50 to .83	2¢
.84 to 1.16	3¢
and so forth.	

6.5% Tax Rate

Sale	Tax
$0.01 to $0.07	No tax
.08 to .23	1¢
.24 to .38	2¢
.39 to .53	3¢
.54 to .69	4¢
.70 to .84	5¢
.85 to .99	6¢
1.00 to 1.15	7¢
and so forth.	

4% Tax Rate

Sale	Tax
$0.01 to $0.12	No tax
.13 to .37	1¢
.38 to .62	2¢
.63 to .87	3¢
.88 to 1.12	4¢
and so forth.	

7% Tax Rate

Sale	Tax
$0.01 to $0.07	No tax
.08 to .21	1¢
.22 to .35	2¢
.36 to .49	3¢
.50 to .64	4¢
.65 to .78	5¢
.79 to .92	6¢
.93 to 1.07	7¢
and so forth.	

5% Tax Rate

Sale	Tax
$0.01 to $0.09	No tax
.10 to .29	1¢
.30 to .49	2¢
.50 to .69	3¢
.70 to .89	4¢
.90 to 1.09	5¢
and so forth.	

7.5% Tax Rate

Sale	Tax
$0.01 to $0.06	No tax
.07 to .19	1¢
.20 to .33	2¢
.34 to .46	3¢
.47 to .59	4¢
.60 to .73	5¢
.74 to .86	6¢
.87 to .99	7¢
1.00 to 1.13	8¢
and so forth.	

5.5% Tax Rate

Sale	Tax
$0.01 to $0.09	No tax
.10 to .27	1¢
.28 to .45	2¢
.46 to .63	3¢
.64 to .81	4¢
.82 to .99	5¢
1.00 to 1.18	6¢
and so forth.	

8% Tax Rate

Sale	Tax
$0.01 to $0.06	No tax
.07 to .18	1¢
.19 to .31	2¢
.32 to .43	3¢
.44 to .56	4¢
.57 to .68	5¢
.69 to .81	6¢
.82 to .93	7¢
.94 to 1.06	8¢
and so forth.	

6% Tax Rate

Sale	Tax
$0.01 to $0.08	No tax
.09 to .24	1¢
.25 to .41	2¢
.42 to .58	3¢
.59 to .74	4¢
.75 to .91	5¢
.92 to 1.08	6¢

and so forth.

¶ 822   Returns, Payments, and Due Dates

Retailers and other persons holding sales tax permits, retailers required or authorized to collect use tax, and contractors liable for excise tax must file sales and use tax returns on forms prescribed and furnished by the Department of Revenue and Regulation (Sec. 10-45-27, Sec. 10-46-27, Sec. 10-46-28, Sec. 10-46A-8, Sec. 10-46B-4, Rule 64:06:01:20). Remittance of tax due must accompany the returns. A taxpayer whose tax liability is at least $1,000 annually must file a return and remit tax by the 20th day of the month following each monthly period, except in the case of taxpayers who remit tax electronically (see below). Other taxpayers file returns and remit tax by the last day of the month following each two-month period. Returns of use tax must be signed by the retailer or its authorized agent and must be certified to be correct (Sec. 10-46-30).

A U.S. Postal Service postmark is evidence of the mailing date for purposes of determining the timely filing of a return, report, or remittance (Se. 10–59–33).

• Extensions

If the due date for a South Dakota return, report, or remittance falls on a Saturday, Sunday, enumerated legal holiday, or day that the Federal Reserve Bank is closed, then that return, report, or remittance is timely filed if mailed, postage prepaid, on the next succeeding day that is not a Saturday, Sunday, enumerated legal holiday, or day that the Federal Reserve Bank is closed (Sec. 10-59-33). Note that this extended due date provision does not apply to a return or report filed, or a payment remitted, using electronic means.

An extension of five days for filing a return and remittance may be granted by the Secretary (Sec. 10-45-27, Sec. 10-46-29).

Any manufacturing, fabricating, or processing business may apply for a six-month extension for remitting sales and use tax on machinery and equipment purchased for direct use in the business if (1) the cost of purchasing and installing the machinery and equipment exceeds $20,000 and (2) the business has applied for an extension permit from the Secretary (Sec. 10-45-27, Sec. 10-45-99—10-45-107).

• Electronic filing

The Secretary of Revenue can authorize payment of taxes or fees by electronic transmission (Sec. 10-59-32). Electronically filed returns are due by the 23rd day of the month following the monthly period, and electronically submitted taxes are due by the second to last day of that month. Prior enrollment in the program is required. Electronic filing and payment is available at **https://apps.sd.gov/RV23EPath/Login.aspx**.

Only those vendors who file returns and remit payments electronically may claim a vendors' allowance credit; see ¶ 825.

- **Direct payment permits**

The Secretary of Revenue may authorize retailers that purchase taxable goods or services to use direct payment permits (Sec. 10-46-67). The holder of a direct payment permit can pay sales and use tax directly to the Department of Revenue and Regulation. A retailer that makes a sale to a direct payment permit holder has no tax liability if the seller has written evidence of the sale indicating the name of the buyer, the product or service purchased, and the amount of the purchase. Retailers must apply in writing to the Secretary in order to obtain authorization to use a direct payment permit.

- **Uniform Sales Tax Administration Act**

South Dakota has enacted the Uniform Sales and Use Tax Administration Act, the product of the Streamlined Sales Tax Project (SSTP) and is a member of the related Streamlined Sales and Use Tax Agreement to simplify and modernize sales and use tax administration in order to substantially reduce the burden of tax compliance for all sellers and for all types of commerce.

The Agreement establishes performance standards for multistate sellers and standards for certification of a certified service provider (CSP), an agent certified by the states to perform all of a seller's sales tax functions, and a certified automated system (CAS), software certified by the states to calculate the tax imposed, determine the amount to remit, and maintain a record of the transaction.

Registration: See ¶ 824.

Sourcing: See ¶ 817.

For additional information on the uniform act, see "Streamlined Sales Tax Project," listed in the Table of Contents.

¶ 823   **Prepayment of Taxes**

There are no provisions regarding prepayment of taxes in South Dakota.

¶ 824   **Vendor Registration**

A retailer or person engaging in business in the state with taxable receipts must file with the Department of Revenue and Regulation an application for a permit or permits on a form prescribed by the Secretary of Revenue (Sec. 10-45-24, Rule 64:06:01:07.01).

Generally, a permit must be obtained for each place of business (Rule 64:06:01:33). However, the Department of Revenue and Regulation can grant a statewide sales tax permit in lieu of requiring a person to obtain a permit for each place of business if each business location has identical ownership, the same federal identification number, the same Standard Industrial Classification number, and the same license type. A business with a statewide sales tax permit must maintain records at one location that clearly show the gross receipts, deductions, and municipal sales for each reported business location (Sec. 10-45-24, Rule 64:06:01:33, Rule 64:06:01:07.02).

A permit cannot be assigned and is valid only for the person in whose name it is issued and at the designated business location (Sec. 10-45-25). Permits are valid until canceled or revoked. A retailer licensed to engage in business in the state is considered to be registered for city sales tax purposes (Rule 64:06:01:30).

Tobacco retailers: In order to sell tobacco products such as cigarettes, cigars, pipe tobacco, and smokeless tobacco, a retailer must possess a South Dakota sales and use tax license and must also register with the state's Department of Revenue and Regulation. There is no fee for this registration. Furthermore, there are no additional taxes, or filing or reporting requirements. The registration simply works in conjunction with the retailer's sales and use tax license.

- **Contractors**

Prior to engaging in business, all contractors or persons subject to the contractors' excise tax must obtain a contractor's excise tax license on forms prescribed by the Secretary of Revenue (Sec. 10-46A-15, Sec. 10-46B-13). A license cannot be assigned, is valid only for the person in whose name it is issued, and is effective until canceled or revoked (Sec. 10-46A-16, Sec. 10-46B-14; *Contractors' Excise Tax Guide,* Department of Revenue, January 2017, CCH SOUTH DAKOTA TAX REPORTS, ¶ 201-160).

- **Online application**

New businesses applying for South Dakota sales and contractors' excise tax licenses can now do so online at the Department of Revenue and Regulation's website at **https://apps.sd.gov/rv23cedar/main/main.aspx**.

- **SST registration**

To register under the Streamlined Sales and Use Tax Agreement (SST), sellers must go to **https://www.sstregister.org**. Sellers can also update previously submitted registration information at this website. The information provided will be sent to all of the full member states and to associate members for which the seller chooses to collect.

When a seller registers under the Agreement, it must select the certified technology model it will be using (or it must select "Other" if it will not be using one of the certified models). The models are the following:

Model One: Certified Service Provider (CSP), an agent certified under the Agreement to perform all the seller's sales and use tax functions;

Model Two: Certified Automated System (CAS), software certified under the Agreement to calculate the appropriate tax (for which the seller retains responsibility for remitting);

Model Three: Certified System (CS), a proprietary automated sales tax system certified under the Agreement.

¶ 825   **Sales or Use Tax Credits**

Credit is allowed against South Dakota use tax for sales and use tax previously paid by the taxpayer to another state or its political subdivisions with respect to the same property or services (Sec. 10-46-6.1, Sec. 10-46-34.1, Rule 64:06:01:34). However, no credit is allowed if the other state or its political subdivision does not grant a reciprocal credit for similar property in South Dakota.

Consumers paying a city sales tax on purchases in one city may offset any subsequent city use tax liability by the amount of tax already paid (Rule 64:06:01:31).

- **Vendor compensation**

For returns filed and taxes remitted after January 1, 2014, sales and use tax monthly filers are authorized to claim a 1.5% credit of the gross amount of the tax due as compensation for their cost of collection (Sec. 10-45-27.2). However, the credit may not exceed $70 per return period. Persons required to file a return and to remit tax more than once within a 30-day period may not receive a collection allowance credit exceeding $70 for all returns filed and all remittances made within the 30-day period.

The credit allowance may be granted only to persons who timely file the return due by electronic means and who timely remit the tax due by electronic means. However, no collection allowance credit may be granted to any person who has outstanding tax returns due or who has outstanding tax payments due. Furthermore, no person who has selected a certified service provider (CSP) as its agent is entitled to the collection allowance credit if the certified service provider receives a monetary allowance for performing the retailer's sales and use tax functions in South Dakota. (Sec. 10-45-27.2)

- **Bad debts**

A credit is allowed for taxes previously paid on worthless accounts that have been charged off for income tax purposes (Sec. 10-45-30). Bad debts include any portion of worthless checks, worthless credit card payments, and uncollectible credit accounts. However interest and financing charges are not included. A seller may deduct bad debts from the total amount upon which the tax is calculated for any return. Bad debts must be deducted within 12 months following the month that the bad debt was charged off for federal income tax purposes.

If a previously deducted bad debt or the amount of a check that was returned and not included as part of gross receipts are collected by the retailer, tax must be paid on the amount collected and reported on a subsequent tax return (Sec. 10-45-30, Rule 64:06:01:03.02).

- **Incentive credits and refunds**

Several incentives in the form or a refund or credit are discussed at ¶ 829.

¶ 826   **Deficiency Assessments**

The Secretary of Revenue will issue a certificate of assessment if it determines that a taxpayer owes tax, penalty, or interest (Sec. 10-46-41, Sec. 10-46-42, Sec. 10-59-8). A copy of the assessment is sent by certified mail to the taxpayer's last known address. A certificate is deemed prima facie correct. The taxpayer, within 60 days from the date of the certificate must either (1) pay the amount of the assessment or make other arrangements agreeable to the taxing authorities to pay the assessment plus any applicable interest, or (2) request a hearing.

Prior to the issuance of a certificate of assessment, the Department of Revenue and Regulation must furnish the taxpayer with a proposed list in writing of taxable items. The Department must hold a conference with the taxpayer to review the list of taxable items, and the taxpayer may protest in writing the inclusion of any of the proposed taxable items. The protest may be included in any appeal of the Department's certificate of assessment.

¶ 827   **Audit Procedures**

The Secretary of Revenue may investigate any taxpayer and examine a taxpayer's books and records (Sec. 10-59-5). Notice of intent to audit must be sent to a taxpayer at least 30 days before commencement of an audit unless the Secretary determines that delay may jeopardize the collection of tax or the 30-day period is waived by consent of both parties. Documents or records that evidence reduction, deduction, or exemption from tax that are not prepared for presentation to the auditor within 60 days from the start of the audit do not have to be considered by the auditor (Sec. 10-59-3, Sec. 10-59-7).

When the gross sales records are inadequate, an auditor may refer to federal income tax returns, bank statements, purchase invoices, gross profit tests based on expenses and withdrawals, and cash transactions (Rule 64:06:01:35.05). A taxpayer's deductions may be verified by invoices for sale for resale, invoices for exempt sales, invoices for out-of-state sales, freight bills showing out-of-state deliveries, invoices for returns and allowances, and worksheets for bad debts.

An auditor may conduct a sample audit instead of a detailed examination of all records (Rule 64:06:01:35.04).

For additional information, see *Audits,* South Dakota Department of Revenue, July 2015, CCH SOUTH DAKOTA TAX REPORTS, ¶ 201-084, or go to **http://dor.sd.gov/Taxes/Audits/**.

¶826   South Dakota

¶ 828   Statute of Limitations

A proceeding, audit, action or jeopardy assessment to determine and collect tax must be commenced within three years from the date a return is filed (Sec. 10-59-16). There is no statute of limitations (1) for any period for which a taxpayer fails to obtain or maintain a required license or permit, (2) for any period for which a taxpayer fails to file a return or files a fraudulent return, (3) for any tax, penalty, or interest first due and payable within three years of the date of mailing of a notice of intent to audit, or (4) for any period for which a taxpayer files a return reporting tax due and fails to remit the reported tax in full.

¶ 829   Application for Refund

A claim for recovery of overpaid tax, penalty, or interest must be filed by a taxpayer on forms prescribed and furnished by the Secretary of Revenue within the earlier of three years from the date the amount was paid or three years from the date the return was due (Sec. 10-59-19, Sec. 10-59-21). Any overpayment that is determined by the Secretary to be recoverable by the taxpayer is credited against the taxpayer's future liability, except that a refund is made if there is no future tax obligation or if the credit is not used within one year (Sec. 10-59-22). The Secretary's determination is considered to be a final decision for purposes of judicial review.

A recovery credit or refund that is not the result of the taxpayer's error includes interest at the same rate the taxpayer would be charged (Sec. 10-59-24).

• Refunds for low-income elderly and disabled

South Dakota provides for a refund of sales taxes paid by any resident person who is 66 years of age or older on or before January 1 in the year for which a claim for refund is made and by any resident disabled person (Sec. 10-45A-2). Claims must be made annually on or before July 1 upon forms prescribed by the Secretary of Revenue (Sec. 10-45A-8). The maximum amount of income that a taxpayer can earn and be entitled to a real property tax refund or a sales and use tax refund is $10,750 for a single-member household and $14,250 for a multiple-member household (Sec. 10-45A-5, Sec. 10-45A-6).

• Refunds to needy families

Resident taxpayers who are heads of households are eligible for a refund of South Dakota sales tax paid on food if their household income is within specified levels (Sec. 10-45A-5; Sec. 10-45A-6). In order to qualify, taxpayers must: (1) live in South Dakota and be a U.S. citizen or have legal status to reside in the U.S.; (2) not reside in a facility where at least 50% of their meals are provided by the facility; and (3) have a household gross monthly income above 130% and below 150% of the federal poverty level. To be eligible to receive the refund, taxpayers must: (1) apply for quarterly refund forms prescribed by the Department of Social services; (2) certify that any refund received will only be used to purchase food; and (3) report quarterly on forms prescribed by the Department to continue eligibility for refunds.

• Contractors of renewable resource small power producers

A contractor that either expands an existing renewable resource small power production facility or constructs a new renewable resource small power production facility is entitled to a 100% refund of realty improvement contractors' excise tax incurred on project costs if the project costs exceeded $500,000 and the taxpayer received a permit from the Secretary of Revenue (Sec. 49-34A-4). A qualifying small power production facility utilizes renewable resources such as wind, geothermal, or biomass to produce electric power.

• Refund for construction of agricultural processing and new business facilities

A refund or credit of contractors' excise tax and sales and use taxes is available for the construction or expansion of an agricultural processing or new business facility if the project costs exceed $10 million (Sec. 10-45B-1 *et seq.*). A "new business facility" is a building or structure, including a power generation facility, that is subject to the contractors' excise tax. However, the definition does not include a building or structure (1) used predominantly for the sale of products at retail, other than the sale of electricity at retail, to individual customers, (2) used predominantly for residential housing or transient lodging, (3) used predominantly to provide health care services, or (4) that is not subject to *ad valorem* real property tax or equivalent taxes measured in gross receipts. Assignment or transfer of the permit or refund claim may be permitted under certain circumstances.

Refund amounts are as follows: (1) for project costs of less than $10 million, there is no refund; (2) for project costs of at least $10 million, but less than $40 million, there is a refund of 45% of the taxes paid; (3) for project costs of at least $40 million, but less than $500 million, there is a refund of 55% of the taxes paid; and (4) for project costs of $500 million or more, there is no refund. (Sec. 10-45B-5.1).

¶ 830   TENNESSEE

¶ 831   Scope of Tax

Source.—Statutory references are to Title 67, Chapter 6, of the Tennessee Code Annotated, as amended to date. Details are reported in the CCH TENNESSEE TAX REPORTS starting at ¶ 60-000.

The Tennessee retailer' sales and use tax is imposed on every person who does any of the following (Sec. 67-6-201):

— engages in the business of selling tangible personal property for retail in the state;

— uses or consumes in Tennessee any article of tangible personal property, irrespective of ownership;

— receives property or services subject to taxation;

— rents or furnishes any property or services subject to taxation;

— stores for use or consumption in Tennessee any article of tangible personal property;

— leases or rents tangible personal property in Tennessee;

— charges taxable admissions, dues, or fees;

— sells space to transient dealers or vendors; or

— charges a fee for cable television or direct-to-home satellite television services.

Digital products: Tax applies to retail sales, leases, licenses, and uses of specified digital products, *i.e.,* electronically transferred "digital audio-visual works," "digital audio works," and "digital books" that would be taxable if sold in tangible form. The statute defines each of these terms (Sec. 67-6-102(87)).

Effective July 1, 2015, the taxability of "specified digital products" is expanded to include "video game digital products" transferred to or accessed by subscribers or consumers in Tennessee (Sec. 67-6-233). For purposes of taxing mobile communication services, a "video game digital product" means the right to access and use computer software that facilitates human interaction with a user interface to generate visual feedback for amusement purposes (Sec. 67-6-102(98)). Possession of the computer software must be maintained by the seller or a third party, regardless of whether the charge for the service is on a per-use, per-user, per-license, subscription, or some other basis. For additional information, see *Important Notice No. 15-13,* Tennessee Department of Revenue, June 2015, CCH TENNESSEE TAX REPORTS, ¶ 401-616.

Tax does not apply to satellite radio services, or to subscriptions to data processing and information services that allow data to be generated, acquired, stored, processed, or retrieved and delivered by electronic transmission to a purchaser, where the purchaser's primary purpose for the underlying transaction is the processed data or information (Sec. 67-6-233). Digital goods provided without charge for less than permanent use are also not taxable. The definition of a "sale" specifically includes the creation of computer software on the premises of the consumer and any programming, transferring, or loading of software into a computer.

Computer software: The sale or use of computer software, including prewritten computer software, is subject to tax, regardless of whether such software is delivered electronically, by use of tangible storage media, or otherwise (Sec. 67-6-231). Computer software repair and installation services are subject to tax, regardless of whether the installation is incidental to a sale of software or tangible personal property, or whether any computer software or tangible personal property is transferred in conjunction with the installation service (Sec. 67-6-205(c)(6)). See also "Services," below.

Beginning July 1, 2015, an exemption is provided for the access and use of software that remains in the possession of the dealer who provides the software or in the possession of a third party on behalf of such dealer, when the software is accessed and used solely by a person or the person's employee exclusively for fabricating software that is both owned by that person and for that person's own use and consumption (Sec. 67-6-387; *Important Notice No. 15-14,* Tennessee Department of Revenue, June 2015, CCH TENNESSEE TAX REPORTS, ¶ 401-617).

The department has created a new Remotely Accessed Software Direct Pay Permit form (RV-F1323107); see *Important Notice No. 15-24,* Tennessee Department of Revenue, December 2015, CCH TENNESSEE TAX REPORTS, ¶ 401-631.

Cloud computing: Charges by a taxpayer for remote storage and virtual computing services (sometimes referred to as "cloud computing") are not subject to Tennessee sales and use tax. The remote storage service allows customers to use a Web-based interface to store their data on the taxpayer's servers. The virtual computing service allows customers to procure computing resources in order to perform a variety of activities, including running applications, monitoring computers and computer usage, and hosting web domains. Both services are accessed through software on the taxpayer's servers, but the taxpayer does not transfer title, possession, or control of the software to customers, and the software is only used in conjunction with the service. The transactions do not involve a sale of tangible personal property or software.

The services fall within the category of data processing and information services, which are specifically excluded from taxable telecommunications services. No use of tangible personal property occurs in Tennessee when customers access the software because all of the servers are located outside Tennessee. Incidental usage fees charged by the taxpayer for services, such as adding or moving files or retrieving data, are also not taxable. (*Letter Ruling No. 13-12,* Tennessee Department of Revenue, September 12, 2013, CCH TENNESSEE TAX REPORTS, ¶ 401-539; see also *Letter Ruling No. 13-15,* Tennessee Department of Revenue, October 14, 2013, CCH TENNESSEE TAX REPORTS, ¶ 401-546; but see *Letter Ruling No. 14-05,* Tennessee Department of Revenue, August 25, 2014, CCH TENNESSEE TAX REPORTS, ¶ 401-584)

Fantasy sports contests: Effective July 1, 2016, a privilege tax is imposed at the rate of 6% on all adjusted revenues of a fantasy sports contest offered by a fantasy sports operator to Tennessee consumers. The tax is due on a quarterly basis. Each fantasy sports operator is required, on or before the 20th day immediately following the end of each calendar quarter, to transmit to the Tennessee Commissioner of Revenue returns that show all receipts derived from offering or providing consumers with any fantasy sports contests taxable under these provisions during the preceding calendar quarter. (Sec. 67-4-3201 *et seq.*)

• **Services**

Specified services are subject to the tax. These include (Sec. 67-6-205):

— providing temporary lodging;

— parking lot or garage services;

— telecommunications services and ancillary services;

— repair services;

— car wash facility services and laundering or dry cleaning of any tangible personal property (excluding coin-operated laundry and bathing of animals by a veterinarian for medical purposes);

— installation of tangible personal property that remains tangible personal property after installation and of computer software, if a charge is made for the installation, regardless of whether the installation is made as an incident to the sale of tangible personal property or computer software, and whether or not any tangible personal property or computer software is transferred in conjunction with the installation service;

— enriching of uranium materials, compounds, or products that is performed on a cost-plus basis or on a toll enrichment fee basis;

— renting or providing space to a vendor without a permanent location in this state, or to persons who are registered at other locations in this state but who are making sales at this location on a less than permanent basis (excluding nonprofit craft, antique, book, and gun fairs; and flea markets, conventions, and trade shows that do not allow the general public to enter for the purpose of making sales or taking orders); and

— effective July 1, 2015, charging a fee for subscription to, access to, or use of television services provided by any electronic means (excluding video programming services or direct-to-home satellite television services sold by persons subject the cable and satellite television user privilege tax).

Sales tax applies to video programming services regardless of the delivery technology utilized (Sec. 67-6-329(a)(20)).

Litigation: The disparate tax treatment of satellite providers and cable providers does not constitute discrimination in violation of the Commerce Clause of the U.S. Constitution for Tennessee sales and use tax purposes, according to the Tennessee Court of Appeals. Tennessee imposes a sales tax on the entire subscription fee billed to satellite customers; however, the first $15 of the subscription fee billed to cable customers is exempt. The taxpayers, direct-to-home satellite service providers, sought a refund of sales and use taxes paid. The taxpayers argued that satellite and cable providers are substantially similar entities because consumers view both as similar and interchangeable, and claimed that the sales tax on satellite television services discriminates both purposefully and in practical effect. The trial court found that the law was violative of the Commerce Clause. The court held that satellite and cable providers are not substantially similar entities for purposes of the Commerce Clause in that, although cable providers are heavily regulated by the federal government, satellite providers are minimally regulated; the bundle of services provided by cable providers differs substantially from the bundle provided by satellite providers; and cable providers are required to offer several public service items including local broadcast stations, educational stations, emergency information, and certain signal quality, whereas satellite providers are not so required. Consequently, the disparate tax treatment of satellite providers and cable providers does not constitute discrimination. (*DirecTV, Inc. v. Roberts,* Tennessee Court of Appeals, No. M2013-01673-COA-R3-CV, February 27, 2015, CCH Tennessee Tax Reports, ¶ 401-601; petition for certiorari denied November 2, 2015, *DIRECTV, Inc. v. Roberts,* U.S. Supreme Court, Dkt. 14-1524)

Service and warranty contracts: Warranty or service contracts for the repair and maintenance of tangible personal property and computer software maintenance contracts are subject to Tennessee sales and use tax when (Sec. 67-6-208(c)):

— the warranty or service contract is sold as part of or in connection with the sale of taxable tangible personal property, or the computer software maintenance contract is sold as part of or in connection with the sale of taxable computer software;

— the warranty or service contract applies to tangible personal property located in Tennessee, or the computer software maintenance contract applies to computer software installed on computers located in Tennessee (if a warranty or service contract applies to tangible personal property located both within Tennessee and outside the state or a computer software maintenance contract applies to computer software installed on computers located both inside Tennessee and outside the state, dealers or users may allocate to Tennessee a percentage of the sales price or purchase price of the warranty or service contract or computer software maintenance contract that equals the percentage of tangible personal property located in Tennessee or computer software installed on computers located in Tennessee); or

— the location of the tangible personal property covered by the warranty or service contract or computer software covered by the computer software maintenance contract is not known to the seller but the purchaser's residential street address or primary business address is in Tennessee.

No additional sales and use tax is due on any repairs or maintenance provided pursuant to a warranty or service contract covering the repair and maintenance of tangible personal property or on any repairs, modifications, updates, or upgrades provided pursuant to a computer software maintenance contract unless the seller makes an additional charge for the repairs, maintenance, modifications, updates, or upgrades. (Sec. 67-6-208(d); *Important Notice No. 15-11,* Tennessee Department of Revenue, June 2015, CCH TENNESSEE TAX REPORTS, ¶ 401-614; *Important Notice No. 15-25,* Tennessee Department of Revenue, December 2015, CCH TENNESSEE TAX REPORTS, ¶ 401-633)

Computer software repair and installation services are taxable (Sec. 67-6-205(c)(6)).

Sales and use tax does not apply to the use, consumption, distribution, or storage in Tennessee of computer software or computer software maintenance contracts if an equal or greater amount of tax has been paid in another state (Sec. 67-6-507(a)).

Internet access: Internet service providers (ISPs) may not collect sales tax from consumers on the sale of Internet access and telecommunications companies may not accept resale certificates from ISPs for the sale of Internet access. (*Important Notice No. 04-03,* Department of Revenue, January 30, 2004; *Letter Ruling No. 08-08,* Tennessee Department of Revenue, February 22, 2008, CCH TENNESSEE TAX REPORTS, ¶ 401-250.)

A publication issued by the Department of Revenue discusses the application of Tennessee sales and use tax to various transactions involving computer connections, telecommunications, and related services (*Revenue Ruling No. #07-05,* Tennessee Department of Revenue, released September 2007, CCH TENNESSEE TAX REPORTS, ¶ 401-210; see also *Letter Ruling No. 08-29,* Department of Revenue, March 24, 2008, CCH TENNESSEE TAX REPORTS, ¶ 401-274).

Web-based services: A taxpayer's sales of web-based services that allow customers to provide remote technical support or computer access are not subject to Tennessee sales and use tax, but services that allow customers to conduct online conferences and training are taxable. The remote support and remote access services are also not taxable telecommunications services and do not involve ancillary services. Because the conferencing and training services link two or more participants of an audio or video conference call, these services are properly considered conference bridging services, which are taxable ancillary services. (*Revenue Ruling No. 12-25,* Tennessee Department of Revenue, October 31, 2012, released January 8, 2013, CCH TENNESSEE TAX REPORTS, ¶ 401-504)

Prepaid calling services: Sales of prepaid calling service and prepaid wireless calling service are taxed at the time of the sale or recharge of the calling card or authorization code. No additional tax is due when the telecommunication service is accessed or received by the user of the calling card or authorization code (Sec. 67-6-230).

• **Legal incidence of the sales and use tax**

Generally, sales tax is imposed on the privilege of engaging in the business of selling at retail or leasing tangible personal property in the state (Sec. 67-6-201, Sec. 67-6-202, Sec. 67-6-204). Use tax is imposed on the privilege of using, consuming, distributing, or storing tangible personal property in Tennessee, unless the property is in interstate commerce (Sec. 67-6-201, Sec. 67-6-203, Sec. 67-6-211). When applied together, the sales and use taxes provide a uniform tax upon either the sale or use of taxable goods and services in Tennessee, regardless of where they are purchased.

The sales or use tax is collected by the state from all dealers making sales within or outside Tennessee of tangible personal property for distribution, storage, use, or other consumption in Tennessee, or for furnishing taxable goods and services (Sec. 67-6-501, Rule 1320-5-1-.95). Although dealers are liable for the tax, they are required, insofar as can be done, to collect the tax from the consumer (Sec. 67-6-502) to protect small retailers against unfair competition by larger retailers' absorption of the tax (*Sam Carey Lumber Co. v. Sixty-One Cabinet Shop, Inc.* (1989, TN Ct App) 773 SW2d 252). Dealers must indicate to their customers whether they are paying any sales tax by posting a sign or by a statement on the receipt (Sec. 67-6-503, Rule 1320-5-1-.90).

Online travel companies: A U.S. District Court granted summary judgment in favor of several online travel companies (OTCs) in a class action suit in which a Tennessee city, on behalf of itself and other Tennessee municipalities, alleged that the OTCs were liable for local hotel occupancy taxes on the difference between the rates the OTCs paid to hotels and the rates they charged their customers. The court held that the OTCs were not "operators" under the ordinance because they had no possessory interest in the hotels. If the Legislature intends to permit political subdivisions to tax the retail rate paid by consumers to the OTCs, the Legislature may do so through appropriate statutory language. (*Goodlettesville, Tennessee v. Priceline.com, Inc.*, U.S. District Court, M.D. Tennessee, No. 3:08-cv-00561, February 21, 2012, CCH Tennessee Tax Reports, ¶ 401-457)

- **Use tax**

The use tax complements the sales tax. It is imposed on taxable transactions on which no sales tax is paid and that would escape taxation otherwise (*Woods v. M.J. Kelley Co.* (1980, Tenn SCt) 592 SW2d 567, cert den (1980, US SCt) 447 US 905, 100 SCt 2987). There can be no duplication of the tax (Sec. 67-6-203).

A merchant who imports quantities of property into the state for resale, but consumes part of the property instead of selling it, is taxable on the property consumed (Sec. 67-6-210(a)).

- **Nexus**

The sales or use tax is collected by the state from all dealers furnishing taxable services or making sales within or outside Tennessee of tangible personal property for distribution, storage, use, or other consumption in Tennessee (Sec. 67-6-501). A "dealer" is defined as every person who does the following (Sec. 67-6-102):

— manufactures or produces tangible personal property for sale at retail, for use, consumption, or distribution, or for storage to be used or consumed in Tennessee;

— imports tangible property from any state or foreign country for sale at retail, for use, consumption, or distribution, or for storage to be used or consumed in Tennessee; – possesses for sale, sells, or offers tangible personal property for sale at retail, or for use, consumption, or distribution, or storage to be used or consumed in Tennessee;

— sold at retail, used, consumed, distributed, or stored for use or consumption in Tennessee, tangible personal property and cannot prove that the applicable tax was paid;

— leases or rents tangible personal property;

— is the lessee or renter of tangible personal property and pays the owner of the property consideration for its use;

— maintains within Tennessee, directly or indirectly, an office, sales room, house, warehouse, distribution center, or other place of business;

— furnishes any taxable property or services;

— has any representative, agent, salesperson, or solicitor operating in Tennessee for the purpose of making sales or taking orders for sales, either permanently or temporarily, regardless of whether a place of business is maintained in Tennessee;

— engages in the solicitation of a consumer market in Tennessee (*Note:* The Tennessee Supreme Court held that imposition of use tax collection liability on a person engaged in the regular or systematic solicitation of a consumer market in Tennessee by means of catalogs, advertising fliers, and the like, was unconstitutional (*Bloomingdale's by Mail, Ltd. v. Huddleston,* 848 S.W.2d 52 (1992)));

— uses tangible personal property in the performance of a contract in Tennessee, unless the property has been previously subject to taxation and the tax due has been paid;

— charges admissions, dues, or fees; or

— rents or provides space to a dealer without a permanent location in Tennessee, or to dealers registered in other locations in Tennessee but who are making sales in a different location on a temporary basis. [*Note:* The latter definition does not apply to flea market operators.]

Out-of-state dealers who engage in the regular or systematic solicitation of consumers in Tennessee through any means and made sales to Tennessee consumers that exceeded $500,000 during the previous 12-month period have substantial nexus with Tennessee and are required to register with the department; see ¶ 839.

The activities of Tennessee schools and teachers were sufficient to create Tennessee sales and use tax nexus for a mail-order bookseller that sells books via marketing materials distributed in schools. The taxpayer's connections with the state were sufficient to establish nexus because the taxpayer created a *de facto* marketing and distribution mechanism within Tennessee schools that it uses to sell books. (*Scholastic Book Clubs, Inc. v. Farr,* Tennessee Court of Appeals, No. M2011-01443-COA-R3-CV, January 27, 2012, CCH TENNESSEE TAX REPORTS, ¶ 401-455; petition for certiorari denied November 26, 2012, *Scholastic Book Clubs, Inc. v. Roberts,* U.S. Supreme Court, Dkt. 12-374,)

Click-through nexus: Effective July 1, 2015, a dealer is presumed to have a representative, agent, salesperson, canvasser, or solicitor operating in Tennessee for the purpose of making sales and is presumed to have a substantial nexus with Tennessee if (Sec. 67-6-520):

— the dealer enters into an agreement or contract with one or more persons located in Tennessee under which the person, for a commission or other consideration, directly or indirectly refers potential customers to the dealer, whether by a link on an Internet website or any other means; and

— the dealer's cumulative gross receipts from retail sales made by the dealer to customers in Tennessee who are referred to the dealer by all residents with this type of an agreement with the dealer exceed $10,000 during the preceding 12 months.

The presumption is rebuttable by evidence that the person with whom the dealer has an agreement or contract did not conduct any activities in Tennessee that would substantially contribute to the dealer's ability to establish and maintain a market in Tennessee during the preceding 12 months. (Sec. 67-6-520; *Important Notice No. 15-12,* Tennessee Department of Revenue, June 2015, CCH TENNESSEE TAX REPORTS, ¶ 401-615)

Commercial printers and mailers: A person does not have nexus with Tennessee for sales and use tax purposes by reason of the relationship between the person and a commercial printer or mailer that has a presence in Tennessee (Sec. 67-6-601(d)).

¶831 Tennessee

• Streamlined Act status

Tennessee is an associate member of the Agreement with a seat on the Governing Board. It has enacted all of the provisions necessary to comply with the Agreement's requirements, but these provisions are not yet in effect (Secs. 67-6-801—67-6-808). As an associate member, Tennessee may not vote on amendments to or interpretations of the Agreement, and sellers registering under the SST system may, but are not required to, collect and remit tax on sales into the state (unless they otherwise legally are required to do so).

Tennessee has postponed the effective date of certain SST conformity provisions until July 1, 2017, and enacted several sales and use tax changes, including provisions affecting electronic payment requirements, computer software fabrication, software maintenance contracts, advertising agency artwork, airline fuel, and municipal stadium admissions, Delayed provisions include the uniform sourcing rules, single article cap limitations, use of a single return covering multiple dealer locations, and the special user privilege taxes that will be imposed in lieu of sales and use tax on items that are taxed at a rate other than the general sales and use tax rate.

SST provisions delayed: SST conformity provisions delayed until July 1, 2017, include (Sec. 3, Ch. 273 (H.B. 95), Laws 2015; *Important Notice No. 15-09,* Tennessee Department of Revenue, June 2015, CCH Tennessee Tax Reports, ¶ 401-613):

— requirements that sales delivered or shipped to the customer be sourced to the delivery or shipping destination;

— modifications to the single article limitation on local option sales taxes;

— use of a single sales and use tax return covering multiple dealer locations; and

— implementation of certain privilege taxes in lieu of sales tax.

¶ 832   Tax Base

The sales tax is levied on the retail sales price from the sale of tangible personal property and on the gross proceeds from the rental or leasing of property (Sec. 67-6-202, Sec. 67-6-204, Sec. 67-6-213, Sec. 67-6-501). The taxable "sales price" of a purchase includes any services that are a part of the sale (Sec. 67-6-102) The use tax is levied on the cost price or fair market value of items not sold, but used, stored, distributed, or consumed in the state (Sec. 67-6-203, Sec. 67-6-501).

Trade-ins: When property is taken in trade as a credit or partial payment on the sale of other property, the basis for the tax is the sales price of the new article less the credit allowed for the trade. Trade-in items must be of a like kind and character as the item purchased and must be indicated as a trade-in on the invoice. This provision also applies to cases where a credit memorandum is given for tangible personal property which is intended to be traded in on the purchase of new articles of tangible personal property. (Sec. 67-6-510; Rule 1320-5-1-.02)

• Selected definitions

"Sales price" is the total amount for which a taxable service or tangible personal property is sold, including any services that are a part of the sale of tangible personal property, valued in money, regardless of whether payment is made in money (Sec. 67-6-102(25)). It also includes any amount for which credit is given to the purchaser by the seller, without any deductions for the cost of the property, materials, labor, services, losses, or any other expenses.

"Gross sales" means the sum total of all retail sales of tangible personal property and all proceeds of taxable services without any deductions, except those deductions provided by law (Sec. 67-6-102(11)).

"Cost price" means the actual cost of the tangible personal property without any deductions for the cost of materials used, labor, services, transportation charges, or other expenses (Sec. 67-6-102(5)).

- **Sourcing of transactions**

Retail sales are sourced according to the following rules (Secs. 67-6-902, 67-6-905):

(1) When a product is received by the purchaser at a business location of the seller, the sale is sourced that business location;

(2) When a product is not received by a purchaser at a business location of the seller, the sale is sourced to the location where receipt occurs by the purchaser or the purchaser's donee, including the location indicated by instructions for delivery to the purchaser, known to the seller;

(3) When the two circumstances above do not apply, the sale is sourced to the purchaser's address that is available from the business records maintained by the seller in the ordinary course of business, when use of this address does not constitute bad faith;

(4) When the three circumstances above do not apply, the sale is sourced to the location of the purchaser's address obtained during consummation of the sale, including the address of a purchaser's payment instrument, if no other address is available, when use of this address does not constitute bad faith;

(5) When none of the previous rules apply, including the circumstance in which the seller does not have sufficient information to apply the previous rules, the sale is sourced to the address from which the tangible personal property was shipped, from which the digital good or the computer software delivered electronically was first available for transmission by the seller (disregarding any location that merely provided the digital transfer of the product sold), or from which the service was provided. In the case of a mobile telecommunications service that is a prepaid telecommunications service, the sale may be sourced to the location associated with the mobile telephone number.

Special sourcing rules apply to leases and rentals and telecommunications.

- **Taxability matrix**

A chart of the taxable status of various items is accessible on the website of the Streamlined Sales Tax Project at **http://www.streamlinedsalestax.org**.

¶ 833 List of Exemptions, Exceptions, and Exclusions

Unless otherwise indicated, the statutory exemptions listed below apply to both sales and use taxes; those applicable to only the sales tax or only the use tax are listed separately. Items that are excluded from the sales or use tax base are treated at ¶ 832, "Tax Base."

Single-member LLCs: A federally disregarded single member limited liability company (SMLLC) whose sole owner has received a determination of exemption from the IRS may also apply for an exemption from Tennessee sales and use tax. The IRS has said that when the sole owner of a federally disregarded SMLLC is exempt from federal income tax, the disregarded SMLLC receives the benefit of the owner's tax-exempt status. The IRS will issue a determination of exemption to the owner, but it will not issue a separate determination to the SMLLC. Because the SMLLC will not have a separate determination of exemption from the IRS, the SMLLC should provide the Department of Revenue with the SMLLC's organizational documents, the owner's determination of exemption, and a copy of the owner's most recent federal annual information return. (*Important Notice No. 14-04,* Tennessee Department of Revenue, May 13, 2014, CCH TENNESSEE TAX REPORTS, ¶ 401-566)

¶833 Tennessee

Tax holiday: An annual three-day tax holiday from sales and use tax begins at 12:01 a.m. on the last Friday of each July and ends at 11:59 p.m. on the following Sunday (Sec. 67-6-393). Clothing and school supplies with a sales price of $100 or less per item and computers with a sales price of $1,500 or less per item are exempt from state and local sales taxes during the tax holiday. The tax holiday does not apply to the following items, which remain taxable: computer software, clothing accessories or equipment, protective equipment, sport or recreational equipment, school art supplies, school instructional materials, school computer supplies, items for use in a trade or business, video game consoles, or leases or rentals.

- **Sales and use tax exemptions, exceptions, and exclusions**

Adjuvants	Sec. 67-6-329(a)(9)
Admissions, certain nonprofit activities	Sec. 67-6-330(a)(6)
Advertising agency sales of preliminary artwork	Sec. 67-6-396
Advertising, direct mail	Sec. 67-6-344
Agricultural products and supplies	Sec. 67-6-207, Sec. 67-6-329(a)(1), Sec. 67-6-329(a)(3)—Sec. 67-6-329(a)(10)
Agri-dust	Sec. 67-6-329(a)(10)
Aircraft repairs, parts and supplies	Sec. 67-6-302, Sec. 67-6-313
Aircraft repair, leases	Sec. 67-6-302(b), Sec. 67-6-313(k)
Aluminum production, natural gas used in	Sec. 67-6-206(b)(7)
Armed forces organizations	Sec. 67-6-322(b)
Atomic weapon parts	Sec. 67-6-209(d)
Automobile adaptive equipment for disabled veterans	Sec. 67-6-353
Aviation fuel used for international flights	Sec. 67-6-349
Barges	Sec. 67-6-345
Blood and plasma	Sec. 67-6-304
Boats, motorboats, and vessels	Sec. 67-6-345
Cable television	Sec. 67-6-714
Charitable organizations	Sec. 67-6-322
Clothing, used, sold by charitable organizations	Sec. 67-6-348
Communications	Sec. 67-6-102(30), Sec. 67-6-342
Computer media exchange services	Sec. 67-6-313 [j]
Computer software developed, fabricated, or repaired for an affiliated company	Sec. 67-6-395
Computer software fabrication for personal use or for fabricating other software	Sec. 67-6-387
Computer software obtained from or repaired by an affiliated company	Sec. 67-6-395
Construction for charitable or nonprofit organizations	Sec. 67-6-209(b)
Construction machinery—transfers between parent and subsidiary corporations	Sec. 67-6-311
Containers or coverings used in agriculture	Sec. 67-6-329(a)(6)
Data centers, equipment used in	Sec. 67-6-102(39)(K)

¶833   Tennessee

Industrial materials . . . . Sec. 67-6-329(a)(12)

Insecticides . . . . Sec. 67-6-329(a)(5)

Insulin and syringes . . . . Sec. 67-6-312

Intercompany communications facilities use charges . . . . Sec. 67-6-342(b)

Interstate commerce . . . . Sec. 67-6-313(a),
Sec. 67-6-313(f)

Leases to aircraft repairers or air carriers . . . . Sec. 67-6-302(b)

Livestock feed, medication, and reproductive substances . . . . Sec. 67-6-329(a)(7),
Sec. 67-6-329(a)(8)

Liquefied gas and compressed natural gas (CNG) taxed as alternative
fuels . . . . Sec. 67-6-329(a)(5)

Local government purchases . . . . Sec. 67-6-329(a)(13)

Magazines and other periodicals . . . . Sec. 67-6-329(a)(16),
Sec. 67-6-329(a)(21)

Manufactured structural metal . . . . Sec. 67-6-339

Manufacturing materials . . . . Sec. 67-6-206

Material handling equipment and racking systems . . . . Sec. 67-6-102(46)(H)(i)

Medical equipment and devices for disabled persons . . . . Sec. 67-6-314

Medical supplies, disposable . . . . Sec. 67-6-320(c)

Motion picture rentals by theater owners . . . . Sec. 67-6-309

Motor fuel: dyed diesel sold to commercial carriers . . . . Sec. 67-4-2503

Motor fuel subject to gallonage tax . . . . Sec. 67-6-329(a)(2)

Motor vehicles removed from state within 3 days . . . . Sec. 67-6-343

Motor vehicles sold to certain Armed Forces members . . . . Sec. 67-6-303

Motor vehicles used in passenger transportation . . . . Sec. 67-6-331

Newspapers . . . . Sec. 67-6-329(a)(21)

Nursery products and supplies . . . . Sec. 67-6-301(a)

Optical labs that sell directly to patients . . . . Sec. 67-6-316

Optometrists, opticians, and ophthalmologists . . . . Sec. 67-6-316

Ostomy products . . . . Sec. 67-6-317

Oxygen . . . . Sec. 67-6-318

Packaging materials . . . . Sec. 67-6-102(24)(E)(ii)

Parking lots provided by state or local governments . . . . Sec. 67-6-102(24)(F)(ii)

Parking privileges sold to students . . . . Sec. 67-6-329(a)(18)

Parts, replacement, for warranty repairs . . . . Sec. 67-6-324

Pesticides . . . . Sec. 67-6-329(a)(5)

Pharmaceutical samples . . . . Sec. 67-6-319

Plastic used in the care of plants . . . . Sec. 67-6-329(a)(6),
Sec. 67-6-329(a)(17)

Pollution control equipment . . . . Sec. 67-6-102(13)(A),
Sec. 67-6-206(a),
Sec. 67-6-329(a)(20)

Poultry feed . . . . Sec. 67-6-329(a)(7)

Prescription drugs . . . . Sec. 67-6-320

Printing . . . . Sec. 67-6-102(24)(E)(iii)

• Exemptions, exceptions, and exclusions applicable only to the sales tax

Book fair booth space	Sec. 67-6-102(24) (F) (viii)
Coin-operated amusement devices	Sec. 67-6-330(a) (10)
Concert admissions, nonprofit community group associations	Sec. 67-6-330(a) (16)
Craft-fair booth space	Sec. 67-6-102(24) (F) (viii)
Dental equipment	Sec. 67-6-314
Film, television, or radio production fees	Sec. 67-6-330(a) (8)
Fishing tournament fees	Sec. 67-6-330(a) (18)
Flea market rental space	Sec. 67-6-102(24) (F) (viii)
Gun shows	Sec. 67-6-310
Health club fees	Sec. 67-6-330(a) (19)
Horse shows	Sec. 67-6-330(a) (20)
Hunting	Sec. 67-6-330(a) (21)
Live entertainment fees for restaurants	Sec. 67-6-330(a) (23)
Lodging over 90 days	Sec. 67-6-102(24) (F) (i)
Medical equipment	Sec. 67-6-320(c)
Membership fees to specific organizations	Sec. 67-6-330(a) (4), Sec. 67-6-330(a) (6)
Museum admissions	Sec. 67-6-330(a) (7)
Occasional sales	Sec. 67-6-102(2), Sec. 67-6-201
Prostheses, crutches, wheelchairs, orthotics	Sec. 67-6-314
Railroad rolling stock	Sec. 67-6-321(a)
Recordings, rental by broadcasters	Sec. 67-6-309
Recreation club assessments to members for improvements	Sec. 67-6-330(a) (14)
Rentals of booth space	Sec. 67-6-102(24) (F) (viii)
Replacement parts under warranty	Sec. 67-6-324
Resales	Sec. 67-6-102(24) (A)
River boating activities	Sec. 67-6-330(a) (9)
Rodeos	Sec. 67-6-330(a) (15)
School event admissions (K-12)	Sec. 67-6-212(b), Sec. 67-6-330(a) (1)
Ticket resales	Sec. 67-6-102(24) (G)
Time-share estates	Sec. 67-6-102(a) (32) (F) (i), Sec. 67-6-212(c)
Tradeshow or exposition space rentals	Sec. 67-6-102(24) (F) (viii)

- ## Exemptions, exceptions, and exclusions applicable only to the use tax

Boats previously registered in another state	Sec. 67-6-219(c)
Construction materials, specified	Sec. 67-6-209(a)
Consumption by a farm family of farm products	Sec. 67-6-301(b)
Fill dirt	Sec. 67-6-209(a) (2)
Manufactured homes brought into state by new residents	Sec. 67-6-210(b)
Motor vehicles brought into state by new residents	Sec. 67-6-210(b)
Nursery products consumed by nursery workers and families	Sec. 67-6-301(b)
Personal automobile, manufactured home, effects imported	Sec. 67-6-210(b)

With the exception of certain items mentioned below, the state sales and use tax rate in Tennessee is 7% (Sec. 67-6-202). The rate is assessed against retail sales (Sec. 67-6-202); taxable services (Sec. 67-6-205); the use, consumption, distribution, or storage of property (Sec. 67-6-203); and the lease or rental of property (Sec. 67-6-204(a)(2), Sec. 67-6-213).

Additional tax on single articles: With respect to the sale or use of any single article of personal property, an additional state tax is imposed at the rate of 2.75% on the amount in excess of $1,600 but less than or equal to $3,200 (Sec. 67-6-202, Sec. 67-6-228). "Single article" applies only to motor vehicles, aircraft, watercraft, modular homes, manufactured homes, or mobile homes (Sec. 67-6-702).

Food and food ingredients: The tax rate for food and food ingredients is 5% (Sec. 67-6-202, Sec. 67-6-228). However, alcoholic beverages, tobacco products, candy, dietary supplements, and prepared food are taxed at the 7% rate.

Water and fuels used in manufacturing: Water used by qualified manufacturers that have registered with the Department of Revenue is taxed at 1%, and energy fuels used by qualified manufacturers are taxed at 1.5%. Energy fuels include gas, electricity, fuel oil, coal, and other fuels (Sec. 67-6-206(b), Rule 1320-5-1-.15). In certain circumstances, manufacturers may be exempt from taxation (Sec. 67-6-206(b)).

Data centers: Electricity purchased by a qualifying data center is taxed at the rate of 1.5% (Sec. 67-6-206(c)).

Common carriers: Common carriers may purchase tangible personal property, excluding fuel, food, and drink, for use outside the state at a reduced state sales tax rate of 3.75% (Sec. 67-6-219). Local sales tax is also applied to the purchase, but the maximum local rate that may be imposed is 1.5% (Sec. 67-6-702(e)) (see also ¶ 835). A certificate from the Commissioner of Revenue is required before purchases may be made at the reduced rate.

Aviation fuel: Aviation fuel actually used in the operation of an aircraft is taxed at a 4.5% rate, subject to certain maximum taxes (Sec. 67-6-217).

Rental car tax: In addition to sales or use taxes, an excise tax of 3% of the contract price is imposed on rentals for periods of 31 days or less of private passenger motor vehicles, trucks with a gross weight rating of 26,000 pounds or less, and trailers (Sec. 67-4-1901).

Manufactured homes: Because manufactured homes are subject to state tax at one-half the regular rate, sales of such homes are subject to a state rate of 3.5%, plus an additional 1.375% state rate on the amount from $1,600.01 to $3,200 for single articles of tangible personal property (*Important Notice,* Tennessee Department of Revenue, July 29, 2002).

Cable and satellite television services: Video programming service, including cable television service, is not subject to sales and use tax but is subject to a 9% special user privilege tax (Sec. 67-4-2401). The tax does not apply to the first $15 of the gross charges for the video programming services. Satellite television service is not subject to sales and use tax but is subject to an 8.25% special user privilege tax (Sec. 67-4-2402).

Vending machines: Sales from vending machines are subject to local sales and use tax at the rate of 2.25% (Sec. 67-6-702(d)). Entities that operate vending machines for the benefit of a charitable nonprofit organization may register with the Department of Revenue and pay a 1.5% gross receipts tax on sales (2.5% on tobacco items) rather than the 7% Tennessee sales tax (Sec. 67-4-506). The market value of the merchandise sold must not exceed 25¢.

Short-term rentals: A property management company engaged in renting or leasing properties for less than 90 days must register as a dealer and collect and remit the tax (*Important Notice,* Department of Revenue, October 2001).

Out-of-state retailers: A rule provides that out-of-state dealers who engage in the regular or systematic solicitation of consumers in Tennessee through any means and made sales to Tennessee consumers that exceeded $500,000 during the previous 12-month period have substantial nexus with Tennessee and are required to register with the department and to collect and remit Tennessee sales and use tax by the first day of the third calendar month following the month in which the dealer met the threshold. In no case will such dealers be required to collect and remit sales and use taxes to the department for periods before July 1, 2017. (Rule 1320-05-01-.63; Rule 1320-05-01-.129)

A registration portal is available at **https://revenue.webapps.tn.gov/ outofstatedealerregistration**.

- **SST registration**

To register under the Streamlined Sales and Use Tax Agreement (SST), sellers must go to **https://www.sstregister.org**. Sellers can also update previously submitted registration information at this website. The information provided will be sent to all of the full member states and to associate members for which the seller chooses to collect.

When a seller registers under the Agreement, it must select the certified technology model it will be using (or it must select "Other" if it will not be using one of the certified models). The models are the following:

Model One: Certified Service Provider (CSP), an agent certified under the Agreement to perform all the seller's sales and use tax functions;

Model Two: Certified Automated System (CAS), software certified under the Agreement to calculate the appropriate tax (for which the seller retains responsibility for remitting);

Model Three: Certified System (CS), a proprietary automated sales tax system certified under the Agreement.

Monetary allowances: For the period of time that Tennessee is an associate member of the Streamlined Sales and Use Tax Agreement, the Commissioner of Revenue will have the authority to provide to volunteer sellers and certified service providers the monetary allowances required to be provided under the Agreement. However, Model 1 sellers under the Agreement will not be entitled to the dealer's deductions for accounting costs (Sec. 67-6-542).

¶ 840   **Sales or Use Tax Credits**

A credit is allowed against Tennessee use tax for sales or use tax paid in another state on tangible personal property or taxable services imported into Tennessee (Sec. 67-6-507(a), Rule 1320-5-1-.91). It should be noted that the statute allowing the credit (Sec. 67-6-507(a)) refers only to tangible personal property, while the rule (Rule 1320-5-1-.91) refers to both tangible personal property and taxable services.

Dealers are allowed credit for sales or use taxes paid under the following circumstances: (1) for taxes paid on property or services that are subsequently resold by the dealer without collection of tax (Sec. 67-6-507(b)); (2) on returned merchandise or in certain other purchase price and sales tax refund situations (Sec. 67-6-507(c), Rule 1320-5-1-.50); (3) on certain repossessed goods, if the balance due exceeds $500 (Sec. 67-6-507(d), Rule 1320-5-1-.52); (4) on bad debts that are worthless and actually charged off for federal income tax purposes (Sec. 67-6-507(e), *Release,* Department of Revenue, June 20, 1974); and (5) on goods improperly purchased at lower tax rates (Sec. 67-6-507(f)).

Dealer's compensation: An out-of-state dealer who voluntarily registers to collect and remit tax on items sold to Tennessee customers may deduct 2% of the first $2,500 and 1.15% of amounts over $2,500 on each report, as long as the report and payment of tax due are not delinquent (Sec. 67-6-509).

• Bad debts

A seller is authorized to deduct bad debt from its taxable sales. In conformity with the Streamlined Sales and Use Tax Agreement, "bad debt" is defined as in IRC Sec. 166. However, the amount calculated under IRC Sec. 166 must be adjusted to exclude (1) finance charges or interest, (2) sales or use tax charged on the sales price, (3) uncollectible amounts on property that remains in the possession of the seller until the full purchase price is paid, (4) expenses incurred in attempting to collect bad debt, and (5) the value of any repossessed property (Sec. 67-6-507(e)).

The Tennessee Supreme Court declined to review a Court of Appeals' decision holding that a taxpayer's claims for a sales tax deduction for bad debts associated with private label and co-branded credit card programs were properly denied (Sears, Roebuck & Co. v. Roberts., Court of Appeals of Tennessee, May 11, 2016, CH TENNESSEE TAX REPORTS, ¶ 401-649; review denied, September 23, 2016, *Sears, Roebuck & Co. v. Roberts,* Tennessee Supreme Court, No. M2014-02567-SC-R11-CV).

• Telecommunications services

A hotel, motel, college, university, or hospital may take as a credit the portion of sales tax paid to a vendor of telecommunication services that are resold with tax collected (Sec. 67-6-507(h)). The credit is limited to the tax paid on the portion of the telecommunication services that is resold.

A credit is also allowed for sales tax properly paid to other states on interstate telecommunications charges taxed by Tennessee unless the charge is made to a service address in the state (Sec. 67-6-507(g)).

• Pollution control

A 100% credit applies to the tax paid with respect to any otherwise ineligible pollution control that is required in order to comply with federal, state, or local law or regulation (Sec. 67-6-346). The credit is not available to persons primarily engaged in processing, treating, or controlling pollution created by others. Effective July 1, 2010, the pollution control equipment credit was expanded to apply to machinery and equipment used to provide electricity in a certified green energy production facility.

In addition, a 100% credit applies to sales or use tax paid with respect to necessary equipment purchased by automobile body paint shops in order to comply with certain federal, state or local governmental emission control standards (Sec. 67-6-507(i)). A 50% credit applies to tax paid with respect to necessary replacement equipment purchased by dry cleaners in order to comply with these same standards (Sec. 67-6-507(j)).

• Fire protection sprinkler contractors

A credit is allowed for any special contractor tax paid in another state on certain materials purchased or used by a fire protection sprinkler contractor (Sec. 67-6-355). The materials must be used by the contractor to fabricate pipe and pipe fittings or valves and pipe fittings for application or use in the performance of a contract outside the state, and the credit is limited to the amount of tax attributable to the value of the materials.

• Bad debts and cash basis dealers

Certain cash basis dealers are allowed a credit for tax paid on worthless accounts on the sales tax return for the period when the account is found to be worthless. However, if the account is collected later, in whole or in part, the amount collected must be included in the first return filed after collection of the account and the sales tax due paid accordingly (Sec. 67-6-507(e)).

¶840   **Tennessee**

- **Common carriers**

A credit is available to common carriers that export for use in another state goods upon which the tax had been paid (Rule 1320-5-1-.85). Also, a dealer may claim a credit for sales and use tax paid on fuel or petroleum products sold to an air common carrier, if the air common carrier subsequently uses the fuel or petroleum products for a flight destined for, or continuing from, a location outside the United States (Sec. 67-6-349).

- **Stolen vehicles**

The most recent *bona fide* purchaser of a motor vehicle is allowed a credit for use taxes paid on the vehicle if the vehicle has been stolen, is recovered by an authorized law enforcement officer, and is not returned to the purchaser (Sec. 67-6-508).

- **Flea market dealers**

Generally, flea market dealers are allowed as a credit against actual annual sales tax liability the amount paid as a registration fee for the applicable registration period (Sec. 67-6-220).

- **Corporate headquarters**

A credit for all sales and use taxes paid, except tax at the rate of 0.5%, is available for the sales or use of building materials, machinery, equipment, fixtures, and furniture used in a qualified, new, or expanded headquarters facility located in Tennessee. The facility must house the international or national headquarters of a corporation, must be newly constructed or expanded through a minimum investment of at least $10 million and must create not less than 100 new full-time employee jobs in conjunction with the construction, expansion, or remodeling of the qualified headquarters facility. In addition, the investment must be made during the period beginning one year before the start of construction and ending one year after the completion of construction and must not exceed six years. The facility must be utilized as a corporate headquarters for at least 10 years from the end of the investment period. The taxpayer is not required to establish its commercial domicile in Tennessee in order to receive the credit. (Sec. 67-6-224)

If determined to be in the best interests of the state, the Commissioner of Revenue and the Commissioner of Economic and Community Development may lower the number of jobs that must be created, but the job creation requirement cannot be lowered by more than 50%. The credit amount will be reduced in direct proportion to the job requirement reduction. (Sec. 67-6-224)

Before July 1, 2015, the credit was available for a regional headquarters facility, in addition to international and national headquarters facilities. Any taxpayer that filed an application and business plan as a regional headquarters facility with the department before July 1, 2015, continues to be eligible for the credit (Sec. 67-6-224(b)(3), (4)).

- **Tobacco buydown credit**

A credit is granted for the amount of sales tax due on tobacco buydown payments included in the sales price of tobacco sold at retail (Sec. 67-6-357). The credit is applied so that sales tax is owed on the sales price of the tobacco less the tobacco buydown payment associated with the sale.

- **Credit for disaster restoration projects**

A credit is allowed for purchases of qualified tangible personal property purchased for use in a qualified disaster restoration project (Sec. 67-6-235). A "qualified disaster restoration project" is a project undertaken in connection with the restoration of real or tangible property located within a declared federal disaster area that suffered damages as a result of that disaster (Sec. 67-6-235(b)(1)). The project must involve a minimum investment of at least $50 million for the restoration of the property. The minimum investment may include the cost of constructing or refurnishing a building and the cost of building materials, labor, equipment, furniture, fixtures, computer software, and other tangible property within the building but does not include land or inventory.

The credit amount is all but 0.5% of the state sales and use tax paid on purchases of qualified tangible personal property, which includes building materials, machinery, equipment, computer software, furniture, and fixtures used exclusively to replace or restore real or tangible personal property damaged as a result of the disaster and purchased or leased prior to substantial completion of the qualified disaster restoration project (Sec. 67-6-235(b)(2)). The term does not include any payments with respect to leases of qualified tangible personal property that extend beyond substantial completion of the project.

¶ 841   Deficiency Assessments

The Commissioner of Revenue's power to collect delinquent taxes comes largely from the Tax Enforcement Procedures Act (Sec. 67-1-1401). The Act applies to every public tax, license, or fee collected by the Commissioner and overrides any other statutes that are inconsistent with its provisions (Sec. 67-1-1402). All assessments must be made within the appropriate limitations period (see ¶ 843).

If a person fails to report or makes an incorrect or fraudulent report, the Commissioner of Revenue is charged with making an estimate of sales and with computing and collecting the tax, interest, and penalties due (Sec. 67-6-517). The Commissioner's estimate is considered *prima facie* correct, with the burden of proving the contrary on the taxpayer. As part of this process, the Commissioner may require a dealer to appear with the dealer's records and give testimony regarding the computation of the tax. If the dealer does not appear, the Commissioner may make the assessment on the basis of available information (Sec. 67-6-517).

Effective January 1, 2015, if it is determined that a taxpayer has failed to pay the correct amount of any tax, a notice of proposed assessment will be issued, together with notice of the right to an informal conference. The notice must provide that when an assessment becomes final, the taxpayer has the right to file suit to challenge the final assessment in the appropriate Tennessee chancery court within 90 days from the date the assessment becomes final. Taxpayers also have the right to request an informal conference within 30 days after the date of the notice of proposed assessment. The informal conference must be held within 10 days from the date of the request, and the decision must be issued within 10 days after the conference. If a taxpayer does not request an informal conference, the proposed assessment becomes final on the 31st day after the notice of proposed assessment. (Sec. 67-1-1438)

Taxpayer Bill of Rights: Under the Tennessee Taxpayer Bill of Rights, the Commissioner of Revenue is required to promulgate rules, regulations, and policies informing taxpayers of their rights and guaranteeing that taxpayers are treated with fairness, courtesy, and common sense (Sec. 67-1-110).

¶ 842   Audit Procedures

The Commissioner of Revenue or a delegate has the authority to examine books and records and require testimony of a taxpayer under oath for the purpose of ascertaining the correctness of any return or the liability of a dealer who has not filed a return or who has filed a false or fraudulent return (Sec. 67-1-1301, Sec. 67-1-1437, Sec. 67-6-517). The dealer is given 10-days' notice in writing to appear with the books and records for the Commissioner to examine and to answer interrogatories under oath (Sec. 67-6-517).

¶ 843   Statute of Limitations

State taxes for which a return is required must be assessed within three years from December 31 of the year in which the return is filed (Sec. 67-1-1501(b)). When no return is filed or a false or fraudulent return is filed, an assessment may be made and collection may begin at any time (Sec. 67-1-1501(b)).

The Commissioner of Revenue and a taxpayer may enter into a written agreement allowing the assessment of taxes after the expiration of the statute of limitations (Sec. 67-1-1501(b)).

Timely assessed taxes may be collected by procedures begun within six years after the assessment of the tax or prior to the expiration of the collection period agreed upon by the Commissioner and the taxpayer (Sec. 67-1-1429(a)).

The filing of a suit by the taxpayer tolls all statutes of limitation as to other people potentially liable to the taxpayer because of the occurrence from which the claim arises until the suit's final determination (Sec. 67-1-1803).

¶ 844   **Application for Refund**

A taxpayer who believes that an assessment of any tax collected or administered by the Commissioner of Revenue is unjust, illegal, or incorrect may either pay the tax due and file a refund claim or file suit within one year challenging the assessment in chancery court (Sec. 67-1-1801). However, generally, the exclusive remedy to appeal a state tax *not* collected or administered by the Commissioner or a county or municipal tax is to pay the tax due under protest and file a refund suit in chancery court (Sec. 67-1-901, Sec. 67-1-911, Sec. 67-1-912). A party must have standing to sue for a refund. For example, a purchaser who pays sales tax to a vendor ("dealer") does not have standing to sue for a refund because the vendor is the taxpayer who bears liability for the tax.

Offsets: The commissioner of revenue is required to offset tax refunds of $200 or more that are not eligible for automatic credit or refund by the amount of any debt owed to a state agency or to a person on whose behalf the agency acts to collect a debt. The priority for offsets is as follows: state tax liabilities, child support, overpayment of certain state benefits or obligations, criminal court fees, incarceration costs, judgments and liens, and other debts. (Sec. 67-1-1802(a)(1)(B))

Any taxpayer requesting a refund of $200 or more that is not eligible for automatic credit or refund must submit a report of debts. If it is determined that a debtor is entitled to a refund or credit, interest is added beginning 90 days from the date the commissioner receives proof that the refund or credit is due and payable. (Sec. 67-1-1802(a)(1)(B)(ii)) The commissioner must provide information to any state agency if the information is necessary to collect debts owed. Taxpayers subject to offset will have an opportunity for a hearing. Suits challenging the denial of a refund must be filed within one year.

Single article cap: For refunds of taxes collected in excess of the local single article cap, see ¶ 835.

Source.—Statutory references are to Title 2, Subtitle E, Chapters 151, 152, and 153 of the Tax Code, as amended to date. Details are reported in the CCH TEXAS TAX REPORTS starting at ¶ 60-000.

The Texas limited sales, excise, and use tax is imposed on sales of "taxable items," except sales for resale, within the state (Sec. 151.005; Sec. 151.006; Sec. 151.302; Sec. 151.051). "Taxable items" include tangible personal property and specified services (Sec. 151.010). The furnishing of natural gas or electricity is a sale of tangible personal property (Sec. 151.009; 34 TAC 3.295(b)).

The Texas use tax is a complementary tax imposed on the storage, use, or other consumption in the state of a taxable item purchased from a retailer (Sec. 151.011; Sec. 151.101).

Digital products: Software, including software delivered over electronic media, and customized programs are considered tangible personal property for sales and use tax purposes and taxed as such. Sales of Internet-delivered digital products, including computer programs and prepaid calling cards, are taxable as sales of tangible personal property (Sec. 151.009). Charges for access to data on a web page are taxable as charges for information service based on the benefit the customer derives in Texas (*CCH Internet/Electronic Commerce Survey,* Texas Comptroller of Public Accounts, September 28, 1999).

Cloud computing: A comptroller letter discusses the sales tax treatment of various "cloud computing" services offered by a Texas company that would allow customers to access computing power, storage capacity, and other information technology infrastructure through the Internet without having to spend capital on servers, support staff, or real estate. The topics addressed include:

 — data processing services, including data storage, manipulation, and retrieval;

 — data transfer fees and incidental usage fees;

 — bulk and transactional email-sending services for businesses and developers;

 — taxable information services, such as gathering data from around the Web and making it available to customers in the form of lists and searchable data;

 — the sourcing of data processing and information services for local tax purposes; and

 — determining the proper local sales tax rate in the event a sales office, technology development office, or data center is created in the state.

(*Letter No. 201207533L,* Texas Comptroller of Public Accounts, July 31, 2012, CCH TEXAS TAX REPORTS, ¶ 403-845).

• Specialized taxes

The sales and use taxes on motor vehicles (Sec. 152.001 *et seq.*), manufactured housing (Sec. 158.001 *et seq.*), boats and boat motors (Sec. 160.021 *et seq.*) and mixed beverages (Sec. 183.041, *et seq.*) are imposed by special laws, as indicated, rather than by the Limited Sales, Excise, and Use Tax Act (Sec. 151.001 *et seq.*), (Sec. 151.308(a)).

Hotel occupancy tax: A tax is levied on the cost of occupancy of any room or rooms in a hotel when charges are $15 or more each day (Sec. 156.051). A "hotel" means any building or buildings in which the public may for a consideration obtain sleeping accommodations. The term includes hotels, motels, tourist homes, houses or courts, lodging houses, inns, rooming houses, or bed and breakfast establishments, but does not include hospitals, sanitariums, nursing homes, or college dormitories (Sec. 156.001; Sec. 351.001; Sec. 352.001; Sec. 334.251, Local Government Code; 34 TAC Sec. 3.161). Occupancies for more than 30 consecutive days are exempt (Sec. 156.101; Sec. 351.002).

Homeowners who lease their homes, apartments, or condominiums to members of the public when an entertainment event is held in their area must collect and remit hotel occupancy tax on the rentals, unless an exemption applies. Homeowners who have not registered for the state hotel occupancy tax must complete and submit a questionnaire (Form AP-102) and pay any tax due on past rentals. They should also contact the county, city, and special purpose district where the rental home is located to determine if any local hotel tax responsibilities apply. See also ¶ 850, "Local Taxes."

Room resellers: When a travel agency or tour operator contracts with a hotel to make rooms available to the public and then marks up the room charge to its customers, the reseller must collect and remit hotel tax on the marked-up room price. Credit may be taken for hotel taxes directly paid by the operator to the hotel on the lower wholesale price of the room. Records must be maintained to link tax paid by customers to the tour operator with tax paid to hotels by the operator. (*Tax Policy News*, Texas Comptroller of Public Accounts, March 2010).

In a class action brought by 172 Texas cities against 11 online travel companies (OTCs), the U.S. District Court of the Western District of Texas, San Antonio Division, held that the OTCs were required to calculate, collect, remit, and report Texas city hotel occupancy taxes based on the total retail amount charged to their customers for a hotel room, including mark-up/margin, breakage, extra person fees, and service fees, rather than on the wholesale price paid by the OTCs to the hotels. The OTCs were held liable for unpaid occupancy taxes on the difference between the retail and the wholesale amounts for the applicable periods. Further, the OTCs were directed to adjust their business practices to ensure that taxes on post-judgment transactions are collected and paid on the retail price of hotel rooms charged to their customers. (*City of San Antonio v. Hotels.Com, L.P.,* U.S. District Court, W.D. Texas, Dkt. SA-06-CA-381-OG, April 4, 2013, CCH TAXAS TAX REPORTS, ¶ 403-895).

• Incidence of tax

Sales tax: The state may proceed against either the purchaser or the seller for unpaid sales tax (Sec. 151.051; Sec. 151.052). Although sellers are responsible for collecting and remitting the tax to the state, the tax is intended to fall on the purchaser and a seller's failure to collect the tax from the purchaser does not relieve the purchaser of its own tax liability. The sales tax is required to be added to the sales price and becomes a debt from the purchaser to the seller recoverable at law in the same manner as the sales price.

Use tax: The incidence of the use tax is on the person consuming, using, or storing the taxable item in the state; the consumer's liability continues until the tax is paid to the state unless the consumer pays the tax to, and obtains a receipt from, the retailer or other person authorized to collect the tax (Sec. 151.101; Sec. 151.102). Retailers engaged in business in the state are responsible for collecting and remitting use taxes and are generally liable for such tax if they fail to do so. Upon the purchase of goods, the use tax becomes part of the sales price and is a debt owed by the purchaser to the retailer. If the tax is unpaid, the retailer may file a lawsuit to recover it (Sec. 151.103).

• Taxable services

Taxable services include the following (Sec. 151.0101(a)):

    — amusement services;

    — cable television services, (*i.e.,* distribution of video programming, with or without the use of wires, to subscribing or paying customers (Sec. 151.0033));

— specified personal services, defined as personal services listed under Group 721, Major Group 72 of the Standard Industrial Classification Manual, 1972 (laundry, cleaning, and garment services), plus three specific services listed under Group 729 (massage parlors, escort services, and Turkish baths) (Sec. 151.0045);

— motor vehicle parking and storage services;

— the repair, remodeling, maintenance, and restoration of tangible personal property other than aircraft, motor vehicles, certain ships, boats, and vessels, and certain computer programs;

— telecommunications services;

— credit reporting services (*i.e.,* the assembling or furnishing of credit history or credit information) (Sec. 151.0034);

— debt collection services, including the service performed for which a processing fee is collected under Ch. 617, Acts of the 68th Legislature, Regular Session, 1983 (Art. 9022, V.T.C.S.) (processing fee of up to $25 chargeable by holder of a dishonored check), but excluding the collection of a judgment by the attorney or law firm that represented the judgment creditor in the action from which the judgment arose, and excluding the collection of court-ordered child support or medical child support (Sec. 151.0036);

— insurance services, including loss or damage appraisal, inspection, investigation, actuarial work, claims adjustment and processing, and loss prevention, but not insurance coverage (Sec. 151.0039);

— information services, including electronic data retrieval and research, and the furnishing of news or other current information except (a) to newspapers and federally licensed radio and television stations, and, (b) information furnished by or on behalf of a homeowners association to one of its members (Sec. 151.0038);

— real property services, such as landscaping, yard work, garbage removal or collection (other than the removal or collection of certain hazardous and industrial solid waste), janitorial and custodial services, certain structural pest control services, and surveying real property (Sec. 151.0048); however, these services are not considered "real property services" if they are purchased by a contractor as part of the improvement of real property while building a new residential structure or an improvement to be used for residential purposes that is adjacent to that structure;

— data processing services, all forms of computerized data storage and manipulation, such as word processing, data entry and retrieval, data search, information compilation, and the rental of a computer or computer time for data processing, no matter who performs the processing service (Sec. 151.0035); data processing services do not include the transcription of medical dictation by a medical receptionist;

— real property repair and remodeling services, other than (a) certain residential realty, (b) improvements adjacent to such realty, and (c) improvements to manufacturing or processing production units in a petrochemical refinery or chemical plant that provides increased capacity in the production unit (Sec. 151.0047);

— private security services for which a license is required under Texas law; and

— telephone answering services.

• **Use tax**

The Texas use tax is a nonrecurring tax complementary to the sales tax (34 TAC Sec. 3.346(a)(3)). In general, the storage, use, or other consumption in Texas of a taxable item that was purchased outside of Texas is subject to the use tax (Sec. 151.101(a); 34 TAC Sec. 3.346(b)(1)). With respect to a taxable service, the term "use" means the derivation in Texas of a direct or indirect benefit from the service (Sec. 151.011(b)).

• Nexus

Every retailer engaged in business in Texas and making sales of taxable items for storage, use, or other consumption in Texas, not otherwise exempted, must collect use tax from the purchaser (Sec. 151.103). A retailer is engaged in business in Texas if the retailer (Sec. 151.107(a); 34 TAC 3.286(a)(2)):

(A) maintains, occupies, or uses in Texas permanently, temporarily, directly, or indirectly or through a subsidiary or agent, an office, distribution center, sales or sample room or place, warehouse, storage place, or any other physical location where business is conducted;

(B) has a representative, agent, salesman, canvasser, or solicitor operating in Texas under the authority of the retailer or its subsidiary for the purpose of selling or delivering or the taking of orders for a taxable item;

(C) derives receipts from the sale, lease, or rental of tangible personal property situated in Texas;

(D) engages in regular or systematic solicitation of sales of taxable items in Texas by the distribution of catalogs, periodicals, advertising flyers, or other advertising, by means of print, radio, or television media, or by mail, telegraphy, telephone, computer data base, cable, optic, microwave, or other communication system for the purpose of effecting sales of taxable items;

(E) solicits orders for taxable items by mail or through other media and under federal law is subject to or permitted to be made subject to the jurisdiction of Texas for purposes of collecting Texas sales and use taxes;

(F) has a franchisee or licensee operating under its trade name if the franchisee or licensee is required to collect Texas sales or use tax;

(G) holds a substantial ownership interest in, or is owned in whole or substantial part by, a person who maintains a location in Texas from which business is conducted and if:

(1) the retailer sells the same or a substantially similar line of products as the person with the location in Texas and sells those products under a business name that is the same as or substantially similar to the business name of the person with the location in Texas; or

(2) the facilities or employees of the person with the location in Texas are used to:

(a) advertise, promote, or facilitate sales by the retailer to consumers; or

(b) perform any other activity on behalf of the retailer that is intended to establish or maintain a marketplace for the retailer in Texas, including receiving or exchanging returned merchandise;

(H) holds a substantial ownership interest in, or is owned in whole or substantial part by, a person that:

(1) maintains a distribution center, warehouse, or similar location in Texas; and

(2) delivers property sold by the retailer to consumers; or

(I) otherwise does business in Texas.

Internet hosting: A person whose only activity in Texas is conducted as a user of Internet hosting is not engaged in business in the state for sales and use tax nexus purposes. "Internet hosting" means providing to an unrelated user access over the Internet to computer services using property that is owned or leased and managed by the provider and on which the user may store or process the user's own data or use software that is owned, licensed, or leased by the user or provider. The term does not include telecommunications services. (Sec. 151.108) Additional information is available on the Comptroller's website at **https://comptroller.texas.gov/taxes/sales/**.

Out-of-state companies doing disaster or emergency work: An out-of-state business entity is not engaged in business in Texas if the entity's physical presence in Texas is solely from the entity's performance of disaster- or emergency-related work during a disaster response period. (Sec. 151.0241; see also ¶ 854)

- **Streamlined Act status**

Texas is not a member of the Streamlined Sales and Use Tax Agreement because, although it has enacted legislation authorizing it to enter into the Agreement (Sec. 142.005), it has not yet enacted all of the changes to its laws necessary to comply with the Agreement's requirements. However, as an Advisor state, it will continue to have input through its representation on the State and Local Advisory Council, which advises the Governing Board on matters pertaining to the administration of the Agreement. For additional information, see ¶ 852.

¶ 847	Tax Base

The sales tax is measured by the sales price of the taxable item (tangible personal property or taxable service) (Sec. 151.010; Sec. 151.051).

Use tax: The use tax is also measured by the sales price of the taxable item purchased for storage, use, or other consumption in Texas (Sec. 151.101; 34 TAC Sec. 3.346(a)(3)).

- **"Sales price" or "receipts" defined**

"Sales price" or "receipts" is the total amount for which a taxable item is sold, leased, or rented, valued in money, without a deduction for the cost of any of the following (Sec. 151.007):

— the taxable item sold, leased, or rented;

— the materials used, labor or service employed, interest, losses, or other expenses; or

— the transportation of tangible personal property or transportation incident to a taxable service.

"Sales price" or "receipts" has a specialized meaning as it applies to sales through vending machines and to memberships in a private club or organization.

Used motor vehicles: The sales price of a used motor vehicle for tax purposes cannot be less than 80% of the used motor vehicle's standard presumptive value unless the purchaser establishes a lower value by obtaining a certified appraisal. If a used motor vehicle is purchased from a dealer, the sales price on the title application or dealer's invoice is used to calculate the tax due (Sec. 152.0412; 34 TAC 3.79).

¶ 848	List of Exemptions, Exceptions, and Exclusions

Unless otherwise indicated, the statutory exemptions listed below apply to both sales and use taxes; those applicable only to the use tax are listed separately. Items that are excluded from the sales or use tax base are treated at ¶ 847, "Tax Base."

Sales tax holidays: School supplies, clothing, and footwear with a sales price of less than $100 per item are exempt each year from Friday through Sunday on a weekend in August that begins at least 15 days before the start of school (Sec. 151.326). The exemption does not include special athletic or protective clothing or footwear; accessories such as jewelry, handbags, wallets, watches, etc.; or the rental of clothing or footwear.

Energy Star and WaterSense sales tax holidays are concurrently in effect over Memorial Day weekend each year, Saturday through Monday. Products that bear the "Energy Star" or WaterSense logos qualify, as do certain other water-conserving products. Additional details are available in Sales Tax Publications 96-1331, 98-490, 98-1017, and 98-1018, Texas Comptroller of Public Accounts, revised February 2017, and on the Comptroller's Web site at **https://comptroller.texas.gov/taxes/sales/**.

Sales of emergency preparation items are exempt from sales tax during a period beginning on the Saturday before the last Monday in April and ending on the last Monday in April. Eligible items include portable generators, storm protection devices for doors or windows, batteries, flashlights, and various other specified items (Sec. 151.3565).

Sales for resale—federal contracts: Effective October 1, 2011, the definition of "sale for resale" was amended to include a sale of tangible personal property to a purchaser who acquires the property for the purpose of transferring it as an integral part of performing a contract, or a subcontract of a contract, with the federal government only if the purchaser (1) allocates and bills to the contract the cost of the property as a direct or indirect cost; and (2) transfers title to the property to the federal government under the contract and applicable federal acquisition regulations. A sale for resale does not include the sale of tangible personal property or a taxable service to a purchaser who acquires the property or service for the purpose of performing a service that is not taxed, regardless of whether title transfers to the service provider's customer, unless the tangible personal property or taxable service is purchased for the purpose of reselling it to the United States in a contract or subcontract with any branch of the Department of Defense, Department of Homeland Security, Department of Energy, National Aeronautics and Space Administration, Central Intelligence Agency, National Security Agency, National Oceanic and Atmospheric Administration, or National Reconnaissance Office to the extent allocated and billed to the contract with the federal government. (Sec. 151.006).

• Agricultural and timber product exemptions

A person claiming a Texas sales tax exemption on certain items used in the production of agricultural and timber products must include a registration number issued by the Comptroller of Public Accounts on the exemption certificate that the person provides to the seller (Sec. 151.1551). Exemptions that require a registration number include the exemptions for (1) fertilizers and herbicides; (2) machinery and equipment related to roads, water facilities, and pollution control equipment; (3) items incorporated in a structure for disposal of chicken carcasses; (4) property used in the production of agricultural products or timber; (5) electricity used in agricultural or timber operations; and (6) services performed on the above exempt items. The registration number is also required for claiming an exemption for the purchase or rental of a machine, trailer, or semitrailer for use primarily for farming, ranching, or timber operations. Additional information is available on the Comptroller's website at **https://comptroller.texas.gov/taxes/sales/**.

• Sales and use tax exemptions, exceptions, and exclusions

Agricultural equipment, machinery, aircraft, supplies	Sec. 151.316(a); Sec. 151.342
Aircraft, commercial	Sec. 151.328
Aircraft maintenance services	Sec. 151.0101(a)(5)(A)
Aircraft repair services	Sec. 151.328
Alcoholic beverages	Sec. 151.308(a)(7)
Ambulances	Sec. 152.087
Amusement services, sold by nonprofit corporation	Sec. 151.3101

¶848   Texas

• Use tax exemptions, exceptions, and exclusions

Processing, fabricating, or manufacturing property into other property or attaching the property to, or incorporating the property into, other property for the purpose of subsequently transporting the property out of state for use out of state . . . . Sec. 151.011

Storage or use of repair or replacement parts that are acquired outside the state and used as repair or replacement parts in the vehicles of licensed or certificated common carriers that transport persons or property . . . . Sec. 151.330(i)

Tangible personal property purchased outside Texas, temporarily stored in Texas but subsequently removed and used solely outside Texas . . . . Sec. 151.330(b)

Transactions subject to the sales tax . . . . Sec. 151.303(a)

Transactions that would be exempt from the sales tax if the item were purchased in Texas . . . . Sec. 151.330(c)

Transfers that occur in the regular course of business . . . . Sec. 151.011

Transportation of property outside the state for use solely outside the state . . . . Sec. 151.011

¶ 849   Rate of Tax

The state sales and use tax rate is 6.25% of the sales price of the item sold (Sec. 151.051). This rate applies to all items subject to tax under the Limited Sales, Excise, and Use Tax Act.

• Special taxes

Special sales and use tax rates and conditions apply to:

— motor vehicles (6.25%) (Sec. 152.001; Sec. 152.021; Sec. 152.022);

— manufactured housing (5%, imposed on only 65% of sales price) (Sec. 158.051; Sec. 158.052);

— boats and boat motors (6.25%) (Sec. 160.021);

— mixed beverages (8.25%) mixed beverages (Sec. 183.041(b)).

Rental of motor vehicles: A tax is imposed on the gross rental receipts from the rental of a motor vehicle at the rate of 10% for rentals of 30 days or less and 6.25% for the rental of a vehicle for longer than 30 days (Sec. 152.026). Tax does not apply to separately stated charges for insurance, charges for damages occurring during the rental period, separately stated charges for motor fuel, or discounts. The total amount of gross rental receipts tax cannot be less than the motor vehicle retail sales or use tax (above). The motor vehicle retail sales and use tax does not apply to a motor vehicle registered as a rental vehicle; the tax on gross rental receipts is imposed instead.

Hotel occupancy tax: The state hotel occupancy tax is imposed at the rate of 6% of the price paid for a room in a hotel (Sec. 156.052). The price of the room does not include the cost of food served by the hotel or the cost of personal services performed by the hotel, except charges for cleaning or readying the room for occupancy (Sec. 156.051).

Special use taxes: In lieu of the specified use tax rates, a flat tax is imposed on new residents of Texas who bring boats or motor vehicles into Texas. The use tax for boats previously purchased and owned in another state is $15 (Sec. 160.023), and the use tax for owned or leased motor vehicles previously registered in another state or foreign country is $90 (Sec. 152.023).

Wireless 911 charges: Retail sellers of prepaid wireless telecommunications service must collect a prepaid wireless 911 emergency service fee from customers. The fee is

2% of the purchase price of each prepaid wireless telecommunication service sold by way of retail transaction or used by a seller in Texas. Prepaid wireless telecommunication service means a mobile telecommunication service that is paid for entirely in advance and allows a person to access 9-1-1 emergency communication services. Vendors must file a quarterly report and pay the fee to the Comptroller on or before the 30th day of the month following each calendar quarter. A seller may deduct and retain 2.0% of the fees it collects during each report period to offset its costs in collecting and remitting the fee. (Sec. 771.0712, Health and Safety Code; 34 TAC Sec. 3.1271).

In addition, three other 911-related charges are imposed monthly: (1) the 911 Emergency Service Fee, (2) the 911 Wireless Emergency Service Fee, and (3) the 911 Equalization Surcharge. Information about these fees can be found on the Comptroller's Web site at **https://comptroller.texas.gov/taxes/sales/**.

- **Texas Emissions Reduction Plan surcharges**

Heavy diesel equipment: A 1.5% (2%, before Sept. 1, 2015) surcharge is imposed in each county on the sale, lease, or rental of new or used off-road, heavy-duty diesel equipment that uses an engine of 50 horsepower or greater and on the storage, use, or consumption of such equipment. The fee is in addition to state and local sales and use taxes that are due on the equipment and is administered and enforced in the same manner as sales or use tax. No surcharge is due if the purchase, lease, or rental is exempt from state sales and use tax. The surcharge expires on August 31, 2013 (Sec. 151.0515). The surcharge applies to equipment purchased out-of-state for use in Texas and equipment purchased by direct payment permit holders (34 TAC Sec. 3.320).

Taxpayers who use off-road, heavy-duty diesel equipment exclusively in the production of timber for sale may claim an exemption from the surcharge (34 TAC Sec. 3.367(f)). In addition, the surcharge does not apply to the following: (1) repair or replacement parts or accessories related to the equipment, unless sold or leased with the equipment; (2) implements of husbandry used solely for agricultural purposes, including equipment used exclusively on a farm or ranch to build or maintain roads or water facilities; (3) processing machinery and equipment eligible for manufacturing exemptions; (4) machinery and equipment exempt from sales and use tax (such as equipment used to construct or operate a water or wastewater system under Sec. 151.355); or (5) equipment used in oil and gas exploration and production at an oil or gas well site (34 TAC Sec. 3.3200).

- **Certain prior contracts exempt from tax rate increases and tax base increases**

Taxable items that are purchased, leased, or rented for use in the performance of a *third-party* contract or bid signed on or before the date provided for prior contracts in the enabling legislation are exempted from the amount of an increase in the *tax rate* (34 TAC Sec. 3.319). Taxable items that are purchased, leased, or rented that are the subject of a contract or bid (not just a *third party* contract or bid) signed on or before the date provided for prior contracts in the enabling legislation are exempted from a change in the *tax base*. A "third-party contract" is a contract between the purchaser of the items for which exemption is claimed and a party other than the seller of the items for which exemption is claimed. "Enabling legislation" refers to a bill enacted into law by the Texas legislature that authorizes an exemption for prior contracts or bids (34 TAC Sec. 3.319).

Local taxes: Similar prior contract exemptions exist for purposes of the municipal sales and use taxes (34 TAC Sec. 3.376) and the transit authority sales and use taxes (34 TAC Sec. 3.426).

¶ 850　　Local Taxes

A Texas municipality may impose a local sales and use tax at any rate that is an increment of ⅛ of 1%, provided that the rate does not result in a combined rate of local sales and use tax rates in excess of the maximum combined rate of 2% in any location.

Also, a municipal tax rate may be reduced or increased to any rate that is an increment of ⅛ of 1%, provided that it does not result in a combined rate that exceeds the 2% maximum combined rate for local taxes. (Sec. 321.103)

Certain municipalities may also impose a tax for crime prevention and control purposes at a rate not to exceed ½% (Sec. 323.105).

Collection responsibilities: A Comptroller letter sets forth four general rules for collecting local Texas sales and use taxes. First, sales tax takes precedence over use tax. Second, a seller can collect no more than 2% in total local taxes for all applicable jurisdictions. Third, if a seller collects a sales tax for a city, county, special purpose district (SPD), or transit authority, the seller may not collect a use tax for another local taxing jurisdiction of the same type. A seller may, however, collect more than one transit or SPD sales tax or multiple transit or SPD use taxes in relation to the same transaction. And fourth, the seller must collect the full amount of a local tax without exceeding the 2% cap; fractional collection is not permitted. In other words, a seller must collect all or none of a jurisdiction's tax (*Letter No. 200710981L,* Texas Comptroller of Public Accounts, October 19, 2007, CCH Texas Tax Reports, ¶ 403-336).

• Development Corporation Act taxes

A city adopting a local sales and use tax for the benefit of an industrial development corporation or municipal development corporation must adopt a rate of ⅛%, ¼%, ⅜%, or ½% (Art. 5190.6, Sec. 4A(d), R.C.S.; Sec. 379A.081). However, the city cannot adopt a rate that would result in a combined sales and use tax imposed by the city or any political subdivision having territory within the city exceeding 2% (Art. 5190.6, Sec. 4B(e), R.C.S.). A city adopting a local sales and use tax for the benefit of a corporation building entertainment and sports facilities must also adopt a rate of ⅛%, ¼%, ⅜%, or ½% (Art. 5190.6, Sec. 4B(e), R.C.S.).

• County sales and use tax

A county that has adopted the sales and use tax authorized by the County Sales and Use Tax Act must impose the tax at the rate of ½%, unless the county includes no territory within the limits of a municipality, in which case it must impose the tax at the rate of 1% (Sec. 323.103; Sec. 323.104). Certain counties may also impose a tax for crime prevention and control purposes at a rate not to exceed ½% (Sec. 323.105). A county tax levied for the purpose of funding health services may be imposed at the rate of only ½% (Sec. 324.022).

• Transit authority sales and use taxes

Metropolitan Rapid Transit Authorities, Regional Transportation Authorities, and County Transportation Authorities are allowed to levy local sales and use taxes at any of the following rates: ¼%, ½%, ¾%, and 1% (Sec. 451.404, Transportation Code, Sec. 452.401, Transportation Code, Sec. 460.056, Transportation Code). City Transit Developments are allowed to levy local sales and use taxes at either ¼% or ½% (Sec. 453.401, Transportation Code).

• Hospital district sales and use taxes

Hospital districts that are authorized to impose ad valorem taxes may adopt a sales and use tax at any rate, in multiples of ⅛%, up to a maximum of 2% (Sec. 285.061, Health and Safety Code). However, a hospital district cannot adopt a rate that would result in a combined rate imposed by the district and other political subdivisions having territory in the district exceeding 2% (Sec. 285.061, Health and Safety Code).

• City, county, or venue district sales and use taxes for "venue projects"

Cities, counties, and venue districts formed by combinations of cities, counties, or both may impose a sales and use tax to finance venue projects at the following rates: ⅛%, ¼%, ⅜%, or ½% (Sec. 334.083, Local Government Code).

¶850 Texas

- **Street maintenance**

Municipalities may adopt a sales and use tax of 0.25%, subject to voter approval, to provide revenue for the maintenance and repair of local streets (Sec. 327.003). However, a municipality may not adopt such a tax if the combined rate of all sales and use taxes imposed by the municipality and other state subdivisions exceeds 2% at any location in the municipality. The tax would be subject to reauthorization by the voters every five years.

- **Hotel occupancy taxes**

Local hotel occupancy taxes may be imposed by municipalities, counties, county development districts, and venue districts at various rates (Sec. 334.251; Sec. 335.001; Sec. 351.001; Sec. 352.002).

- **Sourcing rules**

If a retailer has more than one place of business in Texas, each sale of each taxable item is consummated at the place of business of the retailer in the state where the retailer first receives the order, provided that the order is placed in person by the purchaser or lessee of the taxable item at the place of business of the retailer in Texas where the retailer first receives the order. (Sec. 321.203(c); Sec. 323.203(c))

If a retailer has more than one place of business in Texas and the above sourcing provision does not apply, the sale is consummated at the place of business of the retailer (1) from which the retailer ships or delivers the item, if the retailer ships or delivers the item to a point designated by the purchaser or lessee, or (2) where the purchaser or lessee takes possession of and removes the item, if the purchaser or lessee takes possession of and removes the item from a place of business of the retailer. (Sec. 321.203(c); Sec. 323.203(c)).

An outlet, office, facility, or any location that contracts with a business to process invoices or other records is not considered a "place of business of the retailer" if the Comptroller determines that it exists to avoid tax or exists solely to rebate a portion of taxes to the contracting business. Such an outlet, office, facility, or location does not exist to avoid tax or solely to rebate a portion of taxes if it provides significant business services, beyond processing invoices, to the contracting business, including logistics management, purchasing, inventory control, or other vital business services. (Sec. 321.002(3)(B))

Finally, if a retailer has more than one place of business in Texas and neither sourcing provision above applies, the sale is consummated at (1) the place of business of the retailer where the order is received or (2) if the order is not received at a place of business of the retailer, the place of business from which the retailer's agent or employee who took the order operates. The new sourcing provision does not apply if the taxable item is shipped or delivered from a warehouse that is a place of business of the retailer and the retailer has an economic development agreement with a municipality or county that provides certain prescribed information to the comptroller regarding each warehouse and place of business of the retailer. (Sec. 321.203(c); Sec. 323.203(c))

- **Telecommunications taxes**

A publication that lists over 500 jurisdictions currently imposing a local tax on telecommunications is available on the Texas Comptroller's website at **https:// www.comptroller.texas.gov/taxes/publications/96-339.php**.

Sales of telecommunications services are sourced as follows:

— (1) the sale of telecommunications services sold based on a price that is measured by individual calls is sourced to the location where the call originates and terminates, or the location where the call either originates or terminates and at which the service address is also located (Sec. 321.203(g-1); Sec. 323.203(g-1));

— (2) except as provided below, the sale of telecommunications services sold on a basis other than on a call-by-call basis is sourced to the location of the customer's primary place of use (Sec. 321.203(g-2); Sec. 323.203(g-2));

— (3) a sale of post-paid calling services sold based on a price that is measured by individual calls is sourced to the location of the origination point of the telecommunications signal as first identified by the seller's telecommunications system or by information received by the seller from the seller's service provider if the system used to transport the signal is not that of the seller (Sec. 321.203(g-3); Sec. 323.203(g-3)).

Texas has conformed to the federal Mobile Telecommunications Sourcing Act (Act), P.L. 106-252. All charges for mobile telecommunications services are considered to be provided by the customer's home service provider and sourced to the customer's place of primary use (Sec. 151.061; 34 TAC Sec. 3.344(a)(8)). All such charges are subject to sales tax based on the customer's place of primary use.

The service provider will be held harmless for an error in assigning wireless services to a jurisdiction if it utilizes an electronic database provided by the state or a designated entity, or, if the state has not provided or designated a database, if it utilizes a database that makes assignments based on a nine-digit zip code.

- **Local rate changes**

In conformity with the Streamlined Sales Tax Agreement (¶ 852), a tax rate change must take effect on the first day of a calendar quarter (Sec. 151.012). If the performance of a taxable service begins before the effective date of a rate change, but the performance of the service will not be complete until after the effective date, the rate change applies to the first billing period for the service performed on or after the effective date.

- **Local tax rates**

A sales tax rate locator is available on the website of the Comptroller of Public Accounts at **https://mycpa.cpa.state.tx.us/atj/**. The Comptroller's website also permits viewing local tax rates in book format. City, county, and special district tax rates may be viewed individually or as combined area rates, with local codes and effective dates.

A list of city sales tax rates is available at **https://comptroller.texas.gov/taxes/ sales/city.php**. County sales tax rates are listed at **https://comptroller.texas.gov/ taxes/sales/county.php**

A list of special purpose district tax rates is available at **https://comptroller.texas.gov/taxes/sales/spd.php**.

¶ 851 Bracket Schedule

The Comptroller is authorized to issue a bracket or rate schedule for sales that involve a fraction of a dollar (Sec. 151.053(b)). The statute provides the formula for deriving the bracket schedule (Sec. 151.053(a)): a fraction of one cent that is less than one-half of a cent is not collected, and a fraction of one cent that is equal to or more than one-half of a cent is collected as one cent of tax.

Sales and use tax rate charts for rates 6.25% through 8.25% are available on the Comptroller's website at **https://comptroller.texas.gov/taxes/sales/forms/**.

A local sales tax collection guide for sellers is available on the Comptroller's website at **http://comptroller.texas.gov/taxinfo/taxpubs/tx94_105.pdf**.

- **Individual transactions of less than taxable amount**

Any retailer who can establish that 50% or more of the total receipts arise from individual transactions of less than the taxable amount may exclude such receipts from taxable sales (see ¶ 849).

¶ 852　　　　　　　Returns, Payments, and Due Dates

The following are required to file sales and use tax returns (Sec. 151.403):

— a person subject to the sales tax;

— a retailer engaged in business in Texas who is required to collect the use tax; and

— a person who acquires a taxable item, the storage, use, or consumption of which is subject to the use tax, if the person did not pay the use tax to a retailer or other authorized person.

• Due dates of returns and payments

Generally, sales and use taxes must be paid and reported to the Comptroller by the 20th day of the month following the end of the calendar month being reported, unless a taxpayer reports and pays taxes quarterly or prepays taxes quarterly (Sec. 151.401; 34 TAC Sec. 3.286(e), 34 TAC Sec. 3.286(f)).

Quarterly: If a taxpayer owes less than $500 for a calendar month or $1,500 for a calendar quarter, the taxes are due and payable on the 20th day of the month following the end of the quarter (Sec. 151.401; 34 TAC Sec. 3.286(f)(1)).

Annually: If the taxpayer owes less than $1,000 during a calendar year, the taxpayer may request the Comptroller for authority to file on a yearly basis. If authority is granted, the return and payment are due on or before January 20 of the following calendar year (34 TAC Sec. 3.286(f)(2)).

Weekends and holidays: If the date on which a report or payment is due falls on a Saturday, Sunday, or a legal holiday included on a list published by the Treasurer in the Texas Register, then the due date for the report or payment is the next day that is not a weekend or listed holiday (Sec. 111.053; 34 TAC Sec. 3.286(e)(1)).

Penalty for failure to file tax report: A $50 penalty will be assessed against a person who fails to file a sales and use tax or hotel occupancy tax report as required by law, an owner of a motor vehicle subject to the tax on gross rental receipts who fails to file a tax report on time, and a seller of a motor vehicle sold in a seller-financed sale who fails to file a motor vehicle sales and use tax report on time. The penalty will be assessed without regard to whether the taxpayer subsequently files the report or whether any taxes were due for the reporting period. The former $50 additional penalty imposed on a person who has failed to file a timely sales and use tax report on two or more previous occasions is repealed. (Sec. 151.703(d))

• Collection allowance or discount

Retailers may deduct a discount of 0.5% of the tax due from their returns (Sec. 151.423; 34 TAC Sec. 3.286(g)), provided the return and tax payment are timely. The discount is a reimbursement for the expenses incurred in collecting the sales and use taxes. For retailers who prepay the tax (see ¶ 853), an additional 1.25% discount is available (Sec. 151.424(a); 34 TAC Sec. 3.286(g)).

• Electronic funds transfer requirements

Under the Government Code, the Comptroller must require certain persons to transfer funds that are due to the Comptroller by one or more means of electronic funds transfer (EFT) approved by the state treasurer on or before the payment due date (Sec. 404.095, Government Code). EFT is required if a person paid the Comptroller a total of $10,000 or more in any specified category of taxes during the preceding state fiscal year and if the Comptroller reasonably expects the person to make payments of $10,000 or more in one category of taxes during the current state fiscal year (Sec. 111.0625; 34 TAC Sec. 3.9).

A taxpayer required to pay by EFT must also file returns electronically (Sec. 111.0626).

• Online filing

Businesses may file their sales and use tax returns online using the Comptroller's WebFile system. To use the system, a taxpayer must complete an online sales tax return. Once the form has been submitted, the system scans it for any errors and calculates the amount of sales tax due. The taxpayer may submit payment by a Discover or American Express credit card or may have the payment electronically deducted from the taxpayer's bank account. If the taxpayer remits payment by electronic funds transfer, the taxpayer may select a date, on or before the due date, for the sale tax to be automatically paid.

The WebFile system is accessible through the Comptroller's website at **https:// comptroller.texas.gov/taxes/file-pay/about-webfile.php**.

Alcoholic beverage reporting: Brewers, manufacturers, and package store local distributors must submit electronic files of sales of alcoholic beverages (beer, wine, and distilled spirits) to Texas retailers, such as bars and restaurants. To facilitate this electronic filing requirement, the Comptroller's office has developed a Retail Inventory Tracking System (RITS) and a visual guide that walks filers through the filing process. The RITS visual guide is available on the Comptroller's website at **https://comptroller.texas.gov/taxes/sales/**.

• Uniform Sales Tax Administration Act

Texas has enacted the Uniform Sales and Use Tax Administration Act. Texas also has enacted legislation to conform with many provisions of the Streamlined Agreement. For additional information on the uniform act, see "Streamlined Sales Tax Project," listed in the Table of Contents.

¶ 853   **Prepayment of Taxes**

In addition to the 0.5% collection allowance or discount (Sec. 151.423; 34 TAC Sec. 3.286(g)), an additional 1.25% of the amount due may be retained by monthly or quarterly filers who prepay their tax (Sec. 151.424(a); 34 TAC Sec. 3.286(g)). The prepayment must be a reasonable estimate of the state and local tax liability or at least 90% of the total tax due or the actual net tax that was paid for the same reporting period of the immediately preceding year. Only monthly and quarterly filers may make tax prepayments (34 TAC Sec. 3.286(g)(3)).

Yearly and monthly filing requirements, prepayment procedures, and discounts for timely filing do not apply to holders of direct payment permits (34 TAC Sec. 3.286(m)).

Special prepayment of taxes required in August: This temporary prepayment requirement for 2013 through 2015 is discussed at ¶ 852.

• Due dates of prepayments

Quarterly filers must make their prepayments by the 15th day of the second month of the quarter for which the tax is due (Sec. 151.424(b); 34 TAC Sec. 3.286(g)(3)). Monthly filers must prepay by the 15th of the month.

By the 20th day of the month following the end of the period for which a prepayment was made, the taxpayer must file a return that shows the actual tax liability and must remit any balance due in excess of the prepayment (Sec. 151.424(c); 34 TAC Sec. 3.286(g)(3)(D)). If the prepayment exceeds the actual liability, the taxpayer will receive an overpayment notice or a refund warrant (Sec. 151.424(d); 34 TAC Sec. 3.286(g)(3)(D)).

If the taxpayer fails to file the quarterly or monthly return and payment by the due date, all discounts will be forfeited and a mandatory 5% penalty will be imposed (Sec. 151.425; 34 TAC Sec. 3.286(g)(15)). An additional mandatory 5% penalty will be imposed after 30 days' delinquency. After 60 days' delinquency, interest begins to accrue at the rate of 12% compounded monthly.

¶ 854   Vendor Registration

Every retailer, wholesaler, distributor, manufacturer, or other person who sells, leases, rents, or transfers ownership of taxable items for a consideration in Texas is required to obtain a sales tax permit. In addition, effective January 1, 2012, the definition of a "seller" or "retailer" is expanded to include a person who has been entrusted with the possession of property and has the power to sell, lease, or rent the property without further action by the owner (Sec. 151.008(a)). Out-of-state sellers engaged in business in Texas must obtain a permit for purposes of collecting the use tax.

Occupancy taxes: Texans who temporarily rent their houses or rooms to visitors in town for sporting or entertainment events such as festivals, fairs, rodeos, and races must register to collect and remit Texas hotel occupancy tax from their customers, in the same way a hotel or motel collects the tax from its patrons.

• Sales tax permits

Any person who desires to be a seller in Texas must apply to the Comptroller for a separate permit for each place of business in the state (Sec. 151.202(a); 34 TAC Sec. 3.286(b)). Direct sales organizations are required to hold Texas sales tax permits and to collect Texas tax; however, independent salespersons of such organizations are not required to hold sales tax permits (34 TAC Sec. 3.286(b)).

A person desiring to be a seller in Texas must agree to collect any applicable local use tax that is due from a purchaser even if the retailer is not engaged in business in the local jurisdiction into which the taxable item is shipped or delivered (Sec. 151.202(c)).

The sales tax permit must be displayed conspicuously in the applicant's place of business (Sec. 151.201). A person who operates two or more types of business under the same roof needs only one permit (34 TAC Sec. 3.286(c)(2)). A person who engages in business without a permit is subject to penalties. A person who has traveling salespersons operating from a central location need obtain only one permit (Sec. 151.201; 34 TAC Sec. 3.286(c)(3)).

The permit is valid only for the person and the place of business to which it applies and is not assignable (34 TAC Sec. 3.286(c)(2)). Each legal entity must apply for its own permit.

A sales tax permit is valid indefinitely but may be cancelled if no activity is reported for 12 consecutive months (Sec. 151.2021).

The application for a permit must be on a form prescribed by the Comptroller, include the name and address of the business and other required information, and be signed by the owner (Sec. 151.202(b)). An application filed electronically complies with the signature requirement (Sec. 151.202(c)). The applicant must also file adequate security for the payment of the taxes. The permit is issued without charge (34 TAC Sec. 3.286(c)(1)).

Absorption of tax: A Texas business engaged in making sales over the Internet may not state or indicate that it will pay or absorb any Texas sales and use taxes due on the sales it makes. A criminal penalty is imposed on sellers that advertise, hold out, or state to a customer or to the public that they will assume, absorb, or refund Texas sales tax or will not add the tax to the sales price of a taxable item. (Sec. 151.704).

• Use tax collection permits

A retailer "engaged in business" in Texas who sells a taxable item for storage, use, or consumption in Texas is required to collect the use tax from the purchaser and give the purchaser a receipt in a prescribed form. Upon the purchase of goods, the use tax becomes part of the sales price and is a debt owed by the purchaser to the retailer. If the tax is unpaid, the retailer may file a lawsuit to recover it (Sec. 151.103).

The retailer must register for a use tax collection permit and provide security for payment of taxes (Sec. 151.106). The application must include the name and address of the retailer's agents operating in Texas, the location of all distribution or sales offices and other places of business in Texas, and other information required by the Comptroller.

• **Alcoholic beverages**

Wine sales: Out-of-state wineries must obtain a Texas sales tax permit and a direct shipper's permit in order to sell and deliver wine to Texas consumers. The annual fee for an out-of-state winery direct shipper's permit is $75. Permit holders must maintain complete sales and delivery records for at least five years. Texas consumers who purchase wine from an out-of-state winery may not resell the wine (Sec. 54.01 *et seq.*, Alc. Bev. Code).

• **Out-of-state companies doing disaster or emergency related work in Texas**

Effective June 16, 2015, an out-of-state business entity whose transaction of business in Texas is limited to the performance of disaster- or emergency-related work during a disaster response period is not required to:

    — register with the secretary of state;

    — file a tax report with or pay taxes or fees to Texas or a political subdivision of the state; or

    — pay an ad valorem (property) tax or use tax on equipment that is brought into the state, used only by the entity to perform disaster- or emergency-related work during the disaster response period, and removed from the state following the disaster response period.

Such an out-of-state business entity is not considered a retailer engaged in business in Texas for sales tax nexus or reporting purposes. In addition, the business entity is not required to comply with state or local business licensing or registration requirements, occupational licensing requirements, or related fees. (Sec. 112.004, Business & Commerce Code)

An out-of-state employee whose only employment in Texas is for the performance of disaster- or emergency-related work during a disaster response period is not required to file a tax report with or pay taxes or fees to Texas or a political subdivision of the state. Also, the out-of-state employee is not required to comply with state or local occupational licensing requirements or related fees, if the employee is in substantial compliance with applicable occupational licensing requirements in the employee's state of residence or principal employment. (Sec. 112.005, Business & Commerce Code)

An out-of-state business entity or out-of-state employee as described above would remain subject to Texas motor fuels tax, sales or use tax, hotel occupancy tax, motor vehicle rental tax, and other transaction taxes and fees imposed in state, unless the entity or employee is otherwise exempt from the tax or fee. (Ch. 559 (Sec. 112.006, Business & Commerce Code))

¶ 855   **Sales or Use Tax Credits**

• **Credit for taxes paid to another state**

Texas allows as a credit against Texas use tax any combined amounts of legally imposed sales and use taxes paid on the same property to another state or a political subdivision of another state, if such other state provides a similar credit for Texas taxpayers (Sec. 151.303(c); 34 TAC Sec. 3.338(b), 34 TAC Sec. 3.346(d)(5)).

Sales tax imposed by Texas will not be refunded because of a subsequent payment of use tax to another state (34 TAC Sec. 3.338(b)). However, Texas will refund or credit, to the extent of the payment, use tax that is subsequently paid to another state if the other state's use tax was imposed because the item was used in that state prior to its use in Texas.

¶855   Texas

Credit against Texas use tax will not be allowed for sales tax paid to another state if the tax was not legally due and payable to that state (34 TAC Sec. 3.338(b)). A credit against Texas use tax will not be allowed for any gross receipts tax, imposed on retailers in another state, that is not customarily separated from the sales price and is not passed on directly to customers as tax.

• Credit for tax paid on property subsequently resold

A seller who acquires tangible personal property for storage or use, pays the tax, and subsequently sells, leases, or rents the item in the regular course of business before making a taxable use of the property may take a credit for the amount of tax paid to the supplier (Sec. 151.427(a); 34 TAC Sec. 3.338(c)). The seller must not have made any use of the item other than retaining, displaying, or demonstrating it while holding it for sale. If a credit is taken, the seller's supplier may not receive a credit or refund with respect to that sale (Sec. 151.427(b)).

The purchaser must have a receipt from a Texas retailer or other seller authorized to collect the Texas sales and use tax, reflecting the tax paid and the selling price of the item purchased (34 TAC Sec. 3.338(c)). A purchaser may claim a credit on a return for a later period or by filing an amended return.

• Other credits, refunds, and tax incentives

Enterprise projects: A seller may claim certain sales and use tax refunds for enterprise projects and businesses operating in enterprise zones (Sec. 151.429; 34 TAC Sec. 3.329(c)). An enterprise project is eligible for a refund of sales taxes paid on all taxable items purchased for use at the qualified business site related to the project or activity.

Bad debts: A seller may exclude from tax any amount entered in its books as a bad debt during the reporting period in which the underlying item was sold, leased or rented that is claimed as a deduction for federal income tax purposes during the same or subsequent reporting period (Sec. 151.426(a)). If the seller has paid taxes on an account that is later determined to be a bad debt and is actually charged off for federal income tax purposes, the seller is entitled to a credit or reimbursement of the corresponding portion of the taxes represented by the bad debt (Sec. 151.426(d)(1)).

Returns: A seller is entitled to a credit or reimbursement equal to the amount of sales tax refunded to a purchaser when the purchaser receives a full or partial refund of the sales price of a returned taxable item (Sec. 151.4261).

Providers of cable television, Internet access, or telecommunications services: A sales and use tax refund is available for the consumption of certain tangible personal property directly used and consumed by a provider during the provision of cable television distribution services, Internet access provision services or telecommunications services. (Sec. 151.3186). A provider is entitled to a tax refund for the sale, lease or rental or storage, use, or other consumption of tangible personal property if:

— the property is sold, leased or rented to or stored, used or consumed by a provider or a subsidiary of a provider; and

— the property is directly used or consumed by the provider or subsidiary in or during the distribution of cable television service, the provision of Internet access service, or the transmission, conveyance, routing or reception of telecommunications services.

The owner of property directly used or consumed in or during the provision, creation or production of a data processing service or information service is not eligible for a refund. The amount of a provider's refund for a calendar year is equal to:

— the amount of the tax paid by the provider or subsidiary during the calendar year on property eligible for a refund, if the total amount of tax paid by all providers and subsidiaries that are eligible for a refund is not more than $50 million for the calendar year; or

— a pro rata share of $50 million, if the total amount of tax paid by all providers and subsidiaries that are eligible for a refund is more than $50 million for the calendar year.

The refund is not available for local sales and use taxes. A "provider" is a provider of cable television service, Internet access service or telecommunications services. (Sec. 151.3186).

For additional information on this refund, see 34 TAC Sec. 3.345 and the comptroller's web page at **https://comptroller.texas.gov/taxes/sales/**.

¶ 856　　　　　　　　　Deficiency Assessments

If the Comptroller is not satisfied with a tax return or the amount of tax reported, he or she may recompute the tax due either from the report or from other information and issue a deficiency determination or assessment (Sec. 111.008(a); Sec. 151.501). If no return is filed, the Comptroller may compute the tax due using any information available (Sec. 151.503).

The Comptroller may estimate the receipts of a person subject to the sales tax; the total sales prices of taxable items sold, leased, or rented in Texas; and the total sales prices of items acquired for storage, use, or consumption, without the payment of use tax, for the period in which no report was filed.

If the Comptroller finds that a tax is insecure and specified statutory conditions are met, the Comptroller may require a taxpayer who is delinquent in the payment of the tax to provide security for the payment of the tax or to establish a tax escrow account at a bank or other financial institution (Sec. 111.012). If a taxpayer fails to furnish the security or establish a tax escrow account when required, the Comptroller may sue to enjoin the taxpayer from engaging in business.

¶ 857　　　　　　　　　Audit Procedures

The Comptroller or a representative may examine the books, records, papers, and equipment of any person who sells taxable items or who is liable for use tax, and may investigate the character of the taxpayer's business to verify the accuracy of a report or to determine the amount of tax required to be paid (Sec. 151.023).

Both sellers and purchasers may be audited and assessed relative to any transaction on which tax was due but has not been paid (34 TAC Sec. 3.282(g)) and both remain liable until the tax, penalty, and interest have been paid (Sec. 3.282(h)).

An audit may be conducted at any time during regular business hours at the discretion of the Comptroller or his authorized representative (34 TAC Sec. 3.282(a)). The auditor may examine all transactions in detail or employ sampling or projected audits to determine liability (34 TAC Sec. 3.282(b)). If the taxpayer's records are inadequate, the auditor will determine the best information that is available and base the audit report on that information (34 TAC Sec. 3.282(e)).

Sampling: The Comptroller is authorized to use sample auditing methods to determine tax liability (Sec. 111.0042). Sampling methods are appropriate if the records are so voluminous that a detailed audit is impractical, if the taxpayer's records are incomplete, or if the cost of a detailed audit would be unreasonable in relation to the benefits derived. The sample must reflect as nearly as possible the normal conditions under which the business was operated during the audit period. Before a sample technique may be used to establish a tax liability, the taxpayer must be given written notification of the sampling procedure to be used.

Resale and exemption certificates: Resale and exemption certificates should be available at the time of the audit (34 TAC Sec. 3.282(f)(1)). Certificates acquired after the audit begins are subject to independent confirmation before the deductions will be allowed. If a seller is not in possession of resale or exemption certificates within 60 days after the date on which the Comptroller gives written notice that certificates for particular periods or transactions are required, then any deductions claimed that require resale or exemption certificates will be disallowed (34 TAC Sec. 3.282(f)(2)). Certificates presented after the 60-day period will not be accepted.

Resale and exemption certificates are the only acceptable proof that taxable items are purchased for resale or qualify for exemption (34 TAC Sec. 3.282(f)(3)).

Managed self-audits: Taxpayers approved by the Comptroller may enter into an agreement to conduct their own managed audits of the taxpayer's business to determine the taxpayer's sales and use tax liability for specified transactions occurring during a set period of time (Sec. 151.0231). Penalties will be abated and interest may be waived on any amount identified to be due by the Comptroller's office when verifying the audit results. However, penalties and interest will still be imposed if there is fraud or willful evasion of tax involved or if the taxpayer does not remit to the Comptroller's office any amount of tax actually collected. In determining whether to authorize a taxpayer to conduct managed audits, the Comptroller may consider (1) the taxpayer's history of tax compliance, (2) the amount of time and resources the taxpayer has available to dedicate to the audit, (3) the extent and availability of the taxpayer's records, and (4) the taxpayer's ability to pay any expected liability.

¶ 858   Statute of Limitations

In general, the limitations period for assessing taxes is four years from the date the tax becomes due and payable (34 TAC Sec. 3.339(a)(1)). The deficiency notice must be served or mailed within four years of the last day of the calendar month following the close of the taxpayer's regular reporting period, or after the report is filed whichever is later (Sec. 151.507(a)).

However prior to the expiration of the limitations period, the Comptroller and the taxpayer may agree in writing to an extension. The extension applies only to the period specifically mentioned in the agreement (34 TAC Sec. 3.339(a)(2)). Assessment or refund requests pertaining to periods for which limitations have been extended must be made prior to the expiration date of the agreement.

The statute of limitations does not apply to any period during which a taxpayer's timely filed claim for refund is pending (34 TAC Sec. 3.339(a)(4)).

¶ 859   Application for Refund

Any person may request a refund for any tax overpayment within four years from the tax due date or six months after a deficiency determination becomes final, or six months after a determination would have become final had payment not been made before such final date (34 TAC Sec. 3.325(a)).

The time during which an administrative proceeding is pending before the Comptroller is not counted. Before the expiration of the limitations period, the Comptroller and the taxpayer may agree in writing to extend the period. Failure to file a claim within the limitation constitutes a waiver of any claim on the basis of the overpayment.

The refund request must be in writing, state the specific grounds upon which the claim is founded, and indicate the period for which the claimed overpayment was made (34 TAC Sec. 3.325(a)(4)).

*CAUTION:*Both the prior version of 34 TAC Sec. 3.325(a)(4) (refund request requirements) in effect from July 19, 2011, through January 6, 2013, as well as the current version of subsection (a)(4), in effect since January 7, 2013, were declared invalid because they impose additional burdens, conditions, and restrictions on tax refund claims in excess of specific provisions of the Texas sales tax refund statute (Sec. 111.104) and other tax statutes. (*Hegar v. Ryan, LLC,* Court of Appeals of Texas, Third District, Austin, No. 03-13-00400-CV, May 20, 2015, CCH TEXAS TAX REPORTS, ¶ 404-054).

Taxes, penalties, and interest that have been unlawfully or erroneously collected are first applied against any amount due from the taxpayer (Sec. 111.104). The excess is then refunded.

Procedures: Separate refund claim procedures are provided for (34 TAC Sec. 3.325):

(1) permitted sellers (sellers holding a Texas sales and use tax permit, including their assignees and successors),

(2) permitted purchasers (purchasers holding a Texas sales and use tax permit), and

(3) non-permitted purchasers.

Class actions: A claimant may not file a single refund claim on behalf of a class, and the Comptroller may not administer or grant a class action refund claim. Although there is authority to bring a class action suit for tax paid under protest in district court under Sec. 112.055, there is no such authority for the Comptroller to grant a refund directly to a class. The Legislature did not provide either a judicial or administrative remedy for class action lawsuits concerning refund claims (*Decision, Hearing No. 102,510,* Texas Comptroller of Public Accounts, March 1, 2010, CCH TEXAS TAX REPORTS, ¶ 403-660; see also *Assignees of Best Buy, Office Max, and CompUSA v. Combs,* Court of Appeals of Texas, Third District, Austin, No. 03-10-00648-CV, February 22, 2013, CCH TEXAS TAX REPORTS, ¶ 403-882).

Incentive refunds: For information on refunds or credits for incentive purposes, see ¶ 855.

¶ 860   **UTAH**

¶ 861   Scope of Tax

Source.—Statutory references are to Title 59, Chapter 12, of the Utah Code Annotated, as amended to date. Details are reported in the CCH UTAH TAX REPORTS starting at ¶ 60-000.

The sales and use tax is a general sales tax applicable to all retail sales of tangible personal property that are not specifically excluded or exempted and specified services (Sec. 59-12-103(1)). The tax is levied on the transaction itself and not on the articles or services sold (Rule R865-19S-2). The tax is based upon the amount paid or charged for the articles or services (Sec. 59-12-103(1)).

The Utah sales tax applies to all retail sales of nonexempt tangible personal property and the sale of specified services within Utah (Sec. 59-12-103(1)). The use tax applies to property purchased outside Utah and used in Utah; it is a complementary tax that applies when the Utah sales tax does not (Rule R865-19S-1, Rule R865-21U-2). The sales and use tax is imposed in addition to other taxes and licenses provided for by law (Sec. 59-12-116).

Transient room tax: Effective January 1, 2018, Utah will impose a separate state transient room tax of 0.32% on transactions involving tourist home, hotel, motel, or trailer court accommodations and services that are regularly rented for less than 30 consecutive days (Sec. 59-28-101 *et seq.*). The Tax Commission will administer, collect, and enforce the tax. The tax will be repealed on January 1, 2023 (S.B. 264, Laws 2017).

Digital products: Products that are transferred electronically expressly fall outside the definition of "tangible personal property" (Sec. 59-12-102(94)). Tax applies to the sale of products transferred electronically, and to the repair or renovation of such products, if the product, repair, or renovation would be subject to tax if the product was transferred in a way other than electronically, regardless of whether the sale grants a right of permanent or nonpermanent use. A product transferred electronically or a repair or renovation of a "product transferred electronically" is taxable. A "product transferred electronically" means a product that is transferred electronically that would be subject to tax if that product were transferred in a manner other than electronically, but does not include an ancillary service, computer software or a telecommunications service. (Sec. 59-12-102(82)).

"Repairs or renovation of tangible personal property" means attaching tangible personal property or a product transferred electronically to other tangible personal property if the attachment of tangible personal property or a product transferred electronically to other tangible personal property is made in conjunction with a repair or replacement of tangible personal property or a product transferred electronically (Sec. 59-12-102(92)). "Repairs or renovation of tangible personal property" does not include attaching prewritten computer software to other tangible personal property if the other tangible personal property to which the prewritten computer software is attached is not permanently attached to real property (Sec. 59-12-102(92)(b)).

Cloud-based computing: The Utah State Tax Commission has issued a private letter ruling advising that a company's provision of cloud-based services was subject to sales and use tax because the services involved customers' use of the company's prewritten computer software. Utah does not have an exemption for electronically delivered software. Further, under statute, an electronically delivered product cannot include software.

The commission also ruled that purchases of the services occurred in Utah because sales are made in Utah when the customers are located in Utah. Finally, the company's purchases of hardware and software needed to provide the cloud-based services were nontaxable only because such purchases were made outside of Utah. If the purchases were made inside Utah, they would be taxable but might qualify for the resale exemption. The commission also noted that the cloud-based services are not taxable as telecommunications services. (*Private Letter Ruling*, Opinion No. 13-003, Utah State Tax Commission, December 4, 2013, CCH Utah Tax Reports, ¶ 400-889).

Prepaid calling cards: Sales and use tax applies to a telecommunications service, including a prepaid calling service, other than a mobile telecommunications service, that originates and terminates within Utah (Sec. 59-12-103). As a result, a prepaid telecommunications service sold as a prepaid calling card is taxable for in-state calls. If a card can only be used for international or interstate calls, the card can be sold exempt from tax. See *Publication 62,* Utah State Tax Commission, June 2014, CCH Utah Tax Reports, ¶ 400-960.

• Services subject to tax

The sales tax on services is a limited tax imposed only on specific transactions. The following services are subject to sales and use tax: utilities, including gas, electricity, and telephone for residential and commercial use; meals; any amusement entertainment, recreation, exhibition, cultural or athletic activity for which admission or user fees are paid; use of amusement devices; use of coin-operated car washes; repairs, renovations, or installation of tangible personal property or a product transferred electronicall; cleaning or washing of tangible personal property; lodging for less than 30 days; laundry and dry cleaning services, and escort services (Sec. 59-12-103(1), Rule R865-19S-78). Sexually explicit businesses are subject to a specific tax on certain transactions, including any services provided by the business (see ¶ 864).

Computer software maintenance contracts; repairs and renovations: The purchase of an optional computer software maintenance contract that consists of taxable and nontaxable products that are not separately itemized on an invoice or similar billing document is a bundled transaction that is 40% taxable and 60% nontaxable. A "computer software maintenance contract" is a contract that obligates a seller of computer software to provide a customer with (1) future updates or upgrades to computer software, (2) support services with respect to computer software, or (3) a combination of both. An "optional computer software maintenance contract" is a computer software maintenance contract that a customer is not obligated to purchase as a condition to the retail sale of the computer software. (Sec. 59-12-103; see also *Publication 64,* Utah State Tax Commission, May 2012, CCH Utah Tax Reports, ¶ 400-774).

Taxable repairs or renovations of tangible personal property include the detaching of property or a product transferred electronically from other property if (Sec. 59-12-102):

— the property from which the tangible personal property or product transferred electronically is detached is not permanently attached to real property; and

— detachment of tangible personal property or a product transferred electronically from other property is made in conjunction with a repair or replacement of property or a product transferred electronically.

"Repairs or renovations of tangible personal property" does not include detaching prewritten computer software from other property if the other property is not permanently attached to real property (Sec. 59-12-102(95)).

Cable and satellite services: Amounts paid or charged for cable and satellite television services are subject to a specific state tax (Sec. 59-26-103). See ¶ 864 for the rate. See ¶ 870 for a tax credit.

Professional Employer Organization (PEO): Under the Professional Employer Organization Licensing Act (Sec. 31A-40-101 *et seq.*), effective May 5, 2008, a covered employee whose service is subject to sales or use tax is considered the client's employee for purposes of imposing and collecting sales or use tax on the services that the covered employee performs. The Act may not be interpreted to relieve a client of a sales or use tax liability (Sec. 31A-40-207).

- **Use tax**

The use tax is an excise tax on the storage, use, or other consumption of tangible personal property in Utah on which no sales tax was paid (Sec. 59-12-103(1)(l), Rule R865-21U-1). In addition, the use tax also applies to repair, renovation, and installation services, wherever performed, if the property on which the services are performed is stored, used, or consumed in Utah after the services are rendered (Rule R865-21U-1). The primary purpose of the use tax is to protect Utah merchants from discrimination arising from the state's inability to impose its sales tax on sales made to its residents in interstate commerce or by merchants in other states.

The use tax does not apply to property that is brought into Utah for some purpose other than storage, use, or consumption in Utah (Rule R865-21U-12). For example, steel purchased out of state and brought into Utah for fabrication would be exempt, provided the steel was purchased for intended use in an out-of-state contract and retained its identity through the fabrication process and eventually was used in the intended contract.

- **Incidence of sales and use tax**

The purchaser is liable for paying the sales tax (Sec. 59-12-103(1), Rule R865-19S-2), but vendors are responsible for collecting the tax and remitting it to the state (Sec. 59-12-107(4), Sec. 59-12-107(2), Rule R865-19S-6, Rule R865-19S-4).

The person "storing, using, or consuming" tangible personal property within the state is liable for the use tax (Sec. 59-12-107(3), Rule R865-21U-6). Retailers are responsible for collecting the use tax from consumers (Rule R865-21U-3). However, if a retailer does not have a certificate of registration, the purchaser must pay the Tax Commission directly (Rule R865-21U-6).

Sales and use tax is imposed on the purchaser for amounts paid to any telephone service provider (Sec. 59-12-102, Sec. 59-12-103).

Drop shipments: When all parties are located in Utah, the retailer furnishes a resale certificate to the primary seller, rendering the first sale a nontaxable transaction (Sec. 59-12-107(7)). The retailer then collects sales tax on behalf of the state on the secondary sale to its customer (Sec. 59-12-103). However, different considerations arise when one or more of the parties are not within the state.

Utah exempts a primary sale to an out-of-state retailer by a Utah manufacturer who drop ships the product to the retailer's customer if the retailer furnishes a resale exemption from its state (Sec. 59-12-107(7)). The secondary sale by the retailer to its Utah customer is an exempt interstate sale when the retailer lacks any Utah nexus. When that is the case, the customer is subject to the use tax because no sales tax has been paid (Rule R865-19S-1; Rule R865-21U-16).

Nexus standards: Out-of-state vendors who regularly solicit orders in Utah are required to pay or collect and remit Utah sales and use tax unless the vendor's only activity in Utah is (1) advertising or (2) solicitation by direct mail, electronic mail, the Internet, telephone, or any other similar means (Sec. 59-12-107(1)(a)).

- **Nexus**

The Utah Supreme Court has held that nexus can be determined by looking at more than only the taxed activity, in that the activity the state seeks to tax is not the sole connection that can be considered to determine whether there is "substantial nexus". (*Questar Pipeline Company v. Utah State Tax Commission*, Utah Supreme Court, 817 P.2d 316, August 1, 1991) The activity that creates nexus need not be the activity being taxed. (*Private Letter Ruling*, Opinion No. 08-006, Utah State Tax Commission, May 2009)

A vendor must collect the use tax if one of the following conditions exists (Sec. 59-12-107(1)):

— the vendor has or utilizes an office, distribution house, sales house, warehouse, service enterprise, or other place of business in the state;

— the vendor maintains a stock of goods in the state;

— the vendor regularly solicits sales of tangible personal property in Utah, unless the vendor's only activity in Utah is advertising or solicitation by direct mail, electronic mail, the Internet, telephone, or any other similar means;

— the vendor regularly engages in the delivery of property in the state other than by common carrier or U.S. mail; or

— the vendor regularly engages in any activity directly related to the leasing or servicing of property located within the state.

Affiliate nexus: Utah requires certain out-of-state sellers to collect and remit Utah sales and use tax. A seller is considered to be engaged in the business of selling tangible personal property, a service, or a product transferred electronically for use in Utah, and thus required to pay or collect and remit taxes, if (Sec. 59-12-107(2)(b)):

— the seller holds a substantial ownership interest in, or is owned in whole or in substantial part by, a related seller; and

— the seller sells the same or a substantially similar line of products as the related seller and does so under the same or a substantially similar business name; or

— the place of business of the related seller or an in-state employee of the related seller is used to advertise, promote or facilitate sales by the seller to the purchaser.

A "substantial ownership interest" is an ownership interest in a business entity if that ownership interest is greater than the degree of ownership of equity interest specified in 15 U.S.C. Sec. 78p, with respect to a person other than a director or an officer (Sec. 59-12-107(1)(c)). "Ownership" is direct or indirect ownership through a parent, subsidiary, or affiliate (Sec. 59-12-107(1)(a)). A "related seller" is a seller that (Sec. 59-12-107(1)(b)):

(1) meets one or more criteria requiring the seller to collect and remit sales and use tax; and

(2) delivers tangible personal property, a service, or a product transferred electronically that is sold by a seller that does not meet the same criteria.

The criteria are that the seller has or utilizes in Utah an office, a distribution house, a sales house, a warehouse, a service enterprise or a similar place of business.

If the U.S. Supreme Court or Congress issues a decision or passes legislation, respectively, authorizing a state to require certain sellers to collect a sales tax that Utah does not already require a seller to collect, including the currently enacted affiliated nexus seller requirement, sellers shall collect and remit the authorized tax to Utah.

A seller that is not required to collect tax under this requirement can voluntarily collect and remit the tax.

For additional information on nexus, see *Publication 37*, Utah State Tax Commission, March 2016, CCH Utah Tax Reports, ¶ 401-158.

Out-of-state businesses doing disaster or emergency work in Utah: An out-of-state business temporarily working or providing services in Utah related to a declared disaster or emergency is not considered to have established a level of presence that would subject that business to any state licensing or registration requirements, provided that the out-of-state business is in substantial compliance with all applicable regulatory and licensing requirements in its state of domicile. (Sec. 53-12a-1202 *et seq.*).

A sales and use tax exemption is also available (¶ 863), as well as income and property tax provisions for such businesses and their employees.

- **Streamlined Act status**

Utah is a full member of the Streamlined Sales and Use Tax governing board.

Utah previously enacted SSUTA conformity legislation, then repealed most of the provisions, including the controversial destination-based sourcing changes (S.B. 233, Laws 2006). Recent conformity legislation now addresses many areas, including the sourcing of sales and use transactions, the collection, remittance, and payment of tax on direct mail (H.B. 206, Laws 2008; S.B. 73, Laws 2010; H.B. 35, Laws 2011).

Utah's taxability matrix is located at **http://tax.utah.gov/sales/sst** and on the website of the Streamlined Sales Tax Project at **http://www.streamlinedsalestax.org**.

¶ 862   Tax Base

The sales tax computation in the sales and use tax return is based on total nonexempt cash and charge sales. The use tax computation is based on the total amount of cash and charge sales or purchases for storage, use, or other consumption in Utah (Sec. 59-12-107(10)).

Tax is levied on the amount paid or charged (Sec. 59-12-103(1)). "Purchase price" means the amount charged for tangible personal property or taxable services, excluding cash discounts taken or any excise tax imposed on the purchase price by the federal government (Sec. 59-12-102(15)). "Sales price" may be used interchangeably with "purchase price" (Rule R865-19S-30).

In conformity with the Streamlined Sales and Use Tax Agreement, the definitions of "purchase price" and "sales price" include the seller's cost of a product transferred electronically (Sec. 59-12-102(69)). The terms also include the consideration a seller receives from a person other than the purchaser if the seller actually receives consideration from a person other than the purchaser, and if the consideration is directly related to a discount or price reduction on the sale, the seller is obligated to pass the discount or reduction on to the purchaser, the consideration attributable to the sale is fixed and determined by the seller at the time of the sale to the purchaser, and the purchaser presents a certificate, coupon, or other documentation to the seller to claim a price reduction or discount. "Purchase price" and "sales price" exclude, if separately stated on an invoice, bill of sale, or similar document for the purchaser, a manufacturer rebate on a motor vehicle, a tax or fee legally imposed directly on the consumer, or a carrying charge, financing charge, or interest charge from credit extended on the sale of tangible personal property or services.

In-store discount coupons, trade-ins, and separately stated delivery charges and finance charges are generally excluded from the tax base.

Bundled transactions: A "bundled transaction" is defined as the sale of two or more items of tangible personal property, products, or services if the property, products, or services are distinct, identifiable, and sold for one nonitemized price (Sec. 59-12-102(15)). The term does not include the sale of real property, services to real property, or the retail sale of tangible personal property and services if the property is essential to the use of the service, is provided exclusively in connection with the service, and if the service is the true object of the transaction. "Bundled transaction" does not include the retail sale of certain combinations of two services, or items having a *de minimis* price. The term also does not include retail sales of exempt items and taxable tangible personal property if the sale includes food and food ingredients, drugs, durable medical equipment, mobility enhancing equipment, over-the-counter drugs, prosthetic devices, or medical supplies, and if the seller's purchase price of the taxable property comprises 50% or less of the seller's total purchase or sales price.

Mobile wireless: A private letter ruling issued by the Utah State Tax Commission discusses the Utah sales tax treatment of charges by wireless telephone service providers for plans that offer Internet access services which are bundled with voice services or are sold separately. Intrastate telecommunications services and ancillary services associated with intrastate telecommunications services are taxable when they are sold separately, but interstate telecommunications services and ancillary services associated with interstate telecommunications services are not. Telecommunications services include mobile wireless services, such as unlimited long distance, air time, text messaging and picture messaging. Ancillary services include call waiting and caller ID services. Bundled transactions that include taxable and nontaxable services are generally subject to tax. Nontaxable services, such as data (Internet access) services, sold in a bundled transaction are not subject to tax if the seller can identify from the books and records it keeps in its regular course of business the value of the nontaxable services. (*Private Letter Ruling, Opinion No. 10-002,* Utah State Tax Commission, August 10, 2010, CCH UTAH TAX REPORTS, ¶ 400-687).

• **Sourcing rules**

The Streamlined Sales Tax (SST) Governing Board has amended the SST Agreement to allow states that meet specified requirements to become full members while continuing to source sales on an origin basis. Utah's sourcing provisions are in Sec. 59-12-211 through Sec. 59-12-215.

Sourcing certain software transactions: If a purchaser uses computer software and a copy of that software is not transferred to the purchaser, the location of the transaction is determined in accordance with existing rules for determining the location of a transaction. Further, if a purchaser uses computer software at more than one location, the location of the transaction is determined in accordance with rules issued by the Utah State Tax Commission. (Sec. 59-12-211(12)).

"Point of sale" means that for sellers with one or more fixed places of business, sales will continue to be sourced to the place of business where the sales occur, regardless of where the goods are delivered. For sellers whose place of business is not fixed (*e.g.,* vending machine operators, mobile tool companies), sales will continue to be sourced to where the sales take place. If a business sells merchandise that is shipped from outside Utah direct to a consumer in Utah, and if the seller has nexus with Utah, then the sale is sourced to the location of the purchaser. See *Publication 25,* Utah State Tax Commission, September 2015, CCH UTAH TAX REPORTS, ¶ 401-103.

Updated information can be obtained from the Tax Commission website at **www.tax.utah.gov**, or by calling the Technical Research Unit at **(801) 297-7705** or **1-800-662-4335**, ext. 7705.

¶ 863   List of Exemptions, Exceptions, and Exclusions

Unless otherwise indicated, the statutory exemptions, exceptions, and exclusions listed below apply to both sales and use taxes. Items that are excluded from the sales or use tax base are treated at ¶ 862, "Tax Base."

Exemption certificates: For purposes of accepting exemption certificates, a seller or certified service provider will not be liable to collect tax unless the seller or certified service provider knew or had reason to know at the time the purchaser provided an exemption certificate that the information related to the exemption claimed was materially false or that the seller or certified service provider otherwise knowingly participated in an activity intended to purposefully evade the tax due on the transaction. (Sec. 59-12-106(e)).

• **Sales and use tax exemptions, exceptions, and exclusions**

Access charges to a database	Sec. 59-12-102(78)
Admissions to college athletic events	Sec. 59-12-104(46)
Agricultural sprays and insecticides	Sec. 59-12-104(19)
Agriculture: crops sold by producer during harvest	Sec. 59-12-104(21)

Agriculture: farm machinery, equipment, parts, and supplies	Sec. 59-12-104(18)
Agriculture: finished products exchanged for raw materials	Rule R865-19S-40
Agriculture: hay	Sec. 59-12-104(20)
Aircraft manufactured in Utah	Sec. 59-12-104(31)
Aircraft parts and equipment sold by aircraft manufacturer for installation in an aircraft	Sec. 59-12-104(5)
Aircraft; property sold in repair, maintenance, overhaul of certain types	Sec. 59-12-104(69)
Airlines, commercial; purchases of certain property for sale to passengers	Sec. 59-12-104(4)(b)
Airports, construction materials purchased for	Sec. 59-12-104(69), (70)
Amusement device—coin-operated	Sec. 59-12-104(42)
Amusement equipment	Sec. 59-12-104(76)
Annual membership dues to a private organization	Sec. 59-12-102(1)(b)
Athletic events, college	Sec. 59-12-104(46)
Boat, trailer, and outboard motor sales for export	Sec. 59-12-104(31)
Broadcasting	Sec. 59-12-104(6)
Coins, currency, and other items with a gold, silver, or platinum content of at least 80%.	Sec. 59-12-104(52), (53) Sec. 59-1-1503(2)
Commercials, audio program tapes or records, and video tapes sold to exhibitors, distributors, or broadcasters	Sec. 59-12-104(6)
Disasters or emergencies: purchases or leases of property by an out-of-state business temporarily working or providing services related to a declared disaster or emergency	Sec. 59-12-104(81)
Drilling equipment manufacturers' machinery, equipment, materials and replacement parts	Sec. 59-12-104(83)
Dry-cleaning machine—coin-operated	Sec. 59-12-104(7)
Electricity produced from a new alternative energy source	Sec. 10-1-304(4), Sec. 59-12-104(49)
Energy-related machinery and equipment (exp. 6/30/2019)	Sec. 59-12-102(14)(b), (49), (58), (59)
Enterprise zones and similar tax incentives	Sec. 63-38f-1304
Even exchanges of tangible personal property	Sec. 59-12-104(17)
Financial services electronic payment equipment	Sec. 59-12-102(41), (79)
Farm machinery, equipment, parts, and supplies	Sec. 59-12-104(18)
Food and food ingredients	Sec. 59-12-102(25), Sec. 59-12-104(3), (12), (21)
Food and drinks for in-flight consumption on commercial airlines . . .	Sec. 59-12-104(4)
Food: meals served by certain institutions	Sec. 59-12-104(12)
Food purchased with food stamps or purchased under the USDA's WIC program	Sec. 59-12-104(21), (28)
Food sold by schools	Sec. 59-12-102(32)
Fuel: aviation fuel, motor fuel, and special fuel subject to motor fuel excise taxes	Sec. 59-12-104(1)

Pollution control: property, materials, or services used in certain facilities	Sec. 19-2-124, Sec. 59-12-104(11)
Prescription drugs, equipment	Sec. 59-12-104(10), (36)
Previously taxed property	Sec. 59-12-104(26)
Property purchased or stored for resale, either in its original form or as part of a manufactured product	Sec. 59-12-104(23), (25)
Prosthetic devices	Sec. 59-12-104(55)
Publications sold by government entities	Sec. 59-12-104(41)
Real property and improvements to real property	Sec. 59-12-102(22)
Religious or charitable institutions' sales or purchases in the conduct of regular activities	Sec. 59-12-104(8), Sec. 59-12-104.1
Resales: property purchased for resale or stored in the state for resale	Sec. 59-12-104(23), Sec. 59-12-104(25)
Research and development: property used in coal, oil shale, tar sands technology	Sec. 59-12-104(68)
Intracompany sales of restaurant equipment	Sec. 59-12-104(54) [75]
Sale-leaseback transactions	Sec. 59-12-104(54)
Sales of tangible personal property to persons within state to be shipped out of state	Sec. 59-12-104(9), (30), (31), (61)
Sales relating to schools and fundraising sales	Sec. 59-12-104(35)
Scrap recyclers	Sec. 59-12-102(14)
Semiconductor materials and repair parts	Sec. 59-12-104(46)
Senior citizen centers	Sec. 59-12-104(45)
Ski resorts: electricity used to operate passenger ropeways	Sec. 59-12-104(37)
Ski resorts: passenger ropeways	Sec. 59-12-104(38)
Ski resorts: snowmaking and grooming equipment and repair parts .	Sec. 59-12-104(38)
Sprays and insecticides	Sec. 59-12-104(19)
Tangible personal property used in farming operations	Sec. 59-12-104(18)
Telecommunications equipment	Sec. 59-12-104(64)
Telephone and telegraph services used in compounding taxable telephone and telegraph services	Sec. 59-12-104(28)
Telephone service purchased by companies to provide telephone services to customers	Sec. 59-12-104(32)
Telephone service sales charged to prepaid telephone calling card . .	Sec. 59-12-104(43)
Textbooks for college students sold by college bookstores	Sec. 59-12-104(71)
Trade-in of a vehicle, and trade-in of personal property as payment for a purchase	Sec. 59-12-104(17)
United States government-owned tooling and equipment	Sec. 59-12-104(15)
Vehicle registered for temporary sports event	Sec. 59-12-104(48)
Vehicle exterior cleaning and washing	Sec. 59-12-104[86]
Vehicles sold or leased to carriers	Sec. 59-12-104(33)
Vending machine sales	Sec. 59-12-104(3)
Water in pipes, conduits, and reservoirs	Sec. 59-12-104 (51)
Web search portal, machinery, equipment, and parts	Sec. 59-12-104 (52)

The general sales and use tax rate is 4.7% (Sec. 59-12-103(2)). The composite tax rate for sales of food and food ingredients is 3% statewide. The composite rate includes the state rate of 1.75%, the local option rate of 1%, and the county option rate of 0.25%. In addition, sales for residential use of gas, electricity, heat, coal, fuel oil, or other fuels are taxed at the state rate of 2% plus any applicable local or public transit taxes.

The general sales and use tax rate applies to all transactions other than food and food ingredients, the residential use of utility services, and transactions by certain sexually explicit businesses, as discussed below. Commercial use of utility services is subject to the general tax rate, but industrial use is exempt (Sec. 59-12-103(3); Sec. 59-12-104(39)).

Non-nexus sellers: Sales of nonfood items shipped into the state by sales and use tax filers who do not have a direct or representational presence within Utah ("non-nexus" sellers) are taxed at the combined state and local sales tax rate for the delivery location. (See *Tax Bulletin 12-08,* Utah State Tax Commission, December 15, 2008, CCH Utah Tax Reports, ¶ 400-589).

Supplemental state tax: The state may impose a tax under the Supplemental State Sales and Use Tax Act within a city, town, or the unincorporated area of a county of the first or second class if, on January 1, 2008, there was a public transit district within any part of that county. The state cannot impose this tax in a county of the first or second class if within all of the cities, towns, and the unincorporated area of the county, a 0.30% public transit tax, tax for highways or to fund a system for a public transit system, or tax under Sec. 59-12-1503, Utah Code Ann., is imposed.

Collection discount: See ¶ 870.

• **Food and food ingredients**

The sales and use tax rate on food and food ingredients is 1.75% (Sec. 59-12-103(2)(b)(iii)). Food and food ingredients are subject to local taxes imposed by a county, city, or town.

Bundled transactions: In a bundled transaction involving a sale price attributable to both food and food ingredients and another item of tangible personal property, the entire transaction is taxed at the general state rate plus the applicable local tax rate. Furthermore, food, food ingredients, and prepared food sold at restaurants are subject to the general state rate plus the applicable local tax rate, while such items sold at a location that is not a restaurant are taxed at the 1.75% state rate plus the applicable local tax rate (Sec. 59-12-103(2)(f)).

• **Cable and satellite services**

Amounts paid or charged for cable and satellite television services are subject to a state tax at the rate of 6.25% (Sec. 59-26-103).

• **Sexually explicit businesses**

A person engaged in a sexually explicit business at which nude or partially nude individuals perform any service for the business is liable for a Utah tax of 10% of the amounts charged for the following transactions: an admission fee; a user fee; a retail sale of tangible personal property; the sale of food and beverages; and any services provided by the business (Sec. 59-26-103, Sec. 59-26-104, Sec. 59-26-106).

The tax is also imposed on a person who provides escort services to others at the rate of 10% of the amount charged for providing such services.

The Utah Supreme Court held that the statute imposing the Sexually Explicit Business and Escort Service Tax is a content-neutral law that imposes only incidental burdens on some expression, but is unreasonably vague with respect to the imposition of the tax on escort service providers. (*Bushco v. Utah State Tax Commission*, Utah Supreme Court, No. 20070559, November 20, 2009, CCH UTAH TAX REPORTS, ¶ 400-640).

- **Transient room tax**

Beginning January 1, 2018, Utah imposes a state transient room tax of 0.32% on transactions involving tourist home, hotel, motel, or trailer court accommodations and services that are regularly rented for less than 30 consecutive days (Sec. 59-28-103).

¶ 865   Local Taxes

All 29 of Utah's counties have imposed the local sales and use tax at the rate of 1.0%, so it is collected throughout the state. If a city imposes the tax, it receives revenue from the tax on sales made in that city. If no city tax is imposed, the county collects the tax on sales made in the city. (Sec. 59-12-204, Utah Code Ann.).

Metro townships in Utah may impose local sales and use taxes (Sec. 59-12-203). Effective January 1, 2017, the Utah State Tax Commission must treat metro townships that impose sales and use taxes the same as it treat cities (Sec. 59-12-203). Previously, the law stated that a metro township that imposes sales and use tax must meet the same requirements that a city must meet.

Generally, the maximum local sales and use tax rate is 1% (Sec. 59-12-205, Sec. 59-12-204). However, the rate is higher in certain counties and cities that impose one or more of the following additional taxes: a transient room tax (Sec. 59-12-352, Sec. 59-12-603(1)(b), Sec. 59-12-1301); a motor vehicle rental tax (Sec. 59-12-603(1)(b)); a short term leasing tax (Sec. 59-12-901); a restaurant tax (Sec. 59-12-603(1)(b)); a recreational and zoo tax (Sec. 59-12-703), a public transit tax (Sec. 59-12-501; 59-12-1903), and a resort community tax (Sec. 59-12-401).

The Military Installation Development Authority is authorized to impose certain taxes within a project area described in a project area plan adopted by the Authority under the Military Installation Development Authority Act (Sec 10-1-304(1)(b); Sec. 10-1-403(1)(a)(ii); Sec. 59-12-352(1)(b)). The taxes imposed include a municipal energy sales and use tax, a municipal telecommunications license tax, a transient room tax, and, effective March 2, 2010, a resort communities tax. A municipality cannot levy the taxes within any part of the municipality that is located within such a project area (Sec 10-1-304(5)(a); Sec. 10-1-403(6)(a); Sec. 59-12-352(5)(a)).

- **Telecommunications**

A municipality may levy a maximum 3.5% sales and use tax on a telecommunications service provider's gross receipts. The tax may be levied on intrastate telephone services and on intrastate mobile telecommunications services, only to the extent permitted by the federal Mobile Telecommunications Sourcing Act (discussed below). The tax is administered by the Utah State Tax Commission pursuant to an interlocal agreement between the municipality and the Commission (Sec. 10-1-403, Sec. 10-1-404, Sec. 10-1-405). See also *Publication 62,* Utah State Tax Commission, June 2014, CCH UTAH TAX REPORTS, ¶ 400-960.

Mobile telecommunications: Utah conforms to the federal Mobile Telecommunications Sourcing Act (P.L. 106-252; 4 U.S.C. Secs. 116-126) (Sec. 59-12-102(17), Sec. 59-12-103(1)(b)(ii)(C), Sec. 59-12-207(5)). Under the Act, charges for mobile telecommunications services are taxable only in the state and locality encompassing the street address where the customer resides or maintains its primary business address. Any other state or locality is prohibited from taxing the services, regardless of where the services originate, terminate, or pass through. These provisions do not apply to prepaid telephone calling services or air-ground service.

Limitation on voluntary collections: If a vendor voluntarily chooses to collect and remit use tax (see ¶ 861), the maximum amount of tax to be collected is equal to the usual state rate, plus the sum of (1) the lowest local sales and use tax rate imposed by a Utah county, city, or town under (Sec. 59-12-204), but only if all Utah counties, cities, and towns impose the tax; (2) the lowest local sales and use tax rate imposed by a Utah county, city, or town under (Sec. 59-12-205), but only if all Utah counties, cities, and towns impose the tax; and (3) the Utah county option sales tax, but only if all Utah counties impose the tax (Sec. 59-12-103). All 29 Utah counties impose the 1% sales and use tax under (Sec. 59-12-205), but only 27 of the 29 counties impose the ¼% county option sales tax. However, the state will impose a sales and use tax of 0.25% on taxable transactions in counties that have not enacted a county option sales tax (Sec. 59-12-1802(1)).

• Local sales tax rate schedules and tax rate lookup

Local tax rate schedules and access to an online sales tax rate tool, which allows taxpayers to look up local sales tax rates and jurisdiction codes by address or zip code, are available at **http://tax.utah.gov/sales/rates**. Taxpayers can also use the tool to download point of delivery sales tax rate tables and Streamlined Sales and Use Tax (SST) rate and boundary tables. In addition, the tool will calculate the amount of taxes due on a transaction. The tool should be used only for determining sales tax rates for delivery locations.

¶ 866   Bracket Schedule

The sales and use tax is computed by rounding up to the next cent whenever the third decimal place of the tax liability is greater than four. Taxpayers may compute the tax due on an item basis or invoice basis (Rule R865-19S-117).

Tax rate schedules are available at **http://tax.utah.gov/sales/cards**.

¶ 867   Returns, Payments, and Due Dates

A person responsible for collecting the sales or use tax must file a sales and use tax return regardless of whether any tax is due (Rule R865-19S-12). Most taxpayers must file on a quarterly basis, while certain taxpayers are required to file monthly and others are allowed to file annually.

Taxes are due and payable to the Tax Commission without assessment or notice at the time fixed for filing returns (Rule R865-19S-14). The amount that must be remitted is the greater of the actual tax collections for the reporting period or the amount computed at the rates imposed by law against the total taxable sales for that period (Rule R865-19S-16).

• Due dates for returns

For most taxpayers, sales and use tax returns, accompanied by the tax due, are filed with the Tax Commission on a quarterly basis; the returns must be filed on or before the last day of the month following a calendar quarter (Sec. 59-12-107(4), Rule R865-19S-12).

Annual filing: New businesses that expect annual sales tax collections of less than $1,000 are assigned an annual filing status (Rule R865-19S-12). In addition, a business currently assigned a quarterly filing status may be changed by the Tax Commission to annual filing status provided the business is in good standing and reported less than $1,000 in tax for the preceding calendar year. Annual returns are due on January 31 following the calendar year end. The Tax Commission may revoke the annual filing status of a business if its sales tax collections exceed $1,000 or as a result of a delinquent payment history.

Monthly filing: A taxpayer whose state and local sales and use tax liability was $50,000 or more for the previous year must file sales and use tax returns on a monthly basis (Sec. 59-12-108). The return for each month must be filed on or before the last day of the following month and must be accompanied by the state, local, and public transit sales and use taxes that are required to be collected or paid for the period covered by the return.

The Tax Commission will provide advance notification on a yearly basis to vendors who meet the $50,000 threshold; however, a vendor who meets the threshold but does not receive such notification is not excused from timely monthly filing (Rule R865-19S-86). Vendors who are not required to file monthly may voluntarily do so by contacting the Commission not less than 30 days prior to the beginning of a new fiscal year (Rule R865-19S-86). The election to file on a monthly basis is effective for the immediate fiscal year thereafter unless the vendor notifies the Tax Commission in writing prior to the beginning of a fiscal year that the vendor no longer elects to file monthly.

Monthly filers must also file and remit their waste tire fees and transient room, resort communities and tourism, recreation, cultural, and convention facilities taxes on a monthly basis.

Filing extensions: If the due date for a return falls on a Saturday, Sunday, or legal holiday, the return will be considered timely filed if received on the next business day (Rule R865-19S-12). For a return that is mailed, a legible cancellation mark or the date of registration of certified mail is considered to be the date the return is filed.

Consolidated payment dates for certain fees and taxes: The municipal energy sales and use tax, municipal telecommunications license tax, multi-channel video or audio tax, lubricating oil recycling fee, waste tire recycling fee, statewide emergency services telecommunications charge to fund the Poison Control Center, and additional emergency services telecommunications charge to fund statewide unified E-911 emergency services are payable as follows.

— monthly on or before the last day of the month immediately following the last day of the previous month if the person paying the tax, fee, or charge is required to file a monthly sales and use tax return with the commission or is not required to file a sales and use tax return; or

— quarterly on or before the last day of the month immediately following the last day of the previous quarter if the person paying the tax, fee, or charge is required to file a quarterly sales and use tax return.

Computation of tax for certain contractors: For a sale that includes the delivery or installation of tangible personal property at a location other than a seller's place of business, if the delivery or installation is separately stated on an invoice or receipt, a seller may compute the tax due on the sale by applying a ratio based on the amount the seller receives for that sale during each period for which the seller receives payment for the sale. To compute taxes using the ratio, the seller must be a qualifying purchaser. A qualifying purchaser is a purchaser who is required to remit taxes but is not required to remit them monthly and who converts tangible personal property into real property. A qualifying purchaser can remit the taxes due on property for which it claims certain exemptions based on the period in which the qualifying purchaser receives payment for the conversion of the tangible personal property into real property. The sales tax as computed on the return is based on the total nonexempt sales made during the period for which the return is filed, including both cash and charge sales. To determine the amount of tax to remit, a qualifying purchaser will apply a ratio to the total amount of tax due on the qualifying purchaser's purchase of tangible personal property that was converted into real property. The numerator of the ratio is the payment received in the period for the qualifying purchaser's sale of the tangible personal property that was converted into real property. The denominator is the entire sales price for the qualifying purchaser's sale of the tangible personal property that was converted into real property. (Sec. 59-12-107(9)).

A qualifying purchaser may deduct from the total amount of taxes due the amount of tax it paid on its purchase of tangible personal property converted into real property to the extent that (1) tax was remitted using the ratio method described above; (2) the qualifying purchaser's sale of that tangible personal property converted into real property later becomes bad debt; and (3) the books and records that the qualifying purchaser keeps in the qualifying purchaser's regular course of business identify by reasonable and verifiable standards that the tangible personal property was converted into real property. (Sec. 59-12-107)

Collection allowances: A seller generally may retain each month 1% of any amounts the seller is required to remit to the commission (Sec. 59-12-108(2)(d)). A seller that is not required to collect and remit sales and use tax, such as a remote seller, but that voluntarily collects and remits the tax, may retain a collection allowance of 18% (Sec. 59-12-108(5)(a)).

Sellers collecting the transient room tax may retain, as a commission, 6% of the amount the seller would otherwise remit (Sec. 59-28-104(3)).

• Bad debts

Sellers may claim a deduction or refund for bad debts (Sec. 59-12-107(8)). "Bad debt" is as defined in IRC Sec. 166, except it does not include: (1) an amount included in the purchase price of tangible personal property or a service that is either exempt or not subject to sales or use tax; (2) a financing charge; (3) interest; (4) a state or local sales or use tax on the purchase price of tangible personal property or a service; (5) an uncollectible amount on tangible personal property that is subject to a state or local sales or use tax and that remains in the possession of a seller until the full purchase price is paid; (6) an expense incurred in attempting to collect any debt; or (7) an amount that a seller does not collect on repossessed property.

A seller's certified service provider may make a deduction or claim a refund for bad debt on behalf of the seller if the certified service provider credits or refunds the full amount of the bad debt deduction or refund to the seller (Sec. 59-12-107(8)). A bad debt may be allocated among the states that are members of the Agreement if a seller's books and records support that allocation.

• Electronic funds transfer

Any person whose state, local, and public transit sales and use tax liability was $96,000 or more for the previous year must remit monthly tax payments by electronic funds transfer (EFT) (Sec. 59-12-108). Upon approval of the Tax Commission, vendors may, in lieu of EFT, remit a cash equivalent such as cash, wire transfer, or cashier's check (Rule R865-19S-86). Approval is limited to those vendors that are able to establish that remittance by EFT would result in a hardship to the vendor's organization. The Tax Commission will provide advance notification on a yearly basis to vendors who meet the $96,000 threshold; however, a vendor who meets the threshold but does not receive such notification is not excused from timely remitting the tax by EFT. For additional information, see *Publication 43*, Utah State Tax Commission, July 2014, CCH UTAH TAX REPORTS, ¶ 400-951.

Taxpayers with tax liability of at least $50,000, but less than $96,000, may remit their monthly tax liability by any method permitted by the Commission. All vendors who remit taxes by EFT must file an EFT agreement with the Tax Commission, which will supply the agreement form.

• Internet filing

TaxExpress, the Utah State Tax Commission's online filing and payment system, is available for filing and paying sales and use taxes. Registration is required to use TaxExpress. All sales and use tax forms and schedules are available on the system. In addition, taxpayers can use the system for other tasks, such as checking balances, amending returns, or requesting payment plans. The system is located at **http:// taxexpress.utah.gov**.

¶867 Utah

• **Direct payment**

In conformity with the Streamlined Agreement (see below), Utah enacted direct pay authority. The Commission may issue a direct payment permit to a seller that obtains a license, makes aggregate purchases of at least $1.5 million for each of the three years prior to the year in which the Commission issues the seller the permit, has a record of timely payment of state and local sales and use taxes as determined by the Commission, and demonstrates to the Commission that the seller has the ability to determine the appropriate location of a transaction for each transaction for which the seller makes a purchase using the direct payment permit (Sec. 59-12-107.1). A direct payment permit may not be used in connection with the purchase of prepared food and food and food ingredients; the purchase of accommodations and services; amounts paid for admissions; the purchase of a motor vehicle, an aircraft, a watercraft, or a modular, manufactured, or mobile home; transactions for common carrier or telecommunications services; or sales of gas, electricity, heat, coal, fuel oil, or other fuels for commercial use.

The holder of a direct payment permit must present evidence of the direct payment permit to a seller at the time the holder of the direct payment permit makes a purchase using the direct payment permit (Sec. 59-12-107.1). The holder must also determine the appropriate location of each transaction for which the holder makes a purchase using the direct payment permit and determine the amount of any state and local sales and use tax due on each such transaction. The holder must report and remit to the Commission the appropriate sales and use tax at the same time and in the same manner as the holder of the direct payment permit reports and remits other sales and use taxes. The holder must maintain records that indicate the appropriate location of each transaction for which a purchase is made using the direct payment permit and provide information necessary to determine the amount of tax for each transaction.

A seller that is presented evidence of a direct payment permit at the time of a transaction may not collect state and local sales and use tax on the transaction, but must, for a period of three years from the date the seller files a return with the Commission reporting the transaction, retain records to verify that the transaction was made using a direct payment permit (Sec. 59-12-107.1).

• **Uniform Sales Tax Administration Act**

As discussed at ¶ 861, Utah repealed and then reinstated most of the provisions conforming state law to the provisions of the Streamlined Sales and Use Tax (SST) Agreement. For additional information on the uniform act, see **http://tax.utah.gov/sales/sst** and "Streamlined Sales Tax Project," listed in the Table of Contents.

¶ 868   Prepayment of Taxes

There are no provisions requiring prepayment of Utah sales and use taxes.

¶ 869   Vendor Registration

Any person required to collect the sales or use tax must obtain a sales tax license by filing an application with the Tax Commission, before engaging in business (Sec. 59-12-106(1)). The Commission must notify sales tax license applicants that (1) the purchaser of a business that has outstanding sales and use tax must withhold enough of the purchase price to cover the unpaid tax until the former owner produces either a receipt from the Commission showing that the tax has been paid or a certificate showing that no tax is due, and (2) failure to comply with this requirement makes the purchaser personally liable for payment of unpaid tax collected by the seller.

A separate license is needed for each place of business, but if the same person operates more than one place of business, a single application may be completed (Rule R865-19S-7). The license must be posted in a conspicuous place in the business.

A person who sells exempt tangible personal property or exempt services exclusively is not required to have a sales tax license (Sec. 59-12-106(1)).

A sales tax license holder who discontinues business is required to notify the Tax Commission immediately and return the sales tax license for cancellation (Rule R865-19S-25).

Out-of-state businesses doing disaster or emergency work in Utah: An out-of-state business temporarily working or providing services in Utah related to a declared disaster or emergency is not considered to have established a level of presence that would subject that business to any state licensing or registration requirements, provided that the out-of-state business is in substantial compliance with all applicable regulatory and licensing requirements in its state of domicile. (Sec. 53-12a-1202(1)(a))

¶ 870 Sales or Use Tax Credits

Use tax credits are allowed in many instances for sales taxes paid other states or counties. However, no adjustment is made if the tax paid to the other state exceeds the amount of Utah state and local taxes (Sec. 59-12-104(27)).

Collection discount: A vendor who is required to file and remit taxes on a monthly basis may retain up to 1.31% of the total monthly state sales tax and 1% of the total monthly local, public transit, and municipal energy sales and use tax as compensation for the cost of collecting and remitting the tax on a monthly basis (Sec. 59-12-108). Voluntary monthly and EFT filers, as well as direct-payment filers, also are entitled to this reimbursement (Rule R865-19S-86). However, no reimbursement is allowed for the cost of monthly filing or remittance of waste tire fees or transient room, resort communities or tourism, recreation, cultural, or convention facilities taxes. Additionally, no reimbursement is allowed if the tax payment is late.

Collection discount on food sales: Sellers filing on a monthly basis who remit the reduced tax collected on sales of food and food ingredients may retain an amount equal to the sum of the following (Sec. 59-12-108(d)(2)(a)):

1.31% of the amount the seller is required to remit under the provision imposing the reduced tax rate on food and food ingredients; and

1.31% of the difference between the amounts the seller would have remitted under the provision imposing the general tax rate and the amounts the seller must remit under the provision imposing the reduced tax rate on food and food ingredients.

Bad debts: A refundable deduction for bad debt is available. See ¶ 867.

Cable and satellite services: A nonrefundable tax credit may be claimed by multi-channel video or audio service providers that pass the credit through to their subscribers of multi-channel video or audio service. The credit equals 50% of the amount of municipal or county franchise fees that a provider pays to counties and municipalities within the state that charge franchise fees (Sec. 59-26-104.5). However, satellite TV providers do not pay local franchise fees and, therefore, do not qualify for the credit.

The Utah Supreme Court held that the sales tax credit against local franchise fees available to cable television (TV) providers, but not satellite TV providers, did not violate the U.S. dormant Commerce Clause or the Utah Constitution's Uniform Operation of Laws provision. (*DIRECTV and DISH Network v. Utah State Tax Comm'n,* Utah Supreme Court, No. 20130742, December 14, 2015, CCH Utah Tax Reports, ¶ 401-126)

¶ 871   Deficiency Assessments

If it appears to the Tax Commission that an insufficient amount of tax has been computed on a return, the Commission is authorized to recompute the tax (Sec. 59-12-110(1)) and issue a deficiency assessment (Sec. 59-12-110(5)).

If no return is filed, the Commission can either give written notice that a return must be filed or make an estimate of the taxes due on the basis of any information in its possession regarding the total sales subject to the tax. The Commission's estimate is presumed to be correct (Sec. 59-12-111(1)).

Interest will be added to the deficiency from the date the return was due, excluding extensions (Sec. 59-12-110(1)). The amount of the deficiency assessment (including penalties and interest) is due and payable by the taxpayer within ten days after notice and demand for payment by the Commission, unless the tax is not deemed to be in jeopardy, in which case it is due within 30 days after the Commission mails its notice (Sec. 59-12-110(5)).

In the case of a false or fraudulent return or payment with intent to evade tax (or failure to file a return), the tax can be assessed at any time, without notice of assessment (Sec. 59-12-110(6)).

Each collection remedy of the state is cumulative, and the use of one remedy does not limit the ability to take advantage of other remedies (Sec. 59-12-115(4)).

¶ 872   Audit Procedures

The Tax Commission is required, as soon as practicable after a return is filed, to examine the return and determine the correct amount of the tax (Sec. 59-12-110(1)). If it is found that the correct amount of tax is greater than indicated on the return, a deficiency assessment is to be made and the taxpayer notified in writing (Rule R865-19S-17).

Voluntary disclosure program: This program is designed to help businesses and individuals voluntarily resolve prior business tax liabilities. Companies may anonymously approach the program staff to seek resolution of these liabilities. Generally, companies may benefit from the voluntary disclosure process by not having penalties imposed and by receiving a limited look-back period. For additional information, see *Publication 4,* Utah State Tax Commission, October 31, 2013, CCH Utah Tax Reports, ¶ 400-884.

¶ 873   Statute of Limitations

If a deficiency is due to failure to file a return, filing a false or fraudulent return, or payment with intent to evade tax the tax may be assessed or a proceeding for collection begun at any time (Sec. 59-12-110(6)).

When a return is filed and no fraud is involved, the Tax Commission may assess additional taxes within three years after the return was filed (Sec. 59-12-110(6), Sec. 59-12-115(3)). If taxes are not assessed within this limitations period, they cannot be collected (Sec. 59-12-110(6)).

A limitations period may be extended if the following conditions are met: the Utah State Tax Commission and a taxpayer agree to the extension in writing; they agree to the extension before the original limitations period lapses; and they specify how long the extended period will last. An extension agreement may buy more time for the Commission to assess a tax deficiency against a taxpayer, including penalties and interest, or to start a court proceeding to collect an unpaid tax. It also may allow a taxpayer more time to seek a refund of overpaid taxes.

The statute of limitations for prosecution of criminal violations is six years from the date on which the tax should have been remitted (Sec. 59-1-401(9)).

Application for Refund

If the amount of tax paid is greater than that due, the Tax Commission must refund the difference upon written application of the taxpayer, unless it is determined that the extra amount was submitted for the purpose of investment (Sec. 59-12-110(2); Rule R861-1A-46).

A taxpayer may file a claim for a refund or credit regardless of whether the taxpayer received or objected to a notice of deficiency or a notice of assessment (Sec. 59-12-110(2)). If the Tax Commission denies a claim for a refund or credit, the taxpayer may request a redetermination of the denial by filing a petition or request for agency action with the Tax Commission.

No refund is allowed, however, unless a claim is filed within three years from the date of overpayment (Sec. 59-12-110(2)).

Source. Statutory references are to Title 32 of the Vermont Statutes Annotated, as amended to date. Details are reported in the CCH VERMONT TAX REPORTS starting at ¶ 60-000.

The Vermont sales tax is a general tax on the sale of tangible personal property, including property used to improve, alter or repair the real property of others by a manufacturer or any person who is primarily engaged in the business of making retail sales of tangible personal property, sold at retail in Vermont, unless specifically exempted, and a limited tax on services (Sec. 9771).

The compensating use tax is a general tax on the purchase at retail of any tangible personal property not subject to the sales tax (Sec. 9773).

Digital products: Sales and use tax is imposed on digital audio-visual works, digital audio works, digital books, and ringtones that are transferred electronically to an end user (Sec. 9701(46); Sec. 9771(8); Sec. 9773(4)). The sales and use tax on specified digital products transferred electronically applies regardless of whether the products are for permanent use or less than permanent use and regardless of whether the transfer of products is conditioned upon continued payment from the purchaser. See also *Technical Bulletin No. TB-49*, Vermont Department of Taxes, January 22, 2010, CCH VERMONT TAX REPORTS, ¶ 200-721.

When a billing, payroll, or information service results in the creation and transfer of tangible personal property, such as computer data transferred on disks, tapes, or other media devices, from the vendor to the customer, the transaction is not subject to sales and use tax (*Technical Bulletin TB-54*, Vermont Department of Taxes, November 19, 2010, CCH VERMONT TAX REPORTS, ¶ 200-743).

Software: Canned software is subject to sales tax, regardless of whether it is provided in tangible form or delivered electronically (Sec. 9701(7); Sec. 9771(1)). Prewritten software, or canned software, includes customized software that is compiled though the addition of separate subprograms, subroutines or modules, each prewritten and available for sale to other customers in other combinations (*Technical Bulletin TB-54,* Vermont Department of Taxes).

Custom software, or nonprewritten software, is exempt from sales tax, regardless of whether it is provided in tangible form or delivered electronically (Sec. 9701(7); Sec. 9771). To qualify for exemption, custom software, or nonprewritten software, must be designed and developed to meet the unique requirements of a specific purchaser and sold for that specific purchaser's exclusive use (*Technical Bulletin TB-54*, Vermont Department of Taxes, November 19, 2010, CCH VERMONT TAX REPORTS, ¶ 200-743).

Software delivery method: The sale of prewritten software is generally taxable regardless of whether it is a sale of tangible media such as disks or other memory storage devices, through downloading, or through load and leave contracts (*Technical Bulletin TB-54,* Vermont Department of Taxes, November 19, 2010, CCH VERMONT TAX REPORTS, ¶ 200-743).

Cloud computing: A legislative moratorium on the collection of sales tax on prewritten software accessed remotely expired on June 30, 2013. Effective July 1, 2015, the sales and use tax on charges for the right to remotely access prewritten software (cloud computing) was repealed. Charges for the right to access remotely prewritten software are not considered charges for tangible personal property under Sec. 9701(7); see *Fact Sheet No. FS-1084,* Vermont Department of Taxes, August 2015, CCH VERMONT TAX REPORTS, ¶ 200-937, also accessible at **http://tax.vermont.gov/research-and-reports/publications/fact-sheets**.

Telephone calling cards and authorization numbers: The sale at retail of prepaid telephone calling cards and prepaid telephone authorization numbers (or the reauthorization of either) is subject to sales and use tax. If the sale or recharge of the calling card or authorization number does not take place at the vendor's place of business, it is determined to have taken place at the customer's shipping or billing address (Sec. 9771(6)).

Real property construction, improvement, alteration, or repair:. Manufacturers and retailers that purchase materials and supplies to be used in erecting structures or otherwise improving, altering, or repairing real property are treated as contractors unless they elect, by filing a form with the Department of Taxes, to be treated as a retailer on their purchase of such materials and supplies. If the manufacturer or retailer makes the election, the purchase of such materials and supplies is not considered a retail sale. (Sec. 9701(5); see also *Fact Sheet No. FS-1112,* Vermont Department of Taxes, July 2016, CCH VERMONT TAX REPORTS, ¶ 200-997, also accessible at **http://tax.vermont.gov/research-and-reports/publications/fact-sheets**)

Soft drinks: Effective July 1, 2015, the definition of exempt "food and food ingredients" no longer includes soft drinks (Sec. 9701(31)). "Soft drink" means a nonalcoholic beverage that contains natural or artificial sweeteners (Sec. 9701(54)). The term does not include beverages that contain milk or milk products; soy, rice, or similar milk substitutes; or greater than 50% of vegetable or fruit juice by volume.

Medical marijuana: Medical marijuana is exempt from sales and use tax as a prescription drug under Sec. 9741(2). However, pipes, vaporizers, and other items classified as drug paraphernalia sold in a medical marijuana dispensary are taxable. The fact sheet discusses the rationale behind the exemption; requirements for medical marijuana dispensaries and patients; why exemption certificates are not required; the tax on marijuana-related supplies; and other matters. (*Fact Sheet No. FS-1072,* Vermont Department of Taxes, July 2016, CCH VERMONT TAX REPORTS, ¶ 200-988, also accessible at **http://tax.vermont.gov/research-and-reports/publications/fact-sheets**)

- **Use tax**

The compensating use tax is a general tax on the purchase at retail of any tangible personal property not subject to the sales tax. The use tax also applies to (Sec. 9773):

— any tangible personal property manufactured, processed or assembled by the user, if the user offers the same kind of personal property for sale in the regular course of business;

— any tangible personal property, however acquired if not acquired for resale, upon which taxable production, printing, or fabrication services are performed;

— specified digital products transferred electronically to an end user; and

— effective July 1, 2014, telecommunications services, except coin-operated telephone service, private telephone service, paging service, private communications service, and value-added non-voice data service.

For information on the use tax base, see ¶ 877.

- **Incidence of tax**

The Vermont sales tax is imposed on the receipts from certain sales (Sec. 9771). The use tax is imposed on a taxable "use" made in the state, in effect on the user, in cases where the sales tax was not paid (Sec. 9773).

While Vermont law does not make clear whether the sales tax is imposed on the buyer or the seller, the Vermont Supreme Court has held that the sales tax is imposed on the buyer, with the seller required to collect (*Bud Crossman Plumbing and Heating v. Commissioner of Taxes* (1982, Vt SCt) 455 A2d 799).

¶876 Vermont

- **Responsibility for collection**

The sales tax is paid by purchasers of tangible personal property or taxable services through a system of reimbursements that allows vendors to collect the tax from their customers (Sec. 9772). The use tax is imposed on persons using tangible personal property or taxable services in Vermont that were not subject to the sales tax (Sec. 9773).

Vendor liability: The taxes are collected by vendors of taxable tangible personal property or services, and recipients of entertainment charges (Sec. 9701(14)).

Purchaser liability: Although sellers are primarily responsible for collection and payment of the tax, no claim can be made that the tax is not considered as an element in the price paid by the customer (Sec. 9708). If the tax is not paid to the seller, the purchaser is obligated to pay it directly to the Department of Taxes (Sec. 9705(a)).

Noncollecting vendor notice and annual statement requirements: Noncollecting vendors making sales into Vermont are required to notify certain purchasers that sales or use tax is due on nonexempt purchases from the vendor and that Vermont requires the purchaser to file a sales or use tax return. "Noncollecting vendor" is defined as a vendor that sells tangible personal property to purchasers who are not exempt from Vermont sales tax and that does not collect the tax. (Sec. 9701(54))

The notice to purchasers must be provided by January 31 of each year to Vermont purchasers who have made purchases amounting to $500 or more from the noncollecting vendor in the previous calendar year. The notice must show the total amount paid by the purchaser for Vermont purchases made from the noncollecting vendor in the previous calendar year. Specific requirements are provided for the content and mailing of the notices, including a requirement that the notice must state that Vermont requires a sales or use tax return to be filed and tax to be paid on nonexempt purchases made by the purchaser from the noncollecting vendor. (Sec. 9712)

- **Nexus**

Vermont requires any vendor doing business in Vermont and making retail sales of taxable tangible personal property, services, or amusements to a person in Vermont, the receipts from which are taxed, to collect and remit sales or use tax whether or not the sale is made within the state. (Sec. 9701(7), (9), (14),(15); Reg. 233-1). Vermont sales and use tax law includes in the definition of "vendor" any out-of-state seller making sales with a destination in the state that does not maintain a place of business in the state, and who engages in regular, systematic, or seasonal solicitation of sales of tangible personal property in Vermont (Sec. 9701(9)):

— by the display of advertisements in Vermont;

— by the distribution of catalogs, periodicals, advertising flyers or other advertising by means of print, radio or television media;

— by mail, telegraphy, telephone, computer data base, cable, optic, microwave or other communication systems, for the purpose of effecting sales of tangible personal property; provided such person has made sales from outside Vermont to destinations within Vermont of at least $100,000 or at least 200 sales transactions during any 12-month period preceding the monthly or quarterly period with respect to which the person's liability for tax is determined.

"Click-through nexus": Vermont's click-through nexus law became effective as of October 13, 2015, because the Vermont Attorney General determined that 15 or more other states have adopted requirements that are the same, substantially similar, or significantly comparable to Vermont's "click-through nexus" requirements. Impacted remote sellers were required to register and begin collecting and remitting sales tax on December 1, 2015. (Sec. 9701(9)(I))

Under the "click-through nexus" provision, a person making sales that are subject to sales and use tax is presumed to be soliciting business through an independent contractor, agent, or other representative if the person enters into an agreement with a Vermont resident under which the resident, for a commission or other consideration, directly or indirectly refers potential customers by a link on an Internet website, or by other means, to the person. The presumption applies only if the cumulative gross receipts from sales by the person to customers in Vermont, who are referred to the person by all residents with this type of agreement with the person, exceed $10,000 during the preceding tax year. The presumption can be rebutted by proof that the resident with whom the person has an agreement did not engage in any solicitation in Vermont on behalf of the person that would satisfy the nexus requirements of the U.S. Constitution during the tax year in question. (Sec. 9701(9)(I))

• **Streamlined Act status**

Vermont is a full member of the Governing Board of the Streamlined Sales Tax Project. It has enacted the Uniform (Simplified) Sales and Use Tax Administration Act and legislation to conform the state's laws to the Streamlined Sales and Use Tax Agreement (Sec. 9701). For additional information, see ¶ 882.

Taxability matrix: Vermont maintains a taxability matrix that is also accessible on the SSTP's website at **http://www.streamlinedsalestax.org**.

¶ 877   Tax Base

The sales tax is imposed on the "receipts" from taxable transactions (Sec. 9771). Taxable transactions include (1) retail sales of tangible personal property, (2) retail sales of public utility services, including gas and electricity, but not water and transportation, (3) charges for producing, fabricating, printing, or imprinting property for consumers who furnish the property, (4) entertainment charges, (5) retail sale of telecommunications services, and (6) retail sales and reauthorizations of prepaid telephone calling cards or prepaid telephone authorization numbers.

"Receipts" is defined as the amount of the sales price of any property and the charge for any taxable entertainment valued in money, whether received as money or otherwise, without any deduction for expenses or early payment discount, but excluding any amount for which credit is allowed by the vendor to the purchaser (Sec. 9701(4)). Also excluded from the definition of "receipts" are the following:

— any refund in cash or credit for the return of merchandise under a warranty, and the price of property returned by customers when the full price is refunded by either cash or credit;

— amounts received for labor or services used in installing or repairing the property sold, if separately charged or stated; and

— the cost of transportation from the retailer's place of business or other point from which shipment is made directly to the purchaser, if the cost of transportation is separately stated and occurs by means of common carrier, contract carrier, or the United States mails.

Use tax: The compensating use tax is imposed on the use in Vermont of property not subject the sales tax (Sec. 9773). In the case of the purchase of tangible personal property subject to the use tax, the tax is imposed on the consideration given or contracted to be given, adjusted in the same manner as is the sales price under the sales tax to arrive at "receipts" (Sec. 9774).

The tax on tangible personal property that is purchased by a Vermont resident for use outside Vermont which subsequently becomes subject to the use tax is based on the purchase price of the property, except that if the property was used for more than six months outside the state the tax is based on the current market value of the property at the time of its first use in Vermont, and if property is brought into the state for the performance of a contract or subcontract for less than six months, the tax may be based on the fair rental value for the period of use (Sec. 9774).

¶877   Vermont

¶ 878   List of Exemptions, Exceptions, and Exclusions

Unless otherwise indicated, the statutory exemptions, exceptions, and exclusions listed below apply to both sales and use taxes; those applicable only to the use tax are listed separately. Items that are excluded from the sales or use tax base are treated at ¶ 877, "Tax Base."

The Vermont Department of Taxes publishes a fact sheet that lists examples of items that are exempt from, or subject to, sales and use tax. The information on the fact sheet is meant only as a general guideline. The lists include examples of exempt clothing; taxable clothing accessories or equipment; taxable protective equipment; taxable sport or recreational equipment; exempt over-the-counter (OTC) drugs; taxable grooming and hygiene products; exempt medical equipment and supplies; and taxable supplies. (*Fact Sheet No. FS-1028,* Vermont Department of Taxes, July 2015, CCH VERMONT TAX REPORTS, ¶ 200-913, also accessible at **http://tax.vermont.gov/research-and-reports/publications/fact-sheets**).

- **Sales and use tax exemptions, exceptions, and exclusions**

Agricultural feeds and supplies	Sec. 9741(3)
Agricultural machinery and equipment	Sec. 9741(25)
Agricultural research	Sec. 9741(24)
Aircraft sold to an air carrier and aircraft parts for installation in an aircraft	Sec. 9741(29)
Alcoholic beverages sold for immediate consumption	Sec. 9741(10)
Artificial components of human body	Sec. 9741(2)
Auctioneer sales on the owner's premises	Sec. 9741(48)
Baler twine	Sec. 9741(3)
Bedding	Sec. 9741(3)
Blood or blood plasma	Sec. 9741(2)
Building supplies to charitable or government buildings	Sec. 9743(4)
Building supplies used in construction or expansion of facilities to manufacture tangible personal property for sale	Sec. 9741(39)
Casual sales	Sec. 9741(4)
Charitable organizations transactions	Sec. 9743(3)
Clothing	Sec. 9741(45)
Coin-operated car washes	Sec. 9741(19)
Coin-operated laundries	Sec. 9741(19)
Coin-operated telephones	Sec. 9741(42)
Commercial research	Sec. 9741(24)
Compost, animal manure, manipulated animal manure, and planting mix sold in bulk, and clean, high carbon bulking agents	Sec. 9741(49), (50)
Computer hardware used in manufacturing or high-tech business	Sec. 9741(14), (47)
Computer services excluded from definition of "sale"	Sec. 9741(35)
Corporate transfers of property	Sec. 9742(2), Sec. 9742(3), Sec. 9742(5)
Crutches	Sec. 9741(2)
Dental devices	Sec. 9741(2)

Nonprofit museum admissions . . . . Sec. 9741(20)

Nonprofit organizations' fundraisers (limited exemption) . . . . Sec. 9743(5)

Optical devices . . . . Sec. 9741(2)

Packaging . . . . Sec. 9741(16)

Partnership transfers of property . . . . Sec. 9742(4),
Sec. 9742(6)

Poultry . . . . Sec. 9741(3)

Printing and bookmaking process . . . . Sec. 9741(14)

Professional services . . . . Sec. 9741(35)

Prosthetic devices . . . . Sec. 9741(2)

Publication process . . . . Sec. 9741(14)

Rail line property . . . . Sec. 9741 (44)

Railroad rolling stock . . . . Sec. 9741(30)

Recyclable bags and wrap . . . . Sec. 9741(3)

Regional transit districts . . . . Sec. 5127, Tit. 24, V.S.A.

Repair charges . . . . Sec. 9701(4)

Resales . . . . Sec. 9701(5)

Research—Agricultural, industrial, or commercial . . . . Sec. 9741(24)

Residential utilities . . . . Sec. 9741(26)

Rooms subject to meals and rooms tax . . . . Sec. 9741(9), (10)

Schools . . . . Sec. 9743(6)

Seeds . . . . Sec. 9741(3)

Seeing eye dogs . . . . Sec. 9741(2)

Semen breeding fees . . . . Sec. 9741(3)

Software, custom (non-prewritten) . . . . Sec. 9701(7)
Sec. 9771(1)

Spirituous liquors and malt beverages subject to alcohol tax . . . . . . Sec. 9741(6)

Stair-lift chairs . . . . Sec. 9741(2)

Tracked vehicle (tax not to exceed $1,300; see ¶ 879) . . . . Sec. 9741(38)

Transportation services . . . . Sec. 9701(4),
Sec. 9771(2)

United States transactions . . . . Sec. 9743(2)

Vermont government transactions . . . . Sec. 9743(1)

Veterinary supplies . . . . Sec. 9741(3)

Volunteer ambulance companies, fire departments, and rescue squads
. . . . Sec. 9741(21)

Waste wood use by manufacturer . . . . Sec. 9742(9)

Water . . . . Sec. 9771(2)

Wheelchairs . . . . Sec. 9741(2)

Wholesale transactions between telecommunications service providers
. . . . Sec. 9741(41)

- **Exemptions, exceptions, and exclusions applicable only to the use tax**

Building materials stored for 180 days or less, if purchased by a
    contractor for the construction, reconstruction, alteration,
    remodeling, or repair of real property in a state that has no sales
    and use tax . . . . Sec. 9744(a)(5)

Nonresident's purchase of property used outside Vermont . . . . Sec. 9744(a)(2)

Property donated to government or exempt organizations . . . . Sec. 9744(a)(4)

Sales tax paid in another state that allows corresponding credit for
    Vermont . . . . Sec. 9744(a)(3)

¶ 879   **Rate of Tax**

The sales tax (Sec. 9771) and compensating use tax (Sec. 9773) are both imposed at the rate of 6%.

- **Meals and rooms tax**

Restaurants and lodging facility operators must collect and remit a 9% tax on taxable meals or alcoholic beverages and room occupancies (Sec. 9241). For application of the tax to vending machine sales, see *Fact Sheet No. FS-1085,* Vermont Department of Taxes, July 2016, CCH VERMONT TAX REPORTS, ¶ 200-991, also accessible at **http://tax.vermont.gov/research-and-reports/publications/fact-sheets**).

Beginning October 1, 2016, Airbnb has agreed to collect and remit meals and rooms tax on payments for lodging offered by its hosts. Hosts on Airbnb will not be responsible for any back taxes they have failed to collect. (*Short-Term Rentals,* Vermont Department of Taxes, September 2016)

- **Fuels for home heating**

The fuel gross receipts tax of 0.5% applies to all retail sales of heating oil, kerosene, other dyed diesel fuel, and, effective July 1, 2014, propane, delivered to a residence or business; and all sales of natural gas; electricity; and coal (Sec. 2503). The tax is collected quarterly from the seller and is scheduled to expire June 30, 2016.

Sales of fuels subject to fuel tax are generally exempt from sales and use tax. However, aviation jet fuel and natural gas used to propel a motor vehicle are subject to sales and use tax (Sec. 9741(7)).

- **Motor vehicle purchase and use tax**

The motor vehicle purchase and use tax is imposed on the purchase or use of motor vehicles by Vermont residents and measured by the vehicle's taxable cost (purchase price, less allowance for trade-in or other allowable deductions) (32 V.S.A. Sec. 8902(5)). Motor vehicles taxed under the motor vehicle purchase and use tax are exempt from the state sales and use tax (32 V.S.A. Sec. 9741(12)). Exemptions from the motor vehicle tax are listed at Sec. 8911.

The motor vehicle purchase and use tax is imposed at the rate of 6% of the taxable cost of pleasure cars, motorcycles, motor homes, and other vehicles weighing up to 10,099 pounds, other than a farm truck (32 V.S.A. Sec. 8903(a),(b)). For other motor vehicles, including farm trucks, the rate is 6% of the taxable cost or $2,075, whichever is less.

Tracked vehicles: The maximum Vermont sales and use tax on tracked vehicles is $1,320 from July 1, 2016 through June 30, 2018 (previously, $1,300). The maximum tax is adjusted for inflation in even-numbered years and rounded to the nearest $10. If the sale of a tracked vehicle occurs in a municipality with a local option sales tax, the local option tax applies to the first $22,000 of the sales price of the vehicle. If the sales price of a tracked vehicle is more than $22,000, the local option tax is capped at $220. In such cases, the maximum state plus local tax is $1,540. (*Technical Bulletin TB-52,* Vermont Department of Taxes, June 14, 2016, CCH VERMONT TAX REPORTS, ¶ 200-984)

• Motor vehicle rental tax

A use tax of 9% applies to short-term rental charges for pleasure vehicles. Short term rentals are rentals for less than 30 days in a continuous period of 365 days or for less than 60 days in a continuous period of 730 days. The use tax does not apply, however, to separately stated charges imposed for insurance, recovery, refueling costs, or other separately stated charges not related to the use of the pleasure car. (Sec. 8903(d))

¶ 880	Local Taxes

A Vermont local option sales tax of 1% is authorized conditionally as an alternative method of raising municipal revenues required by 1997 reforms to the method of financing public education. The local option tax cannot be applied to the telecommunications tax. The tax may be imposed only by municipalities that meet certain criteria related to the education property tax rate (Sec. 138, Tit. 24, V.S.A.).

Local option taxes may be imposed on any or all of the following: (1) sales, excluding telecommunications; (2) meals and alcoholic beverages; and (3) rooms.

Mobile telecommunications: Vermont conforms to the provisions of the federal Mobile Telecommunications Sourcing Act (P.L. 106-252, 4 U.S.C. Secs. 116-126) (Sec. 9782). Wireless telecommunications services are sourced to the customer's "primary place of use," which is the residential or primary business address of the customer, and must be located in the service provider's licensed service area. The jurisdiction in which the primary place of use is located is the only jurisdiction that may tax the communications services, regardless of the customer's location when a call is placed or received.

• Localities imposing tax

Current lists of towns imposing the local option sales tax, local option meals tax, and local option rooms tax are available at **http://tax.vermont.gov/business-and-corp/sales-and-use-tax/local-option-tax/municipalities**. See also *Fact Sheet No. FS-1012,* Vermont Department of Taxes, October 2016, CCH VERMONT TAX REPORTS, ¶ 200-999, also accessible at **http://tax.vermont.gov/research-and-reports/publications/fact-sheets**.

• Sourcing of local taxes

Vendors doing business in Vermont must collect Vermont local option sales tax on a destination sales basis. Vendors located within the borders of a town that imposes a local option sales tax must collect the town's tax. In addition, vendors who deliver or send items to a customer in a town that levies a local option tax, and out-of-state vendors who are registered under Streamlined Sales and Use Tax (SST) Agreement provisions, must collect the town's local option tax. Charges for shipping taxable tangible personal property to a customer in a town that levies a local option tax are taxable. However, items shipped from a town that levies a tax to a town that does not levy a tax are not subject to local option sales tax (*Technical Bulletin TB-37,* Vermont Department of Taxes, March 16, 2007, CCH VERMONT TAX REPORTS, ¶ 200-666).

¶ 881	Bracket Schedule

Sales tax must be calculated by multiplying the sales price of all the taxable transactions by 6%, carried to the third decimal place and rounded to the nearest whole cent (Sec. 9772). Schedules are available at **http://tax.vermont.gov/research-and-reports/tax-rates-and-charts/local-option-sales-tax**.

¶ 882 Returns, Payments, and Due Dates

Persons required to collect or pay the sales tax must file monthly returns, due on or before the 25th of the following month (Sec. 9775). Persons whose sales and use tax liability for the immediately preceding calendar year was (or would have been) $500 or less must pay the tax in one annual payment on or before January 25 of each year. Persons whose sales and use tax liability for the immediately preceding calendar year was (or would have been) more than $500, but less than $2,500 must file quarterly returns, on or before the 25th day of the month following the quarter ending on the last days of March, June, September, and December of each year.

When the due date for the filing of a return falls on a federal or state holiday, the due date is the next business day after such holiday. A tax return filed by mail will be accepted as timely filed if (1) it is received by the Department within three business days after the due date, or (2) the taxpayer provides proof satisfactory to the Commissioner that the return was mailed by the due date (Sec. 3201(d), Title 32, V.S.A.).

The Commissioner may permit or require returns to be made covering other periods of time, taking into account the dollar volume of tax as well as the need for insuring the prompt and orderly collection of the taxes imposed.

Integrated tax system (VTax): The Commissioner may allow or require payment by electronic funds transfer (Sec. 9776). Beginning January 1, 2016, the Commissioner requires electronic filing of sales and use and meals and rooms taxes by business owners with multiple locations.

VTax is a modern integrated tax system designed to perform all functions for all Vermont tax types. Taxpayers may use VTax to register a new business, file returns, pay tax bills, and request refunds, in addition to other services. Additional information is available at **https://myvtax.vermont.gov/_/**.

Special provision for building materials: Sales and use taxes that must otherwise be filed monthly may instead be filed quarterly if the taxpayer shows that (1) at least 50% of the immediately preceding calendar year's sales were comprised of building materials sold to contractors to improve real estate, and (2) the building materials were sold by the person required to collect tax, on credit terms allowing an average period of at least 40 days to pay. Failure to timely pay the taxes will result in revocation of the quarterly filing privilege (Sec. 9775).

Local taxes: To compensate the Department of Taxes for the costs of administration and collection of local option taxes, a fee of $9.52 per return is assessed.

Consumer use tax reporting: The Commissioner of Taxes must provide that individuals report use tax on their Vermont individual income tax returns. Effective January 1, 2016, and applicable to tax year 2015 returns, taxpayers reporting their use tax on individual income tax returns may elect to report an amount that is 0.15% (previously, 0.1%) of their Vermont adjusted gross income, as shown on a table published by the Commissioner of Taxes. The taxpayer's use tax liability arising from the purchase of each item with a purchase price in excess of $1,000 must be added to the table amount. (Sec. 5870; see also *Fact Sheet No. FS-1035,* Vermont Department of Taxes, January 2017, CCH VERMONT TAX REPORTS, ¶ 201-007, also accessible at **http://tax.vermont.gov/research-and-reports/publications/fact-sheets**)

• **Uniform Sales Tax Administration Act**

Vermont has enacted the Uniform (Simplified) Sales and Use Tax Administration Act, the product of the Streamlined Sales Tax Project (SSTP), and also has enacted laws to conform to the Streamlined Sales and Use Tax Agreement, effective January 1, 2007 (Act 66 (H.B. 480), Laws 2003; Ch. 152 (H.B. 784), Laws 2004).

— *Exemptions:* All sales of clothing are exempt. The exemption does not apply to sales of clothing accessories or equipment, protective equipment, or sport or recreational equipment. Also, sales of malt beverages and spirituous liquors are no longer exempt from sales and use taxes;

— *Exemption certificates:* The Commissioner of Taxes requires a vendor to obtain an exemption certificate for the following sales: (1) sales for resale, (2) sales to organizations, (3) sales to exempt organizations, and (4) sales that qualify for a use-based exemption. Acceptance of an exemption certificate satisfies the vendor's burden of proving that a transaction is not taxable. A vendor's failure to possess an exemption certificate at the time of a sale is presumptive evidence that a sale is taxable;

— *Telecommunications credit:* The $20 credit for residential purchasers or users of local exchange (telecommunications) services is eliminated;

— *Local taxes:* A local government that adopts a local option tax must use destination-based sourcing. Localities must exempt clothing, but must impose tax on telecommunications services;

SST-registered sellers: A taxpayer registered under the SST Agreement, who does not have to be registered in Vermont and is not a Model 1, 2, or 3 seller, may file a Vermont sales and use tax return within one year of the month of initial registration and may file annual returns in the same month for succeeding years. Also, such a taxpayer must file a return on the 25th of the month following any month when the taxpayer accumulated state and local taxes of $1,000 or more (Sec. 9775).

¶ 883   **Prepayment of Taxes**

Vermont has no tax prepayment requirement.

¶ 884   **Vendor Registration**

Vermont's Department of Taxes, the Secretary of State's office, and the Department of Labor have partnered to bring you an Online Business Service Center at **https://www.vtsosonline.com/online**. Before commencing business or opening a new place of business, any person required to collect the tax and any person purchasing tangible personal property for resale must file for a certificate of registration, using a form prescribed by the Commissioner of Taxes (Sec. 9707). The Commissioner will issue without charge a certificate of authority empowering the retailer to collect the tax. The certificate must state the place of business, and must be prominently displayed.

Persons not required to collect the tax may choose to apply for a certificate of authority to collect the use tax, and the Commissioner has discretion whether to issue or not issue the certificate.

The following are required to file certificates of registration (Reg. 233-1):

— persons making sales of tangible personal property or services, the receipts of which are subject to tax;

— persons maintaining a place of business in Vermont and making sales, whether at that place of business or elsewhere, to persons within Vermont of tangible personal property or services, the use of which is subject to tax;

— persons who solicit business either by employees, independent contractors, agents or other representatives or by distribution of catalogs or other advertising matter and by reason thereof make sales to persons within Vermont of tangible personal property or services the use of which is subject to the tax;

— the state of Vermont or any of its agencies, instrumentalities, public authorities, or public corporations that sell services or property of a kind ordinarily sold by private persons;

— every person purchasing tangible personal property for resale; and

— every person maintaining a place of amusement at which amusement charges are made.

Taxpayers may use VTax to file and pay taxes and to access other services; go to **https://myvtax.vermont.gov/_/**.

Vermont   ¶884

• **Tax relief for disaster responders**

An out-of-state business that conducts operations within Vermont for purposes of performing work or services related to a declared state disaster or emergency during the disaster response period will not be considered to have established a level of presence that either would require the business to register, file, or remit state or local taxes or that would require the business or its out-of-state employees to be subject to any state licensing or registration requirements. This includes any state or local business licensing or registration requirements or state and local taxes or fees, including unemployment insurance, occupational licensing fees, *ad valorem* tax on equipment brought into Vermont temporarily for use during the disaster response period and subsequently removed from Vermont, and Public Service Board or Secretary of State licensing and regulatory requirements. However, disaster responders will be required to pay transaction taxes and fees, including sales and use taxes, as described below, and may be required to provide certain information to the Vermont Secretary of State. (11 V.S.A. Sec. 1701 *et seq.*)

An out-of-state business or out-of-state employee that remains in Vermont after the disaster response period will become subject to Vermont's normal standards for establishing presence, residency, or doing business in Vermont and will therefore become responsible for any business or employee tax requirements that apply.

Income taxes: For purposes of any state or local tax on or measured by, in whole or in part, net or gross income or receipts, all qualified disaster response activity of the out-of-state business that is conducted in Vermont will be disregarded with respect to any filing requirements for such tax, including the filing required for a unitary or combined group of which the out-of-state business may be a part (11 V.S.A. Sec. 1702(a)(1)(C)). For the purpose of apportioning income, revenue, or receipts, the performance by an out-of-state business of any qualified disaster relief work will not be sourced to, or will not otherwise impact or increase the amount of income, revenue, or receipts apportioned to, Vermont. (11 V.S.A. Sec. 1702(a)(1)(D))

Transaction taxes and fees: An out-of-state business and an out-of-state employee will be required to pay applicable transaction taxes and fees incurred during the disaster response period, including fuel tax, sales and use tax, meals and rooms tax, and car rental taxes or fees, unless such taxes are otherwise exempt during a disaster response period. An out-of-state business making retail sales of tangible personal property during the disaster response period will be subject to all sales tax registration, collection, and reporting requirements, as well as other sales and use tax law requirements. (11 V.S.A. Sec. 1702(b))

¶ 885 **Sales or Use Tax Credits**

Use tax credits are allowed in many instances for sales taxes paid other states or counties.

Property (other than property incorporated into real property in performance of a contract or vessels) purchased by the user while a nonresident of Vermont is specifically made tax exempt (Sec. 9744(a)(2)). A use tax exemption is also provided for tangible personal property on which the sales tax has been paid in another state, provided that the other state allows a corresponding credit for the Vermont tax (Sec. 9744(a)(3)).

Collection allowance: Although Vermont does not offer a direct credit for collection of the tax, it allows those collecting the tax to keep the difference between the amount collected under the brackets schedules and the flat 6% tax assessed against total sales.

¶ 886   Deficiency Assessments

If a required return is not filed, or if an incorrect or insufficient return is filed, the Commissioner can determine the amount due from any information available (Sec. 9777(a)).

Notice of the determination is to be given to the person liable for the tax. The determination will serve to irrevocably fix the amount of the tax within 60 days after notice of the determination unless the person receiving notice applies, in writing, to the Commissioner for a hearing, or unless the Commissioner redetermines the tax.

¶ 887   Audit Procedures

If the Commissioner determines the amount of tax due on the basis of information available, the tax can be estimated on the basis of external indices, such as stock on hand, purchases, rental paid (location, scale of rents or charges, comparable rents or charges, type of accommodations and service), number of employees, or other factors (Sec. 9777(a)).

In determining the tax, the Commissioner also has the power to hold hearings, administer oaths and examine under oath any person relating to his or her business or relating to any matter concerning the sales and use tax laws (Sec. 3201(3)). The Commissioner can compel the attendance of witnesses and the production of any books, records, papers, or memoranda of any person the Commissioner has reason to believe is liable for the payment of a tax or any person believed to have information pertinent to any matter under investigation by the Commissioner at any hearing (Sec. 3201(4)).

To aid in the collection of sales and use taxes, there is a statutory presumption that all receipts for taxable property, services or entertainment are subject to the tax until the contrary is established (Sec. 9813). The burden of proving exemption is with the person required to collect the tax.

Furthermore, the Commissioner has the power to treat any salesperson, representative, peddler, or canvasser as the agent of the vendor, distributor, supervisor, or employer under whom the agent operates and to hold such agent jointly and severally responsible with the principal for the collection and payment of tax (Sec. 9704).

• **Notice by commissioner**

Any notice required by the sales and use tax provisions may be given by mailing it to the person for whom it is intended in a postpaid envelope addressed to that person at the address given in the last return filed (Sec. 9815(a)). If no return was filed, any address obtainable can be used. Mailing of the notice is presumptive evidence of its receipt.

¶ 888   Statute of Limitations

No assessment of additional tax can be made after the expiration of more than three years from the later of (1) the date of the filing of a return, or (2) the date the return was due (Sec. 9815(b)). When a return is required by law but none is filed, there is no limitations period.

Court actions to collect taxes must be brought within six years after the taxes are due (Sec. 9812(a)). The six-year limitations period does not apply, however, if the vendor filed a fraudulent return or failed to file a return when the return was due.

¶ 889   Application for Refund

An application for refund of tax can be made by either (1) a customer who has actually paid the tax or (2) a person required to collect the tax, if it is established that the tax was refunded to the customer (Sec. 9781, Reg. 226-14). The refund must be requested within three years of the due date of the tax.

¶ 890

VIRGINIA

¶ 891

Scope of Tax

Source.—Statutory references are to Title 58.1, Chapter 6, of the 1950 Code of Virginia, as amended to date. Details are reported in the CCH Virginia State Tax Reports starting at ¶ 60-000.

The sales tax is a privilege tax imposed on persons engaged in the business of selling at retail, distributing, renting, or furnishing tangible personal property in Virginia (Sec. 58.1-603). It is also imposed on persons who store, lease, or rent property for use or consumption in the state. The tax applies to all property not specifically exempted or excluded by law. The only services taxed are those expressly mentioned by statute; see the discussion of services below.

Real property: A taxpayer's rentals of sports facilities, including pools, indoor gymnasiums *(i.e.,* basketball courts), and outdoor sports facilities *(i.e.,* tennis courts), to various entities were not subject to Virginia retail sales and use tax because the facilities were considered real property, not tangible personal property as defined in Sec. 58.1-602 *(Ruling of Commissioner,* P.D. 10-223, Virginia Department of Taxation, September 22, 2010, CCH Virginia State Tax Reports ¶ 205-337).

Digital products: Sales and use tax applies only to the sale or use of tangible personal property (Sec. 58.1-603, Sec. 58.1-604). Software, data, content, and other information services delivered electronically via the Internet are expressly exempt from Virginia sales and use tax (Sec. 58.1-609.5). Therefore, content such as movies and video games streamed over the Internet is exempt *(Ruling of Commissioner,* P.D. 13-59, Virginia Department of Taxation, May 2, 2013, CCH Virginia State Tax Reports, ¶ 205-815). Likewise, electronic document services are also exempt *(Ruling of Commissioner,* P.D. 14-14, Virginia Department of Taxation, January 30, 2014, CCH Virginia State Tax Reports, ¶ 205-995).

However, software delivered electronically was taxable when it was an integral part of the overall sale to the customer of tangible personal property *(i.e.,* a complete medical system) and was included in the taxable sales price of the system *(Ruling of Commissioner,* P.D. 14-178, Virginia Department of Taxation, October 23, 2014, CCH Virginia State Tax Reports, ¶ 206-096).

Cloud computing: Generally, cloud computing services are treated in the same manner as the electronic transfer of software products. There is typically no transfer or provision to customers of cloud computing services via a tangible medium. Thus, cloud computing services are not taxable. *(Ruling of Commissioner,* P.D. 14-42, Virginia Department of Taxation, March 20, 2014, CCH Virginia State Tax Reports, ¶ 206-015)

Prepaid calling cards: The initial purchase of telephone calling cards is subject to sales and use tax, and such cards are exempt from all other state or utility taxes (Sec. 58.1-602).

- **Use tax**

The use tax is imposed on the use, consumption, or storage of tangible personal property in the Commonwealth or the storage of such property elsewhere for use in the Commonwealth (Sec. 58.1-604, 23 VAC 10-210-6030). A transaction taxed under the sales tax is not subject to the use tax. Also, out-of-state mail order catalog purchases totaling $100 or less during any calendar year are specifically exempt from use tax (Sec. 58.1-604).

Virginia state agencies may not contract for goods or services with a nongovernmental source if the source or an affiliate is required to collect tax under Virginia's sales and use tax nexus statute but fails or refuses to collect and remit Virginia use tax on its sales delivered to locations within Virginia (Sec. 2.2-4321.1). The prohibition does not apply in an emergency or if the nongovernmental source is the only source of specific goods or services.

- **Services subject to tax**

The sales tax applies to the gross sales of specified services (Sec. 58.1-603(5)).

Taxable services: The sales tax applies to charges for the following (23 VAC 10-210-4040):

— services included in or in connection with the sale of tangible personal property;

— fabrication of property for consumers who furnish the materials;

— provision of meals or other property consumed on the premises; and

— lodging for less than 90 days.

- **Communications Tax**

In addition to all other taxes and fees imposed by law, a communications sales or use tax is imposed on customers of communications services (Sec. 58.1-648(A)). The state communications sales and use tax and an E-911 tax on landline telephone service replaced the pre-2007 local consumer utility tax and certain other taxes and fees. For additional information, see *Guidelines and Rules for the Virginia Communications Taxes,* November 1, 2006, CCH VIRGINIA TAX REPORTS, ¶ 204-590.

"Communications services" means the electronic transmission, conveyance, or routing of voice, data, audio, video, or other information or signals, including cable services, to a point or between or among points, by or through an electronic, radio, satellite, cable, optical, microwave, or other medium or method, regardless of the protocol used for the transmission or conveyance. The term includes, but is not limited to, (1) the connection, movement, change, or termination of communications services; (2) detailed billing of communications services; (3) the sale of directory listings in connection with a communications service; (4) central office and custom calling features; (5) voice mail and other messaging services; and (6) directory assistance (Sec. 58.1-647).

Communications services on which the tax is levied do not include the following: (1) information services; (2) the installation or maintenance of wiring or equipment on a customer's premises; (3) the sale or rental of tangible personal property; (4) the sale of advertising, including, but not limited to, directory advertising; (5) bad check charges; (6) billing and collection services; (7) Internet access service, electronic mail service, electronic bulletin board service, or similar services that are incidental to Internet access, such as voice-capable e-mail or instant messaging; (8) digital products delivered electronically, such as software, downloaded music, ring tones, and reading materials; and (9) over-the-air radio and television service broadcast without charge by an entity licensed for such purposes by the Federal Communications Commission. Public safety agencies that were exempt from local consumer utility taxes are exempt from the communications sales and use tax (Sec. 58.1-648(C)).

Activation fees have been held not subject to the communications sales and use tax, regardless of whether the customer buys a telephone from the taxpayer or a separate retail store (*Ruling of Commissioner,* P.D. 14-64, Virginia Department of Taxation, May 14, 2012, CCH VIRGINIA TAX REPORTS, ¶ 206-033). However, the department properly assessed communications sales tax on the taxpayers' activation fees that were exclusively for Internet access service (*Ruling of Commissioner,* P.D. 14-131, Virginia Department of Taxation, August 7, 2014, CCH VIRGINIA TAX REPORTS, ¶ 206-069).

- **Incidence of tax**

The legal incidence of the sales tax is on the purchaser. Although the seller is legally obligated to collect the tax from the purchaser, the tax is a legal debt of the purchaser (*United States v. Forst* (1978, US CA-4) 569 F2d 811).

Drop shipments: When all the parties are located in the state, the retailer furnishes a resale certificate to the primary seller, rendering the first sale a nontaxable transaction.

¶891   Virginia

The retailer then collects sales tax on behalf of the state on the secondary sale to its customer. However, different considerations arise when one or more of the parties are not within the state.

An out-of-state seller registered in Virginia to collect taxes that sells equipment for resale to a company located outside of Virginia, but is directed to ship the equipment to a third party located in Virginia, is not required to collect and remit the sales or use tax on the drop shipment, provided it receives a completed and signed resale exemption certificate from the buyer located outside of Virginia. (*Ruling of Commissioner,* P.D. 98-142, October 8, 1998, CCH VIRGINIA TAX REPORTS, ¶ 204-422) An out-of-state company sells property to Virginia customers and contracts with Virginia merchants for the drop shipment delivery of goods. If the seller is not registered to collect Virginia use tax, Virginia customers are responsible for reporting and remitting the use tax to the Department on its untaxed purchases. The seller may purchase property exempt of the tax from Virginia merchants, provided the seller furnish merchants with a valid resale exemption certificate. (*Ruling of Commissioner,* P.D. 97-95, February 21, 1997, CCH VIRGINIA TAX REPORTS, ¶ 203-350)

- **Nexus**

Any of the following conditions or activities in Virginia by an out-of-state or Virginia dealer will establish that the dealer has sufficient contact with the state to be required to register and collect the sales and use tax (Sec. 58.1-612(C); 23 VAC 10-210-1090):

— maintaining or having within Virginia, directly or through an agent or subsidiary, an office, warehouse, or place of business;

— soliciting business by employees, independent contractors, or representatives;

— advertising in newspapers or other periodicals printed and published in Virginia, on billboards or posters, or through materials distributed by means other than U.S. Mail;

— delivering tangible personal property more than 12 times per year other than by common carrier;

— soliciting business on a continuous, regular, seasonal, or systematic basis through advertising that is broadcast or distributed from within Virginia;

— soliciting business by mail, if done on a continuous, regular, seasonal, or systematic basis and if the dealer benefits from any financial or marketing activities in Virginia or benefits from the presence of authorized installation, servicing, or repair facilities;

— being owned or controlled by the same interests that own or control a business in Virginia;

— having a franchisee (or, licensee) registered and operating under the same trade name in Virginia; or

— owning tangible personal property that is rented, leased, or offered, on approval, to a Virginia consumer.

Remote sellers: Virginia legislation, if and when it becomes effective, would require certain remote sellers that utilize in-state facilities to collect Virginia sales tax (Sec. 58.1-612(D)). The law establishes a presumption that a dealer has nexus with the state if any commonly controlled person maintains a distribution center, warehouse, fulfillment center, office, or similar location in Virginia that facilitates the delivery of tangible personal property sold by the dealer to its customers. The presumption may be rebutted by demonstrating that the activities conducted by the commonly controlled person in Virginia are not significantly associated with the dealer's ability to establish or maintain a market in the state. A "commonly controlled person" means any person that is a member of the same "controlled group of corporations," as defined in IRC Sec. 1563(a), as the dealer or any other entity that bears the same ownership relationship to the dealer as a corporation that is a member of the same controlled group of corporations. For additional information, see *Tax Bulletin 13-11*, Virginia Department of Taxation, August 22, 2013, CCH VIRGINIA TAX REPORTS, ¶ 205-898.

The law takes effect on the effective date of federal legislation authorizing the states to require a seller to collect taxes on sales of goods to in-state purchasers without regard to the location of the seller. (Sec. 2, Ch. 590 (S.B. 597), Laws 2012).

Contingent procedures for collection of tax on remote sales: Procedures have been established for the collection of the state and local sales and use taxes from remote sellers for sales made in Virginia, contingent upon the federal government passing legislation requiring such collection. Specifically, to comply with any provisions in any federal legislation that requires states to simplify the administration of their sales and use taxes as a condition to require remote sellers to collect and remit their state and local sales taxes, the Virginia Tax Commissioner must take all administrative actions deemed necessary to facilitate the Commonwealth's compliance with the minimum simplification requirements, including but not limited to (Sec. 58.1-601(B)):

> (1) providing adequate software and services to remote sellers and single and consolidated providers that identify the applicable destination rate, including the state and local sales tax rate (if any), to be applied on sales on which the Commonwealth imposes sales and use tax;

> (2) providing certification procedures for both single providers and consolidated providers to make software and services available to remote sellers;

> (3) ensuring that no more than one audit be performed or required for all state and local taxing jurisdictions within the Commonwealth; and

> (4) requiring that no more than one sales and use tax return per month be filed with the Department of Taxation by any remote seller or any single or consolidated provider on behalf of such remote seller.

Rate change notice: Prior to any change in the rate of the local sales and use tax, the Tax Commissioner must provide remote sellers and single and consolidated providers with at least 30 days' notice (Sec. 58.1-605(D); Sec. 58.1-606(D)). Any change in the rate of local sales and use tax will only become effective on the first day of a calendar quarter. Failure to provide notice would require the Commonwealth and the locality to hold the remote seller or single or consolidated provider harmless for collecting the tax at the immediately preceding effective rate for any period of time prior to 30 days after notification is provided.

Any remote seller, single provider, or consolidated provider who has collected an incorrect amount of sales or use tax is relieved from liability for such additional amount, including any penalty or interest, if collection of the improper amount is a result of the remote seller, single provider, or consolidated provider's reasonable reliance upon information provided by the Commonwealth, including, but not limited to, any information obtained from software provided by the Department of Taxation. (Sec. 58.1-635(D)).

Fulfillment centers: A ruling holds that online retailers located outside of Virginia that maintain an inventory of their products in warehouses located in Virginia ("fulfillment centers") do not have sufficient activity with Virginia that would require them to register for the collection and remittance of Virginia retail sales and use tax regarding online sales made to Virginia customers. The sellers online sales to Virginia customers were packed and shipped directly to Virginia customers by the fulfillment centers. The sellers maintained no offices, employees, business locations, or warehouses in Virginia. The sellers maintained ownership of their product located in fulfillment centers and could withdraw or increase their inventory at their own discretion. The fulfillment centers never took ownership of the seller's inventory. Sec. 58.1-612(C)(2) provides that a dealer has sufficient activity in Virginia to require registration if such dealer "solicits business in this Commonwealth by employees, independent contractors, agents or other representative." Based on the information provided, the sellers solicited sales in Virginia through online transactions between the sellers and the Virginia customers. The fulfillment centers did not act as independent contractors of the sellers and had not established an agency relationship with the sellers. In addition, there is no statutory requirement that maintaining a resale inventory in Virginia would establish nexus. Thus, the sellers did not have sufficient activity within Virginia to require them to register for the collection and remittance of the Virginia retail sales and use tax regarding online sales made to Virginia customers. (*Ruling of Commissioner,* P.D. 15-194, Virginia Department of Taxation, October 16, 2015, CCH Virginia Tax Reports, ¶ 206-195)

- **Streamlined Act status**

Virginia is not a member of the Streamlined Sales and Use Tax Agreement because, although it has enacted legislation authorizing it to enter into the Agreement, it has not yet enacted the changes to its laws necessary to comply with the Agreement's requirements. However, as one of the SST Advisor States, it will continue to have input through its representation on the State and Local Advisory Council, which advises the Governing Board on matters pertaining to the administration of the Agreement.

¶ 892   Tax Base

The sales tax is imposed on the gross sales price of articles of tangible personal property sold at retail or distributed in Virginia (Sec. 58.1-603). The tax is computed on the following bases:

- gross sales (defined below);
- gross proceeds derived from leases or rentals;
- cost price of stored property;
- gross proceeds from transient accommodations; or
- gross sales of taxable services.

Suppression devices: Effective July 1, 2014, Virginia prohibits and designates as a Class 1 misdemeanor the willful use of a device or software to falsify the electronic records of cash registers and other point-of-sale systems or otherwise manipulate transaction records in order to affect any Virginia state or local tax liability. Violators are subject to a $20,000 state civil penalty, a $20,000 local civil penalty, or both, depending upon whether the software or device is used to affect a state or local tax liability or both. (Sec. 58.1-1814(B))

- **"Sales price" defined**

For purposes of the retail sales and use tax, the term "sales price" means the total amount for which tangible personal property or services are sold, including any services that are a part of the sale (Sec. 58.1-602). The term includes any amount for which credit is given to the purchaser, consumer, or lessee by the dealer, without any deduction on account of the cost of the property sold, losses or any other expenses, but does not include a transfer of title to tangible personal property after its use as tools, tooling, machinery, or equipment, including dies, molds, and patterns, if, at the time of purchase, the purchaser is obligated under a written contract to make the transfer and the transfer is made for the same or a greater consideration to the person for whom the purchaser manufactures goods (Sec. 58.1-602).

- **"Gross sales" defined**

The term "gross sales" means the sum total of all retail sales of tangible personal property or services (Sec. 58.1-602). Excluded from the definition are the federal retailers' excise tax or federal diesel fuel excise tax (if billed separately) and sales and use taxes levied by Virginia or its political subdivisions.

- **"Gross proceeds" defined**

"Gross proceeds" means the charges made or voluntary contributions received for the lease or rental of tangible personal property or for furnishing services, computed with the same deductions, where applicable, as for sales price as defined in this section over the term of the lease, rental, service, or use, but not less frequently than monthly (Sec. 58.1-602).

Effective July 1, 2015, the definition specifically excludes finance charges, carrying charges, service charges, or interest from credit extended on the lease or rental of tangible personal property under conditional lease or rental contracts or other conditional contracts providing for the deferred payments of the lease or rental price.

- **Use or consumption—Cost price**

A tax is imposed on the cost price of each article of tangible personal property used or consumed in Virginia (Sec. 58.1-604). Tangible personal property that has been acquired for use outside Virginia and subsequently becomes subject to the use tax is taxed on the basis of its cost price if the property is brought into Virginia for use within six months of its acquisition. If, however, the property is brought into Virginia six months or more after its acquisition, the property will be taxed on the basis of the current market value (but not in excess of its cost price) of the property at the time of its first use within Virginia. The tax will be based on such proportion of the cost price or current market value as the duration of time of use within Virginia bears to the total useful life of the property.

Gift transactions: For sales qualifying as gift transactions, dealers registered to collect tax in the state of the recipient may, upon approval of the Tax Commissioner, elect to collect either Virginia sales tax or the tax imposed by the state of the recipient (Sec. 58.1-604.6, Code). A "gift transaction" is a retail sale resulting from an order for tangible personal property placed by any means by any person that is for delivery to a recipient, other than the purchaser, located in another state.

- **Communications Tax**

The sales price on which the communications tax is levied does not include charges for any of the following (Sec. 58.1-648(B), Code):

— separately stated excise, sales, or similar taxes levied by the United States or a state or local government on the purchase, sale, use, or consumption of a communications service that is permitted or required to be added to the sales price of such service;

— separately stated fees or assessments levied by the United States or a state or local government, including, but not limited to, regulatory fees and emergency telephone surcharges, that are required to be added to the price of service;

— coin-operated communications services;

— the sale or recharge of a prepaid calling service;

— the provision of air-to-ground radiotelephone services;

— a communications services provider's internal use of communications services in connection with its business of providing communications services;

— charges for property or other services that are not part of the sale of communications services, if the charges are stated separately from the charges for communications services;

— sales for resale; and

— charges for communications services to Virginia, political subdivisions of Virginia, and the federal government or agency or instrumentality of the federal government.

Sourcing: Except for certain defined communication services, the sale of communications service sold on a call-by-call basis must be sourced to Virginia when the call (1) originates and terminates in Virginia or (2) either originates or terminates in Virginia and the service address is also located in Virginia. A sale of communication services sold on a basis other than a call-by-call basis generally must be sourced to the customer's place of primary use (Sec. 58.1-649(C)(1)). Subject to the definitions and exclusions of the federal Mobile Telecommunications Sourcing Act, the sale of mobile communication services must be sourced to the customer's place of primary use (Sec. 58.1-649).

Special sourcing provisions apply to sales of private communications services and postpaid calling services (Sec. 58.1-649(C)).

¶ 893   **List of Exemptions, Exceptions, and Exclusions**

Unless otherwise indicated, the statutory exemptions, exceptions, and exclusions listed below apply to both sales and use taxes. Items that are excluded from the sales or use tax base are treated at ¶ 892, "Tax Base."

Sunset dates for exemptions: The sunset date on any existing sales tax exemption may not be extended beyond June 30, 2022. Any new sales tax exemption enacted prior to the 2021 regular legislative session must have a sunset date not later than June 30, 2022. However, this requirement does not apply to tax exemptions administered by the Department of Taxation for nonprofit entities and for exemptions with sunset dates after June 30, 2022, enacted or advanced during the 2016 session of the General Assembly.

Cigarette wholesalers: Effective January 1, 2018, purchasers of cigarettes for resale must apply for a special cigarette exemption certificate from the Virginia Department of Taxation in order to not be liable for the payment of sales and use tax at the time of purchase. The department will conduct a background investigation for taxpayers applying for the certificate, with a waiting period of at least 30 days. However, a taxpayer shall be eligible for an expedited process to receive a cigarette exemption certificate if the taxpayer possesses, at the time of filing an application for a cigarette exemption certificate, an active liquor or tobacco products license. (Sec. 58.1-623.2)

The legislation sets forth numerous requirements that a taxpayer must meet in order to qualify for a cigarette exemption certificate and establishes processes and procedures for the application (including a fee of up to $50), renewal, denial, suspension, and revocation of the certificates. A cigarette exemption certificate will be valid for five years. The department must develop guidelines regarding the exemption certificate, and must complete the process for issuing cigarette exemption certificates no later than December 31, 2017. The department must ensure that any taxpayer who qualifies under the expedited process prior to December 1, 2017, or applies for a cigarette exemption certificate prior to December 1, 2017, will be issued or denied the cigarette exemption certificate prior to January 1, 2018. (Ch. 112 (Sec. 58.1-623.2))

• **Sales tax holidays**

Beginning in 2015, three sales tax holidays are combined into one, three-day annual holiday that begins on the first Friday in August and ends at 11:59 p.m. on the following Sunday (August 5-7 in 2016). All of the tax holidays are set to expire on July 1, 2022. For additional information, see *Ruling of Commissioner, P.D. 15-149,* Virginia Department of Taxation, July 10, 2015, CCH Virginia Tax Reports, ¶ 206-157.

Exempt products are as follows:

Back-to-school: The exemption applies to (1) school supply items with a selling price of $20 or less including, but not limited to, dictionaries, notebooks, pens, pencils, notebook paper, and calculators; and (2) articles of clothing and footwear with a selling price of $100 or less, designed to be worn on or about the human body. Discounts, coupons, and other credits will be taken into account in determining the selling price. Dealers may choose to absorb taxes on taxable items during the tax holiday and are liable for payment in the same manner as they are for tax collected from purchasers. The prohibition against the absorption of sales or use tax does not apply during the tax holiday or during the 14 days immediately preceding it, for advertisements relating to sales during the tax holiday.

Energy conservation: Energy Star qualified products include dishwashers, clothes washers, air conditioners, ceiling fans, light bulbs, dehumidifiers, programmable thermostats, and refrigerators that have been designated by the United States Environmental Protection Agency and the United States Department of Energy as meeting or exceeding requirements under the Energy Star program. WaterSense qualified products are those that have been recognized as being water efficient by the WaterSense program sponsored by the U.S. Environmental Protection Agency as indicated by a WaterSense label (Sec. 58.1-609.1(18)).

Hurricane preparedness: Items available for exemption during the period include portable generators used to provide light or communications or preserve food in the event of a power outage and certain other hurricane preparedness equipment. The exemption applies to each portable generator with a selling price of $1,000 or less per item, and each other article of hurricane preparedness equipment, with a selling price of $600 or less (Sec. 58.1-611.3).

- **Sales and use tax exemptions, exceptions, and exclusions**

Advertising	Sec. 58.1-602, Sec. 58.1-609.6(4), Sec. 58.1-609.8(2), Sec. 58.1-612(c)(5)
Agricultural commodities, products, and property	Sec. 58.1-609.2(2)
Agricultural produce and eggs sold at farmers' markets and roadside stands	Sec. 58.1-609.2(7)
Air ambulance services for low-income patients	Sec. 58.1-1505
Air carrier providing scheduled air service	Sec. 58.1-1501, Sec. 58.1-1505
Aircraft	Sec. 58.1-1501, Sec. 58.1-1505(C)
Aircraft parts, engines, and supplies for maintenance, repair	Sec. 58.1-609.3(6), Sec. 58.1-609.10(20)
Aircraft sold in Virginia and removed from Virginia within 60 days	Sec. 58.1-1505(D)
Airline property	Sec. 58.1-609.3(6)
Alterations	Sec. 58.1-609.3(4), Sec. 58.1-609.5(4)
Alternative energy (sun, wind) machinery, tools, and equipment used by public service corporations (eff. 1/1/2017; exp. 6/30/2027)	58.1-609.3(2)
Audio or video tapes leased for commercial use (exp. 7/1/2022)	Sec. 58.1-609.6(1)
Audiovisual work incorporated into another such work (exp. 7/1/2022)	Sec. 58.1-609.6(6)
Beer-making machinery, equipment, and supplies	Sec. 58.1-609.3(19)

Blind vendors	Sec. 58.1-3840,
	Sec. 63.1-164(B),
	Sec. 63.1-164(C)
Broadcasting equipment (exp. 7/1/2022)	Sec. 58.1-609.6(2)
Building materials for low-income housing (refund)	Sec. 58.1-608.1
Bullion (gold, silver, platinum) and legal tender coins in excess of $1,000 (exp. 12/31/2022)	Sec. 58.1-609.1(19)
Cable television systems (exp. 7/1/2022)	Sec. 58.1-609.6(2)
Catalogs	Sec. 58.1-604(5),
	Sec. 58.1-609.6(4)
Church materials	Sec. 58.1-609.10(16)
Commercial and industrial exemptions	Sec. 58.1-609.3
Commercial fishing equipment	Sec. 58.1-609.2(4)
Common carriers	Sec. 58.1-609.3(3)
Community diversion programs	Sec. 58.1-609.1(13)
Computers used by handicapped persons	Sec. 58.1-609.10(13)
Computers used in a data center	Sec. 58.1-609.3(17)
	Sec, 58.1-609.10(20)
Contractors, certain exempt property	Sec. 58.1-610(B)
Custom computer programs	Sec. 58.1-602,
	Sec. 58.1-609.5(7)
Data centers, computer equipment and software for use in (exp. 6/30/2035)	Sec. 58.1-609.3(18)
Delivery out of state	Sec. 58.1-609.10(4)
Dialysis drugs and supplies	Sec. 58.1-609.10(11)
Domestic fuel	Sec. 58.1-609.10(1)
Donation of property from inventory	Sec. 58.1-609.10(15)
Drugs	Sec. 58.1-609.10(9), (11),
	(14)
Educational materials	Sec. 58.1-609.6(7)
	Sec. 58.1-609.10(8)
Election materials	Sec. 58.1-609.1(8)
Electronic products delivered over the Internet	Sec. 58.1-609.5
Electrostatic duplicators	Sec. 58.1-609.3(11)
Enterprise zones	Sec. 59.1-270—Sec.
	59.1-284.01
Eyeglasses and contact lenses	Sec. 58.1-609.10(10)
Feed manufacture	Sec. 58.1-609.2(5)
Flags	Sec. 58.1-609.1(7)
Food and beverages sold at nonprofit fundraisers (exemption from local sales and meals taxes only)	Sec. 58.1-3833,
	Sec. 58.1-3840
Food stamps	Sec. 58.1-609.10(5)
Food fabricated and sold to or donated to an exempt organization . . .	Sec. 58.1-609.10(19)
Fuel for home use	Sec. 58.1-609.10(1),
	Sec. 58.1-609.13
Future use for rental	Sec. 58.1-609.10(3)

Watercraft used by government or agencies, insurance companies, or
    volunteer sea rescue squads . . . .   Sec. 58.1-1404(A),
                                                                               Sec. 58.1-1404(E)

Youth organization sponsoring camping assembly . . . .   Sec. 58.1-609.10(5)

¶ 894   Rate of Tax

The general sales and use tax rate is 4.3% (increased from 4%, effective July 1, 2013) (Sec. 58.1-603, Sec. 58.1-604).

Rate reduced for certain food: The state tax rate applied to sales of food for human consumption is 1.5%. The 1% general sales and use tax levied by counties is unaffected, so the combined rate on such food is 2.5% (Sec. 58.1-611.1).

The lower rate generally does not apply to prepared food sold for immediate consumption.

Vending machine sales: Dealers who place vending machines and sell tangible personal property through them are subject to a combined state and local rate of 6.3% (.35% state and 1% local) on the purchase cost or manufacture cost of the tangible personal property sold in the vending machine (Sec. 58.1-614, 23 VAC 10-210-6041). However, any dealer located in any county or city for which the taxes under Secs. 58.1-603.1 and 58.1-604.01 (Planning Districts) are imposed is required to remit an amount based on 6% of wholesale purchases.

The method of accounting used for federal income tax purposes is to be used in determining the cost of purchase or manufacture (23 VAC 10-210-6041). If all of a dealer's machines are under contract to nonprofit organizations, tax at the rate of 5% is imposed on the dealer's gross receipts (23 VAC 10-210-6042). Gross receipts are calculated by deducting all sales of 10¢ or less from gross receipts and dividing the balance by 1.05 (23 VAC 10-210-6042). Tax at the rate of 5% is imposed on the gross taxable sales of dealers who do not place vending machines but who use vending machines at their places of business to sell merchandise (23 VAC 10-210-6043).

Contractors' use tax: The contractors' use tax is imposed at the rate of 4% on all tangible personal property except motor vehicles, aircraft, and watercraft, which are taxed at other rates (Sec. 58.1-604.1).

Motor vehicle sales: A special tax is imposed on the sale, use, or storage of motor vehicles, including manufactured homes (Sec. 58.1-2402(A)(1), (A)(2)).

A rate of 4.15% was phased in over four years as follows (Sec. 58.1-2402(A)(1)):

— 3% through June 30, 2013;

— 4% beginning July 1, 2013, through June 30, 2014;

— 4.05% beginning July 1, 2014, through June 30, 2015;

— 4.1% beginning July 1, 2015, through June 30, 2016; and

— 4.15% beginning on and after July 1, 2016.

The tax is 2% if the motor vehicle is a mobile office. The minimum tax is $35 (Sec. 58.1-2402(A)(3)). The tax does not apply to trucks, tractor trucks, trailers, or semitrailers with a gross vehicle weight rating or gross combination weight rating of 26,001 pounds or more that are sold, used, or stored for use in Virginia.

Motor vehicle rentals: A 4% tax is imposed on the gross proceeds from the rental of any motor vehicle with a gross vehicle weight rating or a gross combination weight rating of 26,000 lbs or less in the Commonwealth (Sec. 58.1-1736 (A-1)). An additional 4% tax and a 2% fee are imposed on the gross proceeds from the rental in Virginia of any daily rental vehicle, regardless of whether the car is required to be licensed in the Commonwealth (Sec. 58.1-1736(A)(2), (3); see *Ruling of Commissioner,* P.D. 13-109, Virginia Department of Taxation, July 1, 2013, CCH VIRGINIA TAX REPORTS, ¶ 205-863).

Exclusions from the motor vehicle rental tax include: cash discounts allowed and actually taken on a rental contract; finance, carrying, and other service charges; charges for motor fuels; charges for optional accidental death insurance; taxes or fees levied or imposed under the motor vehicle sales and use tax (Chapter 24); any violations, citations, or fines and related penalties and fees; delivery charges, pickup charges, recovery charges, or drop charges; pass-through charges; transportation charges; third-party service charges; or refueling charges (Sec. 58.1-1735).

Watercraft and aircraft: A sales and use tax is imposed at the rate of 2% on watercraft (Sec. 58.1-1402) and on aircraft (Sec. 58.1-1502). See ¶ 893 for exemptions.

Digital media fee: Virginia imposes a 10% digital media fee on the price of all in-room purchases or rentals of digital media in hotels, motels, bed and breakfast establishments, inns, and other facilities offering guest rooms rented out for continuous occupancy for fewer than 90 consecutive days (Sec. 58.1-1731). For purposes of the fee, "digital media" means any audio-visual work received through the in-room television for a separate charge, including motion pictures, television or audio programming, or games. The term does not include Internet access or telephone service. The fee must be collected and remitted monthly in the same manner as sales and use taxes (Sec. 58.1-1732). For more information, see *Tax Bulletin 09-5*, Virginia Department of Taxation, May 21, 2009, CCH VIRGINIA TAX REPORTS, ¶ 204-999.

• Communications Tax

The state communications sales or use tax is imposed on customers of communications services at the rate of 5% of the sales price of each communications service sourced to Virginia (Sec. 58.1-648(A), Code). See also ¶ 891.

¶ 895   **Local Taxes**

The local sales and use tax rates are limited to 1.3%. Currently, every city and county in the state imposes a 1% local sales and use tax, so the combined general rate is 5.3% statewide.

Regional tax rates: An additional retail sales and use tax of 0.7% is imposed in the Northern Virginia and Hampton Roads Regions, except for the counties of Gloucester and Surrey; see *Tax Bulletin 13-8,* Virginia Department of Taxation, June 14, 2013, CCH VIRGINIA TAX REPORTS, ¶ 205-832.

The regional rate in Northern Virginia applies to the Cities of Alexandria, Fairfax, Falls Church, Manassas and Manassas Park; and in the Counties of Arlington, Fairfax, Loudoun and Prince William.

The regional rate in Hampton Roads applies to the Cities of Chesapeake, Franklin, Hampton, Newport News, Norfolk, Poquoson, Portsmouth, Suffolk, Virginia Beach and Williamsburg, and the Counties of Isle of Wight, James City, Southampton and York.

Lookup tool: FIPS Codes (or Federal Information Processing Standards codes) are a standardized set of numeric codes to ensure uniform identification of geographic entities such as cities, counties and towns. The Virginia Department of Taxation uses FIPS codes to identify where a business is located and where their sales take place. A FIPS code lookup tool is available at **http://www.tax.virginia.gov/fips.**

Admissions taxes: Certain counties are specifically authorized by statute to levy a tax not to exceed 10% on admissions charged for attendance at any event (Sec. 58.1-3818). The governing bodies of these counties are required to prescribe the terms, conditions, and amounts of these taxes by local ordinance, and are permitted to distinguish between charitable and noncharitable events for purposes of the tax.

Local motor fuels taxes: An additional tax is imposed on wholesale distributors of motor fuels at the rate of 2.1% in a qualifying Planning District. (Sec. 58.1-2295).

• **County food and beverage tax**

Roanoke County, Rockbridge County, Frederick County, Arlington County, and Montgomery County are authorized to levy an additional tax on food and beverages, not to exceed 4% (Sec. 58.1-3833(B)). The amount of the tax may not exceed 8½% when added to the state and local general sales and use tax.

Exemptions from the county food and beverage tax are provided for the following: (1) boarding-houses that do not accommodate transients; (2) cafeterias operated by industrial plants for employees only; (3) churches, fraternal and social societies, and volunteer fire department and rescue squads that hold occasional dinners and bazaars lasting for one or two days; (4) churches that serve meals for their members as a regular part of their religious observances; (5) nonprofit cafeterias in public schools, nursing homes, and hospitals, and (6) a broad range of other businesses, agencies, and organizations that provide food to their employees, volunteers, members, or patients. (Sec. 58.1-3833).

• **County transient occupancy taxes**

Any county may levy a transient occupancy tax on hotels, motels, boarding houses, travel campgrounds, and other facilities offering guest rooms (Sec. 58.1-3819). The tax may not exceed 2% of the amount of the charge for the occupancy of the room or space occupied. However, the tax may be assessed up to 5% in certain counties. Local authorities should be consulted for current rates.

There is also imposed an additional transient occupancy tax at the rate of 2% in each county and city located in a qualifying Planning District (Sec. 58.1-1742).

Combined taxes: Certain counties are allowed to adopt an ordinance imposing a combined transient occupancy and food and beverage tax of up to 4% on bed and breakfast establishments when the establishment does not separately state its room charges and food and beverage charges.

¶ **896** Bracket Schedule

Bracket schedules for various rates are not currently available from the Department of Taxation. A 5% collection schedule is included in *Virginia Retail Sales and Use Tax Rate Increase Guidelines,* Virginia Department of Taxation, August 1, 2004, CCH VIRGINIA TAX REPORTS, ¶ 204-302.

¶ **897** Returns, Payments, and Due Dates

Every dealer required to collect or pay the sales or use tax must file a return (Sec. 58.1-615, 23 VAC 10-210-480, 23 VAC 10-210-485). A return must be filed even if the dealer is not liable to remit any tax for the period covered by the return.

The return must be accompanied by payment of any tax due (Sec. 58.1-616, 23 VAC 10-210-480, 23 VAC 10-210-485).

• **Due dates for dealers**

Every dealer who is required to collect or pay the sales or use tax must, on or before the 20th day of the month, file a return showing the gross sales, gross proceeds, or cost price, as the case may be, arising from all taxable transactions that occurred during the preceding month (Sec. 58.1-615, 23 VAC 10-210-480, 23 VAC 10-210-485).

Communications tax: Communications service providers' returns and payments are due on or before the 20th day of the month following the month in which the tax is billed. Returns must be filed even if tax is not due for the period covered by the return (Sec. 58.1-654).

Timeliness of returns: When the last day on which a tax return may be filed falls on a Saturday, Sunday, or legal holiday, the return may be filed on the next succeeding business day. A "legal holiday" is any day designated as such by Sec. 2.2-3300. A " business day" is any Monday, Tuesday, Wednesday, Thursday, or Friday that is not a legal holiday. (Sec. 58.1-8; 23 VAC 10-20-20).

¶**896** **Virginia**

A mailed return is considered to be timely filed if it is postmarked on or before midnight of the day it is due. State and local taxing officials are required to treat tax returns or payment of taxes that are remitted by means of a recognized commercial delivery service and bearing a confirmation date falling on or prior to the due date the same as returns and payments delivered through the U.S. Postal Service. (Sec. 58.1-9; *Tax Bulletin 11-5*, Virginia Department of Taxation, June 8, 2011, CCH VIRGINIA TAX REPORTS, ¶ 205-493).

• **Due dates for direct payment permit holders**

Except as provided above, direct payment permit holders must file returns by the 20th day of each month for the preceding month, and payment must accompany the return (Sec. 58.1-624(B)).

• **Accelerated June payments**

Retail sales and use tax dealers and direct payment permit holders with $1 million or more of taxable sales and/or purchases in the preceding period (July through June) are required to make an additional payment in June of each year (Ch. 1 (H.B. 5001), Special Session 1, Laws 2014; *Ruling of Commissioner,* P.D. 15-83, April 22, 2015, CCH VIRGINIA TAX REPORTS, ¶ 206-122). Dealers meeting this threshold are required to make a payment in June equal to 90% of the dealer's retail sales and use tax liability for June of the previous year. The accelerated sales tax payment is due on June 25 for dealers paying by mail and on June 30 for dealers paying electronically. In the event that either June 20 or July 20 falls on a Saturday or Sunday, any payment made on or before the next succeeding business day will be considered timely. Each affected dealer is entitled to take a credit for this amount on the return for June of the current year, due July 20 (*Ruling of Commissioner,* P.D. 11-72, May 11, 2011, CCH VIRGINIA TAX REPORTS, ¶ 205-464).

Beginning with the tax payment to be remitted on or before June 25, 2017, if the payment is made by other than electronic fund transfers, and by June 30, 2017, if payments are made by electronic fund transfer, the accelerated sales tax payment provisions apply only to those dealers or permit holders with taxable sales and purchases of $10 million or greater for the 12-month period beginning July 1 and ending June 30 of the immediately preceding calendar year. (Sec. 3-5.06(G)(1), Ch. 780 (H.B. 30), Laws 2016)

Beginning with the tax payment that would be remitted on or before June 25, 2018 (if payments are made by other than electronic funds transfer) or by June 30, 2018 (if payments are made by electronic fund transfer), the accelerated sales tax payment provisions will apply only to those dealers or permit holders with taxable sales and purchases of $25 million or greater for the 12-month period beginning July 1 and ending June 30 of the immediately preceding calendar year. (Sec. 3-5.06(G)(2), Ch. 780 (H.B. 30), Laws 2016)

• **Filing of returns**

Dealers may choose to file returns with the commissioner of the revenue or the treasurer for the locality in which the dealer is located, rather than with the Department of Taxation (Sec. 58.1-615(C), Code). The local official must stamp the date on the return and mail it to the Tax Commissioner no later than the following business day. A return will be deemed to have been filed with the Tax Commissioner on the date that it is delivered by the dealer to the local official and receipt is acknowledged. A local official may collect the cost of postage from the dealer.

Electronic filing and payment: Monthly and quarterly retail sales and use tax filers of Forms ST-9 and ST-9CO must submit their returns and payments electronically. Virginia has three systems, all secure and free of charge, for electronic filing and payment of business returns:

— The Business iFile system is a good choice for businesses with multiple locations. In addition to file/pay features, Business iFile provides access to the business's account history (up to 14 months) with the ability to also update important business address/contact/liability details. However, Business iFile cannot be used to electronically submit W2/1099 wage and income statements. To submit this data electronically, you must use Web Upload or eForms.

— Web Upload allows tax professionals to submit multiple employer withholding and sales tax returns and payments for multiple clients in a single file. Web Upload also lets small business owners submit a single tax return prepared on a program such as QuickBooks or Excel. Web Upload is especially beneficial if the business has multiple returns to file/pay (including employment tax returns) at the same time or accounts that involve schedules for multiple locations.

— The eForms system is allows taxpayers to file and pay state taxes electronically without having to remember a user name and password. The eForms are fillable electronic forms that are designed to look and function similar to the paper version of the tax returns.

Additional information on these systems is available on the Department's web site at **http://www.tax.virginia.gov/content/online-services**.

FIPS code lookup: The Virginia Department of Taxation has an online service to assist businesses in reporting their sales and use tax by identifying the FIPS (Federal Information Processing Standards) code associated with the city/county where their sales took place. The FIPS Code Lookup is available at **http://www.tax.virginia.gov/fips**.

Fillable forms: The tax commissioner must ensure that all required Virginia state tax forms are fillable forms in a portable document format (PDF) and are available on the Department of Taxation's website. The commissioner must also publish guidelines for using fillable forms on the department's website. (Sec. 58.1-202.3)

• Use of credit or debit cards for payment

Payment of taxes, interest, penalties or other fees by use of a credit card or a debit card is acceptable. However, a service charge may be added to the required payment in an amount negotiated and agreed to in a contract with the Department (Sec. 58.1-13.1).

• Collection discount

Some dealers and holders of direct pay permits are allowed a discount as compensation for collecting the tax, contingent on timely payment of the tax (Sec. 58.1-622, 23 VAC 10-210-485). The discount is calculated as a percentage of the first 3% of tax shown on the return, as follows:

— For monthly taxable sales up to $62,500, the discount is 1.6% (discount factor = 0.012; 0.016 for qualifying food);

— For sales of $62,501 to $208,000, the discount is 1.2% (discount factor = 0.009; 0.012 for qualifying food);

— For sales above $208,000, the discount is 0.8% (discount factor = 0.006; 0.008 for qualifying food)

Collection discounts are not available to any dealer required to remit retail sales and use tax by electronic funds transfer or to dealers liable for the tire recycling fee, the communications sales and use tax, the tax for enhanced E-911 service, or certain excise taxes.

To simplify the calculation on returns and worksheets, dealers may use the discount factors. (*Tax Bulletin 10-5,* Virginia Department of Taxation, May 17, 2010, CCH VIRGINIA TAX REPORTS, ¶ 205-181).

The department annually determines which dealers have an average monthly retail sales and use tax liability exceeding $20,000 and notifies those dealers that they are required to remit the tax by EFT. Dealers required to remit the retail sales and use tax by electronic funds transfer (EFT) may not retain a dealer discount.

Quarterly and seasonal filers: The retail sales and use tax dealer discount for quarterly filers and seasonal filers is at the same discount percentages and discount rates as for all other dealers.

Vending machine sales: Dealers required to remit the retail sales and use tax on vending machine sales by EFT may not retain a dealer discount. The dealer discount is allowed on the first 4% of the 5% state retail sales and use tax on vending machine sales and is computed without regard to the number of certificates of registration that a dealer holds. For discounts and factors applicable to vending machine sales, see *Tax Bulletin 10-5,* Virginia Department of Taxation, May 17, 2010, CCH VIRGINIA TAX REPORTS, ¶ 205-181.

• Uniform Sales and Use Tax Administration Act

Virginia has enacted a pared-down version of the Uniform (Simplified) Sales and Use Tax Administration Act, the product of the Streamlined Sales Tax Project (SSTP) Ch. 476 (S.B. 688), Laws 2002. See also ¶ 876.

¶ 898 Prepayment of Taxes

There are no specific provisions relating to prepayment of taxes.

¶ 899 Vendor Registration

Every person who wants to engage in or conduct business as a dealer in Virginia must apply to the Tax Commissioner for a certificate of registration for each place of business in Virginia (Sec. 58.1-613(A), 23 VAC 10-210-290). A dealer making sales through vending machines is required to obtain a certificate of registration in each county or city in which the dealer has machines (Sec. 58.1-614, 23 VAC 10-210-6040—23 VAC 10-210-6043).

Local registration: Local commissioners of revenue may allow dealers seeking to register for the general Virginia retail sales and use tax and out-of-state contractors who are subject to the special use tax in Virginia the option of registering with the local commissioner, rather than registering with the state tax commissioner. The local commissioner of revenue would be required to follow the guidelines, rules, or procedures set forth by the state tax commissioner in providing these services. (Sec. 58.1-604.2; Sec. 58.1-613).

Disaster responders: Out-of-state businesses and employees who come into Virginia solely for the purpose of performing disaster-related or emergency-related work in response to a declared disaster or emergency are not considered to have established residency or a presence in Virginia that would require registration or the filing and paying of certain taxes. Such businesses and employees are not subject to tax withholding and will not be required to file and pay any other Virginia state or local tax or fee during the disaster response period. However, the new provisions do not apply to any applicable transaction taxes and fees, including motor fuels taxes, sales and use taxes, transient occupancy taxes, and car rental taxes or fees, based on purchases, leases, or consumption in Virginia. In addition, the out-of-state employee, or that person's employer, must file and pay income taxes or be subject to tax withholding in the employee's home state on income earned in Virginia during the disaster response period. (Sec. 44-146.28:2)

Remote sellers: See also ¶ 891.

¶ 900   **Sales or Use Tax Credits**

A credit is allowed for sales or use tax paid in another state for tangible personal property used in Virginia (Sec. 58.1-611, 23 VAC 10-210-450). The amount of the credit may not exceed the amount of the Virginia tax. This credit does not require that the state of purchase grant a similar credit for tax paid to Virginia. The credit does not apply to tax erroneously paid to another state (23 VAC 10-210-450). For example, if a person takes delivery in Virginia of tangible personal property purchased from an out-of-state dealer who incorrectly charges out-of-state tax, no credit is available; instead, the purchaser must apply to the dealer for a refund.

Credits are also allowed for motor vehicle sales and use taxes paid to other states, except when that state exempts from tax vehicles sold to residents of a state which does not give credit for the tax (Sec. 58.1-2424), and for aircraft and watercraft sales and use taxes paid to other states (Sec. 58.1-1409, Sec. 58.1-1504).

Modular buildings: A modular building manufacturer that has paid tax on the cost of materials incorporated into a modular building sold without installation may take a credit against the sales tax due from the sale of the modular building in the amount of the tax previously paid (Sec. 58.1-610.1).

¶ 901   **Deficiency Assessments**

If any person fails to make a proper return or fails to pay in full any tax, the Commissioner will assess the tax due, as well as any applicable penalties and interest (Sec. 58.1-1812, 23 VAC 10-20-150). Upon assessment, the Department will send a bill to the taxpayer. The tax, penalties, and interest must be remitted to the Department within 30 days from the date of the bill.

Estimated assessments: Whenever a taxpayerwho is liable under the law to file a state tax return fails or refuses on demand to file a correct and proper return, the Department may make an estimate from any information in its possession of the amount of taxes due the state by the taxpayer and assess the taxes, penalties, and interest (Sec. 58.1-111).

In addition, the Retail Sales and Use Tax Act specifically provides that the Tax Commissioner must make estimated assessments when a dealer files no return or when the return is false or fraudulent (Sec. 58.1-618). For an estimated assessment, 10 days' written notice to appear must be given the dealer. If the dealer fails to file a return, permit an examination of books, records, or papers, or appear and answer questions within the scope of the investigation, the Tax Commissioner may make an assessment based on available information. The estimated assessment is deemed to be *prima facie* correct.

• **Tax amnesty**

A Virginia tax amnesty program will occur during the period of July 1, 2017, through June 30, 2018, and will not last less than 60 nor more than 75 days. The exact dates of the program will be established by the Tax Commissioner. (Sec. 58.1-1840.2)

Any taxpayer required to file a return or to pay any tax administered or collected by the Department of Taxation will be eligible to participate in the amnesty program, subject to certain requirements and guidelines. The Tax Commissioner may require participants to complete an amnesty application and other forms and to furnish any additional information necessary to make a determination regarding the validity of an amnesty application. With certain exceptions, all civil or criminal penalties assessed or assessable, and one-half of the interest assessed or assessable, that are the result of nonpayment, underpayment, nonreporting, or underreporting of tax liabilities, may be waived under the program upon receipt of the payment of the amount of taxes and interest owed. (Ch. 54 (H.B. 2246), Laws 2017)

¶ 902   **Audit Procedures**

To enforce the tax laws, the Tax Commissioner may require the examination of a taxpayer's books and records or the taxpayer's appearance to answer questions (Sec. 58.1-219, Sec. 58.1-618).

¶ 903   **Statute of Limitations**

A tax must be assessed within three years from the date on which it became due and payable (Sec. 58.1-634). However, in cases of false or fraudulent returns or failure to file a return, a tax may be assessed within six years from such date.

The Tax Commissioner may not inspect a person's records after a three-year period unless there is reasonable evidence of fraud or reasonable cause to believe that the person was required by law to file a return and failed to do so.

¶ 904   **Application for Refund**

A dealer may request a refund for sales and use taxes erroneously or illegally collected by the Department of Taxation (23 VAC 10-210-340). It must be shown that the dealer paid the tax and did not pass it on to the consumer or that the dealer collected the tax and later refunded it to the consumer.

Requests for a refund must be made within three years from the due date of the return. If a dealer filed a timely return and deducted the dealer's discount, the amount of the refund is reduced by the dealer's discount taken (see ¶ 897).

Refunds are also allowed when an amended return leads to a reassessment and a finding that excess taxes were paid (Sec. 58.1-1823, 23 VAC 10-20-180).

Motor vehicles returned under warranty: Effective July 1, 2017, a purchaser may be refunded motor vehicle sales and use tax paid if the vehicle is returned pursuant to the Virginia Motor Vehicle Warranty Enforcement Act, or if the vehicle is returned within 45 days of purchase, and the purchase price is refunded, due to a mechanical defect or failure. A person claiming the refund under the Virginia Motor Vehicle Warranty Enforcement Act is required to provide a written statement stating that the vehicle was returned under the Act. A person claiming the refund due to a mechanical defect or failure is required to submit an affidavit to the Commissioner of the Department of Motor Vehicles stating that the vehicle was returned due to a mechanical defect or failure, the purchase price was refunded, the title was assigned to the person accepting the return, and the purchaser no longer has possession of the vehicle. (Sec. 58.1-2403; Sec. 58.1-2423)

¶ 905   WASHINGTON

¶ 906   Scope of Tax

Source.—Statutory references are to Chapters 82.08 and 82.12 of Title 82 of the Revised Code of Washington (RCW), as amended to date. Details are reported in the CCH Washington Tax Reports starting at ¶ 60-000.

The Washington sales tax is imposed on each retail sale or lease in the state of tangible personal property, extended warranties, and specified services (RCW 82.08.020, RCW 82.12.020). The use tax is imposed on every consumer who uses an article of tangible personal property in Washington acquired in a specified manner (RCW 82.12.020).

The sales and use tax is imposed in addition to other licenses, taxes, and excises imposed by Washington and its municipal subdivisions (RCW 82.32.280).

Digital products: Digital products that are transferred electronically, including digital songs, books, games, and movies, are taxable. These digital products, in addition to digital codes and digital automated services, are also taxable when they are accessed remotely or streamed. (RCW 82.04.050; RCW 82.12.010; WAC 458-20-15503; see also *Excise Tax Advisories 3176.2013 and 3177.2013*)

Canned computer software is considered tangible personal property, while information services such as news and information are not considered tangible property (RCW 82-08-050(6); WAC 458-20-15502). Software maintenance agreements, which may include software upgrades and updates, telephone consulting, help desk services, and remote diagnostic services generally are not subject to sales tax; however, if a maintenance agreement sale includes software upgrades or updates that are not separately itemized, it would be considered a bundled transaction subject to retail sales tax if the updates/upgrades represent at least 10% of the total price. *(Tax Topics,* Washington Department of Revenue, March 22, 2017)

The Washington Department of Revenue has concluded that online searchable databases (OSDs) are digital automated services (DAS) and therefore do not qualify for the sales tax exemption for digital goods used only for a business purpose. OSDs, such as legal research services, are DAS as they are transferred electronically and use at least one software application. The department will accept prior reporting of sales as taxable or exempt but will enforce the current policy beginning January 1, 2011. (*Special Notice,* Washington Department of Revenue, November 2, 2010, CCH Washington Tax Reports, ¶ 203-213).

A person's ownership of digital goods or codes residing on servers located in Washington may not be considered as evidence of substantial nexus with the state (RCW 82.32.532).

"Deal of the day" discount vouchers: Upon redemption of a discount voucher, or "deal-of-the-day voucher," a retailer is required to collect sales tax on the total amount paid for the voucher and any other consideration received from the customer (*e.g.,* cash, check, or credit card amount). The purchase of the discount voucher prior to redemption is not taxable.

A discount voucher is an instrument redeemed by a customer that meets the following conditions:

— is obtained by the customer from a discount voucher provider (DVP) that has an agreement with the seller, and the seller has determined the price of the voucher;

— allows the customer to acquire the voucher for less than face value; is redeemable either for a specific good or service or for a certain dollar amount towards the sales price; and

— the seller, at the time of redemption, knows the amount paid by the customer for the voucher.

If the discount voucher is redeemed for a product subject to retail sales tax, the amount paid by the customer is included in the product's taxable sales price. If at the time of sale, the seller does not know the amount paid to obtain the discount voucher, the seller must treat the consideration paid by the customer as equal to the face value of the instrument. (*Special Notice,* Washington Department of Revenue, August 23, 2012, CCH WASHINGTON TAX REPORTS, ¶ 203-443).

Prepaid phone cards: Prepaid telephone calling cards are taxable (Excise Tax Advisory 3093, Washington Department of Revenue).

• **Services**

Taxable services include: (1) installing, repairing, cleaning, altering, improving, constructing, or decorating real or personal property of or for consumers; (2) constructing, repairing, decorating, or improving structures; (3) cleaning, fumigating, razing, or moving structures; (4) automobile towing; (5) furnishing lodging for less than a month; (6) specified personal services; (7) amusement and recreation services; (8) abstract, title insurance, and escrow services; (9) credit bureau services; (10) automobile parking and storage garage services; (11) landscape maintenance and horticultural services; (12) service charges associated with tickets to professional sporting events; (13) renting or leasing tangible personal property; and (14) telephone service. (RCW 82.04.050)

Services that are not taxable include janitorial services, barber services, dental services, physicians' medical services, attorney services, security services, and training services. (RCW 82.04.050(2)(d), WAC 458-20-138 (Rule 138)).

• **Incidence of the sales and use tax**

Sales and use taxes are imposed on the buyer and collected by the seller from the buyer (RCW 82.08.050, RCW 82.12.020). However, the Department may, in its discretion, collect the sales tax directly from the buyer when the buyer has failed to pay the seller.

People who obtain a certificate of registration, maintain a place of business in Washington, maintain a stock of goods in Washington, or engage in business activities within Washington are required to collect use tax from people in Washington to whom they sell tangible personal property at retail and from whom they have not collected sales tax (RCW 82.12.040, WAC 458-20-221(4)). A person in Washington who acts as a selling agent for a person without a valid certificate of registration, and who receives compensation as a result of the sales, is a retailer who must collect tax from the purchasers.

People in Washington who buy articles of tangible personal property at retail are liable for use tax with respect to purchases on which sales tax has not been paid (WAC 458-20-178(4), WAC 458-20-221(3)). The extractor or manufacturer who commercially uses the articles extracted or manufactured, the bailor or donor and the bailee or donee if the tax is not paid by the bailor or donor, the lessee if the tax is not paid by the lessor, and the lessor of equipment with an operator are liable for the use tax (WAC 458-20-178(4)).

A seller who fails to collect or remit the sales or use tax is personally liable to the state for the amount of the tax. Sellers whose activities in Washington are conducted electronically via a website on a server owned or operated by an unaffiliated entity are not required to collect sales or use tax if their activities are limited to: (1) the storage, dissemination, or display of advertising; (2) the taking of orders; or (3) the processing of payments (RCW 82.08.050; RCW 82.12.040).

¶906 Washington

• Use tax

The use tax is imposed on every person who consumes the following property in Washington acquired in any manner (RCW 82.12.020):

— tangible personal property;

— tangible personal property acquired at a casual or isolated sale, and byproducts used by the manufacturer thereof;

— any prewritten software, regardless of the method of delivery, but excluding prewritten software that is either provided free of charge or is provided for temporary use in viewing information, or both;

— extended warranty;

— specified services, excluding access to remote access software that is provided free of charge; and

— digital goods, digital codes, or digital automated services, whether or not the purchaser obtains a right of permanent use, or is obligated to make continued payments.

The use tax supplements the sales tax by taxing the use in Washington of every service defined as a retail sale in RCW 82.04.050(3)(a) and every article of tangible personal property on which sales tax has not been paid (RCW 82.08.050). No use tax is due if the sale or use of tangible personal property by the present user or the bailor or donor has already been subject to Washington sales or use tax, or if the tax has already been paid for property acquired by bailment based on reasonable rental (RCW 82.12.0252, WAC 458-20-178).

Services performed outside Washington: Use tax is imposed on services performed outside Washington on tangible personal property used in the state, including installing, repairing, cleaning, altering, imprinting, or improving tangible personal property (RCW 82.12.010(4)(b)). With respect to these services, the term "use" is defined as the first act within the state by which a taxpayer takes control, as a consumer, over the article of tangible personal property on which the service was performed (RCW 82.12.010(3)).

• Nexus

The sale of tangible personal property by out-of-state vendors to people located in Washington is subject to tax (WAC 458-20-193(8) and (9)). Out-of-state vendors are required to collect and remit sales or use tax on deliveries to Washington customers when the vendor, whether directly or through an agent or other representative, does any of the following in Washington (WAC 458-20-193(7), (9)):

— has or utilizes an office, distribution house, sales house, warehouse, service enterprise, or other place of business;

— maintains a stock of goods;

— regularly solicits orders whether or not such orders are accepted in Washington, (unless the activity in this state consists solely of advertising or of solicitation by direct mail);

— regularly engages in the delivery of property in Washington other than by common carrier or U.S. Mail;

— regularly engages in any activity in connection with the leasing or servicing of property located within Washington;

— performs, directly or by an agent or representative, significant services in relation to establishment or maintenance of sales into Washington, even though the seller may not have formal sales offices or the agent or representative may not be formally characterized as a "salesperson;" and

— installs, either directly or by an agent or representative, products in Washington as a condition of sale.

Trade shows: Effective July 1, 2016, the participation of one or more representatives at a single trade convention per year in Washington is not considered a factor in the nexus determination. The safe harbor does not apply to persons making retail sales at a trade convention. (Sec. 3, Ch. 137 (H.B. 2938), Laws 2016)

Internet sales: A seller is not obligated to collect use tax if its activities in Washington are limited to:

— storing, disseminating, or displaying advertising;

— taking of orders; or

— processing of payments; and

— the activities are conducted electronically by a Web site on a server or other computer equipment located in Washington that is not owned or operated by the seller or an affiliated person.

Persons are "affiliated" with respect to each other where one of the persons has an ownership interest of more than 5%, whether direct or indirect, in the other, or where an ownership interest of more than 5%, whether direct or indirect, is held in each of the persons by another person or by a group of other persons which are affiliated with respect to each other (RCW 82.12.040(5); RCW 82.04.424).

Click-through nexus: Beginning September 1, 2015, a seller is presumed to have substantial nexus with Washington if the seller enters into an agreement with one or more residents under which the resident, for a commission or other consideration, directly or indirectly, refers potential customers, by a link on an Internet website or otherwise, to the seller. (Uncodified Sec. 202, S.B. 6138, Laws 2015)

The presumption requires that the cumulative gross receipts from sales by the seller to customers in the state who are referred to the seller be greater than $10,000 during the preceding calendar year. The presumption may be rebutted by demonstrating that the residents with whom the seller had agreements did not engage in solicitation on behalf of the remote seller that would satisfy the nexus requirements of the U.S. Constitution during the calendar year. A remote seller engaging in such agreements with state residents would also be presumed to have substantial nexus with Washington for purposes of retailing business and occupation (B&O) tax liability. (Uncodified Sec. 202, S.B. 6138, Laws 2015)

If the department determines that a change in the Streamlined Sales and Use Tax Agreement or in federal law taking effect after September 1, 2015 creates a conflict with the click-through nexus provision, the application of that provision terminates. (Uncodified Section 205, S.B. 6138, Laws 2015)

SST registration: A business's mere registration under or compliance with the Streamlined Sales and Use Tax Agreement (SSUTA) does not constitute nexus for purposes of the local government's authority to impose Washington business and occupation tax on the business. Also, a first-class city, second-class city, code city, and town may not require a business to obtain a license based solely upon the business's registration under or compliance with the SSUTA. However, if a firm actually has nexus within the city, it is still potentially subject to registration for local business tax purposes. (RCW 35.102.150; RCW 82.32.530).

• **Streamlined Act status**

Washington is a full member of the Governing Board of the Streamlined Sales and Use Tax Agreement (SSUTA) For additional information, see ¶ 912.

Washington's taxability matrix is available on the Streamlined Sales Tax Governing Board's website at **http://www.streamlinedsalestax.org**.

Whenever the taxability matrix is amended, sellers are relieved from liability due to reliance on the preceding version of the state's matrix until the first day of the calendar month that is at least 30 days after the Department of Revenue submits notice of a change to the matrix to the SST governing board (RCW 82.32.740).

¶ 907	Tax Base

Sales tax is levied on the selling price of each retail sale in Washington (RCW 82.08.020). Use tax is imposed on the value of the article used (RCW 82.12.020).

• Selling price

"Selling price" means the consideration expressed in terms of money paid by a buyer to a seller (RCW 82.08.010(1), WAC 458-20-107). It includes the cost of tangible property sold, the cost of materials, labor costs, interest, discount, delivery costs, taxes, losses, or other expenses, but does not include the value of trade-in property of like kind or the amount of cash discount actually taken by a buyer.

When tangible personal property is rented or leased and the consideration does not represent a reasonable rental, the "selling price" is determined according to the value of such use at the places of use of similar products of like quality and character (RCW 82.08.010(1)).

• Value of the article used

"Value of the article used" means the consideration paid by the purchaser to the seller for the article of tangible personal property, the use of which is taxable (RCW 82.12.010(1), WAC 458-20-178(13)). It includes the amount of any tariff or duty paid, but not the value of trade-in property of like kind. If the article is transferred under conditions such that the purchase price does not represent the true value, the value of the article is determined according to the retail selling price at the place of use of similar products of like quality and character.

The value of articles acquired by bailment is an amount representing a reasonable rental for the use of the article, determined according to the value of the use at places of use of similar products of like quality and character (RCW 82.12.010(1), WAC 458-20-178(13)). If an article acquired by bailment is used for construction, repairs, or improvement and becomes a component of a structure of the United States, its instrumentalities, or a county or city housing authority, the value of the use of the article is determined according to the retail selling price of the articles, according to the retail selling price at place of use of similar products of like quality and character, or on the cost basis.

If an article is owned by a user engaged in business outside Washington and is brought into the state for no more than 180 out of 365 days for temporary business use, the value of the article used is the reasonable rental for the use of the article (RCW 82.12.010(1), WAC 458-20-78(15)).

Articles manufactured and used in the manufacture of products sold to the United States Department of Defense are valued according to the value of the ingredients of the articles (RCW 82.12.010(1)).

• Sourcing

Washington generally uses destination-based sourcing on sales. Special provisions apply to sourcing of leases and rentals and telecommunications services.

Florists: Florists may use origin-based sourcing to determine Washington sales and use tax liability on certain florist sales. Specifically, when one florist takes an order from a customer and then communicates that order to another florist who delivers the items purchased to the place designated by the customer, the location at or from which the delivery is made to the consumer is deemed to be the location of the florist originally taking the order. (RCW 82.32.730(6)).

¶ 908   **List of Exemptions, Exceptions, and Exclusions**

Unless otherwise indicated, the statutory exemptions, exceptions, and exclusions listed below apply to both sales and use taxes; those applicable only to the sales tax or only to the use tax are listed separately. Items that are excluded from the sales or use tax base are treated at ¶ 907, "Tax Base."

Marijuana farmers and producers: For purposes of Washington sales and use tax and business and occupation tax, the terms "agriculture," "agricultural product," "farming," "horticulture," "horticultural," and "horticultural product" may not be construed as including or relating to marijuana, useable marijuana, or marijuana-infused products. Persons involved in the growing or producing of such products therefore do not qualify for numerous existing tax preferences.

The sales and use tax exemptions that are unavailable to persons involved in the marijuana, useable marijuana, and marijuana-infused products industry include the following:

— farm tractors or vehicles from the additional 0.3% tax on the sale of motor vehicles;

— machinery and equipment used directly in a manufacturing operation, research and development operation or testing;

— charges for labor and services rendered in respect to installing, repairing, cleaning, altering, or improving such equipment;

— auction sales made by auctioneers of property used in conducting a farm activity when the seller is a farmer;

— sales to certain nonresidents;

— services relating to the construction of agricultural employee housing and tangible personal property that becomes a component of such housing;

— sales of drugs for human use dispensed pursuant to prescription;

— sales of drugs or devices used for family planning purposes for human use dispensed pursuant to a prescription;

— sales of drugs or devices for family planning purposes for human use supplied by a family planning clinic under contract with the department of health;

— lease of certain irrigation equipment;

— food and food ingredients;

— remittance for wholesalers or third-party warehousers who own or operate warehouses or grain elevators and retailers who own or operate distribution centers; and

— exemption for farm tractors or vehicles from the regional transportation investment district tax.

In addition to the above, the legislation enacts numerous exclusions from preferences under business and occupation taxes, excise taxes, and property taxes. (S.B. 6505, Laws 2014)

Marijuana retailers' exemptions: Beginning July 1, 2016, the following transactions by marijuana retailers with a medical marijuana endorsement qualify for exemption (*Special Notice,* Washington Department of Revenue, May 6, 2016, CCH Washington Tax Reports, ¶ 204-047):

— Sales and donations of marijuana products determined by the Department of Health to be of beneficial medical use to qualifying patients and designated providers who have recognition cards;

— Sales and donations of low-THC products to qualifying patients and designated providers with recognition cards;

— Sales of high-CBD compliant marijuana products to all consumers.

Beginning July 1, 2016, sales and donations of topical, nondigestible low-THC products by certain health care professionals to qualifying patients are exempt from sales and use tax. Health care professionals must still pay retail sales or use tax on their purchases of these products. However, when the health care professional sells or donates low-THC products to a qualifying patient, they can use a reseller permit to purchase these products exempt of tax. The notice also includes instructions on how to complete a tax return and document this exemption. (*Special Notice,* Washington Department of Revenue, May 6, 2016, CCH WASHINGTON TAX REPORTS, ¶ 204-049)

Marijuana cooperatives: For information about exempt products that a cooperative can produce and provide to its members, the process of documenting exemptions, the taxability of marijuana plant purchases from marijuana producers, and the taxability of purchases of other goods or services, see *Special Notice,* Washington Department of Revenue, May 6, 2016, CCH WASHINGTON TAX REPORTS, ¶ 204-050)

• Sales and use tax exemptions, exceptions, and exclusions

Academic transcripts	RCW 82.08.02537, RCW 82.12.0347
Agricultural animal pharmaceuticals	RCW 82.08.880, RCW 82.12.880
Agricultural bedding for chicken coops	RCW 82.08.920, RCW 82.12.920
Aircraft parts (tangible personal property incorporated into)	RCW 82.08.02566, RCW 2.12.02566
Aircraft used in interstate commerce or commuter transportation	RCW 82.08.0262, RCW 82.12.0254
Airplanes, large private; sold to nonresidents (exp. 7/1/2021)	RCW 82.08.215, RCW 82.12.215
Air pollution control equipment	RCW 82.32.393, RCW 82.08.810, RCW 82.12.810, RCW 82.08.811, RCW 82.12.811
Alternative housing for youth in crisis	RCW 82.08.02915, RCW 82.12.02915
Aluminum smelters (exp. 12/31/17)	RCW 82.08.805, RCW 82.12.805
Anaerobic digesters for cattle manure	RCW 82.08.900, RCW 82.12.900
Art exhibits	RCW 82.04.4328, RCW 82.08.031, RCW 82.12.031
Artificial insemination of livestock	RCW 82.08.0272, RCW 82.12.0267
Auctions	RCW 82.08.040
Blood, bone, or tissue banks	RCW 82.04.324, RCW 82.08.02805, RCW 82.12.02747
Boats used in interstate commerce	RCW 82.08.0262, RCW 82.12.0254
Bottled water	RCW 82.08.0293 (2) (f)
Candy	RCW 82.08.0293 (2) (e)

Carbon and other materials used in producing aluminum . . . . RCW 82.08.02568, RCW 82.12.02568

Chemicals used for post-harvest treatment . . . . RCW 82.04.050(8)

Coal to generate electricity . . . . RCW 82.08.811, RCW 82.12.811

Computers used in aerospace design, development, and
    manufacturing, and in providing aerospace services . . . . RCW 82.08.975, RCW 82.12.975

Computers used in printing or publishing . . . . RCW 82.08.806, RCW 82.12.806

Conifer seed for export . . . . RCW 82.08.850, RCW 82.12.850

Construction labor for a political entity . . . . RCW 82.04.050(8)

Construction of aircraft maintenance facilities (exp. 1/1/2027) . . . . . H.B. 2839, Laws 2016

Construction of airplane manufacturing facilities . . . . RCW 82.08.980, RCW 82.12.980

Construction of alternative housing for youth in crisis . . . . RCW 82.08.02915, RCW 82.12.02915

Cover charges for dancing . . . . RCW 82.08.050(3)

Custom computer software . . . . RCW 82.04.050(6)

Data centers, servers and power infrastructure equipment for . . . . . RCW 82.08.986, RCW 82.12.986

Dental appliances . . . . RCW 82.08.0283, RCW 82.12.0277

Delivery charges for direct mail, separately stated . . . . RCW 82.08.010

Deposits on vehicle batteries . . . . RCW 82.08.036, RCW 82.12.038

Diesel fuel used in certain watercraft . . . . RCW 82.08.0298, RCW 82.12.0298

Digital codes, goods, services, (specific) . . . . RCW 82.08.0208 *et seq.*, RCW 82.12.0208 *et seq.*

Disabled veterans or military members, automotive adaptive
    equipment for (exp. 7/31/2018) . . . . RCW 82.08.875, RCW 82.12.875

Distribution centers . . . . RCW 82.08.820, RCW 82.12.820

Drugs . . . . RCW 82.08.0281, RCW 82.12.0275

Electric vehicle batteries, infrastructure . . . . RCW 82.08.816, RCW 82.12.816

Energy, renewable; equipment and labor (exp. 6/30/2020) . . . . RCW 82.08.962, RCW 82.12.962

Farm auctions . . . . RCW 82.08.0257, RCW 82.12.0258

Fitness classes provided by local government . . . . RCW 82.08.0291

Fuel (diesel, biodiesel, aviation) for agricultural use . . . . RCW 82.08.865, RCW 82.12.865

Farm machinery, parts, and repairs sold to nonresidents . . . . RCW 82.08.0268

Farm machinery, replacement parts	RCW 82.08.855, RCW 82.12.855
Farmworker housing	RCW 82.08.02745, RCW 82.12.02685
Federal aid and relief corporations	RCW 82.12.0259
Feed for livestock	RCW 82.08.0294, RCW 82.08.0296, RCW 82.12.0294, RCW 81.12.0296
Feed, seed, fertilizer, and spray materials	RCW 82.04.050(8)
Ferries	RCW 82.08.0285, RCW 82.12.0279
Ferry fuel	RCW 82.08.055, RCW 82.12.0256
Financial information (standard), sold to international financial management companies (exp. 7/1/2021)	RCW 82.08.207, RCW 82.12.207
Floating homes, used	RCW 82.08.034, RCW 82.12.034
Food and food ingredients (for human consumption)	RCW 82.08.0293, RCW 82.12.0293
Food flavoring products sold to restaurants (exp. 7/1/2017)	RCW 82.08.210, RCW 82.12.210
Food stamps	RCW 82.08.0297, RCW 81.12.0297
Form lumber	RCW 82.08.0274, RCW 82.12.0268
Free hospitals	RCW 82.08.02795, RCW 82.12.02745
Government contractors	RCW 82.04.050(8)
Gun clubs; clay targets sold to (exp. 7/1/2017)	RCW 82.08.205, RCW 82.12.205
Gun safes	RCW 82.08.832, RCW 82.12.832
Grain elevators	RCW 82.08.820, RCW 82.12.820
Hog fuel for renewable energy generation (exp. 6/30/2024)	RCW 82.08.956, RCW 82.12.956
Honeybees, feed for (exp. 7/1/2017)	RCW 82.08.200, RCW 82.12.200
Honeybees sold to beekeepers	RCW 82.08.0204, RCW 82.12.0204
Horticultural product packing	RCW 82.08.0311, RCW 82.12.0311
Horticultural services provided to farmers	RCW 82.04.050(3)
Human blood, tissue, organs, bodies, body parts	RCW 82.08.02806, RCW 82.12.02748
Ingredients or components	RCW 82.04.050(1)

¶908   **Washington**

Motor vehicles using clean alternative fuel and plug-in hybrids (exp. 7/1/2019) . . . . RCW 82.08.809; RCW 82.08.813; RCW 82.12.809; RCW 82.12.813

Motor vehicles and trailers sold to nonresidents . . . . RCW 82.08.0264

Motor vehicles and trailers used in interstate commerce . . . . RCW 82.08.0263, RCW 82.12.0254

Motor vehicles sold to tribe or tribal members in Indian country . . . (Sec. 1, Ch. 232 (S.B. 6427), Laws 2016)

Motor vehicles used in ridesharing . . . . RCW 82.08.0287, RCW 82.12.0282

Natural gas or propane used to heat chicken coops . . . . RCW 82.08.910, RCW 82.12.910

Nonprofit organizations' fundraising activities . . . . RCW 82.04.3651

Nonprofit youth organization—amusement and recreation services . RCW 82.04.4271, RCW 82.08.0291

Nonresidents . . . . RCW 82.08.0273

Nonreturnable containers for beverages and food . . . . RCW 82.08.0282, RCW 82.12.0276

Nontaxable sales—by law or constitution . . . . RCW 82.08.0254

Observatory construction . . . . RCW 82.08.02569, RCW 82.12.02569

Organ procurement organization, sales to . . . . RCW 82.08.02807, RCW 82.12.02749

Ostomic items . . . . RCW 82.08.0283, RCW 82.12.0277

Oxygen medically prescribed . . . . RCW 82.08.0283, RCW 82.12.0277

Packing materials for horticultural products . . . . RCW 82.08.0311, RCW 82.12.0311

Park model trailers, used . . . . RCW 82.08.032, RCW 82.12.032

Political subdivisions . . . . RCW 82.08.0278, RCW 82.12.0274

Pollen . . . . RCW 82.08.0277, RCW 82.12.0273

Pollution control facilities . . . . RCW 82.08.035, RCW 82.12.036, RCW 82.34.020, RCW 82.34.050

Poultry . . . . RCW 82.08.0259, RCW 82.08.0267, RCW 82.12.0261, RCW 82.12.0262

Precious metal bullion or monetized bullion . . . . RCW 82.04.062(1), RCW 82.04.062(3)

Prescription drugs . . . . RCW 82.08.0281, RCW 82.12.0275

Property consumed in manufacturing . . . . RCW 82.04.050(1), RCW 82.04.120

Prosthetic and orthotic devices	RCW 82.08.0283, RCW 82.12.0277
Public records	RCW 82.08.02525, RCW 82.12.02525
Public road materials	RCW 82.04.190(3)
Public utilities—gross operating revenue	RCW 82.08.0256, RCW 82.12.0257, RCW 82.16.020(1)
Public utilities—sale of operating property	RCW 82.08.0252, RCW 82.12.0253, RCW 82.16.020
Railroad cars used in interstate commerce	RCW 82.08.262, RCW 82.12.0254
Removal of trees and brush near electric transmission or distribution lines or equipment	RCW 82.04.050(3)
Renewable energy generation (1 kw or more); equipment and labor (exp. 6/30/2020)	RCW 82.08.962, RCW 82.12.962
Renewable energy generation (hog fuel) (exp. 6/30/2024)	RCW 82.08.956, RCW 82.12.956
Resales	RCW 82.04.050(1)(a), RCW 82.04.470
Research and development	RCW 82.08.02565, RCW 82.12.02565
Ridesharing vehicles	RCW 82.08.0287, RCW 82.12.0282
Road construction labor	RCW 82.04.050(6)
Sale/leasebacks of food processing equipment	RCW 82.08.0295, RCW 82.12.0295
Sales to noncontiguous U.S. states, territories, and possessions	RCW 82.08.0269
Sample and display wearing apparel	RCW 82.08.0276, RCW 82.12.0271
Sand, rock, and gravel for public roads	RCW 82.08.0275, RCW 82.12.0269
Semiconductor manufacturing, gases and chemicals (exp. 12/1/2018)	RCW 82.08.9651
Solar energy (10 kw or less); equipment and labor (exp. 6/30/2018) .	RCW 82.08.963, RCW 82.12.963
Special fuel	RCW 82.08.0255(1), RCW 82.12.0256
Transit authorities, sales to	RCW 82.04.050(10)
Vehicle components and labor for construction, repairs, cleaning . . .	RCW 82.08.0262, RCW 82.12.0254
Vessel deconstruction	RCW 82.08.9996, RCW 82.12.9996
Video production business	RCW 82.08.0315, RCW 82.12.0315
Warehouses	RCW 82.08.820, RCW 82.12.820

¶908   Washington

Washington Credit Union Share Guaranty Association . . . . RCW 31.12A.130

Washington Insurance Guaranty Association . . . . RCW 48.32.130

Washington Life and Disability Insurance Guaranty Association . . . . RCW 48.32A.100

Watercraft sold to nonresidents . . . . RCW 82.08.0266

Watercraft sold to residents of foreign countries . . . . RCW 82.08.02665

Watercraft used in interstate commerce . . . . RCW 82.08.0262, RCW 82.12.0254

Watershed protection and flood prevention . . . . RCW 82.08.0271

Wearing apparel used as a sample or display . . . . RCW 82.08.0276, RCW 82.12.0271

Weatherization materials for residences . . . . RCW 82.08.998, RCW 82.12.998

Wind and solar energy facilities . . . . RCW 82.08.02567

• Exemptions, exceptions, and exclusions applicable only to the sales tax

Amusement and recreation services . . . . RCW 82.08.0291

Camps and conference centers . . . . RCW 82.08.830

Casual and isolated sales . . . . RCW 82.04.040, RCW 82.08.0251

Environmental remedial action services . . . . RCW 82.04.050(10)

Lodging for homeless people . . . . RCW 82.08.0299

Newspapers . . . . RCW 82.08.0253

Network telephone service . . . . RCW 82.08.0289

Manufactured gas . . . . RCW 82.08.026, RCW 82.12.023

Natural gas . . . . RCW 82.08.026, RCW 82.12.023

Physical fitness classes provided by a local government . . . . RCW 82.08.0291

Repairs for nonresidents . . . . RCW 82.08.0265

Sale/leasebacks by regional transit authorities . . . . RCW 82.04.834

Trail grooming services sold to nonprofit corporation or the state of Washington . . . . RCW 82.08.0203

Vehicle parking charges . . . . RCW 82.08.02875

• Exemptions, exceptions, and exclusions applicable only to the use tax

Armed Forces household goods, personal effects, and private automobiles . . . . RCW 82.12.0251

Natural gas (compressed or liquefied) sold as a transportation fuel . . Sec. 82.12.022(6)

Credit unions, merging or converting . . . . RCW 82.12.860

Property produced for use in manufacturing ferrosilicon subsequently used to make magnesium for sale . . . . RCW 82.04.050

Use by a bailee of tangible personal property consumed in research and development activities . . . . RCW 82.12.0265

Use by a manufacturer of machinery and equipment used directly in manufacturing or research and development . . . . RCW 82.08.02565, RCW 82.12.02565

Use by a nonprofit charitable organization or state or local governmental entity of certain donated items . . . . RCW 82.12.02595

Use of personal property valued at under $10,000, purchased or
received as a prize in a game of chance from a nonprofit
organization or library (exp. 7/1/2017) . . . .   RCW 82.12.225

Use of computers, components, accessories, or software donated to
schools or colleges . . . .   RCW 82.12.0284

Use of dual controlled vehicle for driver training . . . .   RCW 82.12.0264

Use of effluent water purchased from a government sewage treatment
facility . . . .   RCW 82.08.036

Use of fuel by manufacturer when used directly in operation for the
plant producing the fuel . . . .   RCW 82.12.0263

Use of tangible personal property on which tax has been paid . . . . .   RCW 82.12.0252

Vessel manufacturers and dealers . . . .   RCW 82.12.800, RCW
82.12.801

¶ 909   Rate of Tax

Except as noted below, the sales and use tax in Washington is levied at the rate of 6.5% of the selling price of the article or value of the article used (RCW 82.08.020, RCW 82.12.020, WAC 458-20-237(1) (Rule 237)). For local sales and use taxes that are levied in addition to the state tax and for a chart of the rates, see ¶ 910.

An additional tax of 5.9% is levied on retail car rentals (RCW 82.08.020(2)).

Syrup: An excise tax is imposed on each sale at wholesale of syrup, which means a concentrated liquid that is added to carbonated water to produce a carbonated beverage, at the rate of $1 per gallon (RCW 82.64.010, RCW 82.64.020). No tax is due on the retail sale if the tax has already been paid (RCW 82.64.030).

Alcoholic beverages: Instead of the regular sales and use tax rate, sales of spirits or strong beer in the original package are taxed as follows (RCW 82.08.150):

— the retail sale of spirits or strong beer in the original package, except sales to full service restaurant licensees, is taxed at the rate of 15%;

— the sale of spirits or strong beer in the original package to full service restaurant licensees is taxed at the rate of 10%;

— the retail sale of spirits in the original package is subject to an additional tax at the rate of $1.72 per liter;

— the retail sale of spirits or strong beer in the original package is subject to an additional tax of 14% of the taxes payable as stated above;

— the retail sale of spirits in the original package is subject to an additional tax at the rate of 7¢ per liter;

— the retail sale of spirits in the original package, except sales to full service restaurant licensees, is subject to an additional tax at the rate of 3.4% of the selling price;

— the retail sale of spirits in the original package to full service restaurant licensees is subject to an additional tax at the rate of 2.3% of the selling price; and

— the retail sale of spirits in the original package is subject to an additional tax at the rate of 41¢ per liter;

— an additional tax of $1.33 per liter is imposed on each retail sale of spirits in the original package, excluding sales to spirits, beer, and wine restaurant licensees.

Gas: Natural and manufactured gas are subject to use tax at the rate in effect for the public utility tax on gas distribution businesses (RCW 82.12.022(2)).

Motor vehicles: An additional tax of 0.3% is imposed on retail sales of new and used motor vehicles (RCW 82.08.020). The additional tax does not apply to farm tractors or farm vehicles, off-road and nonhighway vehicles, or snowmobiles.

- **Marijuana**

A marijuana excise tax is collected by the Liquor and Cannabis Board at a rate of 37% of the selling price on each retail sale of marijuana concentrates, usable marijuana, and marijuana-infused products. The tax is paid by the buyer, is separate and in addition to general state and local sales and use taxes, and is not part of the total retail price to which general state and local sales and use taxes apply. (RCW 69.50.535) The tax must be separately itemized from the state and local retail sales tax on the sales receipt. (RCW 69.50.535)

Medical marijuana: Effective January 1, 2016, sales of medical marijuana and specified related products are exempt from sales and use taxes (Uncodified Sec. 208, H.B. 2136, Laws 2015).

Tribal sales of marijuana: The Washington governor is authorized to enter into agreements with federally recognized Indian tribes regarding marijuana regulation. Each such agreement must include a tribal marijuana tax equal to the state marijuana excise tax and state and local sales and use taxes. However, a tribe may exempt sales to the tribe, tribal enterprises, tribal-owned businesses, or tribal members of marijuana that is grown, produced, or processed within Indian country. A tribe may also exempt activities to the extent that they are exempt from the state marijuana excise tax or the state and local sales or use taxes on marijuana sales pursuant to state or federal law. The retail sale of and commercial activities related to the production, processing, sale, and possession of marijuana covered by a tribal-state marijuana agreement are exempt from sales and use taxes and taxes and fees imposed by the Uniform Controlled Substances Act. (H.B. 2000, Laws 2015)

- **Vending machines**

Owners or operators of vending machines through which food products are dispensed are required to report and pay tax based on 57% of the gross receipts from such machines (RCW 82.08.0293, WAC 458-20-244(4)(d)).

¶ 910   Local Taxes

A sales and use tax may be imposed by a county at the rate of 0.5% and by a city at a rate of up to 0.5% of the selling price or the value of the article used (RCW 82.14.030, WAC 458-20-237 (Rule 237)). If a county has imposed the tax, a city in that county may impose a tax of only 0.425%. An additional tax to compensate local government for losses from the phase-out of the property tax on business inventories may be imposed by a county or city at the rate of up to 0.5% of the selling price or the value of the article used. The rate of the sales and use tax imposed by a city may be altered pursuant to a government service agreement (RCW 82.14.032).

Local legislative authorities are authorized to submit additional sales and use tax rate increases of up to 0.3% for voter approval at a primary or general election. Sales of motor vehicles and leases of motor vehicles for up to the first 36 months of the lease are exempt from the additional sales tax (RCW 82.14.450).

Rural counties: A rural county may impose a sales and use tax at the maximum rate of 0.08% of the selling price in the case of a sales tax or value of the article used in the case of a use tax (RCW 82.14.370). The tax must be collected from those persons who are taxable by the state under Chs. 82.08 and 82.12 RCW upon the occurrence of any taxable event within the county. The tax may be collected for up to 25 years after the date that the tax is first imposed. Revenues from the tax must be used for the purpose of financing public facilities in rural counties.

Criminal justice tax: A tax to support criminal justice purposes may be imposed by any county if the tax is subject to repeal by referendum, at the rate of 0.1% of the selling price or value of the article used (RCW 82.14.340).

Transportation taxes: A tax for high capacity transportation services may be imposed at the rate of up to 1% of the selling price or value of the article used (RCW 81.104.170, WAC 458-20-237 (Rule 237)). If a criminal justice tax has also been imposed, the high capacity transportation services tax is limited to a maximum of 0.9% of the selling price or value of the article used.

A tax for public transportation may be imposed at rates ranging from 0.1% to 0.9% of the selling price or value of the article used (RCW 82.14.045, WAC 458-20-237 (Rule 237)).

Three Puget Sound counties are authorized to impose additional local option taxes and fees. Specifically, King, Snohomish, and Pierce counties may, with voter approval, impose some or all of the following taxes and fees: a regional sales and use tax of up to 0.1%, a local option vehicle license fee of up to $100 per vehicle, a parking tax, a local motor vehicle excise tax, an employer excise tax of up to $2 per month, and vehicle tolls on new or reconstructed facilities. An authorized county may create a regional transportation investment district (RTID). The projects that may be funded are capital improvements to highways of statewide significance, as designated by the Transportation Commission or the legislature. Participating counties may choose to impose any remaining high-capacity transportation taxes that have not been used by the regional transit authority (Sec. 82.14.430).

Regional centers: Public facilities districts may impose a sales and use tax of up to 0.033% to provide funds for the costs associated with financing, designing, acquiring, constructing, equipping, operating, maintaining, remodeling, repairing, and reequipping its public facilities or constructing a regional center (RCW 82.14.048, RCW 82.14.390).

Juvenile justice: If approved by the voters, a county with a population of less than one million may impose a sales and use tax for the purpose of financing, designing, acquiring, constructing, equipping, operating, maintaining, remodeling, repairing, reequipping, and improving juvenile detention facilities and jails at the rate of one-tenth of 1% of (1) the selling price, in the case of a sales tax, or (2) the value of the article used, in the case of a use tax (RCW 82.14.350).

Lodging taxes: The legislative body of any county or any city, is authorized to levy and collect a special excise tax that may not exceed 2% on the sale of or charge made for the furnishing of lodging by a hotel, rooming house, tourist court, motel, trailer camp, and the granting of any similar license to use real property, as distinguished from the renting or leasing of real property (RCW 67.28.180). The total combined sales tax rate for lodging may not exceed 12% or any greater rate that was in effect on December 1, 2000 (RCW 82.14.410). An additional local charge of $2 per night may be imposed under certain circumstances (RCW 35.101.020—35.101.050).

Regional transit taxes: Regional transit authorities (RTAs) may be established by two or more contiguous counties, if each county has a population of 400,000 or more, to develop and operate a high capacity transportation system as defined in RCW Ch. 18.104. A regional transit authority may submit an authorizing proposition to the voters for the purpose of imposing a sales and use tax to provide high capacity transportation service (RCW 81.104.170).

Utility use taxes: A tax on the use of natural or manufactured gas within a city may be imposed at the rate in effect for the tax on natural gas businesses under RCW 35.21.870 in the city in which the article is used (RCW 82.14.230).

Rental car tax: Franklin, King, Pierce, and Spokane Counties impose a 1% tax on short term (less than 30 days) rentals of cars.

¶910   Washington

Emergency communications tax: Washington counties are authorized to impose an additional 0.1% sales and use tax for the establishment, maintenance, and improvement of emergency communications systems and facilities (RCW 82.14.420). The tax may be imposed only upon approval by county voters.

Mental health tax: County legislative authorities may impose a Washington local sales and use tax, in addition to other taxes, to provide new or expanded chemical dependency or mental health treatment services and for the operation of new or expanded therapeutic court programs. The tax, if imposed, may be imposed at a rate of 0.1% of the selling price in the case of a sales tax or value of the article used in the case of a use tax. (RCW 82.14.460).

- **Uniform statewide rate**

People who are obligated to collect use tax solely because they are engaged in business activities within Washington may elect to collect local use tax at a uniform statewide rate of 0.5% (WAC 458-20-221 (Rule 221)).

Sourcing of telecommunications charges: Washington has conformed to the federal Mobile Telecommunications Sourcing Act (Act), P.L. 106-252. All charges for mobile telecommunications services are considered to be provided by the customer's home service provider and sourced to the customer's place of primary use (RCW 82.14.020(5)(b)). All such charges are subject to sales tax based on the customer's place of primary use.

The service provider will be held harmless for an error in assigning wireless services to a jurisdiction if it utilizes an electronic database provided by the state or a designated entity, or, if the state has not provided or designated a database, if it utilizes a database that makes assignments based on a nine-digit zip code.

Rate changes: A sales and use tax rate increase imposed on services applies to the first billing period starting on or after the effective date of the increase, and a sales and use tax rate decrease imposed on services applies to bills rendered on or after the effective date of the decrease (WAC 458-20-235).

- **Local tax rates**

The Washington Department of Revenue maintains a tax rate lookup tool on its website at **http://dor.wa.gov/content/FindTaxesAndRates/ SalesAndUseTaxRates/**. Lists of tax rates with location codes are also presented alphabetically by city/county and as cities grouped by county.

Rental car tax.—Franklin, King, Kittitas, Pierce, and Spokane Counties impose a tax on short term (less than 30 days) rentals of cars. Rate information is available at **http://dor.wa.gov/content/FindTaxesAndRates/OtherTaxes/tax_rentalcar.aspx**

Lodging taxes: Tax rates of local lodging taxes are available at **http://dor.wa.gov/ content/FindTaxesAndRates/SalesAndUseTaxRates/**

¶ 911   **Bracket Schedule**

Sellers compute the sales or use tax due by carrying the computation to the third decimal place and rounding up to the next whole cent if the third decimal place is greater than four. Sellers may compute the tax due on an item or an invoice basis. This rounding rule is applied to the aggregated state and local taxes (RCW 82.08.054).

¶ 912   **Returns, Payments, and Due Dates**

Payments of taxes, reports, and returns on forms prescribed by the Department of Revenue are due monthly by the 25th day of the month following the month in which the taxable activities occurred (RCW 82.32.045, WAC 458-20-228, WAC 458-20-22801). The Department of Revenue may allow a longer reporting period of up to a year, in which case the taxes are due on the last day of the month after the end of the reporting period. The Department may also require an annual return. Tax is immediately due and the return is due in ten days when a taxpayer sells or quits the business (RCW 82.32.140). Taxpayers obligated to collect use tax solely because they are engaged in business activities within Washington are not required to file a return and remit tax more frequently than quarterly (WAC 458-20-221(6)).

Taxpayers subject to use tax who are not required to register or report taxes must file returns by the 25th day of the month succeeding the end of the period in which the tax accrued (RCW 82.08.050, WAC 458-20-178(16)).

Taxes and returns are on a calendar year basis or, with permission from the Department of Revenue, a fiscal year (RCW 82.04.020, RCW 82.08.010(4), RCW 82.32.270).

A taxpayer who uses the cash method of accounting may file returns on a cash receipts basis instead of paying tax on all sales made (RCW 82.08.100, RCW 82.12.070, WAC 458-20-199).

A return or remittance transmitted to the Department by U.S. mail is deemed filed on the date postmarked (RCW 82.32.080).

Extensions: The Department of Revenue may, for good cause, extend the time for filing a return for a reasonable period without penalties (RCW 82.32.080, WAC 458-20-228). However, any permanent extension of more than ten days and any extension of more than 30 days is conditional on deposit with the Department of an amount approximately equal to the estimated tax liability for the reporting period for which the extension is granted.

Sales suppression devices: It is unlawful for any person to knowingly sell, purchase, install, transfer, manufacture, create, design, update, repair, use, possess, or otherwise make available, in Washington, any automated sales suppression device or phantomware (RCW 82.32.290(4)).

• **Payment**

Unless electronic filing and payment is required, payment may be made to the Department of Revenue by uncertified check, but if the check is not honored by the bank on which it was drawn, the taxpayer is liable for taxes and penalties as if no check had been tendered (RCW 82.32.080, WAC 458-20-228).

A taxpayer who files a return without remittance of the tax shown to be due is deemed to have failed or refused to file a return (RCW 82.32.080, WAC 458-20-228).

Electronic filing and payment: Electronic filing and payment of taxes by electronic funds transfer (EFT) is required for all taxpayers, but the requirement may be waived by the Department of Revenue (DOR) for taxpayers that are required to file less frequently than quarterly and for any taxpayer for good cause (RCW 82.32.080(2)).

The DOR supports both the EFT credit and EFT debit methods of making payments. EFT debit is the most common option chosen. As an alternative to EFT, the DOR may authorize other forms of electronic payment, such as credit card and e-check. The DOR is authorized to accept payment of taxes by EFT or other acceptable forms of electronic payment from taxpayers that are not subject to the mandatory electronic payment requirement.

Charts of 2016 EFT due dates for monthly, quarterly, and annual filers are available on the Department of Revenue's website at **http://dor.wa.gov/content/File-AndPayTaxes/FilingFrequenciesAndDueDates/doingBus_EFTDueDts_17.aspx**.

The Department of Revenue has issued a publication explaining electronic funds transfer (EFT) options for payment of Washington taxes. Options discussed include EFT debit and EFT credit. The publication can be found on the department's Web site at **http://dor.wa.gov/Docs/Pubs/ExciseTax/FilTaxReturn/EFTGuide.pdf**.

¶912   Washington

Credit card payment: E-filing a tax return provides the option of paying with a credit card. Payment by American Express, VISA, MasterCard, and Discover are available. A fee of 2.5% is charged for processing credit card payments.

- **Direct payment**

Taxpayers whose cumulative tax liability is reasonably expected to be $240,000 or more in the current calendar year or who make taxable purchases in excess of $10 million per year may apply to the Department of Revenue for a direct pay permit authorizing them to remit state and local sales and use taxes directly to the Department rather than to the seller (RCW 82.32.087; *Special Notice*, Washington Department of Revenue, October 27, 2011, CCH WASHINGTON TAX REPORTS, ¶ 203-348).

An agreement for direct payment relieves the seller of the obligation to collect sales or use tax and requires the buyer to pay use tax on tangible personal property and sales tax on retail labor and/or services. The Department may approve or deny an application based on the applicant's capability with regard to local sales and use tax coding, vendor notification, recordkeeping, electronic data, and tax reporting procedures.

- **Deferral of tax**

Deferral of sales and use taxes is used as a business incentive in specific industries. In some cases, the deferred taxes need not be repaid if the taxpayer meets specific program requirements. Taxpayers claiming certain incentives must file an annual survey containing information about their business activities and employment and an annual report (WAC 458-20-268, WAC 458-20-268).

High unemployment counties: Deferral of sales and use taxes is allowed for materials used and labor and services rendered in the construction of qualified buildings and the acquisition of machinery and equipment by manufacturers, research and development laboratories, commercial testing facilities, and persons conditioning vegetable seed in certain distressed areas of Washington (high unemployment counties and Community Empowerment Zones (CEZs)). The recipient of the deferral is required to maintain the manufacturing or research and development activity for an eight-year period. If all program requirements are met, the deferred taxes do not have to be repaid. However, the Department of Revenue may require repayment if the recipient fails to meet reporting requirements or an investment project is found to be ineligible. (RCW 82.60.010; WAC 458-20-24001)

The eligible counties for applications received from July 1, 2016 – June 30, 2018 are the following: Adams, Benton, Clallam, Cowlitz, Ferry, Franklin, Grant, Grays Harbor, Jefferson, Klickitat, Lewis, Mason, Okanogan, Pacific, Pend Oreille, Skagit, Skamania, Stevens, Wahkiakum, and Yakima. The six CEZs are located in Bremeton, Duwamish, Spokane, Tacoma, White Center, and Yakima. (*Special Notice: High Unemployment County Sales and Use Tax Deferral Program,* Washington Department of Revenue, June 19, 2014; *Special Notice,* Washington Department of Revenue, May 2016; WAC 458-20-24001).

The authorization to make applications for deferral of taxes and to issue tax deferral certificates expires July 1, 2020 (RCW 82.60.030; WAC 458-20-24001(11)).

Gas to generate electricity: A deferral is available to direct service industrial customers for their first 60 months' use of natural or manufactured gas to generate electricity in a facility they own. To qualify for the deferral, direct service customers are required to maintain certain average annual employment levels (RCW 82.12.024). The deferred tax is payable over the five years following the first year of deferral.

Alternative fuels: Investment projects for the manufacture of wood biomass fuel, biodiesel fuel, alcohol fuel, and biodiesel feedstock are eligible for deferral of sales and use taxes. Deferred taxes need not be repaid if the Department of Revenue determines that the recipient has met the program requirements for the seven calendar years following certification of completion by the Department (RCW 82.68.010—82.68.080, RCW 82.69.010—82.69.080).

Washington ¶912

Processing, warehousing: Retail sales and use taxes will be deferred for eligible investment projects undertaken for the purpose of fresh fruit and vegetable processing, cold storage warehousing, dairy and seafood product manufacturing, or research and development into such projects (RCW 82.74.030). "Eligible investment project" means an investment in qualified buildings or qualified machinery and equipment, including labor and services rendered in the planning, installation, and construction of the project (RCW 82.74.010(4)). The deferral program is scheduled to expire July 1, 2012 (RCW 82.74.030(2)). An application for deferral must be made before the initiation of construction of the investment project or the acquisition of equipment or machinery. Taxes deferred under the program generally need not be repaid. However, if the Department of Revenue finds that an investment project no longer meets the program criteria during the calendar year when the project is certified as having been operationally completed, or at any time during the seven succeeding calendar years, a portion of the deferred taxes will be immediately due.

In addition, a retail sales and use tax exemption, in the form of a remittance, is enacted for cold storage warehouses having at least 25,000 square feet of space (RCW 82.08.820(3)(a)). The remittance is equal to 100% of the amount of state taxes paid for qualifying construction, materials, service, and labor, as well as qualifying material-handling and racking equipment.

Biotechnology products manufacturing: A state and local sales and use tax deferral is available for investments in qualified buildings or qualified machinery and equipment, including labor and services, used in the manufacturing of biotechnology products and medical devices. Applications must be made to and approved by the Department of Revenue before initiation of construction or acquisition of equipment and machinery. Exemptions are not available for projects that have already received exemptions under the high-technology program or the rural-counties program. The legislation provides for a repayment schedule for deferred taxes if an investment project is used for purposes other than qualified biotechnology product manufacturing or medical device manufacturing activities at any time during the calendar year in which the project was certified as completed or during any of the seven succeeding calendar years (RCW 82.75.010 *et seq.*).

Corporate headquarters in CEZ: A deferral/exemption, effective through December 31, 2020, is available for an eligible investment project involving construction of a new structure or expansion of an existing structure to be used as a corporate headquarters in a Community Empowerment Zone (CEZ) (RCW 82.82.010 *et seq.*). A participant in the deferral program must invest at least $30 million in the corporate headquarters and must employ at the headquarters at least 300 employees, each earning at least the average annual wage in Washington. "Corporate headquarters" means a facility or facilities where corporate staff employees are physically employed, and where the majority of the company's management services are handled either on a regional or a national basis. If a building is used partly for corporate headquarters and partly for other purposes, the applicable tax deferral is determined by apportionment of the costs of construction. Participants must submit an application for deferral of taxes prior to completion of construction of a qualified building.

Generally, deferred taxes need not be repaid. However, a portion of the deferred taxes must be repaid if an investment project no longer meets the requirements of an eligible investment project or if the recipient fails to complete an annual survey as required. Also, all deferred taxes are immediately due if a recipient does not satisfy employment requirements by the end of the second calendar year following the year in which the project is certified as operationally complete (RCW 82.82.010 *et seq.*).

¶912   **Washington**

Employee retraining pilot program: Beginning September 1, 2015, a tax incentive pilot program is established for businesses that invest in manufacturing facilities and reinvest tax savings in employee retraining programs. An eligible investment project is composed of five new, renovated, or expanded manufacturing operations, at least two of which must be located in Eastern Washington. A deferral of sales and use taxes applies to the first $10 million in costs for qualified buildings and machinery. (Sec. 401 *et seq.*, S.B. 6057, Laws 2015; *Special Notice,* Washington Department of Revenue, August 5, 2015, CCH WASHINGTON TAX REPORTS, ¶ 203-914)

The recipient of the deferral must begin repaying the deferred taxes in the fifth year after the date the department has certified the project as complete. Equal annual payments must be made over the course of a 10-year period.

- **Uniform Sales Tax Administration Act**

Washington has enacted the Uniform Sales and Use Tax Administration Act and the related Streamlined Sales and Use Tax Agreement (SSUTA) to simplify and modernize sales and use tax administration in order to substantially reduce the burden of tax compliance for all sellers and for all types of commerce. Washington became the 19th full member on the Streamlined Sales Tax (SST) Governing Board on July 1, 2008. All sellers registered under the SSUTA must collect tax on sales into Washington.

For additional information on the uniform act, see "Streamlined Sales Tax Project," listed in the Table of Contents.

¶ 913   **Prepayment of Taxes**

Washington has no provisions for the prepayment of sales and use taxes.

¶ 914   **Vendor Registration**

Every person who maintains a place of business or stock of goods in Washington or engages in business activities within the state must obtain a certificate of registration (RCW 82.12.040). Any person who does any business or performs any act upon which a tax is imposed must obtain a registration certificate (RCW 82.32.030, WAC 458-20-101). Registration requirements, a business license application, and additional information are available at **http://dor.wa.gov/content/doingbusiness**. Registration for all states that are members of the Streamlined Sales Tax Project is available at **https://www.sstregister.org/**.

Unless a person is a dealer of firearms and dangerous weapons, registration is not required if (RCW 82.32.030(2)).

— the value of products, gross proceeds of sales, or gross income of the business from all business activities taxable under the business and occupation tax is less than $12,000 per year,

— the person's gross income of the business from all activities taxable under the public utility tax is less than $12,000 per year,

— the person is not required to collect or pay to the Department of Revenue any other tax or fee that the Department is authorized to collect, and

— the person is not otherwise required to obtain a license subject to the master application procedure provided by Chapter 19.02 of the Washington Revised Code.

Out-of-state persons required to collect Washington's retail sales or use tax, or who have elected to collect Washington's use tax, even though not required by law, must obtain a tax registration endorsement (WAC 458-20-101).

Place of business: A certificate is required for each place of business and must be posted in a conspicuous place at the place of business for which it is issued (RCW 82.12.040, WAC 458-20-101). If a person has no fixed place of business and sells from one or more vehicles, each vehicle is a "place of business" (RCW 82.08.110). When a taxpayer changes the place of business, a new certificate must be issued for the new place of business. When a business changes ownership, the old certificate must be surrendered to the Department of Revenue for cancellation, and the new owner must obtain a new certificate of registration.

Temporary registration: A temporary revenue registration certificate may be issued to temporary businesses. Temporary businesses, for purposes of registration, are those with (1) definite, predetermined dates of operation for no more than two events per year with each event lasting no longer than one month; or (2) seasonal dates of operation lasting no longer than three months. Each temporary registration certificate is valid for a single event (WAC 458-20-101).

Contractors: For a contractor to qualify for a seller's permit, at least 25% of the contractor's total dollar amount of material and labor purchases for the preceding 12 months must have been for retail construction activity. Instead of a seller's permit, a buyer required to be registered with the Department of Revenue may submit a uniform exemption certificate approved by the Streamlined Sales and Use Tax (SST) Agreement Governing Board. Sellers' permits issued to qualifying contractors are valid for 12 months, and permits issued to other qualifying businesses are valid for a period of 48 months. (RCW 82.08.130)

Rescinding a certificate: When a taxpayer has submitted tax returns for two consecutive years reporting no gross income and no tax liability, the Department of Revenue may notify the taxpayer in writing that it has closed the taxpayer's account and rescinded its certificate of registration (WAC 458-20-101). Within 30 days of receiving the notice, the taxpayer may request in writing that the Department, at its discretion, keep the account active.

Revocation: A certificate of registration may be revoked if a warrant has been issued and is not paid within 30 days after it has been filed with the clerk of the superior court or if the taxpayer is delinquent for three consecutive reporting periods (RCW 82.32.215, WAC 458-20-101). A copy of the order of revocation will be posted in a conspicuous place at the main entrance to the taxpayer's place of business. It is a class C felony for a person to engage in business after revocation of a certificate of registration (RCW 82.12.040, WAC 458-20-101).

The certificate may not be reinstated, nor may any new certificate be issued, until the amount due on the warrant has been paid and the taxpayer has deposited with the Department of Revenue a security for payment of taxes, increases, and penalties due or that may become due (RCW 82.32.215, WAC 458-20-101).

• SST registration

A business's mere registration under or compliance with the Streamlined Sales and Use Tax Agreement (SSUTA) does not constitute nexus for purposes of the local government's authority to impose Washington business and occupation tax on the business. Also, a first-class city, second-class city, code city, and town may not require a business to obtain a license based solely upon the business's registration under or compliance with the SSUTA. However, if a firm actually has nexus within the city, it is still potentially subject to registration for local business tax purposes. (RCW 35.102.150; RCW 82.32.530).

¶ 915   **Sales or Use Tax Credits**

A credit against use tax is allowed in the amount of sales or use tax paid in another state, its political subdivision, foreign country, or its political subdivision prior to the use of the property in Washington (RCW 82.12.035, WAC 458-20-178(12)).

Bad debts: A credit or refund may be taken by the original seller for sales or use tax paid on debts deductible as worthless for federal income tax purposes (RCW 82.08.037,

RCW 82.12.037, WAC 458-20-196). "Bad debts" do not include property that remains in the possession of the seller, expenses of collection, or repossessed property.

A taxpayer that sold its private label credit card accounts to a bank was not entitled to a Washington sales tax refund for bad debts, because the bank was the exclusive owner of the credit card accounts and solely bore the risk of the credit card losses. The agreement between the bank and the taxpayer clearly stated that the bank was the sole owner of the credit card accounts and the taxpayer could not seek repayment from its customers for unpaid credit card charges. Though the taxpayer incurred financial loss in the form of a reduced service fee received from the bank, this loss did not reflect uncollected sales tax. The taxpayer was already compensated for the tax and purchase price of the merchandise by the bank and therefore no longer held any debt "directly attributable" to its sales tax payments to the Department of Revenue. (*Tax Determination No. 13-0178*, Washington Department of Revenue, May 30, 2014, CCH Washington Tax Reports, ¶ 203-680)

Exported fuel: Tax paid on special fuel subsequently established to have been actually used outside Washington in interstate commerce may be claimed as a credit or refund (RCW 82.08.0255(2), WAC 458-20-126).

Imported gas: A credit against the use tax on natural or manufactured gas may be taken in the amount of any tax paid by either the person that sold the gas to the consumer when that tax imposed by another state is a gross receipts tax similar to the public utility tax imposed by Washington or by the person consuming the gas upon which a use tax imposed by another state similar to the use tax imposed by Washington has been paid on the gas (RCW 82.12.022(5)).

- **Annual report**

Taxpayers that receive certain tax incentives are required to file either an annual survey or annual report with the Department of Revenue. The annual report must include information regarding employment, wages, and employer-provided health and retirement benefits for employment positions in Washington in the year the preference was claimed. The survey or report is generally due by April 30 of the following year. Surveys and reports must be electronically filed. (RCW 82.32.585; RCW 82.32.534; WAC 458-20-267; WAC 458-20-268).

¶ 916   Deficiency Assessments

After examination of a return or other information, if a tax or penalty appears to have been underpaid, the Department of Revenue will assess the additional amounts due plus a penalty and interest (RCW 82.32.050). If the tax due on a return is not paid by the due date, a 5% penalty is assessed. A total penalty of 15% applies if the tax is not paid by the last day of the month following the due date, and a total penalty of 25% applies if the tax is not paid by the last day of the second month following the due date. The minimum penalty for late payment is $5. (RCW 82.32.090). The Department must notify the taxpayer by mail of the additional amount, which must be paid within 30 days from the date of the notice, or within such further time as the Department may provide.

The Department may examine the books, records, and papers of the person and may take evidence, on oath, of any person relating to the amount of tax payable or the correctness of a return (RCW 82.32.100, RCW 82.32.110).

If a person fails to file a return or make records available for examination, the Department of Revenue will estimate the tax due on the basis of the information available (RCW 82.32.100). The Department will assess the tax and penalties due on the basis of the estimate, and the taxpayer must pay the tax within 30 days of receiving the notice of assessment from the Department of Revenue. The taxpayer may petition the Department for a correction of an assessment before paying the tax or may pay the tax and appeal the assessment to the superior court.

• **Stay of collection**

When an assessment has been made, the taxpayer may obtain a stay of collection by filing with the Department a bond of not more than twice the amount of the stay (RCW 82.32.200). The bond is conditioned on payment of the assessment plus interest of 1% for each 30 days or portion thereof from the due date thereof until paid. The rate of interest imposed is an average of the federal short-term rate as defined in a federal law plus two percentage points. The interest is imposed for each 30 days or portion thereof from the date the bond is filed until the date of payment.

¶ 917   Audit Procedures

All of a taxpayer's books, records, and invoices must be open for examination by the Department of Revenue at any time (RCW 82.32.070, RCW 82.32.110). Also, anyone who is liable for any fee or tax imposed by RCW Chs. 82.04 through 82.27 and who contracts with another person or entity for work subject to RCW Chs. 18.27 or 19.28 must obtain and preserve a record of the unified business identifier account number for the person or entity performing the work (RCW 82.32.070). An out-of-state taxpayer must produce only the necessary books and records in the state as required by the Department or permit examination by an agent of the Department at the place where the records are kept (RCW 82.32.070).

In addition, the Department may take evidence, on oath, of any person relating to the amount of tax payable or the correctness of a return (RCW 82.32.110). The Department may require the attendance of a person by summons in the same manner as a subpoena, may require testimony, may require production of records, and may administer oaths (RCW 82.32.110, RCW 82.32.120). A person giving false testimony under oath is guilty of first degree perjury, and a person failing to obey a summons or refusing to testify or produce records is subject to contempt proceedings in superior court.

If an audit or examination of the taxpayer's records reveals that excess tax has been paid within the statutory period for assessment, the excess will be credited to the taxpayer's account or refunded to the taxpayer, at the taxpayer's option (RCW 82.32.060).

Managed audits: Washington offers a managed audit program under which taxpayers are allowed to perform some or all of the audit functions. For information about the program, see *Managed Audits,* Washington Department of Revenue, October 2012, CCH WASHINGTON TAX REPORTS, ¶ 203-460.

Voluntary Disclosure Program: The VDP encourages unregistered businesses to comply with Washington's tax laws by voluntarily registering and paying prior tax obligations. Under the program, the following benefits apply:

— the look-back period for tax liability is generally four years plus the current year;

— up to 35% in potential penalties can be waived; and

— the department can summarize the unreported tax liability in a single tax assessment.

For additional information, see **http://dor.wa.gov/content/doingbusiness/registermybusiness/doingBus_vod.aspx**.

¶ 918   Statute of Limitations

No assessment or correction of an assessment for additional taxes due may be made by the Department of Revenue more than four years after the close of the tax year except in the case of a nonregistered taxpayer, fraud or misrepresentation by the taxpayer, or a written waiver of the limitation by the taxpayer (RCW 82.32.050, RCW 82.32.100, WAC 458-20-230).

The Department of Revenue will not give a credit or refund for taxes paid more than four years prior to the beginning of the calendar year in which the refund application is made or examination of records is completed (RCW 82.32.060). A taxpayer claiming a credit or refund for performing a government contract that requires the contractor to refund or credit to the United States the taxes paid, however, must file the claim for refund within one year of the date that the amount due to the United States is finally determined and within four years of the date on which the tax was paid.

Exception for overpayments on leased equipment: An exception to the four-year statute of limitations on credits or refunds is provided with respect to overpayments of sales tax on the purchase of property acquired for leasing (RCW 82.32.062). Taxpayers may take an offset if they were entitled to purchase the property at wholesale and substantiate that they made no intervening use of the equipment. The offset is applied to and reduced by the amount of sales tax owed from the beginning of lease of the property until the offset is extinguished.

¶ 919   Application for Refund

A person who has paid a tax or assessment may apply to the Department of Revenue for a refund by written petition for a correction of the amount paid and for a conference for examination and review of the tax liability (RCW 82.32.170). If the petition is denied, the taxpayer will be notified by mail. If the petition is granted, the Department will notify the taxpayer by mail of the time and place of the conference. After the hearing, the Department will mail a copy of the determination to the taxpayer.

The Department of Revenue will refund to the taxpayer or credit to the taxpayer's account payments determined to be in excess of those properly due (RCW 82.32.060, WAC 458-20-229). The refund will be in the form of vouchers approved by the Department and by the issuance of warrants drawn upon funds provided by the legislature. Taxpayers who are required to pay taxes by electronic funds transfer will have refunds paid by electronic funds transfer.

Interest: Interest will be allowed by the Department of Revenue and by any court on the amount of any refund, credit, or other recovery allowed to a taxpayer for taxes, penalties, or interest paid by the taxpayer (RCW 82.32.060, WAC 458-20-229). Interest allowed is computed at a variable rate that is the federal short-term rate plus two percentage points.

No interest will be paid on refunds or credits to taxpayers performing contracts for the United States that require the contractor to refund or credit to the United States any taxes (RCW 82.32.060).

• Remittance for working families

A working families' tax exemption in the form of a Washington sales tax remittance may be claimed by an eligible low-income person who files a federal income tax return and is granted a federal earned income tax credit (EITC) (RCW 82.08.0206). The person must have resided in Washington for more than 180 days in the year for which the exemption is claimed and must have paid Washington sales tax in that year.

Exemption amount: For remittances made in 2011 and thereafter, the tax exemption for the prior year is equal to the greater of $50 or 10% of the EITC granted. The exemption for any fiscal period must first be approved by the Legislature in the state Omnibus Appropriations Act. (RCW 82.08.0206).

Remittance application and administration: Eligible low-income persons must apply to the Department of Revenue for an exemption remittance in the year following the year for which their federal return was filed. The Department must provide for electronic and alternative methods of filing an application and will issue tax remittances to eligible persons by electronic funds transfer or other means. (RCW 82.08.0206).

¶ 921   Scope of Tax

Source.—Statutory references are to Chapter 11 of the West Virginia Code, as amended to date. Details are reported in the CCH WEST VIRGINIA TAX REPORTS starting at ¶ 60-000.

The West Virginia general consumers sales and service tax is a tax on the privilege of selling tangible personal property or rendering certain selected services (Sec. 11-15-1, Sec. 11-15-3(a)). The use tax is an excise tax levied and imposed on the use in West Virginia of tangible personal property and taxable services (Sec. 11-15A-2(a)). The consumers sales and service tax and the use tax are intended to be complementary (Sec. 11-15-1a, Sec. 11-15A-1a).

Sales and use of custom software are subject to West Virginia tax to the same extent as tangible personal property and taxable services (W.Va. Code Sec. 11-15-3(a)).

• Services subject to tax

In addition to taxing sales of tangible personal property, West Virginia also taxes sales of services not specifically exempted (Sec. 11-15-8, Reg. Sec. 110-15-33.3).

Mobile phone service: The furnishing of prepaid wireless calling services for consideration is included in the definition of "sale" for purposes of West Virginia consumers' sales and service tax (Sec. 11-15-2(b)(17)). "Prepaid wireless calling service" is defined as a telecommunications service that provides the right to use mobile wireless services and other non telecommunications services (including the download of digital products delivered electronically) that are paid for in advance and sold in predetermined dollars or units that decline with use in a known amount. (Sec. 11-15-2(b)(13))

Maintenance contracts and warranties: If a charge is made for the sale of a manufacturer's warranty, extended warranty, or a service or maintenance contract, the sale is subject to consumers' sales and service tax as the sale of a taxable service. The charge for the warranty is a prepayment for future services, and the warrantor may claim the resale exemption when services are performed under the warranty. (Reg. Sec. 110-15-63)

The term "computer software maintenance contract" is defined as a contract that obligates a computer software vendor or other person to provide a customer with future updates or upgrades to computer software, support services related to the software, or both. This term includes contracts sold by a person other than the computer software vendor to which the contract relates. "Mandatory computer software maintenance contract" refers to a computer software maintenance contract that the customer is contractually obligated to purchase as a condition to the retail sale of software. "Optional computer maintenance contract" means a computer software maintenance contract that a customer is not obligated to purchase as a condition to the retail sale of software. (S.B. 430, Laws 2012)

Lodging: Persons engaged in the rental of rooms in hotels, motels, tourist homes, and rooming houses on a daily basis must calculate consumers' sales and service tax on the daily charge. Consumers' sales and service tax is not computed on any local hotel or motel tax. (Reg. Sec. 110-15-38; see also Reg. Sec. 110-15-33.5)

The following are examples of businesses and entities that must collect consumers' sales and service tax when providing lodging, selling tangible personal property, or furnishing services or amusements: bed and breakfasts, inns, boarding houses, cabin rentals, camp grounds, state parks, condominium rentals, hostels, hotels, motels, lodges, private clubs, resorts, public and private sleeping rooms, tourist homes, and YMCA-YWCA facilities. (*TSD-316,* West Virginia State Tax Department, October 2014, CCH WEST VIRGINIA TAX REPORTS, ¶ 401-121)

Construction: A publication provides a general explanation of the sales tax rules for persons in the construction trades. It also lists numerous construction trade activities and materials and specifies whether such activities and materials represent a taxable repair, maintenance, or installation of tangible personal property or an exempt capital improvement. (*TSD-310,* West Virginia State Tax Department, March 2017, CCH WEST VIRGINIA TAX REPORTS, ¶ 401-270)

- **Use tax**

The use tax complements the consumers sales and service tax to bar the avoidance of paying sales tax on tangible personal property or services purchased outside the state and used in-state (Reg. Sec. 110-15-43, *TSD-369,* WVa Dept. of Tax and Revenue, January 1, 2012, CCH WEST VIRGINIA TAX REPORTS, ¶ 400-916). The tax is imposed on every person using tangible personal property or taxable services within the state (Sec. 11-15A-2(b)). It is not imposed in the following situations (Sec. 11-15A-3, Reg. Sec. 110-15-9.5):

    (1) where the sales tax has already been paid;

    (2) where a transaction would be exempt from the consumers sales and service tax;

    (3) where a transaction is not subject to consumers sales and service tax; and

    (4) where a nonresident temporarily brings property into the state for the person's own use.

- **Incidence of consumers sales and service tax**

The law imposes upon vendors the duty to collect sales tax from purchasers and to pay the collected tax to the Tax Commissioner (Sec. 11-15-3(a), Reg. Sec. 110-15-33.1). The amount collected is deemed to be held in trust for the state (Sec. 11-10-5j, Reg. Sec. 110-15-4.5). The sales tax is intended to be passed on to and paid by the ultimate consumer by adding the tax to the sales price (Sec. 11-15-10). The purchaser pays the vendor the amount of the tax which is added to, and constitutes part of, the sales price (Sec. 11-15-4).

Drop shipments: When all the parties are located within West Virginia, the retailer furnishes a resale certificate to the primary seller, rendering the first sale a nontaxable transaction. The retailer then collects sales tax on behalf of West Virginia on the secondary sale to its customer. However, different considerations arise when one or more of the parties are not within the state. (See Sec. 11-15-3)

In the case of drop shipments, a third-party vendor (such as a drop shipper) can claim a resale exemption based on an exemption certificate provided by its customer/reseller (or any other acceptable information available to the third-party vendor showing qualification for a resale exemption) when the sale is sourced to West Virginia. In addition, it is irrelevant whether the customer/reseller is registered to collect and remit sales and use taxes in West Virginia. (Reg. Sec. 11-15B-24(a)(8))

- **Incidence of use tax**

Retailers engaging in business in West Virginia and other retailers authorized by the Tax Commissioner are obligated to collect and remit use tax to the Tax Commissioner (Sec. 11-15A-5). Amounts collected are held in trust for the state (Reg. Sec. 110-15-4.5). Persons not physically engaged in business in the state who provide taxable services to West Virginia customers must collect use tax if they have sufficient nexus with the state (Reg. Sec. 110-15-33.2). Use tax not collected by the retailer must be paid to the Tax Commissioner directly by the purchasers using the property in West Virginia (Sec. 11-15A-5).

- **Nexus**

West Virginia requires any retailer engaging in business in West Virginia to collect and remit sales or use tax. "Retailer engaging in business in this state" or any like term means and includes, but is not limited, to any retailer having, maintaining, occupying, or using, directly or by a subsidiary, an office, distribution house, sales house, warehouse, or other place of business, or any agent operating within West Virginia under the authority of the retailer or its subsidiary. This is regardless of whether such place of business or agent is located there permanently or temporarily, or whether the retailer or subsidiary is admitted to do business within West Virginia. (Sec. 11-15A-1(a)(8))

"Business" or "doing business" includes any purposeful revenue generating activity in West Virginia and includes all activities engaged in with the intent of gain or economic benefit. This includes all activities of West Virginia and its political subdivisions that involve sales of tangible personal property or the rendering of services when those service activities compete with or may compete with the activities of other persons. (Reg. Sec. 110-15-2.9)

- **Streamlined Act status**

West Virginia is a full member of the Agreement with a seat on the Governing Board. It has enacted all of the provisions necessary to comply with the Agreement's requirements and these provisions currently are in effect (Sec. 11-15B-1, *et seq.*). As a full member, it may vote on amendments to or interpretations of the Agreement, and sellers registering under the SST system must collect and remit tax on sales into the state. For additional information, see ¶ 922 and ¶ 927.

West Virginia's taxability matrix can be viewed on the Streamlined Sales Tax website at **http://www.streamlinedsalestax.org**.

¶ 922   **Tax Base**

The tax base for the consumers sales and service tax is monetary consideration as defined in the statute; the tax base for the use tax is purchase price or sales price (Sec. 11-15-3(c), Sec. 11-15A-2(a), Reg. Sec. 110-15-3.4.1). However, if a manufacturer or natural resource producer uses or consumes self-produced or self-manufactured products, the tax is based on the gross value, as defined in the regulations, of the product. The tax on gasoline and special fuel is based on the average wholesale price.

Bundled transactions: A "bundled transaction" is defined as a retail sale of two or more distinct and identifiable products, other than real property and services to real property, sold for one non-itemized price (Sec. 11-15B-2(b)(4). Treatment of bundled transactions is discussed in; *Administrative Notice 2008-27*, West Virginia State Tax Department, December 4, 2008, CCH WEST VIRGINIA TAX REPORTS, ¶ 400-588).

- **"Monetary consideration" and "purchase price" defined**

"Monetary consideration," "purchase price," and "sales price" are synonymous with the term "gross proceeds" (Reg. Sec. 110-15-2.35). "Gross proceeds" is the amount received in money, credits, property, or other consideration from sales and services, without deduction on account of the cost of property sold or for interest or other expenses, but reduced by the value of trade-ins or the amount of any discount at the time of purchase (Sec. 11-15-2(i), Reg. Sec. 110-15-2.35). The regulations define "monetary consideration" as the actual cost to the purchaser after deduction for the value of any trade-in as part of the consideration paid for the tangible personal property or service purchased (Reg. Sec. 110-15-2.51). "Purchase price" is the total amount for which tangible personal property or a taxable service is sold, valued in money, whether paid in money or otherwise, but excluding cash discounts allowed and taken on sales (Sec. 11-15A-1(6), Reg. Sec. 110-15-2.68).

• **Sourcing rules**

In conformity with the Streamlined Sales and Use Tax Agreement, sales are sourced generally to the destination of the product sold, with a default to origin-based sourcing in the absence of that information. Special sourcing rules apply to sales or leases of transportation equipment and telecommunications. The following general sourcing rules apply (Sec. 11-15B-15(a)):

(1) when the tangible personal property or service is received by the purchaser at a business location of the seller, the sale is sourced to that business location;

(2) when the tangible personal property or service is not received by the purchaser at a business location of the seller, the sale is sourced to the location where receipt by the purchaser occurs;

(3) if neither of the above apply, the sale is sourced to the location indicated by an address for the purchaser that is available from the business records of the seller that are maintained in the ordinary course of the seller's business when use of the address does not constitute bad faith;

(4) if none of the above apply, the sale is sourced to the location indicated by an address for the purchaser obtained during the consummation of the sale, including the address of a purchaser's payment instrument, if no other address is available, when use of the address does not constitute bad faith;

(5) if none of the other rules apply, including the circumstance in which the seller is without sufficient information to apply the previous rules, then the location will be determined by the address from which tangible personal property was shipped, from which the digital good or the computer software delivered electronically was first available for transmission by the seller, or from which the service was provided.

Special provisions apply to sourcing of direct mail, telecommunications and ancillary services.

¶ 923   List of Exemptions, Exceptions, and Exclusions

Unless otherwise indicated, the statutory exemptions, exceptions, and exclusions listed below apply to both sales and use taxes; those applicable only to the use tax are listed separately. For additional information, see *TSD-300*, State Tax Department, March 2017, CCH WEST VIRGINIA TAX REPORTS, ¶ 401-268. Items that are excluded from the sales or use tax base are treated at ¶ 922, "Tax Base."

• **Sales and use tax exemptions, exceptions, and exclusions**

Admission charges to school activities	Sec. 11-15-9(a)(21)
Advertising services in connection with the sale of broadcast time	Sec. 11-15-9(a)(12)
Advertisement space	Sec. 11-15-9(a)(12)
Agricultural sales	Sec. 11-15-9(a)(8), Sec. 11-15-9(a)(32)
Aircraft repair and maintenance	Sec. 11-15-9(a)(34)
Artistic services and performances	Sec. 11-15-9(a)(41)
Boy Scouts	Sec. 11-15-9(a)(6)(E)
Brokerage fees and charges	Sec. 31-17-2(b)
Burial lots, opening and closing	Sec. 11-15-9(a)(31)
Camp Dawson facilities sales	Sec. 15-1H-5

Charitable and nonprofit organizations	Sec. 11-15-9(a)(6)(C),
	Sec. 11-15-9(a)(6)(D),
	Sec. 11-15-9(a)(6)(E),
	Sec. 11-15-9(a)(6)(F),
	Sec. 11-15-9(a)(6)(G),
	Sec. 11-15-9(b)(1)
Charitable bingo purchases	Sec. 47-20-6a
Church purchases and sales	Sec. 11-15-9(a)(5),
	Sec. 11-15-9(a)(6)(A),
	Sec. 11-15-9(a)(14)
Clothing (donated) sold by tax-exempt organizations	Sec. 11-15-9l
Commissions paid to manufacturers' representatives	Sec. 11-15-9(a)(38)
Communication activity purchases	Sec. 11-15-9(b)(2)
Computer hardware, software, and services	Sec. 11-15-9h
Construction materials purchased by contractors for certain customers	Sec. 11-15-8d,
	Sec. 11-15-9n
Contracting services	Sec. 11-15-8a(a),
	Sec. 11-15-2(c)
Corporate services to another corporation in control group	Sec. 11-15-9(a)(24)
Corporations subject to Public Service Commission control	Sec. 11-15-8
Day care services	Sec. 11-15-9(a)(13)
Drugs, prescription	Sec. 11-15-2(f),
	Sec. 11-15-9(a)(11),
	Sec. 11-15-9(i)
Educational institutions	Sec. 11-15-9(a)(6)(B),
	Sec. 11-15-9(a)(15)
Electricity	Sec. 11-15-2(w),
	Sec. 11-15-9(a)(1),
	Sec. 11-15-9(b)(2)
Electronic data processing services and software	Sec. 11-15-9(a)(22)
Environmental standards, services for technical compliance with . . .	Sec. 11-15-9(a)(47),
	Sec. 11-15-9c
Farm equipment	Sec. 11-15-9(a)(8)
Feed	Sec. 11-15-9(a)(32)
Fertilizer used in commercial production of agricultural products . . .	Sec. 11-15-9(a)(8)
Flags	Sec. 11-15-9(a)(50)
Food and food ingredients (grocery food) (see also ¶ 924)	Sec. 11-15-3a,
Food purchased or sold by certain organizations or purchased with food stamps	Sec. 11-15-9(a)(5),
	Sec. 11-15-9(a)(20),
	Sec. 11-15-9(a)(25)
Fraternal and social organizations	Sec. 11-15-9(b)(3)
Fundraising sales by volunteer fire departments	Sec. 11-15-9(a)(48)
Funeral services (partial exclusion)	Sec. 11-15-9(a)(31)
Gas	Sec. 11-15-9(a)(1)
Gasoline sold in bulk to interstate motor carriers	Sec. 11-14-5a(a),
	Sec. 11-14-5a(c)

• Exemptions, exceptions, and exclusions applicable only to the use tax

¶ 924   Rate of Tax

The consumers' sales and service tax is imposed at the rate of 6¢ on the dollar of sales or services (Sec. 11-15-3(b)).

The use tax is imposed at the rate of 6% of the purchase price (Sec. 11-15A-2(a), Reg. Sec. 110-15-3.3). The Department of Tax and Revenue indicates that the use tax is to be calculated by using the bracket schedule provided for sales tax (see ¶ 926).

• Motor fuels

Sales and use taxes are imposed at a rate of 5% on the average wholesale price of gasoline and special fuel; the wholesale price may not be less than 2.34¢ per gallon (Sec. 11-15-3(b); Sec. 11-15-18B(b)). Notification of the average wholesale price must be given by the Tax Commissioner at least 30 days before January 1 of each year by filing notice in the state register. The average wholesale price cannot vary by more than 10% from one calendar year to the next (Sec. 11-14C-5(b)(2)).

During 2017, the average wholesale price of gasoline and special fuel is $2.340 per gallon. As a result, the variable fuel tax rate for the period from January 1, 2017, through December 31, 2017, is decreased to 11.7 cents per gallon (previously, 12.7 cents per gallon), for a combined rate of 32.2 cents per gallon.

For liquefied petroleum gas (propane), the average wholesale price for 2017 is 9.85 cents, resulting in a variable fuel tax rate of 4.9 cents per gallon (for a combined total rate of 19.9 cents per gallon).

For compressed natural gas, the wholesale price is $4.911 per 1,000 cubic feet, resulting in a variable fuel tax rate of 24.6 cents per 1,000 cubic feet, or 3.1 cents per gasoline gallon equivalent (for a combined total rate of 23.6 cents per gallon).

For liquefied natural gas, the average wholesale price is 40 cents per gallon, resulting in a variable fuel tax rate of 2 cents per gasoline gallon equivalent (for a combined total rate of 15.2 cents per gallon).

(*Administrative Notice 2016-27*, State Tax Department, November 22, 2016, CCH WEST VIRGINIA TAX REPORTS, ¶ 401-135-243)

• Mobile and manufactured homes

The sale or use of a mobile home used by the purchaser or owner as a principal year-round residence is subject to tax at the rate of 6%, but the tax levied is based on 50% of the sales price of the mobile home (Sec. 11-15-3(f), Sec. 11-15A-3(a)(5)).

A $20 fee is imposed on sales of factory-built homes. The fee is addition to consumers' sales tax and must be collected and remitted to the State Tax Commissioner. (Sec. 11-15-4c)

• Motor vehicles

Sales tax at the rate of 5% applies to all motor vehicle sales to West Virginia residents (Sec. 11-15-3b). It does not apply, however, to the registration of a motor vehicle owned by, and titled to, a new West Virginia resident who was not a resident when purchasing the vehicle.

The sales tax does not apply to the rental of passenger vehicles by daily passenger rental car businesses, sales to certain active duty military personnel, or certain transfers of vehicles between related companies. The sales tax also does not apply with regard to vehicles acquired by tax-exempt senior citizen service organizations, acquired for resale by dealers registered in West Virginia, or acquired by urban mass transit authorities, tax-exempt mass transit providers, the state or its political subdivisions, volunteer fire departments, chartered rescue squads, or ambulance squads. In addition, tax does not apply to Class B trucks, truck tractors, and road tractors registered at a gross weight of 55,000 pounds or greater, or to Class C trailers, semitrailers, full trailers, pole trailers, or converter gear having a weight of 2,000 pounds or greater. (Sec. 11-15-3b(f)).

Leased vehicles: The sales is imposed at the rate of 5% of each monthly lease payment (Sec. 11-15-3b(g)).

¶924   **West Virginia**

- **Food and food ingredients**

The tax on food and food ingredients (grocery food) was completely phased out by July 1, 2014 (Sec. 11-15-3a; *TSD-419,* West Virginia State Tax Department, August 2013, CCH WEST VIRGINIA TAX REPORTS, ¶ 401-025).

Local sales and use taxes on sales of grocery food were also eliminated because the tax base for local sales and use taxes is the same as for the state-level sales and use tax. (Sec. 8-13C-4(c); Sec. 8-13C-5(c)).

¶ 925   Local Taxes

Local governments have no general authority to impose sales and use taxes. However, municipalities with unfunded police and fire pension relief funds may impose municipal sales and use taxes of up to 1%. The authority to impose these taxes is not effective until the municipality presents a plan to the West Virginia Legislature's Joint Committee on Government and Finance to remove unfunded liabilities of pension funds and the necessary changes in West Virginia law have been enacted to allow for implementation of the plan (Sec. 8-13C-2; Sec. 8-13C-4; Sec. 8-13C-11).

Municipalities that do not impose or cease to impose a business and occupation tax may impose additional sales and use taxes not to exceed 1% (Sec. 8-13C-4(b)).

Basis of local taxes: The tax base of a local sales or use tax levied by a local jurisdiction is generally the same as the state-level sales and use tax base. However, there are exceptions for wholesale sales of gasoline or special fuel to power motor vehicles, aircraft, locomotives, or watercraft, and electricity, piped natural or artificial gas, or other fuels delivered by the seller. Also excepted from the local tax base are retail sales or transfers of motor vehicles, aircraft, watercraft, modular homes, manufactured homes, or mobile homes. (Sec. 8–13C-4)

Collection: A publication provides general tax information about local governments' West Virginia sales and use tax collection responsibilities. The publication also contains a chart reflecting the rounding rule applicable to the computation of sales and use tax. (*TSD-301,* West Virginia State Tax Department, March 2017, CCH WEST VIRGINIA TAX REPORTS, ¶ 401-269)

Hotel occupancy tax: Counties and municipalities may impose a hotel occupancy tax at rates that vary from 3% to 6% (Sec. 7-18-2; Sec. 8-13-3).

Resort service fees: The levy of resort service fees is authorized on sales of goods and services by certain establishments located within resort area districts. "Resort service fee" means a fee imposed on the price of goods and services sold within a resort area district by the following types of establishments and on the following specified activities: (1) hotels, motels, campgrounds, lodges, and other lodging or camping facilities; (2) restaurants, fast-food stores, and other food service establishments selling prepared foods; (3) taverns, bars, nightclubs, lounges, and other public establishments that serve beer, wine, liquor, or other alcoholic beverages by the drink; (4) retail establishments; (5) entertainment facilities, including but not limited to theaters, amphitheaters, halls, and stadiums; and (6) recreational facilities and activities, including but not limited to ski resorts, golf courses, water sports, rafting, canoeing, kayaking, rock climbing, and zip lining. (Sec. 7-25-3(q))

- **Economic opportunity development districts**

Counties and municipalities may create economic opportunity development districts to reallocate state sales and use tax revenue by imposing within those districts a special district excise tax at the rate of 6% on sales and services. Counties and municipalities may not levy this tax unless expressly authorized by the Legislature. A special district excise tax generally mirrors the sales and use tax and is intended to stimulate economic growth and job creation within the district. The tax base of a special district excise tax is the same as the tax base of the sales and use tax, and the tax will be collected by the Tax Commissioner in the same manner as the sales and use tax. A special district excise tax becomes effective on the first day of the calendar month that begins 60 days following adoption of the tax unless otherwise specified. (Sec. 7-22-1, Sec. 7-22-9, Sec. 7-22-12, Sec. 8-38-1, Sec. 8-38-9, Sec. 8-38-12).

- **County transportation taxes**

A county commission, with voter approval, may impose a transportation sales and use tax at a rate not to exceed 1% to finance the accelerated construction, upgrading, or modernization of roads and bridges within the county (Sec. 7-27-1 *et seq.*). Two or more counties may contract to share expenses and dedicate county funds or county transportation sales and use tax revenues, on a *pro rata* basis, to facilitate projects.

Tax base: The tax base of a county transportation sales and use tax is generally the same as that of the state consumers sales and service tax and use tax, with some exceptions. (Sec. 7-27-28(c), (d))

Exemptions: County transportation sales and use taxes do not apply to (Sec. 7-27-28(e)):

(1) sales and uses of motor vehicles upon which the 5% consumers sales tax on motor vehicle sales was paid or is payable;

(2) sales and uses of motor fuel upon which the motor carrier road tax and motor fuel excise tax was paid or is payable;

(3) any sale of tangible personal property, sale of custom software, or furnishing of a service that is exempt from state consumers sales and service tax;

(4) any use of tangible personal property, use of custom software, or the results of a taxable service that is exempt from state use tax. However, this exception is not applicable to any use within the county when the state consumers sales and service tax was paid to the seller at the time of purchase but the county's transportation sales tax was not paid to the seller; and

(5) any sale or use of tangible personal property, custom software, or taxable service that the county is prohibited from taxing under federal law or the laws of West Virginia.

Sourcing: The state's Streamlined Sales Tax sourcing laws apply to county transportation sales and use taxes. If state consumers sales tax was paid to the vendor at the time of purchase but the county's sales tax was not paid because the vendor is located in West Virginia but not in the county imposing county transportation use tax, the purchaser who uses the tangible personal property, custom software, or taxable service in the county owes the use tax imposed by that county unless taxation is otherwise exempt. (Sec. 7-27-28(f))

Collection and remission: A vendor selling tangible personal property or custom software or furnishing a taxable service in a county that imposes a county transportation sales tax must collect the county's transportation sales tax from the purchaser at the same time and in the same manner that the consumers sales tax is collected from the customer.

When tangible personal property, custom software, or the result of a taxable service is purchased in a West Virginia county that does not impose county transportation sales and use taxes, and the items or services are used in a county that does impose the tax, then:

(1) a vendor who delivers the tangible personal property, custom software, or taxable service results to a purchaser (or the purchaser's done) located in a county that imposes a county transportation sales and use tax must add the tax to the purchase price and collect the tax from the purchaser (Sec. 7-27-28(f)(1)); and

(2) a person using tangible personal property or custom software in a West Virginia county that imposes a county transportation sales and use tax must remit

the county's use tax to the State Tax Commissioner unless the amount of sales and use taxes imposed by the county in which the tangible personal property, custom software, or taxable service was purchased were lawfully paid (Sec. 7-27-28(f)(2)).

- **Local jurisdiction database**

In conformity with the Streamlined Agreement (see ¶ 927), the state will provide and maintain a database that describes boundary changes and tax rates for all local taxing jurisdictions. The state must also maintain a database that assigns each zip code within the state to the proper rates and jurisdictions. The state must apply the lowest combined rate imposed in a zip code area if the area includes more than one tax rate in any level of taxing jurisdictions. If a nine-digit zip code designation is not available for an address, or if a seller is unable to determine the nine-digit zip code designation of a purchaser after exercising due diligence, the seller may apply the rate for the five-digit zip code area. There is a rebuttable presumption that a seller has exercised due diligence if the seller has attempted to determine the nine-digit zip code by utilizing software approved by Agreement members. The state will participate with other member states in the development of an address-based system for assigning taxing jurisdictions.

Sellers and certified service providers registered in West Virginia under the Agreement are not liable for charging and collecting an incorrect amount of tax as a result of reliance on erroneous data provided by the state concerning tax rates, boundaries, or taxing jurisdiction assignments.

Current rates: Municipal sales and use tax rates are available at **http://tax.wv.gov/ Business/SalesAndUseTax/LocalSalesAndUseTax/Pages/ LocalSalesAndUseTax.aspx**

¶ 926   **Bracket Schedule**

West Virginia has enacted the rounding rule consistent with the Streamlined Sales and Use Tax Agreement (see ¶ 927). The price is multiplied by 6% and calculated to the third decimal place; if the third decimal place is five or greater, then the tax is rounded up to the next whole cent (Sec. 11-15-3).

Despite the enactment of the rounding rule, the West Virginia State Tax Department has issued a tax chart for the 6% rate, as follows (Sec. 11-15-3(c)):

Monetary consideration	Tax
8¢ or less	none
9¢ to 24¢	1¢
25¢ to 41¢	2¢
42¢ to 58¢	3¢
59¢ to 74¢	4¢
75¢ to 91¢	5¢
92¢ to $1.00	6¢

¶ 927   **Returns, Payments, and Due Dates**

Consumers sales and service tax is generally due and payable monthly (Sec. 11-15-16(a), Reg. Sec. 110-15-5.3), except that taxpayers whose average monthly tax liability for the taxable year does not exceed $250 may remit the tax quarterly, and a taxpayer whose annual tax liability does not exceed $600 is required to file an annual return only (Sec. 11-15-20).

The taxpayer must file with the Tax Commissioner, on or before the 20th day of the month following the monthly or quarterly period for which the tax accrued, a signed return that is accompanied by the tax due. The return must show the total gross proceeds of the taxpayer's business for the taxable period, the gross proceeds of the business upon which the tax is based, the amount of tax due, and any other required information necessary to compute and collect the tax. Any taxpayer required to file a consumers' sales and service tax return or a use tax return must complete and file a combined return for consumers' sales and service taxes and use taxes (Sec. 11-15-16).

Annual returns: An annual return must be filed with the Tax Commissioner on or before January 31 consisting of the final monthly or quarterly return for the year, together with payment of any remaining tax due for the preceding year, and showing the total gross proceeds from business for the preceding tax year (Sec. 11-15-21, Reg. Sec. 110-15-5.3).

Consolidated returns: A person operating two or more places of business of like character may file consolidated returns (Sec. 11-15-22, Reg. Sec. 110-15-5.3).

Accelerated payments: Accelerated tax payment is required for consumers sales and service tax (and the complimentary use tax) attributable to the first 15 days of June for taxpayers whose average monthly payments in the previous calendar year exceeded $100,000. Thus, the first accelerated payment of consumers sales and service tax was due on June 20, 2015 (with payments in subsequent years due on June 20), and the first accelerated payment of withholding tax was due June 23, 2015 (with payments in subsequent years due on June 23). (Sec. 11-15-16(g); S.B. 331, Laws 2014)

Electronic funds transfer (EFT) payment: Certain taxpayers may be required to file and pay their sales and use taxes electronically. For tax years beginning on and after January 1, 2016, the tax liability threshold is raised from $10,000 to $25,000. A 3% civil penalty will be applied to any payment received on or after March 1, 2015, that is not made by EFT when EFT payment is required and a waiver has not been obtained. (Sec. 11-10-5t; Reg. Secs. 110-10F-1 through 110-10F-18) Electronic payment is accomplished at **https://mytaxes.wvtax.gov**.

All remittances from sellers under the technology models in the Streamlined Agreement (see ¶ 929) must be remitted electronically, using either the ACH credit or ACH debit method.

Information returns: The Tax Commissioner may require a seller to file an information return containing information required by the sales and use tax act that is not included in any sales and use tax return developed in accordance with the Streamlined Agreement. Such returns may not be required on a more frequent basis than every six months.

Online filing: West Virginia sales and use tax returns (Form WV/CST-200 and Form WV/CST-220) may be filed online. Taxpayers must apply for online filing by completing a business registration application and an electronic funds transfer application. Once the State Tax Department has received this information, it will provide an account number and a PIN for the taxpayer to use when filing online.

Retailers volunteering to remit tax for out-of-state sales made via the Internet must submit a Foreign Retailer Voluntarily Collecting and Remitting Use Tax form and an electronic funds transfer application to register for the program (*Release*, West Virginia State Tax Department, February 11, 2004).

Due dates: if a payment due date falls on a Saturday, Sunday, or legal holiday, the payment (including related payment voucher information) is due on the next business day. Also, if the Federal Reserve Bank is closed on a payment due date, and if this closure prevents a taxpayer from being able to make a payment by ACH debit or credit, the payment will be considered timely if made on the next day the Federal Reserve Bank is open. (S.B. 430, Laws 2012)

• **Quarterly and annual filers**

In lieu of monthly returns, a taxpayer whose average monthly tax liability does not exceed $250 may file a quarterly return on or before the 20th day of the first month in the following quarter (Sec. 11-15-20, Reg. Sec. 110-15-5.3).

Taxpayers whose annual tax liability does not exceed $600 may file an annual return instead of monthly or quarterly returns (Sec. 11-15-20). Reports and payments are due by the 31st day of the first month following the close of a taxpayer's tax year.

• **Use tax**

A person who is required to hold a business registration certificate and who uses tangible personal property or taxable services upon which use tax has not been paid, either to a retailer or directly to the Tax Commissioner, must file a signed return (Form WV/CST-220) with the Tax Commissioner on or before the 15th day of the month following the end of each quarterly filing period, accompanied by the use tax due, showing the information required by the return (Sec. 11-15A-11, Reg. Sec. 110-15-5.5).

Consumers' returns: The State Tax Department has issued Form IT-140 Schedule UT (West Virginia Purchaser's Use Tax Return) and the associated instructions. Schedule UT is filed by individuals who owe use tax on the total purchase price of taxable tangible personal property or taxable services that they used, stored, or consumed within West Virginia for which they have not already paid West Virginia sales or use tax. Use tax applies to transactions such as online purchases, magazine subscription purchases, mail-order transactions, out-of-state purchases, and telephone purchases made from outside the state. The Schedule UT must be filed with the Form IT-140 (West Virginia Personal Income Tax Return) if the taxpayer is reporting use tax due.

Self-produced and self-consumed goods: A manufacturer that uses or consumes its own manufactured products must pay use tax on their gross value, unless the use or consumption is otherwise exempt (Sec. 11-15-7; Sec. 11-15A-2a(a); Reg. Sec. 110-15-3.4.7; Reg. Sec. 110-15-7.2). The gross value or tax base of a product used or consumed by its own manufacturer is equal to the selling price at the place of use or consumption of comparable products offered for sale by persons not related to the taxpayer, or if there are no such sales, the average price of comparable products sold by the manufacturer to its customers. In the absence of sales to customers, the tax base is the cost of the product plus the average markup realized by the manufacturer. If the product is consumed or used away from the place of manufacturing, freight charges are not deductible unless they were considered in the method by which the values were determined. (Sec. 11-15A-2a(b); Reg. Sec. 110-15-3.4.7.1.a; Reg. Sec. 110-15-7.3)

Use tax accrues when the manufacturer first uses or consumes the product in West Virginia in a non-exempt manner (Reg. Sec. 110-15-4.7.2).

• **Direct payment**

An eligible person may use a direct pay permit to purchase tangible personal property or services. Persons using a direct pay permit must pay the tax directly to the Tax Commissioner, and the vendor is not responsible for the collection of the tax (Sec. 11-15-9d(a), Sec. 11-15A-3d(a); *TSD-345*, State Tax Department, revised June 2011, CCH WEST VIRGINIA TAX REPORTS, ¶ 400-835).

An eligible person is one of the following who:

— is engaged in the business of manufacturing, transportation, transmission, communication, or the production of natural resources;

— is subject to the business and occupation tax, the severance tax, or the telecommunications tax;

— is a bona fide charitable organization that makes no charge for its services;

— is a nationally chartered fraternal or social organization whose purchases are used solely for free distribution in public welfare or relief work;

— is a volunteer fire department;

— makes purchases the use of which is unknown to the person at the time of purchase and a reasonably foreseeable use would be exempt from consumers sales and service tax and use tax; or

— makes purchases used in both exempt and taxable manners and apportions the tax.

A direct pay permit holder must file with the Tax Commissioner on or before the 15th day of each month a direct pay permit tax return for the preceding month. Payment of tax accompanies the return.

• **Bad debt deduction**

A refundable deduction for bad debt is allowed (Sec. 11-15B-27). "Bad debt" is as defined in IRC Sec. 166, except it does not include: (1) a financing charge; (2) interest; (3) sales or use tax paid on the purchase price; (4) an uncollectible amount on property that remains in the possession of a seller until the full purchase price is paid; (5) an expense incurred in attempting to collect any debt; or (6) repossessed property.

A seller's certified service provider may make a deduction or claim a refund for bad debt on behalf of the seller if the certified service provider credits or refunds the full amount of the bad debt deduction or refund to the seller. A bad debt may be allocated among the states that are members of the Streamlined Agreement if a seller's books and records support that allocation.

• **Uniform Sales Tax Administration Act**

West Virginia has enacted the Uniform Sales and Use Tax Administration Act, the product of the Streamlined Sales Tax Project (SSTP) (Sec. 11-15B-1, *et seq.*) as well as legislation to conform its sales and use tax laws to provisions of the Streamlined Sales and Use Tax Agreement. The legislation includes:

— adoption of a rule for computation of tax due (¶ 926);

— vendor registration requirements (¶ 929);

— allowance of a deduction for bad debts (see above);

— adoption of sourcing rules in conformity with the Agreement (¶ 922);

For additional information on the uniform act and the NCSL modifications, see "Streamlined Sales Tax Project," listed in the Table of Contents, or go to the SST website at **http://www.streamlinedsalestax.org/**.

¶ 928   **Prepayment of Taxes**

At the time a nonresident contractor registers with the Tax Commissioner, the contractor must deposit the tax on the gross value of the contract (Sec. 11-15-8b, Reg. Sec. 110-15-8b). The money is deposited in the Contractor's Use Tax Fund pending completion of the contract, the determination of the sales and use taxes due, and the payment of tax. The deposit is then refunded.

In lieu of paying the deposit, a nonresident contractor may provide a corporate surety bond for each contract (Sec. 11-15-8b, Reg. Sec. 110-15-8b). A corporate surety bond may also be provided for several contracts or all contracts within a specified period unless the taxpayer has no payment history or record with the Tax Department (Reg. Sec. 110-15-8b).

Performance on the contract may not start until the deposit or corporate bond is approved by the Tax Commissioner (Reg. Sec. 110-15-8b).

Within 30 days after registering with the Tax Commissioner, the contractor must file a statement with the Tax Commissioner itemizing the machinery, materials, supplies, and equipment that will be on hand in the state for performance of the contract and upon which West Virginia sales or use taxes have not been paid (Sec. 11-15-8b, Reg. Sec. 110-15-8b). The statement must include the location outside the state from which the property was or will be brought or shipped. The tax is paid at the time of filing the statement.

Vendor Registration

Any person engaging in a business activity in West Virginia, including foreign retailers engaging in business in the state, must obtain a business registration certificate from the State Tax Commissioner (Sec. 11-12-3(a), Sec. 11-15A-6(b), Sec. 11-15A-6a(b)). Foreign retailers not engaging in business in the state may be issued a permit to collect use tax, provided adequate security is furnished to the Tax Commissioner (Sec. 11-15A-7). See also *TSD-360*, West Virginia State Tax Department, October 2015, CCH WEST VIRGINIA TAX REPORTS, ¶ 401-180.

• Registration under the Streamlined Agreement

A seller that registers to collect West Virginia sales and use taxes using the online sales and use tax registration system established under the Agreement is not required to also register under traditional seller provisions unless the seller has sufficient presence in the state that provides at least the minimum contacts necessary for a constitutionally sufficient nexus for the state to require it. A person appointed by a seller to represent the seller before the states that are members of the Agreement may register the seller under the Agreement. A seller registered under the Agreement may cancel its registration at any time under uniform procedures adopted by the member states (Sec. 11-15B-11).

For information on West Virginia state registration, see *TSD-360 Registration Procedures for Businesses,* West Virginia State Tax Department, October 2015, CCH WEST VIRGINIA TAX REPORTS, ¶ 401-180.

SST registration for sales and use taxes in multiple states is available at **https:// www.sstregister.org/**.

Effect of registration: By registering under the Agreement, the seller agrees to collect and remit sales and use taxes for all taxable sales into West Virginia, as well as for all other states participating in the Agreement (Sec. 11-15B-12(a)). Subsequent withdrawal or revocation of a member state does not relieve a seller of its responsibility to remit taxes previously or subsequently collected. The state may not use registration with the central registration system and the collection of sales and use taxes in West Virginia as a factor in determining whether the seller has a nexus with the state for any tax at any time.

Payment by certain Agreement participants: A seller that is registered under the Agreement and is not otherwise required to collect West Virginia sales or use tax and that does not use one of the technology models for remittance must pay a tax collected to the Tax Commissioner annually on or before the last day of the month immediately following the last day of each calendar year. The Tax Commissioner may require that a tax collected be due and payable on the last day of the month immediately following any month in which the seller has accumulated a total of at least $1,000 in state and local sales and use tax.

• Seller models

The following are the seller models that may be selected when registering under the Agreement:

— "Model I seller" means a seller that has selected a certified service provider as its agent to perform all the seller's sales and use tax functions, other than the seller's obligation to remit tax on its own purchases (Sec. 11-15B-2(b)(21));

— "Model II seller" means a seller that has selected a certified automated system to perform part of its sales and use tax functions, but retains responsibility for remitting the tax (Sec. 11-15B-2(b)(22));

— "Model III seller" means a seller that has sales in at least five member states, has total annual sales revenue of at least $500 million, has a proprietary system that calculates the amount of tax due each jurisdiction, and has entered into a performance agreement with the member states that establishes a tax performance standard for the seller (Sec. 11-15B-2(b)(23)). As used in this definition, a seller includes an affiliated group of sellers using the same proprietary system.

— "Model IV seller" is a seller who is registered under the SST Agreement and who is not a model I seller, a model II seller, or a model III seller.

A seller or certified service provider (CSP) that has charged and collected an incorrect amount of state or local sales or use tax is relieved from liability for state or local penalties when the error is due to reliance by the seller or CSP upon erroneous, state-provided data contained in the state's Streamlined Sales and Use Tax (SST) taxability matrix (see ¶ 922). (*Administrative Notice 2009-26*, West Virginia State Tax Department, October 14, 2009, CCH West Virginia Tax Reports, ¶ 400-662)

¶ 930 Sales or Use Tax Credits

A credit against use tax is allowed for sales tax paid to another state up to the amount of the use tax imposed on the use of the property in West Virginia (Sec. 11-15A-10a, Reg. Sec. 110-15-43). See also ¶ 934.

Other credits include the research and development project credit (Sec. 11-15-9b) and the tourism development project credit (Sec. 5B-2E-5, expires 12/31/2019).

Bad debts: See ¶ 927.

¶ 931 Deficiency Assessments

The Uniform Tax Procedure and Administration provisions apply to the consumers sales and service tax and use tax (Sec. 11-10-3).

The Tax Commissioner may estimate a taxpayer's tax liability and issue an assessment if the taxpayer fails to remit the tax or file a return or if a return is incomplete or erroneous (Sec. 11-10-7). The Commissioner may amend an assessment before it becomes final and issue a supplemental assessment within the period prescribed for assessments.

Exemption certificates: Exemption certificates must be presented to vendors at the time of purchase, unless no certificate is required because the transaction is exempt *per se*, or because the transaction qualifies for a refundable exemption that requires the purchaser to (1) pay the tax and subsequently apply for a tax refund or credit, or (2) provide the vendor with a direct pay permit number. (Sec. 11-15-9; Reg. Sec. 110-15-9.2)

Examples of transactions that the Commissioner by rule has specified are exempt *per se* include sales of electricity, sales of prescription drugs and insulin, and sales of food by public or private schools. See Reg. Sec. 110-15-9.2.

Sellers seeking to be relieved of the duty to remit sales tax but who fail to obtain a fully completed exemption certificate or the required data elements within 90 days following a sale must, within 120 days following a substantiation request from the State Tax Commissioner, obtain a fully completed exemption certificate from the purchaser, taken in good faith. Alternatively, the seller must obtain other information showing that the transaction was not subject to sales tax. (S.B. 430, Laws 2012)

¶ 932 Audit Procedures

The Tax Commissioner may examine any books, papers, records, memoranda, inventory, or equipment relevant to matters required to be included in a return and may make test checks of tax yield (Sec. 11-10-5a). The Commissioner may require the attendance of any person with knowledge of matters contained in a return and may take testimony.

In addition, the Commissioner may examine the books, records, papers, and equipment of any person who is either selling tangible personal property or liable for use tax (Sec. 11-15A-21, Reg. Sec. 110-15-14.2.2). The character of the person's business may be investigated to verify the accuracy of any return or the amount of use tax due. Any books and records must be made available for inspection in West Virginia upon reasonable notice, but if the records must be kept out of state, the person may either bring the records to a place in West Virginia and notify the Commissioner or pay the traveling and living expenses of the Commissioner's representatives who examine the records at the out-of-state place where the records are kept.

Voluntary disclosure agreements: Qualified businesses and individuals may come forward and comply with West Virginia tax laws in exchange for a waiver of civil or criminal penalties or prosecution. A publication addresses qualification requirements, agreement procedures, and advantages of entering into an agreement, as well as contact information for submitting requests for voluntary disclosure agreements. (*TSD-412,* West Virginia State Tax Department, October 2014, CCH WEST VIRGINIA TAX REPORTS, ¶ 401-118, also available at **http://tax.wv.gov/Documents/TSD/tsd412.pdf**)

¶ 933   Statute of Limitations

The period of time in which an assessment or collection may be made, and the time limit for prosecution of a criminal offense, are discussed below.

• Assessment

Any tax, additions to tax, penalties, and interest must be assessed within three years after the date the return was filed (Sec. 11-10-15). Early returns are deemed to have been filed on the last day prescribed by law or regulation for the filing of the return. An assessment may be made at any time if a false or fraudulent return is filed with the intent to evade tax. The execution or preparation of a return by the Tax Commissioner for a taxpayer not filing a proper return does not start the running of the period of limitations on assessment.

A West Virginia consumers' sales and service tax refund claim, which was filed within three years after the due date of the annual reconciliation return, was timely filed. The statute of limitations begins to run on the due date of the annual reconciliation return, rather than on the due date of the monthly or quarterly return (*Decision 05-167,* West Virginia Office of Tax Appeals, June 17, 2005, CCH WEST VIRGINIA TAX REPORTS, ¶ 400-394).

The instructions to the exemption certificate (Form WV/CST-280) state that a purchaser who makes false or fraudulent use of the certificate with intent to evade tax may be assessed for the tax at any time.

• Collection

If an assessment has been issued, proceedings to collect the tax, including penalties and interest, must be brought within ten years after the date the assessment became final (Sec. 11-10-16, Sec. 11-10-17(e)(7)). If an assessment has not been issued, proceedings for collection must be brought within five years after the date the annual return was filed or, if no annual return was required to be filed, within ten years from the date after the latest periodical return was filed.

• Criminal prosecution

Criminal prosecutions must be commenced within three years after an offense was committed (Sec. 11-9-15).

¶ 934   Application for Refund

Certain exemptions from consumers sales and service tax and use tax may only be claimed by the purchaser by either paying the tax to the vendor and then filing a claim for refund or credit with the Tax Commissioner, or by presenting a direct pay permit number to the vendor (Sec. 11-15-9(b), Reg. Sec. 110-15-9.4, Reg. Sec. 110-15-9a.1, Reg Sec. 110-15-9a.4).

Claim for credit: The taxpayer may file a claim for credit within one year from the date of payment of the tax instead of a claim for refund (Reg. Sec. 110-15-9a.5, Reg. Sec. 110-15-9a.8). Sales and use tax overpayments may be credited against the quarterly or monthly remittance of sales and use tax due, and any overpayments remaining may be credited against certain other taxes as provided in the law and regulations. Any claim to a credit made more than one year after the payment of the tax is null and void and the overpayments are forfeited.

• General refund and credit provisions

If there is an overpayment of consumers sales and service tax, use tax, penalties, additions to tax, or interest, a taxpayer must timely file a claim for refund or credit (against the same tax for other periods) on a form (Form WV/CST-240) furnished by the Tax Commissioner in order to receive the refund or credit (Sec. 11-10-14(c), Sec. 11-10-14(h)). The claim must be filed within three years after the due date of the return, including any authorized extension of time for filing the return, or within two years from the date the tax was paid, whichever period expires later, or if no return was filed, within two years from the time the tax was paid (Sec. 11-10-14(*l*)).

Source.—Statutory references are to Subchapter III, Chapter 77, of the Wisconsin Statutes, as amended to date. Details are reported in the CCH WISCONSIN TAX REPORTS starting at ¶ 60-000.

The Wisconsin sales tax is a general sales tax imposed on retailers for the privilege of selling, leasing, or renting tangible personal property at retail in Wisconsin (Sec. 77.52(1)). It is also a limited sales tax imposed on all persons selling, performing, or furnishing certain taxable services at retail to consumers or users in Wisconsin (Sec. 77.52(2)).

Digital goods: Sales and use tax is imposed on specified digital goods and additional digital goods (Sec. 77.51(17x); Sec. 77.51(1a); Sec. 77.52(1d), Sec. 77.52(1)). Taxable digital goods include digital audio works, digital audiovisual works, digital books, greeting cards, finished artwork, newspapers, periodicals, and video or electronic games. Digital goods that would be exempt if sold in tangible form are exempt (Sec. 77.54(50); *Publication 240,* Wisconsin Department of Revenue, May 2016, CCH WISCONSIN TAX REPORTS, ¶ 4021-043).

Computer software: Sales and use tax applies to all prewritten ("canned") computer software sold or used in Wisconsin, regardless of how it is delivered to the purchaser, unless an exemption applies (Sec. 77.51(20); Sec. 77.52(10r)). Custom software is exempt (Sec. 77.51(10r); Sec. 77.52(1)).

Prepaid calling cards: Sales of prepaid phone cards, including prepaid calling services and prepaid wireless calling services, are subject to sales or use tax when sold in Wisconsin or shipped to a Wisconsin address (*Sales and Use Tax Report,* No. 2-14, Wisconsin Department of Revenue, June 2014).

- **Services subject to tax**

The sales tax is levied on the following types of services (Sec. 77.52(2), Rule Sec. Tax 11.001):

— furnishing of rooms or lodging to transients by hotel keepers for less than one month;

— the sale of admissions to amusement, athletic, entertainment, or recreational events and furnishing the privilege of access to clubs or access to, or use of, amusement, entertainment, athletic, or recreational devices or facilities;

— the sale of telecommunication and cable television system services;

— the sale of laundry, dry cleaning, pressing, and dyeing services (except self-service laundry machines and cloth diaper laundering services);

— the sale of photographic services, including film processing;

— the sale of parking services for motor vehicles or aircraft and docking or storage services for boats;

— providing the repair, service, alteration, fitting, cleaning, painting, coating, towing, inspection, and maintenance of items of tangible personal property (but not in residences or residential facilities);

— producing, fabricating, processing, printing, or imprinting services performed on tangible personal property furnished by consumers; and

— the sale of landscaping and lawn maintenance services.

Temp agencies: Generally, if a person sells, licenses, performs, or furnishes a service listed as taxable under statute, the person is liable for sales tax on its sales price from such services. However, if a seller is a "temporary help company," "employee leasing company," or "professional employer organization," and meets certain other criteria, it is considered to be providing nontaxable temporary help services (see *Tax Bulletin No. 165,* Wisconsin Department of Revenue, February 2010, CCH Wisconsin Tax Reports, ¶ 401-280).

Timeshares: The furnishing of rooms or lodging through the sale of a timeshare and the furnishing of recreational facilities in connection with the sale or use of timeshare property are not taxable services (Sec. 77.52(2)(a)1, Sec. 77.52(2)(a)2).

Internet access: Sales of Internet access services are subject to Wisconsin sales and use tax if the customer's place of primary use is in Wisconsin. The federal Internet Tax Freedom Act provides a moratorium on the taxation of Internet access services, but Wisconsin is exempt from the moratorium. Therefore, monthly fees paid by customers to access the Internet, including monthly fees paid for high-speed digital subscriber line (DSL) services, are taxable. For additional information, see *News for Tax Professionals— Internet Access Services are Taxable in Wisconsin,* Wisconsin Department of Revenue, July 12, 2012, CCH Wisconsin Tax Reports, ¶ 401-592.

Cloud computing: For treatment of software-as-a-service and similar services, see *Frequently Asked Questions—Sales and Use Tax Treatment—Computer Hardware, Software, Services,* Wisconsin Department of Revenue, January 25, 2013, CCH Wisconsin Tax Reports, ¶ 401-678.

Online travel companies: A Wisconsin Court of Appeals determined that markup amounts collected by an online travel company (OTC) as part of its reservation facilitation services were not subject to sales tax. The tax was imposed on the furnishing of rooms or lodging to transients by hotelkeepers, motel operators, and other persons furnishing accommodations available to the public. The court agreed with the Tax Appeals Commission's conclusion that the term "furnishing" in the statute (Sec. 77.52(2)(a)1) was ambiguous since it was unclear whether the term encompassed those who, like the online travel company, facilitated reservation arrangements with hotelkeepers and motel operators. The court found that, in light of such ambiguity, it was reasonable for the commission to interpret the statute as not imposing sales tax on the online travel company. The court also upheld the commission's conclusion that the statute did not impose tax on the selling of the service of making hotel room reservations, because the statute did not indicate that the sale of the furnishing of rooms or lodging was taxable. (*Wisconsin Department of Revenue v. Orbitz, LLC,* Court of Appeals of Wisconsin, District IV, No. 2015AP200, February 11, 2016, CCH Wisconsin Tax Reports, ¶ 402-040)

- **Use tax**

The use tax complements the sales tax, protecting Wisconsin merchants from discrimination arising from the inability of the state to impose the sales tax on out-of-state purchases by Wisconsin residents. It is imposed on the storage, use, or other consumption in Wisconsin of tangible personal property or taxable services purchased from any retailer and is computed on the basis of the purchase price of the property or services (Sec. 77.53(1)). It is not imposed in situations where the sales tax has already been applied (Sec. 77.56(1)).

- **Incidence of tax**

The sales tax is imposed on retailers (Sec. 77.52(1)) and persons providing taxable services (Sec. 77.52(2)); however, the retailer, service provider, or the Department of Revenue can collect the sales tax from the consumer or user (Sec. 77.52(3)).

The use tax is imposed on any person who stores, uses, or otherwise consumes tangible personal property or taxable services in Wisconsin (Sec. 77.53(2)) but this liability is extinguished with a receipt from a retailer required or authorized to collect the tax showing that the tax has been paid.

The sale, license, lease, or rental of a product may be taxed only once under the sales and use tax law, regardless of whether the sale, license, lease, or rental is subject to taxation under more than one provision (Sec. 77.61(20)).

"Retailer" defined: the term "retailer" includes every seller who makes any sale, regardless of whether the sale is mercantile in nature, of tangible personal property, or items, property, or goods under Sec. 77.52(1)(b), (c), or (d), or a service specified under Sec. 77.52(2)(a). (Sec. 77.51(13)(intro))

Distribution facilities: The definition of "retailer" does not include persons or their affiliates who operate a distribution facility and sell tangible personal property or certain collectors' coins and stamps on behalf of a third-party seller that owns the items sold and is disclosed to the customer. To qualify for the exclusion, the person or affiliate operating the distribution facility cannot make any sales for which the customer takes possession of the item sold at a location operated by the person or affiliate. This exclusion does not apply to sales at auction; sales of collectors' coins and stamps previously owned by the distribution facility operator or affiliate; and sales of motor vehicles, aircraft, snowmobiles, recreational vehicles, trailers, semitrailers, all-terrain vehicles, utility terrain vehicles, or boats. (Sec. 77.51(13b)(b))

• Nexus

Wisconsin requires any retailer engaged in business in Wisconsin and making sales of tangible personal property or other taxable items or taxable services to collect and remit sales or use tax (Sec. 77.53(3); Rule Sec. Tax 11.97). A "retailer engaged in business in this state" includes any person who has an affiliate in Wisconsin if the person is related to the affiliate and uses facilities or employees in Wisconsin to advertise, promote, or facilitate the establishment of or market for sales of items by the related person to purchasers in Wisconsin or for providing services to the related person's purchasers in Wisconsin, including accepting returns of purchases or resolving customer complaints. Persons are "related" if any of the following apply (Sec. 77.51(13g)(d)):

— One person, or each person, is a corporation and one person and any person related to that person in a manner that would require a stock attribution from the corporation to the person or from the person to the corporation under IRC §318 owns at least 50% of the corporation's outstanding stock value.

— One person, or each person, is a partnership, estate, or trust and any partner or beneficiary; and the partnership, estate, or trust and its partners or beneficiaries, own in the aggregate at least 50% of the profits, capital, stock, or value of the other person or both persons.

— An individual stockholder and the members of the stockholder's family, as defined in IRC §318, owns, in the aggregate at least 50% of both persons' outstanding stock value.

The definition of "retailer engaged in business in this state" also includes the following nexus-creating activities (Sec. 77.51(13g)):

— any retailer owning any real property in Wisconsin;

— any retailer leasing or renting out any tangible personal property (including coins or stamps) in Wisconsin;

— any retailer maintaining, occupying, or using, permanently or temporarily, directly or indirectly, or through a subsidiary, an agent, or some other person, an office, place of distribution, sales or sample room or place, warehouse or storage place, or other place of business in Wisconsin;

— any retailer having any representative, including a manufacturer's representative, agent, salesperson, canvasser, or solicitor operating in Wisconsin under authority of the retailer or its subsidiary for the purpose of selling, delivering, or the taking orders for any tangible personal property or services;

— persons servicing, repairing, or installing equipment, tangible personal property, or other taxable items in Wisconsin;

— persons delivering tangible personal property or certain collectors' items into Wisconsin in the seller's vehicle; and

— persons performing construction activities in Wisconsin.

• **Streamlined Act status**

Wisconsin sales and use tax laws are conformed to the SSUTA, effective October 1, 2009 (Act 2 (S.B. 62), Laws 2009). Wisconsin became a full member, with a seat on the Governing Board, on October 1, 2009. Materials on the SSUTA that were used to train audit staff of the Department of Revenue are available on the department's website at **http://www.revenue.wi.gov/sstp/training.html**.

Wisconsin's SST taxability matrix and certificate of compliance are available on the website of the SSTP at **http://www.streamlinedsalestax.org/otm**.

¶ 937 **Tax Base**

The sales tax is based on the "gross receipts" from the sale of nonexempt tangible personal property or taxable services (Sec. 77.52). Generally, use tax is based on the "sales price" of tangible personal property or taxable services stored, used, or consumed in the state (Sec. 77.53(1)), but also including certain "self-produced" property whether manufactured inside or outside the state.

• **Sourcing**

Retail sales must be sourced as follows (Sec. 77.522):

— When the product is received by the purchaser at a business location of the seller, the sale is sourced to that business location.

— When the product is not received by the purchaser at a business location of the seller, the sale is sourced to the location where receipt by the purchaser, or the purchaser's designated donee, occurs, including the location indicated by instructions for delivery to the purchaser or donee.

— If neither of the above apply, the sale is sourced to the location indicated by an address for the purchaser that is available from the business records of the seller that are maintained in the ordinary course of the seller's business when use of this address does not constitute bad faith.

— If none of the above apply, the sale is sourced to the location indicated by an address for the purchaser obtained during the consummation of the sale, including the address of a purchaser's payment instrument, if no other address is available, when use of this address does not constitute bad faith.

— If none of the other rules apply, including the circumstance in which the seller is without sufficient information to apply the previous rules, then the location will be determined by the address from which tangible personal property was shipped, from which the digital good or the computer software delivered electronically was first available for transmission by the seller, or from which the service was provided. Any location that merely provided the digital transfer of the product sold is disregarded.

Special sourcing provisions apply to direct mail, florists, Internet access, online sales, and telecommunications.

Certain vehicles: For local sales and use tax purposes, single payment or lump-sum leases and rentals (*i.e.,* those that do not require recurring periodic payments) of certain motor vehicles, boats, recreational vehicles, and aircraft are to be sourced on the basis of the location where the customer receives the property (previously, where the motor vehicle, boat, recreational vehicle, or aircraft was customarily kept). (Sec. 77.71(4))

Drop shipments: A manufacturer or other seller may accept an exemption certificate claiming resale from an out-of-state purchaser, even when the manufacturer or other seller is directed to ship the product to a consumer in Wisconsin and the out-of-state purchaser does not have a Wisconsin seller's permit or Wisconsin use tax registration certificate.

• "Gross receipts" defined

"Gross receipts" means the total amount of the sale, lease, or rental price from sales at retail of tangible personal property or taxable services, valued in money, whether received in money or otherwise, without any deduction for any of the following (Sec. 77.51(4)(a), Rule Sec. Tax 11.32):

— the cost of the property sold;

— the cost of the materials used, labor or service cost (*e.g.,* charges for customer alterations, handling services, small orders, returned merchandise, restocking, and split shipments), interest paid, losses, or any other expenses;

— the cost of transportation of the property prior to its sale to the purchaser; and

— certain excise or other taxes imposed upon retailers.

"Gross receipts" specifically includes the following (Sec. 77.51(4)(c)):

— all receipts, cash, credits, and property except traded-in property;

— any services that are a part of the sale of tangible personal property, including amounts charged in lieu of a tip or gratuity;

— the entire sales price of credit transactions, included in the reporting period in which the sale is made; and

— the price received for installing or applying tangible personal property (unless it becomes part of real property).

Intercompany transfers of assets: The definitions of "gross receipts," "purchase," "sale," and related terms provide that transactions in which the taxpayer's books and records show that the transferee has an obligation to pay a certain amount of money or show an increase in accounts payable are subject to sales and use tax. Transactions in which the taxpayer's books and records show that the transferor has a right to receive a certain amount of money or show an increase in accounts receivable are also taxable. Thus, intercompany transfers of assets are subject to tax (Sec. 77.51(4), (12), (14)).

The amendments relating to the tax on intercompany transfers of assets also provide that the following are taxable unless specifically exempt (Sec. 77.52):

— all sales, leases, or rentals of tangible personal property at retail in Wisconsin;

— the selling, performing, or furnishing of taxable services at retail in Wisconsin; and

— the storage, use, or other consumption in Wisconsin of all tangible personal property, and the use or other consumption in Wisconsin of a taxable service, purchased from any retailer.

• "Sales price" defined

"Sales price" means the total amount for which tangible personal property is sold, leased, or rented, valued in money, whether paid in money or otherwise, without any deduction for any of the following (Sec. 77.51(15)(a), Sec. 77.51(15)(c), Rule Sec. Tax 11.32):

— the cost of the property sold;

— the cost of the materials used, labor or service cost, interest paid, losses or any other expenses;

— the cost of transportation of the property prior to its purchase; and

— certain separately stated excise or other taxes imposed upon retailers that may be passed on to the user or consumer.

"Sales price" specifically includes the following (Sec. 77.52(15)(a), Sec. 77.52(15)(c)):

— any services that are a part of the sale of tangible personal property, including amounts charged in lieu of a tip or gratuity; and

— the amount charged for installing or applying tangible personal property sold (unless when installed it would become part of real property).

¶ 938   List of Exemptions, Exceptions, and Exclusions

Unless otherwise indicated, the statutory exemptions, exceptions, and exclusions listed below apply to both sales and use taxes; those applicable only to the sales tax or only to the use tax are listed separately. Items that are excluded from the sales or use tax base are treated at ¶ 937, "Tax Base."

Products provided free of charge: A person who provides a product or service that is not distinct and identifiable because it is provided free of charge to a purchaser who must also purchase another taxable product from that person in the same transaction may purchase the product or service that is to be provided free of charge without tax, for resale. (Sec. 77.52(21); Sec. 77.52(2m))

• Sales and use tax exemptions, exceptions, and exclusions

Adaptive equipment for handicapped (motor vehicles)	Sec. 77.54(22)(g)
Admissions to county fairs	Sec. 77.52(2)(a)
Admissions to nonprofit youth sports activities	Sec. 77.52(2)(a)
Admissions to public school activities	Sec. 77.54(9)
Advertising and promotional direct mail	Sec. 77.54(59)
Advertising transactions	Sec. 77.52(2)(a)(11), Sec. 77.54(25)
Affiliated group members, sales among	Sec. 77.54(49)
Agricultural equipment and supplies	Sec. 77.54(3), Sec. 77.54(3m)
Aircraft licensed for use in interstate commerce	Sec. 77.53(17r)
Aircraft (as specified), parts, maintenance and repair services	Sec. 77.52(2)(a)(10), Sec. 77.54(5)(a)(3)
Aircraft purchased out-of-state	Sec. 77.53(17r)
American Legion baseball sales	Sec. 77.54(35)
Animal tags and samples, sales by Department of Agriculture	Sec. 77.54(42)
Animals (including microorganisms) for research; machinery and equipment used to raise	Sec. 77.54(57)
Auction sales, household goods and farm property	Sec. 77.51(9)(e)
Biomass, used for residential fuel	Sec. 77.54(30)
Bird hunting preserves: live game birds and clay pigeons	Sec. 77.54(47)
Bottled water	Sec. 77.54(20)(a)
Broadcasting, certain property and equipment used in	Sec. 77.54(23n)
Burial vaults	Sec. 77.54(21)

Camping fees, state parks	Sec. 77.54(10)
Caskets	Sec. 77.54(21)
Cemeteries, property and services used exclusively by a nonprofit cemetery	Sec. 77.52(9a)(i)
Community-based residential facilities, food served by	Sec. 77.54(20)(c)(4)
Component parts, property consumed or destroyed	Sec. 77.54(2)
Constitutionally or federally protected transactions	Sec. 77.54(1)
Construction: contractor's purchases of materials incorporated into government or nonprofit exempt property	Sec. 77.54(9m)
Construction: property and services that are less than 10% of a one-price contract	Sec. 77.54(60)
Construction supplies and equipment for home stadium of professional athletic team	Sec. 77.54(41)
Containers	Sec. 77.54(6)(b)
Currency, U.S., sales at face value	Sec. 77.51(20)
Deer (farm raised), sold to a hunting preserve or game farm	Sec. 77.54(62)
Diabetes treatment supplies	Sec. 77.54(28)
Diaper cleaning services	Sec. 77.52(2)(a)(6), Sec. 77.51(3m)
Diapers, cloth	Sec. 77.51(1m), Sec. 77.54(40)
Digital goods, if the tangible form would be exempt	Sec. 77.54(50)
Elastic hose and stockings	Sec. 77.54(22)(f)
Electricity for residential or farm use	Sec. 77.54(30)(a)(3)
Energy: alternative energy products	Sec. 77.54(56)
Eyeglasses	Sec. 77.54(22)(d)
False teeth	Sec. 77.54(22)(c)
Farm medicine	Sec. 77.54(33)
Fertilizer, feed milling, and grain drying equipment, supplies, and building materials	Sec. 77.54(6)(am), (bn),(cn)
Fire trucks and equipment for volunteer fire departments	Sec. 77.54(16)
Fishing boats (commercial)	Sec. 77.54(13)
Flags (US and Wisconsin)	Sec. 77.54(46)
Food and beverages provided to restaurant employees	Sec. 77.54(20)(c)(4m)
Food and beverages sold from vending machines	Sec. 77.54(20)(c)(6)
Food and food ingredients sole by various nonprofit organizations	Sec. 77.54(20n)(b)
Food for human consumption off premises	Sec. 77.54(20)
Football, seat licenses	Sec. 77.54(45)
Fuel and electricity for manufacturing use	Sec. 77.54(30)
Fuel converted to electric energy, gas, or steam	Sec. 77.54(6)(c), Sec. 77.54(6r)
Fuel for residential or farm use	Sec. 77.54(30)(a)
Fuel for sportfishing boats for hire	Sec. 77.54(30)(a)7
Government transactions	Sec. 77.55(1), Sec. 77.54(9)(a)—(h)

Occasional sales to family members or transferor-owned corporation, motor vehicles	Sec. 77.54(7)(b)1
Occasional sales to family members or transferor-owned corporation, transportation equipment	Sec. 77.54(7)(b)
Oxygen for medical use	Sec. 77.54(14s)
Printers: computers and certain property stored for use out of state	Sec. 77.54(61)
Printed material for out-of-state publishers; catalogs	Sec. 77.52(2)(a)(11), Sec. 77.54(25),(25m)
Printing and imprinting services	Sec. 77.52(2)(a)(11)
Prosthetic devices and medical aids	Sec. 77.54(22)(a), Sec. 77.54(22)(b)
Public benefits fees charged by electric utilities	Sec. 77.54(44)
Public or private university food	Sec. 77.54(20)(c)(5)
Public records, copies of	Sec. 77.54(32)
Railroad rolling stock	Sec. 77.54(12)
Repossessions	Sec. 77.51(14g), Sec. 77.51(14g)(d), Sec. 77.51(14g)(e), Sec. 77.51(14g)(em), Sec. 77.51(14g)(f)
Resale, purchases for	Sec. 77.51(14), Sec. 77.52
Research, biotechnology or manufacturing	Sec. 77.54(57), Sec. 77.54(57d)(b)
School sales	Sec. 77.54(9a), Sec. 77.54(4)
Semen used for artificial insemination of livestock	Sec. 77.54(27)
Shoppers guides	Sec. 77.54(15)
Snowmaking and trail grooming machines and equipment, fuel, and electricity	Sec. 77.54(58)
Snowmobile trail groomers used by club	Sec. 77.54(38)
State and local transactions	Sec. 77.54(9a)
Telecommunications services, rights to purchase	Sec. 77.54(46)
Time-share property and services	Sec. 77.51(4), Sec. 77.52(2)(a)1, Sec. 77.52(2)(a)2
Tractors and machinery used in farming	Sec. 77.54(3)
Transfers pursuant to business formations, reorganizations, or liquidations	Sec. 77.51(14g)
Transmission facilities, transfer to transmission company	Sec. 77.51(14g)(fm)
Trucks sold to common carriers	Sec. 77.54(5)(b)
Used mobile homes	Sec. 77.54(31)
Vegetable oil and animal fat converted into exempt personal motor vehicle fuel	Sec. 77.54(11m)
Vessels used in commerce	Sec. 77.54(13)
Veterinary services	Sec. 77.52(2)(a)(10)
Waste reduction or recycling machinery and equipment	Sec. 77.54(26m)

Waste treatment facility component parts . . . . Sec. 77.54(26)
Water delivered through mains . . . . Sec. 77.54(17)
Wheelchairs . . . . Sec. 77.54(22)(e)
Wood residue used as fuel . . . . Sec. 77.54(30)(a)

• Exemptions from sales tax only

Common carrier equipment for out-of-state use . . . . Sec. 77.55(2)
Exports outside United States . . . . Sec. 77.55(3)
Insurance charges separately stated on invoice . . . . Sec. 77.54(8)
Railroad crossties for out-of-state use . . . . Sec. 77.55(2m)
Sales to the United States government . . . . Sec. 77.55(1)

• Exemptions from use tax only

Donation of property purchased for resale . . . . Sec. 77.56(3)
Driver education vehicle donations . . . . Sec. 77.56(2)
Foreign publishers . . . . Sec. 77.51(13h)
Property purchased for resale used for demonstration or display . . . Sec. 77.52(15),
                                                                Sec. 77.53(12)
Purchases by nonresidents . . . . Sec. 77.53(17),
                                                                Sec. 77.53(18)
Raw materials used in printed materials . . . . Sec. 77.51(18),
                                                                Sec. 77.51(22)
Transactions on which sales tax has been paid . . . . Sec. 77.56(1)

¶ 939   Rate of Tax

The state sales tax rate is 5% of the gross receipts from sales of tangible personal property (Sec. 77.52(1)) and taxable services (Sec. 77.52(2)), and the state use tax rate is 5% of the sales price (Sec. 77.53(1)).

• Vehicle rental fee

A state vehicle rental fee is imposed at the rate of 5% of gross receipts from vehicle rentals for a period of 30 days or less by an establishment that is primarily engaged in short term rentals of vehicles without drivers (Sec. 77.995). The fee is not imposed on re-rentals or the rental of a vehicle as a service or repair replacement vehicle, nor is it imposed on rentals of motor trucks, road tractors, truck tractors, semi-trailers, trailers, or motor buses.

• Manufactured homes; modular homes

The sales price of a new manufactured home for tax purposes does not include 35% of the sales price, excluding trade-ins. This provision does not apply to a lease or rental. (Sec. 77.51(15b)(b)7; Rule Sec. Tax 11.32(7)(a); Rule Sec. Tax 11.88(4)(b))

A retailer of a modular home has the option to exclude from the sales price or purchase price either (a) 35% of the sales price of the modular home or (b) an amount equal to the sales price of the home minus the cost of materials that become an ingredient or component part of the home (Sec. 77.51(15b)(b)8; Rule Sec. Tax 11.32(8)). No credit is allowed on trade-ins if the sales price or purchase price is reduced under this provision. Once a retailer reduces the sales price or purchase price by the amount in either (a) or (b), the retailer must continue to use that method of reduction for all sales of modular homes that are tangible personal property when sold, unless the Department of Revenue provides written approval of the use of the other method (Rule Sec. Tax 11.32(8)).

Sales of manufactured and modular homes to a contractor-consumer for use in real property construction activities outside Wisconsin are exempt from sales and use tax (Sec. 77.54(5)(am)).

A publication provides guidance regarding sales of manufactured homes, mobile homes, and modular homes; carports, decks, garages, ramps, and steps; leases and rentals of manufactured and mobile homes; tax rates; and other matters (*Publication No. 231,* Department of Revenue, June 2012, CCH WISCONSIN TAX REPORTS, ¶ 401-582)

- **Rate increases: construction contracts**

Increases in sales or use tax rates do not apply to building materials purchased by persons engaged in the business of constructing, altering, or improving real estate for others when the materials are affixed to real property pursuant to a written contract entered into or a bid made before the tax increase, when the contract does not allow for a change in price or the bid cannot be altered or withdrawn (Sec. 77.535).

¶ 940   Local Taxes

Counties may levy a sales and use tax at a rate of 0.5%. The Department of Revenue Web site has a look-up tool for finding state, county, and stadium sales tax rates at **https://ww2.revenue.wi.gov/STRB/application**. Taxpayers can find the state, county, and stadium sales tax rates applicable to specific transactions by entering the date of the transaction and either the nine-digit or five-digit ZIP code applicable to the location of the transaction. A chart of sales tax rates by county is available at **http://www.revenue.wi.gov/faqs/pcs/taxrates.html#txrate4**.

Mobile telecommunications: Wisconsin sales and use tax laws regarding telecommunications services conform to the federal Mobile Telecommunications Sourcing Act (MTSA) (P.L. 106-252), 4 U.S.C. Secs. 116-126. Thus, Wisconsin sales and use tax applies to mobile telecommunications services provided to customers whose primary place of use of the services is in Wisconsin, as determined under the MTSA (Sec. 77.52(2)(a)5). For local tax purposes, sales of mobile telecommunications services have a situs at the customer's primary place of use, which means a street address within the licensed service area of the home service provider (Sec. 77-522(4)(a)(9)).

- **Football stadium tax**

Until October 1, 2015, Brown County imposed a local professional football stadium district sales and use tax at the rate of 0.5% on the sale, storage, use, or consumption of tangible personal property and taxable services in the county.

- **Baseball park tax**

A local professional baseball park district imposes a 0.1% "special district" sales and use tax in five Wisconsin counties (Milwaukee, Racine, Washington, Ozaukee, and Waukesha) (Sec. 77.705, Sec. 77.71).

Retailers located in other parts of the state may be subject to the stadium tax if they (1) deliver taxable goods or services to a consumer located in one of the five counties and are engaged in business in that county, or (2) sell autos, boats, and other licensed vehicles that will customarily be kept in one of the five counties, even if the sale occurs in another part of the state (*Releases,* Department of Revenue, November 28, 1995, and December 5, 1995).

- **Premier resort area tax**

Either a county or a municipality within the county, but not both, may impose by ordinance a 0.5% or 1% premier resort area sales tax (Sec. 77.994). Municipalities that imposed a premier resort area tax effective before 2000 may increase the tax to 1.25% if approved by a majority of voters (Sec. 77-944(3)(b)(1)).

The following municipalities impose the premier resort area tax at the rates indicated:

Municipality	Effective date
City of Rhinelander (0.5%)	
City of Bayfield (0.5%)	
City of Eagle River (0.5%)	
City of Wisconsin Dells (1.25%)	
Village of Lake Delton (1.25%)	
Village of Stockholm (0.5%)	

For additional information, see **https://www.revenue.wi.gov/faqs/pcs/ premier.html**.

- **Milwaukee Exposition District**

The Milwaukee Exposition Center Tax District imposes a food and beverage tax, a room tax, and a rental car tax pursuant to its taxing authority. The District is made up of all municipalities located wholly or partially in Milwaukee County. The taxes fund the exposition center and are administered by the Department of Revenue on behalf of local authorities (Sec. 229.44(15); *Publication 410,* Department of Revenue, July 2015, available at **https://www.revenue.wi.gov/html/taxpubs.html#sales**).

Food and beverage tax: The District's food and beverage tax is 0.5% on sales in Milwaukee County. Generally, if the food and beverages are subject to the state sales tax, they are also subject to the District tax (Sec. 77.981; *Publication No. 410*, Wisconsin Department of Revenue; July 2015, available at **https://www.revenue.wi.gov/html/ taxpubs.html#sales**).

Room taxes: The District's basic room tax is 2% on the furnishing of rooms or lodging to any person residing for a continuous period of less than one month in a hotel, motel, or other furnished accommodations available to the public. An additional room tax of 7% is imposed on room rentals located within the city of Milwaukee (Sec. 66.75).

Rental car tax: The District's rental car tax is 3% on the receipts from the rental, for 30 days or less, of automobiles without drivers within the District's jurisdiction. The rental is considered to take place at the location where the automobile comes into the lessee's possession (Sec. 77.99).

¶ 941   Bracket Schedule

A retailer must use a straight mathematical computation to determine the amount of the tax that the retailer may collect from the retailer's customers. The retailer calculates the tax amount by combining the applicable tax rates and multiplying the combined tax rate by the sales price or purchase price of each item or invoice, as appropriate. The retailer must calculate the tax amount to the 3rd decimal place, disregard tax amounts of less than 0.5¢, and consider tax amounts of at least 0.5¢ but less than 1¢ to be an additional cent. The use of a straight mathematical computation does not relieve the retailer from liability for payment of the full amount of the tax. (Sec. 77.61(3m)).

The Department has provided the brackets by regulation (Rule Sec. Tax 11.32(5); see *Publication 229,* Wisconsin Department of Revenue, October 2016, CCH WISCONSIN TAX REPORTS, ¶ 402-099, also available at **https://www.revenue.wi.gov/html/ taxpubs.html#sales**):

When more than one taxable item is sold in a single transaction, the tax is computed on the aggregate sales price of the taxable items sold (Rule Sec. Tax 11.32(5)).

¶941   Wisconsin

Returns, Payments, and Due Dates

Every "seller," as defined by Sec. 77.51(17), is required to file a sales tax return, and every retailer engaged in business in Wisconsin, as defined by Sec. 77.51(13g), is required to file a use tax return (Sec. 77.58). Persons purchasing tangible personal property or taxable services the storage, use, or consumption of which is subject to the use tax must file a use tax return unless the tax was paid to a retailer required to collect the tax. Persons who purchase motor vehicles, boats, snowmobiles, mobile homes not exceeding 45 feet in length, trailers, semitrailers, all-terrain vehicles, or aircraft from vendors who are not licensed or registered Wisconsin dealers of such property must file sales tax returns and pay any tax due on the purchase prior to registering or titling the property in Wisconsin (Sec. 77.61(1)).

Disregarded entities: A single-owner entity that is disregarded as a separate entity for income or franchise tax purposes is also disregarded as a separate entity for sales and use tax purposes. Owners of disregarded entities may elect to file separate sales and use tax returns for each disregarded entity. (Sec. 77.58(3)(a))

Agreements with out-of-state marketers: The Department of Revenue may enter into agreements with out-of-state direct marketers requiring them to collect Wisconsin state, county, and stadium sales and use taxes (Sec. 77.63). An out-of-state direct marketer that collects taxes pursuant to such an agreement may retain 5% of the first $1 million of the taxes collected in a year and 6% of the taxes collected in excess of $1 million in a year. This provision does not apply to out-of-state direct marketers who are otherwise required to collect Wisconsin taxes.

Sales and use tax provisions relating to returns, payments, deficiency and refund determinations, interest, and penalties apply to the direct marketer agreements, except the Department may negotiate payment schedules and audit procedures with the direct marketers (Sec. 77.63).

• Due dates for returns and payments

In general, sales and use tax returns are filed and tax payments are made on a quarterly basis (Sec. 77.58). The due date for quarterly returns and payments is the last day of the month following the end of a calendar quarter. However, monthly returns and payments may be required. If the amount of tax (Sec. 77.58):

— exceeds $1200, the Department may require by written notice to the taxpayer that taxes imposed each month be paid, and a return for those taxes filed, by the last day of the following month; and

— exceeds $3,600, the Department may require by written notice to the taxpayer that taxes imposed each month be paid, and a return for those taxes filed, by the 20th day of the following month.

The Department of Revenue can require returns and payments for other periods if necessary to ensure payment or facilitate the collection of the tax (Sec. 77.58(5)). A retailer holding a regular seller's permit that, during the previous calendar or fiscal year, had a sales and use tax liability not exceeding $600 will be notified by the department that it must file only one sales and use tax return for the following year (Rule Sec. Tax 11.93). Such retailers that want to continue filing quarterly must contact the department.

• Payment by EFT

General, county, and stadium sales and use taxes must be paid by electronic funds transfer (EFT) if the aggregate amount due in the prior calendar year was $300 or more (Rule Sec. Tax 1.12). To be considered timely, an EFT payment must have a settlement date on or before the due date of the payment. Any person not required to use the EFT payment method may elect to pay taxes by EFT. The Department will notify a person when EFT payments are required. The first required EFT payment will be due on the first payment due date following the end of a 90-day registration period. The Department may waive the EFT payment requirement if the payer establishes that the requirement will cause an undue hardship.

An online service for business taxpayers called "My Tax Account" is available on the DOR's website at **https://tap.revenue.wi.gov/mta/_/#1**. The service allows businesses and their authorized representatives to electronically file personal income tax withholding, sales and use, premier resort area, local exposition center, and rental vehicle tax returns. Taxpayers may make payments through electronic funds transfer (EFT) or by credit card; view their return filing and payment history, demographics, and balance due; view and reprint selected Department correspondence; and submit requests for demographic changes and installment payment agreements.

Overdue accounts: Taxpayers making installment agreement payments to the Department of Revenue on overdue Wisconsin tax accounts must pay by electronic funds transfer (EFT) if (1) the initial overdue balance was at least $2,000, (2) the installment agreement is for more than two years, (3) the agreement was requested by an entity with an active business permit, (4) the agreement is for a person with an out-of-state account, and (5) the payment history of the account dictates that it would be in the Department's best interest to require payment by EFT (Rule Sec. Tax 1.12).

- **Payment by other means**

Credit card: The Department of Revenue accepts credit card payments of sales and use taxes through the Official Payments Corporation. American Express, Discover, Master Card, and Visa are accepted. More information on this payment method is available at the Official Payments Corporation website, , or by calling the Official Payments Corporation at 1-800-272-9829.

Telephone and Internet: Taxpayers filing their sales and use tax returns by telephone through the Sales TeleFile service may pay their taxes by electronic funds transfer (EFT), credit card, money order, or direct withdrawal from a taxpayer's account. For TeleFile instructions, go to **http://www.revenue.wi.gov/eserv/e-sales.html**.

Taxpayers filing their sales and use tax returns over the Internet through My Tax Account may pay their taxes by EFT, check, or money order. Taxpayers filing their sales and use tax returns using the File Transmission service may submit an authorization for an electronic funds transfer (EFT) payment within the File Transmission file. File Transmission information is on the Department's website at **http://www.revenue.wi.gov/eserv/file/index.html**. (*Publication No. 129,* Wisconsin Department of Revenue, October 2007, CCH Wisconsin Tax Reports, ¶ 401-071).

Payment on individual income tax returns: Individuals who owe Wisconsin sales or use tax on tangible personal property or taxable services purchased from an out-of-state seller that does not charge sales tax may report and pay the tax on their individual income tax return Form 1, 1A, WI-Z, or 1NPR. The Department conducts various audit projects to identify individuals who may not be properly reporting sales and use tax due on out-of-state purchases (Rule Sec. Tax 11.01; *Tax Bulletin No. 146,* Wisconsin Department of Revenue, February 2006, CCH Wisconsin Tax Reports, ¶ 400-882).

- **Collection discount**

Retailers may deduct 0.5% of the tax payable or $10, whichever is greater, as administration expenses if the payment is not delinquent. The collection discount is limited to $1,000 for each reporting period (Sec. 77.61(4)(c)).

- **Retailer absorption of tax**

A provision that prohibited retailers from advertising that they will absorb or assume Wisconsin sales and use tax was repealed, effective June 8, 2011. The repealed provision also prohibited retailers from advertising that the tax would not be added to the selling price or, if added, that the tax would be refunded. Retailers who advertise that the tax will be absorbed or assumed by the retailer, or that the tax will not be added to the sales price, remain responsible for payment of the tax. (Former Sec. 77.52(4); Act. 18 (S.B. 12), Laws 2011)

- **Mailing of returns**

Documents and payments are considered timely filed if they are mailed in a properly addressed envelope with the postage prepaid if the envelope is postmarked before midnight of the due date and if the document or payment is received within five days after the prescribed date (Sec. 77.58, Sec. 77.61(14)).

- **Uniform Sales Tax Administration Act**

Wisconsin has enacted the Uniform Sales and Use Tax Administration Act, the product of the Streamlined Sales Tax Project (SSTP) (Sec. 77.65). The following provisions became effective October 1, 2009, except as noted:

— Certified service provider.—An agent that is certified jointly by the states that are signatories to the SST Agreement, and that performs all of a seller's sales tax and use tax functions related to the seller's retail sales, except that a certified service provider is not responsible for a retailer's obligation to remit tax on the retailer's own purchases (Sec. 77.51(1g));

— Certified automated system.—Software that is certified jointly by the states that are signatories to the SST Agreement, and that is used to calculate the sales tax and use tax on a transaction by each appropriate jurisdiction, to determine the amount of tax to remit to the appropriate state, and to maintain a record of the transaction (Sec. 77.524(1)(am));

— Collection compensation for CSPs, CASs, and sellers using qualified proprietary systems.—The following persons may retain a portion of sales and use taxes collected on retail sales in an amount determined by the Department of Revenue and by contracts that the Department enters into jointly with other states as a member state of the SST Governing Board pursuant to the SST Agreement (Sec. 77.63):

(1) a certified service provider (CSP);

(2) a seller that uses a certified automated system (CAS); or

(3) a seller that sells tangible personal property, taxable items, or taxable services in at least five states that are signatories to the SST Agreement; that has total annual sales revenue of at least $500 million; that has a proprietary system that calculates the amount of tax owed to each taxing jurisdiction in which the seller sells tangible personal property, taxable items, or taxable services; and that has entered into a performance agreement with the states that are signatories to the SST Agreement.

— Sellers registered through SST central registration system.—Except for a seller who uses a certified service provider, a seller that registers through the SST Governing Board's central registration system, and indicates at the time of registration that it anticipates making no sales in Wisconsin, is not required to file a Wisconsin return until it makes a taxable sale that is sourced to Wisconsin. Once such a seller makes a taxable sale sourced to Wisconsin, that seller must file a return. The return is due by the last day of the month following the last day of the calendar quarter when the sale occurred, and the seller must continue to file such quarterly returns unless the Department of Revenue notifies the seller of a different filing frequency. (Sec. 77.58(2)(d))

"Seller" includes an affiliated group of sellers using the same proprietary system to calculate the amount of tax owed in each taxing jurisdiction in which the sellers sell tangible personal property, taxable items, or taxable services (Sec. 77.63).

¶ 943 **Prepayment of Tax**

Wisconsin has no tax prepayment requirements. However, the Department of Revenue is authorized to require certain taxpayers to make a security deposit to ensure the prompt payment of tax.

¶ 944 **Vendor Registration**

Generally, every person making retail sales or rentals of tangible personal property or selling, performing, or furnishing taxable services at retail in Wisconsin must obtain from the Department of Revenue a seller's permit for each place of operation. Permits are issued to persons holding valid business tax registration certificates under Sec. 73.03(50). The permits are not assignable and are valid only for the person who originally obtains them and only at the designated place of operation (Sec. 77.52(9), Sec. 73.03(50)). Although the permits do not automatically expire, the *certificates* must be renewed every two years for a fee (Sec. 73.03(50)).

New businesses may register in Wisconsin at **https://www.revenue.wi.gov/businesses/new-business/index.html**.

Existing businesses may register for tax purposes at **https://tap.revenue.wi.gov/services/_/#1**.

Disregarded entities: If a business owner elects to file a separate electronic return for each of the owner's disregarded entities, each disregarded entity must obtain a business tax registration certificate (Sec. 73.03(50)(d)). If an owner elects to file a separate electronic return for each of its disregarded entities, each disregarded entity is an applicant for a seller's permit (Sec. 77.52(7)). For a single-owner entity that is disregarded as a separate entity under Wisconsin income tax laws, the requirement to hold a seller's permit is satisfied if the seller's permit is in the name of either the disregarded entity or its owner (Sec. 77.61(11)).

• **Use tax registration**

Every out-of-state retailer who is engaged in business in Wisconsin and not required to hold a seller's permit or who is not engaged in business in the state but elects to collect use tax for the convenience of its Wisconsin customers must register with the Department of Revenue and obtain a valid business registration certificate (Sec. 77.53(9), Sec. 77.52(9m)). A retailer who is required to obtain a certificate must provide the Department of Revenue with the names and addresses of all agents operating in the state, the locations of all distribution or sales houses, offices, or other places of business in the state, and such other information the Department may require (Sec. 77.53(9)).

A person who is not required to have a seller's permit or registration certificate and who regularly owes use tax because purchases are made without sales or use tax being charged must obtain a consumers use tax registration certificate (Rule Sec. Tax 11.002).

The Wisconsin Secretary of Revenue must determine and periodically certify to the Wisconsin Secretary of Administration the names of persons and their affiliates who make taxable sales of tangible personal property and services but who are not registered to collect and remit Wisconsin sales and use tax or, if registered, do not collect and remit the tax (Sec. 77.66).

SSUTA conformity: Wisconsin sales and use tax laws are conformed to the Streamlined Sales and Use Tax Agreement (SSUTA), effective October 1, 2009 (Act 2 (S.B. 62), Laws 2009).

Multistate businesses may register for all SST states at **https://www.sstregister.org/**.

• **Out-of-state disaster responders**

Out-of-state businesses that perform disaster relief work in Wisconsin are not required to register with the Department of Revenue for sales or use tax purposes, are not required to obtain a sales tax seller's permit, and are not required to obtain a business tax registration certificate for sales made during the disaster period (Sec. 77.53(9)(b)). In addition, use tax does not apply to tangible personal property that is purchased outside Wisconsin by an out-of-state business, brought into Wisconsin, and used solely for disaster relief work (Sec. 77.53(19)).

Effective November 13, 2015, the following definitions apply (Sec. 323.12(5)):

— "Disaster relief work" means work, including repairing, renovating, installing, building, or performing other services or activities, relating to infrastructure in Wisconsin that has been damaged, impaired, or destroyed in connection with a state of emergency declared by the governor.

— "Disaster period" means the time that begins 10 days before a declared state of emergency and ends 60 days after the declared state of emergency ends.

— "Out-of-state business" means a sole proprietorship, partnership, limited liability company (LLC), joint venture, corporation, or other organization or enterprise, whether operated for profit or not for profit, that is not organized under Wisconsin law and that, except for disaster relief work during a disaster period, was not doing business in Wisconsin during the three taxable years immediately preceding the disaster period or the current taxable year when the declared state of emergency occurs.

Additional information is available in *Publication No. 411,* Wisconsin Department of Revenue, July 2016, CCH WISCONSIN TAX REPORTS, ¶ 402-083.

¶ 945   Sales or Use Tax Credits

When the purchase, rental, or lease of tangible personal property or a service subject to Wisconsin use tax was subject to a sales tax by another state where the purchase was made, the amount of the sales tax paid the other state may be claimed as a credit against the Wisconsin use tax (Sec. 77.53(16)). For purposes of this credit, "sales tax" includes a use or excise tax imposed on the use of tangible personal property or a taxable service by the state in which the sale occurred, and "state" includes the District of Columbia but does not include Puerto Rico or any U.S. territory. The amount of the credit may not exceed the amount of Wisconsin use tax otherwise due. For additional information, see *Tax Release,* Wisconsin Department of Revenue, July 2008, CCH WISCONSIN TAX REPORTS, ¶ 401-116.

Tax paid to Native American tribes: A credit is available against the use tax equal to the amount of sales, use, or excise tax paid to a federally recognized Native American Indian tribe or band if the purchase, rental, or lease of the tangible personal property or service occurred on tribal lands. The credit is allowed only as determined by an agreement between the Department of Revenue and the tribal council, and the credit applies only if the tribal tax was imposed before imposition of the use tax. (Sec. 77.53(16m))

Exemption certificate late reporting: A retailer that receives an exemption certificate after reporting a sale covered by the exemption certificate as taxable, that has paid the tax to the Department of Revenue, and that has returned to the buyer in cash or in credit all tax previously paid by the buyer may claim a deduction for the sales price or purchase price previously reported as taxable. This deduction is claimed on the return filed for the reporting period in which the exemption certificate is received. This provision does not apply if the reporting period in which the exemption certificate is received is in a taxable year of the retailer that is subsequent to the taxable year of the retailer in which the sale covered by the exemption certificate occurred. For purposes of this provision, the taxable year of the retailer is the same as the retailer's taxable year for income tax purposes. (Sec. 77.585(10))

• Bad debts

If accounts are found to be worthless and have been charged off for income or franchise tax purposes, a retailer who has previously paid the sales tax on these amounts may take as a deduction from the measure of the tax the amount found to be worthless (Sec. 77.51(4)(b)(4), Sec. 77.52(6), Sec. 77.53(4), Rule Sec. Tax 11.30).

Effective July 1, 2017, debt-collection expenses, which are excluded from the definition of "bad debt," do not include dual purpose credit debts and private label credit debts (Sec. 77-585(11)).

"Dual purpose credit debt" means accounts and receivables that result from credit sale transactions using a dual purpose credit card, but only to the extent the account or receivable balance resulted from purchases made from the seller whose name or logo appears on the card. "Dual purpose credit card" means a credit card that may be used as a private label credit card or to make purchases from persons other than the seller whose name or logo appears on the card or the seller's affiliates or franchisees, if the credit card issuer is able to determine the sales receipts of the seller and the seller's affiliates or franchisees apart from any sales receipts of unrelated persons. (Sec. 77-585(11)(a)(2))

"Private label credit debt" means accounts and receivables that result from credit sale transactions using a private label credit card, but only to the extent the account or receivable balance resulted from purchases made from the seller whose name or logo appears on the card. "Private label credit card" means any charge card or credit card that identifies a seller's name or logo on the card and that may be used only for purchases from that seller or from any of the seller's affiliates or franchisees. (Sec. 77-585(11)(a)(4))

A seller may claim as a deduction the amount of any bad debt that the seller or lender writes off as uncollectible in the seller's or lender's books and records and that is eligible to be deducted as a bad debt for federal income tax purposes, regardless of whether the seller or lender is required to file a federal income tax return. A seller who claims this deduction must claim the deduction on the return that is submitted for the period in which the seller or lender writes off the amount of the deduction as uncollectible in the seller's or lender's books and records and in which that amount is eligible to be deducted as bad debt for federal income tax purposes. If the seller or lender subsequently collects all or part of any bad debt for which a bad debt deduction is claimed, the seller must include the amount collected in the return filed for the period in which the amount is collected and must pay the tax with the return. Also, "bad debt" means the portion of the sales price or purchase price that the seller has previously reported as taxable, and for which the seller has paid the tax, and that the seller or lender may claim as a deduction under IRC Sec. 166. Previously, lenders were not included in these provisions.

"Lender" means any person who owns a private label credit debt, an interest in a private label credit debt, a dual purpose credit debt, or an interest in a dual purpose credit debt, if the person purchased the debt or interest directly from a seller who remitted the sales and use tax or from a third party or if the person originated the debt or interest pursuant to the person's contract with the seller who remitted the tax or with a third party. The term "lender" includes any person who is a member of the same affiliated group, as defined under IRC Sec. 1504, as a lender or who is an assignee or other transferee of a lender. (Sec. 77-585(11)(a)(3))

Sellers may compute their bad debt deduction using an estimate if the Department of Revenue approves the method for computing the estimate (Sec. 77-585(11)(c)(2)).

¶ 946   Deficiency Assessments

The Department of Revenue may determine by audit the sales or use tax, penalties, and interest required to be paid to the state (Sec. 77.59(1), Sec. 77.59(2), Sec. 77.59(10)). A deficiency determination is presumed to be correct, and the burden of proving it incorrect is on the person challenging its correctness.

When the Department determines that sales tax is owed by more than one person, it may assess the entire amount of tax due to each person, specifying that the assessment is in the alternative (Sec. 77.59(9m)). In addition, when a liability is for either sales tax or use tax, an assessment may be made for both taxes, specifying once again that the assessment is in the alternative.

Written notice of a determination must be given to a taxpayer within the applicable statute of limitations period (generally four years) (Sec. 77.59(3)). Service of the notice by publication is authorized when the Department is unable to obtain service by mail. In general, the Department of Financial Institutions is deemed to be the lawful attorney upon whom notices and other legal processes may be served for nonresidents who transact business or perform personal services in the state (Sec. 71.80(12), Sec. 77.62).

In general, a determination by the Department is final unless, within 60 days of receiving the determination notice, the taxpayer (or a person directly interested) petitions the Department for a redetermination (Sec. 77.59(6)).

¶ 947   Audit Procedures

The Department of Revenue may conduct office audits (Sec. 77.59(1)) or field audits (Sec. 77.59(2)) in order to determine the tax required to be paid or any refund due. Both office audit determinations and field audit determinations may be made upon the basis of facts contained in a return or any other information in the Department's possession. A field audit determination may also be made on the basis of sampling, regardless of whether the person being audited has complete records of transactions or whether the person consents (Sec. 77.59(2)).

During the course of a field audit, the Department may examine and inspect the books, records, memoranda, and property of any person in order to verify the tax liability of that person or of another person (Sec. 77.59(2)). The Department may subpoena any person to testify under oath or to produce books, records, or memoranda. Reconciling differences between the gross receipts reported for franchise/income tax and sales/use tax purposes is one of the most common issues addressed in a field audit.

One or more office audit determinations may be made of the amount due for any period (Sec. 77.59(1); see also *Publication 505,* Wisconsin Department of Revenue, February 2017, CCH WASHINGTON TAX REPORTS, ¶ 402-138). However, once a field office determination becomes final, the tax liability of the taxpayer for the period audited may not be subsequently adjusted, unless the taxpayer files a refund claim with respect to the audited period or the Department determines that a return filed for the audited period was false or fraudulent (Sec. 77.59(2); see also *Publication No. 506,* Wisconsin Department of Revenue, March 2016, CCH WASHINGTON TAX REPORTS, ¶ 402-059).

The notice of a determination must specify whether the determination is an office audit or a field audit determination (Sec. 77.59(3)).

Additional information on audits is available at **https://www.revenue.wi.gov/faqs/ise/audit.html**.

- **Failure to file return**

If a person fails to file a return, the Department of Revenue can make an estimate of the amount of the appropriate tax base (Sec. 77.59(9)). The estimate is based on any information in the Department's possession. The tax is calculated on the basis of this estimate and a 25% penalty added.

¶ 948   Statute of Limitations

No determination of tax liability of a person may be made unless written notice is given to the taxpayer by the later of the following (Sec. 77.59(3)): within four years after the due date of the taxpayer's Wisconsin income or franchise tax return (or, if exempt, within four years of April 15th of the year following the close of the calendar or fiscal year); within four years of the dissolution of a corporation; or within four years of the date any sales and use tax return required to be filed for any period in that year was filed. The notice must specify whether the determination is an office audit or a field audit determination.

The limitations period may be extended if the taxpayer consents in writing prior to the expiration of the limitations period (Sec. 77.59(3m)).

There is no limitations period in cases where a required return is not filed, or where a false or fraudulent return is filed with the intent to defeat or evade the tax (Sec. 77.59(8)).

Assessments and refunds: Effective March 3, 2016, the four-year limitations periods refer to the due date of the person's Wisconsin income or franchise return that corresponds to the date the sale or purchase was completed (Sec. 77.59(4)(a)). Previously, the limitations periods referred to the due date of the Wisconsin income or franchise tax return or the corresponding Wisconsin income franchise tax return.

A provision regarding claims for refunds that are not passed along to customers, which provides a two-year statute of limitations for refund claims after an audit determination, is amended to provide that claims for refund are not allowed with regard to items that were not adjusted in the office audit or field audit (Sec. 77.59(4)(b)). Previously, the provision disallowed refund claims for any tax self-assessed by the taxpayer.

¶ 949   **Application for Refund**

The Department of Revenue may, by office or field audit, determine a sales or use tax refund due to any person (Sec. 77.59(1), Sec. 77.59(2)). When the Department has not made an office audit or field audit determination, a seller (or a buyer, under certain circumstances) may file a claim for refund within a specified time period (Sec. 77.59(4)). A claim for refund is regarded as a request for a determination, and the Department must make the determination within one year after receiving the claim unless the taxpayer consents to an extension of the one-year period. If both a buyer and a seller file a valid claim for the same refund, the Department may pay either claim.

Due date: A seller may file a claim for refund at any time within four years after the due date of its corresponding Wisconsin income or franchise tax return (Sec. 77.59(4)(a)). If the seller is exempt from income and franchise taxes, the refund must be claimed within four years of the 15th day of the fourth month of the year following the close of the calendar or fiscal year for which the seller files the claim. The same time frames apply to the filing of a buyer's claim for refund, although the four-year period is calculated from the *unextended* due date of the buyer's corresponding income or franchise tax return.

If a taxpayer has consented to an extension of the period of time during which the Department may give a notice of determination, which period is basically the same as the period for filing a refund claim, the taxpayer may file a claim for refund at any time prior to the expiration of the extended period (Sec. 77.59(3m)).

Audited taxpayers: When the Department makes an office audit or field audit determination that the taxpayer does not protest by filing a petition for redetermination, the taxpayer may file a claim for refund at any time within two years of the determination if the refund will not be passed along to the taxpayer's customers (Sec. 77.59(4)(b)). This, however, enables the Department to make an additional assessment with respect to any item that was a subject of the prior assessment.

Setoffs: A taxpayer does not have any right to or interest in tax refunds until the setoff of amounts owed by the taxpayer to government entities has been completed (Sec. 77.59(5)).

- **Refund claims by buyers**

A buyer may file a claim for refund of sales or use tax paid to a seller under any of the following conditions (Sec. 77.59(4)(a)):

— the claim is for at least $50;

— the seller has ceased doing business;

— the buyer is being field audited; or

— the seller may no longer file a claim.

The $50 threshold requirement may be satisfied by aggregating into one claim separate transactions on which tax refunds are claimed, if the total refund claimed equals or exceeds $50.

Refund from seller: A seller who erroneously collects tax from a buyer but does not remit the tax, or who is entitled to a refund that is offset to pay a deficiency, must, within 90 days, refund the tax and related interest to the buyer from whom the tax was collected or pay it to the Wisconsin Department of Revenue if the seller cannot locate the buyer (Sec. 77.59(5m)).

Additional information: See *Publication No. 216,* Wisconsin Department of Revenue, October 2012, CCH WISCONSIN TAX REPORTS, ¶ 401-623.

¶ 950

¶ 951

Source.—Statutory references are to Title 39 of the Wyoming Statutes, as recodified in 1998 and amended to date. Details are reported in the CCH WYOMING TAX REPORTS starting at ¶ 60-000.

The Wyoming sales tax is an excise tax levied on retail sales or leases of tangible personal property and specified services on the basis of the sales price (Sec. 39-15-103). The use tax is a complementary tax and does not apply in situations when the sales tax is collected (Sec. 39-16-105(a)(v)(A)).

Digital products: Tax is imposed on digital books, audio and audio-visual products transferred to the end user if the purchaser has permanent use of the products (Sec. 39-15-103(a)(i)(A)).

Software: Prewritten or canned computer software is subject to sales and use tax regardless of whether it is sold on tangible storage media or delivered by the seller electronically (Sec. 39-15-103(a)(i)(O); Sec. 39-16-103(a)(iii); Rule Ch. 2, Sec. 15(d)).

The service of creating custom software for a person is not subject to sales tax. The person performing the service is considered the consumer of all tangible personal property or services purchased to perform the service (Rule Ch. 2, Sec. 15(d)). For additional information, see *Publication—Computer Sales and Services,* Wyoming Department of Revenue, July 1, 2014, CCH WYOMING TAX REPORTS, ¶ 201-209.

- **Services subject to tax**

The sales tax is levied on the following services (Sec. 39-15-103(a)(i)(A-O)):

— intrastate telephone services (including equipment);

— intrastate transportation of passengers;

— furnishing of public utility service, including gas, electricity or heat;

— furnishing of meals (including cover charges);

— furnishing of lodging in hotels, motels, tourist courts and similar establishments providing lodging for transient guests;

— admissions to places of amusement;

— charges for repair, alteration or improvement of tangible personal property;

— contract seismographic surveying, contract geophysical surveying and other contract geophysical exploration operations used in searching for oil or gas; and

— mobile telecommunications services if the calls originate and terminate in a single state and are billed to a customer with a place of primary use in Wyoming.

Online travel companies (OTCs): The Wyoming Supreme Court has affirmed that several online travel companies (OTCs) were vendors and liable for collecting and remitting Wyoming sales and lodging taxes on the total amount paid to them by guests who used their online reservation services to book hotel rooms in Wyoming. The total amount consisted of the discounted room rate (net rate) that the OTCs agreed to pay to the hotel plus a service or facilitation fee (mark-up) that the OTCs argued, unsuccessfully, was not subject to tax.

The court held that the markup was not exempt as a service or transaction fee but rather was part of the sales price. Guests could not obtain a hotel room unless it paid the OTCs' charges. Thus, the charges were for "services necessary to complete the sale," which could not be deducted from the taxable sales price. Even though they were not hotels, the OTCs were held to be vendors for tax purposes because they contracted with hotels to assign rooms and they had the authority to rent those rooms at a price they established. Moreover, the OTCs, not the hotels, controlled the financial aspects of the transaction. For example, customers seeking a refund or cancellation could do so only through the OTC.

Finally, application of Wyoming sales tax to the OTCs did not violate the Dormant Commerce Clause, the Equal Protection Clause, or the Due Process provisions of the U.S. Constitution or the federal Internet Tax Freedom Act. (*Travelocity.Com LP, et al. v. Wyoming Department of Revenue,* Wyoming Supreme Court, No. S-13-0078, April 3, 2014)

For additional information, see *Important Notice: Process for Remitting Sales and Lodging Tax for Businesses and Hotels Utilizing the "Merchant Model" to Facilitate Reservations of Hotel Accommodations in Wyoming,* Wyoming Department of Revenue, December 2, 2014, CCH WYOMING TAX REPORTS, ¶ 201-226.

- **Use tax**

Use tax is imposed on the purchase or lease of tangible personal property outside Wyoming for use, storage, or other consumption within Wyoming, provided the same transaction would have been subject to sales tax if the transaction had occurred within Wyoming (Sec. 39-16-103, Rule Ch. 2, Sec. 4(f)). Tangible personal property that is sold by any person for delivery in Wyoming is deemed sold for storage, use, or consumption in the state unless the seller receives a resale certificate from the purchaser (Sec. 39-16-103(a)(ii)).

The use tax is not imposed when the Wyoming sales tax has already been paid or when a transaction is specifically exempted (Sec. 39-16-105). For additional information about Wyoming use tax, see *Sales and Use Tax Bulletin #21,* Wyoming Department of Revenue, July 1, 2013, CCH WYOMING TAX REPORTS, ¶ 201-194.

- **Incidence of tax**

Although the sales tax is "paid" by the purchaser, vendors are required to collect the tax and are liable for the entire amount (Sec. 39-15-104(a), Sec. 39-15-103(c)(i)). However, sales tax provisions also include a secondary liability provision requiring that the sales tax be paid to the Department of Revenue by the purchaser unless the purchaser paid the taxes to a vendor (Sec. 39-15-103(c)(ii)).

The use tax is similarly paid by the purchaser, but collected by the vendor, who is required to give the purchaser a receipt (Sec. 39-16-103(c)(i)). Persons actually storing, using, or consuming tangible personal property are liable for the use tax (Sec. 39-16-103(c)(ii)). This liability is not extinguished until the tax has been paid, although presentation of a receipt showing that the tax has been paid to a registered vendor will relieve the purchaser of liability.

To aid in collecting the use tax, there is a statutory presumption that tangible personal property sold for delivery in Wyoming is sold for storage, use, or consumption in the state and subject to the tax (Sec. 39-16-103(a)(ii)).

Drop shipments: A bulletin examines the Wyoming sales and use tax treatment of third party drop shipping transactions in which a vendor purchases a product from a supplier and, to avoid double shipping, arranges for the supplier to ship the product directly to the vendor's customer in Wyoming. The first transaction, between the vendor and supplier, is considered a purchase for resale and is not subject to Wyoming sales tax if the vendor provides the supplier with a properly completed Streamlined Sales Tax Agreement Certificate of Exemption. The supplier would then be relieved of any tax obligation on this transaction. The second transaction, between the vendor and the vendor's customer, is a taxable retail transaction unless an exemption exists. If the vendor holds a Wyoming sales/use tax license, he or she must collect and remit Wyoming sales tax on this transaction. If the vendor is not required to hold a Wyoming sales/use tax license, he or she is not required to collect and remit Wyoming sales tax; however, the customer must pay Wyoming use tax directly to Wyoming based on the sales tax rate in the county in which the product is delivered, with an offsetting credit for any tax paid to another state. The supplier is not subject to any tax liability on the second transaction; it is merely acting as a shipping agent delivering products that have been purchased by the Wyoming customer. (*Sales Tax Bulletin #20,* Wyoming Department of Revenue, July 1, 2013; CCH Wyoming Tax Reports, ¶ 201-193).

• Nexus

Every vendor, including remote sellers, must register with the Department and collect the use tax (see ¶ 959). "Vendor" is defined as any person making retail or wholesale sales of tangible personal property who has or maintains within Wyoming (directly or through any subsidiary) an office, distribution house, sales house, warehouse, or other place of business. "Vendor" also includes persons making sales who have agents operating, soliciting sales, or advertising within Wyoming under the authority of the vendor or its subsidiary, regardless of whether the place of business or agent is located in the state permanently or temporarily or whether the vendor or subsidiary is qualified to do business within the state. Agents acting under the authority of the vendor include (but are not limited to) truckers, peddlers, canvassers, salespersons, representatives, employees, supervisors, distributors, delivery persons, or any other persons performing services in Wyoming (Sec. 39-16-101(a)(x)).

Any out-of-state vendor may voluntarily register with the Department and if registered must collect and remit Wyoming use tax (Sec. 39-16-107(a)(vi)).

Remote sales: A seller without a physical presence in Wyoming must remit sales tax on its sales of tangible personal property, admissions, or services delivered into Wyoming once the seller meets either of the following requirements in the current or preceding calendar year (Sec. 39-15-501):

    (1)   the seller's gross revenue from such sales exceed $100,000 or

    (2)   the seller sold such items in 200 or more separate transactions.

The Department of Revenue may bring an action to obtain a declaratory judgment that the seller is obligated to remit sales tax (Sec. 39-15-501(b)). "Vendor" is amended to include a remote seller (Sec. 39-15-501101(a)(xv)).

Regular solicitation of sales by advertising: The use tax definition of "vendor" also includes any person who engages in regular or systematic solicitation by three or more separate transmittances of advertising in any 12-month period in a consumer market in Wyoming by the distribution of catalogs, periodicals, flyers, or other advertising, or by means of print, radio or television or other electronic media, by mail, telegraph, telephone, computer data base, cable, optic, microwave, satellite, or other communication system for the purpose of effecting retail sales of tangible personal property. (Sec. 39-16-101(a)(x))

• Streamlined Act status

Wyoming is a full member of the Streamlined Sales Tax (SST) Governing Board, effective January 1, 2008. It has enacted the provisions necessary to comply with the Agreement's requirements (Sec. 39-15-401—Sec. 39-15-408). As a full member, it may vote on amendments to or interpretations of the Agreement, and sellers registering under the SST system are required to collect and remit tax on sales into the state. For additional information, see ¶ 957.

¶ 952   **Tax Base**

The sales tax is imposed on the sales price of taxable sales of property or services and the gross rental paid on taxable leases (Sec. 39-15-103(a)). For sales tax purposes, "sales price" is defined as the consideration paid by the purchaser of tangible personal property, excluding any trade-ins allowed and any federal taxes or Wyoming sales tax imposed (Sec. 39-15-101(a)(vi)).

For use tax purposes, "sales price" means the consideration paid by the purchaser, excluding any trade-ins allowed (Sec. 39-16-101(a)(iv)). In conformity with the Uniform Sales and Use Tax Administration Act, the term "sales price" includes consideration received by a seller from a third party if the amount of the consideration attributable to the sale is fixed and determinable by the seller at the time of the sale of the item to the purchaser and if other conditions are met. The term also includes consideration received by a seller from third parties in connection with a price reduction or discount when the purchaser presents a coupon, certificate, or other documentation to the seller or when the purchaser identifies himself or herself as a member or a group or organization entitled to a price reduction or discount (Sec. 39-16-101(a)(viii)(C)).

"Consideration" means recompense or payment that includes anything of value to the parties to a sale (Rule Ch. 2, Sec. 3(e)). Consideration is not limited to cash. Assumption of debt is a form of consideration.

"Gross rental" means the total consideration paid to enjoy and maintain temporary possession of tangible personal property, but does not include taxes imposed by the federal government, the Wyoming sales/use tax, or the Wyoming surcharge on rental vehicles (Rule Ch. 2, Sec. 13(j)). Pick up and delivery charges for delivery of rental equipment are part of the tax base of the rental (Rule Ch. 2, Sec. 6(k)). Charges for moving rental equipment for the lessee within the term of the lease are not part of the tax base of the rental.

• Sourcing rules

Retail sales must be sourced as follows (Sec. 39-15-104; Sec. 39-16-104):

— when the product is received by the purchaser at a business location of the seller, the sale is sourced to that business location;

— when the product is not received by the purchaser at a business location of the seller, the sale is sourced to the location where receipt by the purchaser, or the purchaser's designated donee, occurs, including the location indicated by instructions for delivery to the purchaser or donee;

— if neither of the above apply, the sale is sourced to the location indicated by an address for the purchaser that is available from the business records of the seller that are maintained in the ordinary course of the seller's business when use of this address does not constitute bad faith;

— if none of the above apply, the sale is sourced to the location indicated by an address for the purchaser obtained during the consummation of the sale, including the address of a purchaser's payment instrument, if no other address is available, when use of this address does not constitute bad faith;

— if none of the other rules apply, including the circumstance in which the seller is without sufficient information to apply the previous rules, then the location will be determined by the address from which tangible personal property was shipped, from which the digital good or the computer software delivered electronically was first available for transmission by the seller, or from which the service was provided. Any location that merely provided the digital transfer of the product sold is disregarded.

Sales of services: Wyoming sources sales tax on services to the location where the customer makes first use of the service after it is rendered (Sec. 39-16-103). Prior to July 1, 2014, Wyoming sourced taxable sales of services to the location where the service was performed. This change on the sourcing of taxable services brings Wyoming in line with other states that participate in the Streamlined Sales Tax (SST) Project. This change will not affect the sourcing of retail sales, leases, or rentals of tangible personal property. Examples are provided in the *Policy Statement on Sourcing of Sales Tax on Services*, Wyoming Department of Revenue, January 31, 2014, CCH WYOMING TAX REPORTS, ¶ 201-202.

Other taxable sales: Special sourcing rules apply to leases and rentals, direct mail, and telecommunications (Sec. 39-15-104; Sec. 39-16-104).

• Taxability matrix

The Wyoming matrix is available on the SST Governing Board's website at **http://www.streamlinedsalestax.org**.

¶ 953   List of Exemptions, Exceptions, and Exclusions

Unless otherwise indicated, the statutory exemptions, exceptions, and exclusions listed below apply to both sales and use taxes; those applicable only to the use tax are listed separately. Items that are excluded from the sales or use tax base are treated at ¶ 952, "Tax Base."

Exemption certificates: Wyoming utilizes the Streamlined Sales Tax Agreement Certificate of Exemption, which requires the purchaser's name, address, tax ID number, type of business, reason for exemption, and signature; the seller's name and address; and the state(s) in which the exemption is claimed. The purchaser must provide a fully completed exemption certificate at the time of sale, or if not at the time of sale, within 90 days of the date of sale. Sellers must keep exemption certificates in their records for three years. The buyer may issue a blanket certificate if the buyer makes recurring purchases from the same seller and claims the same exemption. Special instructions apply to exemption certificates provided by the federal government, foreign diplomats (Personal Tax Exemption Cards and Mission Tax Exemption Cards), the State of Wyoming and its political subdivisions, and Native American Tribes. (*Sales and Use Tax Bulletin—Exemption Certificate,* Wyoming Department of Revenue, May 2016, CCH WYOMING TAX REPORTS, ¶ 201-246)

• Sales and use tax exemptions, exceptions, and exclusions

Admissions to public recreation facilities and swimming pools	Sec. 39-15-105(a)(iv)(E)
Agricultural purchases	Sec. 39-15-105(a)(iii)(B), Sec. 39-16-105(a)(iii)(B)
Aircraft	Sec. 39-15-105(a)(ii)(B), Sec. 39-16-105(a)(ii)(A)
Aircraft parts and repair services, air carriers	Sec. 39-15-105(a)(viii)(J), Sec. 39-16-105(a)(viii)(B)
Apprenticeship programs	Sec. 39-15-105(a)(ii)(D), Sec. 39-16-105(a)(ii)(B)
Assistive devices for disabled	Sec. 39-15-105(a)(vi)(B)
Carbon dioxide used in tertiary production of oil or gas	Sec. 39-15-105(a)(viii)(F), Sec. 39-16-105(a)(viii)(A)
Chemicals used in manufacturing	Sec. 39-15-105(a)(iii)(A), Sec. 39-16-105(a)(iii)(A)
Churches	Sec. 39-15-105(a)(iv)(B), Sec. 39-16-105(a)(iv)(B)
Constitutionally protected transactions	Sec. 39-15-105(a)(i)(A), Sec. 39-16-105(a)(i)(A)
Computer equipment for a data processing center	Sec. 39-15-105(a)(viii)(S), Sec. 39-16-105(a)(viii)(H)
Construction, coal facility equipment	Sec. 39-15-105(a)(viii)(R), Sec. 39-16-105(a)(viii)(G)
Contact lenses	Sec. 39-15-105(a)(vi)(B), Sec. 39-16-105(a)(vi)(A)

¶953   Wyoming

Livestock	Sec. 39-15-105(a)(iii)(B), Sec. 39-16-105(a)(iii)(B)
Lottery tickets and equipment	Sec. 39-15-105(a)(viii)(T), Sec. 39-16-105(a)(viii)(J)
Manufacturing machinery (exp. 12/31/2027)	Sec. 39-15-105(a)(iii)(A), Sec. 39-16-105(a)(iii)(A)
Manufacturing machinery	Sec. 39-15-101(a), Sec. 39-15-105(a)(viii)(O), Sec. 39-16-101(a), Sec. 39-16-105(a)(viii)(D)
Meals for senior citizens by nonprofit organizations	Sec. 39-15-105(a)(iv)(B)
Meals furnished to employees of a food establishment	Sec. 39-15-105(a)(iii)(J)
Medical equipment and supplies used in direct patient care	Sec. 39-15-105(a)(vi)(C), Sec. 39-16-105(a)(vi)(C)
Mobile homes, if attached to realty	Sec. 39-15-105(a)(v)(B)
Motor fuel subject to fuel tax	Sec. 39-15-105(a)(v)(C), Sec. 39-16-105(a)(v)(B)
Motor vehicle purchased by nonresident	Sec. 39-15-105(a)(ix)(B), Sec. 39-16-105(a)(x)(B)
Motor vehicle vendors' inventory and demonstrators	Sec. 39-15-107(b)(iii)
Newspapers	Sec. 39-15-105(a)(viii)(D)
Nonprofit organizations	Sec. 39-15-105(a)(iv)(B), Sec. 39-16-105(a)(iv)(B)
Occasional sales	Sec. 39-15-101(a)(v), Sec. 39-16-101(a)(iii)
Occasional sales by charitable or religious organizations	Sec. 39-15-105(a)(iv)(C)
Outfitters—Temporary shelter	Sec. 39-15-105(a)(viii)(G)
Oxygen for medical use	Sec. 39-15-105(a)(vi)(B), Sec. 39-16-105(a)(vi)(A)
Paging services, one way	Sec. 39-15-105(a)(viii)(K)
Passenger buses	Sec. 39-15-105(a)(ii)(B), Sec. 39-16-105(a)(ii)(A)
Professional drilling services	Sec. 39-15-105(a)(viii)(B)
Prosthetic devices	Sec. 39-15-105(a)(vi)(B), Sec. 39-16-105(a)(vi)(A)
Public recreation facilities and swimming pools	Sec. 39-15-105(a)(iv)(E)
Railroad rolling stock, purchases of; property and services for repair (exp. 7/1/2021)	Sec. 39-15-105(a)(ii)(B), Sec. 39-16-105(a)(ii)(A), Sec. 39-15-105(a)(viii)(F), Sec. 39-16-105(a)(viii)(Q)
Repair of government property	Sec. 39-15-105(a)(iv)(F), Sec. 39-16-105(a)(iv)(D)
Repossession of motor vehicle	Sec. 39-15-105(a)(vii)(B), Sec. 39-16-105(a)(ix)
Repossession of personal property by a chattel mortgage holder . . .	Sec. 39-16-101(a)(iii)(J)
Resales	Sec. 39-15-101(a)(xiii), Sec. 39-15-105(a)(iii)(F)

Sales to raise funds for schools	Sec. 39-15-105(a)(vii)(M)
School annuals	Sec. 39-15-105(a)(viii)(C)
Seeds	Sec. 39-15-105(a)(iii)(B), Sec. 39-16-105(a)(iii)(B)
Telecommunications—Interstate transmissions	Sec. 39-15-103(a)(i)(C)
Transfers between related entities	Sec. 39-15-101(a)(v)(A—M), Sec. 39-16-101(a)(iii)
Transportable homes, if attached to realty	Sec. 39-15-105(a)(v)(B)
Transportation fuel	Sec. 39-15-105(a)(iii)(E)
Trucks, truck-tractors, trailers, semitrailers	Sec. 39-15-105(a)(ii)(B), Sec. 39-16-105(a)(ii)(A)
Water delivered by pipeline or truck	Sec. 39-16-105(a)(vi)(D)
Wheelchairs	Sec. 39-15-105(a)(vi)(B), Sec. 39-16-105(a)(vi)(A)
Water sold to tenants for allocation purposes	Sec. 39-15-101(a)(vi)(H)(VIII)
Wholesale sales	Sec. 39-15-105(a)(iii)(F)
Wyoming film and video reward account (tax refund)	Sec. 9-2-306

- **Exemptions, exceptions, and exclusions applicable only to the use tax**

Motor vehicle previously registered by same nonresident owner in another state	Sec. 39-16-107(b)(ii)
Property subject to sales tax	Sec. 39-16-105(a)(v)(A)

¶ 954   Rate of Tax

All taxable sales in Wyoming are subject to a 3% general state sales tax plus a 1% additional tax, for a combined state tax of 4%. Wyoming use tax is imposed at the same rate (Sec. 39-16-103(c)(i)).

The additional tax may be reduced. If it is determined before April 1 of any year that the unappropriated general fund balance at the end of the current budget period, less any expected shortfall in school foundation program revenue for the following year, will exceed $35 million, the 1% additional tax will be reduced to 0.5% on July 1 of that same year (Sec. 39-15-104(d)).

Rental vehicle surcharge: A vehicle rental agency must collect a surcharge of 4% of the amount of a vehicle rental contract for 31 days or less (Sec. 31-19-105).

Prepaid wireless 911 tax: Beginning July 1, 2016, a statewide 911 emergency tax of 1.5% is imposed on every retail sale of prepaid wireless communications access in Wyoming (Sec. 16-9-109). A service supplier who sells prepaid wireless communications access must collect the tax from the purchaser, who is considered a service user. The amount of the tax must be separately stated on an invoice, receipt, or other similar document or be otherwise disclosed to the service user.

"Prepaid wireless communications access" means wireless communications access that requires advance payment that is sold in predetermined units or dollars of which the number declines with use in a known amount. A retail sale of prepaid wireless communications access occurs in Wyoming if the transaction would be sourced to Wyoming under existing sales tax sourcing rules for prepaid calling services and prepaid wireless calling services. (Sec. 16-9-109)

The 911 emergency tax is not imposed on sales of prepaid wireless communications access intended for resale or upon any state or local governmental entity.

A service supplier must remit the collected 911 taxes to the Department of Revenue at the times and in the manner required for Wyoming sales tax, and the tax is subject to the penalty and enforcement provisions and audit and appeal procedures applicable to the state sales tax. The service supplier may deduct and retain 3% of the taxes collected as the cost of administration for collecting the taxes. (Sec. 16-9-109)

For additional information, see *Sales and Use Tax Bulletin—Wyoming Prepaid Wireless Tax,* Wyoming Department of Revenue, May 2, 2016, CCH WYOMING TAX REPORTS, ¶ 201-248.

¶ 955   Local Taxes

Wyoming counties are authorized to impose voter-approved sales and use taxes at a rate of up to 2% for general revenue purposes and up to 2% for specific revenue purposes that do not include ordinary local government operations (Sec. 39-16-203(a), Sec. 39-16-204(a)). The total sales and use tax imposed by any county for general revenue and/or special purposes (excluding lodging tax) may not exceed 3%.

Economic development: With voter approval, local governments may use and impose local sales and use taxes for the purpose of economic development. The sale, storage, use, and consumption of tangible personal property, as well as admissions and services, may be taxed. The rate of tax can be in increments of ¼% (0.25%), but cannot exceed 1% (Sec. 39-15-204(a)(iii) and (vi); Sec. 39-16-204(a)(v)).

Resort taxes: Resort districts may impose general purpose local option sales and use taxes in increments of 0.5% (not to exceed a rate of 3%) on retail sales of tangible personal property, admissions, and services, or on the storage, use, and consumption of tangible personal property. The taxes may be imposed by the board of the resort district, but are subject to approval by a majority of voters in the resort district (Sec. 39-16-204(a)(iv)).

Lodging taxes: A city or town may impose a tax on the price paid for lodging services in increments of 1% (not to exceed 4%) (Sec. 39-16-204(a)(ii)).

Sourcing rules: See ¶ 952.

Mobile telecommunications: Wyoming sales and use tax is imposed on intrastate calls from mobile telecommunications services if the calls originate and terminate in a single state and are billed to a customer with a place of primary use in Wyoming. The definitions and provisions of the federal Mobile Telecommunications Sourcing Act, 4 U.S.C. Secs. 116—126, are applicable in administering the tax (Sec. 39-15-103(a)(i)(C)).

• Local tax rates

A local tax rate or boundary change takes effect on the first day of a calendar quarter after 60 days notice has been given to a vendor. In the case of a vendor selling from a printed catalog, a new tax rate takes effect on the first day of the calendar quarter following 120 days notice provided to the vendor (Sec. 39-15-207(c); Sec. 39-16-207(c)).

Local sales, use, and lodging tax rates are available on the website of the Wyoming Department of Revenue at **http://revenue.wyo.gov/Excise-Tax-Division/sales-use-tax-rates**. Local rate charts are published quarterly.

¶ 956   Bracket Schedule

Tax computation must be carried out to the third decimal place and rounded to the nearest whole cent, rounding up whenever the third decimal place is greater than four. (Rule Ch. 2, Sec. 4, WyDR),

The following schedules for selected tax rates are made available by the Wyoming Department of Revenue. See also the Vendor Manual at **http://revenue.wyo.gov/Excise-Tax-Division/vendor-manual**.

4% State Rate

Amount of Sale	Amount of Tax
$ .01— $ .37	.... 1¢
.38— .62	.... 2¢
.63— .87	.... 3¢
.88— 1.12	.... 4¢
and so forth.	

5% State and Local Rate

Amount of Sale	Amount of Tax
$ .01— $ .29	.... 1¢
.30— .49	.... 2¢
.50— .69	.... 3¢
.70— .89	.... 4¢
.90— 1.09	.... 5¢
and so forth.	

6% State and Local Rate

Amount of Sale	Amount of Tax
$ .01— $ .24	.... 1¢
.25— .41	.... 2¢
.42— .58	.... 3¢
.59— .74	.... 4¢
.75— .91	.... 5¢
.92— 1.08	.... 6¢
and so forth.	

¶ 957   Returns, Payments, and Due Dates

Vendors are required to remit the tax on the last day of the month following the month in which they were collected or as required by the Department of Revenue (Sec. 39-15-107(a)). Also required of sales tax vendors is a return showing the preceding month's gross sales. In the case of a use tax vendor, the required return must show total sales of tangible personal property subject to the Wyoming use tax.

• Reporting period

The Department of Revenue will assign vendors a frequency for filing reports (either monthly, quarterly, or annually) at the time of licensing on the basis of the volume of sales/use tax collected and other criteria (Rule Ch. 2, Sec. 6(a)). As appropriate, if the total tax to be remitted by the vendor in any month is less than $150, quarterly or annual returns may be filed on or before the last day of the month following the end of the quarter or year, respectively (Sec. 39-15-107). "Quarterly return" is defined as any three consecutive months using the business starting date as the beginning month of the quarter (Sec. 39-15-101(a)(iii), Sec. 39-16-101(a)(i)).

• Due date of return

Vendors must submit sales/use tax returns on or before the last day of the month following the last month in the reporting period in which tax was collected (Rule Ch. 2, Sec. 6(c)).

Consumers, including contractors, remitting tax not paid to the vendor must remit the tax on or before the last day of the month following the month of purchase.

The postmark date recorded by the Department will be deemed the date of filing. Persons remitting tax in person will receive a receipt indicating the amount of tax paid and the date received. Hand delivered returns will be date stamped at the time received and this will serve as the filing date.

Discount for early payment: Vendors and direct payers who pay Wyoming sales and use taxes on or before the 15th day of the month that the taxes are due arbe allowed a credit for expenses incurred for the accounting and reporting of taxes. See "Vendor compensation: at ¶ 960.

Direct payment: Any person liable for the payment of sales tax or a licensed vendor may apply to the director of the Wyoming Department of Revenue for issuance of a permit authorizing the applicant to make direct payment of sales tax to the department rather than to the selling vendor. The director will have sole discretion in issuing a direct pay permit, and the decision is not appealable. A direct payment permit may be revoked by the department at any time upon 90 days written notice to the permittee. (Sec. 39-15-107.1)

• Uniform Sales Tax Administration Act

Wyoming has enacted the Uniform Sales and Use Tax Administration Act and, with some exceptions, the related Streamlined Sales and Use Tax Agreement. Many conforming definitions have been adopted, including those relating to telecommunications (Sec. 39-15-101(a)(xxxix), Sec. 39-16-101(a)(xvii)) and "bundled transactions" (Sec. 39-15-101(a)(xl)). Most conforming provisions became effective January 1, 2008.

Sourcing rules: See ¶ 952.

SST registration: See ¶ 959.

For additional information on the uniform act, see "Streamlined Sales Tax Project," listed in the Table of Contents or go to **http://www.streamlinedsalestax.org/**.

¶ 958   **Prepayment of Taxes**

Wyoming does not require prepayment of sales or use taxes.

¶ 959   **Vendor Registration**

Every vendor, including remote sellers (see ¶ 951), must obtain a sales tax license to conduct business in Wyoming (Sec. 39-15-106, Sec. 39-16-106). An application for a license must state the name and address of the applicant, the character and location of the proposed business, and other information required by the Department of Revenue. An out-of-state vendor may voluntarily apply for a license.

A license is not transferable, and a separate license is required for each place of business, where it must be posted in a conspicuous place (Sec. 39-15-106). A change in business ownership requires a new license application (Rule Ch. 2, Sec. 5). There are provisions for the cancellation, revocation, and suspension of a license (Sec. 39-15-106, Rule Ch. 2, Sec. 5). The Department must comply with certain notice and hearing procedures before suspending or revoking a vendor's license (Rule Ch. 2, Sec. 14).

License fee: A new vendor in Wyoming is required to pay a $60 license fee (Sec. 39-15-106, Sec. 39-16-106). Licenses are valid without further payment of fees until revoked. The license may be forfeited if a vendor fails to timely file any return and a $60 fee may be charged for reinstatement of the license.

Contractors: Any nonresident prime contractor and any resident prime contractor who hires a nonresident subcontractor must register a project with the Department of Revenue not more than 15 days after the start of the project. The nonresident prime contractor must provide a properly executed bond or a cash deposit of not less than 4% of the total payments due under the contract. The cash deposit will be refunded to the contractor upon the Department's receipt of a surety bond or upon satisfactory completion of the project. A failure to register a project on time will result in a penalty assessment of 1% of the total payments due under the contract (Sec. 39-15-303(b)(iv) and Sec. 39-16-303(b)(iv)).

• Use tax registration

Use tax vendors must also register with the Department, giving the name and address of all agents operating in the state and the location of all places of business (Sec. 39-16-106, Rule Ch. 2, Sec. 5). New vendors in Wyoming must pay the license fee discussed above.

• Voluntary disclosure agreements

The Department of Revenue may enter into a voluntary disclosure agreement with any person who has sufficient contact with the state to qualify as a vendor (Sec.

39-15-107.2). However, such an agreement may not be made with a person who is under investigation or audit. Interest and penalties may be waived as part of a settlement.

• **SST registration**

To register under the Streamlined Sales and Use Tax Agreement (SST), sellers must go to **https://www.sstregister.org/**. Sellers can also update previously submitted registration information at this website. The information provided will be sent to all of the full member states and to associate members for which the seller chooses to collect.

When a seller registers under the Agreement, it must select the certified technology model it will be using (or it must select "Other" if it will not be using one of the certified models). The models are the following:

Model One: Certified Service Provider (CSP), an agent certified under the Agreement to perform all the seller's sales and use tax functions;

Model Two: Certified Automated System (CAS), software certified under the Agreement to calculate the appropriate tax (for which the seller retains responsibility for remitting);

Model Three: Certified System (CS), a proprietary automated sales tax system certified under the Agreement.

¶ 960   **Sales or Use Tax Credits**

Wyoming allows a credit for sales tax paid to another state on a purchase, equal to but not exceeding the Wyoming use tax liability on that purchase (Rule Ch. 2, Sec. 4(f)). Claims for the offsetting credit must be substantiated with invoices showing the sales tax paid. No offsetting credit is allowed for use tax paid to another state.

Erroneously paid sales or use tax, penalties, or interest will be credited against the taxpayer's subsequent tax liability or may be refunded (Sec. 39-15-109(c), Sec. 39-16-109).

• **Bad debts**

Taxes paid on accounts that have been written off as bad debts may be credited against a vendor's sales and use tax liability. The vendor must document that customary debt collection procedures have been taken or that the debt qualifies for a bad debt federal income tax deduction under IRC Sec. 166 (Sec. 39-15-107(a)(x)). If the bad debts exceed the taxable sales for a subsequent period, the vendor may request a refund of the tax on the bad debt from the department so long as the claim is made within three years of the date of the return on which the bad debt could first be claimed (Sec. 39-15-107(a)(x)). For additional information, see Bulletin #3, Wyoming Department of Revenue, July 1, 2013, CCH WYOMING TAX REPORTS, ¶ 201-177.

• **Vendor compensation**

Vendors and direct payers who pay Wyoming sales and use taxes on or before the 15th day of the month that the taxes are due are allowed a credit for expenses incurred for the accounting and reporting of taxes (Sec. 39-15-107(b); Sec. 39-16-107(b)).

For the first $6,250 of tax due, the credit is equal to 1.95% of the amount of tax due. For any tax due in excess of $6,250, the credit is 1% of that additional amount. The total credit may not exceed $500 in any month. The credit must be deducted on forms prescribed by the Wyoming Department of Revenue.

Service suppliers subject to the 911 emergency tax (see ¶ 954) may deduct and retain 3% of the taxes collected as the cost of administration for collecting the taxes (Sec. 16-9-109).

All of the vendor's returns currently due must be filed and paid in full, and the account may not have any outstanding balances. If a vendor has entered into a payment